GEORGINA CAMPBELL'S
ireland

the guide

2007

The best places to eat, drink and stay

Georgina Campbell Guides

Editor: Georgina Campbell
Production Editor: Bob Nixon

Epicure Press,
PO Box 6173
Dublin 13
Ireland

website: www.ireland-guide.com
email: info@ireland-guide.com

The contents of this book are believed to be correct at the time of going to press. Nevertheless the publisher can accept no responsibility for errors or omissions or changes in the details given.

Front cover photographs:	Dunraven Arms Hotel, Co Limerick
	Isaacs Restaurant, Cork City
	Glassdrumman Lodge, Co Down
Back cover top, (left to right):	Bushmills Inn, Co Antrim
	The Morrison Hotel, Dublin
	Borris Weir (WM Nixon)
	Heritage Hotel, Killenard
	Rathsallagh House, Co Wicklow
Back cover bottom, (left to right):	Nellie in Donegal
	Moyglare Manor, Co Kildare
	Ahernes Seafood Restaurant, Co Cork
	Moyglare Manor, Co Kildare
	Macreddin, Co Wicklow (WM Nixon)
Spine:	Rathmullan House, Co Donegal

Design and Artwork by Brian Darling of The Design Station, Dublin
Printed and bound in Spain
Images of 'Fishy Fishy Café' courtesy of Richard Bradfield
First published 2006 by Georgina Campbell Guides Ltd.

ISBN: 1-903164-23-0

Georgina Campbell Guides Awards

Mount Juliet Conrad
Hotel of the Year

MacNean House & Bistro
Restaurant of the Year

Stefan Matz
Chef of the Year

The Roundwood Inn
Pub of the Year

Ballymore Inn
Féile Bia Award

Fishy Fishy Café
Seafood Restaurant of the Year

The full list of awards is on page 9

AWARD WINNER

How to Use the Guide

Location /Establishment name

- Cities, towns and villages arranged in alphabetical order within counties, with the exception of Dublin, Cork, Belfast, Galway and Limerick which come first in their categories
- Establishments arranged alphabetically within location
- In Dublin city, postal codes are arranged in numerical order. Even numbers are south of the River Liffey, and uneven numbers on the north, with the exception of Dublin 8 which straddles the river. Dublin 1 and 2 are most central; Dublin 1 is north of the Liffey, Dublin 2 is south of it (see map). Within each district, establishments are listed in alphabetical order.

Telephone numbers

- Codes are given for use within the Republic of Ireland / Northern Ireland. To call ROI from outside the jurisdiction, the code is +353 (or +44 for NI), then drop the first digit (zero) from the local code.
- To call Northern Ireland from the Republic, replace the 028 code with 048.

Rating for outstanding cooking, accommodation or features

☆ - Demi star: restaurant approaching star status

★ - For cooking and service well above average

★★ - Consistent excellence, one of the best restaurants in the land

★★★ - The highest restaurant grade achievable

- Outstanding accommodation of its type

- Deluxe hotel

- Pub star: good food and atmosphere

- Denotes establishment committed to the Féile Bia Charter

- Identifies inclusion in the BIM Seafood Circle programme

€ - 'Best Budget' denotes moderately priced establishment (max approx €50 pps for accommodation, €35 for 3-course meal without drinks)

- Outstanding location, building or atmosphere

E - Editor's Choice; a selection of establishments outside the standard categories that should enhance the discerning travellers experience of Ireland

N - Establishments that are new to this edition of the Guide

- Previous award winner in earlier editions of our guides

◇ - Confirmation of times/prices not received at time of going to press

Maps are intended for reference only: Ordnance Survey maps are recommended when travelling; available from Tourist Information Offices.

PRICES & OPENING HOURS

PLEASE NOTE THAT PRICES AND OPENING HOURS ARE GIVEN AS A GUIDELINE ONLY, AND MAY HAVE CHANGED; CHECK BEFORE TRAVELLEING OR WHEN MAKING A RESERVATION.

Prices in the Republic of Ireland are given in Euro and those in Northern Ireland in pounds Sterling.

Thanks and acknowledgements

The publication of this guide would not have been possible without the support and encouragement of a large number of organisations, companies and individuals. Particular thanks must go to the sponsors, of course, an also to the many individuals who have given invaluable assistance: sincere thanks to you all.

Georgina Campbell, Editor.

CONTENTS

GEORGINA CAMPBELL'S ireland

The Best of the Best

STARRED RESTAURANTS

★★ / ★ / ☆

REPUBLIC OF IRELAND

2 Star: ★★
Dublin, Restaurant Patrick Guilbaud
Dublin, Thornton's

1 Star: ★
Dublin, Chapter One
Dublin, The Tea Room @ The Clarence Hotel
Dublin, l'Ecrivain
Dublin, One Pico Restaurant
Co Cavan, MacNean Bistro, Blacklion
Co Clare, Dromoland Castle
Co Cork, Ballymaloe House, Shanagarry
Co Kerry, Park Hotel Kenmare
Co Kerry, Killarney Park Hotel, Killarney
Co Kerry, Sheen Falls Lodge, Kenmare
Co Mayo, Ashford Castle, Cong
Co Sligo, Cromleach Lodge, Castlebaldwin
Co Waterford, The Tannery, Dungarvan

Demi-Star: ☆
Dublin, Bang Café
Dublin, Mermaid Café
Dublin, Mint
Dublin, Pearl Brasserie
Dublin, Roly's Bistro
Dublin, The Merrion Hotel
Co Dublin, King Sitric Seafood Restaurant & Accommodation, Howth
Cork City, Café Paradiso
Cork City, Fleming's
Cork City Isaacs
Cork City, Jacob's on the Mall
Cork City, Jacques
Co Cork, Blairs Cove House, Durrus
Co Cork, Casino House, Kilbrittain

Demi-Star (continued): ☆
Co Cork, Good Things Café, Durrus
Co Cork, Longueville House, Mallow
Co Cork, Otto's Creative Catering, Mallow
Co Cork, Toddies, Kinsale
Co Carlow, Sha-Roe Bistro, Clonegal
Co Cavan, The Olde Post Inn, Cloverhill
Co Clare, Cherry Tree Restaurant, Killaloe
Co Clare, Sheedy's Hotel, Lisdoonvarna
Co Galway, St. Clerans Country House, Craughwell
Co Kerry, The Chart House Restaurant, Dingle
Co Kerry, The Lime Tree Restaurant, Kenmare
Co Kerry, Mulcahys Restaurant, Kenmare
Co Kerry, Packie's Restaurant, Kenmare
Co Kerry, Restaurant David Norris, Tralee
Co Kildare, Kildare Hotel, Straffan
Co Limerick, The Mustard Seed @ Echo Lodge, Ballingarry
Co Mayo, The Park Inn, Mulranny
Co Monaghan, The Nuremore Hotel, Carrickmacross
Co Tipperary, The Old Convent Gourmet Hideaway, Clogheen
Co Westmeath, Left Bank Bistro, Athlone
Co Westmeath, Wineport Lodge, Glasson
Co Wexford, Dunbrody House, Arhurstown
Co Wexford, Marlfield House, Gorey
Co Wexford, La Riva, Wexford

NORTHERN IRELAND

2 Star: ★★
Belfast, Restaurant Michael Deane

Demi-Star: ☆
Belfast, James Street South

DELUXE HOTELS

REPUBLIC OF IRELAND

Dublin, Berkeley Court, Ballsbridge
Dublin, The Clarence, Temple Bar
Dublin, Four Seasons Hotel, Ballsbridge
Dublin, The Merrion, Merrion Street
Dublin, The Morrison, Ormond Quay
Dublin, The Shelbourne, St. Stephen's Green
Dublin, The Westbury, Grafton Street
Dublin, The Westin Hotel, College Green
Cork City, Hayfield Manor Hotel
Co Clare, Dromoland Castle, Newmarket-on-Fergus
Co Galway, The G Hotel
Co Galway, Glenlo Abbey Hotel
Co Kerry, Aghadoe Heights Hotel, Killarney
Co Kerry, Killarney Park Hotel, Killarney
Co Kerry, Hotel Europe, Killarney
Co Kerry, Dunloe Castle Hotel, Killarney
Co Kerry, Park Hotel Kenmare
Co Kerry, Sheen Falls Lodge, Kenmare
Co Kildare, Kildare Hotel, Straffan
Co Kilkenny, Mount Juliet Conrad, Thomastown
Co Limerick, Adare Manor, Adare
Co Mayo, Ashford Castle, Cong
Co Wexford, Marlfield House, Gorey

NORTHERN IRELAND

Co Down, Culloden Hotel, Holywood

OUTSTANDING PUBS (for good food & atmosphere)

REPUBLIC OF IRELAND

Dublin, Café en Seine
Dublin, Clarendon Café Bar
Dublin, The Porterhouse
Dublin, The Purty Kitchen, Monkstown
Co Carlow, Lennon's Café Bar, Carlow
Co Clare, Vaughans Anchor Inn, Liscannor
Co Cork, Bushe's Bar, Baltimore
Co Cork, Mary Ann's Bar & Restaurant, Castletownshend
Co Cork, Hayes' Bar, Glandore
Co Cork, The Bosun, Monkstown
Co Galway, Moran's Oyster Cottage, Kilcolgan
Co Kerry, QC's Seafood Bar & Restaurant, Cahirciveen
Co Kerry, Lord Baker's Restaurant & Bar, Dingle
Co Kildare, The Ballymore Inn, Ballymore Eustace
Co Kilkenny, Marble City Bar, Kilkenny
Co Leitrim, The Oarsman Bar & Café, Carrick on Shannon
Co Mayo, Gaughans, Ballina
Co Offaly,The Wolftrap, Tullamore
Co Roscommon, Keenans Bar & Restaurant, Tarmonbarry
Co Waterford, The Glencairn Inn, Lismore
Co Wicklow, Roundwood Inn, Roundwood

NORTHERN IRELAND

Belfast, Crown Liquor Salon
Co Down, Grace Neill's, Donaghadee
Co Down, The Plough Inn, Hillsborough
Co Down, Balloo House, Killinchy

For further accreditations, see symbols on listed entries.

Introduction

by Georgina Campbell, Editor

Welcome to the 2007 edition of '*the* guide' – this is our ninth annual guide to the best of Irish hospitality and, once again, we have trawled the length and breadth of the country to find the best: wherever you may find yourself, whether on business or leisure, we suggest the best choices for your needs. This is the only guide of its kind, offering recommendations across a very wide range of categories and price ranges – and, very importantly, our selections are made entirely on merit: unlike most other 'guides', establishments do not pay to be included in any of the Georgina Campbell guide books.

The last year has again seen a huge amount of change and, although we have tried to make the guide more compact by including more 'Round-Up entries, and a significant number of establishments previously recommended no longer feature for various reasons (closure, change of ownership, a drop in standards), it is our biggest guide to date, and includes well over 150 new recommendations. These are of every type, and distributed all over the country, but it is remarkable how many very luxurious new hotels and country houses have opened this year, some of them in remote and beautiful areas – a testament to the level of demand from discerning travellers, both visitors and Irish, and the enduring appeal of this lovely country.

Promising new restaurants continue to open at a brisk pace too – and, while there have been some very significant openings in Dublin (including the arrival of RhodesD7), it is satisfying to see exciting developments, including Richard Corrigan's new restaurants at The Lyons Demesne in County Kildare, taking place outside the capital. There seems to be a lot of luxury around at the moment, but fortunately, you don't have to spend a large amount of money to enjoy this new quality culture: for every smart new hotel or restaurant at the top end of the scale, there are plenty of smaller operators who share the 'hospitality gene' but like to do things their own way, in the many excellent guest houses, farmhouses, B&Bs, owner run restaurants and quality-led cafés that are flourishing all over the country.

And, although prosperity has brought rapid development in recent years, don't forget that stunningly beautiful countryside still lies beyond the bustle of urban centres: lakes, rivers, picturesque villages, and the gentler pace of life in rural Ireland are there for your enjoyment.

I hope that you will enjoy using the guide – and don't forget to check our website (www.ireland-guide.com), where you will find constant updates.

Awards of Excellence

Annual awards for outstanding establishments and individuals

Georgina Campbell Guides
gratefully acknowledges the support of the following sponsors:

Bord Bia
Irish Food Board

BIM Ireland

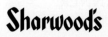

Sharwood's

Taste and Tradition
Rudd's

AWARD WINNER

GEORGINA CAMPBELL'S ireland

Hotel of the Year

Mount Juliet Conrad

Co. Kilkenny

See page 343

2006 WINNER:

Hayfield Manor Hotel, Cork

GEORGINA CAMPBELL'S ireland

Restaurant of the Year

MacNean House & Bistro

Co. Cavan

See page 155

2006 WINNER:

Restaurant Patrick Guilbauld, Dublin

AWARD WINNER

GEORGINA CAMPBELL'S ireland

Business Hotel of the Year

Brooks Hotel

Dublin

See page 61

2006 WINNER:

Conrad Dublin Hotel, Dublin

GEORGINA CAMPBELL'S ireland

Chef of the Year

Stefan Matz

Ashford Castle,
Cong, Co. Mayo

See page 385

2006 WINNER:

Mark Anderson, Cherry Tree Restaurant, Co Clare

AWARD WINNER

AWARD WINNER

Bord Bia

Irish Food Board

Féile Bia Dish of theYear

Dunbrody Country House Hotel

Co. Wexford

See page 459

Bord Bia

Irish Food Board

Féile Bia Award

Ballymore Inn

Ballymore Eustace, Co. Kildare

See page 324

2006 WINNER:

Richmond House, Cappoquin, Co Waterford

AWARD WINNER

Seafood Bar of the Year

Aherne's Seafood Bar & Restaurant

Youghal, Co. Cork

See page 235

BIM Ireland

Seafood Restaurant of the Year

Fishy Fishy Café

Kinsale, Co. Cork

See page 219

2006 WINNER:

The King Sitric Fish Restaurant, Howth, Co Dublin

AWARD WINNER

GEORGINA CAMPBELL'S ireland

Natural Food Award

Farmgate
Midleton, Co. Cork

See page 227

2006 WINNER:

Neven Maguire, MacNean Bistro, Blacklion, Co Cavan

Sharwood's

Ethnic Restaurant of the Year

Rasam
Dun Laoghaire, Co. Dublin

See page 133

2006 WINNER:
Hô Sen, Temple Bar, Dublin

AWARD WINNER

GEORGINA CAMPBELL'S ireland

Newcomer of the Year

Sha-Roe Bistro

Clonegal, Co. Carlow

See page 150

2006 WINNER:

Aldridge Lodge, Duncannon, Co Wexford

GEORGINA CAMPBELL'S ireland

Hideaway of the Year

Gregans Castle Hotel

Ballyvaughan, Co. Clare

See page 161

2006 WINNER:

Stella Maris Hotel, Ballycastle, Co Mayo

AWARD WINNER

GEORGINA CAMPBELL'S ireland

Wine Award of the Year

Ely CHQ
IFSC, Dublin

See page 54

2006 WINNER:

The French Paradox, Dublin

GEORGINA CAMPBELL'S ireland

Pub of the Year

Roundwood Inn

Roundwood, Co. Wicklow

See page 483

2006 WINNER:

Vaughans Anchor Inn, Co Clare

GEORGINA CAMPBELL'S ireland

Hosts of the Year

Seamus & Aoife Brock

Teach de Broc, Ballybunion, Co. Kerry

See page 287

2006 WINNER:

Mrs. Vi McDowell, Gray's Guesthouse, Co Mayo

GEORGINA CAMPBELL'S ireland

Atmospheric Restaurant of the Year

La Péniche

Grand Canal, Mespil Road, Dublin

See page 107

2006 WINNER:

Toddies Restaurant, Co Cork

AWARD WINNER

GEORGINA CAMPBELL'S ireland

B&B of the Year

Killyon House
Navan, Co. Meath

See page 398

2006 WINNER:

Quay House, Clifden, Co Galway

GEORGINA CAMPBELL'S ireland

Country House of the Year

Rathmullan House

Rathmullan, Co. Donegal

See page 251

2006 WINNER:

Delphi Lodge, Leenane, Co Galway

AWARD WINNER

AWARD WINNER

GEORGINA CAMPBELL'S ireland

Farmhouse of the Year

Glasha

Ballymacarbry, Co. Waterford

See page 437

2006 WINNER:

Glendine House, Arthurstown, Co Wexford

GEORGINA CAMPBELL'S ireland

AWARD WINNER

Family Friendly Hotel of the Year

Dingle Skellig Hotel

Dingle, Co. Kerry

See page 293

2005 WINNER:

Kelly's Resort Hotel, Rosslare, Co Wexford

TASTE AND TRADITION

Rudd's

SPONSORS OF

Georgina Campbell's Irish Breakfast Awards

— Hotel —

Portaferry Hotel

Portaferry, Co. Down

— Country House —

Ballinderry Park

Ballinasloe, Co. Galway

— Guesthouse —

Glenogra House

Dublibn

— B&B —

Killyon House

Navan, Co. Meath

— Café —

Farmgate Café

Cork

TASTE AND TRADITION

Rudd's

SPONSORS OF

Georgina Campbell's Irish Breakfast Awards — National Winner —

Farmgate Café

English Market, Cork

See page 182

2006 WINNER:

Quay House, Clifden, Co Galway

A Taste of Ireland

Irish Hospitality

Visitors to contemporary Ireland find a prosperous country where urban life is fast paced and city streets traffic laden - but, although the Irish are under increasing pressure of work, they still enjoy the good things in life, especially good food and breaks taken with family and friends.

Irish hospitality is legendary and, although the pace of modern life does take its toll, there are many people offering food, drink and accommodation all over Ireland who love nothing better than getting to know their guests and helping them to get every last drop of enjoyment out of a visit to this conntry and - most patricularly - to their own area. They say all politics is local and the same is true of hospitality - in a world of increasing sameness, it's the local differences that count and the most rewarding way to travel in Ireland is by visiting the people who care about the area they live in. And, despite the huge amount of development that has taken place in recent years, you will still find that, beyond the bustle of urban centres, lies stunningly beautiful countryside: lakes, rivers, picturesque villages, and the gentler pace of life in rural Ireland.

Trends

Ireland cannot claim to be a low cost destination, but independent travellers visiting this country today will find that the quality of accommodation and food is generally high, and that a growing number of estabishments are specialising in providing for the most discerning of guests, and giving value at all price levels - as the wide-ranging entries in this guide clearly demonstrate, this is true at every level, whether you seek a luxurious place to stay, a small but special retreat, a fine meal for a special occasion or a bite to eat based on the highest local and speciality foods.

Courtesy of Sharwood's

Irish society is becoming increasingly cosmoplitan and this - plus the influence of international food fashion - has led to a multi-cultural cooking style in many restaurants, and rapid growth in the number and variety of ethnic restaurants and shops. All the main food cultures are well represented and the best rstaurants - where you will find an emphasis on authenticity, rather than westernised versions of ethnic cuisines - are included in the guide. While Italian and Chinese restaurants are common in every corner of the island, you'll also find many others including regional French, Spanish tapas (blossoming of late), Indian, Thai, Nepalese and, since the enlargement of the Euopean Union, an increasing number of Eastern European cuisines.

On the other hand there is enormous interest in Irish food and, particularly, the artisan food products thaat are flourishing throughout the country. Over the last fifteen years, the influence and strength of Euro-toques (The European Community of Chefs) has been a real force for good in reawakening interest and pride in the value of locally produced, traditional foodstuffs and the leading chefs have put a creative, often innovative, spin on traditional Irish dishes. The result is a contemporary Irish cuisine that is "entirely itself"-an Irish idiom that indicates our high regard for an individual approach to life and living.

Style & Value

Some welcome current trends result from the higher value placed on seasonal and local food - including a move away from the very complex dishes that have been fashionable in recent years, towards a simpler style with more emphasis on the taste and flavour of top quality ingredients. The growth of interest in wine is also very noticeable, many restaurants have expanded the number of good value house wines and half bottles on their wine lists - and, most interestingly, many more are now offering a wide range of wines by the glass. Giving value for money is also a high priority and visitors who wish to eat well without breaking the budget will often find that the best value is offered on early dinner menus and fixed price two-course menus- and lunchtime remains the least costly way of enjoying a meal in our leading restaurants, where a stunning meal may often be found at a surprisngly reasonable price. A Sunday curiosity worth keeping an eye out for is the extended lunch hour, sometimes running from noon to seven in the evening.

The Irish Breakfast

Traditional Irish breakfasts known as "the full Irish" are substantial and lingering over a leisurely breakfast remains an essential part of being on holiday. In some establishments the traditional morning meal of oatmeal and fruit followed by bacon, sausage, black and white pudding, eggs, mushrooms, and tomatoes accompanied by Irish soda bread and scones, has become but one choice from an elaborate menu. You'll also be offered fresh or smoked fish dishes, vegetarian dishes, local farmhouse cheeses, traditional cured hams and other cured meats and salamis.

Potato Pancakes with Fried Eggs & Bacon

These traditional potato cakes are delicious just served warm with a knob of butter: Makes 8-10 pancakes approx.

Potato Pancakes

4 large potatoes, cooked and mashed
2 eggs, beaten
3 tablesp. flour
1 teasp. baking powder
Salt and pepper
125-250ml ($^1/_3$-$^1/_2$ pt) milk
Butter for frying
4 eggs
4 rashers of bacon, back or streaky

To Cook

Place the potatoes in the food processor. Add the eggs, flour, baking powder and seasoning. Blend everything together, then gradually add the milk - just enough to give you a thick batter. Heat a non-stick pan, and butter lightly. Place spoonfuls of the mixture on the hot pan and cook gently for 2-3 minutes on each side until fully cooked and nicely browned. Remove from the pan and keep warm.

Fry the eggs and bacon and serve with the potato pancakes.

Artisan and speciality foods

Our siren call "Ireland the food island" is more than a clever sales slogan. We are a food producing nation-far more than we can eat ourselves. In support of their mission to promote Irish food, Bord Bia (The Irish Food Board) has initiated programmes that have had a genuinely beneficial effect on the quality and diversity of Irish foods available to chefs and their customers. The Féile Bia programme (a celebration of food) is a partnership initiative between Bord Bia, The Restaurants Association of Ireland and The Hotels Federation of Ireland, supported by the farming community. The scheme covers beef, lamb, pork, bacon, chicken and eggs, produced under Quality Assurance schemes, mainly (although not exclusively) by large scale food producers.

The developments in promotion of food and horticulture as a result of the amalgamation of Bord Bia and Bord Glas (Irish Horticulture Board) allows the joint expertise of both organisations to promote and market food and horticulture at home and abroad and to provide an integrated offering to consumers. Certainly, it's likely to underpin the trend towards offering

creative vegetarian dishes, the increased use of seasonal fruit and vegetables from named local growers, and the increasing popularity of organic vegetables.

An initiative to support the development of small food producers is also in operation, the TASTE Council (acronym for traditional, artisan, speciality, trade expertise) is coordinated by Bord Bia. Its main aim is to support the growing number of craft food producers to develop, distribute and market their products; also to offer a focus for small food producers that allows them to draw on expertise within the group itself. Membership of the council includes small food producers, organic growers, representatives of relevant organisations like Cáis (the Irish Farmhouse Cheesemakers Association), Euro-Toques (The European Community of Chefs), and retailers and distributors who specialise in traditional, artisan and speciality foods.

Bord Bia works with over 300 small speciality food producers (just part of a growing number of artisan food producers), a sector that continues to expand, driven by consumer demand at home and abroad. EU agricultural reforms, particularly de-coupling, has concentrated farmers' minds on ways and means to survive in the leaner, meaner climate. Those who believe they have the capacity to expand profitably can do so without the need to acquire quotas, or rights to trade. Adaptable farmers see this as an opportunity to cut out the middle man and sell direct to the customer by turning their produce into consumer goods that can be sold locally and at food markets. Markets are a great place for producers and farmers to get mutual support from fellow producers, to get feedback on their produce and ideas for improvement, and just interact with consumers in a way that Irish farmers have not done for generations.

The Local Food Market Revolution

The widespread revival of local food markets has been one of the most exciting achievements of the last few years. If you come from anywhere else in Europe you will wonder why they were in need of reviving. For historical reasons (you'd almost need a degree in Irish history to understand them) local food markets, widespread and highly organised since Norman times had, apart a few, all but died out. Now to the delight of food lovers all that has changed. For a nation that treasures individualism there is a remarkable degree of mutual support between artisan food producers and other interested parties. The Irish Food Market Traders Association addresses the many and varied needs of food market traders - spread around the country by their very nature, there was little contact with each other, so the association was set up to

give strength, structure and negotiating power to this disparate group of individuals and protect their historical and legal rights to sell food direct to the public at local markets. They have established a safety committee who try to maintain meaningful dialogue with local health and safety officers; Bord Bia lend a helping hand with a web-based service offering advice and assistance for people wishing to establish a market and also (via the internet) promoting the thirty-two regular farmers' markets and one held in September during the Food At Farmleigh month - this is one of the events when the state guest house (normally devoted to offering hospitality to state guests) is open to the public.

Irish Farmers Markets

Markets are a wonderful way of experiencing Irish food - a chance to buy food for a picnic, to taste traditional and innovative food products from traditional smoked wild salmon, trout, mackerel, smoked mussels, or smoked scallops, fish patés, seafood soups and seaweeds (an ancient tradition in Ireland). Farmhouse cheeses are one of the glories of artisan producers and there about 70 farmhouse cheesemakers, each producing cheeses that are unique to the family and farmland. Here, too, you will find distinctive Irish breads, biscuits and cakes. A surprising Irish speciality is handcrafted chocolates filled with cream and Irish liqueurs; fine examples are winners of Irish Food Writers Guild Chocolate Lovers' Awards: Gallwey's made in Co Waterford and Eve's made in Cork. Soft fruit and wild berries are often made into gorgeous preserves and chutneys. Traditional dry cures of bacon and ham are found alongside innovative smoked and cured meats, like the award-winning smoked Connemara lamb and smoked Irish beef, both innovative creations of young craft butcher James McGeough of Oughterard. This year he won both the top prize at The Irish Food Writers Guild Food Awards and The Craft Butchers Speciality Foods Competition.

Bord Bia guide - farmers food markets, held regularly in many cities, towns & villages:

CO ANTRIM
- Origin Farmers Market Castlecroft, Main St, Ballymoney. Last Saturday of month 11-2pm.
- City Food And Garden Market, St George's Street, Belfast. Saturday 9-4pm.
- Lisburn Market, Every Saturday.

CO ARMAGH
- Portadown Market. Last Saturday of month.

CO CARLOW
- Carlow Farmers Market, Potato Market, Carlow, Saturday 9-2pm.

CO CLARE
- Ballyvaughan Farmers Market, The Old Schoolhouse, Ballyvaughan. *Check details: Jenny Morton - 065 7077941.
- Ennis Farmers Market, Car Park, Upper Main Street. Friday 8-2pm.
- Killaloe Farmers Market , Between the Waters. Sunday 11-3pm.
- Kilrush Farmers Market, The Square. Thursday 9-2pm.
- Shannon Farmers Market, Drumgeely Shopping Area. Friday 12.30-7pm.

CO CORK
- Ballydehob Food Market, Community Hall. Friday 10.30-12pm. Bandon Market, Bandon. Friday 10.30-1pm.
- Bantry Market, Main Square, 1st Friday of month.
- Castletownbere, 1st Thursday of month.
- Clonakilty Farmers Market, McCurtain Hill. Thursdays & Sundays 10-2pm.
- Cobh Market, Sea Front, Friday 10-1pm.
- Cornmarket Street Market, Cornmarket Street, Saturday 9-3pm. Douglas Food Market, Douglas Community Park, Saturday 9.30-2pm.
- Dunmanway, The Old Mill, Castle St, Fridays 10-2pm.
- English Market Cork, entrances on Princes St & Grand Parade. Daily

- Fermoy Farmers Market, Opposite Cork Marts, Saturday 9-1pm.
- Inchigeelagh Market, Creedons Hotel, Last Saturday of month.
- Mahon Point Farmers Market, West Entrance, Mahon Point, Shopping Centre, Thursday 10-2pm.
- Macroom Farmers Market, The Square, Tuesday 9-3pm.
- Mallow - Blackwater Valley Farmers Market, Nano Nagle Centre, Every 2nd Saturday 10.30-1pm.
- Midleton Farmers Market, Hospital Road, Saturday.
- Mitchelstown Farmers Market, Main Square, Saturday 9-1pm
- Schull Farmers Market, Car Park Near Pier, Sunday 10-3pm.
- Skibbereen Farmers Market, Old Market Square, Saturday 10-2pm.

CO LONDONDERRY

- Guildhall Country Fair, Last Sat in month.

CO DONEGAL

- Ballybofey Farmers Market GAA grounds, Friday 12-4pm.

CO DOWN

- Newry-Dundalk Farmers Market, Newry Marketplace, John Mitchell Place, Friday 9am-2pm

CO DUBLIN

- Dalkey Market, Dalkey Town Hall, Fri 10-4pm.
- Dundrum Farmers Market, Airfield House, Saturday 10-4pm.
- Dun Laoghaire Harbour Market, Sat 10-4pm.
- Dun Laoghaire People's Park Market, People's Park, Sunday 11-4pm.
- Dun Laoghaire Shopping Centre, Thursdays 10-5pm.
- Farmleigh Food Market, Farmleigh House, 2007 dates TBC.
- Fingal Food Fayre, Fingal Arts Centre, Last Sunday every month.
- Howth Harbour Market, The Harbour, Howth, Sunday 10-3pm.
- Leopardstown Farmers Market, Leopardstown Racecourse, Friday 11-7pm.
- Malahide Market, Garden Centre, Saturday 11-5pm.
- Marley Park Food Market, Marlay Park Craft Courtyard, Saturday 10-4pm.
- Monkstown Village Market, Monkstown Parish Church, Saturday 10-4pm.
- Pearse Street Market, St Andrews Centre, Saturday 9.30-3pm.
- Ranelagh Market, Multi Denominational School, Sunday 10-4pm.
- Temple Bar Market, Meeting House Square, Saturday 9-5pm.

CO GALWAY

- Ballinasloe Farmers Market, Croffy's Centre, Main Street, Fridays, 10-3pm.
- Galway Market, Beside St Nicholas Church, Saturday, 8.30-4pm & Sunday 2-6pm.

CO KERRY

- Cahirciveen Market, Community Centre, Thursday 10-2pm (Jun-Sept).
- Caherdaniel Market, Village Hall, Friday 10-12am (Jun-Sept & Christmas).
- Dingle Farm Produce & Craft Market, by the fishing harbour near bus stop. Friday 9.30-4pm
- Kenmare Farmers Market, Wed - Sun 10-6pm (7 days Jul-Aug).
- Listowel Food Fair, Seanchai Centre, Thursday 10-1pm.
- Milltown Market, Old Church, Sat 10-2pm.
- Milltown Market, Organic Centre, Tuesday - Friday, 2-5pm.
- Sneem Market, Community Centre, Tuesday 11-2pm (Jun-Sept & Christmas).
- Tralee Farmers Market, Friday 9-5pm.

CO KILDARE

- Athy Farmers Market, Emily Square, Sunday 10-2pm.
- Larchill Market, Larchill Arcadian Gardens, 3rd Sunday in month
- Naas Farmers Market, The Storehouse Restaurant, Saturday 10-3pm.
- Newbridge Farmers Market, The Courtyard Shopping Centre, Friday 10-3pm.

CO KILKENNY

- Kilkenny Farmers Market, Gowran Park, 1st & 3rd Sunday of month.

CO LEITRIM

- Origin Farmers Market (Manorhamilton), Beepark Resource Centre, Last Friday of each month.

CO LIMERICK

- Abbeyfeale Farmers Market, Parish Hall, Friday 9-1pm.
- Kilmallock Farmers Market, The Kilmallock GAA Club, Friday 9-1pm.
- Limerick Milk Market, Saturday 8-1.30pm.

CO LONGFORD

- Longford Farmers Market, Temperance Hall, Saturday 9.30-1pm.

CO LOUTH

- Castlebellingham Farmers Market, Bellingham Castle Hotel, 1st Sunday of month.
- Dundalk Farmers Market, The County Museum, Jocelyn St, Saturday 10am-2pm.

CO MEATH

- Kells Farmers Market, FBD Insurance Grounds, Saturday 10-2pm

CO MONAGHAN

- Monaghan Farmers / Country Market, Castleblayney Livestock Salesyard,
- Last Saturday of month, 9-1pm.

CO OFFALY

- The Full Moon Market, The Chestnut Courtyard, Every 3rd Sunday
- Tullamore Country Fair, Millenium Square, Saturday 9-4pm.

CO ROSCOMMON

- Origin Farmers Market (Boyle), Grounds of King House, Saturday, 10-2pm.

CO SLIGO

- Origin Farmers Market (Sligo) IT Sports Field Car Park. Saturday.

CO TIPPERARY

- Cahir Farmers Market, Beside The Craft Granary, Saturday 9-1pm.
- Clonmel Farmers Market, St Peter & Paul's Primary School, Kickham Street, beside Oakville Shopping Centre, Saturday 10-2pm.
- Carrick-on-Suir, Heritage Centre, Main St, Friday 10-2pm.
- Nenagh Farmers Market, Teach an Lean, 1st Saturday of month 10-2pm.

CO TYRONE

- Origin Farmers Market (Strabane), The Score Centre, Dock Rd. Last Sat of month.
- Tyrone Farmers Market, Dungannon, Tesco Carpark, 1st Saturday of month 8.30-1pm.

CO WATERFORD

- Dunhill Farmers Market, Parish Hall, Last Sunday of month 11.30-2pm.
- Dungarvan Farmers Market, Scanlon's Yard (beside Friary St & Mary St), Thursday 9.30-2pm.
- Lismore Farmers Market, Blackwater Valley, Stradbally Community Market, 1st Saturday of month, 10-12.30pm.
- Waterford Farmers Market, Jenkins Lane, Saturday 10-4pm.

CO WESTMEATH

- Athlone Farmers Market, Market Square, Athlone, Saturday 10-3pm.
- Mullingar Farmers Market, Harbour Place Shopping Centre,1st & 3rd Sunday of Month.

CO WEXFORD

- New Ross Farmers Market, Conduit Lane, Saturday 9-2pm.
- Wexford Farmers Market, Dunbrody, Dunbrody Abbey Centre, Sun 12-3.30pm.
- Wexford Farmers Market Community Partnership, The Abbey Square Carpark, Saturday 9-2pm.
- Wexford Farmers Market, Trimmers Lane West (beside La Dolce Vitae Restaurant), Friday 9-2pm.

CO WICKLOW

- Brooklodge Organic Market, Macreddin Village, 1st & 3rd Sunday of month.
- Glendalough Farmers Market, Brockagh Resource Centre, 2nd Sun of month 11-6pm.
- Kilcoole, Saturdays, 10.30 - 11.30am.
- Powerscourt Waterfall Market, Farmyard, almost next to Powerscourt Waterfall 2nd and 4th Sunday of every month.
- Bray, Killarney Road near the Boghall Road, Saturday 10-3pm.
- Bray Seafront Market, Albert Avenue, just across from the aquarium. Friday & Sunday weekly

NB: Times, days and locations of markets do sometimes change; be sure to check locally or log on to: www.bordbia.ie/go/Consumers/Buying_Food/farmers_markets

FÉILE BIA- CERTIFIED FARM TO FORK

Féile Bia is a year round programme that emphasises the importance of food sourcing in hotels, restaurants, pubs and workplaces throughout the country. Féile Bia was introduced in 2001 in response to growing consumer concerns on the origins of food offered when eating out. Féile Bia is the consumer's reassurance that the fresh beef, lamb, pork, bacon, chicken and eggs being served are fully traceable from farm to fork and have been produced under a Quality Assurance Scheme.

When you see the Féile Bia logo displayed in a restaurant, hotel or pub you can be sure of the origin of the food being served. There are 1,300 members so far and the number is growing all the time. Those establishments recommended by the guide which have signed up to the charter are listed below and are identified within the body of the guide by the use of the Féile Bia logo.

THE FÉILE BIA AWARD

Each year, in the Guide, we single out for the Féile Bia Award an establishment that we feel is interpeting the Féile Bia message especially well and not only putting into practice the principles of Quality Assurance and traceability, but doing so in a creative and pro-active manner, with the enthusiastic inclusion of local and speciality foods on their menus. This year's winner is The Ballymore Inn, at Ballymore Eustace, Co Kildare - and these recipes are typical of the delicious food they serve in the bar and café-restaurant.

Lamb Pizza with Yogurt and Mint

At the Ballymore Inn, they are renowned for their crisp homemade thin-based pizzas, although you could use a ready-made pizza base for this at home if you wish. In this pizza they use Slaney lamb for its quality and flavour - it makes a popular starter to share in the café, or enjoyed with a pint in the 'Back Bar'!

Mince topping: (you can make as much as you like, it also makes a great pasta sauce). Sauté some chopped onion, add the minced lamb and brown well together. Add chopped garlic, tomatoes, a pinch of cinnamon and seasoning. Cook and set aside.

Pizza: Set the oven to maximum. Spread a pizza base with some chopped tomatoes, olive oil and chopped basil. Sprinkle with Parmesan, then add the lamb topping and a few pieces of chopped mozzarella. Bake in the hot oven until crispy on the base and well cooked. Just before serving, drizzle with some natural yogurt and chopped mint.

Crispy Beef Stirfry with Broccoli, Chili and Lime

Beef used at The Ballymore Inn is all prime quality Irish beef, and aged for 3 weeks to guarantee tenderness. Serves 2.

STIRFRY:
1 tablesp. oil
300g beef fillet, thinly sliced
1 dessertsp. cornflour plus seasoning
Broccoli, mushrooms, & mange tout, chopped
A little garlic and fresh ginger root, chopped

DRESSING:
Juice of 2 limes
2 teasp. sugar
1 tablesp sweet chilli sauce
1 tablesp. soy sauce

To cook:

Heat a wok until very hot. Add the oil. Coat the beef in the seasoned cornflour and stir-fry until crispy. Add in the vegetables. Stir-fry for a minute or two with the garlic and ginger. Add in the dressing ingredients and boil for another minute, then serve.

The Ballymore Inn Lemon Tart

Each day there's a 'tart of the day' on the menu. Saturday night is Lemon Tart - the best! Serves 8.

PASTRY:
180g butter
75g icing sugar
2 egg yolks
225g plain flour

FILLING:
300g sugar
9 eggs
5 lemons, juice and rind
350mls cream, lightly whipped

TART TIN: 28cm diameter x 3cm deep

To Prepare:

PASTRY: Mix the butter, icing sugar and egg yolks together in the processor, add in the flour. Gather up the pastry and chill for an hour. Set oven at 180°c, roll out the pastry as thinly as possible and line the tin. Bake blind for 25mins.

FILLING: Lightly beat the sugar and eggs together. Add in the lemon juice and rind. Fold in the cream and mix well. Pour the filling into the pastry case, reduce the heat to 150°c and bake for 45 minutes, or until just set.

Cool before slicing, then serve with sliced figs in caramel, or any seasonal fruit.

EURO-TOQUES
(The European Community of Chefs)

Local sourcing from small, artisan producers is central to the ethos of Euro-toques chefs. One of their principal aims is to protect the quality, diversity and flavour of our food and to promote indigenous and traditional production methods. Euro-toques have been diligent in representing the interests of their own members but also those of the network of small producers who supply them and the consumers they cater for. With over two hundred members and an energetic and vibrant organisation presently led by Martin Dwyer, Commissioner-General of Euro-toques Ireland. The Euro-toque ethos has been of immeasurable value in the creation of a unique contemporary Irish cuisine that many Irish people now take for granted. Creative and dedicated they may be, but they come out of their kitchen when needs be. For example they have been active in lobbying (and encouraging other organisations to lobby) against any threat to the diversity and quality of Irish food. At a recent annual Food Forum they tackled the dangers of introducing genetically modified food crops into Ireland. Calling on the government to make Ireland a GM-free zone, the Euro-Toques statement said: "Cross contamination of organic and conventional crops will inevitably occur and consumers will have no choice about eating GM foods. In our experience people are increasingly looking for traditionally and naturally produced foods. They simply don't want GM foods." Euro-toques are also diligent in developing young chefs, nurturing the particularly talented through the annual Bailey's/Euro-toques Young Chef of the Year Competition and coaching Ireland's representatives at international cooking competitions including the prestigious Bocuse d'Or.

The Small Foods Initiative is another interesting programme that has run over the last two years. Focused on the border counties and Northern Ireland, it is an INTERREG IIIA project (Ireland/Northern Ireland) to foster communication between chefs and small food producers and develop the latter's ability to supply and aid chefs in sourcing quality ingredients. They hope, in time, this will have a positive influence on the standard of food generally available in Ireland.

Slow Food

The international Slow Food Movement has caught the imagination of food lovers. Despite the name it's a fast-growing movement and over the last year many more local convivia have been established. The movement's emblem, the snail (a small, cosmopolitan and prudent animal), stands as the symbol of a movement that exists to spread awareness of food culture, to safeguard agricultural heritage techniques, to defend biodiversity in crops, craft techniques, food traditions, and eating places. Members are free to attend international Slow Food events but, probably, what appeals even more to the Irish independence of spirit is that local activities are led from the bottom up-local convivia meet regularly to explore with like-minded people their own small corner. It provides a meeting ground with artisan food producers, with growers and traditional farmers, to share knowledge and support those who work in harmony with the principles of the movement.

Bord Iascaigh Mhara (BIM)

Located at the outermost edge of Europe with clean Atlantic waters warmed along much of the coast by the Gulf Stream, these waters yield a wonderful harvest of seafood. Bord Iascaigh Mhara (The Irish Sea Fisheries Board-BIM) is dedicated to the development of the seafood industry working closely with all sectors from fisherman to fish farmer, processor, retailer and chef. As well as safeguarding Ireland's fishing waters, BIM plays a role in the development of aquaculture, supporting the trend towards environmentally friendly and organic fish farming, as well as the cultivation of shellfish like oysters, clams, scallops and mussels.

IRISH SEAFOOD - SOMETHING SPECIAL.

Luscious Dublin Bay prawns, succulent oysters, melt in the mouth mussels, tempting smoked salmon, mouth-watering mackerel, tantalising monkfish...just some of the delicious seafood you'll find on menus right round Ireland. Irish people love to eat seafood when dining out; in fact, unlike our European neighbours, we eat more seafood outside the home (perhaps this is a testament to the quality of our restaurants). Visitors to Ireland also place a high value on the range and quality of Irish seafood. For many, a trip to Ireland wouldn't be complete without sampling a few oysters and sinking a pint of the black stuff.

Wonderful seafood is found in a vast range of establishments, from award winning restaurants to hotels, little bistros and pubs. Locally caught seafood is especially good and is often flagged on the menu. Seafood is incredibly versatile, allowing chefs to creative innovative dishes suitable for all meal occasions whether it's a breakfast, light lunch, quick snack or gourmet dinner. Irish seafood is renowned for its quality and flavour and is much sought after in markets worldwide. Smoked Irish salmon finds a ready market in France, Italy and Germany while Irish mussels are enjoyed as far afield as the west coast of America. Pub goers in Toyko are snacking on Irish crab, salmon and mussels and in Spain monkfish and hake from Irish waters are snapped up.

BIM Seafood Circle

The BIM Seafood Circle initiative was initially set up as programme encouraging pubs to serve seafood dishes at lunchtime, a meal at which many people prefer to choose lighter, healthier dishes. This has been further developed in conjunction with Georgina Campbell Guides to encompass not only pubs but also restaurants and hotels. The programme also covers fish retailers. Check out the listings in this guide and you'll find top quality, innovative, delicious seafood dishes in the establishments carrying the distinctive Seafood Circle logo.

And if you fancy yourself as seafood chef then watch out for the Seafood Circle specialist/seafood counter logos in fish shops around the country or check www.bim.ie/seafoodcircle for a listing. Shops displaying the logo offer a range of top quality seafood and you'll be assisted by knowledgeable, professional staff.

Nutritionists recommend we eat seafood at least twice a week. They are packed with protein, minerals and vitamins, seafood provides many of the nutrients we need for good health. BIM has developed a range of information materials on the health benefits of fish consumption. Visit www.bim.ie/wellbeing for nutritional information and great recipe ideas.

Garlic Stuffed Mussels

Mussels grow in the wild all around the Irish coast, and they are also farmed - through a very natural process whereby mussels attach themselves to ropes provided in clean tidal waters; there they feed naturally, and can then be harvested easily and cleanly. This classic recipe is one of the most popular dishes served in the many restaurants and bars offering Irish seafood, and is easy to make at home. Serves 4.

INGREDIENTS
2 kilos Irish mussels
A little white wine
250g butter
4 / 5 cloves garlic - crushed or finely chopped
2 tablespoon chopped fresh parsley
Juice and zest of one lemon
120g / 4 handfuls fine white breadcrumbs
Salt and pepper

METHOD

Remove the mussel beards, and wash the mussels well, discarding any that do not close when tapped, and drain. Steam in a large saucepan with a splash of white wine for 3 or 4 minutes until they open. Discard any which remain closed. Remove the top shell from each mussel. Arrange the bottom shell and flesh on an ovenproof dish or baking tray.

Melt the butter, add crushed garlic, parsley and lemon juice. Mix through the breadcrumbs and season with salt and pepper. Use a spoon or clean hands to place a small amount of the crumb mixture onto each mussel, just covering the meat. Grill or bake until golden brown and crispy (Approx 2/3 minutes)

Serve with a lemon wedge, and a fresh herb garnish of your choice.

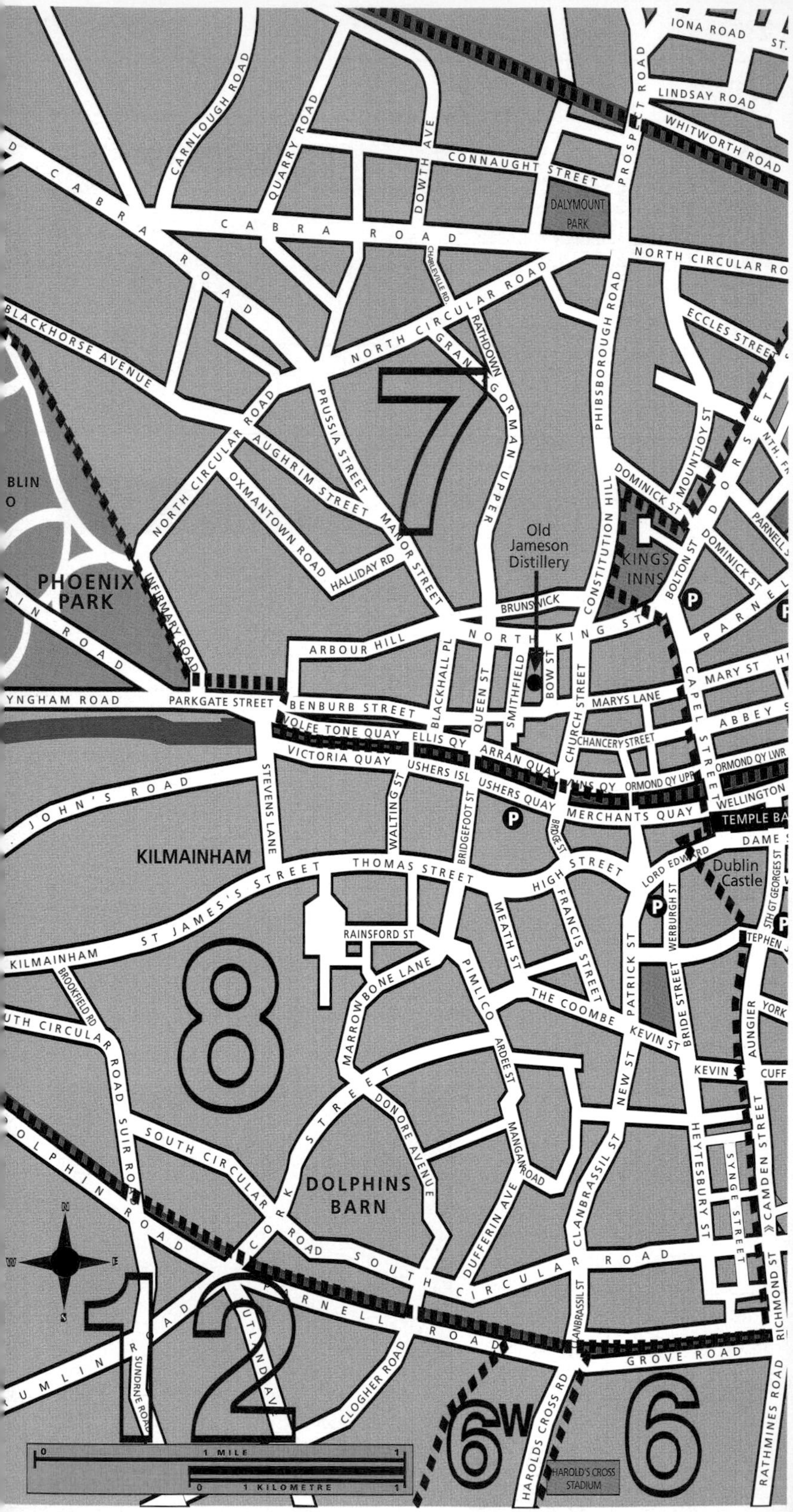
PHOENIX PARK
KILMAINHAM
DOLPHINS BARN
Old Jameson Distillery
KINGS INNS
Dublin Castle
TEMPLE BAR
DALYMOUNT PARK
HAROLD'S CROSS STADIUM
CABRA ROAD
NORTH CIRCULAR ROAD
PHIBSBOROUGH ROAD
PRUSSIA STREET
MANOR STREET
NORTH KING ST
ARBOUR HILL
PARKGATE STREET
BENBURB STREET
WOLFE TONE QUAY
VICTORIA QUAY
ARRAN QUAY
USHERS QUAY
MERCHANTS QUAY
THOMAS STREET
ST JAMES'S STREET
HIGH STREET
CORK STREET
SOUTH CIRCULAR ROAD
PARNELL ROAD
GROVE ROAD
DOLPHIN ROAD
CRUMLIN ROAD
CONNAUGHT STREET
CAPEL STREET
DORSET ST
PATRICK ST
NEW ST
CLANBRASSIL ST
RATHMINES ROAD
THE COOMBE
1 MILE
1 KILOMETRE
7
8
12
6W
6

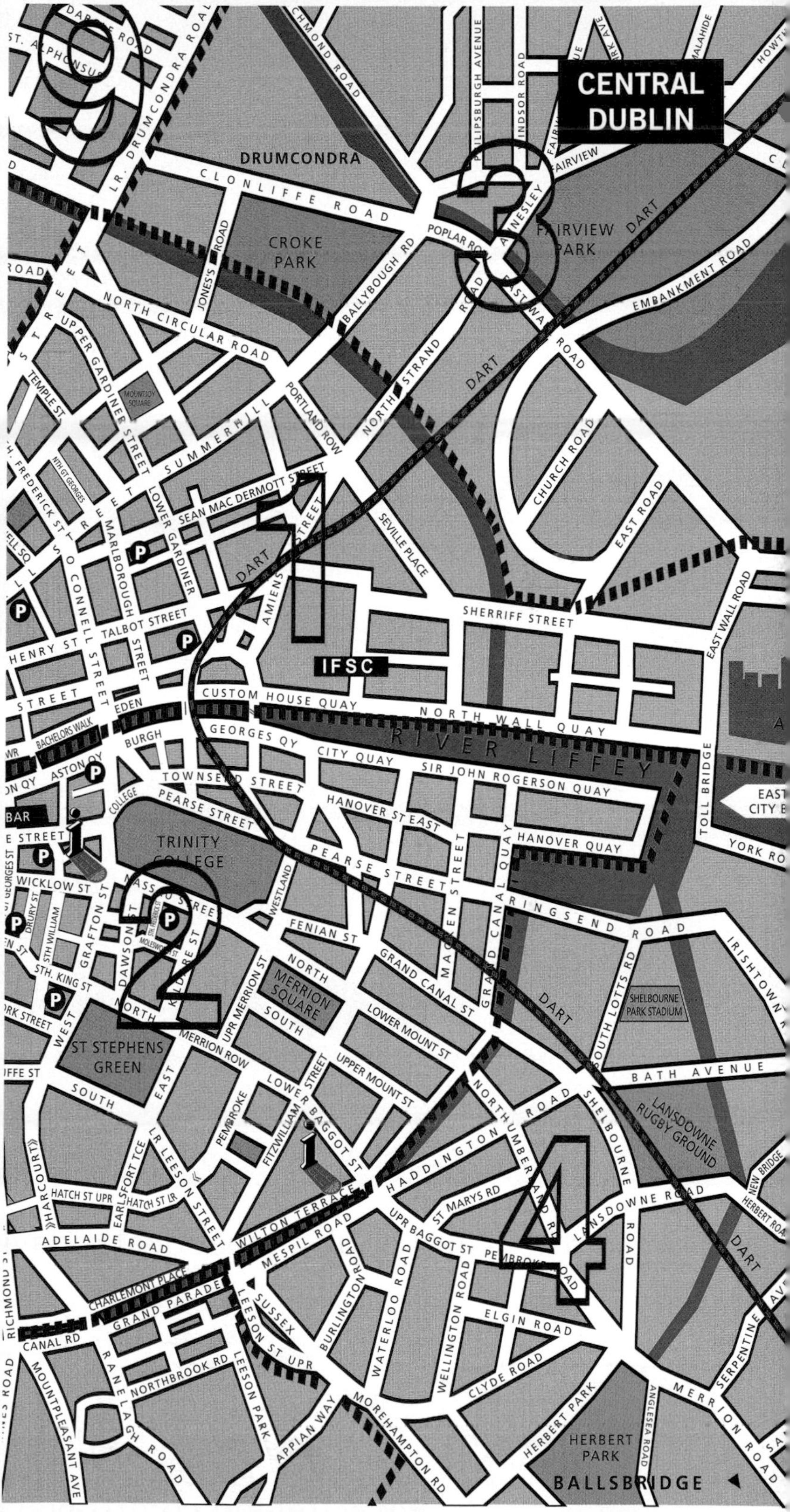
CENTRAL DUBLIN
DRUMCONDRA
CLONLIFFE ROAD
CROKE PARK
FAIRVIEW PARK
FAIRVIEW
DART
EMBANKMENT ROAD
POPLAR ROW
ANNESLEY
BALLYBOUGH RD
NORTH CIRCULAR ROAD
JONES'S ROAD
LR. DRUMCONDRA ROAD
ST. ALPHONSUS
UPPER GARDINER STREET
MOUNTJOY SQUARE
TEMPLE ST
SUMMERHILL
PORTLAND ROW
NORTH STRAND
EAST WALL ROAD
CHURCH ROAD
EAST ROAD
SEAN MAC DERMOTT STREET
SEVILLE PLACE
AMIENS STREET
SHERRIFF STREET
LOWER GARDINER
MARLBOROUGH
O CONNELL STREET
TALBOT STREET
HENRY ST
IFSC
CUSTOM HOUSE QUAY
NORTH WALL QUAY
RIVER LIFFEY
GEORGES QY
CITY QUAY
SIR JOHN ROGERSON QUAY
TOWNSEND STREET
HANOVER ST EAST
HANOVER QUAY
PEARSE STREET
TRINITY COLLEGE
BACHELORS WALK
ASTON QY
BURGH
EDEN
COLLEGE
TOLL BRIDGE
YORK RO
WICKLOW ST
GRAFTON ST
DAWSON ST
KILDARE ST
WESTLAND
FENIAN ST
MACKEN STREET
GRAND CANAL QUAY
RINGSEND ROAD
IRISHTOWN
SOUTH LOTTS RD
SHELBOURNE PARK STADIUM
GRAND CANAL ST
MERRION SQUARE
LOWER MOUNT ST
UPPER MOUNT ST
UPR MERRION ST
MERRION ROW
ST STEPHENS GREEN
STH. KING ST
DRURY ST
STH WILLIAM
LOWER BAGGOT ST
FITZWILLIAM ST
PEMBROKE
LR LEESON STREET
EARLSFORT TCE
HATCH ST UPR
HATCH ST LR
HARCOURT
ADELAIDE ROAD
WILTON TERRACE
HADDINGTON ROAD
NORTHUMBERLAND ROAD
BATH AVENUE
LANSDOWNE RUGBY GROUND
LANSDOWNE ROAD
SHELBOURNE ROAD
NEW BRIDGE
HERBERT ROAD
ST MARYS RD
UPR BAGGOT ST
PEMBROKE ROAD
MESPIL ROAD
CHARLEMONT PLACE
GRAND PARADE
CANAL RD
SUSSEX
LEESON ST UPR
BURLINGTON ROAD
WATERLOO ROAD
WELLINGTON ROAD
ELGIN ROAD
CLYDE ROAD
HERBERT PARK
ANGLESEA ROAD
MERRION ROAD
SERPENTINE AVE
NORTHBROOK RD
LEESON PARK
RANELAGH ROAD
MOUNTPLEASANT AVE
RICHMOND ROAD
APPIAN WAY
MOREHAMPTON RD
BALLSBRIDGE
EAST CITY

Sunset, Lough Erne

DUBLIN

A Town for our Times

As one of Europe's fastest expanding economic centres, Dublin's commercial and creative energy is matched by the vibrancy of its everyday life and hospitality. At its heart is an old town whose many meandering stories have interacted and combined to create today's busy riverside and coastal metropolis. Through a wide variety of circumstances, it has become an entertaining place suited to the civilised enjoyment of life in the 21st Century. That said, there's no doubting the edge there is to life in Dublin today, with the daily business news and movements in property values attracting as much popular interest as sport and politics.

Dubliners tend to wear their city's history lightly, despite having in their environment so much of the past in the way of ancient monuments, historic buildings, gracious squares and fine old urban architecture that still manages to be gloriously alive. This if anything is emphasised by the city's impressive modern developments, seen particularly in the area around the International Financial Services Centre and across the Liffey on George's Quay and around the Grand Canal Harbour. Further regeneration is taking place along the Liffey towards the bay, while the city's spirit is expressed dramatically in the Spire in O'Connell Street, and in the Gaelic Athletic Association's national headquarters at Croke Park, the third largest stadium in Europe.

Dubliners may not quite take their city's dynamic interaction of classic and modern for granted, but nevertheless they have to get on with life. Indeed, these days they've a vigorous appetite for it. So they'll quickly deflate any visitor's excessive enthusiasm about their city's significance with a throw-away line of Dublin wit, or sweep aside highfalutin notions of some legendary figure of established cultural importance by recalling how their grandfathers had the measure of that same character when he was still no more than a pup making a nuisance of himself in the neighbourhood pub.

The origins of the city's name are in keeping with this downbeat approach. From the ancient Irish there came something which derived from a makeshift solution to local inconvenience. Baile Atha Cliath - the official name today - means nothing more exciting than "the townland of the hurdle ford". Ancient Ireland being an open plan sort of place without towns, the future city was no more than a river crossing.

But where the Irish saw inconvenience, the Vikings saw an opportunity. When they brought their long-ships up the River Liffey, they found a sheltered berth in a place which the locals of the hurdle ford called Dubh Linn - "the black pool". Although the name was to go through many mutations as the Vikings were succeeded by the Normans who in turn were in the business of becoming English, today's name of Dublin is remarkably similar to the one which the Vikings came upon, although the old Irish would have pronounced it as something more like "doo-lin".

The modern pre-eminence of that name makes sense, for it was thanks to the existence of the black pool that Dublin became the port and trading base which evolved as the country's natural administrative centre. Thus your Dubliner may well think that the persistent official use of Baile Atha Cliath is an absurdity. But it most emphatically isn't the business of any visitor to say so, for although Dublin came into existence almost by accident, it has now been around for a long time, and Dubliners have developed their own attitudes and their own way of doing things.

As for their seaport, it is still very much part of the city, and has never been busier – with forty major ship movements every day, sea and city are closely intertwined. That said, Dubliners' perception of themselves is starkly defined by whether they live north or south of the Liffey – for a relatively narrow river, it is a remarkable divide.

Located by a wide bay with some extraordinarily handsome hills and mountains near at hand, the city has long had as an important part of its makeup the dictates of stylish living, and the need to cater efficiently for individual tastes and requirements. From time to time the facade has been maintained with difficulty through periods of impoverishment, but even in the earliest mediaeval period this was already a major centre of craftsmanship and innovative shop-keeping. Today, the Dublin craftsmen and shop-keepers and their assistants are characterful subjects worthy of respectful academic study. And in an age when "going shopping" has become the world's favourite leisure activity, this old city has reinvented herself in the forefront of international trends.

For Dublin virtually shunned the Industrial Revolution, or at least its decision-makers took some care to ensure that it happened elsewhere. The city's few large enterprises tended to be aimed at personal needs and the consumer market, rather than some aspiration towards heavy industry. Typical of them was Guinness's Brewery, founded in 1759. Today, its work-force may be much slimmed in every sense, but it still creates the black nectar, and if a new mash is under way up at the brewery and the wind is coming damply across Ireland from the west, the aroma of Guinness in the making will be wafted right into the city centre, the moist evocative essence of Anna Livia herself, while the imaginatively renovated Guinness Storehouse - with its interactive museums, restaurants and bars - provides a visitor centre of international quality

Although some of the vitality of the city faded in the periods when the focus of power had been moved elsewhere, today Dublin thrives as one of Europe's more entertaining capitals, and as a global centre of the computer, communications and financial services industries. While it may be trite to suggest that her history has been a fortuitous preparation for the needs of modern urban life in all its variety of work and relaxation, there is no denying Dublin's remarkable capacity to provide the ideal circumstances for fast-moving people-orientated modern industries, even if those same people find at times that their movement within the city is hampered by weight of traffic. Nevertheless it's a civilised city where the importance of education is a central theme of the strong family ethos, this high level of education making it a place of potent attraction in the age of information technology.

Such a city naturally has much of interest for historians of all kinds, and a vibrant cultural life is available for visitors and Dubliners alike. You can immerse yourself in it all as much or as little as you prefer, for today's Dublin is a city for all times and all tastes, and if you're someone who hopes to enjoy Dublin as we know Dubliners enjoy it, we know you'll find much of value here. And don't forget that there's enjoyment in Dublin well hidden from the familiar tourist trails.

When Dublin was starting to expand to its present size during the mid-20th Century, with people flocking in from all over Ireland to work in the city, it was said that the only "real Dub" was someone who didn't go home to the country for the weekend. Today, with Dublin so popular with visitors, the more cynical citizens might well comment that the surest test of a real Dub is someone who avoids Temple Bar...

But it is rather unfair of any Dubliner to dismiss that bustling riverside hotbed of musical pubs, contemporary cafes, ethnic restaurants, cultural events and nightclubs as being no more than a tourist ghetto. After all, in addition to its many places of entertainment and hospitality, Temple Bar is also home to at least 1,300 people, their needs being served locally by useful happenings such as the Natural Food Fair, held every Saturday (10am to 6pm) in Cow's Lane, with organic foods and the freshest of produce from land and sea matching the gourmet quality of the exotic products sold through the Specialist Market in Meeting House Square.

So there's real life here too. And at the very least, it is Temple Bar which maintains the Dubliner's international reputation as a round-the-clock party animal. Now that the area has settled down and achieved a certain mellowness in its new role, you will definitely meet "real Dubs" here, though in today's very cosmopolitan city, just how we'd define a "real Dub" is a moot point.

Nevertheless, come nightfall and your discerning Dubliner is more likely to be found in a pleasant pub or restaurant in one of the city's many urban villages, delightfully named places such as Ranelagh or Rathmines or Templeogue or Stoneybatter or Phibsborough or Donnybrook or Glasnevin or Ringsend or Dundrum or Clontarf or Drumcondra or Chapelizod, to name only a few. And then there are places like Stepaside or Howth or Glasthule or Foxrock or Dalkey which are at sufficient distance as scarcely to think of themselves as being part of Dublin at all. Yet that's where you'll find today's real Dubs enjoying their fair city every bit as much as city centre folk. Happy is the visitor who is able to savour it all, in and around this town for our times.

Local Attractions & Information

Abbey & Peacock Theatres, Lower Abbey Street	01 878 7222
Andrew's Lane Theatre, off Exchequer Street	01 679 5720
The Ark Arts Centre, Eustace St., Temple Bar D2	01 670 7788
Bank of Ireland (historic), College Green	01 661 5933
Botanic Gardens, Glasnevin, D9	01 837 4388
Ceol - Irish Traditional Music Centre, Smithfield	01 817 3820
Christchurch Cathedral, Christchurch Place, D8	01 677 8099
City Arts Centre, 23-25 Moss St., D2	01 677 0643
Croke Park, GAA Stadium and Museum D3	01 855 8176
Drimnagh Castle (moat, formal 17c gardens) Longmile Rd	01 450 2530
Dublin Airport	01 814 4222
Dublin Castle, Dame Street	01 677 7129

Dublin Film Festival (April)	01 679 2937
Dublin Garden Festival, RDS (June)	01 490 0600
Dublin International Horse Show, RDS, (August)	01 668 0866
Dublin International Organ & Choral Fest. (June)	01 677 3066
Dublin Theatre Festival (October)	01 677 8439
Dublin Tourism Centre (restored church) Suffolk St.	1850 230 330
Dublin Writer's Museum, Parnell Square	01 872 2077
Dublinia (living history), Christchurch	01 475 8137
Farmleigh House, Phoenix Park	01 815 5900
Farmleigh House Boathouse Restaurant	01 815 7255 / 815 7250
Gaiety Theatre, South King Street	01 677 1717
Gate Theatre, Cavendish Row	01 874 4045
Guinness Brewery, St Jame's Gate	01 453 6700 ext 5155
Guinness Storehouse	01 408 4800
Helix DCU Performing Arts Centre, Collins Avenue, D9	01 700 7000
Hugh Lane Municipal Gallery, Parnell Square	01 874 1903
Irish Antique Dealers Fair, RDS (October)	01 285 9294
Irish Film Centre, Eustace Street	01 679 3477
IFSC Farm Market (Mayor Sq., Wed 10.30am-4pm)	087 611 5016
Irish Museum of Modern Art/Royal Hospital Kilmainham	01 671 8666
Irish Music Hall of Fame, Middle Abbey Street	01 878 3345
Irish Tourist Board/Failte Ireland, Baggot St Bridge	01 602 4000
Iveagh Gardens, Earlsfort Terrace	01 475 7816
Jameson Distillery, Smithfield, D7	01 807 2355
Kilmainham Gaol, Kilmainham	01 453 5984
Lansdowne Road Rugby Ground, Ballsbridge	01 668 4601
Mother Redcaps Market nr St Patricks/Christchurch Fri-Sun 10am-5.30pm	
National Botanic Gardens, Glasnevin	01 837 7596
National Concert Hall, Earlsfort Terrace	01 671 1888
National Gallery of Ireland, Merrion Square West	01 661 5133
National Museum of Ireland, Kildare Street	01 677 7444
National Museum of Ireland, Collins Barracks	01 677 7444
Natural History Museum, Merrion Street	01 677 7444
Newman House, St Stephen's Green	01 475 7255
Northern Ireland Tourist Board, Nassau Street	01 679 1977
Number 29 (18c House), Lower Fitzwilliam Street	01 702 6155
Old Jameson Distillery, Smithfield, D7	01 807 2355
Olympia Theatre, Dame Street	01 677 7744
Pearse St Market (St Andrew's Cntr.), Sats 9am-3pm	01 873 0451
Point Depot (Concerts & Exhibitions), North Wall Quay	01 836 6000
Powerscourt Townhouse, South William Street	01 679 4144
Pro Cathedral, Marlborough Street	01 287 4292
Project Arts Centre, 39 East Sussex St, D2	01 679 6622
RDS (Royal Dublin Society), Ballsbridge	01 668 0866
Royal Hospital, Kilmainham	01 679 8666
St Michans Church (mummified remains), D7	01 872 4154
St Patrick's Cathedral, Patrick's Close	01 453 9472
Shaw birthplace, 33 Synge St., D8	01 475 0854
Shelbourne Park Greyhound Stadium	01 668 3502
Temple Bar Foodmarket, Sat morning	01 677 2255
The Dillon Garden, 45 Sandford Rd, Ranelagh, D6	01 497 1308
The Old Jameson Distillery, Smithfield, D7	01 807 2355
Tivoli Theatre, Francis Street	01 454 4472
Trinity College (Book of Kells & Dublin Experience)	01 608 2308
Viking Adventure, Essex St W, Temple Bar,	01 679 6040
Viking Splash (Amphibious Tours)	01 453 9185
War Memorial Gardens (Sir Edwin Lutyens) Islandbridge	01 677 0236
Zoological Gardens, Phoenix Park	01 677 1425

DUBLIN 1

New to the area are budget hotels **Comfort Inn** (Parnell Square; **01 873 7700**) and **Jurys Inn** (Parnell Street; **01 878 4900**); the Hugh Lane Gallery on Parnell Square has a restaurant, **Blas** (Mon-Sat 10-6 pm, Sun 10.30-5) and there is also a café at the **Writers' Museum** (Mon-Sat 10-5). The Moore Street/Parnell Street area is well known for its street markets and specialist food shops catering for an increasingly cosmopolitan population - it has become a hothouse of international flavours and is a place to wander for authentic, keenly priced food from different cultures. The area has many great value ethnic restaurants, including: **Bangkok Café** (Parnell Street; **01 878-6618**). **Cactus Jack's** (Millennium Way; **01 874 6198**): one of a small chain of above average Tex-Mex restaurants (also at Tallaght & Galway City). **China House** (Parnell Street, **01 873 3870**); friendly, authentic, very good value Chinese; **Hanyang** (Parnell Street **01 874 6144**): authentic Korean cuisine & hospitality, beside the **Ice Bar Asian** pub. **Fayruz** (Middle Abbey Street; **01 872 3336**) good budget Lebanese. **Radha Govinda's** (Middle Abbey Street; **01 872 9861**) Hare Krishna restaurant serving wholesome, inexpensive vegetarian food.

IFSC

D.One Restaurant (North Wall Quay; **01 856 1622**): a contemporary glass cube, this restaurant takes full advantage of its waterside location and can be very busy at lunchtime. **Il Fornaio** (Valentia House Square; **01 672 1852**): new and equally informal branch of the long-established authentic Italian pizzeria/restaurant in Kilbarrack, Dublin 5. **Insomnia** (Lr Mayor St, Custom House Quay; **01 671 8651**): one of an excellent small chain of speciality coffee outlets around Dublin (some under the Bendini & Shaw brand, whose complementary speciality is sandwiches. Also at: Charlotte Way, Dublin 1; Ballsbridge, Dublin 4; Main Street Blackrock, Co Dublin; Pavilion SC Swords. **Milano** (Clarion Quay; **01 611 9012**): north quays branch of the stylish and reliable pizza & pasta restaurant chain. **WWW.IRELAND-GUIDE.COM FOR THE BEST PLACES TO EAT, DRINK & STAY**

Dublin 1

RESTAURANT

101 Talbot Restaurant

100-102 Talbot Street Dublin 1

Tel: 01 874 5011 Fax: 01 878 1053 Email: Web: www.101talbot.com

féile bia Good cooking, good value and menus that promise something different from the ubiquitous fashionable offerings elsewhere are at the heart of Margaret Duffy and Pascal Bradley's ground breaking northside restaurant - and they were here a decade ahead of the current gold rush to service the growing needs of the new "city" area in and around the maturing International Financial Services Centre. Its potential may be more obvious today but it is they who created the buzz. While the nearby Abbey and Gate Theatres and the constantly changing art exhibitions in the restaurant are partly responsible for drawing an interesting artistic/theatrical crowd, it is essentially their joyfully creative and healthy food that has earned the 101 such a fine reputation and it is heartening to see standards maintained in a busy city centre restaurant when so many around take the easier option. Mediterranean and Middle Eastern influences explain the uniquely enjoyable wholesomeness across the complete range of dishes offered on hand written menus with six to eight choices on each course, always including strong vegetarian options, such as celeriac rösti topped with spinach & blue cheese, with a sage cream sauce - and dietary requirements are always willingly met. Interesting food, nice little details - friendly staff who welcome arriving guests promptly, the good complimentary breads offered at table, helpful advice with menu choices - and very reasonable prices ensure the continuing success of this popular restaurant. Just don't expect lavish decor - and try to ignore the drabness of Talbot Street, which seems to creep in a little up the lino-clad stairs. Children welcome before 8pm. **Seats 80.** Open Tue-Sat, 5-11. A la carte. Early D €21.50 (5-8, all evening Wed), Set D 2/3 course € 30/35. House Wine €18.95. Closed Sun & Mon, Christmas. Amex, MasterCard, Visa, Laser. **Directions:** 5 minutes walk between Connolly Station and O'Connell Street. Straight down from the spire.

BLOOMS LANE

Known variously as the Italian Quarter (reflecting the collection of of Italian-inspired establishments that have congregated here), occasionally, as 'Quartier Bloom', sometimes as 'Mick Wallaces' (after the inspired developer who created it), or, more usually, simply by its address, this stylish food court off the north quays is home to some interesting restaurants, cafes and shops. It's at its best on Friday night or Saturday lunchtime; on Saturday evening (unless the Italians have won the World Cup that day) it's more 'gloom' than 'Bloom' the street is dark and uninviting, and some atmospheric lighting is needed, to dispel a spooky 'Victorian Whitechapel' feeling. **Enoteca delle Langhe** (01 888 0834), an appealing shop-cum-wine bar, was one of the first to open; food, while not exactly incidental, plays second fiddle to the wines here, but they carry a good range of dried Italian meats, cheeses, panini etc, and you can sit at a sturdy wooden table and have something by the glass (or choose any bottle, plus 10%), and a bite from a limited but interesting selection of quality food, which includes some hot dishes (limited hours) and you can always have cold deli plates, or plates of bruschetta with toppings like sundried tomato pesto, fresh tomato & sautéed courgettes, mortadella & black olive tapénade and perhaps a dessert of hazelnut biscuits with apricots & peaches in amaretto. It's all very relaxed and sociable, prices are reasonable - and it's a pleasant way to shop for wine. Nearby you will also find other like-minded outlets like **Wallaces Italian Food Shop, Café Cagliostro** (great coffees), a juice café and **Taverna di Bacco** (01 873 0040), a dark and atmospheric restaurant, which offers an interesting menu and authentic ingredient-led Italian food, including great antipasta, unusual variations on risotto, handmade pasta dishes and really good coffees And many people head here specially to eat in **Bar Italia** (01 874 1000) chaotic, warm, real food, great coffee, it's the essence of Italy minus cheap local wine. With good restaurants, an excellent deli and the bustling daytime café, Blooms Lane makes a great addition to the atmospherics of Dublin.

WWW.IRELAND-GUIDE.COM FOR THE BEST PLACES TO EAT, DRINK & STAY

Dublin 1

★RESTAURANT

Chapter One Restaurant

18/19 Parnell Square Dublin 1

Tel: 01 873 2266 Fax: 01 873 2330

Email: info@chapteronerestaurant.com Web: www.chapteronerestaurant.com

féile bia In an arched basement beneath the Irish Writers Museum, one of Ireland's finest restaurants is to be found in the former home of the great John Jameson of whiskey fame. Together with an exceptional team including head chef Garrett Byrne, restaurant manager Declan Maxwell and sommelier Ian Brosnan, the proprietors - chef-patron Ross Lewis and front of house manager Martin Corbett - have earned an enviable reputation here, for outstanding modern Irish cooking and superb service from friendly and well-informed staff. The original granite walls and old brickwork of this fine Georgian house contrast with elegant modern decor to create atmospheric surroundings, and special features include a beautiful carved oyster counter in the reception area, where a champagne menu allows you to choose the perfect bubbly to accompany the noble bivalve. The cooking - classic French lightly tempered by modern influences - showcases specialist Irish produce whenever possible, notably on a magnificent charcuterie trolley, which demonstrates particularly the skills of West Cork producer Fingal Ferguson and is a treat not to be missed, and also an unusual fish plate which is a carefully balanced compilation of five individual fish and seafood dishes, served with melba toast. Other specialities include slow cooked meat - a sweet-flavoured shoulder of spring lamb, for example, with creamed onion and curry spice, roast carrot and garlic, kidney, and boulangère potato - and, of course, a cheese menu offering farmhouse cheeses in peak condition. But many guests will stall at dessert, as an utterly irresistible choice of half a dozen delectable dishes is offered, each with its own dessert wine or champagne... An excellent wine list leans towards the classics and offers many fairly priced treats for the wine buff - and also carefully selected house wines and wines by the glass, including a range of dessert wines. Another special treat is the perfectly timed pre-theatre menu, for which Chapter One is rightly renowned: depart for one of the nearby theatres after your main course, and return for dessert after the performance - perfect timing, every time. Like the lunch menu, early dinner offers outstanding value. Chapter One was our Restaurant of the Year in 2001, and it has been on our Awards shortlist every year since then. Small conferences. Air conditioning. Children welcome. **Seats 85** (private rooms,14 & 20). L Tue-Fri, 12.30-2.15, D Tue-Sat, 6-10.45. Set L €32.50. Pre-theatre menu €32.50 (6-6.30); D à la carte (Tasting Menu, for entire parties, €70). House wine €24. SC discretionary. Closed L Sat, all Sun & Mon, 2 weeks Christmas, 2 weeks August. MasterCard, Visa, Laser. **Directions:** Top of O'Connell Street, north side of Parnell Square, opposite Garden of Remembrance, beside Hugh Lane Gallery.

Dublin 1

HOTEL/RESTAURANT

Clarion Hotel Dublin IFSC

Excise Walk IFSC Dublin 1

Tel: 01 433 8800 Fax: 01 433 8801

Email: info@clarionhotelifsc.com Web: www.clarionhotelsireland.com

féile bia This dashing contemporary hotel on the river side of the International Financial Services Centre was the first in the area to be built specifically for the mature 'city' district and its high standards and central location have proved very popular with leisure guests, as well as business guests and the financial community, especially at weekends. Bright, airy and spacious, the style is refreshingly clean-lined yet comfortable, with lots of gentle neutrals and a somewhat eastern feel that is emphasised by the food philosophy of the hotel - a waft of lemongrass and ginger in the open plan public areas entices guests through to the Kudos Bar, where Asian wok cooking is served; the more formal restaurant, Sinergie, also features world cuisine, but with more European influences. Uncluttered suites and bedrooms have everything the modern traveller could want, including a high level of security, air conditioning, generous semi-orthopaedic beds and excellent bathrooms with top quality toiletries. There is a sense of thoughtful planning to every aspect of the hotel, and helpful, well-trained staff show a real desire to ensure the comfort of guests. Clarion Hotel Dublin IFSC was our Business Hotel of the Year in 2002. **Rooms 163** (17 suites, 50 executive, 80 no smoking, 8 disabled, 5 family rooms). B&B €132.50 pps. Room rate €265, no SC. Kudos Bar & Restaurant: Mon-Fri,12-8; Sinergie Restaurant: L Mon-Fri 12.30-2.30, D daily, 6-9.45. Set L €12.95; Early D €19.95 (6-7.30); D €19.95-€24.95, also à la carte. House wines, from €23. Sinergie closed L Sat. Kudos no food Sun. [* Comfort Inn, Talbot Street (Tel: 01-874 9202) is in the same group and offers budget accommodation near the IFSC.] Amex, Diners, MasterCard, Visa, Laser. **Directions:** Overlooking the river Liffey in the IFSC.

Dublin 1

ely chq

N RESTAURANT/WINE BAR

CHQ IFSC Dublin 1 **Tel: 01 672 0010**

WINE AWARD OF THE YEAR

féile bia

In contrast to the cosy atmosphere of Erik and Michelle Robson's original Ely Wine Bar in a four-storey Georgian building just off St Stephen's Green (see entry), Ely CHQ (Customs House Quay) is a brave new northside venture on Georges Dock. There's an old building in there alright most obviously in the vast vaulted basement area, which has less appeal in summer than the bright, open ground floor space or, particularly, a covered terrace where tables are in great demand but the style reflects the dashing contemporary architecture of the IFSC rather than the maritime history of the area; an understandable, and stylish choice, although blending in the nautical theme might have brought extra depth and character to the design. However, the successful Ely theme of simple organic food appealingly presented (including meats from the Robson family farm in County Clare) has been continued at the new venue: the burger is quite simply the best in town; no other gives you quite as much of that 'this is meat in its prime' feeling. Likewise, in the guide's experience, seafood is zingingly sea-fresh and although there were some service problems in the settling phase you could even be lucky enough to have a pleasant and efficient young Italian waiter who can commandeer an 'espresso' with thick crema that would be appreciated in Naples or Milan, let alone Dublin's northside. But it is their great wine list and, especially, an unrivalled choice of nearly a hundred wines offered by the glass - that makes Ely such as exceptional dining destination. This allows diners to taste a huge range of wines that might otherwise be inaccessible - and every dish offered on the lunch and a la carte menus (although not on the evening menu when, perhaps, bottles are more likely to appeal) has a suggested glass of wine to accompany: thus a glass of Domaine Alary, La Brunote, Ciaranne at €8.50 could accompany their renowned 'cold charger' selection of cured meats, cheese and home pickled vegetables (available as a starter or main course €9.50/17.50), and a glass of Domaine de la Janasse, Cotes du Rhône at €6.65, might complement the ultimate comfort dish of 'our very own' bangers & mash (€15.50) The wine list runs to over 500 bottles and mirrors that of the original Ely, being both well thought out and comprehensive, with many old favourites such as Domaine Baumard Savennieres and Ferd Max Richter Riesling available; although a little light on choice at the lower end, there is some very interesting drinking once you get among the thirty-somethings, much of it unavailable elsewhere. There is also a carefully selected beer list and you can even buy a Laguiole corkscrew ('guaranteed for life') and machine washable wine glasses to take home. *Another branch, **Ely HQ,** is planned for the south quays soon. Of the three choices, the best place to dine is outside if the weather is at all clement, with bright views across the open square and of the Liffey. Inside on the ground floor is fine but we fear the stygian catacombs may not appeal. **Seats 150** (private rooms to 100, outdoors, 50); children welcome before 7pm; L&D daily: Mon-Sat 12-3 & 4.30-11.30; Sun 1-4 & 6-10; a la carte; SC 12.5% on groups 6+. Closed Christmas week. Amex, Diners, MasterCard, Visa, Laser. **Directions:** On the banks of the Liffey, overlooking Georges Dock, 2 mins from Connolly Station.

EPICUREAN FOOD HALL

On the corner of Liffey Street and Middle Abbey Street, The Epicurean Food Hall is a collection of small units with a common seating area where you will find a wide range of gourmet foods, cooked and uncooked - and the wines to go with them. The hall is open during the day every day (opens later on Sunday, remains open for late shoppers on Thursday evening); it's an enjoyable place to browse -

there are lots of lovely little shops and cafes in the hall, including a good choice of ethnic ones, and they quite often change so these long-established tenants are just a taster: **La Corte** (01 873 4200) is one of two north river outposts of Stefano Crescenzi and David Izzo's smart Italian café (see entry). **Itsabagel** (Tel 01 874 0486): Domini and Peaches Kemps' classy bagel bar offeres authentic New York bagels, savoury breads with fillings, juices, muffins and cookies and is very popular with discerning lunchtim browsers (also at The Pavilion, Dun Laoghaire).

Dublin 1

Expresso Bar Café IFSC

RESTAURANT

6 Custom House Square IFSC Dublin 1
Tel: 01 672 1812 Fax: 01 672 1813 Email: jcathcart@ireland.com

Sister of the Expresso Bar Café in Ballsbridge - Anne Marie Nohl and Jane Cathcart have applied the same winning formula to this stylish little contemporary restaurant in Dublin's financial heartland. Breakfasts worth getting in early for kick off with freshly squeezed orange juice and lead on to a wonderful menu of temptations, from the best of traditional fries through the likes of pancakes with crispy bacon and syrup, or freshly baked pastries. Lunches are in a class of their own too, offering lots of lovely, colourful dishes - sweet mustard salmon with dill, new potatoes & fennel salad is a typical summer example, or stuffed chicken breast with roast veg, white wine & rosemary - all based on the best ingredients, impeccably sourced. Desserts are given daily on a board and there's a wide choice of coffees, minerals and a compact, well-selected wine list. Takeaway bagel menu also available. **Seats 85.** Reservations accepted. Open Mon-Fri, 8am-3pm; Sat & Sun brunch, 10am-4pm. Air-conditioning. Closed 25 Dec, bank hols. Amex, MasterCard, Visa, Laser. **Directions:** On corner, left of Custom Square, IFSC.◇

Dublin 1

The Gresham

HOTEL/RESTAURANT

23 Upper O'Connell Street Dublin 1
Tel: 01 874 6881 Fax: 01 878 7175
Email: info@thegresham.com Web: www.gresham-hotels.com

féile bia This famous hotel has been at the centre of Dublin society since the early nineteenth century and is one of the city's best business hotels. A recent makeover has transformed the ground floor, including the lobby lounge, which is a favourite meeting place and renowned for its traditional afternoon tea, and also the Gresham and Toddy's Bars, both popular rendezvous for a pint. The hotel, which takes commendable pride in the quality of its staff, has always been a popular choice for business guests - who will also appreciate the recently refurbished bedrooms: 108 rooms have been transformed in executive contemporary style, and all 288 rooms now have Quadriga digital entertainment system (internet/movies/TV/jukebox). Dining options in the hotel include the contemporary restaurant "23": smart and welcoming, it offers good cooking and interested service. Knowledgeable young staff make this a useful place to know about, and the 2-course 'city' dinner menu offers especially good value. Conference/banqueting (350/280). Business centre; secretarial services; video conferencing. Fitness suite. Wheelchair access. Secure multi-storey parking. No pets. **Rooms 288** (4 suites, 2 junior suites, 96 executive, 60 no-smoking, 3 disabled); Children welcome (u12s €40 sharing with parents); Lifts. B&B €175pps, ss up to €175. [Restaurant "23":D Mon-Sat 5.30-10.15, Early D €26 5.30-7, also á la carte] Hotel open all year. Amex, Diners, MasterCard, Visa, Laser. **Directions:** City centre, on north side of the River Liffey.

Dublin 1

The Harbourmaster Bar and Restaurant

BAR/RESTAURANT

IFSC Dublin 1 **Tel: 01 670 1688** Fax: 01 670 1690

féile bia In a waterside setting at Dublin's thriving financial services centre, this old Dock Offices building has genuine character and makes a fine restaurant and bar. The bar itself is very busy at times, but there is also an impressive contemporary upstairs restaurant, The Greenhouse, in a modern extension which has been designed in sympathy with the original building. Most tables have an interesting (and increasingly attractive) view of the development outside but, as there are now several dining areas, it is wise to ensure you get to the right one on arrival. For fine weather, there's also a decked outdoor area overlooking the inner harbour and fountain, with extra seating. The Harbourmaster has that indefinable buzz that comes from being in the financial centre of a capital city and, while not necessarily a destination dining experience, the food is appropriately international and contemporary in style. **The Greenhouse Restaurant:** L, Mon-Fri. Restaurant closed evenings and weekends (except for functions). Bar open Mon-Wed, noon-closing daily (Sun 12.30-11) Brasserie food all day, daily. Closed 25 Dec & Good Fri. Amex, Diners, MasterCard, Visa. **Directions:** In IFSC, near Connolly train station.◇

Dublin 1
CAFÉ/RESTAURANT/PUB

John M Keating

Former St. Mary's Church Mary Street Dublin 1
Tel: 01 828 0102 Email: reservations@jmk.ie Web: www.jmk.ie

Keating's was well known as a welcoming pub for many a Dubliner until it disappeared a while ago in the massive wave of reconstruction that has taken place around the Mary Street area, and now it has a stunning new home in this converted church. A striking ultra-modern see-through entrance tower outside the church sets the tone for an impressive contemporary interior which includes a function room with great views of the city, as well as a large ground floor bar (with a restaurant area in the surrounding gallery), and a cellar bar & café. Although, initially at least, it seems to have missed the mark on the food side, the sleek minimalist bar would be well worth a visit for the sheer quality of the restoration work alone. The old has been meticulously restored and the new sits easily against it, a testament to brilliant design. Bar food: Mon-Wed, 12-9.30pm, Thur-Sat, 12-10pm, Sun, 12.30-8pm; Cafe: Mon-Sat, 12-10pm, Sun, 12.30-8pm; Restaurant: Mon-Wed, 12-10pm, Thurs-Sat, 12-11pm, Sun, 12.30-10pm; SC 12.5% on parties 6+.

Dublin 1
HOTEL

Jurys Custom House Inn

Custom House Quay Dublin 1
Tel: 01 607 5000 Fax: 01 829 0400

féile bia Right beside the International Financial Services Centre, overlooking the Liffey and close to train, Luas and bus stations, this hotel meets the requirements of business guests with better facilities than is usual in budget hotels. Large bedrooms have all the expected facilities, but with a higher standard of finish than most of its sister hotels; fabrics and fittings are good quality and neat bathrooms are thoughtfully designed, with generous shelf space. As well as a large bar, there is a full restaurant on site, plus conference facilities for up to 100 and a staffed business centre. No room service. Adjacent multi-storey car park has direct access to the hotel. **Rooms 239.** Room Rate from c. €108 (max 3 guests); breakfast c. €8-10. Closed 24-26 Dec. Amex, Diners, MasterCard, Visa. **Directions:** IFSC, overlooking River Liffey.◇

Dublin 1
HOTEL/RESTAURANT

The Morrison Hotel

Lower Ormond Quay Dublin 1
Tel: 01 887 2400 Fax: 01 874 4039
Email: reservations@morrisonhotel.ie Web: www.morrisonhotel.ie

féile bia Centrally located on the north quays, close to the Millennium Bridge over the River Liffey, this luxurious contemporary hotel is within walking distance of theatres, the main shopping areas and the financial district. When it opened in 1998 it was a first for Dublin, with striking 'east meets west' interiors created by the internationally renowned designer, John Rocha, and the same team has recently overseen a huge development programme with the addition of 48 new bedrooms and extensive conference and meeting facilities - designed around a calm Courtyard Garden, which makes an attractive venue for receptions, or pre-dinner drinks. Stylish public areas include the cool but comfortable Café Bar - just the place for a cappuccino or cocktails - and a new spa opened in 2006, offering holistic and relaxation treatments. Simple, cool bedroom design - the essence of orderly thinking - contrasts pleasingly with the more flamboyant style of public areas, and there is a welcome emphasis on comfort (Frette linen, Aveda toiletries, air conditioning); all rooms have complimentary broadband, Apple Mac plasma screen with keyboard, wireless mouse and surround sound, iPod docking stations and CD players, safe and mini-bar. Exceptionally friendly and helpful staff make every effort to provide the best possible service for guests, and complimentary room upgrades to studios and suites are given when available. Conference/banqueting (240/90); video conferencing (by arrangement). Children welcome (under 12 free in parents' room, cot available without charge, babysitting arranged). Pets permitted by arrangement. **Rooms 138** (12 suites, 6 junior suites, 38 shower only, 5 for disabled, 80 no smoking). Lift. Room service (limited hours). Room rate €285 (SC incl). No private parking (arrangement with nearby car park). Closed 23-27 Dec. **Halo:** This popular restaurant is now next to the riverside entrance of the hotel, allowing diners a view over the river and the busy thoroughfare on the quays. The new restaurant lacks the warm opulence of the old Halo setting but, although the décor sends mixed messages (minimalist oriental stools set beside Georgian style claw-footed tables) it is a more relaxed and informal space and, under head chef Andrew O'Gorman, this change of policy is seen in a quite rustic cooking style. Menus are not too long, top quality ingredients are a feature and hearty dishes with unusual flavour combinations suggest an imaginative but unpretentious chef; breads are all home made, and specialities include traditional short rib beef (served on a big board with crisp potatoes and onion rings), and old-fashioned dessert like vanilla & cinnamon rice pudding with tapioca & strawberry jam. An all day tapas menu includes oysters various ways, smoked salmon & Guinness bread and Irish cheeses, served with oatmeal biscuits, and there's a walk-in glass wine cellar, where you can browse and take your pick (although no half bottles). The homely quality of the cooking may seem at odds with the décor of this trendy hotel, but many guests will welcome a style that is not too refined. As elsewhere in the hotel, very good service is a special feature: all male staff are dressed in black are very courteous and knowledgeable. The wine list offers about 50 bottles, including three dessert wines; about half of the selection is French, six are offered by the glass, and there is plenty of choice and good quality in the €24 to €40 range. **Seats 90.** Air conditioning. L& D daily (Sun D only), Served all day 12-10, à la carte; house wine from €18.50; sc 12.5% on groups 6+. Amex, Diners, MasterCard, Visa, Laser, Switch. **Directions:** Located on the quays near the city centre beside the Millennium Bridge.

Dublin 1

Panem

€ CAFÉ

Ha'penny Bridge House 21 Lower Ormond Quay Dublin 1
Tel: 01 872 8510 Fax: 01 872 8510

Ann Murphy and Raffaele Cavallo's little bakery and café has been delighting discerning Dubliners - and providing a refuge from the thundering traffic along the quays outside - since 1996. Although tiny, it just oozes Italian chic - not surprisingly, perhaps, as Ann's Italian architect husband designed the interior - and was way ahead of its time in seeing potential north of the Liffey. Italian and French food is prepared on the premises from 3 am each day: melt-in-the-mouth croissants with savoury and sweet fillings, chocolate-filled brioches, traditional and fruit breads, filled foccacia breads are just a few of the temptations on offer. No cost is spared in sourcing the finest ingredients (Panem bread is baked freshly each day using organic flour) and special dietary needs are considered too: soups, for example, are usually suitable for vegans and hand-made biscuits - almond & hazelnut perhaps - for coeliacs. They import their own 100% arabica torrisi coffee from Sicily and hot chocolate is a speciality, made with the best Belgian dark chocolate. Simply superb. Open Mon-Fri, 8-6, Sat, 9-6 & Sun, 10-4.30. Closed 24 Dec-8 Jan. **No Credit Cards. Directions:** North quays, opposite Millennium Bridge. ◇

Dublin 1

Ristorante Romano

RESTAURANT

12 Capel Street Dublin 1 **Tel: 01 872 6868**

Long before there was as much as a hint of fashionable restaurants opening on Capel Street, Romano's was widely recognised as one the best value Italian restaurants in town, especially at lunch. Friendly and generous-spirited, this is a simple cafe-style restaurant (in the old-fashioned sense) and gives great home cooking with a little extra oomph - and good value wines too. Expect lovely big home prepared pastas, generous side salads with DIY dressing, good steaks, homemade desserts and moreish espressos. Great value, great little place - we need more like this. Open 7 days. Wines from €19. **Directions:** North end of Capel Street.

Dublin 1

Soup Dragon

CAFÉ

168 Capel Street Dublin 1 **Tel: 01 872 3277** Fax: 01 872 3277

This tiny place offers a stylish way to have a hot meal on a budget: a daily choice of soups and stews is available in three different sizes, with a medium portion and a selection of delicious home-made breads and a piece of fruit starting at about €6. Some change daily, while others stay on the menu for a week or a season. Choose from dahl (Indian lentil), potato & leek or carrot & coriander soup; or opt for something more substantial like beef chilli or a very fine Thai chicken curry from the blackboard menu. In keeping with their healthy philosophy, a range of wholesome and innovative breakfasts is offered, and also a range of freshly squeezed drinks (Red Dragon: strawberry, raspberry and cranberry or home-made lemon & lime lemonade) and smoothies, all made to order so they taste fresh and vibrant. Desserts include old favourites like rice pudding (served with cream) and a range of unusual home-made ice creams. Food to go is also available. **Seats 10.** Open Mon-Fri 8-5.30 & Sat 11-5. Closed Sun, bank hols, Christmas. [Opening times not confirmed at time of going to press.] **No Credit Cards. Directions:** Bridge at Capel Street.

Dublin 1

The Vaults

BAR/RESTAURANT

Harbourmaster Place IFSC Dublin 1 **Tel: 01 605 4700**
Fax: 01 605 4701 Email: info@thevaults.ie Web: www.thevaults.ie

These ten soaring vaulted chambers underneath Connolly Station were built in the mid-19th century to support the railway between Amiens Street and the Royal Canal and have since found many uses, including the storage of Jameson whiskey, which used to occupy a tunnel running from Connolly to Westland Row! In 2002 this wonderful space entered a new and exciting era when Michael Martin - previously best known for his culinary expertise as head chef of the Clarence Hotel restaurant, The Tea Room - opened it as a multi-purpose venue. Despite the size - and a ceiling height of four metres - the atmosphere is surprisingly intimate: the Portland Stone floor is warm and welcoming and the vaults, which have been treated individually in styles ranging from sleek contemporary (brown leather booth seating) to neo-classical (salvaged lamps, aged sculptures) add up to a stylish and highly versatile space. Each has its own entrance, allowing a number of events to take place simultaneously and, in addition to high-resolution digital projectors allowing cinema quality audio-visual effects, surround sound and drop-down screens in three of the vaults, others have plasma screens - ideal for sports events (seats bookable in advance). Given Michael Martin's background, culinary expectations are high at The Vaults and head chef Fraser O'Donnell ensures that everything is made from scratch, including pasta, ice cream and breads; menus are simple - mainly grills, pizzas and pastas - but brilliantly executed and beautifully presented on plain white modern crockery. This place encapsulates the dramatic changes taking place north of the Liffey: simply stunning. **Seats 180** (private room 90). (All spaces available to hire, for business or pleasure). Reservations accepted. Food served Mon-Fri 12-8, Sat 1-8. Various menus - lunch, afternoon/evening, Saturday brunch and Sunday roast - à la carte. Vegetarian dishes on main menu. SC 10%. House wine €19. Late night bar & club Fri/Sat to 02.30. Closed Sun, 24-30 Dec, Good Fri, Bank Hols. Amex, MasterCard, Visa, Laser. **Directions:** Under Connolly station; last stop on Luas red line.

Dublin 1

The Winding Stair

(N) (E) RESTAURANT

40 Lower Ormond Quay Dublin 1 **Tel: 01 872 7320**
Email: info@winding-stair.com Web: www.winding-stair.com

Closure of the old Winding Stair Bookshop & Café a while ago provoked much muttering about the end of an era so what a delightful surprise for old fans to discover that this much-loved café overlooking the Ha'penny Bridge is back and better than ever. Although now a proper restaurant with gleaming wine glasses and a fine new La Marzocco coffee machine, something of the old café atmosphere is still to be found in the wooden floorboards, bentwood chairs and simple tables and, under the direction of Elaine Murphy, good management will ensure that you'll also find friendly staff - and a talented young chef, Aine Murphy, who is clearly putting heart and soul into the job and intent on making a mark by sourcing the best possible ingredients and allowing sound cooking and simplicity to take its course. There's plenty of 'the organic and real' on menus that could include superb starters such as an Irish charcuterie plate (Connemara dry cured lamb and beef, salamis from the Gubbeen smokehouse in County Cork, accompanied by home made chutney & capers), and main dishes including outstanding renditions of classics such as bacon and cabbage with parsley sauce, and great seafood: mussels and prawns, tasty fresh sardines - and specials, such as whole sea bream, or undyed smoked haddock with a delicious white cheddar mash and onions. To finish, there's an excellent Irish farmhouse cheese selection and delicious seasonal desserts which, like the rest of the menu, are very fairly priced. An unusually interesting wine list is clearly put together by enthusiasts, and sourced from a variety of quality suppliers and you could finish with a superb ristretto, pulled by someone who knows how to use the coffee machine. The Winding Stair is that rarity among Irish restaurants, serving simple, high quality food and it has a lovely ambience. Aided by nostalgia, it also has personality in spades and will quickly attract a following - book a window table for a view of the river. Children welcome; **Seats 100;** food served daily, 12.30-10.30pm; a la carte; house wine €21. Closed 25-26 Dec, 1 Jan. Amex, Diners, MasterCard, Visa, Laser. **Directions:** Beside Ha'penny bridge.

DUBLIN 2

Dublin 2

Acapulco Mexican Restaurant

RESTAURANT

7 South Great Georges St Dublin 2 **Tel: 01 677 1085**

You'll find reliable Tex-Mex fare at this bright, cheap and notably cheerful place on the edge of Temple Bar. Recently refurbished in warm tones of red, pinks and green, the decor matches the food which is authentic Mexican - nachos with salsa & guacamole, enchiladas, burrito, sizzling fajitas - and good coffee. **Seats 70.** Open 7 days: L 12-3pm, D 6-10.30pm (Fri 12-4pm & 6-11pm, Sat & Sun 2-10.30pm). Affordable wines, from about €17.95. 10% SC on parties of 6+. Amex, MasterCard, Visa, Laser. **Directions:** Bottom of South Gt George's St (Dame Street end).◇

Dublin 2

Alexander Hotel

HOTEL

Merrion Square Dublin 2 **Tel: 01 607 3700** Fax: 01 661 5663
Email: alexanderres@ocallaghanhotels.ie Web: www.ocallaghanhotels.ie

féile bia Very well situated at the lower end of Merrion Square within a stone's throw of Dáil Éireann (Government Buildings), the National Art Gallery and History Museum as well as the city's premier shopping area, this large modern hotel is remarkable for classic design that blends into the surrounding Georgian area. In contrast to its subdued public face, the interior is strikingly contemporary and colourful, both in public areas and bedrooms, which are all to executive standard, spacious and unusual. Perhaps its most positive attribute, however, is the exceptionally friendly and helpful attitude of the hotel's staff, who immediately make guests feel at home and take a genuine interest in their comfort during their stay. Conference/banqueting (400/400). Business centre. Secretarial services. Video conferencing. Gym. Children welcome (Under 2s free in parents' room; cots available). No pets. **Rooms 102** (4 suites, 40 no-smoking, 2 for disabled). Lift. B&B about €105. Room-only rate about €295 (max. 2 guests). Open all year. Amex, Diners, MasterCard, Visa. **Directions:** Off Merrion Square.◇

Dublin 2

Ar Vicoletto Osteria Romana

RESTAURANT

5 Crow Street Temple Bar Dublin 2 **Tel: 01 670 8662**

Genuine little Italian restaurant, doing authentic, restorative food in a relaxing atmosphere and at very moderate prices - a set two-course lunch which includes a glass of wine and tea or coffee, is particularly good value. Friendly helpful staff too - one of the pleasantest spots in Temple Bar. Children welcome. **Seats 35.** L &D daily. Children welcome. Air conditioning. Closed 24-25 Dec. Amex, MasterCard, Visa. **Directions:** In Temple Bar.

Dublin 2

Avoca Café

€ RESTAURANT

11-13 Suffolk St Dublin 2 **Tel: 01 672 6019** Fax: 01 672 6021
Email: info@avoca.ie Web: www.avoca.ie

féile bia City sister to the famous craftshop and café with its flagship store in Kilmacanogue, County Wicklow (see entry), this large centrally located shop is a favourite daytime dining venue for discerning Dubliners. The restaurant (which is up rather a lot of stairs, where queues of devotees wait patiently at lunchtime) has low-key style and an emphasis on creative, healthy cooking that is common to all the Avoca establishments. Chic little menus speak volumes - together with careful cooking, meticulously sourced ingredients like Woodstock tuna, Hederman mussels, Gubbeen bacon and Hicks sausages lift dishes such as smoked fish platter, organic bacon panini and bangers & mash out of the ordinary. All this sits happily alongside the home baking for which they are famous - much of which can be bought downstairs in their extensive delicatessen. Licensed. Meals daily, in shop hours. **Seats 100;** toilets wheelchair accessible; opening hours: 10am-5.30pm Mon-Sat (hot food served until 4.30pm Mon-Fri), 11am-5pm Sun; à la carte. Bookings accepted but not required. SC 10%. Closed 25/26 December, 1 Jan. Amex, Diners, MasterCard, Visa. Amex, Diners, MasterCard, Visa. **Directions:** Turn left into Suffolk St. from the bottom of Grafton St.◇

Dublin 2

Aya Restaurant & Sushi Bar

RESTAURANT

49/52 Clarendon Street Dublin 2 **Tel: 01 677 1544** Fax: 01 677 1607
Email: mail@aya.ie Web: www.aya.ie

This contemporary Japanese restaurant was Dublin's first conveyor sushi bar, restaurant and food hall - it's owned by the Hoashi family, who established Dublin's first authentic Japanese restaurant, Ayumi-Ya, in 1983 - and was a runaway success from the day it opened, in 1999. Wall-to-wall style is the order of the day - and the menu includes a wide range of sushi, all authentically Japanese, and also some hot food, including Asian and Japanese tapas, as well as tempura and teriyaki dishes and additions with broader Asian flavours to tempt a wider range of customers. The sushi conveyor belt has stools and also booths for communal diners, as well as restaurant seating for the à la carte."Sushi 55" at the sushi bar allows unlimited food from the conveyor for 55 minutes, including 1 drink and 1 miso soup, all for €29 plus a €2 seat charge per person. Some products are available to takeaway from the Aya Deli. Children welcome before 7pm. **Seats 60** (sushi bar & restaurant). Air conditioning. Open daily - Sushi Bar: 12.30-10 (to 11 Fri/Sat); Restaurant: L 12.30-3 (Sat to 4), D 5-10 (Sat to 11, Sun to 9). Set L €19; Set D €30, Early D €18.95 5-7. Also à la carte. House wine from €22. SC 12.5%. Closed 25-26 Dec. Amex, MasterCard, Visa, Laser. **Directions:** Directly behind Brown Thomas off Wicklow Street.

Dublin 2

The Bailey

PUB

2-3 Duke Street Dublin 2 **Tel: 01 670 4939**

Although it's now more of a busy lunchtime spot and after-work watering hole for local business people and shoppers, this famous Victorian pub has a special place in the history of Dublin life - literary, social, political - and attracts many a pilgrim seeking the ghosts of great personalities who have frequented this spot down through the years. Closed 25 Dec & Good Friday. **Directions:** Off Grafton Street.

Dublin 2

Bang Café

☆RESTAURANT

11 Merrion Row Dublin 2 **Tel: 01 676 0898**
Fax: 01 676 0899 Web: www.bangrestaurant.com

Stylishly minimalist, with natural tones of dark wood and pale beige leather complementing simple white linen and glassware, this smart restaurant is well-located just yards from the Shelbourne Hotel. It is on two levels with a bar in the basement; upstairs, unstressed chefs can be seen at work in one of the open kitchens: an air of calm, relaxed and friendly professionalism prevails. Head chef Lorcan Cribben's menus offer innovative, modern food: a starter of perfectly cooked foie gras served atop a crisp onion bahji with Sauternes jus is typical and well-balanced main course options include a signature dish of bangers & mash (made with Hicks sausages) now also on the menu at the newer Clarendon Café Bar; also great fish dishes (seared scallops are especially popular) - using fresh fish from Bantry, in West Cork. Tempting desserts include several fruity finales (Scandinavian iced berries are a speciality) as well as the ever-popular dark chocolate treats, or there's an Irish farmhouse cheese selection. Attention to detail is the keynote throughout and this, seen in carefully sourced food and skilful cooking combined with generous servings and professional service under the management of Kelvin Rynhart, ensures an enjoyable dining experience and value for money (especially at lunch time). **Seats 99** (private room, 36); reservations required; air conditioning; L&D Mon-Sat 12.30-3pm, 6-10.30pm; à la carte L&D. House wine €21. 12.5% sc on parties of 6+. Closed Sun, bank hols, 25 Dec-3 Jan. MasterCard, Visa, Laser. Amex, MasterCard, Visa, Laser. **Directions:** Just past Shelbourne Hotel, off St Stephen's Green.

Dublin 2

Bewley's - Mackerel & Café Bar Deli

€ CAFÉ/RESTAURANT

Bewleys Building 78-79 Grafton Street Dublin 2
Tel: 01 672 7720 Fax: 01 677 4585
Email: info@mackerel.ie Web: www.sherland.ie

Established in 1840, Bewley's Café had a special place in the affection of Irish people. Bewleys on Grafton Street was always a great meeting place for everyone, whether native Dubliners or visitors to the capital 'up from the country'. It changed hands amid much public debate in 2005 but, despite renovations, it has somehow retained its unique atmosphere together with some outstanding architectural features, notably the Harry Clarke stained glass windows. The popular Café-Bar-Deli chain has taken over most of the seating area now, but the coffee shop at the front remains, and also the in-house theatre (phone for details); and, if you go through the coffee shop and up steep stairs to the right, you'll find a new fish restaurant, called simply Mackerel. While far from luxurious, this little restaurant has struck a chord with discerning Dubliners: smart-casual decor - wooden floors, small green marble tables, chandeliers - has youthful appeal and, while there is a printed menu for everything else, the fish dishes are posted on a blackboard menu daily. The range of fish offered is wide, including starters like seafood chowder, Pacific oysters, smokies (with natural smoked haddock), tuna carpaccio, and main courses such as organic salmon, roast whole seabass with an avocado salsa and Howth pier mackerel with apple & shallot compôte- and the cooking is outstanding. Modern classic is the style and it is achieved with panache; accompanying vegetables have real flavour, classic desserts are delicious (hazelnut pannacotta, chocolate fudge cake), and cheeses served in perfect condition on a wooden platter come from Sheridans cheesemongers just across the road. An interesting wine list and good value complete a very attractive package - and the fact that they are open for dinner has transformed the atmosphere of Grafton Street at night. **Mackerel: Seats 48** (outdoor, 8); Toilets wheelchair accessible, Air con, Children welcome until 6pm; L daily 12-4, D daily 5-10. **Cafe**

Bar Deli: Seats 350 open for food all day 8am-11pm. Café open for food all day 8am-11pm. Closed 25/6 Dec, Bank Hols. Amex, MasterCard, Visa, Laser. **Directions:** Halfway up Dublin's premier shopping street.

Dublin 2

RESTAURANT/WINE BAR

Bleu Bistro Moderne

Dawson St Dublin 2 **Tel: 01 676 7015**
Fax: 01 676 7027 Web: www.bleu.ie

féile bia A younger sister to Eamonn O'Reilly's excellent flagship restaurant One Pico (see entry), this modern bistro is now known generally as simply 'Bleu' or even 'Blue' and, at its best, can be impressive. Smartly laid tables are rather close together (paper napkins at lunch time - linen at night) and hard surfaces make for a good bit of noise which adversely affects the dining ambience. But Head Chef Shane O'Neill's food is based on carefully sourced quality ingredients, skilfully cooked and pleasingly presented on plain white plates: signature dishes include salmon fish cakes with cucumber pickle & saffron aïoli and loin of lamb stuffed with boudin noir, with fondant potato and mushroom & Madeira onion tart. Portions are on the small side, which may make value on the plate seem less than it looks on the menu (vegetables, salads etc charged as extras). The long opening hours are an advantage - there's a very nice little afternoon menu offered, with an appealing list of wines by the glass, which could make an enjoyable late lunch or early evening meal - and an outdoor seating area was completed in summer 2006. Good wine list, with a dozen or so wines by the glass (from €5.50). **Seats 60** (outdoor seating 14). Reservations advised. Air conditioning. Open all day Mon-Sat 9am-midnight, L 12-5, D 5-12, Sun - L 12-4, D 5-10; Set L 2/3 course €21.50/25. Early D €29 (5-7.30), Set D €20, also á la carte L&D. House wine from €22. Closed bank hols. Amex, MasterCard, Visa, Laser. **Directions:** At top of Dawson St. off St. Stephen's Green.

Dublin 2

Ⓝ RESTAURANT

Brasserie Sixty6

66-67 South Great Georges Street Dublin 2
Tel: 01 400 5878 Fax: 01 400 5879
Email: info@brasseriesixty6.com Web: www.brasseriesixty6.com

Although it has a narrow street frontage this is a large restaurant, high-celinged and extending way back into an old building - and the stylish deli next door is also part of it. Décor is unfussy modern, for the most part wooden floors, simple bare-topped tables and leather 'bus seat' banquettes or chairs that would look at home in a country kitchen. Aside from a very large chandelier and some unusual artwork, the main decorative theme is a whole wall of mismatched plates, echoing the traditional kitchen dresser, a good idea that lends warmth and informality; it adds up to a comfortably stylish setting for menus that are strong on house specialities and offer something different from the standard fare. Starters include a crisp and tasty house rendition of deep-fried squid and there may also be unusual dishes such as marrowbone with toasted brioche, while the signature main course is rotisserie chicken served with corn on the cob, coleslaw and cornbread or mash another good retro idea, using top notch chicken that is cooked with a different marinade each day. Good steaks come with proper homemade chips, there are several versions of bangers and mash, or you might go mad with lobster, or even whole suckling pig for a group, on occasion Service is pleasant and helpful (although it can be disorganised), and you can also expect updated classic desserts, good coffee, a short but well-chosen wine list (plus beers, cocktails and freshly squeezed juices), plus a bill that won't break the bank. Toilets wheelchair accessible; air conditioning; children welcome; open all day 8am-11.30pm (from 10am Sat & Sun), L 12-5, D 5-11.30, set L €14.95, also a la carte; house wine €19.50; SC 12.5% on groups 6+. Closed 25-26 Dec, 1 Jan, Good Fri. Amex, MasterCard, Visa, Laser. **Directions:** Opposite Georges Street arcade.

Dublin 2

HOTEL/RESTAURANT

Brooks Hotel

59-62 Drury Street Dublin 2
Tel: 01 670 4000 Fax: 01 670 4455
Email: reservations@brookshotel.ie Web: www.sinnotthotels.com

BUSINESS HOTEL OF THE YEAR

féile bia One of Dublin's most desirable addresses, especially for business guests, the Sinnott family's discreetly luxurious hotel is a gem of a place - an oasis of calm just a couple of minutes walk from Grafton Street. A ground floor bar, lounge and restaurant all link together, making an extensive public area that is quietly impressive on arrival - the style is a pleasing combination of traditional with minimalist touches, using a variety of woods, some marble, wonderful fabrics and modern paintings - and, while a grand piano adds gravitas, there's a welcome emphasis on comfort (especially in the residents' lounge, where spare reading glasses are thoughtfully supplied). Efficient service ensures you are in your room promptly, usually with the help of Conor, the concierge, who never forgets a face or a name. All bedrooms have exceptionally good amenities, including a pillow menu (choice of five types) and well-designed bathrooms with power showers as well as full baths (some also have tile screen TV), and many other features. Boardrooms offer state-of-the-art facilities for meetings and small conferences, and there is a 26-seater screening room. Fitness suite & sauna. Children welcome (under 2 free in parents' room; cots available without charge, baby sitting arranged). No pets. **Rooms 98** (1 suite, 2 junior suites, 3 executive, 87 no-smoking, 5 semi-invalid). Lift. Air conditioning throughout. 24 hr room service. B&B €190pps, ss €65. *Special breaks offered - details on application. Arrangement with car park. Open all year. **Francescas:** Pre-dinner drinks are served in a lovely little cocktail bar, Jasmine, and the restaurant has a youthful contemporary look, and a welcoming ambience - an open plan kitchen has well positioned mirrors allowing head chef Patrick McLarnon and his team to be seen at work. Tables are elegantly appointed with classic linen cloths and napkins, and waiting staff, smartly attired in black, look after customers with warmth and professionalism. Patrick sources ingredients with great care (wild salmon, organic chicken, dry aged steak, wild boar sausage), his cooking is generally imaginative - and there's a strong emphasis on fish and seafood. Tasty pan-fried mackerel with a sweet gooseberry and apple salsa attracted praise on a recent visit, although the fish of the day (red snapper on a bed of couscous) was a little bland. Unusual meat dishes may include a starter of McGeough's air-dried Connemara lamb (subject to availability) and a main course peat smoked loin of Wexford lamb, with caramelised shallots, tomato fondue and champ, with a rosemary jus. Finish, perhaps, with a zingy home-made lemon tart served with a delicious strawberry or raspberry sorbet and a classy individually packed infusion, or coffee. A nice wine selection includes good quality wines available by the glass. The early dinner offers good value, and breakfast offers a wide variety of juices, cereals and nuts, yoghurt, pastries, meat, cheeses and fruit. A good range of hot dishes includes pancakes with maple syrup, kippers with poached egg and full Irish breakfast as you like it, although service can be slow. [*Informal meals also available10 am-11.30 daily.] **Seats 60.** Reservations advised. Children welcome. Air conditioning.Toilets wheelchair accessible. D daily, 6-9.30 (Fri/Sat to 10). Early D € 18.50 (6-7); also à la carte. Closed to non-residents 24/25th December. Amex, MasterCard, Visa. Amex, MasterCard, Visa, Laser. **Directions:** Near St Stephen's Green, between Grafton and Great St. Georges Streets; opposite Drury Street car park.

Dublin 2

Brownes Hotel

HOTEL

22 St Stephen's Green Dublin 2 **Tel: 01 638 3939** Fax: 01 638 3900
Email: info@brownesdublin.com Web: www.brownesdublin.com

Stylish conversion of this fine period house on the stretch of St Stephen's Green between Grafton Street and the Shelbourne Hotel makes an impressive and exceptionally well-located small hotel. Up a short flight of granite steps, you pass through a reception area and there is a small drawing room area furnished with antiques (where aperitifs and digestifs can be served for the restaurant). The house has something of the atmosphere of a private home about it. The present owners, the Stein Group, have invested heavily in on refurbishment of the premises, including the spacious accommodation. **Brownes Restaurant** - This is one of Dublin's loveliest dining rooms yet, despite good food and a great location, it seems to be something of a well-kept secret when other well-known restaurants nearby are impossible to get into, there may well be spare tables here. The menu and food are appealing and well presented, although they do perhaps lack the 'wow' factor demanded by the 'tiger cub' generation, who also have a well known aversion to eating in hotels. But the ambience is lovely and the cooking sound, backed up by good, professional staff perhaps it's the ideal destination for discerning diners who wouldn't wish to be labelled 'tiger cubs' Small conference/banqueting (24/70). Children welcome (under 6 free in parents' room, cot available without charge). No pets. **Rooms 12** (2 suites). Lift. 24 hour room service. B&B about €200 pps. *Short breaks / golfing breaks offered. L Sun-Fri & D daily. Closed Christmas/New Year. Amex, Diners, MasterCard, Visa, Laser. **Directions:** Stephens Green North, between Kildare & Dawson Streets. ◇

Dublin 2

Buswells Hotel

HOTEL

23 Molesworth Street Dublin 2 **Tel: 01 614 6500** Fax: 01 676 2090
Email: buswells@quinn-hotels.com Web: www.quinn-hotels.com

Home from home to Ireland's politicians, this 18th century townhouse close to the Dail (parliament) has been an hotel since 1921 and is held in great affection by Dubliners. Since major refurbishment several years ago, it now offers a fine range of services for conferences, meetings and private dining. Accommodation is comfortable in the traditional style with good amenities for business guests and it's just a few yards from the city's prime shopping and cultural area, making it an ideal base for private visits - and the lobby and characterful bar make handy meeting places. Conference/banqueting (85/50). Business centre, secretarial services, video conferencing. Children welcome (Under 3s free in parents' room; cots available). No pets. **Rooms 67** (2 junior suites, 7 shower only, 40 no smoking, 1 for disabled). Lift. B&B €90pps, ss €45. 24 hr room service, Lift. **Trumans:** This elegant, well-appointed restaurant has a separate entrance from Kildare Street, or access from the hotel. Quite extensive menus feature modern dishes such as a starter of asaparagus & wild mushroom risotto with Parmesan chips, or Trumans own bang bang chicken salad, and have the little touches that endear guests to an establishment, such as a tasty appetiser presented before the meal 'compliments of the chef'. Wisely, given the likely clientèle, simpler dishes are always an option - notably steaks presented various ways, or grilled Dover sole on the bone - and vegetarian dishes are creative. Finish with a classic dessert like strawberry tart with crème anglaise - or Irish cheeses, perhaps. The wine list includes half a dozen house wines, all under €20, and a good choice of half bottles. Children welcome. **Seats 80** (private room, 50). Reservations advised. L 12-2.30 (carvery), D 6-9.45. à la carte. House wine €18.75. SC discretionary. Closed 24-27 Dec. Amex, Diners, MasterCard, Visa, Laser. **Directions:** Close to Dail Eireann, 5 minutes walk from Grafton Street.

Dublin 2

Butlers Chocolate Café

CAFÉ

24 Wicklow Street Dublin 2 **Tel: 01 671 0599** Fax: 01 671 0480
Email: chocolate@butlers.ie Web: www.butlerschocolates.com

Butlers Irish Handmade Chocolates combine coffee-drinking with complimentary chocolates here - an over-simplification, as the range of drinks at this stylish little café also includes hot chocolate as well as lattes, cappuccinos and mochas and chocolate cakes and croissants are also available. But all drinks do come with a complimentary handmade chocolate on the side - and boxed or personally selected loose chocolates, caramels, fudges and fondants are also available for sale. Open 7 days: Mon-Fri 8am-7pm, Sat 9am-7pm, Sun 11am-6pm. Closed 25-26 Dec, Easter Sun & Mon. Also at: 51 Grafton Street (Tel: 01 671 0599); 9 Chatham Street (Tel: 01 672 6333); 18 Nassau Street (Tel: 01 671 0772), 31 Henry Street (Tel 01 874 7419); Heuston Station; Dundrum Shopping Centre; Dublin Airport; 30 Oliver Plunkett St, Cork; 40 William St, Galway. All of the above have similar opening times to the Wicklow Street branch, except Nassau St, Grafton St & Henry St open at 7.30 am on weekdays. Amex, MasterCard, Visa, Laser. **Directions:** 5 city centre locations & Dublin Airport.

Dublin 2

Cafe Bar Deli

RESTAURANT

13 South Gt George's Street Dublin 2 **Tel: 01 677 1646**
Fax: 01 677 6044 Email: georgesstreet@cafebardeli.ie Web: www.cafebardeli.ie

Despite its obvious contemporary appeal - paper place mat menus set the tone by kicking off with Tasters, the first of which is home-made breads with three dips and marinated olives - the friendly ghosts of the old Bewleys Café are still alive and well in Jay Bourke and Eoin Foyle's inspired reincarnation of one of Dublin's oldest and best-loved comfort zones. Even the name is a play on what was the essence of a café in the old-fashioned sense - steaming pots of tea and milky coffee, with scones or a traditional fry; today it suggests a very different character. Tables may be old café style, with simple bentwood chairs, the original fireplace and a traditional brass railing remain, but a smartly striped awning over the the large street window signals the real nature of the place from the outset. Imaginative salads are packed with colourful, flavoursome treats in the modern idiom - Parmesan, anchovies, goat's cheese, hazelnuts, couscous and hummus are the vocabulary of this menu - with pizza and pasta menus continuing in the same tone. The ten or so pizzas offered include a Café Bar Deli special, changed daily, as do the pastas - and there are also family sized bowls available (serves two for about €25). Spelt bread is available, and all pasta dishes can be made with gluten/wheat free pasta. A sensibly limited wine list combines quality and style (sparkling and dessert wines included) with value; service is friendly and efficient and prices remarkably moderate - an attractive formula for an informal outing, and treating a family won't break the bank. Branches at: Ranelagh, Dublin 6 (Tel 01 496 1886); Cork (Bodega); and Sligo (Garavogue). Children welcome; air conditioning. **Seats 160;** open 7 days: Mon-Sat, 12.30-11; Sun 2-10pm; A la carte. House wine €23 (litre). No reservations. Closed 25-27 Dec, Good Fri. Amex, MasterCard, Visa, Laser. **Directions:** Next door to the Globe Bar.

Dublin 2

Café en Seine

CAFÉ/PUB

40 Dawson Street Dublin 2 **Tel: 01 677 4567** Fax: 01 677 4488
Email: cafeenseine@capitalbars.com Web: www.capitalbars.com

The first of the continental style café-bars to open in Dublin, Café en Seine is still ahead of the fashion - the interior is stunning, in an opulent art deco style reminiscent of turn-of-the-century Paris. Not so much a bar as a series of bars (your mobile phone could be your most useful accessory if you arrange to meet somebody here), the soaring interior is truly awe-inspiring with a 3-storey atrium culminating in beautiful glass-panelled ceilings, forty foot trees, enormous art nouveau glass lanterns, and statues and a 19th century French hotel lift among its many amazing features. No expense has been spared in ensuring the quality of design, materials and craftsmanship necessary to create this beautiful Aladdin's cave of a bar. Lush ferns create a deliciously decadent atmosphere and the judicious mixture of old and new which make it a true original - and its many 'bars within bars' create intimate spaces that are a far cry from the impersonality of the superpub. Appealing food is a feature too: menus offering simple bar food are left on tables - there's a sociable combination platter serving four people and hot dishes like steak sandwiches, scampi and quiches with salads are popular; everything is spotlessly clean and, while simple, the food is really tasty. There's also a snack bar offering desserts and takeaway sandwiches & baguettes with coffee, and an informal range of contemporary dishes is available over lunchtime every day, light bites all day and a popular Jazz Brunch every Sunday. Little wonder that so many people of all ages see it as the coolest place in town. Small al fresco covered section at front seats about 30. Lunch daily, 12-3; (Sun brunch 1-4). D daily: Sun-Wed, 5-9; Thu-Sat, 5-10. Wheelchair access. Bar open 10.30am-2.30am daily. Carvery lunch 12-3. Snack menu 4-10. Closed 25-26 Dec & Good Fri. Amex, MasterCard, Visa, Laser. **Directions:** Upper Dawson Street, on right walking towards St Stephen's Green (St Stephen's Green car park is very close). ◇

Dublin 2

Café Mao

RESTAURANT

2-3 Chatham Row Dublin 2 **Tel: 01 670 4899** Fax: 01 670 4993
Email: chathamrow@cafemao.com Web: www.cafemao.com

In simple but stylish surroundings and undergoing a complete refurbishment at the time of going to press, Mao Café Bar brings to the Grafton Street area the cuisines of Thailand, Malaysia, Indonesia, Japan and China - about as 'Asian Fusion' as it gets. The atmosphere is bright and very buzzy, and interesting food is based on seasonal ingredients; the standard of cooking is consistently good and so is value for money, although the bill can mount up quickly if you don't watch the number of Asian beers ordered. Chilli squid, Nasi Goreng and Malaysian chicken are established favourites, also tempura sole with stir-fried vegetables in a citrus sauce; vegetarians might try a starter of Jakarta salad (crisp vegetables and fruits in a piquant chilli dressing) followed by Thai green vegetable curry, with Jasmine rice. Chilli strength is considerately indicated on the menu, also vegetarian and low fat dishes, dishes containing nuts. A compact but wide-ranging drinks menu includes cocktails, fresh juices and smoothies, a range of coffees and teas and speciality beers as well as wines. While authenticity may not always be guaranteed, the cooking is generally good here. No reservations. Fully wheelchair accessible. Children welcome. **Seats 110.** Air conditioning. Open Mon-Thur 12-8.30, Fri-Sat 12-11pm, Sun 1-10pm. Menu à la carte. House wine from about €18; Asian beers from about €4.50. SC discretionary. CLOSED FOR REFURBISHMENT UNTIL SPRING 2007. MasterCard, Visa, Laser. **Directions:** City centre - just off Grafton Street at the Stephen's Green end.

Dublin 2

Caife Úna

Ⓝ RESTAURANT

46 Kildare St Dublin 2 **Tel: 01 670 6087**
Email: caifeuna@hotmail.com Web: www.caifeuna.com

Visitors to Ireland often ask where they can go to eat in a traditional, homely Irish atmosphere and except for pubs, which were usually the most reliable source until the 'gastropub' concept swept the scene with its new modern broom, it can be tricky enough thinking of somewhere to suggest. Enter Una NicGabhann's restaurant, which is walking a tightrope between traditional cooking and more contemporary fare (presumably to avoid scaring off local business that might not find the idea of old-fashioned cooking appealing), but is an exceptionally friendly and welcoming place and holds an unusual trump card in that it's bilingual: you don't have to speak Irish to eat here, but it's encouraged and many people will find that hearing the language in use, even in Dublin, adds a lot to a meal out. It's a semi-basement and, with a bare floor, and simple wooden tables and chairs - quite sparse, but warmed by the soft pinks of old brickwork. The menu is short and, perhaps surprisingly, quite international, but it will probably include Irish Stew, comfort food like roast chicken with black pudding mash and less usual ingredients like ling once a staple food in Irish coastal areas, but very rarely seen on a menu these days. Admirable details include home-made brown bread and, at its best, it's quite like good home cooking which, in Ireland today, is pretty international and it's good value too. Free broadband WI/Fi. **Seats 40** (outdoors, 2); children welcome before 8pm; food served daily 11am-10pm (close at 5pm Mon); house wine €18.50. Closed Sun & Bank Hols. MasterCard, Visa, Laser. **Directions:** Turn off Nassau St. and is the second business on the right - basement.

Dublin 2
RESTAURANT

Chatham Brasserie

Chatham Street Dublin 2
Tel: 01 679 0055 Web: www.chathambrasserie.ie

Just off Grafton Street, the large glass frontage and dainty tables and chairs outside Chatham Brasserie are welcoming - this is a handy place to take a break from shopping. Indoors, the chunky wooden tables with a single flower on each, bentwood chairs and a soothing combination of browns and creams give the room a slightly French elegance, underlined by effective lighting and a display of modern paintings. Menus highlight responsible sourcing of key ingredients and offer something for everyone - there's a Kids Menu as well as a wide range of popular fare like pasta, pizzas, burgers etc. Starters include one or two retro dishes like breaded & fried fishcakes (updated with grilled lime, rocket & sweet chilli mayo accompaniments), and main courses such as Cape Malay chicken curry (with poppadom, raita, chutney & rice, €16.95), and grilled organic Irish salmon fillet (with chive mash & caper butter, €17.95) are well thought out complete dishes, with delicious vegetables and salads. Dishes suitable for vegetarians and coeliacs are highlighted, also those unsuitable for anyone with nut allergies; some bottled beers are offered in addition to a short but interesting wine list. This is wholesome, satisfying fare, served by friendly (mainly French) staff - not a place for a romantic night out, perhaps, but ideal for refuelling after shopping. **Seats 80** (outdoor dining + 8), Air con. Value L Mon-Fri 11-4 €10; Early Bird D Mon-Fri 5-7 €17.95/21.95 2/3 courses. House wine €19. Open daily from 11 am - 11pm. Closed 25-26 Dec. Amex, MasterCard, Visa, Laser. **Directions:** Off Grafton Street.

Dublin 2
RESTAURANT

Chez Max

1 Palace St Dublin 2
Tel: 01 633 7215

Everyone loves Max Delaloubie's friendly brasserie, an almost too-perfect reproduction of 1940's Paris, opening onto a cobbled street at the entrance to Dublin Castle. The food, too, has that ring of Parisian authenticity - rillettes, frogs' legs, cassoulet although there is concern amongst devotees that such dishes may not have many takers in an essentially conservative city and this could bring changes to the menu, however subtle. But there is plenty there for everyone including lots of less contentious treats like Croque Monsieur and Croque Madame, Salade Parisienne, good pastries and a range of classic home-made desserts. Meanwhile, the proprietor continues to make people welcome and wannabe Parisians of every generation can groove to music that stretches from Henri Krein, Brassens and Piaf to St Etienne. The shortish wine list offers few surprises, but overall both wine and food offer very good value for money. **Seats 66** (outdoor, 25); children welcome; open for breakfast from 7.30; tea/ coffee and pastries served all day; L & D daily 12-3.30 and 5.30-10.30 (to 10 on Sun); House wine €22.50. Closed 25 Dec, 1 Jan. MasterCard, Visa, Laser. **Directions:** on the right of the Dame St. entrance to Dublin Castle.

Dublin 2
RESTAURANT

Chili Club

1 Anne's Lane South Anne Street Dublin 2
Tel: 01 677 3721 Fax: 01 635 1928

This cosy restaurant, in a laneway just off Grafton Street, has great charm; it was Dublin's first authentic Thai restaurant and is still as popular as ever a decade later. Owned and managed by Patricia Kenna, who personally supervises a friendly and efficient staff, it is small and intimate, with beautiful crockery and genuine Thai art and furniture. Supot Boonchouy, who has been head chef since 1996, prepares a fine range of genuine Thai dishes which are not 'tamed' too much to suit Irish tastes. Set lunch and early evening menus offer especially good value. Children welcome. **Seats 40** (private room, 16) L Mon-Fri 12.30-2.30, D daily 6-11. Set L €14. Early D from €14 (6-7pm), Set D €30. A la carte also available. House wine €19. SC discretionary (10% on parties 6++. Closed L Sat, Sun, 25-31 Dec. Diners, MasterCard, Visa, Laser. **Directions:** Off Grafton Street.

Dublin 2
★ HOTEL/RESTAURANT

Clarence Hotel & Tea Room Restaurant

6-8 Wellington Quay Dublin 2
Tel: 01 407 0800 Fax: 01 407 0820
Email: reservations@theclarence.ie Web: www.theclarence.ie

Dating back to 1852, this hotel has long had a special place in the hearts of Irish people - especially the clergy and the many who regarded it as a home from home when 'up from the country' for business or shopping in Dublin - largely because of its convenience to Heuston Station. Since the early

'90s, however, it has achieved cult status through its owners - Bono and The Edge of U2 - who have completely refurbished the hotel, creating the coolest of jewels in the crown of Temple Bar. No expense was spared to get the details right, reflecting the hotel's original arts and crafts style whenever possible. Accommodation offers a luxurious combination of contemporary comfort and period style, with excellent amenities including mini-bar, private safe, PC/fax connections (fax available on request), remote control satellite television and video and temperature control panels. Public areas include the clublike, oak-panelled Octagon Bar, which is a popular Temple Bar meeting place, and The Study, a quieter room with an open fire. Parking is available in several multi-storey carparks within walking distance; valet parking available for guests. Conference/banqueting (60/70); video conferencing on request. Beauty treatments, massage, Therapy @ The Clarence (also available to non-residents). Children welcome (Under 12s free in parents' room, cots available without charge, baby sitting arranged). No pets. **Rooms 49** (5 suites, incl 1 penthouse; 21 executive, 4 family rooms, 6 no smoking, 1 for disabled). Lift. 24 hr room service, Turndown service. Room rate €340; SC discretionary. **The Tea Room:** The restaurant, which has its own entrance on Essex Street, is a high-ceilinged room furnished in the light oak which is a feature throughout the hotel. Pristine white linen, designer cutlery and glasses, high windows softened by the filtered damson tones of pavement awnings, all combine to create an impressive dining room. Head chef Fred Cordonnier, previously at a number of distinguished kitchens including Restaurant Patrick Guilbaud, took the helm in the autumn of 2005 and all the signs are that he is now running a happy ship. Table d'hôte lunch and dinner menus are changed daily, and are fairly priced for an hotel of this calibre, and an à la carte menu is also offered. There is no separate reception area for the restaurant so you will be shown to your table before considering choices from a well-balanced selection of about nine dishes on each course, all demonstrating top class cooking skills and ingredients, and many of them luxurious: terrine of foie gras with black fig chutney & warm brioche toast is a typical starter for example, although more unusual dishes might include braised pigs head with roasted shrimps, confit tomatoes and broad beans. Other dishes which attracted praise on a recent visit included a beautifully presented risotto of ceps and rocket served under a cloud of Parmesan emulsion, and a main course of Wicklow lamb marinated in Vandouvan spice with preserved lemon and lamb jus split with Colombo curry oil - a lovely dish, not over spiced Even traditional sole on the bone is given a new take, when served with (boned) confit chicken wings and baby vegetables : an unpromising combination, perhaps, but it works - although low lighting could make it hard to deal with the fish bones. Finish, perhaps, with a plate of six well presented and ripe cheeses with home made biscuits & mustard fruits, or a perfect chocolate fondant, from a classic dessert menu. A well-chosen, if expensive, wine list includes a selection of very good wines by the glass, and wine service is knowledgeable. *Lighter menus are also available in the hotel - an informal Evening Menu, for example, Afternoon Tea, and The Octagon Bar Menu, offering a light à la carte and a different main course dish every day of the week. **Seats 90.** Toilets wheelchair accessible. L Sun-Fri 12.30-2.30, D daily 7-10.30 (Sun to 9.30). Set L €24, Set D €47.50/55. also a la carte L & D. House wine from €27. SC Discretionary. Octagon Bar Menu,12-10pm daily. Closed L Sat and 24 Dec-27 Dec. Amex, Diners, MasterCard, Visa. **Directions:** Overlooking the River Liffey at Wellington Quay, southside, in Temple Bar.

Dublin 2

Clarendon Café Bar

CAFÉ/BAR

Clarendon Street Dublin 2 **Tel: 01 679 2909** Fax: 01 670 6900

The Stokes brothers' stylish contemporary café-bar just off Grafton Street is a sister to Bang Café and has a chic exterior with a large glass frontage and some simple little aluminium tables and chairs outside. It's a big place, with bars spread over several storeys, but subtle decor - dark wooden floors, pale walls, chrome bars, comfortable wicker chairs - soft background music, and a warm and friendly welcome create a lovely ambience and there's a very nice buzz about it. And, as in Bang, there's a commitment to interesting food, promised on menus that name suppliers and are not over-extensive yet offer a wide range of tempting dishes: starters might include seafood like smoked haddock and cod fish cakes, or seared scallops with chorizo and roasted red pepper for example, then there are pannini for busy lunch times (and sandwiches made to order), and mains like corn-fed chicken & chive mash with smoked bacon lardons, all scrumptious bangers & mash with a piquant shallot & mustard jus. Great char-grilled steaks are served with classic béarnaise & fries, and there's an accurate description of the cooking, eg 'rare; very red, cool centre' etc, which is a must to avoid confusing orders and make life a lot easier in the kitchen. The wine list is short, but makes up in interest anything it may lack in length - and an exceptional choice is offered by the glass. If this is the way that modern bars are going in Ireland, we're all for it. Open 10-11. Food served: Mon-Sat, 12-8; Sun 12-6. No reservations. Air conditioning. Toilets wheelchair accessible. A la carte. Wines from €15.50. Closed 25 Dec, Good Fri. Amex, MasterCard, Visa, Laser. **Directions:** From St Stephen's Green, walking down Grafton Street - 1st street on left, 100yards.

Dublin 2

Conrad Hotel Dublin

HOTEL

Earlsfort Terrace Dublin 2 **Tel: 01 602 8900** Fax: 01 676 5424
Email: dublininfo@conradhotels.com Web: www.conradhotels.com

Situated directly opposite the National Concert Hall and just a stroll away from St Stephen's Green, this fine city centre hotel celebrated its twentieth anniversary in 2005 with the completion of a €15 million refurbishment programme which saw the entire hotel renovated and upgraded, and was the Guide's Business Hotel of the Year in 2006. This is an extremely comfortable place to stay - friendly staff are well-trained and helpful, and many of the pleasantly contemporary guestrooms enjoy views of the piazza below and across the city; nice touches include providing an umbrella in each room - and also a laminated jogging map of the area with one- and three-mile routes outlined. The Conrad has particular appeal for business guests, as all of the bedrooms also double as an efficient office, with ergonomic workstation, broadband, dataports, international powerpoints and at least three direct dial telephones with voice-mail - and the hotel also has extensive state-of-the-art conference and meeting facilities, a fitness centre and underground parking. Public areas include a raised lounge, which makes an ideal meeting place, and the popular Alfie Byrne's Pub, which is home to locals and visitors alike and opens on to a sheltered terrace. Conference/banqueting (320/280). Executive boardroom (12). Business centre; secretarial services; video conferencing. Underground carpark (100). Children welcome (under 18s free in parents' room, cots available, baby sitting arranged). **Rooms 192** (16 suites, 7 junior suites, 165 no-smoking, 1 for disabled). Lift. 24 hr room service. Turndown service. Room rate €270, no SC. Open all year. **Alex:** A new head chef, Brian Meehan, now leads the kitchen team at The Conrad's seafood restaurant, Alex. The decor is contemporary classic - a bright open plan room, with Elizabeth Cope paintings and low music, has polished tables with crisp white runners, and smart modern place settings - and menus are divided into choices from Land or Sea. Fish choices are quite extensive, balanced by a handful of meat and vegetarian choices. Delicious home-made breads (including a lovely Guinness bread) begin your meal and, although the tone is international, there are some dishes with an Irish slant - a starter terrine of ham hock and Savoy cabbage, for example: the aim is to offer seasonal dishes based on top quality ingredients and cooked simply, using as little added fat and salt as possible. Sometimes special culinary events are arranged - in the autumn of 2006, for example, Brian Meehan and his team were joined by Chef Sam Ang from the award-winning Conrad Singapore for "A Taste of Asia", a week-long celebration of Asian cooking: Tom Yum Goong soup, Seared Rare Marlin with Soba Noodles, Fillet of Barracuda were among the Asian seafood dishes offered. But, at any time, Brian Meehan's confident cooking and attentive service from friendly staff should ensure that dining here is an enjoyable experience. **Alex Restaurant: Seats 90;** air conditioning, children welcome. Food served all day, Mon-Sat, 7am-10pm, Sun L 1-2.30pm, Sun D, 5.30-9.30pm. Set L €28, set 3 course Sun L €40 (inc glass of champagne); early D €29, 5.30-8pm; set 2/3 course D €29/38; house wine from €24. Restaurant closed D 25 Dec, 26 Dec. Amex, Diners, MasterCard, Visa, Laser. **Directions:** On the south-eastern corner of St Stephen's Green, opposite the National Concert Hall.

Dublin 2

Cookes Restaurant

RESTAURANT

14 South William Street Dublin 2 **Tel: 01 679 0536** Fax: 01 679 0537
Email: cookes1@eircom.net Web: www.cookesrestaurant.com

Cookes has one of the pleasantest locations of any Dublin restaurant, and was among the first to offer tables outside, on the pedestrianised street under the trademark dark green awning. Johnny Cooke is a great chef and was probably also the first to present the real essence of The Med to Dublin diners. It's a place that's had its ups and downs but is now back on form; as always, the very best ingredients provide the basis for stylish food, ensuring that a starter such as duck foie gras ravioli, for example, not only looks ravishing but tastes even better. A fish special of the day - John Dory en papillotte, perhaps, simply surrounded by cooked cherry tomatoes and palourdes - enchants with its freshness, and (always renowned for the quality of his beef), you can expect a really good steak, although you may have difficulty in getting the chef to agree if you like yours well done. Salads and breads are invariably excellent, desserts are usually superb and cheeses are served in perfect condition with grapes, crisp apples and a decent selection of biscuits. Service is very friendly (some might feel it over familiar); wine service, in recent experience, is outstanding. Avoid the upstairs room unless you are in a large group - eat downstairs, and try and get a table from which to 'people-watch', especially in the afternoon. **Seats 90** (outdoor seating 40). L & D daily; L 12-4.30, D 6-10.30, Value L&D avail €24.50 (Value D 6-7pm). MasterCard, Visa, Laser. **Directions:** On corner of Castle Market and South William Street.

Dublin 2
Ⓝ RESTAURANT

Coopers Restaurant

62 Lr Leeson St Dublin 2
Tel: 01 676 8615 Fax: 01 676 8089
Email: info@coopersrestaurant.ie Web: www.coopersrestaurant.ie

Situated near Leeson Street Bridge in a very attractive old cut-stone coach house, this restaurant offers a lot of the old favourites. Prawns pil pil, Caesar salad and beef tomato & mozzarella salad are typical starters, for example, and you may expect steaks various ways, lamb cutlets, a fish dish of the day and a vegetarian pasta dish. The restaurant is on two levels and, although simply set up, the natural stone walls and the character of the building give it a pleasing atmosphere for enjoying their mid-range food. In summer, especially, it is a place worth knowing about for the outdoor seating, which is comfortably set up with plants around and an awning to protect diners from extremes of weather a pleasant spot to enjoy the light lunch menu (€15), perhaps, or the early evening menu (from €20). **Seats 120** (outdoors, 30); children welcome; L Mon-Fri, 12-3, Set L €18.50; D Mon-Sat, 5.30- "late," early D €20, 5.30-7; also a la carte L&D; house wine €18.50; 10% SC on groups 6+. Closed 25-27 Dec, Good Fri. Amex, Diners, MasterCard, Visa, Laser. **Directions:** Just before Leeson St. bridge coming from town centre.

Dublin 2
RESTAURANT

Cornucopia

19 Wicklow Street Dublin 2 **Tel: 01 677 7583**
Fax: 01 671 9449 Email: cornucopia@eircom.net

You don't have to be vegetarian to enjoy this long-established wholefood restaurant, which is well located for a wholesome re-charge if you're shopping around the Grafton Street area, but it might be a good idea to go with someone who is on a first visit. It was originally a wholefood store with a few tables at the back and, although it has now been a dedicated restaurant for some time, a waft of that unmistakable aroma remains. It may give out mixed messages in various ways - the smart red and gold frontage and pavement screen seem inviting in a mainstream way, but the atmosphere is actually quite student / alternative so don't expect a trendy modern restaurant. It is very informal, especially during the day (when window seats are well placed for people watching), and regulars like it for its simple wholesomeness, redolent of good home cooking. Vegetarian breakfasts are a speciality (lots of freshly squeezed juices to choose from) and all ingredients are organic, as far as possible. Yeast-free, dairy-free, gluten-free and wheat-free diets catered for and no processed or GM foods are used. Organic wines too. **Seats 48.** Mon-Sat 8.30am-8pm (Thu to 9pm), Sun 12-7. All à la carte (menus change daily); organic house wine about €16 (large glass about €3.95). Closed 25-27 Dec, 1 Jan, Easter Sun/Mon, Oct Bank Hol Sun/Mon. MasterCard, Visa, Laser. **Directions:** Off Grafton St. turn at Brown Thomas.

Dublin 2
RESTAURANT

Da Pino

38-40 Parliament Street Dublin 2
Tel: 01 671 9308 Fax: 01 677 3409

Just across the road from Dublin Castle, this busy youthful Italian/Spanish restaurant is always full - and no wonder, as they serve cheerful, informal, well cooked food that does not make too many concessions to trendiness and is sold at very reasonable prices. Paella is a speciality and the pizzas, which are especially good, are prepared in full view of customers. Children welcome. **Seats 75.** Open 12-11.30 daily. 2-course L (Mon-Fri), €7.40; special D €18 (all evening), also à la carte. Wine from €15.90. Closed Christmas & Good Fri. Amex, Diners, MasterCard, Visa, Laser. **Directions:** Opposite Dublin Castle.

Dublin 2
Ⓝ RESTAURANT

Darwins

16 Aungier Street Dublin 2 **Tel: 01 475 7511**
Fax: 01 475 9881 Email: darwinsrestaurant@eircom.net

Proprietor Michael Smith's own butchers shop supplies certified organic meats to this restaurant in an area known for its butchers but not, until recently, so much as a dining destination. But, together with a strong team of head chef Arter Ston and restaurant manager, Amy O'Brien, who both joined the team in 2005, Michael has opened up a whole new area for Dublin's discerning diners - and, building on their early success, the restaurant has acquired an extensive collection of original art work. Flavoursome cooking that pleases the eye as much as the taste buds combines sophistication with generosity, making the most of well-sourced ingredients, including excellent vegetables and delicious fish. Given Michael's background, you may expect excellent meats - especially great steaks - but it may be more of a surprise to find that vegetarians are so well looked after, and that one of the house specialities is a delicious vegetarian risotto of wild mushrooms and sun-dried tomato. Finish with a choice of gorgeous puddings - a well-made classic lemon tart perhaps - or mature farmhouse cheeses (attractively presented plated with fresh fruit and oatcakes) and a wack of irresistible Illy coffee. Good, reasonably priced house wines set the tone for a fair wine list - with interesting food, great service and competitive pricing too, it is no surprise that this restaurant is doing well. **Seats 50;** Air Con; Children welcome before 7; D Mon-Sat, 5.30 to 11; Early D daily 5-7 €19.50; also à la carte. Closed Sun, 25-26 Dec & Bank Hols. Amex, MasterCard, Visa, Laser. **Directions:** Opposite Carmelite Church.

Dublin 2

HOTEL

The Davenport Hotel

Merrion Square Dublin 2 **Tel: 01 607 3900** Fax: 01 661 5663
Email: davenportres@ocallaghanhotels.ie Web: www.ocallaghenhotels.ie

féile bia On Merrion Square, close to the National Gallery, the Dail (Parliament Buildings) and Trinity College, this striking hotel is fronted by the impressive 1863 facade of the Alfred Jones designed Merrion Hall, which was restored as part of the hotel building project in the early '90s. Inside, the architectural theme Is continued in the naming of rooms - Lanyon's Restaurant, for example honours the designer of Queen's University Belfast, and the Gandon Suite is named after the designer of some of Dublin's finest buildings, including the Custom House. The hotel, which is equally suited to leisure and business guests, has been imaginatively designed to combine interest and comfort, with warm, vibrant colour schemes and a pleasing mixture of old and new in both public areas and accommodation. Bedrooms are furnished to a high standard with orthopaedic beds, air conditioning, voicemail, modem lines, personal safes and turndown service in addition to the more usual amenities - all also have ample desk space, while the suites also have fax and laser printer. Above all, perhaps, The Davenport is known for the warmth and helpfulness of its staff, and it makes a very comfortable base within walking distance of shops and galleries; it is the flagship property for a small group of centrally located hotels, including the Alexander Hotel (just off Merrion Square) and the Stephen's Green Hotel (corner of St Stephen's Green and Harcourt Street). Conference/banqueting (380/400). Business centre. Gym. Children welcome (Under 2s free in parents' room; cots available, baby sitting arranged). No pets. **Rooms 115** (2 suites, 10 junior suites). Lift. 24 hr room service. B&B about €97.50pps. Open all year. Amex, Diners, MasterCard, Visa. **Directions:** just off Merrion Square. ◇

Dublin 2

PUB

Davy Byrnes

21 Duke Street Dublin 2 **Tel: 01 677 5217**
Fax: 01 671 7619 Web: www.davybyrnes.com

féile bia Just off Grafton Street, Davy Byrnes is one of Dublin's most famous pubs - references in Joyce's Ulysses mean it is very much on the tourist circuit. Despite all this fame it remains a genuine, well-run place and equally popular with Dubliners, who find it a handy meeting place. The bar food offered is quite traditional, providing 'a good feed' at reasonable prices (most meals, with hearty vegetables, are under €15). Oysters with brown bread & butter, Irish stew, beef & Guinness pie and deep-fried plaice with tartare sauce are typical and there's always a list of daily specials like sautéed lambs liver with bacon & mushroom sauce, pheasant in season - and, in deference to the Joycean connections, there's also a Bloomsday Special (gorgonzola and burgundy). Half a dozen wines are available by the glass, and about twice that number by the bottle. Not suitable for children under 7. Outside eating area. Bar food served daily, 12-9 (winter to 5). Eoin Scott - Irish roots, trad and contemporary songs 9-11pm Sun-Tue. Closed 25-26 Dec & Good Fri. MasterCard, Visa, Laser. **Directions:** 100 yards from Grafton Street.

Dublin 2

(N) RESTAURANT/WINE BAR

Dax Restaurant

23 Upper Pembroke Street Dublin 2
Tel: 01 676 1494 Email: olivier@dax.ie Web: www.dax.ie

Olivier Meisonnave - who will be warmly remembered by many in his previous role as restaurant manager at Thornton's - named his own venture after his home town in Les Landes, and this appealing wine bar-cum-restaurant is the culmination of a longheld ambition. Flagged floors, light-toned walls and upholstery that set off simple contemporary darkwood furniture in the bar and restaurant areas, and an open plan lounge area with comfortable seating for those who prefer a casual bite - it all adds up to a tone of relaxed contemporary elegance. Specialties like sautéed foie gras with apple and whole roasted seabass with herbs, feature on chef Pól ó Héannraich's menus that change weekly and offer a carefully judged selection of dishes that can make up a standard 3-course meal, or stand alone as a light plate to enjoy with wine - a growing trend in Dublin at the moment, and a welcome one.

Charcuterie and tapas style plates, for example which serve as starter or stand-alone dishes, and also substantial main courses (in the cuisine grand-mère style, perhaps - perfect for a chilly day), good puddings and an exceptional range of European cheeses - French, Italian, Spanish and, of course, Irish - on a trolley that is also available to anyone who drops in for a glass of wine between lunch and dinner. An extensive European wine list includes a large selection by the glass. **Seats 70** (Private room seats 14); Tapas menu avail in the bar; Children welcome (over 3 yrs). No wheelchair access but help available (6 steps) and no steps inside. Air con. Open Tue-Sat, L 12.30-2.30; D 6-10.30, Set L €24, D á la carte; also open during the day as a wine bar. Closed Sun, Mon, 24 Dec - 4 Jan. Amex, Diners, MasterCard, Visa, Laser.

Dublin 2

RESTAURANT

Diep Le Shaker

55 Pembroke Lane Dublin 2 **Tel: 01 661 1829** Fax: 01 661 5905
Email: info@diep.net Web: www.diep.net

This fashionable two-storey restaurant is elegantly appointed with comfortable high-back chairs, good linen and fine glasses, while sunny yellow walls and a long skylight along one side of the upper floor create a bright, summery atmosphere and the ambience is always lively - especially when the in-house cocktail wizard Paul Lambert and a team of "mixologists" are at work, creating cocktails with panache. Head chef Taweesak Trakoolwattana, who has experience in five star hotels in Thailand, has been leading the kitchen team since 2002 and at its best the cooking is excellent; the Chinese dishes previously listed have all but disappeared as a team of Thai chefs has developed the newer Royal Thai Cuisine to replace them: signature dishes include Lab Gai (spicy minced chicken salad with roasted crushed rice, shallots, chili powder, mint and fresh lime juice, served with crunchy vegetables and sticky rice) and seafood dishes like Gaeng Goong Maprow Oon (red tiger prawn curry served in young coconut) and Pla Thod Kratiem Prik Thai (crispy whole sea bass with crispy garlic, sea salt & mixed crushed peppercorn crust). Service is invariably charming and solicitous. Not suitable for children after 9 pm. Air conditioning. Toilets wheelchair accessible. Jazz Tue & Wed night. **Seats 120.** Reservations accepted. L Mon-Thu 12.15-2.30 (Fri 12-5.30), D Mon-Wed 6.15-10.30, D Thu-Sat 6.15-11.15. L & D à la carte. House wine from €21. SC 12.5% on parties 6+. Closed L Sat, Sun, bank hols, 25-29 Dec. Amex, MasterCard, Visa, Laser. **Directions:** First Lane on left off Pembroke Street.

Dublin 2

RESTAURANT

Dobbins Wine Bistro

15 Stephens Lane Dublin 2
Tel: 01 661 3321 Fax: 01 661 3331

féile bia This restaurant hidden away near Merrion Square is something of a Dublin institution, and it was run since 1978 by the late John O'Byrne and manager Patrick Walsh. Now a major revamp has transformed the restaurant - gone are the famous old Nissen hut and sawdust-strewn floors of old, here instead we have a sleek new look with smart leather banquettes and chairs, and contemporary lighting. But has it really changed so very much? A visit to this unique oasis has always been a treat for great hospitality, food which was consistently delicious in a style that showed an awareness of current trends without slavishly following them, and a love of wine. Now, while old hands may miss the cosiness of the previous Dobbins, the hospitality and professionalism has not changed and, although the presentation may be slicker, the cooking should still please. Ingredients are sourced with care, and reflect the locality: Dublin Bay prawns (not the ubiquitous tiger prawns found in so many establishments that should know better), and pork that is served with crackling indicate the philosophy and you'll find good value here too. Children welcome. Air conditioning. **Seats 120** (private room, 40). L Mon-Fri 12.30-2.30, D Tue-Sat 7.30-10.30. Set L €24.50, D à la carte. House wine from €20. SC discretionary. Closed L Sat, all Sun, D Mon, bank hols, Christmas week. Amex, Diners, MasterCard, Visa, Laser. **Directions:** Between Lower & Upper Mount Street. ◇

Dublin 2

PUB

Doheny & Nesbitt

5 Lower Baggot Street Dublin 2
Tel: 01 676 2945 Fax: 01 676 0655

Only a stone's throw from Toner's (see entry), Doheny & Nesbitt is another great Dublin institution, but there the similarity ends. Just around the corner from the Dail (Irish Parliament), this Victorian pub has traditionally attracted a wide spectrum of Dublin society - politicians, economists, lawyers, business names, political and financial journalists - all with a view to get across, or some new scandal to divulge, so a visit here can often be unexpectedly rewarding. Like the Horseshoe Bar at the nearby Shelbourne Hotel which has a similar reputation and shares the clientèle, half the fun of drinking at Nesbitt's is the anticipation of 'someone' arriving or 'something' happening, both more likely than not.

Although it has been greatly extended recently and is now in essence a superpub, it has at its heart the original, very professionally run bar with an attractive Victorian ambience and a traditional emphasis on drinking and conversation. Closed 25 Dec & Good Fri.

Dublin 2

The Dome Restaurant

RESTAURANT

St Stephens Green Shopping Centre St Stephens Green Dublin 2
Tel: 01 478 1287

At the top of the shopping centre, this bright and airy daytime restaurant has a lot going for it before you take a bite: beautiful views over St Stephen's Green, a friendly atmosphere, fresh flowers - and sometimes even live background music. On entering there is a self-service section with a full chalk board description above, and a full salad bar opposite. Everything on display is very appetising and friendly chefs are at hand behind the counter to assist your choices. The food style is basically French and Mediterranean, also a full breakfast which is served from 8 am, and afternoon meals every day. Main courses like steak Wellington, braised lamb shank and cod au gratin should tempt the most determined sandwich muncher - and there are lovely desserts supplied by the Mardi Cake Shop, next door. Children are made very welcome too, with high chairs, changing facilities and bottle warming available. And they even have live music sometimes. Great value for money too. Children welcome. **Seats 200.** Air conditioning. Open Mon-Sat, 8-6 (Sun 10-6, Thu to 8). A la carte. Wines (1/4 bottles) from €5.20. SC discretionary. Closed 25-26 Dec. MasterCard, Visa, Laser. **Directions:** Top floor of St Stephens Green Shopping Centre.

Dublin 2

Dunne & Crescenzi

RESTAURANT

14 & 16 South Frederick Street Dublin 2
Tel: 01 677 3815 Fax: 01 664 4476
Email: dunneandcrescenzi@hotmail.com Web: www.dunneandcrescenzi.com

This Italian restaurant and deli very near the Nassau Street entrance to Trinity College delights Dubliners with its unpretentiousness and the simple good food it offers at reasonable prices. It's the perfect place to shop for genuine Italian ingredients - risotto rice, pasta, oils, vinegars, olives, cooked meats, cheeses, wines and much more - and a great example of how less can be more. How good to sit down with a glass of wine (house wine is a remarkable €12, and bottles on sale can be opened for a small corkage charge) and, maybe, a plate of antipasti - with wafer-thin Parma ham, perhaps, several salamis, peppers preserved in olive oil, olives and a slice of toasted ciabatta drizzled with extra virgin olive oil... There are even a couple of little tables on the pavement, if you're lucky enough to get them on a sunny day. Indoors or out, expect to queue: this place has a loyal following. **Seats 60** (outdoor, 20). Air conditioning. Open Mon-Sat 8-11, Sun L only 12-6. Á la carte; wine from €12. Amex, MasterCard, Visa, Laser. Amex, MasterCard, Visa, Laser. **Directions:** Off Nassau Street, between Kilkenny and Blarney stores.

Dublin 2

Eden

RESTAURANT

Meeting House Square Temple Bar Dublin 2
Tel: 01 670 5372 Fax: 01 670 5373
Email: eden@edenrestaurant.ie Web: www.edenrestaurant.ie

A highlight of the Temple Bar area, this spacious two-storey restaurant was designed by Tom de Paor and has its own outdoor terrace on the square - and terrace tables have the best seats for the free movies screened on the square on Saturdays in summer; modern, with lots of greenery and hanging baskets, there's an open kitchen which adds to the buzz and a fresh, contemporary house style is seen quite extensive seasonal menus that make use of organic produce where possible, in updated classics which suit the restaurant well. Head chef Michael Durkan's menus are clear and to the point: specialities include a deliciously simple starter of smokies (smoked haddock with spring onion, crème fraîche and melted cheddar cheese), a fresh-flavoured crab salad, and down to earth dishes like beef & Guinness stew, and belly of pork. Organic beef is a feature - an excellent chargrilled sirloin with red onion, chips and a classic béarnaise sauce, perhaps - and vegetables, which always include a vegetable of the day, are exceptionally varied and imaginative. A three-course pre-theatre menu, offering four choices on each course, is great value at E25. A well-balanced and fairly priced wine list offers several wines by the glass. Great food and atmosphere, efficient service and good value too - Eden continues to fly the flag for Temple Bar. Children welcome, but not after 8pm. **Seats 96** (private room, 12-30; outdoor seating, 32). Air conditioning. L daily,12.30-3 (Sun 12-3). D daily 6-10.30 (to 10 Sun). Set L & Sun L €24, Early Bird D €25 (6-7, Sun-Thu), also à la carte. House wine €23. SC 12.5% on groups 6+. Closed bank hols, 25 Dec - 2 Jan. Amex, Diners, MasterCard, Visa, Laser. Amex,

Diners, MasterCard, Visa, Laser. **Directions:** Next to the Irish Film Theatre, opposite Diceman's Corner.

Dublin 2
RESTAURANT

Elephant & Castle

18 Temple Bar Dublin 2
Tel: 01 679 3121 Fax: 01 679 1399

This buzzy Temple Bar restaurant was one of the first new-wave places in the area and, although not quite what is was in the early days, its specialities remain the same: big, generous and wholesome salads (their special Caesar salad is renowned), pasta dishes, home-made burgers and great big baskets of chicken wings. Not a place to drop in for a quick bite - waiting staff are usually foreign students and, although willing and friendly, it can take longer than anticipated to finish a meal; however, the lively atmosphere is perhaps the strongest attraction here, so the time passes agreeably. Children welcome. Air conditioning. **Seats 85.** Open Mon-Fri, 8am-11.30pm; Sat, 10.30am-11.30pm, Sun from 12. Toilets wheelchair accessible. Closed Christmas & Good Fri. Amex, Diners, MasterCard, Visa. **Directions:** Behind Central Bank, Dame Street. ◇

Dublin 2
CAFÉ/RESTAURANT/WINE BAR

Ely Winebar & Café

22 Ely Place Dublin 2
Tel: 01 676 8986 Fax: 01 678 7866
Email: elywine@eircom.net Web: www.elywinebar.ie

Erik and Michelle Robson's unusual wine bar and café is in an imaginatively renovated Georgian townhouse just off St Stephen's Green and, since opening in 1999, they have built on their commitment to offer some of the greatest and most interesting wines from around the world - and earned a well-deserved reputation for a wine list that is a likely contender to be the most comprehensive in Ireland. They update their list every year, to offer customers what is best at the time - at the time of going to press they are listing over 500 wines, with about 90 available by the glass a (plus bottles on sale, which can be opened for a small corkage charge), thus providing the opportunity to taste wines which would otherwise be completely unaffordable to most people. And this exceptional wine list is backed up by other specialities including a list of premium beers and, on the food side, organic produce, notably pork, beef and lamb from the family farm in County Clare, are a special feature - and not just premium cuts, but also products like home-made sausages and mince, which make all the difference to simple dishes like sausages and mash or beefburgers. Recent refurbishment has created lots more room and greater comfort for adventurous sippers - and a sister establishment, the much bigger 'ely chq', opened in the IFSC in 2006, in a 10,000 sq ft grade one listed building built in 1821, and formerly known as Stack A (see entry). **Seats 100.** Open Mon-Sat 12 noon-12.30 am. L 12-3 (1-4 Sat), D 6-10.30 (11 Fri/Sat). Bar open to midnight. Wines from €26. SC 12.5% on groups of 6+. Closed Sun, Christmas week, bank hols. Amex, Diners, MasterCard, Visa, Laser Amex, Diners, MasterCard, Visa, Laser. **Directions:** Junction of Baggot Street/Merrion Street off St Stephens Green.

Dublin 2
Ⓔ Ⓝ RESTAURANT

Fallon & Byrne

11-17 Exchequer Street Dublin 2
Tel: 01 472 1000 Web: www.fallonandbyrne.com

Although it was one of Dublin's highest profile recent openings, this chic, contemporary French restaurant could easily be missed given its location above their ground floor speciality grocery and food market (which simply begs you to browse). But once up the flight of stairs or lift professionalism prevails as diners are swiftly greeted at the door and escorted to their table. Except for large flower arrangements displayed against the rear wall, decoration is minimal high ceilings, white walls, no paintings but oddly it doesn't feel stark, but has that special French bistro ambience. Two islands of warm burgundy leather upholstered seating dominate the central area, surrounded by simply laid dark-wood tables and chairs. There's a definite buzz to this bright and airy restaurant and, if you can find a free stool, a bar along one end provides a reception area where you can have a drink while waiting for your table an agreeable interlude, as you watch the extremely attentive staff at work. Once seated, breads, butter and water are presented, along with appealing menus offering a refreshingly simple and well balanced choice of meats, poultry, fish and salads - and you can look forward to authentic French bistro cooking here: a deliciously sweet French onion soup, for example, or seared foie gras with cinnamon brioche, or summer truffle brulée to start, followed by main courses with an equally French tone such as a lean and succulent loin of rabbit with fig & onion tart, morel mousse & cherry sauce. Even the long and mysterious trek to the toilets on the top floor (not an unusual experience in this area) will not dent enthusiasm for Fallon & Byrne with its central location, simple and well executed menu, great tasting food, ultra professional staff and good value. Afterwards, spend a little time looking around what has become Dublin's favourite food store downstairs you are unlikely to leave empty-handed. **Directions:** Above grocery shop on Exchequer Street. ◇

Dublin 2

Fire

N RESTAURANT

The Mansion House Dawson Street Dublin 2
Tel: 01 676 7200 Fax: 01 676 7530
Email: enquiries@mansionhouse.ie Web: www.mansionhouse.ie

The Mansion House has been the official residence of the Lord Mayor of Dublin since 1715 - the only mayoral residence in Ireland, it is older than any mayoral residence in Britain. A very large room previously known as The Supper Room is now used as a restaurant - the room itself is of sufficient interest to be worth a look even if you haven't time to eat, although the unusual Celtic themed contemporary décor of the current occupant, 'Fire', is unexpected in this graceful old room. The central feature that inspires the name is a huge wood-burning stove which also influences the menus, as most of the food is cooked in it; what you may expect here is an emphasis on quality ingredients and simple char-grilled dishes such as a speciality 'Tuscan' lamb cutlets (marinated in olive oil with rosemary and lemon, then char-grilled and served with roast aubergine, hummus and gremolata), char-grilled chicken and good steaks. Desserts tend to be a high point, service is smart and a fairly priced wine list includes above-average quality house wines at under-average prices. D Mon-Sat, 5.30-10pm, Sat, Jazz L, 1-4pm. Closed Sun. **Directions:** Half way up Dawson Street. ◇

Dublin 2

Fitzers Restaurant

RESTAURANT

51 Dawson Street Dublin 2 **Tel: 01-677 1155** Fax: 01-670 6575
Email: eat@fitzers.ie Web: www.fitzers.ie

féile bia A very popular meeting place after work or when shopping in town, Fitzers offers reliable Cal-Ital influenced cooking in a smart contemporary setting, and has a heated al fresco dining area on the pavement. **Seats 90;** Open daily 11am-11pm; Early D €17.95, 5-7pm; set D €40; house wine €22; SC 12.5% on parties 6+. Closed Dec 25/26, Good Friday. Amex, Diners, MasterCard, Visa. Also at: *Temple Bar Square, Tel: 01-679 0440(12-11 daily, cl 25 Dec & Good Fri) *National Gallery, Merrion Square Tel: 01-663 3500 Mon-Sat 9.30-5, Sun 12-4.30, closed Gallery Opening days). **Directions:** Halfway up Dawson Street, on the right heading towards St Stephen's Green.

Dublin 2

The Fitzwilliam Hotel

HOTEL

St Stephens Green Dublin 2 **Tel: 01 478 7000** Fax: 01 478 7878
Email: enq@fitzwilliamhotel.com Web: www.fitzwilliamhotel.com

This stylish contemporary hotel enjoys a superb location on the north-western corner of St Stephen's Green. Behind its deceptively low-key frontage lies an impressively sleek interior created by Sir Terence Conran's design group CD Partnership: public areas combine elegant minimalism with luxury fabrics and finishes, notably leather upholstery and a fine pewter counter in the bar, which is a chic place to meet in the Grafton Street area. In addition to the hotel's premier restaurant, Thornton's (see separate entry), breakfast, lunch and dinner are served daily in their informal restaurant Citron, on the mezzanine level. Bedrooms, while quite compact for a luxury hotel, are finished to a high standard with air-conditioning, safe, fax/modem point, stereo CD player and minibar, and care has been lavished on the bathrooms too, down to details such as designer toiletries. There's an in-house hair & beauty salon, Free Spirit, and the hotel has a great hidden asset - Ireland's largest roof garden is to be found here. Conference/banqueting (80/60). 3 conference rooms. Secretarial services. Children welcome; (under12s free in parents' room; cots available free of charge). 24 hour room service. **Rooms 128** (2 suites, 128 executive, 90 no-smoking, 4 for disabled). Lift. B&B about €160pps No service charge. Open all year Amex, Diners, MasterCard, Visa, Laser. **Directions:** On St. Stephen's Green. ◇

Dublin 2

Franks Bar & Restaurant

BAR/RESTAURANT

The Malting Tower Grand Canal Quay Dublin 2
Tel: 01 662 5870 Email: eat@franksbarandrestaurant.com

féile bia First impressions are of a somewhat sombre exterior, and the idea of eating virtually underneath a railway bridge in an artificially lit tunnel-like room (a little like a low Nissen hut) may not seem especially appealing - but, once inside John Hayes and Elizabeth Mee's popular restaurant, it all makes sense (this is, after all, the team that brought the punchy flavours of the original Elephant & Castle to Dublin): there is a smart horseshoe shaped bar, modern and sleek, with window tables - and, behind it, a pleasant dining room, furnished with stylishly designed furniture and discreet lighting reflected in long mirror strips. A sassy bistro menu offers so many tempting dishes that the big problem is deciding what to order - it's a craftily constructed all-day menu covering every possible dining eventuality from brunch right through to dinner, when an evening Specials menu is also offered. Starters kick off simply enough with rock oysters or smoked salmon, then a little French chic kicks in with more unusual choices like potted shrimps with poilane toast. Superb salads (mostly available in small or large portions) might include a luscious combination of roasted beetroot with goats cheese, French beans and rocket, with a walnut oil vinaigrette, then there are great main courses including lots of good red meat, in classic steak tartare, for instance, and juicy home made beef burgers. And how good it is to find fruit and vegetables featuring in virtually every dish as prime ingredients rather than presenting the sad 'national flag' trio of side vegetables as happens in thousands of restaurants throughout Ireland. Francophiles will be delighted to find that the mouthwatering range of sandwiches offered includes old favourites like croque m'sieu and croque m'dame... and here's even an omelette menu - what a place to go for brunch. An interesting and informative wine list makes a great read and includes out-of-the-ordinary house wines. **Seats 70.** Reservations accepted. Air conditioning. Toilets wheelchair accessible. Open 11.30 -11 pm daily (Sat/Sun from 12.30). Children welcome. Closed 24-26 Dec, Good Fri. Amex, MasterCard, Visa, Laser. **Directions:** First right after Kitty O'Shea's - just across canal bridge (on D2 side of Grand Canal).

Dublin 2

Good World Chinese Restaurant

RESTAURANT

18 South Great Georges Street Dublin 2
Tel: 01 677 5373 Fax: 01 677 5373

One of a cluster of interesting ethnic restaurants around Wicklow Street and South Great George's Street, this was one of the first and is popular with the local Chinese community, who appreciate the high standard of their Dim Sums - a selection of which can be had after 6pm at about €5 per item. A more interesting and authentic Chinese menu is available as well as the standard one, offering unusual dishes such as 'Fish Slices Congee' - a sort of rice porridge not often seen even in London - other variations are beef, chicken, salted eggs and pickle. Another satisfying concoction consists of assorted meats (chicken, pork etc and also seafood including squid, prawns and scallops) with tofu, mushrooms and Chinese leaf - delicious and a real bargain at about €14. The restaurant prides itself on an especially full range of Chinese dishes, suitable for both Chinese and European customers, and service is both friendly and efficient. **Seats 95.** Open 12.30pm-midnight daily. Closed 25-26 Dec. Amex, Diners, MasterCard, Visa, Laser. **Directions:** Corner of Sth Gt George's St & Wicklow Street.

Dublin 2

Gotham Café

RESTAURANT

8 South Anne Street Dublin 2
Tel: 01 679 5266 Fax: 01 679 5280

A lively, youthful café-restaurant just off Grafton Street, the Gotham does quality informal food at reasonable prices and is specially noted for its gourmet pizzas - try the Central Park, for example, a Greek style vegetarian pizza with black olives, red onion & fresh tomato on a bed of spinach with feta & mozzarella cheeses and fresh hummus, which is just one of a choice of sixteen tempting toppings. Other specialities include Caesar salad, baby calzoni (two miniatures - one with chèvre, prosciutto, basil & garlic; the other with baby potato, spinach, caramelised red onion, mozzarella & fresh pesto) and Asian chicken noodle salad (satay chicken fillets on a salad of egg noodles tossed in a light basil & crème fraîche dressing). There's a good choice of pastas too - and it's a great place for brunch on Sundays and bank holidays; consistent quality at fair prices. At the time of going to press Gotham Cafe was undergoing a complete renovation and will then be introducing some new menu items. [*A sister outlet, The Independent Pizza Company, is at 28 Lr Drumcondra Road, Dublin 9]. Children welcome. Air conditioning. **Seats 65** (outdoor seating, 10). Open daily: Mon-Sat 12 -12 (L 12-5, D 5-12); Sun, 12-11. A la carte. House wine €17.50. SC discretionary (10% on parties of 6+). Closed 2 days Christmas & Good Fri. Amex, MasterCard, Visa, Laser. **Directions:** Just Off Grafton Street.

Dublin 2

The Grafton Capital

HOTEL

Stephens Street Lower Dublin 2 **Tel: 01 648 1100** Fax: 01 648 1122
Email: info@graftoncapital-hotel.com Web: www.capital-hotels.com

In a prime city centre location just a couple of minutes walk from Grafton Street, this attractive hotel offers well furnished rooms and good amenities at prices which are not unreasonable for the area. Rooms are also available for small conferences, meetings and interviews. The popular 'Break for the Border' night club next door is in common ownership with the hotel. Small conferences (22). Business centre. Wheelchair access. Parking by arrangement with nearby carpark. Children welcome (Under 12s free in parents' room; cots available; baby sitting arranged). No Pets. **Rooms 75** (3 junior suites, 19 no-smoking, 4 for disabled). Lift. B&B about €100pps, ss €40. Short breaks offered. Closed 24-26 Dec. Amex, Diners, MasterCard, Visa, Laser. **Directions:** Near St. Stephen's Green (opposite Drury Street carpark).◇

Dublin 2

Harrington Hall

GUESTHOUSE

69/70 Harcourt Street Dublin 2 **Tel: 01 475 3497** Fax: 01 475 4544
Email: harringtonhall@eircom.net Web: www.harringtonhall.com

Conveniently located close to St Stephen's Green and within comfortable walking distance of the city's premier shopping areas, Trinity College and the National Concert Hall, Henry King's fine family-run guesthouse was once the home of a former Lord Mayor of Dublin and has been sympathetically and elegantly refurbished, retaining many original features. Echoes of Georgian splendour remain in the ornamental ceilings and fireplaces of the well-proportioned ground and first floor rooms, which include a peaceful drawing room with an open peat fire. Although there are some smaller, more practical bedrooms at the back, the main guestrooms are beautiful and relaxing with sound-proofed windows, ceiling fans and lovely marbled bathrooms. Service can be a little reserved but housekeeping is a strong point, and good breakfasts are served in a sunny yellow room with pictures of Dublin streetscapes to ensure a bright start to your day. All round this is a welcome alternative to a city-centre hotel, offering good value, handy to the Luas (tram), and with the huge advantage of free parking behind the building; luggage can be stored for guests arriving before check-in time (2pm). Small conferences (12). Children welcome (under 3s free in parents' room, cot available without charge). Staff are friendly and helpful. Parking (10). **Rooms 28** (2 junior suites, 3 shower only, 6 executive, 2 Family Rooms, all no smoking). Lift. 24 hour room service. B&B €86.50, ss €20. Open all year. Free wireless internet available. Amex, Diners, MasterCard, Visa, Laser. Amex, Diners, MasterCard, Visa, Laser. **Directions:** Off southwest corner of St Stephens Green (one-way system approaches from Adelaide Road).◇

Dublin 2

Hilton Dublin

HOTEL

Charlemont Place Dublin 2 **Tel: 01 402 9988** Fax: 01 402 9966
Email: allan.myhill@hilton.com Web: www.dublin.hilton.com

féile bia Overlooking the Grand Canal, this modern hotel is just a few minutes walk from the city centre and caters well for the business guest. Each double-glazed bedroom provides a worktop with modem point, swivel satellite TV and individual heater as well as the usual facilities. A buffet-style breakfast is served in the well-appointed Waterfront Restaurant. Conference/banqueting (350/270). Underground carpark. Children welcome (Under 12s free in parents' room; cots available). No pets. Lift. **Rooms 189** (78 no-smoking, 8 for disabled). Room rate from about €110 (max. 2 guests). Weekend specials from €176. Open all year. Amex, MasterCard, Visa. **Directions:** Off Fitzwilliam Square.◇

Dublin 2

Hô Sen

RESTAURANT

6 Cope Street Temple Bar Dublin 2 **Tel: 01 671 8181**
Email: timcostigan@hotmail.com Web: www.hosen.ie

Ireland's first authentic Vietnamese restaurant was our Ethnic Restaurant of the Year for 2006; the chefs are are trained in Vietnam and take pride in bringing their cuisine to this pleasingly simple restaurant - and in introducing this lighter, clear-flavoured Asian cooking style at prices which are very reasonable by Dublin standards, and especially for Temple Bar where restaurants are often over-priced - so word spread like wild fire and, from the outset, this has been a busy place. Dimmed lights and candles create an appealing atmosphere from the street and, with comfortably-spaced tables, gentle background jazz and chopsticks supplied as well as western cutlery, the scene is set for an interesting evening. Vietnamese cooking has a reputation for being among the healthiest in the world and, although the familiar Asian styles feature - spring rolls, satays, stir fries and pancake dishes, for example - fresh herb flavours of coriander and lemongrass are dominant, and there is a light touch to both the flavours and the cooking. An extensive menu is shorter than it seems, as it includes many variations on a theme, and dishes are explained quite clearly. Examples attracting praise on a recent visit included an unusual cold shredded beef dish, Bò Tái Chanh, which is a refreshing speciality from Ho Chi Minh city, flavoured with coriander and lime juice, and and Cá Kho Tô, a hotpot made with your choice of fish from the catch of the day, in which a generous amount of fish is cooked in a rich-flavoured 'pork marinade' with mushrooms, ginger root, lemongrass and a mixture of Vietnamese herbs and spices, including chilli. Choosing an appropriate wine might be a little problematic - perhaps beer or tea would be a more suitable choice. Although the presentation isn't fancy, everything is appetising, and service is lovely - pleasant, helpful and efficient. And, as the cooking here is as exciting as the welcome is warm, this place is a little gem - and its growing popularity is a reassuring sign that Dubliners appreciate quality and value when they find it. **Seats 120** (private room available seats 20). L Thu-Sun 12.30-2.30 (3 Sun) Value L €10.80; D Tue-Sat 5-10.30 (9 Sun), Early Bird D €16.95 (5-6.30). Wines from €16.95. Closed Mon, 17 Mar, 25 Dec. MasterCard, Visa, Laser. **Directions:** In Temple Bar, behind the Central Bank.

Dublin 2
N HOTEL/RESTAURANT

Holiday Inn Dublin

98-107 Pearse Street Dublin 2
Tel: 01 670 3666 Fax: 01 670 3636
Email: info@holidayinndublin.ie Web: www.holidayinndublincitycentre.ie

féile bia The Holiday Inn brand may possibly summon up the wrong images for independent travellers, but this centrally located hotel is not only a convenient place for visitors to stay, but has earned a particularly good reputation on several counts as a venue for business meetings and conferences (parking available), for food that is well above the standard expected from a mid-range hotel, and for its helpful staff. The accommodation offers all that would be expected (plus a gym for residents' use), and The Green Bistro offers appealing food, freshly cooked to order pizzas, pastas, fish and (excellent) steaks and is good value. Conferences/Banqueting (400), car parking, business centre, gym. **Rooms 101;** B&B from €50-150 pps, open all year. **Directions:** Pearse Street, City Cente.

Dublin 2
RESTAURANT

Il Primo Ristorante

16 Montague Street Dublin 2
Tel: 01 478 3373 Email: alto.primo@iolfree.ie

Dieter Bergman's cheery little two storey restaurant and wine bar between Harcourt Street and Camden Street was way ahead of current fashions when it opened in 1991. Separate air conditioned dining rooms are simply furnished, but the essentials are right: warm hospitality and good, imaginative, freshly cooked modern Italian food that includes gourmet pizzas (with smoked salmon & spinach, for example), excellent pastas and lovely salads (try the insalata misto, with mixed leaves, cheese, olives & French beans). Unusual speciality dishes include Ravioli Il Primo - open ravioli filled with chicken breast, parma ham and wild mushrooms, in a cream sauce - and lasagne with crabmeat and leek. The wines are Dieter's special passion: the list is impressive (mainly Italian and French, with a little nod to the rest of the world), and Dieter also organises regular wine tastings and dinners. Food prices are quite moderate - except for steaks, most main courses are under about €20 - but the bill can mount alarmingly if you don't watch the wine orders closely. Fresh flavours and buzz sum up Il Primo best - a visit here is always fun. Separate dining/function rooms available (30). Children welcome. **Seats 80.** Air conditioning. L Mon-Sat, 12.30-3, D daily 6-11 (Sun to 10); à la carte. House wines €25 per litre. SC10%. Closed L Sun. Amex, Diners, MasterCard, Visa, Laser. **Directions:** 5 mins from Stephens Green between Harcourt Street & Wexford Street. ◇

Dublin 2
RESTAURANT

Imperial Chinese Restaurant

12A Wicklow Street Dublin 2 **Tel: 01 677 2580**
Fax: 01 677 9851 Email: imperial@hotmail.com

Mrs Cheung's long-established city centre restaurant has enjoyed enduring popularity with Dubliners and has also a clear vote of confidence from the local Chinese community, who flock here for the Dim Sum at lunchtime - a good selection of these delectable Cantonese specialities is available between 12.30 and 5.30 daily: beef tripe is very enjoyable and Fried Seafood Noodles also attract regular praise: lots of succulent prawns, scallops and squid with Pak Choi. Crispy aromatic duck is another speciality from a wide-ranging selection of Chinese dishes. Children welcome. **Seats 180.** Private room available. Open daily 12.30-11.30 (L12.30-2.10 Mon-Sat). Set L about €12, Set D about €30. Also à la carte. House wine about €17. SC 10%. Closed 25-26 Dec. Amex, MasterCard, Visa, Laser. **Directions:** On Wicklow Street near Brown Thomas. ◇

Dublin 2
PUB

The International Bar

23 Wicklow Street Dublin 2 **Tel: 01 677 9250**

Just a minute's walk from Grafton Street, this unspoilt Victorian bar makes a great meeting place - not a food spot, but good for chat and music. Closed 25 Dec. & Good Friday. **Directions:** Corner of Wicklow Street & St Andrew Street.

Dublin 2

Jacobs Ladder

RESTAURANT

4 Nassau Street Dublin 2 **Tel: 01 670 3865** Fax: 01 670 3868
Email: dining@jacobsladder.ie Web: www.jacobsladder.ie

féile bia Adrian and Bernie Roche's smart contemporary restaurant is up a couple of flights of stairs and has a fine view, overlooking the playing fields of Trinity College. The decor is on the minimalist side with a wooden floor (which can be noisy) and paintings for sale by new Irish artists; good-sized tables with classic white linen and comfortable high-back chairs bode well for the meal ahead. Adrian's cooking style is creative modern Irish and, while there is a slight leaning towards fish - a summer dish of pan fried red mullet & scallops with tomato & aubergine, scallion risotto & pepper stew was well received on a recent visit by the Guide - his wide ranging seasonal menus always include some less usual meat dishes: steamed loin of rabbit, perhaps, with its kidney and livers - and imaginative vegetarian dishes - which, along with 'healthy eating' dishes, are considerately highlighted. Several menus are offered including a compact à la carte selection at lunch, and an early 2 or 3-course set dinner which is very good value. An appealing 8-course tasting menu, for complete parties, is also offered. Service can sometimes be a little slow but food is cooked to order and it's worth allowing time to finish off with a classic dessert (poached meringue with summer fruits and pineapple & ginger sorbet, perhaps) or Irish farmhouse cheeses, which come from Sheridans cheesemongers, and are served with tomato chutney & oat biscuits. The wine selection has character and includes half a dozen well chosen house wines, and a fair number of half bottles. *A revamp of the interior is about to take place as we go to press. Children welcome. **Seats 80** (private room, 50). L Tue-Sat 12.30-2.30; D Tue-Sat, 6-10; Early D €21/26.75 2/3 courses (6-7); Set D €44;Tasting menu €80, also à la carte. House wine from €21. No SC. Closed Sun & Mon, 25 Dec - 6 Jan, 17 Mar, Good Friday & 1 week Aug. Amex, Diners, MasterCard, Visa, Laser. **Directions:** City centre overlooking Trinity College.

Dublin 2

Jaipur

RESTAURANT

41-46 South Great Georges Street Dublin 2 **Tel: 01 677 0999**
Fax: 01 677 0979 Email: info@jaipur.ie Web: www.jaipur.ie

féile bia This custom-built restaurant is named after the "Jewel of Rajasthan" and offers a different, more contemporary image of ethnic dining. It's a cool and spacious place, with a large modern spiral staircase leading up to an area that can be used for private parties and the main restaurant below it. Although the modern decor may seem strange in comparison with traditional Indian restaurants, warm colours send the right messages and it is a pleasing space. Head chef Armit Wadhwan is keen to make the most of Irish ingredients, notably organic lamb (Khato Ghosth - Wicklow lamb braised in yoghurt with carom seeds & mustard oil, finished with asafoetida and dried mango powder - is a signature dish), while importing fresh and dried spices directly. Menus offer an attractive combination of traditional and more creative dishes - try Jaipur Jugalbandi, an assortment of five appetisers, to set the tone. Service is invariably attentive and discreet and Jaipur is a fine restaurant - and it was the first ethnic restaurant in Ireland to devise a wine list especially suited to spicy foods. *Jaipur may relocate to a new city centre premises during 2007. **Seats 110.** D daily, 5.30-11.30. Set D from €20. A la carte. House wine from €15. Closed 25-26 Dec. * Also at: 21 Castle Street Dalkey, Co.Dublin, Tel: 01 285 0552; 5 St.James' Terrace, Malahide, Co.Dublin, Tel: 01 845 5455. Amex, MasterCard, Visa, Laser. **Directions:** At the corner of Sth Great Georges St. and Lower Stephens Street.

Dublin 2

John Mulligan

PUB

8 Poolbeg Street Dublin 2 **Tel: 01 677 5582**

One of Dublin's oldest and best-loved pubs, Mulligan's 'wine & spirit merchant' is mercifully un-renovated and likely to stay that way - dark, with no decor (as such) and no music, it's just the way so many pubs used to be. The only difference is that it's now so fashionable that it gets very crowded (and noisy) after 6pm - better to drop in during the day and see what it's really like. Closed 25 Dec & Good Fri.

Dublin 2

Kehoe's

PUB

9 South Anne Street Dublin 2 **Tel: 01-677 8312**

One of Dublin's best, unspoilt traditional pubs, Kehoe's changed hands relatively recently and added another floor upstairs, but without damaging the character of the original bar. Very busy in the evening - try it for a quieter daytime pint instead. Closes 25 Dec and Good Friday. **Directions:** Off Grafton Street.

Dublin 2
CAFÉ/RESTAURANT

Kilkenny Restaurant & Café

5-6 Nassau Street Dublin 2 **Tel: 01 677 7075**
Fax: 01 670 7735 Email: info@kilkennyshop.com

féile bia Situated on the first floor of the shop now known simply as Kilkenny, with a clear view into the grounds of Trinity College, the Kilkenny Restaurant is one of the pleasantest places in Dublin to have a casual bite to eat - and the experience lives up to anticipation: ingredients are fresh and additive-free (as are all the products on sale in the shop's Food Hall) and everything has a home-cooked flavour. Salads, quiches, casseroles, home-baked breads and cakes are the specialities of the Kilkenny Restaurant and they are reliably good. They also do an excellent breakfast: fresh orange juice to start and then variations combinations of the traditional fare. [Kilkenny was the Dublin winner of our Irish Breakfast Awards in 2003.] A range of Kilkenny preserves and dressings - all made and labelled on the premises - is available in the shop. Air conditioning. Children welcome. **Seats 190.** Open Mon-Sat, 8.30-5.30 (Thu to 7), Sun 11-5.30. Breakfast to 11.15, lunch 11.30-3. A la carte. Licensed. Air conditioning. Closed 25-26 Dec, 1 Jan, Easter Sun. Amex, Diners, MasterCard, Visa. Amex, Diners, MasterCard, Visa. **Directions:** Opposite TCD playing fields.

Dublin 2
★RESTAURANT

L'Ecrivain

109a Lower Baggot Street Dublin 2
Tel: 01 661 1919 Fax: 01 661 0617
Email: sallyanne@lecrivain.com Web: www.lecrivain.com

féile bia On two levels - spacious and very dashing - Derry and Sallyanne Clarke's acclaimed city centre restaurant has lots of pale wood and smoky mirrors - and lovely formal table settings which promise seriously good food. The upstairs seating has recently been extended, to include a conservatory complete with awning which also acts as a functional, airy and comfortable smoking area. Derry's cooking style - classic French with contemporary flair and a strong leaning towards modern Irish cooking - remains consistent, although new ideas are constantly incorporated and the list of specialities keeps growing. Special treats to try might include a speciality starter of baked rock oysters with York cabbage & crispy cured bacon, with a Guinness sabayon - perhaps followed by a main course of loin and cutlet of spring lamb with organic turnip cream, lamb faggot & vegetable broth. Thoughtful little touches abound - a fine complimentary amuse-bouche before your first course, for example - and there are some major ones too, like the policy of adding the price of your wine after the 10% service charge has been added to your bill, instead of charging on the total as most other restaurants do: this is an expensive restaurant (minimum spend €70 per person) but a gesture like this endears it to customers who happily dig deep into their pockets for the pleasure of eating here. Seafood, lamb, beef and game, in season, are all well-represented, but menus could also include neglected ingredients like rabbit, which is always appealingly served. Pastry chef Jenny Inkle's wonderful puddings are presented with panache and might include a warm chocolate fondant with pistachio ice cream & zabaglione cream, or cherry & mascarpone parfait with chocolate stuffed cherries & chocolate sauce; a special wine is suggested for each dish on the dessert menu and an extensive tea and coffee menu is offered. Presentation is impressive but not ostentatious, and attention to detail - garnishes designed individually to enhance each dish, careful selection of plates, delicious home-made breads and splendid farmhouse cheeses - is excellent. Lunch, as usual in top rank restaurants, offers outstanding value although service can sometimes be a little slow. A fine wine list is augmented by a tempting selection of digestifs - all of which up to a very caring approach and an exceptional restaurant. **Seats 100.** (private room, 20. outdoor seating, 25) L Mon-Fri 12.30-2, D Mon-Sat 7-10.30, Set L €45. Set D €75 (Vegetarian Menu about €50). Tasting Menu €120. House wine €30. 10% SC (on food only). Closed L Sat, all Sun, Christmas & New Year, Easter, bank hols. Amex, MasterCard, Visa, Laser. **Directions:** 10 minutes walk east of St Stephens Green, opposite Bank of Ireland HQ.

Dublin 2
E RESTAURANT

L'Gueuleton

1 Fade Street Dublin 2
Tel: 01 675 3708 Fax: 01 635 9902

This no-frills French restaurant took Dublin by storm when it opened in the autumn of 2004 - so much so that, in a very short time, it became necessary to extend. The format: simple premises and no-nonsense French bistro decor, with tightly packed table and a few seats at the bar (with views into the kitchen), plus a menu that makes no distinction between courses and offers a combination of less usual dishes (roquefort & snail pithviers with herb salad) and the classic (blanquette of lamb). Add to this great cooking, a short, all French wine list (by Simon Tyrrell), pretty efficient service and terrific value for money - and you have the kind of restaurant that Dubliners have been praying for. Small wonder it has already doubled in size. The only downside is the continuing no reservations policy. **Seats 75.** Open Mon-Sat, L 12.30-3, D 6-10. Closed Sun. A la carte. House wines €19. No reservations. MasterCard, Visa, Laser. **Directions:** At Hogans Bar, off Georges Street.

Dublin 2
RESTAURANT/WINE BAR

La Cave Wine Bar & Restaurant

28 South Anne Street Dublin 2
Tel: 01 679 4409 Fax: 01 620 5255
Email: lacave@iol.ie Web: www.lacavewinebar.com

féile bia Wine bars were originally not a noticeable feature of Dublin's hospitality scene, but Margaret and Akim Beskri have run this characterful place just off Grafton Street since 1989 and it's well-known for its cosmopolitan atmosphere, late night opening and lots of chat. An excellent wine list of over 350 bins (predominantly French) includes over 15 bubblies, an exceptional choice of half bottles and a separate list of wines by the glass. With its traditional bistro atmosphere, classic French cooking ("food for the gourmet at reasonable prices"), it makes a handy place to take a break from shopping, for an evening out, or for a party. Classic menus with the occasional contemporary twist make a refreshing change from the ubiquitous eclectic fare that has taken over the restaurant scene in recent years: paté de campagne, moules marinieres, Wicklow lamb cutlets with a thyme jus, warm salad of kidneys, and tarte tatin with cinnamon & vanilla ice cream all indicate the style (although it is a pity to see tiger prawns listed here, beside West Coast oysters...). Many of the dishes are perfect for a one plate light meal - ideal for a shopping break. A private room upstairs (with bar) is suitable for parties and small functions - Christmas parties are a speciality, but it's ideal for any kind of party, family reunions or even small weddings. No children after 9pm. **Seats 28** (private room, 28). Air conditioning. Open Mon-Sat 12.30-11, Sun 5.30-11. Set L €13.50. Early D €15.95, Set D €32. Also à la carte. House wine from €17.50. SC discretionary. Closed L Sun, 25-26 Dec, Good Fri. Amex, Diners, MasterCard, Visa, Laser. **Directions:** Just off Grafton Street.

Dublin 2
€ CAFÉ

La Maison des Gourmets

15 Castle Market Dublin 2 **Tel: 01 672 7258**

In a pedestrianised area handy to car parks and away from the hustle and bustle of nearby Grafton Street, this French boulangerie has a smart little café on the first floor and also a couple of outdoor tables on the pavement for fine weather. Home-baked bread is the speciality, made to a very high standard by French bakers who work in front of customers throughout the day, creating a wonderful aroma that wafts through the entire premises. The speciality is their award-winning sourdough bread, which is used as the base for a selection of tartines - French open-style sandwiches served warm - on the lunch menu (about €12): baked ham with thyme jus and smoked bacon cream, perhaps, or vegetarian ones like roast aubergine with plum tomato, fresh parmesan & basil pesto. Add to this a couple of delicious soups (typically, French onion with Emmental croûtons), a hot dish like classic beef bourguignon with potato purée, one or two salads - and a simple dessert like strawberries with balsamic reduction and fresh cream - and the result is as tempting a little menu as any discerning luncher could wish for. Portions are on the small side, which suits most lunch time appetites, and service can be a little slow; but everything is very appetising, the atmosphere is chic and you can stock up on bread and croissants from the shop as you leave - just don't think in terms of a quick bite. **Seats 28.** Open Mon-Sat, 9-5.30 (L12-4). Set L €18.50; also A la carte. SC discretionary. House wine €19. Closed Sun, bank hols, 4 days Christmas. Amex, Diners, MasterCard, Visa, Laser. **Directions:** Pedestrianised area between Georges Street Arcade and Powerscourt Shopping Centre. ◇

Dublin 2
RESTAURANT

La Mère Zou

22 St Stephen's Green Dublin 2 **Tel: 01 661 6669** Fax: 01 661 6669
Email: info@lamerezou.ie Web: www.lamerezou.ie

Eric Tydgadt's French/Belgian restaurant is situated in a Georgian basement on the north side of the Green and has recently undergone a complete refurbishment - the style is leaner-lined and fresher, but fans will be pleased to know that the essence of the old restaurant is still there. Likewise, the food - although there are some concessions to current cuisine (especially on the lunch menu), this establishment's reputation is based on classic French/Belgian country cooking, as in rillette of pork with toasted baguette or confit duck leg with braised lentils; specialities include steamed mussels (various ways) with French fries, and prices are reasonable - a policy carried through to the wine list too. The lunch menu - which offers a choice of three dishes on each course - also suggests six or seven more luxurious seafood dishes from the à la carte, so you can make a feast of it if time allows or, at the other extreme, they offer a range of Big Plates, with a salad starter and a main course served together on a king size plate which is great value and ideal if you're in a hurry. This is one of Dublin's pleasantest and most reliable restaurants, and they have recently opened a sister 'establishment', La Péniche, on the Grand Canal (see entry). [*The associated business, **Supper's Ready** - an enlightened takeaway doing real food like navarin of lamb and potée paysanne - now has three outlets: 51, Pleasant Street, Dublin, 8. (Tel: 01-475 4556); 58 Clontarf Road, Dublin 3 (Tel: 01 853 3555) and Monread Avenue, Naas, Co. Kildare (Tel: 045 889554). Check the website for further details: www.suppersready.ie] **Seats 60** (private room, 8, outdoor, 6); Live jazz Fri-Sat 9-11; L Mon-Fri, 12-2.30. D 6-10.30 (Sun to 9.30). Early D €24.50 (6-7), Set L €24.50; also à la carte. House wine €21.50. SC discretionary. Closed L Sat, L Sun, 25 Dec - 1st Fri Jan. Amex, Diners, MasterCard, Visa, Laser. **Directions:** Beside Shelbourne Hotel.

Dublin 2
HOTEL/RESTAURANT

La Stampa

35 Dawson Street Dublin 2
Tel: 01 677 4444 Fax: 01 677 4411
Email: dine@lastampa.ie Web: www.lastampa.ie

Reminiscent of a grand French belle époque brasserie, La Stampa is best known as a restaurant and it is one of Ireland's finest dining rooms - high-ceiling, with large mirrors, wooden floor, candelabra, Victorian lamps, plants, flowers and various bits of bric-a-brac, the whole noisily complemented by a constant bustle. It is a fun and lively place, offering international brasserie-style food in delightful surroundings. Hotel: More recently, La Stampa has been developed as an hotel, and very attractive rooms have sumptuous fabrics, echoing the ambience of the restaurant and bar below. No children under 12 after 8pm. Air conditioning. **Seats 230** (private room, 70). L daily, 12-3; D daily, 6-12.30am. Set menus offered; also à la carte. SC10%. **Rooms 30.** Room rate about €135. Open all year. ***Tiger Becs,** a mainly Thai restaurant downstairs, is under the same management. Seats 130, D Mon-Sat 6-12.30. ***Sam Sara Bar and Café** is also part of the La Stampa complex Amex, Diners, MasterCard, Visa, Laser. **Directions:** Across Dawson Street from the Mansion House. ◇

Dublin 2
RESTAURANT

Layla Turkish Restaurant

31-32 Lr Pembroke Street Dublin 2 **Tel: 01 662 2566**
Fax: 01 662 2567 Email: info@layla.ie Web: www.layla.ie

Upstairs, over the Pembroke Bar where 'The Pemboke Restaurant' used to be, this new Turkish restaurant now offers ethnic quality and great value (delicious mezze platters, grilled skewered meats, the slow-cooked lamb dishes typical of the area, and sweet desserts with nuts and honey). The food is excellent and it's a relaxed, fun place for a meal - and the occasional presence of a belly dancer no doubt contributes to Layla's popularity. A short international wine list includes raki, available by the glass or bottle. Children welcome. **Seats 60** (outdoors, 40); L&D served Mon-Sat, 12-4 & 6-12; a la carte L&D, house wine €20. Closed Sun, Christmas and New Year. MasterCard, Visa, Laser. **Directions:** Off Lower Baggot street.

Dublin 2
RESTAURANT

Les Frères Jacques

74 Dame Street Dublin 2 **Tel: 01 679 4555** Fax: 01 679 4725
Email: info@lesfreresjacques.com Web: www.lesfreresjacques.com

One of the few genuinely French restaurants in Dublin, Les Frères Jacques opened beside the Olympia Theatre in 1986, well before the development of Temple Bar made the area fashionable. Most of the staff are French, the atmosphere is French - and the cooking is classic French. The decor is soothing - all the better to enjoy seasonal menus that are wide-ranging and well-balanced but - as expected when you notice the lobster tank on entering - there is a strong emphasis on fish and seafood; game also features in season, although there will always be prime meats and poultry also. Lunch at Les Frères Jacques is a treat (and good value) but dinner is a feast. The à la carte offers classics such as west coast oysters (native or rock) and grilled lobster, individually priced, and probably game in season. Finish with cheeses (perhaps including some Irish ones) or a classic dessert like warm thin apple tart (baked to order), with cinnamon ice cream and crème anglaise. The wine list naturally favours France and makes interesting reading. Children welcome. Air conditioning.* **Seats 60** (private room, 40). L Mon-Fri, 12.30-2.30; D Mon-Sat, 7-10.30 (to 11pm Fri/Sat). Set 2/3 courese L €17.50/22.50; Set D €36; D also à la carte. House wine €20.50. SC 12.5%. Closed L Sat, all Sun, 24 Dec-2 Jan. Amex, MasterCard, Visa, Laser. **Directions:** Next to Olympia Theatre. ◇

Dublin 2

The Long Hall Bar

PUB

51 South Great George's Dublin 2 **Tel: 01-475 1590**

A wonderful old pub with magnificent plasterwork ceilings, traditional mahogany bar and Victorian lighting. One of Dublin's finest bars and well worth a visit. Closed 25 Dec & Good Fri.

Dublin 2

Longfields Hotel

HOTEL

10 Lower Fitzwilliam Street Dublin 2 **Tel: 01 676 1367** Fax: 01 676 1542
Email: info@longfields.ie Web: www.longfields.ie

Located in a Georgian terrace between Fitzwilliam and Merrion Squares, this reasonably priced hotel is more like a well proportioned private house, furnished with antiques in period style - notably in elegant public areas. Comfortable bedrooms are individually furnished, some with four-posters or half-tester beds, although they vary considerably in size as rooms are smaller on the upper floors. Small conferences (22). 24 hour room service. Children welcome (cots available). No pets. Lift. **Rooms 26** (2 junior suites, 19 shower only). B&B about €87.50pps, ss about €47.50 Open all year. Amex, MasterCard, Visa, Laser. **Directions:** On corner of Fitzwilliam Street & Baggot Street.

Dublin 2

M J O'Neill's Public House

PUB

2 Suffolk Street Dublin 2 **Tel: 01 679 3656** Fax: 01 679 0689
Email: mike@oneillsbar.com Web: www.oneillsbar.com

A striking pub with its own fine clock over the door and an excellent corner location, this large bar has been in the O'Neill family since 1920 and is popular with Dubliners and visitors alike. Students from Trinity and several other colleges nearby home into O'Neill's for its wide range of reasonably priced bar food, which includes a carvery with a choice of five or six roasts and an equal number of other dishes (perhaps including traditional favourites such as Irish Stew) each day; finish off with some home-made rhubarb pie, perhaps. There is also a well-presented sandwich/salad bar. Carvery 12 - 10.15 Daily. Also extensive à la carte bar menu. Live traditional music every Mon night at 9pm. Wheelchair access. No children after 9pm. Closed 25 Dec, Good Fri. Amex, MasterCard, Visa, Laser. **Directions:** On the corner of Suffolk St and Church Lane, opposite the DublinTourist Centre.

Dublin 2

Market Bar & Tapas

BAR

Fade Street Dublin 2 **Tel: 01 613 9090** Fax: 01 677 4585
Email: info@tapas.ie Web: www.tapas.ie

A fairly recent addition to the chain of bars operated by Jay Bourke and Eoin Foyle, this large bar is is located in the Victorian redbrick block best known for the George's Street Market Arcade that runs through its centre. It's an attractive space with lofty ceilings (high enough to allow the addition of a mezzanine floor) and simple, stylish furnishings - a little too simple perhaps, as the wooden floor and hard surfaces bounce noise around and there's precious little to absorb it. It was an immediate hit with young Dubliners however and the food, which is cooked in an open kitchen, has given it a broader attraction as The Market Bar has earned a reputation for serving some of the best tapas in Dublin. The menu is loosely Spanish, offering nibbles like olives, smoked almonds and anchovies, and more substantial dishes which can be ordered as small or large portions (about €6-10 each) and include appealing renditions of Spanish classics like tortilla, morcilla inchos and patatas bravas. Alowing a little licence for local tastes, and providing you don't mind eating in a busy bar (even a designated restaurant area is likely to feel crowded), this could be a good choice for casual eating while socialising. Toilets wheelchair accessible, bar access via ramp; children welcome before 7pm; air conditioning. Food daily: Mon-Sat 12-10; Sun 4-10. Closed 25-26 Dec, Good Fri. Amex, MasterCard, Visa, Laser. **Directions:** Off Georges St.

Dublin 2

McDaids

PUB

3 Harry Street Dublin 2

Established in 1779, McDaids more recently achieved fame as one of the great literary pubs - and its association with Brendan Behan, especially, brings a steady trail of pilgrims from all over the world to this traditional premises just beside the Westbury Hotel. Dubliners, however, tend to be immune to this kind of thing and drink there because it's a good pub - and, although its character is safe, it's not a place set in aspic either, as a younger crowd has been attracted by recent changes. History and character are generally of more interest than food here, but sandwiches are available. Open Mon-Wed,10.30am-11.30pm; Thu-Sat, 10.30am-12.30am; Sun 12.30-11. Closed 25 Dec & Good Fri.

Dublin 2

☆RESTAURANT

The Mermaid Café

69-70 Dame Street Dublin 2
Tel: 01 670 8236 Fax: 01 670 8205
Email: info@mermaid.ie Web: www.mermaid.ie

Ben Gorman and Mark Harrell's unusual restaurant on the edge of Temple Bar is not large, but every inch of space is used with style in two dining areas and a wine lounge. They celebrated a decade in business in 2005 and, during that time, they've achieved well-earned recognition for a personal style of hospitality, imaginative French and American-inspired cooking and interesting one-off decor. Innovative, mid-Atlantic, seasonal cooking can be memorable for inspired combinations of flavour, texture and colour - and specialities like New England crab cakes with piquant mayonnaise, the Giant Seafood Casserole (which changes daily depending on availability) and pecan pie are retained on daily-changing menus by popular demand. Vegetables, always used imaginatively, are beautifully integrated into main courses - rump of lamb with roast vegetable & couscous tart, aubergine & cumin purée is a good example, and there are many more like it on each day's menus. Then delicious desserts, wonderful Irish cheeses (like the deeply flavoured Gabriel and Desmond from West Cork, served with apple chutney) and coffees with crystallised pecan nuts: attention to detail right to the finish. Lunch menus are extremely good value, and Sunday brunch is not to be missed if you are in the area. Wines are imported privately and are exclusive to the restaurant. Children welcome. **Seats 60** (private room, 24). Reservations required. Air conditioning. Toilets wheelchair accessible. L 12.30-2.30 (Sun brunch to 3.30), D 6.00-11 (Sun to 9). Set L €21.95/25.95 2/3 courses, also á la carte; D á la carte. House wine €22.95. SC discretionary execept tables 5+. Closed Christmas, New Year, Good Friday. *Next door, Gruel (Tel 01 670 7119), is a quality fast-food bistro (60 seats) under the same management, with a large & loyal following; open Mon-Sat 11-10.30; Sun 11-9. Amex, MasterCard, Visa, Laser. **Directions:** Next door to Olympia Theatre, opposite Dublin Castle.

Dublin 2

☆HOTEL/RESTAURANT

Merrion Hotel

Upper Merrion Street Dublin 2
Tel: 01 603 0600 Fax: 01 603 0700
Email: info@merrionhotel.com Web: www.merrionhotel.com

Right in the heart of Georgian Dublin, opposite Government Buildings, this luxurious hotel comprises four meticulously restored Grade 1 listed townhouses built in the 1760s and, behind them, a contemporary garden wing overlooks formal landscaped gardens. Public areas include three interconnecting drawing rooms (one is the cocktail bar with a log fire), with French windows giving access to the gardens; Irish fabrics and antiques reflect the architecture and original interiors with rococo plasterwork ceilings and classically proportioned windows - and the hotel owns one of the most important private collections of 20th-century art. Maintenance is immaculate - refurbishment of soft furnishings, for example, is so skilfully effected that it is completely unnoticeable. Beautifully furnished guest rooms and suites have sumptuous bathrooms (all with separate bath and shower) and all the extras expected in a hotel of this calibre, including broadband. Discreet, thoughtful service is an outstanding feature of the hotel and staff, under the excellent direction of General Manager Peter MacCann, are exceptionally courteous and helpful - likewise, the pamper-factor in the splendid leisure complex, The Tethra Spa - which is romanesque, with classical mosaics - is predictably high. Dining options match standards elsewhere in the hotel: choose between the elegant vaulted Cellar Restaurant (see below) and Restaurant Patrick Guilbaud (see separate entry), which is also on site. Conference/banqueting (60/50). **Rooms 143** (20 suites, 10 junior suites, 80 no smoking, 5 for disabled). Children welcome (under 2s free in parents' room, cot available free of charge, baby sitting arranged). Air conditioning. Lift. 24 hr room service, B&B €160 pps. Complimentary underground valet parking. Open all year. **Cellar Restaurant:** Warm, friendly staff swiftly seat arriving guests at beautiful classically appointed tables in this elegant vaulted dining-room, and explain well-balanced menus which are changed daily and have a refreshingly straightforward tone. With comfortable furniture and thoughtfully designed lighting and ventilation, this is a very relaxing room - and the philosophy is to source the best ingredients and treat them with respect in a simple style that shows the food to advantage without over-emphasis on display. Merrion fish & chips with mushy peas and tartare sauce somehow seems a most appropriate signature dish in a restaurant where accomplished cooking goes without saying, and delicious flavours, excellent service and great value for the quality of food and surroundings are the priorities. A good wine list also offers value, including wines by the glass. *In fine summer weather the hotel also offers dining outdoors on the terrace. The Cellar Restaurant: **seats 80;** air con; children welcome; D daily 6-10, early D 6-7 Mon-Thurs €32.50, also á la carte; L Mon-Sat 12.30-2, Set L €24.95; Sun Brunch 12.30-2.30, €29.50/35 2/3 course. Open all year. Amex, Diners, MasterCard, Visa, Laser. Amex, Diners, MasterCard, Visa, Laser. **Directions:** City centre, opposite Government Buildings.

Milano

Dublin 2

RESTAURANT 38 Dawson Street Dublin 2 **Tel: 01 670 7744** Fax: 01 679 2717

This stylish contemporary restaurant at the top of Dawson Street is best known for its wide range of excellent pizzas (it's owned by the UK company Pizza Express), but it's more of a restaurant than the description implies. Children are welcome and they run a very popular crèche facility on Sunday afternoons (12-4.30pm). Branches also in Temple Bar, and Cork & Galway. **Seats 140** (private room 80). Air conditioning. Open daily,12 noon-12 midnight (Sun to 11.30). Menu à la carte. House wine about €17. SC discretionary (10% on parties of 7+). Closed Dec 25 & 26. Amex, Diners, MasterCard, Visa, Laser. **Directions:** Opposite Mansion House, just off Stephens Green.

Mont Clare Hotel

Dublin 2

HOTEL Merrion Square Dublin 2 **Tel: 01 607 3800** Fax: 01 661 5663

Email: montclareres@ocallaghanhotels.ie Web: www.ocallaghanhotels.ie

A few doors away from the National Gallery, this well-located and relatively reasonably priced hotel is in common ownership with the nearby Davenport and Alexander Hotels. The hotel is imaginatively decorated in contemporary style - except the old stained glass and mahogany Gallery Bar, which has retained its original pubby atmosphere. Compact bedrooms are well furnished and comfortable - and executive rooms for business guests have full marbled bathrooms and good amenities, including air conditioning, three direct line phones, a personal safe, ISDN lines and fax - and multi-channel TV with video channel. Business centre; use of gym (at Davenport Hotel). Conference/banqueting. (200). Children welcome (Under 2s free in parents' room; cots available free of charge). No pets. **Rooms 80** (40 no-smoking). Lift. Room rate about €245. Open all year. Amex, Diners, MasterCard, Visa, Laser. **Directions:** Corner of Clare Street, just off Merrion Square. ◇

Montys of Kathmandu

Dublin 2

Ⓔ RESTAURANT 28 Eustace Street Temple Bar Dublin 2

Tel: 01 670 4911 Fax: 01 494 4359

Email: montys@eircom.net Web: www.montys.ie

Shiva Gautham's modest-looking restaurant opposite the Irish Film Centre is the only one in Ireland's to specialise in Nepalese cuisine, and the food here can have real character - at agreeably moderate prices. The chefs are all from Nepal and although all the familiar Indian styles are represented- tandoori, curry etc - the emphasis is on Nepalese specialities and varying standard dishes by, for example, using Himalayan spices. The menu is quite extensive and includes a platter of assorted starters which is a good choice for a group of four, allowing time to consider the rest of the menu without rushing; there's also a fair selection of vegetarian dishes, including a traditional Nepali mixed vegetable curry which can be served mild, medium or hot. Friendly staff are happy to offer suggestions, or to choose a well balanced meal for you, including specialities like Kachela (a starter of raw minced lamb with garlic, ginger, herbs and spices which is said to be a favourite amongst the Newars in Kathmandu, served with a shot of whiskey) and Momo - these Nepalese dumplings served with a special chutney require 24 hours notice and are 'the most popular dish in Kathmandu'. But you will also find sound renditions of old favourites here, including Chicken Tika Masala: moist pieces of tender boneless chicken cooked in the tandoori, and served in a creamy masala sauce. This can be a really rewarding restaurant and, in addition to a very adequate wine list and drinks menu, they even have their own beer, 'Shiva', brewed exclusively for the restaurant. Children welcome. **Seats 60** (private room, 30) L Mon-Sat, 12-2.15; Set L €17, D from €20; D daily 6-11.30, (Sun to 11), Tasting Menu about €30-45. L&D à la carte available. SC discretionary. House wine from about €17. Closed L Sun, 25-26 Dec, 1 Jan & Good Fri. Amex, MasterCard, Visa, Laser. **Directions:** Temple Bar - opposite the Irish Film Centre (IFC). ◇

Morgan Hotel

Dublin 2

HOTEL 10 Fleet Street Temple Bar Dublin 2 **Tel: 01 679 3939** Fax: 01 679 3946

Email: sales@themorgan.com Web: www.themorgan.com

In deepest Temple Bar, this unusual boutique hotel is characterised by clean simple lines and uncluttered elegance. Bedrooms have 6' beds in light beech, with classic white cotton bed linen and natural throws, while standard bedroom facilities include satellite TV and video, CD/hi-fi system, mini-bar, safe, voicemail and Internet access. The stylish Morgan Bar is open all day and offers an oasis of comfort and relaxation amongst the hustle and bustle of Temple Bar - try an exotic Morgan Mai Tai, perhaps? Casual dining is available in the Morgan Bar, where an excellent (and extensive) tapas menu is served all day (12.30pm until 9.30pm). Children welcome (cots available without charge, baby sitting arranged). **Rooms 66** (1 suite, 1 junior suite, 15 executive, 30 shower only, 33 no-smoking). Lift. Room rate €220. Closed Christmas. Amex, Diners, MasterCard, Visa, Laser. **Directions:** off Westrmoreland Street. ◇

Dublin 2

Neary's

PUB

1 Chatham Street Dublin 2 **Tel: 01 677 8596** Fax: 01 677 7371

This unspoilt Edwardian pub off Grafton Street has been in the present ownership for over half a century and is is popular at all times of day - handy for lunch or as a meeting place in the early evening and full of buzz later when a post-theatre crowd, including actors from the nearby Gaiety Theatre, will probably be amongst the late night throng in the downstairs bar. Traditional values assert themselves through gleaming brass, well-polished mahogany and classics like smoked salmon and mixed meat salads amongst the bar fare. Open Sun-Thu 10.30-11.30 (to 12.30 Fr & Sat). Bar food: Mon-Sat, 10.30-2.45. Closed 25 Dec & Good Fri. MasterCard, Visa, Laser. **Directions:** Off Grafton Street.

Dublin 2

Nude Restaurant

CAFÉ

21 Suffolk Street Dublin 2 **Tel: 01 672 5577**
Fax: 01 672 5773 Email: niamh@nude.ie

Nude offers fantastic very fresh food - organic whenever possible - in an ultra-cool, youthful environment. Just off Grafton Street it's a great place for a quick snack, with plenty of room to sit down at long canteen-style tables. Queue up, order and pay at the till, then collect your food if it's ready or it will be delivered to your table. If you eat with your eyes, just looking at the fresh fruit and vegetables hanging or racked up in the open kitchen should revive you while you wait! A choice of soups includes seafood chowder, chunky vegetable and Thai chicken broth, all served with freshly baked breads; there are hot wraps - chicken satay or vegetarian Jumping Bean, for example - and panini, including one with Gubeen cheese, or try the chill cabinet for salads like Caesar or tomato & mozzarella, and cold wraps such as hummus or spinach & peppers, or soft bread rolls (e.g. smoked salmon & cream cheese). Freshly squeezed juices, smoothies and organic Fair Trade coffees, teas and herbal teas are all very popular (drinks can be made up to order) and the menu caters for vegetarians, people with nut allergies and other dietary requirements. **Seats 40.** Open daily 7.30am-9pm (to 10pm Thurs, 8pm Sun). MasterCard, Visa, Laser. **Directions:** Near Dublin Tourism office. ◇

Dublin 2

Number 31

Ⓔ GUESTHOUSE

31 Leeson Close Lr Leeson Street Dublin 2
Tel: 01 676 5011 Fax: 01 676 2929
Email: number31@iol.ie Web: www.number31.ie

Formerly the home of leading architect Sam Stephenson, Noel and Deirdre Comer's hospitable 'oasis of tranquillity and greenery' just off St Stephen's Green makes a relaxing and interesting city centre base, with virtually everything within walking distance in fine weather. Public areas of the house are spacious and very comfortable, and fresh, elegant bedrooms have good bathrooms and nice little extras including complimentary bottled water as well as phones, TVs and tea/coffee trays. Breakfasts served at communal tables inside, and in the conservatory are not to be missed - freshly baked breads and delicious preserves, and lovely hot dishes like kippers or mushroom frittata cooked to order... Prices are moderate for central Dublin, and secure parking adds greatly to the attraction of a stay here. Not suitable for children under 10. No pets. Rooms at the back are quieter. **Rooms 20** (all en-suite & no smoking). B&B from about €75, ss €25. Open all year. Amex, MasterCard, Visa. Amex, MasterCard, Visa. **Directions:** From St. Stephens Green onto Baggot St., turn right on to Pembroke St. and left on to Leeson Street. ◇

Dublin 2

O'Donoghue's

PUB

15 Merrion Row Dublin 2 **Tel: 01 676 2807**

O'Donoghues has long been the Dublin mecca for visitors in search of a lively evening with traditional music - live music every night is a major claim to fame - but a visit to this famous pub near the Shelbourne Hotel at quieter times can be rewarding too. Closed 25 Dec & Good Fri.

Dublin 2

O'Neill's Pub & Guesthouse

PUB/GUESTHOUSE

37 Pearse Steet Dublin 2 **Tel: 01 677 5213** Fax: 01 8325218
Email: oneilpub@iol.ie Web: www.oneillsdublin.com

Established in 1885, this centrally located pub on the corner of Pearse Street and Shaw Street is easily recognised by the well-maintained floral baskets that brighten up the street outside. Inside, this cosy bar has kept its Victorian character and charm (two bars have lots of little alcoves and snugs) and serves a good range of reasonably priced home-cooked food - typically steak champignon with red wine sauce, served with French fries and an attractive salad; lamb filo parcels with mint yoghurt and chilli con carne - all good value (under €15). (Accommodation is available in en-suite rooms, with breakfast served in a pleasant room above the pub; rather expensive for simple accommodation at about €45 pps midweek - a little more at weekends - but conveniently located.) Bar food: L 12.30-2.30, D 5.30-8. Closed Christmas & Good Fri. Amex, MasterCard, Visa, Laser. **Directions:** Opposite Pearse Street side of Trinity College.

Dublin 2

Odessa Lounge & Grill

E BAR/RESTAURANT

13/14 Dame Court Dublin 2 **Tel: 01 670 7634**
Fax: 01 670 4195 Email: info@odessa.ie Web: www.odessa.ie

Tucked away just a few minutes walk from Grafton Street, this has long been a favourite haunt for Dublin's bright young things and was one of the first places in Dublin to do brunch - a smart entrance gives way to a fashionably furnished restaurant and, downstairs, a more clubby room with comfy leather chairs, subdued lighting, and plenty of room to spread out and read the papers in peace is an appealing place to be after a late night on the town. Menus, which were ahead of fashion when Odessa opened in 1994, haven't changed in years yet they still seem fresh and have an emphasis on seasonal ingredients - fresh seafood includes Galway Bay lobster and wild Irish crab, when available, and a summer speciality is glazed rump of lamb with mint crushed potatoes and balsamic jus. Skilful cooking, very good value for the quality of food and style of restaurant, and Irish staff who combine efficiency with good humour make this a great place to dine. *The Odessa Club (www.odessaclub.ie) is a private Members Bar with screening facilities on the second floor, and is affiliated with Societe De Kring (www.kring.nl) in Amsterdam; wine tasting dinners are held regularly, and Odessa Club members are offered a special rate for accommodation nearby at Grafton House (www.graftonguest-house.com; Tel 01 679 2041), 26/27 South Great George's Street. **Seats 190** (private room, 60). Air conditioning. Sat & Sun open brunch 11.30-4.30; D daily 6-10.30, Early bird D €18.50 (Sun-Fri, 6-7); Set D €28/40 2/4 course. House Wine €20. SC 12.5%. Closed Bank Hols, 25/26 Dec. * Odessa Private Members Club also opened upstairs Amex, MasterCard, Visa, Laser. **Directions:** Just off George's Street / Exchequer Street.

Dublin 2

The Old Mill

RESTAURANT

14 Temple Bar Dublin 2 **Tel: 01 671 9262**

Long before this area became trendy Temple Bar, Moroccan chef-patron Lahcen Iouani had a loyal following in the area - since the mid-80s, in fact, when this restaurant delighted discerning Dubliners in an earlier guise as 'Pigalle'. The name change has relevance to local history (you can read all about it on the back of the menu) but other things have thankfully remained the same and Lahcen continues to offer good French cooking at refreshingly modest prices. The place has a homely feeling, like stepping back in time to an old French restaurant - giving good value to the customer is something he feels strongly about. A blackboard menu offers traditional starters like paté de foie de canard and salade niçoise, and classic main courses such as boeuf Bourginonne and sole meunière are unusually well-priced. Vegetarian dishes are offered and there's also a good value early menu. **Seats 50.** Reservations accepted. Air conditioning. Open Mon-Sun, 12.30-11.30; L 12.30-4, D 5-11. Set L €16.95, value D from 5-7.30pm, also à la carte. House wine from about €19. SC discretionary except on parties of 8+ (12.5%). MasterCard, Visa, Laser, Switch. **Directions:** Above Merchants Arch on Temple Bar Square (behind Central Bank).

Dublin 2

The Old Stand

PUB

37 Exchequer Street Dublin 2 **Tel: 01 677 7220**

This fine traditional pub, which is a sister establishment to Davy Byrnes, off Grafton Street, occupies a prominent position on the corner of Exchequer Street and St Andrew Street and lays claim to being "possibly the oldest public house in Ireland"! Named after the Old Stand at the Lansdowne Road rugby grounds, it has a loyal following amongst the local business community, notably from the 'rag trade' area around South William Street, and also attracts a good mixture of rugby fans and visitors, who enjoy the atmosphere. They offer no-nonsense traditional bar food (12.15-9 daily), but its warm and friendly atmosphere is a bigger draw than the food. Not suitable for children after 8. Closed 25-26 Dec & Good Fri. Amex, MasterCard, Visa, Laser. **Directions:** Off Grafton Street.

Dublin 2

One Pico Restaurant

★RESTAURANT

5-6 Molesworth Place Schoolhouse Lane Dublin 2
Tel: 01 676 0300 Fax: 01 676 0411 Web: www.onepico.com

féile bia Quietly located in a laneway near St Stephen's Green, just a couple of minutes walk from Grafton Street, Eamonn O'Reilly's One Pico is one of Dublin's most popular fine dining restaurants. The surroundings are elegant, with crisp white linen and fine china and glassware, and the cooking is exceptionally good: sophisticated, technically demanding dishes are invariably executed with confidence and flair. The range of menus offered includes lunch and pre-theatre menus which, as usual in restaurants of this calibre, represent great value, an 8-course Tasting Menu, a vegetarian menu (on request), and an à la carte, with about ten quite luxurious dishes offered on each course, plus optional side dishes which should not be necessary as each main course is individually garnished. There is an occasional small nod to Irish traditions, but this is classical French cooking with a modern twist, albeit based for the most part on the very best local ingredients. Specialities include creative seafood dishes - roasted skate wing is accompanied by crisp potato with crab, spinach purée and herb butter, for example - and there are also upbeat versions of traditional meat dishes such as a braised beef daube with roasted vine tomatoes. Eamonn O'Reilly cooks with first class ingredients, turning them into classic dishes with lovely clean flavours, and his own unique style on each dish. To finish, it is difficult to decide between an innovative and delicious cheese menu, or beautifully presented desserts that taste as good as they look - and include refreshing choices like a summer creation of luscious Wexford strawberries with creme patissiere, crisp tartine & strawberry granité. This is a fine restaurant and has earned its place among the city's best. *A sister restaurant is Bleu Bistro Moderne - see entry. **Seats 85** (private room, 46). Air conditioning. L& D Mon-Sat: L12-3, D 6-11. Set L €30, Early D €38 (6-7.30); Set D €38, Tasting Menu €90, also à la carte. House wine €28. SC discretionary. Closed Sun, bank hols, 24 Dec-5 Jan. Amex, Diners, MasterCard, Visa, Laser. **Directions:** 2 mins walk off St Stephens Green/Grafton Street near government buildings.

Dublin 2

The Palace Bar

PUB

21 Fleet Street Dublin 2 **Tel: 01 671 7388**

The Palace has had strong connections with writers and journalists for many a decade. Its unspoilt frosted glass and mahogany are impressive enough but the special feature is the famous sky-lighted snug, which is really more of a back room. Many would cite The Palace as their favourite Dublin pub. Closed 25 Dec & Good Fri. **Directions:** Temple Bar.

Dublin 2

Pasta Fresca

RESTAURANT

2-4 Chatham Street Dublin 2
Tel: 01 679 2402 Fax: 01 668 4563

This long-established Italian restaurant in the Grafton Street shopping area specialises in fresh pasta, and is known for its consistent standards; their popular all-day menu is based on good home-made pastas, thin-based crispy Neapolitan pizzas, a wide range of interesting salads with well-made dressings. There are plenty of vegetarian dishes on offer - bruschetta rosso, with fresh tomatoes & mozzarella, for example, or fettucine al broccoli - and a speciality pasta salad (with Tuscan beans, sweetcorn, fresh vegetables, shaved Parmesan & house dressing). A shorter list of grills includes fish of the day and several chicken dishes: their own Pollo Pasta Fresca, for example, is well worth trying - chicken breast filled with mozzarella cheese and spinach, wrapped in bacon the baked in its on juices and served with herby mashed potatoes and salad. Evening menus offer a wider choice and shoppers and diners alike can also buy Italian groceries, fresh pasta and sauces made on the premises from their deli counter. Children welcome. **Seats 150** (outdoors, 20). Air conditioning. Open all day Mon-Sat, 12-12, Sun 1-12. Set L €9.95 (11-5); D also à la carte. House wine from €17.95. SC discretionary. Closed 25 Dec, 1 Jan. Amex, Diners, MasterCard, Visa, Laser. **Directions:** Off top of Grafton Street. ◇

Dublin 2

Pearl Brasserie

☆RESTAURANT/WINE BAR

20 Merrion Street Upper Dublin 2
Tel: 01 661 3572 Fax: 01 661 3629
Email: info@pearl-brasserie.com Web: www.pearl-brasserie.com

Just a few doors away from The Merrion Hotel, Sebastien Masi and Kirsten Batt's stylish basement restaurant has an open peat fire and colourful blue banquettes picking up tones from an aquarium that runs the length of the bar, where aperitifs and a light bar menu are served. The style is contemporary international, with a classic French base and a pleasing emphasis on clean flavours highlighting the high quality of ingredients. Several menus are offered, including an attractive vegetarian menu, and there is a leaning towards towards fish and seafood, which Sebastien cooks with accuracy and flair - a fresh crab meat & guacamole starter is served with tomato & gazpacho & potato galette, for example - and specialities from the land include luscious pan-fried foie gras with toasted brioche with strawberry & rhubarb compôte (and an optional glass of Montbazillac, which is hard to resist); main courses include prime meats - pan-fried fillet beef with fondue of spinach and roquefort croquette potato, is a speciality - and there are less usual luxurious dishes such as squab pigeon Rossini, with pan-fried foie gras and black truffle mashed potato. Desserts are a highlight and include particularly good ices, and coffee is served with home made chocolates. Charming, efficient and well informed service complements Sebastien Masi's unusual and beautifully presented meals. The wine list is a good match for the food, favouring France and including a good choice of half bottles. *Separate Wine Bar area serving nibbles & light bar menu. Also available for cocktails and apperitif and digestif drinks. Children welcome. **Seats 80** (private area, 10); Air-conditioning. L Tue-Fri 12-2.30, D daily 6-10.30. 'Value' L €26, D à la carte. House wine €21. SC discretionary. Closed bank hols. Amex, MasterCard, Visa, Laser. **Directions:** Opposite Government Building, near Merrion Hotel.

Dublin 2

The Pembroke

PUB

31/32 Lower Pembroke Street Dublin 2 **Tel: 01 676 2980**
Fax: 01 676 6579 Email: info@pembroke.ie Web: www.pembroke.ie

There was consternation amongst traditionalists when this fine old pub was given a complete makeover some years ago, creating the bright and trendy bar that it is now - it even has a cyber café in the basement. But, if the cosiness of old has now gone for ever, the spacious new bar that took its place has character of its own and, along with some striking design features (notably lighting), the atrium/conservatory area at the back brings the whole place to life and there is space for a large number of outdoor tables. Meeting the needs of those who get in to work before the traffic builds up, bar food begins with an impressive breakfast menu offering everything from cereals or muesli to the Full Irish, with all sorts of more sophisticated treats like scrambled egg with smoked salmon and eggs benedict (ham) or florentine (spinach) in between. Later menus are appealing too, offering, for example, hot sizzler dishes like strips of sirloin beef teriyaki, served with stir-fried noodles, peppers & beansprouts - and a range of bar snacks including grilled crostini or omelettes with fries and rocket leaves. **Seats 200** (private room 60, outdoor seating 80). Food served Mon-Sat, 7.30am-8pm. Closed Sun, Christmas & Good Fri. *Layla Turkish restaurant upstairs, see entry. Amex, Diners, MasterCard, Visa, Laser. **Directions:** Near St Stephen's Green - off Lr Baggot Street.

Dublin 2

Peploe's Wine Bistro

Ⓔ RESTAURANT

16 St Stephen's Green Dublin 2 **Tel: 01 676 3144**
Fax: 01 676 3154 Email: info@peploes.com Web: www.peploes.com

In the basement of the Georgian terrace than runs along the north side of St Stephen's Green, Peploe's is very handy to both the Grafton Street area and the nearby offices - perfect territory for a laid-back wine bar. The retro décor is reminiscent of a chic 1950s New York brasserie and creates a warm and inviting atmosphere, complete with neat table settings and stylishly-dressed staff. Although the dining room appears cramped, it is comfortable and the service is pleasant and professional. The menu offers a good variety of dishes, if only for an appetiser or two (from a choice of ten starters) to accompany your wine, and the dozen or so main courses are well-balanced between pasta, meat and fish, plus the chef's specials which are notified at the table. A choice of tasty breads gets your meal off to a good start, followed by quite unusual dishes such as carpaccio of veal with aioli, or lightly-crusted Brie which is set off well by marinated Pruneaux d'Agen. An autumn menu might include venison loin, cooked to your taste, girolle mushrooms and balsamic jus while the chef's special is likely to be deliciously fresh fish. A generous apple & blackberry crumble would be enough for two people and delightfully fruity, or you may finish with a choice of French and Irish cheeses, and good coffee. An extensive wine list includes a dozen or more champagnes and about thirty wines by the glass. Service is smart, the atmosphere is great and the cooking has style - all this and a reasonable bill too. **Seats 95.** Reservations required. Air conditioning. Toilets wheelchair accessible. Children welcome. Open 12.30-3.45 & 6-10.15 daily; Set D €45, also à la carte. Closed 25 Dec, Good Fri. Amex, MasterCard, Visa, Laser, Switch. **Directions:** On St. Stephen's Green. ◇

Dublin 2

The Port House

Ⓝ RESTAURANT/WINE BAR

64a South William Street Dublin 2
Tel: 01 677 0298 Fax: 01 677 0298
Email: info@porthouse.ie Web: www.porthouse.ie

This new venture by the team who created The Porterhouse (Parliament Street and branches), bears all their hallmark attention to detail - the wine bottles on high shelves, warm brick walls, remains of an old fireplace, flagged floors and simple mismatched modern furniture make this basement wine bar highly atmospheric, especially when seen in candlelight. But, although that's a great start, there's more to this little place than atmosphere and they have begun well on the food side too, bringing a taste of Spain to South William Street. Menus offer a couple of dozen tapas size items (think 'small starter'), divided into hot and cold 'pinchos' and mostly under €5; order a few to share and see how it goes, depending on whether you're just having a drink and a nibble or want the equivalent of a light meal. There are some tempting items on offer, some more familiar than others: nibbles like toasted almonds with paprika, less usual offerings such foie gras or mini sirloin steaks, and regional Spanish cheeses and tasty renditions of many of the well known tapas classics like calamares rabas (squid in batter), tostas de setas (mushrooms with garlic butter), tortilla (Spanish omelette) and patatas bravas (deep fried potato cubes with tomato sauce). Cooking is good and it's fun. There are some value wines, and also some interesting Basque bottled beers too (the ale and lager are perhaps better than the stout). Not suitable for children under 10 yrs; no reservations accepted. **Seats 50** (private room, 6, outdoors, 6); Air conditioning; Tapas served daily, all day 11-1am (Sun to 11pm); house wine from €3.50 per glass. Closed 25-26 Dec. MasterCard, Visa, Laser. **Directions:** A few doors up from the corner of Exchequer St and South William Street.

Dublin 2

The Porterhouse

PUB

16-18 Parliament Street Temple Bar Dublin 2
Tel: 01 679 8847 Fax: 01 670 9605
Email: oliver@theporterhouse.ie Web: www.theporterhouse.ie

Dublin's first micro-brewery pub opened in 1996 and, although several others have since set up and are doing an excellent job, The Porterhouse was at the cutting edge. Ten different beers are brewed on the premises and connoisseurs can sample a special tasting tray selection of plain porter (a classic light stout), oyster stout (brewed with fresh oysters, the logical development of a perfect partnership), Wrasslers 4X (based on a West Cork recipe from the early 1900s, and said to be Michael Collins' favourite tipple), Porter House Red (an Irish Red Ale with traditional flavour), An Brain Blasta (dangerous to know) and the aptly named Temple Brau. But you don't even have to like beer to love The Porterhouse. The whole concept is an innovative move away from the constraints of the traditional Irish pub and yet it stays in tune with its origins - it is emphatically not just another theme pub. The attention to detail which has gone into the decor and design is a constant source of pleasure to visitors and the food, while definitely not gourmet, is a cut above the usual bar food and, like the pub itself, combines elements of tradition with innovation: Carlingford oysters, Irish stew, beef & Guinness casserole are there, along with the likes of homemade burgers and a good range of salads. This is a real Irish pub in the modern idiom and was a respected winner of our Pub of the Year award in 1999. No children after 9pm. **Seats 50.** Open noon - 11.30 daily (Thu-Sat to 12.30). Bar food served 12-9.30 daily (Sun from 12.30). Closed 25 Dec & Good Fri. [*The original Porterhouse is located on Strand Road on the seafront in Bray, Co. Wicklow and, like its sister pub in Temple Bar, it offers bar food daily from 12.30-9.30. Tel/Fax: 01 286 1839. There is also a Porterhouse in London, at Covent Garden.] MasterCard, Visa. **Directions:** South side of Ha'penny Bridge. ◇

POWERSCOURT TOWNHOUSE CENTRE

South William Street Dublin 2

Built in 1774 as a Town House for Lord Powerscourt, it was extensively refurbished and opened as a Shopping Centre in 1981. It is right in the middle of the Grafton Street/Georges Street shopping area and, whilst offering interesting shops, Powerscourt Townhouse is also home to a selection of bars, restaurants and cafés, some within a lovely central atrium that can be particularly restful especially when there is a pianist playing. Promising places to drop into for a bite include **Café Fresh** (01 671

9669), well known for its delicious vegetarian and vegan food; **La Corte** (01 633 4477), from the **Dunne & Crescenzi** stable (see entries), provides simple Italian food and great coffee; **Ba Mizu** (01 674 6712) is a stylish bar/restaurant serving an appealing contemporary menu, and **Mimo** (01 679 4160) - a sister establishment - is on the top floor, serving coffee, food and wine in an informal, relaxed and spacious environment. For more information on Powerscourt Townhouse see their website, www.powerscourtcentre.com.

WWW.IRELAND-GUIDE.COM - FOR THE BEST PLACES TO EAT, DRINK & STAY.

Dublin 2

Queen of Tarts

€ CAFÉ

4 Cork Hill Dame Street Dublin 2 **Tel: 01 670 7499**

Behind Yvonne and Regina Fallon's quaint traditional shopfront near Dublin Castle lies an equally quaint traditional tea room, with warmly welcoming friendly and efficient staff, and wonderful smells wafting across the room as they struggle to make space for new arrivals to the comfortable, lived-in little room. Yvonne and Regina both trained as pastry chefs, but there's nothing 'cheffy' about the good home baking that you'll find here - the emphasis is on wholesomeness and real flavour. Service begins with breakfast (including a vegetarian cooked breakfast) which is served until the lunch/afternoon menu takes over at noon. Home-made scones, buttermilk brown bread, roast chicken & coriander tartlets, warm plum tarts with cream, chocolate fudge cake, orange chocolate pinwheel cookies and much else besides taking their place on a surprisingly extensive menu, which includes some seriously good sandwiches and salads - most people pop in for a snack, but you could just as easily have a 3-course lunch. Inexpensive, consistently excellent food, lovely atmosphere and great service - what more could anyone ask? [*Also at: City Hall, Dame St. Tel 01 672 2925. Open museum hours: Mon-Sat 10-4.30, Sun 2-5.] **Seats 25.** Air conditioning. Toilets wheelchair accessible. Children welcome. Open daily: Mon-Fri 7.30-7 (L12-7); Sat/Sun 8.30-7. Closed 24 Dec-02 Jan, bank hols. **No Credit Cards. Directions:** Opposite the gates of Dublin Castle. ◇

Dublin 2

Relax Café @ Habitat

N RESTAURANT

6-10 Suffolk Street Dublin 2 **Tel: 01 677 1433**

At the time of the Guide's visit, shortly before publication, a new team had taken over this popular mezzanine café and an entirely new menu had been introduced. The aim is to deliver authentic Irish style food using organic ingredients where possible. The menu offers a traditional cooked breakfast which happily includes kidneys and home baked soda bread (€12.50); French toast and omelettes are also on offer, as are starters, salads and more substantial main courses. Some interesting sounding dishes (beetroot jelly with Cashel blue cream cheese, toasted hazelnuts and drizzled honey (€7), and the cucumber Neapolitana with roasted stuffed tomatoes (€7.50) were unavailable on our visit, and others were perhaps in need of further development. However, promising dishes included baked leek, hazelnut & Gubbeen crepe; pan fried Barbary duck breast with kumquat compote & French beans; and organic pork and leek sausages with scallion champ sautéed onions. Although there was still some work to be done to match the high standards of the previous incumbent, the menu offers promise and this remains a popular place to meet for an informal meal. **Seats 54.** Lift. House wines €15, €3.75 glass. No SC. Open all week 9.15 am to 6pm. MasterCard, Visa, Laser. **Directions:** Entrance is by College Green, other entrance Suffolk Street.

Dublin 2

Restaurant Patrick Guilbaud

★★RESTAURANT

21 Upper Merrion Street Dublin 2 **Tel: 01 676 4192**
Fax: 01 661 0052 Email: restaurantpatrickguilbaud@eircom.net
Web: www.restaurantpatrickguilbaud.net

For almost a quarter of a century this spacious, elegant restaurant in a Georgian townhouse adjoining the Merrion Hotel has been the leading French restaurant in Ireland. Approached through a fine drawing room, where drinks are served, the restaurant is a bright, airy room, enhanced by an outstanding collection of Irish art, and opens onto a terrace and landscaped gardens which make a delightful setting for drinks and al fresco dining in summer. Head chef Guillaume Lebrun has presided over this fine kitchen since the restaurant opened and is renowned for exceptional modern classic cuisine, based on the best Irish produce in season: his luxurious, wide-ranging menus include a wonderfully creative 9-course Tasting Menu (€130), themed as 'Sea & Land', perhaps, and celebrating traditional Irish themes with Gallic flair; at the other end of the spectrum, a daily table d'hôte lunch menu offers the best value fine dining in Dublin. Contemporary French cooking at its best, combined with the precision and talents of a team of gifted chefs, produces dishes of dexterity, appeal and flavour: a speciality starter of lobster ravioli, for example, is made from Clogherhead lobster coated in a coconut scented lobster cream and served with hand made free range egg pasta, toasted almonds and lightly curry-flavoured olive oil. The main course house speciality is a magnificent dish of Challan duck (for two people) and, in due course, an assiette of chocolate ends your meal in spectacular fashion, with a plate of no less than five cold and hot chocolate desserts. Consistent excellence is the order of the day: cheeses are supplied by Sheridan's cheesemongers, breads are home-made, and the mostly French wine list includes some great classics, alongside some reasonably-priced offerings. A visit here is always an experience to treasure, each dish a masterpiece of beautiful presentation, contrasting textures and harmonious flavours, all matched by faultless service - under the relaxed supervision of Restaurant Manager Stéphane Robin, service is invariably immaculate, and Patrick Guilbaud himself is usually present to greet guests personally. Every capital city has its great restaurant and this is Dublin's gastronomic heaven: Restaurant Patrick Guilbaud continues to set the standard by which all others are judged. Children welcome. **Seats 80** (private room, The Roderic O'Conor Room is available for up to 25 people). Air conditioning. L Tue-Sat 12.30-2.15, D Tue-Sat 7.30-10.15. Set L €33/45 for 2/3 courses. Vegetarian Menu (Main courses from €28). 9-course Tasting Menu €130. L&D à la carte available. House wine from €38. SC discretionary. Closed Sun & Mon, bank hols, Christmas week. Amex, Diners, MasterCard, Visa, Laser. **Directions:** Opposite Government Buildings.

Dublin 2
RESTAURANT

Saagar Indian Restaurant

16 Harcourt Street Dublin 2
Tel: 01 475 5060 / 5012 Fax: 01 475 5741
Email: info@saagarindianrestaurants.com Web: www.saagarindianrestaurants.com

Meera and Sunil Kumar's highly-respected basement restaurant just off St Stephen's Green is one of Dublin's longest established Indian restaurants and, although it is an old building with an interesting history (Bram Stoker, author of Dracula, once lived here), it has a contemporary feel, with wooden flooring and restrained decor - and a music system featuring the latest Indian music. It is an hospitable place and you will be warmly welcomed - and probably offered a drink in the little bar while choosing from the menu. The cooking is consistently good, offering a wide range of speciality dishes, all prepared from fresh ingredients and considerately coded with a range of one to four stars to indicate the heat level. Thus Malai Kabab is a safe one-star dish, while traditional Lamb Balti and Lamb Aayish (marinated with exotic spices and cooked in a cognac-flavoured sauce) is a three-star and therefore pretty hot. Beef and pork are not served but this is balanced by a good vegetarian selection, and the side dishes such as Naan breads, which are made to order in the tandoori oven, are excellent. Customer care is a high priority here, and service is always knowledgeable and attentive. The Kumars also have restaurants in Athlone and Mullingar. Children welcome, but not very young babies (under 1), or after 10pm. **Seats 60.** Toilets wheelchair accessible. L Mon-Fri, 12.30-2.30; D 6-11 daily. L&D à la carte available. House wine about €16. SC discretionary. Closed L Sat, L Sun & Christmas week. Amex, Diners, MasterCard, Visa, Laser, Switch. **Directions:** Opposite Children's Hospital on Harcourt Street (off Stephen's Green). ◇

Dublin 2
RESTAURANT

Salamanca

1 St Andrew's Street Dublin 2 **Tel: 01 670 8628**

Although many have since followed suit, the idea of partnering wine with nibbles that are more interesting and nourishing than crisps and peanuts was new to Dublin when John Harvey opened this atmospheric tapas bar and Spanish restaurant in the heart of Dublin several years ago, and it immediately struck a chord with Dubliners, who enjoyed the informality. It has no waiting space for new arrivals, but the entrance is pleasant - past a bar with flowers on the counter - and welcoming staff show you straight to a simple marble-topped table. The menu - which is in Spanish with English explanations - is flexible enough to suit anything from a light lunch to a full dinner and plenty of choices: three tapas plates will make a generous lunch for two. Although they might not pass on absolute authenticity with flying colours, Spanish staples are generally well-handled: garlic roast chicken, langoustines with serrano ham, squid in chilli butter and patatas bravas are all tasty and presentation is simple and traditional, with nice little touches like fresh parsley and drizzles of sour cream to set off the food. A handy location, tasty food, delightful staff and good value make this place busy at peak times, so be prepared to wait. The wine list includes a range of sherries by the glass, the traditional accompaniment for tapas, and their lovely frothy-topped mocha served in a tall glass is a great reviver. Meals: Mon-Thu, 12 noon-11 pm, Fri & Sat to midnight. Closed Sun. MasterCard, Visa. **Directions:** Near Dublin Tourism. ◇

Dublin 2
RESTAURANT

Shanahan's on the Green

119 St. Stephen's Green Dublin 2
Tel: 01 407 0939 Fax: 01 407 0940
Email: sales@shanahans.ie Web: www.shanahans.ie

féile bia This opulent restaurant was Dublin's first dedicated American style steakhouse - although, as they would be quick to reassure you, their wide-ranging menu also offers plenty of other meats, poultry and seafood. However, the big attraction for many of the hungry diners with deep pockets who head for Shanahan's is their certified Irish Angus beef, which is seasoned and cooked in a special broiler, 1600-1800F, to sear the outside and keep the inside tender and juicy. Steaks range from a 'petit filet' at a mere 8 oz/225g right up to The Shanahan Steak (24 oz/700g), which is a sight to gladden the heart of many a traditionally-minded Irishman - and, more surprisingly perhaps, many of his trendier young friends too. Strange to think that steak was passé such a short time ago. There is much else to enjoy, of course, including a dramatic signature dish of onion strings with blue cheese dressing. The wine list includes many special bottles - with, naturally, a strong presence from the best of Californian producers. Not suitable for children. **Seats 100.** Reservations required. Air conditioning. L Fri only (except for groups), 12.30-2. D daily, 6-10.30. Set L €45; otherwise à la carte. (SC discretionary, but 15% on parties of 6+). House wine €30. Closed Christmas period. Amex, Diners, MasterCard, Visa, Laser. **Directions:** On the west side of St Stephen's Green, beside Royal College of Surgeons.

Dublin 2
HOTEL/RESTAURANT

Shelbourne Hotel

27 St Stephen's Green Dublin 2 **Tel: 01 663 4500**
Fax: 01 661 6006 Web: www.shelbourne.ie

Now in new ownership and under major restoration, The Shelbourne Hotel is expected to re-open in early spring 2007. Amex, Diners, MasterCard, Visa. **Directions:** Landmark building on north side of St Stephen's Green.

Dublin 2
CAFÉ

Silk Road Café

Chester Beatty Library Dublin Castle Dublin 2
Tel: 01 407 0770 Fax: 01 407 0788
Email: silkroadcafe@hotmail.com Web: www.silkroadcafe.ie

In a fine location in the heart of the city centre, Dublin Castle provides wonderful gardens and historic architecture which greatly enhance the enjoyment of a visit to this unusual restaurant, which is situated in the clock tower beside the Chester Beatty Library (European Museum of the Year in 2002, and one of the few Dublin museums offering free entry). Middle Eastern, Mediterranean, vegetarian and organic are the themes brought together by Abraham Phelan and his small but dedicated team, who create inspired versions of classics like Greek moussaka, Moroccan cous cous, falafel and spinach & feta pie to the delight of their many returning customers. Fresh organic herbs are used in all dishes and, in line with halal/kosher rules, all dishes are made without the use of pork or beef. Prices are very reasonable - an average main course served with rice or salad is around €10. Toilets wheelchair accessible. Children welcome. **Seats 65** (private room 30). Air conditioning. Open Mon-Fri, 10-5; à la carte. No service charge. MasterCard, Visa, Laser. **Directions:** Beside Chester Beatty Library in Dublin Castle.

Dublin 2
PUB

The Stag's Head

1 Dame Court Dublin 2 **Tel: 01 679 3701**

In Dame Court, just behind the Adams Trinity Hotel, this impressive establishment has retained its original late-Victorian decor and is one of the city's finest pubs. It can get very busy at times but this lovely pub is still worth a visit. Closed 25 Dec & Good Fri. **Directions:** Just off Exchequer Street.

Dublin 2
GUESTHOUSE

Stauntons on the Green

83 St Stephen's Green Dublin 2 **Tel: 01 478 2300** Fax: 01 478 2263
Email: stauntonsonthegreen@eircom.net Web: www.stauntonsonthegreen.ie

Well-located with views over St Stephen's Green at the front and its own private gardens at the back, this guesthouse - which is in an elegant Georgian terrace on the south of the Green and has fine period reception rooms - offers moderately priced accommodation of a good standard, with all the usual amenities. Maintenance could be a little sharper and front rooms would benefit from sound-proofing from traffic noise, but it's in the heart of the business and banking district and the Grafton Street shopping area is just a stroll across the Green. Meeting rooms are available, with secretarial facilities on request - and there's private parking (valet parking service offered - it would be wise to phone ahead with your time of arrival to arrange this, as there is no parking at the door). Children welcome. No pets. **Rooms 38** (all en-suite, 24 shower only). B&B about €76 pps, ss €20. Closed 24-27 Dec. Amex, Diners, MasterCard, Visa, Laser. **Directions:** On south side of the Green.

Dublin 2

Stephen's Green Hotel

HOTEL

St Stephen's Green Dublin 2 **Tel: 01 607 3600** Fax: 01 661 5663
Email: stephensgreenres@ocallaghanhotels.ie Web: www.ocallaghanhotels.ie

This striking landmark hotel on a south-western corner site overlooking St Stephen's Green is the newest of the O'Callaghan Hotels group (Alexander, Davenport, Mont Clare - see entries). Public areas include an impressive foyer and, in memory of the writer George Fitzmaurice who used to live here, 'Pie Dish' restaurant and 'Magic Glasses' bar - both named after titles from his work. It's a great location for business or leisure and bedrooms have exceptionally good facilities, particularly for business travellers, including air conditioning, 3 direct line telephones, voice mail and modem line, desk, mini-bar as standard. Small conference/meeting rooms. Business centre. Gym. Children welcome (Under 2s free in parents' room; cots available). No pets. **Rooms 75** (9 suites, including 2 studio terrace suites, 3 penthouse suites, junior suites; 40 no-smoking rooms, 2 for disabled). Lift. 24 hour room service. Room rate about €295, max. 2 guests). Open all year. Amex, Diners, MasterCard, Visa, Switch. **Directions:** Corner of Harcourt Street and St. Stephen's Green. ◇

Dublin 2

Stephen's Hall Hotel & Suites

HOTEL

14-17 Lower Leeson Street Dublin 2 **Tel: 01 638 1111** Fax: 01 638 1122
Email: stephens@premgroup.com Web: www.stephens-hall.com

Conveniently located just off St Stephen's Green, this 'all-suite' hotel consists of units (bedroom, bathroom, living room, kitchenette) each with modem point, fax machines and CD players. **Rooms 33** (all suites, 9 no-smoking). Wheelchair access. Lift. Room rate from about €165. Free underground parking. Open all year. **Romanza:** George Sabongi took over this attractive semi-basement adjacent to the hotel in 2001 and with him came the piano bar concept for which he is well-known in Dublin. An enclosed coffee terrace at the back creates a pleasantly summery 'outdoor' atmosphere and, as the restaurant is accessible directly from the hotel and nearby offices, it's a popular lunchtime venue - and very convenient to the National Concert Hall in the evening too. Moderately priced menus include informal Italian fare like quality pizzas and pastas, but there's also a range of antipasti and substantial main courses like charcoal grilled rib eye of beef and barbecue leg of lamb, and Egyptian influence showing in a vegetarian dish such as koushery, which is based on black lentils. You can also just have a drink at the bar (10am-midnight); there's quite an extensive cocktail list and a short bar food menu,10.30-5.30. Live music at weekends. L Mon-Fri, 12.30-3; D Mon-Sat 5-12. A la carte. House wine about €16. 10% s.c. on parties of 6+. Closed L Sat, all Sun. [Times/prices not confirmed at time of going to press.] Amex, Diners, MasterCard, Visa, Laser. **Directions:** Just off St.Stephen's Green, on Lower Leeson Street. ◇

Dublin 2

Steps of Rome

RESTAURANT

1 Chatham Street Dublin 2 **Tel: 01-670 5630**

One of a cluster of inexpensive little Italian places specialising in pizza around Balfe and Chatham Streets, each with its following, this authentic one-room café just beside Neary's pub is a favourite lunch spot for many discerning Dubliners. A good place to take a break. (Branch at: Ciao Bella Roma, Parliament St.) **Seats 18.** Open 12 noon-11pm Mon-Sat, Sun 1-10pm. House wine about €14. No service charge. **No Credit Cards. Directions:** Just off top of Grafton Street. ◇

Dublin 2

Temple Bar Hotel

HOTEL

Fleet Street Temple Bar Dublin 2 **Tel: 01 677 3333** Fax: 01 677 3088
Email: reservations@tbh.ie Web: www.templebarhotel.com

This pleasant hotel is relatively reasonably priced, and handy for both sides of the river. Spacious reception and lounge areas create a good impression and bedrooms are generally larger than average, almost all with a double and single bed and good amenities. Neat, well-lit bathrooms have over-bath showers and marble wash basin units. Room service menu (6-10pm). No parking, but the hotel has an arrangement with a nearby car park. Conference/banqueting (70/60). Wheelchair access. Children welcome (Under 12s free in parents' room, cots available without charge).

No pets. **Rooms 129** (35 no-smoking, 2 for disabled). Lift. B&B about €100pps, ss €60. Closed Christmas. Amex, Diners, MasterCard, Visa, Laser. **Directions:** Near Fleet Street car park.

Dublin 2

Thornton's Restaurant

★★RESTAURANT 128 St Stephen's Green Dublin 2 **Tel: 01 478 7008** Fax: 01 478 7009
Email: thorntonsrestaurant@eircom.net Web: www.thorntonsrestaurant.com

Although rumours in the press about a possible relocation persist, Kevin and Muriel Thornton's renowned restaurant is still to be found on the top floor of the Fitzwilliam Hotel, overlooking St Stephen's Green. You can take a lift up through the hotel, but it is best approached from its own entrance on the Green: mounting the wide staircase, deep-carpeted in dark blue, conveys a sense of occasion. Once inside, the decor is simple and elegant: pale walls washed with colour reflected from heavy primrose silk curtains highlight a series of subtle oil paintings, and understated linen-clad tables leave you in no doubt that the food is to be the star here: A welcoming team of waiting staff set a tone of friendly professionalism from the outset, offering an aperitif at the neat reception area, or the maître d' - Kevin's brother, Garret Thornton - may show you straight to your table to consider a menu which, literally, bears the hand of the master on the cover. Kevin Thornton offers creative cooking of the highest class: he has a perfectionist's eye for detail with a palate to match, and uses only the very best seasonal ingredients. Menus offered include a concise lunch menu, a vegetarian menu and a table d'hôte dinner menu, in addition to a shortish à la carte offering about eight luxurious choices on each course - Kevin Thornton has a name for generosity with truffles and he will not disappoint: a vegetarian first course of warm white asparagus is served with truffle hollandaise and green asparagus bavarois for example, and among the seafood dishes you will find a luxurious signature dish of sautéed prawns with prawn bisque, and truffle sabayon. Other signature dishes include roast suckling pig, and trotter served with glazed turnip and a light poitin sauce - and variations on these creations appear throughout an 8-course Surprise Menu (€125). Although beautifully presented, this is not show-off food - the cooking is never less than sublime and the emphasis is always on flavour. Service is impeccable, from the moment breads are offered to the final presentation of assorted petits fours accompanying coffees and teas. Sommelier Emilie Balvay has made revisions to the extensive wine list, which now includes a choice of 16 house wines. Thornton's offers a wonderful experience and good value at all levels - and at lunch it is exceptional. Reservations required. Children welcome. Air conditioning. **Seats 90** (private area, 33). L Tue-Sat, 12.30-2; D Tue-Sat, 7-10. Set L €30/40. Set D €65, Surprise Menu €125, A la carte also offered. House wine from €27-40. SC discretionary. Closed 25 Dec, 17 Mar. Amex, Diners, MasterCard, Visa, Laser. **Directions:** On St Stephen's Green (corner at top of Grafton Street); entrance beside Fitzwilliam Hotel.

Dublin 2

Toners

PUB 139 Lower Baggot Street Dublin 2 **Tel: 01 676 3090** Fax: 01 676 2617

One of the few authentic old pubs left in Dublin, Toners is definitely worth a visit (or two). Among many other claims to fame, it is said to be the only pub ever frequented by the poet W.B. Yeats. Closed 25 Dec & Good Fri. **Directions:** On Baggot Street, Stephen's Green end.

Dublin 2

Town Bar & Grill

Ⓔ RESTAURANT 21 Kildare Street Dublin 2 **Tel: 01 662 4800** Fax: 01 662 3857
Email: reservations@townbarandgrill.com Web: www.townbarandgrill.com

Just off St Stephen's Green and across the road from the side entrance to the Shelbourne Hotel, Ronan Ryan and Temple Garnier's New York/Italian style restaurant beneath Mitchell's wine merchants is very much 'town'. A delicate hand with the decor - warm floor tiles, gentle lighting and smart but not overly-formal white-clothed tables with promising wine glasses - creates a welcoming tone on arrival in the L-shaped basement, and warmly professional staff are quick to offer the choice of a drink at the bar or menus at your table. Starters include a really excellent antipasti plate and dishes rarely seen elsewhere, such as grilled fresh sardines, while house versions of classics like Italian sausage amatriacana, with gnocchi or pappardelle, appear among main courses which will also offer several interesting fish dishes and, in season, game such as crown of pheasant - served with confit leg, soft polenta and glazed shallots, perhaps. An Irish and Italian cheeseboard is offered and moreish desserts may include classics like gooseberry fool, served with with pistachio biscotti; combinations are sometimes unusual, and flavours are delicious. Interested, well-informed staff add greatly to the enjoyment of a meal here, and the cooking is generally confident and accurate, set off handsomely by simple presentation on plain white plates. Prices are fair for the high quality of food and service offered, with lunch and pre-theatre menus offering very good value. There is also - perhaps uniquely in a city centre restaurant of this calibre - a special children's menu, offering healthy low-salt and low-sugar 'real' food such as char-grilled chicken breast bruschetta with buffalo mozzarella & tomato salsa, and home-made fish fingers with oven roasted chips. *A sister restaurant **'South Bar & Grill'** is due to open in the Beacon South Quarter, Sandyford, in spring 2007. Free Broadband WI/FI; Children welcome. **Seats 80.** Air conditioning. Open daily: L 12-5.30, D 5.30-11 (to 10 on Sun); set L €26.95; pre-theatre menu € 29.95, Mon-Thurs 5.30-7.15; Set 3 course D € 55.95, also à la carte. House wine €21.95. Pianist Thu-Sat from 8pm, Jazz on Sun from 8. Closed 25 Dec, Good Fri. Amex, MasterCard, Visa, Laser. **Directions:** Opposite side door of Shelbourne, under Mitchell's wine shop.

Dublin 2

HOTEL

Trinity Capital Hotel

Pearse Street Dublin 2 **Tel: 01 648 1000** Fax: 01 648 1010
Email: info@trinitycapital-hotel.com Web: www.capital-hotels.com

A stylish hotel right beside the headquarters of Dublin's city centre fire brigade (inspiring the name 'Fireworks' for its unusual club-style bar) and opposite Trinity College. Very centrally located for business and leisure, the hotel is within easy walking distance of all the main city centre attractions on both sides of the Liffey and the lobby wine and coffee bar make handy meeting places. Rooms have a safe, interactive TV, phone, data ports, hair dryer, trouser press, tea/coffee trays, comfortable beds and good bathrooms -junior suites suites have jacuzzi baths, hi-fi system and mini-bar. The Siena Restaurant offers an above-average expereince for an hotel dining room, providing an appealing alternative for guests who prefer to dine in (D daily, 6-9.30). Guests have free admission all the bars and clubs in the city centre owned by Capital Bars, including the adjacent Fireworks night club. Conference/banqueting 40/80. Meeting rooms; secretarial services. Children welcome (under 12s free in parents' room; cots available without charge, baby sitting arranged). **Rooms 82** (4 suites, 4 junior suites, 24 no-smoking, 3 shower only. Lift. 24 hour room service. B&B about €106.50 pps, ss €30. (Room only about €199). Amex, Diners, MasterCard, Visa, Laser. **Directions:** City centre. ◇

Dublin 2

GUESTHOUSE

Trinity Lodge

12 South Frederick Street Dublin 2 **Tel: 01 617 0900**
Fax: 01 617 0999 Email: trinitylodge@eircom.net Web: www.trinitylodge.com

As centrally located as it is possible to get, this well-signed and attractively maintained guesthouse offers a high standard of accommodation at a reasonable price just yards away from Trinity College. As is the way with Georgian buildings, rooms get smaller towards the top so the most spacious accommodation is on lower floors. The reception area is a little tight, and there is no residents' lounge, but guest rooms have air conditioning and are stylishly furnished in keeping with the age of the building, and most have bath and shower; as it is a listed building it is not permissible to install a lift, a point worth bearing in mind if stairs could be a problem. An extensive breakfast is served in a bright, boldly decorated basement and, although no dinner is offered, there are numerous good restaurants nearby and, for light meals, guests are directed across the road to George's Wine Bar, where tapas and desserts are available (Tue-Sat, from 5pm). No private parking (multi-storey carparks nearby). Air-conditioned rooms have a safe, direct-dial phone, tea/coffee making facilities, multi-channel TV, trouser press and iron. Children welcome (under 5 free in parents' room; cots available). No pets. **Rooms 16** (6 family, 1 ground floor, all shower only and no-smoking). Room service (limited hours). B&B €80pps. Closed 23-27 Dec. Amex, Diners, MasterCard, Visa, Laser. **Directions:** Off Nassau Street, near Trinity College.

Dublin 2

RESTAURANT

Trocadero Restaurant

3/4 St Andrew Street Dublin 2 **Tel: 01 677 5545**
Fax: 01 679 2385 Web: www.restaurantsindublin.ie

The Dublin theatrical restaurant par excellence with deep blood-red walls and gold-trimmed stage curtains, black and white pictures of the celebrities who've passed through the place dimly lit, intimate tables with individual beaded lampshades and snug, cosy seating, the 'Troc' is one of Dublin's longest-established restaurants and has presided over St. Andrew Street since 1956. It has atmosphere in spades, food and service to match. Comforting menus reminiscent of the '70s offer starters like French onion soup, deep-fried brie, chicken liver pâté and avocado prawn Marie Rose, followed by ever-popular grills - fillet steak (with Cashel Blue cheese perhaps), Wicklow rack of lamb and sole on the bone are the mainstays of the menu, also wild Irish salmon and Dublin Bay Prawns from Clogherhead, naturally all with a sprinkling of freshly chopped parsley. Desserts include apple and cinnamon strudel and wicked chocolate and Baileys slice, and a better-value winelist will be hard to find. There's privacy too sound-absorbing banquettes and curtains allow you to hear everything at your own table with just a pleasing murmur in the background. Lovely friendly service too: magic. **Seats**

100. Air conditioning. Children welcome (up to 9pm). D Mon-Sat, 5-12. Pre-theatre D from 5pm - about €18, but table to be vacated by 8pm - also à la carte,. House wine from about €18.50. Closed Sun, 25-26 Dec, 31 Dec, Good Fri. Amex, Diners, MasterCard, Visa, Laser. **Directions:** Beside Dublin Tourism Centre. ◇

Dublin 2

RESTAURANT

Tulsi Restaurant

17a Lr Baggot Street Dublin 2 **Tel: 01 676 4578** Fax: 01 676 4579
Email: sharmin@gofree.indigo.ie Web: www.tulsi-indian.com

One of a small chain of authentic Indian restaurants, this bustling place has a compact reception area leading into a pleasingly elegant restaurant with echoes of the Raj in the decor. Tables are set up with plate warmers, fresh flowers, sauces and pickles and service is brisk so you will quickly be presented with menus offering a broad range of Indian styles - there's a slight leaning towards Punjabi style cooking, with its use of nuts and fruit in sauces, but also tandoori, tikka, biryani, balti and an extensive vegetarian menu. A selection of naan breads is offered and the food quality overall is consistently high; this, together with good value, make booking at both lunch and dinner advisable. A range of special menus offers variety and value; Indian beer available. **Seats 64** (outdoor,8). L Mon-Sat, 12-2.30, D daily, 6-11. Set L €24.95. Set D €24.95, also à la carte. House wine €17.50. Closed L Sun, L bank hols; 25-26 Dec. * Tulsi has a number of branches, including: 4 Olive Mount Terrace, Dundrum Road, Dundrum (01 260 1940); Lr Charles St., Castlebar, Co Mayo (Tel: 094 25066); Buttermilk Way, Middle St., Galway Tel: 092-564831). Sister restaurants 'Shanai Indian' at Cornelscourt S.C. and Old Bray Road, Foxrock, Co Dublin. Amex, Diners, MasterCard, Visa, Laser. **Directions:** 2 minutes walk east from St Stephens Green (Shelbourne Hotel side).

Dublin 2

Ⓔ RESTAURANT

Unicorn Restaurant

12B Merrion Court off Merrion Row Dublin 2
Tel: 01 676 2182 Web: www.unicornrestaurant.com

In a lovely, secluded location just off a busy street near St. Stephen's Green, this informal and perennially fashionable restaurant is famous for its antipasto bar, piano bar and exceptionally friendly staff. It's particularly charming in summer, as the doors open out onto a terrace which is used for al fresco dining in fine weather - and the Number Five piano bar, which extends to two floors, is also a great attraction for after-dinner relaxation with live music (Weds-Sat 9pm-3am). Aside from their wonderful display of antipasto, an extensive menu based on Irish ingredients (suppliers are listed) is offered, including signature dishes such as risotto funghi porcini (which is not available on Monday), and involtini 'saltimbocca style' - pockets of veal stuffed with Parma ham, mozzarella and sage, braised in white wine and lemon sauce; good regional and modern Italian food, efficient service and great atmosphere all partially explain The Unicorn's enduring success - another element is the constant quest for further improvement. There is always something new going on - the 'Unicorn Foodstore' round the corner, on Merrion Row, is a relatively recent addition to the enterprise, for example, also the Unicorn Antipasto/Tapas Bar - and food service has been extended with the introduction of a bar menu in the piano bar, which is a fair indication of the popularity of this buzzing restaurant. Many of the Italian wines listed are exclusive to The Unicorn: uniquely, in Ireland, they stock the full collection of Angelo Gaja wines and also the Pio Cesare range. Not suitable for children after 9pm. **Seats 80** (private room 30; outdoor 30). Reservations required. Air conditioning. Open Mon-Sat, L12.30-4.30, D 6-11 (Fri/Sat to 11.30), Fri open all day. A la carte. House wine €23. SC discretionary. Closed Sun, bank hols, 25 Dec-2 Jan. Amex, Diners, MasterCard, Visa, Laser. **Directions:** Just off Stephen's Green, towards Baggot Street.

Dublin 2

Ⓝ RESTAURANT

Venu Brasserie

Annes Lane Dublin 2 **Tel: 01 670 6755**
Fax: 01 633 4559 Web: www.venu.ie

Following in the footsteps of a father who has run the best restaurant in Ireland for over a quarter of a century can't be easy but, although the level of public anticipation must have been a nightmare for Charles Guilbaud, there was a great deal of goodwill toward his big new restaurant. It is situated rather unglamorously (but very conveniently) in the basement of an office building, and aims to offer good, simple food at fair prices - a concept familiar in France, of course, but still rare in Dublin. Whether or not you like the décor some find it depressingly canteen-like, while others see the plainness of the rather boxy wooden furniture and red leather banquettes as the height of cool, you're bound to love the affordable all day menus and a concise, fairly priced wine list that includes four well-chosen house wines at under €20. Although by no means an exclusively French menu, head chef Sebastien Geber offers many dishes that will bring back the best kind of memories: think gratinated onion soup with croutons (a vegetarian variation of the classic, no less), or a white potato soup with watercress, and vegetarians might also think green leaf salad with roasted vegetables. Several starters are also available as main courses - duck leg confit, with Lyonnaise potatoes, for example (€9.50/17.50 respectively), wild Galway mussels mariniere, or toasted goats cheese tart with onion marmalade (both €8.50/13.50). Quite what tiger prawns are doing in a cocktail here is hard to understand, however - is there no getting away from them? Main courses tread a carefully chosen path, offering a great choice from steak & chips (one of several steak options) or traditional fish & chips (€17/15 respectively), to spicy dishes like grilled lamb skewers with cumin & coriander spices (€16) and the luxury of grilled Irish lobster with cepes, tarragon & potato stuffing and garlic butter, which is also offered as a starter or main course (€25/45). This is good simple food, and desserts like bread and butter pudding or home made ice creams mainly follow in the same vein, although there are some surprises too. Together with long opening hours and smart service, the great cooking and value here will earn many happy fans for Venu. Toilets wheelchair accessible. Children welcome. **Seats 120;** air conditioning. Food served daily: from a la carte menu all day, 12-11pm; House wine €19. Closed 25/26 Dec, 1 Jan, Easter. Amex, MasterCard, Visa, Laser. **Directions:** From Grafton Street on to South Anne street, take 1st right.

Dublin 2

RESTAURANT

Wagamama

Unit 4B South King Street Dublin 2
Tel: 01 478 2152 Fax: 01 478 2154
Email: dublin@wagamama.ie Web: www.wagamama.ie

The Dublin branch of this popular London-based noodle bar is full of groovy young things, who find it cool - both for the food and the interior, which is a huge basement canteen, simple and functional, but strikingly designed with high ceilings. The generous portions of noodles consist of ramen (thread noodles), udon (fat noodles) or soba (a round buckwheat noodle) served in soups or pan-fried, well seasoned and colourfully decorated with South Asian ingredients. The large menu gives plenty of information about ingredients and dishes - and also explains how orders are taken (kids love the electronic notepads used by servers); it includes a few Japanese dishes such as teriyaki (little kebabs) and edamame (freshly steamed green soya beans, served sprinkled with salt), also a selection of fruit and vegetable juices, some rice dishes and plenty of vegetarian options. All food served in Wagamama noodle bars is GMO free, and Sake and interesting soft drinks such as kombucha take their place on the drinks menu alongside wines and coffees. Service is friendly and efficient. It's noisy, and not a place for those who value comfort - or privacy (not an intimate venue at all) - but kids love it. No reservations, but queues move quickly. Also at: South Main Street, Cork. Multi-storey carpark nearby. Children welcome. **Seats 110.** Air conditioning. Open daily, 12-11 (Sun to 10). A la carte. SC discretionary. Closed 25-26 Dec. Amex, Diners, MasterCard, Visa, Laser. **Directions:** Opposite Gaiety Theatre.

Dublin 2

HOTEL/RESTAURANT

The Westbury Hotel

Grafton Street Dublin 2
Tel: 01 679 1122 Fax: 01 679 7078
Email: westbury@jurysdoyle.com Web: www.jurysdoyle.com

Possibly the most conveniently situated of all the central Dublin hotels, the Westbury is a very small stone's throw from the city's premier shopping street and has all the benefits of luxury hotels - notably free valet parking - to offset any practical disadvantages of the location. Unashamedly sumptuous, the hotel's public areas drip with chandeliers and have accessories to match - like the grand piano on The Terrace, a popular first floor meeting place for afternoon tea, and frequently used for fashion shows. Accommodation is similarly luxurious, with bedrooms that include penthouse suites and a high proportion of suites, junior suites and executive rooms. With conference facilities to match its quality of accommodation and service, the hotel is understandably popular with business guests, but it also makes a great base for a leisure break in the city. Laundry/dry cleaning. Mini-gym. Conference/banqueting (220/200). Business centre. Secretarial services, video conferencing, broadband Wi/Fi.Children welcome. No pets. **Rooms 205** (4 suites, 14 junior suites, 25 executive rooms, 160 no-smoking, 2 for disabled). Lifts. B&B from €218 pps. SC 15%. Car park. Open all year. **Restaurants:** After a drink in one of the hotel's bars - the first floor Terrace bar and the Sandbank Bistro, an informal seafood restaurant and bar accessible from the back of the building - the Russell Room offers classic dining, with some global cuisine and modern Irish influences. **Seats 85.** Air conditioning. SC 15%. L daily, 12.30-2.30; D daily 6.30-10.30 (Sun to 9.30). Set L €28.50, Set D €55, also à la carte. House wine from €22 Amex, Diners, MasterCard, Visa, Laser, Switch. **Directions:** City centre, off Grafton Street; near Stephens Green.

Dublin 2

HOTEL

The Westin Dublin

21 College Green Westmoreland Street Dublin 2
Tel: 01 645 1000 Fax: 01 645 1234
Email: reservations.dublin@westin.com Web: www.westin.com/dublin

féile bia Two Victorian landmark buildings provided the starting point for this impressive hotel, and part of the former Allied Irish Bank bank was glassed over to create a dramatic lounging area, The Atrium, which has a huge palm tree feature and bedroom windows giving onto it like a courtyard (effective, although rather airless). The magnificent Banking Hall now makes a stunning conference and banqueting room, and the adjacent Teller Room is an unusual circular boardroom - while the vaults have found a new lease of life as The Mint, a bar with its own access from College Street. It's an intriguing building, especially for those who remember its former commercial life, and it has many special features including the business traveller's 'Westin Guest Office', designed to combine the efficiency and technology of a modern office with the comfort of a luxurious bedroom, and the so-called 'Heavenly Bed' designed by Westin and 'worlds apart from any other bed'. A split-level penthouse suite has views over Trinity College (and a private exercise area). Very limited parking (some valet parking available, if arranged at the time of booking accommodation). Fitness room. Conferences/Banqueting (250/170); business Centre, video conferencing, broadband Wi/Fi. **Rooms 163** (17 suites, 7 junior suites, 19 for disabled). Lift. 24 hour room service. Room rate about €359 (max 2 guests). Children welcome (under 17s free in parents room, €45 for roll away bed, cot available at no charge, baby sitting arranged). **The Exchange:** An elegant, spacious room in 1930s style, the restaurant continues the banking theme and, with a welcome emphasis on comfort, it simply oozes luxury. Everything about it, from the classily understated decor in tones of cream and brown to the generous-sized, well-spaced tables and large carver chairs says expensive but worth it. And, in the Guide's experience, that promise generally follows through onto the plate in well-executed menus - a fairly contemporary style, and confident, unfussy cooking endear this restaurant to visitors and discerning Dublin diners alike. Westin Smart Dining options (moderate in calories and fat) and vegetarian options are highlighted on menus. Friendly service from knowledgeable young waiting staff. There is live music on Saturday night and at Sunday Brunch, which is quite an institution and, like the pre-theatre dinner menu, offers good value. **Seats 70.** Breakfast daily 6.30-10, L Mon-Fri 12-2.30, D daily 6-10, Early D €24/28 2/3 course 6-7. Sun Brunch 12-4.30, €40; live music (jazz) Sat D & Sun brunch. Restaurant closed L Sat, D Sun. Hotel open all year Amex, Diners, MasterCard, Visa, Laser. **Directions:** On Westmoreland Street, opposite Trinity College.

DUBLIN 3

CLONTARF / FAIRVIEW

Fairview and its more fashionable shoreside neighbour, Clontarf, are a few miles from central Dublin and convenient to attractions such as the Croke Park stadium; championship golf at the Royal Dublin Golf Club, walking, bird watching, kite surfing and many other activities on Bull Island, a large sand island in Dublin Bay. There are also sites of historical significance such as the Casino at Marino and Fairview Crescent, a former home of Bram Stoker, author of Dracula. In Fairview, casual dining is available at **Ristorante da Enzo** (01 855 5274), a basic little restaurant known for its warm and friendly staff, great food and atmosphere - and terrific value; across the road is **Canters** (01 833 3681), a new sister restaurant to **The Washerwomans Hill In Glasnevin** (see entry). A little further out, Clontarf is an affluent suburb, with all the shops, pubs, restaurants and cafés to be expected in such an area. Of special interest is **Hemmingways** (01 833 3338), a new deli with an informal seafood & tapas bar and a wet fish bar, that is proving extremely popular; nearby, **Picasso** (01 853 1120) is a popular local Italian restaurant - both are near the seafront on Vernon Avenue.

VISIT WWW.IRELAND-GUIDE.COM FOR THE BEST PLACES TO EAT, DRINK & STAY.

Dublin 3

HOTEL

Clontarf Castle Hotel

Castle Avenue Clontarf Dublin 3 **Tel: 01 833 2321** Fax: 01 833 2279
Email: info@clontarfcastle.ie Web: www.clontarfcastle.ie

This historic 17th century castle is located near the coast, and convenient to both the airport and city centre. The hotel has been imaginatively incorporated into the old castle structure, retaining the historic atmosphere; some rooms, including the restaurant and the old bar, have original features and the atrium linking the old castle to the hotel is an impressive architectural feature. Clontarf Castle has extensive conference and banqueting facilities along with luxurious bedrooms furnished to a high standard and well equipped for business guests with wireless broadband, voicemail and US electrical sockets in addition to the usual amenities found in an hotel of this standard. Bathrooms are well designed, and all south-facing rooms have air conditioning. Although it is a pity that so little of the original grounds now remain, welcoming, friendly staff contribute to the atmosphere and major recent investment has ensured that it remains at the cutting edge for business guests. Conference/banqueting (550/490). Secretarial services. Children welcome (Under 5 free in parents' room; cots available, baby sitting arranged). No pets. **Rooms 111** (3 suites, 2 junior suites, 4 executive rooms, 41 no-smoking, 3 for disabled). Lift. 24 hr room service. B&B €142.50 pps. Templars: D Mon-Sat, 6.30-10.30 (Sun 6-9); L Sun only, 1-3. Closed 24-25 Dec.* There is a sister hotel, the Crowne Plaza, at Dublin Airport. Amex, Diners, MasterCard, Visa, Laser. **Directions:** Take M1 from Dublin Airport, take a left on to Collins Avenue, continue to T junction, take left on to Howth Road. At second set of lights, take a right on to Castle Avenue, continue to roundabout, take right into hotel. ◇

Dublin 3

N HOTEL

Jurys Croke Park Hotel

Jones's Road Dublin 3 **Tel: 01 871 4444** Fax: 01 871 4400
Email: crokepark@jurysdoyle.com Web: www.jurysdoyle.com

The first major hotel to be built in this area, Jurys has brought much-needed facilities and is a welcome newcomer for business guests and fans attending events at Croke Park stadium. The design is pleasant and very practical, with extensive public areas including a very large foyer/reception with good seating arrangements and several sections conducive to quiet conversation - and a vast bar has a predictably large screen. There's an inner courtyard, which comes into its own in sunny weather, and a a gym for guests' use. A room card key is required to operate the lift (which can be annoying, but is is a useful security measure), and accommodation is well-equipped with everything required by the business traveller; light sleepers should request a quietly-located room as some overlook the railway line, which may be disturbing. Staff are not always very experienced but cheerful and willing and, although this is not a dining destination, food in the hotel's restaurant is adequate. **Rooms 232;** room rate from €104 per night. **Directions:** From North Circular Road - Continue on along the road until Russell Street turn left, cross The Royal Canal and Jurys Croke Park Hotel is on your left.

Dublin 3

RESTAURANT

Kinara Restaurant

318 Clontarf Road Dublin 3 **Tel: 01 833 6759** Fax: 01 833 6651
Email: info@kinara.ie Web: www.kinara.ie

This smart two-storey restaurant specialising in authentic Pakistani and Northern Indian cuisine enjoys a scenic location overlooking Bull Island. Fine views - especially from the first floor dining room - are a feature at lunch time or on fine summer evenings, and there's a cosy upstairs bar with Indian cookbooks to inspire guests waiting for a table or relaxing after dinner. A warm welcome from the dashing Sudanese doorman, Muhammad, ensures a good start, and the restaurant has a very pleasant ambience, with soft lighting, antiques, interesting paintings, the gentlest of background music and streamlined table settings. The menu begins with an introduction to the cuisine, explaining the four fundamental flavours known collectively as 'pisawa masala' - tomato, garlic, ginger and onions - and their uses. Each dish is clearly described, including starters like kakeragh (local crab claws with garlic, yoghurt, spices and a tandoori masala sauce) and main courses such as the luxurious Sumandari Badsha (lobster tails with cashew nuts, pineapple, chilli and spices). There is a declared commitment to local produce - notably organic beef, lamb and chicken - and a section of the menu devoted to organic and 'lighter fare' main courses (typically Loki Mushroom, a vegetarian dish of courgettes and mushrooms in a light spicy yoghurt sauce). The kitchen team have over 80 years experience between them and the quality of both food and cooking is exemplary: dishes have distinct character and depth of flavour, and everything is appetisingly presented with regard for colour, texture and temperature - and fine food is backed up by attentive, professional service and fair prices. Care and attention marks every aspect of this comfortable and attractive restaurant, earning it a loyal following. [Kinara was the Guide's Ethnic Restaurant of the Year in 2004.] **Seats 77** (private room 20). Air conditioning. Children welcome. L Thu, Fri & Sun, 12.30-2.45; D daily, 6-11.30. Set L €14.95; early D €19.95 (Mon-Thu, 6-7.30pm); also à la carte L&D. House wine €18.50. Closed 25-26 Dec, 1 Jan. Amex, MasterCard, Visa, Laser. **Directions:** 3km (1.5 m) north of city centre on coast road to Howth (opposite wooden bridge).

DUBLIN 4

Dublin 4
GUESTHOUSE

Aberdeen Lodge

53 Park Avenue Ballsbridge Dublin 4
Tel: 01 283 8155 Fax: 01 283 7877
Email: aberdeen@iol.ie Web: www.halpinsprivatehotels.com

Centrally located (close to the Sydney Parade DART station) yet away from the heavy traffic of nearby Merrion Road, this handsome period house in a pleasant leafy street offers all the advantages of an hotel at guesthouse prices. Elegantly furnished executive bedrooms and four-poster suites offer air conditioning and all the little comforts expected by the discerning traveller, including a drawing room with comfortable chairs and plenty to read, and a secluded garden where guests can relax in fine weather. Staff are extremely pleasant and helpful (tea and biscuits offered on arrival), housekeeping is immaculate - and, although there is no restaurant, a Drawing Room menu offers a light menu (with wine list), and you can also look forward to a particularly good breakfast of fresh and stewed fruits, home-made preserves, freshly-baked breads and muffins, big jugs of juice and hot dishes cooked to order - including delicious scrambled eggs and smoked salmon, kippers and buttermilk pancakes with maple syrup, as well as numerous variations on the traditional Irish breakfast. Guests may join residents for breakfast - a useful service for early morning meetings - and the spa at the nearby sister property, Merrion Hall, is available for guests' use. [Aberdeen Lodge was the Dublin winner of our Irish Breakfast Awards in 2004.] Boardroom, business and fitness facilities for business guests - and mature secluded gardens. Small conferences/banqueting (50/40). Children welcome. No pets. **Rooms 17** (2 suites, 6 executive rooms, all no-smoking).24 hour room service. B&B €75 pps, ss E35. Residents' meals available: D (Drawing Room Menu) €22 + all-day menu. House wines from €30. Open all year. Amex, Diners, MasterCard, Visa. **Directions:** Minutes from the city centre by DART or by car, take the Merrion Road towards Sydney Parade DART station and then first left into Park Avenue.

Dublin 4
GUESTHOUSE

Anglesea Townhouse

63 Anglesea Road Ballsbridge Dublin 4
Tel: 01 668 3877 Fax: 01 668 3461

Helen Kirrane's guesthouse brings all the best 'country' house qualities to urban Dublin - a delightful building and pleasant location near Herbert Park, Ballsbridge; comfortable, attractive bedrooms; good housekeeping; a warm, welcoming drawing room with a real period flavour and wonderful breakfasts that prepare guests for the rigours of the most arduous of days. Thoroughly recommended for its creativity and perfectionism in redefining what a guesthouse can be, Anglesea Townhouse was the winner of our 1999 Irish Breakfast Award. Garden. Children welcome (Under 3s free in parents' room; cots available without charge). No pets. **Rooms 7** (5 shower only, all no-smoking). B&B about €65 pps, no ss. Closed Christmas and New Year. Amex, MasterCard, Visa, Laser. **Directions:** Located off Merrion Road, near the RDS; south of the city centre. ◇

Dublin 4
RESTAURANT

Baan Thai

16 Merrion Road Ballsbridge Dublin 4 **Tel: 01 660 8833**

Delicious aromas and oriental music greet you as you climb the stairs to Lek and Eamon Lancaster's well-appointed first floor restaurant opposite the RDS. Friendly staff, Thai furniture and woodcarvings create an authentic oriental feeling and intimate atmosphere - and, as many of the staff are Thai, it's almost like being in Thailand. A wide-ranging menu includes various set menus that provide a useful introduction to the cuisine (or speed up choices for groups) as well as an à la carte. The essential fragrance and spiciness of Thai cuisine is very much in evidence throughout and there's Thai beer as well as a fairly extensive wine list. [*Also at: Leopardstown, 01 293 6996]. D only, Sun-Thu 6-11, Fri & Sat to 11.30. Amex, Diners, MasterCard, Visa, Laser. **Directions:** Opposite RDS. ◇

Dublin 4
RESTAURANT

Bahay Kubo

14 Bath Avenue Sandymount Dublin 4
Tel: 01 660 5572 Fax: 01 668 2006

Don't be put off by trains rumbling overhead as you approach this unusual Filipino restaurant - once you get upstairs past the rather worn carpeted entrance and stairway, you will find yourself in a clean-lined modern room with a spacious, airy and welcoming atmosphere. Friendly staff seat new guests immediately and bring iced water with menus that are well organised with explanations about dishes

- which are probably very necessary as most guests will not be familiar with the cuisine, which is related to Chinese food, with Malaysian, Indonesian and Thai influences. Several set menus are offered (a good choice on a first visit, perhaps), and an à la carte which is, by oriental standards, quite restrained; anyone who likes Chinese food should enjoy the Filipino versions, which are similar but with generally fresher flavours of lemongrass, ginger, chilli and coconut; no MSG is used and soups are refreshingly free of cornstarch. As in some other oriental cuisines, the weakness is in the dessert menu, so make the most of the excellent savoury dishes instead. Service is attentive, making up in willingness anything it may occasionally lack in training. **Seats 80.** Reservations required. D Tue-Sat, 6-11 (Sun 5-10), L Thu & Fri, 12-2.30. Set Menu from €29, also à la carte Live music Thu & Sat. Closed Mon Amex, MasterCard, Visa, Laser. **Directions:** Above Lansdowne Bar, at railway bridge. ◇

Dublin 4

Bella Cuba Restaurant

RESTAURANT

11 Ballsbridge Terrace Dublin 4 **Tel: 01 660 5539** Fax: 01 660 5539
Email: info@bella-cuba.com Web: www.bella-cuba.com

féile bia Juan Carlos & Larissa Jimenez's bright and warm-toned restaurant is decorated with dramatic murals by a Cuban designer, bringing the atmosphere of that unique country to Dublin - and Juan Carlos's cooking demonstrates the Spanish, Caribbean and South American influences on Cuba's food. It's a healthy cuisine as most dishes are slow cooked, with very little deep frying and no heavy sauces, characterised by aromatic spices and herbs - predominantly garlic, cumin, oregano and bay. Informative menus give the names of dishes in two languages, with a full description of each, and it's well worth a visit to experience something genuinely different: begin with a famous Cuban cocktail like a Daiquiri or Mojito and then try a speciality of Caribbean rack of lamb or red snapper with coconut cream. The wine list, which offers a choice fairly balanced between the old world and the new, includes a pair of Cuban bottles. Unusually, the early evening 'Value Menu' allows you to choose from a limited selection on the à la carte. Not suitable for children after 7pm. **Seats 30.** D daily, 5 - 11 (to 10.30 Sun). L Thu & Fri, 12-3. Value L €10.50, Early D €25 (5-7). Also à la carte. House wine €19.50. SC discretionary. Closed Christmas. Amex, MasterCard, Visa, Laser. **Directions:** Middle of Ballsbridge.

Dublin 4

Berkeley Court Hotel

HOTEL/RESTAURANT

146 Pembroke Road Ballsbridge Dublin 4
Tel: 01 665 3200 Fax: 01 661 7238
Email: berkeleycourt@jurysdoyle.com Web: www.jurysdoyle.com

féile bia Set in its own grounds, yet convenient to the city centre, this luxurious hotel has long been a haunt of the rich and famous when in Dublin. The tone is set by a spacious chandeliered foyer, which has groups of seating areas arranged around it, with bars, restaurants and private conference rooms leading off. The hotel is known for its high standards of service and accommodation, and all suites and executive rooms were refurbished in 2005/6. Berkeley Room: A fine hotel restaurant with very professional staff and some reliable specialities - seafood dishes are especially good and they are renowned for their roast beef. **Seats 60.** Air conditioning. L daily, 12.30-2.30pm; D Mon-Sat, 7-10.30. A la carte. Toilet wheelchair accessible. Restaurant closed D Sun. On-site facilities include health & beauty treatments, a barber shop and giftshop/newsagent. Conference/banqueting (450/370) Video conferencing, business centre, broadband Wi/Fi. **Rooms 186** (1 penthouse suite, 6 luxury suites, 24 executive rooms, 35 no-smoking, 4 for disabled). Lift. Car Park. B&B about €190 pps, sc15%. Open all year. Amex, Diners, MasterCard, Visa, Laser. **Directions:** Near Lansdowne Road rugby stadium; approx 13 Km from Airport.

Dublin 4

Berman & Wallace

RESTAURANT

Belfield Office Park Beaver Row Clonskeagh Dublin 4 **Tel: 01 219 6252**
Fax: 01 219 6219 Web: www.bermanandwallace.com

féile bia This pavilion-style restaurant, in a courtyard surrounded by office buildings, supplies the local business community with wide-ranging high quality brasserie style daytime food. Choose from such all-time favourites as Irish Stew, fish and chips, bangers and mash (made with Hicks sausages) and baguettes filled with chargrilled steak and garlic mayonnaise, to pasta dishes, lamb passanda, chicken piri-piri with herb risotto and a great deal more. There are also several revitalising or detoxing juices and smoothies for the diet conscious, and there is a daily health lunch special on offer. Wines by the glass or by bottle. Full breakfast; takeaway/corporate platters. Delivery and party menus available. Restaurant available for evening functions. Parking for 20 cars. **Seats 80** (outdoor 20). Open Mon-Fri, 7.30-3. Closed Sat/Sun, Christmas, Easter, bank hols. Amex, MasterCard, Visa,

Laser. **Directions:** From Donnybrook, turn at Bus Station up Beaver Road towards Clonskeagh. Turn left at second set of lights into business park and follow signs.

Dublin 4

Bewley's Hotel, Ballsbridge

HOTEL

Merrion Road Ballsbridge Dublin 4 **Tel: 01 668 1111** Fax: 01 668 1999
Email: bb@bewleyshotels.com Web: www.bewleyshotels.com

This modern hotel is cleverly designed to incorporate a landmark period building next to the RDS (entrance by car is on Simmonscourt Road, via Merrion Road or Anglesea Road; underground carpark). Bedrooms are spacious and well-equipped with ISDN lines, iron/trouser press, tea/coffee facilities and safe, making a good base for business or leisure visits. Like its sister hotels at Newlands Cross, Leopardstown and Dublin Airport, you get a lot of comfort here at a very reasonable cost. *Restaurant: See entry for O'Connells in Ballsbridge. Children welcome (free in parents' room up to 16; cots available without charge, baby sitting arranged). No pets. Garden; walking. Parking. **Rooms 304** (10 shower only, 64 family rooms, 254 no smoking, 12 for disabled, 50 ground floor). Lift. No room service. Room rate €99 (max. 2 adult guests, or 2 adults & 2 children). Closed 24-26 Dec. Amex, Diners, MasterCard, Visa, Laser. **Directions:** At junction of Simmonscourt and Merrion Road.

Dublin 4

Blakes Townhouse

GUESTHOUSE

50 Merrion Road Ballsbridge Dublin 4
Tel: 01 668 8324 Fax: 01 668 4280
Email: blakestownhouse@iol.ie Web: www.halpinsprivatehotels.com

One of Pat Halpin's small group of quality guesthouses, Blakes is very handily situated for anyone attending exhibitions in Dublin, as it's directly opposite the RDS, and offers an attractive alternative to hotel accommodation. Comfortable bedrooms are well-equipped for business and professional travellers and executive rooms and four-poster suites also have whirlpool spa baths. A high level of service for a guesthouse - and, like all the Halpin establishments, very good breakfasts. Drawing Room and room service menu available all day (selection of quality wines, from €25); 24 hour room service. Children welcome (under 3 free in parents' room. No pets. Complimentary use of nearby leisure centre. Private parking. **Rooms 12** (2 suites,10 executive, all no smoking). B&B €70 pps, ss €40; SC 10%. *Short breaks, including golf breaks, offered. Open all year. Amex, Diners, MasterCard, Visa, Laser. **Directions:** Opposite the RDS in Ballsbridge. ◇

Dublin 4

Brownes

Ⓝ RESTAURANT

18 Sandymount Green Sandymount
Tel: 01 269 7316

Previously a daytime café - mini Irish breakfasts, good sandwiches, 'melts', quiche and soup Brownes has recently undergone a menu revamp under the energetic Peter Bark, who introduced interesting new sandwiches, (crayfish tails; rare beef, horseradish and rocket) and transformed it into a good neighbourhood restaurant by opening in the evening and serving simple, classical French-inspired food. Décor is still minimal, with good paintings by local artists and simple bentwood chairs (that would not encourage you to linger), but now Cathal Brugha Street trained chef Neil Hawley cooks things like a mean moules mariniere (starter or main - nice fat mussels in a wine and cream sauce), and great meats including aged sirloin (crusty on the outside and pink within, served with chunky, crispy 'real' chips) and pan-fried rack of lamb, cooked medium rare and served on a bed of flageolet beans, with tasty, slightly waxy, continental style new potatoes. Finish with a well-made traditional dessert (creme brulée, crumble) or excellent home-made ice creams and sorbets. BYO wine a small corkage charge is levied "unless you offer us a glass of something nice". Coffee could be the weak point, so call for the (surprisingly modest) bill and have it at home. **Seats 22;** €32-35 for 3 courses.

Dublin 4

Burlington Hotel

HOTEL

Upper Leeson Street Dublin 4 **Tel: 01 660 5222** Fax: 01 660 8496
Email: burlington@jurysdoyle.com Web: www.jurysdoyle.com

féile bia

Ireland's largest hotel, the Burlington has more experience of dealing with very big numbers efficiently and enjoyably than any other in the country. All bedrooms have been recently refurbished and banquets for huge numbers are not only catered for but can have a minimum choice of three main courses on all menus. Good facilities for business guests: a high proportion of bedrooms are designated executive, with ISDN lines, fax machines and air conditioning. Conference/banqueting (1500/1200). Business centre. Secretarial services. Video conferencing. No pets. Special offers often available. **Rooms 500.** B&B about €145 pps, ss €115. Open all year. Amex, Diners, MasterCard, Visa, Laser. **Directions:** Leeson Street.

Dublin 4
GUESTHOUSE

Butlers Town House

44 Lansdowne Road Ballsbridge Dublin 4
Tel: 01 667 4022 Fax: 01 667 3960
Email: info@butlers-hotel.com Web: butlers-hotel.com

On a corner site in Dublin's 'embassy belt' and close to the Lansdowne Road stadium, this large townhouse/guesthouse has been extensively refurbished and luxuriously decorated in a Victorian country house style and is a small hotel in all but name. Public rooms include a comfortable drawing room and an attractive conservatory-style dining room where breakfast is served; an attractive all-day menu is also offered. Rooms are individually decorated and furnished to a high standard, some with fourposter beds. Private parking (15). Wheelchair accessible. Not suitable for children. No pets. **Rooms 19** (3 superior, 1 disabled, all no smoking). 24 hr room service. Turndown service offered. B&B about €95, ss €45; no SC. Closed 21 Dec-5 Jan. Amex, Diners, MasterCard, Visa, Laser, Switch. **Directions:** Corner of Lansdowne Road and Shelbourne Road. ◇

Dublin 4
€ RESTAURANT

Canal Bank Café

146 Upper Leeson Street Dublin 4
Tel: 01 664 2135 Fax: 01 664 2719
Email: info@tribeca.ie Web: www.tribeca.ie

Trevor Browne and Gerard Foote's well-known almost-canalside restaurant is a rather sleek modern reinterpretation of Dish, their original arty-simple restaurant in Temple Bar. The format is designed to meet the current demand for quality informal food or 'everyday dining', but the original philosophy still applies and only the best ingredients are used - organic beef and lamb, free-range chicken and a wide variety of fresh fish daily. The menu is user-friendly, divided mainly by types of dish - starters like crispy fried calamari with lemon mayonnaise, big salads (Caesar, niçoise) and, for those who need a real feed, steaks various ways and specialities like Brooklyn meatloaf with spinach, onion gravy & mashed potatoes, and there's also a good sprinkling of vegetarian dishes. A carefully selected, compact wine list includes a good choice of house wines - and a range of brunch cocktails too.] Children welcome. **Seats 70.** Air conditioning. Open 11.30am-11pm daily. A la carte. House wine about €20.95. SC 10% on parties of 6+. Closed 24-28 Dec & Good Fri. Amex, Diners, MasterCard, Visa, Laser. **Directions:** Near Burlington Hotel. ◇

Dublin 4
N RESTAURANT

The Courtyard Restaurant & Piano Bar

1 Belmont Avenue Donnybrook Dublin 4
Tel: 01 283 0407 Fax: 01 283 0420
Email: info@thecourtyardcafe.ie Web: www.thecourtyardcafe.ie

Set well back from the road and approached through the courtyard that inspired the name, this popular neighbourhood restaurant is a relaxed spot with some style where good food combines attractively with reasonable prices and a pleasing ambience. It's not a place that visitors are likely to find by chance, but useful to know about, especially as they are open from late afternoon every day so you can enjoy a leisurely early evening meal before going on to a concert or the theatre in town. Piano in the evening. **Seats 170** (private room, 70, outdoors, 40); air conditioning; children welcome; D Mon-Sat, 5.30-10.30 (Sun 5-9); L Sun only, 5-9; Early D €17, 5.30-7; Sun L €23; House wine €18-20. SC 10%. Closed 25 Dec, Good Fri. Amex, Diners, MasterCard, Visa, Laser. **Directions:** Behind Madigans pub.

Dublin 4
N RESTAURANT

DonnyBrook Fair Café

89a Morehampton Road Donnybrook Dublin 4 **Tel: 01 614 4849**
Fax: 01 667 1187 Email: Web: www.donnybrookfair.ie

Situated above what many regard as Ireland's smartest supermarket, this café is popular with the ladies who lunch. The look is clean-lined, with a few stools at the bar and the rest of the room set up with chic white tables dressed only with black place mats, a cutlery bundle and a proper no-gimmick pepper mill, which seems to bode well. Day menus offer an appealing range of light dishes (pastries, chowder, salads) and a few more substantial ones (pan-fried sea trout, risotto, 6 oz rib-eye steak), some 'indulgences' (including Murphy's of Dingle ice creams) and quite an extensive drinks menu. Evening menus include dressed up versions of the more substantial day dishes, plus some extras. Although the cooking can be inconsistent, this is a useful place to know about for its location and long opening hours and the salads, especially, are appealing - also some of the meat dishes, including the homemade burger. The wine list is extensive (presumably supplied by the boutique supermarket below), and includes a range of about 30 fairly moderate 'quick pick' wines, all available by the glass. Toilets wheelchair accessible; children welcome. **Seats 80** (private room, 25); air conditioning; reservations accepted Sat/Sun L; food served all day, Mon-Sat, 7.30am - 9.30pm; Sun brunch 12-7.30; set L €23.95; early D €23.95 5.30-7, Sun-Fri, also a la carte L&D; house wine from €18; SC on groups of 10+. Closed Christmas. MasterCard, Visa, Laser. **Directions:** City side of Donnybrook village, AIB on corner.

Dublin 4

Dunne & Crescenzi Sandymount

RESTAURANT

11 Seafort Avenue Sandymount Dublin 4 **Tel: 01 667 3252**
Email: dunneandcrescenzi@hotmail.com Web: www.dunneandcrescenzi.com

Genuine Italian fare is what you'll find at this small restaurant, a younger branch of the well-known Dublin 2 establishment. Like its older sister, it's a quality ingredients-led place with tightly packed tables, an extensive Italian wine list and a menu that dispenses with the idea of courses, offering instead a selection of charcuterie plates, panini and other light dishes like insalata caprese, and some hot dishes so you can have a light bite or a full meal as appetite dictates. House wine €11. **Directions:** Next to O'Reilly's pub.

Dublin 4

Dylan

HOTEL/RESTAURANT

Eastmoreland Place Dublin 4 **Tel: 01 660 3000**
Fax: 01 660 3005 Email: justask@dylan.ie Web: www.dylan.ie

It feels as if it's in a peaceful backwater, yet this splendid Victorian building is just yards from one of Dublin's busiest city centre roads. Formerly the Hibernian Hotel, it is now in new ownership and has been spectacularly renovated - arrival at the gates of Dylan is an experience in itself, especially in the evening, when it is magically lit by old fashioned lamps outside the main entrance, where doormen greet you. A modern wing sits comfortably with the original building and the lobby offers a foretaste of the edgy design beyond. Leather padded walls, over-sized floral motifs and tactile wallpaper along with ultra-modern seating and creative lighting are just some of the quirky elements that create an atmosphere of decadent elegance. The edgy look continues in the individually designed bedrooms which are fitted to a very high specification. Standard rooms are laptop compatible and include a plasma screen TV, MP3 players, safes, cordless phones with voicemail and speakerphone, customised 7th Heaven Beds, Frette linen, air conditioning, under floor heated bathrooms, power showers, robes & slippers, Etro toiletries, mini bar and twice daily housekeeping. Even the most demanding international traveller would be hard pressed to complain at this five star boutique hotel. Not suitable for children. Business centre, secretarial services, free broadband Wi/Fi. **Rooms 44** (6 suites, 38 executive, 15 shower only, 1 disabled, all no smoking); Lift; 24hr room service. B&B from €395 per room for Dylan Luxury (€275 off peak, other rooms discounted depending on availability), Dylan Style €440, Dylan Experience €690, one Dylan Signature Suite €800. Lifts. Non-smoking hotel. Open all year except 25-26 Dec. Amex, Diners, Mastercard, Visa, Laser & Switch. **The Still:** This strangely named bright, white dining room is filled with no less then nine glittering chandeliers, luxurious cream and white chairs, wildly curved furnishings, a pale padded wall and a baby grand piano. The ambience is lavish 1940s Hollywood decadence and there were plenty of big Irish names to be spotted on the Guide's visit. The menu is also indulgent, but perhaps slightly more restrained in style. Some faultless dishes singled out for praise on our visit included fresh lasagne with Dublin Bay prawns, white leek, salsify and roasted scallops (€22); roasted venison with pureed parsnip and root vegetable terrine (€35); and beautifully handled fillet of sea bream with braised salsify, sauce lie de vin and girolles mushrooms (€36). The pear tatin with Poire William ice cream, spun sugar, and vanilla syrup was something of a master class in the skills of a good patisserie chef (€14). The very extensive wine list leans heavily towards classic super stars with prices to match although some less noble wines are at more accessible prices. Attentive service is a hallmark of this smart hotel - doors are held open for guests, and highly knowledgeable waiting staff explain each course. A champagne cocktail will set you back €20 but this is not a place people visit to count the pennies: Dylan is very much a place to be seen, so the prices match the opulent stage setting. **Restaurant: Seats 44** (private room, 12, outdoors, 20); air conditioning; L daily, 12.30-2.30pm, D Mon-Wed, 6-10.30pm, Thu-Sat, 6-11pm, D Sun, 6-10pm; set 3 course L €38, also a la carte L&D. Average starter €21, main courses €35, desserts €15. Tasting Menu of 8 courses €110. House wine from €20.95. SC discretionary. Amex, Diners, Mastercard, Visa, Laser & Switch. Amex, MasterCard, Visa, Laser. **Directions:** Just off Upper Baggot Street before St. Marys Road.

Dublin 4
€ CAFÉ

Expresso Bar Café

1 St Mary's Road Ballsbridge Dublin 4
Tel: 01 660 0585 Fax: 01 660 0585

Great flavour-packed food, good value and efficient service attracts a loyal following to Ann-Marie Nohl's clean-lined informal restaurant, which is renowned for carefully sourced ingredients that make a flavour statement on the plate. An all-morning breakfast menu offers many of the classics, often with a twist: thus a simple poached egg on toast comes with crispy bacon and relish, porridge is a class act topped with toasted almonds and honey, and French toast comes with bacon, or winter berries and syrup. Lunch and dinner menus tend to favour an international style, but the same high standards apply: whether it's a Dublin Bay Prawn pil pil with chili, coriander, char-grilled lime and crusty bread, or panfried cornfed chicken breast stuffed with goats cheese sundried tomato and Mediterranean vegetables & red pepper coulis, or just a vegetarian pasta, it's the quality of the ingredients and cooking that make the food here special. An informative and well-chosen wine list offers a fair choice by the glass. Weekend brunch is a must. Also at: Custom House Square, IFSC, Dublin 1 (01 672 1812). Not suitable for children after 8pm. Air conditioning. **Seats 60.** Open Mon-Fri, 7.30am-9.15pm (B'fst 7.30-11.30, L12-5, D 5-9.15), Sat 9am-9.15pm, Sun brunch 10am-5pm. Closed D Sun, 25 Dec, 1 Jan, Good Friday. MasterCard, Visa, Laser. **Directions:** Opposite Dylan Hotel, off Upper Baggot Street. ◇

Dublin 4
HOTEL/RESTAURANT

Four Seasons Hotel

Simmonscourt Road Dublin 4
Tel: 01 665 4000 Fax: 01 665 4099
Email: reservations.dublin@fourseasons.com Web: www.fourseasons.com/dublin

féile bia Set in its own gardens on a section of the Royal Dublin Society's 42-acre show grounds, this luxurious hotel enjoys a magnificent site, allowing a sense of spaciousness while also being convenient to the city centre - the scale is generous throughout and there are views of the Wicklow Mountains or Dublin Bay from many of the sumptuous suites and guest rooms. A foyer in the grand tradition is flanked by two bars - the traditional wood-panelled Lobby Bar and the newer Ice, which is deliciously contemporary. Accommodation is predictably luxurious and, with a full range of up-to-the-minute amenities, the air-conditioned rooms are designed to appeal equally to leisure and business guests. A choice of pillows (down and non-allergenic foam) is provided as standard, the large marble bathrooms have separate bath and shower, and many other desirable features - and there's great emphasis on service, with twice daily housekeeping service, overnight laundry and dry cleaning, one hour pressing and complimentary overnight shoe shine: everything, in short, that the immaculate traveller requires. But the Spa in the lower level of the hotel is perhaps its most outstanding feature, offering every treatment imaginable - and a naturally lit 14m lap pool and adjacent jacuzzi pool, overlooking an outdoor sunken garden. Outstanding conference and meeting facilities make the hotel ideal for corporate events, business meetings and parties in groups of anything up to 550. Conferences/Banqueting (550/450), business centre, secretarial services, video conferencing (on request), broadband Wi/Fi. Children welcome (under 18s free in parents' room, cot available free of charge, baby sitting arranged). **Rooms 196** (16 suites, 26 junior suites, 178 no-smoking, 13 for disabled). 24 hr room service, Lift, Turndown service. Room rate €315 (max. 3 guests). No SC. Open all year. **Seasons Restaurant:** This spacious, classically-appointed restaurant overlooks a leafy courtyard and no expense has been spared on the traditional 'grand hotel' decor - the style is a matter of debate (the ultra modern Ice Bar more recently added has attracted high praise from Dubliners), but nobody denies that this is an extremely comfortable restaurant - and, more importantly, that the service is exceptional. Executive Head Chef Terry White's contemporary international menus have their base in classical French cooking and offer a wide-ranging choice of luxurious dishes, with a considerate guide to dishes suitable for vegetarians, 'healthier fare' and dishes containing nuts. A 7-course Tasting Menu is offered - and a speciality dish is an unusual Irish scallop tasting, prepared with Parmesan with creamy spicy sauce, jalapeno salsa or natural, with caviar. The standard of cooking is high and, while it may not rival the city's top independent restaurants as a cutting edge dining experience, this is a fine hotel restaurant with outstanding service, and a good pricing policy ensuring value for money in luxurious surroundings. Sommelier Simon Keegan's excellent wine list includes some very good wines by the glass. *Informal menus are also available at varying times in The Café (daily), and in Ice Bar (Tue-Sat); Afternoon Tea, served daily in the Lobby Lounge, includes an extensive menu of classic teas and infusions. Air conditioning. **Seats 90** (private room, 12). Breakfast 7-11 daily, L 12.30-2.30 daily, D 6.30-9.30 daily. Set L from €35; à la carte also available D. House wine from €33. Amex, Diners, MasterCard, Visa. **Directions:** Located on the RDS Grounds on corner of Merrion and Simmonscourt Roads.

Dublin 4

RESTAURANT/WINE BAR

The French Paradox

53 Shelbourne Road Ballsbridge Dublin 4
Tel: 01 660 4068 Fax: 01 663 1026
Email: pch@chapeauwines.com Web: www.thefrenchparadox.com

On a busy road near the RDS, this inspired and stylish operation brings an extra dimension (and a whiff of the south of France) to the concept of wine and food in Dublin. French Paradox combines a wine shop, a large and atmospheric ground floor wine bar (where weekly wine tastings are held) and a room on the first floor, which gains atmosphere from the irresistible charcuterie on display close beside the tables. The main emphasis is on the wide range of wines available by the glass - perhaps 65 wines, kept in perfect condition once open using a wine sommelier, with inert gas. Pierre and Tanya Chapeau are renowned for their directly imported wines and food is, in theory, secondary here; but, although the choice is deliberately limited (a small à la carte offers a concise range of dishes, as single or shared charcuterie plates), the quality is exceptional and everyone just loves specialities like the foie gras, the smoked duck salad and the 'Bill Hogan', made with the renowned thermophilic cheeses from west Cork...and sitting outside on a sunny summer day, enjoying a plate of charcuterie with any one of the dozens of wines available by the glass, you could be lunching in the south of France. Classic desserts - chocolate terrine, crème brulée - and excellent coffees to finish. Wines offered change regularly (the list is always growing), and food can be purchased from the deli-counter to take home. Not suitable for children under 7 after 7pm. **Seats 25** (+25 in tasting room, +12 outside). Air conditioning. Toilets wheelchair accessible. L&D Mon-Thu, 12-3 & 6-9.30; open all day Fri & Sat, 12-9.30. Set L €14.95; Set D €29. A la carte. House wines (6) change monthly, from €18.95. Closed Sun (except for "Rugby Match" Sundays), Christmas, Bank Hols. Amex, MasterCard, Visa, Laser. **Directions:** Opposite Ballsbridge Post Office.

Dublin 4

RESTAURANT

Furama Restaurant

G/F Eirepage House Donnybrook Dublin 4
Tel: 01 283 0522 Fax: 01 668 7623
Email: info@furama.ie Web: www.furama.ie

In the sleek black interior of Rodney Mak's long-established restaurant, Freddy Lee, who has been head chef since the restaurant opened in 1989, produces terrific food with an authenticity which is unusual in Ireland. Even the menu does not read like other Chinese restaurants - dishes aren't numbered, for a start, and they are also presented and described individually. They do offer Set Dinners, which are more predictable - and many traditional Chinese dishes on the à la carte menu - but the option is there to try something different. Specialities include steamed seafood, roasted duck and Chinese vegetables. Service, under the supervision of Rodney Mak and manager Paul Fung, is friendly and efficient. A Special Chinese Menu can be arranged for banqueting with one week's notice (up to 30 people) and outside catering is also available. Parking. **Seats 70.** Mon-Fri: L 12.30-2pm, D 6pm-11.30pm, Sat D only 6pm-11.30pm, Sun open 1.30pm-11pm; D Various set menus from about €35. A la carte available. House wine from about €19. Air conditioning. SC 10%. Closed Sat L, 24-26 Dec & Good Fri. Amex, Diners, MasterCard, Visa, Laser. **Directions:** Opposite Bective Rugby Ground in Donnybrook, near RTE. ◇

Dublin 4

GUESTHOUSE

Glenogra House

64 Merrion Road Ballsbride Dublin 4
Tel: 01 668 3661 Fax: 01 668 3698
Email: info@glenogra.com Web: www.glenogra.com

GUESTHOUSE BREAKFAST OF THE YEAR

Conveniently located for the RDS and within 3 minutes walk of the Sandymount DART station, this well known guesthouse has recently been taken over by new owners, Peter and Veronica Donohoe, who are doing an excellent job. The public areas have all been refurbished and, from the minute you arrive there is a great sense of welcome and hospitality - lovely fresh flowers in the large hall, someone to carry your bags to your room and explain the facilities, the security of knowing there is safe parking. The bedrooms are not furnished in the latest style - expect to find darkwood furniture, fringed lampshades and little dressing table mirrors - but they are comfortable and clean, and offer some welcome extras, including smart white bathrobes and portable radios. Moreover, you'll get a really good breakfast, with plenty of choice, (including scrambled egg with smoked salmon) leaf tea and exceptionally delicious home-made muesli. Children welcome (cots available free of charge). No pets. **Rooms 13** (2 shower only, 1 family room, all no-smoking). B&B €59.50 pps, ss €30. Closed 22 Dec - 10 Jan. Amex, Diners, MasterCard, Visa, Laser. **Directions:** Opposite Four Seasons Hotel, RDS.

Dublin 4
HOTEL

Herbert Park Hotel

Ballsbridge Dublin 4 **Tel: 01 667 2200** Fax: 01 667 2595
Email: reservations@herbertparkhotel.ie Web: www.herbertparkhotel.ie

féile bia This large, privately-owned contemporary hotel is attractively located in an 'urban plaza' near the RDS and the public park after which it is named. It is approached over a little bridge, which leads to an underground carpark and, ultimately, to a chic lower ground foyer and the lift up to the main lobby. Public areas on the ground floor are impressively light and spacious, with excellent light meals and drinks provided by efficient waiting staff. The bright and modern style is also repeated in the bedrooms, which have views over Ballsbridge and Herbert Park and are stylishly designed and well-finished, with a high standard of amenities. Team building, jazz events, golf packages and special breaks are all offered. A good choice for the business guest or corporate events as well as private guests, this hotel is also reasonably priced for the standard of accommodation and facilities offered. Conference/banqueting (100/220). Business centre. Video conferencing. Gym. Garden. Children welcome (under 2 free in parents' room, cots available free of charge, playground). No pets. **Rooms 153** (2 suites, 40 executive rooms, 34 no-smoking, 8 for disabled). Lift. 24 hr room service. Turndown service. B&B €115pps. SS €85. No SC. Open all year. **Pavilion Restaurant:** In a bright, elegant, contemporary room which is pleasingly devoid of hard-edged minimalism and overlooks a garden terrace (where tables can be set up in fine weather), head chef Henry Jonkers presents wide-ranging international menus with, perhaps, a slight leaning towards fish and seafood: fresh lobster cooked to order is a speciality. Prices are reasonable, especially when seen in comparison with nearby competition, and the lunch menu offers particularly good value. **Seats 200.** Breakfast 7-10 (Sat & Sun to 10.30, Sun from 8); L 12.30-2.30; D Tue-Sat 6-9.30. Set L €25.50 (Buffet Sun L €39.50); D à la carte. House wine €22.50. Closed D Sun, D Mon. Amex, Diners, MasterCard, Visa. **Directions:** In Ballsbridge, shortly before RDS heading out of city.

Dublin 4
N E RESTAURANT

Itsa4

6a Sandymount Green Sandymount Dublin 4
Tel: 01 219 4676
Email: itsa4@itsabagel.com Web: www.itsabagel.com

féile bia This smart contemporary place has a 'New York Diner' feel, appropriate given the American connections of Domini and Peaches Kemp, the talented and hard-working sisters who are already well known for the 'Itsa Bagel' cafés - but this is a fully-fledged restaurant and not an extension of the bagel concept. Quality ingredient-led menus have a strong emphasis on provenance and no obvious distinction between starters and main courses; you might start, for example, with a platter of Terry Butterly's excellent pale smoked salmon, served in a portion generous enough to serve two easily, or perhaps a portion of potato skins with cheddar, dry-cured bacon and a sour cream dip as another nibbling option to share. The daily pasta dishes are invariably excellent and dishes which attracted special praise on a recent visit included a superb dry-aged rib-eye beef, which is served with a gorgeously rich béarnaise sauce and great vegetables (from Gold River Farm, in Co Wicklow); the house 'organic' chips (which are unpeeled) have instigated debate as many feel that they have 'more flavour but less crispness' than regular chips. As usual in the organic debate, it is the organic/traditional farming question rather than the variety (or even its locality) that comes under scrutiny given the correct variety, organic chips will be just as crisp as any other. Excellent desserts include gorgeous home-made ice creams and sorbets, and perfectly matured Sheridans cheese is served simply on a wooden platter with warm biscuits and grapes. Java Republic organic Fairtrade coffees are good (and served with excellent breakfasts too try the eggs Benedict), service is friendly and efficient, and there's an interesting well-priced wine list which includes unusual bottles from specialist suppliers. Toilets wheelchair accessible. Free broadband WI/FI. Children welcome before 8.45pm. **Seats 55** (outdoor, 10); air conditioning; L & D daily: Mon-Sat, 12-4 and 6-10; Sun 11-4 and 5-9; house wine €17. Closed 25-26 Dec, Good Fri, Easter Sun. MasterCard, Visa, Laser. **Directions:** On Sandymount Green.

Dublin 4
HOTEL

Jurys Ballsbridge Hotel & The Towers

Pembroke Road Ballsbridge Dublin 4
Tel: 01 660 5000 Fax: 01 660 5540
Email: ballsbridge@jurysdoyle.com Web: wwwjurysdoyle.com

féile bia Centrally located in the Ballsbridge area, and always busy, Jurys has the distinction of being both an international hotel providing high levels of service to business and leisure guests, while remaining a popular local hotel for Dubliners. Rooms and service are of a high standard (24 hour room service and laundry and dry cleaning services) and executive rooms also have a mini-bar and many extras particularly useful to business guests. The facilities offered by the hotel generally are excellent - Jurys was the first Dublin hotel to have a swimming pool; the leisure centre currently also has a whirlpool, sauna and gym, and there's a health & beauty salon, hairdresser and newsagent on site. [* The Towers is a quieter, more exclusive section of the main Jurys Hotel in Ballsbridge, a hotel within a hotel located to the rear of the main block, with its own entrance on Lansdowne Road and a high level of security]. There are two restaurants, Raglans (**Seats 98.** Air conditioning. Open for L&D daily. Toilets wheelchair accessible.) and the informal Coffee Dock; two bars: the larger Dubliner Bar is a popular meeting place. Conference/banqueting (850/600). Business centre, secretarial services. No pets. Special offers often available. **Rooms 396** (3 junior suites, 103 executive rooms, 150 no-smoking, 2 for disabled). Lifts. B&B from about €153.50pps, ss €116.50. SC12.5%. Open all year. Amex, Diners, MasterCard, Visa, Laser. **Directions:** About 11 km from the airport & 1 km from city centre.

Dublin 4

Jurys Montrose Hotel

HOTEL

Stillorgan Road Dublin 4 **Tel: 01 269 3311** Fax: 01 269 3376
Email: montrose@jurysdoyle.com Web: www.jurysdoyle.com

féile bia This south-city hotel near the University College campus has recently undergone extensive refurbishment, including completely updating the exterior; more rooms are now offered to executive standard, and also some wheelchair friendly accommodation. All rooms have quite good facilities (direct dial phone, multi-channel TV, tea/coffee-making facilities and trouser press/iron) and there's 12 hour room service and laundry/dry cleaning services. Executive rooms also have a modem line and complimentary newspaper and business magazines. The hotel's Belfield Restaurant is open for lunch and dinner every day and offers traditional food such as roasts, sole on the bone and roast duck (pianist on Fridays). Although conference facilities are not extensive (max. 70 delegates), there's a business centre, seven meeting rooms and free parking, making this an attractive venue for small events. Children welcome (cots available). **Rooms 178** (3 suites, 35 executive). B&B from €101pps, ss about €74; weekend specials available. Open all year. Amex, Diners, MasterCard, Visa, Laser. **Directions:** On Stillorgan dual carriageway near RTE studios.

Dublin 4

Kites Restaurant

RESTAURANT

15-17 Ballsbridge Terrace Ballsbridge Dublin 4
Tel: 01 660 7415 Fax: 01 660 5978 Email: kites@eircom.net

Lots of natural light with white painted walls, dark wooden fittings and a rich, dark carpet create a good first impression at this split-level Ballsbridge restaurant, and a mix of diners (Chinese and non-Chinese, business and pleasure) gives the place a nice buzz. The cuisine is a combination of Cantonese, Szechuan, Peking and Thai - predominantly Cantonese - and menus range from the standard set meals to a decent list of specials. For the indecisive, a house platter of appetisers makes a good beginning, offering a selection of spring rolls, wontons, sesame prawn toasts, spare ribs along with some more unusual additions. Duckling and seafood are specialities: half a crispy aromatic duck comes with fresh steaming pancakes, while a combination dish of salt & pepper jumbo king prawns and a stir-fry chicken is interesting. Stir-fried lamb with ginger & spring onion (one of the few Peking dishes) is to be recommended. Desserts are not a strong point, but courteous, good humoured and charming service adds considerably to the experience. **Seats 100** (private room, 40).Air conditioning. L daily 12.30-2, D daily 6.30-11.30. Set L €19,50, set D €34; also à la carte. House wine from €22. SC 10%. Closed 25-26 Dec. Good Fri. Amex, Diners, MasterCard, Visa, Laser. **Directions:** In the heart of Ballsbridge.

Dublin 4

La Péniche

(N) RESTAURANT

Grand Canal Mespil Road Dublin 4 **Tel: 087 790 0077**
Email: info@lapeniche.ie Web: www.lapeniche.ie

ATMOSPHERIC RESTAURANT OF THE YEAR

Dining afloat is an attraction in many European cities but, until recently, Dublin has remained stubbornly out of the loop so perhaps it should come as no surprise that it is Eric Tydgat and his team at the popular French/Belgian restaurant 'La Mere Zou' who have finally introduced the city to this entertaining experience. The barge, which is moored on the south bank of the Grand Canal near the Mespil Hotel, is smartly got up with red velvet couches and seat covers, and gleaming varnished tables complete with a small lamp and button to call for service. It's quite a squeeze when fully booked, but that's all part of the fun. The menu is based on authentic French bistro dishes, and the idea is that you can have a full four-course meal, a simple charcuterie plate or just a dessert with coffee. Typical sharing dishes include Galway Oysters, a platter of duck rillette, saucisson, paté de campagne & cured ham), and a similar plate offering a combination of charcuterie and cheese; (all available, like many of the dishes, as a small or large portion, around €9.95/€14.95 respectively). Homely hot dishes range from good soups (potato & leek, perhaps) and rustic classics such as flavoursome Toulouse sausage with basil pesto mash, to a prawn & smoked fish pie, with white wine sauce & pomme purée. There's a special too, and vegetarians can look forward to salads (buffalo mozzarella & roast vine tomato with sun-dried tomato pesto, virgin olive oil & balsamic vinegar, perhaps) and hot dishes like mushroom vol-au-vent with mixed salad (small or large). The atmosphere is helped along by very friendly and helpful service and, as well as a good choice of (mainly French) wines, there's a small list of French beers and ciders. On Thursdays dinner is even more fun, eaten under way as La Péniche cruises the canal. The barge is a great place for a party, and can be hired exclusively, with live music if requested. All round it's a hugely entertaining addition to the Dublin dining scene, and adds a new dimension to the city. Children welcome. **Seats 45** (outdoors, 40); L & D Tue-Sat, 12-3pm & 6-10.30pm; Sun L only, 2pm-5pm; value set L €9.95; also a la carte L&D. Closed Mon, 1 Jan - 15 Jan. MasterCard, Visa, Laser. **Directions:** Boat on Grand Canal - Mespil Road.

Dublin 4

The Lobster Pot

E RESTAURANT

9 Ballsbridge Terrace Ballsbridge Dublin 4 **Tel: 01 660 9170**
Fax: 01 668 0025 Email: Web: www.thelobsterpot.ie

On the first floor of a redbrick Ballsbridge terrace, conspicuously located near the Herbert Park Hotel - and just a few minutes walk from all the major Ballsbridge hotels - this long-established restaurant has lost none of its charm or quality over the years. The whole team - owner Tommy Crean, restaurant manager (and sommelier) John Rigby and head chef Don McGuinness - have been working here together since 1980 and the system is running very sweetly. How good it is to see old favourites like dressed Kilmore Quay crab, home-made chicken liver paté and fresh prawn bisque on the menu, along with fresh prawns mornay and many other old friends, including kidneys turbigo and game in season. The menu is a treat to read but there's also a daily fish tray display for specials - dishes are explained and diners are encouraged to choose their own combinations. All this and wonderfully old-fashioned service too, including advice from John Rigby on the best wine to match your meal. If only there were more places like this - long may it last. D Mon-Sat, 6.30-9.30. House wine about €22.50. SC 12.5%. Closed Sun, 24 Dec-4 Jan, bank hols. Amex, Diners, MasterCard, Visa, Laser. **Directions:** In the heart of Ballsbridge adjacent to the US embassy.

Dublin 4

Merrion Hall

GUESTHOUSE

54 Merrion Road Ballsbridge Dublin 4
Tel: 01 668 1426 Fax: 01 668 4280
Email: merrionhall@iol.ie Web: www.halpinsprivatehotels.com

This adapted Edwardian property opposite the RDS is one of the small group of Halpin guesthouses; handy to the DART (suburban rail), it makes a good base for business or leisure. At the time of our most recent visit (summer 2006). it was in the throes of expansion, and a large number of new rooms should be operative for the 2007 season. The transition is a little disruptive (particularly noticeable in the lobby, and the rear carpark), but this has not affected efficiency or the welcome. Large, comfortable rooms have TV, period furniture (some have 4-posters), fine original windows and bathrobes - and bathrooms are well-appointed, with in-bath jacuzzi and quality cosmetics. There's a well-stocked library, a comfortable big drawing room, and a fine, airy, spacious, basement dining room and outside patio, with tables in summer. In common with other Haplin establishments, good breakfasts are served here - an attractiive buffet and well-presented fry. This is a very comfortable guest house - hopefully it will function as well when the accommodation is almost doubled. Off-street parking at the back. Small conference/private parties (50/50). Garden. Children welcome (under 3s free in parents' room, cots available free of charge). No pets. **Rooms 34** (8 junior suites,10 executive, 4 family rooms, 4 ground floor, all no smoking, 2 disabled). Lift. 24 hr room service. Turndown service. B&B €75 pps, ss €35. Drawing Room/room service menu available 7am-9pm daily; house wine €25. Open all year. Amex, Diners, MasterCard, Visa. **Directions:** Opposite the RDS in Ballsbridge. ◇

Dublin 4

Merrion Inn

PUB

188 Merrion Road Dublin 4 **Tel: 01 269 3816** Fax: 01 269 7669
Email: themerrioninn@gmail.com

féile bia The McCormacks are a great pub family (see separate entry for their Mounttown establishment) and this attractive contemporary pub on the main road between Dublin and Dun Laoghaire makes a handy meeting place. It is a spacious place on two floors, with various quiet sections on the ground floor and an attractive covered outdoor section at the back to relax in relative peace, away from the busy bars. What you can expect to get here is above average pub fare: a hot and cold buffet is served at lunch time and there's a well balanced dinner menu with vegetarian and gluten free dishes marked up. Dishes enjoyed on a recent visit included starters of stuffed shitake mushroom with melted goats cheese, sun-dried tomatoes & rocket, and Irish oak-smoked salmon with red onion, capers & homemade brown bread. Main course choices offer quite an extensive range of popular dishes salads, chicken dishes, omelettes, bangers & mash, several fish dishes, steaks various ways - then there are homemade desserts, which change daily. There's a large function room with bar upstairs, and a partially covered heated patio area is available for smokers. Bar food served daily 12-10 (L12-3, D 3.30-10). Buffet / à la carte. House wine from €14.95. Closed 25 Dec & Good Fri. Amex, Diners, MasterCard, Visa, Laser. **Directions:** Opposite St. Vincent's Hospital.

Dublin 4

Mespil Hotel

HOTEL

Mespil Road Dublin 4 **Tel: 01 488 4600** Fax: 01 667 1244
Email: reservations@leehotels.com Web: www.mespil.com

This fine modern hotel enjoys an excellent location in the Georgian district of the city, overlooking the Grand Canal and within walking distance of St Stephen's Green and all the city centre attractions in fine weather. Public areas are spacious and elegant in an easy contemporary style, and bright, generously-sized bedrooms are comfortably furnished with good amenities including fax/modem connection and voicemail. Dining options include the 200-seater 'Glaze Restaurant, which is open for lunch and dinner daily and offers a well-balanced choice of traditional and contemporary fare based on carefully sourced ingredients at fair prices, and the Terrace Bar, where lunch and light snacks are served. The hotel takes pride in the friendliness and efficiency of the staff and is moderately priced for the area; special breaks offer especially good value. Small meeting and seminars (35). Children welcome (Under 12 free in parents' room; cots available free of charge, baby sitting arranged). No pets. **Rooms 255** (15 for disabled). Lift. Room service (limited hours). Room rate €155 (max. 3 guests). Closed 24-26 Dec. Amex, MasterCard, Visa, Laser. **Directions:** On the Grand Canal at Baggot St. Bridge.

Dublin 4

O'Connells Restaurant

RESTAURANT

Bewleys Hotel Merrion Road Dublin 4
Tel: 01 647 3304 Fax: 01 647 3398
Email: info@oconnellsballsbridge.com Web: www.oconnellsballsbridge.com

Located in a large semi-basement under Bewley's Hotel, this remarkable restaurant strives to provide quality ingredient-driven modern Irish cooking - simple food, with natural flavours, often emphasised by cooking in a special wood-fired oven. It has dark wood-panelled walls and floor to ceiling windows overlooking a courtyard used for al fresco dining and barbecues in summer - arriving by the courtyard steps rather than through the hotel helps the ambience considerably. The restaurant is run by Tom O'Connell, a brother of Darina Allen, of Ballymaloe Cookery School, and of Rory O'Connell, previously of Ballymaloe House, who visits regularly and works closely with the kitchen team. More recently Rosemary Kearney, author of 'Healthy Gluten Free Eating', has joined the team as a consultant, and O'Connell's is probably Ireland's most coeliac-friendly restaurant, offering home-baked gluten-free bread and a dinner menu that is almost entirely gluten free. Menus are a hymn to quality ingredients, stating that pork, beef, eggs and catering supplies are sourced using Bord Bia's Quality Assurance Schemes, and also naming a number of individual artisan producers and suppliers, often in dishes that have become house specialities - typically, a starter salad is made with Fingal Ferguson's Gubbeen smoked bacon, from Schull in Co. Cork, and Ashe's Black Pudding, from Annascaul, Co. Kerry served with sautéed potatoe, Bramley Apple and Mustard Sauce. Fish is from Castletownbere, specially aged Slaney beef comes from Wexford, organic pork is from Tipperary and Gold River Farm in Co Wicklow supply vegetable; Irish farmhouse cheese, matured on the premises, is served with home-made biscuits and classic desserts include (genuinely) home-made ice creams - a nice idea here is to offer two little desserts from a choice of eight: just the job after a filling meal. A highly informative wine list, which includes an extensive selection of by-the-glass and 24 house wines, reflects the same philosophy and gives details of vintage, region, grape, grower/shipper, merchant, taster's notes, suggested food partnership, bottle size (including some magnums) and price - invariably moderate for the quality offered - for every wine on the list; even the house water, Tipperary, (served by the carafe at Ireland's lowest price, €1.50 per litre) gets 'the treatment' (region, taster's notes...) Recent visits have seen an improvement in service and this remains an unique restaurant, offering meals based on the very highest quality ingredients - and the set menus plus a restructured buffet system now give more of a sense of occasion at very moderate prices. Fully wheelchair accessible. **Seats 180** (summer courtyard, 60). Air conditioning. Buffet L daily 12.30-2.30 (Sun to 4). D daily 6-10 (Sun to 9.30). Sun Buffet & Early D (6-7) €19.75. Set D €28.50. Also à la carte D available. SC 10%. House wines from €19.85. Closed eve 24- eve 27 Dec. Amex, Diners, MasterCard, Visa, Laser. **Directions:** Off Merrion Road at Simmonscourt Road, opposite the Four Seasons Hotel.

Dublin 4

Ocean Bar

BAR

Charlotte Quay Dock Ringsend Road Dublin 4 **Tel: 01 668 8862**
Fax: 01 6677435 Email: info@oceanbar.ie Web: www.oceanbar.ie

Dramatically situated on the water's edge with lots of glass on two sides, and extensive outdoor patio seating to take full advantage of views over the Grand Canal Basin, Ocean has great atmosphere and makes an excellent meeting place for people of all ages. The trendy modern furnishings are not quite as spruce as they once were, but the location, style, friendliness of the staff and comfortable lounging couches all make it a great place to relax - and a particularly good choice for visitors to the city. There's a choice of three bars and dining areas and, while menus offering a wide range of contemporary favourites may not contain many surprises, food is freshly prepared and competently cooked - and the ambience is exceptional. Three good sized private function rooms are available, one on the ground floor next to the bar and two downstairs. Ingredients are carefully sourced, and it would be interesting to see details on menus. Tables are laid as you order - simple cutlery, paper napkins - and food is served modern bistro style on big white plates. Food with an international tone is pleasant rather than outstanding, but what makes for a special feeling is the location - and the Sunday jazz brunches are a particular success. Conference/banqueting. Children welcome. **Seats 180** (private room, 80; outdoor seating, 80). Air conditioning. Toilets wheelchair accessible. Food served daily, 12 -10. House wine €21. Closed 25 Dec, Good Fri. Amex, MasterCard, Visa, Laser. **Directions:** On Pearse Street/Ringsend Road bridge (Grand Canal Basin).

Dublin 4

Orchid Szechuan Chinese Restaurant

N RESTAURANT

120 Pembroke Road Dublin 4
Tel: 01 660 0629

This long established restaurant has a faithful following not surprisingly, as the food is of very high quality and provides for both conservative and adventurous tastes, whilst the service is admirably efficient and friendly. Once you have braved the entrance (which can be a little off-putting) the interior is warm, welcoming and typically Chinese with smoky mirrors and black-painted walls decorated with simple floral designs. Fresh flowers and linen napkins set the tone for clearly presented menus that offer many Szechuan specialities but also some Cantonese and even a few Thai dishes. Try the light and crispy deep-fried scallops, served with a simple ight soy dip, and follow with Yin-yang Prawn two prawn dishes (one hot and spicy, the other a mild fresh flavoured stirfry) served side-by-side, both delicious and pretty or popular roast duck in plum sauce, prettily garnished with an orchid.. 'House dinners' are good-value (each about €35) one is dedicated entirely to Dim Sum, which is served in the evening here and includes some eight dishes as well as jasmine tea or (very good) coffee The wine list is on the pricey side, but offers a good choice. **Directions:** Pembroke Road.

Dublin 4

Pembroke Townhouse

E GUESTHOUSE

90 Pembroke Road Ballsbridge Dublin 4
Tel: 01 660 0277 Fax: 01 660 0291
Email: info@pembroketownhouse.ie Web: www.pembroketownhouse.ie

Conveniently located close to the RDS and Lansdowne Road, this fine guesthouse has all the amenities usually expected of an hotel. There's a drawing room and study for residents' use and comfortably furnished, individually designed rooms have a safe and facilities for business guests (wi-fi is available in all areas), as well as direct dial phone, cable television, tea/coffee facilities and trouser press (but no tea / coffee making facilities). Breakfast is the only meal served, but it offers a full buffet and less usual dishes like sautéed lambs liver served on a bed of sautéed onions and topped with bacon, as well as the traditional cooked breakfast. When arriving by car, it is best to go the carpark at the back, as you can then take a lift with your luggage (avoiding heavy traffic and steep steps to the front door). Wine licence (coffee, snacks, minerals and wine available from reception). Private parking at rear. **Rooms 48** (1 suite, 2 family, 3 shower only, 2 disabled, 24 no smoking). Lift. Limited room service. B&B €65 pps, ss €25. *High Speed WI FI Internet access is now available in all areas of the Pembroke Townhouse Amex, Diners, MasterCard, Visa, Laser. **Directions:** Pembroke Road leads onto Baggot St. On the right hand side going towards town.

Dublin 4

RESTAURANT

Poulot's Restaurant

Mulberry Gardens Donnybrook Dublin 4 **Tel: 01 269 3300**
Fax: 01 269 3260 Email: toptable@mac.com Web: www.poulots.ie

Tucked away down a laneway and easy to miss, Lorna Jean and Jean Michel Poulot's restaurant is in the premises previously occupied by Ernie's, a Dublin institution named after the late Ernie Evans and famously filled with paintings of his beloved Kerry. The L-shaped dining-room overlooks a pretty courtyard garden, floodlit at night, and the decor now is much simpler - a warm neutral scheme opens the area up and makes it seem much larger. Jean Michel brought with him a reputation for his time at Halo at the Morrison and, before that, at a number of other important kitchens including Ballylickey Manor in County Cork, where Lorna Jean was also working at the time. Jean Michel's menus offer detailed descriptions of a range of luxurious dishes, including French classic like seared duck foie gras (served with brioche and a fig compôte) and more unusual specialities such as a fennel and Parmesan risotto with yellow fin tuna and shellfish cream; among the main course specialities you will find a very refined loin of venison - little cylinders of tender, lean meat, served with celeriac cream, wild mushrooms and a game jus flavoured with juniper and black pepper. Classic desserts include an excellent creme brulée, and Valrhona chocolate fondant - served, perhaps, with a superb hazelniut ice cream. Presentation on huge white plates is dramatic and, like the oversized menus, acts as a reminder that this is definitely fine dining dining, and not for those days when you're in the mood for something simple. The atmosphere, however, is relaxed, helped by by service which has retained an old-style professionalism. An extensive wine list is Lorna Jean's special interest and, although it naturally lean towards France, it offers a careful selection from all over the world. Children welcome. Air conditioning. **Seats 70.** Open Mon-Sat, L12-3, D 7-10.30. Closed Sun, Mon; Bank Hols. Amex, Diners, MasterCard, Visa, Laser. **Directions:** Behind K Pub in Donnybrook.

Dublin 4

HOTEL/RESTAURANT

Radisson SAS St Helen's Hotel

Stillorgan Road Dublin 4
Tel: 01 218 6000 Fax: 01 218 6030
Email: info.dublin@radissonsas.com Web: www.dublin.radissonsas.com

Set in formal gardens just south of Dublin's city centre, with views across Dublin Bay to Howth Head, the fine 18th century house at the heart of this impressive hotel was once a private residence. Careful restoration and imaginative modernisation have created interesting public areas, including the Orangerie Bar and a pillared ballroom with minstrels' gallery and grand piano. Bedrooms, in a modern four-storey block adjoining the main building, all have garden views (some of the best rooms also have balconies) and air conditioning, and are well-equipped for business guests. Rooms are comfortably furnished to a high standard in contemporary style, although some are less spacious than might be expected in a recent development. Conference/banqueting (350/220); also St Helen's Pavilion (600/800) in summer. Business centre, video conferencing, free broadband Wi/Fi. Fitness centre; beauty salon. Garden. Ample parking. Children welcome (under 18s free in parents' room, cots available without charge, baby sitting arranged). **Rooms 151** (25 suites, 70 no-smoking, 8 for disabled). 24 hr room service, Lift, Turndown service. Room rate from €170 (max. 3 guests). Open all year. **Talavera:** In four interconnecting rooms in the lower ground floor, this informal Italian restaurant is decorated in warm Mediterranean colours and, with smart wooden tables dressed with slips, modern cutlery, fresh flowers and Bristol blue water glasses, it is atmospheric when candle-lit at night. A well-balanced menu offers a balanced choice of dishes inspired by tradition and tailored to the modern palate. Head chef Ciaran Hickey's skilful cooking is matched by a good atmosphere and caring service from friendly, efficient staff, under the supervision of Restaurant Manager Primiano Sese. The wine list offers a strong selection of regional Italian bottles to match the food. *Lighter menus are also offered all day in the Orangerie Bar and Ballroom Lounge. **Seats 140.** Air conditioning, toilets wheelchair accessible. D daily 6-10.30. Set menus from €35; also a la carte. Amex, Diners, MasterCard, Visa, Laser. **Directions:** Just 5.5km (3 miles) south from the city centre, on N11.

Dublin 4

☆RESTAURANT

Roly's Bistro

7 Ballsbridge Terrace Ballsbridge Dublin 4
Tel: 01 668 2611 Fax: 01 660 3342
Email: ireland@rolysbistro.ie Web: www.rolysbistro.ie

This bustling Ballsbridge bistro has been a smash hit since the day it opened. Chef-patron Colin O'Daly (one of Ireland's most highly regarded chefs) and head chef Paul Cartwright present imaginative, reasonably priced seasonal menus at lunch and an early dinner, and also an evening à la carte menu - and the chef's art is not confined to the plate: Colin's paintings adorn the walls and the menu card has a delightful reproduction of his "Sensitive study of a young dancer in morning light". A lively interpretation of classical French cooking gives more than a passing nod to Irish traditions, world cuisines and contemporary styles, and carefully sourced ingredients are the sound foundation for cooking that never disappoints. The breads bear special mention: a trio of sliced yeast loaves, bacon & onion, tomato and pesto flavours, gluten free bread and brown soda. (All breads and confectionery made in-house, under the direction of pastry chef David Walsh, are also sold through Rolys bakery service.) Dublin Bay Prawns are always in demand (and may be served Neuberg, a speciality that comes with a tian of mixed long grain and wild rice), and an upbeat version of traditional Kerry lamb pie is another favourite. Service is efficient but discreet, cooking is invariably excellent, everyone loves the buzz, and Rolys has always given great value for money - they were the first to offer a good range of wines at an accessible price, for example, and famously ran a whole selection at £10; now they offer a Euro version which doesn't have quite the same ring to it but it's a good deal all the same., and also applies to wines available by the glass. Offering quality with good value has been the philosophy of the restaurant from the outset; it continues to fulfil this promise well and the set menus - lunch, pre-theatre and the table d'hôte - all offer particularly good value. **Seats 220.** Air conditioning. L daily 12-2.45 (to 3 Sun), D daily 6-10; Set L €19.95; Early D €21.95 (Mon-Thu, 6-6.45), Set D €42; L&D also à la carte. SC10%. Closed Good Fri & 25-27 Dec inc. Amex, Diners, MasterCard, Visa, Laser. **Directions:** Heart of Ballsbridge, across the road from the American Embassy.

Dublin 4

Schoolhouse Hotel

HOTEL

2-8 Northumberland Road Ballsbridge Dublin 4
Tel: 01 667 5014 Fax: 01 667 5014
Email: reservations@schoolhousehotel.com Web: www.schoolhousehotel.com

Dating back to its opening in 1861 as a school, this canalside building at Mount Street Bridge has seen many changes, culminating in its opening in 1998 as one of Dublin's trendiest small hotels. The Schoolhouse Bar is always a-buzz with young business people of the area, and the classroom theme continues to the restaurant, Canteen, where had chef Kevin Arundel has earned an enviable reputation for smart cooking - local lobster with cajun spiced butter, herb salad & chips is a current favourite. Rooms are finished to a high standard, with air conditioning, power showers and the usual amenities expected of a quality hotel, and all were completely refurbished in 2006. Small conference/banqueting (18/85). Wheelchair accessible. Parking. Children welcome (Under 5s free in parents room; cots available with no charge). No pets. Lift. **Rooms 31** (30 no-smoking, 10 ground floor, 2 for disabled). B&B from about €99 pps. SC discretionary. Closed 24-26 Dec. Amex, Diners, MasterCard, Visa. **Directions:** Southbound from Trinity College, at the end of Mount St. across the Grand Canal.

Dublin 4

Waterloo House

GUESTHOUSE

8-10 Waterloo Road Ballsbridge Dublin 4
Tel: 01 660 1888 Fax: 01 667 1955
Email: info@waterloohouse.ie Web: www.waterloohouse.ie

Evelyn Corcoran's pair of Georgian townhouses make a luxurious and reasonably priced base in a quiet location, which is very convenient to the city centre and also Lansdowne Road (rugby), RDS (equestrian & exhibitions) and some of the city's most famous restaurants. Excellent breakfasts are a high point of any stay. Equally attractive to the business or leisure traveller. Conservatory & Garden. Wheelchair access. Own parking. Children welcome (under 4 free in parents' room, cot available). No pets. Garden. **Rooms 17** (1 disabled). Lift. B&B about €60 pps, ss about €20. Closed Christmas. MasterCard, Visa, Laser. **Directions:** South on Stephens Green on Merrion Row for 1 mile. First turn right after Baggot Street Bridge. ◇

DUBLIN 5

RAHENY AREA

Raheny is a pleasant suburb with some excellent amenities including St. Anne's Park, once home to the Guinness family; this is one of the finest parks in North Dublin - stretching from Raheny village down to the coast at Bull Island, and then along to the edges of Clontarf, it has extensive parkland walks, famous rose gardens and playing fields. A protected Victorian red brick stable yard (1885) has recently been renovated and converted into artists studios, a gallery and the **Rose Café** (087 671 7791), which overlooks the park and offers wholesome home-made fare; it is situated in a spacious (if very bright and, perhaps, hot) first floor conservatory, and also has some tables out in the courtyard in fine weather. There will be an artisan food market here every Saturday, and there are plans for a monthly arts & crafts market (on a Sunday). At the Kilbarrack end of Raheny, just off the road to Howth, **Il Fornaio** (01 832 0277) is a great little restaurant/bakery serving simple, ingredient led authentic Italian food in casual surroundings; their pizzas are renowned and it's the ideal place to pick up the makings of a picnic.

WWW.IRELAND-GUIDE.COM - FOR THE BEST PLACES TO EAT, DRINK & STAY.

DUBLIN 6

Dublin 6

Antica Venezia

RESTAURANT

97 Ashfield Road Ranelagh Dublin 6 **Tel: 01 497 4112**

A real throw-back in time and refreshingly so: this entirely Italian-run restaurant has a classic Italian 70's interior with stained wooden floors and ceiling beams, Venetian trompe-l'oeil scenes on the walls and candlewax-dripped Chianti bottles on every table. The food is also traditional Italian, with a menu that could easily date back to the Seventies too: old-fashioned favourites like stuffed mushrooms and antipasto misto of Italian meats are followed by classics like chicken breast with mushroom and white wine sauce, salmon with lemon butter sauce, pork with marsala sauce and a choice of pasta dishes and pizzas, with predictable but good desserts such as banoffi, tiramisu and cassata as well as a selection of ice creams. Consistently good food, with service that is laid back but attentive - a perfect recipe for a popular neighbourhood restaurant. **Seats 45.** Reservations advised. Air conditioning. Children welcome. D daily, 5-11, L Fri only 12-2.30. A la carte. House wine €18.50. SC discretionary, but 10% on parties of 6+. MasterCard, Visa, Laser. ◇

Dublin 6

Bijou Bistro

RESTAURANT

47 Highfiield Road Rathgar Dublin 6 **Tel: 01 496 1518**
Fax: 01 491 1410 Email: bijourestaurant@eircom.net

A distinctly French atmosphere prevails at this neighbourhood restaurant and, despite recent developments which have virtually doubled its size, it is still advisable to book a table. It's appealingly decorated in a gently modern style, with soft neutral tones and good lighting, and the well-tried system still applies - casual dining is offered in a comfortably furnished area on the ground floor and there's a more formal restaurant upstairs. Well made breads accompany an innovative menu with a dozen or so choices on each course and several fish specialities each evening (typically chargrilled loin of swordfish with chive mash and spiced chickpea salsa); other specialities include risotto of spiced cajun chicken with parmesan herb salad, while more traditional tastes will welcome dishes like pork fillet with sage & bacon potato cake, apple & raisin chutney and Vermouth cream, cooked with accuracy and style - and served on plates decorated with a colourful art deco flourish. Finish with classic desserts or an Irish cheese selection with muscat grapes. A good wine list, plus a couple of weekly specials. Children welcome. **Seats about 100** (private room, 14). Air conditioning. Times on application. SC discretionary. Closed Christmas/ New Year. Amex, Diners, MasterCard, Visa, Laser. **Directions:** Rathgar crossroads. ◇

Dublin 6

Diep Noodle Bar

RESTAURANT

19 Ranelagh Dublin 6 **Tel: 01 497 6550** Fax: 01 497 6549
Email: info@diep.net Web: www.diep.net

Younger sister to Diep le Shaker off Fitzwilliam Square, this colourful little place quickly gained a reputation as the in place for discerning young things to meet. It has a great atmosphere, chic, clean-lined decor and - as if a mixture of Thai and Vietnamese food weren't fashionable enough - a cocktail bar too. Closely packed tables reach a long way back down the long narrow room, and you can be fairly sure it will be packed, any night of the week, which adds to the ambience. Service is a strong point from the moment you arrive and the menu - which offers plenty of noodle dishes, and much else besides - points out that no monosodium glutamate is used and that food arrives, Asian style, just as soon as it's ready, rather than in courses. Whether the freefall attitude to meal structure works is, perhaps, a matter of luck - if you order well, it's fine and adds to the fun, but you could end up with too much or too little of one thing, or a feeling that dishes are arriving in the wrong order. Individual dishes are not expensive - a classic Phad Thai, for example, is around €13.95, Tom Yaam Goong (hot & sour soup with prawns) €6.95, Vietnamese noodle soups all around €9-10, and curries and stir-fries in the €15-16 region; but by the time you've had a couple of cocktails, ordered a bit of everything and had an Asian beer or a bottle of wine with your food it can add up surprisingly fast. There's a sense of excitement to this little restaurant - it's a place to have fun; so first time out, order carefully - old hands know how to work the menu. Open 7 days: L 2.30-5.30, D 5.30-11.30. 2/3 course Set L. €11.50/14.50. Early D from €24.50 (5.30-7.30); also à la carte. Wine from about €17.50. Closed Mon to 5.30, 24-31 Dec (re-opens 1 Jan at 5.30). Amex, MasterCard, Visa, Laser.

Dublin 6

Mint

☆RESTAURANT

47 Ranelagh Village Dublin 6
Tel: 01 497 8655 Fax: 01 282 7018

This highly regarded restaurant in Ranelagh village has recently had both a revamp and a change of chef, and appears to have come through both with flying colours. The décor remains classy and understated, lending an air of spaciousness to a small area, but it's a little softer and more welcoming. Friendly, professional staff quickly bring you to your stylish, white-clothed table - there is no room for a reception area, which is a small downside, but new arrivals are quickly settled in. Dylan McGrath has taken over as Head Chef now that Oliver Dunne, who established Mint's reputation, is opening his own restaurant in Malahide; it was a hard act to follow but the changeover has been achieved with flair and, although both food and wine are expensive - this is very much a fine dining place - some brilliant cooking is going on at Mint. Menus offered are a little confusing and, at the time of going to press, they do not include an a la carte, making an outing here not only expensive but, perhaps, daunting for those with small appetites. Value for money is not in doubt, however: at lunch time a set price menu with two choices on each course is a snip at €31.50; at the other end of the spectrum, a Tasting Menu is available to complete tables, at €95, and would certainly be a wonderful experience for a special occasion. There is also a more accessible 3-course menu, at €65 - yet there are so many extras included that this bears no resemblance to the normal expectation: a range of little foams, amuse-bouche delicacies and delicious breads all arrive before your starter, then there are little treats between courses, and superp petits fours - and the cooking throughout is exceptionally creative and skilfully executed. Luxurious ingredients sit cheek by jowl beside fashionably 'rustic' ones and the cooking style is refined and intricate, yet the combinations of flavours and textures are so skilfully judged that it works - so, providing you have sufficient appetite to enjoy an extensive dining experience, you will come away feeling that your money was well spent. A pricey wine list offers little under €30. Childen welcome, but not suitable after 8pm. **Seats 45.** Reservations advised. L Tue-Sun, 12-3; D Tue-Sun, 6-10. Set 1-3 course L €15-25; Early D €27 (6-6.45); D also à la carte. Wines from €19. Closed Mon, bank holidays. Amex, MasterCard, Visa, Laser. **Directions:** Centre of Ranelagh Village.

Dublin 6

Ouzo

RESTAURANT

1 Sandford Road Ranelagh Dublin 6
Tel: 01 491 2253 Fax: 01 667 0780

féile bia The entrance to Ouzo is not obvious as it's somewhat concealed beside the doors to McSorley's pub. Once discovered however, you'll find yourself in a one-off restaurant. Two large rooms, basically furnished and decorated, make up the buzzing restaurant: no frills, but this is reflected in the price list. Though steaks are equally popular, it is the high quality fresh fish (caught by their own Dingle-based, 21-foot fishing boat MFV Phoenix) that draws the attention: everything that comes out of the kitchen is well cooked and served at very reasonable prices. Add willing, friendly service that reflects genuine (but today not always observed) 'old-fashioned' Irish hospitality, and you have an unusual restaurant for these times. Very limited wine list. * Also at 11, Upper Baggot Street, Dublin 4 (Tel 01 667 3279). **Seats 80.** Children welcome - children's menus available. Wheelchair access difficult. Open 12-"late" daily. Closed Good Fri & 25-26 Dec. Amex, Diners, MasterCard, Visa, Laser. **Directions:** Above McSorleys pub.

Dublin 6

Poppadom Indian Restaurant

RESTAURANT

91a Rathgar Road Dublin 6
Tel: 01 490 2383 Fax: 01 411 1155

féile bia Behind a neat but unremarkable frontage in a row of modern shops lies Poppadum, a colourful and airy new wave Indian restaurant, with linen-clad tables, comfortable chairs and a bar. The aim here is to demonstrate the diversity of Indian cooking and offer some appealingly unusual dishes. Complimentary poppadoms with fresh chutney dips are brought before menus which offer regional specialities including a starter of Karwari Prawns - deep-fried jumbo prawns marinated in ginger, garlic, yoghurt, garam masala and barbecued in the tandoor, then served with a fresh mint chutney - and main courses ranging in heat from Chicken Avadh, a mild and creamy dish with nuts that was a speciality of the erstwhile Avadh empire of central India, to Lamb Chettinad, a fiery festive dish of the Chettiyar clan in Tamil Nadu. Vegetarians have plenty of dishes available as main courses or side orders, and variations like garlic, onion & coriander naan and lime rice offer a subtle change from the standard accompaniments. Food presentation is contemporary and service solicitous. Make a point of trying the masala tea, made with leaf tea and cardamom pods. The wine list helpfully begins with some advice on the styles that partner spicy food well, wisely suggesting Alsace wines, notably Gewurztraminer as the best all-rounder. Children welcome. **Seats 45.** Reservations advised. Air conditioning. D daily, 6-12. A la carte. Wines from about €17. SC discretionary. Closed 25 Dec. Amex, MasterCard, Visa, Laser, Switch. **Directions:** 1 minute from Comans Pub, Rathgar. ◇

Dublin 6

TriBeCa

RESTAURANT 65 Ranelagh Village Dublin 6 **Tel: 01 497 4174** Fax: 01 491 1584

An outpost of the Canal Bank Café (see entry), this New York style restaurant was a hit from the start for its good fast food and relaxed, casual feel, with bright and airy decor and wooden floors and tables. It's just right for food like carefully sourced burgers (made from 100% organic beef), salads, omelettes and chicken wings, which take their place beside the fusion inspired dishes that keep the more adventurous diners happy. It's not cheap, but it is wholesome fare - and portions are generous so it works out as quite good value for money. Children welcome. **Seats 70** (outside seating 16). Reservations advised. Air conditioning. Toilets wheelchair accessible. Open daily, 12-11. Set L €9.50/15 (12-5); otherwise à la carte, plus daily blackboard specials. House wine€17.50. Closed Dec 24-26, Good Fri. MasterCard, Visa, Laser. **Directions:** Heading southbound from city centre, halfway along Ranelagh main street, on right. ◇

Dublin 6W

Vermilion

RESTAURANT

94-96 Terenure Road North Terenure Dublin 6W
Tel: 01 499 1400 Fax: 01 499 1300
Email: mail@vermilion.ie Web: www.vermilion.ie

This purpose-built restaurant on the first floor above the Terenure Inn pub opened to some acclaim in 2001 and the decor - a contemporary, smart interior in soft primary colours - reflects a forward-looking food philosophy, which offers colourful, beautifully presented and updated versions of many Indian favourites. Nibbles include little bowls of various condiments such as a rich tomato sauce, a vibrantly yellow, fragrant custard dip and grated carrots with ginger and black mustard seeds. The menu includes specialities from Kerala, Tamil-Nadu and Goa and pride is clearly taken in the quality of ingredients and cooking. A small selection of desserts is more tempting than is usual in oriental restaurants (although only the kulfi is an Indian speciality). Each summer, from June to September, Vermilion hosts an Indian Summer Festival, following a culinary trail around India - from the fiery southern dishes and curries with cooling coconut, to the Punjabi and Kashmiri styles of the north, and from western hot and spicy dishes to the rich and creamy dishes from the central Mogul region - complete with Bollywood movie clips and belly dancing. Although the menu gives detailed explanations of each dish, some of which are well known, this is not a traditional Indian restaurant, so come with an open mind and don't expect the usual, familiar experience of 'popular' Indian food. Service is friendly and solicitous. **Seats 90** (private area 35). Reservations advised. Air conditioning. D daily 5.30-10, L Sun only, 1-3.30. Set Menu, €20 (available L Sun Sep-May & D 5.30-7 Sun-Thu & to 6.30 Fri & Sat). D also à la carte. Indian Summer Menu €38 inc 1/2 bottle wine). House wine from €17.50. Closed 25-26 Dec, Good Fri. Amex, Diners, MasterCard, Visa, Laser, Switch. **Directions:** 200 yards from Terenure crossroads. ◇

DUBLIN 7

Dublin 7

Hanley at the Bar

Ⓝ RESTAURANT

The Distillery Building May Lane Dublin 7
Tel: 01 878 0104 Fax: 01 878 1105

Well known caterer Claire Hanley's smart daytime restaurant near the Jameson Distillery has always been popular with the lawyers from the nearby Law Library and the Four Courts, but was otherwise a well-kept secret until this area began its recent phase of rapid development. High stools at the bar provide a comfortable perch if you are waiting for a table (it gets very busy at lunch time), but it's worth a little patience as you may expect good contemporary cooking in very chic surroundings.

Dublin 7
PUB

The Hole in the Wall

Blackhorse Avenue Phoenix Park Dublin 7
Tel: 01 838 9491 Fax: 01 868 5160

PJ McCaffrey's remarkable pub beside the Phoenix Park is named in honour of a tradition which existed here for around a hundred years - the practice of serving drinks through a hole in the wall of the Phoenix Park to members of the army garrison stationed nearby. Today the Hole in the Wall also claims to be the longest pub in Ireland - and it is certainly one of the most interesting. They do food too - there's a carvery lunch, and a bar menu available throughout the day offers a wide choice including traditional Irish dishes like Beef & Guinness Pie, Dublin Coddle and Irish Stew. Children welcome. Pets allowed in certain areas. Music nightly and all day Sun. Wheelchair access. Parking. Bar menu served daily (12-9). Closed 25 Dec & Good Fri. Amex, MasterCard, Visa, Laser. **Directions:** Beside Phoenix Park.

Dublin 7
RESTAURANT

Kelly & Ping, Bar & Restaurant

Smithfield Village Dublin 7 **Tel: 01 814 8583**
Fax: 01 817 3841 Web: www.kellyandping.com

This colourful, glass-fronted restaurant is popular locally for its informality and eclectic menus. The style is broadly Asian, mainly Thai, and many of the popular dishes are offered - chicken satay, vegetable spring rolls, Thai style sweet & sour pork, Nasi Goreng - along with many less well-known dishes, and a range of Kelly & Ping Thai curries which can be ordered red (hot), green (medium) or yellow (mild). There's also a sprinkling of international bistro dishes like goats cheese & home-dried tomato salad, baked salmon with caramelised onion mash and smoked chicken & mango quesadilla, all offered in generous portions and well-priced. As well as a moderately priced wine list, there's a good choice of Asian beers. **Seats 100** (outdoor, 50). Open Mon-Fri 12-10 (L12-3, D 4-11), Sat 5pm-10pm. Closed Sat L, Sun, bank hols. Amex, MasterCard, Visa, Laser, Switch. **Directions:** Behind the Four Courts, beside Old Jameson Distillery.

Dublin 7
PUB

The Old Jameson Distillery

Bow Street Smithfield Dublin 7 **Tel: 01 807 2355** Fax: 01 807 2369
Email: reservations@ojd.ie Web: www.whiskeytours.com

While most visitors to Dublin will visit the restored Old Jameson Distillery to do the tour (which is fascinating), it's also a good spot for a bite to eat. There are special menus for groups (including evening functions, when the Distillery is not otherwise open) but The Stillroom Restaurant is also open to individuals - light food served all day and lunch, featuring Irish specialities like John Jameson beef casserole, roast loin of pork with apple & Jameson sauce, and Jameson farmhouse whiskey cake - and the standard of cooking is generally high. Downstairs, the 1780 Bar is open from 12 noon daily, with bar food (mainly modern international - chicken Caesar, panini etc) available at lunchtime (12.30-3). **Restaurant Seats 103.** Reservations accepted. Open 9-5 daily; L 12.30-2.30. House wine €18. Closed 25 Dec, Goood Fri. Amex, MasterCard, Visa, Laser. **Directions:** On northside of Quays, off Arran Quay, near Four Courts. Well signed.

Dublin 7
RESTAURANT

Rhodes D7

The Capel Building Mary's Abbey Dublin 7
Tel: 01 804 4444 Fax: 01 804 4445
Email: info@rhodesD7.com Web: www.rhodesd7.com

Dublin's most-hyped recent opening, Rhodes D7 is in a part of town which is only just beginning to blossom (but, by a happy chance, is handy to the Law Library), immediately sparking off debate as to whether the celebrity chef was ill-advised or just ahead of the game. The restaurant is set back from the street a little, allowing for tables at a terrace along the front, which is perfect for smokers, and those who enjoy watching local children dodging the Luas trams, although the space is tight for comfort and ease of service. Inside, the basic structure is modern but the designers have gone for a mixum-gatherum of styles which has attracted a pretty comprehensive thumbs-down: the interior is dominated by some specially commissioned and very colourful large modern paintings (cows, produce) which you will love or loathe but, with an antique table here, trellis-back chairs there, modern table settings, and some vaguely old-fashioned light fittings, it doesn't add up to a 'look'. But this is the perfect time to bring stylish yet well-priced dining to Dublin, and it is on the food and wine and service - that Rhodes will be judged. Although this is essentially a franchise - Gary Rhodes was very upfront from the start that he would not personally be cooking - head chef Paul Hargraves worked with him as sous chef for six years before coming to Dublin, and his cooking is impressive. The menu is well-judged, offering plenty of choice from a dozen or so appealing starters and main courses including specialities such as haddock rarebit and gammon steak (the speciality dessert is a Baileys crème brulée). Decent wines from an interesting list beginning at €16 should certainly please (there's a good choice by the glass too). The concept here has been adapted from the UK prototype and some feel that there's an 'Englishness' which seems stilted in Dublin but the (rightly) well-regarded Rhodes menus have been adapted with care and there's a full-on commitment to using Irish produce where possible, as there would be to local produce in other locations. The cooking is generally excellent and, although service has been inconsistent in the early days, this promises to become a favourite with Dubliners. Children welcome; Toilets wheelchair accessible. **Seat 248** (private room, 50, outdoors, 50); air conditioning; band Thurs-Sun, 8.30-11pm. Food served Mon-Sat, 12-10.15pm (closed Mon D), Sun L 12-4pm, all a la carte. Closed Sun & Mon D, Bank Hols. Amex, MasterCard, Visa, Laser. **Directions:** Junction of Capel St. and Mary's Abbey.

DUBLIN 8

Dublin 8

Bar Italia Essex Quay

CAFÉ/RESTAURANT

Lr Exchange Street Essex Quay Dublin 8

Tel: 01 679 5128 Email: acrobat_ltd@yahoo.it Web: www.baritalia.ie

In a modern office block on the edge of Temple Bar and close to the Civic Offices known disparagingly to Dubliners as 'The Bunkers', this little Italian trattoria style restaurant has floor-to-ceiling glass to make the most of a splendid view across the Liffey towards the magnificent Four Courts - and there's plenty of space outside to enjoy lunch 'al fresco' when the weather's right. Attentive Italian waiters quickly seat new arrivals, service throughout is quick and professional and the banter lends a relaxed atmosphere - matched by colourful, flavoursome food, simply presented. The minestrone soup can be memorable, paninis and pasta dishes are the business, and it's a place worth seeking out for their espressos alone. And it's great value too. **Seats 25.** Outdoor seating. Open every day: Mon-Fri, 8-6, Sat 9-6, Sun 12-6. A la carte. Closed Christmas/New Year. Also at: Bar Italia, 26 Lower Ormond Quay, Dublin, 1 (Tel 01 874 1000). MasterCard, Visa. **Directions:** South quays, west end of Temple Bar (near Dublin Corporation head office).

Dublin 8

Brazen Head

PUB

20 Lower Bridge Street Dublin 8 **Tel: 01 677 9549** Fax: 01 670 4042

Email: info@brazenhead.com Web: www.brazenhead.com

Dublin's (possibly Ireland's) oldest pub was built on the site of a tavern dating back to the 12th century - and it's still going strong. Full of genuine character, this friendly, well-run pub has lots of different levels and dark corners. Food is wholesome and middle-of-the-road at reasonable prices - visitors will be pleased to find traditional favourites like beef & Guinness stew and Irish stew, but there are also more contemporary dishes like stuffed breast of chicken with sage & sausage meat, wrapped in bacon - and a lot of seafood. Live music nightly in the Music Lounge. **Seats 80** (private room 40, outdoor seating 40). Open every day,12-10: L12-6 & D 6-10 daily (Bar meals 12-9). Closed 25 Dec & Good Fri. Amex, MasterCard, Visa, Laser. **Directions:** Opposite the Four Courts.

Dublin 8

Chorus Café

CAFÉ

Fishamble Street Dublin 8 **Tel: 01 616 7088** Fax: 01 616 7088

A small restaurant with a big heart, this bright and friendly little place is near the site of the first performance of Handel's Messiah, hence the name - and some features of the decor. Interesting breakfasts (Danish pastries, home-made scones and bagels with imaginative fillings, for example, as well as the 'full Irish'), are followed by an all-day procession of good things. Gourmet ciabatta and panini, and old favourites like tuna melts, jostle for space alongside wonderful salads: a useful daytime place to know about if you're visiting anywhere in the Christchurch area. **Seats 24.** Open Mon-Fri, 7.30am-4.30pm, Sat 10-4.30. Closed Sun, Christmas, New Year. **No Credit Cards. Directions:** Opposite Dublin Corporation Offices, at Christchurch end of Fishamble Street. ◇

Dublin 8
CAFÉ

Gallic Kitchen

49 Francis Street Dublin 8
Tel: 01 454 4912 Fax: 01 4733972 Email: galkit@iol.ie

This little spot in Dublin's "antique" district has been delighting locals and visitors alike for some years now. Patissière Sarah Webb is renowned for quality baking (quiches, roulades, plaits, tartlets, wraps) and also salads and delicious little numbers to have with coffee. A judicious selection from an extensive range is offered to eat in the shop: sourcing is immaculate, cooking skilful and prices reasonable, so you may have to queue. Outside catering offered (with staff if required). Open Mon-Sat, 9-4.30. * Sarah also has a stall at several markets: Temple Bar (Sat, 9-5); Dun Laoghaire (Thu, 10.30-5); Leopardstown (Fri, 11-5); Laragh, Co Wicklow (one Sun each month). MasterCard, Visa, Laser. ◇

Dublin 8

Guinness Storehouse

St James Gate Dublin 8 **Tel: 01 471 4261**
Email: sinead.staunton@diageo.com Web: www.guinness.com

The most spectacular pint of Guinness in Dublin - indeed, in all Ireland - awaits you in Gravity, the modern glass-walled bar providing panoramic views of the city from its unique position atop the impressive Guinness Storehouse, a handsome 1904 building. The Storehouse is commodious - with 170,000 square feet of floor space, it is one of the choicest pieces of real estate in Dublin. The space is imaginatively used to house the Guinness Museum, the story - told with fascinating high tech exhibits - of the famous company's 250-plus years in business. It also includes (on Level 5) the traditional Brewery Bar, serving nourishing Irish fare (seafood chowder, beef & Guinness stew) and the contemporary-style Source Bar. Slightly more formal evening menus, including a short children's menu, are available in Jul-Aug. Opened in the autumn of 2000, the Guinness Storehouse has long since welcomed its millionth visitor: it has so much to offer that some folk spend an entire day there. The Storehouse is open daily, 9.30-5. Entrance fees apply. Bureau de Change. Free parking. Brewery **Bar Seats 120.** Food served 12-4 daily. Closed 25 Dec, Good Fri. Amex, MasterCard, Visa, Laser. **Directions:** James Street, Guinness storehouse.

Dublin 8
CAFÉ

Havana Tapas Bar

3 Camden Market Grantham Street Dublin 8
Tel: 01 476 0046 Email: info@havana.ie Web: www.havana.ie

This compact tapas bar is tucked away on a little street off Camden Street and is a favourite with locals and people working in the area. Home-cooked food is freshly made on the premises: chorizo & lentil stew, tortilla, paella, Serrano ham and delicious breads from the famous Bretzel Bakery is the kind of food you'll get, along with tapas like marinated jumbo prawns. Prices are reasonable. [* A newer Havana is now open on South Great George's Street, and is extremely popular (01 400 5990; www.havana.ie)]. For music, be there on Friday and Saturday nights at 10 o'clock (until "late") for salsa music. **Seats 60** (private room 20). Open Mon-Sat 12-11.30 (Fri-Sat to 2 am, last orders 1.30). Tapas from about €6.50. Set Menu €13 (available all day Mon-Wed). House wine about €15. SC 12%. Closed Sun, bank hols, 1st 2 weeks Aug. Amex, MasterCard, Visa, Laser. **Directions:** Adjacent to Cassidy's Pub, Camden Street. ◇

Dublin 8
HOTEL

Jurys Inn Christchurch

Christchurch Place Dublin 8 **Tel: 01 454 0000** Fax: 01 454 0012
Email: info@jurysdoyle.com Web: www.jurysdoyle.com

féile bia Jurys Inn Christchurch is well placed for both tourist and business travellers, offering reasonably priced accommodation within walking distance of the main city centre areas on both sides of the Liffey and close to Dublin Castle and events in Temple Bar. Rooms are comfortable and spacious, with large, well positioned work desks, and practical bathrooms with economy baths and overbath showers. A large multi-storey car park at the rear has convenient access to the hotel. **Rooms 182.** Room rate from €108 (up to 3 adults or 2 adults & 2 children); weekend rate €117, rising to €225 on rugby weekends. Breakfast from about €10. Closed 24-26 Dec Amex, Diners, MasterCard, Visa, Laser. **Directions:** Follow signs to city centre; opposite Christchurch Cathedral.

Dublin 8

Locks Restaurant

RESTAURANT

1 Windsor Terrace Portobello Dublin 8
Tel: 01 454 3391 Fax: 01 453 8352

féile bia In an old building with a lovely canal-side setting, this two-storey restaurant has long been a favourite with Dubliners. It has a warm and elegant style with soft lighting, open fires and there's a timelessness about it which is refreshing. Accomplished cooking, caring service and a warm ambience make this a pleasing place to be and, in the Guide's experience, the dining experience has always been enjoyable. Children welcome. **Seats 55** (private room, 24). L Mon-Fri,12.30-2; D Mon-Sat, 6.30-10. Reservations essential. Closed L Sat, all Sun, bank hols, Christmas week. Amex, Diners, MasterCard, Visa, Laser. **Directions:** Half way between Portobello and Harold's Cross Bridges.

Dublin 8

The Lord Edward

E RESTAURANT

23 Christchurch Place Dublin 8 **Tel: 01 454 2420** Fax: 01 454 2420
Email: ledward@indigo.ie Web: www.lordedward.ie

Dublin's oldest seafood restaurant/bar spans three floors of a tall, narrow building overlooking Christchurch Cathedral. Traditional in a decidedly old-fashioned way, The Lord Edward provides a complete contrast to the current wave of trendy restaurants that has taken over Dublin recently, which is just the way a lot of people like it. If you enjoy seafood and like old-fashioned cooking with plenty of butter and cream (as nature intended) and without too many concessions to the contemporary style of presentation either, then this could be the place for you. While certainly caught in a time warp, the range of fish and seafood dishes offered is second to none (sole is offered in no less than nine classic dishes, for example), and the fish cookery is excellent, with simplest choices almost invariably the best. There are a few non-seafood options - traditional dishes like Irish stew, perhaps, or corned beef and cabbage - and desserts also favour the classics. This place is a one-off - long may it last. Bar food is also available Mon-Fri, 12-2.30. Children welcome. **Seats 35.** L Mon-Fri, 12.30-2.30, D Mon-Sat 6-10.45. 5 course D €35; also à la carte. House wine from €19.50. Reservations required. Closed Sun, 24 Dec-2 Jan, bank hols. Amex, Diners, MasterCard, Visa, Laser. **Directions:** Opposite Christchurch Cathedral.

Dublin 8

Nonna Valentina

N RESTAURANT

1-2 Portobello Road Dublin 8 **Tel: 01 454 9866** Fax: 01 633 4476
Email: acrobat_ltd@yahoo.it Web: www.dunneandcrescenzi.com

A recent addition to the group of restaurants run by the members of the Dunne and Crescenzi families (Dunne & Crescenzi, Bar Italia, La Corte, L'Officina), this attractively located two-storey restaurant is named after Stefano Crescenzi's grandmother and enjoys a pleasant outlook over the Grand Canal. Simple rooms with hardwood flooring and white clothed tables are given a sense of occasion by neat chandeliers and smart chair covers but, although this is at the fine dining end of the restaurants in the group, the main emphasis - as in all of the Dunne & Crescenzi restaurants - is on immaculately sourced ingredients, great service and the buzz created by rooms full of happy diners. Concise menus in Italian and English may include old favourites like bruschette, buffalo mozzarella (stuffed with salty anchovies) or breseola (served with rocket and Parmesan) while others, such as carpaccio of Donegal tuna, may be less familiar. Specialities include delicious home-made pastas ('primi piatti' on the menu, but positioned to bridge the gap between the Italian tradition of serving them as a starter and the Irish preference for pasta as a main course), deeply-flavoured sauces, and a short choice of main courses ranging from simple excellence in a perfectly cooked organic fillet steak to some quite sophisticated dishes, including poultry and game. And sweet-toothed diners would do well to leave a little room for delicious home-made desserts which include some unusual ices and an exceptional rendition of that great classic, tiramisu. All this plus excellent coffee, a short but carefully selected wine list, great service and very fair prices - no wonder this restaurant has been a hit since it opened, in late summer 2005. Toilets wheelchair accessible. **Seats 60** (private room, 20); Air con; Food served all day 12-11; Early D €20, 5-7, also á la carte; House wine €18. Closed 25 Dec. Amex, MasterCard, Visa, Laser. **Directions:** On the banks of the canal.

Dublin 8

Ryan's of Parkgate Street

PUB

28 Parkgate Street Dublin 8 **Tel: 01 677 6097** Fax: 01 677 6098

féile bia Ryan's is one of Ireland's finest and best-loved original Victorian pubs, with magnificent stained glass, original mahogany bar fixtures and an outstanding collection of antique mirrors all contributing to its unique atmosphere. Bar food is available every day except Sunday and, upstairs, there's a small restaurant, FXB at Ryans, serving food which is a step up from bar meals. Street parking only (can be difficult, but Pay & Display nearby). Pub food: Mon-Fri, 3-11.30, Fri & Sat, 12-10. Restaurant: L Fri & Sat from 12 noon; D Mon-Sat 5-9.30 (last orders). Closed 25 Dec, Good Fri, first 2 wks Jan & bank hols. MasterCard, Visa, Laser. **Directions:** On the quays - across the river from Heuston Station.

Dublin 8

The Grass Roots Café

CAFÉ

Irish Museum of Modern Art Royal Hospital Kilmainham Dublin 8
Tel: 01 612 9900

This self-service café is a pleasant place for an informal meal, whether or not you are visiting the museum - it has good parking facilities and the spacious room, which is attractively located overlooking a garden area, has a pleasingly cool modern ambience. An appetising small menu offers home-made soup, salads and quiches, tarts and cakes plus several hot dishes - tortellini with pesto cream, perhaps, or tasty pork tacos, generously served - and about half the daily selection is vegetarian. Food quality and presentation is good (large white plates), cafeteria style service is efficient - and it's a handier choice for a quick lunch than city centre venues, perhaps. Wine choices are restricted to a few quarter bottles. Open: Mon-Sat 10-5, Sun 12-5. MasterCard, Visa. **Directions:** At Royal Hospital Kilmainham museum.

DUBLIN 9

Dublin 9

Addison Lodge

PUB

Botanic Road Glasnevin Dublin 9 **Tel: 01 837 3534**
Fax: 01 837 5942 Email: addison@eircom.net

A useful place to know about if you're visiting the Botanic Gardens, just across the road: this friendly family-run pub with accommodation is just the spot for wholesome, freshly-prepared food. Snacks like soup and sandwiches are available from opening time onwards and lunch-time brings hot food, probably including traditional favourites like Irish stew and bacon & cabbage, which are especially welcome. Not suitable for children after 7pm. Food served daily, 12.30-8 (Sun to 6). Closed 25 Dec, Good Fri. Amex, MasterCard, Visa. **Directions:** Opposite entrance to the Botanic Gardens. ◇

Dublin 9

Andersons Food Hall & Café

E CAFÉ/WINE BAR

3 The Rise Glasnevin Dublin 9 **Tel: 01 837 8394**
Email: info@andersons.ie Web: www.andersons.ie

Previously a butchers shop, and still with its original 1930s' tiled floor, high ceiling and façade, Noel Delaney and Patricia van der Velde's wonderful delicatessen, wine shop and continental style café is quietly situated on a side road, so the unexpected sight of jaunty aluminium chairs and tables outside - and a glimpse of many wine bottles lining the walls behind the elegant shopfront - should gladden the hearts of first-time visitors sweeping around the corner from Griffith Avenue. Oak fittings have been used throughout, including the wine displays, and the chic little marble-topped tables used for lighter bites suit the old shop well - in the extension behind it, there are larger tables and space for groups to eat in comfort. Now, where cuts of meat were once displayed, there's a wonderful selection of charcuterie and cheese from Ireland and the continent: an Irish Plate offers a selection of ham, pastrami, Irish stout cured beef and Irish farmhouse cheeses, for example, while The Iberian Selection comprises Serrano ham, chorizo salamis, Mediterranean vegetables, olives and Manchego sheep's milk cheese - all served with speciality breads - and a Children's Selection educates the younger palate with the likes of hot panini with smoked turkey and Emmenthal cheese. A short blackboard menu of hot dishes and specials (penne pasta with tomato, spicy meat & aubergine for example), plus a daily soup, a range of salads, gourmet sandwiches, wraps, hot paninis, pastries and classic café desserts (and luscious ice creams from Murphys of Dingle) complement the charcuterie and cheese which have the gravitas to balance the collection of wines lining the walls - and, in addition to the wine list, which changes regularly, you can choose any bottle to have with your food at a very modest corkage charge. There's also an extensive drinks menu, offering speciality coffees and teas, and some unusual beverages, like Lorina French lemonade. * Also at: Andersons Crêperie (01 830 5171), Carlingford Road, Drumcondra, Dublin 9, where the speciality is buckwheat pancakes, but they also offer charcuterie, cheeses etc. **Seats 43** (outside seating 18); No reservations, children welcome, toilets wheelchair accessible. Open daily: Mon-Wed, 9-7, Thu-Sat 9-8.30, Sun 9-7 (last food orders half an hour before closing). 14 House Wines (€16.95-€23.95) & 160 wines available from the wine shop at €6 corkage. Closed 4 days over Christmas, Good Fri & Easter Sun. MasterCard, Visa, Laser. **Directions:** Off Griffith Avenue, near junction with Mobhi Road.

Dublin 9

Egans House

GUESTHOUSE

7-9 Iona Park Glasnevin Dublin 9 **Tel: 01 830 5283** Fax: 01 830 3312
Email: info@eganshouse.com Web: www.eganshouse.com

Within walking distance of the Botanic Gardens and convenient to the airport, north Dublin golf clubs, Dublin City University, the Helix (DCU Performing Arts complex, Dublin port and the city centre, the Finn's family-run guesthouse offers comfortable, well-maintained accommodation at a reasonable price. All rooms are en-suite, with full bath, phone, tea/coffee trays. Work desk, internet access, safe. Wine licence. Wheelchair access. Parking. Children welcome (Under 3s free In parents' room; cots available). No pets. Garden. **Rooms 23** (22 shower only, 14 no-smoking, 13 ground floor, 4 family rooms). B&B €55, ss€10. Closed 22-28 Dec. MasterCard, Visa, Laser. **Directions:** North of city centre - Dorset Street - St. Alphonsus Road- Iona Park.

Dublin 9

Independent Pizza Company

RESTAURANT

28 Lr Drumcondra Road Dublin 9
Tel: 01 830 2044 Fax: 01 830 3952

A sister restaurant of the popular Gotham Café just off Grafton Street (see entry), the Independent Pizza Company is in smart new premises and the menu includes many of the Gotham favourites, so you can expect to find designer salads and contemporary pasta dishes, for example, alongside the excellent range of gourmet pizzas for which they are best known. Family-friendly (crayons, colouring books provided) and a handy place for a meal on the way to the airport. Lunchtime specials are good value and there's a good drinks menu, including speciality coffees. Air conditioning. Wheelchair friendly. **Seats 50** (Max table size 8). Open daily, 12 noon-midnight (Sun to 11). House wine €15; beer licence. A la carte; sc discretionary (except 10% on groups of 6+ adults). Closed Christmas, Good Fri. Amex, MasterCard, Visa, Laser. **Directions:** On the airport road - under the bridge at Drumcondra railway station.

Dublin 9

John Kavanagh (Grave Diggers)

PUB

1 Prospect Square Glasnevin Dublin 9 **Tel: 01 830 7978**

John Kavanagh's lays claim to being the oldest family pub in Dublin - it was established in 1833 and the current family are the 6th generation in the business. Also known as "The Gravediggers' because of its location next to the Glasnevin cemetery and its attached folk history, this is a genuine Victorian bar, totally unspoilt - and it has a reputation for serving one of the best pints in Dublin. No music, "piped or otherwise". Theme pub owners eat your hearts out. No children after 7pm. Bar food (home made soups & sandwiches 'with a twist'), 12-3 Mon-Fri (except Bank Hols). Closed Good Fri & Christmas. **Directions:** Old Glasnevin Cemetery Gate, off Botanic Road.

Dublin 9

Porterhouse North

PUB

Cross Guns Bridge Glasnevin Dublin 9 **Tel: 01 830 9922**
Fax: 01 830 9920 Web: www.porterhousebrew.com

Originally the Iona Garage, owned by the Cahill family (who were also associated with the aviation industry), Porterhouse North is a large white canalside building with a copper sign above the door - hard to miss, although parking nearby may not be so easy in this busy area. It has been redeveloped to retain some of the original art deco features - notably the stepped badge detail in the middle of the pediments, which have been preserved, stripped back to the original plaster and clad with black and white terrazzo and copper banding. Inside it is a very trendy pub - on four different levels, with outdoor seating at the back and side - and the building's history is echoed in materials associated with the era (terrazo flooring, leather on the counter, rippled glass walls with copper banding and ceramic column castings; with large flat screen TV, an open kitchen with pizza oven on the first floor and a buzzy atmosphere giving it obvious youth appeal. Menus offer a range of popular dishes but, although interesting as a bar, it's not really a food place (perhaps with the exception of pizzas), more a place to drop in for a drink. Wheelchair accessible. Open usual pub hours (to 12.30am Fri & Sat). Food served daily: Sun-Fri, 12-10pm; Sat 12-9.30. Closed 25 Dec, Good Fri. **Directions:** At Cross Guns Bridge. ◇

Dublin 9

The Washerwomans Hill Restaurant

RESTAURANT

60a Glasnevin Hill Glasnevin Dublin 9 **Tel: 01 837 9199**
Fax: 01 837 9492 Email: washerwomanrestaurant@eircom.net

Situated on a busy road, just across from the Met Office and convenient to the Botanic Gardens and the airport area, first impressions of this popular neighbourhood restaurant may be a little dusty but a prompt welcome and (if you are lucky) the offer of a choice of tables should help new arrivals warm to it. Traditional, slightly old-world in style, this charming restaurant is quite dimly-lit and cosy in a country kitchen style, with simply-laid darkwood tables and the work of a local artist displayed on the walls. Well-balanced traditional table d'hôte and à la carte menus offer the popular dishes that people of all ages feel comfortable with, sometimes with a contemporary twist, and the cooking style is quite homely. Some suppliers are listed on the menu and special diets can be accommodated. The ambience on the ground floor is warmer and more relaxed than a first floor room, which has rather gimmicky decor. A recent visit by the Guide was most enjoyable, and the early dinner is excellent value. [*A sister restaurant, **Canters,** has recently opened in Fairview (01 833 3681)] Children welcome (not after 10pm). **Seats 70** (private rom, 35). Air conditioning. L Sun-Fri 12.30-3.30 (Sun 1.30-4); D daily 6-10. Set L €20, Set Sun L €26, early D €26 (6-8). Set D €35; also à la carte. House wine €17.50. Closed Sat L. 25-26 Dec, Good Fri. Amex, MasterCard, Visa, Laser. **Directions:** Past Bon Secours hospital, opposite the Met Office.

DUBLIN 14

Dublin 14

Indian Brasserie

RESTAURANT

Main Street Rathfarnham Dublin 14 **Tel: 01 492 0261**

Samir Sapru's Indian Brasserie is just a minute's walk from Rathfarnham Castle, at the Butterfield Avenue end of the village. The restaurant, which is run as a buffet, offers freshly prepared wholesome food, aiming to make it the nearest to home cooking that can be achieved in a restaurant. The selection usually includes around eight starters, five or six salads and seven or eight main courses, with each dish individually prepared from scratch and the selection worked out so that all the dishes complement each other. Breads - which are baked quickly at a very high temperature - are cooked to order. The hospitality is intended to make each guest feel as if they are visiting a private house - customers are encouraged to try a little of everything that has been prepared on the night. Own parking. No children after 7pm. **Seats 50.** Air conditioning D 5-11 daily. L Sun only 12.30-4 or 5pm. Set D about €20; early D, 5.30-7.30pm. House wine about €14. SC discretionary. Toilets wheelchair accessible. Closed 25-26 Dec. Amex, Diners, MasterCard, Visa. **Directions:** At the Butterfield Ave. end of Rathfarnham village, under TSB Bank. ◇

Dublin 14

The Yellow House

PUB

1 Willbrook Road Rathfarnham Dublin 14
Tel: 01 493 2994 Fax: 01 494 2441

Named after the unusual shade of the bricks with which it is built, the landmark pub of Rathfarnham makes a perfect rendezvous, with no chance of confusion. The tall and rather forbidding exterior gives little hint of the warmth inside, where pictures and old decorative items relevant to local history repay closer examination. (Traditional bar food is served in the lounge and there's a restaurant upstairs serving evening meals and Sunday lunch.) Closed 25-6 Dec & Good Fri. Amex, Diners, MasterCard, Visa, Laser. **Directions:** Prominent corner building in Rathfarnham Village.

DUBLIN 15

Dublin 15

Ashbrook House

COUNTRY HOUSE

River Road Ashtown Castleknock Dublin 15
Tel: 01 838 5660 Fax: 01 838 5660 Email: evemitchell@hotmail.com

Although it is only a 15 minutes drive from the airport (and a similar distance from the city centre), Eve Mitchell's lovely Georgian country house is in a countryside location beside the Tolka River. Set in 10 acres of grounds, with a grass tennis court, walled garden and many garden paths to wander, it is also just beside the Phoenix Park and within a few minutes' drive of seven golf courses. There are two magnificent drawing rooms, and the large beautifully furnished bedrooms are very comfortable, with phone, tea/coffee facilities and en-suite power showers; two family rooms have a single bed as well as doubles. TV lounge. Children welcome (baby sitting arranged) No pets. No smoking house. B&B about €45 pps. Single supplement about €15. Closed Christmas/New Year. MasterCard, Visa, Laser. **Directions:** Off N3, 15 minutes from airport; similar distance from city centre. ◇

Dublin 15

N HOTEL

Castleknock Hotel & Country Club

Porterstown Road Castleknock Dublin 15
Tel: 01 640 6300 Fax: 01 640 6303
Email: reservations@chcc.ie Web: www.towerhotelgroup.com

This new hotel just outside Castleknock Village is a welcome addition to the limited accommodation and amenities in the area. With its own golf course, extensive conference facilities and countryside views, it makes a pleasant base for both business and leisure guests. Spacious, comfortably furnished bedrooms are not over-decorated and have cable TV, radio, telephone with voice mail, high speed internet access, in room safe, tea/coffee facilities and trouser press as standard, and bathrooms have separate shower and bath. Non-smoking bedrooms are available on request (subject to availability), and there are also a number of interconnecting rooms for families. The hotel offers formal dining in The Park restaurant, and an informal option in The Brasserie, where breakfast is also served. Conferences/Banqueting, golf, leisure centre. Ample parking. **Rooms 144;** B&B from €75 pps. Closed 24-26 Dec.

Dublin 15

N RESTAURANT

Cilantro

Above Brady's Pub Old Navan Road Castleknock Dublin 15
Tel: 01 824 3443 Fax: 01 821 8763

Brady's Inn - a large but pleasant pub - is a local landmark in Castleknock, and above it you will find this very agreeable owner-run Indiian restaurant. Modern, clean lined and smartly decorated, with black leather fireside seating in the reception area, and generous white-clothed tables set up with with crisp linen napkins, generous fine wine wine glasses and fresh flowers, it creates a good first impression - enhanced by a warm welcome from friendly Indian staff. A well balanced wine list (including some Indian beers) and menus are promptly presented, and apreritifs follow swiftly - an auspicious start. Poppodums and an array of chutneys make tasty nibbles to begin with, while looking through menus that offer a wide range of dishes, including many of the traditional favourites, but also less known dishes such as starters of ajwaini machli (marinated whole mackerel cooked in a clay oven) and shami kebab (beef patties flavoured with rosewater, accompanied by a tomato & apple chutney). Tandoori specialities feature on the main course choices, and a mixed tandoori dish especially enjoyed on a recent visit brought together pieces of lamb, chicken and beef, cooked over charcoal in the tandoor to produce a delicious contrast between the crusty exterior and succulent meat within, served with a tomato sauce; various creamier dishes are offered too, plus tempting naan breads and an unusual range of side vegetables. Desserts are not likely to be any better than in most Indian restaurants, so finish with a refreshing lassi (a traditional, slightly salty, mixture of yoghurt and water) instead. Sister establishments: Tulsi (Galway, Dublin), Kasturi (**Seats 90;** D daily 5-11.30pm. **Directions:** Over Brady's Pub. ◇

Dublin 15

HOTEL/BAR/RESTAURANT

The Twelfth Lock

Castleknock Marina The Royal Canal Castleknock Dublin 15
Tel: 01 860 7400 Fax: 01 860 7401
Email: info@twelfthlock.com Web: www.twelfthlock.com

The Twelfth Lock is a gem of a bar, with views out over the picturesque Royal Canal, a warm, friendly atmosphere and good informal meals. The main bar is modern, light and airy, with a variety of high and low wooden tables dotted around, and a fine fire that would warm up the coldest evening - and, there's also a sizeable heated deck with canopy covers and views out over the canal. Interesting bar menus offer a good range of quality food including meats like lamb loin chops with creamed potato & port wine sauce and a mixed salad garnish, and vegetarians visiting in summer will be pleased with a big Greek Salad; there's also a good choice of fish - grilled salmon steak with fresh house salad, roasted peppers & basil mash, perhaps, and goujons of fresh cod with red pepper & caper mayonnaise, served with a tossed salad and wedges. Friendly and helpful staff are always on hand and cope well even when the bar is busy, which it tends to be even midweek as it is understandably popular with locals. *The Bar Bistro offers a slightly more formal evening dining experience, Wednesday-Saturday only. **Accommodation:** The ten guest rooms are on lower ground floor and a little dark, but furnished to a high standard. Children are welcome, but not allowed in bar after 7pm. **Rooms 10** (1 disabled). Lift. Room service (limited hours). Room rate €115 (with breakfast); weekend rates available. Bar Meals Mon-Thurs, 12 noon-9:30pm; Fri-Sun 12 noon-8:30pm. Outside eating. Wheelchair accessible. Bar Bistro open Wed-Sat from 7pm(to 11:30am midweek, 12:30am Fri & Sat). Amex, MasterCard, Visa, Laser. **Directions:** On Royal Canal, at Twelfth Lock near Brady's Castleknock Inn Pub. ◇

DUBLIN 16

Dublin 16

Café Mao

Ⓝ RESTAURANT

The Mill Pond Civic Square Dundrum Shopping Centre Dublin 16
Tel: 01 296 2802 Fax: 01 296 2813
Email: dundrum@cafemao.com Web: www.cafemao.com

This modern, airy two story restaurant is the latest addition to the Café Mao stable in Dublin. Conveniently located in a restaurant piazza to the rear of the shopping centre, it provides a perfect place to drop the bags down following a hard days shopping. The atmosphere is bright and very buzzy, and interesting food is based on seasonal ingredients; the standard of cooking is consistently good, offering simple, tasty food that is served quickly and at a reasonable price. Chilli squid, Nasi Goreng and Malaysian chicken are established favourites, also tempura sole with stir-fried vegetables in a citrus sauce; vegetarians might try a starter of Jakarta salad (crisp vegetables and fruits in a piquant chilli dressing) followed by Thai green vegetable curry, with Jasmine rice. Chilli strength is considerately indicated on the menu, also vegetarian and low fat dishes, dishes containing nuts. A compact but wide-ranging drinks menu includes cocktails, fresh juices and smoothies, a range of coffees and teas and speciality beers as well as wines. Like its its sister restaurants, Café Mao Dundrum shopping centre offers healthy food, good value and friendly efficient service. Fully wheelchair accessible; Children welcome before 7pm; **Seats 120** (outdoor, 50); serving food daily 12.00-23.00 and Sun 12.00-10.00; Value L €10, value D €15, 5-7; House Wine €18. Closed 25/26 Dec. **Directions:** At the back of Dundrum shopping centre next to the Old Mill Pond.

Dublin 16

Harvey Nichol's First Floor Restaurant

Ⓝ RESTAURANT

Dundrum Shopping Centre Sandyford Road Dublin 16 **Tel: 01 291 0488**
Fax: 01 291 0489 Web: www.harveynichols.com

The concept of fine dining in a department store is quite alien to most Dubliners but the First Floor Restaurant & Bar at Harvey Nichols has a separate entrance and express lift so, having whizzed up, most are willing to admit that the scene has been set pretty impressively. The interior - designed by French interior architect Christian Biecher - is contemporary cool, with vibrant pinks taking the lead in the bar (where in-house mixologists are at hand to create the perfect cocktail...) and a combination of warm plummy pinks and yellows linking into the restaurant too, where high-backed couches and banquettes are balanced by slouchy leather carver chairs and crisp, white-clothed classic modern table settings. Head chef Thomas Haughton arrived at Dundrum via a lot of prestigious kitchens, most recently Luttrellstown Castle, so the modern classic menus offered should come as no surprise: dishes on a typical dinner menu could include luxurious starters such as panfried foie gras wih black pudding & apple compôte, or a rillette of fragrant crab with tartare of avocado & lime yoghurt, and main courses like slow roasted belly of pork with caramelised parsnip and turnip purée and a speciality HN 'sandwich of seabass with black olive and tomato dressing. Despite the hype, stylish dishes are quite simply presented and clean-flavoured - and one of the most appealing aspects of this smart new dining venue is that lunch (and the early evening 'Value Diner') make it so accessible. At the other end of the spectrum, a Tasting Menu, at €75, allows this talented chef to strut his stuff, and is perfect for a special occasion. Similarly, an impressive wine list offers treats for the connoisseur and also a choice of eight good, well-priced house wines. Although it may take some time to find its level alongside the city's established leaders, 'The First Floor' is heading in the right direction - and you can take all sorts of treats home with you too, from their Foodmarket & Wineshop. Toilets wheelchair accessible; Children welcome before 9pm. **Seats 80** (private room, 12); air conditioning; L daily, 12-3; Set L €25, set Sun L €27.50; D Mon-Sat, 6-10, value D €25, 6-7.30pm, Set D €19.95/25, 2/3 courses, Gourmet D €75, also a la carte D; house wine €18; SC 12.5%. Closed Sun D and 25/26 Dec. Amex, Diners, MasterCard, Visa, Laser. **Directions:** Above Harvey Nichols department store in the Dundrum Shopping Centre.

Dublin 16
Ⓝ RESTAURANT

L'Officina by Dunne & Crescenzi

Dundrum Shopping Centre Dundrum Dublin 16
Tel: 01 216 6764 Fax: 01 216 6765
Email: dunneandcrescenzi@hotmail.com Web: www.dunneandcrescenzi.com

Located in an informal dining piazza to the rear of Dundrum shopping centre, this younger sister to the well-known Dunne & Crescenzi restaurants offers al fresco dining alongside the fountains in the Old Mill pond - a fine spot on a sunny day for a light meal, or to quell a shopping driven thirst (they have a fine selection of wine by the glass or bottle), and also for a wholesome and satisfying evening meal. Decorated in tune with the style of food service simple, no-fuss, efficient there's a buzzy atmosphere, and an impressive display of wine balances the simplicity of paper place mats and minimal table settings. Italian staff are quick to greet and seat arriving guests (when possible this is a busy place, and seats are often at a premium); menus and wine list are promptly presented, along with an outline of the mouthwatering daily blackboard specials - speedy, attentive service which allows relaxation on even the shortest lunch break. As would be expected of any Dunne & Crescenzi outlet, impeccably sourced ingredients form the backbone of healthy menus at L'Officina, where the use of D.O.P. products (an EU guarantee certifying the authenticity of artisan foods) is proudly highlighted and there are plenty of classic Italian dishes on offer such as Anti Pasti e Piatti Freddi Caprese con bufala campana (buffalo mozzarella, ripe tomatoes and fresh basil drizzled with extra virgin olive oil, €8.50); Panini (lunch only); Insalate Insalata capricciosa (mixed salad dressed with extra virgin olive oil, artichokes, sundried tomatoes, olives and asiago alpine cheese, €7.50); Piatti Caldi Minestrone di Verdure (fresh home made vegetable soup, €5.50). Menus also include platters that are particularly good for sharing perfect for hungry shoppers, who can sample several dishes. Evening menus are a little more extensive, offering fish (€20) or organic fillet of beef (€22) with a side order, for example, and plenty of choice for vegetarians. Finish with a treat from a selection of home made desserts (€2.00-7.50), partnered with some of Ireland's finest coffee. All round, L'Officina offers great quality at a fair price and the staff are terrific. **Directions:**

DUBLIN 18

DUBLIN 18

Bordering onto Stillorgan (sometimes Dublin 4, or Co Dublin) and Blackrock (Co Dublin), Dublin 18 is a chameleon area, with edges a little blurred and, it seems, sometimes shifting... But one thing is certain, and it's that the burgeoning business parks have ensured the choice of interesting places to eat and comfortable places to lay your head are on the increase: a lively business area, it now has the 352 bedroom **Bewleys Hotel** (**01 293 5000**; www.bewleyshotels.com), for example, offering a high level of comfort (and links to the airport) for as little as €89; and also the newer, design-led 82-room contemporary **Beacon Hotel** (**01 291 5000**; www.thebeacon.com), offering something a little different from a round €120. Dining options in the area include old favourites like **Bistro One** (see entry) and the newer **Fado Restaurant & Bar** (**01 289 1000**; www.fado.ie), at Leopardstown Racecourse.

Dublin 18
RESTAURANT

Bistro One

3 Brighton Road Foxrock Village Dublin 18
Tel: 01 289 7711 Fax: 01 207 0742 Email: bistroone@eircom.net

féile bia This popular neighbourhood restaurant can get very busy but there is a bar on the way in, where guests are greeted and set up in comfort, and the attitude throughout is laid back but not without care. Ingredients are carefully sourced - fresh produce comes from organic farmers' markets, cheeses from Sheridan's cheesemongers, smoked fish from Frank Hederman's smokehouse in Cobh, Co Cork. Seasonal menus - which considerately indicate dishes containing nuts or nut oil - offer eight or ten tempting choices per course. Starters will almost certainly include the ever-popular Bistro One's salad with pancetta, rocket & pine nuts - while the pasta and risotto selection can be starter or main course as preferred: typically, spaghetti with organic meatballs & fresh basil, perhaps, or Carnaroli risotto with green pea and organic mint. Main courses include classics - in seafood dishes, maybe, or roast duck - and organic meats, perhaps in an old fashioned dish like pan fried lambs liver & organic streaky bacon with a red onion mash. There are generous side vegetables and a choice of French and Irish cheese; home-made ice creams or classic puddings to finish. Children welcome. **Seats 75.** D Tue-Sat 6-10.30, L 12-2.30. A la carte. House wine €22. SC 10%. Closed Sun, Mon & 25 Dec - 2 Jan. MasterCard, Visa, Laser. **Directions:** Southbound on N11, first right after Foxrock church.

Dublin 18
RESTAURANT

The Gables Restaurant

The Gables Foxrock Village Dublin 18
Tel: 01 289 2174 Fax: 01 289 2167
Email: value@mccabeswines.ie Web: www.mccabeswines.ie

This imaginative venture by McCabes Wines, whose shop is part of the restaurant, offers a wine experience in addition to brunches and stylish contemporary food. The wine list (which begins at about €17) offers quality wines at an unusually low mark-up - and you can have any wine from about 800 available in the shop at a moderate corkage charge. The list, which is organised by grape variety, offers a good range of wines by the glass - and a novel 'try before you buy' offer, which would be hard to resist: you taste a wine before ordering it and, if you like it, you can add it to your bill and have a case put into your car (at a very favourable price) while dining at The Gables: easy peasy. Head chef, Chris Allen came to the Gables with experience at some impressive English restaurants, including Harrods and The Ivy, under his belt and is now doing a good job here. **Seats 70** (outdoor, 20). Open 8am-10pm daily (Sun 10-9). L 12.30-4 (Sun brunch 10-5); D 6-9.30 (Sun 5-10). Á la carte. House wine €17. SC discretionary. Closed 25 Dec, Good Fri. Amex, Diners, MasterCard, Visa, Laser. **Directions:** Travelling into the city on N11, turn off left for Foxrock Village.

DUBLIN 22

DUBLIN 22

Dublin 22, on the western edges of the city, is a busy commercial area known mainly for its industrial estates and business parks- and the huge Lifey Valley Shopping Centre. Hotels which service the needs of the area well include the landmark **Red Cow Moran Hotel** on the Naas Road (01 459 3650; www.moranhotels.com), with outstanding conference facilities; **Bewleys Hotel Newlands Cross** (01 464 0140; www.bewleyshotels.com), offering a lot of space and comfort at a modest pirce; and the newer **Clarion Hotel Liffey Valley** (01 625 8000; www.clarionhotelliffeyvalley.com), cleverly disguised as a warehouse but actually quite stylish within.

COUNTY DUBLIN

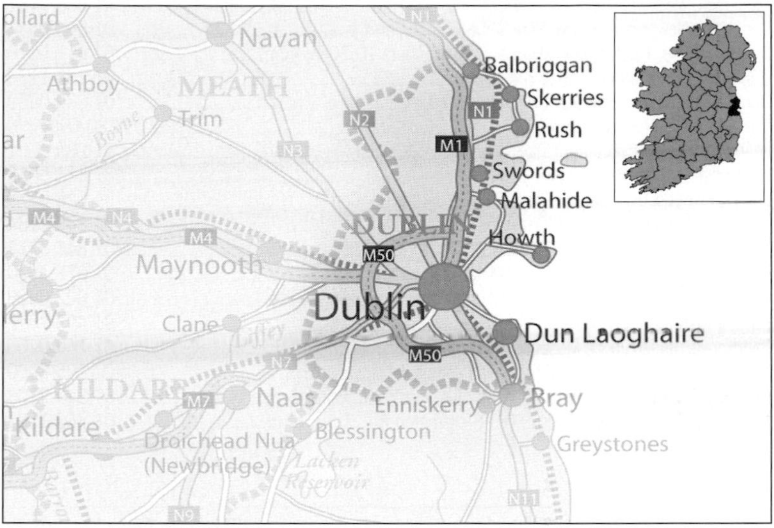

Dublin County is divided into the three administrative "sub-counties" of Dun Laoghaire-Rathdown to the southeast, South Dublin to the southwest, and the large territory of Fingal to the north. However, although these regions are among the most populous and economically active in all Ireland, the notion of Greater Dublin being in four administrative parts is only slowly taking root - for instance, all postal addresses still either have a Dublin city numbered code, or else they're simply "County Dublin".

Inevitably, it is in the countryside and towns in the Greater Dublin Region that some of the pressures of the success of the Irish economy continue to be most evident. But although Dubliners of town and county alike will happily accept that they're part of a thrusting modern city, equally they'll cheerfully adhere to the old Irish saying that when God made time, He made a lot of it. So most folk are allowing themselves all the time in the world to get used to the fact that they are now either Fingallions, or South Dubliners, or indeed Hyphenators out in Dun Laoghaire-Rathdown.

This relaxed approach is good news for the visitor, for it means that if you feel that the frenetic pace of Dublin city is just a mite overpowering, you will very quickly find that nearby, in what used to be - and for many folk still is - County Dublin, there continue to be oases of a much more easy-going way of life waiting to be discovered.

Admittedly, the fact that the handsome Dublin Mountains overlook the city in spectacular style means that, even up in the nearby hills, you can be well aware of the city's buzz. But if you want to find a vigorous contrast between modern style and classical elegance, you can find it in an unusual form at Dun Laoghaire's remarkable harbour, where one of the world's most modern ferryports is in interesting synergy with one of the world's largest Victorian artificial harbours.

A showcase marina in the harbour, expensively built so that its style matches the harbour's classic elegance, has steadily developed, while the harbour area of Dun Laoghaire town beside it continues to be improve in quality and vitality, with a weekly Farmer's Market on the waterfront (Thursdays, 10.0am to 4.30pm) providing an intriguing interaction between sea and land.

Should you head northward into Fingal, you'll quickly discover an away from-it-all sort of place of estuary towns, fishing ports, offshore islands alive with seabirds, and an environment of leisurely pace in which it's thought very bad form to hasten over meals in restaurants where portion control is either unknown, or merely in its infancy.

Life in Fingal was much improved by the completion of the M1 Motorway northward across the county, removing the pressure of through traffic on local roads. It's interesting to note that connoisseurs of this intriguing region reckon that one of its long established features, the Dublin-Belfast mainline railway - first used in 1838 - effectively creates a "land island" on the Donabate-Portrane peninsula, as there are only two road crossings into this sandy territory with its four golf courses.

Local Attractions and Information

Balbriggan/Skerries, Ardgillan Castle	01 849 2212
Blackrock, Deepwell House & Gardens	01 288 7407
Donabate, Newbridge House, Park & Traditional Farm	01 843 6534
Dun Laoghaire, Farm Market (Harbour Plaza, Thurs 10.30am-4pm)	087 611 5016
Dun Laoghaire, Harbour Office (24 hours)	01 280 1130
Dun Laoghaire, National Maritime Museum, Haigh Terrace	01 280 0969
Dun Laoghaire, Tourist Information	01 280 6984/5/6
Leopardstown, Racecourse	01 289 3607
Leopardstown, Farm Market Fri 11am-7pm	087 611 5016
Lucan, Primrose Hill Garden (house attrib. James Gandon)	01 628 0373
Malahide, Malahide Castle & Demesne	01 846 2184
Malahide, Fry Model Railway (Malahide Castle)	01 846 3779
Malahide, Talbot Botanic Gardens (Malahide Castle)	01 872 7530
Naul (Fingal), Seamus Ennis Centre (Traditional Music)	01 802 0898
Rathfarnham, Marlay Demesne gardens	01 493 7372
Sandycove, James Joyce Museum (Martello Tower)	01 280 9265
Sandyford, Fernhill Gardens (Himalayan species)	01 295 6000
Skerries, Skerries Mills - Working Windmills, Craft and Visitor Centre	01 849 5208
Tallaght, Community Arts Centre, Old Blessington Rd	01 462 1501

Blackrock
RESTAURANT

Dali's Restaurant

63-65 Main Street Blackrock Co Dublin
Tel: 01 278 0660 Fax: 01 278 0661

Just across the road from the Library, these premises have been home to several of Dublin's most successful restaurateurs and Dali is no exception, having a loyal local clientèle and a reputation beyond the immediate area. There's a chic little bar just inside the door and a dining area, at a slightly higher level, beyond - all very attractively set up in a style that is contemporary but without hard-edged minimalism. Menus are appealingly light and colourful, including first course classics like a pretty ham terrine and a good bit of fresh seafood (seared scallops, Dublin Bay scampi); balanced main course choices could include some unusual variations on old favourites, and it's worth saving some appetite for tempting desserts and a good cheese selection. Good, honest cooking based on quality ingredients and offering excellent value for money has them beating a path to the door, so booking is essential, especially at weekends. Set lunch menus offer a choice of four or five dishes on each course and are particularly good value. Professional, efficient service and a good wine list complete an appealing package. Children welcome. Air conditioning. **Seats 65.** L Tue-Sat, 12-3, Sun L, 12.30-3.30pm; D Tue-Sat 6-10pm. Set L from about €15. A la carte L&D available; house wine about €20, sc discretionary except 10% on parties of 6+. Closed D Sun, all Mon, 25-27 Dec. Amex, Diners, MasterCard, Visa, Laser. **Directions:** Opposite Blackrock Library. ◇

Blackrock
CAFÉ/BAR

Tonic

5 Temple Road Blackrock Village Co Dublin **Tel: 01 288 7671**
Fax: 01 288 7150 Email: mail@tonic.ie Web: www.tonic.ie

This smart designer bar brings some welcome style to Blackrock village with its cool walnut woodwork, cube chairs, cream leather banquettes and artwork for sale on exhibition - all of which, plus a big screen upstairs, have made it the in place for the trendy young crowd. Informal menus are offered through the day - brunch, daytime and evening bistro - and there's a patio area for al fresco dining in fine weather; however perhaps it's more a place to drop into for a drink in stylish surroundings. Toilets wheelchair accessible. **Seats 100.** Open 12am-12pm; food served all day 12-11, L12-4, D 4-11. Closed 25 Dec & Good Fri. Amex, MasterCard, Visa, Laser. **Directions:** Centre of Blackrock village.

Dalkey
PUB

Daniel Finnegan

2 Sorrento Road Dalkey Co Dublin **Tel: 01 285 8505**

This is a pub of great character and much-loved by locals and visitors alike. It's comfortable and cosy, with wood panelling and traditional Irish seating in 'snugs', and the large extension built a few years ago has now 'blended in'. Food is served at lunchtime only - a full hot bar lunch, including starters such as baked Dalkey crab, brie fritters with apple coulis and main courses like roast stuffed pork steak, honey roast half duck and grilled cod steak, followed by traditional desserts like apple pie and lemon cheesecake. The fresh fish (from the harbour nearby) is excellent, the vegetables predictable but tasty and good value. No reservations - get there early to avoid a long wait. Carpark nearby. Bar food 12.30-3pm Mon-Sat. Closed 25 Dec, Good Fri & & New Year. Amex, Diners, MasterCard, Visa, Laser. **Directions:** Near Dalkey DART station. ◇

Dalkey

IN

CAFÉ/BAR

115-117 Coliemore Road Dalkey Co Dublin
Tel: 01 275 0007 Fax: 02 275 0009

This stylish contemporary café-bar in the centre of Dalkey has retained a special niche, offering something rather different from pubs and restaurants in the area. The atmosphere is relaxed and what you get here is informal dining in comfortable, pleasant surroundings: menus offer a choice ranging from the ubiquitous steak, and bistro dishes like lamb shank (deliciously tender) or crisp confit of duck; a range of platters for groups of four to eight (about €20-40), is an good idea. Specialities include Kimchee prawns - fish is purchased daily from local markets - and an interesting (possibly unique) house speciality is home-raised Irish bison! **Seats 80** (+15 Outdoors; Private room 40); Toilets wheelchair accessible; Live Piano Jazz classics Thu - Sun 10-1am. Open 10 am-11pm (Fri & Sat to 1.30). Bar meals daily: 10-11. Meals Daily - L 12-4, D 5-10. Set L €9.95, Value D Thu-Sun, all night, €19.95. Á la Carte L&D also avail. Amex, Diners, MasterCard, Visa, Laser. **Directions:** At the end of Dalkey's main street.

Dalkey

Jaipur Restaurant Dalkey

RESTAURANT

20 Castle Street Dalkey Co Dublin **Tel: 01 285 0552**
Fax: 01 284 0900 Email: info@jaipur.ie Web: www.jaipur.ie

This stylish south County Dublin branch of the small chain of well-regarded progressive Indian restaurants has become well-established as a favourite in the area. (See entries under Dublin 2 and Malahide). The trademark modern decor is a refreshing change from traditional Indian restaurants - warm colours send the right messages and it is a pleasing space. Menus offer an attractive combination of traditional and more creative dishes - try Jaipur Jugalbandi, an assortment of five appetisers, to set the tone. Fresh and dried spices ar directly imported but proprietor Asheesh Dewan and long-serving head chef Mahipal Rana are keen to make the most of Irish ingredients, notably organic lamb (in Khato Ghosth, perhaps: Wicklow lamb braised in yoghurt with carrom seeds & mustard oil, finished with asafoetida and dried mango powder) and seafood (Hakli Sukka , a speciality dish of lightly battered baby squid with chilli & dried shrimps. Jaipur is a fine restaurant - and was the first ethnic restaurant in Ireland to devise a wine list especially suited to spicy foods. Service is attentive and discreet. **Seats 70;** Air con; D daily, 5-11; Early D €20, 5-7; Set D from €30, also à la carte. House wine €19. Closed 25 Dec Amex, MasterCard, Visa, Laser. **Directions:** On Dalkey's main street.

Dalkey

Nosh

RESTAURANT

111 Coliemore Road Dalkey Co Dublin **Tel: 01 284 0666**
Fax: 01 281 4489 Email: comments@nosh.ie Web: www.nosh.ie

Samantha and Sacha Farrell's bright, contemporary restaurant is next to the famous Club Bar and, with its clean lines and lightwood furniture, no-nonsense menus and quality ingredients, it has a special place in the Dalkey dining scene. Head chef Eilish Murphy's contemporary seasonal menus have a slight bias towards fish and vegetarian food, and change throughout the day: their great weekend brunch menu has become very popular, and offers hot dishes (anything from the traditional Irish 'Nosh brunch', or bagels with scrambled eggs and smoked salmon, to omelettes, buttermilk pancakes with grilled bananas and maple syrup, to fish pie with mash) and a wide range of coffees and other hot and cold drinks, including home-made lemonade). For lunch there's some overlap from the Brunch menu and a dozen or so other choices, ranging up to the "Posh Nosh" special of the day. In the evening, you might begin with prawn pil-pils in sizzling garlic & chilli oil (an enduring favourite) and proceed to beer battered cod with home-made chips, pea purée & tartare sauce (another speciality) or an appealing vegetarian dish such as sweetcorn fritters with mixed bean ragoût. Desserts are home-made and there's a limited but well-chosen wine list, with a few half bottles, offered throughout the day. Not suitable for children after 8pm. Wheelchair accessible. Air conditioning. **Seats 45.** L Tue-Fri, 12-4 (Sat & Sun, Brunch 12-4); D Tue-Sun 6-10. A la carte. House wine €18.50. Closed Mon, bank hols. MasterCard, Visa, Laser. **Directions:** End of Dalkey town, take left.

Dalkey
RESTAURANT/PUB

The Queen's Bar & Restaurant

12 Castle Street Dalkey Co Dublin **Tel: 01 285 4569**
Fax: 01 285 8345 Email: queens@clubi.ie

The oldest pub in Dalkey, and also one of the oldest in Ireland, The Queen's was originally licensed to 'dispense liquor' as far back as 1745, and renovations and improvements in recent years have been done with due respect for the age and character of the premises. It's attractively done up, with dark wood, little alcoves and a raised level breaking up the space, and there's also a small section outside at the front to go if the weather's fine (the section at the back was closed on our most recent visit). Good bar fare is available and the more contemporary Queen's Restaurant is next door, offering popular evening meals like steaks (€21.95), fish (€18.95), pizzas (€12.50) and pastas (€12.95). The Queen's has had its ups and downs, and changed hands fairly recently; a recent visit by the Guide was enjoyable and, at the time of going to press it seems to be on form. Good bar food: chowders, salads, pies, steak sandwiches etc also available every afternoon and and evening, and can be served to patio areas at the back and front in fine weather. Wheelchair accessible. Restaurant **Seat 70;** D daily from 6pm; early D 6-7.30. Bar menu Mon-Fri, 12-4 & 5-7.30; Sat 12-4; Sun 12.30-3.45. Closed 25 Dec & Good Fri. Amex, Diners, MasterCard, Visa, Laser. **Directions:** Centre of town,beside Heritage Centre. ◇

Dalkey
RESTAURANT

Ragazzi

109 Coliemore Road Dalkey Co Dublin **Tel: 01 284 7280**

Possibly Dublin's buzziest little bistro, this is the pizza place where everyone goes to have their spirits lifted by theatrical Italian waiters and great value. Lovely pastas, luscious bruschettas - but best of all the pizzas, renowned for their thin, crisp bases and scrumptious toppings. But it's the atmosphere that counts - every town should have a place like this. D served daily, 5.30-10.30pm. ◇

Dalkey
RESTAURANT

Thai House Restaurant

21 Railway Road Dalkey Co Dublin **Tel: 01 284 7304**
Email: tony@thaihouse.ie Web: www.thaihouse.ie

Established in 1997, well before the current vogue for Thai food, Tony Ecock's bustlig two-storey restaurant has earned a loyal following and head chef Wilai Khruekhcai has maintained a reputation for including dishes that do not pander too much to bland western tastes. In typical oriental style, a number of set menus are offered for groups of various sizes and there is also an extensive à la carte which offers a wider choice. After an aperitif in the wine bar/reception area, begin, perhaps, with the Thai House Special Starter Pack, a sampling plate of six starters, well-balanced in flavour and texture and including some vegetarian options: Thai prawn toast, chicken satay with peanut sauce, deep-fried corn cakes with herbs & curry paste, crispy vegetarian spring rolls, deep-fried prawn cakes with sweet chilli sauce; service can be under pressure at times, so it is a good plan to get this shared starter (and your drinks) ordered as soon as possible. After this you can relax and take more time to consider the options; soup choices include the famous Tom Yam Gung (spicy prawn soup with lemon grass and chilli) and Tom Yam Rumit - a spicy soup with prawns, squid, crab and mussels - which is perhaps the most interesting. Main courses include a range of curries - a speciality is fresh monkfish dumplings in green curry sauce with wild ginger - and vegetarian dishes are listed separately. Groups of four can share a dessert platter (usually with coconut and/or banana). The wine list includes a page of house favourites (all under €25) and a Thai beer. Not suitable for children after 8pm. Air conditioning. **Seats 34.** D Tue-Sun. Closed Mon. Amex, Diners, MasterCard, Visa, Laser. **Directions:** 100 metres from Dalkey DART Station. ◇

Dublin Airport
HOTEL

Clarion Hotel Dublin Airport

Dublin Airport Co Dublin **Tel: 01 808 0500** Fax: 01 844 6002
Email: info@clarionhoteldublinairport.com Web: www.clarionhoteldublinairport.com

féile bia This large, comfortable hotel is right at the airport and has recently been taken over by Clarion hotels, and undergone extensive refurbishment; there is complimentary wifi in the lobby, bar and restaurant. It makes an ideal meeting place and guests may use the ALSAA Leisure Complex swimming pool, gymnasium and sauna free of charge. Bedrooms all have TV and pay movies, and mini-bar. Well-equipped meeting rooms/conference suites available for groups of up to 300. Courtesy bus to and from the airport terminal (24 hr). A new bar and restaurant (Kudos) have recently been introduced, in line with other Clarion hotels. Parking. Children welcome (Under 12s free in parents' room; cots available without charge). Wheelchair accessible. **Rooms 248** (15 executive rooms,

4 family rooms, 2 for disabled). Lift. 24 hour room service. Room rate about €250. Closed 24-25 Dec. Amex, Diners, MasterCard, Visa, Laser. **Directions:** In airport complex, on the right when entering airport.

Dublin Airport
HOTEL

Great Southern Hotel Dublin Airport

Dublin Airport Co Dublin **Tel: 01 844 6000** Fax: 01 844 6001
Email: res@dubairport-gsh.com Web: www.greatsouthernhotels.com

féile bia This spacious modern hotel in the airport complex is just two minutes drive from the main terminal building (with a coach service available); at the time of going to press, sale of the Great Southern Hotel group was being completed and the new branding of this hotel was not yet confirmed. Rooms are all double-glazed and include a high proportion of executive rooms (12 of which are designated lady executive). It's a good choice for business guests and, should your flight be delayed, the large bar and Potters Bistro on the ground floor could be a welcome place to pass the time. Conference/banqueting (450/300); video conferencing; business centre; secretarial service. Children welcome (under 10s free in parents' room; cots available free of charge). **Rooms 229** (2 suites, 3 junior suites, 116 executive rooms, 184 no-smoking, 2 rooms for disabled, 2 family rooms) Lifts. Room service (24 hr). Room rate about €270 (1 or 2 guests). Closed 24-25 Dec. Amex, Diners, MasterCard, Visa, Laser. **Directions:** Situated in airport complex.

DUBLIN AIRPORT AREA

A number of new hotels have sprung up around Dublin airport recently, but they are not always as close as you might expect. **The Clarion** and **Great Southern** hotels are on site (see entries), and the following are in the locality. Budget accommodation is available at the **Tulip Inn** (01 895 7777; www.tulipin-ndublinairport.ie), and **Travelodge** (01 807 9400; www.travelodge.ie). Nearby hotels offering more extensive facilities and a higher level of service include: **Bewleys Hotel** (01 871 1000; www.bewleyshotels.com), **Carlton Dublin Airport Hotel** (01 866 7500, www.carlton.ie), **Crowne Plaza Hotel** (01 862 8888; www.cpdublin-airport.com), and **Hilton Dublin Airport** (01 866 1800; www.hilton.co.uk/dublinairport). **Roganstown Golf & Country Club Hotel** and **Belcamp Hutchinson** country house are also convenient to the airport (see entries). The nearest town is Swords, where you will find **Wrights cafe bar** (01 840 6760; bar food available) and **The Old Borough Pub** (01 895 7685), both centrally located, and you could eat at **Indie Spice** restaurant (01 807 7999; www.indiespicecafe.com), or the owner-chef run **Treetop Restaurant** (01 8409911; www.thetreetop.ie) in an area of the town known as Applewood Village. The attractive coastal town of Malahide is also convenient to Dublin airport, and offers a wide range of restaurants and bars (see entries).
WWW.IRELAND-GUIDE.COM FOR THE BEST PLACES TO EAT, DRINK & STAY

Dun Laoghaire
RESTAURANT

Brasserie Na Mara

1 Harbour Road Dun Laoghaire Co Dublin **Tel: 01 280 6767**
Fax: 01 284 4649 Email: brasserienamara@irishrail.ie

féile bia The old Kingstown terminal building beside the Dun Laoghaire DART station makes a fine location for this harbourside restaurant. Part of Irish Rail's art collection graces the walls - a Nora McGuinness, a Lambe, a Leech - and the current contemporary decor is stylish, with high ceilings and tall windows complemented by linen-covered tables, glistening glasses and a single fresh flower on each table - and the bar faces in towards the reception area, so you look out over the harbour while enjoying your aperitif. Interesting menus are in a bright, modern style to suit the decor and, while there is always plenty of choice, there is a special emphasis on seafood as one would expect: starters like shrimp & cod chowder, pan seared scallops, or sesame crusted mackerel with stewed tomatoes, basil & onion, for example, and main courses of classic black sole meunière, pan fried monkfish with red wine risotto, braised leeks & spring onion and a pancetta jus - or a speciality dish of grilled seabass, served with sauce vierge, French beans & herb mashed potatoes. Popular meat and poultry dishes include baked ham with champ potatoes and roast breast of duck served oriental style with vegetable spring roll, coconut rice and ginger & chilli syrup; vegetarian dishes are always included - goats cheese, asparagus & sun dried tomato ravioli is typical. Tempting desserts like chocolate cookie millefeuille with mascarpone ice cream & strawberry compôte are well executed. Service is friendly, and pleasing surroundings, quality ingredients, accomplished cooking and good value ensure the popularity of this well-located restaurant. A well-priced wine list includes an unusually good choice of half bottles. **Seats 64** (private room, 45). Reservations advised. L Mon-Fri 12.30-2.30; D Mon-Sat, 6.15-10; Sun 1pm-5pm. [Mon-Fri: Set L €25; Set 'Value' D €35.] D also à la carte; house wine about €21. SC 12.5%. Closed L Sat & D Sun, 25-26 Dec & 1 Jan, bank hols. Amex, Diners, MasterCard, Visa, Laser. **Directions:** Coast road, beside DART, opposite the Pavilion.

Dun Laoghaire
RESTAURANT

Café Mao

The Pavilion Dun Laoghaire Co Dublin
Tel: 01 214 8090 Fax: 01 214 7064
Email: dunlaoghaire@cafemao.com Web: www.cafemao.com

féile bia This large, informal contemporary café-restaurant near the harbour is a younger sister establishment to the popular Café Mao in the city centre, which was one of Dublin's first - and enduringly successful - fusion cafés. It is run on the same lines, with the philosophy of providing simple, quick and healthy food, with youthful appeal, at a reasonable price - and there's always a good buzz. Dishes with nuts are highlighted on the menu, also chilli strength, low fat and vegetarian dishes. There are house specialities including Nassi Goreng, Malaysian chicken and five spiced chicken; daily specials are particularly good value, and there's a daily cake selection - e.g. cappuccino with walnut gateau, toffee & apple gateau, pecan pie & Mississippi mud pie - and an interesting drinks menu. It's a good place for brunch, with tables outside for fine weather. **Seats 120** (outdoor seating, 30); fully wheelchair accessible; children welcome until 7pm; large parties welcome. Open daily 12 - 11 (to 10 Sun); Early D €15 5-7; Bookings accepted. Closed 25 Dec, Good Fri. MasterCard, Visa, Laser. **Directions:** Dun Laoghaire seafront, near station.

Dun Laoghaire
RESTAURANT

Cavistons Seafood Restaurant

59 Glasthule Road Dun Laoghaire Co Dublin **Tel: 01 280 9245**
Fax: 01 284 4054 Email: info@cavistons.com Web: www.cavistons.com

Caviston's of Sandycove has long been a mecca for lovers of good food - here you will find everything that is wonderful, from organic vegetables to farmhouse cheeses, cooked meats to specialist oils and other exotic items. But it was always for fish and shellfish that Cavistons were especially renowned - even providing a collection of well-thumbed recipe books for on-the-spot reference. At their little restaurant next door, they serve an imaginative range of healthy seafood dishes influenced by various traditions and all washed down by a glass or two from a very tempting little wine list. Cavistons food is simple, colourful, perfectly cooked - it speaks volumes for how good seafood can be. Start with Cavistons smoked salmon plate, perhaps, or tasty panfried crab and sweetcorn cakes with red pepper mayonnaise, then follow with seared king scallops with a saffron and basil sauce - or a more traditional panfried haddock fillet with tartare sauce. Gorgeous desserts include timeless favourites like chocolate brownies with chocolate sauce & cream, or you can finish with a selection of Cavistons cheeses (they sell a great range in the shop). Don't expect bargain basement prices though - this may be a small lunch time restaurant, but the prime ingredients are costly - and it's a class act. Children welcome. **Seats 28.** L 3 sittings: Tue-Fri - 12, 1.30 and 3pm, Sat 12, 1.45, 3.15pm A la carte. SC discretionary. Closed Sun, Mon & Christmas/New Year. Amex, Diners, MasterCard, Visa, Laser. **Directions:** Between Dun Laoghaire and Dalkey, 5 mins. walk from Glasthule DART station.

Dun Laoghaire
PUB

Eagle House

18 Glasthule Road Dun Laoghaire Co Dublin **Tel: 01 280 4740**

This fine traditional establishment is full of interest and a great local. The interior is dark, but has a fascinating collection of model boats, ships and other nautical bric-à-brac and is arranged in comfortably sized alcoves and 'snugs' on different levels. Bar meals, available at lunchtime and in the evening, can be very good. Closed 25 Dec & Good Fri. Amex, MasterCard, Visa, Laser. **Directions:** 5 mins walk from Glasthule DART station, opposite Caviston's. ◇

Dun Laoghaire
RESTAURANT/PUB

The Forty Foot

Pavilion Centre Dun Laoghaire Co Dublin
Tel: 01 284 2982

féile bia Named after a well-known local swimming place, this ultra-modern two-storey bar and restaurant in the Pavilion Centre is designed to make the most of views over the harbour and Dublin Bay - particularly from the first floor restaurant - and to impress. Bright, spacious and airy, with acres of wood and huge windows the restaurant, especially, is a lovely space and (except at very busy times when you may be directed down to the bar), you can settle into a comfortable sofa to read the menu before being shown to a table simply laid with good linen and cutlery and handsome, plain glasses. The choice is wide and the menu reads well: colourful, fresh-sounding starters are offered - typically mozzarella with roasted peppers & rocket salad, or tian of salmon & crab with crème fraîche; main courses in a similar vein: expect pleasant, attractively presented food and you will not be disappointed; well-informed, attentive staff will, together with the pleasing ambience, ensure you wish to return. If you hit it on a sunny day, the large terraces outside both the bar and restaurant might also be a draw Closed 25 Dec, Good Fri. MasterCard, Visa. **Directions:** At Pavilion Centre. ◇

Dun Laoghaire
PUB

P. McCormack & Sons

67 Lr Mounttown Rd Dun Laoghaire Co Dublin
Tel: 01 280 5519 Fax: 01 280 0145

This fine pub (and 'emporium') has been run by the McCormack family since 1960. It's one of the neatest pubs around, with a landscaped car park creating a pleasant outlook for an imaginative conservatory extension at the back of the pub. The main part of the pub is full of traditional character and the whole place has a well-run hum about it. Good bar food cooked to order includes fresh fish available on the day as well as classics like home-made hamburger (with mixed leaf salad, fries & a choice of toppings), hot sandwiches and salads. Evening menus offer tasty light dishes: warm crispy bacon and croûton salad, and steak sandwiches alongside more substantial dishes including a fish special, a 10 oz sirloin steak (with mushroom and Irish whiskey sauce perhaps) or pasta dishes with fresh parmesan. No children after 7pm. Wheelchair accessible. Bar food daily, 12-3 & 4-10. Closed 25 Dec, Good Fri. Amex, Diners, MasterCard, Visa, Laser, Switch. **Directions:** Near Dun Laoghaire at Monkstown end.

Dun Laoghaire
Ⓔ RESTAURANT

Rasam

18-19 Glasthule Road Dun Laoghaire Co Dublin **Tel: 01 230 0600**
Fax: 01 230 1000 Email: info@rasam.ie Web: www.rasam.ie

ETHNIC RESTAURANT OF THE YEAR

Above The Eagle pub in Glasthule, this is an appealing restaurant, impressively decorated in dark teak, with traditional Balinese furnishings and generous, well-spaced tables. Rasam offers something different from other Indian restaurants, as the cuisine is lighter and more varied - the menu is laid out like a wine list, with the name of the dish and a brief (but clear) description, and the name of the region it comes from alongside the (surprisingly reasonable) price. Two head chefs are from Bengali and Kerala regions, so the food reflects that as well as other regions. You might begin with samosas which are delightfully served, or Sarson Jhinga, a wonderfully subtle dish of grilled jumbo prawns from Kolkatta, flavoured with kasundi (yellow mustard paste) and lemon juice. Main courses might include a relatively simple Kori Gassi, from Coorg, which is a long-established dish at Rasam - chicken is simmered in a spicy masala of brown onions and tomatoes, with a special blend of coorgi masala; this is not dressy, but a homely dish with honest flavours. Other meats are well represented - Pork Sobotel, from Goa, is an aromatic example, flavoured with tamarind, garlic, pickled onion potatoes, black peppercorn & coriander seeds. Shakahari Thali, served on a great silver dish, is a memorable mixture of five lentils, cooked with spinach, tempered with mustard seeds and curry leaf, shrimp curry, eggplant and pepper, mushroom, and onion relish. Many special ingredients are used in the cooking here, including rare herbs and spices unique to the restaurant, all ground freshly each day; everything is made on the premises, including the poppodums. Great accompaniments include delicious naan bread and chapatti, and there is an extensive range of side dishes. Indian restaurants are not known for their desserts but, in addition to some western dishes like millefeuille of strawberries & almonds and baked alaska, there's an interesting 'Falooda' kulfi with saffron & pistachio, which is served on a bed of sandalwood syrup - and an otherwise classic creme brulée is 'easternised' with rose petal flavouring. An extensive wine and drinks menu is thoughtfully selected for compatibility with Indian food, and solicitous staff ensure that everything is as it should be. All round, for a great Indian dining experience, Rasam has earned its place right at the top of the league. Children welcome. **Seats 75.** Reservations required; D daily, 5.30-11.30 (Sun to 11); Early D €19.95 5.30-6.30, Set D €35, also a la carte. Closed 25-26 Dec, Good Fri. MasterCard, Visa, Laser. **Directions:** Over The Eagle pub.

Dun Laoghaire
Ⓝ HOTEL

Rochestown Lodge Hotel

Rochestown Avenue Dun Laoghaire Co Dublin
Tel: 01 285 3555 Fax: 01 285 3914
Email: info@rochestown.com Web: www.rochestown.com

Well set back from the busy road, this smartly painted modern hotel has a café-bar alongside it with tables outside, giving it a welcoming feeling and not too many cars at the door, thanks to the underground car park. It has recently been completely refurbished and a large, stylishly furnished reception area sets the tone for bright, spacious public areas and comfortable guestrooms - which offer a range of options from family rooms to junior and executive suites and, with power showers and internet access, they are well set up for business guests. Good leisure facilities include an air conditioned gym,

15m heated pool, hydro therapy pool, steam room and sauna - and a luxurious new spa, 'Replenish', which offers a unique range of therapies. There's an intimate Snug bar, and menus in the minimalist café-bar offer a variety of steaks and a balanced range of seafood, poultry and meats - and appetising starters/light dishes like smoked salmon & crab open sandwich with dressed leaves and spring onions, or pan fried prawns, with potato rosti, julienne of cabbage & carrot and garlic butter. Underground parking (complimentary); wheelchair accessible. Standard B&B room rack rate €140 per night. Café Bar food opened Mon-Fri, 5.30-9.30pm, Sat, 12-3pm & 5.30-9.30pm, Sun 12-9.30pm. Replenish Spa opening hours. Mon-Fri, 10am-8pm, Sat 9am-6pm, Sun 10am-6pm. ◇

Dun Laoghaire
E RESTAURANT

Roly @ The Pavilion

8 The Pavilion Dun Laoghaire Co Dublin
Tel: 01 236 0286 Fax: 01 236 0288

Roly Saul's purpose-built restaurant just across from the Royal St George Yacht Club is full of light, with gleaming contemporary decor balanced by some traditional gilded mirrors and light and dark leather upholstery (ageing to a deep burgundy); different levels and a mixture of banquettes and high-back chairs are used to break the area up and give it interest and semi-private areas. It's a favourite haunt of many from the area (and beyond) who appreciate both the hospitality and the work of a youthful kitchen team, who relish the challenge of creating international cuisine. True to his philosophy of offering an accessible wine list and real value, Roly has managed to keep the (French) house wines (and many other good bottles) at fair prices. The set lunch menu is especially good value. Outside eating area. Air conditioning. Not Suitable for children under 7 after 7 pm. **Seats 100.** Tue-Sat: L 12-3pm, light menu 3-5.30pm, D 6-10pm (pre-theatre menu 6-7pm); Sun L menu all day, noon-8pm. Closed Mon, 25-27 Dec, Good Fri. Amex, MasterCard, Visa, Laser. **Directions:** Opposite Railway Station. ◇

Dun Laoghaire
N RESTAURANT

Tribes

57a Glasthule Road Glasthule Dun Laoghaire Co Dublin
Tel: 01 236 5971 Fax: 01 236 5971 Email: tribes@yahoo.com

This newish restaurant aims to offer top quality at reasonable prices, something that attracted attention from the outset, and the fact that head chef Karl Whelan came to Glasthule via some respected kitchens (including Mulcahys in Kenmare and The Belfry near Mullingar) heightened expectations. It's a pleasing restaurant, modern but not too sharp-edged, with comfortable high-backed leather chairs and warm-toned lampshades over some of the tables, softening the lighting. Despite some early hype, however (comparisons with Gordon Ramsay were unwisely made in a press release), this is essentially a neighbourhood restaurant: lunchtime menus offer wholesome down to earth dishes like baked fish with colcannon or steak sandwiches, and homely puddings like fruit crumbles; on evening menus, the tone gears up (steak sandwich might graduate to fillet of beef, for example, vanilla ice cream to milk sorbet) and it becomes a more elegant experience, with more refined cooking and a sense of occasion. Staff are very pleasant, helpful and efficient, it's a pleasant place to be and prices are reasonable - a good neighbourhood restaurant, and an asset to the area. ***Valaparaiso** (01 280 1992), a popular Spanish/Mediterranean restaurant over Goggins pub in Monkstown, is a sister restaurant. Children welcome; **Seats 60** (outdoors, 10); air conditioning; L Mon-Sun, 12.30-3pm (to 4pm Sun), D Mon-Sun, 5.30-11 (from 6pm Sat, to 10pm Sun); house wine €19; SC 10%. Closed 25-26 Dec, 1 Jan, Good Fri. Amex, MasterCard, Visa, Laser. **Directions:** Just past Dun Laoghaire heading South.

Glencullen
PUB

Johnnie Fox's Pub

Glencullen Co Dublin **Tel: 01 295 8911**
Fax: 01 295 8911 Email: info@jfp.ie Web: www.jfp.ie

Nestling in an attractive wooded hamlet in the Dublin Mountains, south of Dublin city, this popular pub dates back to the eighteenth century and has numerous claims to fame, including the fact that Daniel O'Connell was once a regular, apparently (he lived in Glencullen at one time), and it's "undoubtedly" the highest pub in the land. Whatever about that, it's a warm, friendly and generally well run place just about equally famous for its food the "Famous Seafood Kitchen" and its music "Famous Hooley Nights" (booking advisable). Unlike so many superficially similar pubs that have popped up all over the world recently, it's also real. Kitsch, perhaps, but real nonetheless the rickety old furniture is real, the dust is real and you certainly won't find a gas fire here there's a lovely turf or log fire at every turn. It's a pleasant place to drop into at quieter times too, if you're walking in the hills or just loafing around, and Dubliners find it an amusing place to take visitors from abroad. Reservations recommended for food. Own parking. Children welcome (under supervision, not after 7.30pm).

Traditional Irish music and dancing. **Seats 352** (private room, 55, outdoor 60). Open daily, food 12.30-9.30; all menus à la carte, house wine €19.50. No SC. Closed 24-25 Dec & Good Fri. Amex, Diners, MasterCard, Visa, Laser. **Directions:** In Dublin Mountains, 30 minutes drive from Dublin city centre.

HOWTH

The fishing port of Howth is easily accessible by DART from Dublin, and is an interesting place to wander around. The fish shops along the west pier attract a loyal clientèle, and for many a year it's been a tradition to come out from town after work on a Thursday to buy fish for the fast day on Friday - while that is largely a thing of the past, the shops still stay open later on Thursday evenings, which gives the place a special buzz in summer, when people stay on for a walk around the harbour or a bite to eat before going home. A Farmers' & Fishermen's Market is held on the pier every Sunday, and there are several interesting food shops around the village too: on the seafront, **Cibo** (01 839 6271) is a great place for real home-cooked food to take home, and up in the village, **Baily Wines** (01 832 2394) is not only an interesting owner-run wine shop but also offers a carefully selected choice of deli products, including some of the finest Irish artisan foods. Then up beside the church, there's **Main Street Flowers & Country Market** (01 839 5575) for flowers, fresh produce and some specialist groceries. An ever-growing selection of restaurants includes a smart fish restaurant, **Deep** (01 806 3921) on the west pier and, newly opened just as we go to press, a casual fish restaurant **The Oar House** (01 839 4562) includes a wet fish bar; a sister restaurant, on the harbour front, is **Casa Pasta** (01 839 3823), known for its great atmosphere and inexpensive food appealing to all age groups. There are a few ethnic restaurants: **Lemongrass** (01 832 4443) above the impressive and popular Findlaters Bar, the long-established **El Paso** (01 832 3334) and a stylish Indian, **The Green Chilli** (01 832 0444), which are all on the front. Also on the harbour front you will find the **Waterside Bar** and the more traditional **Wheelhouse Restaurant** (01 839 0555) which is known for its steaks. Up in Howth village **Ella** (01 839 6264) is a chic restaurant/wine bar and **Cibo** (01 839 6344) offers ingredients led all day food. For accommodation: the village centre **Baily Hotel** (01 832 2691; www.baily.com) is under energetic young management and has been re-styled as a boutique hotel (the cool Bá Mizu next door is attached to the hotel); up the hill - above Howth castle and with spectacular sea and coastal views over Irelands largest public golf complex, but with rather dated accommodation - is the **Deer Park Hotel** (01 832 2624; www.deerpark-hotel.ie).

WWW.IRELAND-GUIDE.COM FOR THE BEST PLACES TO EAT, DRINK & STAY

Howth

Abbey Tavern

RESTAURANT/PUB

Abbey Street Howth Co Dublin **Tel: 01 839 0307** Fax: 01 839 0284
Email: info@abbeytavern.ie Web: www.abbeytavern.ie

Just 50 yards up from the harbour, part of this famous pub dates back to the 15th century, when it was built as a seminary for the local monks (as an addition to the 12th century Chapter House next door). Currently owned by James and Eithne Scott-Lennon - James' grandfather bought it in 1945 - the entire establishment was refurbished in 1998 but this well-run and immaculately maintained pub retains features that have always made the Abbey special - open turf fires, original stone walls, flagged floors and gas lights. In 1960 the Abbey started to lay on entertainment and this, more than anything else, has brought the tavern its fame: it can cater for groups of anything between two and 200 and the format, which now runs like clockwork, is a traditional 5-course dinner followed by traditional Irish music. It's on every night but booking is essential, especially in high season. Bar food such as Howth seafood chowder, smoked salmon with home-made brown bread, and a hot traditional dish such as corned beef and cabbage is available at lunchtime, but this is really a place visited for its atmosphere. In 1956 a restaurant was opened, quite a novel move in a pub at the time; it is now called The Abbot and, with its old stone walls and open fires, it has a welcoming ambience; the food here has its ups and downs and, at its best it can be very enjoyable - fresh fish from the harbour is a speciality, and simplest choices are usually the best. **Seats 70** (private room, 40). Reservations required. Air conditioning. L&D 12-3 / 7-10 Tue-Sat, (Bar Sun L 12.30 - 4); Set D 2/3 course € 33/38, also à la carte, house wine €18. SC discretionary. Children welcome; carpark on harbour. Restaurant closed Sun, Mon; establishment closed 25 Dec & Good Fri. Amex, Diners, MasterCard, Visa, Laser. **Directions:** 15km (9 m) from Dublin, in the centre of Howth.

Howth

Ann's

Ⓝ B&B

5 East Pier Howth Co Dublin **Tel: 01 832 3197**
Email: annsofhowth@eircom.net Web: www.annsofhowth.com

Situated right on the harbour front, Una and Jonathan Cooke's hospitable B&B is very comfortable and conveniently situated, with the bonus of a wonderful location. Rooms have Velux windows to catch the harbour and island view - very nice to wake up to - and are attractively furnished with wooden floors, double bed, dressing table, a small wardrobe and tea/coffee making facilities, and a small but nicely decorated en-suite shower room. Breakfast is served in a lovely seafacing lounge/dining room - a gorgeous fresh fruit plate, with interesting fruits, a very well cooked breakfast, and good tea and coffee as well. Una and Jonanthan are very friendly and informative and it's a pleasure to stay here. Sea angling, walking, hill walking, golf nearby, garden visits nearby, newsagent. Children welcome (under 2's free in parents' room, no cots avail); Pets permitted by prior arrangement. **Rooms 4** (all power shower only, all no smoking); B&B €40-50 pps, ss €10. Open all year.Amex, MasterCard, Visa, Laser. **Directions:** Howth seafront, opposite East Pier.

Howth

Aqua Restaurant

RESTAURANT

1 West Pier Howth Co Dublin
Tel: 01 8320 690 / 1850 34 64 64 Fax: 01 8320 687
Email: dine@aqua.ie Web: www.aqua.ie

Previously a yacht club, this is now a fine contemporary restaurant with plenty of window tables to take advantage of sea views westwards, towards Malahide, and take in the island of Ireland's Eye to the north. Behind a glass screen, a team of chefs provide entertainment as well as colourful food that is cooked with panache and thoughtfully, but quite simply, presented - a refreshing change from the over-worked presentation in many restaurants at the moment. What was once a snooker room is now a characterful bar with a unique blend of original features and modern additions - with an open fire and comfortable seating, it has retained a cosy, clubby atmosphere and is a lovely place to relax before or after your meal. The style of cooking is strong, simple and modern; given the location, seafood is the natural choice but dry-aged steak - with grilled peppers, roasted baby potatoes, balsamic vinegar and extra virgin olive oil, perhaps - is also a speciality. Unchanging menus offer a pleasing repertoire of broadly Cal-Ital origin - crostini of Serrano ham with rocket, asparagus & extra virgin oil, char-grilled breast of chicken with roasted corn salsa, red pepper coulis, herb oil - occasional new dishes, or some daily specials, would be welcome to give fresh choices to a loyal local clientèle. The waterside location, well-sourced ingredients, good cooking and solicitous service all make dining at Aqua a pleasure; à la carte menus are pricey, but the set menu offered for early dinner, lunch and the popular jazz lunch on Sunday, is very good value. **Seats 100.** D Tue-Sun 5.30-10.30, Sun 6-9.30; L Sun 12.30-4 (Bar L Tue-Sat, 1-3). Early D €29.95 (5.30-7), Set Sun L €29.95. Also à la carte. House wine €21.95, SC discretionary. Closed Mon, 25-27 Dec, Good Fri. Amex, MasterCard, Visa, Laser. **Directions:** Left along pier after Howth DART Station. ◇

Howth

King Sitric Fish Restaurant & Accommodation

☆ RESTAURANT WITH ROOMS

East Pier Howth Co Dublin
Tel: 01 832 5235 Fax: 01 839 2442
Email: info@kingsitric.ie Web: www.kingsitric.ie

Named after an 11th century Norse King of Dublin who had close links with Howth and was a cousin of the legendary Brian Boru, Aidan and Joan MacManus' striking harbourside establishment is one of Dublin's longest established fine dining restaurants. The bright and airy first floor restaurant takes full advantage of the sea and harbour views, which are especially enjoyable on summer evenings and at lunch time and, from this East Pier site, chef-patron Aidan MacManus can keep an eye on his lobster pots in Balscadden Bay on one side and the fishing boats coming into harbour on the other. Aidan is well known for his dedication to quality produce, and informative notes on menu covers state the restaurant's commitment to local producers, some of whom are named - and gives a listing of Irish fish in six languages. Specialities worth travelling for include a luscious red velvet crab bisque, crab mayonnaise, and calmar frites with tartare or tomato sauce; less well known seafood, such as locally fished razor shell clams in garlic butter, often shares the menu with classics like sole meunière and Dublin lawyer (lobster with whiskey sauce) - and, in winter, lovers of game also went their way here for treats on both lunch and dinner menus. Farmhouse cheeses and lovely desserts are always worth leaving room for - the house dessert, meringue Sitric, may even be seen by some as a challenge. And Aidan MacManus oversees one of the country's finest wine lists, with special strengths in Chablis, Burgundy and Alsace. A special feature of the King Sitric is a temperature controlled wine cellar on the ground floor, where tastings are held. It is cleverly incorporated into the reception area, with only a glass door between them, so diners can enjoy the ambience while having an aperitif. The house wine, Pinot Blanc Cuvée Les Amours Hugel (a special reserve for the King Sitric) is outstanding for both quality and value, and a perfect match for his delicious fish cooking. Although this is a fine dining restaurant, Aidan and Joan MacManus work hard to keep prices accessible - lunch is especially good value, also their Special Value Menu (D Mon-Thu, no time restriction). The King Sitric was the Guide's Seafood

Restaurant of the Year in 2006 ,and received the Wine List of the Year Award in 2001; the restaurant operates a Food & Wine Club off-season. Banqueting (70). **Seats 70** (private room, 28). Air conditioning. L Mon-Sat,12.30-2.15; D Mon-Sat, 6.30-10. Set L from €29. 'Value' D €35 (Mon-Thu all year, no time restrictions); 4-course Set D €55; also à la carte; house wine from €23; SC discretionary (12.5% parties 8+). Closed Sun, bank hols, last 2 weeks Jan, Christmas. **Accommodation:** There are eight lovely rooms, all with sea views and individually designed bathrooms. **Rooms 8** (2 superior, 1 family room, all no-smoking). B&B from €72.50 pps, ss €32.50. Amex, MasterCard, Visa, Laser, Switch. **Directions:** Far end of the harbour front, facing the east pier.

Howth/Sutton Area

Marine Hotel

HOTEL

Sutton Cross Dublin 13 **Tel: 01 839 0000** Fax: 01 839 0442
Email: info@marinehotel.ie Web: www.marinehotel.ie

Well-located on the sea side of a busy junction, this attractive hotel has ample car parking in front and a lawn reaching down to the foreshore at the rear. Public areas give a good impression: a smart foyer and adjacent bar, an informal conservatory style seating area overlooking the garden and a well-appointed restaurant. Bedrooms, some of which have sea views, have recently been refurbished. A popular venue for conferences and social gatherings, especially weddings, the Marine is also the only hotel in this area providing for the business guest. Business centre; secretarial services. Conference/banqueting (200/190). Golf nearby. Garden. Children welcome (under 3 free in parents' room; cots available without charge). No pets. **Rooms 48** (1 junior suite, 6 shower only, 31 executive rooms, 12 no-smoking, 2 disabled). Lift. Limited room service. B&B €90 pps, ss €30. Meridian Restaurant: L&D daily; bar meals available, 5-8pm daily. Closed 25-26 Dec. Amex, Diners, MasterCard, Visa, Laser. **Directions:** Take coast road towards Howth from city centre, on right at Sutton Cross.

Killiney

Fitzpatrick Castle Hotel Dublin

HOTEL

Killiney Co Dublin **Tel: 01 230 5400** Fax: 01 230 5430
Email: jenna.shortall@fitzpatricks.com Web: www.fitzpatrickshotels.com

Located in the fashionable suburb of Killiney, this imposing castellated mansion overlooking Dublin Bay dates back to 1741. It is surrounded by landscaped gardens and, despite its size and grand style, has a relaxed atmosphere. Spacious bedrooms combine old-world charm with modern facilities, and a fitness centre has a 22 metre pool, jacuzzi, spa and relaxation deck. Although perhaps best known as a leading conference and function venue, Fitzpatrick's also caters especially well for business guests and 'The Crown Club', on the 5th floor functions as a 'hotel within a hotel', offering pre-arranged private transfer from the airport and a wide range of facilities for business guests. Five championship golf courses, including Druid's Glen, are nearby. Garden. Lift. **Rooms 113.** Room rate about €130. Closed 24-26 Dec. Amex, Diners, MasterCard, Visa, Laser. **Directions:** Take M50 from the airport, follow signs for Dun Laoghaire ferry port; south to Dalkey - top of Killiney hill. ◇

Leixlip

Becketts Country House Hotel

HOTEL/RESTAURANT

Cooldrinagh House Leixlip Co Dublin
Tel: 01 624 7040 Fax: 01 624 7072

A handsome house on the County Dublin side of the river that divides Leixlip, this house was once the home of Samuel Beckett's mother and it is now an unusual hotel, offering a personalised service for business guests: from the moment you arrive a butler looks after all your needs, whether it be dining, laundry, limousine facilities or tailored requirements for meetings or conferences. Imaginatively converted to its present use, luxurious accommodation includes four boardroom suites and six executive suites, all furnished to a high standard in a lively contemporary style. All have a workstation equipped for computers, including modem/Internet connection and audio visual equipment, private fax machines etc. are also available on request. Public areas, including a bar and an attractive modern restaurant, have a far less business-like atmosphere. Cooldrinagh House overlooks the Eddie Hackett-designed Leixlip golf course, for which golf tee off times may be booked in advance. Conference/banqueting (350/250) Business centre/secretarial services. Golf. Wheelchair accessible. No pets. **Rooms 10** (4 suites, 6 executive rooms) B&B from about €75. Open all year except Christmas. **Restaurant:** Atmosphere is the trump card in this stylish restaurant, with its stone walls, old wooden floors and soft lighting - and an exceptionally warm and genuine welcome. Pristine white tablecloths, gleaming silverware and glasses, and candlelit tables create an romantic atmosphere, helped by the way that three large alcoves overlooking a courtyard divide the dining area into intimate spaces. Arriving guests are shown to their table promptly, and menus quickly follow, along with a basket of home-made breads. The a la carte - which is very expensive - is available every night (the signature dish is Beckett's Aromatic Duck, with sultana, ginger & sage stuffing, and classic orange sauce), but it is worth getting here in time for the early dinner, which is a set menu and offers much better value; typical starters might include classic Caesar salad or a (rather bland) smoked haddock & mussel seafood chowder, followed by mains like delicious pan-seared sea bream with fennel & avocado salad, or pan-roasted rack of lamb with a rosemary demi-glaze and herb mash. An impressive range of wines (seen across the back wall as you enter the restaurant) is another attractive feature - and all this, plus the warm and efficient service that is part of the charm at Beckett's, ensures a strong local following, so booking is advisable. **Seats 130.** L Mon-Fri 12.30-2.15 & Sun 12.30-6; D daily: Early D Mon-Fri 6-7.30, €27.50; a la carte D daily 6-10. Closed L Sat. Amex, Diners, MasterCard, Visa. **Directions:** Take N4, turn off at Spa Hotel, next left after Springfield Hotel. ◇

Lucan

Finnstown Country House Hotel

HOTEL

Newcastle Road Lucan Co Dublin **Tel: 01 601 0700** Fax: 01 628 1088
Email: manager@finnstown-hotel.ie Web: www.finnstown-hotel.ie

Approached by a long tree-lined driveway, this fine old manor house is set in 45 acres of woodland and (despite a large, blocky extension), is full of charm. It may not be immediately obvious where the hotel reception is, but an open fire in the foyer sets a welcoming tone and all of the large, well-proportioned reception rooms - drawing room, restaurant, bar - are elegantly furnished in a traditional style well-suited to the house. Although quite grand, there is a comfortable lived-in feeling throughout. Bedrooms vary and include some studio suites, with a small fridge and toaster in addition to the standard tea/coffee making facilities; although most rooms have good facilities including full bathrooms (with bath and shower), some are a little dated, and the view can be disappointing if you are looking over the extension - and light sleepers should ensure a quiet room is allocated if there is a wedding or other function taking place. Residential golf breaks are a speciality. Conference/banqueting (300/200). Business centre; secretarial services. Leisure centre. Swimming pool. Tennis. Snooker; pool. Shop. Children welcome (Under 12 free in parents' room; cots available without charge, baby sitting arranged). Pets permitted. Parking (200). Wheelchair accessible. **Rooms 77** (28 executive, 10 no-smoking, 1 for disabled). B&B €65, ss €45. Open all year. **The Dining Room:** As in the rest of the house, the decor of this comfortable room, is pleasantly quirky - and, with good lighting and ventilation and lovely piano playing, the atmosphere is relaxing. Tables are a little cluttered, perhaps, but nicely set up with fresh flowers, and menus are not over-ambitious, offering about five choices on each course; most are familiar but there are may be some surprises (a starter ragout of venison in a red wine and juniper jus in a puff pastry case, for example), and what arrives on the plate is far from the average hotel meal: quality ingredients are used and down to earth cooking has the emphasis on flavour - and food is attractively presented without ostentation, all making for an enjoyable meal that is also good value for money. **Seats 100** (private room, 30). L daily 12.30-2pm (Sun 1-5pm); D daily 7.30-9.30; set Sun L €29.95. set D, €42. L&D also à la carte. House wine €21.95. House closed Christmas. *Long term accommodation also available in apartment suites. Amex, Diners, MasterCard, Visa, Laser. **Directions:** Off main Dublin-Galway Road (N4): take exit for Newcastle off dual carriageway.

Lucan

La Banca

Ⓝ RESTAURANT

Main Street Lucan Village Co Dublin **Tel: 01 628 2400**
Fax: 01 628 2444 Web: www.labanca.ie

This pleasant neighburhood restaurant off Lucan's winding main street is well positioned near the Italian Embassy. Moving swiftly through the dark and distinctly tatty entrance area, you will be pleasantly surprised by a bright, modern and well presented restaurant, where arriving guests are welcomed by friendly Italian staff - who show you to your table promptly and immediately present a comprehensive Italian menu, good bread and gorgeous garlic infused olive oil. It can be hard to make choices from very long menus but a wide choice of antipasti dishes includes a delicious plate of Parma ham, salami, mortadella, olives & buffalo mozzarella a sociable choice if dining out with friends. Main course choices include all the Italian staples, including pasta dishes like cannelloni alla carne and pizzas but, although not necessarily local, the fish could well be a good choice - for example, you might try perfectly cooked sea bass and swordfish (served with well chosen side vegetables). As is often the case in Italian restaurants service is good, with friendly Italian waiters always ready to be of assistance. *The Vault Bar is a small downstairs area (you have to brave the dark entrance area again to reach it or the toilets); it opens on Friday & Saturday nights and is available for private parties. Live music in Vault Bar Fri-Sat night. Opening hours Tue-Sat 4-10.30pm, Sun 2-9.30pm. ◇

MALAHIDE

The attractive coastal town of Malahide offers plentiful accommodation - the large and ever-growing **Grand Hotel** (01 845 0000; www.thegrand.ie) has every facility - and there's quality shopping and an abundance of things to do. There's a Farmers' Market held here every Saturday, and the town is alive with bars, cafés and restaurants. In New Street, **Gibneys** pub (01 845 0863) is a first port of call for many; this characterful place has a large beer garden at the back for fine weather, and offers contemporary bar food and an interesting wine selection (including a blackboard menu by the glass); next door is their award-winning wine shop & off-licence. In a first floor premises on The Green, and overlooking the marina area, the relaxed **Ciao Ristorante** (01 845 1233) can claim one of the best views in town. Meanwhile, gardeners - and many who are just having a day out - head up to the garden centre, **Gardenworks** (01 845 0110), where wholesome food is served every day in the **Café** (Mon-Sat, 10-5; Sun & bank hols, 12-5), or to nearby **Malahide Castle** (01 846 2184), where there is extensive parkland, the Talbot Botanic Gardens, the Fry Model Railway and also an informal restaurant/tea rooms.
WWW.IRELAND-GUIDE.COM FOR THE BEST PLACES TO EAT, DRINK & STAY

Malahide

Bon Appetit

Ⓝ RESTAURANT

9 St James Terrace Malahide Co Dublin **Tel: 01 8450 314**
Fax: 01 8450 314 Email: info@bonappetit.ie Web: www.bonappetit.ie

féile bia In a Georgian terrace near the marina, this renowned restaurant was made famous by one of Ireland's finest classical chefs, Patsy McGuirk, and it is fitting that it should now have come into the ownership of one of this country's most highly regarded younger chefs, Oliver Dunne - who (like Patsy before him, a quarter of a century ago) has moved out of town to establish his new business in this delightful town. At the time of going to press renovation work on the four-storey building is nearing completion, and re-opening is imminent - the new set-up includes an informal brasserie-café serving casual daytime meals, and a contemporary fine dining restaurant where fans of Oliver's superb cooking at the Ranelagh restaurant Mint will be hoping to find some of his great dishes - and fans of the old Bon Appetit wonder if they might rediscover some of the wonderful dishes associated with this building, like the fresh prawn bisque with cognac, Sole Creation McGuirk (whole boned black sole, filled with turbot and prawns, in a beurre blanc sauce), a dish so gloriously old-fashioned that it's now come full circle and (with a little tweaking perhaps) could take retro pride of place on any contemporary menu. Whatever dishes end up on the menu, Dunne's reputation as a first class chef virtually guarantees that diners will enjoy a memorable experience here. Amex, Diners, MasterCard, Visa, Laser. **Directions:** Coming from Dublin go through the lights and turn left into St James's Terrace at Malahide Garda Station.

Malahide

Cape Greko

Ⓝ RESTAURANT

Unit 1 First Floor New Street Malahide Co Dublin **Tel: 01 845 6288**
Fax: 01 845 6289 Email: info@capegreko.ie Web: www.capegreko.ie

This friendly first floor restaurant offers a genuinely relaxed big Greek Cypriot experience and it's a fun, good value place for a group outing. It's a simple room decorated in blue cool and white to match the Greek flag that takes pride of place over the wine rack (no Greek wine on the Guide's most recent visit, alas, but that is not always the case), with high-backed lightwood chairs and tables simply laid with runners and plain cutlery. but you can be sure of a warm welcome, and friendly staff are quick to take orders from menus that offer a good selection of the classics - tzatsiki (the cucumber and yoghurt dip with garlic), hummus with pitta bread, crisp nakopita (triangular pastry parcels of baby spinach with feta cheese), grilled halloumi (sheep's cheese) with tomato & onion salad and pitta bread, calamari, and deep-fried breaded squid with lemon. Favourites from the main courses include lamb kleftiko (meltingly tender lamb shank slow cooked with onions, tomatoes, cinnamon and olive oil - a winner, served with crisp roast Greek potatoes), mixed souvlaki (a combination of pork meatballs, onion, parsley & spices) and chicken kebabs served with tzatsiki. A range of side orders includes the ubiquitous Mediterranean lettuce and tomato salad, of course, along with other staples such as couscous and roasted peppers, but it's worth checking whether you need to order extras as some dishes are very generous. There is live music on Friday nights too, which makes it a real night out. *A second branch was recently opened in **Bray** (01 286 0006). D Mon-Thu, 5-midnight, Fri-Sun, 12.30 - midnight (Sun to 11pm). **Directions:** At the corner of New Street above Marios Pizzas.

Malahide
RESTAURANT

Cruzzo Bar & Restaurant

The Marina Village Malahide Co Dublin **Tel: 01 845 0599**
Fax: 01 845 0602 Email: info@cruzzo.ie Web: www.cruzzo.ie

Built on a platform over the water, this attractive bar and restaurant is large and stylish in Florida style, with views over the marina. Approaching from the carpark over a little bridge creates a sense of anticipation, and the interior is dashing, with a large piano bar on the lower floor and a rather grand staircase rising to the main dining areas above, which are comfortable and well-appointed, with well-spaced tables in interesting groupings - although it is worth ensuring a table with a view when booking, as there is always something interesting going on in daylight, and the seawater all around is impressively lit at night; an elevated section at the front has the best tables in the house. Contemporary menus hold no great surprises but offer a varied choice of perhaps eight or ten dishes on each course, including attractively presented starters like a specialty tian of avocado with Boston prawn, with lemon vinaigrette, or simple chicken liver pate, served with a delicious date chutney and crostini. Main courses offer imaginatively dressed up versions of popular dishes (fillet steak may be served with herbed potato cake and an unusual prune & fig sauce, for example, or chicken breast with field mushrooms, chorizo and creamed leeks). The cooking has had its ups and downs, but recent visits have found it running sweetly, and the location and ambience always give a sense of occasion - especially at weekends, when a band or pianist playing downstairs adds to the atmosphere. Although prices on the à la carte are quite high (and vegetables are charged extra), the early dinner menu is very good value, and there is a nice little 'grown up' children's menu too. Not suitable for children after 9pm, lift, toilets wheelchair accessible, air conditioning. **Seats 260;** L Mon- Fri, 12-2.30, Sun 12.30-3.30; D Mon-Fri 6-10pm, Sat, 5.30-10.30pm, Sun 6.30-9.30pm. Early D € 16.50/22, 2/3 courses, Mon-Fri, 6-7pm, Sat, 5.30-6.30pm; L & D also à la carte. Live music (Jazz & Sinatra), Tue, Fri, Sat evening. House wine from €20. SC 12.5% on parties 6+. Closed Sat L, Bank Hol Mon D, 25-26 Dec,1 Jan, Good Fri. Amex, Diners, MasterCard, Visa, Laser. **Directions:** From Malahide Village through arch into Marina.

Malahide
RESTAURANT

Jaipur Restaurant Malahide

St James Terrace Malahide Co Dublin **Tel: 01 845 5455**
Fax: 01 845 5456 Email: malahide@jaipur.ie Web: www.jaipur.ie

This chic new-wave Indian restaurant is the third Jaipur - the others are in Dublin 2 and Dalkey (see entries); it's in the basement of a fine Georgian terrace and, although Malahide is particularly well-served with interesting eating places, it has earned a loyal following. Cooking is crisp and modern - a contemporary take on traditional Indian food; head chef Kuldip Kumar came from the 5* Imperial Hotel in New Delhi and it shows in colourful, well-flavoured dishes that have a lot of eye appeal. Vegetarian choices are particularly appealing, old favourites like tandoori prawns take well to the contemporary treatment and even desserts - usually a total no-no in ethnic restaurants - are worth leaving room for. Meals: D daily, 5-11. Early D, €20 (5-7pm). Set menus €25-45 (incl 4-course Tasting Menu). House wine €20. Closed 25-26 Dec. Amex, MasterCard, Visa, Laser. **Directions:** In Georgian terrace facing the tennis club in Malahide.

Malahide
RESTAURANT

Siam Thai Restaurant

1 The Green Malahide Co Dublin **Tel: 01 845 4698**
Fax: 01 845 4489 Email: siam@eircom.net Web: www.siamthai.ie

This was one of Dublin's earlier Thai restaurants and was consistently popular in its previous out-of-the-way premises, so the recent move to a much more public (and glamorous) location overlooking the Green should mark the beginning of an even more successful phase. The new restaurant has a smart blue-covered heated terrace at the front and a spacious interior in three sections, with a full bar; the back is subtly lit and ideal for private parties or a large table, and the front area is very pleasant, with views out over the marina. A typically warm Thai welcome gets guests into the mood, and there is a pianist on some nights, which adds to the atmosphere. Sutchan Sutchudthad, who has been with the restaurant since 1994, presents menus that offer many of the Thai classics on an extensive à la carte as well as the set menus and, although perhaps blanded down a bit for local tastes, there's a willingness to vary the spiciness according to personal preference. No monosodium glutamate is used. Menus are very extensive so it is wise to order an aperitif and allow plenty of time to decide - or the indecisive might begin with Siam Combination Appetisers (including chicken satay, spring rolls, special coated prawns, marinated pork ribs, prawns wrapped in ham and bags of golden wonton with plum sauce), followed perhaps by main courses like Ghung Phad Phong Garee (Tiger prawns with scallions, mushrooms and basil leaves and a spicy sauce) and Ped Makham (boneless crisp-skinned duck with crispy noodles and plum sauce). Outstandingly warm and friendly staff are knowledgeable and efficient. Children welcome. Air conditioning. Live music (piano or live Thai band) most nights. **Seats 120** (private room, 45, outdoor, 30); L daily 11.30-5; D daily 5-12. Early D €21 (5-7.30 Sun-Thu); Set D €32/36 2/3 coure; à la carte also available. House wine €20. Closed 25-26 Dec. Amex, Diners, MasterCard, Visa, Laser. **Directions:** In Malahide village, near marina; turn left at Church to end of road.

Malahide

Silks

RESTAURANT

5 The Mall Malahide Co Dublin **Tel: 01 845 3331**

This smart Chinese restaurant is spacious, modern and airy, with cheerful decor, and staff who are friendly and helpful, to match. The long menu is predictable, offering all the familiar set menus and dishes - the sizzlers and sweet & sours are there, along with Peking duck with pancakes, spiced chicken, and shared starter platters (spring rolls, chicken satay, spare ribs, wontons) followed, perhaps, by Garlic Prawn, Sweet & Sour Chicken, Duck Cantonese Style and Beef with Green Peppers, along with side dishes like Yung Chow Fried Rice. Desserts are unsurprising: banana fritters with an above average vanilla ice cream, perhaps, or a simple bowl of lychees. Silks may not be the first port of call for those seeking genuinely authentic chinese cuisine - there is a sense that the cooking has been 'dumbed down' for the Irish palate - but this has never been an issue with the loyal customers of this enormously popular neighbourhood restaurant, who have always enjoyed the busy atmosphere and friendly service. Reservations are essential as this restaurant is busy every night of the week. **Seats 90** (private room 20). Air conditioning. D daily: Mon-Sat 6-12.30. Sun 5-11. A la carte. **Directions:** Opposite Garda Station. ◇

Malahide Area

Belcamp Hutchinson

COUNTRY HOUSE

Carrs Lane Malahide Road Balgriffin Dublin 17
Tel: 01 846 0843 Fax: 01 848 5703
Email: belcamphutchinson@eircom.net Web: www.belcamphutchinson.com

Dating back to 1786, this impressive house just outside Malahide takes its name from the original owner, Francis Hely-Hutchinson, 3rd Earl of Donoughmore. It is set in large grounds, with interesting gardens, giving it a very away-from-it-all country atmosphere - yet Belcamp Hutchinson is only about half an hour from Dublin city centre (off peak) and 15 minutes to the airport. The present owners, Doreen Gleeson and Karl Waldburg, have renovated the house sensitively: high ceilinged, graciously proportioned rooms have retained many of their original features and are furnished and decorated in keeping with their age. Bedrooms are very comfortable, with thoughtfully appointed bathrooms and views over the gardens and countryside. Although its convenient location makes this an ideal place to stay on arrival or when leaving Ireland, a one-night stay won't do justice to this lovely and hospitable place. No dinner is served, but the restaurants (and good shopping) of Malahide are nearby. Walled garden; maze. Golf, equestrian, walking, garden visits, tennis and sailing are all nearby. Not suitable for children under 10. Pets welcome. **Rooms 8** (all with full bath & overbath shower). B&B €75 pps, no ss. Closed 20 Dec-1 Feb. MasterCard, Visa, Laser. **Directions:** From city centre, take Malahide Road; past Campions pub, 1st lane on left (sign on right pointing up lane).

Monkstown

The Purty Kitchen

CAFÉ/PUB

3-5 Old Dunleary Road Monkstown Co Dublin
Tel: 01 284 3576 Fax: 01 284 3576
Email: info@purtykitchen.com Web: www.purtykitchen.com

Established in 1728 - making it the second oldest pub in Dublin (after The Brazen Head) and the oldest in Dun Laoghaire - this attractive old place has seen some changes, but its essential character remains, with dark wooden floors, good lighting, large mirrors and a good buzz. It's well set up for enjoyment of the bar food for which it has earned a fine reputation, with shiny dark wooden tables (a candle on each) and inviting menus which still have old favourites like the famous Purty Seafood Chowder and Purty Seafood Platter. But, although best known for seafood - and a wide range is offered, including crayfish, lobster and fresh crab in season and lovely dishes like crisp, fresh-tasting calamari with a sweet chilli dressing, or a seafood tempura selection (calamari, prawns & hake served with sweet chilli, soy & home made spiced marie rose dips) - head chef Sheenagh Toal also applies her creativity to a large selection of dishes for non seafood eaters, including vegetarians. Lovely fresh food with a home cooked flavour, presented attractively on different shaped plates, make this an unusually enjoyable informal dining experience. A list of House Favourites also includes some dishes that have stood the test of (considerable) time, such as a traditional breakfast, home-made beef burgers and seafood quiche, all at reasonable prices. A garden terrace offers a pleasing outdoor alternative in fine weather, and the Food & Wine Emporium next door specialises in artisan Irish foods. *A new Purty Kitchen is due to open in Temple Bar during 2007. A la carte menu available Mon-Fri 12-9.45, Sat-Sun, 12.30-9.45. Veg menu also available. Purty Kitchen Food & Wine Emporium open every day (pub hours). Toilets wheelchair accessible. House wine from about €16.50 (€4.50 per glass). Live music Tue & Fri evenings. Closed 25 Dec, Good Friday. Amex, Diners, MasterCard, Visa, Laser. **Directions:** On left approaching Dun Laoghaire from Dublin by the coast road. ◇

Mount Merrion
Ⓝ RESTAURANT

Michael's Food & Wine

57 Deerpark Road Mount Merrion Co Dublin
Tel: 01 278 0377 Fax: 01 278 0377

Well maintained hanging baskets and a few tables for alfresco dining set a welcoming tone outside Michael and Mary Lowe's wine shop, Italian deli and little trattoria style restaurant. You'll notice bottles of wine in view as you arrive and, in the shop, find the walls lined from floor to ceiling with Michael's collection of specially imported Italian wine; a table displaying speciality foods (pastas, Italian sauces etc) takes centre stage and a deli counter at the back of the shop offers charcuterie, great cheeses, olives, and other treats to take home. At the back, a small room is simply furnished with wooden tables and chairs and small candles, and a blackboard notice sums up the philosophy of this little place very well: "No salt or sugar added, 99% ingredients & 1% skill"! A blackboard menu offers a small selection of dishes (some available in two sizes) including a must-try and totally delicious antipasta dish with bruschetta, sun blushed tomatoes, salami, prosciutto, red and green pesto, olives, a pair of handmade Italian cheeses and a choice of salads. Main dishes, costing about €9.95, normally include a hot special such as pizzaiola - mozzarella, aubergine, bruschetta, red pesto, regato and parmesan, and vegetarians will also enjoy the 'veggie snack' of focaccia, courgette, aubergine, pesto, red peppers, mozzarella, layered and served with fresh rocket leaves wrapped in a slice of roasted aubergine. Tempting desserts are displayed in a glass cabinet in the wine shop where you may may choose a bottle to enjoy with your meal for a corkage fee of just €5.75 and, on bottles over €30, there is no corkage charge. The quality of ingredients used and generous portions make for very good value, and friendly service and advice is always at hand. Cheese & Wine night on Wednesdays, 7pm onwards. **Seats 24;** D Thurs-Fri, 7-9.30pm, L Sat only 12-3pm; cheese & wine from 7pm on Wed. MasterCard, Visa, Laser. **Directions:** Situated off Fosters Avenue on Deerpark Road just past Kiely's of Mount Merrion. ◇

Portmarnock
HOTEL/RESTAURANT

Portmarnock Hotel & Golf Links

Strand Road Portmarnock Co Dublin
Tel: 01 846 0611 Fax: 01 846 1876
Email: sales@portmarnock.com Web: www.portmarnock.com

Originally owned by the Jameson family of whiskey fame, Portmarnock Hotel and Golf Links enjoys a wonderful beachside position overlooking the islands of Lambay and Ireland's Eye. Convenient to the airport, and only eleven miles from Dublin city centre, the hotel seems to offer the best of every world - the peace and convenience of the location and a magnificent 18 hole Bernhard Langer-designed links course. Extension and renovation work is in progress at the time of going to press, so the hotel is not looking its best but the interior is bright and spacious, with modern decor in most areas, and a relaxed atmosphere. The Jameson Bar, in the old house, has character and there's also an informal Links Bar and Restaurant next to the golf shop (12-10 daily). Accommodation is imaginatively designed so that all rooms have sea or golf course views, and all - including some in the original house which are furnished with antiques, two with four-posters and executive rooms with balconies or bay windows - are furnished to a high standard of comfort, with good bathrooms. Conference/banqueting (350/250) Business centre. Golf (18). Oceana, health & beauty: gym, sauna, steam rooms & a wide range of treatments. Children welcome (under 4 free in parents' room, cots available without charge, baby sitting arranged). No pets. Garden. **Rooms 98** (14 executive, 61 no-smoking, 32 ground floor, 3 disabled). Lift. 24 hour room service. B&B about €157.50 pps, ss about €75. Open all year. **Osborne Restaurant:** Named after the artist Walter Osborne, who painted many of his most famous pictures in the area including the view from the Jameson house, the restaurant is in a semi-basement overlooking gardens at the side of the hotel - and first-time visitors may not find it easily, so inquire at reception. The room is in a traditional style, with rather too many busy patterns for contemporary tastes, but tables are beautifully appointed; when the restaurant first opened in 1996 it was an important addition to a sparse north Dublin dining scene, and a succession of distinguished chefs put the this formal dining room firmly on the map, but it is now less a culinary destination and more a fine dining option for resident guests and a 'special occasion' restaurant for local residents. Menus are constructed with the international traveller in mind, offering about eight dishes on each course, and fish features strongly, reflecting the coastal location. Sophisticated dishes offered include starters of lobster ravioli on a curry lemon grass velouté (€16), grilled tiger prawns with goat's cheese foam and fried baby aubergines (€15), and warm gazpacho with avocado, as well as an optional sorbet of the day (€4.50). Main courses range from €24.50 to €32: fish comes with unusual accompaniments such as sea bream with green asparagus, tomato confit and ginger potato fritter; monkfish confit with red onion tarte tatin, parsley root mash and beurre rouge; and seared tuna with paprika and lemon butter. Traditionalists will be satisfied by Barbary duck, Kerry lamb and Irish beef and there's also a vegetarian option, such as goats' cheese strudel on a wild mushroom risotto (€18.50). An extensive wine list is offered, and friendly service takes the edge off the formality. Air conditioning. **Seats 80** (private room, 20). D only Tue-Sat, 7-10. Set D from €47, Tasting Menu from €50-60. A la carte available; house wine from €19.85; SC discretionary. Closed Sun, Mon. Links Brasserie open 12-10 daily Amex, MasterCard, Visa, Laser. **Directions:** On the coast in Portmarnock. ◇

Saggart

Citywest Hotel Conference Leisure & Golf Resort

HOTEL

Saggart Co Dublin **Tel: 01 401 0500** Fax: 01 401 0945
Email: info@citywesthotel.com Web: www.citywesthotel.com

féile bia Only about 25 minutes from the city centre and Dublin airport (traffic permitting), this large hotel was planned with the needs of the rapidly expanding western edge of the capital in mind. It is set in its own estate, which includes two 18-hole golf courses and a comprehensive leisure centre with a large deck level swimming pool and a wide range of health and beauty facilities. The other big attraction is the hotel's banqueting, conference and meeting facilities, which include a convention centre catering for 4,000 delegates, making Citywest one of the largest venues in the country. All round, a valuable amenity for West Dublin. Conference/banqueting (4,000/2,000); secretarial services, video-conferencing. Leisure centre, swimming pool. Hairdressing/beauty salon. Children welcome (under 6 free in parents' room, cots available free of charge). Restaurant: L Mon-Fri, D daily. **Rooms 892** (19 suites, 759 no smoking). Lift, room service 24 hr. B&B about €75 pps, ss €30. Open all year.Amex, Diners, MasterCard, Visa, Laser. **Directions:** Off Naas Road - N7 (from Dublin, take left after Independent printers & follow road for about a mile.

SKERRIES

So far remarkably unspoilt, Skerries is not completely undeveloped but its essential atmosphere has remained unchanged for decades (perhaps because it does not yet have marina and all its attendant development) and it makes a refreshing break from the hurly-burly of Dublin city. The harbour is renowned for its fishing, notably Dublin Bay prawns (langoustine), and the surrounding area is famous for market gardening, so it has always been a good place for a very subtstantial bite to eat - and there are several pubs of character along the harbour front to enjoy a pint before your meal - or the Coast Inn, just across the road from the Red Bank (see entry), does a great line in cocktails. Olive Coffee & Wine is a very attractive little place opposite Gerry's Supermarket, there are a couple of ethnic restaurants, and **Russell's** (01 849 2450) is a friendly neighbourhood restaurant. While in the area, allow time to visit **Skerries Mills** (working windmills (Tel: 01 849 5208)) and **Ardgillan Castle and Victorian Gardens** (Tel: 01 849 2212) nearby at Balbriggan, both of which have tea rooms.
WWW.IRELAND-GUIDE.COM FOR THE BEST PLACES TO EAT, DRINK & STAY

Skerries

Red Bank House & Restaurant

Ⓔ RESTAURANT/GUESTHOUSE

5-7 Church Street Skerries Co Dublin
Tel: 01 849 1005 Fax: 01 849 1598
Email: sales@redbank.ie Web: www.redbank.ie

féile bia Golfing breaks are a speciality at Terry McCoy's renowned restaurant with accommodation in the characterful fishing port of Skerries. The restaurant is in a converted banking premises, which adds to the atmosphere (even the old vault has its uses - as a wine cellar) and Terry is an avid supporter of local produce, with fresh seafood from Skerries harbour (including local razor fish) providing the backbone of his menu. Menus, written in Terry's inimitable style, are a joy to read and a statement at the end reads: "All items on the menu are sourced from Irish producers and suppliers. There are too many items for us to list all ingredients after each dish but you can take my word for it, we use local Irish because it's the freshest & so the best." Just so - a few places taking pride in 'organics' that have come half way round the world before arriving on the plate could learn a lot from Terry. Dishes conceived and cooked with generosity have names of local relevance - grilled goat's cheese St. Patrick, for example, is a reminder that the saint once lived on Church Island off Skerries - plainly cooked food is also provided on request, and dishes suitable for vegetarians are marked on the menu. The dessert trolley is legendary - a large space should be left if pudding is to be part of your meal. An informative, fairly priced wine list includes a wide selection of house wines, and a good choice of half bottles - and the early dinner and Sunday lunch menus offer great value. **Seats 60** (private room,10). D Mon-Sat, 6.30-9.45; L Sun only, 12.30-4.30. Early D €30 (Mon-Fri, 6.30-7.30); Set D €36/40, Gourmet Menu €45. A la carte also available. 4 house wines €20; no sc. Children welcome. Closed D Sun. Restaurant only closed 24-27 Dec. **Accommodation:** 18 fine, comfortably furnished guest rooms have all the amenities normally expected of an hotel. While in the area, allow time to visit Skerries Mills (working windmills (Tel: 01 849 5208)) and the beautifully located Ardgillan Castle and Victorian Gardens (Tel: 01 849 2212) nearby, where there are tea rooms. Facilities for private parties (50). Gourmet Golf breaks - up to 40 golf courses within 20 minutes drive. Children under 4 free in parents' room (cots available free of charge). Pets permitted in certain areas. **Rooms 18** (all superior & no-smoking). B&B €60 pps, ss €15 (DB&B rate is good value at €90 pps). Accommodation open all year. Amex, Diners, MasterCard, Visa, Laser. **Directions:** Opposite AIB Bank in Skerries. ◇

Skerries
BAR/RESTAURANT

Stoop Your Head

Harbour Road Skerries Co Dublin
Tel: 01 849 2085 Fax: 01 849 1144

After a quiet off season drink a few doors along at Joe May's, there can be no greater pleasure in north Dublin than to slip into 'Stoops' for some of Andy Davies' mainly seafood cooking. 'Fresh, simple and wholesome' is how he describes his food, and who could want any more than that? If it's busy you may have to wait at the little bar - where you can opt to eat if you like, or have a look at the menu while waiting for a table (they seem to turn over fairly fast). The surroundings are simple - chunky wooden tables, closely packed - and the menu is not elaborate but there is plenty to choose from, and there are blackboard specials every day too; what could be more delightful than starters of dressed crab, or moules marinière - or perhaps a classic fresh prawn Marie Rose? Prawns - which means Dublin Bay prawns (langoustines) - are landed in Skerries and a speciality; and, like the crab claws, they are offered as starters or main courses, in irresistible garlic butter. You don't have to eat seafood here - there are other choices like Asian chicken salad, or pasta dishes or even fillet steak medallions - but it would be a pity to miss it. Super fresh and deliciously simple, it's a treat. Toilets wheelchair accessible. **Seats 50** (outdoor seating, 20). No reservations. Children welcome. L & D daily: L 12-3, D 5.30-9.30 (Sun D 4-8). House wine €17. Closed 25 Dec & Good Fri. MasterCard, Visa, Laser. **Directions:** On the harbour front in Skerries.

Stillorgan
RESTAURANT

Beaufield Mews Restaurant & Gardens

Woodlands Avenue Stillorgan Co Dublin
Tel: 01 288 0375 Fax: 01 288 6945
Email: beaumews@iol.ie Web: www.beaufieldmews.com

Dublin's oldest restaurant is located in a characterful 18th century coachhouse and stables - and, as the name implies, it is surrounded by beautiful mature gardens where guests can have an aperitif on the lawn before dinner, or take coffee afterwards, as the gardens are lit up by night. The effect in a built-up area is quite startling, as you are just a few hundred yards off one of Dublin's busiest roads and yet, with its mature trees, spacious surroundings and old-fashioned feeling in both the buildings and gardens, you could be forgiven for thinking you have been mysteriously transported to the country - there's even an antique shop where guests are encouraged to have a browse before dining (Open 3-9pm). This impression has been reinforced by recent changes - including the installation of a new 'Hayloft' bar and a new 'garden' look for the restaurant: atmosphere really is the trump card at this legendary restaurant and the cooking style and courteous service are in tune with the old-fashioned surroundings. A lovely outdoor patio area overlooking the gardens has recently been added too. Good wine list. Not suitable for children after 6.30pm. **Seats 200** (private room, 60; outdoor seating, 20). D Tue-Sat, 6.30-9.30; L Sun only, 12.30-2.30. Early D €20 (6.30-7.30); Set D €30.95; also à la carte. Closed Mon, bank hols, Good Fri. Amex, Diners, MasterCard, Visa, Laser. **Directions:** 4 miles from city centre, off Stillorgan dual carriageway. ◇

Stillorgan
RESTAURANT

China Sichuan Restaurant

4 Lower Kilmacud Road Stillorgan Co Dublin
Tel: 01 288 0882 Fax: 01 288 4817

Despite well-publicised plans to move to a new location in nearby Sandyford, this Dublin favourite is still in its original unprepossessing setting of a suburban shopping centre, cheek by jowl with a late night convenience store and buzzing even on weekday nights with fans of the authentic Chinese cuisine. With smiling welcomes and friendly accommodating service, the Hui family have been presiding over what many rate as the best Chinese restaurant in the country for over 20 years. Old favourites like the tea-smoked duck, sizzling and shredded dishes and three styles of dumpling are still there along with an impressive range of seafood which includes scallops, squid and cuttlefish. A mention of soft-shelled crabs enjoyed previously were promptly offered on a recent visit even though they weren't on the menu. Star dessert is the plate of toffee banana fritters, sent piping hot from the kitchen to the table, where the accomplished waiters deftly dip each toffee coated morsel into iced water and arrange the crisp fritter alongside vanilla ice cream. Brisk lunchtime business features a well-priced table d'hôte and fast service while the evening attracts a more leisured mix of regular diners, celebratory groups and a fair representation of suits entertaining out of towners. Well selected wine list with a good price range. Children welcome. **Seats 100** (outdoor, 20). Reservations required. Air conditioning. L Mon-Fri 12.30-2, L Sun 1-2.30. D daily 6-11. Set L €16 (Sun €17), Set D €36; à la carte available; house wine €20; SC10%. Closed L Sat, 25-27 Dec & Good Fri. Amex, MasterCard, Visa, Laser. **Directions:** Above shops on Kilmacud Road.

Stillorgan

Stillorgan Park Hotel

HOTEL

Stillorgan Road Stillorgan Co Dublin **Tel: 01 200 1800** Fax: 01 283 1610
Email: sales@stillorganpark.com Web: www.stillorganpark.com

This fine hotel on the Stillorgan dual carriageway is a sister establishment to the famous Talbot Hotel in Wexford; great improvements have been made in recent years and it is furnished in a lively modern style throughout. Public areas include the stylish reception and lounge areas, and bedrooms - some with views of Dublin Bay - are spacious, attractively decorated in a bright contemporary tone, with well-finished bathrooms. Ample free parking is an attraction and good facilities for business guests include work space and fax/modem lines in rooms. Conference/banqueting (500/400); business centre, secretarial services. Children welcome (under 4 free in parents' room, cots available without charge). **Rooms 125** (4 suites, 121 executive rooms, 50 no-smoking, 4 for disabled) Lift. B&B from €65 pps, ss €44. No SC. **The Purple Sage Restaurant**: An attractive, informal restaurant with seating in several areas, and welcoming staff. Menus are appealing in a fairly contemporary style - grilled seabass with citrus fruits, saffron potatoes & baby fennel is typical. Imaginative vegetarian cooking has always been a feature and the hotel regularly runs special themed dining weeks, including one when 'healthy options' are highlighted on the menu. Children welcome. **Seats 146.** Reservations unnecessary. Air conditioning. Toilets wheelchair accessible. L & D daily, 12-2 & 5.45-9.30. Set L €27.95, Set Sun L €25; Early D €27.95 5.45-7.30, Set D €36.50; à la carte D also available; house wine €19; no SC. Amex, Diners, MasterCard, Visa, Laser. **Directions:** Situated on main N11 dual carriageway.

Swords

Roganstown Golf & Country Club Hotel

Ⓔ HOTEL/RESTAURANT

The Naul Road Swords Co Dublin
Tel: 01 843 3118 Fax: 01 843 3303
Email: info@roganstown.com Web: www.roganstown.com

Built around the original Roganstown House and situated conveniently for all the many golf courses in the area and only a few minutes' drive from Dublin Airport, this recently opened hotel enjoys a country setting and is the only golf hotel in the area also offering gym / leisure facilities and beauty therapies - a great amenity for local residents as well as an appealing base for golfers or those using the airport. The Christy O'Connor Junior designed course ('a masterpiece of skill and tactical design') is a major attraction, but the restaurant, McLoughlins, is also attracting favourable attention - add a high level of comfort and something of a country house ambience and it's easy to see why this new hotel is already making a mark. Business and conference facilities available. Conferences/banqueting (300/250), business centre, free Broadband WI/FI. Children welcome (cots avail free of charge, baby sitting arranged). Golf (18), leisure centre with 'pool, spa, beauty salon. **Rooms 52** (3 shower only, 16 executive, 1 junior suite, 43 no smoking, 20 groundfloor, 3 for disabled); Room service limited hours; Lift. B&B €85-137.50 pps, ss €40. Midweek specials offered. Closed 24-26 Dec. Helipad.Amex, Diners, MasterCard, Visa, Laser. **Directions:** Take Ashbourne road from Swords village, take right turn for Naul, 500m on the left. ◇

COUNTY CARLOW

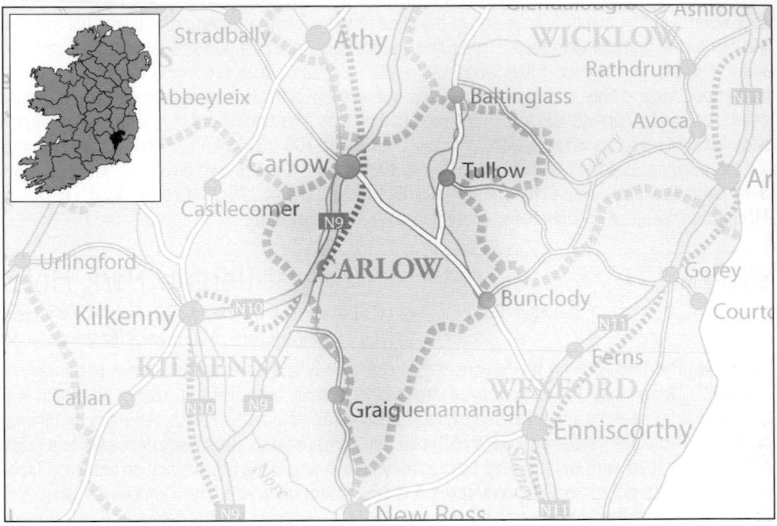

Carlow's character and charm is within easy reach of Dublin, yet the metropolitan commuter spread seems only to touch its northern fringes Although it is Ireland's second smallest county, it confidently incorporates such wonderful varieties of scenery that it has been memorably commented that the Creator was in fine form when He made Carlow. Whether you're lingering along the gentle meanderings of the waterway of the River Barrow, or enjoying the upper valley of the River Slaney while savouring the soaring outlines of the Blackstairs Mountains as they sweep upwards to the 793 m peak of Mount Leinster, this gallant little area will soon have you in thrall.

There's history a-plenty if you wish to seek it out. But for those who prefer to live in the present, the county town of Carlow itself fairly buzzes with student life and the energetic trade of a market centre which is also home to a micro-brewery that, among other admirable products, is the source of the award-winning O'Hara's Stout. A more leisurely pace can be enjoyed at riverside villages such as Leighlinbridge and Bagenalstown. Leighlinbridge - pronounced "Lochlinbridge" – has for many years been Carlow's most community-conscious riverside village, the holder of a Tidy Towns Gold Medal. There are also welcome improvements taking place to fulfill Bagenalstown's potential as a proper miniature river port, while the hidden hillside village of Borris is an enchantment in itself.

Local Attractions and Information

Carlow, Eigse – Arts Festival (June) 059 914 0491
Carlow town, Tourist Information 059 913 1554
Carlow county, Carlow Rural Tourism .... 059 913 0411 / 913 0446
Carlow, Craft Brewery Micro-brewery 059 913 4356
Tullow, Altamont Gardens 059 915 9444

Bagenalstown
COUNTRY HOUSE

Kilgraney House

Borris Road Bagenalstown Co Carlow
Tel: 059 977 5283 Fax: 059 977 5595
Email: info@kilgraneyhouse.com Web: www.kilgraneyhouse.com

In a lovely site overlooking the Barrow Valley, Bryan Leech and Martin Marley's charming late Georgian house - which (encouragingly) takes its name from the Irish 'cill greíne', meaning 'sunny hill or wood' - is set in extensive wooded grounds that feature, amongst many other delights, a croquet lawn and fine cut-stone outbuildings. It is a serene and restful place with beautiful walks, and Altamont gardens nearby; Bryan and Martin have a great love of gardens - a recent project has been the development of their monastic herb gardens, and the kitchen garden provides plenty of good things for Bryan to transform into delicious dinners. His cooking style is creative and contemporary, making full use of local and artisan produce, including Lavistown cheese from nearby Kilkenny. Six-course menus begin with an amuse bouche (crab & cucumber roll with soy & lime dressing, perhaps) and, although there are various influences at work, there's a leaning towards Japan, notably in specialities like their own home-smoked duck (with noodle salad and soy & mirin dressing, perhaps) and a very beautiful dish of wild Slaney salmon wrapped in nori and wasabi. You'll also find flavours closer to home, of course, in dishes like smoked loin of Callan bacon with cider sauce, and your breakfast next morning will showcase local foods, including cheeses, more traditionally. But it is for the sheer sense of style pervading the house that it is most famous - Bryan and Martin's enjoyment in its restoration and furnishing is abundantly clear: elegant, yes, but with a great sense of fun too. Dinner can be shared with other guests at a communal table, or served at separate tables; a short, informative wine list is chosen with care - and non-residents are welcome by reservation. An aroma spa offers a range of therapies and massages, for both men and women, including pregnancy treatments. Self-catering accommodation is also available, in two courtyard suites, the gate lodge and a recently restored cottage. Herbal treatment room (massage & aromatherapy). Small conferences. Not suitable for children under 12. **Rooms 8** (2 suites, 3 shower only, 1 ground floor, all no smoking). No pets. B&B €85, ss about €35. D (non-residents welcome by reservation), 8 pm. Set 6-course D, €48-50. (Vegetarian meals or other special dietary requirements on request.) Wines from about €20. Closed Mon-Tue and mid Nov-Feb. Helipad. Amex, MasterCard, Visa, Laser. **Directions:** Just off the R705, halfway between Bagenalstown and Borris.

Bagenalstown

Ⓔ COUNTRY HOUSE

Lorum Old Rectory

Kilgraney Bagenalstown Co Carlow

Tel: 059 977 5282 Fax: 059 977 5455

Email: enquiry@lorum.com Web: www.lorum.com

Bobbie Smith's mid Victorian cut stone granite rectory was built for the Rev. William Smyth-King in 1864, and it now makes a warm and welcoming family home. Elegant and homely, there's a library as well as a lovely drawing room where guests can gather around the fire and relax; spacious accommodation includes one particularly impressive guest room with a four-poster- and all rooms are very comfortable, with big beds, phones and tea/coffee trays. But it is Bobbie Smith's easy hospitality that keeps bringing guests back: Bobbie, who is a member of the international chefs' association, Euro-Toques, is committed to using local produce and suppliers whenever possible and is renowned for delicious home cooking using mainly organic and home grown ingredients; rack of local lamb is a speciality, cooked with a honey, mustard & rosemary glaze, and residents have dinner at a long mahogany table, where wonderful breakfasts are also served. This relaxed place was the guide's Pet Friendly Establishment for 2000 and guests are still welcome to bring their own dogs, by arrangement. This area make as an ideal base for exploring the lush south-east of Ireland, and is close to many places of interest, including medieval Kilkenny, Altamont Gardens, New Ross (where river cruises are available, and you can see the famine ship Dunbrody), Kildare's National Stud and Japanese Gardens. Also close by is Gowran Park racecourse and activities such as golf and a riding school (offering both outdoor and indoor tuition). Dinner must be booked by 3 pm; a concise, well priced wine list with tasting notes is offered. Private parties/small conferences (10). Cycling. Own parking. Garden. Not suitable for children under 10 years. **Rooms 5** (all en-suite, all shower only and no smoking). B&B from €75 pps, ss €20. Dinner for residents by arrangement(8pm) €45. Closed Dec/Jan/Feb. Amex, MasterCard, Visa, Laser. **Directions:** Midway between Borris & Bagenalstown on the R705.

Ballon

HOTEL/RESTAURANT

Ballykealey Manor Hotel

Ballon Co Carlow **Tel: 059 915 9288** Fax: 059 915 9297

Email: ballykealeymanor@eircom.net Web: www.ballykealeymanorhotel.com

Seat of the Lecky family for three centuries, the present house was designed by Thomas A Cobden (designer of Carlow cathedral) and built in the 1830s as a wedding present. Gothic arches and Tudor chimney stacks take you back to the architectural oddities of the time, but the house is set in well-maintained grounds and promising first impressions are well founded. The property moved into energetic new hands in 2003 and the owners, Edward and Karen Egan, have completely refurbished the hotel with considerable style, and improvements continue on an ongoing basis. Bold decorative touches in the entrance hall set a confident tone that is carried through into spacious reception rooms which are furnished in a pleasingly elegant mixture of contemporary style and period features, combining comfort with a friendly atmosphere. Individually designed bedrooms, which are very pleasing to the eye, are luxuriously furnished decorated in keeping with the character of the house and have all the expected amenities, including direct-dial phones and multi-channel TV. *A further 30 rooms are under construction at the time of going to press. Conferences/banqueting (20-250). Wheelchair access; children welcome (under 6 free in parents' room, cot available without charge).

Pets by arrangement. **Rooms 12** (1 junior suite, 4 shower only, 2 non-smoking). B&B about €70pps, ss about €20; no SC. Closed 24 Dec. **Seats 32** (private room 32). D daily, 7-9.30; L Sun only 12.30-3.30. D A la carte, Set Sun L €25.50. House wines €18. A la carte bar menu available 12.30-9.30. Closed 24 Dec. MasterCard, Visa, Laser. **Directions:** 10 miles from Carlow on the N80. ◇

Ballon
RESTAURANT

The Forge Restaurant

Kilbride Cross Ballon Co Carlow
Tel: 059 915 9939 Email: theforgekilbride@eircom.net

Jordan's unpretentious daytime restaurant. Off the road but handy to it and with ample parking at the back, the granite building dates back to the 1700s and it makes a great place to break a journey, or for a wholesome bite before or after walking or visiting local attractions such as nearby Altamont Gardens. Mary takes pride in sourcing ingredients from local suppliers and her menus offer just the kind of food everybody loves on a day out - home-made vegetable soup with soda bread scones, ploughman's sandwiches and comforting hot lunch time favourites like baked ham, roast beef or lamb, and freshly made lasagne. Outside lunch service times you can always get simple treats like fresh scones with home-made jam for morning coffee or after noon teas - and they have a tourist information point as well as local art and craft work for sale. Walkers welcome and packed meals supplied on request. All round, a great little place for a break. Wheelchair friendly. Children welcome. Parking. **Seats 45** (outdoor, 30, private room, 120. Open 9.30-5 daily (Sun to 3.30), L 12.45-2.30 (Sun to 3.30). Late opening by arrangement; Set 3 course L €15.95, set Sun L €18.30, also A la carte. House wine €17.95 (€4.50 per glass). Closed 10 days at Christmas. MasterCard, Visa, Laser. **Directions:** Off the N80, between Ballon and Bunclody.

Ballon
€ COUNTRY HOUSE

Sherwood Park House

Kilbride Ballon Co Carlow **Tel: 059 915 9117** Fax: 059 915 9355
Email: info@sherwoodparkhouse.ie Web: www.sherwoodparkhouse.ie

Built around 1700 by a Mr Arthur Baillie, this delightful Georgian farmhouse has sweeping views over the countryside and is next to the famous Altamont Gardens. Patrick and Maureen Owens, who have welcomed guests here since 1991, accurately describe it as "an accessible country retreat for anyone who enjoys candlelit dinners, brass and canopy beds, and the relaxing experience of eating out while staying in". Spacious accommodation is furnished in period style and thoughtful in the details that count - and Maureen takes pride in offering guests real home cooking based on the best of local produce, including "best locally produced Carlow beef and lamb, from Ballon Meats" and fish from Kilmore Quay. There's a lovely garden, Altamont Gardens are on the doorstep (just 5 minutes away on foot) and it's a good area for walking - and fishing the Slaney. Dinner is served at 8pm and is mainly for residents, although non-residents are welcome when there is room - and guests are welcome to bring their own wine and any other drinks. (Please give advance notice if you would like dinner.) Children welcome (no cot available). Pets permitted by arrangement. Garden. D €35 (BYO wine); non-residents welcome by reservation. **Rooms 5** (all en-suite & no smoking). B&B €50 pps, ss €10. Amex, MasterCard, Visa. **Directions:** Signed from the junction of the N80 and N81.

Borris
N ATMOSPHERIC PUB

M O'Shea

M O'Shea Borris Co Carlow **Tel: 059 977 3106**

Halfway up the steep main street of Borris, this unspoilt old-world grocery-pub is well worth a visit. The old grocery section at the front links into a modern-day shop next door - a very practical arrangement that brings past and present together in a delightful way. Conversions and extensions towards the back allow for several larger rooms, where food can be served or music sessions held, and there's a paved area at the back for fine weather. Absolutely charming. Sandwiches, weekday lunches available. Music every fortnight or so: "it's a bit random". Closed 25 Dec & Good Fri. **Directions:** Middle of Borris. ◇

Borris
€ HOTEL

The Step House

66 Main Street Borris Co Carlow **Tel: 059 977 3209** Fax: 059 977 3395
Email: cait@thestephouse.com Web: www.thestephouse.com

Stylishly decorated and furnished in period style, with antiques throughout, James and Cait Coady's attractive old house has well-proportioned reception rooms including a fine dining room (used for breakfast) and a matching drawing room that overlooks the back garden. Comfortable, elegant bedrooms include one with a four-poster and all are furnished to a high standard with smart shower rooms, TV and tea/coffee facilities. The renovation and upgrading of this fine old house has been accomplished beautifully, including the conversion of the whole of the lower ground floor to make a magnificent kitchen of character, and a relaxed living room area with direct access to the garden - and a sunny decking area beside the dining room allows guests to enjoy breakfast outdoors on fine mornings. *At the time of going to press, The Coadys (who also own one of Ireland's finest classic pubs, Tynans Bridge Bar, in Kilkenny city) are developing a hotel and restaurant, due for completion in time for the 2007 season; meanwhile, The Step House will continue as before and guest accommodation is also available in a number of self-catering houses and apartments, used for short term letting, or B&B. NB: there are several flights of stairs, including steps up to the front door. Not suitable for children. Pets permitted by arrangement. Fishing, walking, garden. **Rooms 20** (2 suites, 2 family rooms, all no-smoking). B&B about €45pps, ss10. Closed 25 Dec. MasterCard, Visa, Laser. **Directions:** From main Carlow-Kilkenny road, take turning to Bagenalstown. 16km (8 miles) to Borris.

Carlow

€ GUESTHOUSE

Barrowville Townhouse

Kilkenny Road Carlow Co Carlow
Tel: 059 914 3324 Fax: 059 914 1953
Email: barrowvilletownhouse@eircom.net Web: www.barrowvillehouse.com

féile bia Dermot and Anna Smyth's exceptionally comfortable guesthouse is just a few minutes walk from the town centre. It is fine period house, set in lovely gardens and there is also a particularly pleasant and comfortable residents' drawing room, with an open fire and plenty to read. The house is immaculately maintained and bedrooms - which inevitably vary in size and character due to the age of the building - are comfortable and stylishly furnished with a mixture of antiques and fitted furniture, as well as direct dial phones, tea/coffee trays and television, and thoughtfully designed, well-finished bathrooms. Breakfast is served in a handsome conservatory (complete with a large vine) overlooking the peaceful back garden. Garden. Private parking (10). Not suitable for children. No pets. **Rooms 7** (1 shower only, all no-smoking). B&B €55pps, ss €20. Closed 24-26 Dec. Amex, MasterCard, Visa. **Directions:** South side of Carlow town on the N9.

Carlow

E RESTAURANT

The Beams Restaurant

59 Dublin Street Carlow Co Carlow
Tel: 059 913 1824 Email: the.beams@ireland.com

Originally a coaching inn, this characterful building was restored by Betty and the late Peter O'Gorman, who opened it as a restaurant in 1986. Massive wooden beams are a reminder of the building's long history (it has held a full licence since 1760) and it retains a quaint charm that is carried through to the bar - where aperitifs and menus are promptly offered - and a general sense of old-world hospitality. This charming restaurant is now open only for dinner on Saturday but it is well worth bearing in mind: classic French cuisine is the speciality of French chef Romain Chall, who has been at The Beams since it opened and was deservedly described by Peter O'Gorman as a "master craftsman". Not surprisingly - as they have their own wine shop to draw on - the wine list is a special feature. **Seats 40.** Only open Sat to 10 pm (or will open for private parties during the week); Set D €40, also à la carte; service discretionary. Closed Christmas week (from 24 Dec). Amex, MasterCard, Visa, Laser. **Directions:** Town centre, on main street - entrance under an archway beside Beams wine shop. ◇

Carlow

ATMOSPHERIC PUB

Lennon's Café Bar

121 Tullow Street Carlow Co Carlow **Tel: 059 913 1575**
Fax: 059 913 1579 Email: lennonscafebar@eircom.net

féile bia Sinéad Byrne runs this attractive modern café-bar with her husband, Liam, and their stylish contemporary design and deliciously healthy, reasonably priced food has clearly been a hit with both locals and visitors to the town. In a manner reminiscent of that great Kerry speciality, the pub that gradually develops into a restaurant at the back without actually having a dedicated restaurant area, the design of the bar - which has a striking metal spiral staircase at the back - helps the atmosphere to shift into café gear as you move through it. Simple, uncluttered tables and speedy service of jugs of iced water bode well for menus that include a host of wholesome dishes: home-made soups; open sandwiches (on freshly-baked home-made bread); ciabattas, wraps, some very tempting salads (fresh salmon with home-made fresh herb mayo perhaps) and a range of hot specials like steak & kidney pie topped with pastry & served with champ, or cod & mussel bake. Dishes suitable for vegetarians are highlighted, gluten free bread is available for coeliacs and everything is really wholesome and freshly made to order from top quality ingredients (some local sources are named on the menu).

Home-made desserts too - hazelnut meringue roulade with raspberry sauce, perhaps, or hot apple crumble. This is well-balanced good home cooking and was a worthy winner of our Happy Heart Eat Out Award for 2003. Children welcome; Toilets wheelchair accessible. Breakfast Mon-Sat 9.30-11; L Mon-Fri,12-3pm, Sat 12-4pm; D Thu-Fri 5.30-9pm a la carte menu.Closed 25 Dec, Good Fri. MasterCard, Visa, Laser. **Directions:** At Junction of Tullow Street & Potato Market.

Clonegal
N ☆RESTAURANT

Sha-Roe Bistro

Main Street Clonegal Co Carlow
Tel: 053 937 5636 Email: sha-roebistro@hotmail.com

NEWCOMER OF THE YEAR

Away from the main road to anywhere, the delightfully pretty and well-preserved village of Clonegal on the borders of Wexford and Carlow is now home to one of our best young chefs. Even in a village with many exceptionally lovely houses (next door is a traditional pub which is equally perfect) this beautifully maintained 18th century building stands out - and former head chef at Marlfield House, Henry Stone, and his partner Stephanie Barrillier's small but beautifully appointed restaurant promises a dining experience well worth a detour. Although they have already earned a following from a wide area, the exceptional quality of Henry's beautifully presented food will be a delightful surprise to those who are not already aware of this chef's gifts. A lovely sitting room acts as reception area and simple décor throughout - warm cream walls, pale wooden floors, plain darkwood tables, comfortable chairs, the warm glow of night lights - provides a pleasing backdrop for rather good paintings, which are for sale. Original features are intact, including a huge open stone fireplace now with a wood burning stove installed which is the focal point in one room, and, by contrast, a pretty courtyard provides a retreat for smokers, or for dining in fine weather. Good management is evident from the moment of arrival - behind the warm welcome lies a professional efficiency that allows guests to relax and feel confident that everything will run smoothly. Menus based on seasonal foods might begin with lightly-seared scallops on a pea purée accompanied by a delicately flavoured pea soup with smoked bacon, or a smoked duck breast spring roll with crisp vegetables, guacamole and a lightly-cooked plum. Of the main courses (accompanied by platters of freshly cooked vegetables), beef - matured for seven weeks - is a delight, simply served with mushrooms and pearl onions, perhaps, or there might be a gorgeously tender rump of lamb with courgettes, aubergine, pepper and roasted tomatoes. A fillet of monkfish may be offered with summery asparagus and cherry tomato, or vegetarians might enjoy an organic sweetcorn risotto with baby spinach. Desserts, many featuring seasonal fruits, are tempting: blueberry crème brulée with butter biscuit; a gratin of late summer berries with a shot of homemade elderflower lemonade; or a rich chocolate marquise with superbly delicate vanilla ice cream and an orange reduction are all typical. Or you may want to try the local cheese plate: mature Edam from Carlow, St Killian from Wexford and goats milk Camembert from Co Kilkenny, served with rhubarb chutney and homemade crackers. A short but well chosen wine list includes a good fairly-priced house selection (at about €19) as well as a number of wines and dessert wines by the glass. This is a serious kitchen producing faultless cooking, and offers superb value for the quality of food and service. Space is limited so reservations are essential especially in summer.* After Sunday lunch, a visit to historical Huntington Castle (just around the corner from Sha-Roe) might be recommended. Not suitable for children after 8pm. **Seats 24.** D Wed-Sat, 6.30-9.30, a la carte; L Sun only, 12.30-3.30, set Sun L €28.50; house wine €19.50. Closed Sun D, Mon, Tue and Jan. MasterCard, Visa, Laser. **Directions:** Off N80 Enniscorthy-Carlow road, 8 km from Bunclody, on Main St.

Leighlinbridge
HOTEL/BAR/RESTAURANT

The Lord Bagenal Inn

Main Street Leighlinbridge Co Carlow
Tel: 059 972 1668 Fax: 059 972 2629
Email: info@lordbagenal.com Web: www.lordbagenal.com

The Lord Bagenal is beautifully situated on the River Barrow and it's a useful place to break a journey or make your base for exploring this fascinating area - there's a very pleasant riverside walk nearby and a fine harbour and marina right beside the inn. Although now more of an hotel than the pub that is fondly remembered by many regular patrons, proprietors James and Mary Kehoe have taken care to retain some of the best features of the old building - notably the old end bar, with its open fire and comfortably traditional air, and the restaurant section beside it - while incorporating new ideas. (A novel - and highly practical one - is a supervised indoor playroom, which is in the bar but behind glass so that, in time-honoured fashion, offspring can be seen and not heard). Bar meals include a lunchtime carvery/buffet, but it is the evening restaurant that draws diners from a wide area and, and fortunately there is no need to travel far after dinner, as the spacious new bedrooms are just a few yards away: comfortably furnished in a neutral "hotel" style with phones, TV and tea/coffee facilities. *A new development, including 27 rooms and conference rooms, is under construction at the time of going to press. Golf & equestrian nearby; fishing boats for hire. Marina (30 berths). Conferences/ banqueting (300/350). Garden, fishing, walking. Children welcome; playroom. No pets. **Rooms 39** (all en-suite, 1 for disabled). B&B from €65 pps, ss €45.* Special breaks offered. **Restaurant:** A new restaurant is to be included in the redevelopment, but the existing one is appealingly set up with polished tables, crisp linen napkins, fresh flowers and candles and - as elsewhere in the Lord Bagenal - the owners' collection of Irish art casts its spell and, helped buy good lighting, open fires and classic music, the atmosphere is very relaxed. Well-balanced menus offer plenty of choice; the style is eclectic, based on well-sourced produce including Dunmore East seafood and local farmhouse cheeses. Allow time to browse through James Keogh's famed wine list; this labour of love runs to 60 pages, with excellent tasting notes, and offers very good value. Restaurant D only 6-10; Set D from €27.50, also à la carte. House wine €18. Bar food 12-10 daily. Closed 25 Dec. Amex, Diners, MasterCard, Visa, Laser. **Directions:** Just off the main N9 Dublin/Waterford Road in Leighlinbridge. 12km (8 m) Carlow/32 km (20 m) Kilkenny.

Leighlinbridge
CAFÉ

Mulberry's Restaurant

Arboretum Garden Centre Kilkenny Road Leighlinbridge Co Carlow
Tel: 059 972 1558 Fax: 059 972 1642
Email: arboretum@eircom.net Web: www.arboretum.ie

This pleasant self-service restaurant is in the main hall of the garden centre at the Arboretum, and offers an attractive selection of wholesome, freshly-prepared food. Tables are simply set up, but every second table has fresh flowers; in addition to a blackboard menu, a self-service counter presents an appetising display of salads and quick-serve dishes - everything is fresh and home-made with good ingredients, and there's a nice flair in the desserts (banoffi pie is a house speciality). Not really a wine place, but there's wine by the glass from the fridge, and a few quarter bottles, also fruit drinks (including apple juice) and minerals. A good place to break a journey, as there's a pleasant ambience and a browse around is relaxing. Ample parking (150). Wheelchair friendly. Children welcome. Wine licence. Open 9-5 Mon-Sat, Sun 11-5. Closed 25 Dec & 1 Jan. Amex, Diners, MasterCard, Visa, Laser. **Directions:** From Carlow, take N9 towards Leighlinbridge. ◇

St Mullins
B&B

Mulvarra House

St Mullins Graiguenamanagh Co Carlow
Tel: 051 424 936 Fax: 051 424 969
Email: info@mulvarra.com Web: www.mulvarra.com

Harold and Noreen Ardill's friendly and well-maintained modern house is in a stunning location overlooking the River Barrow above the ancient and picturesque little harbour of St Mullins and, although it may seem unremarkable from the road, this relaxing place is full of surprises. Comfortably furnished bedrooms have balconies to take full advantage of views of the romantic Barrow Valley, for example, and, not only is there the luxury of (limited) room service, but even a range of treatments (massage, mud wraps, refresher facials) to help guests unwind from the stresses of everyday life and make the most of this magical place. Noreen - a keen self-taught cook - prepares dinners for residents to enjoy in the dining room which also overlooks the river: quality produce, much of it local, is used in home-made soups, seafood paté, fresh Barrow salmon, stuffed loin of pork and Baileys bread & butter pudding, all of which are favourites, although menus are varied to suit guests' preferences. Genuinely hospitable and reasonably priced, this is a tranquil place where the hosts want their guests to relax and make the most of every moment. Special breaks available (eg 2 nights B&B, 1D & 2 treatments, from about €165 pps). Walking; fishing; treatments/mini spa (must be pre-booked). Pets permitted by arrangement. Garden. Children welcome (under 3s free in parents' room; cot available without charge; baby sitting arranged). Room service (limited hours). **Rooms 5** (all en-suite & no-smoking, 1 family room). B&B €40, ss €6. Residents D nightly, €30 (7.30pm, by reservation). House wine €20. Closed Mid Dec-Mid Jan. MasterCard, Visa, Laser. **Directions:** 7km (4.5 m) from Graiguenamanagh; take R702 from Borris, turn right in Glynn; signposted from Glynn.

Tullow
HOTEL

Mount Wolseley Hilton Hotel

Tullow Co Carlow **Tel: 059 915 1674**
Fax: 059 915 2123 Web: www.mountwolseley.ie

This new hotel attached to the Christy O'Connor designed championship course presents an immaculate exterior, a good impression immediately reinforced by friendly, helpful staff who set a welcoming tone that is noticeable throughout the hotel. Accommodation has been completed to four star standard and the food standard in the restaurant is much higher than is usual in hotels: a comfortable, airy dining room and smartly appointed tables with crisp white linen and fresh flowers provide an appropriate background for imaginative contemporary cooking backed up by helpful, well-informed service, and the set dinner menus offer very good value. There's plenty to do both in the area and on site, including spa pampering. Golf. Spa. **Rooms 142.** Lift. Open all year except Christmas. ◇

Tullow

CAFÉ

Rathwood

Rath Tullow Co Carlow **Tel: 059 915 6285** Fax: 059 915 6239
Email: info@rathwood.com Web: www.rathwood.com

This award-winning garden centre and shopping emporium near Tullow is a good place for a journey break (or even a day out) as, in addition to an exceptionally wide range of quality goods for garden and home (including classy gift items), there is good wholesome food available all day. Going well beyond what might be expected in a garden centre café, an extensive deli menu is offered, using all fresh local Irish produce in, for example, an open sandwich of roast chicken on home-made brown bread. And there are a more substantial meals too: Atlantic salmon with baby spinach & wild rocket is a speciality, and there are lovey home-made deserts including a moreish lemon mousse cake - a useful place to know about. Country walks. Outdoor play area. Open 7 days: Mon-Sat 9.30am-6pm (including bank hols); Sun 12-6; L daily 12.30-2.30 (to 3 Sun). MasterCard, Visa, Laser. **Directions:** Just over an hour from Dublin, off Blessington-Tullow road - well signed in the area.

COUNTY CAVAN

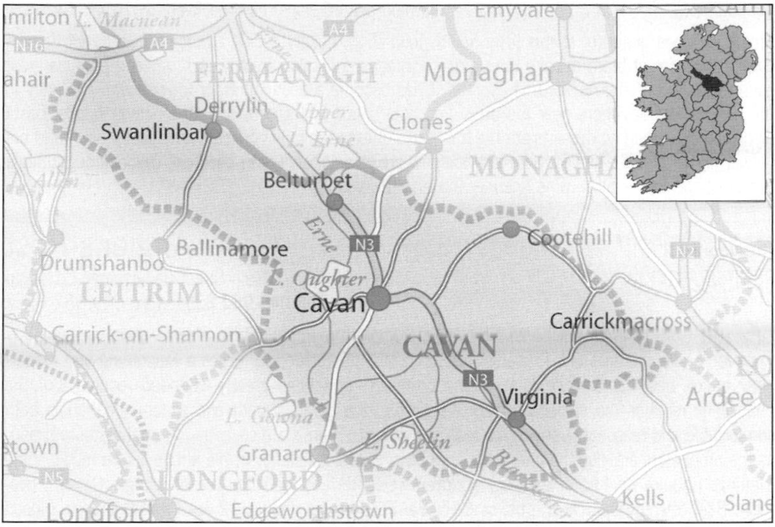

Cavan is one of Ireland's most watery counties. This is classic drumlin country, interwoven with more lakes than they know what to do with. But the very fact that the meandering waterways dictate the way of the roads means that much of Cavan is hidden. In today's intrusive world, this is a virtue. It is a place best discovered by the discerning visitor. Much of it has quiet and utterly rural charm, seemingly remote. But it isn't so very far from Belfast or Dublin, and modern Cavan is noted for an economic vibrancy and entrepreneurial flair typical of modern Ireland.

Yet if you take your time wandering through this green and silver land - particularly if travelling at the leisurely pace of the deservedly renowned Shannon-Erne Waterway which has joined Ireland's two greatest lake and river systems - then you'll become aware that this is a place of rewardingly gentle pleasures. And you'll have time to discover that it does have its own mountain, or at least it shares the 667 m peak of Cuilcagh with neighbouring Fermanagh. No ordinary mountain, this - it has underground streams which eventually become the headwaters of the lordly River Shannon.

In fact, Cavan is much more extensive than is popularly imagined, for in the northeast it has Shercock with its own miniature lake district, while in its southeast it takes in all of Lough Ramor at the charming lakeside village of Virginia. It also shares Lough Sheelin, that place of legend for the angler, with Westmeath and Meath, while in the far northwest its rugged scenery hints at Donegal. And always throughout its drumlin heartlands you can find many little Cavan lakes which, should the fancy take you, can be called your own at least for the day that's in it.

Local Attractions and Information

Bailieboro, Tourism Information	042 966 6666
Ballyjamesduff, Cavan County Museum	049 854 4070
Ballyjamesduff, International Pork Festival (June)	049 854 4242
Belturbet, Tourist Office	049 952 2044
Cavan town, Cavan Crystal	049 433 1800
Cavan town, Tourist Information	049 433 1942
Cootehill, Maudabawn Cultural Centre	049 555 9504
Killykeen, Equestrian Centre	049 436 1707
Mullagh, Lakeview Gardens	046 42480
Shannon-Erne Waterway (Ballinamore-Ballyconnell)	078 45124

Bailieborough
CAFÉ

Planet Earth Café

Lower Main Street Bailieborough Co Cavan **Tel: 042 966 5490**
Email: diane@planet-earth.ie Web: www.planet-earth.ie

Small is indeed beautiful at this little health food shop, bakery & café , which is run by an English couple, who rise at 5 am to bake their range of breads and cakes freshly each day and produce great gourmet foods on site. As word has spread it has become a destination for foodies who are likely to find themselves anywhere near the area. Foccacia bread is a speciality and delicious salads, pasta dishes and outstanding desserts are the hallmarks of exceptionally honest, flavoursome food - and not only is Fairtrade coffee served, but Fairtrade gifts are on sale too. Lucky people of Bailieborough! **Seats 21;** open Tue-Sat, 9-5pm, wine licence. Closed Sun, Mon. ◇

Ballyconnell
RESTAURANT/PUB

Angler's Rest

Main Street Ballyconnell Co Cavan
Tel: 049 952 6391 Fax: 049 952 6777

Golf, fishing, walking and cycling are among the pursuits that attract visitors to this lovely lakeland area and Francis McGoldrick's characterful pub makes a welcoming and moderately priced base for a relaxing stay. The premises have been greatly extended recently but the philosophy remains the same: staff are hospitable, the bar has spirit and accommodation is both comfortable and reasonably priced - a real inn, in fact. There's a pleasantly informal restaurant and, as the proprietors are also the chefs, you can be sure of consistency in the kitchen. Live music some evenings (inquire for further details.) Children welcome; cot available free of charge. Garden; pool table. B&B offered, about €35 pps, ss €15. Bar Food served daily, L 12.30-3 pm, D 6-9pm. Closed 25 Dec & Good Fri. Mastercard, Visa. **Directions:** On N3, main street in Ballyconnell village. ◇

Ballyconnell
RESTAURANT

Pól O'D Restaurant

Main Street Ballyconnell Co Cavan
Tel: 049 952 6228 Email: polod@oceanfree.net

Owner-chef Paul O'Dowd's cottagey little restaurant consists of two small rooms on two floors with the country character of stripped pine, old brick and stonework - all of which suit its daytime persona. But Paul's talents really come into play at dinner time, when he presents imaginative contemporary menus - typically a warm smoked duck salad with quails eggs, main courses like medley of seafood with prawn & lemon sauce, and an accomplished dessert selection - all cooked with a flair and confidence. Old favourites too, like good steaks, lamb and crispy duck. A new dining room upstairs, with simple white table linen and candlelight, has added a pleasing space and comfort. Reasonable prices together with consistently good cooking and friendly, helpful service under the direction of Geraldine O'Dowd make this a great asset to the area. Children welcome. Wheelchair accessible. **Seats 50.** Open Wed-Sat 6-9.30; Thu-Sat. Set D about €35, early menu €25 (5-6.30), set D €35/39.50 2/3 courses, also à la carte; house wine €19. Bookings strongly recommended. Closed Sun - Tue. Amex, MasterCard, Visa, Laser. **Directions:** On main street of Ballyconnell village.

Ballyconnell
HOTEL

Slieve Russell Hotel & Country Club

Ballyconnell Co Cavan **Tel: 049 952 6444** Fax: 049 952 6046
Email: slieve-russell@quinn-hotels.com Web: www.quinn-hotels.com

Close to the attractive town of Ballyconnell, this striking flagship of the Sean Quinn Group is named after a nearby mountain and set amongst 300 acres of landscaped gardens and grounds, including 50 acres of lakes. Everything is on a generous scale - and it's very much the social and business centre of the area. In the foyer, seating areas are arranged around the marble colonnades and a grand central staircase, flanked by a large bar on one side and two restaurants at the other. All bedrooms have pleasant country views, extra large beds and spacious marble bathrooms as well as the usual amenities (direct dial, phone tea/coffee tray, TV, trouser press). Recent developments, include the addition of 60 superior rooms and two presidential suites, plus a new conference centre, and Ciúin Spa & Wellness Centre. The hotel's Conall Cearnach Restaurant is quite traditional - the newer contemporary restaurant, Setanta, offers a less formal atmosphere and a continental/Asian style menu. Outstanding leisure facilities include the Golf and Country Club - the championship golf course is one of Ireland's top golfing venues and there's a putting green, practice area and nine hole, par 3 course. Off-season value breaks. Children under 3 free in parents' room, cot available free of charge; crèche, playroom; baby sitting arranged. Conference/banqueting (1500/625). Leisure centre; swimming pool. Golf (18/9), tennis, snooker, garden. Spa/treatment centre; hairdresser. Shop. Garden. No pets. **Rooms 219** (22 suites, incl 2 presidential, 6 executive; 146 executive rooms; 2 for disabled). Lift. 24-hr room service; turn-down service. B&B from €140 pps, single €140. Helipad. Open all year. Amex, Diners, MasterCard, Visa, Laser. **Directions:** Take N3 from Dublin to Cavan, proceed to Belturbet then Ballyconnell. ◇

Belturbet
RESTAURANT/GUESTHOUSE

International Fishing Centre

Loughdooley Belturbet Co Cavan
Tel: 049 952 2616 Fax: 049 952 2616
Email: michelneuville@eircom.net Web: www.angling-holidays.com

At this lovely waterside location, the Neuville family offers residential fishing holidays, which are especially popular with continental guests; however the restaurant is open to non-residents coming in off the river, when there is room, and several fine new wooden 'cabins' offer comfortable accommodation for up to six and have a large sitting room opening out onto a deck overlooking the river, making an attractive option for a family holiday whether fishing or not. The centre is like a little corner of France, with all signage in French, and neatly manicured lawns sweeping down to the river where, in typical French style, the menu is clearly displayed. When the weather allows, tables are set out on the terrace and the restaurant provides an excellent facility for holidaymakers on river cruisers, as there are pontoons at the bottom of the garden. Short French-style menus offer a range of traditional French dishes, many of them from Alsace, and great value: a no-choice 4-course dinner at 7pm is only €18, and a later menu offering several choices is about €25. A compact French wine selection is also keenly priced, so it all adds up to a refreshingly reasonable bill. Charmant. **Rooms 18** (B&B about €45 pps en-suite, standard €40; details of cabins for groups available on request). Restaurant seats 35. Max preferred table size 10. (Private Room, 8, outdoor seating, 12). Set D 7-9pm daily, €18 & €25. House wine from €16. No s.c. Closed 1 Dec-1 Mar. MasterCard, Visa.

Belturbet
ATMOSPHERIC PUB

Seven Horseshoes

Belturbet Co Cavan **Tel: 049 952 2166**

This old pub in the centre of town is full of character, with an unusual wattle hurdle ceiling, plenty of local history, an open fire for cold days and the pleasingly dim atmosphere that makes Irish pubs so relaxing. This makes it very popular with boating folk, who also head up from the river for hearty home cooking at reasonable prices: steaks, mixed grills, lamb cutlets and pan-fried plaice are the order of the day. Just right for appetites fired up by plenty of fresh air. Accommodation is also offered, in comfortably appointed modern en-suite rooms. Food available daily: L 12.30-3 (Sun 1-4), evenings 5-9. Amex, MasterCard, Visa, Laser. **Directions:** Town centre. ◇

Blacklion
★RESTAURANT WITH ROOMS

MacNean House & Bistro

Main Street Blacklion Co Cavan
Tel: 071 985 3022 Fax: 071 985 3404

RESTAURANT OF THE YEAR

Some of the best cooking in Ireland is to be found at Neven Maguire's family restaurant in this little border town, and the prospect of a meal here brings devotees from all over Ireland, and beyond. Despite his popularity as a TV chef, author of best-selling cookbooks and celebrity supporter of food events all over Ireland, Neven shows no sign of being distracted from the restaurant and his cooking is better than ever: exact, perfectly judged food, that makes the most of meticulously sourced ingredients from the local and artisan producers he so strongly advocates, is an experience to treasure. Menus, which are admirably simply worded, include a wonderful 10-course Tasting Menu, (with fish and vegetarian variations available), as well as Dinner Menus that offer great value for cooking of this calibre, and a keenly priced a Sunday lunch which draws admirers from all over the country. The restaurant is not large but it has recently been refurbished, with elegant high-backed chairs, immaculate linen and restrained creamy white crockery, and will have a small bar for the 2007 season, all creating the right ambience for full enjoyment of Neven's exquisite food. Specialities are too numerous to mention, but main dishes are interspersed with all the treats that are part of the dining experience in the grandest restaurants - meals begin with an absolutely gorgeous assortment of warm yeast breads and dipping oil, and there will also be pre-starters (a delicately flavoured parsnip served in little cups, perhaps), pre-desserts (possibly a dinky trio of panna cotta, mango jelly & a mini brulée) and superb petits fours. To give just one typical dish: caramelised pork belly is a speciality, and might be served with with foie gras, celeriac remoulade and apple sorbet - an inspired dish, marrying a Cinderella cut of meat with the richness of foie gras, and the lightly spiced apple sorbet is a stroke of genius. Desserts have always been a particular passion for Neven and it's a must to leave a little room for one of his skilfully crafted confections - the grand finale is just that in this case and, here again, an extra selection of Chef's Specials is offered, as well as the regular dessert menu. This is outstanding cooking, served with charm by family members including Neven's wife, Imelda, who is efficient and very pleasant front of house - and it is exceptionally good value too, especially for Sunday lunch which combines elements of the traditional meal with more typical choices from other menus. An accessible, informative wine list leans towards France and includes a dozen house wines (all €20), and eight half bottles. Moderately priced guest rooms (most of which have recently been refurbished) is also offered. A genuine enthusiasm for good food combined with exceptional creativity and skill, generosity and hospitality mark this restaurant out as special - MacNean House is nothing short of a national treasure. **Seats 40.** D Thu-Sun (Wed-Sun in high season) 7-9.30pm; L Sun only, 12.30-3.30, €29; set D € 45; Gourmet D €55; vegetarian menu €35; also à la carte. House Wine from €20. Service discretionary. **Accommodation: Rooms 6** (all en-suite and no smoking), €60 pps. Tea/coffee tray & TV in rooms. Children welcome; cot available free of charge. Pets allowed by arrangement. Establishment closed 23 Dec - 1 Feb. MasterCard, Visa, Laser. **Directions:** On N17, main Belfast-Sligo road.

Cavan

Cavan Crystal Hotel

HOTEL/RESTAURANT

Dublin Road Cavan Co Cavan **Tel: 049 436 0600** Fax: 049 436 0699
Email: info@cavancrystalhotel.com Web: www.cavancrystalhotel.com

This impressive modern hotel on the Dublin side of Cavan town is a great asset to the area, bringing a state-of-the art health and fitness club, conference and banqueting facilities and a focal point for local activities. In common ownership with the adjacent Cavan Crystal Showroom and Visitor Centre, it can offer guests the opportunity to tour the crystal factory - and even to cut your own crystal. The striking contemporary design is not immediately obvious from the outside, but the tone is set in the foyer and public areas, including a three story atrium area which provides an impressive setting for the hotel's Atrium Bar. Bedrooms are luxuriously appointed fitted out and, in addition all the usual facilities, bathrobes, complimentary bottled water & newspaper plus iron & ironing board are in all rooms as standard. In addition to good leisure facilities in the Zest Health & Fitness Club, there's also a hair & beauty clinic. Conference/banqueting (500/350). 18m swimming pool, sauna, jacuzzi, steam room, gym. Children welcome (discounts available; children's meals; baby sitting). **Rooms 85** (3 suites incl. 1 Presidential, 66 executive; smoking rooms on request; 9 ground floor, 6 disabled); Lift. B&B €90 pps, ss €25. Closed 24 & 25 Dec. **Opus One Restaurant:** The restaurant is off the central atrium area, and has a smart but comfortable feeling, created by native Irish wood and mellow brickwork combined with contemporary furnishings. Chef Dave Fitzgibbon has cut a bit of a culinary dash here and balances more traditional dishes with some epicurean adventures. Grilled rib eye steak with a shallot and bacon dumpling, confit of pearl onion, café de Paris butter and veal jus will satisfy most, as will a roulade of chicken with Stilton and pear stuffing, potato blinis glazed baby turnip and cabbage with chorizo sausage. However, some real imagination can also be found in dishes like a starter of baked goats cheese and pumpkin seed tartlet with white onion mousseline and beetroot ice. Other starters include confit of duck leg with candied onion, chilli, parsnip crisps and a squash and veal jus. Vegetarian options are always on menu -coral and fennel scented ravioli with a radicchio filling served with roasted scallops and a cherry tomato dressing is a particularly memorable example, and other interesting dishes include a celeriac and potato soufflé with warm chick pea and semi-sun dried tomato gateau. An accessible wine list from the old and new world is mostly priced around the €24 mark but there are some real treats on offer too, as well as a very good half-bottle selection. Friendly staff are well trained and well informed, making dinner at Opus One a real treat - though be warned that the lunch menu is quite different. **Seats 90.** D Mon-Sun, 6-10; L daily 12.30-3.30. Fine dining dinner menu a la carte only (average starter €8, main courses €20, desserts €7). Tasting menu or set menu available for large parties. Set L €22. Service discretionary. Amex, MasterCard, Visa, Laser. **Directions:** On N3, a few minutes from town centre in Dublin direction.

Cavan

The Side Door

RESTAURANT

Drumalee Cross Cootehill Road Cavan Co Cavan **Tel: 049 433 1819**
Fax: 049 433 1819 Email: debbie@chuig.com

féile bia

A younger sister restaurant to two successful and admirably consistent restaurants in Navan (The Loft) and Kells (The Ground Floor), The Side Door is based on the same principles of accessibility (good quality international food at a fair price), funky surroundings that make for an informal atmosphere that appeals equally to different age groups - and well-trained staff, who greet guests promptly on arrival and provide watchful service throughout. All fresh meat and poultry used is Irish and fully traceable - good to know when you're tucking into tasty meals that include popular starters like spicy chicken wings, and old main course favourites like char-grilled steaks and home-made burgers. Popular dishes from around the world include pastas, pizzas and a good selection of salads; specialities include vegetarian dishes - a Green Thai curry, perhaps - and there's a daily specials board, including fish specials, also changed daily. **Seats 90.** D daily 5.30 -10.30 (Sat to 11.30, Sun 4-9), early D €18.50 (Tue-Sat, 5.30-7.30), otherwise à la carte; L Sun only,12.30-4. House wine about €17.95. 10% SC. Closed Mon; 25 & 26 Dec, Sun hours on Bank Hols. MasterCard, Visa, Laser. **Directions:** On the Cootehill Road, 1km from Cavan town, above the Orchard Bar.

Cavan Area
HOTEL

Radisson SAS Farnham Estate Cavan

Farnham Estate Cavan Co Cavan
Tel: 049 437 7700 Fax: 049 437 7701
Email: info.farnham@radissonsas.com Web: www.farnhamestate.com

A winding driveway through lush parkland brings you to the dramatic entrance of Farnham Estate Hotel. The reception is in a giant glass atrium linking the simple classical building dating from 1810 to the striking 21st extension. You leave your car several hundred metres from the entrance and use a courtesy bus - a sign of the times, perhaps, but some guests may be less than happy to forfeit the convenience of having easy access to their cars. The hotel is a stunning marriage of the ancient and modern. The old house has eight suites which have been cleverly restored with a sensitive eye to the past and some real modern flair. Traditional fabrics cover exotic seats and old-fashioned shapes are given quirky colours and patterns. Rooms in the extension are sleek, modern and comfortable with walk-in showers and bath tubs. All rooms have wireless high-speed internet access, robes, irons, hairdryer, mini bar, coffee making facilities, simple heat control and complicated interactive flat screen TV & radio. The 1,250 acre estate has a private lake for fishing, seven kilometres of walks and a partially constructed 18 hole golf course (due to be open in mid 2008). There are three stunning drawing rooms in the house itself and The Wine Goose Cellar Bar is atmospherically situated underground, in tunnels. The hotel had only just opened at the time of our visit, and the Botanica Restaurant was still finding its feet - and the health spa had yet to open. The spa promises to have nineteen treatment rooms, a thermal suite, a relaxation room, an indoor-outdoor infinity pool and its own restaurant. The Redwood Suite has ten meeting rooms and can take up to 440 delegates. Although the scarred parkland may take some time to mature the hotel itself sets a new standard in stylish country house hospitality. **Rooms 158** (8 suites in the old house, 4 new suites, non-smoking rooms available, 12 disabled.) Lifts. B & B from €65 pps midweek, €85 pps weekend, ss €105 midweek, €125 weekend. Prices will change when spa open (due to open 1st weekend in October). **Restaurant: Seats 220** (private room, 40); Children welcome; L served daily 12.30-3, D served daily 7-9.30. Set L €25, Gourmet D €48, D also á la carte. Open all year. Amex, MasterCard, Visa, Laser. **Directions:** From Dublin, N3 to Cavan town, then take the Killeshandra Road for 3km to the gates of the estate. The hotel is a 1.7km drive from the gates.

Cloverhill
☆RESTAURANT WITH ROOMS

The Olde Post Inn

Cloverhill Co Cavan **Tel: 047 55555** Fax: 047 55111
Email: gearoidlynch@eircom.net Web: www.theoldepostinn.com

féile bia Gearoid and Tara Lynch's restaurant is in an old stone building in a neatly landscaped garden which served as a post office until 1974 and, since then, has made an attractive and popular inn. Gearoid is a talented young chef and, with Tara managing front of house with efficiency and charm, they make a good team and, since taking over here in 2002, have earned a reputation for fine food and genuine hospitality that draws guests from well beyond the region. There's a pleasant rural atmosphere about the place, which has a proper bar to enjoy your pre/post-prandial drinks and an old-world style throughout, with bare walls, dark beams and simple wooden furniture - but, comfortably rustic as it may seem, that is far from the case in the kitchen, and elegantly-appointed tables with crisp white linen and gleaming glasses are a hint of the treats to come. Gearoid's route to Cloverhill has included time in some fine establishments - at least one of which lives on here, in a house speciality: 'Le Coq Hardi' chicken breast (stuffed with potato, apple, bacon & herbs, wrapped in bacon and served with an Irish whiskey sauce). A committed Euro-Toques chef, Gearoid sources ingredients with great care and his respect for regional and seasonal foods shows in many ways, notably in adaptations of traditional themes such as a delicious speciality starter of warm bacon and cabbage terrine with a baby leek cream sauce. This is a happy ship and the talent and dedication of a good kitchen team can produce some excellent cooking - made all the more enjoyable by the friendly, helpful service provided by local staff. The Olde Post Inn was the our Newcomer of the Year in 2004. Ample parking. **Seats 100** (private room, 25); toilets wheelchair accessible. D Tue-Sun, 6.30-9.30 (Sun to 8.30), L Sun only, 12.30-3. Set D €53, also à la carte, Gourmet Menu €75. Set Sun L €28. Closed Mon. **Accommodation:** There are seven en-suite rooms at the inn; while not esecially luxurious or large, they are convenient for diners who don't wish to travel far from the dinner table, and most have full baths. Children welcome, under 4s free in parents' room, baby sitting can be arranged. No pets. **Rooms 7** (2 shower only, 1 family room, all no smoking), B&B €50 pps, ss €10.

Closed 24-26 Dec.Amex, MasterCard, Visa, Laser. **Directions:** 9km (6 m) north of Cavan town: take N54 at Butlersbridge, 2.5km (2 m) on right in Cloverhill village.

Kingscourt
HOTEL

Cabra Castle Hotel & Golf Club

Kingscourt Co Cavan **Tel: 042 966 7030** Fax: 042 966 7039
Email: sales@cabracastle.com Web: www.cabracastle.com

Formerly known as Cormey Castle and renamed Cabra Castle in the early 19th century, this impressive hotel is set amidst 100 acres of garden and parkland, with lovely views over the Cavan countryside, famous for its lakes and fine fishing. (The nearby Dun A Ri Forest has many walks and nature trails on land once part of the Cabra estate.) Although initially imposing, with its large public rooms and antique furnishings, the atmosphere at Cabra Castle is relaxing. Due to the age of the building, the bedrooms vary in size and outlook, but all are comfortable and individually decorated. Accommodation includes some ground floor rooms suitable for less able guests and, in addition to rooms in the main building, the newer rooms in an extension are particularly suitable for families. There are also some romantic beamed rooms, in a courtyard that has been converted to provide modern comforts without sacrificing character. The combination of formal background and easy ambience make this a good venue for private and business functions; it is popular for both weddings and conferences (250/500 respectively). Garden, walking, golf (9), fishing. Off-season value breaks. Children welcome (under 2s free in parents' room, cots available without charge, baby sitting arranged); pets permitted by arrangement. **Rooms 86** (2 suite, 2 junior suites, 26 shower only, 4 family rooms, 40 no smoking, 1 disabled). All day room service (7am-10pm). B&B €130pps, ss €20. Closed at Christmas. Amex, MasterCard, Visa, Laser. **Directions:** Dublin - N2 - Navan - R162 - Kingscourt.

Kingscourt
ATMOSPHERIC PUB

Gartlans Pub

Main Street Kingscourt Co Cavan **Tel: 042 966 7003**

This pretty thatched pub is a delightfully unspoilt example of the kind of grocery/pub that used to be so typical of Ireland, especially in country areas. Few enough of them remain, now that the theme pub has moved in, but this one is real, with plenty of local news items around the walls, a serving hatch where simple groceries can be bought, all served with genuine warmth and hospitality. The Gartlans have been here since 1911 and they have achieved the remarkable feat of appearing to make time stand still. Closed 25 Dec & Good Fri. **Directions:** On the main street in Kingscourt village.

Mountnugent
FARMHOUSE

Ross House

Mountnugent Co Cavan **Tel: 049 854 0218** Fax: 049 854 0218
Email: rosshouse@eircom.net Web: www.ross-house.com

In mature grounds on the shores of Lough Sheelin, Peter and Ursula Harkort's old manor house enjoys a very lovely location and offers a good standard of accommodation at a modest price. Bedrooms, which are distinctly continental in style, have telephone, TV and tea/coffee trays and some unusual features: three have their own conservatories, four have fireplaces (help yourself to logs from the shed) and most have unusual continental style showers. Peace and relaxation are the great attraction, and there's a fine choice of activities at hand: a pier offers boats (and engines) for fishermen to explore the lake, there's safe bathing from a sandy beach, and also tennis. Ross House is also an equestrian centre, with all facilities including riding lessons, cross country riding, shows and breeding. An additional outdoor arena and warm-up area was recently completed, and there are plans for a large indoor arena soon. Ulla cooks for everyone, making packed lunches, sandwiches, high tea and a 4-course dinner (€22; wine list from about €11). Equestrian, fishing, tennis. Children welcome;cot available (€5); pets permitted. **Rooms 6** (all en-suite & shower only). B&B €38 pps, ss €10. SC discretionary. MasterCard, Visa, Laser. **Directions:** From Dublin Airport: M50, then N3 to Navan-Kells- Mountnugent. 5 Km from Mountnugent, signposted.

VIRGINIA

This attractive town is on the the northern side of beautiful Lough Ramor, which has wooded shores and a great reputation for coarse fishing. It makes a good base for a fishing holiday, or simply exploring an attractive and unspoilt part of the country. For travellers between Northern Ireland and Dublin it's the ideal spot to take a break - up at **The Park Hotel** (049 854 6100), perhaps, which isn't quite what it used to be but it's set in well-maintained parkland and its own golf course and you can get a bite in the bar then take a stroll along the shore; or - the preferred choice for discerning diners - at **The Cinnamon Stick** (049 854 8692) a clean-lined coffee shop in the village, where they do a mean Illy coffee and serve wholesome home-made food. Another option, in a waterside position right on the Dublin road, is the **Lakeside Manor Hotel** (049 854 8200; www.lakesidemanor.ie) which has been earning compliments for good food lately - but don't expect a manor house.

COUNTY CLARE

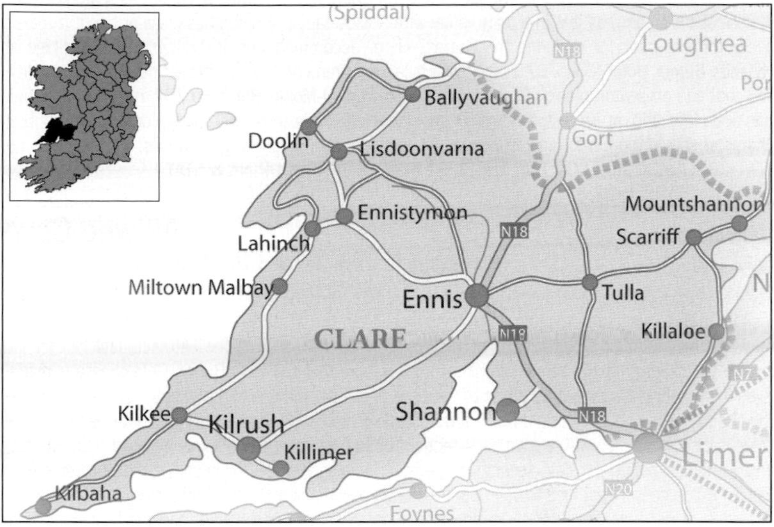

Clare is impressive, a larger-than-life county which is bounded by the Atlantic to the west, Galway Bay to the north, the River Shannon with Lough Derg to the east, and the Shannon Estuary to the south. Yet it's typical of Clare that, even with its boundaries marked on such a grand scale, there is always something extra added.

Thus the Atlantic coasts includes the astonishing and majestic Cliffs of Moher, and also one of Ireland's greatest surfing beaches at Lahinch – equally renowned for its golf - on Liscannor Bay. As for that Galway Bay coastline, it is where The Burren, the fantastical North Clare moonscape of limestone which is home to so much unexpectedly exotic flora, comes plunging spectacularly towards the sea around the attractive village of Ballyvaughan.

To the eastward, Lough Derg is one of Ireland's most handsome lakes, but even amidst its generous beauty, we find that Clare has claimed one of the most scenic lake coastlines of all. As for the Shannon Estuary, well, Ireland may have many estuaries, but needless to say the lordly Shannon has far and away the biggest estuary of all. It is the port of call for the largest freight ships visiting Ireland, and on its northern shore is Shannon International Airport. Yet the Estuary is also home to a numerous and remarkable friendly dolphin population, with Kilrush the most popular port for dolphin-watching.

The county town of Ennis has seen steady expansion, yet it is managing itself so well that it is the holder of a Gold Medal in the National Tidy Towns competition. Places like Ennistimon, Milltown Malbay, Corofin and Mountshannon - they all have a very human and friendly dimension. For this is a county where the human spirit defines itself as being very human indeed, in the midst of scenic effects which at times seem to border on the supernatural.

Local Attractions and Information

Ballyvaughan, Aillwee Cave	065 707 7036
Bunratty, Bunratty Castle & Folk Park	061 360 788
Cliffs of Moher, Tourist Information	065 708 1171
Corofin, Clare Heritage Centre	065 683 7955
Ennis, Tourist Centre	065 682 8366
Killimer, Killimer-Tarbert Ferry	065 53124
Kilrush, Kilrush Heritage Centre	065 905 1577
Kilrush, Scattery Island Interpretive Centre	065 905 2139
Kilrush, Vandeleur Walled Garden	065 905 1760
Quin, Craggaunowen (Celts & Living Past)	061 360 788
Quin, Knappogue Castle	061 360 788
Shannon Airport, Tourist Information	061 471 664

BALLYVAUGHAN

This attractive little port is best known for its major attraction, the Aillwee Cave, but its seafood comes a close second - and, as it is in a leafy valley with a wide range of amenities close at hand, it makes a comfortable base for exploring the Burren. Hotel accommodation is available in the village at **Hylands Burren Hotel** (065 707 7037; www.hylandsburren.com), who offer all day food (speciality: seafood) and off-season breaks. Of the pubs, the traditional **Monks Bar** (065 707 7059), on the pier, has open fires and, at its best, a name for good seafood, while those with a yen for a real old pub of character should drop in for a jar at nearby O'Loughlins, family-run for generations.
WWW-IRELAND-GUIDE.COM FOR THE BEST PLACES TO EAT, DRINK & STAY

Ballyvaughan

Aillwee Cave

CAFÉ

Ballyvaughan Co Clare **Tel: 065 707 7036** Fax: 065 707 7107
Email: info@aillweecave.ie Web: www.aillweecave.ie

Visitors to this 2-million-year-old cave will see more than the amazing illuminated tunnels and waterfalls, for there is much of interest to food lovers as well. Driving up to the entrance, look out for the sign to the cheese-making demonstrations - for it is here that the local Burren Gold cheese is made. Even if the process is in a quiet phase at the time of a visit, there is still plenty to see - and buy - as the cheesemaking takes place alongside a well-stocked food shop. Just inside the entrance to the cave there is a souvenir shop with a good book section (including travel and cookery books of Irish interest) and a themed potato bar café serving inexpensive, wholesome fare - typically baked potatoes with Burren Gold cheese. Fast food (coffee, panini etc) also available outside - and a mountain trail "guaranteed to work up an appetite". A garden centre has recently been added, and the Liscannor Rock Shop is a sister enterprise (see entry) - it also provides wholesome, inexpensive food in its little café (and goodies, such as home-made preserves and fudge, to take home too). Children welcome. Café **Seats 60.** Wheelchair access (to building only, not the cave). Meals all day Mon-Sun (10-6.30). Closed mornings in Dec; Christmas. Diners, MasterCard, Visa, Laser. **Directions:** 4.5 km (3 miles) south of Ballyvaughan.

Ballyvaughan

An Fear Gorta (Tea & Garden Rooms)

CAFÉ

Ballyvaughan Co Clare **Tel: 065 707 7157** Fax: 065 707 7127

Approached from the harbour side through a lovely front garden, Katherine O'Donoghue's delightful old stone restaurant dates back to 1790, when it was built as a residence for 'coast security officers'. Having been rebuilt by the present owners in 1981, it is now just the spot for a light bite to eat. In fine weather the beautiful back garden or the conservatory can be idyllic; otherwise the homely dining room offers comfort and shelter, with its informal arrangement of old furniture and a tempting display of home-baked fare. This is the speciality of the house - all laid out on an old cast-iron range and very reasonably priced - beginning at only €1.50 for scone, butter & home-made jam. Speciality teas are available as well as savoury choices including farmhouse cheeses, home-baked ham and Tea Room Specials including Open Smoked Salmon Sandwich on Brown Bread. 2-3 course lunch specials are available at around €10 and there's home-made jam and marmalade to take away. Open Jun-Sep, Mon-Sat:11-5.30 (L 12-4.30). Closed Oct-May. **No Credit Cards. Directions:** On the harbour front in Ballyvaughan. ◇

Ballyvaughan

Drumcreehy House

GUESTHOUSE

Ballyvaughan Co Clare **Tel: 065 707 7377** Fax: 065 707 7379
Email: info@drumcreehyhouse.com Web: www.drumcreehyhouse.com

Just along the road beyond the Whitethorn restaurant and craftshop, Armin and Bernadette Grefkes' attractive purpose-built guesthouse makes a comfortable and moderately-priced base for a break in this lovely area and is a delightful place to stay. The furnishing style is a mixture of old and new with antiques and newer country furnishings blending well; front bedrooms have sea views across Galway Bay while those at the back have a pleasant outlook over the Burren - and all have phones and television. There's also a comfortable sitting room with an open fire available for guests' use and everything is spotless and full of character. A very good breakfast includes local cheese, from Annaliese Bartelink in Kilnaboy, gravadlax, smoked salmon and unsusual hot dishes such as herrings with horseradish sauce as well as the more usual options. Beach nearby (10 minute walk). Garden. **Rooms 10** (all en-suite & no smoking, 2 family, 2 ground floor). Children welcome (cot available without charge, baby sitting arranged); Pets permitted. B&B €50 pps, ss€16. Closed Nov-Feb. (Open on request off-season.) MasterCard, Visa, Laser. **Directions:** 2 km (1 mile) outside Ballyvaughan village - N67 in Galway direction; house on right.

Ballyvaughan

RESTAURANT/COUNTRY HOUSE

HIDEAWAY OF THE YEAR

Gregans Castle Hotel

Ballyvaughan The Burren Co Clare
Tel: 065 707 7005 Fax: 065 707 7111
Email: stay@gregans.ie Web: www.gregans.ie

Gregans Castle has a long and interesting history, going back to a tower house, or small castle, which was built by the O'Loughlen clan (the region's principal tribe) between the 10th and 17th centuries and is still intact. The present house dates from the late 18th century and has been added to many times; it was opened as a country house hotel in 1976 by Peter and Moira Haden who (true to the traditions of the house) continued to develop and improve it, together with their son Simon, who is now Managing Director. The exterior is grey and stark, in keeping with the lunar landscape of the surrounding Burren - the contrast between first impressions and the warmth, comfort and hospitality to be found within is one of the great joys of arriving at Gregans Castle, which is now a place with a uniquely serene atmosphere. Peace and quiet are the dominant themes: spacious rooms are furnished to a very high standard, with excellent bathrooms and lovely countryside views - and deliberately left without the worldly interference of television. Yet this luxurious hotel is not too formal or at all intimidating; non-residents are welcome to drop in for lunch or afternoon tea In the Corkscrew Bar - named after a nearby hill road which, incidentally, provides the most scenic approach to Ballyvaughan. In fine weather guests can sit out beside the Celtic Cross rose garden and watch patches of sun and shade chasing across the hills. In the morning, allow time to enjoy an excellent breakfast - there is a delicious buffet set up with fresh juices and fruits, dried fruit compotes, organic cereals and yogurts, freshly baked breads and home-made preserves, local Burren Smokehouse organic smoked salmon, Burren Gold organic cheese and Limerick ham, plus a range of teas, infusions and coffees, plus a menu of hot dishes, which reads very simply - but the secret is in the quality ingredients, which sing with flavour. Children welcome (no concessions, but cot available, €15). No pets. All day room service. **Rooms 21** (3 premier suites, 3 junior suites) B&B €115 pps; ss €75. No service charge. **The Dining Room:** The restaurant is decorated in a rich country house style and elegantly furnished in keeping with the rest of the house. Most tables have lovely views over the Burren (where there can be very special light effects as the sun sets over Galway Bay on summer evenings) and dinner is often accompanied by a pianist or, more unusually, a hammer dulcimer. A commitment to using local and organic produce, when available, is stated on the menu - all fish is caught locally around Galway Bay, and Burren lamb and beef come from local butchers. Head chef Adrian O'Farrell's wide-ranging menus reflect this philosophy in fresh, colourful dishes that blend traditional values and contemporary style - in a speciality starter of home cured gravadlax, for example, that is served with a caper & rocket salad, sesame tuile and lime coriander dressing, or a main course of slow braised shank of Burren lamb, with pommes mousseline, brochette of garden vegetables and rosemary glaze. Delicious desserts may include their Irish Mist Mousse (which features in the Blue Book Recipe Collection, 'Irish Country House Cooking'), and there is always a fine selection of local cheeses, with home-made biscuits. The wine list is an interesting read and includes an impressive selection of organic and biodynamic wines, leading off with the Spanish house wines. Dinner is a treat at Gregans Castle, but they also offer an attractive short à la carte lunch menu (served in The Corkscrew Bar) and delicious Afternoon Teas too. **Seats 50** (Private Room, 34). Children welcome. D daily, 6.30-8.30; Á la Carte. House wines from €24. Service charge discretionary. Short à la carte lunch is available in the Corkscrew Bar, 12-2.30 daily. Afternoon Tea, 3-5 daily. Hotel closed 29 Oct - 4 Apr. Amex, MasterCard, Visa, Laser. **Directions:** On N67, 3.25 miles south of Ballyvaughan.

Ballyvaughan

GUESTHOUSE

Rusheen Lodge

Knocknagrough Ballyvaughan Co Clare
Tel: 065 707 7092 Fax: 065 707 7152
Email: rusheen@iol.ie Web: www.rusheenlodge.com

John and Rita McGann swapped houses with their daughter Karen, who now runs Rusheen Lodge to the high standards for which it is well known, and they live next door so there's no shortage of experienced hands nearby for very busy times - and, as it was John McGann's father, Jacko McGann, who discovered the Aillwee Cave, an immense network of caverns and waterfalls under the Burren which is now a major attraction in the area, the McGanns understand better than most the popularity of Ballyvaughan as a visitor destination. Fresh flowers in both the house and garden create a riot of colour in contrast to the overall green-greyness of the surrounding Burren, suggesting an oasis in a wilderness - which is just what Rusheen Lodge aims to provide. A 3-room executive suite introduced in 2002 has proved popular and all of the generously proportioned, well-appointed bedrooms have phones, tea/coffee trays, TV, trouser press and good bathrooms; all this, plus spacious public rooms, good food and warm hospitality make Rusheen Lodge a particularly pleasant place to stay. While evening meals are not provided, the pubs and restaurants of Ballyvaughan are only a few minutes' walk and breakfast - whether traditional Irish or continental - is a major feature of a stay. Children welcome (under 3s free in parents' room, cot available without charge, baby sitting arranged). No pets. Garden. **Rooms 9** (2 suites, 1 executive room, 1 family room, 3 ground floor, all no-smoking). B&B €50pps, ss€20. Closed mid Nov-mid Feb. MasterCard, Visa, Laser. **Directions:** 0.75 km from Ballyvaughan village on the N67, Lisdoonvarna road.

BUNRATTY

With its famous medieval Castle and Folk Park, Bunratty attracts vast numbers of visitors and there is plenty of competition here when it comes to accommodation, restaurant and, of course, entertainment: of the hotels, the best known are the **Bunratty Castle Hotel** (061 478700; www.bunrattycastlehotel.com), a modern hotel on a rise overlooking Bunratty Castle and Folk Park which is attractively designed to reflect its Georgian origins, and the **Bunratty Shannon Shamrock Hotel** (061 361177; www.dghotels.com) which was built in the 1960s at the time when the castle was restored; it has good conference and leisure facilities and offers special breaks. **Avoca Handweavers** (061 364029) also have an outlet at Bunratty and, with wholesome daytime café food available, this can be a good place to break a journey.

Bunratty

Durty Nelly's

RESTAURANT/PUB

Bunratty Co Clare **Tel: 061 364 861** Web: www.durtynellys.ie

féile bia Although often seriously over-crowded with tourists in summer, this famous and genuinely characterful old pub in the shadow of Bunratty Castle somehow manages to provide cheerful service and above-average food to the great numbers who pass through its doors. All-day fare is served downstairs in the bar (all day) and Oyster Restaurant (lunch and dinner), upstairs there is a more exclusive restaurant, The Loft, open in the evening only (Mon-Sat, 6-10). Both areas offer à la carte menus. Closed 25 Dec, Good Fri. Amex, MasterCard, Visa, Laser, Switch. **Directions:** Beside Bunratty Castle.

Bunratty

The Red Door Restaurant

Ⓝ RESTAURANT

Bunratty House Hill Road Bunratty Co Clare
Tel: 061 466 993 Web: www.thereddoorrestaurant.com

This semi basement restaurant is at the back of the Bunratty estate, with some windows overlooking Bunratty Park and the castle; as you drive through tall iron gates and up the drive to Bunratty House, you can't miss the banner signs proclaiming that you've arrived at The Red Door Restaurant - and there is a warmth to the welcome that makes red a good colour choice for this recently established venture. Open for lunch, early evening meals and for dinner, it's a hive of activity (so popular that there are some signs of stretch in the kitchen), but the reason it has attracted a following so quickly is an undoubted will to please the customer. There's a bar as you enter, with sofas to relax in and views across the park, and the labyrinth of small rooms in the downstairs restaurant are well furnished, with red and cream brick walls subtly lit, cool jazz in the background and comfortable leather dining chairs - there's an intimate, relaxed ambience to the place. Typical lunch dishes might include blackened Cajun chicken salad with guacamole and sour cream or a lamb's liver, bacon and wild mushroom salad, while the Early Bird menu offers main courses such as roast stuffed pork steak with glazed pears. A more ambitious dinner menu informs diners that the beef is sourced from a local butcher (perhaps served as individual fillets of beef Wellington) and there are always fish dishes, too, such as turbot or cod. Offering diners the choice of sitting outside in good weather or snuggling down in the cosy rooms below, is an example of a willingness to please, which is always welcome. A short wine list, grouped by country, is reasonably priced. L&D Tue-Sun, 12-3.30pm & 6.45-9.30pm; early bird D, 5.30-6.45pm. Closed Mon. ◇

Carron

Burren Perfumery Tea Rooms

€ CAFÉ

Carron Co Clare **Tel: 065 708 9102** Fax: 065 708 9200
Email: burrenperfumery@eircom.net Web: www.burrenperfumery.com

When touring Clare you will be pleased to find this charming spot - the perfumery is beautifully laid out, with a herb garden (where many native plants are grown - and later used in the organic herbal teas), pleasing old buildings and lovely biodynamic scents. The little tea rooms open onto a courtyard, opposite the perfumery shop - and beside the distillation room, where essential oils are extracted in a traditional still. Although small and simple, the tea rooms are pretty, with floral waxed tablecloths, fresh flowers and cups and saucers all creating a happy mismatch of pastels - and what they do is of high quality, made freshly on the premises, and uses local organic produce. At lunch time there might be summer minestrone & herbs soup with brown bread, or salad plates - a home-made organic goat's cheese & spinach quiche served with mixed salad - or, from a range of traditional home baking, you could just have a home-made scone with butter and Maureen's jam. All kinds of teas and tisanes are offered, also natural juices - and coffee is served in individual cafetières. In July & August Sunday lunch is offered, with special dishes available (booking required). **Tea Rooms: Seats 20,** open daily 9-4.30 (to 5 on Sun), Apr-Sep; open weekend only winter, please call ahead in Jan. [Perfumery open daily 9am-5pm all year (except Christmas); high season (Jun-Sep) open to 7pm.] MasterCard, Visa, Laser. **Directions:** In the Burren, east of Gort - off R480 & N67.

Corofin

Fergus View

FARMHOUSE

Kilnaboy Corofin Co Clare **Tel: 065 683 7606** Fax: 065 683 7192
Email: deckell@indigo.ie Web: www.fergusview.com

Mary Kelleher runs a very hospitable house and the care taken to ensure guests enjoy their visit to the full is shown in details like the the information packs on the area compiled by her and left in each bedroom. Locally sourced quality foods and home-grown fruits, vegetables and herbs are showcased in interesting breakfasts that include home-made yogurt, freshly squeezed juice, home-made muesli, Anneliese Bartelink's excellent local Poulcoin cheeses and a wide range of teas as well as cooked breakfasts with free range eggs. Rooms are comfortable although a little on the small side, as often happens when family homes are converted to include en-suite facilities, but they are thoughtfully furnished and, as well as a comfortable sitting room, there is a relaxing conservatory which opens onto the garden and has extensive views. Constant improvement and refurbishment is the norm here, and there's also a lovely stone cottage next door, Tigh Eamon, which has been charmingly converted for self-catering accommodation. *No evening meals, but Mary will direct you to the best local choices. Children welcome (under 12s free in parents room; cot available, €12). Walking. Garden. No pets. **Rooms 6** (5 en-suite with shower only,1 with private bathroom, all no-smoking). B&B about €36 pps; ss €15. Closed end Oct-March. **No Credit Cards. Directions:** Follow R476 to Corofin - 2 miles north, on Kilfenora Road.

DOOLIN

Most famous for its music, and as a ferry port for visits to the nearby Aran Islands, Doolin also makes a good base for exploring the area, or a journey break when touring the Burren. Useful places to know about include the **Doolin Crafts Gallery** (Tel 065 707 4309), which is just outside Doolin, beside the cemetery , and has a pleasant café as well as a shop selling quality crafts and home-made fare. Also on the edge of Doolin - at the top of the hill - the **Aran View House Hotel** (065 707 4061; www.aranview.com) is a family-run hotel with dramatic sea views across to the islands. And everyone loves Deirdre Clancy & Niall Sheedy's **Doolin Café** (065 824 505460), which is open for lunch and dinner every day in summer.

WWW.IRELAND-GUIDE.COM FOR THE BEST PLACES TO EAT, DRINK & STAY

Doolin

Ballinalacken Castle Country House & Restaurant

RESTAURANT/COUNTRY HOUSE

Doolin Co Clare **Tel: 065 707 4025** Fax: 065 707 4025
Email: ballinalackencastle@eircom.net Web: ballinalackencastle.com

Well away from the bustle of Lisdoonvarna, and with wonderful views of the Atlantic, Aran Islands, Cliffs of Moher and the distant hills of Connemara, Ballinalacken is easily identified by the 15th century castle still standing beside the hotel. In the O'Callaghan family ownership since opening in 1940, Ballinalacken has retained a Victorian country house atmosphere with its welcoming fire in the hall and well-proportioned public rooms comfortably furnished with antiques. Public rooms and some bedrooms enjoy magnificent views and recent renovations have upgraded the accommodation, which includes two suites - one with panoramic views, the other an historic room with a fireplace and a rather grand bathroom. The grounds - which are substantial - are gradually being improved. Children welcome (under 3s free in parents' room, cot available without charge). Pets permitted by arrangement. **Rooms 12** (2 suites, 1 room shower only; all no-smoking). B&B about €65pps, ss €55. Closed end Oct-mid Apr. **Restaurant:** with lovely views from window tables, this traditional restaurant provides a fine setting for modern cooking which, although the style is international, is based firmly on the best local produce.

Flavoursome food is cooked with skill - and served with well-chosen accompaniments. Good home-made breads set the tone and well-balanced menus will include local seafood (a starter tian of fresh crabmeat, perhaps), good soups, and a vegetarian option such as goat cheese & pesto wontons. Well-balanced flavours and accurate cooking make the most of prime ingredients like local scallops and Burren lamb - seafood dishes demonstrate particular confidence. Good coffee, served at the table or in the drawing room, rounds off the evening nicely and refills are automatically offered. Eating here is a happy event and staff seem pleased to make your evening enjoyable. Open to non-residents. D Wed-Mon, 6.45-8.45. A la carte. House wine about €20 Service discretionary. Restaurant closed Tue. Amex, MasterCard, Visa. **Directions:** Coast road, R477 North of Doolin Village. ◇

Doolin

Cullinan's Seafood Restaurant & Guesthouse

RESTAURANT/GUESTHOUSE

Doolin Co Clare **Tel: 065 707 4183** Fax: 065 707 4239
Email: cullinans@eircom.net Web: www.cullinansdoolin.com

Proprietor-chef James Cullinan and his wife Carol, who looks after front of house, have earned a loyal following at their comfortable dining room overlooking the Aille river at the back of the house. Menus include an attractive early dinner which has three or four choices on each course (including vegetarian dishes) and is very good value, and the à la carte is available at any time from opening. Local produce - including Burren smoked salmon, Inagh goats cheese, Doolin crabmeat and Aran scallops - is credited on the menu, providing a sound base for fairly modern Irish cooking with some French influence, as in starter terrines and main course specialities like pan-seared Aran scallops - with garden spinach & saffron juices, perhaps. Carnivores are well looked after too, of course - duo of local Clare lamb cutlet and loin is a speciality - and there is always a vegetarian dish of the day. Tempting desserts - rhubarb trifle or home-made ice cream, perhaps - or farmhouse cheeses to finish. A quite extensive wine list includes a fair choice of half bottles. Children welcome. **Seats 25** D Thu-Tue, 6-9. A la carte; 2/3 course early D €24/30 (6-7pm). House wines €20. SC discretionary. Closed Wed & 25-26 Dec. **Accommodation**: Warm hospitality, comfortable beds and a tasty breakfast make this a good place to stay. Cheerful modern rooms have all the necessities, including phones and tea/coffee trays - at a reasonable price. Children welcome (under 3s free in parents' room, cot available without charge). Garden. No pets. **Rooms 8** (3 shower only, 2 family rooms, 3 ground floor, all no-smoking); all day room service. B&B about €40 ss €20. Closed Christmas. MasterCard, Visa, Laser. **Directions:** Centre of Doolin.

Doonbeg

Doonbeg Lodge

HOTEL/RESTAURANT

Doonbeg Co Clare **Tel: 065 905 5602**
Email: reservations@doonbeggolfclub.com Web: www.doonbeggolfclub.com

In May 2006, the long-awaited luxury accommodation, The Lodge, opened at at Doonbeg Golf Club on Doughmore Bay - and, although it is a private club, there is limited visitor access to both golf and accommodation when available. You could hardly wish for a more moodily romantic backdrop for the Greg Norman-designed golf course, and the contrast between the wild Clare land- and sea-scape and the luxurious interiors of The Lodge heightens the experience still further. Appropriately reminiscent on first approach to a baronial Scottish castle, closer inspection reveals a cluster of more intimate buildings and, in acknowledgment of Irish tradition, all are slated-roofed and built in local stone. It has an Irish 'great house' feel with an American opulence - 'a relaxed country house atmosphere with an unparalleled level of the service' is the aim and, with the apparent ease born of long experience, House Manager Bernie Merry (previously at nearby Moy House, Lahinch) ensures the atmosphere and service are always right. And then there is the White Horses Spa, designed by the US-based Irish designer Clodagh: offering every possible kind of pampering, the design is inspired by the local environment (the walls of the fitness room, for example, feature a continuous image of the beach at Doonbeg) and non-golfers, especially, could pass many an agreeable hour here. **Restaurants**: Good food is another high priority at The Lodge, and there are three choices: Darby's is for everybody, a great spacious pub-like bar where you can have good food like fish and chips, prawn salads, and steaks. Meals are also offered in the members' bar where the ambience is elegant yet clubby and fine dining is offered in The Long Rooms, an intimate restaurant with its own bar, antique mirrors and a great bay window looking on to the ocean. Much-lauded American chef Tom Colicchio, the force behind New York City's Grammercy Tavern, is a consultant, and the kitchen team is led by Aidan McGrath, formerly of Sheen Falls Lodge, who is doing a tremendous job. Spa; golf shop. Accommodation from €210-390 per courtyard room (ocean and river view available at greater cost). **Directions:** Just outside Doonbeg. ◇

Doonbeg
BAR/B&B/RESTAURANT

Morrissey's Seafood Bar & Grill

Doonbeg Co Clare **Tel: 065 905 5304** Fax: 065 905 5142
Email: info@morrisseysdoonbeg.com Web: www.morrisseysdoonbeg.com

This attractive grey stone family-run bar in Doonbeg village has recently entered a new and energetic phase with the involvement of the next generation. Hugh Morrissey now runs this lively seafood bar & grill and it has a new look that is refreshing and young. Some of the charm of the old bar has been kept and the new extension onto the River Cree has added light to the dining room and views of the river and lovely country side. Smart, simply presented menus are just the right length with seafood chowder, Carrigaholt crab claws and Atlantic jumbo prawns for starters and Angus sirloin steak with homemade onion rings and garlic butter or pepper sauce among six main meat dishes. Half a dozen popular fish main courses are offered, too - homemade scampi with homemade tartare sauce, fresh fillet of salmon with warm baby potato salad and fresh herb relish. Winter will bring a change to the menu with Roasted monk fish and some meat casseroles. A useful place to know about when playing Doonbeg, or when touring the area. **Accommodation:** Seven pleasingly simple bedrooms are bright and pristine clean, with good facilities - phone, ISDN, TV, iron/trouser press. Children welcome (under 3s free in parents room, cot available at no cost) **Rooms 7** (all en-suite, 2 Executive, 1 Junior Suite, all no smoking); B&B about €50, SS €20. **Seats 70** (private room, 30; outdoor dining for 30); Toilets Wheelchair Accessible; Children welcome but not suitable after 10pm; L 12-2.30; D 6-9.30; House Wine about €18. Closed Mon and Nov, Jan, Feb. MasterCard, Visa, Laser. **Directions:** In Doonbeg village.

ENNIS

The county town - and the main road junction of County Clare - Ennis has a venerable history, dating back to 1241 when Ennis Abbey was founded by Donough Cairbeach O'Brien for the Franciscans. It became a famous seat of learning so it is appropriate that this characterful old town with winding streets is equally notable for its progressiveness in some areas of enterprise. Comfortable hotels in the area include the **Best Western West County Hotel** (065 682 8421; www.bestwestern.ie) is a short walk from the centre of town and is renowned for its exceptional business and conference facilities; also a short distance from the town centre, **Auburn Lodge** (065 682 1247)is a pleasant owner-managed hotel, with traditional music in the bar every night. **The Woodstock Hotel & Golf Club** (065 684 6600; www.woodstockhotel.com) is predominantly a golfing hotel located a few km outside Ennis; it is built around a 19th century manor house on around 200 acres, now mostly utilised by the golf course; **Halpino's Restaurant,** previously on the High Street, has moved to Woodstock Hotel - and has been replaced in the town centre by **Zucchini** (065 686 6566; www.zucchini.ie), a friendly, buzzy restaurant where owner-chef Colm Chawke is taking pride in showcasing local produce.
WWW.IRELAND-GUIDE.COM FOR THE BEST PLACES TO EAT, DRINK & STAY

Ennis
RESTAURANT

Kasturi

Carmody Street Ennis Co Clare **Tel: 065 684 8065** Fax: 065 684 8068

This friendly restaurant is a sister establishment to the successful Tulsi restaurants in Dublin and Galway. Although smartly decorated in royal blue, there is little about the decor (except a perforated back-lit elephant frieze) to give it an Indian atmosphere; however, it has earned a good reputation for its authentic Indian cooking and helpful, friendly service, and is a useful place to know about. **Seats 74.** L Fri, 12-2.30 Sun 1-4; D daily: Mon-Sat 5-11.30, Sun 4-10.30. MasterCard, Visa. **Directions:** Ennis town centre - next to ESB. ◇

Ennis
FARMHOUSE

Newpark House

Ennis Co Clare **Tel: 065 682 1233** Fax: 065 682 1233
Email: newparkhouse.ennis@eircom.net Web: www.newparkhouse.com

Strange as it may seem to find a genuine farmhouse in a country setting within easy walking distance of the pubs and restaurants of Ennis, the Barron family home is the exception that defies easy description. This 300 year old house is of great historic interest and has large homely rooms, furnished with old family furniture and a quiet atmosphere - and bedrooms which vary in size and character, as old houses do, but they are comfortable and full of interest. The en-suite bathrooms also vary considerably (remember this is a farmhouse), and first-time guests may need a fairly independent spirit in order to get into the ways of the house as information is not always forthcoming. However, regular guests adore the place and its exceptionally convenient location makes it a useful base for touring the area, following country pursuits (golf, horse riding, fishing, walking) or genealogy - there's a lot of useful material in the house and the Barrons can give advice on researching your roots. Local record centres - the library and courthouse - are just a few minutes' walk. Children welcome (under 4s free in parents' room, baby sitting arranged); pets permitted by arrangement. **Rooms 6** (all en-suite & no smoking, 1 shower only; 4 triple rooms, 2 family rooms). B&B €50 pps, ss €10. Closed 1 Nov-1 Mar. MasterCard, Visa, Laser. **Directions:** 1 mile outside Ennis; R352, turn right at Roselevan Arms.

Ennis

HOTEL

Old Ground Hotel

O'Connell Street Ennis Co Clare **Tel: 065 6828127**
Fax: 065 6828112 Email: oghotel@iol.ie Web: www.flynnhotels.com

This ivy-clad former manor house dates back to the 18th century and, set in its own gardens, creates an oasis of calm in the bustling centre of Ennis. One of the country's best-loved hotels, the Old Ground was bought by the Flynn family in 1995 and has been imaginatively extended and renovated by them in a way that is commendably sensitive to the age and importance of the building. Despite the difficulties of dealing with very thick walls in an old building, major improvements were made to existing banqueting/conference facilities in the mid '90s, and extra storeys have since been added to provide fine new rooms - as the famous ivy-clad frontage continues to thrive, the external changes are barely noticeable to the casual observer, and major refurbishment has also taken place throughout the interior of the hotel, including all the older bedrooms - which have good amenities and well-designed bathrooms. A traditional style bar, Poet's Corner (bar menu 12-9) features traditional music on some nights. *Town Hall Café (see entry), is an informal contemporary restaurant in an historic building adjacent to the hotel. Children welcome (under 2 free in parents' room, cot available without charge, baby sitting arranged). Conference/banqueting (130/200). No pets. Garden. **Rooms 114** (12 suites, 6 junior suites, 50 executive rooms, 20 no-smoking, 1 for disabled.) Lift. 24 hour room service; turndown service. B&B about €85pps; ss €32. Closed 24-26 Dec. **O'Brien Room Restaurant:** The hotel's formal dining room is at the front of the hotel and has warmth and charm, in an elegant old-fashioned style. Today's kitchen team has been part of the hotel since 1980, and they take pride in using local produce in enduring specialities dishes such as Burren lamb with rosemary & honey glaze or fillets of turbot with lemon & chive beurre blanc, followed by homely desserts like seasonal fruit crumbles. **Seats 65** (private room, 70). Toilets wheelchair accessible. Air conditioning. L&D daily: L12-2.30, D 6.30-9.15. Closed 25-26 Dec. Amex, Diners, MasterCard, Visa, Laser. **Directions:** Town centre. ◇

Ennis

HOTEL

Temple Gate Hotel

The Square Ennis Co Clare **Tel: 065 682 3300** Fax: 065 682 3322
Email: info@templegatehotel.com Web: www.templegatehotel.com

This family-owned hotel was built in the mid '90's on the site of a 19th century convent, to a design that retains the older features including a church. Existing Gothic themes have been successfully blended into the new throughout the hotel, creating a striking modern building which has relevance to its surroundings in the heart of a medieval town, and succeeds in providing the comfort and convenience demanded by today's travellers, at a reasonable price. 'Preachers' pub offers a bar menu (12-9.30 daily) and traditional music every weekend - and the shops and many famous music pubs of the town centre are just a short walk across a cobble-stoned courtyard. Conference/banqueting (190/160). 24hr room service. **Rooms 73** (2 suites, 39 no smoking, 3 family rooms, 13 ground floor). Lift. B&B €89 pps, ss €35. **Restaurant:** JM's Bistro is located in a lovely high ceilinged room with lots of character. With comfortable seating and professional, attentive and friendly service, it's a relaxing place to linger after an active day and the hustle and bustle of the town. International influences are seen in starters such as a colourful red pepper soup and, perhaps, crisp crab dumplings, warm black pudding salad, or tempura of local goats cheese. Main courses may include a speciality of prime oven-roasted monkfish on spring onion colcannon, or Burren rack of lamb with fresh herb crust and tomato & mint chutney. An attractive dining-in option for residents, and an enjoyable experience for all. JM's Bistro: D, L & D daily - 7-9.45, 12.45-3 & 7-9.45 (to 9.15 Sun). Closed 25-26 Dec. Amex, Diners, MasterCard, Visa, Laser. **Directions:** Town Centre Location - In Ennis, follow signs to tourist office: hotel is beside it.

Ennis

RESTAURANT

Town Hall Café

O'Connell Street Ennis Co Clare **Tel: 065 682 8127** Fax: 065 682 8112
Email: oghotel@iol.ie Web: www.flynnhotels.com

Adjacent to (and part of) The Old Ground Hotel, the Town Hall Café has a separate street entrance and this contemporary space in no way feels like a 'hotel restaurant'. The old town hall has been well restored and the restaurant is in an impressive high-ceilinged room with sensitively spare decor - large art works which will be loved or loathed, big pots and simple table settings allow the room to speak for itself. Daytime menus are concise but varied, a mixture of modern bistro-style dishes and tea-room fare - just what people need to re-charge during a day's shopping it seems, as the cooking is good, service swift and value excellent. In the evening it all moves up a notch or two, when a shortish à la carte menu comes on stream, offering about half a dozen choice per course. Baked Inagh goat's cheese, beer-battered monkfish with organic leaves and prime 10oz sirloin steak with a grain mustard & Irish whiskey sauce are all typical. Desserts from a daily selection. Not fine dining, but stylish and great value - the best restaurant in Ennis, many would say. Reservations recommended except for snacks. **Seats 80.** Open from 10am daily: L 10-4.45pm, D 6-9.30pm. House wines from €17. Closed 24-26 Dec. Amex, Diners, MasterCard, Visa, Laser. **Directions:** On main street of Ennis town.

Ennistymon

Byrne's Restaurant & Accommodation

RESTAURANT WITH ROOMS

Main Street Ennistymon Co Clare
Tel: 065 707 1080 Fax: 065 707 2103
Email: byrnesennistymon@eircom.net Web: www.byrnes-ennistymon.com

Located in a fine period house at the top of this old market town, Byrne's is a wonderfully stylish high-ceilinged restaurant with views of Ennistymon's famous cascading river at the back of the building. Contemporary style and genuine hospitality are wedded to ambitious standards of food and a visit here should not disappoint. Menus are in the modern mode (warm salads and gravadlax are typical starters, with lamb shank and marinaded monkfish popular main courses), but servings are generous and the early bird offers very good value. Dinner menus are weighted towards dishes using carefully sourced local fresh fish: cod, turbot, scallops mussels and wild salmon are usually bolstered by specials of the day; vegetarians are also well looked after. *A "pub" in the cellar provides good bar food (call to check times). Air conditioning. Not suitable for children after 8 pm. **Seats 60** (outdoor, 40, private room, 15). D only, Mon-Sat; Set D €30/35 2/3 course, also à la carte. House wines from €20. Closed Sun (except bank hol weekends), Christmas, Nov and Feb. Phone to check opening off season. *Accommodation is offered in spacious superior rooms. **Rooms 6** (all en suite, 3 family rooms). B&B €60 pps, ss €20. Amex, MasterCard, Visa, Laser. **Directions:** Large, prominent building at the head of the main street.

Ennistymon

Holywell Italian Café

Ⓝ RESTAURANT

Ennistymon Co Clare **Tel: 065 707 7322** Fax: 065 707 7323
Email: info@holywell.net Web: www.holywell.net

This white-washed building in the centre of Ennistymon is one of two descendants of the much-loved Italian cafe, previously at Ballyvaughan. You enter a tiny hall and there is a corridor-bar, with two spacious rooms to the right and left. The familiar Tyrolean style interior has been reproduced - tiled floor, a lot of dark wood, dark upholstered benches, café style chairs - and both rooms have large windows letting in plenty of light. It's a comfortable place to eat, and wines offered by the glass are generous. Menus are similar to those offered at Ballyvaughan - all vegetarian, specialising in simple dishes like pastas and pizzas - and a recent visit confirms that dishes such as the bruschetta and mozzarella & tomato salad remain on form. However it seems that the philosophy of 'simple excellence' may have slipped a little as the famous pizza had a slightly gritty texture that was disappointing, and salads were watery. Nonetheless, it might have been an off-day and it is a useful place to know about, with long opening hours in summer. Open 11am-11pm daily. Phone to check opening off season. MasterCard, Visa.

Fanore

Italian Trattoria

RESTAURANT

Craggagh Fanore Co Clare **Tel: 065 707 6971** Fax: 065 707 2465

This new venture is one of two descendants of the well-known vegetarian Italian café, previously at Ballyvaughan - and, as the mother restaurant did, it is now earning a following for its simple style, the integrity of the cooking and reasonable prices. There is a fundamental difference, however, as the menu here includes meat - and has also moved away from the famous pizzas, towards a more balanced trattoria menu. Although there is still a strong leaning towards vegetarian dishes, and vegetarian options are offered on some of the meat dishes, the minestrone now includes diced beef, the antipasti plate includes stuffed Parma ham rolls and chicken liver paté, and home-made pasta is offered with with seafood bolognese sauce - and you can even have a succulent grilled meats plate. The chef previously at Ballyvaughan is cooking here and it shows in delicious, well-presented food based on high quality ingredients. It's a relaxed, cosy place with an easy ambience, and wonderful views at sunset. Staff are very friendly and efficient, there's a short, well-selected list of Italian wines (also beers and minerals), outstanding coffees - and it's great value.

KILFENORA

One of the most famous music centres in the west of Ireland, traditional Irish music and set dancing at **Vaughan's Pub** (Tel: 065 708 8004; www.vaughanspub.com) and (previously thatched) barn attract visitors from all over the world; it's been in the family since about 1800 and serves traditional Irish food (seafood chowder, bacon & cabbage, beef & Guinness stew)based on local ingredients. Discerning travellers looking for a snack head for the nearby Visitor Centre, which does a very nice line in good home baking.

WWW.IRELAND-GUIDE.COM FOR THE BEST PLACES TO EAT, DRINK & STAY

KILKEE

Aside from its appeal as a base for golfing holidays, Kilkee is a traditional family holiday destination - many would say there is nowhere else to be during the long Irish summer holidays. if staying in a large impersonal hotel is not your thing, consider **Stella Maris Hotel** (Tel 065 9056455; www.stellamarishotel.com), a long established family-run hotel with a warm and friendly atmosphere and rooms that is gradually being upgraded: guest rooms are being refurbished and a lift is to be installed for the 2007 season.

WWW.IRELAND-GUIDE.COM FOR THE BEST PLACES TO EAT, DRINK & STAY

Kilkee

HOTEL

Halpins Townhouse Hotel

Erin Street Kilkee Co Clare **Tel: 065 905 6032** Fax: 065 905 6317
Email: halpinshotel@iol.ie Web: www.halpinsprivatehotels.com

Adapting the original Victorian building of the Halpin family's small townhouse hotel to provide en-suite bathrooms has meant that bedrooms are neat rather than spacious, but they are comfortable and well-appointed with direct-dial phone, TV, hospitality tray with mineral water as well as tea/coffee-making facilities and a laundry service. There's a characterful basement bar with an open fire where visitors, including the many who come to play the adjacent Kilkee Golf Course get together after dinner at the hotel's restaurant, Vittles. In common ownership with Aberdeen Lodge, Blakes Townhouse and Merrion Hall (see Dublin entries.) Conference/banqueting (50). Own parking. Off-season value breaks. Children welcome (under 3 free in parents' room, cots available without charge, baby sitting arranged). **Rooms 12** (2 suites, all en-suite, all no smoking) B&B €50 pps, ss €30. Bar food available 11-9 daily, L 11-3 (Sun 11-2), D 6.30-9; Set D €35, à la carte also available L&D; house wine €25. Closed 15 Nov-15 Mar. Amex, Diners, MasterCard, Visa. **Directions:** Centre of Kilkee.

Kilkee

RESTAURANT

Murphy Blacks

The Square Kilkee Co Clare
Tel: 065 905 6854 Email: murphy-blacks@iol.ie

Having previously run a successful bar here, Cillian Murphy and Mary Redmond had the opportunity to acquire the premises next door a couple of years ago, and set up Murphy Blacks Restaurant. It's in a Victorian building, and, although the restaurant is quite modern, they've kept as many period features as possible to retain the atmosphere of the pub it was for 150 years. Cillian, an ex fishing skipper who uses his fishing connections to ensure the freshest fish possible, is in charge of front of house and Mary, a graduate of Dublin's famous Cathal Brugha Street catering college and the fourth generation of her family involved in the hospitality trade in Kilkee, provides all the necessary skills in the kitchen. The combination has proved a winning one and in a very short time Murphy Blacks has become one of the best places to eat on the west coast of Clare. They both believe the secret to good food is in the buying, and a considerable effort goes into ensuring they get the best from all suppliers and this commitment to quality shows, in succulent, well-flavoured food. Menus have a natural leaning towards seafood, especially the starters, and dishes singled out for special praise on a recent visit include a starter of prawn tempura with chilli dip (super fresh prawns, perfectly seasoned and cooked), and a superb main course of cannelloni of plaice (fillets of plaice stuffed with crabmeat & baked in a cream sauce). But non-fish eater will be happy too, with classics like rack of lamb and steaks various ways, and there is always a vegetarian choice. Generous portions mean you may not get as far as dessert, but everything is home-made and the selection changes monthly. A balanced wine list is accessibly priced and includes eight half bottles. **Seats 37** (outdoors, 12); D Mon-Sat, 6-9pm. Closed Sun. Reservations advised. MasterCard, Visa, Laser. **Directions:** Middle of Kilkee.

KILLALOE / BALLINA

At the southern end of Lough Derg - a handsome inland sea set in an attractive blend of mountain and hillside, woodland and farm - Killaloe straddles the Shannon with two townships - Ballina in Tipperary on the east bank, and Killaloe in Clare, with the ancient cathedral across the river to the west. However, while it's all usually known as Killaloe (Co Clare), establishments of interest to the guide happen to be on the east (Tipperary) side of the river. The aptly named **Lakeside Hotel** (061 376122; www.lakeside-killaloe.com) is popular for its location and facilities, while **Liam O'Riain's** (061 376722) is a traditional unspoilt pub. Then there's **Gooser's,** an attractive almost-riverside pub; it gets very busy in summer but makes a pleasant off-season stop and, at its best, the food can be enjoyable. (See also entry for **Cherry Tree Restaurant**.)

WWW.IRELAND-GUIDE.COM FOR THE BEST PLACES TO EAT, DRINK & STAY

Killaloe

☆RESTAURANT

Cherry Tree Restaurant

Lakeside Ballina Killaloe Co Clare **Tel: 061 375 688**
Fax: 061 375 689 Web: www.cherrytreerestaurant.ie

féile bia Harry McKeogh's impressive modern restaurant is a favourite weekend destination for discerning Limerick residents, who enjoy the lovely waterside location and consistently excellent contemporary cooking. The setting is charming, with just a stretch of grass between the restaurant and the River Shannon, and the high-ceilinged room with well-spaced, classically appointed tables makes a fine restaurant. As you arrive, Chef de Cuisine Mark Anderson and his team are at work in the kitchen, which is reassuringly on view, and Harry or one of his staff will show you to a small reception area nearby or straight to your table, where menus, iced water and delicious home-baked breads will quickly follow. Carefully sourced ingredients have always been the star here, providing a sound basis for a wide range of dishes - many of them admirably simple. Mark Anderson, who was our Chef of the Year in 2006, changes menus monthly and is clearly committed to using the best of local ingredients, many of them organic; menu notes state the philosophy and credit suppliers. Simply worded menus offer a wide, often luxurious, choice of dishes - perhaps eight on each course on the à la carte, which is peppered with ingredients like truffles, foie gras and diver caught scallops; but simpler foods are just as good - the Cherry Tree's salads are legendary (a starter of fried mushrooms with lemon shallot batter, 'petite salade' of Helga's organic leaves & garlic emulsion is a nice addition to the repertoire), and an outstanding ingredient that has inspired more than one speciality dish is their superb beef; the Cherry Tree received the Guide's Irish Beef Award in 2001, and beef dishes here remain a treat, especially perfectly cooked dry-aged steaks served with changing accompaniments - chickpea onion rings, black bean & chorizo cassoulet and red pepper marmalade is a recent variation. Crab is a favourite ingredient in season - in a favour-packed starter of fresh crab & naturally smoked cannelloni with a fine purée of garden peas, shaved fennel & orange and crab bisque froth - and excellent puddings. each with a suggested dessert wine to accompany, might include a luscious seasonal 'trifle' of black cherries & organic strawberries with a fresh berry coulis, crushed pistachio nuts and vanilla cream. There's a fine Irish farmhouse cheese plate too, and an interesting, carefully chosen wine list includes seven half bottles and offers plenty of treats. Set menus - especially Sunday lunch - offer outstanding value. **Seats 60** (private room, 10). Toilets wheelchair accessible. Children welcome until 8pm. D 6-10 Tue-Sat. Set D €44; also à la carte. House wines €18. Sun L 12.30-3, Sun L €29. Closed Sun D, Mon, 24-26 Dec, last week Jan, 1st week Feb. Amex, MasterCard, Visa, Laser. **Directions:** At Molly's Pub in Ballina turn down towards the Lakeside Hotel, the Cherry Tree Restaurant is just before the hotel, on the left.

Lahinch

RESTAURANT

Barrtra Seafood Restaurant

Lahinch Co Clare **Tel: 065 708 1280**
Email: barrtra@hotmail.com Web: www.barrtra.com

féile bia Views of Liscannor Bay from Paul and Theresa O'Brien's traditional, whitewashed cottage on the cliffs just outside Lahinch can be magic on a fine evening - and pleasingly simple decor and large windows allow them to take centre stage. Local seafood is the other star attraction - Barrtra was our Seafood Restaurant of the Year in 2002 - and Theresa's excellent, unfussy cooking makes the most of a wide range of fish, while also offering a choice for those with other preferences. Several menus are offered in high season, starting with their famous 5 O'clock Menu which is a real snip - giving value has always been a priority here and local seafood is all offered at customer-kindly prices; lobster is a speciality, when available, and is very reasonably priced - on the dinner menu it only attracts a €10 supplement. Otherwise expect dishes like richly flavoured chowders, glorious crab salads with home-made mayonnaise and bread, and perfectly cooked fish with excellent sauces; exact timing and perfect judgement of flavourings enhances while always allowing the fish to be "itself". Vegetarian dishes are highlighted on menus, and vegetables generally are another strong point, a deliciously flavoursome combination that will include beautiful Clare potatoes is served on a platter. Paul manages front of house with easy hospitality, and is responsible for an interesting and keenly priced wine list, which includes a wide choice of house wines and half bottles, several sherries and a beer menu. Quality and outstanding value are the hallmarks of this great little restaurant - for the third year in succession prices remain the same. Children welcome before 7pm. **Seats 40.** D only, Tue-Sun (Also Mon Jul & Aug) 5-10. Early D (3-course) 5-6.30, €26; Set 6-course D €37; also à la carte. House wines from €20. s.c. discretionary. Closed Mon (except Jul-Aug) & Jan-Feb. Phone to check opening hours off season. MasterCard, Visa, Laser. **Directions:** 3.5 miles south of Lahinch N67.

Lahinch

COUNTRY HOUSE

Moy House

Lahinch Co Clare

Tel: 065 708 2800 Fax: 065 708 2500

Email: moyhouse@eircom.net Web: www.moyhouse.com

This stunning house just outside Lahinch was our Country House of the Year in 2003. It's on a wooded 15 acre site on the river Moy and enjoys a commanding position overlooking Lahinch Bay, with clear coastal views. It is one of Ireland's most appealing (and luxurious) country houses and, although it appears to be quite a small, low building as you approach, its hillside position allows for a lower floor on the sea side - a side entrance below has direct access to the dining room and lower bedrooms (useful for anyone who might have difficulty with the narrow spiral staircase which joins the two floors internally). A large, elegant drawing room on the entrance level has an open fire and honesty bar, where guests are free to enjoy aperitifs before going down to dine, or to relax after dinner. Decor, in rich country house tones, uses rugs and beautiful heavy fabrics to great advantage and bedrooms, which all have sea views, are wonderfully spacious and luxuriously appointed, and lovely bathrooms have underfloor heating; one of the bedrooms has recently been upgraded to make a unique suite with private conservatory overlooking the Atlantic. Residents' dinner and breakfast are served at separate tables in a dining room (also with a conservatory), that is elegant, yet also cosy in wild weather. A 4-course dinner menu is offered, with several well-balanced choices on each course - grilled local St Tola goats cheese with tossed salad and grilled sea bass with lemon butter sauce are typical dishes. There's a short but interesting wine list and, all round, this lovely house offers a unique experience. Children welcome (cot available at no charge; baby sitting arranged). **Rooms 9** (3 shower only, 2 family rooms, 1 suite, 1 for disabled, all no smoking) B&B €125 pps, ss €40. D 7-8.45 (residents only, reservations required), €50. House wine €24. Closed Jan. Helipad. Amex, Diners, MasterCard, Visa, Laser. **Directions:** On the sea side of the Miltown Malbay road outside Lahinch.

Lahinch

E HOTEL

Vaughan Lodge

Ennistymon Road Lahinch Co Clare

Tel: 065 708 1111 Fax: 065 708 1011

Email: info@vaughanlodge.ie Web: www.vaughanlodge.ie

Michael and Maria Vaughan's new hotel offers peace and relaxation within easy walking distance of the town centre, and was purpose-built to high specifications, mainly with the comfort of golfers in mind - you don't have to be a golfer to enjoy staying here, but it must help. Michael Vaughan brought considerable experience in the hospitality industry to this new venture, and it shows in pleasing contemporary design, quality materials and great sense of space in large, clean-lined bedrooms and public areas - including a clubby bar with leather easy chairs and sofas which golfers, in particular, are sure to enjoy; the ambience throughout is of a comfortable gentleman's club, and it is most noticeable in the bar. A drying room is available for golfers' or walkers' wet clothing. Children welcome (under 12 free in parents' room; cot available without charge). No pets. **Rooms 22** (1 junior suite, 4 executive, 6 ground floor, 1 shower only, 1 disabled, all no smoking); B&B €115 pps, ss €40. All day room service. Lift. Ample parking space. **Restaurant:** The intention from the outset was to operate the restaurant for the public as well as residents, so it is large in comparison with the rest of the building and situated just off the foyer at the front of the building, giving it a separate identity. Polished tables with linen runners, gleaming glassware and stylish cutlery set the tone, and Philippe Farineau (previously head chef at Hayfield Manor Hotel, in Cork) presents predictably sublime menus listing a wide range of equally desirable dishes based on local products. The 5-course dinner menu allows for substitution from the a la carte (any surcharges are marked on the carte). Menus are in French and English and, with the superb quality of local ingredients, especially seafood, as their foundation Philippe Farineau devises dishes that are right up to the minute in style: current house favourites, for example, include a cute starter tasting plate of fresh Galway prawns (crème brulée, risotto, consommé and wonton), and a luxurious main course of shelled lobster set on a butternut squash crème brulee, with baby spinach & lobster froth. Diners not in the mood for seafood will enjoy dishes like a delightful crumble of St Tola goats cheese with all kinds of good things including a fig chutney, and Burren rack of lamb with a fresh herb crust, served with haricot beans and boulangere potato. There's an excellent cheese selection, and gorgeous desserts include a number of serious indulgences, but also something simpler based on seasonal fruit, such as pear & rhubarb crumble, with a blueberry & crème fraîche ice cream: not fussy, simply packed with flavour. A wine list grouped by price offers a good choice of house wines and half bottles. Good value is offered throughout, service is excellent and there's a welcome emphasis on pleasing the customer. **Seats 70.** D daily 6.30-9.30 (set D €39) House wine €22. No SC. Closed Nov - Mar. Amex, Diners, MasterCard, Visa, Laser. **Directions:** On N85 just at the edge of Lahinch on the left.

Liscannor
CAFÉ

Liscannor Rock Shop Café

Derreen Liscannor Co Clare
Tel: 065 708 1930 Fax: 065 708 1944

A useful place for anyone touring Clare to know about, the café is on the premises of the Liscannor Stone Story and The Rock Shop which are both extremely interesting and worth allowing some time to visit (especially if the weather is poor). It's a sister operation to the Aillwee Cave at Ballyvaughan (see entry) and makes a good place to factor in a bite to eat - not a major meal, perhaps, but a light lunch or a tea or coffee break. The café, which overlooks the stones and the hills, has a terrace outside for fine weather; it's quite simply set up with a servery display area, but everything is freshly home-made on the premises, giving dishes like cottage pie, Irish stew and (vegetarian) lasagne much more appeal - there's a blackboard menu offering the day's home-made soup, various salads (served with French bread), a range of hot dishes such as poached salmon, honey coated bacon with cabbage & jacket potatoes. Home-made scones, cakes (well-displayed and tempting by the slice) and desserts are lovely for morning or afternoon breaks - and you can also buy their home-made preserves to take home. **Seats 75.** Self service. Open daily 10-6. Tea rooms closed Sep-May. MasterCard, Visa, Laser. **Directions:** On road from Liscannor to Cliffs of Moher. ◇

Liscannor
RESTAURANT/PUB

Vaughans Anchor Inn

Main Street Liscannor Co Clare
Tel: 065 708 1548 Fax: 065 708 6977
Email: info@vaughansanchorinn.com Web: www.vaughansanchorinn.com

The Vaughan family's traditional bar has great character, with open fires and lots of memorabilia - it was our Pub of the Year in 2006 and it's just the place for some seriously good seafood at fair prices, either in the bar or in a newer restaurant area at the back. Although famed locally for their seafood platters (and they are delicious - and great value) there's much more to the menu than that: Denis Vaughan is a creative chef who cooks everything to order and patience is quite reasonably requested on this score, as it gets very busy and everything really is fresh - they offer about twenty varieties of fish, and the menu may even be changed in mid-stream because there's something new coming up off the boats. However, you don't have to eat seafood to eat well here - vegetarian options are offered and they do excellent steaks too. Cooking combines old-fashioned generosity with some contemporary (and, in some cases, sophisticated) twists: succulent fresh salmon, for example, may be a pan seared fillet with mussel, pea and fresh herb risotto & shell fish oil, while perfectly seared scallops may come with buttered samphire, smoked haddock & spring onion potato cake with truffled white wine & caviar butter. It's understandably very popular and they don't take bookings so, get there early - lunch time (when some more casual dishes, like open sandwiches, are also offered) might be worth a gamble but, if you want to have a reasonably quiet dinner without a long wait, get there before seven o'clock. Good bread, good service - and great value. Children welcome. **Seats 106.** Food served 12-9.30 daily. Toilets wheelchair accessible. Accommodation also available. Closed 25 Dec. (Open Good Fri for food, but bar closed.) MasterCard, Visa, Laser. **Directions:** 2.5 miles from Lahinch on Clifs of Moher route.

Lisdoonvarna

☆🏛 HOTEL/RESTAURANT/COUNTRY HOUSE

Sheedys Country House Hotel & Restaurant

Lisdoonvarna Co Clare
Tel: 065 707 4026 Fax: 065 707 4555
Email: info@sheedys.com Web: www.sheedys.com

John and Martina Sheedy run one of the west of Ireland's best loved small hotels - it offers some of the most luxurious accommodation and the best food in the area, yet it still has the warm ambience and friendly hands-on management which make a hotel special. The sunny foyer has a comfortable seating area - and an open fire for chillier days - and all the bedrooms are spacious and individually designed to a high standard with generous beds, quality materials and elegant, quietly soothing colours; comfort is the priority, so bathrooms have power showers as well as full baths and there are bathrobes, luxury toiletries and CD music systems, in addition to the usual room facilities. Fine food and warm hospitality remain constant qualities however - and an original feature has already enhanced the exterior in a way that is as practical as it is pleasing to the eye: the gardens in front of the hotel have been developed to include a rose garden, and also a potager (formal vegetable and herb garden), which supplies leeks, Swiss chard, beetroot and cabbage to the kitchen: a delightful and practical feature. Not suitable for children, except babies (cot available free of charge). No pets. **Rooms 11** (3 junior suites, 2 with separate bath & shower, 1 for disabled, all no smoking). B&B €70 pps, ss €25. **Restaurant:** The combination of John Sheedy's fine cooking and Martina's warmth and efficiency front of house make Sheedy's a must-visit destination for discerning visitors to the area. A stylishly subdued olive-grey, curtainless dining room with plain candle-lit tables provides an unusual setting for carefully-presented meals that showcase local products, especially seafood; amuse-bouches sent out from the kitchen while you are choosing your dinner (delicious little bites likes parsnip crisps, semi dried tomatoes and black olives in spiced oil) sharpen the anticipation of delights to come. And everything on John's well-balanced menus just seems so appetising: tender and perfectly cooked fresh Atlantic prawns in crisp spring roll pastry, with a dense lightly spiced tomato & chilli jam on the side make a wonderful house starter, for example, and main courses will include local meats - a perfectly pink, deeply flavoured roast rack of Burren lamb, with an olive & mustard crust, for example. Vegetarian dishes are equally appealing - risotto of asparagus and wild mushrooms is typical, served with parmesan cheese and basil pesto. Finish with a gorgeous dessert such as lemon posset with fresh fruit - rhubarb, perhaps, or raspberries - and crisp shortbread. A carefully selected wine list complements the cooking and prices are very fair for the quality provided. The same high standards apply at breakfast, where scrambled eggs with smoked salmon from the nearby Burren Smokehouse is a particular hit (Sheedy's was the Munster winner of our Irish Breakfast Awards in 2004). Not suitable for children after 7.30pm. **Seats 25.** D daily, 7-8.30. A la carte. House wine €19.50. SC discretionary. MasterCard, Visa, Laser. **Directions:** 200 metres from square of town on road to Sulphur Wells.

Miltown Malbay

B&B/RESTAURANT

Berry Lodge Restaurant & Cookery School

Annagh Miltown Malbay Co Clare **Tel: 065 708 7022** Fax: 065 708 7011
Email: info@berrylodge.com Web: www.berrylodge.com

Near the coast of west Clare, between Kilkee and Lahinch, this Victorian country house is the family home of Rita Meade, who has run it as a restaurant with accommodation since 1994 and, more recently, also as a cookery school. The restaurant is open for dinner every night in high season and at other times by request, including events such as birthdays and small weddings. Although there is no formal reception area, the restaurant is set up welcomingly in an informal country style with pine furniture and is quite extensive, with a conservatory area at the back of the house, overlooking the garden. Wide-ranging menus offer local seafood of course but meats, from a local butcher, are exceptional and a simple dish like roast lamb can be memorable; poultry is another strength - an updated classic of slow roast spiced duckling with Guinness honey & orange sauce & red onion marmalade is a speciality. Menus are interesting and food quality is very high - a combination which makes for an enjoyable dining experience. *Golf breaks available (transfer to Lahinch or Doonbeg Golf Clubs arranged on request). **Seats 30.** D daily 7-9, by reservation. Set D €34/40, 2/3 courses. House wines €20. SC discretionary. Closed 1 Jan-1 Mar. **Accommodation:** Neat en-suite bedrooms are furnished with an attractive country mixture of old and new, including Irish craft items. Children welcome. No pets. **Rooms 5** (all shower only). B&B about €38 pps, ss about €10. MasterCard, Visa, Laser. **Directions:** N87 from Ennis to Inagh, R460 to Milltown Malbay, N67 to Berry Lodge over Annagh Bridge, second left, first right to Berry Lodge.

Miltown Malbay

Black Oak

RESTAURANT

Rineen Miltown Malbay Co Clare **Tel: 065 708 4403**

Set on a hillside with views over Liscannor Bay, this large modern house may not look like a restaurant (and the sign at the gate is small, although it is well-signed from Lahinch), but it is well-established and very comfortable, with plenty of sofas and chairs in a smallish reception area - a policy of seating guests quickly and taking orders from the table prevents overcrowding. The dining room is decorated in warm tones, with well-spaced, well-appointed tables - fresh flowers, good linen and glasses, comfortable chairs - setting a positive tone ahead of the meal. While not especially innovative, moderately priced menus offer a very fair choice, with starters like St Tola goat cheese, crab in filo pastry and mussels in wine then main courses such as rack of lamb and Seafood Pot (a house speciality - a generous and perfectly cooked selection of fish cooked in a tomato, leek, saffron & garlic sauce and served in its own pot), well-presented with a selection of side vegetables. Desserts tend towards the classics - lemon tarte, variations on crème brûlée. This restaurant delivers what it promises: good fresh food, with a high level of comfort and service at reasonable prices - and is predictably popular, so booking is essential. Air conditioning. **Seats 65** (Max table size, 10). D Tue-Sun, 6-10 pm. Early D about €20; Set D about €30. Closed Mon & Christmas-April. MasterCard, Visa. **Directions:** 7 km outside Lahinch village on the Miltown road. ◇

Miltown Malbay

The Admiralty Lodge

RESTAURANT/GUESTHOUSE

Spanish Point Miltown Malbay Co Clare
Tel: 065 708 5007 Fax: 065 708 5030
Email: info@admiralty.ie Web: www.admiralty.ie

Golfers - and, indeed, anyone who seeks peace - will love this luxurious guesthouse and restaurant just minutes away from Spanish Point Links Course, and very convenient to Doonbeg and Lahinch. A sweeping entrance leads to the smartly maintained building - there's an old 1830s lodge in there somewhere, with various extensions in different finishes creating the rather pleasing impression of a cluster of buildings - and, once inside, a large reception area with matt cream marble floors, mahogany desk, deep purple chaise longue and two huge elephant feet plants set the tone, and a spacious air of luxury takes over. Smart, comfortable and restful public areas continue in the same vein and large, airy bedrooms have a similar sense of style and generosity, with king size four-posters and sumptuous marbled bathrooms with bath and power shower, flat screen TV and stereo. Children welcome (under 3s free in parents' room). Pets by arrangement. Garden, walking. Golf nearby. **Rooms 12** (1 superior, all no smoking, 1 ground floor, 1 disabled). Air conditioning. Room service (all day). Turndown service. B&B €100pps, ss €60. Closed Nov-Mar. **Piano Room:** The restaurant is a long room decorated in warm tones with beautiful Waterford crystal chandeliers, a grand piano, and French doors leading to a large garden. Immaculate table settings set the tone for cooking by head chef Nadine Le Gallo, previously of Ballylickey Manor in Co Cork, who joined the team in 2005. Her menus are quite simple in style, although the execution is sophisticated: a crab starter, for example is served in three variations - a rillette of crab and beetroot emulsion, a jelly of crab & green asparagus, and crab claws in aromatic stock, Japanese style. Quite hearty main courses include a choice of sirloin or fillet steaks - meeting the requirements of hungry golfers, perhaps - and another intriguing trio may appear among the dessert, this time a trio of crème brulées, flavoured with herbs. An Irish cheese selection includes some less known cheeses, such as Wicklow Blue, Dingle Peninsula and Baylough. An informative wine list, includes a couple of dessert wines and some half bottles. Early dinner and lunch menus offer particularly good value. **Seats 55** (private room, 30); air conditioning; toilets wheelchair accessible. Pianist weekends or nightly in summer. D Tue-Sun 6.30-9.30 (Mon residents only); Lounge Menu L daily, 12-3 (except Sun). Early D €30 (6-7), Set D €39. House wine €24. SC discretionary. Restaurant closed Sun L; also on Mon night (except for residents). Helipad.Amex, MasterCard, Visa, Laser. **Directions:** From Ennis take Lahinch road into Miltown Malbay, on to Spanish Point.

Mountshannon

Mountshannon Hotel

(N) HOTEL

Main Street Mountshannon Co Clare **Tel: 061 927162** Fax: 061 927272
Email: info@mountshannon-hotel.ie Web: www.mountshannon-hotel.ie

This attractive spot is one of very few south-facing waterside villages in the area - and the harbour is just a short stroll from this modest and friendly family-run hotel. There's a welcoming fire in the bar and the many fans who were disappointed by the recent closure of Noel Lyons' restaurant in the village, will be delighted to find that he has since opened The Harbour Restaurant in the hotel. (Booking well ahead will be necessary). With the traditional Keane's pub and shop also across the road, too, it's a village worth knowing about when visiting the area. Banqueting (200); **Rooms 14** (all en-suite). Bar meals 12.30-9 daily. Restaurant: D Thu-Sun, 6.30-9; L Sun only 1-3. Amex, Diners, MasterCard, Visa, Laser. **Directions:** Centre of Mountshannon ◇

New Quay

Mount Vernon

Best COUNTRY HOUSE/CASTLE/HISTORIC HOUSE

Flaggy Shore New Quay Co Clare
Tel: 065 707 8126 Fax: 065 707 8118
Email: mtvernon@eircom.net Web: www.hidden-ireland.com/mountvernon

Set back from the flag-stone shore and looking onto the cliffs of Aughinish, you enter another place at Mount Vernon, a magical country house whose owners, Mark Helmore and Aly Raftery, seem to have a special empathy with it. Named after George Washington's residence in Virginia, it was built in the 18th century for his friend Colonel William Presse of Roxborough, who served in the American War of Independence. The three tall cypress trees in the walled garden are thought to be a gift from George. At the end of the 19th century it became the summer home of Sir Hugh Lane, the noted art collector, and then to his aunt Lady Augusta Gregory of Coole Park, Co. Galway. Many of the leaders of Ireland's cultural renaissance stayed and worked here, including WB Yeats, AE (George Russell), Sean O'Casey, Synge and GB Shaw. The lovely reception rooms have fine antique furniture, paintings and batiks and painted panels from Sir William Gregory's' time as Governor of Ceylon; three fireplaces were designed and built by the Pre-Raphelite painter Augustus John. The bedrooms are spacious and interesting with views to the sea, or the wonderfully tended gardens. There is a leisurely feel here and meals are an event with drinks and conversation at 7.30 and dinner at 8.00pm. There's an emphasis on organic and local foods, especially seafood like crab, lobster, salmon and monkfish in summer, moving towards game and other meats in the cooler months. Although conveniently located, only 20 miles from Galway city, this is a world apart. Golf links at Lahinch and Doonbeg are within comfortable driving distance. Guided walks on the Burren available locally. Not suitable for children under 12. Equestrian, fly fishing, golf and hunting/shooting all nearby. **Rooms 5** (4 en-suite, 1 with private bathroom, all no smoking); B&B €99 pps, ss €30. Residents D 8-10pm nightly, €49, must be booked by noon on the previous day, house wine €22. Closed 1 Jan-1 Apr. MasterCard, Visa, Laser. **Directions:** New Quay is between Kinvara and Ballyvaughan.

Newmarket-on-Fergus

Dromoland Castle Hotel

★ HOTEL/RESTAURANT

Newmarket-on-Fergus Co Clare
Tel: 061 368 144 Fax: 061 363 355
Email: sales@dromoland.ie Web: www.dromoland.ie

féile bia The ancestral home of the O'Briens, barons of Inchiquin and direct descendants of Brian Boru, High King of Ireland, this is one of the few Irish estates tracing its history back to Gaelic royal families, and it is now one of Ireland's grandest hotels, and one of the best-loved. Today's visitor will be keenly aware of this sense of history yet find it a relaxing hotel, where the grandeur of the surroundings - the castle itself, its lakes and parkland and magnificent furnishings - enhances the pleasure for guests, without overpowering. It is an enchanting place, where wide corridors lined with oak panelling are hung with ancient portraits and scented with the haunting aroma of wood smoke, and it has all the crystal chandeliers and massive antiques to be expected in a real Irish castle. Guest rooms and suites vary in size and appointments, but are generally spacious, have all been refurbished recently and have luxurious bathrooms. The Brian Boru International Centre can accommodate almost any type of gathering, including exhibitions, conferences and banquets. Conference/banqueting (250/300); business centre; secretarial services on request. Leisure centre (indoor pool, spa, beauty salon, hairdressing); golf (18); fishing, tennis, cycling, walking. Snooker, pool table. Gift shop, boutique. No pets. Children welcome; under 12's free in parents' room (cot available free of charge, baby sitting arranged). **Rooms 100** (6 suites, 8 junior suites, 13 executive, 48 separate bath & shower, all no smoking, 1 disabled). Lift. 24 hr room service. Room rate €430 (max 2 guests), SC inc. Breaks offered. Open all year. **Earl of Thomond Restaurant:** Dining here is a treat by any standards - it is a magnificent room, with crystal, gilding and rich fabrics, and has a lovely view over the lake and golf course. And outstanding food and service match the surroundings, and then some: begin with an aperitif in the Library Bar, overlooking the eighth green, before moving through to beautifully presented tables and gentle background music provided by a traditional Irish harpist. David McCann, who has been doing a superb job as executive head chef since 1994, presents a table d'hôte menu, a vegetarian menu, and an à la carte offering a wonderful selection of luxurious dishes. The table d'hôte is more down-to-earth - a little less glamorous than the carte but with the same quality of ingredients and cooking. Although the style is basically classic French (with some of the current international influences) some dishes highlight local ingredients and are more Irish in tone: a starter like Inagh goats cheese salad. with red onion compôte, for or example, or a main course duo of Irish lamb, cutlet &

loin, with Savoy cabbage, potato puree & glazed carrots with shallot sauce. The cooking is invariably superb, all the little niceties of a very special meal are observed and service, under the direction of restaurant manager Tony Frisby, is excellent. Delicious desserts include a number of variations on classics (hot brown bread soufflé with brown bread ice cream is a nice example); there's an excellent range of Irish farmhouse cheeses, and a good Sunday lunch menu offers a wide choice of interesting dishes - often including a special Dromoland version of Irish Stew. The wine list - about 250 wines, predominantly French - is under constant review. (House wines from about €27). The breakfast menu includes a number of specialities - buttermilk pancakes with lemon & maple syrup, Limerick ham with mushrooms, poached eggs, toast & cheddar cheese - as well as a well-laden buffet, and the traditional Irish cooked breakfast. A 15% service charge is added to all prices. **Seats 90** (private room 70). D daily, 7-9, L Sun only 12.30-1.30; Set Sun L €40; Set D €65; Vegetarian menu €56à la carte D also available. *The Gallery Menu offers a lighter choice of less formal dishes throughout the day (11.30-6.30), including Afternoon Tea. *Beside the castle, the Dromoland Golf and Country Club incorporates an 18-hole parkland course, a gym, a Health Clinic offering specialist treatments, also the Green Room Bar and Fig Tree Restaurant (6.30-9.30), which provide informal alternatives to facilities in the castle, including excellent food (9am-9.30pm). Open all year. Helipad.Amex, Diners, MasterCard, Visa, Laser. **Directions:** 26km (17 m) from Limerick, 11km (8 m) from Shannon. Take N18 to Dromoland interchange; exit & follow signage.

NEWMARKET-ON-FERGUS/SHANNON

Useful places to know about in the Shannon / Newmarket-on-Fergus / Dromoland area include several hotels which are right at Shannon airport: **Oakwood Arms Hotel** (Tel 061 361500; www.oakwood arms.com) is a neat owner-managed hotel with good facilities, including conference facilities; **Shannon Court Hotel** (previously Quality Hotel Shannon, Tel 061 364 588; www.irishcourthotels.com) offers modern accommodation at a reasonable price; the **Great Southern Hotel Shannon Airport** (061 471122; www.greatsouthernhotels.com) is directly accessible from the main terminal building at Shannon Airport, the and is in an unexpectedly lovely location overlooking the estuary and, with its views and rather gracious atmosphere, it retains a little of the old romance of flight.

WWW.IRELAND-GUIDE.COM FOR THE BEST PLACES TO EAT, DRINK & STAY

QUIN

Quin is an historic village about 15 km from Ennis, and is home to a heritage site, **Craggaunowen** (061 630 788; open daily in summer); telling how the Celts arrived and lived in Ireland, it includes replicas of dwellings and forts, and the ancient castle is also an attraction. A major feature is the Brendan Boat built by Tim Severin who sailed from Ireland to Greenland, re-enacting the voyage of **St. Brendan,** reputed to have discovered America centuries before Columbus. **The Gallery Restaurant** (065 682 5789; www.thegalleryquin.com) is located on the Main Street opposite Quin Abbey and operated by owner-chef Gerry Walsh, who takes pride in showcasing local produce (D Tue-Sun, also L Sun). **Zion Coffee House & Restaurant** (065 682 5417;www.zion.ie) is a more casual restaurant beside the Abbey, offering good breakfasts and lunches, and light refreshments throughout the day - also popular locally for informal evening meals.

WWW.IRELAND-GUIDE.COM FOR THE BEST PLACES TO EAT, DRINK & STAY

Scariff

Mac Ruaidhri's

N RESTAURANT

The Square Scariff Co Clare **Tel: 061 921 999**
Email: info@macruaidhris.com Web: www.macruaidhris.com

On the square at the top of this hilly little country town you'll find MacRuaraidh's, a neatly presented and attractive restaurant run by local man Manus Rodgers and talented head chef Peter Martin. Expect a warm welcome, good service and a concise, keenly priced early dinner at this pleasant restaurant and a wide range of choices on a later menu. Specialities include seafood, and roast rack of Burren lamb. Reservations advised. Children welcome; Toilets wheelchair accessible. **Seats 60** (outdoors, 6); reservations required; air conditioning; D Wed-Sat. 6-9.15 (open Tue D Jul-Sep), Sun L only, 12-2.30; house wine €19. Closed Sun D, Mon, and Tue in winter. MasterCard, Visa, Laser. **Directions:** From Ennis follow signs for Tulla/Scariff until Bodyke village, turn right, 5km (3 miles), going straight through Tuamgraney. On Scariff square.

Tulla

Flappers Restaurant

RESTAURANT

Main Street Tulla Co Clare **Tel: 065 683 5711**

Jim and Patricia McInerney's simple little split-level restaurant is refreshingly free of decoration, except for a pair of striking pictures and fresh flowers on the tables. Lunchtime sees the emphasis on fairly hearty food and good value but, although the menu is limited, you can easily work up to a rather smart 3-course meal if you wish: organic mixed greens with honey mustard dressing to start, perhaps, lemon peppered chicken (breast of chicken grilled with a light lemon pepper sauce) and a home-made dessert such as fresh fruit meringues with banana cream. In the evening the mood changes and there's a pleasing, fairly priced à la carte menu offering a well-balanced choice of dishes which are a little out of the ordinary and make a change from the repetitive menus in the vast majority of restaurants. Specialities like a starter salad of fresh crabmeat with lemon tomato salsa & curried crème fraîche and a main course of roast rack of lamb with creamy flageolet beans or carrot & parsnip purée are deservedly popular, also tempting vegetarian choices like a red onion and goats cheese tartlet (using local Bluebell Falls soft goats cheese). But don't forget to leave room for delicious desserts - who could resist a tangy lemon mousse with sautéed raspberries and hazelnut shortbread cookies, for instance? A well-chosen wine list is well priced - and there's even a take-away service, which must be a boon for anyone in self-catering accommodation. **Seats 40.** Air conditioning; wheelchair access to toilets. B Mon-Fri 9.30am-noon, L Mon-Sat 12-3pm, D Fri-Sat, 7-9.15pm. A la carte; house wine about €17; SC discretionary (except 10% on groups of 8+). Closed Sun, bank hols; 2 weeks Nov & Jan. MasterCard, Visa, Laser. **Directions:** Main street Tulla village, 10 miles from Ennis. ◇

CORK CITY

It is Cork, of all Ireland's cities, which most warmly gives the impression of being a place at comfort with itself, for it's the heart of a land flowing in milk and honey. Cork is all about the good things in life. While it may be stretching things a little to assert that the southern capital has a Mediterranean atmosphere, there's no doubting its Continental and cosmopolitan flavour, and the Cork people's relaxed enjoyment of it all.

The central thoroughfare of St Patrick's Street is comfortably revitalised in a handsome and mainly pedestrianised style which is continued in the bustling urban network radiating from it. This fine thoroughfare was a river channel until 1783, as the earliest parts of Cork city were built on islands where the River Lee meets the sea. But for more two centuries now, it has been Cork's main street, affectionately known to generations of Corkonians as "Pana". Designed by Catalan architect Beth Gali, the regeneration project brought a flavour of Barcelona's Ramblas to a city which responded with enthusiasm and pride. Oliver Plunkett Street has received the same improvement, and Grand Parade is being up-graded to create a city centre with attractive pedestrian priorities.

Cork's unique qualities, and its people's appreciation of natural produce, make it a favoured destination for connoisseurs. Trading in life's more agreeable commodities has always been what Cork and its legendary merchant princes were all about. At one time, the city was known as the butter capital of Europe, and it continues to be unrivalled for the ready availability of superbly fresh produce, seen at its best in the famous English Market where Grand Parade meets Patrick Street, while the Cork Free Choice Consumer Group (021 7330178) meets each month to promote the cause of quality food.

The way in which sea and land intertwine throughout the wonderfully sheltered natural harbour, and through the lively old city itself, has encouraged waterborne trade and a sea-minded outlook. Thus today Cork is at the heart of Ireland's most dynamically nautical area, a place world-renowned for its energetic interaction with the sea, whether for business or pleasure.

In the city itself, we find two Irish stouts being brewed - Murphy's and Beamish. Each has its own distinctive flavour, each in turn is different from Dublin's Guinness, and it is one of life's pleasures - in a characterful Cork pub - to discuss and compare their merits while savouring the Cork people's delightful line in deflationary and quirky humour.

Local Attractions and Information

Cork Airport	021 431 3031
Cork Arts Society	021 427 7749
Cork City Gaol	021 430 5022
Cork-European Capital of Culture	021 455 2005
Cork Farmers Market Cornmarket St Sats 9am-1pm	021 733 0178
Cork Tourist Information	021 427 3251
Guinness Cork Jazz Festival (late October)	021 427 8979
Cork International Choral Festival (April/May)	021 430 8308
Cork International Film Festival (October)	021 427 1711
Cork Public Museum	021 427 0679
Crawford Gallery, Emmett Place	021 427 3377
English Market (covered, with specialty food stalls), corner between Grand Parade & Patrick Street	021 427 4920 / 086 240 0153
Firkin Crane Dance Centre, Shandon	021 450 7487
Frank O'Connor House (Writers Cntr) 84 Douglas St	021 431 2955
Glucksman Gallery, UCC	021 490 1844
Good Food In Cork (Consumer Group)	021 733 0178
Opera House	021 427 0022
Railway Station	021 450 4888
Tig Fili, Arts Centre & Publishers, MacCreddin St	021 450 9274
Triskel Arts Centre, Tobin St off Sth Main St	021 427 2022

Cork City
RESTAURANT

A Taste of Thailand

8 Bridge Street Cork Co Cork **Tel: 021 450 5404**
Fax: 021 450 5404 Email: maryan@iol.ie

This authentic Thai restaurant has contemporary style and a loyal following, giving it a lively atmosphere, even early in the week. The familiar set menus ('banquets') for groups of various sizes are offered, as well as an à la carte which has a more interesting selection of dishes; vegetarians are catered especially well for as most dishes are vegetarian based, and some European dishes are also offered. All the well known Thai styles are represented - Pad Thai and red curry are among the house specialities and there are always a few appealing specials offered: Thai style ducking, for example, is half a farmyard duckling - crispy style and boneless - served on a bed of Thai spicy soft noodles. Fresh ingredients are all Irish, except for exotics, and mainly come from the English Market. Making everything to order (mild, medium or hot to suit personal preference), sound cooking and attractive presentation add up to an appealing package: good food, service and value explain this restaurant's popularity. **Seats 48** (private room, 8). D Mon-Sat, 6-11 (from 5pm Sat); Early D €18-20 (6-7 pm); Set menus ('banquets') from €23.50, otherwise à la carte. House wine from €17.95 (beers, including Thai beers, available; BYO allowed - corkage €5.95). Closed 25-27 Dec. MasterCard, Visa, Laser. **Directions:** 1 minute walk from city centre.

Cork City
RESTAURANT

Amicus

14 A French Church Street Cork Co Cork
Tel: 021 427 6455 Fax: 021 422 3547

Tucked into a small space in Cork's Huguenot district, Ursula and Robert Hales' restaurant looks interesting from the (pedestrianised) street and has some tables outside in fine weather. It's bright and modern, with large prints and paintings on the walls - and, although small and tightly packed with tables (which adds to the sense of buzz), well placed mirrors give an impression of space. Arriving guests are promptly seated and offered quite extensive laminated menus featuring popular international dishes: salads (Cajun chicken), bruschetta (roasted vegetable with goat's cheese, olives & pesto), gourmet sandwiches and wraps, pastas on the daytime menu with some overlap onto the evening menu which offers more substantial dishes, notably seafood (grilled lemon sole, herb butter & pesto). Real, uncomplicated food, fair pricing and a youthful atmosphere add up to an attractive package which is clearly popular with locals and visitors alike. Service, under Ursula's direction is efficient, with children made welcome. **Seats 40** (outside seating, 26). Open Mon-Sat 8am-10.30pm, Sun 11.30am-10pm; L 12-6, D 6-10.30; house wine about €15. Closed 25-26 Dec. MasterCard, Visa, Laser, Switch. **Directions:** Just off the centre Patrick Street, between the Modern & the Ulster Bank. ◇

Cork City
Ⓝ RESTAURANT

Arco-Irish

7 Washington Street Cork Co Cork
Tel: 086 351 9290 Web: www.oarco.tk

This unrepetentious little café/restaurant describes itself as a tasca, which is perhaps best translated as the Portuguese equivalent of a Spanish tapas bar although the dishes here are more substantial. Bright and welcoming, with tiled floor, walls decorated with football mementoes and a television over the bar, this friendly place is a first for Cork and offers simple, authentic food. Short menus list a range of unpretentious dishes salads, various rissoles and traditional dishes, plus a few specials; some of these dishes - such as Corela/Entrecosto (pork ribs) and Arroz de marisco (seafood rice) are only available on Sundays, or by prior arrangement all are very reasonably priced. An appetiser of bread and chouriço is presented (and charged for if eaten), and good quality fresh ingredients go into wholesome dishes such as Bife special (steak with ham & cheese), served with a typical Portuguese garnish of rice, potatoes and a simple salad. A brief list of Portuguese wines offers excellent quality and great value. **Seats 30.** Open: Tue-Thu & Sun 10.30am-10pm, Fri & Sat 10.30am-11pm. Closed Mon.Open all day. **No credit cards. Directions:** Near Grand Parade end of Washington Street opposite church.

Cork City
CAFÉ/BAR

Bodega

46-47 Cornmarket Street Cork Co Cork **Tel: 021 427 2878**
Fax: 021 427 2897 Email: info@bodega.ie Web: www.bodega.ie

Outdoor tables with overhead canopies alongside the entire front of this old warehouse building, make for an inviting entrance. Inside, a large open space with high ceilings and old mirrors resembles a large Amsterdam brown-café, with people of all ages coming in for a drink, to play chess, read their papers or meet with friends over a coffee or a light meal. There is a laid-back and relaxed atmosphere without any pressures to order or finish one's meal. Food is not ambitious but what they do, they do well: a generous portion of good nachos will be freshly made to order and served hot, for example, or a honey roast duck wrap is well made and delicious. Different menus are offered through the day: lunch may offer soup and sandwiches, a Greek lamb and chickpea casserole or a vegetarian pasta dish. Dinner may range from from quesadillas or deep-fried crab toes to steaks and burgers, (and a choice of simple desserts) whilst for Sunday brunch you may choose to share a correctly made Eggs Benedict with friends. There is also a healthy options and a children's menu. Friendly staff, moderate prices and a relaxing atmosphere make bodega a place for everyone, no matter what age, to chill out. Parking in the area is not difficult after 6.30pm. **Seats 80** (private room, 50). Open all day, 12-9: Daytime food, Mon-Sat 12-5 (L12-3); also Sat & Sun brunch. D Wed-Sun 5 -10.30. Set L from €7.50; set D €18.50. Also à la carte. House wine €14.50; quarter bottles, €4.30. Establishment closed 25 Dec, Good Fri. Amex, Diners, MasterCard, Visa, Laser. **Directions:** 2 minutes from Grand Parade in the historic Irish Market. ◇

Cork City

Boqueria

Ⓝ PUB/WINE BAR

6 Bridge St Cork Co Cork **Tel: 021 455 9049**
Fax: 021 455 8072 Email: tapas@boqueriasixbridgest.com

Located in an attractive former pub in an old building on a busy one-way thoroughfare, this pleasant and welcoming place caused quite a stir when it opened a couple of years ago, and has now settled comfortably into the Cork dining scene. A long, narrow premises with upholstered bar stool and comfortable seating at tables towards the back, the character of the original bar has been retained but brightened up with a new black marble topped bar, wine racks and large, unframed modern oil paintings. The menu offers a mixture of genuine Spanish tapas dishes along with some Irish variations - smoked salmon, black pudding and Irish cheeses appear in some tapas - so you might get an attractive selection of mixed Spanish and Irish cheeses, for example, served with membrillo (Irish quince jelly). Some of these little dishes are uncooked products such as charcuterie or smoked fish, served cold and dependent on well-sourced products for success (Hedermans wild salmon and Stauntons black pudding are credited, and many ingredients are described as organic or free range), whilst others are freshly cooked and served hot. Many of the familiars are here - tortilla espana, patatas bravas, and piquillos but there are lots of interesting hybrids too, and the offering varies according to the day and time. There's a full licence, and a list of about 40 Spanish wines includes quarter bottles, and sherries by the glass. Not suitable for children after 7pm. **Seats 40;** air conditioning; food served Mon-Sat, 8.30am - 11pm, Sun 5.30pm-10pm; house wine €19.50. Closed Good Fri, 24-25 Dec. MasterCard, Visa, Laser. **Directions:** Between Patrick St. and MacCurtain St. on Bridge St.

Cork City

Café Gusto

CAFÉ

3 Washington Street Cork Co Cork **Tel: 021 425 4440**
Fax: 021 425 4440 Email: info@cafegusto.com Web: www.cafegusto.com

Big ideas are evident in this little designer coffee bar near Singer's Corner, which specialises in gourmet rolls, wraps and salads, either to go or to eat on the premises. The brainchild of Marianne Delaney, previous manager of The Exchange on George's Quay, and her Ballymaloe-trained partner Denis O'Mullane, who take pride in sourcing the very best quality ingredients - small is indeed beautiful here, where coffee is made by baristas trained to master standard, using 100% arabica beans from the Java Roasting Company. The same philosophy applies to the food in this tiny café, in a short menu ranging from Simply Cheddar (freshly baked Italian bread filled with with beef tomato, white onion & relish) to The Flying Bacon (filled with chicken, bacon, Emmenthal, honey Dijon, lettuce & tomato). Food prices are not much more than supermarket sandwiches and the extensive selection of coffees, teas, herbal teas etc are keenly priced too. A breakfast menu lays the emphasis on healthy options. Great value, popular local meeting place - if only there were more like this. *A sister restaurant, Liberty Grill, has recently opened on Washington Street (see entry), and another newer restaurant beside the Clarion Hotel on Lapps Quay. Air conditioned. **Seats 20.** Open Mon-Sat, 7.45 am-6pm. Closed Sun, bank hols. **No Credit Cards. Directions:** On corner of Washington Street & Grand Parade.

Cork City

Café Paradiso

☆RESTAURANT

16 Lancaster Quay Western Road Cork Co Cork
Tel: 021 427 7939 Fax: 021 427 4973
Email: info@cafeparadiso.ie Web: www.cafeparadiso.ie

Devotees travel from all over Ireland - and beyond - to eat at Denis Cotter and Bridget Healy's groundbreaking vegetarian restaurant, where they produce such exciting mainstream cooking that even the most committed of carnivores admit to relishing every mouthful. House specialities that people cross the country for include delicious deep-fried courgette flowers with a fresh goats cheese & pinenut stuffing, olive & caper aoili and basil courgettes, which is a brilliant example of the cooking style at this colourful little restaurant. It's a modest place with a busy atmosphere (and a slighlty well-worn look these days); staff, under the direction of Bridget Healy, are not only friendly and helpful but obviously enthusiastic about their work. Seasonal menus based on the best organic produce available are topped up by daily specials; dishes attracting praise on a recent visit include potato gnocchi in a cream cheese & sweet pepper sauce, a vegetable risotto and an aubergine & spinach dish, all of them vibrantly full of taste. The bowl of new potatoes with minty butter were, alone, worth travelling for, and desserts of blackberry fool and a mountainous strawberry Pavlova were also gorgeous. A well-priced global wine list features an exceptional choice in New Zealand wines (from Bridget's home country) and a number of organic wines; carafes of New Zealand wines (St. Clair Sauvignon Blanc, Marlborough, and Brookfields Cabermet Sauvignon, Hawkes Bay) at €14. and €12.5 represent quality at a fair price. The cooking is never less than stunning - and significantly, in this era of "cheffy" food and big egos, the creator of this wonderful food describes himself simply as "owner cook"; many of Denis Cotter's creations are featured in his acclaimed books: Café Paradiso Cookbook and Café Paradiso Seasons. Café Paradiso may be small, but it packs a mighty punch. ***Paradiso Rooms:** accommodation over the restaurant for dinner guests, at a room rate of about €160. **Seats 45** (outdoor seating, 6). Toilets wheelchair accessible. L Tue-Sat, 12-3, D Tue-Sat 6.30-10.30. A la carte. House wines from €22. Service discretionary. Closed Sun, Mon, Christmas week. Amex, MasterCard, Visa, Laser. **Directions:** On Western Road, opposite Jurys Hotel.

Cork City
RESTAURANT

Citrus Restaurant

Barrycourt House East Douglas Village Cork Co Cork
Tel: 021 436 1613 Fax: 021 489 1269

Harold Lynch and Beth Haughton's restaurant is a lovely bright space, with windows on two sides and simple uncluttered tables - not a lot to absorb the sound of lots of happy people enjoying Harold's cooking, but there's a good buzz. The style is international but as much as possible is based on local produce: meats and fish come from the famous butchers, O'Flynns, and fishmongers, O'Connells, for example, both at the English Market. Laminated menus are usually a big turn-off, but Harold's read simply and are full of things you'd love to try - and a plate of anti pasta (a selection of salamis, prosciutto, olives, cheese & crostini) makes a good start with your aperitif, while making the main choices. Starters are particularly attractive and many regulars choose two starters: a mildly spicy fish soup with rouille(€5.95) and seared beef salad with rustic potatoes, blue cheese dressing & French fried onions (€10.95) might make an agreeable lunch combination, for example. There will usually be one or two tempting vegetarian dishes, such as goats cheese & roasted vegetable pannini with pesto, and updated classics such as salmon & potato cakes with a spinach butter sauce; excellent raw materials are generally allowed to speak for themselves. Tempting desserts tend to be variations on favourite themes - chocolate & rum roulade with poached mix berries is typical- and a well-chosen wine list is short but sweet. Service, under Beth's supervision, is charming and efficient. **Seats 60.** Toilets wheelchair accessible. Children welcome before 9pm. Mon-Sat: L12-3.30, D 5.30-10, Sun D only, 5-9. House wine €18.50. SC discretionary. Closed L Sun, Christmas Day. Amex, MasterCard, Visa, Laser. **Directions:** Through Douglas village, 1st left after Bully's Restaurant. ◇

Cork City
HOTEL

Clarion Hotel Cork

Lapps Quay Cork Co Cork **Tel: 021 422 4900**
Email: info@clarionhotelcorkcity.com Web: wwwclarionhotelsireland.com

Those who like ultra-modern hotels and enjoy the buzz of the city centre will love the new Clarion. In a briliant central location with a wide terrace and boardwalk along the River Lee, this striking modern hotel embodies many of the best features of other recently built Clarion hotels and has excellent amenities including state-of-the-art conference facilities, spa, swimming pool, and gym. The entrance foyer is highly dramatic, with a atrium soaring right up the a glass roof, and rooms off galleries which overlook the foyer, and well-appointed accommodation includes riverside suites and a penthouse suite. A choice of dining is offered the well-appointed Sinergie restaurant offers an international menu, good cooking and attentive service, while the Kudos bar provides an informal alternative and serves Asian food to 10pm (weekends to 8pm). Conferences/Banqueting (350/190), business centre, secretarial services. Leisure centre with pool, fitness room, spa. **Rooms 191** (2 suites, 10 for disabled, 5 family rooms, 95 no smoking); limited room service; Lift, children welcome (u 12s free in parents room, cots avail at no charge, baby sitting arranged). B&B €125pps, ss€125. Amex, Diners, MasterCard, Visa, Laser. **Directions:** Corner of Clontarf St. and Lapps Quay. Diagonally across from City Hall.

Cork City
€ RESTAURANT

Crawford Gallery Café

Emmet Place Cork Co Cork
Tel: 021 427 4415 Fax: 021 465 2021
Email: crawfordinfo@eircom.net Web: www.ballymaloe.ie

This fine 1724 building with a large modern extension houses an excellent collection of 18th- and 19th-century landscapes. And this is also home to the Crawford Gallery Café, one of Cork city's favourite informal eating places, which is managed by Isaac Allen, grandson of Myrtle and the late Ivan Allen, founders of Ballymaloe House - and, by a remarkable coincidence, also a descendant of Arthur Hill, architect of a previous extension to the gallery, completed in 1884. Menus in this striking blue and white room reflect the Ballymaloe philosophy that food is precious and should be handled carefully, so Isaac Allen's freshly prepared dishes are made from natural local ingredients, and he also offers Ballymaloe breads and many of the other dishes familiar to Ballymaloe fans. Except for a few specialities too popular to take off (such as their spinach & mushroom pancakes), the menu changes weekly but the style - a balanced mixture of timeless country house fare and contemporary international dishes featuring carefully sourced meats, fish from Ballycotton and the freshest of seasonal vegetables - remains reassuringly constant. Substantial dishes, such as classic sirloin steak and chips, with béarnaise sauce - or a big vegetarian option like Mediterranean bean stew with coriander & basmati rice - are great for a real meal, and the home-made pickles, relishes, chutneys and preserves are delicious details. And, for a lighter bite, the home baking is outstanding. A short well-balanced wine list offers some half bottles. Conference/banqueting: available for private parties, corporate entertaining, lectures etc in evenings; details on application. **Seats 60.** No reservations. Toilets wheelchair accessible. Open Mon-Fri, 10am-4.30pm, Sat, 9.30am-4pm, L 12.30-2.30. Set L €20; also à la carte. House wine €17.50. Service discretionary. Closed Sun, 24 Dec-7 Jan, bank hols. Amex, MasterCard, Visa, Laser. **Directions:** City centre, next to Opera House. ◇

Cork City
ATMOSPHERIC PUB

Dan Lowrey's Tavern

13 McCurtain Street Cork Co Cork **Tel: 021 450 5071**

This characterful pub beside the Everyman Palace Theatre was established in 1875 and is named after its founder. Long before the arrival of the "theme pub", Lowrey's was famous for having windows which originated from Kilkenny Cathedral, but it also has many of its own original features, including a fine mahogany bar. It has been run by Anthony and Catherine O'Riordan since 1995 and Catherine oversees the kitchen herself, so it's a good place for an inexpensive home-cooked meal - popular dishes like home-made quiche or lasagne served with salad or fries, for example, or seafood bake, filled with salmon, monkfish & cod, topped with creamed potatoes and toasted breadcrumbs. It's popular with local business people at lunch time. A new outdoor seating area was recently introduced. Not suitable for children after 9pm. **Seats 30** (plus outdoor seating for 10) L & D daily: 12-3.30 & 7-9, Sun L 12.30-5 €12.50. (Sandwiches available all day). Closed 25 Dec & Good Fri. **No Credit Cards. Directions:** Next to Metropole Gresham Hotel, across from Isaacs Restaurant.

ENGLISH MARKET

It is hard to imagine a visit to Cork without at the very least a quick browse through the English Market and - although it is most famous for its huge range of fresh food stalls selling everything from wet fish, and almost forgotten vegetables to cheeses, freshly baked breads and, these days, imported produce like olives - there's a growing choice of places to top up the browser's energy levels along the way. The premier spot is **Farmgate Café** on the first floor (see entry), but a growing number of stalls are offering nourishment on the go: Mary Rose's **Café Central** stall is well-known to regulars - she used to sell pork & bacon there but converted it to a coffee stall about 5 years ago, and now does a roaring trade in croissants, coffees and confectionery. A couple of years ago **Juice Boost** came along, serving fresh juices, soon followed by **The Sandwich Stall,** which serves filled rolls & coffee. And, most recently, there is **Joup,** offering more substantial fare, including breakfast and lunches (mainly soups & salads) and also coffee & other beverages during the day.

WWW.IRELAND-GUIDE.COM FOR THE BEST PLACES TO EAT, DRINK & STAY

Cork City
CAFÉ

Farmgate Café

English Market Cork Co Cork **Tel: 021 427 8134**
Fax: 021 427 8134 Email: knh@eircom.net

IRISH BREAKFAST AWARDS - NATIONAL WINNER

BEST CAFÉ BREAKFAST AWARD

féile bia A sister restaurant to the Farmgate Country Store and Restaurant in Midleton, Kay Harte's Farmgate Café shares the same commitment to serving fresh, local food - and, as it is located in the gallery above the English Market, where ingredients are purchased daily, it doesn't come much fresher or more local than this. The atmosphere is lively and busy, with constant movement (especially in the self-service area) as people come and go from the market below, giving a great sense of being at the heart of things. With its classic black and white tiles, simple wooden furniture and interesting art work there's a combination of style and a comfortably down to earth atmosphere which suits the wholesome food they serve and, having highlighted the freshness of local ingredients for some time in dishes that were a mixture of modern and traditional, Kay Harte and her team now offer regional dishes using the food they buy in the market, and have introduced lesser known foods such as corned mutton to their menus alongside famous old Cork ones with a special market connection, like tripe & drisheen and corned beef & champ with green cabbage. Menus depend on what is available in the English Market each day, including "oysters to your table from the fish stall" and other fish - used, for example, in a chowder that market regulars keep coming back for. And, however simple, everything is perfectly cooked - including superb breakfasts. Either full cooked or continental breakfast is offered, with self-service or table service available. Quality is excellent and at €6.50 the mini-Irish breakfast is marvellous value; for this you get:bacon, sausage, black & white pudding, tomato, lovely toast and marmalade and abundant first rate coffee. All this and delicious home-baked cakes and breads too, whether as a bite to accompany a coffee, or to finish off a meal, a wonderfully home-made seasonal sweet such as a classic raspberry sponge is always a treat. This is an interesting and lively place to enjoy good food - and it's great value for money. **Seats 110.** Meals Mon-Sat, from 8.30am - 5pm: B'fast 8.30-10.30, L 12-4. Licensed. Closed Sun, bank hols, Dec 25-3 Jan. Diners, MasterCard, Visa, Laser. **Directions:** English Market - off Oliver Plunkett Street and Grand Parade. ◇

Cork City
RESTAURANT

Fenns Quay Restaurant

5 Sheares Street Cork Co Cork **Tel: 021 427 9527**
Fax: 021 427 9526 Web: www.fennsquay.ie

féile bia Situated in a 250-year old listed building, this is a bright, busy restaurant with a welcoming atmosphere and simple decor enlivened by striking modern paintings. Both lunch and dinner menus offer plenty of interesting choices, including a number vegetarian options (highlighted) and daily specials, including seafood sourced daily from the nearby English Market. Carefully sourced ingredients are local where possible (including meat from the owners' own business, which is a point of pride) presented in a pleasing bistro style. Specialities include char-grilled fillet steak "Wellie Style", an enduring favourite which comes with house cut potato chips. An interesting wine list offers variety at reasonable prices, with several by the glass - good value is a feature of both food and drink. A new, very comfortable, outdoor seating area opened in 2006; refurbishments have enabled wheelchair access to the restaurant but not to toilets, unfortunately, as it is a listed building. Air conditioning. Children welcome. On street parking can be difficult during the day, but is easy to find after 6.30. **Seats 60** (outdoor seating, 10). Open all day Mon-Sat 10am-10pm; L 12.30-3, D 6-10. L Deal €10 (12.30-5), also à la carte; early D 6-7.30 Mon-Fri, €20/25; Set D €31, à la carte also available. House wine €18. Service discretionary. Closed Sun, 25 Dec, bank hols. Amex, MasterCard, Visa, Laser. **Directions:** Central city - 2 minutes from the Courthouse.

Cork City
☆RESTAURANT WITH ROOMS

Flemings Restaurant

Silver Grange House Tivoli Cork Co Cork
Tel: 021 482 1621 Fax: 021 482 1800
Email: info@flemingsrestaurant.ie Web: www.flemingsrestaurant.ie

Clearly signed off the main Cork-Dublin road, this large Georgian family house is home to Michael and Eileen Fleming's excellent restaurant with rooms. On a hillside overlooking the river, the house is set in large grounds, including a kitchen garden which provides fruit, vegetables and herbs for the restaurant during the summer. It is a big property to maintain and the entrance can seem a little run down, but this is quickly forgotten when you enter the light, airy double dining room, which is decorated in an elegant low-key style that highlights its fine proportions, while well-appointed linen-clad tables provide a fine setting for Michael Fleming's classical and modern French cooking. Seasonal table d'hôte and à la carte menus offer a wonderful choice of classics, occasionally influenced by current international trends but, even where local ingredients feature strongly, the main thrust of the cooking style is classical French - as in a superb speciality starter of pan fried foie gras de canard with Timoleague black pudding & glazed apple, or a home-made summer tomato consommé. Less usual choices might include seared rabbit in pancetta with white onion risotto. Vegetables are imaginative in selection and presentation. Desserts may include a deep apple pie served with home made ice cream - and a selection of cheese is served traditionally, with biscuits and fruits. Michael's cooking is invariably excellent, presentation elegant, and service both attentive and knowledgeable. A great antidote to the sameness of modern multicultural restaurants - a visit to a classic restaurant like this is a treat to treasure. Good wine list - and good value all round. *A large basement area has recently been converted to make a comfortable bar/lounge seating up to 70. Banqueting (90). **Seats 80** (private room 30; outside seating, 30). Children welcome. L&D daily, 12.30-3, 6.30-10; reservations not necessary. Set L €28.50, D à la carte. House wine about €22. SC discretionary. **Accommodation:** There are four spacious en-suite rooms, comfortably furnished in a style appropriate to the age of the house (B&B €55 pps, ss €33). Closed 24-27 Dec. Amex, MasterCard, Visa, Laser. **Directions:** Off main Cork-Dublin route, 4km from city centre.

Cork City
HOTEL

Great Southern Hotel Cork Airport

Cork Airport Cork Co Cork
Tel: 021 494 7500 Fax: 021 494 7501
Email: res@corkairport-gsh.com Web: www.gshotels.com

féile bia This stylish modern hotel is very handily located, within walking distance of the terminal. Ideal for a first or last night's stay, it's also a useful meeting place and is well equipped for business guests. Like its sister airport hotels in Dublin and Shannon, it aims to provide a tranquil haven for travellers amid the hustle and bustle of a busy airport; its success can be judged by its popularity with a discerning local clientèle as well as travellers passing through. Rooms have voice mail, fax/modem lines, desk space and TV with in-house movie channel as well as more usual facilities like radio, hair dryer, tea/coffee trays and trouser press. Leisure centre. Parking (150). Business centre. Conference/banqueting (100). Children welcome (under 12 free in parents' room; cot available without charge). **Rooms 81** (81 executive, 38 no smoking, 4 disabled). Lift. B&B about €59 pps, ss €25.* Short breaks offered. Closed 23 Dec-2 Jan. Amex, MasterCard, Visa, Laser. **Directions:** Off Cork-Kinsale road; situated within airport complex. ◇

Cork City
HOTEL

Gresham Metropole Hotel & Leisure Centre

MacCurtain Street Cork Co Cork **Tel: 021 450 8122** Fax: 021 450 6450
Email: info@gresham-metropolehotel.com Web: www.gresham-hotels.com

féile bia This imposing city-centre hotel next door to the Everyman Palace Theatre and backing on to the River Lee, celebrated its centenary in 1998. Always popular with those connected with the arts and entertainment industry, there are many displays (photos and press cuttings) of stars past and present in the public areas and the atmospheric, traditionally-styled Met Tavern. Many of the hotel's original features remain, including the marble facade, exterior carved stonework and plaster ceilings. Recent refurbishment has greatly improved the bedrooms, most of which now combine a period feel with modern facilities, and care has been taken to bring previously neglected areas back to their former elegance by, for example, correcting ceiling heights which had been changed in previous 'improvements'. Conference and meeting facilities have air conditioning and natural daylight. (450). Children welcome (under 2 free in parents' room, cot available without charge, baby sitting arranged). No pets. Arrangement with nearby car park. **Rooms 113** (2 junior suites, 44 executive rooms,10 shower only, 55 no-smoking, 1 for disabled). B&B about €127.50pps. Open all year. Amex, Diners, MasterCard, Visa, Laser. **Directions:** City centre hotel. ◇

Cork City
HOTEL/RESTAURANT

Hayfield Manor Hotel

Perrott Avenue College Road Cork Co Cork
Tel: 021 484 5900 Fax: 021 431 6839
Email: enquiries@hayfieldmanor.ie Web: www.hayfieldmanor.ie

féile bia Set in two acres of gardens near University College Cork, the city's premier hotel provides every comfort and a remarkable level of privacy and seclusion, just a mile from the city centre. Although quite new, it has the feel of a large period house, and is managed with warmth and discreet efficiency. Public areas include a choice of restaurants, both excellent of their type - the formal Orchids, which overlooks gardens at the back, and the newer smart-casual Perrotts - and a redesigned bar that skilfully links the contrasting traditional and contemporary styles of the interior.

On-site amenities include a leisure centre with indoor pool and beauty treatments. Spacious suites and guest rooms vary in decor, are beautifully furnished with antiques and have generous marbled bathrooms, all with separate bath and shower. *Hayfield Manor was our Hotel of the Year in 2006. 24 hr room service. Lift. Turndown servvice. **Rooms 88.** (4 suites, 4 interconnecting, disabled); children under 12 free in parents' room, cot available free of charge. Lift. B&B €140, ss €65. **Orchids:** Since the refurbishment of Hayfield's Bar - a judicious blend of traditional and contemporary, resulting in the cosy atmosphere of a traditional bar, with chic modern touches - it has become an appealing place for an aperitif before going in to this fine dining restaurant, which overlooks the walled garden at the back of the hotel and has recently been completely refurbished in a contemporary style that works well with the old style of the building. Well spaced tables are very comfortably arranged in three sections, with the main area opening onto the garden, and a raised section beside it. Emphasising the relative formality - Orchids is normally an evening restaurant, although open for lunch when there is demand - tables are set up classically, with pristine white linen and gleaming glasses. Alan Hickey, who has been head chef since 2005, bases his menus on local produce where possible, and continues the tradition of fairly classical cuisine with an occasional contemporary twist for which this restaurant is well known. Although the new restaurant was only recently open at the time of our visit, and the kitchen had not fully settled, it was a generally pleasing and relaxing meal, enhanced by professional and caring service. An extensive (and expensive) wine list offers around 120 wines from around the world (house wines €31.75; 14 table wines available by the glass), but the list is to be revised. **Perrotts:** In a new conservatory area at the front of the hotel, this smart and relaxing contemporary restaurant offers an informal alternative to dining in Orchids. Open for lunch and dinner daily, it has a bright and airy atmosphere and plenty of greenery, and quickly became established as a favoured destination with discerning Corkonians who enjoy the ambience and stylish bistro cooking, which offers dishes ranging from updated classics, to international lunchtime favourites like Perrotts home made burger with bacon and Emmenthal cheese, spicy guacomole and tomato relish dip, and hand cut chips. Stylish surroudings, varied menus, confident cooking and helpful, attentive service make for a very enjoyable dining experience. Orchids: **Seats 90.** D daily, 7-10. Set D €45/55, 2/3 course, also à la carte. House wine from €31.75. SC in restaurant of 10% on parties of 8+. Perrotts Restaurant, 12.15-2.30 & 6-10 daily. Amex, Diners, MasterCard, Visa, Laser. **Directions:** Opposite University College Cork - signed off College Road.

Cork City

HOTEL/RESTAURANT

Hotel Isaacs

48 MacCurtain Street Cork Co Cork

Tel: 021 450 0011 Fax: 021 450 6355

Email: greenes@isaacs.ie Web: www.isaacscork.com

Opposite the Everyman Palace Theatre and approached through a cobbled courtyard, this attractive hotel offers comfort in spacious rooms at a fairly reasonable price. Recent major renovations included the replacement of all front windows, which reduced traffic noise, and the addition of 14 superior bedrooms; all the existing bedrooms have since been refurbished. The furnishing style is appealing and different from most hotels: bedrooms have free-standing pine furniture and an unusually homely feeling. Conferences(55); secretarial services available (from reception), video conferencing by arrangement. Children welcome (under 3 free in parents room, cot available free of charge). All day room service. Car park nearby. No pets. Garden (courtyard). Self-catering apartments available (open all year; due for refurbishment winter 2004/5). **Rooms 47** (14 executive, 4 shower-only, 37 no-smoking, 2 for disabled). Lift. Room service (meal times). B&B €65 pps, ss €25. Closed 24-27 Dec. **Greene's:** Despite being next door to the well-known Isaacs restaurant (with the confusion of the hotel's similar name) Greene's Restaurant has established itself successfully and earned a following. The approach from the street is very attractive, under a limestone arch to a narrow courtyard with a waterfall - which is floodlit at night, making an unusual feature when seen from the restaurant. The reception and two restaurant areas have character and the atmosphere is more like an independent restaurant than an hotel dining room. Head chef Frederic Desormeaux's menus are quite adventurous, offering modern renditions of classic dishes, sometimes with a French slant and often based on local ingredients, especially seafood. Starters might include a pretty smoked Salmon rillette with grilled baguette and salad, for example, or creamy Ballycotton mussel & leek soup, while main courses include classics like pan-fried T-bone steak with homemade chips. Finish perhaps with a a trio of ice-creams in a pistachio tuile bowl, or a treat devised to make the most of seasonal fruits. Accurate cooking, attractive presentation and friendly, helpful service - plus a lively atmosphere and quite reasonable prices - should ensure an enjoyable meal. The early dinner menu is especially good value. **Seats 100** (private room, 36, outdoor, 30). L Mon-Sat, 12.30-3; D daily 6-10 (Sun & Bank hols to 9.30), L Sun 12.30-4. Early D €27 (6-7pm); Set D €45; also à la carte. Set L €12-15. Set Sun L €25. House wine from about €18. SC10% on groups 10+. Closed 24-27 Dec. Amex, Diners,

MasterCard, Visa, Laser, Switch. **Directions:** 400 m down MacCurtain Street, on left; entrance opposite Everyman Palace Theatre, through cobblestone archway.

Cork City
CAFÉ

Idaho.Café

19 Caroline Street Cork Co Cork **Tel: 021 427 6376**

féile bia This friendly and exceptionally well-located little café hits the spot for discerning shoppers, who appreciate Mairead Jacob's wholesome food - this is good home cooking based on the best of ingredients. The day begins with breakfast, and a very good breakfast it is too: everything from lovely hot porridge with brown sugar and cream to warm Danish pastries, muffins, or Belgian waffles with organic maple syrup and the option of crispy bacon. You can choose from this menu up to noon, when they ease into lunch, with tasty little numbers like a house special of gratinated potato gnocchi with smoky bacon & sage or, equally typical of the treats in store, crispy duck, spring onion and Irish brie quesadillas or sheperdess's pie (using organic beef). But best of all perhaps, as baking is a speciality, are the 'Sweet Fix' temptations which are just ideal for that quick morning coffee or afternoon tea break - the coeliac friendly 'orange almond' cake has developed a following, and there's a wide of range hot and cold drinks, including 'Hippy' specialist teas. Dishes which are vegetarian, or can be adapted for vegetarians, are highlighted on the menu at this great little place. Great service, and great value too: full marks. **Seats 30.** Toilets not wheelchair accessible. Children welcome. Open Mon-Thu, 8.30-5, Fri/Sat 8.30-6pm; B'fst 8.30-12, L 12-4.30. House wine from €16.50 or from 2.95 a glass, specialist beers from about €3.75. Closed Sun, Bank Holidays, 24-26 Dec. **No Credit Cards. Directions:** Directly behind Brown Thomas, Cork. ◇

Cork City
HOTEL

Imperial Hotel

South Mall Cork Co Cork **Tel: 021 427 4040** Fax: 021 427 5375
Email: info@imperialhotelcork.ie Web: www.flynnhotels.com

This thriving hotel in Cork's main commercial and banking centre dates back to 1813 and has a colourful history - Michael Collins spent his last night here, no less, and that suite now bears his name. However, it's the convenient location - near the river and just a couple of minutes walk from the Patrick Street shopping area - that makes this hotel so popular for business and pleasure, also the free car parking available for residents. It has been run by the Flynn family (of the famous Old Ground Hotel in Ennis, Co Clare) since 1998. Recent developments have seen refurbishment of some public areas including the hotel's popular Pembroke Restaurant which is now airy and spacious; a new spa and beauty salon has also opened. There are plans for 30 new bedrooms, but guest rooms currently vary considerably in size and appointments and it would be wise to discuss requirements when booking. Live jazz in the bar on Friday nights is popular with guests and locals alike. Attractive weekend and off-season rates are offered. Conference/banqueting (280/220). Private car park. Children welcome (cots available without charge). No pets. **Rooms 130** (20 suites, 20 executive, 8 shower-only, 2 for disabled). Lift. 24 hour room service. B&B €87.50 pps, ss €45. Closed 24-27 Dec. Amex, Diners, MasterCard, Visa, Laser. **Directions:** City centre location.

Cork City
☆RESTAURANT

Isaacs Restaurant

48 MacCurtain Street Cork Co Cork
Tel: 021 450 3805 Fax: 021 455 1348

féile bia In 1992 Michael and Catherine Ryan, together with partner/head chef Canice Sharkey, opened this large, atmospheric modern restaurant in an 18th-century warehouse and it immediately struck a chord with people tired of having to choose between fine dining and fast food, and became a trend-setter in the modern Irish food movement. The combination of international influences and reassuring Irish traditions was ahead of its time, and it quickly gained a following of people who enjoyed both the informal atmosphere, and the freshness of approach in Canice Sharkey's kitchen: a homely mushroom soup might sit easily on the menu alongside tempura of prawns, scallions & aubergine with soy dipping sauce, and a traditional seafood chowder could be garnished with garlic croûtons. In a quiet, low-key way, this restaurant has played a leading role in the culinary revolution that has overtaken Ireland over the last decade or two. Their original blend of Irish and international themes, together with a policy of providing great food and good value in an informal, relaxed ambience has attracted endless imitations. But the idea behind this restaurant was no gimmick and the Isaacs team have retained the restaurant's original style and - most importantly - its policy of delivering quality at a fair price. Ingredients are carefully sourced, the cooking is consistently accomplished and menus are freshened by occasional inspired introductions (a plate of tapas, for example, which is offered as a starter in the evening, but also makes a lovely light lunch was introduced relatively recently and has become a firm favourite). A list of about seven specials changes twice daily, and most dishes are available with little oil and no dairy produce, on request. The service is terrific too, and a visit here is always great fun. The wine list - which is considerately arranged by style ('dry, light and fresh', 'full bodied' etc) follows a similar philosophy, offering a good combination of classics and more unusual bottles, at accessible prices, and Isaacs coffee is organic and Fair Trade. **Seats 120.** L Mon-Sat 12.30-2.30, D daily 6-10 (Sun to 9). Short à la carte and daily blackboard specials; vegetarian dishes highlighted. House wine from €18. Service discretionary. Closed - L Sun, Christmas week, L Bank Holidays. Amex, Diners, MasterCard, Visa, Laser. **Directions:** 5 minutes from Patrick Street; opposite Gresham Metropole Hotel.

Cork City

RESTAURANT

Ivory Tower

The Exchange Builldings Princes Street Cork Co Cork

Tel: 021 427 4665

Seamus O'Connell, one of Ireland's most original culinary talents, runs this unusual restaurant upstairs in an early Victorian commercial building; the entrance to the dowdy building is uninspiring (although, once inside, the stairs and landing have been brightened up of late) and, you arrive in the high-ceilinged room with its slightly faded decor, eclectic ornaments and modern paintings, you will receive a warm and friendly welcome, and soon be impressed by the efficient service and outstanding food and cooking. Tables sporting a crescent moon and star motif are simply laid with linen napkins and good cutlery and glasses. Very best quality ingredients (all local and organic or wild, including game in season), creative menus and excellent details like delicious home-baked breads and imaginative presentation are the hallmarks of The Ivory Tower - and vegetarian dishes interesting enough to tempt hardened carnivores are always a feature. Varied international 5-course dinner menus with a strong Japanese leaning start off with a "surprise taster" to set the mood and follow with a choice of about eight starters: a perfectly light battered tempura of squash, shiitake & pepper; Korean style bacon & cabbage; salad of aromatic duck confit, girolles & mesclun; selection of nigri sushi are all typical; a middle course then offers a sorbet (gin & tonic, perhaps) and a choice of seasonal soups, such as white miso & oyster or courgette & fennel. Among the ten or so main courses, you will find many treats such as salmon on samphire, with sorrel sauce, fillet steak teriyaki with onion tempura and unusual vegetarian dishes like Morrocon aubergine charlotte & tzatziki, or gnocchi with truffle, girolles, asparagus & parmesan. To finish there are indulgences like dark chocolate silk cake with liquorice & coffee, exotic fruits, and cheeses served with fresh figs. About 50 wines from a variety of interesting regions offer fair value for a restaurant of this quality (no half bottles). Not suitable for children under 5. Private room available. **Seats 35.** L Tue-Sat, 12-3, D Tue-Sat, 6.30-10 (Tue is Sushi Night). 5-course D €60; Surprise Menu about €75. House wine from about €18. SC discretionary. Closed Mon-Wed. Amex, MasterCard, Visa, Laser. **Directions:** Corner of Princes/Oliver Plunkett street. ◇

Cork City

☆RESTAURANT

Jacobs On The Mall

30A South Mall Cork Co Cork

Tel: 021 425 1530 Fax: 021 425 1531

Email: info@jacobsonthemall.com Web: www.jacobsonthemall.com

Its location in the former Turkish baths creates a highly unusual and atmospheric contemporary dining space for what many would regard as Cork's leading restaurant. Head Chef Mercy Fenton is doing a consistently excellent job: modern European cooking is the promise and, with close attention to sourcing the best ingredients allied to outstanding cooking skills, the results are commendably simple and always pleasing in terms of balance and flavour. Details like home-made breads are excellent, and fresh local and organic produce makes its mark in the simplest of dishes, like delicious mixed leaf salads. Reflecting the availability of local produce, lunch and dinner menus change daily and are sensibly brief - offering a choice of about half a dozen dishes on each course, notably seafood and vegetables in season: a simple meal of Ballycotton crab salad with ginger and lime mayonnaise, and sirloin steak with lyonnaise potatoes, green beans, garlic butter and red wine jus could be memorable, for example. Creativity with deliciously wholesome and colourful ingredients, accurate cooking, stylish presentation and efficient yet relaxed service all add up to an outstanding dining experience. Finish on a high note - with a delectable date and butterscotch pudding, with vanilla ice cream, perhaps, or farmhouse cheeses, which are always so good in Cork, served here with fruit and home-made oatcakes. An interesting and fairly priced wine list includes some organic wines and a good choice of half bottles.* Major developments are expected soon, as Jacobs is developing a building at the back of the restaurant. Children welcome. Special diets willingly accommodated with advance notice. **Seats 130** (Private room, 50, with own bar). Air conditioning. Toilets wheelchair accessible. L Mon-Sat 12.30-2.30, D Mon-Sat 6.30-10pm. A la carte. House wines from €19.50;

sc10% (excl L). Closed Sun, 25/26 Dec, L on bank hols. Amex, Diners, MasterCard, Visa, Laser. **Directions:** Beside Bank of Ireland, at the Grand Parade end of the South Mall.

Cork City
☆RESTAURANT

Jacques Restaurant

Phoenix Street Cork Co Cork
Tel: 021 427 7387 Fax: 021 427 0634
Email: jacquesrestaurant@eircom.net Web: www.jacquesrestaurant.ie

An integral part of Cork life since 1982, sisters Eithne and Jacqueline Barry's delightful restaurant has changed with the years, evolving from quite a traditional place to the smart contemporary space that it is today. But, while the surroundings may go through periodic re-makes, the fundamentals of warm hospitality and great food never waiver and that is the reason why many would cite Jacques as their favourite Cork restaurant - and it is hard to envisage a visit to the city without a meal here. There is always a personal welcome and, together with Eileen Carey, who has been in the kitchen with Jacque Barry since 1986, this team has always a put high value on the provenance and quality of the food that provides the basic building blocks for their delicious meals. Menus are based on carefully sourced ingredients from a network of suppliers built up over many years and this care, together with skill and judgement in the kitchen, shows particularly in having the confidence to keep things simple and allow the food to speak for itself. You could start your meal in delectably civilised fashion with a half bottle of Manzanilla, served with nuts and olives, while considering choices from menus that are refreshingly short, which allows this skilled team to concentrate on the delicious cooking that is their forte. Moreish starters like warm salad of chicken, crispy bacon, nuts & rustic potatoes, with tomato vinaigrette are also available as a main course, and there are numerous wonderful speciality dishes including, perhaps, Hake with a mustard and honey glaze, purple sprouting broccoli and celeriac gratin. Ultra fresh fish, simply cooked on or off the bone, is a highlight - and the producers and suppliers who mean so much to this magic restaurant are listed on the back of the menu. Delicious desserts could include rhubarb and custard tart or, if you have a savoury tooth, you might choose Cashel Blue cheese with prune & apple jelly and a walnut biscuit. An interesting, informative wine list matches the food, includes some organic wines, a wine of the month and a god choice of half bottles. Consistently good cooking in stylish, relaxed surroundings and genuinely hospitable service are among the things that makes Jacques special - and it's excellent value too, especially the lunch and early dinner menus. **Seats 62.** Air conditioning. An interesting, fairly priced wine list includes some organic wines and about ten half bottles. Food served all day Mon-Sat 12-10.30. Set L €15.90; D Mon-Sat 6-10.30. Early D 6-7, €21.90. Also à la carte. House wine €19.90. SC discretionary. Closed Sunday, Bank Hols, 24 Dec - 27 Dec. Amex, MasterCard, Visa, Laser. **Directions:** City centre, near G.P.O.

Cork City
HOTEL

Jurys Inn Cork

Andersons Quay Cork Co Cork **Tel: 021 494 3000**
Fax: 021 427 6144 Web: www.jurysdoyle.com

In a fine central riverside site, this conveniently located budget hotel has all the features that Jurys Inns are well known for: room prices include comfortable en-suite accommodation for up to two adults & two children (including a sofa bed) and there is space for a cot (which can be supplied by arrangement). No room service. Arrangement with nearby car park (fee payable). **Rooms 133** (2 suitable for disabled guests, 36 family rooms). Room rate from €89. Innfusion Restaurant serves lunch and dinner every day. Bar serves food 1-10, there's a late bar (to 1.30am, residents only) every night. (Bar closed on Good Friday). Closed 24-27 Dec. Amex, MasterCard, Visa. **Directions:** City centre, on quays.

Cork City
HOTEL/RESTAURANT

Kingsley Hotel

Victoria Cross Cork Co Cork
Tel: 021 480 0500 Fax: 021 480 0526
Email: info@kingsleyhotel.com Web: www.kingsleyhotel.com

Conveniently situated in an attractive location alongside the River Lee, just minutes from both Cork airport and the city centre, this modern hotel has been built and furnished to a high standard and is especially appealing to business visitors, for whom it quickly becomes a home from home. A large, comfortably furnished foyer has a luxurious feel to it - both it and an informal restaurant area a few steps up from it (and overlooking the weir), make good meeting places. This feeling is noticeable throughout the hotel, from the moment guests are greeted on arrival, and accommodation is personally decorated and well-planned to make a good base away from home. Spacious rooms offer traditional comfort and are designed with care: air conditioning, work station with ISDN and modem, interactive TV with message facilities, safes, trouser press with ironing board and same day laundry Recent developments have added a further 75 rooms, plus short-stay apartments, spa, a private dining & conference suite, and an underground carpark. Conference/banqueting (230/200); business centre, broadband, secretarial services; video conferencing, on request; 24 hour room service. Leisure centre (recently refurbished & gym equipment renewed), swimming pool; treatment rooms, beauty salon. Children welcome (under 12s free in parents' room; cot available without charge, baby sitting arranged). Garden. Riverside walks. Pets permitted by arrangement. Parking. **Rooms 131** (71 separate bath & shower, 4 suites, 6 for disabled, all no smoking). Air conditioning. Lift. B&B €80 pps, ss €65. Open all year. **Weir:** Good food has always been a feature of this hotel and the new "Weir" restaurant is sure to provide an attractive dining option for residents and non-residents alike. Service is professional and, as elsewhere in the hotel, outstandingly friendly and helpful. **Seats 140** (private room 20). L & D daily: L 12.30-3, D 5.30-10 (Sun 6-10). Set L €30; Early Bird D 5.30-7.30 €26. set D €50; D also à la carte. House wine from around €17. SC discretionary. *Lounge and bar food also available through the day. Open all year. HelipadAmex, Diners, MasterCard, Visa, Laser. **Directions:** On main N25 Killarney road by Victoria Cross.

Cork City
GUESTHOUSE

Lancaster Lodge

Lancaster Quay Western Road Cork Co Cork
Tel: 021 425 1125 Fax: 021 425 1126
Email: info@lancasterlodge.com Web: www.lancasterlodge.com

This modern purpose-built guesthouse has plenty of parking in its own well-maintained grounds and, together with prompt, friendly and efficient reception, creates an excellent first impression. It was built with vision, to offer hotel quality accommodation, with personal supervision, at a moderate price - and recent visits by the Guide have found everything in tiptop order, with many thoughtful little touches that make a stay here a real pleasure - bottled water on each floor, newspapers in the breakfast room and pleasing surroundings throughout, including original art works. Spacious guest rooms are furnished to a high standard (with free broadband, safes, 12 channel TV, trouser press, tea/coffee facilities and room service as well as the more usual facilities) and the bathrooms, some with jacuzzi baths, are well-designed. Excellent breakfasts are served in an attractive contemporary dining room - a bright and airy space, with light oak floors, high quality modern furnishings and art pieces on the walls. A tempting buffet display offers all manner of juices, fresh and dried fruits, yoghurts and so on, while hot dishes - including dishes like pancakes and wild salmon & scrambled eggs as well as the traditional Irish Breakfast and its many variations - are cooked to order. At the time of going to press an additional 9 bedrooms and a meeting room are almost complete. Children welcome (under 5s free in parents' room, cot available, baby sitting arranged). Free secure parking. 24 hour reception. **Rooms 48** (2 executive rooms, 5 shower only, 2 for disabled, all no smoking, 2 family rooms). Lift. B&B from €65 pps. ss €35 Closed 24-28 Dec. Amex, Diners, MasterCard, Visa, Laser. **Directions:** On Western Road, opposite Café Paradiso.

Cork City
E RESTAURANT

Les Gourmandises Restaurant

17 Cook Street Cork Co Cork
Tel: 021 425 1959 Web: www.lesgourmandises.ie

Just off South Mall, this simple little restaurant feels like an outpost of France - the menu in the window will draw you in and you'll be glad you noticed it. It's run by Patrick and Soizic Kiely - both previously at Restaurant Patrick Guilbaud but, although that says a lot about the key standards, this is an utterly down to earth place far more reminiscent of family-run restaurants in France. The long, narrow room is bright and functional but, although the décor remains rather spare, there can be quite a buzz as the restaurant fills up. Staff - who are mainly French - are pleasant and helpful, swiftly bringing simple menus in the French style, and a lovely wine list. The nearby English market supplies many of the ingredients and a tasting plate of starters is a great idea to get things going (including sample portions of classic dishes like terrine of braised ham, foie gras and roasted sweetbread and tian of crab with roasted cherry tomato & tapenade, perhaps); typical dishes on a lunch menu may include a classic boeuf bourguignon with smoked bacon, mushrooms & pomme purée - which is marinated and very slowly braised, producing superb flavour and melting texture. To finish, there's a good French & Irish cheese selection, a dessert tasting plate and some seasonal dishes - a vanilla & blackcurrant vacherin (with toasted almonds, swiss meringue & blackcurrant sauce), perhaps - as well as the timeless classic like caramelised lemon tart. Presentation is beautiful and the details are excellent - good bread, lovely coffee. A compact, informative list of about 20 wines gives a well-balanced selection from throughout the country and includes several half bottles; excellent house wines are available by the glass. The early dinner menu is more limited than the a la carte, but offers the same high standards at a very reasonable price. Terrific food and good value: a great all-round dining experience. Children over 6 welcome. **Seats 30.** L Fri only (also all of the week before Christmas), 12-2. D Tue-Sat, 6-9.30. Early D, 2/3 course: €27.50/31.50. Also à la carte. House wine €22. Closed Sun, Mon; Mar, Sep. MasterCard, Visa, Laser, Switch. **Directions:** City centre - access to Cook Street from South Mall. ◇

Cork City

Liberty Grill

RESTAURANT

32 Washington Street Cork Co Cork **Tel: 021 427 1049**
Email: dine@libertygrillcork.com Web: www.libertygrillcork.com

This recently-opened restaurant is a sister establishment to Café Gusto on Washington Street (see entry), so you may expect the same philosophy of offering quality ingredients led food, where possible organic and locally sourced. It's situated on the renovated ground floor of an early Victorian block - you'll notice menus displayed on a lectern outside the door - and it's an attractive room, with some exposed stonework, darkwood floor and modern designer chairs & leatherette banquettes; lighting is well done, and a brilliant white ceiling reflects light too, giving it a pleasantly bright and spacious atmosphere. Comfortably spaced tables are set up bistro style with paper napkins and good quality stainless cutlery, and a youthful clientele creates a buzz. Searate menus are offered for brunch, lunch and dinner. The extensive brunch menu is very appealing, and worth knowing about for breakfast, especially if you are staying 'room only' in the area, although it is actually an all day menu. There is some overlap in the afternoon - lunch and dinner menus major in a choice of burgers (including a vegetarian option) and salads, and of course there are grills - fresh fish from the English Market, with salad & fries, for example, or organic sirloin steak. An appropriately small wine list is offered. All round Liberty Grill offers real, tasty food and good value in pleasant surroundings. **Seats 40.** Open Mon-Fri 8am-9pm, Sat 8-10. A la carte. House wine €16. Closed Sun. MasterCard, Visa, Laser. **Directions:** On Washington Street in block between North Main Street and Courthouse.

Cork City

Lotamore House

GUESTHOUSE

Tivoli Cork Co Cork **Tel: 021 482 2344** Fax: 021 482 2219
Email: lotamore@iol.ie Web: www.lotamorehouse.com

Sidney and Geri McElhinney's large period house is set in mature gardens and, although not overly grand, it was built on a generous scale. Spacious, airy rooms have air conditioning, phones, TV and trouser press (tea/coffee trays on request), and they're comfortably furnished, with room for an extra bed or cot, and all have full bathrooms. A large drawing room has plenty of armchairs and an open fire and, although only breakfast and light meals are offered, Fleming's Restaurant (see entry) is next door. The whole house has recently been refurbished. Small conferences by arrangement (25). Children welcome (cot available). Own parking. **Rooms 19** (All no-smoking, 1 family room). Garden. No pets. B&B €65 pps, ss €20. Closed 22 Dec-5 Jan. MasterCard, Visa, Laser. **Directions:** On N8, 10 minutes drive from Cork City.

Cork City

Maryborough House Hotel

HOTEL

Maryborough Hill Douglas Cork Co Cork
Tel: 021 436 5555 Fax: 021 436 5662
Email: info@maryborough.ie Web: www.maryborough.com

féile bia This hotel, which is quietly situated on the south of the city and very convenient to Cork airport and the Jack Lynch tunnel, has a fine country house at its heart and is set in its own gardens. The main entrance is via the original flight of steps up to the old front door and as a conventional reception area would intrude on the beautifully proportioned entrance hall, guests are welcomed at a discreetly positioned desk just inside the front door. The original house has many fine features and is furnished in period style with antiques; spacious public areas now extend from it, right across to the new accommodation wing through the Garden Room, a spacious contemporary lounge furnished with smart leather sofas. The new section of the hotel - which is modern and blends comfortably with the trees and gardens surrounding it - includes excellent leisure facilities, the main bar and restaurant, and guest accommodation. Guest rooms and suites are exceptionally attractive in terms of design - simple, modern, bright, utilising Irish crafts: rooms are generously-sized, with a pleasantly leafy outlook and good amenities; bathrooms have environmentally friendly toiletries, small baths and towels, and suggestions on saving water by avoiding unnecessary laundry - they are, however, well-finished and well-lit, with plenty of marbled shelf space. Conference/banqueting (500/400). Leisure centre (swimming pool); beauty salon. A new spa development, ESPA opened shortly before the guide went to press. Children welcome (under 2s free in parents room, cots available without charge, baby sitting arranged). No pets. **Rooms 93** (2 suites, 3 junior suites, 88 executive rooms, 37 no-smoking, 8 for disabled). Lift. 24 hour room service. B&B €85 pps, ss €25. Closed 24-26 Dec. **Zings:** Creative use of lighting separates areas within this design-led dining area without physical divisions - and the tables are considerately spot lit (ideal for lone diners who wish to read). Gerry Allen, who has been head chef since the hotel opened in 1997 and has earned a local following, offers European cuisine with Mediterranean flavours on quite extensive menus. Although international influences dominate, local produce is used - pretty desserts that are worth leaving room for include a commendable number of choices using seasonal fruits, for example, and local farmhouse cheeses are also a strong option. An unusually wide selection of house wines is offered, all moderately priced. Not suitable for children after 5pm. **Seats 120.** Air conditioning. L daily 12.30-2.30, D 6.30-9.30. Set L €27, D à la carte. House wines from €20. SC discretionary. Amex, Diners, MasterCard, Visa, Laser. **Directions:** Near Douglas village & adjacent to Douglas Golf Club; signed from roundabout where Rochestown Road meets Carrigaline Road.

Cork City
RESTAURANT

Milano

8 Oliver Plunkett Street Cork Co Cork
Tel: 021 427 3106 Fax: 021 427 3107

This spacious modern restaurant is one of a small chain operated in Ireland by the UK company PizzaExpress. Like its sister restaurants (see Dublin) it specialises in providing good moderately priced Italian food - mainly, but not exclusively, authentic pizzas and pastas - in stylish surroundings. Consistency and good service are their strong points and they're happy to cater for large parties, drinks receptions and so on. Live jazz on Wednesday nights. **Seats 120.** No smoking area; air conditioning. Toilets wheelchair accessible. Children welcome. Open daily, noon-midnight (Sun to 11); à la carte. House wine €16.60. Closed 25-26 Dec. Amex, Diners, MasterCard, Visa, Laser. **Directions:** City centre. ◇

Cork City
Ⓝ HOTEL

The Montenotte Hotel

Montenotte Co Cork **Tel: 021 453 0050** Fax: 021 453 0060
Email: reservations@themontenottehotel.com Web: www.themontenottehotel.com

Previously the Country Club Hotel, the 'new' Montenotte opened just as we went to press - perched high over the city in a fashionable residential area, it offers a chic alternative to city centre accommodation. Public rooms include The Vista Bar and Merchants Bistro, both with city views of Cork; lunch (carvery) and light evening food is available in the bar, and the stylish Merchants Bistro offers contemporary cooking in the evening. Bright en-suite bedrooms have all the facilities expected of a modern hotel, including complimentary tea & coffee making service and complimentary wi-fi internet access. Good leisure facilities include a gym, 18m swimming pool, sauna, steamroom and Jacuzzi. For longer stays, The City Suites 2 bedroom apartments offer all the services of a hotel, with more space and privacy. **Rooms 108.** B&B from €139 per double room, or €99 single. **Directions:** From Patrick's Street in the City Centre cross Patrick's Bridge and travel along Mc Curtain Street. At the lights take a left turn up Summerhill North to St. Luke's Cross, at the St. Luke's Cross junction turn right to proceed along the Middle Glanmire Road. The Montenotte Hotel is on your right just after the first bend in the road.

Cork City
RESTAURANT

Nakon Thai Restaurant

Tramway House Douglas Village Cork Co Cork **Tel: 021 436 9900**
Fax: 021 488 8002 Web: www.nakonthai.com

Efficient reception by smiling staff gets guests off to a good start at this smart restaurant in Douglas village. The aim is to provide traditional Thai cuisine in a relaxed and friendly atmosphere and and several menus offer wide range of dishes, including all the popular Thai dishes - house specialities include hot & sour prawn soup - but also some lesser-known dishes. Everything is freshly cooked, without any artificial flavourings or MSG and, although the flavours typical of Thai cuisine - coriander, lime, chilli, saltiness - seem to have been tamed somewhat, presumably to meet local demand, several dishes met with high approval on a recent visit, including Pla Muk Gratjiem Prik Thai (tender squid marinated in garlic and black pepper, stir-fried with Thai herbs) and, from a simple dessert selection that includes exotic Thai fruit salad for a refreshing finish, and a delicious Thai custard. An informative fairly priced wine list deserves investigation (a gewurtztraminer partners Thai food exceptionally well, for example); imported Thai beers are also available. Children welcome. **Seats 42.** Air conditioning. D daily: Mon-Sat 5.30-11, Sun 5-10. Set menus from €19.50; à la carte also available. House wine from €17.95. SC discretionary. Closed 24-28 Dec, Good Fri. Amex, Diners, MasterCard, Visa, Laser. **Directions:** Douglas Village opposite Rugby Club.

Cork City
RESTAURANT

Proby's Bistro

Proby's Quay Crosses Green Cork Co Cork
Tel: 021 431 6531 Fax: 021 497 5882
Email: info@probysbistro.com Web: www.probysbistro.com

féile bia Handier to the city centre than it first appears, this is a pleasant spot for a bite to eat during the day (tables outside for fine weather) as well as in the evening, when menus are more likely to include less usual dishes, such as a main course house speciality of duck confit with foie gras and caramelised onion, sauteed potatoes & green cabbage with bacon lardons. Although the style - established before the current wave and competently executed - is global cuisine, with an emphasis on things Mediterranean, plenty of local produce is used: West Cork black pudding is a favourite in starters, for example and fish from Ballycotton. Fast lunch (€8.50 for a gourmet sandwich with a choice of soup, fried or salad) and early dinner menus offer especially good value. A compact, well-chosen wine list offers about 40 wines, including a pair of appealing French house wines, plus quite an extensive menu of aperitifs, beers and after dinner drinks. An extended, covered terrace was recently completed. Private parties/banqueting (120). Children welcome. **Seats 120** (private room 50; outdoor seating, 20). Air conditioning. Open 6 days: Mon-Fri, 10 am-10pm (L 12-5, D 6-10); Sat D only, 6-10. Value L €8.50, Early D €25 (6-7.30), set D €25/30 2/3 courses, also à la carte; SC discretionary (except 10% on parties of 8+). House wine €19.50. Closed Sun, bank hol Mons, 24-27 Dec. Amex, MasterCard, Visa, Laser. **Directions:** Adjacent to St. Finbarre's Cathedral and Beamish & Crawford brewery.

Cork City
N HOTEL

Radisson SAS Hotel & Spa Cork

Ditchley House Little Island Cork Co Cork
Tel: 021 429 7000 Fax: 021 429 7101
Email: info.cork@radissonsas.com Web: www.radissonsas.com

Unlike most of the Radisson hotels, which tend to be centrally located, this one is situated just east of Cork city, adjacent to an industrial estate - and near the Jack Lynch tunnel, which gives easy access across to the airport. However, it is set in 9 acres of landscaped gardens, and follows the familiar practice of adding a well-designed modern build to an old property, with stylish contemporary interiors including pleasingly spacious public areas. Designed to appeal to both leisure and business guests, the attractive Banks Bar is equally suitable for a relaxing drink, or for business business meetings, and The Island Grillroom offers an intimate dining area. Accommodation is to the usual high standard for new Radisson hotels, offering very comfortable rooms in two distinct styles, Urban or Ocean, which gives guests the choice of warm or cool tones in the decor. In addition to other facilities expected of an hotel of this standard, free WiFi internet access is complementary throughout the hotel. 'The Retreat' leisure facilities include a Spa, with nine treatment rooms and a relaxation suite, and a Fitness Centre with hydrotherapy pool and state of the art gymnasium. The hotel has 9 meeting rooms, a ballroom and pre-conference area - and can equally well accommodate a meeting for two or an event for 450 people. Conference/banqueting (450). **Rooms 129.** B&B from €80 pps. Open all year. **Directions:** Signed off main Cork-Midleton road. ◇

Cork City
HOTEL

Rochestown Park Hotel

Rochestown Road Douglas Cork Co Cork
Tel: 021 489 0800 Fax: 021 489 2178
Email: info@rochestownpark.com Web: www.rochestownpark.com

féile bia Formerly a home of the Lord Mayors of Cork, this attractive hotel stands in lovely grounds and the original parts of the building feature gracious, well-proportioned public rooms. Since opening in 1989 the hotel has seen many changes under the watchful eye of General Manager Liam Lally. Rooms are furnished to a high standard with all the comforts - including air conditioning and safe in executive rooms, as well as the more usual conveniences like tea/coffee trays, multi-channel TV and trouser press, all of which make this a popular base for business guests, who are well looked after in an executive wing. Facilities include a fine leisure centre with a Roman style 20-metre swimming pool, sauna, steam room and computerised gymnasium, as well as a Thalasso Therapy centre which predates the current fashion for spas by a good few years. Conference and meeting facilities are amongst the best in the country. Conference/banqueting (700/500); video conferencing on request. Children welcome (under 6 free in parents' room; cots available free of charge, baby sitting arranged). Leisure centre, swimming pool, beauty salon. Garden. Parking (500). No pets. **Rooms 163** (1 suite, 4 junior suites, 100 executive rooms, 25 no smoking, 3 for disabled). Lift. 24 hour room service. B&B €70 pps, ss €25. SC 12.5%. Thalassotherapy breaks offered, also short breaks (W/E:

2B&B/1D €135). Long stay self-catering available. Open all year except Christmas. L&D daily 12.30-2.30 & 6-10. Bar menu 10-9 daily. SC 12.5%. Amex, Diners, MasterCard, Visa, Laser. **Directions:** Second left after Jack Lynch Tunnel, heading in Rochestown direction.

Cork City
HOTEL

Silver Springs Moran Hotel

Tivoli Cork Co Cork **Tel: 021 450 7533**
Fax: 021 450 7641 Web: www.moranhotels.com

A sister hotel of the Red Cow Moran Hotel in Dublin, this landmark hotel is situated in 25 acres of landscaped gardens about five minutes drive from the city centre; built on a steeply sloping site just above the main Cork-Dublin road, it has the natural advantage of views across Cork harbour from many public areas and bedrooms. Thanks to a major makeover, overseen by John Duffy Design and completed without the hotel closing at any time, it has now shaken off its blocky 1960s concrete image and this stylish "new" hotel is once again an attractive choice for discerning travellers and the business community. Conferences/Banqueting (1,500/1,050). A well-equipped leisure centre with a 25-metre pool. **Rooms 109** (5 suites, 2 mini-suites, 29 executive rooms, 16 no-smoking rooms and 5 for disabled). B&B about €100 pps.Closed 25-26 Dec. Amex, Diners, MasterCard, Visa, Laser. **Directions:** At the Tivoli flyover above the main Cork Dublin road and clearly signed off it. (From Cork, take first left then right at the flyover.)

Cork City
RESTAURANT

Star Anise

4 Bridge Street Cork Co Cork **Tel: 021 455 1635** Fax: 021 455 1635
Email: staranise@eircom.net Web: www.star-anise-cork.com

A smartly painted frontage and cool frosted glass windows create a good impression on arrival at this chic contemporary restaurant - a feeling quickly confirmed by an attractive interior, with clean-lined modern table settings (linen napkins, gleaming glasses), mellow lighting, judiciously placed plants and some very attractive paintings and prints. Although too small for a dedicated reception area, Virginie Sarrazin's welcome is speedy and hospitality genuine: a choice of table (if available), water with ice and lemon brought without asking and tempting menus promptly presented. Proprietor-chef Lambros Lambrou's pleasingly seasonal, accurately described menus are well-balanced - with imaginative choices for vegetarians, and also some daily specials - and the reading is made all the more enjoyable by the arrival of a complimentary amuse-bouche (a shot glass of tomato infused with basil, perhaps) and speedily delivered bread. Speciality dishes tend to favour seafood - Mediterranean fish stew, for example, or pan fried fillet of wild sea bass with basil ratatouille. Carnivores will love the slow cooked lamb wrapped in filo pastry. Classic desserts to finish: Poire Belle Hélène, Tarte tatin, crème brulée (with chocolate & orange perhaps). Imaginative food, sassy service, and an interesting wine list too; wines by the glass chalked up on a board start at about €5 and include a sparkling wine. Good call. Children welcome. **Seats 35.** Air conditioning. L Tue-Sat, 12-3; D Tue-Sat, 6-10. A la carte. House wine from €20.50. Open all year. Diners, MasterCard, Visa, Laser. **Directions:** Between Patrick's Bridge and McCurtain Street.

Cork City
Ⓝ RESTAURANT

Wagamama Cork

4-5 South Main St Cork Co Cork
Tel: 021 427 8872 Web: www.wagamama.ie

A Cork branch of the popular Japanese chain (see entry in Dublin), Wagamama noodle bar offers healthy, inexpensive meals, including an extensive choice of meat, seafood and vegetarian pan Asian dishes, all cooked to order and promptly serves. **Seats 120.** Open 12-11 daily.

COUNTY CORK

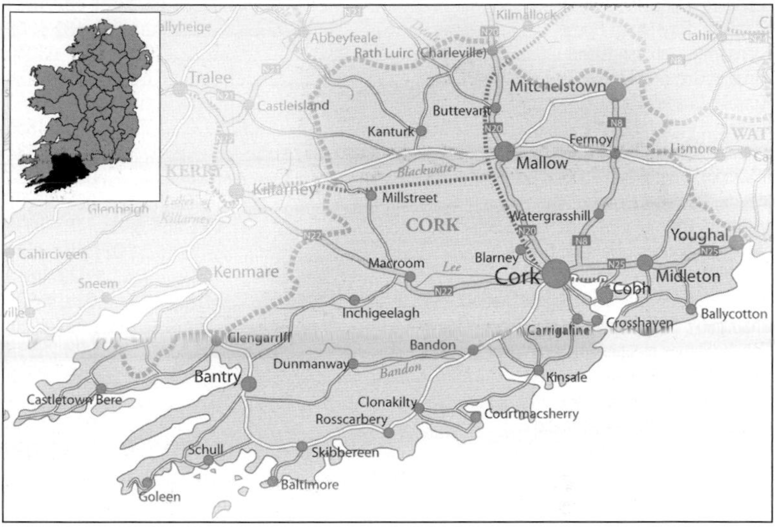

Cork is Ireland's largest county, and its individualistic people take pride in this distinction as they savour the variety of their territory, which ranges from the rich farmlands of the east to the handsome coastline of West Cork, where the light of the famous Fastnet Rock swings across tumbling ocean and spray-tossed headland.

In this extensive county, the towns and villages have their own distinctive character. In the west, their spirit is preserved in the vigour of the landscape. By contrast, East Cork's impressive farming country. radiating towards the ancient estuary port of Youghal, is invitingly prosperous.

The spectacularly located township of Cobh - facing south over Cork Harbour - asserts its own identity, with a renewed sense of its remarkable maritime heritage being expressed in events such as a Sea Shanty Festival, while the town's direct link with the Titanic – Cobh was the ill-fated liner's last port of call – is also commemorated in many ways.

Different again in character is Kinsale, a bustling sailing/fishing port which is home to many intriguing old buildings, yet is a place which is vibrantly modern in outlook.

The county is a repository of the good things of life, a treasure chest of the finest farm produce, and the very best of seafood, brought to market by skilled specialists. Not surprisingly, it is County Cork which is at the forefront in developing the very commendable international Slow Food Movement in Ireland (028-31179)

As Ireland's most southerly county, Cork enjoys the mildest climate of all, and it's a place where they work to live, rather than live to work. So the arts of living are seen at their most skilled in County Cork, and they are practised in a huge territory of such variety that it is difficult to grasp it all, even if you devote your entire vacation to this one county.

Local Attractions and Information

Ballydehob, Nature Art Centre	028 37323
Bantry, Bantry House	027 50047
Bantry, Murphy's International Mussel Fair (May)	027 50360
Bantry, Tourism Information	027 50229
Blarney, Blarney Castle	021 438 5252
Cape Clear Island, International Storytelling Festival (early September)	028 39157
Carrigtwohill Fota Estate (Wildlife Park, Arboretum)	021 481 2728
Castletownbere, Mill Cove Gallery (May to Sept.)	027 70393
Castletownroche, Annes Grove (gardens)	022 26145
Clonakilty, Lisselan Estate Gardens	023 33249
Cobh, The Queenstown Story	021 4813591

Cobh, Sirius Arts Centre	021 481 3790
Cork Airport	021 431 3131
Glanmire, Dunkathel House	021 482 1014
Glanmire, Riverstown House	021 482 1205
Glengarriff, Garinish Island	027 63040
Kinsale, Gourmet Festival (early October)	c/o 021 477 2234
Kinsale, Charles Fort	021 477 2263
Kinsale, Desmond Castle	021 477 4855
Kinsale, Tourism Information	021 477 2234
Macroom, Brierly Gap Cultural Centre	026 42421
Mallow, Cork Racecourse	022 50207
Midleton, Farm Market Sats 9am-1.30pm	021 464 6785 / 463 1096
Midleton, Jameson Heritage Centre	021 461 3594
Millstreet, Country Park	029 71810
Mizen Head, Mizen Vision Signal Station	028 35591
Shanagarry, Ballymaloe Cookery School Gardens	021 464 6785
Schull, Ferries to Sherkin, Cape Clear and Fastnet	028 28278
Schull, Schull Planetarium	028 28552
Skibbereen, Creagh Gardens	028 22121
Skibbereen, Tourism Information	028 21766
Skibbereen, West Cork Arts Centre	028 22090
Slow Food Ireland, (c/o Glenilen Farm, Drimoleague)	028 31179
Youghal, Myrtle Grove	024 92274

Ahakista

Hillcrest House

€ FARMHOUSE

Ahakista Durrus Bantry Co Cork **Tel: 027 67045**
Email: hillcrestfarm@ahakista.com Web: www.ahakista.com

Hospitality comes first at this working farm overlooking Dunmanus Bay, where Agnes Hegarty's guests - including walkers, who revel in the 55 mile "Sheep's Head Way" - are welcomed with a cup of tea and home-baked scones on arrival. It is a traditional farmhouse with some recent additions, and makes a comfortable base for exploring the area, or a traditional family holiday - there's a swing and a donkey on the farm, rooms are big enough for an extra child's bed and it's only five minutes' walk to the beach. There's a sitting room for guests, with television and an open fire, and bedrooms - either recently refurbished or in a new extension - have power showers or bath, very comfortable beds, electric blankets, hair dryers, tea/coffee making facilities and clock radios. Two new rooms are on the ground-floor, with direct access to a sheltered patio, and parking close by. Fine cooked-to-order breakfasts will set you up for the day, and moderately priced evening meals are available if required - although there are plenty of good restaurants nearby, also pub with traditional Irish music. Hillcrest House was our Farmhouse of the Year in 2001. **Rooms 4** (3 en-suite & no-smoking, 3 shower only) B&B €32-34 pps (cot available without charge.) Evening meals by arrangement (7 pm; €22); light meals also available. *Self-catering cottage and farmhouse also available, all year - details on the website. Closed 30 Nov - 6 Jan. MasterCard, Visa, Laser. **Directions:** 3 km from Bantry, takeN71 and turn off for Durrus, then Ahakista - 0.25km to Hillcrest.

Ahakista

The Tin Pub

ATMOSPHERIC PUB

Ahakista Durrus Bantry Co Cork **Tel: 027 67337**
Email: mail@tinpub.com Web: www.tinpub.com

Tom Harrington runs one of the most relaxed bars in the country: known affectionately as "the tin pub" because of its corrugated iron roof, it has a lovely rambling country garden going down to the water at the back, where children are very welcome to burn off excess energy. Other than succumbing to the telephone a year or two ago after years of resistance, it's a place that just doesn't change. Normal pub hours don't apply in this part of the world, but they're open from 12 noon in summer and evenings all year (open Mon-Fri 5, Sat 4, Sun 3 - bar food available any time), except 25 Dec & Good Fri. **Directions:** Sheeps Head direction, from Durrus.

Ballycotton
HOTEL/RESTAURANT

Bayview Hotel

Ballycotton Co Cork **Tel: 021 464 6746** Fax: 021 464 6075
Email: res@thebayviewhotel.com Web: www.thebayviewhotel.com

Overlooking Ballycotton Harbour, John and Carmel O'Briens' hotel enjoys a magnificent location on the sea side of the road, with a path down to the beach through its own gardens - and there are miles of sandy beaches nearby. The O'Briens completely rebuilt the hotel in the 1990's, keeping the building fairly low and in sympathy with the traditional style and scale of the surrounding buildings and harbour, and its immaculate grounds, classy cream paintwork and smart black railings create an excellent first impression. The style is quite traditional throughout and comfortable, homely public areas include a very pleasant bar with clubby leather furniture and a cosy atmosphere - and friendly, helpful staff do their best to make guests feel at home. Well-furnished bedrooms all have sea views although they vary according to their position in the building - first floor rooms include two corner suites (with jacuzzi) and they all open onto small balconies, while those on the top have smaller dormer windows (and may seem cosy or a little claustrophobic, depending on your taste). All rooms and bathrooms have recently been completely refurbished. Small conferences/banqueting (40/90). Children welcome (under 12 free in parents' room, cot available without charge, baby sitting arranged). No pets. Garden, tennis, fishing, walking. *The nearby **Garryvoe Hotel** is in the same family ownership and has recently undergone impressive redevelopment; its beachside location makes it a popular base for family holidays (see website above for details.) **Rooms 35** (2 suites, 5 no-smoking rooms). B&B €86pps, ss€32. Closed Nov-Apr. **Capricho at the Bayview**: Head chef Ciaran Scully has been at the Bayview since 1996 and his creative cooking has earned a loyal following. The restaurant is smartly furnished, with a nice traditional feel; the best tables have lovely harbour and sea views, although you may not be guaranteed a window table when booking. However, whether for dinner or Sunday lunch, you can safely anticipate an interesting and satisfying dining experience, complemented by caring service. Menus, changed daily, are developed from a classic French base, with some contemporary international overtones - but the cooking is increasingly influenced by local produce and the tone is refreshingly straightforward, reflecting the confidence of a talented chef whose cooking style is modern Irish. Unusual speciality dishes in Ciaran's repertoire include 'Fishy, Fishy, Fishy' - a trio of ketafi coated prawns with avocado salsa & chilli sauce; seared brochette of organic salmon & teriyaki sauce; and smoked tuna loin with wasabi mayonnaise and Japanese salad - and 'Three Little Pigs', a trio of: braised pigs cheek with swede purée; honey & mustard baked bacon belly with cabbage; and faggot of sausage meat, pudding and caramelised apple. Vegetarian dishes are not always listed on the menu, so you may have to ask for a special dish to be made to order - but main courses are imaginatively garnished. delicious desserts may include refreshing fruit sushi, with a selection of sorbets and sauces, and farmhouse cheeses are served with a terrine of dried figs. Ciaran Scully is a committed chef - his menu leads off with an introduction to local produce, in which he takes great pride, and finishes with a list of suppliers; but there's also a sense that this chef has fun in the kitchen, creating new dishes, which is exciting for all concerned - not least the fortunate guest. In fine weather, light meals may be served in the garden. A nice, informative wine list includes an unusually good choice of half bottles. Children welcome. **Seats 45** (private room 28) D 7-9 daily, L Sun only, 1-2. D à la carte; Set Sun L €23. Wines from about €23. (Bar meals available daily 12.30-6). Amex, Diners, MasterCard, Visa, Laser. **Directions:** At Castlemartyr, on the N25, turn onto the R632 in the direction of Garryvoe - Shanagarry - Ballycotton.

Ballydehob
E RESTAURANT

Annie's Restaurant

Main Street Ballydehob Co Cork
Tel: 028 37292

Anne and Dano Barry have been running their famous restaurant since 1983 - and, for many, a visit to West Cork is unthinkable without a meal here. Extending into the building next door a while ago allowed them to upgrade the whole restaurant so all facilities, including disabled toilets, are on the ground floor - but it's still the same Annie's, just a bit bigger. Annie is a great host, welcoming everybody personally, handing out menus - and then sending guests over to Levis' famous old pub across the road for an aperitif. Then she comes over, takes orders and returns to collect people when their meals are ready - there has never been room for waiting around until tables are ready, so this famous arrangement works extremely well. As to the food at Annie's, there's great emphasis on local ingredients and everything is freshly made on the day: wild smoked salmon comes from Sally Barnes nearby at Castletownhend; fresh fish is delivered every night; meat comes from the local butcher (who kills his own meat); their famous roast boned duck is from nearby Skeaghanore Farm; their west Cork farmhouse cheeses include one of Ireland's most renowned cheeses, Gubbeen, which is made by Annie's sister-in-law Giana Ferguson; smoked foods come from the Gubbeen Smokehouse, where nephew

Fingal Ferguson smokes bacon and cheese; and all the breads, ice creams and desserts for the restaurant are made on the premises. And Dano's cooking is simple and wholesome, the nearest to really good home cooking you could ever hope to find in a restaurant. Dano cooks fish like a dream and there is nowhere else like Annie's. Prices are very fair - the 4-course dinner menu is priced by choice of main courses and there's a carefully chosen wine list, with the majority of bottles under €30; annual tasting sessions decide on the six wines selected as House Wines for the year - interesting choices, and all great value at about €20. Not suitable for children after 9 pm. Toilets wheelchair accessible. Air conditioning. **Seats 45.** D Tue-Sat 6.30-10, Set D €36/47 2/3 courses, à la carte also offered. House wines €20. SC Discretionary. Closed Sun, Mon & 14 Oct - 1 Dec. MasterCard, Visa, Laser, Switch. **Directions:** Street-side, midway through village.

Ballydehob

Levis' Bar

ATMOSPHERIC PUB

Corner House Main Street Ballydehob Co Cork **Tel: 028 37118**

The Levis sisters ran this 150-year-old bar and grocery for as long as anyone can remember - sadly, Julia died in 2006, but Nell is still welcoming visitors as hospitably as ever. It is a characterful and delightfully friendly place, whether you are just in for a casual drink or using the pub as the unofficial 'reception' area for Annie's restaurant across the road (see entry for Annie's above). Closed 25 Dec & Good Fri. **Directions:** Main street, opposite Annie's.

Ballylickey

Seaview House Hotel

HOTEL/RESTAURANT

Ballylickey Bantry Co Cork
Tel: 027 50462 Fax: 027 51555
Email: info@seaviewhousehotel.com Web: www.seaviewhousehotel.com

féile bia A warm welcome and personal supervision are the hallmarks of Kathleen O'Sullivan's restful country house hotel close to Ballylickey Bridge. Public rooms, which are spacious and well-proportioned, include a graciously decorated drawing room and a cocktail bar, both overlooking lovely gardens at the front of the house, and with outdoor seating for fine weather, also a cosy library and television room. Rooms vary, as is the way with old houses, and the most luxurious accommodation is in junior suites in a new wing; but many rooms have sea views, all are generously sized and individually decorated, and most have good bathrooms. Family furniture and antiques enhance the hotel, and standards of maintenance and housekeeping are consistently outstanding. Children welcome (cot available, baby sitting arranged). Pets permitted in some areas by arrangement. **Rooms 25** (6 junior suites, 2 family rooms, 5 ground floor rooms, 1 shower only, 2 disabled, all no smoking). No lift. B&B €95 pps, ss €25. **Restaurant:** Overlooking the garden, with views over Bantry Bay, the restaurant is elegant and well-appointed with antiques, fresh flowers and plenty of privacy. Set five-course dinner menus change daily and offer a wide choice on all courses; the style is country house cooking, with the emphasis firmly on local produce, especially seafood, in dishes like simple fresh Bantry Bay crab salad with Marie Rose sauce, chicken & celery consommé, baked fillet of lemon sole with tartare sauce or (an all time favourite) roast rack of lamb with rosemary. Choose from classic desserts - strawberry meringue roulade, crème brulée - or local cheeses to finish. Tea or coffee and petits fours may be served out of doors on fine summer evenings. A carefully selected, very informative, wine list offers an extensive range of well chosen house wines, a generous choice of half bottles - and many treats. Service, as elsewhere in the hotel, is caring and professional. **Seats 50.** Children welcome. Toilets wheelchair accessible. D 7-9 daily, L Sun only 12.45-1.30; Set D €30/40, 2/3 courses. House wines from €18. 10% sc. Hotel closed mid Nov-mid Mar. Amex, MasterCard, Visa, Laser. **Directions:** 10 mins drive from Bantry, on N71 to Glengarriff.

BALTIMORE AREA

Baltimore village has grown a lot of late, although it still retains its unique laid-back holiday atmosphere. The Jacob family - originally known for the Breton seafood restaurant **Chez Youen** (028 20136; www.youenjacob.com) - now operates several establishments in the village so it is necessary to group them together: in addition to Chez Youen, **Baltimore Bay Guesthouse** (028 20600) & the informal restaurant below it, La Jolie Brise, are run by Youen Jacob the younger and, adjacent to it, you will find **The Waterfront** (028 20159), a pub acquired by the family in 2004. Just a 10-minute trip ferry from Baltimore harbour Sherkin Island is a small island 3.5 miles long and 1.5 miles wide, with a population of only a hundred or so and three lovely safe beaches. **The Islanders Rest Hotel** (Tel 028 20116; wwww.islandersrest.ie) would make a comfortable base for a break, and an unusual choice for a traditional family holiday - and wholesome fare is available to those taking the ferry to the isalnd for the day. Those preferring a smaller, quieter base might consider **Windhoek** (Tel 028 20275;

www.windhoeksherkin.com), a beautifully renovated farmhouse that reaches down to the waterfront and is close to two deserted beaches.

WWW.IRELAND-GUIDE.COM FOR THE BEST PLACES TO EAT, DRINK & STAY

Baltimore

Baltimore Harbour Hotel

HOTEL

Baltimore Co Cork **Tel: 028 20361** Fax: 028 20466
Email: info@baltimoreharbourhotel.ie Web: www.baltimoreharbourhotel.ie

féile bia Quietly located off the road, yet just a couple of minutes' walk from the village/harbour area, this privately owned hotel on enjoys a lovely position overlooking Roaring Water Bay and is well located for garden visits, deep sea fishing, visiting the nearby islands, including Sherkin and Cape Clear, or as a base for exploring the area. having been extensively redesigned and improved in recent years, the hotel is now the centre of a compact complex that offers various types of accommodation including a block of 2- and 3-bedroom suites that are ideal for groups or families - cleverly designed to include a traditional arch which now leads through to the carpark - and a leisure centre, which has a wide range of facilities including a 16-metre swimming pool, gymnasium. Modern furnishings, with plenty of light wood and pastel colours, create a sense of space in public areas - notably the Garden Room lounge, a pleasant west-facing room which has access to an attractive garden - and regular refurbishment keeps the decor fresh. Accommodation includes family rooms and suites, and all rooms are comfortably furnished, with neat bathrooms and sea views; the larger ones have double and single beds. The hotel's Clipper Restaurant caters for a wide range of tastes, and offers a children's menu. Public areas include a bar that can be reversed to serve the Sherkin Room (banqueting/conferences for 150) and a bright semi-conservatory Garden Room for informal meals and drinks. Children are well looked after - there's a playroom, a children's club in school holidays and under 5s are free in parents' room (cots available without charge, baby sitting arranged). Off-season breaks are good value. No pets. Lift. **Rooms 64.** B&B about €84 pps, ss about €25. *Various packages and short breaks are offered; details on application. Closed Christmas-New Year. Amex, Diners, MasterCard, Visa. **Directions:** Signposted on the right as you enter Baltimore on the R595 from Skibbereen.

Baltimore

Bushe's Bar

BAR/B&B

The Square Baltimore Co Cork **Tel: 028 20125** Fax: 028 20596
Email: tom@bushesbar.com Web: www.bushesbar.com

Everyone, especially visiting and local sailors, feels at home in this famous old bar. It's choc-a-bloc with genuine maritime artefacts such as charts, tide tables, ships' clocks, compasses, lanterns, pennants et al - but it's the Bushe family's hospitality that makes it really special. Since Richard and Eileen took on the bar in 1973 it's been "home from home" for regular visitors to Baltimore, for whom a late morning call is de rigeur (in order to collect the ordered newspapers that are rolled up and stacked in the bar window each day). Now, it's in the safe hands of the next generation - Tom, Aidan and Marion Bushe - so all is humming nicely. Simple, homely bar food starts early in the day with tea and coffee from 9.30, moving on to Marion's home-made soups and a range of sandwiches including home-cooked meats (ham, roast beef, corned beef), salmon, smoked mackerel or - the most popular by far - open crab sandwiches, served with home-baked brown bread. And all under €9. This is a terrific pub, at any time of year, and was a very worthy recipient of our Pub of the Year Award in 2000. Children not allowed after 10pm. Bar food served 9.30am-8pm daily (12.30-8 Sun). Bar closed 25 Dec & Good Fri. **Accommodation:** Over the bar, there are three big, comfortable bedrooms, all with a double and single bed, bath & shower, TV and a kitchenette with all that is needed to make your own continental breakfast. There are also showers provided for the use of sailors and fishermen. No pets. **Rooms 3.** B&B €25/30 pps, single rate €35. Amex, MasterCard, Visa, Laser. **Directions:** In the middle of Baltimore, on the square overlooking the harbour.

Baltimore

Casey's of Baltimore

HOTEL

Baltimore Co Cork **Tel: 028 20197** Fax: 028 20509
Email: info@caseysofbaltimore.com Web: www.caseysofbaltimore.com

féile bia The Casey family's striking dark green hotel is just outside Baltimore as you approach and enjoys dramatic views over Roaring Water Bay to the islands beyond. It has grown, organically it seems, from the immaculately maintained bar/restaurant that the Caseys had run for twenty years to the characterful hotel they operate today. The old back bar and restaurant have been ingeniously developed to extend the ground floor public areas and make best use of the view; local seafood has always been the main draw, on both bar and restaurant menus, but there is always a balanced choice including local meats and poultry, and at least one vegetarian dish . Bedrooms are spacious and well-furnished, with good facilities (phone, TV, tea/coffee tray, trouser press) neat bathrooms with full bath and shower - and those wonderful views. Friendly, helpful staff create a relaxed atmosphere and there are well-organised outdoor eating areas for bar food in fine weather. On less favoured days, the open fires are very welcome - and there's traditional music at weekends. Small conferences/banqueting (35/80). Incentive packages; short breaks. Children welcome (under 3s free in parents' room, cots available without charge), but not in public areas after 7 pm. No pets. **Rooms 14** (1 shower only) B&B €87.50 pps, ss €20. Bar meals daily 12.30-3 & 6.30-9. **Restaurant Seats 80:** Air conditioning. L & D daily: L12.30-3, D 6.30-9. Set L (Sun) €25. à la carte L&D also available; house wine from €19.75; service discretionary. Closed 20-27 Dec. Amex, Diners, MasterCard, Visa, Laser. **Directions:** From Cork take the N71 to Skibbereen & then R595 to Baltimore; on right entering the village.

Baltimore

Customs House

N E RESTAURANT

Baltimore Co Cork

Tel: 028 20200 Web: www.thecustomshouse.com

New owners took over this renowned restaurant in 2006 - a hard act to follow - and it is greatly to the credit of Gillian Oliva (the host, who is originally from Baltimore) and her American husband Billy (who is the chef) that they have achieved a smooth changeover and The Customs House continues to please with good cooking and value. You ring the doorbell to go into the restaurant which is in two interconnecting rooms and has a classy and relaxed feeling, with very low music, a subtle shade of yellow on the walls, oil paintings, venetian blinds and floorboards painted rather funkily with (sound-absorbent) red rubber. There's delicious home made ciabatta bread on the table, water is brought without asking (efficient service is a strong point here) and two menus are offered a very short €30 menu and more choice, including a vegetarian option, such as grilled summer vegetable risotto with shaved Parmesan & white truffle essence, for €40. Local seafood is dominant, of course, but you'll also find alternatives such as Skeaghanore duck, and really good dry aged Hereford beef. Starters may include a fresh-flavoured Seafood Tasting - céviche of local seafood, crab claws, marinated tiger prawns (hardly local, but almost universal in Irish restaurants now, alas) - which comes with claw crackers and a piquant mustardy dressing for the salad garnish. Creative combinations like herb roasted monkfish 'Romesco' (with organic tomato and Parmesan polenta, balsamic reduction) and 'barbecue glaze' local wild salmon (with smoked bacon, cabbage and sweetcorn broth) offer new takes on classics and it is a treat to find Dover sole on the bone on a menu in this price range without a supplement charged; it is given a little contemporary lift with extra virgin olive oil, roasted tomatoes and lemon, but not enough innovation to ruin the classic simplicity which this delicious fish deserves. Flavoursome vegetables might include crushed potatoes fried with garlic, fine carrot strips, green beans and sugar peas (and are not charged extra) and an Irish cheese selection offers lesser known cheeses such as Ardagh Castle and Crozier Blue as well as some of the more famous local ones. Pride is taken in the cooking here, and upbeat classic desserts, such as lime & basil pannacotta with raspberry sorbet, and all are all home made. The wine list offers a fair choice and includes some half bottles and pudding wines, but none by the glass. **Seats 34.** D, 7-11. Set D €40; not suitable for children under 13. Opening times & days vary, please call in advance off season. Closed Oct-Apr. **No Credit Cards. Directions:** Beside the Garda Station 50 metres from the pier.

Baltimore

Glebe House Gardens

CAFÉ

Glebe Gardens Baltimore Co Cork **Tel: 028 20232**

Email: glebegardens@eircom.net Web: www.glebegardens.com

Jean and Peter Perry's wonderful gardens just outside Baltimore attract a growing number of visitors each year and, in 2004, they opened a café for those in need of a restorative bite; it's all very wholesome - and they generously allow you to bring your own picnic too, if preferred. The menu is sensibly short but the food, using organically grown ingredients from the garden and from named local craft suppliers, is unpretentious, and cooked (to order) to a very high standard indeed. For example, you might try a four fish chowder (angler, smoked haddock, fresh salmon and mussels -the latter cooked briefly and added just before serving), accompanied by delicious homemade brown bread and the lightest, fluffiest white scone you are likely to find anywhere. A scrumptious four cheese (Irish farmhouse) and tomato tart accompanied by a delicately dressed salad (about ten different leaves and flowers from the garden) and beetroot cake - one of four equally enticing home made cakes - is a highlight. Other possibilities include smoked mackerel with a leaf salad and oatcakes, or Gubbeen sausage with ash & onion gravy - and all this at a surprisingly reasonable cost. Simply delicious. Gardens open weekends Eater-June and Wed-Sun Jun-Aug. **Directions:** Off Skibbereen-Baltimore road: entrance directly opposite 'Baltimore' sign as you enter the village.

Baltimore

CAFÉ/RESTAURANT WITH ROOMS

Rolf's Restaurant & Wine Bar

Baltimore Co Cork **Tel: 028 20289** Fax: 028 20930
Email: rolfsholidays@eircom.net Web: www.rolfsholidays.com

It's a bit of a trek up from the village if you are on foot, but a visit to Rolf's is well worth the effort. The Haffner family have been here for over 20 years and, although part of the business is still a holiday hostel, it's a hostel with a difference; the complex has been extensively renovated and sensitively developed over the last few years, to include some en-suite rooms, and self-catering accommodation with character - and the restaurant and wine bar, which has earned a loyal following. Discerning locals appreciate both the food and the fact that it remains open after the summer visitors have left and, for the casual visitor, the café is open during the day and serves an à la carte lunch. A more extensive dinner menu is offered in the Restaurant 'Café Art' - which has views over Baltimore harbour, and is named after the contemporary art exhibitions held in the restaurant. Euro-Toques chef Johannes Haffner uses as much home-grown, organic and local produce as possible and all pastries, desserts and breads are home-made; wide-ranging menus include quite a few classics and retro dishes - starters like house paté with cranberry sauce & toast and smoked salmon with crusty brown bread for example, or main courses such as beef stroganoff (authentically cooked with vodka), which sit easily beside updated dishes such as steamed mussels with lemongrass and fresh ginger (starter or main course) and stunningly fresh fish simply cooked in the contemporary style; vegetarians are well looked after (dishes highlighted on the menu) and there's also a better choice than in most other restaurants in the area for carnivores. Desserts include some continental treats - Flemish apple tart, "Linzer" almond tart - and coffees are delicious. The wine bar - with an open fire - is just the place for a drink before (or after) dinner; many wines not given on the wine list are available here by the glass. Garden terrace and sea view terrace available for fine weather. Self-catering accommodation also available, and Rolf's can provide home-cooked dishes and wines to take away. **Accommodation: Rooms 14** (10 en-suite, shower only, 6 with private bathrooms - not connecting, 4 family rooms, all no smoking). €40-70 per room (double). Children welcome (cot available without charge, baby sitting arranged). Pets permitted by arrangement. Garden. Walking. **Restaurant: Seats 75** (also outdoor 40). Toilets wheelchair accessible. L 12.30-2.30, D 6-9.30 (to 9 off-season). A la carte. House wine €20. Open all week. Reservations advised. Closed 24-26 Dec. MasterCard, Visa, Laser. **Directions:** On Baltimore Hill, 10 minute walk from village.

Baltimore

B&B

Slipway

The Cove Baltimore Co Cork **Tel: 028 20134** Fax: 028 20134
Email: theslipway@hotmail.com Web: www.theslipway.com

Quietly located away from the bustle around the square, but within easy walking distance of several excellent restaurants, Wilmie Owen's unusual house has uninterrupted views of the harbour and distant seascape from all the bedrooms, and also the first floor breakfast room, which has a balcony (a delightful room but, unfortunately, not available to guests, except at breakfast time). There's a lovely garden and also a charming oyster bar in a converted outbuilding; very much intended for residents, it is only open when Wilmie's husband, Dave, is not away on his travels. A self-catering cottage is also available for weekly rental (sleeps 2); details on application. Not suitable for children under 12; no pets. Garden. **Rooms 4** (all shower only & no-smoking, 1 family room, 2 groundfloor). B&B €37.50 pps, ss €27.50. Closed Nov-Mar officially, but phone to check, open over New Years. **No Credit Cards.** **Directions:** Through Baltimore village, to the Cove, 500 metres.

Baltimore

RESTAURANT

The Mews

Baltimore Co Cork **Tel: 028 20390** Fax: 028 20390

Owner-chef Denis Connolly's hospitable and atmospheric restaurant is a romantic spot, with white linen-clad candlelit tables and strategically placed plants, stone walls and an adjacent conservatory that is bright and fresh for early dining, turning into an equally romantic setting by candle light as darkness falls. Menus are contemporary and the cooking is based on carefully sourced fresh ingredients in generous and light dishes inspired by international influences. Freshly-baked breads and tapenade get the evening off to a good start, and starters like a house seafood chowder, or a goats cheese parcel with sweet roasted cherry tomatoes should not disappoint. Main courses will include several seafood dishes, a vegetarian choice - such as a filo basket filled with stir fried vegetables with a light blue cheese sauce - and a variation on traditional themes, such as fillet steak with a parsnip crisps and sala verde. Desserts include home made ice creams, or you could finish with a European cheese plate and freshly brewed coffee. **Seats 32.** D only, 6-10; à la carte. House wine €21.95. Closed Oct-May. **No Credit Cards.** **Directions:** In village of Baltimore (signed in laneway just before the harbour).

Baltimore Area
(E) RESTAURANT

Island Cottage

Heir Island Skibbereen Co Cork **Tel: 028 38102**
Fax: 028 38102 Web: www.islandcottage.com

Just a short ferry ride from the mainland yet light years away from the "real" world, this place is unique. Hardly a likely location for a restaurant run by two people who have trained and worked in some of Europe's most prestigious establishments - but, since 1990, that is exactly what John Desmond and Ellmary Fenton have been doing at Island Cottage. Everything about it is different from other restaurants, including the booking policy: a basic advance booking for at least six people must be in place before other smaller groups of 2 to 4 can be accepted - not later than 3pm on the day; changes to group numbers require 24 hours notice and a booking deposit of about €15 per head is required to reserve a table (you post a cheque or postal order). The no-choice 5-course menu (about €40) depends on the availability of the fresh local, organic (where possible) and wild island ingredients of that day, which might include wild salmon, shrimp and crab. A typical menu might be: marinated wild salmon on a bed of mayonnaise, with homemade brown bread; roast duck leg (made using hand-reared ducks "of exceptional quality" from Ballydehob) with béarnaise sauce & roast potatoes with rosemary; green salad with a little Gubbeen cheese; hot lemon soufflé; filter coffee. Off season cookery courses offered; also cottages for rent - details from the restaurant. **Seats 24** (max table size 10; be prepared to share a table). Set Menu - no choice, no exceptions D €40. Wed-Sun, 8.15-11.45 pm; one sitting served at group pace. Wine from €20. Off-season: groups of 16-24 by arrangement. Closed Mon & Tue, and mid Sep-mid May (please phone to check off season opening days/times). No credit cards. *Off season cookery courses available. **No Credit Cards. Directions:** From Skibbereen, on Ballydehob road, turn left at Church Cross, signposted Hare Island and Cunnamore. Narrow winding road, past school, church, Minihan's Bar. Continue to end of road, Cunnamore car park. Ferry (blue boat) departs Cunnamore pier at 7.55 returns at 11.55 (journey: 4 minutes.) For ferry, contact John Moore / Richard Pyburn Tel: 086 809 2447.

Bandon
(N) B&B

Kilbrogan House

Bandon Co Cork **Tel: 023 44935**
Email: fitz@kilbrogan.com Web: www.kilbrogan.com

This elegant three-storey Georgian townhouse, built in 1818, faces out onto Kilbrogan Hill, a quiet, mostly residential street in Bandon town. In 1992 brother and sister Catherine and David Fitzmaurice bought it in a dilapidated state and, following sympathetic restoration, including the large sash windows, opened as a guesthouse in 2004. You get the feeling the house, which is listed, has changed little, if at all, since it was built. At the back a large lawn is surrounded by shrubs and tall trees and the stables behind the house, which have been converted into holiday flats rented out by the owners, add to the olde worlde atmosphere. Inside, the hall is large with a wooden floor and a winding staircase. There is a drawing room on the ground floor for guests' use, as well as a sitting room on the first floor with a piano, and a conservatory half way up the stairs at the back of the house. It feels more like a private house than a guesthouse, and guests can help themselves to shoe polish from a small room on the ground floor, watched by the owners' quiet collie dog. Some of the bedrooms look out onto Kilbrogan Hill and the hills beyond the rooftops, others onto the gravel parking area and the lawn and trees at the back; all have mod cons such as flat-screen TV, broadband internet connection and hairdryer, but are elegantly furnished with antiques (including very comfortable beds with lovely starched cotton sheets), and interesting prints decorate the walls; well appointed bathrooms have full bath and power shower, and heated towel rails. Blue and white check cotton napkins and tablecloth on the breakfast table give a cheerful country feel, and David is a trained chef, so you can look forward to a delicious cooked breakfast - just a little let down by commercial juices and the cereal selection, but very enjoyable nonetheless. This is a lovely place to stay, and a great asset to the area. Not suitable for children under 12 yrs; Broadband WI/Fi. **Rooms 4** (all no smoking); B&B €40-50 pps, ss €10. Closed Dec, Jan. *Self catering also available, rates on application. Amex, MasterCard, Visa, Laser. **Directions:** Turn right at Methodist church, follow signs for Macroom.

BANTRY

Delightfully situated at the head of Bantry Bay, this historic town has much to offer the visitor - notably the mid 18th century Bantry House, which is still a family home; set in lovely grounds and gardens, it houses the French Armada Museum. The main hotel in the town is the **Westlodge Hotel** (027 50360; www.westlodgehotel.ie) which, with its extensive amenities, makes a good base for a family holiday; by contrast, the offering is modest at the O'Callaghan family's **Bantry Bay Hotel** (027 50062; www.bantrybayhotel.net) on Wolfe Tone Square, but there is warm family hospitality.

Bantry
BAR/RESTAURANT

O'Connor's Seafood Restaurant & Bar

The Square Bantry Co Cork **Tel: 027 50221** Fax: 027 51094
Email: oconnorseafood@eircom.net Web: www.oconnorseafood.com

This long-established seafood restaurant is right on the main square (site of Friday markets and the annual early-May mussel festival) and, after over thirty years in the O'Connor family, the business was taken over by Peter and Anne O'Brien in 2003. But the entire staff stayed on, the O'Briens kept everything as it was, and everything worked out just fine. And there's actually an even longer family connection here, as Anne's great-grandmother was the original owner of the bar licence back in 1914, which makes for pretty good continuity by any standards. However, in 2006 Peter and Anne decided it was time to make some changes, so the whole place has been refurbished - emerging with a more modern, but very comfortable look. And it's the same old story - the same staff, the same food - and, best of all, the same prices apply. So, you will still find the lobster and oyster fish tank sending all the right messages and Bantry Bay mussels, cooked all ways, remain a speciality - the O'Connor's Selection is quite something, cooked four ways as a main course, or a starter of them grilled with herbs and lemon butter fits the bill perfectly, followed perhaps by fresh scallops and monkfish gratin, baked in white wine sauce with a cheese & breadcrumb crust, and served with an abundance of fresh vegetables. You could splash out and have lobster, when available, and there's a fair choice of non-fish dishes available too, all using local produce - roast rack of local lamb is another speciality (served with a port & thyme jus), also crispy roast Skeaghamore duck, with ginger & orange sauce. At lunchtime you can have soup and a sandwich in the bar, or daily-changing dishes off the blackboard. Children welcome before 8 pm. **Seats 48.** Air conditioning. L 12.15-3, D 6-10 (Sun to 9). Early D €23.50 (6-7pm); Set D €26. Also à la carte. House wine €18.50. SC discretionary. Closed 25 Dec, Bank Hols, Sun Oct-May, but telephone to confirm opening times off-season. MasterCard, Visa, Laser, Switch. **Directions:** Town centre; prominent location on square.

Bantry
PUB

The Snug

The Quay Bantry Co Cork **Tel: 027 50057**

Maurice and Colette O'Donovans' well-named bar is a cosy and welcoming place, bustling with life and ideal for a wholesome bite at moderate prices. Maurice is the chef and takes pride in using local produce and giving value for money; his menus feature a wide range of popular dishes, many of which are in the house style. At lunch time, home-made soups - chicken & leek, perhaps, or carrot & coriander - top the bill and are followed by other equally good things like poached fresh wild salmon, traditional Irish stew, home-made beefsteak & onion pie and vegetarian lasagne "house style". More extensive evening menus offer dressier dishes as well, including starters like Bantry Bay prawn cocktail or oak smoked salmon salad, and a good choice of main courses like steaks, home-made beefburgers and local Skeaghamore duck with orange sauce as well as a number fish dishes - including Bantry Bay mussels, of course. This wholesome fare is good value. Children welcome (but not after 9pm). Food served daily, 10.30am-9pm (Sun 12.30-9). Closed 25 Dec & Good Fri. MasterCard, Visa, Laser. **Directions:** Beside Garda Station, on the quay as you enter Bantry.

Bantry Area
RESTAURANT WITH ROOMS

Larchwood House Restaurant

Pearsons Bridge Bantry Co Cork
Tel: 027 66181

The gardens are a special point of interest here, complementing the restaurant, which is in a relatively modern house with both the traditionally-furnished lounge and dining room enjoying lovely views. Sheila Vaughan, a Euro-Toques chef, presents seasonal dinner menus: smoked salmon with citrus salad, an unusual soup such as carrot & peach, quite traditional main courses such as loin of lamb with lemon and mint, and classical desserts like ice cream terrine or warm chocolate cake with caramel sauce - good cooking and, while the pace is leisurely, the view of the garden is a treat. This is a haven for garden lovers, who often make it a base when visiting the many gardens in the locality; here, the Ouvane River flows through the three acre woodland garden, which includes an island accessible via a footbridge and stepping stones. B&B accommodation is also offered, €40 pps, no ss. Gardens open Mon-Fri 9am-5pm, also several Sundays in June (phone to check dates). **Seats 25.** D Mon-Sat, 7-9.30. Set D €45. House wine €22. SC discretionary. Closed Sun & Christmas week. (Limited opening in winter). Amex, Diners, MasterCard, Visa. **Directions:** Take the Kealkil Road off N71 at Ballylickey; after 2 miles signed just before the bridge. ◇

BLARNEY

Blarney, 5 miles (8km) north of Cork city, is world famous for its castle and the Blarney Stone, with its traditional power of conferring eloquence on those who kiss it... Although it attracts a lot of tourists, its convenience to the city also also make it a good base for business visitors. **The Blarney Park Hotel** (021 438 5281) has excellent facilities for business and leisure, and is a popular conference centre; those who prefer a smaller but lively establishment may like the **Muskerry Arms** (021 438 5200), a traditional pub and guesthouse with traditional music in the bar each evening.

WWW.IRELAND-GUIDE.COM FOR THE BEST PLACES TO EAT, DRINK & STAY

Blarney

GUESTHOUSE

Ashlee Lodge

Tower Blarney Co Cork

Tel: 021 438 5346 Fax: 021 438 5726

Email: info@ashleelodge.com Web: www.ashleelodge.com

Anne and John O'Leary's luxurious purpose-built guesthouse is just a couple of miles outside Blarney and within very easy striking distance of Cork city. (A bus from the city will drop you outside their door.) Everything is immaculate, from the impressive reception area with highly polished floor to bedrooms which, while they may not have views, compensate with king size beds and all the latest technology - wide screen TV, radio and CD unit, direct dial phones with modem access, personal safe and individually controlled air conditioning - as well as tea/coffee facilities, trouser press, hairdryer and (just the thing for padding along to the hot tub on the first floor) bathrobes and towelling slippers. The O'Learys are exceptionally helpful hosts and are willing to assist guest in every way possible - notably with local knowledge of the many golf courses nearby; they arrange tee times, provide transport to and from golf courses and generally act as facilitators. They take pride in giving a good breakfast too - an impressive buffet offers lots of juices, cereals and fresh fruits in season, then there are freshly-baked breads, real honeycomb on every table, and a wide range of hot dishes cooked to order - and prettily presented too. Everything is pristine although, on the down side, the hard flooring used throughout can be noisy.*Dinner is now offered- Anne is the chef, and she offers an appealing choice of about five starters and half a dozen main courses (crostini of St Tola goats cheese with plum & redcurrant compôte, perhaps, followed by Bantry Bay cod with roasted pine nuts, pesto & lemon parsley butter). There's also a choice of 14 wines, all available by the glass and preserved by 'La Verre de Vin' system. Spa with Hot tub, massage. Free broadband; Garden; fishing nearby. Golf breaks. **Rooms 10** (4 suites, 1 shower only, 6 ground floor, 1 for disabled, all no smoking). B&B €70 pps, ss €25. Closed 24 Dec - 20 Jan. Amex, MasterCard, Visa, Laser. **Directions:** Cork side of Blarney.

Blarney

RESTAURANT/PUB

Blairs Inn

Cloghroe Blarney Co Cork **Tel: 021 438 1470**

Email: blair@eircom.net Web: www.blairsinn.ie

John and Anne Blair's delightful riverside pub is in a quiet, wooded setting just outside Blarney yet, sitting in the garden in summer, you might see trout rising in the Owennageara river, while winter offers welcoming open fires in this comfortingly traditional country pub. It's a lovely place to drop into for a drink or a session - and the Blairs have built up a special reputation for their food. Anne supervises the kitchen personally, and care and commitment are evident in menus offering a wide (but not over-extensive) range of interesting but fairly traditional dishes including seafood (from Kenmare and Dingle); old favourites like corned beef with champ & cabbage & parsley sauce, casserole of beef & stout and Irish stew sit easily alongside some fancier fare and make a pleasing change from many other menus; there's always a vegetarian dish on, and game in season too. Lunch is served in the restaurant and bar area; later, there's a separate evening bar menu and à la carte dinner, which can be booked in the candlelit Snug or Pantry dining areas. Outdoor seating is provided in a newly covered patio area, with bar. Children welcome before 8 pm. **Seats 45** (restaurant/bar) & 100 in garden. Bar menu 12.30-9.30 daily. Restaurant L 12.30-4, D 6.30-9.30. A la carte. House wine €21. Service discretionary. Closed 25 Dec & Good Fri. Amex, Diners, MasterCard, Visa, Laser. **Directions:** 5 minutes from Blarney village, on the R579.

Blarney

HOTEL

Blarney Castle Hotel

Village Green Blarney Co Cork **Tel: 021 438 5116** Fax: 021 438 5542

Email: info@blarneycastlehotel.com Web: www.blarneycastlehotel.com

This attractive family-run hotel overlooks the village green in the centre of Blarney, just beside the castle. It has been in the Forrest family since 1837 but, with the exception of the restaurant, reception area and a very characterful old bar with original Victorian tiling and an open fire, they completely rebuilt the hotel a couple of years ago. The new accommodation is very pleasing: spacious, bright bedrooms have a view over the green or a pleasant outlook at the back and all have both a double and single bed, wide screen TV, tea/coffee-making; well-finished bathrooms have classic black and white tiles and full bath. Helpful, friendly staff create a welcoming atmosphere and prices are reasonable for the high standard offered. The adjacent Lemon Tree Restaurant has a separate entrance but is clearly part of the hotel. While it does not carry through the anticipated Mediterranean theme , it offers meals that are above the standard expected in hotel dining rooms and, as elsewhere in the hotel, staff are very hospitable. Short breaks available all year. Golfing breaks offered; numerous golf courses nearby and tee-off times, transport etc arranged for guests. Children welcome (under 5 free in parents' room, cot available without charge, baby sitting arranged.) Pool table. Private parking. **Rooms 13** (1 junior suite,1 shower only, all no smoking). No lift. B&B about €60 pps, ss €20. [Meals: The Lemon Tree Restaurant: D 6.30-9.30. Bar food 12-9.30 daily.] Closed 24-25 Dec. Amex, MasterCard, Visa, Laser. **Directions:** Centre of Blarney, on village green (next to Blarney castle entrance). ◇

Butlerstown

Atlantic Sunset

B&B

Dunworley Butlerstown Bandon Co Cork **Tel: 023 40115**

Mary Holland provides comfortable accommodation and a genuinely warm welcome in her neat modern house with views down to the sea at Dunworley. The house is wheelchair accessible and the ground floor rooms are suitable for less able guests. The breakfast room and some bedroom windows have sea views and, weather permitting, the sight of the sun setting over the Atlantic can indeed be magnificent. Sandy beaches and coastal walk nearby. **Rooms 4** (2 en-suite, shower only). B&B about €28-31pps. Closed Christmas/New Year. **Directions:** From Bandon Road R602 to Timoleague, then Butlerstown Village, Atlantic Sunset 1 km. ◇

Butlerstown

O'Neill's

ATMOSPHERIC PUB

Butlerstown Bandon Co Cork **Tel: 023 40228**

Butlerstown is a pretty pastel-painted village, with lovely views across farmland to Dunworley and the sea beyond. Dermot and Mary O'Neill's unspoilt pub is as pleasant and hospitable a place as could be found to enjoy the view - or to admire the traditional mahogany bar and pictures that make old pubs like this such a pleasure to be in. O'Neill's is now a popular stopping off point for the "Seven Heads Millennium Coastal Walk" so it may be useful to know that children (and well-behaved pets) are welcome. *A point of historical interest: the anchor from the S.S. Cardiff Hall, which sank off the nearby coast in 1925, has found a permanent home on a platform beside the pub. Closed 25 Dec & Good Fri. **No Credit Cards**. **Directions:** On the Courtmacsherry - Clonakilty coast road.

Butlerstown

Otto's Creative Catering - O.C.C.

☆RESTAURANT WITH ROOMS

Dunworley Butlerstown Bandon Co Cork
Tel: 023 40461 Email: ottokunze@eircom.net
Web: www.ottoscreativecatering.com

Very close to the spot where they originally started the famous Dunworley Cottage restaurant many years ago, Hilde and Otto Kunze have created a dream of a place here, with the help of their talented son who lives nearby and is a creative and practical woodworker. The house is unusual and only reveals its true personality once you are inside; words cannot do it justice, so you must go and see it for yourself. Deeply committed to the organic philosophy, Otto and Hilde are members of both Euro-Toques and the Slow Food movement - and their vegetable gardens provide a beautiful and satisfying view from the vine-clad dining room, where meals of wonderful simplicity cooked by Otto are presented by Hilde. Take time to marvel at the sheer originality and ingenuity of their home over a drink (brought with you, if you like - no corkage is charged - or chosen from a short list of biodynamically produced wines) in the sitting room, while also pondering a unique menu that offers several choices on each course. Their own organic farm supplies many of the ingredients for the kitchen, and a comprehensive list of producers and suppliers is presented with the menu. Typically your meal may start with a vegetarian salad platter, with organic leaves and several dips or, perhaps, a plate of Anthony Cresswell's smoked organic salmon. Freshly baked breads and butter will be left temptingly close by on the table - try to resist as there are still marvellous soups (based on whatever vegetable is especially prolific at the time, or perhaps Otto's wonderful beef consommé), before you even reach the main courses. Here Otto moves up another gear and, as well as classics - wild salmon caught off the Seven Heads, panfried and served with, perhaps, a lobster cream, or organic T-bone steak well hung in local butcher Dan Moloney's cold room, pan-fried and served with its own gravy, mushrooms, onions and garlic butter -

there are unusual choices like braised ox tongue with a rich red wine gravy and a vegetarian dish such as white organic asparagus with mustard greens and a freshly whisked sauce béarnaise. A magnificent selection of vegetables, with potatoes and rice, accompanies the main course and everything is presented with originality and palpable pleasure. Then there are desserts - apfelstrudel with vanilla ice cream, perhaps, or rhubarb fool with real vanilla custard. Or, if your visit is well-timed, there might be freshly picked top fruit, warm from the trees in the growing tunnels - cherries, plums, apricots, white peaches... This wonderful food needs no embellishment, it is outstanding value for the quality given - and it clearly gives Otto and Hilde great satisfaction to see their guests' appreciation. This place is a must for any food lover travelling in west Cork. *O.C.C. received our Natural Food Award in 2002, presented jointly by the Guide and Euro-Toques. Organic farm. **Seats 30** (max table size 14). D Wed-Sat, 7.30-9. €55, by reservation (24 hours notice if possible); L Sun only, 1.30-3 pm; Set Sun L €40. Organic house wine from €25, or BYO (no corkage). Closed Mon, Tue; Jan & Feb. **Accommodation:** The bedrooms (four) share the fresh originality of the rest of the house and are furnished in a simple Scandinavian style which, like the cleverly designed shower rooms, is intensely practical. And, of course, you will wake up in a most beautiful place - and have more of that superb food to look forward to, at a breakfast that counts home-made sausages and home-produced rashers among its gems. Children welcome (under 4 free in parents' room, cot available without charge.) Pets by arrangement. Walking, fishing. Garden. *Wheelchair access to dining room, toilet & 1 bedroom only. **Rooms 4.** B&B €65 pps, ss €45. MasterCard, Visa, Laser. **Directions:** Bandon to Timoleague to Dunworley.

Butlerstown

COUNTRY HOUSE

Sea Court

Butlerstown Bandon Co Cork

Tel: 023 40151 / 40218 Email: seacourt_inn@yahoo.com

Set in 10 acres of beautiful tiered parkland (source of the fallen trees used in the construction of Otto's Creative Catering, nearby) Sea Court is at the heart of an unspoilt wonderland for bird-watchers and walkers - and a restful retreat for any discerning traveller. Since 1985, David Elder - an American academic who spends his summers in Ireland - has devoted his energies to restoring this gracious Georgian mansion and, while the task is nowhere near completion, the achievement is remarkable - and ongoing. Recent improvements - installing a shower in the family room, restoring the Georgian library, adding antique pieces - are all part of the long-term plan and, having visited regularly for some years, it is pleasing to see this labour of love unfolding. The grounds and exterior generally are always a credit to him and, although it is wise not to expect too much luxury, what Sea Court has to offer guests is comfortable and reasonably priced accommodation in a real and much-loved country house; bedrooms are, for the most part, elegantly proportioned with bathrooms that are already adequate and gradually being upgraded. Breakfast, cooked by David himself, is served at a long dining table, where dinner is also available if there are advance reservations - and, after dinner, guests can chat around the fire in the drawing room, or browse through David's books. The house is also available for small conferences or celebrations (16-20) and for rental off-season (21 Aug-31 May; sleeps 8-12). **Rooms 6** (5 en-suite, 1 with private bathroom). B&B €50, no ss. D 8pm, €40 (by arrangement - book by noon). No SC. Closed 21 Aug-early June. **No Credit Cards**. **Directions:** Butlerstown is signposted from Timoleague.

Carrigaline

HOTEL

Carrigaline Court Hotel & Leisure Centre

Main Street Carrigaline Co Cork

Tel: 021 485 2100 Fax: 021 437 1103

Email: reception@carrigcourt.com Web: www.carrigcourt.com

féile bia Recent developments have increased the size and amenities of this conveniently-located modern hotel but it is the hands-on management and friendly, attentive staff that really make the difference. Fresh primrose yellow paintwork creates a good first impression which is carried through into bright, spacious public areas - and interesting contemporary furniture is an attractive feature throughout, in both public areas and bedrooms. Accommodation includes several suites and all bedrooms are pleasingly decorated and well-equipped for business guests with work desks, ISDN lines and safes as well as the more usual amenities (TV, tea/coffee making, trouser press); smart marbled bathrooms are quite luxurious, with good quality toiletries. * Bar to be totally redesigned for the 2006/7 season. Conference/banqueting facilities (350/300), also smaller meeting rooms; secretarial services; video conferencing. Leisure centre; swimming pool, crèche, beauty salon. Children welcome (under 5s free in parents' room, cot available without charge, baby sitting arranged). Weekend offers and golf breaks offered. No pets. **Rooms 88** (2 suites, 1 junior suite, 1 for disabled). Lift. 24 hour room service. Turndown service offered. B&B €89 pps, ss €20. Closed 25-26 Dec. Good wine list. Air conditioning. Toilets wheelchair accessible. Children welcome. **Seats 150** (private room, 50). D Mon-Fri 4-9.45, D Sat 6-9.45, D Sun 4-8.45, L Sun only 12.30-2.15. D à la carte; Set Sun

L €25. House wines €18. Closed 25-26 Dec. Amex, Diners, MasterCard, Visa, Laser. **Directions:** Follow South Link Road and then follow signs for Carrigaline.

Carrigaline
GUESTHOUSE

Glenwood House

Ballinrea Road Carrigaline Co Cork
Tel: 021 437 3878 Fax: 021 437 3878
Email: info@glenwoodguesthouse.com Web: www.glenwoodguesthouse.com

This well-respected guesthouse is in purpose-built premises, very conveniently located for Cork Airport and the ferry and set in gardens, where guests can relax in fine weather. Comfortable, well-furnished rooms (including one designed for disabled guests) have all the amenities normally expected of hotels, including ISDN lines, TV with video channel, trouser press/iron, tea/coffee facilities and well-designed bathrooms. Breakfast has always been a strong point - fresh fruits and juices, cheeses, home-made breads and preserves as well as hot dishes (available from 7am for business guests, until 10 am for those taking a leisurely break). A guest sitting room with an open fire makes a cosy retreat on dark winter evenings. Golf nearby. *An extra 5 rooms have recently been added. Children welcome (Under 5 free in parents' room, cot available without charge). No pets. Garden. **Rooms 15** (3 shower only, 1 for disabled, 13 no smoking, all ground floor). Room service (limited hours). B&B €50pps, ss €9. Private parking (15). Closed mid Dec-mid Jan. MasterCard, Visa, Laser. **Directions:** Entering Carrigaline from Cork, turn right at Ballinrea roundabout.

CASTLETOWNBERE

The fishing port of Castletownbere makes a good base for exploring the beautiful south-western tip of the Beara peninsula: Tim Marks and Mary Berry's **Cottage Heights Guesthouse & Seafood Restaurant** (027 71743; www.cottage-heights.com) is on an elevated site at Derrymiham - and **Adrienne MacCarthy's** (027 70014) atmospheric 19th century pub and grocery is close by in the town.
WWW.IRELAND-GUIDE.COM FOR THE BEST PLACES TO EAT, DRINK & STAY

Castletownshend
€ B&B

Bow Hall

Main Street Castletownshend Co Cork
Tel: 028 36114 Email: dvickbowhall@eircom.net

Castletownshend is one of west Cork's prettiest villages and this very comfortable 17th century house on the hill is a wonderful place to stay if you enjoy a civilised atmosphere and old-fashioned comforts. With a pleasant outlook over beautiful well-tended gardens to the sea, excellent home-cooking and a warm welcome by enthusiastic hosts, Dick and Barbara Vickery (who 'retired' here from Minnesota 25 years ago), a visit to this lovely home is a memorable experience. The house is full of interest - books, photographs, paintings - but its most outstanding feature is perhaps the food, which is not only imaginative but much of it is home-grown too. Dinner for residents is by reservation only, when available, and is cooked by Barbara; however this treat would be a truly seasonal meal for a special occasion, based on their own produce fresh from the garden - potatoes, courgettes, swiss chard, salads, fresh herbs and fruit - picked just before serving, and cooked with other local specialities such as fresh crab or salmon. Breakfasts are also a highlight, with freshly squeezed orange juice, Barb's 'just out of the oven scones', home-baked breads and muffins, home-made sausages, bramble jelly and other home-made preserves, pancakes, home-made sausage patties with rhubarb sauce, and eggs Florentine among the many delights. On nights when she is not cooking, Barbara directs guests to good restaurants nearby. Non-smoking house. Children welcome (under 2 free in parents' bedroom, cot available without charge; children's playground nearby). Garden. Walking. Newsagent, tennis & fishing in village. No pets. **Rooms 3** (1 en-suite, 2 with private bath or shower rooms, all no smoking), B&B €50, ss €5; min 2 night stay preferred. Advance bookings essential, especially in winter. Residents D 8 pm, by reservation; €38 (no wine licence). Closed Christmas week. **No Credit Cards. Directions:** 8km (5 miles) from Skibbereen, on main street. Down the hill on the right hand side. Corner House.

Castletownshend
BAR/RESTAURANT

Mary Ann's Bar & Restaurant

Castletownshend Skibbereen Co Cork
Tel: 028 36146 Fax: 028 36920
Email: maryanns@eircom.net Web: www.maryannsbarrestaurant.com

Mention Castletownshend and the chances are that the next words will be 'Mary Ann's', as this welcoming landmark has been the source of happy memories for many a visitor to this picturesque west Cork village over the years. (For those who have come up the hill with a real sailor's appetite from the little quay, the sight of its gleaming bar seen through the open door is one to treasure.) The pub is as old as it looks, going back to 1846, and has been in the energetic and hospitable ownership of Fergus and Patricia O'Mahony since 1988 - but any refurbishments at Mary Ann's have left its original character intact. The O'Mahonys have built up a great reputation for food at the bar and in the restaurant, which is split between an upstairs dining room and The Vine Room at the back, which can be used for private parties; alongside it there is a garden which has been fitted with retractable awning over the tables, allowing for all-weather dining. Seafood is the star, of course, and comes in many guises, usually along with some of the lovely home-baked brown bread which is one of the house specialities. Another is the Platter of Castlehaven Bay Shellfish and Seafood - a sight to behold, and usually including langoustine, crab meat, crab claws, and both fresh and smoked salmon. Much of the menu depends on the catch of the day, although there are also good steaks and roasts, served with delicious local potatoes and seasonal vegetables. Desserts are good too, but local West Cork cheeses are an excellent option. The O'Mahonys also have an art gallery on the first floor, and it is proving a great success. Restaurant **Seats 30** (outside, 100, private room 30). Toilets wheelchair accessible. Children welcome. D daily in summer, 6-9; L 12-2.30. A la carte. House wine from €17.95. SC discretionary. *Bar food 12-2.30 & 6-9 daily. Closed Mon Nov-Mar, 25 Dec, Good Fri & 3 weeks Jan. Amex, MasterCard, Visa, Laser. **Directions:** Five miles from Skibbereen, on lower main street.

CLONAKILTY

A quaint town of narrow streets, brightly coloured houses and hanging baskets, the unlikely product that Clonakilty is most famous for today is black pudding - specifically, Edward Twomey's delicious grainy black pudding. It is now available from every supermarket and good food store throughout the country and, of course, you can buy it (and many other excellent meats) from their fine butchers shop, in Pearse Street. - a good choice if you are in self-catering accommodation in the area. You will, of course, find local black pudding on every breakfast menu in the area - including, no doubt, the traditional **Emmet Hotel** (023 33394; www.emmethotel.com), which is situated on a lovely Georgian Square and has a separate restaurant, **O'Keeffe's** attached; and **Quality Hotel & Leisure Centre** (Tel 021 490 8278; www.choicehotelsireland.ie), which is a little out of the town and could be a good base for family holidays.

WWW.IRELAND-GUIDE.COM FOR THE BEST PLACES TO EAT, DRINK & STAY

Clonakilty

BAR/B&B/RESTAURANT

An Sugan

41 Wolfe Tone Street Clonakilty Co Cork
Tel: 023 33498 Fax: 023 33825
Email: ansugan4@eircom.net Web: www.ansugan.com

The O'Crowley family has owned An Sugan since 1980 and they have done a great job: it's always been a friendly, well-run place and, although it can be very busy at times, their reputation for good food is generally well-deserved. Menus changes daily and are very strong on seafood - specialities include smoked salmon parfait, baked crab and An Sugan seafood basket (prawns, salmon, scallops & monkfish in a dill cream sauce, served in a filo basket) while daily fish specials could include a choice of ten, ranging from cod on a bed of champ to lobster An Sugan (fresh lobster flamed in a brandy & tomato sauce, with mushrooms & shallots) If you're not in the mood for seafood you might try a terrine of the famous Clonakilty puddings or a prime Hereford sirloin steak. Lunch menus are shorter and simpler, but also offer a wide choice of seafood - and some traditional comfort food, like bacon & cabbage. *A new restaurant is under development, to open for the 2007 season. [*B&B accommodation is also available, about €35 pps - call 023 33719 for details.] No private parking. **Seats 42.** Food served 12-9.30 daily; L12-4.30, D 5-9.30. Set Sun L €28, Set D €30/35, also A la carte. House wine from €18. Service discretionary. Restaurant reservations advised. Closed 25/26 Dec & Good Fri. MasterCard, Visa, Laser. **Directions:** From Cork, on the left hand side as you enter Clonakilty.

Clonakilty

HOTEL

Dunmore House Hotel

Muckross Clonakilty Co Cork **Tel: 023 33352** Fax: 023 34686
Email: dunmorehousehotel@eircom.net Web: www.dunmorehotel.com

The magnificent coastal location of the O'Donovan family's hotel has been used to advantage to provide sea views for all bedrooms and to allow guests access to their own stretch of foreshore. Comfortable public areas include a traditional bar and lounges so the dining room - which is light, bright, much more contemporary and home to a fine collection of paintings - is quite a contrast. Bedrooms, which all have sea views, are furnished to a high standard and make a comfortable base for the numerous leisure activities in the area including angling and golf - green fees are free to residents on the hotel's own (highly scenic) nine hole golf course - cycling, horse-riding and watersports; packed lunches are provided on request. Hands-on owner-management, a high standard of maintenance and housekeeping (down to the fresh flowers ordered for the hotel on a weekly basis) and a professional and exceptionally friendly and helpful staff make this a hotel that guests return to again and again. Conference/banqueting 200/250. Wheelchair accessible. Children welcome (under 3 free in parents' room, cot available without charge; junior evening meal 5.30-6.30). Golf, fishing, walking. Dogs allowed in some areas. **Rooms 23** (2 junior suites, 4 shower only, 1 for disabled). B&B about €75 pps, ss €10. Bar food available all day (12-8.30). Restaurant **Seats 80.** Toilets wheelchair accessible. Air conditioning D daily, 7-8.30 (c. €40), L Sun only, 1-2.30 (c. €25). Closed Christmas; 19 Jan-11 Mar. Amex, Diners, MasterCard, Visa, Laser. **Directions:** 4 km from Clonakilty town, well signed. ◇

Clonakilty

Gleeson's

RESTAURANT

3 Connolly Street Clonakilty Co Cork **Tel: 023 21834** Fax: 023 21944
Email: reservations@gleesons.ie Web: www.gleesons.ie

Robert and Alex Gleeson's fine restaurant has a discreet frontage and rather mysterious interior, with dark woods and deep, rich tones in furnishings which exude quality and include many original touches (such as beautifully simple slate place mats). Robert's cooking style is modern French and his experience in famous kitchens - The Dorchester, for example and, closer to home, The Lodge & Spa at Inchydoney Island - should give an idea of what to expect. His menus, which offer about seven choices on each course on the à la carte and three on the early dinner menu, are not over-elaborate but this is emphatically fine dining. Local produce, like Skeaghanore duck, from Ballydehob, is showcased in dishes such as a starter terrine of duck confit, cornfed chicken & woodland mushrooms - or you might try a luxurious main course of Clonakilty Bay lobster with a creamy lobster & herb broth, baby vegetables & saffron potatoes. Not everything is so high fallutin' however, as more down to earth ingredients are used in a speciality dish of pan fried calf's liver with smoked Gubbeen bacon (from the Gubbeen Smokehouse at Durrus), which is served with colcannon mash and onion gravy - dressed up comfort food at its best; side orders are offered but it is pleasing to find that each dish is individually garnished. Vegetarian dishes are imaginative (crisp feta & spinach parcels on a ragoût of chickpeas & tomato, with a lightly spiced beurre blanc) and desserts classical; local farmhouse cheeses, served with home-made crackers, are a tempting alternative. Cooking and service both measure up to the high level of expectation: this is a fine restaurant and is deservedly earning a loyal following. A wide-ranging, informative wine list offers an interesting and well-balanced house selection. Not suitable for children under 7 yrs. **Seats 45.** D Tue-Sat, 6-9.30, L Thu-Fri & Sun only, 12-2.30 (to 3 Sun). Early D €32.50 (6-7pm & all eve Wed); also à la carte. House wine from €19.50. SC discretionary. Closed Sun eve & Mon; 24-26 Dec, 3 weeks Jan/Feb. Amex, MasterCard, Visa, Laser. **Directions:** Town centre; next door to Scannels Pub.

Clonakilty

Harts Coffee Shop

CAFÉ

8 Ashe Street Clonakilty Co Cork
Tel: 023 35583

Good home cooking is the attraction at Aileen Hart's friendly coffee shop in the town centre. A nifty little menu offers all kinds of healthy meals - ranging from a breakfast ciabatta with bacon, eggs & cheese, through warm baguettes (peppered steak strips, perhaps, with lettuce and mayo), sandwiches toasted and cool - all served with side salad & home-made vinaigrette dressing - to specials such as a west Cork salmon plate with home-made brown bread or an Irish cheese plate with a choice of crackers or bread. A Specials board suggests additions to the regular menu - soups (vegetables, perhaps, or pea & mint) based on home-made stocks, which are also used in traditional stews (beef & Beamish, perhaps), available in regular or large portions. But best of all, perhaps, is the choice of home-baked scones just like your granny used to make, served with home-made jam, and tarts - everything from a vegetarian quiche to an old-fashioned apple tart served with cream - and cakes ranging from healthy carrot cake to gooey orange chocolate drizzle cake. Simple, wholesome, home-made: just lovely! Great selection of drinks too, including freshly squeezed juices teas and Green bean coffees. Wine licence. **Seats 30.** Children welcome. Open Mon-Sat, 10-5. Closed 3 weeks Christmas, Sun & bank hols. **No Credit Cards. Directions:** Clonakilty town centre.

Clonakilty

HOTEL/RESTAURANT

The Lodge & Spa at Inchydoney Island

Inchydoney Island Clonakilty Co Cork
Tel: 023 33143 Fax: 023 21164
Email: reservations@inchydoneyisland.com Web: www.inchydoneyisland.com

This hotel enjoys great views over the two 'Blue Flag' beaches at Inchydoney, which bring crowds to the area in summer, so many guests will prefer this as an off-season destination. The building is architecturally uninspired, but it has mellowed as landscaping of the large carpark on the seaward matures - and once inside the hotel (as opposed to the adjacent Dunes Pub), that pampered feeling soon takes over. Dramatic artworks in the spacious foyer are impressive, and other public areas include a large, comfortably furnished first-floor residents' lounge and library, with a piano and extensive sea views, and a soothing atmosphere. Most of the generously sized bedrooms have sea views and all are furnished and decorated in an uncluttered contemporary style, with air conditioning, safe and all the more usual amenities; refurbishment and the addition of balconies is planned for 2007. Exceptional health and leisure facilities include a superb Thalassotherapy Spa (extending at the time of going to press), which offers a range of special treatments and makes Inchydoney a particularly attractive venue off-season, when this a very relaxing place. Special breaks are a major attraction - fishing, equestrian, golf, therapies, or simply an off-season weekend away - and its romantic location ensures its popularity for weddings. Conferences/banqueting (250). Self-catering apartments available (with full use of hotel facilities). Thalassotherapy spa (24 treatment rooms); beauty salon; swimming pool; walking; snooker, pool table. Children welcome (under 4 free in parents' room, cots available, baby sitting arranged). **Rooms 67** (3 suites, 1 junior suite,10 no smoking). Lift. B&B €155, ss €45. SC10%. Open all year except Christmas. **Gulfstream Restaurant:** Located on the first floor, with panoramic sea views from the (rather few) window tables, this elegant restaurant offers fine dining in a broadly Mediterranean style. Fresh local produce, organic where possible, features on seasonal menus that always include imaginative vegetarian options - and willingly caters for any other special dietary requirements. Lighter dishes for spa guests are also offered, with nutritional information outlined. **Seats 70** (private room 250). Non-residents welcome by reservation. Children welcome. Toilets wheelchair accessible. Air conditioning. D 6.30-9.45; Set D €49, also à la carte. House wine €20. SC10%. [*Informal/ bar meals also available 12-9 daily.] Amex, MasterCard, Visa, Laser. **Directions:** N71 from Cork to Clonakilty , then causeway to Inchydoney.

Clonakilty

RESTAURANT/WINE BAR

Malt House Granary Restaurant

30 Ashe Street Clonakilty Co Cork **Tel: 023 34355**
Fax: 023 34355 Email: malthousegranaryrestaurant@eircom.net

The name of Elaine McCarthy's pleasing restaurant and wine bar is inspired by the history of the building. The interior style is modern classic, with warm colours and quality materials giving it a classy feeling - and her interesting, accessible menus confirm that impression. Clonakilty black pudding features, of course - in a starter dish with Gubbeen salami (from Fingal Ferguson's Gubbeen Smokehouse at Durrus) & Italian hams - and so does other local produce: Skeaghanore duckling breast, from Ballydehob, features in an unusual main course (with poached pears) for example, while Bantry Bay mussels are cooked in the classic style, with white wine, and served with a delicious Guinness bread. This restaurant has its heart in the right place, the service is friendly and attentive and it gives good value for money. The wine list, which is interesting, well-priced and informative, includes half a dozen house wines from old and new world countries. **Seats 60** (private room, 15). Reservations accepted but not required. Air conditioning. Toilets wheelchair accessible. Children welcome. L & D daily, 12-4 & 5-10. A la carte. House wines €16.90. Closed Sun L 25 Dec & 1 Jan. MasterCard, Visa, Laser. **Directions:** Town centre, on main street.

Clonakilty

BAR/RESTAURANT

Richy's Bar & Bistro

Wolfe Tone St Clonakilty Co Cork
Tel: 023 21852 Email: richysbarandbistro@eircom.net
Web: www.richysbarandbistro.com

Situated in the centre of Clonakilty, close to a little park, Richy's is one of those relaxed places where today's specials are chalked up on a blackboard you'll find a real cross-section of people, from families with young children to retired couples treating themselves to a night out. It's spacious and appealingly furnished with smart (but not sound-absorbent) window blinds and wooden floors giving a clean, modern feeling, warm yellow walls and paintings well lit in little recessed alcoves. Well-spaced tables, banquettes along one wall and a bar in one of the two eating areas create a comfortable setting for food that ranges widely around the Mediterranean, with a leaning towards

Spain - and locally sourced ingredients may include less usual food like samphire, as well as local lamb and fish. A reasonably priced wine list includes wines by the glass, and other drinks are available from the bar, which is handy for families with young children. If you're really keen on the place, you can buy an apron with Richy's logo, or even a Richy's cookbook, displayed in a glass case in the middle of the restaurant. A useful place to know about, especially when on a family holiday. Children welcome before 8pm. **Seats 80.** Open daily in Summer 11.30am - 10pm; Thu-Mon in winter 5-10pm. Early D Mon-Thu, 5-7; also a la carte. €24.95; House wine €19.95. Closed 25 Dec and Tue, Wed in Jan&FebAmex, MasterCard, Visa, Laser. **Directions:** Next to tourist office.

Clonakilty Area

BAR/RESTAURANT

Deasy's Harbour Bar & Seafood Restaurant

Ring Village Clonakilty Co Cork **Tel: 023 35741**

Just across the road from the water in the pretty village of Ring, this former pub has a decking area at the front and large windows taking advantage of the view of Clonakilty Bay and the boats moored nearby and, inside, brick walls are decorated with nautical bric-a-brac including a fishing net and a ship's wheel, and wooden model ships. With candlelight as well as sea views, it's an atmospheric setting for fine seafood, and lone diners are certain to find something of interest browsing through the coffee table books on marine themes. Tables are simply set and the focus is on menus which are a little international in style (no house or local specialities mentioned), but offer a wide range of seafood including less usual varieties such as shark, with a red pepper and olive sauce, perhaps, as well as fairly classic prime fish dishes like monkfish medallions wrapped in prosciutto with seared scallops and dill creme fraîche. Piquant dips and sauces are out of the ordinary, adding a new dimension to familiar dishes wasabi mayonnaise to complement a crabcake, for example, or a Vietnamese dipping sauce with excellent fish spring rolls; as well as some token offerings of meat or poultry for carnivores, vegetarians are offered an interesting alternative such as polenta with nero di Toscana, basil, pine nuts and parmesan. Good cooking is also seen in tasty vegetables and delicious desserts (vanilla panna cotta with strawberries; lime & coconut cheesecake) and details like lovely breads and thoughtful presentation. With an informal relaxed atmosphere, interesting food and a lovely setting, this has become a popular spot so book well ahead, especially in high season. Not suitable for children after 7pm. **Seats 50;** D Wed-Sat 6-9.30; L Sun only, 1-3; set Sun L €28; house wine €20. Closed Sun D, Mon, Tue and 24-26 Dec. MasterCard, Visa, Laser. **Directions:** 2km outside Clonakilty.

Cloyne

BAR/RESTAURANT

Harty's of Cloyne

Church Street Cloyne Co Cork **Tel: 021 465 2401** Fax: 021 465 2853
Email: akennedy@cork.bonsecours.ie Web: www.hartysrestaurant.com

This attractive pub has a long narrow bar of some character, where bar meals are available every day - and there's a welcoming open fire for colder times: a useful place to break a journey, perhaps. The restaurant - which is next door and accessible from the bar and directly from the street - offers middle of the road food with some exotic options (wild boar, kangaroo, even crocodile sometimes...); staff are pleasant and welcoming and prices quite reasonable. [B&B is under development at the time of going to press.] **Seats 100** (private room, 30, outdoors, 60). Bar meals daily, 12-9; Rest D daily 5-9, L Sun only 12-3.30. Early D €28.50, 5-7pm; Sun L €24.50; house wine from €18.50. Closed 25 Dec & Good Fri. MasterCard, Visa, Laser. **Directions:** Approaching from Midleton, straight through cross in centre of town (Ballycotton is indicated to the left); pub/restaurant 50m on left.

Cobh

COUNTRY HOUSE

Knockeven House

Rushbrooke Cobh Co Cork
Tel: 021 481 1778 Fax: 021 481 1719
Email: info@knockevenhouse.com Web: www.knockevenhouse.com

Clearly signed on the outskirts of Cobh, and at the end of a long winding driveway overhung by tall trees, you will find John and Pam Mulhaire's large and peacefully situated 1840s house. Its rather plain exterior, tarmac parking area and low-maintenance garden give no hint of the luxurious interior which is revealed when the front door opens onto a huge hall, where a deep red carpet and dramatic flower arrangement set on an antique desk set the tone for a house that offers guests best of every world: lavish decor and facilities worthy of a top-class hotel, along with great hospitality, and reasonable prices. The Mulhaires have lived here for 20 years, but only opened for guests in 2004 - Pam is very chatty, relaxed and friendly, a natural hostess who treats her guests to tea and homemade scones on a silver tray on arrival, and on request at any time. An impressive drawing room has plenty of comfortable seating and an open fire and, like the rest of the house, the bedrooms are also decorated with sumptuous good taste (although lovers of old houses will be disappointed by the practical PVC double-glazed windows). Accommodation is very comfortable, with generous beds and immaculate en-suite bathrooms that have power showers (no full bath) and many thoughtful details, including pristine white bathrobes and Molton Brown toiletries. A good breakfast served on white Villeroy & Boch china, with pristine white cotton napkins includes a delicious fresh fruit salad as fresh orange juice, good-quality cereals, yogurts, ham and cheese as well as a sound rendition of the traditional hot breakfast. This is an exceptionally comfortable place to stay and, although no dinner is offered, the restaurants of Midleton (or Monkstown, just across the ferry) are not too far away. Children welcome (cot available). **Rooms 4** (all en-suite and no smoking); limited room service. B&B €60pps, single about €75. **Directions:** On the outskirts of Cobh.

Cobh

N HOTEL

Sheraton Fota Island Golf Resort & Spa

Fota Island Cobh Co Cork **Tel: 021 467 3000** Fax: 021 467 3456
Email: reservations.fota@sheraton.com Web: www.sheraton.com/cork

A beautiful long tree-lined driveway, with glimpses of the water to the right, has always been the entrance to Fota Island Golf Club (which, except for the shared access, is not connected with the hotel), and in no way prepares first time visitors for what awaits around the last corner: whilst the newly planted trees will eventually soften this controversial building, it is easy to see why there was such local opposition to the development. However, as is often the case, things are different when you're on the inside looking out; a concierge desk at the entrance is a good start, as you are met at the door and immediately feel welcome as you move through a large lobby/reception that opens into a spacious high-ceilinged area, with warm lighting, an open fire at and lots of comfy seating. Off this, a bar looks over lawns to the front with a decking area for fine weather; arranged with the bar along one side and windows opposite, this comfortable and appealing room has an open fire which is shared with the adjacent restaurant - also overlooking the grounds, it's a clean-lined room, with bare hardwood tables, white linen napkins, softened by warm lighting. Accommodation is luxurious, as would be expected, with a high proportion of suites and superior rooms, and many rooms enjoying panoramic views over woodlands or golf course; all are spacious and extremely comfortable, with huge beds and big flat screen tv, in addition to the usual facilities, and beautiful bathrooms have double-ended bath with head rests and separate walk in shower. Dining options include the Fota Restaurant, offering a smart option for all day meals, The Cove seafood grill room for evening dining, and The Amber Bar for light meals at any time. Although the hotel had not been open long at the time of our visit, both food and service were impressive. Complimentary wireless internet available in all public areas. * The Island Spa is open and the other big attraction is golf - it can sometimes be difficult to get enough tee times at the adjacent Fota Island Golf Club, but it is hoped that a new 9-hole course which is almost ready for play will allow more flexibility. Championship golf course (18), spa, fitness room, swimming pool. Fly fishing, sea angling and equestrian nearby. Children welcome (cots available at no charge, baby sitting arranged); Conferences/Banqueting (400/280), business centre, secretarial services, Free Broadband. **Rooms 131** (8 suites, 8 junior suites, 40 executive); B&B room rate €165; 24 hr room service; Lift. Open all year. Restaurant: **Seats 80** (outdoor, 30), serves food daily, 12.30-10.30; "The Cove" seafood grill room, seats 40, open Tue-Sat, 7pm-10pm; Barfood served 12.30-8 daily. Helipad. Amex, Diners, MasterCard, Visa, Laser. **Directions:** N25 east from Cork. Approx. 8 km (5m) later take a left and follow signs for Fota island.

CROSSHAVEN

On the west side of Cork Harbour, 17 km from Cork city, Crosshaven is a favourite seaside resort for Cork people and an important yachting centre. The seasonal nature of the town means that restaurants tend to come and go but there are several pubs of character including **The Moonduster Inn** (021 483 1610; www.moondusterinn.com), which also has an attractive first floor restaurant with views cross the water to Currabinny.

WWW.IRELAND-GUIDE.COM FOR THE BEST PLACES TO EAT, DRINK & STAY

Doneraile

Creagh House

Main Street Doneraile Co Cork **Tel: 022 24433** Fax: 022 24715
Email: info@creaghhouse.ie Web: www.creaghhouse.ie

Michael O'Sullivan and Laura O'Mahony left a perfectly normal home to take on this Regency town-house in need of renovation in 2000; since then, they have been giving it enormous amounts of TLC on an ongoing basis so that it may, one day, reach its full potential glory. A listed building, with notable historical and literary connections, stately reception rooms and huge bedrooms, its principal rooms are among the largest from this period outside Dublin, and have beautiful restored plasterwork. Yet it is a relaxed family home and place of work (Michael and Laura both have offices in restored outbuildings), and this hospitable couple clearly thrive on the challenge of the restoration process. Accommodation is wonderful, in vast rooms with huge antique furniture, crisp linen on comfortable beds, little extras (bowls of fruit, bottled water, tea/coffee/hot chocolate making facilities), and bathrooms to match - bath and separate shower, and big, soft towels. All modern partitions have been removed to restore the original scale, and 19th century furniture is used throughout, with 18th and 19th century prints and modern paintings. Anyone interested in architecture and/or history is in for a treat when staying here and Doneraile is well-placed for exploring a wide area - Cork, Cashel, Lismore and Killarney are all within an hour's drive. Garden lovers will be fascinated by the 2-acre walled garden behind Creagh House, which is under restoration ("black topsoil four feet deep!") and the house is beside Doneraile Court, which has 600 acres of estate parkland, free to the public. Golf nearby. Children welcome (under 3s free in parents room, cot available free of charge). No pets. Garden. **Rooms 3** (all en suite, with separate bath and shower, all no smoking). Residents' supper (2-course dinner, €30) available with 24 hours notice. B&B €100-120 pps, no ss. Closed Oct-MarAmex, MasterCard, Visa. **Directions:** Take N20 (Limerick road) from Mallow - 12.5km (8 m).

Durrus

☆RESTAURANT WITH ROOMS

Blairs Cove House

Durrus Bantry Co Cork
Tel: 027 61127 Fax: 027 61487
Email: blairscove@eircom.net Web: www.blairscove.ie

Philippe and Sabine de Mey's beautiful property enjoys a stunning waterside location at the head of Dunmanus Bay. Although additions over the years have enlarged the restaurant considerably - including an elegant conservatory overlooking a courtyard garden - the original room at this remarkable restaurant is lofty, stone-walled and black-beamed. However, while characterful, any tendency to rusticity is immediately offset by the choice of a magnificent chandelier as a central feature, gilt-framed family portraits on the walls, generous use of candles - and the superb insouciance of using their famous grand piano to display an irresistible array of desserts. They have things down to a fine art at Blairs Cove - and what a formula: an enormous central buffet displays the legendary hors d'oeuvre selection, a speciality that is unrivalled in Ireland. Main course specialities of local seafood or the best of meat (rib eye of beef, perhaps) and poultry are char-grilled at a special wood-fired grill right in the restaurant and, in addition to those desserts on the piano, full justice is done to the ever-growing choice of local farmhouse cheese for which West Cork is rightly renowned. An extensive wine list favouring France a little offers a balanced selection in a wide price range, including a good choice of house wines and half bottles. The food is terrific, service friendly and efficient and, as a tribute to its memorable ambience, Blairs Cove was selected as our Atmospheric Restaurant of the Year in 2003. **Seats 80.** Reservations required. D 7.30-9.30 Tue-Sat. Set D €55; house wine €18, SC discretionary. Closed Sun, Mon & Nov-Mar. **Accommodation:** Three small apartments, offered for self-catering or B&B, are furnished in very different but equally dashing styles and there is also a cottage in the grounds. Children welcome, cot available. B&B €110 pps, ss €30; no SC. Amex, Diners, MasterCard, Visa. **Directions:** 3km (1.5 m) outside Durrus on Mizen Head Road, blue gate on right hand side.

Durrus

Ⓝ B&B

Carbery Cottage Guest Lodge

Durrus Bantry Co Cork **Tel: 027 61368**
Email: carberycottage@eircom.net Web: www.carbery-cottage-guest-lodge.net

With well-maintained gardens, plenty of parking and beautiful views, this purpose-built B&B and adjoining self-catering cottage creates a great first impression and a warm welcome extends to your four-legged friends too, with kennels provided, and large grassed penned areas for dogs to run. Owners Mike Hegarty and Julia Bird will be known to many as previous owners of the unique Tin Pub at Ahakista, and they have brought the unique laid-back charm associated with it to this new venture, which offers a home from home with all sorts of hospitable gestures such as a well-stocked drinks fridge where you replace what you take, or use it to store your own. A very comfortable guest sitting room has lots of books, DVDs and games, and there's a sheltered patio for guests; tea and coffee is always available in the dining room where residents' evening meals are served at a big wooden table: seafood dinners are a speciality but the menu also includes other choices including home made soup (served with freshly baked yeast bread) and steak, perhaps, or a casserole, and various home made puddings all for €30. Bedrooms are spacious, simply furnished and modern not the height of luxury but very comfortable; two are en-suite with separate bath and shower, the third has a similar bathroom across the corridor. Full breakfast are available all morning, packed lunches can be arranged. This is a real can-do place, and would make a wonderfully relaxed holiday base. Fishing nearby, walking, short breaks, free broadband WI/Fi, dogs very welcome. Children welcome (under 12's free in parents' room, cot avail.). **Rooms 3** (2 en-suite, 1 with private bathroom, 2 family rooms, 1 ground floor, 1 partially equipped for disabled). B&B €40 pps, no ss. Open all year. Residents D, Mon-Sat, 6-8, €30. *Self catering also avail. **No Credit Cards. Directions:** Between Durrus and Ahakista.

Durrus

Good Things Café

☆CAFÉ

Ahakista Road Durrus Co Cork **Tel: 027 61426** Fax: 027 61426
Email: info@thegoodthingscafe.com Web: www.thegoodthingscafe.com

Great ingredients-led contemporary cooking is the magnet that draws those in the know to Carmel Somers' simple little café-restaurant just outside Durrus village. Well-placed to make the most of fine west Cork produce, she also sells some specialist foods from Ireland and abroad and a few books including the great little guide to Local Producers of Good Food in Cork, produced by Myrtle Allen and Cullen Allen for the Cork Free Choice Consumer Group, which details many of the artisan producers who supply Good Things Café. The daytime café menu offers a concise list including great salads (mixed leaves with fresh beetroot, fresh broad beans, cherry tomatoes, smoked salmon, quails eggs among the goodies), West Cork fish soup (available, like most dishes on the daytime menu, as a starter or main course), West Cork Ploughmans (a trio of local cheeses served with an onion cassis compôte), Durrus cheese, spinach & nutmeg pizza (a thin-based, crisp pizza with a delicious gourmet topping)...then there are irresistible desserts to choose from a display (raspberries and cream, St Emilion chocolate cups...) Dinner brings a more formal menu, with a choice of four on each course, and will feature some of the daytime treats along with main courses like turbot with dill sauce with wilted spinach and local spuds, or beef fillet with pesto, on a bed of wilted spinach, chard, courgette & beetroot. Service is prompt and attentive from the moment a choice of breads and iced water is brought to your table to the arrival of home-made chocolate truffles with your coffee. Ingredients are invariably superb and, at its best, a meal here can be memorable; this place is a one-off and it is well worth planning a stop when travelling in West Cork, especially during the day, when the bright atmosphere and white café furniture seems more appropriate. An interesting, well-priced wine list includes seven well-chosen house wines, and a good choice of half bottles. *Cookery classes also available; details from the restaurant. Wheelchair Accessible. Ample parking. Children welcome. **Seats 40** (plus 10 outdoor in fine weather). In summer, open all day (11-9) Wed-Mon (daily in Aug & during Bantry Music Festival), L 12.30-3; D (7-9). A la carte. House wine about €18. Closed Tue and Sep-Easter. Reservations advised for dinner; a call to check times is wise, especially off-season. MasterCard, Visa, Laser. **Directions:** From Durrus village, take Ahakista/Kilcrohane Road.

Farnanes

Thady Inn

ATMOSPHERIC PUB

Farnanes Co Cork **Tel: 021 733 6379**

Formerly a barracks for British soldiers, this small pub is set well back from the road and the present owners, Den and Martha O'Flaherty, have kept it simple, just as the previous generation did for 30 years before them. They offer a small menu and do a limited number of well-known dishes well: egg mayonnaise, smoked salmon, home-cooked chicken, ham or tongue salad and - the dish that has really made their reputation - great steaks, served with perfectly cooked crispy chips - rounded off with homely apple tart and cream. A good place to break a journey - it's refreshing to visit a pub that hasn't been done up and concentrates on the business of being an inn - looking after wayfarers well. Open 10.30am-12.30am; food available from 4pm daily (last orders 10pm). **No Credit Cards. Directions:** Off N22 between Macroom and Cork.

Farran

Farran House

COUNTRY HOUSE

Farran Co Cork **Tel: 021 733 1215** Fax: 021 733 1450
Email: info@farranhouse.com Web: www.farranhouse.com

Set in 12 acres of mature beech woodland and rhododendron gardens in the rolling hills of the Lee valley, Patricia Wiese and John Kehely's impressive house was built in the mid-18th century, although its present elegant Italianate style only dates back to 1863. It is beautifully situated with views over the medieval castle and abbey of Kilcrea and its location west of Cork city makes this a good base for exploring Cork and Kerry. Since 1993 Patricia and John have painstakingly restored the house to its former glory and, although there are some contemporary touches as well as antiques, none of its original character has been lost - there's a fine drawing room for guests' use (complete with grand piano) and a billiard room with full size table. Despite its considerable size, there are just four bedrooms - all exceptionally spacious and decorated with style (one room is redecorated each year); dinner is offered on most nights, by prior arrangement, and a speciality is home-produced lamb, bred and raised at Farran House; when dinner is unavailable, guests are directed to an interesting old pub nearby where good food is served. The house is available all year for private rental by groups and this is, perhaps, its most attractive use. Broadband. Games room. Office facilities. Golf nearby (six 18 hole courses within 20 km). Children welcome (under 8s free in parents' room, cot available without charge). No pets. Garden. **Rooms 4** (all en-suite, 2 with separate bath & shower; all no smoking); B&B from €85 pps, ss €30 (advance bookings only - 10% discount on 3 night stays; off-season rates reduced); residents D €45 (24 hours notice; not available Sun or Mon, but Thady Inn nearby does good meals). Self-catering coach house (4-6 people, from €500 pw); house also available for self-catering (groups of 8-9, from about €3,500 pw). Closed 1 Nov-31 Mar. MasterCard, Visa, Laser. **Directions:** Just off N22 between Macroom & Cork: heading west, 8km (5 miles) after Ballincollig, turn right to Farran village, up hill, 1st gate on left.

FERMOY

If you need to break a journey in Fermoy, head for **Munchies Gourmet Coffee Shop**, on Lower Patrick Street (Tel: 025 33653); this simple café has an old-fashioned style, but food is well-sourced and freshly cooked with care - and they have a great coffee and tea menu. Open Mon-Sat, all day (9-5). Or, if you are in the mood for something spicier, you might try **Thai Lanna** (025 30900) on McCurtain Street.

WWW.IRELAND-GUIDE.COM FOR THE BEST PLACES TO EAT, DRINK & STAY

Fermoy

La Bigoudenne

RESTAURANT

28 MacCurtain Street Fermoy Co Cork **Tel: 025 32832**

At this little piece of France in the main street of a County Cork town, Noelle and Rodolphe Semeria's hospitality is matched only by their food, which specialises in Breton dishes, especially crèpes - both savoury (made with buckwheat flour) and sweet (with wheat flour). They run a special pancake evening once a month or so, on a Saturday night. But they do all sorts of other things too, like salads that you only seem to get in France, soup of the day served with 1/4 baguette & butter, a plat du jour and lovely French pastries. Opening times are a little complicated, but it's worth taking the trouble to work them out as it's a lovely spot - and even the bill is a pleasant surprise. **Seats 36.** D Tue-Fri, 5.45-9.30, D Sat-Sun, 6.45-9.30: Early D Tue-Thu 5.45-7 (about €21), later D €35 & à la carte; L Thu only, 12.30-3.30. Set D €35, also à la carte. House wine €16.80. Closed Mon & 1-15 Oct. Amex, MasterCard, Visa. **Directions:** On the main street, opposite ESB.

Fermoy Area

Ballyvolane House

COUNTRY HOUSE

Castlelyons Fermoy Co Cork

Tel: 025 36349 Fax: 025 36781

Email: info@ballyvolanehouse.ie Web: www.ballyvolanehouse.ie

The Greene family's gracious mansion is surrounded by its own farmland, magnificent wooded grounds, a trout lake and formal terraced gardens, all carefully managed and well maintained - garden lovers will find a stay here especially rewarding; an information leaflet detailing the garden and walks is available to guests, also one on other walks in the locality. The Italianate style of the present house - including a remarkable pillared hall with a baby grand piano and open fire - dates from the mid 19th century when modifications were made to the original house of 1728. Jeremy and the late Merrle Green first welcomed guests to their home in 1983, and is now run by their son Justin and his wife Jenny; Justin has management experience in top hotels and they are an extremely hospitable couple, committed to ensuring that the standards of hospitality, comfort and food for which this lovely house is renowned will be maintained. And it is a very lovely house, elegantly furnished and extremely comfortable, with big log fires, and roomy bedrooms furnished with family antiques and looking out over beautiful grounds. Ballyvolane has private salmon fishing on 8km of the great River Blackwater, with a wide variety of spring and summer beats, so it is logical that delicious food should be another high point at Ballyvolane, where memorable modern Irish dinners are served in style around a long mahogany table (where breakfast is also served). There is much of interest in the area, making this an excellent base for a peaceful and very relaxing break. Exciting plans are afoot at Ballyvolane at the time of going to press - the Drawing Room is under restoration, and five extra bedrooms ,in the form of Mongolian Yurts, are almost complete in the walled garden, an unobtrusive development that allows the homely house party atmosphere of the main house to be retained. A self-catering cottage is also available. French is spoken. Conferences/Banqueting (50). Children welcome (cot available, free of charge, baby sitting arranged). Pets permitted in some areas. Garden; fishing; walking, cycling. **Rooms**

6 (1 shower only, 1 ground floor, 1 for disabled, all no smoking). B&B €85 pps ss €30. Residents D €50 at 8pm, book by 10am; menu changes daily. Wine list, from €23. Closed 24 Dec - 1 Jan. Amex, Diners, MasterCard, Visa, Laser. **Directions:** Turn right off main Dublin-Cork road N8 just south of Rathcormac (signed Midleton), following house signs on to R628.

GLANDORE / UNION HALL

The attractive village of GLANDORE is beautifully situated in a sheltered location overlooking Glandore Harbour and its guardian rocks, Adam and Eve. The all year population is small and it will never be a place for mass tourism but there is comfortable accommodation to be found at guesthouses in the area and at the family-run **Marine Hotel** (028 33366), right beside the little harbour in the village; the hotel has undergone reconstruction recently, and has now re-opened. And the same family also own the beautifully located period house, The Rectory, which is used mainly for weddings and private functions but is occasionally open as a restaurant as well, if not booked to capacity. Glandore is also fortunate in its pubs, which have different characters and are all special in their own way: The **Glandore Inn,** for example, acts as unofficial clubhouse for the local sailing community (and serves sound food), while the old-fashioned **Casey's** (at the 'top of the town') only opens in the evenings and is a place for impromptu sessions and late-night craic. Across the bridge, in UNION HALL, **Dinty's Bar** (028 33373) and **Casey's** (028 33590) both do bar meals, and there is comfortable B&B accommodation to be found at **Shearwater** (028 33178) and **Ardagh House** (028 33571; www.ardaghhouse.com), which also has a restaurant.

Glandore

Hayes' Bar

PUB

The Square Glandore Co Cork **Tel: 028 33214**
Email: dchayes@tinet.ie Web: www.hayesbar.ie

Hayes Bar overlooks the harbour, has outdoor tables - and Ada Hayes' famous bar food. The soup reminds you of the kind your granny used to make and the sandwiches are stupendous. Everything that goes to make Hayes' special - including the wines and crockery collected on Declan and Ada's frequent trips abroad has to be seen to be believed; their travels also also affect the menu, inspiring favourites like Croque Monsieur - and, never ones to stand still, they've now introduced a tapas menu, offering Manchego cheese, Serrano ham, chorizo Pamplona and so on, with fino sherry and Spanish wines and beer. Wine is Declan's particular passion and Hayes' offers some unexpected treats, by the glass as well as the bottle, at refreshingly reasonable prices. Great reading too, including a lot of background on the wines in stock - and you can now see some of Declan's paintings exhibited, from June to August. By any standards, Hayes' is an outstanding bar. Meals 12-5, Jun-Aug; Tapas Menu 6-9; weekends only off-season. Closed weekdays Sep-May except Christmas & Easter. **No Credit Cards. Directions:** The square Glandore.

Glanmire

The Barn Restaurant

RESTAURANT

Glanmire Co Cork **Tel: 021 486 6211** Fax: 021 486 6525

féile bia

This long-established neighbourhood restaurant has earned a devoted local clientèle for its good French/Irish cooking and professional service. An attractive entrance conservatory leads to a comfortable lounge/reception area, where the welcome is warm and you can choose from menus which offer a good choice of quite traditional dishes - starters like home-smoked salmon with a dill mayonnaise, duet of chef's duck & chicken liver patés with Cumberland sauce and main courses of roast farmyard duckling with port and orange sauce, steaks various ways, fillet of sole & prawns topped with puff pastry lattice are all typical. Comfort is a high priority throughout this large restaurant, which is divided up into several dining areas, with well-spaced tables attractively set up with fresh flowers. While not aiming to be in any way cutting edge, everything is cooked to order, with the emphasis on flavour and wholesomeness - and professional, attentive service; all round a reassuringly old-style approach which makes a welcome contrast to the sameness of many contemporary restaurants. Vegetarians are well looked after, saucing and presentation are good, and accompaniments are carefully selected. Sunday lunch is very popular and menus are similar in style. Car park. Reservations advised (essential at weekends). **Seats about 160.** D daily, 6-9.30, L Sun only 12.30-2.30. Set D about €36, Set Sun L about €22. House wine about €22. Closed Ash Wed & Good Fri. Amex, Diners, Visa, Laser, Switch. **Directions:** On the edge of Cork city, on the old Youghal road at Glanmire. ◇

GLENGARRIFF

Famous for its mild Gulf Stream climate and lush growth - especially on nearby Garinish Island, with its beautiful gardens - Glengarriff has been a popular tourist destination since Victorian times and a little of that atmosphere still exists today. The rather grand looking **Eccles Hotel** (027 63319 www.eccleshotel.com) overlooks the harbour and is perhaps most obviously associated with that era (although it actually dates as far back as 1745), while the smaller, moderately priced and very hospitable family-run **Casey's Hotel** (027 63010) nearby, was established in 1884 and has been run by the same family ever since.

WWW.IRELAND-GUIDE.COM FOR THE BEST PLACES TO EAT, DRINK & STAY

Goleen

RESTAURANT WITH ROOMS

The Heron's Cove

The Harbour Goleen Co Cork
Tel: 028 35225 Fax: 028 35422
Email: info@heroncove.ie Web: www.heronscove.com

féile bia When the tide is in and the sun is out there can be few prettier locations than Sue Hill's restaurant overlooking Goleen harbour. The Heron's Cove philosophy is to use only the best of fresh, local ingredients and there's a natural leaning towards seafood - typically in wholesome starters like plump, perfectly cooked Bantry Bay moules marinières or, more unusually, West Cork smoked sprats, served with organic leaves and horseradish cream. Main course specialities include fillet of John Dory in a caper butter sauce - or there might be perfectly cooked Roaring Water Bay scallops, pan-fried and served with a smoked bacon cream sauce. If you're not in a fishy mood, there might be Goleen lamb cutlets (served on a bed of champ, with rosemary jus, perhaps) or crispy roast duckling, and there's always at least one vegetarian dish. More-ish desserts include the Heron's Cove signature dessert, a baked chocolate & vanilla cheesecake, and a wide selection of home-made ice creams - passion fruit, blackcurrant, blackberry, rum & Michigan cherry (to name a few of the less usual ones). Great ingredients, cooking which is generally pleasing, and friendly attentive service should make for an enjoyable meal - and, considering the quality of ingredients, main courses at €18-25, are fairly priced. An unusual Wine on the Rack system offers a great selection of interesting, well-priced wines that change through the season - they are listed but the idea is that you can browse through the bottles and make your own selection. Children welcome at discretion of the management. **Seats 30** D daily in summer, 7-9.30 (bookings essential Oct-Mar); à la carte. SC discretionary Closed Christmas & New Year. **Accommodation:** Comfortable en-suite rooms, some with private balconies, have satellite TV, phones, tea/coffee-making facilities and hair dryers. Garden. **Rooms 5** (4 shower only, all no smoking, 1 family room). B&B €40 pps, ss €10-30. Open for dinner, bed & breakfast all year except Christmas/New Year, but it is always advisable to book, especially off-season. Amex, Diners, MasterCard, Visa, Laser. **Directions:** Turn left in middle of Goleen to the harbour, 300 m from village.

Goleen Area

FARMHOUSE

Fortview House

Gurtyowen Toormore Goleen Co Cork **Tel: 028 35324**
Email: fortviewhousegoleen@eircom.net Web: www.fortviewhousegoleen.com

Violet & Richard Connell's remarkable roadside farmhouse in the hills behind Goleen is immaculate. It is beautifully furnished, with country pine and antiques, brass and iron beds in en-suite bedrooms (that are all individually decorated) and with all sorts of thoughtful little details to surprise and delight. Richard is a magic man when it comes to building - his recent work around the house includes a lovely conservatory dining room that he has completed with great attention to detail. For her part, Violet loves cooking, and provides guests with a great choice at breakfast - including Tom & Giana Ferguson's Gubbeen cheese, made down the road - and she provides residents' dinners, by arrangement, to the great delight of her guests. *Self-catering cottages also available. Children under 2 free in parents' room. No pets. Garden. **Rooms 5** (4 shower only, 1 family room, 3 ground floor, all no smoking). B&B €45 pps, no ss. Closed 1 Nov-1 Mar. **No Credit Cards**. **Directions:** 2 km from Toormore on main Durrus-Bantry road (R591).

Gougane Barra

HOTEL/RESTAURANT

Gougane Barra Hotel

Gougane Barra Macroom Co Cork
Tel: 026 47069 Fax: 026 47226
Email: gouganebarrahotel@eircom.net Web: www.gouganebarra.com

féile bia In one of the most peaceful and beautiful locations in Ireland, this delightfully old-fashioned family-run hotel is set in a Forest Park overlooking Gougane Barra Lake (famous for its monastic settlements). The Lucey family has run the hotel since 1937, offering simple, comfortable accommodation as a restful base for walking holidays - rooms are comfortable but not over-modernised, all looking out on to the lake or mountain, and there are quiet public rooms where guests like to read. None of this has altered very much over the years, and that's just the way people like it, but 2005 brought a gentle change of direction as Neil Lucey and his wife Katy have taken over management of the hotel from Neil's parents. Their energy is bringing a fresh approach though walking holidays will remain an important part of the business, but there's now a new cultural edge too as Neil opened a little theatre in the hotel and they host a production each summer. And, while the spirit of the place will thankfully remain unchanged, many improvements have been made recently. Visitors are encouraged to drop in for informal meals - Katy's delicious bar menus include specialities like a moreish warm chicken salad, the superb house chowder which she brought from her father's kitchen in Lahinch, where her parents ran Mr Eamon's famous restaurant for many years - and her lovely rich walnut and treacle bread. More formal meals, including breakfast are served in the lakeside dining room. This is a magical place - as ever, the monks chose well. No weddings or other functions are accepted. Shop. Garden, walking. No pets. Children welcome (cots available at no charge). **Rooms 26** (all en-suite & no smoking, 8 shower only, 1 family room, 8 ground floor). B&B €70 pps, No SS. Closed Oct - Apr. MasterCard, Visa, Laser. **Directions:** Situated in Gougane Barra National Forest; well signposted.

Kilbrittain

☆RESTAURANT

Casino House

Coolmain Bay Kilbrittain Co Cork **Tel: 023 49944**
Fax: 023 49945 Email: chouse@eircom.net

féile bia Kerrin and Michael Relja's delightful restaurant is just a few miles west of Kinsale and it is well worth the effort of getting here, as it is one of the best in an area which takes great pride in the excellence of its food. It's a lovely old house and it has an unusually cool continental style in the decor, but Kerrin's hospitality is warm - and Michael's food is consistently excellent, in wide-ranging seasonal menus based on the finest local ingredients: Ummera smoked organic salmon, fresh seafood from nearby fishing ports (don't miss his wonderful speciality lobster risotto) and Ballydehob duck all feature - a starter dish of four variations of duck is another speciality. Tempting vegetarian dishes are often listed ahead of the other main courses - spaghetti with basil oil, lamb's lettuce & feta cheese is typical - and nightly specials will include extra seafood dishes, all with individual vegetable garnishes and deliciously simple seasonal side vegetables. Variations on classic desserts are delicious (a delectable rhubarb & shortbread tartlet, with white chocolate & hazelnut crème and almond ice cream, for example) and local cheeses are always tempting in this area... An al fresco early summer dinner, or Sunday lunch, can be an especially memorable experience. Casino House was our Restaurant of the Year in 2005. *There are plans to add more accommodation, hopefully in 2007. *Casino Cottage: sleeps two €85 per night (or €155 for 2 nights), everything provided except break-fast - which can be supplied if needed. Longer stays discounted; weekly & winter rates available. **Seats 35** (private room 22; outdoor dining 16). D Thu-Tue, 7-9, L Sun only,1-3; all à la carte; house wine from €20.90. Closed Wed, and 1 Jan-17 Mar. Amex, MasterCard, Visa, Laser. **Directions:** On R600 between Kinsale and Timoleague.

Kilbrittain

FARMHOUSE

The Glen Country House

The Glen Kilbrittain Co Cork
Tel: 023 49862 Fax: 023 49862
Email: info@glencountryhouse.com Web: www.glencountryhouse.com

Although classified (correctly) as a farmhouse, Guy and Diana Scott's home is an elegant period house and they have recently renovated it to a high standard for guests. It is quietly located in a beautiful area, and the four large double bedrooms have lovely views across Courtmacsherry Bay. There's even a family suite (consisting of a double room and children's room, with interconnecting bathroom) and guests have the use of a comfortable sitting room, and a dining room where breakfasts are served - a buffet with fresh and poached seasonal fruits, freshly squeezed orange juice, organic muesli and organic yoghurt, and a menu of hot dishes including free range eggs from their own hens. It's a relaxed place, where dogs are welcome to join the two house spaniels (guests' horses are welcome too!) and, although there are no dinners, evening meals and baby sitting are offered for children, allowing parents to go out to one of the excellent local restaurants - Casino House, Otto's at Dunworley and Dillon's of Timoleague are all nearby. Free broadband. Children welcome (under 4s free in parents' room, cot available without charge, baby sitting arranged). Garden. Pets permitted outdoors. **Rooms 5** (all en-suite & no smoking, 4 shower only, 1 family room). B&B €65 pps, ss €10. Closed Nov-Easter. Heli-pad. *Self catering apartment also available, sleeps 4. MasterCard, Visa, Laser, Switch. **Directions:** Signposted off the R600, midway between Kinsale and Clonakilty.

Kilbrittain
Ⓝ BAR/RESTAURANT

The Pink Elephant

Harbour View Kilbrittain Co Cork **Tel: 023 49608**
Email: info@pinkelephant.ie Web: www.pinkelephant.ie

féile bia This low pink-painted bungalow-style building is set on a superb site overlooking the sea and across the bay to Courtmacsherry and, as it is open for lunch as well as dinner in the summer, this lively and unusual restaurant is a very useful place to know about. Picnic tables overlook a lawn towards the sea, or you can eat inside in a large room which is not particularly stylish except for the piano, which has been painted exuberantly in swirling shades of pink a sign of things to come in the evening, when one of the staff tinkles the ivories and sings, along with one of the waitresses. Lunch dishes are marked up on a blackboard in the bar and some may be taken from the evening menu and, encouragingly, another blackboard offers a good range of wines available, in two sizes, by the glass. Delicious food naturally favours local seafood - evening dishes depend on 'whatever the fishermen drop in', with (well priced) lobster and brill on the menu on a recent visit - and the home made breads (sourdough with a salty crust and brown bread made with molasses and seeds) are outstandingly good. Lunch choices might include an excellent Provençal fish soup, served with all the correct aooompaniments, and a moreish home-made ham hock terrine that is chunky and full of flavour, served with a well-dressed salad and more homely choices like Cumberland sausages with onion gravy and mash. An interesting wine list makes a good read, and includes a choice of half bottles and dessert wines, also well-priced bin ends. Laid-back but efficient and charming service matches up to everything else at the Pink Elephant simply brill. Children welcome before 9pm; Toilets wheelchair accessible. **Seats 70** (outdoors, 30); pianist in the evening; L daily 12-2.30 (Sun from 12.30), D daily 6-9; Sun L €25, L&D a la carte; house wine from €17. Open 7 days in summer, phone for opening times in winter. MasterCard, Visa, Laser. **Directions:** On R600 coast road near Kilbrittain.

KINSALE

One of Ireland's prettiest towns, Kinsale has the old-world charm of narrow winding streets and medieval ruins tucked in around Georgian terraces - all contrasting with the busy fishing harbour and marina of today. It was known several decades ago as the 'gourmet capital of Ireland' and, while that claim would now be hotly disputed by several other contenders, it is on the up and up again, offering a remarkable variety of good restaurants and and an exceptionally active programme of culinary activities- and, less widely recognised but of equal interest to the visitor, some of the best accommodation in the country. In the town, **The White Lady Hotel** (021 477 2737) offers moderately priced accommodation and a restaurant with pizzas, pastas and burgers as well as fresh seafood and steaks - a good choice for families. Outside the town, **Innishannon House Hotel** (Tel 021 477 5121; www.innishannon-hotel.ie) is a romantic riverside 'petit chateau' style house in lovely gardens and - also in the Innishannon direction - the recently restored 13-bedroom **Ballinacurra House** (087 2867443; www.ballinacurra.com) is a luxurious venue, available for private parties, small weddings, golfing groups and corporate events. Also outside the ton, the new **Carlton Kinsale Hotel** (021 470 6000; www.carltonkinsalehotel.com)is due to open shortly after we go to press. The town's many pubs offer a judicious mixture of music and food - especially seafood; across the bridge, towards the west, Castle Park has a sandy south-facing beach and **The Dock Bar** (Tel: 021 477 2522) is a friendly pub.
WWW.IRELAND-GUIDE.COM FOR THE BEST PLACES TO EAT, DRINK & STAY

Kinsale
HOTEL

Actons Hotel

Pier Road Kinsale Co Cork **Tel: 021 477 9900** Fax: 021 477 2231
Email: information@actonshotelkinsale.com Web: www.actonshotelkinsale.com

féile bia Overlooking the harbour and standing in its own grounds, this attractive quayside establishment is Kinsale's most famous hotel, dating back to 1946 when it was created from several substantial period houses. Extensive renovations recently included a ground floor extension and creation of a new lobby and additional lounges, the refurbishment of other public areas (which now include a new look modern bar, Waterfront Bar & Bistro) and a contemporary makeover for the restaurant, as well as refurbishment of bedrooms. A new Health & Fitness Club offers a brand new swimming pool with separate children's pool, hot tub, sauna, steam room and whirlpool spa; there's also a gym (with Technogym equipment), aerobics room, solarium and treatment facilities. Good conference/banqueting facilities too (300/250). Children welcome (under 4 free in parents' room, cots available without charge, baby sitting arranged.) No pets. Wheelchair access. Lift. Garden. **Rooms 73** (2 junior suites, 14 executive, 1 shower only, 2 for disabled, 50 no smoking). B&B €100 pps, ss €40 (wide range of special breaks available). Captain's Table Restaurant, L&D daily (speciality: the 'Derek Davis' steamed local seafood platter). Bar food available daily, 12-9.30. Closed 24-26 Dec, all Jan. Amex, MasterCard, Visa, Laser. **Directions:** On the waterfront, short walk from town centre. ◇

Kinsale

Blindgate House

E GUESTHOUSE

Blindgate Kinsale Co Cork **Tel: 021 477 7858** Fax: 021 477 7868
Email: info@blindgatehouse.com Web: www.blindgatehouse.com

Maeve Coakley's purpose-built guesthouse is set in its own gardens high up over the town and, with spacious rooms, uncluttered lines and a generally modern, bright and airy atmosphere, Blindgate makes a refreshing contrast to the more traditional styles that prevail locally. All bedrooms are carefully furnished with elegant modern simplicity, have full en-suite bathrooms and good facilities including fax/modem sockets as well as phones, satellite TV, tea/coffee trays and trouser press. Maeve is an hospitable host - and well-known in Kinsale for her skills in the kitchen, so breakfast here is a high priority: there's a buffet displaying all sorts of good things including organic muesli, fresh fruits and juices, farmhouse cheese and yoghurts, as well as a menu of hot dishes featuring, of course, the full Irish Breakfast alongside catch of the day and other specialities - so make sure you allow time to enjoy this treat to the full. Broadband. Children over 7 welcome (baby sitting arranged). No pets. Garden. **Rooms 11** (all en-suite & no smoking, 5 ground floor, 2 for disabled); room service (all day). B&B €72.50 pps, no ss. Closed late Dec-mid Mar.Amex, MasterCard, Visa, Laser, Switch. **Directions:** From Fishy Fishy Café: Take left up the hill, keeping left after St Multose Church. Blindgate House is after St Joseph's Primary School, on the left.

Kinsale

The Blue Haven Hotel

N HOTEL/RESTAURANT

3/4 Pearse Street Kinsale Co Cork
Tel: 021 477 2209 Fax: 021 4774268
Email: bluehavenkinsale.com Web: www.bluehavenkinsale.com

féile bia This famous hotel has an attractive exterior, with its name emblazoned in blue and white stained glass above the entrance and flags hanging from poles giving it a cosmopolitan look. It came into energetic new ownership recently, and proprietor Ciaran Fitzgerald is now doing everything possible to restore is previously great reputation. Due to the nature of the building, public areas are quite compact, but the lounge/lobby and the bar areas are well planned and comfortable. A major refurbishment programme was recently completed, and all the bedrooms have double glazing to offset the street noise that is inevitable in a central location. However, both the well-appointed rooms and their neat bathrooms make up in thoughtful planning anything they lack in spaciousness and there is extra accommodation available a few doors away at The Old Bank House (see entry), which is now in common ownership. **Restaurant:** The restaurant can be accessed from the hotel or by a separate entrance, underling the sense of it being more than an hotel dining room. The decor is restful, lifted by interesting features such as a five-foot silver candelabra in one corner and a piano in another. Each table has a single flower and nightlight, giving a pleasant soft atmosphere, and simple but pleasing table settings that are a little let down by the use of paper napkins. A lobster tank at the entrance to the restaurant sets the tone for menus that have the emphasis on seafood, balanced by steak, chicken and vegetarian dishes - and there is a separate children's menu. A typical menu might include starters like prawn, avocado and crab timbale in a light plum tomato and red pepper essence, and main courses such as baked monkfish rubbed with chilli and coriander pesto served on a prawn and coconut rice - or, for carnivores, an 8 oz sirloin steak with potato gratin, slow roasted plum tomatoes, pesto and a light jus. Cooking is sound, great care is taken with presentation, and the flavours live up to the first impressions. Good service from well-trained, knowledgeable staff, and an extensive wine list add to the pleasure of a meal here. Children welcome (unders 8s free in parents' room, cots available, baby sitting arranged). No pets. Street parking. **Rooms 17** (4 shower only). Room rate €60-220. Restaurant: **Seats 80.** D 6-10 daily, Set D about €40, à la carte available. House wine from about €20; sc 10%. Open all year.Amex, Diners, MasterCard, Visa, Laser. **Directions:** In the centre of town. ◇

Kinsale

Chart House

B&B

6 Denis Quay Kinsale Co Cork **Tel: 021 477 4568** Fax: 021 477 7907
Email: charthouse@eircom.net Web: www.charthouse-kinsale.com

Billy and Mary O'Connor's delightful 200 year old house has been completely renovated, with commendable attention to period details, and now offers luxurious accommodation. Beautifully furnished bedrooms have orthopaedic mattresses, phone, TV, hair dryer and a trouser press with iron; tea and coffee are served by the fire in a cosy reception/sitting room. An imaginative breakfast menu is served communally on a fine William IV dining room suite. Not suitable for children. No pets. **Rooms 4.** (2 suites with jacuzzi baths, 2 shower only, all no-smoking). B&B from €60 pps (depending on room), single occupancy 75%; single room €50. Closed Christmas week. Amex, MasterCard, Visa, Laser. **Directions:** On Pier Road between Actons and Trident Hotels, turn right after Actons, last house on right.

Kinsale
RESTAURANT/WINE BAR

Crackpots Restaurant

3 Cork Street Kinsale Co Cork **Tel: 021 477 2847**
Fax: 021 477 3517 Email: crackpts@iol.ie Web: www.crackpots.ie

Carole Norman's attractive and unusual restaurant has a lot going for it - not only can you drop in for a glass of wine at the bar, as well as the usual meals, but all the pottery used in the restaurant is made on the premises so, if you take a fancy to the tableware, you can buy that too. Menus are imaginative and considerate, with really attractive options for vegetarians, and many of the specialities are seafood, notably shellfish: moules marinière, crab toes (in a coconut & lemongrass sauce), seared scallops, and whole sautéed prawns in their shells, with a chilli, garlic & lemongrass oil and old favourites like chowder and smoked salmon are sure to make an appearance. If you feel like a change from fish there might be organic roast duck, with a Calvados & prune sauce, or a classic fillet steak on the evening menu. Children welcome. **Seats 50.** Air conditioning. L Sun winter only 12-3; D Mon-Sat 6-10 (Fri-Sat winter). Early D €25 (6-7); otherwise à la carte, house wines €18. Amex, MasterCard, Visa, Laser. **Directions:** Between Garda Station and Wine Museum.

Kinsale
(N) CAFÉ/RESTAURANT

Fishy Fishy Café

Crowley's Quay Kinsale Co Cork
Tel: 021 470 0415

SEAFOOD RESTAURANT OF THE YEAR

Martin and Marie Shanahan's eagerly anticipated mark two Fishy Fishy Café is a very big restaurant, by West Cork standards, yet they've been full to capacity at peak times in their first summer of opening, and they have kept the original Fishy Fishy (which has a wet fish bar) open too. The new premises was previously an art gallery and has been fitted out by a locally based and internationally renowned team of designers who are more accustomed to working on yacht interiors, creating a seriously atmospheric interior on two levels. It makes a design statement from the outset, with wooden gates opening onto a decking path leading to the front door - a bit like a zen garden, it is fitted into a neat rectangle with rounded beach stones filling the gaps. The interior is bright, airy and stylishly simple, with a smart little bar area, unpretentious café-style darkwood furniture and plenty of doors opening out onto the patio and balcony. It is a delightful place especially, perhaps, when it's warm enough to eat outside: a large paved outdoor seating area is enclosed by a hedge and, set up mainly with aluminium chairs and tables and seriously businesslike parasols, it has a continental air of dedication to the comfortable enjoyment of good food. The Shanahans' reputation for offering the widest possible range and freshest of fish is unrivalled throughout Ireland and there's only one word for the fish here, whether sole, hake, tuna, black bream or whatever: that word is superb. Shellfish lovers might be lucky enough to feast on a lunch of oysters, mussels and perhaps even Christy Turley's crab cocktail - Christy is a local food hero, a third generation Kinsale fisherman who supplies much of Fishy Fishy's catch. Prices are very fair for the quality offered and that includes the wine the Reserve Alsace Pinot Gris is quite a steal at €26, for example. True to their original style Fishy Fishy is almost as famous for its celebrity spangled queues as for the fabulous fish no reservations are accepted, so get there early or be prepared for a long wait. **Seats 150** (private room, 40, outdoors, 60); no reservations accepted; air conditioning; children welcome; open daily 12-4.30; a la carte menu. Closed Christmas 3 days. **No credit cards.**

Kinsale
CAFÉ

Fishy Fishy Cafe @ The Gourmet Store

Guardwell Kinsale Co Cork
Tel: 021 477 4453

This delightful fish shop, delicatessen and restaurant is a mecca for gourmets in and around Kinsale and was our Seafood Restaurant of the Year in 2001. There's an agreeably continental air and, although all sorts of other delicacies are on offer, seafood is the serious business here - and, as well as the range of dishes offered on the menu and a specials board, you can ask to have any of the fresh fish on display cooked to your liking. Not that you'd feel the need to stray beyond the menu, in fact, as it makes up in interest and quality anything it might lack in length - and you can have anything you like from seafood chowder or smoked salmon sandwich to grilled whole prawns with lemon garlic & sweet chilli sauce or fresh lobster, crayfish or crab. Vegetarian dishes available on request. [See also entry for the new Fishy Fishy]. Not suitable for children under 7. Wheelchair accessible. No reservations. **Seats 36.** Tue-Sat 12-3.45; à la carte; house wines from about €18. Closed Sun & Mon, 3 days Christmas. **No Credit Cards. Directions:** Opposite St Multose church, next to Garda station.

Kinsale

Friar's Lodge

Ⓝ GUESTHOUSE

Friar's Street Kinsale Co Cork
Tel: 021 477 7384 Fax: 021 477 4363
Email: mtierney@indigo.ie Web: www.friars-lodge.com

Maureen Tierney's friendly and exceptionally comfortable purpose-built guesthouse is very professionally operated, and offers an attractive alternative to hotel accommodation in the centre of Kinsale - it even has private parking, which is a big bonus in this busy little town, and there is a drying room for wet golfing gear (tee times can be arranged). The style is a pleasing combination of traditional and modern, and the spacious, pleasingly furnished, guest rooms have well-designed bathrooms - most with full bath and shower; rooms also have computer/internet connection, safe and TV with DVD as well as the more usual tea/coffee making, hair dryer and ironing facilities. (Minibar and fax & photocopying is also available - details on request.) Guests have use of a spacious, comfortable and elegantly furnished sitting room with an open fire and, although evening meals are not offered, a good breakfast is served in a pleasant dining room. This is a very pleasant place to stay and offers good value too, in comparison with hotels. Children welcome (under 5s free in parents' room, cot available at no charge). **Bedrooms 18** (2 executive, 2 shower only, 2 family rooms, 16 no smoking); lift; B&B €65 pps, ss €15. Closed 22-27 Dec. MasterCard, Visa, Laser. **Directions:** Centre of Kinsale, next to parish church.

Kinsale

Harbour Lodge

GUESTHOUSE

Scilly Kinsale Co Cork **Tel: 021 477 2376** Fax: 021 477 2673
Email: relax@harbourlodge.ie Web: www.harbourlodge.ie

Raoul de Gendre's waterfront guesthouse is extremely comfortable and the position, away from the bustle of the town centre, is lovely and peaceful; some bedrooms have balconies and there's a large conservatory "orangerie" for the leisurely observation of comings and goings in the harbour, and also a sitting room with an open fire for chilly days. An extensive breakfast is offered - and not only does it bid guests a good morning in four languages, but even offers Japanese breakfast items by arrangement. Thoughtfully furnished bedrooms have top of the range beds and bedding and luxurious bathrooms (with the largest, thickest possible towels and bathrobes - and in-house laundry to take care of them). A high level of personal attention and service is the aim, including the arrangement of transport to and from M. de Gendre's restaurant, The Vintage, for guests wishing to dine there. Simple meals are available on request - salads, sandwiches, soup, steaks, moules marinière - and there's a limited laundry and pressing service. Walking, cycling. Golf and many other activities nearby. Special breaks offered. Children welcome. Garden. **Rooms 9** (1 suite, 1 family room, 1 shower only, all no smoking). B&B from €99 pps. Open all year. Amex, Diners, MasterCard, Visa, Laser. **Directions:** Scilly waterfront: 1km (0.5 mile) from town centre, beside the Spinnaker.

Kinsale

Jim Edwards

Ⓝ RESTAURANT/PUB

Short Quay Kinsale Co Cork
Tel: 021 477 2541 Fax: 021 477 3228
Email: info@jimedwardskinsale.com Web: www.jimedwardskinsale.com

This characterful old place in the heart of Kinsale is known for its atmosphere and the consistent quality of the hearty food served in both pub and restaurant. It's cosy, even at lunchtime or on bright summer evenings, as windows let in plenty of light but not so much as to kill the pub atmosphere and some tables have electric "oil" lamps above them, which add to the atmosphere. The décor - a polished wood floor with inset patterned tiles, a mustard and maroon colour scheme, and curios (such as a large conch shell) on display - works really well, for a relaxed pub atmosphere. Seafood is the speciality, but there's plenty to please everyone on all menus, from spicy chicken wings, chicken liver pate & salad or crab claws in garlic butter to sirloin steak, lamb chops and seafood au gratin on the extensive bar menu and lunch menu - and then the treats of scampi, fresh lobster, sole on the bone, rack of lamb or roast duck on the a la carte. Everything is carefully prepared and really tasty even popular dishes like the much-maligned lasagne, or deep-fried plaice come in for praise here, for quality and good cooking, and side dishes are well above average too. Impeccably dressed staff are very professional and efficient, and it's excellent value. What more could you ask for? Children welcome. **Seats 70;** food served daily 12.30-10pm; L 12.30-3.30 (to 3pm Sun), set Sun L €24.90; D 6-10pm; Set 2/3 course D, €16/22, also a la carte L&D; house wine €21. Amex, MasterCard, Visa, Laser. **Directions:** Town centre.

Kinsale
RESTAURANT

Le Bistro

Main Street Kinsale Co Cork
Tel: 021 477 7117 Fax: 021 477 7117
Email: eat@lebistrokinsale.com Web: www.lebistrokinsale.com

Jean-Marc Tsai and Jacqui St John-Jones' popular town centre premises is embellished by murals by local artist Sheila Kern and, in this lively and attractive 'Paris bistro style' restaurant, Jean-Marc offers a unique mélange of classic French and Asian food in the evening, and French bistro style for lunch; Jean-Marc is one of Ireland's great chefs and all who remember the fine dining experience at Chez Jean-Marc, or his superb Asian food at the Chow House will be delighted with this new venture: Vietnamese spring rolls, baked sea bass, 'trou normand' (apple sorbet with calvados), it's all here, on daily-changing menus. Jean-Marc is always in the kitchen and Jacqui is always out at the front, otherwise they are closed. The wine list changes every three months, and offers organic and chemical-free wines - also imported French beers. Off season, Asian nights (Vietnamese, Chinese and Thai) are held on Sundays, for local residents. Gorgeous food, great service, good value - and an enjoyable ambience: this place has it all. **Seats 60.** Children welcome, but not after 8pm. D Daily 6 - 10, Early Bird D €20 before 7.30. House Wine from €19.50. Closed Feb. MasterCard, Visa, Laser. **Directions:** In the centre of Kinsale, corner of Market St.

Kinsale
RESTAURANT

Man Friday

Scilly Kinsale Co Cork **Tel: 021 477 2260**
Fax: 021 477 2262 Web: www.man-friday.net

High up over the harbour, Philip Horgan's popular, characterful restaurant is housed in a series of rooms. It has a garden terrace which makes a nice spot for drinks and coffee in fine weather. Philip presents seasonal à la carte menus that major on seafood but offer plenty else besides, including several vegetarian choices and duck, steak and lamb. While geared to fairly traditional tastes, the cooking is generally sound and can include imaginative ideas - and there's usually a good buzz, which adds hugely to the enjoyment of a meal. Simple, well-made desserts include good ice creams. Service is, for the most part, cheerful and efficient and, unlike many other restaurants in the area, which are seasonal, Man Friday is open in the winter. **Seats 130** (private room, 40). Not accessible to wheelchairs. D Mon-Sat, 6.45-10; gourmet D €40; also à la carte, house wine from €20; sc discretionary. Closed Sun, Dec 24-26. Amex, MasterCard, Visa, Laser. **Directions:** Overlooking the inner harbour, at Scilly.

Kinsale
RESTAURANT

Max's Wine Bar

48 Main Street Kinsale Co Cork
Tel: 021 477 2443 Fax: 021 477 2443

Max's is closed for renovations until March/April 2007, so it should be even better for the summer season. It is run by a young couple, Olivier and Anne Marie Queva, the chef and restaurant manager respectively. They have earned a loyal following in the locality and it's a happy find for visitors too, especially as they offer an attractive light snack lunch and a short set menu that's available at lunch or in the early evening, as well as the main dinner menu. It's a characterful little place with stone walls at the bar end, varnished wooden tables and a pretty conservatory area at the back. Olivier's seasonal menus change regularly (some seasonal, others daily - you might even be lucky enough to find that lobster is the daily special) and offer a balance of meats and poultry, as well as the seafood from the pier - langoustines and oysters (in season), mussels, black sole and so on - which is always so much in demand. Roast rack of Irish lamb is a consistent favourite - or cutlets may be cut from the rack and served with an unusual accompaniment such as confit of butter beans. Menus offer a pleasing balance of luxurious ingredients (foie gras, scallops) and the more homely (beef bourguignon, baked stuffed apple) and appealing vegetarian dishes are always offered too. An informative wine list offers a range of house wines (available by the glass), an above average choice of half bottles and a range of aperitifs, dessert wines and ports. Not suitable for children under 5 after 7pm. **Seats 30.** L Wed-Mon,12.30-3 (Sun 1-3), D Wed-Mon, 6.30-10. Set L/Early D (6.30-7.30) €19.20; à la carte available; house wine €16.90, SC discretionary. Closed Tue; 31 Oct-1 Mar. Amex, MasterCard, Visa, Laser, Switch. **Directions:** Street behind the petrol station on pier.

Kinsale

GUESTHOUSE

The Old Bank House

11 Pearse Street Kinsale Co Cork
Tel: 021 477 4075 Fax: 021 477 4296
Email: info@oldbankhousekinsale.com Web: www.oldbankhousekinsale.com

féile bia

This fine townhouse in the centre of Kinsale has a great reputation, and is now in common ownership with the Blue Haven Hotel. It has an elegant residents' sitting room, a well-appointed breakfast room and comfortable bedrooms with good amenities, antiques and quality materials. All rooms are furnished and decorated to the same impeccable standard, with lovely bathrooms. Children welcome, cot €20. Golf-friendly: tee-off times, hire of clubs, transport to course, golf tuition can all be arranged; golf storage room. **Rooms 17** (1 suite, 3 junior suites, 2 family rooms, all no smoking). Lift. Room service (all day). B&B €85 pps. Closed 23-28 Dec. Amex, MasterCard, Visa, Laser. **Directions:** On right hand side at start of Kinsale, next to the Post Office.

Kinsale

B&B

The Old Presbytery

43 Cork Street Kinsale Co Cork **Tel: 021 477 2027** Fax: 021 477 2166
Email: info@oldpres.com Web: www.oldpres.com

This old house in the centre of the town has provided excellent accommodation for many years and the current owners, Philip and Noreen McEvoy have kept up this tradition well. Bed and breakfast is offered in the original bedrooms, which have character - stripped pine country furniture and antique beds - and have been recently refurbished, and the McEvoys have also added three self-catering suites, each with two en-suite bedrooms, sitting room, kitchenette and an extra bathroom. The new rooms are well-proportioned and furnished in the same style and to the same high standard; they can be taken on a nightly basis (minimum stay 2 nights), sleeping up to six adults. The top suite has an additional lounge area leading from a spiral staircase, with magnificent views over the town and harbour. Children welcome (cot available without charge). **Rooms 6** (3 suites, 2 shower only, 2 family rooms, 1 ground floor, all no-smoking). B&B €80 pps. Self-catering apartments, from €170 per night (min 2 nights). Closed 1 Dec-mid Feb. Amex, MasterCard, Visa, Laser. **Directions:** Follow signs for Desmond Castle - in same street.

Kinsale

Perryville House

Long Quay Kinsale Co Cork **Tel: 021 477 2731** Fax: 021 477 2298
Email: sales@perryville.iol.ie Web: www.perryvillehouse.com

One of the prettiest houses in Kinsale, Laura Corcoran's characterful house on the harbour front has been renovated to an exceptionally high standard and provides excellent accommodation only 15 minutes from the Old Head of Kinsale golf links. Gracious public rooms are beautifully furnished, as if for a private home. Spacious, individually decorated bedrooms vary in size and outlook (ones at the front are most appealing, but the back is quieter) and all have extra large beds and thoughtful extras such as fresh flowers, complimentary mineral water, quality toiletries, robes and slippers. The suites have exceptionally luxurious bathrooms although all are well-appointed. Breakfasts include home-baked breads and local cheeses; morning coffee and afternoon tea are available to residents in the drawing room and there is a wine licence. No smoking establishment. Own parking. Not suitable for children. No pets. **Rooms 26** (5 junior suites, 8 superior, all no-smoking). B&B from €100 pps, No SC. Closed Nov-1Apr. *Wireless internet throughout the house. Amex, MasterCard, Visa, Laser. **Directions:** Central location, on right as you enter Kinsale from Cork, overlooking marina. ◇

Kinsale

GUESTHOUSE

Pier House

Pier Road Kinsale Co Cork **Tel: 021 477 4475** Fax: 021 477 4475
Email: pierhouseaccom@eircom.net Web: www.pierhousekinsale.com

Ann and Pat Hegarty's newly refurbished guesthouse is a recent addition to the choice of quality accommodation in Kinsale, and can be entered from the pier or, at the other side of the block, from Main Street. A professionally landscaped enclosed garden on the harbour side of the house gives a good first impression - it has a barbecue area and wood burning stove, and catches the evening sun - and the house is stylishly decorated. Unexpected extras include a hot tub and sauna room, which has been cleverly squeezed into a balcony area; a communal room with laundering and ironing facilities; and also an ice machine, glasses and openers for guests' use - all thoughtful additions which can be a real bonus when travelling. A gallery seating area for guests' use features highlighted paintings done by Pat's brother Michael, an accomplished artist - creating a bright, airy atmosphere. Bedrooms vary somewhat in size and outlook, but all have television (many in cabinets), direct dial phones and ISDN connections for laptops; most have harbour views and some have small private balconies (where smoking is allowed). Some bathrooms are quite small (with power showers rather than baths) and they lack the small luxuries like a range of complimentary toiletries, but they have the comfort of under floor heating, good shaving mirrors, heated mirrors and towel rails. Breakfast times are arranged with Anne the night before, to avoid a last-minute rush. Children welcome (under 4s free in parents room, cot available, baby sitting arranged). Garden. **Rooms 10** (9 shower only, 1 with family room, all no smoking). B&B €70pps, ss €70. Open all year except Christmas & New Year. MasterCard, Visa. **Directions:** At the top of Pier Road, opposite Tourist Office.

Kinsale

The Spaniard Inn

RESTAURANT/PUB

Scilly Kinsale Co Cork **Tel: 021 477 2436** Fax: 021 477 3303
Email: thespaniard@eircom.net Web: www.thespaniard.ie

Who could fail to be charmed by The Spaniard, that characterful and friendly old pub perched high up above Scilly? Although probably best known for music (nightly), it offers bar food all year round and there's a restaurant in season. Popular traditional fare (Spaniard seafood chowder, smoked salmon platter, Oysterhaven mussels and oysters) for which The Spaniard is well known is served informally in the bar alongside more contemporary dishes such as a gourmet sandwich of warm spicy chicken in ciabatta with coconut cream chilli sauce. Evening meals in the restaurant - which has its own separate bar - are more extensive, offering about ten choices on each course; some, such as the starters of Oysterhaven mussels and oysters, overlap with the bar menu, but there are also luxurious main courses such as a dish of monkfish & scallops, poached in a saffron and chive cream sauce. Desserts can be tempting (passion fruit crème brulée, flourless chocolate torte...) and there are Irish cheeses. Bar meals:L 12.30-3 (to 5.30 Sat/Sun); average main dish about €12.50; Restaurant D: 6.30-10 (main courses about €24). House wines (6), €19.50. Closed 25 Dec & Good Fri, 2 weeks Nov & Jan. Amex, MasterCard, Visa, Laser. **Directions:** At Scilly, about 0.5 kilometre south-east of Kinsale, overlooking the town.

Kinsale

The Vintage Restaurant

RESTAURANT

50 Main Street Kinsale Co Cork **Tel: 021 477 2502** Fax: 021 477 4828
Email: vintagerestaurant@eircom.net Web: www.vintagerestaurant.ie

féile bia Diana and Frank Ferguson have taken over at one of Kinsale's oldest and most famous restaurants, The Vintage - and how appropriate that their chef, Ciáran Faherty, should have previous experience at Drimcong House, until recently run by Gerry Galvin, who first brought The Vintage (and, indeed, Kinsale) to prominence in the heady 1970s days of the emerging 'gourmet capital'... And how good to find that they have a mission to move away from its recent 'expensive exclusivity' and provide a relaxed place to dine, with good, tasty food that is more accessibly priced. The cottagey charm has been retained, however - old stonework and ancient oak beams are the perfect starting point for the gentle pink theme seen in carpets, soft furnishing and table linen, and it is very cosy, especially in the tiny bar/reception area just inside the door. But menus have certainly seen changes and are much shorter and to the point, offering about eight starters and nine main courses plus two daily specials; the emphasis is on fish, although you will find appealing old favourites for non fish eaters, such as dry-aged steak, and roast duck, which is quite traditionally prepared with an apricot & sage stuffing and Grand Marnier sauce. Prices are very fair, starting about €13.95 for a vegetarian pasta dish to €26 for a dish of panfied prawns with garlic crab claws & white wine velouté. Although it would be good to see some mention of provenance on the menu (an opportunity missed), it is clear in the tasting that good quality ingredients are used, and food preparation is careful and simple and skilful cooking is seen in even the simplest dishes - a delicious soup pf roasted mushroom with tarragon, for example; presentation is attractive and - like the quality of service - professional without being over fussy. A shortish wine list offers a mixture of big names and lesser known wines (more information would be helpful), but only the house wine by the glass no half bottles. All round a meal here should be very enjoyable - an good value too. **Seats 60** (private room 20). D daily, 6-10; à la carte. House wine from €25. Closed Mon & Jan-Feb. Amex, MasterCard, Visa, Laser. **Directions:** From the Post Office, turn left at the Bank of Ireland - restaurant is on the right.

Kinsale
☆RESTAURANT

Toddies Restaurant

Kinsale Brewery The Glen Kinsale Co Cork
Tel: 021 477 7769 Email: toddies@eircom.net
Web: www.toddieskinsale.com

This bustling down town restaurant and bar was our Atmospheric Restaurant of the Year in 2006. The address may give the impression that Pearse and Mary O'Sullivan's restaurant is 'out of town' but if you walk down Pearse Street (away from the harbour) and turn right at the T junction, you'll see their sign across the road, outside a fine limestone archway. It's above the Kinsale Brewery, with whom there is a strong working relationship as they pump their Kinsale lager, wheat beer and stout directly up to Toddies bar. From the courtyard, exterior stairs lead up to the restaurant, pausing at the large and stylish al fresco dining area provided by two terraces before arrival at the bar and a smart split-level dining room. It's an exciting enterprise, and word quickly spread to a growing fan club who love not only Pearse's fine modern Irish cooking, but also the inside-or-out table arrangements, great service by Mary and her bubbly staff, and the whole atmosphere of the place. Seafood is, of course, the star - home-made ravioli of lobster with a cherry tomato sauce & shaved parmesan is one of many speciality dishes that had already established Toddies as a leading restaurant in the area - but Pearse's high regard for local meats (and west Cork cheeses), ensures a balanced choice. **Seats 42** (terrace, 60). Children welcome. D daily 5-10.30 (from 6.30 Sat & Sun). Early D €24.95, Mon-Fri 5-6.45, also á la carte. House wine from €23.50. SC discretionary. Closed 15 Jan-end Feb. *Guests can eat at the bar, or in the restaurant. MasterCard, Visa, Laser. **Directions:** Drive to the end of Pearse St., take right turn, Toddies is second on the left through limestone arch and into courtyard.

Kinsale
HOTEL

Trident Hotel

Worlds End Kinsale Co Cork **Tel: 021 477 9300** Fax: 021 477 4173
Email: info@tridenthotel.com Web: www.tridenthotel.com

This blocky, concrete-and-glass 1960s waterfront hotel enjoys an exceptional location and, under the watchful management of Hal McElroy, has long been a well-run, hospitable and comfortable place to stay. Recent development has now seen major changes including a new facade, new and entrance foyer, refurbished conference/ banqueting rooms and - most importantly from the guest comfort point of view - the addition of 30 new front-facing executive rooms, all with king size beds and air conditioning as standard, and separate bath and shower. Older bedrooms are quite spacious and comfortable, with phone, TV and tea/coffee trays (iron and board available on request) and small but adequate bathrooms. The genuinely pubby Wharf Tavern is unchanged and remains one of the town's most popular good meeting places. Conference/banqueting (220/200); video-conferencing on request. Sauna, gym, steam room, jacuzzi. Children welcome (under 3 free in parents room, cot available without charge, baby sitting arranged). No pets. Lift. **Rooms 66** (2 suites, 2 wheelchair accessible). B&B €95 pps, ss €33; no SC. **Seats 80.** D daily, 6.30-9, L Sun only 1- 2.30. Set Sun L €23; Set D €28, D also à la carte; Bistro menu avail 4-9; Bar Menu 12-9. House wine from €19. SC discretionary. Toilets wheelchair accessible. Amex, MasterCard, Visa, Laser. **Directions:** Take the R600 from Cork to Kinsale - the hotel is at the end of the Pier Road.

Kinsale
ATMOSPHERIC PUB

W G Dalton's

3 Market Street Kinsale Co Cork
Tel: 021 477 7957 Email: fedalton@eircom.net

Frances and Colm Dalton's cheerful little red-painted town-centre bar has a characterful, traditional-look interior with green & white floor tiles and lots of wood - and is well worth seeking out for good home cooking. It's a friendly spot and they make a good team - Colm is chef, while Frances is the baker - providing wholesome lunches which are more restaurant meals than usual bar food, five days a week. While there's plenty of choice, the menu is sensibly limited to eight or nine dishes, plus a couple of specials each day - tandoori lamb and steak & kidney pie, for example); there's an understandable emphasis on seafood - steamed mussels, crab cakes, smoked salmon with home-baked brown bread, warm seafood salad - and a sprinkling of other dishes, mostly chicken. Good quality, fresh ingredients and real home cooking make for some delicious flavours - and desserts (apple & blackberry crumble perhaps) are all home-made. Outside lunchtime, Daltons operates normally, as a bar. **Seats 30.** L Mon-Fri 12.30-4. **Directions:** Entering Kinsale from Cork, straight on past Blue haven Hotel, left at end; Daltons on left, opposite Market Place.

Kinsale Area
BAR/RESTAURANT

The Bulman

Summercove Kinsale Co Cork
Tel: 021 477 2131 Fax: 021 477 3359
Email: info@thebulman.com Web: www.thebulman.com

Uniquely situated on the outskirts of Kinsale it looks across towards the town and has a sunny western aspect - The Bulman is a characterful maritime bar (though this is definitely not a theme pub). It's a great place to be in fine weather, when you can wander out to the seafront and sit on the wall beside the carpark, and it's cosy in winter when you can sip local beer from the Kinsale Brewery beside the fire in the downstairs bar and drink in the hospitable atmosphere. The first floor restaurant specialises in seafood, much of it locally caught, including less usual fish like sea bream. Portions are generous (something of a feature of Kinsale dining) and you may find a lot happening on the plate a delicious whole fish may have accompaniments like mango salsa, falafel and chard salad vying for attention - but somehow, like the threads of a symphony, it all manages to come together. Own carpark. **Seats 50.** (Phone for food service times). Closed 25 Dec & Good Fri. Not suitable for children under 12. Toilets wheelchair accessible, restaurant upstairs isn't. Restaurant: seats 51; L Mon-Sat, 12.30-3pm, Sun L only, 1-4pm, D Tue-Sat, 6-9.30pm; earlybird menu 6-7pm, €21.95/25.95 2/3 course, also a la carte; house wine €20. Bar food also available Mon-Sat, 12.30-3pm. Restaurant closed D Sun & Mon.Amex, MasterCard, Visa, Laser. **Directions:** Beside Charles Fort, short distance from Kinsale.

Kinsale Area
COUNTRY HOUSE

Glebe Country House

Ballinadee nr Kinsale Bandon Co Cork
Tel: 021 477 8294 Fax: 021 477 8456
Email: glebehse@indigo.ie Web: http://indigo.ie/~glebehse/

Set in two acres of beautiful, well-tended gardens (including a productive kitchen garden), this charming old rectory near Kinsale has a lovely wisteria at the front door and it is a place full of interest. The building dates back to 1690 (Church records provide interesting details: it was built for £250; repairs and alterations followed at various dates, and the present house was completed in 1857 at a cost of £1,160). More recently, under the hospitable ownership of Gill Good, this classically proportioned house has been providing a restful retreat for guests since 1989, and everybody loves it for its genuine country house feeling and relaxing atmosphere. Spacious reception rooms have the feeling of a large family home, and generous, stylishly decorated bedrooms have good bathrooms, phones and tea/coffee making facilities. The Rose Room, on the ground floor, has French doors to the garden. A 4-course candle-lit dinner for residents, much of it supplied by the garden, is served at a communal table (please book by noon). Although unlicensed, guests are encouraged to bring their own wine. Breakfasts are also delicious, and this can be a hard place to drag yourself away from in the morning although there are many things to do nearby, including golf, and it is well placed for exploring the area. The whole house may be rented by parties by arrangement and several self-catering apartments are also available. Children welcome (under 10s free in parents' room, cots available without charge, baby sitting arranged.) Pets permitted. **Rooms 4** (2 shower only, all no-smoking), B&B €55 pps, ss €15. Residents' D Mon-Sat, €35, at 8pm (please book by noon). No D on Sun. BYO wine. Closed Christmas. *Indoor heated swimming pool. Diners, MasterCard, Visa, Laser. **Directions:** Take N71 west from Cork to Innishannon Bridge, follow signs for Ballinadee 9km (6 miles). After village sign, first on right.

Macroom
BAR/RESTAURANT

The Mills Inn

Ballyvourney Macroom Co Cork **Tel: 026 45237** Fax: 026 45454
Email: millinn@eircom.net Web: www.millinn.ie

féile bia One of Ireland's oldest inns, The Mills Inn is in a Gaeltacht (Irish-speaking) area and dates back to 1755. It was traditionally used to break the journey from Cork to Killarney - and still makes a great stopping place as the food is good and freshly cooked all day - but is now clearly popular with locals as well as travellers. New owners took over in 2003 and they are continuing to develop the premises while retaining its old-world charm and a genuine sense of hospitality - work recently completed was impressive. Toilets wheelchair accessible. L&D daily. Closed 25 Dec. **Accommodation:** Rooms vary considerably due to the age of the building, but all are comfortably furnished with neat bathrooms and good amenities - and, like the rest of the premises, are still undergoing refurbishment at the time of going to press. The newer rooms feel quite spacious and, like the rest of the inn, have charm and a strong sense of style. A large ground-floor room is suitable for less able guests, who can use the residents' car park right at the door - in a courtyard shared with a vintage car and an agricultural museum. Full room service is available for drinks and meals. **Rooms 13** (some shower only, 1 for disabled). B&B about €45pps, no ss. Amex, Diners, MasterCard, Visa, Laser. **Directions:** On N22, 20 minutes from Killarney. ◇

Macroom
HOTEL

The Castle Hotel & Leisure Centre

Macroom Co Cork **Tel: 026 41074** Fax: 026 41505
Email: castlehotel@eircom.net Web: www.castlehotel.ie

féile bia In the ownership of the Buckley family since 1952, this well-managed hotel is ideally located for touring the scenic south-west and is equally attractive to business and leisure guests. Major recent developments include the addition of superior executive bedrooms and suites, an extensive new foyer and reception area, an impressive new bar and the stylish 'B's' Restaurant. Extensive leisure facilities include a fine swimming pool (with children's pool, spa and massage pool), steam room, solarium and gym. Conferences/banqueting (150/150). Special breaks are offered, including golf specials (tee times reserved at Macroom's 18-hole course). **'The Next Door Café'** has a separate entrance from the street and offers informal continental-style fare; it is a popular meeting place for locals and visitors alike. Friendly staff take pride in making guests feel at home. Children welcome (under 3s free in parents' room, cots available without charge; playroom; baby sitting arranged). Conference/banqueting (150). No pets. **Rooms 60.** B&B €75 pps, ss €25. Food available 9.30am-9pm. ('B's' Restaurant 12-3 & 6-8.45; 'Next Door Café' 9.30-5.30; bar food 12-9.30) Closed 24-28 Dec. Amex, MasterCard, Visa, Laser. **Directions:** On N22, midway between Cork & Killarney.

Mallow
RESTAURANT/COUNTRY HOUSE

Longueville House

Mallow Co Cork
Tel: 022 47156 Fax: 022 47459
Email: info@longuevillehouse.ie Web: www.longuevillehouse.ie

When Michael and Jane O'Callaghan opened Longueville House to guests in 1967, it was one of the first Irish country houses to do so. Its history is wonderfully romantic, "the history of Ireland in miniature", and it is a story with a happy ending: having lost their lands in the Cromwellian Confiscation (1652-57), the O'Callaghans took up ownership again some 300 years later. The present house, a particularly elegant Georgian mansion of pleasingly human proportions, dates from 1720, (with wings added in 1800 and the lovely Turner conservatory - which has been completely renovated - in 1862), overlooks the ruins of their original home, Dromineen Castle. Very much a family enterprise, Longueville is now run by Michael and Jane's son William O'Callaghan, who is the chef, and his wife Aisling, who manages front of house. The location, overlooking the famous River Blackwater, is lovely. The river, farm and garden supply fresh salmon in season, the famous Longueville lamb, and all the fruit and vegetables. In years when the weather is kind, the estate's crowning glory is their own house wine, a light refreshing white, "Coisreal Longueville" - wine has always been Michael O'Callaghan's great love, and he has recently started using their abundant apple supply to make apple brandy too. Public rooms include a bar and drawing room, both elegantly furnished with beautiful fabrics and family antiques, and accommodation is equally sumptuous; although - as is usual with old houses - bedrooms vary according to their position, they are generally spacious, superbly comfortable and stylishly decorated to the highest standards. Dining here is always a treat (see below) and breakfast is also very special, offering a wonderful array of local and home-cooked foods, both from the buffet and cooked to order; Longueville was the National Winner of our Irish Breakfast Awards in 2003, and it's worth dropping in even if you can't stay overnight - what a way to break a journey! As well as being one of the finest leisure destinations in the country, the large cellar/basement area of the house has been developed as a conference centre, with back-up services available. The house is also available for small residential weddings throughout the year. Conference/banqueting (50/110). Children welcome (under 2s free in parents' room, cot available). No pets. **Rooms 20.** (4 suites, 2 junior suites, 1 superior room, 3 family rooms; all no-smoking). B&B €118pps, ss €32. Closed early Jan-mid Mar. Shooting weekends available in winter; telephone for details). **Presidents Restaurant:** Named after the family collection of specially commissioned portraits of all Ireland's past presidents (which made for a seriously masculine collection until Ireland's first woman president, Mary Robinson, broke the pattern) this is the main dining room and opens into the beautifully renovated Turner conservatory, which makes a wonderfully romantic setting in candlelight; there is a smaller room alongside the main restaurant, and also the Chinese Room, which is suitable for private parties. William O'Callaghan is an accomplished chef, and home- and locally-produced food is at the heart of all his cooking. An 8-course Menu Gourmand is offered for complete parties, and there are daily dishes (which will include a vegetarian choice) in addition to well-balanced dinner menus. Home-produced and local ingredients star, in starters like house smoked salmon, or salad of crab with dry cured Longueville ham and, main courses of Longueville lamb and home reared pork loin. Home produce influences the dessert menu too, as in a croustade of caramelised apple with Longueville apple brandy ice cream, for example, and it is hard to resist the local farmhouse cheeses. Delicious home-made chocolates and petits fours come with the coffee and service, under Aisling O'Callaghan's direction, is excellent. A fine wine list includes many wines imported directly by

Michael O'Callaghan. Children welcome. **Seats 110** (private room 12). D daily, 6.30-9; early D €40 (6-6.45, Sun-Thu), Set 2/3 course D €40/60, Menu Gourmand €85; light meals 12.30-5 daily. House wine about €29, sc discretionary (SC added to parties of 8+). Closed 7 Jan - 16 Mar. Amex, MasterCard, Visa, Laser. **Directions:** 5km (3 m) west of Mallow via N72 to Killarney.

MIDLETON

Midleton is a busy market town and home of the Jameson Heritage Centre at the **Old Midleton Distillery** (021 461 3594; www.whiskeytours.ie), where you can find out all you every wanted to know about Irish whiskey, and get a bite to eat too. The first choice for accommodation in the town centre is **Midleton Park Hotel & Spa** (021 463 5100; www.mildletonpark.com), with all facilities, and food lovers will enjoy the Farmers Market on Saturday mornings (one of the best in the country). Midleton is well-placed for visiting Cork city, and also exploring the whole of east Cork, including Cobh (last port of call for the Titanic), Fota Wildlife Park & Arboretum and Youghal, famed for its connections with Sir Walter Raleigh. The pretty fishing village of Ballycotton merits a visit, and offers good coastal walking.
WWW.IRELAND-GUIDE.COM FOR THE BEST PLACES TO EAT, DRINK & STAY

Midleton

Farmgate

€ RESTAURANT

The Coolbawn Midleton Co Cork
Tel: 021 463 2771 Fax: 021 463 2771

NATURAL FOOD AWARD

féile bia This unique shop and restaurant has been drawing people to Midleton in growing numbers since 1985 and it's a great credit to sisters Maróg O'Brien and Kay Harte. Kay now runs the younger version at the English Market in Cork, while Maróg looks after Midleton. The shop at the front is full of wonderful local produce - organic fruit and vegetables, cheeses, honey - and their own super home baking, while the evocatively decorated, comfortable restaurant at the back, with its old pine furniture and modern sculpture, is regularly transformed from bustling daytime café to sophisticated evening restaurant (on Friday and Saturday) complete with string quartet. A tempting display of fresh home bakes is the first thing to catch your eye on entering and, as would be expected from the fresh produce on sale in the shop, wholesome vegetables and salads are always irresistible too. Maróg O'Brien is a founder and stall holder of the hugely successful Midleton Farmers Market, which is held on Saturday mornings. Open Mon-Sat, 9-5pm, L 12-4, D Thu-Sat, 6.45 - 9.30pm. Closed Sun, Bank Hols, 24 Dec-3 Jan. MasterCard, Visa, Laser. **Directions:** Town centre. ◇

Midleton

Finíns

BAR/RESTAURANT

75 Main Street Midleton Co Cork
Tel: 021 463 1878 Fax: 021 463 3847

Finín O'Sullivan's thriving bar and restaurant in the centre of the town has long been a popular place for locals to meet for a drink and to eat some good wholesome food. This attractive, no-nonsense place offers a wide range of popular home-made dishes, mostly based on local produce notably fresh seafood from Ballycotton harbour; roast duckling and steaks are also specialities. Bar food available Mon-Sat 10.30am-10pm, specials available noon-6.30pm; Restaurant D Mon-Sat, 7-9.45pm. Bar menu à la carte; D from €25. House wine €18. Closed Sun, bank hols. **Directions:** Town centre. ◇

Midleton

Loughcarrig House

COUNTRY HOUSE

Midleton Co Cork **Tel: 021 463 1955** Fax: 021 461 3707
Email: info@loughcarrig.com Web: www.loughcarrig.com

Bird-watching and sea angling are major interests at Brian and Cheryl Byrne's relaxed and quietly situated country house, which is in a beautiful shore side location. Comfortable rooms have tea/coffee making facilities and there's a pleasantly hospitable atmosphere. Children welcome. Pets permitted by arrangement. Sea fishing, walking, Garden. **Rooms 4** (all en-suite. shower only & no smoking). Closed 16 Dec-16 Jan. B&B €35 pps, ss €10. SC discretionary. **No Credit Cards**. **Directions:** From roundabout at Midleton on N25, take Whitegate Road for 2 miles.

Midleton

O'Donovan's

RESTAURANT

58 Main Street Midleton Co Cork **Tel: 021 463 1255**

An attractive limestone-fronted building on the main street, Pat O'Donovan's highly-regarded restaurant sends out slightly mixed messages with the decor - some features have been retained from its previous use as a pub (a dark wooden service counter and bench seating, for example), tables are traditional with white linen cloths and napkins, and original modern oil paintings adorn the walls; strangely it all adds up to a slightly staid atmosphere. But this is quickly forgotten once you get stuck into Ian Cronin's mouthwateringly promising hand-written menus. Ian - who came to O'Donovans via such illustrious establishments as Aherne's of Youghal and Park Hotel Kenmare - offers a wide choice of top notch dishes on both lunch and dinner menus: a typical lunch menu, for example, offers a couple of soups and a citrus cocktail, then an appealing range of starter / light main course dishes - a warm salad of lambs kidneys with crispy bacon on champ potato, Ballycotton crab mayonnaise on brown bread and salad, roast duck confit on a spring onion mash, panfried fillets of mackerel with hollandaise - all well-priced around €9-12. Dinner menus then offer many of these as starters, following with a choice of around ten main courses. Some dishes are quite unusual - baked pork steak en croûte, for example, is stuffed with a sausage mousse is brushed with Dijon mustard and served on a Bramley apple purée with a wholegrain mustard sauce, and crispy fillet of monkfish is wrapped in potato strings and served on a courgette chutney, with lemon & blue poppy seed dressing. Cooking and presentation are consistently excellent, backed up by efficient service by attentive and informative staff. Delicious desserts are quite traditional - a luscious strawberry meringue roulade, for example, with red fruit coulis, or gorgeously boozy bread & butter pudding with rum-soaked raisins and rum & raisin ice cream - or there's a cheeseboard. A good wine list includes some interesting, unusual wines, and a fair choice of half bottles. Once discovered, Ian Cronin's confident, adventurous cooking, the caring service and good value will have guests planning a return visit here as soon as possible. **Seats 60.** D Mon-Sat, 6-9.30. Closed Sun. MasterCard, Visa, Laser. **Directions:** Travelling eastwards, at eastern end of Main Street, on right-hand side - oppositr entrance to Midleton Distillery. ◇

Midleton Area

★ HOTEL/RESTAURANT

Ballymaloe House

Shanagarry Midleton Co Cork
Tel: 021 465 2531 Fax: 021 465 2021
Email: res@ballymaloe.ie Web: www.ballymaloe.com

Ireland's most famous country house hotel, Ballymaloe was one of the first country houses to open its doors to guests when Myrtle and her husband, the late Ivan Allen, opened The Yeats Room restaurant in 1964. Accommodation followed in 1967 and since then a unique network of family enterprises has developed around Ballymaloe House - including not only the farmlands and gardens that supply so much of the kitchen produce, but also a craft and kitchenware shop, a company producing chutneys and sauce, the Crawford Gallery Café in Cork city, and Darina Allen's internationally acclaimed cookery school. Yet, despite the fame, Ballymaloe is still most remarkable for its unspoilt charm: Myrtle - now rightly receiving international recognition for a lifetime's work "recapturing forgotten flavours, and preserving those that may soon die"- is ably assisted by her children, and now their families too. The house, modestly described in its Blue Book (Irish Country House & Restaurants Association) entry as "a large family farmhouse", is indeed at the centre of the family's 400 acre farm, but with over thirty bedrooms it is a very large house indeed, and one with a gracious nature. The intensely restorative atmosphere of Ballymaloe is remarkable, and there are few greater pleasures than a fine Ballymaloe dinner followed by a good night's sleep in one of their thoughtfully furnished (but not over decorated) country bedrooms - including, incidentally, Ireland's most ancient hotel room which is in the Gate House: a tiny one up (twin bedroom, with little iron beds) and one down (full bathroom and entrance foyer), in the original medieval wall of the old house: delightful and highly romantic! Ground floor courtyard rooms are suitable for wheelchairs. Conferences/banqueting (25/50). Children welcome (cot available; baby sitting arranged). Pets allowed by arrangement. Outdoor swimming pool, tennis, walking, golf (9 hole). Gardens. Shop. **Rooms 33** (4 ground floor, 1 disabled, 2 shower only, all no smoking). B&B €130pps, ss €25. SC discretionary. Room service (limited hours). No lift. Self-catering accommodation also available (details from Hazel Allen). **Restaurant:** The restaurant is in a series of domestic-sized dining rooms and guests are called to their tables from the conservatory or drawing room, where aperitifs are served. A food philosophy centred on using only the highest quality ingredients is central to everything done at Ballymaloe, where much of the produce comes from their own farm and gardens. The rest, including seafood from Ballycotton and Kenmare, comes from leading local producers. Jason Fahey has been head chef at Ballymaloe since 2004 and continues the house tradition of presenting simple, uncomplicated food in the 'good country cooking' style, which allows the exceptional quality of the ingredients to speak for themselves. This is seen particularly at Sunday lunchtime when - apart from the huge range of dishes offered, which would obviously be beyond the home cook - the homely roasts and delicious vegetables are as near to home cooking you are ever likely to find in a restaurant, and what a joy that is. Then things move up a number of notches in the evening, when daily 7-course dinner menus (with vegetarian dishes given a leaf symbol) offer more sophisticated dishes - but there is still a refreshing homeliness to the tone which, despite very professional cooking and service, is perhaps more like a dinner party than a smart restaurant experience. Ballymaloe brown bread, crudités with garlic mayonnaise, a tart of locally smoked fish with tomato & chive beurre blanc, superb roast lamb with rosemary & garlic and chateau potatoes, Irish farmhouse cheeses with home-made biscuits and a dessert trolley that include rhubarb compôte and vanilla ice cream are typical of dishes that invariably delight - and, as if a 7-course dinner isn't enough, second helpings of the main course are offered too. The teamwork at Ballymaloe is outstanding and a meal here is a treat of the highest order. Finish with coffee or tea and home-made petits fours, served in the drawing room - and perhaps a drink from the small bar before retiring contentedly to bed. Children welcome at lunchtime, but the restaurant is not suitable for children under 7 after 7pm. (Children's high tea is served at 5.30.) Buffet meals only on Sundays. **Seats 100.** L daily 1-1.15, D daily 7-9.15 (Sun 7.30-8); Set D €62, Set L €38. House wine from €22. Service discretionary. Reservations essential. House closed 23-26 Dec, 2 weeks Jan. Helipad. * Self Catering Accommodation also available. Amex, Diners, MasterCard, Visa, Laser. **Directions:** Take signs to Ballycotton from N 25. Situated between Cloyne & Shanagarry.

Midleton Area

CAFÉ

Ballymaloe Shop Café

Ballymaloe House Shanagarry Co Cork **Tel: 021 465 2032**
Fax: 021 465 2096 Email: ballymaloeshop@eircom.net

At the back of Wendy Whelan's magnificent crafts, kitchenware and gift shop at Ballymaloe House, there is a very nice little family-run café selling wholesome home-bakes and just the kind of light, nourishing fare that is needed to sustain you through a shopping expedition that may well be taking longer than you had planned. So take the weight off your feet, settle down with an aromatic cup of coffee and a taste of Alison Henderson's delicious home cooking. She offers a simple menu of salads, light lunches, cakes and biscuits - goats cheese, potato & mint tart, Alison's chocolate tart, and pistachio macaroons are specialities. Everything is based on locally sourced fresh ingredients as far as possible, including smoked seafood from Frank Hederman in Cobh, local organic salads, Bill Casey's Shanagarry smoked salmon, and Gubbeen smoked bacon. * Wendy has a charming self-catering cottage, Rockcliffe House, in Ballycotton; details from the shop. Open 10-5 daily, L 12.30-4. House wine €4.50 per glass. Closed 23-27 Dec. Amex, MasterCard, Visa, Laser. **Directions:** 3.5km (2 m) beyond Cloyne on Ballycotton road.

Midleton Area

RESTAURANT/COUNTRY HOUSE

Barnabrow Country House

Barnabrow Cloyne Midleton Co Cork
Tel: 021 465 2534 Fax: 021 465 2534
Email: barnabrow@eircom.net Web: www.barnabrowhouse.com

féile bia John and Geraldine O'Brien's sensitive conversion of an imposing seventeenth century house optimises on stunning views of Ballycotton, and the decor is commendably restrained. Innovative African wooden furniture (among items for sale in an on-site shop) is a point of interest and spacious bedrooms are stylishly decorated and comfortable (although only two have a bath). Some bedrooms are in converted buildings at the back of the house, but (good) breakfasts are served in the main dining room, at a communal table. Recent developments have increased the dining capacity at Barnabrow, so they can now cater for weddings and other functions (up to 150) as well as normal private dining; word has clearly got out to discerning would-be-weds that weddings at Barnabrow are conducted with style and personal interest, as this is now such an important side of the business that it can be difficult for independent guests to obtain a booking. Head chef Gary Masterson took on cooking for the Trinity Rooms Restaurant in 2004 after working on the Queen Mary, and continues the philosophy and cooking style that has earned a fine reputation. Local produce stars, with gratin of cod with cheddar Imokilly cheese & mustard topping an enduring speciality dish.) Children welcome (cots available, free of charge, baby sitting arranged). Pets permitted in some areas. Conference/banqueting (150/150)/ **Rooms 19** (17 shower only, all no smoking). B&B €85pps, ss €20. D 7-9 Thu-Sun, L Sun Only 1-2.30; D à la carte; Set Sun L €27. House wine from €22; service discretionary (10% on parties of 10+). Restaurant closed Mon-Wed; house closed 23-27 Dec. Diners, MasterCard, Visa, Laser. **Directions:** From Cork N25 to Midleton rounddabout, right for Ballinacurra, left for Cloyne, then on to Ballycotton road for 1.5 miles.

Mitchelstown

CAFÉ

O'Callaghan's Delicatessen, Bakery & Café

19/20 Lower Cork Street Mitchelstown Co Cork
Tel: 025 24657 Fax: 025 24657
Email: ocalhansdeli@eircom.net Web: www.ocallaghans.ie

féile bia The ideal place to break a journey, O'Callaghans have an impressive deli and bakery as well as tasty fare for a snack or full meal in the café, where lovely things to look forward to include monkfish & salmon kebabs, Caesar salad, BBQ steak panini, goats cheese on a croûton, garlic mussels and a lovely vegetarian focaccia with herbed feta, mozzarella, red onion, pepper, black olives & pesto mayo... If you're going home to an empty house, this is the place to stock up with delicious home-baked breads and cakes, home-made jams and chutneys - and, best of all perhaps, there's a range of home-made frozen meals. They do a range of seasonal specialities too - and if you have a wedding coming up in the family, ask about their wedding confectionery, made to order. There's also a great home-made gluten free range, offering everything from soda breads and sweet and savoury tarts to Christmas cakes, Christmas puddings and mince pies (telephone orders accepted).A new sun deck was added recently, to accommodate smokers (and non smokers), and has a covered area. To avoid the busy main street, park around the corner on the road to the creamery - or, coming from Dublin, parking is also available on the new square (on right after second set of lights); but remember the square is not available for parking on Thursday - market day. Restaurant **Seats 140** (outdoor 20). Food served Mon-Sat, 8.30 am- 5 pm; L 12.3-5.00. Closed Sun, bank hols, 25-27 Dec. Amex, Diners, MasterCard, Visa, Laser. **Directions:** On main street, right side heading towards Dublin.

Monkstown

The Bosun

BAR/RESTAURANT WITH ROOMS

The Pier Monkstown Co Cork
Tel: 021 484 2172 Fax: 021 484 2008
Email: info@thebosun.ie Web: www.thebosun.ie

Nicky and Patricia Moynihan's waterside establishment close to the both the car ferry across to Cobh and the Ringaskiddy ferries (France and Wales) has grown a lot over the years, with the restaurant and accommodation becoming increasingly important. Bar food is still taken seriously, however; seafood takes pride of place and afternoon/evening bar menus include everything from chowder or garlic mussels through to real Dingle Bay scampi and chips, although serious main courses for carnivores such as beef with brandy & peppercorn sauce and beef & Guinness casserole are also available. Next to the bar, a well-appointed restaurant provides a more formal setting for wide-ranging table d'hôte and à la carte menus - and also Sunday lunch, which is especially popular. Again seafood is the speciality, ranging from popular starters such as crab claws or oysters worked into imaginative dishes, and main courses that include steaks and local duckling as well as seafood every which way, from grilled sole on the bone to medallions of marinated monkfish or a cold seafood platter. There's always a choice for vegetarians and vegetables are generous and carefully cooked. Finish with home-made ices, perhaps, or a selection of Irish farmhouse cheeses. Not suitable for children after 7pm. Restaurant **Seats 80** (max table size 12). Private room 25/30. Air conditioning. Toilets wheelchair accessible. D daily 6.30-9, L Sun 12-2.30, Set D €45, Set Sun L €28.50; à la carte also available; house wine €22, sc discretionary. Bar food available daily 12-9.30). Closed 24-26 Dec, Good Fri. **Accommodation:** Bedrooms are quite simple but have everything required (phone, TV, tea/coffee trays); those at the front have harbour views but are shower only, while those at the back are quieter and have the advantage of a full bathroom. Fota Island Golf Course is only 12 minutes away, also Fota House and Wildlife Centre. **Rooms 15** (9 shower only, all no smoking). Lift. B&B €55 pps, ss €10. Children welcome (under 5s free in parents' room, cot available without charge). No pets. Closed 24-26 Dec, Good FridayAmex, Diners, MasterCard, Visa, Laser. **Directions:** On sea front, beside the Cobh ferry and near Ringaskiddy port ferry.

Oysterhaven

Finders Inn

RESTAURANT

Nohoval Oysterhaven Co Cork
Tel: 021 477 0737 Web: www.findersinn.com

Very popular with local people (but perhaps harder for visitors to find) the McDonnell family's well-named old-world bar and restaurant is in a row of traditional cottages east of Oysterhaven, en route from Crosshaven to Kinsale. It is a very charming place, packed with antiques and, because of the nature of the building, broken up naturally into a number of dining areas (which gives it an air of mystery). Seafood stars, of course - smoked salmon, Oysterhaven oysters, bisques, chowders, scallops and lobster are all here (grilled fillet of salmon and seafood cassoulet attracted prise on a recent visit), but there are a few other specialities too, including steaks, lamb and lovely tender crisp-skinned duckling with an orange-sage sauce, and the cooking, by brothers Rory and Cormac MacDonnell, is excellent. Good desserts, caring service (under the direction of a third brother Donough, who also runs the bar) and a great atmosphere. In addition to the current very successful operation - evening restaurant and atmospheric local bar - there are plans to introduce interesting bar food too. Well worth taking the trouble to find. Not suitable for children under 8 after 8 pm. **Seats 90** (private room, 70). D Tue-Sat (also bank hol Sundays), 7-9.30. A la carte; sc discretionary. Toilets wheelchair accessible. Closed Sun (except bank hol weekends) & Mon; Christmas week. MasterCard, Visa, Laser. **Directions:** From

Cork, take Kinsale direction; at Carrigaline, go straight through main street then turn right, following R611 to Ballyfeard; about 700 metres beyond Ballyfeard, go straight for Nohoval (rather than bearing right on R611 for Belgooly). ◇

Oysterhaven
RESTAURANT

Oz-Haven Restaurant

Oysterhaven Co Cork **Tel: 021 477 0974**
Fax: 021 477 0974 Web: www.ozhaven.com

In a delightful waterside location at the head of Oysterhaven creek, the colourful exterior of Australian Paul Greer's cottage restaurant warns guests to expect something highly individual. There's a great sense of fun about the whole idiosyncratic approach (including a giant fish tank with two huge Amazon fish) and, despite its modernism, the wacky decor works surprisingly well with the old building. The restaurant is divided between three separate areas, with open fires in two; well-spaced tables have comfortable high-back carver chairs and are simply laid in quality contemporary style, with generous wine glasses and white plates decorated only with the restaurant logo. Underlying the wordy descriptions, the best of local ingredients - Oysterhaven mussels and oysters, Gubbeen cheese, local meats - are to be found alongside less likely ones, such as crocodile, kangaroo and ostrich. World flavours weave in and out through the menu (well their motto is 'a fusion of world cuisine') and diners looking for an unusual experience should not be disappointed. Service is under the personal direction of Paul Greer, who takes pride in getting to know everyone - and continuing to present food with a difference, in entertaining surroundings. **Seats 55** (private room 25, outside dining 25). Toilets wheelchair accessible. Children welcome. D Mon-Sat, 7-9.30; L Sun & bank hols, 1-5. Set D €39.95 (€29.95 in winter), also à la carte, Set Sun L €26.95. House wine around €19.95. Closed D Sun, 25-26 Dec. Amex, MasterCard, Visa, Laser. **Directions:** 30 min from Cork city, turn left for Oysterhaven just before Kinsale.

Oysterhaven
COUNTRY HOUSE

Walton Court

Oysterhaven Co Cork **Tel: 021 477 0878** Fax: 021 477 0932
Email: enquiry@waltoncourt.com Web: www.waltoncourt.com

Walton Court dates back to 1645 and when Paul and Janis Rafferty took it over on their return from Kenya in 1996, it was derelict. Five years of restoration work brought this listed building back to its former glory and the courtyard has been converted to provide stylish bedrooms and self-contained cottages, each with its own personality. There is also a small conference room (ISDN, video & lecture facilities), and a little bar with an open fireplace for guests' use. A plant-filled courtyard conservatory at the back of the house is used for breakfast and, perhaps, dining, as an alternative to the restored Georgian dining room. As members of the Slow Food movement, Paul & Janis prepare everything using fresh organic and home-grown ingredients. This unusual place will please those who value character above the hotel conveniences (television, room service) and it helps to like animals as you will certainly be greeted by the dogs as well as their owners, and quite probably cats and other household animals too. When the Guide visited in summer 2004, the main focus of energy was at the waters edge, where a small marina was under construction. Small conferences/banqueting (25). Indoor exercise pool, sauna, treatment rooms. Pets permitted by arrangement. **Rooms 6** (5 shower only, all no smoking). B&B from €75 pps, ss €20. D by arrangement. Children welcome (under 4s free in parents room, cot available). Closed Nov-Feb inc. *Self catering apartments also available. MasterCard, Visa, Laser. **Directions:** 9km (6 m) from Kinsale (Cork side); R600 to Belgooly, signs to Oysterhaven. ◇

Rosscarbery
E RESTAURANT

O'Callaghan-Walshe

The Square Rosscarbery Co Cork **Tel: 023 48125**
Fax: 023 48125 Email: funfish@indigo.ie

This unique restaurant on the square of a charming village (well off the busy main West Cork road) has a previous commercial history that's almost tangible - exposed stone walls, old fishing nets and glass floats, mismatched furniture, shelves of wine bottles and candlelight all contribute to and its unique atmosphere - which is well-matched by proprietor-host Sean Kearney's larger-than-life personality. Then there's the exceptional freshness and quality of the seafood - steaks theoretically share the billing, but West Cork seafood 'bought off the boats at auction' steals the scene. Martina O'Donovan's menus change daily but specialities to look out for include the famous Rosscarbery Pacific oysters. of course, of course, also a superb West Cork Seafood Platter, char-grilled prime fish such as turbot, and grilled whole lobster. Ultra-freshness, attention to detail in breads and accompaniments - and a huge dose of personality - all add up to make this place a delight. O'Callagan Walsh was the Guide's Atmospheric Restaurant of the Year for 2004. An interesting wine list includes a good choice of half bottles. Not suitable for children after 7 pm. **Seats 40.** D Tue-Sun 6.30-9.15. D à la carte, house wine €19.70, sc discretionary. Closed Mon, open weekends only in winter (a phone call to check is advised). MasterCard, Visa, Laser. **Directions:** Main square in Rosscarbery village.

Rosscarbery

Pilgrim's Rest

CAFÉ

The Square Rosscarbery Co Cork **Tel: 023 31796**

A charming café just across the square from O'Callaghan Walshe, The Pilgrim's Rest gives out all the right vibes (delicious Illy coffee and lovely home-bakes) and is well worth checking out for a journey break. Off season menus are quite restricted - just coffee and cakes in winter - but there is much more choice of wholesome light meals in summer. Open 6 days in summer, Tue, 12-5pm, Wed-Sun, 10-5pm; more limited opening off season, please call ahead to confirm. Closed Mon. MasterCard, Visa. **Directions:** Off N71, on main square od Rosscarbery village.

Schull

Corthna Lodge Country House

GUESTHOUSE

Air Hill Schull Co Cork **Tel: 028 28517** Fax: 028 28032
Email: info@corthna-lodge.net Web: www.corthna-lodge.net

Situated up the hill from Schull, commanding countryside and sea views, Martin and Andrea Mueller's roomy modern house just outside the town is one of the best located places to stay in the area. Although fairly compact bedrooms are comfortable with good amenities (and new beds), and there's plenty of space for guests to sit around and relax - both indoors, in a pleasant and comfortably furnished sitting room and outdoors, on a terrace overlooking the lovely garden towards the islands of Roaring Water Bay. House computer available for guests' internet access; unusually, there's also a gym, a hot tub, a barbecue area - and a putting green. Gym. Hot tub. Children over 5 welcome. **Rooms 6** (all shower only & no smoking). B&B €47.50 pps, ss €22.50. Closed 15 Oct-15 April. MasterCard, Visa, Laser. **Directions:** Through village, up hill, first left, first right - house is signposted.

Schull

Grove House

RESTAURANT WITH ROOMS

Colla Road Schull Co Cork **Tel: 028 28067** Fax: 028 28069
Email: katarinarunske@eircom.net Web: www.grovehouseschull.com

Overlooking Schull Harbour, this beautifully restored period house offers quality, relaxed accommodation and great food just a few minutes walk from the main street, and is now run by Katarina Runske (previously at Dunworley Cottage, Butlerstown) and her family. The approach is less than immaculate, but landscaping is beginning to mature and slight untidiness around the house is not typical of the interior, where housekeeping is exemplary. There is plenty of parking, and a terrace set up attractively with garden furniture and parasols overlooking the harbour and all the activity on the pier, where you can relax with a glass of wine or lunch. It is a pleasing house, and any period features have been retained in well-proportioned reception rooms and bedrooms, which are large, with individual character and well-finished shower rooms. Katarina also teaches piano so there is music in the house, with a grand piano in the green room. A lovely dining room, set up stylishly with simple contemporary linen and cutlery, is used for delicious breakfasts and has now come into its own as a restaurant - earning a new following for unique ingredients-lead cooking with a distinctive Swedish flavour. About seven choices are offered on each course at dinner, and there are nightly seafood specials. Katarina's signature dish - herrings three ways - is sure to be among the starters, and main courses will include other firm favourites like local duck in plum & red wine sauce, and Swedish meatballs. Puddings are a highlight (a dense, richly-flavoured almond cake, perhaps), also local cheeses - and excellent homemade breads may include an unusual light rye style brown, and a white yeast loaf. A good wine list is quite extensive - it includes some treats, and wine service is informative. Children welcome. Pets permitted by arrangement. Garden. **Rooms 5** (all en-suite, & no smoking, 3 ground floor); B&B about €50 pps, ss €10. Accommodation open all year round. Retaurant L 12.30-3.30, D 6.30-10.30, closed L Sun - but times of opening not confimed at time of going to press, so phone ahead to check. Open weekend only off season, but can be opened on request. Amex, MasterCard, Visa, Laser. **Directions:** On right beyond Church of Ireland Colla Road, 4 mins walk from village. ◇

Schull

New Haven (La Coquille)

RESTAURANT

Main Street Schull Co Cork **Tel: 028 28642**

Where Jean Michel Caher's restaurant, La Coquille, used to be you will now find the New Haven, which is in the same ownership but re-styled as an all-day restaurant with a wider range of food offered if you have children in tow, you will find good value children's meals, and pizzas a-plenty. Although recently refurbished, ventilation is poor, and bare tables are set up with nothing more than salt, pepper and a bottle of (homemade) vinaigrette; a knife and fork and thin paper napkin is brought with each plate. However, the saving grace for adults is that menus still include some of the fresh fish and seafood for which Jean Michel is best known and, if the Guide's visit was typical, this is still by far the best choice: daily specials offer excellent fresh fish dishes, served with good chips. Prawns in the shell with mayo are also good (and value too, at €8 for ten big prawns, ie langoustines); but beware the avocado with shrimp, made with frozen shrimp. **Seats 35.** Open 12noon to 10.30pm in summer and 12 noon to 9pm in winter. No reservations. Amex, Diners, MasterCard, Visa. **Directions:** In the village, across from the church. ◇

Schull

Stanley House

B&B

Schull Co Cork **Tel: 028 28425** Fax: 028 27887
Email: stanleyhouse@eircom.net Web: www.stanley-house.net

Nancy Brosnan's modern house provides a west Cork home from home for her many returning guests. Compact bedrooms are comfortably furnished with tea/coffee making facilities and there's a pleasant conservatory running along the back of the house, with wonderful sea views over a field where guests can watch Nancy's growing herd of deer and sometimes see foxes come out to play at dusk. Good breakfasts too. Children welcome (under 3s free in parents' room, cots available without charge). No pets. Garden. **Rooms 4** (all shower only, all no-smoking, 2 ground floor). B&B €32 pps, ss €12.50. Closed 31 Oct-1 Mar. MasterCard, Visa, Laser. **Directions:** At top of main street. follow signs for Stanley House.

Schull

T J Newman's

CAFÉ/PUB/WINE BAR

Main Street Schull Co Cork **Tel: 028 27776** Fax: 028 27776
Email: info@tjnewmans.com Web: www.tjnewmans.com

Just up the hill from the harbour, this characterful and delightfully old-fashioned little pub has been a special home-from-home for regular visitors, especially sailors up from the harbour, as long as anyone can remember. The premises was bought by John and Bride D'Alton in 2003 but, although Kitty Newman is missed, the old bar remains much as it always has been. There's a big change next door since then, however, as the D'Alton's new Café / Wine Bar, **Café West,** has replaced the old off-licence and introduced a new flavour to the informal dining options in Schull. Offering lovely food and great value in immaculate premises, they have a second first-floor room that doubles as an art gallery, and provide newspapers for a leisurely browse over an excellent cup of coffee. A cleverly thought out menu offers all sorts of tempting bits and pieces, notably the Newman's West Gourmet Choice which includes West Cork salamis (€5.90)., Irish whiskey gravad lax (€45.90) and Irish cheeses (€6.70), served with salad and lovely brown bread and butter. Delicious desserts might include a more-ish summer pudding (€4.50). Every tourist town should have a place like this. Broadband Wi/Fi. Children welcome. **Seats 50.** Toilets wheelchair accessible. Food served all day 9-12 (Sun to 11). House wines (16), €15.90 (€4 per glass). Closed 25 Dec. **No Credit Cards. Directions:** Main West Cork route to Mizen Head.

Schull Area

Rock Cottage

COUNTRY HOUSE

Barnatonicane Schull Co Cork
Tel: 028 35538 Fax: 028 35538
Email: rockcottage@eircom.net Web: www.rockcottage.ie

Garden-lovers, especially, will thrill to the surroundings of Barbara Klotzer's beautiful slate-clad Georgian hunting lodge near Schull, which is on a south-facing slope away from the sea, which is nearby at Dunmanus Bay. A fascinating combination of well-tended lawns and riotous flower beds, the rocky outcrop which inspired its name - and even great estate trees in the 17 acres of parkland (complete with peacefully grazing sheep) that have survived from an earlier period of its history create a unique setting. The main house has style and comfort, with welcoming open fires and bright bedrooms which - although not especially large - have been thoughtfully furnished to allow little seating areas as well as the usual amenities such as tea/coffee making facilities, and recently refurbished en-suite power showers. There's a sheltered courtyard behind the house and also some appealing self-catering accommodation, in converted stables. And Barbara is an accomplished chef - so you can look forward to a dinner based on the best of local produce, with starters like fresh crab salad or warm Ardsallagh goats cheese, main courses of Rock Cottage's own rack of lamb, monkfish kebab, or even lobster or seafood platters (prices for these options on request), beautiful vegetables and classic desserts like home-baked vanilla cheesecake or strawberry fool. Extensive breakfast choices include a Healthy Breakfast and a Fish Breakfast as well as traditional Irish and continental combinations - just make your choice before 8pm the night before. Barbara also offers laundry facilities - very useful when touring around, (€9 per load for washing and drying). Not suitable for children under 10. No pets. garden. walking. **Rooms 3** (2 with en-suite showers, 1 with private bathroom, all no smoking). B&B from €65 pps, ss €30. Breakfast, 8.30-9.30 (order by 8pm the night before). Residents D Mon-Sat, €48, at 7.30; house wine €20. No D on Sun. Open all year. MasterCard, Visa, Laser. **Directions:** From Schull, 10km, at Toormore, turn into R591 after 2km. Sign on left.

Skibbereen
RESTAURANT

Kalbo's Bistro

48 North Street Skibbereen Co Cork
Tel: 028 21515 Fax: 028 21515

Siobhan O'Callaghan and Anthony Boyle continue to a great job at this bright, buzzy town-centre restaurant. It's informal but there has always been an air of quality about it - staff are quick and helpful and Siobhan's simple food is wholesome and flavoursome in a light contemporary style - lovely home-made soups, pastas, tarts, ciabattas, and scrumptious salads at lunchtime and more serious dishes of local seafood, rack of lamb, steaks and so on in the evening. Home-made burgers come with a choice of toppings and vegetarian options are imaginative. The dishes are popular, but this is real food; consistently delicious, it is well-sourced, accurately cooked, appetisingly presented - and has real flavour. Whether for a quick lunchtime bite or a more leisurely meal, Kalbo's is a great choice - and good value too. **Seats 42.** Open daily in summer: L Mon-Sat, 12-3, D daily, 6.30-9.30. A la carte; house wine €16.95, sc discretionary. Closed Sun; Christmas & Good Fri. Amex, Diners, MasterCard, Visa, Laser. **Directions:** In town centre.

Skibbereen
RESTAURANT

Thai @ Ty ar Mor

46 Bridge Street Skibbereen Co Cork **Tel: 028 22100** Fax: 028 22834
Email: info@tyarmor.com Web: www.tyarmor.com

Chef-patron Michel Philippot and his wife and front-of-house manager, Rosaleen O'Shea, earned a great reputation for their delightful little Breton restaurant in the centre of Skibbereen, which was our Seafood Restaurant of the Year in 2003. However, despite having a lively atmosphere and giving great value for money for high quality of ingredients, cooking and service, the business was very seasonal and a visit to Thailand a couple of years ago inspired Michel to increase the choice offered by extending the restaurant into the first floor, which became Thai @ Ty Ar Mor. This proved such a success that the ground floor was then given over to a shop specialising in Thai food products, cookery books, furnishings, and gifts; this has now been extended to include a delicatessen counter, with daily specialities, and dishes are also available to take home. Thai staff, brought to Ireland especially to work here, ensure a real taste of Thailand and you will still fine plenty of local seafood here, particularly among the daily specials - and Michel is also delighted to make his wonderful Breton specialities on request. Both food and atmosphere are authentic, and a Khantok room offers a choice of the traditional Thai low tables and cushions, in addition to the western furniture in the main dining room. Not suitable for children under 12. **Seats 30** (private room, 10). Open for D, 6-9pm, Mon-Sat peak season, Wed-Sat when open off season; Set D €25/33, 2/3 course. House wine from €17.50. Closed mid Sep - end Nov & Jan-Mar. For exact dates check website or phone. MasterCard, Visa, Laser. **Directions:** Skibbereen town centre, towards road to Schull.

Skibbereen
HOTEL

West Cork Hotel

Ilen Street Skibbereen Co Cork **Tel: 028 21277** Fax: 028 22333
Email: info@westcorkhotel.com Web: www.westcorkhotel.com

This welcoming hotel enjoys a pleasant riverside site beside the bridge, on the western side of the town, and recent refurbishment has been completed with style. The entrance is quite small, but the hotel opens up behind the foyer, to reveal a bright and airy bar along the river side of the hotel, and a pleasant modern restaurant, where breakfast is served to residents, as well as main meals. Bedrooms are not especially large, but they are comfortably furnished in a gently contemporary style and have all the necessary amenities (phone, tea/coffee tray, TV) and neat, well-designed en-suite bathrooms - this would make a good base from which to explore this beautiful area. Rooms at the back are quieter and have a pleasant outlook over trees and river. Conference/banqueting (300/250). Children welcome (cot available without charge). Pets permitted in some areas by arrangement. Garden. Private parking. **Rooms 30** (7 junior suites, 4 shower only). B&B €80, ss €6. Food available in restaurant and bar: 12.30-2.30 & 6-9. Closed 22-28 Dec. Amex, Diners, MasterCard, Visa, Laser, Switch. **Directions:** Follow signs N71 to Bantry through Skibbereen.

YOUGHAL

Best known for its associations with Sir Walter Raleigh, Youghal is an historic town on the estuary of the Blackwater, and was once the second largest port in Europe. Today, thanks to a recently opened by-pass, the town is more accessible for leisurely visits and it is well worth lingering a little to take in the historical walking tour which visits a number of diversely interesting old buildings, including the famous 1777 Clock Gate over the main street. **Old Imperial Hotel with Coachhouse Bar & Restaurant** (024 92435; www.theoldimperialhotel.com): at the front of this recently renovated town centre hotel is a wonderful old-world bar, previously known as D.McCarthy; while the rest of the hotel provides the usual facilities, this is a lovely little low-ceilinged bar of great character, with an open fire and a long history to tell - it's worth calling here for this alone. On the western end of the town, the popular **Tides Restaurant** (024 93127; www.tidesrestaurant.ie) is a useful place to know about, not least for its long opening hours; accommodation is also available.

WWW.IRELAND-GUIDE.COM FOR THE BEST PLACES TO EAT, DRINK & STAY

Youghal

RESTAURANT WITH ROOMS

Aherne's Seafood Restaurant & Accommodation

163 North Main Street Youghal Co Cork
Tel: 024 92424 Fax: 024 93633
Email: ahernes@eircom.net Web: www.ahernes.com

SEAFOOD BAR OF THE YEAR

Now in its third generation of family ownership, one of the most remarkable features of Aherne's is the warmth of the FitzGibbon family's hospitality and their enormous enthusiasm for the business which, since 1993, has included seriously luxurious accommodation. It is for its food - and, especially, the ultra-fresh seafood that comes straight from the fishing boats in Youghal harbour - that Aherne's is best known, however. While John FitzGibbon supervises the front of house, his brother David reigns over a busy kitchen. Bar food tends pleasingly towards simplicity - oysters, chowder, Yawl Bay smoked salmon and oysters make for great snacks or starters (all served with the renowned moist dark brown yeast bread), and you'll find at least half a dozen delicious hot seafood main course dishes like baked cod wrapped in bacon (served with salad, salsa & sauté potatoes) and gorgeous prawns in garlic butter - its sheer freshness tells the story. Restaurant meals are naturally more ambitious and include some token meat dishes - rack of lamb with a rosemary jus or mint sauce, char-grilled fillet steak with mushrooms and shallot jus or pepper sauce - although seafood is still the undisputed star of the show and David is not afraid of simplicity when it is merited. Specialities like pan-fried scallops with spinach, bacon & cream, or fresh crab salad can make memorable starters, for example, and who could resist a main course hot buttered Youghal Bay lobster? These are, in a sense, simple dishes yet they have plenty of glamour too. It is well worth planning a journey around a bar meal at Aherne's - or, if time permits, a relaxed evening meal followed by a restful night in their luxurious accommodation. A wine list strong on classic French regions offers a good selection of half bottles and half a dozen champagnes. **Seats 60** (private room, 20). Toilets wheelchair accessible. D 6.30-9.30 daily; fixed price 2-course set D €35; 3-course €45; also à la carte; house wine about €22, sc discretionary. *Bar food daily, 12-10. **Accommodation:** The stylish rooms at Aherne's are generously sized and individually decorated to a high standard; all are furnished with antiques and have full bathrooms. Housekeeping is exemplary, as elsewhere at Aherne's, and excellent breakfasts are served in a warm and elegantly furnished residents' dining room. Studio apartments more recently added are equipped to give the option of self-catering if required. Conference room (20). Safe & fax available at reception. Children under 5 free in parents' room (cot available without charge, baby sitting arranged). Pets permitted in certain areas. **Rooms 13** (4 junior suites, 2 family rooms, 3 ground floor, 1 for disabled). B&B €105 pps, ss €25. Wheelchair access. Closed 24-28 Dec. Amex, MasterCard, Visa. **Directions:** on N25, main route from Cork-Waterford.

Youghal

FARMHOUSE

Ballymakeigh House

Killeagh Youghal Co Cork **Tel: 024 95184** Fax: 024 95523
Email: ballymakeigh@eircom.net Web: www.ballymakeighhouse.com

Winner of our Farmhouse of the Year Award in 1999, Ballymakeigh House provides a high standard of comfort, food and hospitality in one of the most outstanding establishments of its type in Ireland. Set at the heart of an east Cork dairy farm, this attractive old house is immaculately maintained and run by Margaret Browne, who is a Euro-Toques chef and author of a successful cookery book. The house is warm and homely with plenty of space for guests, who are welcome to use the garden and visit the farmyard. The individually decorated bedrooms are full of character and equally comfortable, and Margaret's hospitality is matched only by her energetic pursuit of excellence - ongoing improvements and developments are a constant characteristic of Ballymakeigh. Margaret Browne has a national reputation for her cooking; an impressive dinner menu is offered every night, and non-residents are very welcome in the restaurant. Garden, walking. Off-season value breaks, special interest breaks. Self-catering accommodation is also available nearby, in a restored Victorian house. Children welcome (under 3 free in parents' room, cot available). Pets allowed in some areas by arrangement. **Rooms 6** (all en-suite & no smoking, 3 shower only, 1 family room). B&B €65 pps, ss €10. D daily, 7-8, residents only; Set D €40-45; house wine from €20; SC discretionary. House closed Nov 1-Feb1. MasterCard, Visa, Laser. **Directions:** Off N25 between Youghal & Killeagh (signed at Old Thatch pub).

COUNTY DONEGAL

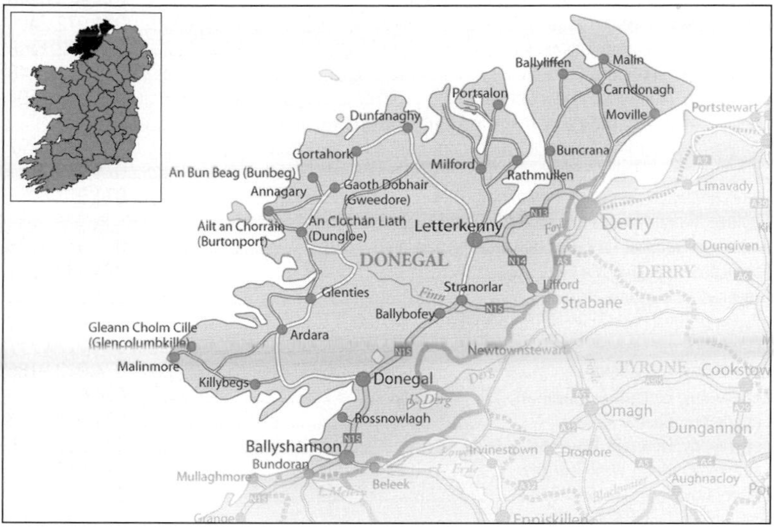

Golden eagles are no mere flight of fancy in Donegal. Glenveagh National Park in the northern part of the county is the focal point of a programme for the re-introduction of this magnificent bird to Ireland – it was last seen here in 1912. The first six Scottish-born chicks of the new wave were released at Glenveagh in June 2001, and by the end of 2004, 15 adult birds were soaring over Donegal, with a further nine sightings to the south in Sligo and Leitrim. Over a five year period, 50 birds have been released, and there are high expectations of success for the project.

Travel at sea level is also an increasingly significant element in visits to Donegal, one of Ireland's most spectacularly beautiful counties. It is much-indented by the sea, but the introduction of local car ferry services is shortening journeys and adding interest. The ferry between Greencastle and Magilligan across the narrow entrance to Lough Foyle has become deservedly popular, and another car ferry – between Buncrana and Rathmullan across Lough Swilly – adds to the travel options, albeit at a more leisurely pace.

For many folk, particularly those from Northern Ireland, Donegal is the holiday county par excellence. But in recent years, despite the international fluctuations of trading conditions, there has been growth of modern industries and the re-structuring of the fishing, particularly at the developing harbour of Killybegs, home port for the largest fishing vessels. This Donegal entrepreneurial spirit has led to a more balanced economy, with the pace being set by the county town of Letterkenny, where the population has increased by 50% since 1991.

But much and all as Donegal county is increasingly a place where people live and make a living, nevertheless it is still a place of nature on the grand scale, where the landscape is challenged by the winds and weather of the Atlantic Ocean if given the slighest chance. Yet at communities like Bundoran and Rossnowlagh, where splendid beaches face straight into the Atlantic, enthusiastic surfers have demonstrated that even the most demanding weather can have its sporting uses.

For most folk, however, it is the contrast between raw nature and homely comfort which is central to Donegal's enduring attraction. For here, in some of Ireland's most rugged territory, you will find many sheltered and hospitable places whose amenities are emphasised by the challenging nature of their broader environment. And needless to say, that environment is simply startlingly utterly beautiful as well.

Local Attractions and Information

Arranmore Ferry, Burtonport-Arranmore	074 952 0532
Ballintra, Ballymagroarty Heritage Centre	074 973 4966
Buncrana, Lough Swilly Ferry	074 938 1901
Buncrana, National Knitting Centre	074 936 2355
Bundoran, Tourism Information	071 984 1350

Churchill, Glebe House & Gallery (Derek Hill) 074 913 7071
Donegal Airport, Carrickfin 074 954 8232
Donegal Highlands, Hillwalking/Irish lang.(adults) 074 973 0248
Donegal town, Donegal Castle 074 972 2405
Donegal town, Tourism information 074 972 1148
Donegal town, Waterbus Cruises 074 972 1148
Dunfanaghy, Workhouse Visitor Centre 074 913 6504
Dungloe, Mary from Dungloe Int. Festival (July/August)
Dungloe, Tourism Information 074 952 1297
Glencolumbcille, Folk Museum 074 973 0017
Glencolumbcille, Tourism Information 074 973 0017
Glenties, Patrick Mac Gill Summer School (August)
Glenveagh National Park (Castle, gardens, parkland) 074 913 7088
Greencastle, Lough Foyle Ferry 074 938 1901
Greencastle, Maritime Museum 074 938 1363
Inishowen, Inishowen Tourism (Carndonagh) 074 937 4933
Letterkenny, An Grianan Theatre 074 912 0777
Letterkenny, Arts Centre 074 912 9186
Letterkenny, Earagail Arts Festival 074 912 9186
Letterkenny, County Museum 074 912 4613
Letterkenny, Newmills Watermill 074 912 5115
Letterkenny, North West Tourism 074 912 1160
Lifford, Cavanacor Historic House 074 914 1143
Rathmullan, Lough Swilly Ferry 074 938 1901
Tory Island Ferry 074 953 1320

Annagry
RESTAURANT WITH ROOMS

Danny Minnie's Restaurant

Annagry Co Donegal **Tel: 074 954 8201**
Web: www.dannyminnies.com

The O'Donnell family has run Danny Minnie's since 1962, and a visit is always a special treat. There's nothing about the exterior as seen from the road to prepare first-time visitors for the atmosphere of this remarkable restaurant: hidden behind a frontage of overgrown creepers a surprise awaits when, after a warm welcome from Terri O'Donnell, guests are suddenly surrounded by antiques and elegantly appointed candle-lit tables. The menu is presented in both Irish and English, and Brian O'Donnell's cooking is a good match for the surroundings - fine, with imaginative saucing, but not at all pompous. On the wide-ranging à la carte menu, seafood stars in the main courses - lobster and other shellfish, availability permitting - and there is also a strong selection of meats including Donegal mountain lamb, typically served with honey, garlic and rosemary gravy, and Donegal beef, served various ways including classic Beef Wellington. Vegetables are a strength and gorgeous desserts, such as lemon and lime pannacotta with a refreshing rhubarb and strawberry compôte, can be relied on to create an appropriately delicious finale. And, under Terri's direction, friendly and attentive waitresses provide lovely service. There's nowhere quite like Danny Minnie's, winner of the Guide's Atmospheric Restaurant of the Year in 2000. Not suitable for children after 9pm. Reservations required. **Seats 80.** Air conditioning. D daily in summer, 6-10. Set D about €40; also à la carte; house wine from about €25; no sc. (Phone ahead to check opening hours, especially off peak season) Closed 25/26 Dec, Good Fri & early week off season. [Accommodation is also offered in eight non-smoking rooms, five of them en-suite and one suitable for disabled guests]. MasterCard, Visa, Laser. **Directions:** R259 off N56 - follow Airport signs. ◇

Ardara
B&B

The Green Gate

Ardvally Ardara Co Donegal **Tel: 074 954 1546**
Web: www.thegreengate-ireland.com

Paul Chatenoud's amazing little B&B is a one-off. Above Adara, up a steep and twisting boreen (follow his unique signing system) that will reward you with a stunning view on arrival, Paul offers simple but comfortable accommodation in his unspoilt traditional cottage and converted outbuildings. It's a far cry from the Parisian bookshop he once ran, but this little place is magic. In the morning (or whenever you wake up - he will be working around his lovely garden and is happy to stop at any time it suits his guests), he cooks up breakfast while you take in the laid-back homeliness of his cosy cottage sitting room. If the morning is fine he may serve breakfast in the garden (just where is that beautiful music coming from?) while he regales you with stories of famous people who have fallen in love with The Green Gate. Just be glad you found it, because he's probably right - it may well be "the most beautiful place anywhere in Ireland". Just leave the Merc at home - and come with an open mind. [Paul asks guests to visit his website and be sure they understand the simplicity of the place they plan to visit before he can accept reservations.] Children welcome (cot available and baby sitting arranged), but some parents may feel it is rather remote for young children. Pets permitted by arrangement. **Rooms 4** (all with en-suite bathrooms, bath only). B&B €35pps, single €60. Open all year. **No Credit Cards. Directions:** One mile from Ardara on the hill (past Woodhill restaurant and follow white arrow)

Ardara

BAR

Nancy's Bar

Front Street Ardara Co Donegal **Tel: 074 954 1187**

This famous pub, in the village renowned for its tweeds and handknits, is a cosy, welcoming place in its seventh generation of family ownership, with five or six small rooms packed with bric à brac and plenty of tables and chairs for the comfortable consumption of wholesome home-made food, especially seafood. Famous for their chowder - maybe try it with a "Louis Armstrong" (smoked salmon on brown bread topped with grilled cheese) and finish with an Irish coffee. Or there's "Charlie's Supper", a speciality of prawns and smoked salmon warmed in a chilli & garlic sauce. Live music too. Bar food served daily 12-9, from Easter to September. Wheelchair access. Closed 25 Dec & Good Fri. **No Credit Cards. Directions:** In Ardara village; half an hours drive from Donegal Town.

Ardara

BAR/RESTAURANT/COUNTRY HOUSE

Woodhill House

Woodhill Ardara Co Donegal
Tel: 074 954 1112 Fax: 074 954 1516
Email: yates@iol.ie Web: www.woodhillhouse.com

Formerly the home of Ireland's last commercial whaling family, John and Nancy Yates' large country house is set in its own grounds overlooking the Donegal Highlands and the hard restoration work they have put in over more than fifteen years is now bearing fruit. This hospitable house has a full bar and offers accommodation in the main house and nearby converted outbuildings - rooms are all en-suite, but vary greatly in position, size and character so it is worth spending a few minutes discussing your preferences when booking. There's also a restaurant (booking recommended as it's very popular locally) offering quite traditional food based on local ingredients at reasonable prices: specialities include local wild salmon, Donegal mountain lamb, duck off the bone and carrageen pudding. The gradual restoration of the gardens (including a walled kitchen garden) is perhaps Nancy's greatest challenge and it's turning out beautifully, not only on the kitchen garden side but as a pleasure garden too. Renovations, on both the main house and some fine outbuildings, continue on an on-going basis; six new rooms, overlooking the old walled garden, have recently been completed, one with wheelchair accessibility. Small conferences/ private parties (50). Children welcome (cot available without charge). Pets permitted in some areas. **Rooms 14** (6 shower-only, 1 family room, 4 ground floor, 1 for disabled). B&B €60 pps, ss €15. **Restaurant: Seats 50** (private room, 15). Children welcome. Reservations accepted. D 6.30-10 daily, Set D €39; Sun L 1-5.30, set Sun L €29; house wine €18.50; sc discretionary. Bar open normal hours (no food). House closed 20-27 Dec. Amex, Diners, MasterCard, Visa, Laser. **Directions:** 500m from Ardara village.

Ballybofey

HOTEL

Jackson's Hotel

Ballybofey Co Donegal **Tel: 074 913 1021** Fax: 074 913 1096
Email: bjackson@iol.ie Web: www.jacksons-hotel.ie

Although it has a town centre location, this attractive family-run hotel is set in its own gardens and enjoys a tranquil position alongside the River Finn. The spacious, elegantly furnished foyer (with open fire) creates a good first impression and this is followed through in other public areas including the restaurant, which overlooks the garden. Major development has been taking place recently and, with the addition of 50 new rooms (including 11 suites), a large conference centre and meeting rooms, and an underground carpark, the hotel is now a major venue for conferences and other large events. But it remains an appealing place for leisure guests; all bedrooms are furnished to a high standard, and are very comfortable with direct-dial phones, tea/coffee trays and TV/DVD and the best have river views. It's just a 40 minute drive to Glenveigh National Park and Castle. Conference/banqueting (1,400/500); business centre, ISDN lines, secretarial services. Leisure centre (22m pool). Snooker, pool table. Children welcome (under 2 free in parents' room, cots available without charge, baby sitting arranged, playroom). Special breaks offer good value. Horse-riding, golf, fishing and bike hire all nearby. Pets permitted in some areas. Garden. **Rooms 120** (2 suites, 5 executive rooms, 50 no smoking, 10 disabled, 10 family rooms). Wheelchair access. Lift. 24 hour room service. B&B €80 pps, ss €20. *Food available all day at the Ballybuffet self-service bistro/restaurant (9am-10.30pm); Garden Restaurant: D 6-9.15 daily, Sun L 12.30-4. Open all year. Amex, Diners, MasterCard, Visa, Laser. **Directions:** Beside the river, in the centre of town.

Ballybofey

Kee's Hotel

HOTEL

Stranorlar Ballybofey Co Donegal **Tel: 074 913 1018** Fax: 074 913 1917
Email: info@keeshotel.ie Web: www.keeshotel.ie

This centrally located, all-year hotel has an unusually long line of continuous family ownership, having been in the Kee family since 1892. Public areas have recently undergone radical renovations, including a new foyer, meeting rooms and a lift. Bedrooms are regularly refurbished and have good bathrooms; those at the back of the hotel, with views of the Blue Stack Mountains, are most desirable as they are away from the road. Residents have direct access from the hotel to a fine leisure centre, with swimming pool. Golf and fishing nearby. Conference/banqueting (200/250). Children welcome, under 3 free in their parents' room; cots and high chairs available, baby sitting arranged. Special breaks offered by the hotel, and offering very good value, include golfing holidays, bank holiday break-aways and a novel "Post Christmas Recovery Break". No pets. **Rooms 53** (1 junior suite, 30 executive rooms, 39 no smoking, 1 for disabled). Lift. Room service (limited hours). B&B €84 pps, ss €15. **The Looking Glass:** Good food has been a particular attraction at Kee's for some years in both the informal Old Gallery bistro, and this fine dining, which is decorated with hand-worked tapestries made by Arthur Kee's mother It's a pleasant warm-toned restaurant in two areas, with plenty of alcoves for privacy - a comfortable setting for enjoying daily-changing menus offering the best of local produce - usually with a French accent, as recent head chefs have been French. Children welcome. Toilets wheelchair accessible. **Seats 75** (private room, 60). D 6.30-9.30 daily, L Sun only, 12.30-3, Set Sun L €23.50; 'Value' D €22 (5.30-9.30); house wine about €17. SC discretionary. [Informal bistro style meals served in the Old Gallery, 12.30-3 and 5.30-9.30 daily.] Amex, Diners, MasterCard, Visa, Laser. **Directions:** On the main street in the village of Stranorlar.

Ballyliffin

Ballyliffin Lodge and Spa

HOTEL

Shore Road Ballyliffin Co Donegal **Tel: 074 937 8200** Fax: 074 937 8985
Email: info@ballyliffinlodge.com Web: www.ballyliffinlodge.com

This impressive hotel in Ballyliffin village is a great asset to the area - with a beautiful view, space and comfort. Public areas include a traditional bar, Mamie Pat's, and the spacious guest rooms are finished to a high standard with many extras, including safes. General Manager Cecil Doherty, who is also a joint-proprietor of the hotel, has considered every detail including excellent on-site leisure facilities with swimming pool and spa treatments. Discounts are available for hotel guests at Ballyliffin GC, and short breaks are offered. The hotel also accepts wedding parties (remember the Donegal catch-phrase is 'up here it's different'). Conference/banqueting 500/400; secretarial service. Children welcome (under 5 free in parents' room, free cot available). **Rooms 40** (12 junior suites, 4 superior, 4 disabled, all no smoking). B&B €90 pps, ss €20. Lift. Room service (limited hours). Open all year except 25 Dec & Good Fri. **Holly Tree Restaurant:** There is a classic and intimate feel to this rather small exclusive room, and it is not just a golf hotel dining room: head chef Kwanghi Chan is well known in Ireland for his accomplished modern European cuisine; he and his team produce classic dishes, sometimes with an Asian twist - and people travel specially to eat here. You can choose between the set dinner (which is particularly good value), and an a la carte; unusual appetisers include an iced water melon soup with balls of cantaloupe melon & whit coconut jelly, and there may also be a delicious roasted breast of quail wrapped with pancetta, confit leg, and celeriac puree & potato rosti. But the specialty of the house is fresh whole fish and the dish attracting highest praise on a recent visit was whole sea bream with lemongrass, ginger, & soy sauce reduction - perfectly cooked, really fresh fish and not a contrived chef's dish but naturally Asian. Desserts are also very good, notably a brilliant steamed lemon pudding with lemon sauce & vanilla ice cream. A well thought out wine list includes plenty of half bottles, and service is excellent. **Restaurant:** Children welcome. **Seats 55,** reservations required, toilets accessible for wheelchairs, air conditioning, vegetarian menu available. D daily, 6.30-9.30. L Sun only, 12.30-4. Set D €40, Set Sun L 18. D also a la carte. Bar meals, 12.30-9 daily. House Wine €18. Closed 25 Dec, Good Friday. Residents can get a discount on local golf. Helipad Amex, Diners, MasterCard, Visa, Laser, Switch. **Directions:** In Ballyliffin village (signed).

Ballyliffin Area

RESTAURANT/COUNTRY HOUSE

Glen House

Straid Clonmany Co Donegal
Tel: 074 937 6745 Email: glenhouse@hotmail.com

Beautifully located and with an ocean view, this large B&B has a charming 18th century house at its heart and would make a moderately priced and hospitable base for golf and the many other activities this lovely area offers - including visiting the nearby waterfall, a fine beach, hill walks (starting at Glen House), and summer festivals that highlight the music and culture of the area Attentive staff are usually family, making guests feel at home, and there's a comfortable sitting room, with paintings by some young local artists on the walls. The eight spacious bedrooms are attractively furnished in quiet tones, and have tea & coffee facilities and good sized bathrooms with power showers. Dinner is available to residents all year, and the restaurant is also open to non residents at weekends (Thursday to Sunday); guests also like The Rusty Nail pub, nearby at Clonmany. Restaurant **Seats 35** (Private Room available seats 16); D daily (non-residents welcome by reservation); Outdoor Dining Area (10); Toilets accessible by wheelchair. Food usually served all day (8-9), D (5-9) but phone to check meal availability. Special Hill Walking breaks available. Open all year. MasterCard, Visa. ◇

Ballyshannon

Ⓝ BAR/RESTAURANT

Soprano's

Main Street Ballyshannon Co Donegal
Tel: 071 985 1415

Newly opened bang in the centre of Ballyshannon town is a genuine Italian (family) run establishment-Sopranos Bar and Restaurant. Open for lunch (great value traditional Italian set menu) and dinner (a keenly priced a la carte), it's proving an enormous hit with the locals and has a great buzz - booking is recommended, especially in the evenings. The main first-floor restaurant (above a ground floor bar) is unexpectedly elegant in décor and style. Cool, soft greys, wooden tables and comfortable chairs - the sort of place you could settle down in for a relaxing evening. The menu features classic Italian dishes carefully and correctly cooked, and served with Italian panache. It's exceptionally child friendly, and teenagers could happily decamp to the downstairs pizzeria. Take away pizza also available. **Directions:** On the left as you come over the bridge-look out for a startling bright blue building. Public car parking is close by and well signed.

Bruckless

B&B/FARMHOUSE

Bruckless House

Bruckless Co Donegal
Tel: 074 973 7071 Fax: 074 973 7070
Email: bruc@bruckless.com Web: www.bruckless.com

Clive and Joan Evans' lovely 18th-century house and Connemara pony stud farm is set in 18 acres of woodland and gardens overlooking Bruckless Bay - an ideal place for people who enjoy quiet countryside and pursuits like walking, horse-riding and fishing. The gardens are not too formal but beautifully designed, extensive and well-maintained - they really enhance a visit here, as does the waterside location: guests have direct access to the foreshore at the bottom of the garden. Family furniture collected through a Hong Kong connection adds an unexpected dimension to elegant reception rooms that have views over the front lawns towards the sea, and the generous, comfortably furnished bedrooms. Accommodation include two single rooms and there is a shared bathroom - although the house is large, the guest bedrooms are close together, so they are ideal for a family or a group travelling together. Enjoyed home-produced eggs at breakfast, which is the only meal served - guests are directed to local restaurants in the evening. Self-catering accommodation is also available all year, in a two-bedroomed gatelodge. Garden, equestrian, walking, fishing. **Rooms 4** (2 en-suite, all no-smoking) B&B €60pps, no ss. Weekly rates also offered. Pets permitted in certain areas. *A two-bedroom Gate Lodge, sleeping four, is available for self-catering. Closed 1 Oct-31 Mar. Amex, MasterCard, Visa. **Directions:** On N56, 12 miles west of Donegal.

Bunbeg

HOTEL

Ostan Gweedore

Bunbeg Co Donegal **Tel: 074 953 1177** Fax: 074 953 1726
Email: reservations@ostangweedore.com Web: www.ostangweedore.com

Although its blocky 1970s' architectural style may not be to today's taste, Ostan Gweedore was built to make the most of the location - and this it does exceptionally well. Spacious public areas, including the aptly named Ocean Restaurant and the Library Bar ("the most westerly reading room on the Atlantic seaboard") have superb views over the shoreline and Mount Errigal - as does the Sundowner Wine & Tapas Bar, which offers a wide range of wines by the glass and a menu of small tapas-style dishes to nibble while you watch the sun sinking in the west. The hotel takes pride in the restaurant - extensive menus offer a wide range of dishes based mainly on local produce, especially seafood and Donegal mountain lamb - and it has a strong local following. Most of the bedrooms have panoramic sea views, and although some may seem a little dated, they are all are comfortable. It's a very relaxing place for people of all ages and in high season it is especially ideal for families, with its wonderful beach and outdoor activities, including tennis, pitch & putt and day visits to nearby islands Tory, Gola and Arranmore. If you enjoy fresh air and exercise, ask at reception for the booklet Walks in the Bunbeg Area, which was specially commissioned by the hotel and details a variety of planned walks and cycle paths in the locality. Wet days are looked after too, with excellent indoor leisure facilities including a 19-metre swimming pool, Jacuzzi and gym, supervised by qualified staff, and a new health and beauty spa which offers all the current pamper treatments. This romantic setting is predictably popular for weddings; (conferences/banqueting 300/350). Leisure centre; spa. Fishing and golf (9 hole) available locally. Children welcome (Under 5s free in parents' room at managements discretion, cot available without charge, baby sitting arranged). *Donegal Airport, Carrickfin is nearby. **Rooms 36** (3 suites, 6 family rooms, 3 ground floor). **Ocean Restaurant:** D daily, 7-8.45, à la carte; Sundowner Tapas bar: 7-9.30 daily. B&B €85 pps, single €96. Closed Nov-Feb. Amex, MasterCard, Visa, Laser. **Directions:** From Letterkenny, take coast road past hospital.

BUNDORAN

A popular seaside resort on the southern shore of Donegal Bay, Bundoran looks across to the hills of Donegal in the north and is backed by the Sligo-Leitrim mountains to the south. Of the many hotels in and around the town, the best located by far is the **Great Northern Hotel** (071 984 1204; www.greatnorthernhotel.com) which is situated at the centre of an 18 hole championship golf course overlooking Donegal Bay; it also offers a new conference centre and good leisure facilities, And, if you enjoy traditional pubs, make a point of calling in at **Brennans / Criterion Bar** on Main Street - it's as fine an unspoilt Irish pub as you'll find anywhere: "no television, just conversation".

WWW.IRELAND-GUIDE.COM FOR THE BEST PLACES TO EAT, DRINK & STAY

BURTONPORT

BURTONPORT (Ailt an Chorrain) is a small fishing port and sea angling centre in The Rosses, renowned for its catches of salmon, lobster and crab in the summer months - fresh seafood which (along with many other varieties) finds its way onto menus in family-run pubs such as **Skippers Tavern** (074 954 2234) and **The Lobster Pot** (074 954 2012) both of which have a national reputation for fresh home-cooked food and warm hospitality. Just off the town, the island of Arranmore has now got an hotel, **Arranmore House Hotel** (074 952 0918; www.arranmorehousehotel.ie), which is open all year; the island is accessible by frequent car ferries.

WWW.IRELAND-GUIDE.COM FOR THE BEST PLACES TO EAT, DRINK & STAY

Culdaff

HOTEL/BAR/RESTAURANT

McGrory's of Culdaff

Culdaff Inishowen Co Donegal

Tel: 074 93 79104 Fax: 074 93 79235

Email: info@mcgrorys.ie Web: www.mcgrorys.ie

féile bia In an area that has so much to offer, in terms of natural beauty and activities like golf, angling and walking, McGrory's would make an ideal base. An inn in the true sense of the word, offering rest and refreshment to travellers, this north-western institution was established in 1924 and remains in the active care of the McGrory family, who set great store by the traditions of hospitality and personal care while also keeping an eye on changing tastes and the requirements of a fast-moving society. It is now a pleasing combination of old and new which is easy on the eye and includes an evening restaurant as well as the bar where informal meals are served. Accommodation is offered in comfortable bedrooms that vary in size and outlook but are attractively furnished in a classic contemporary style; all have well-planned bathrooms and all the necessary amenities (phone, tea/coffee tray, TV); seven new rooms and a lift have recently been added. For anyone touring the Inishowen peninsula this is a logical place to take a break, as popular bar food is available throughout the day. But it is probably for music that McGrory's is most famous - as well as traditional sessions in The Front Bar on Tuesday and Friday nights, Mac's Backroom Bar (constructed on the site of the old outhouses of McGrory's shop) is a major venue for live shows featuring international names. (Live music Wednesday and Saturday; events listings on the web.) Conference/banqueting (100/150). Special interest/off season breaks offered (midweek; weekend; golf - special rates with Ballyliffin Golf Club, early breakfast arranged.) Children welcome (under 4 free in parents' room; cot available free of charge, baby sitting arranged). No pets. **Rooms 17** (all en-suite, 4 shower only, 4 family rooms, 17 no smoking). Lift. Room service (limited hours). B&B €55-65, ss €10. Restaurant: D Tue-Sun, L Sun. Bar meals daily, 12.30-8.30. Car park. Restaurant closed Mon; establishment closed 24-26 Dec. Amex, MasterCard, Visa, Laser. **Directions:** On R238 around Inishowen Peninsula.

DONEGAL TOWN

Donegal Town was originally a plantation town and is now best known as the main centre for the tweed industry and crafts. A visit to the area would be unthinkable without calling into **Magee's** on The Diamond where there are hand loom weaving demonstrations; wholesome fare is available at the in-store restaurant, **The Weavers Loft**, and also at **The Blueberry Tea Room**, just off The Diamond, on Castle Street. **The Craft Village**, on the edge of the town, is well worth a visit and there's a very nice little coffee shop, **Aroma** (see entry), serving good home cooking, notably baking.

WWW.IRELAND-GUIDE.COM FOR THE BEST PLACES TO EAT, DRINK & STAY

Aroma

Donegal
Ⓝ CAFÉ

The Craft Village Donegal Town Co Donegal
Tel: 074 972 3222 Email: paddyrast@eircom.net

Tom Dooley's smart little cafe at the Craft Village just outside Donegal Town has won a lot of friends for its warm and friendly atmosphere an excellent freshly cooked food that offers much more than would be expected of a coffee shop. Tempting cakes, desserts and breads are all homemade and chef Arturo de Alba Gonzalez's menus include a frequently-changed blackboard offering cooked-to-order dishes like real vegetable soups, fried polenta, prosciutto, garlic mushrooms and mixed leaves or white wine risotto with chargrilled chicken and seared asparagus also salads like smoked chicken & avocado and, for the hungry young Mexican, chimichangas. Everything looks and tastes delicious the quality of ingredients, and good cooking both show on the plate Service, under Tom's supervision is knowledgeable and efficient and, with good espresso coffee and an extensive tea menu to go with the great home bakes, this makes a good daytime stop. And, although the coffee shop is small, there's a large outdoor eating area for fine weather. Children welcome. **Seats 30** (outdoors, 16); open 9.30am-5pm (L 12-4); set L €17.50; SC disc. MasterCard, Visa, Laser. **Directions:** 1.6km (1m) outside town on old Ballyshannon road.

Saint Ernan's House Hotel

Donegal
CASTLE/HISTORIC HOUSE

Donegal Co Donegal
Tel: 074 972 1065 Fax: 074 972 2098
Email: res@sainternans.com Web: www.sainternans.com

Set on its own wooded island, connected to the mainland by a causeway built after the famine by tenants as a gesture of thanks to a caring landlord, Brian and Carmel O'Dowd's lovely Victorian country house hotel on the edge of Donegal Town is remarkable for its sense of utter tranquillity. This atmosphere is due, in part, to its unique location - and also, one imagines, to the kindly ghosts who seem to reside here, especially the spirit of John Hamilton, that young landlord who built the house in 1826. That other-worldliness remains there is an almost tangible sense of serenity about the place that makes it the perfect retreat from the stresses of modern life. The spacious public rooms have log fires and antique furniture - plenty of space for guests to read, or simply to relax in front of the fire - and the individually decorated bedrooms echo that restfulness; as in all old houses, they vary in size and position but most also have lovely views and all are furnished to a high standard with antiques, and have good amenities including (surprisingly perhaps) television. Many guests would see no need to leave the island during their stay, but there is much to do and see in the area: the craft shops of Donegal Town are almost on the doorstep, for example, and Glenveagh National Park is just a short scenic drive away. The dining experience at Saint Ernans follows the same philosophy of quiet relaxation and is only for resident guests; simple country house-style dinner menus offer two or three choices on each course and are based on local produce, with vegetarian dishes on request. **Rooms 6** (3 suites, all no smoking). D Residents Only. Seats 16, D 7-8 daily, Set D €52 (semi-à la carte, priced by course); house wine €25. Closed end Oct-mid Apr. MasterCard, Visa, Laser. **Directions:** 1.5 mile south of Donegal Town on R267.

Downings
HOTEL

Rosapenna Hotel & Golf Resort

Downings Co Donegal **Tel: 074 915 5301** Fax: 074 915 5128
Email: rosapenna@eircom.net Web: www.rosapenna.ie

Discerning golfers may think they've died and gone to heaven when staying at Frank and Hilary Casey's fine hotel on the shores of Sheephaven Bay. Although large and impressive, with comfortable and exceptionally spacious public areas and guest rooms and suites that have been thoughtfully designed down to the very last detail to ensure the comfort of their visitors, it is a very hospitable and relaxing place to stay, and not at all intimidating. And, of course, as virtually every guest is bound to be a golfer, residents make up a sort of community of golfers with all the sociability that implies, either in the hotel, or at the superb new golf pavilion. The restaurant is open to non-residents but, in practice, it is usually filled to capacity by hotel guests (lobster thermidor is the house speciality, so no wonder everyone dines in). Golf breaks offered. Golf (18), residents' green fees €30, angling, snooker, indoor 'pool, tennis. Children welcome (baby sitting arranged, cots available at no charge). **Rooms 53** (1 suite, 5 junior suites, 4 family rooms, 3 shower only, 27 ground floor, all no smoking); all day room service; pets permitted in some area by prior arrangement. B&B €90pps, ss €20. Restaurant: **seats 100;** D daily 7.15-8.30, children welcome, reservations required. Hotel closed end Oct-mid Mar. Amex, Diners, MasterCard, Visa, Laser. **Directions:** 36km (23m) northwest of Letterkenny, R425 to Carrigart then 2.5km.

DUNFANAGHY

Many people will have a soft spot for this traditional holiday area, often recalling family holidays spent at the famous old **Arnold's Hotel** (074 913 6208; www.arnoldshotel.com), which has been in the same family for three generations. By contrast the nearby restaurant, **The Cove** (074 913 6300), is a relative newcomer although it has quickly earned an enviable reputation - and it wisely offers a very different style from the well established restaurant of the area, **The Mill** (see entry).
WWW.IRELAND-GUIDE.COM FOR THE BEST PLACES TO EAT, DRINK & STAY

Dunfanaghy
E RESTAURANT WITH ROOMS

The Mill Restaurant

Figart Dunfanaghy Letterkenny Co Donegal
Tel: 074 913 6985 Fax: 074 913 6985
Email: themillrestaurant@oceanfree.net Web: www.themillrestaurant.com

Beautifully located on the shore of the New Lake, which is a special area of conservation, the mill was the home of Susan Alcorn's grandfather and, as they are a family of accomplished painters, the walls are hung with wonderful water colours. Susan and her husband Derek, who is the chef, have earned a dedicated following here, as the location is superb, the welcome warm and the cooking both imaginative and assured - and they offer very good value. The dining room is on two levels, with plenty of windows framing the views, fresh flowers on the tables, soft lighting and some well-placed antiques - a room of character and atmosphere. Menus are based firmly on the best ingredients, local where possible, and change every 4-6 weeks. While based on the classics, the house style is quite contemporary: soups are often unusual (purée of vine tomato & sweet pepper with parsley pesto, for example), while roast rack of lamb may be served with delicious boxty pancake and roast parsnip. Seafood is well-represented, of course, and a speciality upside down fish pie is anything but humble, with its filling of lobster, crab claws and john dory in a brandy cream sauce. Gorgeous desserts might include a seasonal fruit crumble tart with custard & ginger ice cream, or there's a good Irish cheese plate. (Lovely breakfasts too.) Children welcome. **Seats 50.** Air conditioning. D Tue-Sun 7-9pm, Set D €39; house wine €18; sc discretionary. Closed Mon, Jan-Feb (open weekends only Nov Dec & Mar). Accommodation is offered in six individually decorated rooms. The decor is simple but stylish, with good new beds and some antique pieces, and there's also a lovely little sitting room off the dining room, with comfy big chairs and sofas to relax in. Children welcome (cot available without charge). No pets. Garden. Walking; cycling. Free Broadband. **Rooms 6** (all en-suite & no-smoking, 2 shower only). B&B €45 pps, ss €15. Establishment closed mid Dec - mid Mar. Amex, MasterCard, Visa, Laser. **Directions:** N56 from Letterkenny to Dunfanaghy. 1km (1/2 m) outside Dunfanaghy on Falcarragh road on right hand side at the lake.

Dunkineely

HOTEL/RESTAURANT

Castle Murray House Hotel

St. John's Point Dunkineely Co Donegal
Tel: 074 973 7022 Fax: 074 973 7330
Email: info@castlemurray.com Web: www.castlemurray.com

Martin and Marguerite Howley's beautifully located clifftop hotel has wonderful sea and coastal views over the ruined castle after which it is named. It is a comfortable and relaxing place to stay, with a little bar, a residents' sitting room and a large verandah that can be covered with an awning in a good summer, so meals may be served outside. Bedrooms have a mixture of modern and older pieces that give each room its own character, and are gradually being refurbished; most have sea views and all are quite large with a double and single bed, recently refurbished bathrooms (some with full bath) and facilities including digital TV as well as phone and tea/coffee trays. A sun area on the sheltered flat roof at the back of the building has direct access from some bedrooms. Lovely breakfasts are served in the restaurant, and there's an appealing bar menu Banqueting (60). Children welcome (cots available, baby sitting arranged). Pets permitted by arrangement. Garden. Walking. Off-season value breaks. **Rooms 10** (6 shower only, all no smoking). B&B €65pps, ss €20. **Restaurant:** The restaurant is on the seaward corner of the hotel overlooking the sea and the castle (which is floodlit at night), and an open fire makes for real warmth in this dramatic location, even in winter. Remy Dupuis, who has been head chef since 1994, works alongside Marguerite Howley and there is a consistent house style, with a strong emphasis on local produce. Multi-choice menus (basically 3-course, plus options of soup and sorbet), are sensibly priced according to the choice of main course and there is plenty to choose from, including vegetarian dishes. Seafood is the speciality of the house in the summer months - Remy has dedicated fishermen who fish lobster, monk, scallops and other fish for him (although red mullet, seabass and seabream are sourced from Greece). Mouthwatering menus open with starters like a house specialities prawns & monkfish in garlic butter, and also offer a duo of Inver & Bruckless Bay oysters - and non-fishy treats like pan-fried foie gras; main courses choices are extensive, including less usual dishes like stuffed rabbit saddle with black pudding & Calvados, roast pheasant (in season), and at least one vegetarian option as well as seafood dishes - and it's good value too, even the supplement for lobster, from McSwynes Bay, is very reasonable. In winter, when seafood is less plentiful, there are more red meats, poultry and game. Service, under the direction of restaurant manager Caroline Gallagher, is excellent - and the wonderful location, helpful staff and consistently good cooking make this a place people keep coming back to. The wine list leans towards the Old World, particularly France, and offers good house wines, some non-alcoholic wines, extensive selection of champagnes and plenty of half bottles. **Seats 60.** Not suitable for children. D daily in summer 6.30-9.30 (to 8.30 Sun), L Sun only 1.30-3.30; D from €48.00 (depending on choice of main course); Set Sun L €27; house wine €21; No SC. Bar menu also available - phone to check times. Restaurant closed Mon & Tue low season. Hotel closed mid Jan-mid Feb. MasterCard, Visa, Laser. **Directions:** Situated on the N56, 8km from Killybegs, 20 km from Donegal Town on the coast road to St Johns Point; first left outside Dunkineely village.

GLENVEAGH NATIONAL PARK

Glenveagh National Park (Tel: 074 9137090; www.heritageireland.ie) is open to visitors all year, although visitor facilities are seasonal (mid March-early November). The Victorian castle, which is the focal point for visitors to the Park, was donated to the State by the last private owner, Henry Plummer McIlhenny, together with most of its contents - and the gardens are among the most interesting in Ireland, with many unusual and rare plants displayed in a series of garden rooms - the Pleasure Grounds, the Walled Garden, the Italian Garden and so on; garden tours are given regularly by experienced gardeners, but guests are also free to wander freely. The Interpretative Centre includes a restaurant, but there's a treat in store if you go to the **Tea Rooms** at the castle itself; they are in an attractive stone courtyard attached to the castle and specialise in excellent home baking.

WWW.IRELAND-GUIDE.COM FOR THE BEST PLACES TO EAT, DRINK & STAY

Greencastle

BAR/RESTAURANT

Kealys Seafood Bar

The Harbour Greencastle Co Donegal **Tel: 074 938 1010**
Fax: 074 938 1010 Email: kealys@iol.ie

féile bia

The ferry between the fishing port of Greencastle and Magilligan Point in Northern Ireland brings many new visitors to an area that used to seem quite remote - and those in the know plan their journeys around a meal at James and Tricia Kealy's excellent seafood restaurant. It's a low key little place where simplicity has always been valued and, even if it's just to pop in for a daytime bowl of Greencastle chowder and some home-baked chowder, don't miss the opportunity of a visit to Kealys - if we did an award for seafood chowder, theirs would take the prize! James's approach to seafood is creative and balanced, seen in dishes which are modern in tone but also echo traditional Irish themes, and in which delicious local organic vegetables are used with fish to make the most of both resources. Typical dishes might include baked fillet of hake on braised fennel with a tomato & saffron butter sauce and, perhaps, a classic Irish partnership of baked Atlantic salmon with a wholegrain mustard crust served on Irish spring cabbage and bacon. There will be at least one meat or poultry dish offered every day and there's always an imaginative vegetarian dish too - Gubbeen cheese & almond fritters, on a seasonal salad with honey & mustard dressing, for example. James is also a great baker and makes a variety of breads - you might find that one of them makes a perfect partner for one of their range of Irish farmhouse cheeses, typically Gubbeen, St Killian, Boilié and Cashel Blue. Service, under Tricia's direction, is smart and friendly - and a compact but appealing wine list offers good value, and includes a small selection of half and quarter bottles. Children welcome until 9pm. **Seats 65.** L Tue-Sun high season and Sat-Sun low season, 12.30-2.45pm; D Tue-Sun high season, Fri- Sun low season, 7-9.30pm (Sun to 8.30pm); Set D €35, also à la carte. House wine €15. Closed Mon, 2 weeks Nov, 25 Dec, Good Friday. Amex, MasterCard, Visa, Laser. **Directions:** On the harbour at Greencastle, 20 miles north of Derry City. ◇

KILLYBEGS

Killybegs is Ireland's premier deep sea fishing port and a popular sea angling centre. For comfortable modern town centre accommodation try the well-established **Bayview Hotel** (074 973 1950; www.bayviewhotel.ie), with swimming pool and leisure centre, or the stylish newer **Tara Hotel** (074 974 1700;www.tarahotel.ie). Dining options in the area include the 200 year old farmhouse restaurant, **Kitty Kellys** (074 973 1925; www.kittykellys.com), outside the town at Largy, which has special appeal for traditionalists - in both ambience and food.

WWW.IRELAND-GUIDE.COM FOR THE BEST PLACES TO EAT, DRINK & STAY

Kincasslagh

Iggy's Bar

BAR

Kincasslagh Co Donegal **Tel: 074 954 3112**

Just a short walk up from the harbour - it's also called the Atlantic Bar - Ann and Iggy Murray have run this delightfully unspoilt pub since 1986 and it's an all year home-from-home for many a visitor. The television isn't usually on unless there's a match and Ann makes lovely simple food for the bar, mainly seafood - home-made soups, delicious crab sandwiches and Rombouts filter coffee. Children welcome. Bar open 10-12.30 daily, light food available 12-6, Mon-Sat. No food on Sundays. Closed 25 Dec & Good Friday. **No Credit Cards. Directions:** On the corner of the Main Street, where the road turns off to the harbour.

Laghey

Coxtown Manor

RESTAURANT/COUNTRY HOUSE

Laghey Co Donegal
Tel: 074 973 4575 Fax: 074 973 4576
Email: coxtownmanor@oddpost.com Web: www.coxtownmanor.com

Just a short drive from the county town, this welcoming late Georgian house set in its own parkland is in a lovely, peaceful area close to Donegal Bay. Belgian proprietor, Edward Dewael - who fell for the property some years ago and is still in the process of upgrading it - personally ensures that everything possible is done to make guests feel at home. A pleasant wood-panelled bar with an open fire is well-stocked, notably with Belgian beers and a great selection of digestifs to accompany your after dinner coffee - and it extends into a pleasant conservatory on one side and a drawing room on the other. Accommodation is divided between a recently converted coach house at the back where the new bedrooms are very spacious, with plenty of room for golf kits and large items of luggage, and have excellent bathrooms to match - yet many guests still prefer the older rooms in the main house, for their character; some have countryside views and open fireplaces and they are large, comfortable and well-proportioned, with updated bathrooms. Children welcome (under 16 free in parents' room; cot available without charge, baby-sitting arranged). Walking; garden. No pets. **Rooms 9** (2 junior suites, all en-suite, 1 shower only, 5 no smoking, 2 ground floor). B&B €85 pps, ss €29. Breakfast buffet 8-10am; (cooked options include delicious Fermanagh dry-cured black bacon.) **Dining Room:** The elegant and well-appointed period dining room is the heart of the house, and is - like the food served here - attractive yet not too formal. Friendly staff promptly offer aperitifs and menus which are priced by course and offer about four mostly classic dishes with an emphasis on seafood (scallops from Donegal Bay, clams and mussels from Lissadell, for example), also Thornhill duck and local Charolais beef - a sound foundation for proficient cooking: starters will certainly include at least one shellfish dish (trio of Donegal Bay lobster, fresh crab and prawns on organic salad, perhaps); main course choices are also likely to favour seafood (wild Donegal Bay salmon with creamy herb sauce), but may include less usual dishes like squab pigeon (served de-boned, with caramelised apples, perhaps). The produce is mostly local - and of superb quality - but the style is Belgian, offering a different experience from other dining options in the area. Belgian chocolate features strongly on the dessert menu but there are lighter options. Good food and lovely service from friendly staff ensure that a meal here will be a special experience. Restaurant open to non-residents by reservation when there is room. **Seats 28.** D Tue-Sun, 7-9pm; set D €45; also short a la carte. House wine €21.50. Restaurant closed Mon, house closed Nov, 6 Jan - 6 Feb. Amex, MasterCard, Visa, Laser. **Directions:** Main sign on N15 between Ballyshannon & Donegal Town.

LETTERKENNY

The Letterkenny area - including Rathmullan and Ramelton - provides a good central location for exploring the county; a ferry between Rathmullan and Bundoran operates in summer (45 minutes). Originally a fishing village, which developed on the banks of Lough Swilly, Letterkenny town is now one of the largest and most densely-populated towns in Donegal - and one of the fastest-growing towns in Ireland. The Donegal County Museum is in the town and, for those who need accommodation in an hotel with leisure facilities, the new **Holiday Inn Letterkenny** (Tel: 074 812 4369; www.holidayinnletterkenny.net) is a good choice, conveniently situated on the edge of town. For moderately-priced town centre hotel accommodation, try the **Quality Hotel Letterkenny** (Tel:021 490 8278; www.quality-donegal.com), or the new **Ramada Encore** (074 912 3100; www.encoreletterkenny.com).
WWW.IRELAND-GUIDE.COM FOR THE BEST PLACES TO EAT, DRINK & STAY

Letterkenny
HOTEL/RESTAURANT

Castle Grove Country House Hotel

Letterkenny Co Donegal
Tel: 074 915 1118 Fax: 074 915 1118
Email: reservation@castlegrove.com Web: www.castlegrove.com

Parkland designed by "Capability" Brown in the mid 18th-century creates a wonderful setting for Raymond and Mary Sweeney's lovely period house overlooking the lough. Castlegrove is undoubtedly the first choice for discerning visitors to the area, especially executives with business in Letterkenny: it is, as Mary Sweeney says, an oasis of tranquillity. Constant improvement is the policy and recent years have seen major changes, including a new conservatory, and a larger new restaurant; an adjoining coach house was also developed to make seven lovely bedrooms - all carefully designed and furnished with antiques to feel like part of the main house - and a small conference room. The original walled garden is under restoration as part of an on-going development of the gardens which will continue for several years. Bedrooms are spacious and elegantly furnished to a high standard with antiques, and bathrooms are gradually being upgraded where practical, to provide walk-in showers as well as full bath. Good breakfasts include a choice of fish as well as traditional Irish breakfast, home-made breads and preserves. Mary Sweeney's personal supervision ensures an exceptionally high standard of maintenance and housekeeping and staff are friendly and helpful. Two boats belonging to the house are available for fishing on Lough Swilly and there is a special arrangement with three nearby golf clubs. Conference/banqueting (25/50). House available for private use (family occasions, board meetings etc) Not suitable for children under 12. No pets. **Rooms 14** (1 suite, 2 junior suites, 2 shower only, 2 disabled, all no-smoking) B&B a€80 pps, no ss. *Weekends/ short breaks available. Open all year except Christmas. **The Green Room:** This large room is in a recent extension, but furnished in keeping with the original house. Generous, well-spaced tables are classically appointed and several dinner menus are offered - table d'hôte, à la carte and vegetarian - in a style that neatly combines classic French and modern Irish cooking. Carefully sourced specialist and local ingredients are used: many of the herbs, vegetables and soft fruit are home grown, the seafood - such as wild salmon and Swilly oysters - is local, and local meats are regularly used in, for example, a speciality dish of pan fried fillet of beef with grilled horseradish polenta and caramelised chicory which is an enduring favourite. Desserts might include a juicy rhubarb tart with home-made ice cream, or crème caramel with orange segments and fresh cream - well-balanced treats that make a refreshing ending to a fine meal. Not suitable for children under 10 after 7pm. **Seats 50** (private room, 15). B'fst 8-10 daily, L 12.30-2 Mon-Sat, D 6.30-9 daily. Set L from €23, light L about €15; Set D about €30-49.50, D also à la carte; house wines from €18; sc discretionary. Reservations required. Closed L Sun; 23-29 Dec. Amex, Diners, MasterCard, Visa, Laser. **Directions:** R245 off main road to Letterkenny. ◇

Letterkenny
Ⓝ RESTAURANT

Lemon Tree Restaurant

39 Lower Main Street Letterkenny Co Donegal
Tel: 074 912 5788

féile bia With its pretty lemon canopies, lemon painted and tiled frontage and colourful hanging flower baskets, this family run restaurant in the centre of Letterkenny is inviting and even on a Monday night you need to book, as it is popular with both locals and visitors. Terracotta tiles, wooden tables and chairs and peach sponged walls lend warmth - and one wall has all the chefs' awards certificates framed and on show: brothers, Garry and Christopher Molloy are both chefs who trained at the renowned Killybegs Tourism College before going on to work in well known kitchens and achieve success in culinary competitions. This is a restaurant with an open kitchen so there is a buzz about it. The food is traditional Irish and French classic, influenced by country house cooking: it is Féile Bia certified and all meats are Irish sourced, fresh fish is a special feature and all breads, pastries, pastas and desserts are made freshly on site. A choice of about 14 starters (six of them fish) might include hand made ravioli of Irish cheeses with roast vegetables and a fresh pepper coulis, or a roulade of chicken and wild mushroom, with red onion marmalade and tossed leaves and, among the dozen or so main courses, there may be an unusual a tasting plate of grilled fish, served with creamed potato mousseline, fresh herbs and lemon butter. An early dinner menu includes home baked pizzas as well as a wide selection of seafood, poultry and meats. (*The Lemon Tree has a new sister restaurant in the town and offers the same menu, but adds a bistro style menu during the day). Open 7 days from 5pm. **Directions:** Centre of town. ◇

Letterkenny
HOTEL

Radisson SAS Hotel Letterkenny

The Loop Road Letterkenny Co Donegal
Tel: 074 919 4444 Fax: 074 919 4455
Email: martina.gallagher@radissonsas.com Web: www.radissonsas.com

féile bia This fine modern hotel on the edge of Letterkenny town may seem to be in something of an industrial wilderness, but is actually within easy walking distance of shops, theatre etc. Inside, it is a pleasing contemporary building: an atrium lobby with maple panelling and smart leather furniture lends a great sense of space and sets the tone for the rest of the hotel, which is bright and clean-lined throughout - a pleasingly contemporary approach which is equally suited to business or leisure. There's a mix of suites and deluxe, family, and business class rooms, all featuring individual temperature control, satellite TV and quite luxurious bathrooms as well as all the usual facilities, and Business Class rooms also have a desk area with broadband, bathrobe & slippers, daily newspaper, turndown service - and complimentary breakfast. The hotel's TriBecCa Restaurant was an immediate success - not surprisingly, perhaps, given General Manager Ray Hingston's background in fine dining (L'Ecrivain, Dublin) as well as experience in several other top hotels. And the breakfast offered in this hotel is also way above average; like other Radisson hotels, a wide-ranging buffet offers numerous options, including various fruits, cold meats and cheeses as well as the familiar Irish choices, and everything here is particularly fresh and appealing. Well-placed for short breaks in one of Ireland's most beautiful areas, this hotel is an asset to Letterkenny. Children welcome (cot available free of charge). No pets. Golf, gardens, walking, wind surfing etc nearby. Parking (200). Business centre. Conference/banqueting (450/300). Leisure centre (17m swimming pool, steam room, sauna.) **Rooms 114** (1 suite, 2 junior suites, 3 shower only, 6 disabled.) Lift. 24 hr room service. B&B €74.50, ss €14.50. TriBeCa Restaurant: **Seats 80.** D Tue-Sat, 6-9.30; L Sun only 12.30-3. Set D €32.50, also à la carte; Set Sun L €21.50. House wine €21. SC discretionary. Bar meals available 12.30-8 daily. Amex, MasterCard, Visa, Laser. **Directions:** Drive to Letterkenny town, turn left at Tourist Office - hotel on right. ◇

Lough Eske
HOTEL/RESTAURANT

Harvey's Point Country Hotel

Lough Eske Donegal Co Donegal
Tel: 074 972 2208 Fax: 074 972 2352
Email: info@harveyspoint.com Web: www.harveyspoint.com

Blessed with one of Ireland's most beautiful locations, on the shores of Lough Eske, this hotel was first opened by the Gysling family in the late 1980s, with chalet-style buildings linked by covered walkways and pergolas creating a distinctly alpine atmosphere reminiscent of their native Switzerland - a style that suited the site well, with the open low-level design allowing views of the lough and mountains from most areas of the hotel. Guests re-visiting today will find many changes, and a far more luxurious establishment: rooms in the new forty room extension do not all have a lake view, but acres of space, six foot beds and a circular bath the size of a small swimming pool will please many guests.

However, the older rooms - which are tucked away in front of the extension, along the ground floor corridor - may be of much more interest to those in the know; although less luxurious, they will appeal if you would enjoy being closer to the countryside, and with access to the lough. Conference/banqueting 300/400; video conferencing. Treatment rooms (hair, beauty, holistic). Not very suitable for children (no facilities). Pets permitted. Garden. **Rooms 42** (4 suites, 38 junior suites, 20 ground floor, 2 disabled). Lift. Turndown service. Open all year. **Restaurant:** The bar and restaurant areas are unchanged: a welcoming log fire sets the tone in the bar, where menus are promptly offered by friendly staff, and the restaurant - a large room, extending right down to the foreshore, where classically appointed tables are set up to take advantage of the beautiful view - seems more appealing than ever. Menus offer an extensive choice and, while there are no surprises, the tone is refreshingly classical. The restaurant is also open for lunch, every day except Saturday. **Seats 100** (private room, 50). Air conditioning. Toilets wheelchair accessible. L 12.30-2.30 (Sun 12-4) & D daily 6.30-9.30. Set D €55, Set L €29; house wine from €19.50; no SC. Off season (Nov-Mar), closed D Sun, all Mon & Tue. MasterCard, Visa, Laser. **Directions:** N15 /N56 from Donegal Town - take signs for Lough Eske & hotel. (6km from Donegal Town.)

Lough Eske

Rhu-Gorse

€ B&B

Lough Eske Co Donegal **Tel: 074 972 1685** Fax: 074 972 1685
Email: rhugorse@iol.ie Web: www.lougheske.com

Beautifully located, with stunning views over Lough Eske (and windows built to take full advantage of them), Grainne McGettigan's modern house may not be not architecturally outstanding but it has some very special attributes, notably the warmth and hospitality of Grainne herself, and a lovely room with picture windows and a big fireplace, where guests can relax. Bedrooms and bathrooms are all ship-shape and residents can have afternoon tea as well as breakfast, although not evening meals; however Harvey's Point is very close,(see entry), and Donegal town is only a short drive. Animals are central to Rhu-Gorse, which is named after a much-loved pedigree dog bred by Grainne's father-in-law (a descendant now follows her around everywhere), and one of her special interests is breeding horses: not your average B&B, but a comfortable, hospitable and very interesting base for a walking holiday or touring the area, and Donegal town is only a short drive. Golf nearby. Children welcome (under 3s free in parents' room). Pets allowed in some areas. Garden. **Rooms 3** (2 shower only, 1 family room, all no smoking). B&B from €40, ss €10. Closed 31 Oct-31 Mar. MasterCard, Visa, Laser. **Directions:** Take N15/N56 from Donegal Town. Take signs for Lough Eske & Harvey's Point Hotel. Pick up signs for Rhu-Gorse.

Malin

Malin Hotel

HOTEL

Malin Co Donegal **Tel: 074 937 0606** Fax: 074 937 0770
Email: info@malinhotel.ie Web: www.malinhotel.ie

féile bia This attractive hotel came into energetic new ownership in 2003 and has been extensively refurbished, and extended to provide four new bedrooms and a lift. The friendly bar is a popular meeting place for visitors and locals alike, and neat bedrooms have phones, tea/coffee making facilities and TV (local stations); the older rooms have been redesigned and, along with their bathrooms, completely refurbished. About half have full bathrooms, with over bath shower, and while some rooms are not very large, they are inviting and comfortable - offering a friendly and moderately priced base for exploring this beautiful area. The hotel's Jack Yeats restaurant is earning a good reputation in the locality. Food hours are variable due to the seasonal nature of the business (bar meals usually all day from 12 noon in high summer, with dinner daily from 6pm); the midweek dinner menu (Wed-Fri, 6 -9.15) offers great value at €18. Conference/banqueting 200/330. Walking. Children welcome (under 4s free in parents' room, cot available free of charge, baby sitting arranged). No pets. **Rooms 18** (1 suite, 7 executive, 11 shower only, 1 family room, 1 for disabled, all no smoking). Children welcome (under 4s free in parents' room, cot available free of charge, baby sitting arranged.) Limited room service. B&B €65 pps, ss €10. MasterCard, Visa, Laser. **Directions:** Overlooking the village green in Malin town.

Ramelton

Ardeen

COUNTRY HOUSE

Ramelton Co Donegal **Tel: 074 915 1243** Fax: 074 915 1243
Email: ardeenbandb@eircom.net Web: www.ardeenhouse.com

Overlooking Lough Swilly, set in its own grounds on the edge of the heritage town of Ramelton and well-located for touring Donegal and Glenveagh National Park, Anne Campbell's mid-nineteenth century house is not too grand and has the comfortable atmosphere of a family home. Individually decorated bedrooms with views over the Lough or nearby hills all have their own character and are charmingly furnished (Anne is very handy with a sewing machine and time available in the winter is well used for guests' comfort). The drawing room and dining room are both furnished with antiques and have open fires, making this a very warm and comfortable place to return to after a day out. No dinners, but Anne can recommend pubs and restaurants nearby. Children welcome (under 2 free in parents' room, cots available free of charge). Garden, tennis. No pets. *Self-catering also available in the 'Old Stables'; details on request. **Rooms 5** (4 en-suite with shower, 1 twin has private bathroom, all no smoking, 1 family room). B&B €35 (standard); en-suite €40 pps, ss €10. Closed Oct-Easter. MasterCard, Visa. **Directions:** Follow river to Town Hall, turn right; 1st house on right.

Ramelton

Frewin

COUNTRY HOUSE

Rectory Road Ramelton Co Donegal
Tel: 074 915 1246 Fax: 074 915 1246
Email: flaxmill@indigo.ie Web: www.frewinhouse.com

Thomas and Regina Coyle have restored this unspoilt Victorian house with the greatest attention to period detail and guests have the opportunity to drink in the atmosphere on arrival while having a cup of tea in the little book-lined library, where the old parish safe is still set in the wall. Beautifully furnished bedrooms have snowy white bedlinen and a robe provided in case of night-time forays along the corridor (one bathroom is private, but not en-suite). Two bathrooms have recently been refurbished which, in a reverse of the usual improvements, meant removing the baths and replacing them with showers. A delicious breakfast, including freshly baked breads warm from the oven, is taken communally at a long polished table; no dinner is offered but Regina directs guests to the best local restaurants. This beautiful house is most unusual, notably because Thomas Coyle specialises in restoring old buildings and is a collector by nature - much of his collection finds a place in the house, some is for sale in an outbuilding at the back. Not suitable for children under 8. No pets. Garden. **Rooms 4** (3 shower only, 1 with private bath, 1 family room, all no smoking). B&B €75-80, ss €15. D about €35 (by arrangement). Closed 23 Dec-1 Jan. MasterCard, Visa. **Directions:** Take R245 from Letterkenny. Travel 7 miles approx and take right turn on approach to Ramelton. Located 400 yards on right.

Rathmullan

Fort Royal Hotel

HOTEL/RESTAURANT

Rathmullan Co Donegal **Tel: 074 91 58100** Fax: 074 91 58103
Email: fortroyal@eircom.net Web: www.fortroyalhotel.com

Overlooking the sea, and with direct access to a sandy beach, the Fletcher family's attractive Victorian hotel is set in 19 acres of lawn and woodland above Lough Swilly - and has perhaps the best location of any establishment in the area. It's a comfortable, quiet base for family holidays or visiting places of local interest, including Glenveagh National Park and Glebe House, the late artist Derek Hill's former home, which has a museum and gallery next door. Public rooms, which include a recently refurbished bar, are spacious, well-proportioned and comfortably furnished in country house style, with big armchairs and open fires. Well-appointed bedrooms (all en-suite, most with bath and shower, a few bath only) are designed for relaxation and enjoy a pleasant outlook over wooded grounds. Croquet, tennis, golf, pitch & putt are available on the premises, and activities such as riding and fishing are nearby. As there are no conferences or functions held here, this is an ideal place for those seeking a quiet break. Special interest breaks offered. (A 3-day mid-week golf package includes a round of golf at Rosapenna and one at Portsalon, €340-395 depending on the season.) Children welcome (under 4 free in parents' room, cot available without charge, baby sitting arranged). Pets permitted. Garden.* Three attractive self-catering cottages are available in the hotel grounds; details on application. **Rooms 15** (all en-suite & no smoking). Children welcome (under 5s free in parents' room, cot available without charge, babysitting arranged). Pets permitted in some area. Garden. B&B €95pps, ss €35. Hotel closed Nov-Mar. **Restaurant:** This attractive traditional dining room overlooking lawns and woodland is well-appointed with crisp white linen and fresh flowers - just the right setting for good country house cooking. Much of the food at Fort Royal comes from the hotel's own walled gardens and is cooked by Tim Fletcher, who has been head chef since 1995 and proprietor since 2000. His nightly dinner menus offer about five classic choices on each course, considerately priced to allow two- or three-course options. Typical examples from a summer menu include a starter of cornets of smoked salmon filled with smoked trout mousse; grilled fillets of Killybegs plaice meunière (and vegetable selection) and panna cotta with mixed berry compôte. Tea or coffee is served in the lounge afterwards - or, on fine evenings, you could take it outside and enjoy the view down over the lough. Staff are very pleasant and helpful. An informative, fairly priced wine list offers several dessert wines and half a dozen well-chosen half bottles. **Seats 50.** Not suitable for children under 10. D daily, 7.30-9 (Sun D is a cold buffet). Set D €45. House wine €16.50. *Light lunches may be available in the bar or at tables in the garden, 12-2 daily. Phone ahead to check availability. Amex, Diners, MasterCard, Visa, Laser. **Directions:** Ramelton road from Letterkenny, straight on to Rathmullan.

Rathmullan

COUNTRY HOUSE

Rathmullan House

Rathmullan Co Donegal
Tel: 074 915 8188 Fax: 074 915 8200
Email: info@rathmullanhouse.com Web: www.rathmullanhouse.com

COUNTRY HOUSE OF THE YEAR

féile bia Set in lovely gardens on the shores of Lough Swilly, this gracious nineteenth century house is fairly grand, with public areas which include three elegant drawing rooms, but it's not too formal - and there's a cellar bar which can be very relaxed. It was built as a summer house by the Batt banking family of Belfast in the 1800s, and has been run as a country house hotel since 1961 by the Wheeler family. Recently, under the current energetic management of William and Mark Wheeler, and Mark's wife, Mary, an impressive extension has been completed. The design is in sympathy with the surroundings and they now have ten very desirable, individually decorated new bedrooms, and The Gallery, a state of the art conference facility for up to 80 delegates. Bedrooms in the original house vary in size, decor, outlook and cost, but all are comfortably furnished in traditional country house style. Donegal has an other-worldliness that is increasingly hard to capture in the traditional family holiday areas and, although now larger, Rathmullan House still retains a laid-back charm and that special sense of place - and it is greatly to their credit that the Wheeler family have developed their business (and extended the season) without compromising the essential character of this lovely place. Conference/banqueting (80). Swimming pool, steam room, tennis. Children welcome;(free under 6 months, cot €15, baby sitting arranged. Pets permitted by arrangement. Pets permitted by arrangement (special pet-friendly room available). Gardens. **Rooms 32** (19 with separate bath & shower, 9 ground floor, 2 for disabled). B&B €115 pps, ss €45, SC 10%. **The Weeping Elm:** The dining room was revamped and extended as part of the recent development, but the famous tented ceiling (designed by the late Liam McCormick, well known for his striking Donegal churches) has been retained. It is a pleasing room that makes the most of the garden outlook - including a formal garden beside the extension, which is maturing nicely - and provides a fine setting for Tommi Tuhkanen's modern Irish cooking, as well as the tremendous breakfasts for which Rathmullan is justly famous. Cooking here is upbeat traditional and meticulously-sourced menus are based on the very best of local and artisan foods - and fresh produce from their own restored walled garden; the choice offered is wide and includes many beautifully conceived combination dishes - look forward to specialities like Fanad Head crab plate, assiette of Pat Patton's Rathmullan lamb, with loin, braised shoulder, kidney and mini shepherd'ss pie, with rosemary gravy, roast carrots fennel and, perhaps, a fine farmhouse cheese selection or a refreshing compôte of garden fruits with carrageen pudding. (Both cheeses and carrageen are equally at home as part of the legendary Rathmullan breakfast too.) And a particularly attractive feature of Rathmullan is the Children's Menu - a proper little person's version of the adult menu, with lots of choices and no concessions to 'popular' fare, this is education on a plate. Like everything else here, the wine list is meticulously sourced and informative; it includes half a dozen organic & bio-dynamic wines, lots of lovely bubblies and a wide choice of half bottles. All this plus caring service and a beautiful location... Rathmullan is on a roll. **Seats 100** (private room, 30); D daily 7-8.45 (to 9.30 Fri/Sat); Set D €47.50/50, 2/3 courses; house wine from €23; SC 10%. *Informal meals are available in Batts Bar & Café and the Cellar Bar: L, 1-2.30pm daily; Early D is also available in The Cellar Bar, 5-8pm daily in summer; children's menu available. Closed 7 Jan-9 Feb. Amex, MasterCard, Visa, Laser. **Directions:** Letterkenny to Ramelton - turn right to Rathmullan at the bridge, through village and turn right to hotel.

Rathmullan

N RESTAURANT WITH ROOMS

The Water's Edge

Rathmullan Co Donegal
Tel: 074 915 8182 Email: thewatersedge@eircom.net
Web: www.silvertassiehotel.com/html/watersedge

Neil and Mandy Blaney's large bar and restaurant with rooms is a brand new conversion of an old building and really lives up to its name diners in the vast dining room on the edge of Lough Swilly can gaze out at one of the finest views to be had anywhere, across the water to the Inishowen Peninsula. Arriving guests get a warm welcome (attentive service is a highlight of a visit here) and, although everything is gleaming glass, light polished wood and shiny steel, carpeted floors keep the noise down and soft lighting from walls and overhead beams soften the atmosphere. Tables are set up simply but attractively (except let down by unpleasant manmade napkins), and almost all tables have a view; menus crediting plenty of local foods offer a range of dishes divided evenly between meat and fish, with something imaginative for vegetarians; the cooking was fairly classic at the time of our visit, offering dishes like Donegal sirloin steak with fondant potatoes, roast garlic butter and a peppercorn sauce, or roast tail of monkfish with deep fried Portavogie scampi with aioli and pan juices, but there's a plan to introduce a more modern twist to the cooking style food, with oriental influences. A well-balanced wine list holds no surprises but, like the food, offers good value. **Accommodation**: Well-appointed rooms complete with flat screen television offer fine views, and the spacious en suite bathrooms are sparkling, although the baths in some of the rooms are inexplicably small. A welcome addition to this lovely area. **Rooms 10;** B&B from €55 pps. Open all year. **Directions:** On your right as you enter Rathmullan from the Letterkenny direction. ◇

Rossnowlagh

HOTEL/RESTAURANT

Sand House Hotel

Rossnowlagh Co Donegal
Tel: 071 985 1777 Fax: 071 985 2100
Email: info@sandhouse.ie Web: www.sandhouse.ie

féile bia Perched on the edge of a stunning sandy beach two miles long, the Britton family's famous hotel lost its trademark crenellated roof-line a few years ago, but emerged with an extra storey and an elegant new look, reminiscent of a French chateau. Wonderful sea views and easy access to the beach have always been the great attractions of The Sand House, which started life as a fishing lodge in the 1830s and completed its latest metamorphosis with a new floor of bedrooms, a panoramic lift (who will bother with the stairs when the lift has the best view in the house?), a new boardroom and a marine spa, where seaweed products are used for a range of exclusive body and skincare treatments. Existing bedrooms were also refurbished and upgraded recently and many have a superb outlook; all are very comfortable, with excellent bathrooms - and everyone can enjoy the view from the sun deck which allows a sheltered retreat from which to soak in the sea view. Things that never change at the Sand House include the ever-burning welcoming fire in the foyer, exceptional housekeeping - and the hospitality of the Britton family and staff, which is the real appeal of this remarkable hotel. Golf is a major attraction for guests at The Sandhouse, which is a member of The Emerald Triangle (three strategically places establishments offering great golf experiences: the other two are Rathsallagh, Co Wicklow, and Glenlo Abbey, Co Galway, see entries). Also partners in 'Play 3 Great Golf Courses in Ireland's North-West' (Donegal GC, Bundoran, Castle Hume). Spa; fishing, cycling, tennis, walking, tennis on site; horse riding, boating and many other activities available nearby. Details on application. Conferences (100). Children welcome (under 5s free in parents' room, cots available without charge, baby sitting arranged). Pets permitted by arrangement. **Rooms 50** (1 suite, 2 junior suites, 5 executive, 5 shower only, 25 no-smoking, 1 disabled). Lift. 24 hour room service. B&B €100pps, no ss. SC discretionary. Closed Dec & Jan. **Seashell Restaurant:** The restaurant is rather unexpectedly at the front of the hotel (and therefore faces inland) but is well-appointed, in keeping with the rest of the hotel. John McGarrigle, who has been with the hotel since 2000, presents seasonal 5-course dinner menus, changed daily; fresh seafood and locally sourced lamb and beef (also game, in season) provide the foundation for a traditional repertoire which is quite conservative but offers plenty of choice on all courses. Finish with a choice of Irish cheeses or hotel-style desserts. Staff are helpful and attentive. Good choice of wines by the glass. *Soup and sandwiches are also available in the bar at lunchtime, every day except Sunday. **Seats 80.** Children welcome. D daily 7-8.30, L Sun only, 1-2.30. Set Sun L €30; house wines from €20. SC discretionary. Closed Dec & Jan. Amex, MasterCard, Visa, Laser. **Directions:** Coast road from Ballyshannon to Donegal Town.

TORY ISLAND

The Gaeltacht (Irish-speaking) island of Tory lies eight miles off the north-west corner of Donegal and, in spite of its exposed position, has been inhabited for four thousand years. Perhaps not surprisingly, this other-worldly island managed quite well without an hotel until recently, but once Patrick and Berney Doohan's **Ostan Thoraig** (074 913 5920) was built in 1994 it quickly became the centre of the island's social activities - or, to be more precise, The People's Bar in the hotel quickly became the centre. The hotel is beside the little harbour where the ferries bring in visitors from mainland ports. Although simple, it provides comfortable en-suite accommodation with telephone and television. The hotel is open from Easter to October. A special feature of the island is its 'school' of primitive art (founded with the support of well-known artist the late Derek Hill of nearby Glebe House and Gallery, Church Hill). It even has a king as a founder member: the present King of the Tory is Patsy Dan Rogers, who has exhibited his colourful primitive paintings of the island throughout the British Isles and in America. A tiny gallery on Tory provides exhibition space for the current group of island artists. Tory is accessible by ferry (subject to weather conditions) from several mainland ports: telephone 074 913 1320 for details, or ask at the hotel. MasterCard, Visa.

Tremone
FARMHOUSE

Trean House

Tremone Lecamy Inishowen Co Donegal
Tel: 074 936 7121 Fax: 074 936 7227
Email: treanhouse@oceanfree.net Web: www.treanhouse.com

Way out on the Inishowen peninsula, Joyce and Mervyn Norris's farmhouse is tucked into a sheltered corner in stone-walled countryside beside the sea. Surrounded by a large garden with mature trees and welcoming flowers, it is a substantial house and offers a comfortable base for a relaxing away-from-it-all holiday in a homely atmosphere. Guests have the use of a cosy sitting room with an open fire and simple country bedrooms have everything that is needed - the only room without an en-suite shower room has a private bathroom nearby - and, if any other guest prefers a bath, it can be used by arrangement. Joyce's home cooking is another attraction - breakfasts to set you up for the day, evening meals by arrangement. Children welcome (under 3s free in parents' room' cot available without charge). Pets permitted in some areas by arrangement. Garden. **Rooms 4** (all en-suite, 1 with bath & separate shower, 3 shower only & no smoking). B&B €32, ss €12. No SC. Open all year except Christmas. MasterCard, Visa. **Directions:** From Moville follow R238 5kms, turn right & follow house signs.

COUNTY GALWAY

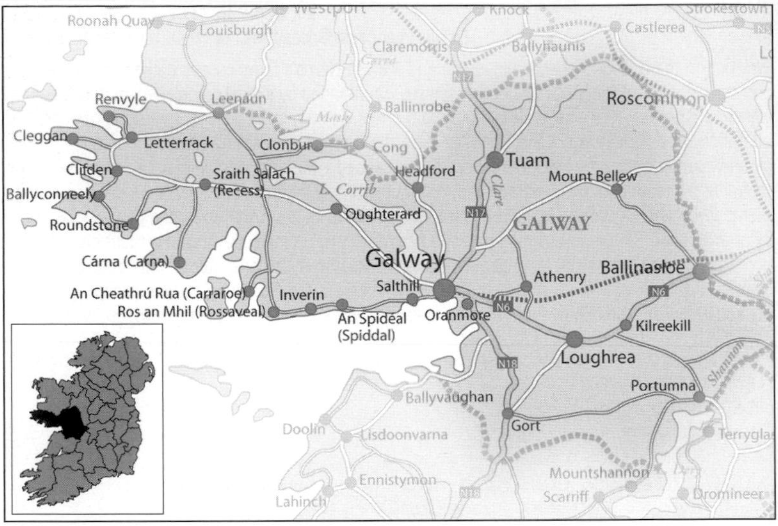

Galway surpasses many other parts of Ireland in the spectacular variety and charm of its many scenic routes. But it also has more to offer in the way of slightly offbeat expeditions and experiences.

Visiting the Aran Islands across the mouth of Galway Bay, for instance, can be done by air as well as by sea. However, as the much-visited Aran Islands have shown, the presence of an air service doesn't seem to lessen the popularity of the ferries, and people often seem to think that you haven't properly visited an island unless you go there by boat. Then, too, there are many coastal boat trips, including an informative seaborne tour from Killary Harbour, Ireland's only genuine fjord, while Lough Corrib is also served by miniature cruise liners.

As for sport ashore, the Galway Races at the end of July have developed into a seven day meeting which is firmly established as Ireland's premier summer horse racing event, while the Ballinasloe International Horse Fair in the Autumn is simply unique. It dates back more than 280 years.

This has to be Ireland's most generous county, for in effect you get two counties for the price of one. They're neatly divided by the handsome sweep of island-studded Lough Corrib, with the big country of many mountains to the west, and rolling farmland to the east. As a bonus, where the Corrib foams into Galway Bay, we find one of Ireland's - indeed, one of Europe's - most vibrant cities. Galway is a bustling place which cheerfully sees itself as being linked to Spain and the great world beyond the Atlantic.

The theme of double value asserts itself in other ways. As Autumn ripeness makes its presence felt, the county and city provide not one, but two, Oyster Festivals. Once September has ushered in the traditional oyster season, Galway's long and distinguished connection with the splendid bivalve mollusc is celebrated first with the Clarenbridge Oyster Festival on the southeast shore of Galway Bay, and then a week or so later, right in the heart of the city with the International Galway Oyster Festival itself, a celebration going back more than half a century.

Lough Corrib is both a geographical and psychological divide. East of it, there's flatter country, home to hunting packs of mythic lore. West of the Corrib - which used itself to be a major throughfare, and is now as ever a place of angling renown - you're very quickly into the high ground and moorland which sweep up to the Twelve Bens and other splendid peaks, wonderful mountains which enthusiasts would claim as the most beautiful in all Ireland.

Their heavily indented coastline means this region is Connemara, the Land of the Sea, where earth, rock and ocean intermix in one of Ireland's most extraordindary landscapes. Beyond, to the south, the Aran Islands are a place apart, yet they too are part of the Galway mix in this fantastical county which has its own magical light coming in over the sea. And yet, all its extraordinary variety happens within very manageable distances – Galway is a universe all within one day's drive.

Local Attractions and Information

GALWAY CITY

Arts Centre, 47 Dominick St	091 565 886
Galway Airport	091 752 874
Galway Arts Festival (July)	091 565 886
Galway Crystal Heritage Centre	091 757 311
Galway Races (late July/early August, Sept & Oct)	091 753 870
Galway International Oyster Festival (late September)	091 527 282 / 522 066
Kenny's Bookshops & Art Galleries, High Street	091 562 739
O'Brien Shipping (Aran Island Ferries)	091 563 081
Tourist Information	091 563 081
Town Hall Theatre	091 569 755

CO GALWAY

Aran Islands, Heritage Centre	099 61355
Aran Islands, Ferries from Rossaveal	091 568 903 / 561 767
Aran Islands, Flights from Inverin Airport	091 593 034
Aughrim, Battle of Aughrim Centre	090 967 3939
Ballinasloe, International Horse Fair (Sept/Oct)	090 964 3453
Clarenbridge, Oyster Festival (September)	091 796 342
Clifden, Connemara Pony Show (mid August)	095 21863
Clifden, Connemara Safari - Walking & Islands	095 21071
Gort, Thoor Ballylee (Yeats' Tower)	091 631 436
Inishbofin, Arts Festival (Biennial, September)	095 45909
Inishbofin Ferries, (Cleggan)	095 44642
Inisheer, Duchas Inis Oirr (Arts Centre)	099 735 576
Killary, Cruises on Connemara Lady	091 566 736
Kinvara, Dungaire Castle	061 360 788
Letterfrack, Connemara Bog Week (May)	095 43443
Letterfrack, Connemara Sea Week (October)	095 43443
Letterfrack, Kylemore Abbey & Gardens	095 41146
Loughrea, Dartfield Horse Museum	091 843 968
Roundstone, Roundstone Arts Week (July)	095 35834
Roundstone, Traditional bodhran makers	095 35808
Tuam, Little Mill (last intact cornmill in area)	093 25486

Galway City
Ⓝ RESTAURANT

Abalone Restaurant

53 Dominick Street Galway Co Galway
Tel: 091 534 895

Round the corner from the Bridge Mills, an off-the-street entrance with a tiny porch leads to Alan Williams' smartly appointed little restaurant: gently minimalist décor, subdued lighting and gentle background music (Sinatra, Nat King Cole) set a romantic tone and tables are promisingly set up with spotless white linen and simple glassware. A small dispense bar doubles as reception desk, where arriving gusts are greeted and quickly settled in with menus and an aperitif. 31 year-old Alan Williams is a dedicated chef and, while his menu may be short and conventional, he is a good cook with a clear idea of what he wants to achieve. Begin with an amuse bouche (a fine chicken liver canapé, perhaps) then starters, which are fairly priced at around €8.50, may include a good clam chowder with diced potato, smoked bacon & parsley, and a crisp homemade duck spring roll, deliciously filled with sweet peppers and duck, with a tart apple chutney alongside. Main courses are around €28, and a dish attracting praise on a recent visit was a generous, flavoursome chargrilled veal cutlet with gratin potatoes, crisp fresh asparagus and a rich Madeira cream sauce. Another option was scallops wrapped in smoked applewood bacon (the bacon rather powerful for the delicate scallops, perhaps). Pleasing desserts (€6.50) might include a wild berry crème brulée or a good chocolate mousse, nicely presented in a demi-tasse. Good coffee to finish. Service is brisk and enthusiastic, and a very short but (apart from Australia), representative wine list includes a couple of half bottles. **Seats 20;** D Mon-Sat, 6-10pm; house wine €17.50; 10% sc on parties 8+. Closed Sun. MasterCard, Visa. ◇

Galway City

Antons

CAFÉ

12 Father Griffin Road Galway Co Galway **Tel: 091 582067**

Antons is a popular, family-run Galway café, a five minute walk from Jurys Inn over the bridge. It's a simple place, a long room with local artists' paintings and a lot of wood - floors, tables, chairs and benches - mugs and unmatching ware. It has been feeding a loyal lunch time trade for many years, so it's just the kind of place visitors need to know about. The menu is pretty constant - soup (tomato and basil with brown bread and butter) sandwiches (made with home-made foccacia and served with mixed leaves and tomato - chicken, spinach and walnut is typical); salads (eg smoked duck and raspberry vinaigrette). Particularly recommended for home baking, consistently good salads and desserts (Raspberry and almond tart, Italian chocolate cake) in an unfussy atmosphere. Great coffees, teas, infusions and freshly squeezed juice too. **Seats 30.** Open all day Mon-Sat. Closed Sun. **Directions:** Over the bridge from Jurys Inn, towards Salthill. ◇

Galway City

Ard Bia

RESTAURANT

2 Quay Street Galway Co Galway **Tel: 091 539 897**
Email: ardbia@gmail.com Web: www.ardbia.com

Ard Bia, literally High Food an appropriate moniker for the latest incarnation upstairs over Naughton's pub on Quay Street. Under Aoibheann MacNamara's direction for a couple of years now, this is an artfully simple daytime restaurant and a fine dining venue at night. Open from 10am, it offers good sandwiches such as cheese & tomato chutney or chicken with relish & organic leaves and day-long hot and cold specials including a generous Ard Bia hamburger and veggie burger. Teas have a special little menu of their own, and juices like Moroccan orange & celery, lime, or tomato & cucumber are freshly squeezed at the bar counter. Ices and sorbets, bought in, are also good as is the daily soup - carrot & coriander perhaps - and a side table displays a small selection of cakes, tarts and scones. The room itself is an awkward space, long and narrow, but the plain wooden tables cleverly arranged to allow views over busy Quay Street and a recessed alcove seats a small group of about eight; in summer there are a couple of tables outside on the street. Evenings bring a short but interesting menu, well executed; there can be delays at dinner time due to high demand, and there is little waiting space but this bustling, well-managed restaurant is currently one of Galway's best and, even though the kitchen is on a higher floor again, service is consistently good. Children welcome. **Seats 40;** air conditioning; open daily - Mon-Sat, 10-10.30pm (closed 5-6): L 12-4, D 6-10.30; Sun 12-6; menus a la carte; house wine €5-6 per glass; SC10% on groups 6+. Closed 25/26 Dec. MasterCard, Visa, Laser. **Directions:** Above Tigh Neachtains pub.

Galway City

Ardawn House

GUESTHOUSE

College Road Galway Co Galway **Tel: 091 568 833** Fax: 091 563 454
Email: ardawn@iol.ie Web: wwwgalway.net/pages/ardawn-house/

Mike and Breda Guilfoyle's hospitable guesthouse is easily found, just a few minutes walk from Eyre Square. Accommodation is all en-suite and rooms are comfortably furnished, with good amenities. Although it may seem expensive for a guesthouse, Mike and Breda make Ardawn House special - they take great pride in every aspect of the business, (including an extensive breakfast) and also help guests to get the very best out of their visit to Galway. Children welcome. Pets permitted by arrangement. **Rooms 8** (all shower only & no-smoking). B&B €75pps, ss €35. Closed 21-28 Dec. MasterCard, Visa, Laser. **Directions:** Off N6, take city east exit; follow signs to city centre. First house on right after greyhound track.

Galway City

Ardilaun House Hotel

HOTEL/RESTAURANT

Taylors Hill Galway Co Galway
Tel: 091 521 433 Fax: 091 521 546
Email: info@ardilaunhousehotel.ie Web: www.ardilaunhousehotel.ie

féile bia Ardilaun House Hotel has an interesting history - it dates back to about 1840, when it was built as a townhouse for prominent members of Galway society, the Persse family (Augusta Persse became Lady Gregory, co-founder of the Abbey Theatre) - and has been over 40 years in the ownership of the Ryan family, who opened it as an hotel in 1962. While convenient to the city, its wooded grounds give it a country feeling. Friendly, helpful staff make a good impression on arrival and everything about the hotel - which has recently been extensively renovated, extended and refurbished - confirms the feeling of a well-run establishment. Public areas are spacious, elegantly furnished and some - notably the dining room - overlook gardens at the back. Bedrooms are traditionally furnished to a high standard and regularly refurbished; amenities are in line with expectation in a hotel of this standard, and include modem lines. Excellent in-house leisure facilities include snooker and a leisure centre with indoor swimming pool, gym, solarium, beauty salon and treatment rooms. It is a popular wedding venue, and purpose-built conference facilities offer a wide range of options for large and small groups, with back-up business services, including video conferencing on request. Off-season and special interest breaks are offered (details on application.) *A major redevelopment programme is under way at the time of going to press. Conference/banqueting (400/270). Children welcome (under 3s free in parents' room, cots available without charge, baby sitting arranged). Pets permitted in some areas. Gardens. **Rooms 89** (1 suite, 2 junior suites, 9 executive rooms, 6 shower only, 24 no-smoking, 3 for disabled). Lift. B&B about €120 pps, ss €25. No SC. Open all year except Christmas. **Camilaun Room: Seats 140** (private room 30). L&D daily: L1-2.15, D 7-9.15. Set L €20.50. Set D from €23 (5-course Set D €39), D also à la carte. House wine €17.50. SC 10%. Closed 22 -27 Dec. Amex, Diners, MasterCard, Visa, Laser. **Directions:** 1 mile west of city centre (towards Salthill). ◇

Galway City
RESTAURANT

Da Roberta

169 Upper Salthill Galway Co Galway **Tel: 091 585 808**
Fax: 091 583 455 Email: daroberta@eircom.net

Roberta and Sandro Pieri see their tightly-packed little restaurant is Salthill as 'a piece of Italy' - and they convey this so successfully that queues regularly form at the door. Sunny, yellow walls are hung with still life prints and posters of "Touring Club Italiano", tables sport linen cloths with peach paper covers, it's child-friendly and buzzes with the chatter of happy diners. Roberta smiles as she takes orders, Sandro moves from table to table with bottles of wine exchanging wry banter with customers as he pours wine, stuffing corks in his pocket. The menu offers many familiar Italian dishes (also available to take away) starting with a daily soup (€4, home-made) rising to a maximum of about €16 for a speciality main course Involtini alla Roberta (veal stuffed with Parma ham, baked with cheese & cream sauce). Between lie many authentic dishes : prosciutto and salad leaves with soft cheese and a salad of rocket with olives, capers and parmesan can both be excellent, for example, also pizzas with thin, crisp bases and a good choice of toppings (Luisa, with sun-dried tomatoes, rosemary, feta and mozzarella, for example) although fritto misto di Mare may disappoint, if consisting of canned squid rings, mussels and tiny prawns sautéed with tomatoes. Desserts - not a strong point and augmented by the familiar plastic card of ice creams - come with good coffee and an appropriate all-Italian wine list (upgraded to 280 bottles in 2006) also offers Italian beer. So what you get here is charming hospitality, an authentic Italian atmosphere and good value - a great recipe for success. *A sister restaurant, **Osteria da Roberta,** has opened nearby (open Mon-Sat 5-11, Sun 12.30-11). **Seats 46.** Open daily 12.30-11. A la carte. House wine €18.50. Reservations required. Amex, MasterCard, Visa, Laser. **Directions:** Central Salthill, opposite the Church.

Galway City
B&B

Devondell

47 Devon Park Lr Salthill Galway Co Galway **Tel: 091 528 306**
Email: devondell@iol.ie Web: www.devondell.com

Although quite unremarkable from the road, Berna Kelly's immaculate house has won many admirers and it's easy to see why: a warm welcome, pretty bedrooms with crisp white linen and many homely touches and Berna's special breakfasts served in a fine dining room overlooking the back garden, are just a few of the reasons guests keep coming back. It's a little difficult to find on the first visit, but well worth the effort. Garden. **Rooms 4** (all en-suite & no smoking, 3 shower only). B&B €45-50 pps, no ss. Closed 1 Nov-1 Mar. **No Credit Cards. Directions:** Fr Griffin Road to T Junction-take left after 400 - 500 metres,Take right at Devon Park House, go to fork 100 metres up, take left and sharp left.

Galway City
HOTEL/RESTAURANT

The G Hotel

Wellpark Galway Co Galway
Tel: 091 865 200 Fax: 091 865 203
Email: info@monogramhotels.ie Web: www.monogramhotels.ie

An unimpressive facade gives no indication of the stunning interior of this new hotel: internationally renowned milliner Phillip Treacy, a native of Galway, was given carte blanche to indulge his quirky creativity by owner, Galwayman, Gerry Barrett and he has given the western capital a stunning new hotel. Eyecatching colour combinations, lighting, furniture, carpets, fireplaces make the public rooms both comfortable and delightfully varied. What might have been an intimidating (all black) lobby and reception area, is cleverly enlivened by a wall-mounted, exotic fish tank featuring the strangest creatures: sea horses, born and bred in Connemara. Accommodation is luxurious, as would be expected and this is a fun place, that brings a smile to people's faces. **Restaurant:** The stylish restaurant, brainchild of London restaurateur Laura Santini, offers refined Italian cooking far removed from the cucina rustica one might expect from a high street trattoria. It's a kind of hybrid: international hotel cuisine with Italian undertones: simple starters, good veal dishes including osso bucco and pastas, very good lamb cutlets and deepfried zucchini as well as a range of predictable desserts. The kitchen and service was still finding its feet at the time of our visit, but there is a real sense that management is working hard to reach a very high standard, as it must to maintain the 5 stars already bestowed on the hotel. Boardroom/Banqueting (20/65), theatre facility next door for 40-150; media centre, broadband, secretarial services; Spa; Golf & equestrian nearby. Wheelchair accessible. **Rooms 101** (3 suites, 26 junior suites, all others deluxe or superior); children welcome (baby sitting arranged) rooms from €200. Helipad. **Directions:** From Oranmore - N6 for Galway East, at Skerrit roundabout take Dublin Road. Proceed to the Ffrench roundabout, take the 4th exit: the g is located immediately on the left. ◇

Galway City

Galway Bay Hotel

HOTEL

The Promenade Salthill Galway Co Galway **Tel: 091 520 520** Fax: 091 520 530
Email: info@galwaybayhotel.net Web: www.galwaybayhotel.net

féile bia

This well-named hotel has clear views over Galway Bay to the distant hills of County Clare from public rooms on the ground floor as well as many of the spacious, well-equipped bedrooms - which have all been lavishly refurbished recently. The large marbled foyer and adjacent public areas are very spacious and facilities for both business and leisure are particularly impressive. Although equally attractive for business or leisure, it's a highly regarded conference centre and a good choice for business guests - as well as the usual facilities, all rooms have modem points and interactive TV for messages, Internet and preview of the bill. Off-season and special interest breaks are offered - details on application. Conference/banqueting (1000/500). Leisure centre, swimming pool, gym; beauty salon. Children welcome (free in parents' room under 2, cot available, baby sitting arranged; playroom) Rooftop garden. Ample parking (inc underground). No pets. **Rooms 153** (2 suites, 2 junior suites, 4 executive, 50 no smoking, 2 for disabled). Lifts. B&B €125 pps, ss €55. Open all year. Amex, MasterCard, Visa, Laser. **Directions:** Located on Salthill Road beside Leisureland, overlooking Galway Bay.

Galway City

Glenlo Abbey Hotel

HOTEL/RESTAURANT

Bushypark Galway Co Galway
Tel: 091 526 666 Fax: 091 527 800
Email: info@glenloabbey.ie Web: www.glenlo.com

féile bia

Originally an eighteenth century residence, Glenlo Abbey is just two and a half miles from Galway city yet, beautifully located on a 138-acre estate, with its own golf course and Pavilion, it offers all the advantages of the country. Although it is not a very big hotel, the scale is generous: public rooms are impressive, and large, well-furnished bedrooms have good amenities and marbled bathrooms. The old Abbey has been restored for meetings and private dining, with business services to back up meetings and conferences. For indoor relaxation the Oak Cellar Bar serves light food and, in addition to the classical River Room Restaurant - a lovely bright room with tables tiered to take full advantage of lovely views over Lough Corrib and the surrounding countryside. Conference/banqueting 120/160. Golf (9 & 18 hole); fishing, equestrian, cycling, walking. Children welcome (cot available, baby sitting arranged). No pets. Garden. Boutique. **Rooms 46** (3 suites, 1 junior suite, 17 executive, 1 shower only, 1 for disabled, all no-smoking). Wheelchair access. Lift. Room rate from €140 (max 2 guests). Ample parking. Helipad. Open all year except Christmas. **Pullman Restaurant:** This is perhaps the country's most novel dinner venue and was our Atmospheric Restaurant of the Year in 2005: four carriages, two of them from the original Orient Express that featured in scenes from "Murder on the Orient Express", filmed in 1974. Adapting it to restaurant use has been achieved brilliantly, with no expense spared in maintaining the special features of a luxurious train. There is a lounge/bar area leading to an open dining carriage and two private 'coupes' compartments, each seating up to six. Background clackity-clack and hooting noises lend an authenticity to the experience and the romance is sustained by discreetly piped music of the 1940s and 50s. The view from the windows is of a coiffeured golf course, Lough Corrib and Connemara hills in the distance. Welcome by smart staff is pleasant, service throughout exemplary. Tables are set up as on a train, with silver cutlery, simple glassware and white linen (although napkins are paper); the food is suitably inclined to Asian influences and, while not cutting edge, it is very enjoyable. In line with the fun of the theme, you could begin your meal with a Pullman Summer Salad - and even end it with Poirot's Pie (apple tart); more typically, try an excellent 'Assiette of Oriental Appetisers' includes sushi,sashimi, prawn tempura, smoked salmon, and mini spring roll soy sauce and wasabi - and follow with a main course of 'Beijing Kao Ya', deliciously crisp-skinned roast half duck with a home-made barbecue & pomegranate sauce. Short, well-chosen wine list. Recommended as much for its unique, special occasion experience as for the fare - but the cooking is reliable and a visit is always enjoyable. **Pullman Restaurant: Seats 66;** open for D daily 7-9.30. **River Room Restaurant: Seats 60.** D daily 7-10; set D €45; gourmet menu €65; also á la carte; house wine €25. River Room closed Sun, Mon. House closed 24-27 Dec. Amex, Diners, MasterCard, Visa, Laser. **Directions:** 4 km from Galway on N59 in the Clifden direction.

Galway City

€ CAFÉ

Goya's

2/3 Kirwans Lane Galway Co Galway **Tel: 091 567010**
Email: info@goyas.ie Web: www.goyas.ie

If only for a cup of cappuccino or hot chocolate and a wedge of chocolate cake or a slice of quiche, a restorative visit to this delightful contemporary bakery and café is a must on any visit to Galway. There's something very promising about the cardboard cake boxes stacked up in preparation near the door, the staff are super, there's a great buzz and the food is simply terrific. What's more, you don't even have to be in Galway to enjoy Emer Murray's terrific baking - contact Goya's for her seasonal mail-order catalogues "Fabulous Festive Fancies" (Christmas cakes, plum pudding, mince pies etc) and "Easter Delights" (simnel cake and others); wedding cakes also available. If you're wondering where to start, why not try a speciality: Goyas 3-layer chocolate gateau cake. *At the time of going to press Goya's is planning to move to new premises, and to expand the range offered. with an emphasis on deli products. **Seats 56** (outdoor, 20), wheelchair accessible. Open all day Mon-Sat (L 12.30-3). MasterCard, Visa, Laser. **Directions:** Behind McDonaghs Fish Shop, off Quay Street.

Galway City

HOTEL

Great Southern Hotel Galway

Eyre Square Galway Co Galway **Tel: 091 564 041** Fax: 091 566 704
Email: res@galway-gsh.com Web: www.greatsouthernhotels.com

Overlooking Eyre Square right in the heart of Galway, this historic railway hotel was built in 1845; at the time of going to press, it has just been sold and there may be a change of name. Prior to the sale, a major refurbishment programme had been completed, intended mainly to reinstate the grandeur and elegance of its 19th century heyday; this has been achieved, most notably in the public areas, where marble flooring, high ceilings, chandeliers and rich fabrics have all contributed to re-creating the grandeur of old. Accommodation has been treated similarly - the wide corridors (designed so that ladies in hooped dresses could pass without inconvenience) are especially impressive in these days of compact modern buildings and all the rooms are spacious and opulently decorated, with bathrooms to match; however, light sleepers might be advised to ask for a quiet room as the traffic on Eyre Square can be disturbing. On the top storey, a health spa has panoramic views over Galway city and harbour (interesting rather than scenic); facilities include a Canadian hot tub, hydrotherapy baths, jacuzzi and steam room, a state of the art gym and fitness area - and treatment rooms offering a wide cantly but O'Flaherty's Pub, which is in the basement of the hotel and also has direct access from the street, is now modern, with a big screen and a high-tech sound system. Conference/banqueting (300); business centre. Leisure centre, indoor swimming pool. Children under 2 free in parents' room, cots available without charge, baby sitting arranged. No pets. 24 hour room service. [* A sister hotel, the **Corrib Great Southern** (Tel 091 7555281; www.gshotel.com) is nearby on the main Dublin road entering the city. Larger & newer with extensive conference & leisure facilities, it is especially suitable for conference/banqueting and family breaks.] **Rooms 99** (13 suites, 8 junior suites, 36 executive, 46 no-smoking, 2 for disabled). Lift. B&B about €140 pps, ss €30. Closed 23-27 Dec. Amex, Diners, MasterCard, Visa, Laser. **Directions:** In heart of the city overlooking Eyre Square.

Galway City

HOTEL

Harbour Hotel

New Docks Road Galway Co Galway **Tel: 091 569 466**
Fax: 091 569 455 Email: info@harbour.ie Web: www.harbour.ie

This contemporary style hotel is conveniently situated at the heart of the city and offers comfortable, if expensive accommodation with secure parking adjacent. Functional bedrooms with all the usual facilities (TV, trouser press) and well-fitted bathrooms have already been refurbished less than two years after the hotel opened - and also an extension has been added, to provide extra dining space, a separate breakfast room and a residents lounge: a clear indication of Galway's current popularity as a holiday destination. Conference/banqueting 80/75; business centre, secretarial services. Spa. Children welcome (under 12s free in parents' room, cot available without charge, baby sitting arranged). No pets. **Rooms 96** (14 executive, 4 for disabled, 55 no smoking). B&B about €180 pps, ss about €50. Open all year except Christmas. Amex, Diners, MasterCard, Visa, Laser, Switch. **Directions:** Beside the docks in Galway, 5 mins from Eyre Square. ◇

Galway City

Ⓝ BAR/RESTAURANT/GUESTHOUSE

The Huntsman Inn

164 College Road Galway Co Galway
Tel: 091 562 849 Fax: 091 561 985
Email: info@huntsmaninn.com Web: www.huntsmaninn.com

Within walking distance of the city centre and easily accessible by car (there is ample parking), this busy spot is equally suitable for a quick bite or a full meal. It looks like a pretty row of houses and, with its colourful hanging baskets, the façade cleverly disguises a large interior including a restaurant, bars and accommodation. Contemporary décor and muted colours complement an airy atmosphere, and it's a relaxed place for no-nonsense, flavoursome food at a reasonable price, served in comfortable surroundings. Well-groomed, smiling staff, simple table settings and uncomplicated menus reflect a refreshingly down to earth philosophy, and service is efficient without any sense of being rushed. The range of food offered varies, with more choice during the week than on Sundays (when it's a favourite for family outings); typical starters might include popular dishes like fish cakes with citrus salsa, light and crunchy spring rolls with a sweet chilli dip, and deep-fried brie with Cumberland sauce. Main courses also sound standard enough - char-grilled steak burger, chicken Caesar salad, medallions of salmon - but, although details might be improved (menu descriptions are not always accurate, for example, and it would be nice to see hand cut chips), careful cooking and attractive presentation generally lifts the generously portioned dishes. A short dessert menu is also predictable but tasty, and there's ever-reliable Illy coffee to finish. The New World dominates a compact wine list, which is short on information but offers a wide range of styles (including a Moet et Chandon house champagne by the bottle, half bottle or snipe) at fair prices, and matches the food well. **Accommodation:** The twelve smart, contemporary en-suite bedrooms offer all the usual conveniences plus satellite TV and computer facilities a good base for business guests. Live music (Fri & Sat). **Seats 200** (outdoors, 50); air conditioning; toilets wheelchair accessible; not suitable for children after 9pm; L daily 12.15-3, D daily 5.30-9.30. Bar food served daily, 12.30-9.30pm. Live Funky Jazz on Thurs from 6.45 pm. Closed Good Fri, Establishment closed 23 Dec - 29 Dec. Amex, MasterCard, Visa, Laser. **Directions:** Follow signs for Galway East, just before Eyre Square.

Galway City

RESTAURANT

K C Blakes

10 Quay Street Galway Co Galway
Tel: 091 561 826 Fax: 091 561 829

K C Blakes is named after a stone Tower House, of a type built sometime between 1440 and 1640, which stands as a typical example of the medieval stone architecture of the ancient city of Galway. The Caseys' restaurant, with all its sleek black designer style and contemporary chic could not present a stronger contrast to such a building. Proprietor-chef John Casey sources ingredients for K C Blakes with care and cooks with skill in wide-ranging menus that offer something for every taste: traditional Irish (beef and Guinness stew), modern Irish (pan-fried scallops and black pudding with potato purée and basil cream, perhaps, or breast of chicken with morel and tarragon stuffing with creamy mash and port jus), classical French (sole meunière) to global cuisine (a huge choice here - oriental duck with warm pancakes stuffed with cucumber and spring onion, perhaps, tiger prawns in filo or pasta dishes such as tagliatelle carbonara). Very professional service, creative cooking and smart surroundings make for quite a sense of occasion - yet this remarkable operation is aimed at a wide market and fairly priced. The upstairs dining room is a more cheerful choice - unless you prefer a people-watching window table downstairs. D daily, 5-10pm. Closed 25 Dec. Amex, MasterCard, Visa. **Directions:** City centre, near Spanish Arch. ◇

Galway City

COUNTRY HOUSE

Killeen House

Bushy Park Galway Co Galway
Tel: 091 524 179 Fax: 091 528 065
Email: killeenhouse@ireland.com Web: www.killeenhousegalway.com

Catherine Doyle's delightful, spacious 1840s house enjoys the best of both worlds: it's on the Clifden road just on the edge of Galway city yet, with 25 acres of private grounds and gardens reaching right down to the shores of Lough Corrib, offers all the advantages of the country, too. Catherine's thoughtful hospitality and meticulous standards make a stay here very special, beginning with tea on arrival, served on a beautifully arranged tray with fine linen and polished silver - a house speciality extending to the usually mundane tray provided in your bedroom. Guest rooms are luxuriously and individually furnished, each in a different period, e.g. Regency, Edwardian and (most fun this one) Art Nouveau; the bedding is exquisite, bathrooms are lovely and there are many small touches to make you feel at home. And, although the menu is not exceptionally extensive, breakfast is a delight. Not suitable for children under 12. Garden; walking. No pets. *Killeen House was our Guesthouse of the Year in 2003. **Rooms 6** (1 shower only). Lift. B&B €90pps, ss €50. Closed 23-27 Dec. Amex, Diners, MasterCard, Visa. **Directions:** On N59 between Galway city and Moycullen village.

Galway City
Ⓔ RESTAURANT

The Malt House Restaurant

Olde Malt Mall High Street Galway Co Galway
Tel: 091 567 866 Fax: 091 563 993
Email: fergus@themalthouse.ie Web: www.malt-house.com

féile bia This old restaurant and bar in a quiet, flower-filled courtyard off High Street is a cosy oasis, away from the often frenetic buzz of modern Galway. It has character - enhanced by low lighting, candles, background jazz and the sound of happy diners at night - and is well-managed, with bar and waiting staff coping seamlessly, even at the busiest of times. Informal meals are served in the bar, and the restaurant is comfortably set up with well-spaced tables smartly dressed in white and maroon (the Galway colours). Brendan Keane, who has been head chef since 1997, offers several menus (including a 5-course Seafood Sampler menu) and, although fairly traditional, there are occasional contemporary notes; and the restaurant is developing areas of speciality - beginning, perhaps, with the range of cocktails offered as aperitifs in the bar, then in menus which demonstrate a desire to offer a genuine choice from the usual line-up, including gluten-free dishes and vegetarian choices. Native Galway oysters are properly served, with a small salad and excellent breads, brown soda and walnut; other good dishes include oven roasted duck breast with sautéed sweet potatoes, caramelised oranges and Grand Marnier sauce, classic Dover sole on the bone, and a feathery chocolate fondant, with tarragon crème anglaise. Service is swift and attentive - and wine buffs will enjoy mulling over a wide-ranging list, presented by grape variety, with extensive notes; there are some bargains to be had, often including each week's featured wine. In addition to the main dinner menus, there is an evening bar menu, a lunch menu that extends through the afternoon and a pre-theatre menu that offers outstanding value. A fine new kitchen was installed in 2006, and there is a sense of something ambitious at work here - and it remains a relaxed restaurant, where people come to have a good time. **Seats 100** (private room, 20; also outdoor dining for 30). Children welcome. Air conditioning. Food served all day Mon-Sat: L 12-5, Set L €24.50 (value L €10.95). D 5-10, early bird €19.90 (5-7pm) Also à la carte L&D available, house wine from €19.90; no SC. Closed Sun, Bank Hols & Dec 25-Jan 2. Amex, MasterCard, Visa, Laser. **Directions:** Located in a courtyard just off High Street.

Galway City
Ⓔ RESTAURANT

Oscars Restaurant Galway

Dominick Street Galway Co Galway **Tel: 091 582 180**
Email: oscarsgalway@eircom.net Web: www.oscarsgalway.com

féile bia This is a love-it-or-loathe-it place: the decor is wildly wacky, with overloud jazz and dim lighting giving it a night clubby atmosphere - but few would question Michael O'Meara's position as Galway's most innovative chef. The menu, in an old-fashioned wine list cover, is extensive: cooking influences are eclectic, leaning towards Thailand and the East, although some dishes are quite European in style (roast rabbit with prunes) or even traditional Irish (fish cakes in an oatmeal crust); a starter platter for two might consist of onion bajhi, spiced chicken wings, mushrooms in garlic butter, fish cake, spare ribs and dip, yet Japanese style chicken yakatori is another option. Staff are very interested and attentive - and, while it's difficult to know what to make of the place at first, all the signs indicate something serious going on in the kitchen. Dishes enjoyed on a recent visit include a starter of tiger prawns tossed in garlic and lemon butter, with toasted rice and salad and, another prawn dish, a Malaysian style prawn and chilli samble - served very dramatically, as is the house style; but, despite the high drama, the cooking is very good, flavours are delicious and less adventurous diners can rely on a really good steak, or rack of Connemara lamb (served boulangère perhaps, with a wild crabapple reduction). Portions are large, including desserts which tend more towards the classics: nectarines poached with star anise and cinnamon, with a raspberry compôte and vanilla ice cream, perhaps. Good service, under the supervision of restaurant manager, Sinead Hughes, who is responsible for the wine list, which favours Europe, but also has some choice also from Australia, Chile, and California. Despite the wackiness of the room and presentation, everything on Oscars' extensive menu is prepared and cooked to order - and Michael O'Meara's expressive, confident cooking has earned a following in Galway. **Seats 45.** D Tue-Sun, 6.30-10 (5.30 Sat/5.30-9 Sun). Earlybird D €20 until 7 (6.30 Sat); also A la carte. House wines from about €19.50. MasterCard, Visa, Laser.

Galway City
HOTEL

Park House Hotel

Forster St Eyre Square Galway Co Galway
Tel: 091 564 924 Fax: 091 569 219
Email: parkhousehotel@eircom.net Web: www.parkhousehotel.ie

This hotel just off Eyre Square has the individuality that comes with owner-management and provides an exceptionally friendly and comfortable haven from the bustle of Galway, which seems to be constantly in celebration. Warmly decorated public areas include a well-run bar with lots of cosy corners where you can sink into a deep armchair and relax, and a choice of dining options - The Park for formal dining, and The Blue Room for informal meals. Guest rooms are spacious, very comfortably furnished and well-equipped for business travellers, with a desk, internet access and safe; generous, well-planned bathrooms are quite luxurious, with ample storage space and Molton Brown toiletries. Good breakfasts include a buffet selection (with a delicious fresh fruit salad), plus a choice of hot dishes, including fish - a perfectly cooked plaice, and undyed smoked haddock attracted praise on a recent visit. And you know you're in Galway when you find oysters on the room service menu... If you want a thoroughly Irish welcome in the heart of Galway, you could not do better than stay at this cosy and central hotel: the prices are very reasonable - and private parking for residents is a real plus. **Park Room Restaurant** (D & L Mon-Sat 12-3/6-9.30, D&L Sun 12.30-9); bar food L&D daily 12-9.30. Children welcome (under 12s free in parents' room, cots available free of charge). No pets. **Rooms 84** (5 junior suites, 3 for disabled, 3 family rooms). Lift. All day room service. B&B €115 pps, ss €115. Closed 24-26 Dec. Amex, MasterCard, Visa, Laser. **Directions:** Located adjacent to Eyre Square.

Galway City
HOTEL

Radisson SAS Hotel Galway

Lough Atalia Road Galway Co Galway
Tel: 091 538 300 Fax: 091 538 380
Email: sales.galway@radissonsas.com Web: www.radissonhotelgalway.com

Ideally situated on the waterfront, overlooking Lough Atalia, this fine contemporary hotel is more central than its scenic location might suggest, as the shops and restaurants off Eyre Square are only a few minutes walk. An impressive foyer with unusual sculptures, audacious greenery and a glass-walled lift raise the spirits, and attractive public areas include the cosy Backstage Bar and a pleasant lounge, in a sunny position looking over the roman-style leisure centre towards Lough Atalia. Guest rooms are furnished to a very high standard throughout with excellent bathrooms and facilities; luxurious 'Level 5' suites have superb views, individual terraces and much else besides - all of which, plus services such as 3-hour express laundry, make this the ideal business accommodation. [Radisson SAS Hotel Galway was our Business Hotel of the Year for 2005]. Excellent facilities for conferences and meetings are matched by outstanding leisure facilities, including a destination spa, Spirit One, which offers a range of beauty treatments, pamper programmes and spa break packages (details on application). Friendly, helpful staff are a great asset in every area of the hotel. Children welcome (under 16s free in parents' room; cot available without charge, baby sitting arranged) Conference/banqueting (1000/680). Video-conferencing, business centre. Leisure centre (17m pool, children's pool, gym, sauna, steam bath, Jacuzzi, outdoor hot tub); spa, beauty salon. No pets. Underground car park. Helipad. **Rooms 217** (2 suites, 2 junior suite, 16 executive, 184 no smoking, 11 for disabled.) Lift. B&B €120, ss €100. **Restaurant Marinas:** The dining experience in this large split-level restaurant has an understandably Scandinavian tone (including a buffet option), but decor in blues and browns is inspired by Lough Atalia and there is a sense of style and confidence about the room that is reflected in capable, friendly service. An extensive à la carte menu is international in style and flavours, although non fish eaters will find enduring favourites like chargrilled beef fillet, rack of lamb, and a vegetarian dish such as couscous stuffed bell peppers. Although there is little mention of local produce, wheat free and vegetarian dishes are highlighted, and also healthy eating options for guests attending Spirit One spa. But Marinas also offers the less usual option of a Scandinavian style buffet, which is an attractive choice if you are dining early, while everything is fresh. The best thing about the buffet is the varied selection of marinated salads and vegetables, cold meats, smoked fish, served with a wide choice of condiments and dressings; although some dishes will deteriorate while keeping hot, the buffet is good value and an enjoyable experience in such pleasant surroundings. The wine list is well thought out and includes about a dozen wines by the glass and nine half bottles - a boon for business guests dining alone. The restaurant works equally well next morning, for its famous Scandinavian buffet breakfast. *The Atrium Bar Menu has a more Irish tone, and offers an informal dining option, including a very reasonably priced 4-course buffet lunch. **Seats 220** (private room 80). Air conditioning. Toilets wheelchair accessible. Children welcome. D daily, 6-10.30, L Daily 12.30-3. D à la carte. House wines from €24. Guests dining in the hotel are entitled to a 35% discount on usual rates in the underground car park. Amex, Diners, MasterCard, Visa, Laser. **Directions:** By lane from Lough Atalia, 3 minutes walk from bus & train station.

Galway City
Ⓝ PUB

Sheridan's on the Dock

Galway Docks Galway Co Galway **Tel: 091 564 905**

A lovely stone building on the corner of the docks nearest the city, this is one of Galway's oldest pubs dating back to at least 1882, when the writer Padraic O'Conaire was born there. A sailor's pub, it still has local clientele and is now owned by the Sheridans of cheese fame, and managed by Seamus Sheridan It has been completely refurbished with black slate floors, white walls, pine tables, little stools and moss green window seats. It is a pub with - according to Seamus - the cheapest pint in Galway, the biggest selection of beers (30 bottled beers) and the biggest selection of wines 40 to date. Added to this is the best Honduras coffee and a small menu of some of the foods from their shop in the city. There are plans for a restaurant upstairs early in 2007. Chef Enda McEvoy operates the wine bar over Sheridans shop in Churchyard Street and some of the food is prepared there at the time of going to press, and Marianne Krause, who originally worked with Sheridans, is joining the team. At the time of our visit, soon after opening, the kitchen had not settled and, although the menu was short, dishes such as a ham hock, chorizo & bean stew and smoked seafood board were not yet fulfilling their potential however, everything is based on the finest ingredients, and the food has promise perhaps it would have been wiser to opt for the cheese board, which is offered in two sizes, using their best cheeses. *Also at: **Sheridans shop & The Winebar,** 14-16 Churchyard Street (091 564832; opposite St Nicholas' Church), where wine classes, readings, private parties and events can be held. Food served: 4.30-9.30pm Mon-Fri, from 12.30 Sat. Closed Sun. *Plans for extended opening hours at time of going to press. Amex, Diners, MasterCard, Visa, Laser. ◇

Galway City
ATMOSPHERIC PUB

Tigh Neachtain

Cross Street Galway Co Galway
Tel: 091 568 820 Fax: 091 563 940

Tigh Neachtain (Naughton's) is one of Galway's oldest pubs - the origins of the building are medieval and it has been in the same family for a century - the interior has remained unchanged since 1894. Quite unspoilt, it has great charm, an open fire and a friendly atmosphere - and the pint is good too. But perhaps the nicest thing of all is the way an impromptu traditional music session can get going at the drop of a hat. (Ard Bia restaurant is on the first floor - see entry). Closed 25 Dec & Good Fri. **Directions:** Situated on crossroads Quay Street/Cross Street/High Street. ◇

GALWAY

Galway is a vibrant, youthful city with an international reputation for exceptional foods - notably the native Irish oysters, which are a speciality of the Clarenbridge area and celebrated at the annual Oyster Festival there in September. The area is renowned for its seafood, especially shellfish, and speciality produce of all kinds - including local cheeses, fruit and vegetables, and specialities that do the rounds of other markets around the country - is on sale at the famous city centre Saturday Market. Restaurants in the area showcase local produce, and - although there is at present no major dining destination here - there are many good places to eat in both city and county. In addition to the establishments described, it may be useful to know about the following: **Westwood House Hotel** (091 521 442; www.westwoodhousehotel.com)is on the edge of the city and set back from the road - the N59 for Clifden; this well-managed hotel offers a good standard of accommodation for business or leisure at fairly reasonable prices. For budget accommodation, consider the city centre **Jurys Inn** (091 566 444;www.jurysinn.com) which is in a superb riverside location beside Spanish Arch, and adjacent to a mutlistorey carpark. East of the city, on the Tuam road, **Travelodge** (091 781 400; www.travelodge.ie) offers simple, clean, budget accommodation without service. Interesting restaurants in Galway are very numerous, but some offering a different experience from those described separately include **Kirwans's Lane Restaurant** (091 568 266), a stylish modern city centre restaurant in common ownership with O'Grady's of Barna (see entry); **Martine's Quay Street Wine Bar** (091 091 565 662; www.winebar.ie), which is in the same family ownership as the famous **McDonagh's** fish shop and restaurant, also on Quay Street; **Viña Mara Restaurant & Wine Bar**, Middle Street (091 561 610; www.vinamara.com) which brings a flavour of Spain to the city and specialises in seafood. For good Indian food, **Tulsi**, on Buttermilk Walk, Middle Street (091 564 831;www.tulsiindian.com) is a sister restaurant of the reliable Dublin restaurant of the same name; and, for style and informal fare (pizzas, pastas etc) at a reasonable price, head for **Milano** on Middle Street (091 568 488).

Aran Islands

An Dún

B&B/Restaurant

Inis Meain Aran Islands Co Galway **Tel: 099 73047** Fax: 099 73047
Email: anduninismeain@eircom.net Web: www.inismeainaccommodation.com

A short jump from Inis Mor, this interesting island is the most traditional of the group - very few cars, wonderful walks, and some people still wearing traditional clothes; by contrast the Inis Meain Knitting Co. factory and showroom offers great bargains on unique products only to be found in specialist outlets in Milan and Japan. At the foot of Dun Conchubhar (Connor's Fort) is Teresa and Padraic Faherty's restaurant and B&B, An Dún, which was the home of Padraig's grandfather and was the first restaurant on the island when it opened in 1989. In 2000 it was refurbished and extended to include en-suite bedrooms (modern, well fitted out, comfortable, great views), a new dining room and a mini-spa; Teresa is qualified in aromatherapy and can arrange packages for the new spa, especially off-season. Once you get here you may not be in a hurry to leave - one Swiss lady came for a week and stayed 31 days...The island's pretty traditional pub is just five minutes' walk. Mini-spa; aromatherapy. Shop. Children welcome (under 3 free in parents' room, cot available without charge, baby sitting can be arranged). No Pets. Garden. Walking, cycling. **Rooms 4** (all en-suite & no smoking). B&B €35-40, ss €5 (advance booking only in winter). No smoking establishment. **Restaurant:** There are two dining rooms - the inner one is original and cottagey, while a modern extension has wooden floors and windows on two sides, with wonderful sea and mountain views. The style and atmosphere is homely and everything is genuinely home-made - some of the best traditional food on the islands is to be found here. Local foods star: fish straight from currachs, (sometimes in time for breakfast); their own floury Inis Meain potatoes, fertilised in the traditional manner, with seaweed; freshly squeezed orange juice for breakfast... scones, crumbles and tarts using local fruits. Specialities include fish dishes like home-made chowder or a trio of ultra fresh mackerel, pollock and wild salmon on a lemony apricot sauce, then there's local lamb shank served with fresh herbs and interesting desserts like Baileys or brandy carrageen or blackberry tart. A short wine list includes a Concannon, from the Livermore vineyard in California, which has local connections. Children welcome. **Seats 40** (private room 12, outdoor seating 10). Reservations required (non-residents welcome). Wheelchair accessible. D daily in summer, 6.30-10. Set D available for residents (about €25), otherwise à la carte. House wine €16-18. Open all year except 1-2 weeks taken off-season. MasterCard, Visa. **Directions:** Centre of island, near church. ◇

Aran Islands

Kilmurvey House

GUESTHOUSE

Kilronan Inis Mór Aran Islands Co Galway
Tel: 099 61218 Fax: 099 61397
Email: kilmurveyhouse@eircom.net Web: www.kilmurveyhouse.com

This 150 year old stone house stands out as a beacon at the foot of the island's most famous attraction, Dun Aonghasa. On the west side of the island away from the bustle of Kilronan, it is just 3 minutes' walk from the island's only blue flag beach (ideal for a swim before breakfast) and a brisk 15-minute walk to the nearest pub. It's a fine house, with a large high-ceilinged hall and wide stairs giving a feeling of space and grandeur; it has been extended to provide extra en-suite accommodation - all with unrestricted views - and four extra bedrooms and a small function room are available for the 2007 season. The house is steeped in history - with portraits of the ferocious O'Flahertys, who owned it and the lands around, and one of the godfather of Oscar Wilde (Oscar O'Flaherty Fingall Wilde) hanging in the sitting room. Well kept, with neat manicured front garden and a feeling of space all around it, it has a walled garden at the back where vegetables, salads and herbs are grown - residents' dinners, served about five evenings each week, are based on home-grown and local produce: wonderful Inis Mór floury potatoes, wild salmon, home-made soups, fruit tarts... Short, but well-chosen, wine list too. Comfortable accommodation, good food, and Treasa Joyce's warm and chatty personality that make this an ideal place to stay for a cycling or walking holiday, or just to relax. Conferences (60). Children welcome (under 5s free in parents' room, cots available free of charge). No pets. Garden; walking. **Rooms 12** (all en-suite, 4 shower only, 1 family room, all no smoking), B&B €45-50, ss €15. Residents' D: €30, 7pm, by arrangement - please check when booking. House wine €18.50. Closed 31 Oct-1 Apr.* **Café An Sunda Caoch** (The Blind Sound) is a café at the Dun Aonghusa visitor centre, run independently by Treasa Joyce. An impressive long stone building in keeping with its surrounding craft shops, it serves delicious home-made food - notably good home baking - every day in summer, 11am-5pm. MasterCard, Visa, Laser. **Directions:** 7km (4.5 m) from Kilronan (take minibus from harbour, or rent bicycles).

Aran Islands
RESTAURANT

Mainistir House

Inis Mor Aran Islands Co Galway **Tel: 099 61169**
Email: mainistirhouse@eircom.net Web: www.mainistirhousearan.com

It's over fourteen years since Joel d'Anjou opened this long single storey whitewashed building on a hill overlooking Galway Bay as a hostel and restaurant, and it is still the most talked about place on the islands. Despite the hostel-type outer hall with lots of notices on the walls - the emphasis is shifting as there are not only small dormitories now, but 12 twin and double rooms and also two studio apartments; guesthouse comfort at a hostel rate is the offer and that's what it delivers, although you'd probably need to be a good mixer to get the most from this type of accommodation. But you don't even have to be staying here to experience Joel's famous 'Vaguely Vegetarian Buffet' which is served nightly and written on a blackboard. It's a quirky system, which everybody loves; on arrival you wait at a table outside, or on the wall, and mix with visitors from around the world until you're called through at 8 o'clock sharp. Six large tables are set up with checked cloths and everyone is served a starter - say a delicious lentil soup - then there are half a dozen dishes displayed on a big round table: a great white dish of wild salmon, paella, one of steaming puy lentils, fresh mixed salad leaves, green beans and great hunks of olive and onion foccacia with a wonderful home-made pesto sauce - and all this for about €12. If you want to push out the boat and spend another three or four euro you can finish off with home-made ice creams - a delicious espresso cream, perhaps, or classic brown bread - or a baked cheesecake. The actual dishes change daily, but this inventive and enthusiastic cook should not disappoint. Service is prompt (and colourful), this is great food - and amazing value. Bring your own wine. Christmas and New Year packages available. Restaurant **Seats 45.** D daily, 8pm. Set Menu €12. BYO wine. **Accommodation:** (8 private rooms plus hostel accommodation for up to 70; all no smoking). B&B €22.50pps, ss €7.50 (includes a simple breakfast of porridge/cereals & freshly baked bread each morning). MasterCard, Visa. **Directions:** 1 mile along the main road from the harbour. ◇

Aran Islands
€ B&B/RESTAURANT

Man Of Aran Cottages

Kilmurvey Inis More Aran Islands Co Galway
Tel: 099 61301 Fax: 099 61324
Email: manofaran@eircom.net Web: www.manofarancottage.com

Despite its fame - this is where the film Man of Aran was made - Joe and Maura Wolfe make visiting their home a genuine and personal experience. The cottage is right beside the sea and Kilmurvey beach, surrounded by wild flowers, and Joe has somehow managed to make a productive garden in this exposed location, so their meals usually include his organically grown vegetables (even artichokes and asparagus), salads, nasturtium flowers and young nettle leaves as well as Maura's home-made soups, stews and freshly-baked bread and cakes. Dinner is served in the little restaurant but there are benches in the garden, with stunning views across the sea towards the mountains, where you can enjoy an aperitif, or even eat outside on fine summer evenings. Packed lunches are available too. **Seats 20.** D at 7.30 (one sitting) is mainly for residents, but non-resident guests are also welcome by reservation. Set D about €35; wine list, about €16-33. No SC. No regular weekly closures, but check availability of meals when booking. Closed Nov-Feb. **Accommodation:** The three little bedrooms are basic but full of quaint, cottagey charm and they're very comfortable, although only one is en-suite. Breakfast will probably be a well cooked full-Irish - made special by Joe's beautifully sweet home-grown cherry tomatoes if you are lucky - although they'll do something different if you like. Children welcome (under 4s free in parents room). No pets. Children welcome (under 4s free in parents' room). No pets. Garden, walking. **Rooms 3** (1 en-suite, all no smoking). B&B €40, ss €10. Closed Nov-Feb. **Directions:** Mini bus or cycle from Kilronan, 6.5km (4 m).

Aran Islands
RESTAURANT/GUESTHOUSE

Pier House Guest House

Kilronan Inishmor Aran Islands Co Galway
Tel: 099 61417 Fax: 099 61122 Email: pierh@iol.ie

In a new building, right on the pier where the boats arrive, Maura & Padraig Joyce run this large well-kept guesthouse. As you walk from the ferry you will be offered tours of the island (mini-bus or pony and trap) or invited to hire one of the thousand or so bikes available on the island. Kilronan is the action centre of the island and Pier House is around the corner from pubs, cafés, a supermarket and the local hall; the attractive beach is round the next corner. While perhaps less characterful than some of the older houses, rooms are comfortable, with more facilities than most island accommodation (TV and phones as well as communal tea/coffee making facilities downstairs to use at any time) and views over sea and hills, and flag-stoned fields at the back. There's also a large residents' lounge and the house generally is comfortable and well-run. The restaurant is currently leased (see entry). *Four attractive self-catering apartments are also offered. Children welcome (under 5s free in parents' room). **Rooms 10** (all en-suite & no smoking, 1 ground floor). B&B €60 pps, ss about €20. MasterCard, Visa, Laser. **Directions:** Galway to Rosamhil thenFerry, 30 minutes to Island.

Aran Islands

N RESTAURANT

Pier House Restaurant

Kilronan Inis Mor Aran Islands Co Galway

Tel: 099 61811 Fax: 099 61122 Email: ddomalley@gmail.com

Brothers Damien and Ronan O'Malley, who are originally from Clifden, run this fine restaurant beside the pier it is in the same building as the Pier House Guest House (see entry) but they are run quite separately. It would be hard to imagine a better situation for an island restaurant, as it so close to the ferry and all the life of Kilronan village, and has beautiful views across the harbour. The only danger is that you might rush past it in your hurry to see the rest of the island but you would be missing a treat, and the hours are long, so it should be possible to have a quick bite here before you set off to see the sites, or a more leisurely meal if you are staying on the island, or before taking the ferry back to the mainland. The setting is very relaxing and, with seating equally divided between inside and outdoor tables, it's a good place to be whatever the weather. Damien and Ronan share the cooking, which is modern Irish in style and, naturally enough, features locally caught fresh fish and seafood (lobster thermidor, king scallops caramelised in olive oil with butternut squash, pea & parmesan risotto, perhaps, or baked fillet of Clare Island organic salmon with leeks & béarnaise sauce), although this is balanced by plenty of other choices - including an imaginative vegetarian dish, and meat such as braised Connemara lamb shank. Details, like good homemade breads, are excellent and delicious desserts include those updated classics like the house crème brulée that are so hard to resist. An extensive drinks menu offers spirits and beer as well as wine list. The brothers have earned a loyal following and Pier House Restaurant - which is regarded buy locals as 'the' place for a special evening out brings people back time and time again, both from the island and beyond. **Seats 44** (+outdoor 40, private room 12); Children welcome until 8; Open Daily L 12-5, D 6-10. Set Value D Sun-Thu €27, also a la carte. House wine €18. Closed mid Oct - mid Mar. MasterCard, Visa, Laser. **Directions:** Overlooking pier and bay 50 metres from the ferry point.

Aran Islands

B&B/GUESTHOUSE

Radharc An Chlair

Castle Village Inis Oirr Aran Islands Co Galway

Tel: 099 75019 Fax: 099 75019 Email: bridpoil@eircom.net

Brid Poil's welcoming dormer house looks over the Cliffs of Moher, with views of Galway Bay on the left, and has a great reputation for many years - she came over from Clare twenty years ago when she married Peadar and thought this would be a nice thing to do. Her many regular guests clearly agree - when the ferry from Doolin started, all Clare came over and are still coming so you need to book a month ahead. A keen cook, Brid makes all sorts of treats for different times of day (prune and apricot compôtes, tea and scones, home-made grapefruit marmalade, strawberry pavlova, bread and butter pudding...) and makes dinner for guests by arrangement. Children over 3 welcome. No pets. Garden; walking. **Rooms 6** (5 with en-suite shower, 1 bath, all no smoking). B&B €30-35, ss €5. Residents' D about €20. **No Credit Cards. Directions:** At Castle Village, overlooking Cliffs of Moher.

BALLINASLOE

Hayden's Hotel (090 964 2347; www.lynchotels.com) has been welcoming guests since 1803 and is still very much the centre of local activities; a useful place to break a journey as food is available all day Mon-Sat. For lunch and evening meals, try the surprisingly named **Kariba's Restaurant** (090 964 4830) on Society Street.

WWW.IRELAND-GUIDE.COM FOR THE BEST PLACES TO EAT, DRINK & STAY

Ballinasloe

BAR/RESTAURANT

Tohers Bar & Restaurant

18 Dunlo Street Ballinasloe Co Galway

Tel: 090 964 4848 Fax: 090 964 4844

féile bia This family-run pub on the main street is very attractive, with a traditional style bar on the ground floor and the restaurant in three separate dining rooms upstairs. A tempting bar lunch menu offers simple but tasty fare: if you can hit Ballinasloe at the right time, this is the spot to be and it's only a short walk up from the new marina too. Restaurant evening meals offer a wide choice of interesting international dishes - including specialities like chargrilled Asian-spiced salmon fillet with mascarpone leeks and tiger prawns with a roast pepper salsa & wasabi cream - and other timeless dishes with flavours closer to home, such as rack of local lamb with a herb crust, served on a bed of basil mash with a blackberry jus. Evening menus, including the early dinner menu, are also served in the bar. *At the time of going to press new developments at Tohers were not yet complete. Open 12 noon - normal closing time. Bar meals: L & D Mon-Sat, 12-3 & 6-9.30. Restaurant: D only, Tue-Sat, 6-9.30. L à la carte; early D €25 (Tue-Fri, 6-7pm); set D available for parties of 10 or more, €35; otherwise à la carte. Closed all Sun & D Mon, 25-26 Dec, Good Fri, 2 weeks Oct. MasterCard, Visa, Laser. **Directions:** Town centre, just off market square. ◇

Ballinasloe Area

Ballinderry Park

Ⓝ COUNTRY HOUSE/CASTLE/HISTORIC HOUSE

Kilconnell Ballinasloe Co Galway
Tel: 090 968 6796
Email: george@ballinderrypark.com Web: www.ballinderrypark.com

COUNTRY HOUSE BREAKFAST AWARD

At the end of a winding track, a smallish but perfectly proportioned early Georgian house comes into view. Recently rescued from dereliction, the house still demands more to be done, but George Gossip and his wife Suzie have worked wonders so far, creating a comfortable house out of a ruin. All the interior walls are clad in panelling not reclaimed, but new and designed by George. The effect is of timeless elegance and the palette of colours used in the various rooms is strikingly beautiful, especially the intense blue of the dining room. The bedrooms (two doubles with en suite bathrooms plus one twin room with shower only) are spacious, with comfortable beds and lots of light. While there are some eccentricities (hot water comes out of the cold tap in one of the bathrooms, for example) these only add to the special nature of a stay at Ballinderry Park. The books and photographs, old framed silhouettes and antique maps that one finds throughout the house clearly speak of the owners' own taste, rather than that of some interior designer. In the evening guests are invited to help themselves to a drink from a well-stocked cupboard then sit beside the log fire to peruse an interesting wine list that is both short and remarkably good value. George is not only a thoughtful host but well known in Ireland as a terrific cook, who seeks out the best ingredients and dreams up meals that are imaginative but don't strive for effect. And he will send you on your way with a wonderful breakfast as a warm memory of your stay: warm griddle cakes, superior sausages, rashers, delectable, buttery scrambled egg, field mushrooms and more, with home made jam and marmalade and cream to go with the peach-flavoured muesli And, before you leave the area, there is a particularly fine ruined abbey awaiting your attention in nearby Kilconnell village. Children welcome (under 3s free in parents' room, cots available free of charge). Cookery classes, fly fishing, walking, special interest breaks on site; Golf and hunting nearby. **Rooms 4** (2 shower only, all no smoking); Dogs permitted in certain areas. Residents' D at 8pm, €48. Closed 1 Nov - 31 Mar - but will open over winter weekends for groups. Amex, MasterCard, Visa, Laser. **Directions:** R348 from Ballinasloe, through Kilconnell, take left for Cappataggle, immediately left.

Ballyconneely

Emlaghmore Lodge

COUNTRY HOUSE

Ballyconneely Co Galway **Tel: 095 23529** Fax: 095 23860
Email: info@emlaghmore.com Web: www.emlaghmore.com

Built in 1862 as a small fishing lodge, Nicholas Tinne's magically located house is situated halfway between Roundstone and the 18-hole links golf course at Ballyconneely, in an Special Area of Conservation. It has been in the Tinne family for over 75 years and is quite a modest house in some ways, but it is comfortably (and interestingly) furnished in keeping with its age. It feels gloriously remote and has its own river running through the garden with fly fishing for sea trout, brown trout and even the occasional salmon, yet it is only a few hundred yards from sandy beaches and there are good pubs and restaurants nearby. Not that you will necessarily feel the need to wander in search of sustenance as Nick (who may be remembered from his famous restaurant, Snaffles, in Dublin) cooks dinner for residents: seafood treats like lobsters and mussels, rack of Connemara lamb and fillet of beef béarnaise... Not suitable for children. No pets. Golf, pony trekking, windsurfing nearby. Walking, fishing, garden. *Self-catering cottage also available nearby. **Rooms 4** (2 en-suite, 1 shower only; 2 with private bathrooms; all no smoking). B&B €80, €40. Residents D, €50 at 8.30 (please book by 10am.). House wine €20. Closed 1 Nov-Easter. MasterCard, Visa, **Directions:** Turn inland off coast road 100 metres on Roundstone side of Callow Bridge. 10 km (6 m) from Roundstone, 4km (2.5m) from Ballyconneely.

BARNA

Just west of Galway city, Barna is known for its fine beach, the Silver Strand; the village is clustered around an attractive little harbour and it's a popular place of escape for Galwegians at weekends and on summer evenings. Recent developments have brought a major change of scale, but, amongst the new builds, you will find **'The Twelve'** (091 764112; www.thetwelvehotel.ie); named after Connemara's famous Twelve Bens mountains, this contemporary boutique hotel is due to open shortly after the guide goes to press, and it promises to bring cutting edge glamour to an area renowned for its quiet, traditional style - the contrast will be interesting.

WWW.IRELAND-GUIDE.COM FOR THE BEST PLACES TO EAT, DRINK & STAY

Barna

Donnelly's of Barna

PUB

Barna Co Galway **Tel: 091 592 487**

Although Barna has now become so built up, Donnelly's of Barna is still a landmark at the crossroads, which leads down to the little harbour. Established in 1892, this seafood restaurant and bar, serves food all day and always seems to be full of both locals and visitors. It is a comfortable old world pub with little snugs, comfy corners and bric a brac as well as a more formal dining area looking on to a small car park. The same bar menu is served throughout the house (no distinction between bar and restaurant meals) and the atmosphere is a casual friendly pub rather than formal dining. The menu offers a lot of seafood starters like moules marinière, pan fried crab claws and timbale of marinated crayfish, and main courses of haddock mornay and fillet of salmon 'in a fisherman's net' are all regulars - balanced by other favourites like oven roast duckling and sirloin steak. Although not inexpensive, all hot main courses are complete (served with a selection of vegetables or fresh garden salad) and the combination of good cooking, friendly attentive service and a relaxing ambience make this good value. Desserts - homemade chocolate brownie with vanilla ice cream & raspberry sauce and passion fruit crème brulee among them - are enticing and the wine list is not too pricey with recommended house wines Libertas Cabernet Sauvignon 2005 from South Africa €18. ◇

Barna

O'Grady's on the Pier

RESTAURANT

Sea Point Barna Co Galway **Tel: 091 592 223**
Fax: 091 590 677 Web: www.ogradysonthepier.com

In a stunning position, with views over the harbour and beach to distant mountains, Michael O'Grady's charming seafood restaurant is popular among Galway diners, and especially so for Sunday lunch. It is a lovely spot on a fine summer's day, with pretty blue and yellow tables set up outside the restaurant, and old boats around the harbour adding to the atmosphere. Inside, the restaurant is low key - 'shabby chic' perhaps describes it, although broken tiles in the (very clean) loos take this a bit far; there are some contemporary elements (especially on the first floor) but tradition has also been allowed its place - the old fireplace has been kept, for example, which bodes well for cosy sessions in wild weather - and Michael's aim is for his seafood to be "simply prepared and very fresh as my father did it years ago". This he and his team are doing very well, although world cuisine is allowed a little space, notably among the daily blackboard specials. Interesting dinner menus offer a wonderful choice of perhaps 14 starters, 11 mains and 8 desserts plus daily specials. The kitchen can sometimes come under pressure at very busy times but, at its best, the skill and cooking style is impressive - dishes enjoyed on a recent visit included starters of gloriously fresh-tasting steamed Galway mussels in a white wine and garlic cream, and a tian of Galway Bay lobster and crab, with lime crème fraîche & quenelles of guacamole - delicious and so simply put together. But the dish attracting particular praise was a main course special Tasting Trio of Seafood, composed of seared king scallops, with pepper basmati rice, white wine & fennel velouté; pan-fried fillet of sea bass, with creamy mash, sweet chilli & chive sauce; and grilled fillet of sea-trout, with curry mash and sun-dried tomato cream sauce. Whew! And, while it may sound OTT, it is skilfully judged, and one of the most delicious seafood dishes you are likely to encounter anywhere. (Ever innovative, Michael was winner of our Creative Seafood Dish Award in 2001.) There's always some choice for non seafood eaters, and desserts are delicious too - if you can find room, a vanilla nut icecream cluster with chocolate & caramel sauce might be tempting. Service, under the direction of the host, is attentive, and there's an extensive wine list. Children welcome. **Seats 95** (private room 25, outdoor seating 25). Air-conditioning. D daily 6-10, L Sun only 12.30-2.45. Set Sun L €24.50, D à la carte; house wine €18.50. Closed Christmas week. Amex, MasterCard, Visa, Laser. **Directions:** 4 miles west of Galway city on the Spiddal Road. ◇

Cashel

Cashel House Hotel

HOTEL/RESTAURANT/COUNTRY HOUSE

Cashel Connemara Co Galway
Tel: 095 31001 Fax: 095 31077
Email: res@cashel-house-hotel.com Web: www.cashel-house-hotel.com

Dermot and Kay McEvilly were among the pioneers of the Irish country house movement when they opened Cashel House as an hotel in 1968. The following year General and Madame de Gaulle chose to stay for two weeks, an historic visit of which the McEvillys are justly proud - look out for the photographs and other memorabilia in the hall. The de Gaulle visit meant immediate recognition for the hotel, but it did even more for Ireland by putting the Gallic seal of approval on Irish hospitality and food. The beautiful gardens, which run down to a private beach, contribute greatly to the atmosphere, and the accommodation includes especially comfortable ground floor garden suites, which are also suitable for less able guests (wheelchair accessible, but no special grab rails etc in bathrooms). Relaxed hospitality combined with professionalism have earned an international reputation for this outstanding hotel and its qualities are perhaps best seen in details - log fires that burn throughout the year, day rooms furnished with antiques and filled with fresh flowers from the garden, rooms that are individually decorated with many thoughtful touches. Service (with all day room service, including all meals) is impeccable, and delicious breakfasts include a wonderful buffet display of home-made and local produce (Cashel House was the Connaught winner of our Irish Breakfast Awards in 2001). Conference/banqueting (15/80). Children welcome; cot available (€10); baby sitting arranged; playroom. Pets permitted in some areas. Walking, tennis. Gardens (open to the public). Well-located for local horse shows (Justice Connemara Pony & Irish Sport Horse Stud Farm is located within the hotel grounds; guests may view).* Self-catering accommodation is also available nearby; details on application. **Rooms 32** (13 suites, 4 family rooms, 6 ground floor, 1 shower only). B&B €135pps, no ss; SC12.5%. **Restaurant:** A large conservatory extension makes the most of the outlook onto the lovely gardens around this well-appointed split-level restaurant, which is open to non-residents. Although ably assisted by a well-trained staff, including Arturo Amit who has been head chef since 2003, Dermot McEvilly has overseen the kitchen personally since the hotel opened, providing a rare consistency of style in five-course dinners that showcase local produce, notably seafood. Despite occasional world influences - in a tasting plate of seafood in a green chilli and coconut broth, for example - the tone is classic: roast Connemara lamb is an enduring favourite and there is an emphasis on home-grown fruit and vegetables, including some fine vegetarian dishes and homely desserts, such as rhubarb or apple tart, or strawberries and cream - then farmhouse cheeses come with home-baked biscuits. The personal supervision of Kay McEvilly and restaurant manager Ray Doorley ensures caring service, and an extensive and informative wine list includes many special bottles for the connoisseur - yet there are also plenty of well-chosen, more accessible wines (under €30), and a good choice of half bottles. *A short à la carte bar lunch menu offers interesting snacks and sandwiches, but also delicious hot meals, including Irish stew or even lobster if desired; afternoon teas are also served daily in the bar. (Bar L12.30-2.30, Afternoon Tea 2.30-5). Restaurant **Seats 85.** D daily 7-9, L 12-2.30. Set D €51. Set Sun L €30; also à la carte. House wine €25. 12.5% s.c. Closed 2 Jan-2 Feb. Amex, MasterCard, Visa, Laser. **Directions:** South off N59 (Galway-Clifden road), 1 mile west of Recess turn left.

Cashel

HOTEL/RESTAURANT

Zetland Country House

Cashel Bay Cashel Co Galway
Tel: 095 31111 Fax: 095 31117
Email: zetland@iol.ie Web: www.zetland.com

Originally built as a sporting lodge in the early 19th century, Zetland House is on an elevated site, with views over Cashel Bay and still makes a good base for fishing holidays. This is a charming and hospitable house, with a light and airy atmosphere and an elegance bordering on luxury, in both its spacious antique-furnished public areas and bedrooms which are individually decorated in a relaxed country house style, and include two lovely newer rooms, more recently opened. The gardens surrounding the house are very lovely too, greatly enhancing the peaceful atmosphere of the house. Its unusual name dates from the time when the Shetland Islands were under Norwegian rule and known as the Zetlands - the Earl of Zetland (Lord Viceroy 1888-1890) was a frequent visitor here, hence the name. Conference/banqueting (30/75). Tennis, cycling, walking. Snooker, Children welcome (cot available, €10; baby sitting arranged). Pets permitted by arrangement in certain areas. Garden. **Rooms 20** (2 family rooms, 1 shower only, 3 ground floor, all no smoking) B&B €120pps, ss €45. **Restaurant:** Like the rest of this lovely hotel, the dining room is bright, spacious and elegant. Decorated in soft, pretty shades of pale yellow and peach that contrast well with antique furniture - including a fine sideboard where plates and silver are displayed - the restaurant is in a prime position for enjoying the view and makes a wonderful place to watch the light fading over the mountains and the sea. A warm welcome and quietly efficient service from staff who are clearly happy in their work greatly enhances the pleasure of dining here. The kitchen makes good use of the vegetables and herbs grown in the hotel garden, along with the best of local produce, notably lobster - and also game in season. From a menu offering about five equally enticing dishes on each course, a typical meal might be Connemara crab & cucumber risotto, pink grapefruit and gin sorbet and chargrilled rump of lamb (served, perhaps, with a goats cheese and potato mousse and tapenade jus); finish with Irish cheeses with apple chutney, or a classic dessert such as warm dark chocolate fondant with whiskey ice cream. Excellent breakfasts are also served in the restaurant - home-made preserves are an especially delicious feature. **Seats 45;** Non residents welcome by reservation; children welcome. D daily 7-9; gourmet D €56. *Snack lunches available, 12-2 daily. Restaurant SC 12.5%. Amex, Diners, MasterCard, Visa, Laser. **Directions:** N59 from Galway. Turn left after Recess.

CLAREGALWAY

Just north-east of Galway on the junction of the N17 and N18 roads, Claregalway is now a fast-growing satellite town for Galway city. Business guests visiting the area will find all the required facilities at the large **Claregalway Hotel** (091 738300; www.claregalwayhotel.ie), or at the smaller more intimate hotel, **The Arches** (www.arches-hotel.com). Only 10km from the city, the town is very convenient to Galway airport.

WWW.IRELAND-GUIDE.COM FOR THE BEST PLACES TO EAT, DRINK & STAY

Clarinbridge

RESTAURANT

The Old School House Restaurant

Clarinbridge Co Galway **Tel: 091 796 898**
Fax: 091 796 117 Web: www.oldschoolhouserestaurant.com

féile bia Although it is beside the main road, Kenneth Connolly's old schoolhouse restaurant is behind a high wall in its own garden, and has parking to the rear, so it has a pleasantly rural feel. The dining room is spacious and full of character: bright and tall-windowed, with quality china and linen napkins, interesting prints on the walls - and welcoming staff who offer menus promptly, in the bar/reception area or at your table. The choice offered is wide and well-organised - perhaps a dozen starters (with local oysters getting a little section to themselves) and at least as many main courses. It's the kind of menu that can be difficult to choose from as everything seems equally appealing, with some really tempting first courses (trio of organic Aran Island smoked salmon & Marie Rose sauce, perhaps, or a vegetarian salad of mixed leaves, with Mediterranean vegetables & herb vinaigrette. Seafood is predictably strong (although it is disappointing to find imports like tiger pawns lurking amongst the local catches), but there will also be some attractive meat and poultry dishes (a choice off fillet or T-bone steak, for example, or pan-fried supreme of chicken, with champ and herb & mushroom sauce), and several creative vegetarian options. The cooking style is not especially adventurous, but carefully sourced quality Irish produce is used for the most part and portions are generous and appealingly presented. To finish, the well-chosen Irish cheeseboard (served with a home-made chutney) is a good bet. A fairly priced wine list offers a wide range of styles. Efficient service, from knowledgeable and attentive staff, adds to the pleasure of a meal here. **Seats 60** (private room, 30, outdoor, 16). Toilets wheelchair accessible. D Tue-Sun, 6.30-10; L Sun only 12.30-2.30. Early D €25, 6.30-7.30. D à la carte. Set Sun L, €24 (children's menu €10). House wine €18.50. Closed Mon, 24-27 Dec, 31 Dec-3 Jan. Amex, MasterCard, Visa, Laser. **Directions:** 9km (6 miles) from Galway city, on N18 Galway-Limerick road.

CLIFDEN

The main town of Connemara, Clifden nestles on the edge of the Atlantic with a dramatic backdrop of mountains. Although it has been somewhat over-developed recently, it remains an excellent base for exploring this exceptionally scenic area; the quality of food and accommodation available in and around the town is very high, and there is plenty to do: walking, horse riding, and bathing are all on the doorstep, the Connemara Garden Trail is relaxing and educational, and the island of Inishbofin can be visited by ferry from Cleggan. For those who require a leisure centre and/or conference facilities, **The Clifden Station House Hotel** (095 21699; www.clifdenstationhouse.com) is built on the site on the old railway station and has everything required; the complex also includes a railway museum and a range of upmarket shops and boutiques. Outside the town, the beautifully located **Rock Glen Country House Hotel** (095 21035;www.rockglenhotel.com) offers space and a peaceful atmosphere.

WWW.IRELAND-GUIDE.COM FOR THE BEST PLACES TO EAT, DRINK & STAY

Clifden

HOTEL

Abbeyglen Castle Hotel

Sky Road Clifden Co Galway **Tel: 095 21201** Fax: 095 21797
Email: info@abbeyglen.ie Web: www.abbeyglen.ie

Set romantically in its own parkland valley overlooking Clifden and the sea, Abbeyglen is family-owned and run in a very hands-on fashion by Paul and Brian Hughes. It's a place that has won a lot of friends over the years and it's easy to see why: from the minute arriving guests meet the parrot at reception it's clear that this place is different; it's big and comfortable and laid-back - and there's a generosity of spirit about the place which is very charming. Complimentary afternoon tea for residents is a particularly hospitable speciality, served in a spacious drawing room or in front of an open peat fire in the relaxing, pubby bar, where many a late night is spent. A major building programme has recently been completed, adding six new superior rooms - and the existing bedrooms (all with good bathrooms) are quite big and have been recently refurbished, as part of the improvement programme. Live music. Snooker. Tennis. Pitch & putt. Outdoor swimming pool. Not suitable for children. No pets. Garden. Wheelchair accessible. Lift. Helipad. **Rooms 45** (25 superior, 20 standard, all en-suite). Room service (limited hours). B&B €101pps, ss €30. 12.5% s.c. Closed 7 Jan-2 Feb Amex, Diners, MasterCard, Visa, Laser. **Directions:** About 300 metres / yards out of Clifden on the Sky Road, on the left.

Clifden

HOTEL/RESTAURANT

Ardagh Hotel & Restaurant

Ballyconneely Road Clifden Co Galway
Tel: 095 21384 Fax: 095 21314
Email: ardaghhotel@eircom.net Web: www.ardaghhotel.com

féile bia

Beautifully located, overlooking Ardbear Bay, Stephane and Monique Bauvet's family-run hotel is well known for quiet hospitality, low key comfort and good food. Public areas have style, in a relaxed homely way: turf fires, comfortable armchairs, classic country colours, and a plant-filled conservatory area upstairs are pleasing to the eye and indicate that peaceful relaxation is the aim here. Bedrooms vary according to their position but are well-furnished with all the amenities required for a comfortable stay, and have been recently renovated. (Not all have sea views - single rooms are at the back, with a pleasant countryside outlook). Bedrooms include some extra large rooms, especially suitable for families. Children welcome (cot available without charge, baby sitting arranged). Pets permitted. Garden, walking; snooker, pool table. **Rooms 17** (2 suites, 4 shower only, 2 family rooms, all no smoking). Room service (all day). B&B €87.50 pps, ss €30.* Short / off-season breaks available. **Restaurant:** This long-established restaurant is a well-appointed light-filled room on the first floor, with stunning lake and mountain views - and a warm reception is sure to set the tone for an enjoyable evening. Monique Bauvet's menus are wide-ranging: an excellent choice of local seafood usually includes oysters, mussels, scallops, wild salmon, crab, lobster, and a variety of fish including black (Dover) sole, and there will be a fair choice of meats too, including local lamb - a roast rack, perhaps, with roasted celeriac mash and a rosemary & thyme jus - along with some poultry and at least one imaginative vegetarian choice. Cooking is generally reliable and delicious home-made breads, well-flavoured soups (including the creamy house chowder), interesting vegetables, home-grown salads and home-made ice creams are among the details that stand out, and there is also a good cheese selection, served with grapes, celery and crackers. Home-made petits fours will follow with your coffee (or tea/tisane). Relaxed service, under the direction of Stéphane Bauvet, contributes to an atmosphere of confident professionalism that greatly enhances a meal here. A fairly priced wine list strong on old world wines, especially Bordeaux and Burgundy, also has an interesting choice from South Africa and offers eight half bottles and several magnums. **Seats 60.** D 7.15-9.30 daily (Sun D 7.30-9.15), Set D €50, à la carte also available; house wine €21.50; sc discretionary. Closed Nov-Mar. Amex, Diners, MasterCard, Visa, Laser. **Directions:** 3 km outside Clifden on Ballyconneely Road.

Clifden

COUNTRY HOUSE

Dolphin Beach Country House

Lower Sky Road Clifden Co Galway
Tel: 095 21204 Fax: 095 22935
Email: stay@dolphinbeachhouse.com Web: www.dolphinbeachhouse.com

The Foyle family's stunning beachside house is set in 14 acres of wilderness, which makes a wonderful contrast to the style and comfort within. The house, which has an early 19th century farmhouse at its heart, was renovated and extended by Billy and Barbara Foyle, who then opened for guests in 1998. Those familiar with the old Foyle magic (Rosleague Manor, Quay House) will find it a-plenty here, where the family talent for creating original interiors is seen especially in Billy's unusual woodwork - bedheads, mirror frames, anything that takes his fancy - which brings a delightfully quirky element to the fresh style of this warm and friendly house. There's a wonderful feeling of quality throughout: bedrooms are finished to a very high standard, with antique furniture, pristine bedlinen, lovely bathrooms and underfloor heating; television and tea/coffee making facilities are available on request. Now that Billy and Barbara's daughters Clodagh (managing) and Sinead (cooking) have key roles, they bring new energy and enthusiasm to this unique house and the atmosphere is delightful. The family grow their own organic vegetables too, and these, together with other local produce, notably seafood and Connemara lamb, are used for Sinead's lovely evening meals, which are served in a dining room overlooking the beach (ask about dinner when booking your room). Breakfast follows the same philosophy

- you can even collect your own free-range eggs for breakfast. (Dolphin Beach was winner of our Irish Breakfast Award for Connacht in 2003). D residents only; small wine list, all under €33. Not suitable for children under 12. Pets permitted by prior arrangement. Walking, garden, safe swimming off rocky beach. **Rooms 9** (5 shower only, all no smoking). B&B €70 pps, ss €20. D 7-8pm, €38 (booking essential, residents only); house wine €24. Closed 15 Dec-1 Feb. MasterCard, Visa, Laser. **Directions:** Left off Sky Road, about 5km (3 miles) from Clifden.

Clifden

G's Restaurant (formerly The Spice Club)

Ⓝ RESTAURANT

The Square Market St Clifden Co Galway **Tel: 095 22323**

A fairly recent arrival on the Clifden restaurant scene, this restaurant has a striking black and maroon shopfront set back from a corner of the square (and with menus clearly displayed outside), and is popular with discerning locals in the know. A small reception area leads to a long restaurant with well spaced tables and maroon, black and cream painted walls decorated with mirrors and oriental print; while not very atmospheric, a window at one end overlooks the estuary - and, once your food arrives, it will take centre stage, notably due to excellent seafood cooking: lovely appetisers of deep-fried mini Thai fish cakes, perhaps, or tasty crab lasagne, and main courses like crisp pan-fried sea bass on a tangy base of ratatouille, garlic, spinach and a little grain mustard butter sauce, or scallops seared to perfection with a butter sauce flavoured with smoked bacon. The à la carte menu is supplemented by a list of daily specials, desserts include refreshing fruity options, and there's a well-priced list of about two dozen wines. **Seats 64.** Open D only, Daily in summer. Closed 25/26 Dec, 2 weeks Jan & Mon-Wed low season. Ringing to check opening times off season is highly recommended. MasterCard, Visa, Laser. **Directions:** In centre of Clifden. ◇

Clifden

Mitchell's Restaurant

RESTAURANT

Market Street Clifden Connemara Co Galway
Tel: 095 21867 Fax: 095 21770

féile bia This attractive and well-managed family-run restaurant offers efficient, welcoming service and very agreeable "good home cooking" all day, every day throughout a long season - and they have been doing so, with admirable consistency, since 1991. An all-day menu offers a wide range of lightish fare - everything from sandwiches and wraps to seafood chowder and seafood tagliatelle; the international flavours are there but how refreshing it is to find old friends like deep-fried Gubbeen cheese and bacon & cabbage there amongst the home-made spicy fish cakes and fresh crab salad with home-made brown bread. There's some overlap onto an à la carte evening menu, which offers a judicious selection from the snack menu but the choice is much wider and includes half a dozen appealing meat and poultry dishes (traditional Irish stew made with Connemara lamb, for example, and roast half duckling with sage & onion stuffing and red wine gravy) and a vegetarian dish of the day as well as eight or nine seafood dishes and a choice of main course salads. This is a very fair place, offering honest food at honest prices: half dozen local oysters at about €10, for example, and a seafood platter for about €20. **Seats 70.** Air conditioning. Not suitable for children after 6 pm. Open daily, 12-10; set D €26.50, 3 course; also à la carte. House wine from €18.50. Closed Nov-Feb. Amex, Diners, MasterCard, Visa, Laser. **Directions:** Next to SuperValu supermarket.

Clifden

The Quay House

GUESTHOUSE

Beach Road Clifden Co Galway
Tel: 095 21369 Fax: 095 21608
Email: thequay@iol.ie Web: www.thequayhouse.com

In a lovely location - the house is right on the harbour, with pretty water views when the tide is in - The Quay House was built around 1820. It has the distinction of being the oldest building in Clifden and has also had a surprisingly varied usage: it was originally the harbourmaster's house, then a convent, then a monastery; it was converted into a hotel at the turn of the century and finally, since 1993, has been relishing its most enjoyable phase as a guesthouse, in the incomparable hands of long-time hoteliers, Paddy and Julia Foyle. It's a fine house, with spacious rooms - including a stylishly homely drawing room with an open fire, that makes a relaxing place to read, or to come back to after an evening out. And the accommodation is exceptionally comfortable, in airy, wittily decorated and sumptuously furnished rooms that include not only two wheelchair-friendly rooms, but also seven newer studio rooms, with small fitted kitchens, balconies overlooking the harbour and, as in the original rooms, all have excellent bathrooms with full bath and shower. Breakfast is served in a charming conservatory, decorated with a collection of silver domes and trailing Virginia creeper criss-crossing the room on strings, and it is simply superb - treats include a buffet laid out to tempt you as you enter, with fresh and dried fruits, yoghurt and cheeses, freshly baked breads and home-made preserves...and (how nice to see the priorities here) orders for your tea or coffee are taken even before you sit down at a table beautifully set up with individual jugs of freshly squeezed orange juice. Hot dishes - a perfectly cooked traditional Irish, scrambled eggs with smoked salmon, kedgeree and pan-fried lemon sole - are all served with crisp toast (crusts removed), and fresh top-ups of tea and coffee. Although officially closed in winter it is always worth inquiring. *The Quay House was our Guesthouse of the Year for 2006, and also the national winner of the Irish Breakfast Awards. Children under 12 free in parents' room (cots available without charge). No pets. Garden. Walking. **Rooms 14** (all with full bathrooms, 2 on ground floor, all no smoking, 1 for disabled). B&B €75pps, ss €40. Closed Nov-mid Mar. MasterCard, Visa, Laser. **Directions:** 2 minutes from town centre, overlooking Clifden harbour - follow signs to the Beach Road.

Clifden

Sea Mist House

B&B

Clifden Connemara Co Galway **Tel: 095 21441**
Email: sgriffin@eircom.net Web: www.connemara.net/seamist

Sheila Griffin's attractive house was built in 1825, using local quarried stone. Major renovations undertaken over the last few years have retained its character while adding modern comforts, allowing her to offer stylish and comfortable accommodation. A recently added conservatory has made a lovely, a spacious room overlooking the garden, where guests can relax - and fruit from the garden is used in spiced fruit compôtes and preserves which appear at breakfast along with home-made breads, American-style pancakes with fresh fruit salsa and scrambled eggs with smoked salmon and a special of the day which brings an element of surprise to the menu each morning. The cottage garden adjacent to the house has been developing over the years and is now reaching maturity - guests are welcome to wander through it and soak in the tranquil atmosphere. There are also many other gardens to visit nearby (the Connemara Garden Trail). Private parking (3). No pets. Garden. **Rooms 4** (all shower only & no-smoking, 1 family room). B&B €50pps, ss €20. Closed Christmas, also mid-week off season. MasterCard, Visa, Laser. **Directions:** Left at square, a little down on right.

Clifden

Two Dog Café

€ CAFÉ

1 Church Hill Clifden Co Galway **Tel: 095 22186** Fax: 095 22195
Email: kennel@twodogcafe.ie Web: www.twodogcafe.ie

This smashing little café just off the square in Clifden is a gem, combining home-made cakes, gourmet sandwiches and aromatic Illy coffee with charming service, a laid-back newspaper-reading atmosphere and an Internet cafe upstairs. Ingredients are carefully sourced, using fresh local produce where possible (often from the local farmers' market), and everything is freshly made on the premises. They do several imaginative soups - an unusual sweet potato & mulato soup with honey and cream came is a favourite when we visit - and a wide range of gourmet sandwiches, wraps, panini and quiches just the sort of thing for a light daytime bite. Try their quesadillas (tangy cheddar cheese, sliced scallions & chopped chillis & fresh coriander pan-toasted between two four tortillas, then served with soured cream and spicy salsa dips) or chicken Caesar salad - with romaine lettuce, smoked chicken, bacon, parmesan, homemade croutons and a freshly-prepared Caesar dressing, perhaps. But, luscious as all the wholesome savoury choices may be, it's really the display of home bakes that proves irresistible to any with the slightest hint of a sweet tooth. Scones, brownies, pan-roasted pear cake, orange & almond cake (flourless - ideal for coeliacs) and light and tasty raspberry cake...Just like granny used to make magic! A must for daytime visitors to Clifden. Children welcome. **Seats 28.** Open daytime 10.30-4.30 (Sun, Aug only 12.30-4). No reservations. Closed Sun all year except Aug, Mon Dec- May & all Nov, last week in Apr. MasterCard, Visa, **Directions:** Behind the Alcock & Brown Hotel in Market Square.

CLONBUR

This attractive village is a popular base for walking holidays, and fishing on Lough Corrib and Lough Mask. The Lynch family's refurbished (Victorian) **Fairhill House Hotel** (094 954 6176; www.fairhill-house.com) is comfortable and friendly - and everybody loves **John J Burke's** Atmospheric pub/restaurant, which is renowned for both food and music.

WWW.IRELAND-GUIDE.COM FOR THE BEST PLACES TO EAT, DRINK & STAY

Clonbur

FARMHOUSE

Ballykine House

Clonbur Co Galway **Tel: 094 954 6150** Fax: 094 954 6150
Email: ballykine@eircom.net Web: www.ballykinehouse-clonbur-cong.com

Comfortable accommodation and Ann Lambe's warm hospitality make this an appealing base for a peaceful holiday. There are guided forest walks from the house, angling on Lough Corrib, an equestrian centre (at nearby Ashford Castle) and bikes for hire locally. It's also well-placed for touring Connemara. Moderately priced rooms have TV, tea/coffee making facilities and hairdryers. No evening meals but the pubs and restaurants of Clonbur - are all within walking distance, and so is Ashford Castle. On fine evenings guests often like to walk to the pub or restaurant of their choice and get a lift back later. There's plenty of comfortable seating in the sitting room and conservatory for lounging and chatting, also a pool table - and a drying room for anglers. A new library room for visitors was recently completed. Garden. **Rooms 5** (4 with en-suite shower; 1 with private bath, restricted use), B&B €30, ss €10. Closed 1 Nov-17 Mar. **No Credit Cards**. **Directions:** 3 km from Cong, on Cong/Clonbur Rd - R345.

Craughwell

☆COUNTRY HOUSE

St. Clerans Country House

Craughwell Co Galway
Tel: 091 846 555 Fax: 091 846 600
Email: info@stclerans.com Web: www.stclerans.com

Once the home of the film director John Huston, St Clerans is a magnificent 18th century manor house on 45 acres of gardens and grounds, beautifully located in rolling countryside. It was carefully restored some years ago by the current owner, the American entertainer Merv Griffin, and decorated with no expense spared to make a sumptuous, hedonistically luxurious country retreat and restaurant. There's a great sense of fun about the furnishing and everything is of the best possible quality; reception rooms include a magnificently flamboyant drawing room and spacious bedrooms that are individually decorated and have peaceful garden and countryside views; most are done in what might best be described as an upbeat country house style, while others - particularly those on the lower ground floor, including John Huston's own favourite room, which opens out onto a terrace with steps up to the garden - are restrained, almost subdued, in atmosphere. All are spacious, with luxuriously appointed bathrooms (one has its original shower only) and a wonderful away-from-it-all feeling. Housekeeping is immaculate, and there was a discernible sense of purposeful new management on recent visits by the Guide. **Rooms 12** (6 junior suites, 6 executive. 1 shower only, 4 gound floor). B&B €200 pps, no ss. Children under 11 years free in parents room; cots available free of charge; baby sitting arranged. Closed 24-26 Dec. **Restaurant:** The restaurant, which is open to non-residents by reservation, provides an elegant setting for cooking by Japanese head chef Hisashi Kumagai (Kuma). The room has lovely views of pastoral east Galway, including a fine tree which dominates a near meadow, and is floodlit at night; a crimson carpet and heavy, matching drapes set a slightly decadent tone but appointments are otherwise quite classical, with plain white linen-clad tables, fine glassware, silver, and china and gold candle holders. Aperitifs are served in the drawing room by a turf fire, to muted strains of Chopin and Beethoven (but not from the grand piano that suits the room so well). Unpriced 4-course set dinner menus, printed on parchment-like paper tied with ribbon, offer a choice of 4 or 5 dishes on each course. Kuma is an accomplished chef, ingredients are always the very best and his food is beautifully presented. A spring roll of oak-smoked salmon and avocado with sesame seed & hoisin sauce is an outstanding example of Kuma's oriental/western fusion cooking, and an equally exceptional main course is roulade of local lamb with prosciutto ham with mint-scented rosemary sauce - a stunning tribute to Connemara lamb, and the inclusion of old fashioned floury new potatoes with a modern al dente selection is delightful. Desserts might include an unusual green tea ice cream. The wine list is shortish for an establishment of this status, but includes a good choice of half bottles. Service by local staff is charming and attentive and, overall, local diners are fortunate to have this rare gem within striking distance of Galway city. **Seats 30.** D 7-9pm daily, €65. SC discretionary. Closed 24-26 Dec. Amex, MasterCard, Visa, Laser. **Directions:** 4km (2 miles) off N6 between Loughrea and Craughwell.

Furbo

HOTEL/RESTAURANT

Connemara Coast Hotel

Furbo Co Galway **Tel: 091 592 108** Fax: 091 555 065
Email: info@connemaracoast.ie Web: www.sinnotthotels.com

féile bia This beautifully located hotel is an attractive building which makes the best possible use of the site without intruding on the surroundings: set on the sea side of the road, in its own extensive grounds, it is hard to credit that Galway city is only a 10 minute drive away. An impressive foyer decorated with fresh flowers sets the tone on entering, and spacious public areas include a mezzanine and library (which is a lovely space), and a new patio area with a gazebo at the front.

Facilities are particularly good too - a fine bar, two restaurants, a children's playroom and a leisure centre (which has a Canadian hot tub) among them. A policy of constant refurbishment and upgrading of facilities ensures that the hotel has a warm, well-cared for atmosphere; there was major refurbishment of rooms in 2004, and upgrading is continuing throughout. This most likeable of hotels is understandably popular for conferences - the facilities and service are both excellent, and the location is magic. A range of special breaks is offered both here and at its fine sister hotel, Brooks Hotel, in Dublin (details on application). Conference/banqueting (400/250). Children welcome (under 3 free in parents' room; cots available without charge, baby sitting arranged; playroom; crèche). Leisure centre, indoor swimming pool; beauty salon. Playground; pool table. No pets. Walking, tennis, garden. **Rooms 112** (1 suite, 9 executive rooms, 7 ground floor, 25 family rooms, 1 for disabled, 80 no smoking). B&B €120pps, ss €40. 24 hr room service. **Restaurant:** There are two dining rooms - one modern with a grand piano in the centre - and the food is seriously good, helped by staggered dining times that allow the kitchen to present every dish at its best. Although the tableware, glasses and do not match the quality of the food (there are plans for change here, we are told), welcoming details such as proper butter curls and good nutty breads are promising. Appealing menus name head chef Ulriche Hoeche from Germany, also Patrick Kelly, restaurant manager and sommelier - and offer a wide range of dishes, notably local seafood - braised monkfish in a fennel, celery & tomato fondue, with smoked bacon, is a speciality and local meats are represented by roast rack of lamb, cooked pink, with a herb & mustard crust. A new style a la carte menu had just been introduced at the time of a recent visit, and dishes attracting special praise included coconut prawns with tequila lime dip ('delicious and wonderful prawns in tempura batter') and slow braised pork belly served with an aniseed jus & smoked aubergine caviar - a superb dish of meltingly tender pork, although definitely a 'man's' portion. Conference/banqueting (400/250). Children welcome (under 3 free in parents' room; cots available without charge, baby sitting arranged; playroom; crèche). Leisure centre, indoor swimming pool; beauty salon. **Gallery Restaurant,** D 7-9.30pm daily (not suitable for children under 16); informal D, Daly's 7-9.30 daily; bar food daily 12.30-6.30 (1-4 Sat/Sun). Open all year. Amex, MasterCard, Visa, Laser. **Directions:** 9km (6 m) from Galway city on Spiddal road.

Headford

Lisdonagh House

COUNTRY HOUSE

Caherlistrane nr Headford Co Galway **Tel: 093 31163** Fax: 093 31528
Email: cooke@lisdonagh.com Web: www.lisdonagh.com

Situated about 15 minutes drive north of Galway city in the heart of hunting and fishing country, Lisdonagh House is on an elevated site with beautiful views overlooking Lake Hackett. It is a lovely property, with large well-proportioned reception rooms, and a fine staircase; very comfortable bedrooms are furnished with antiques (some have four-posters) and decorated in period style, with impressive marbled bathrooms to match - although not necessarily with the little extras, such as bottled water, that today's guests demand in this price range (and restricted choice of television channels). The drawing room is welcoming in the evening, with a log fire and honesty bar encouraging guests to relax before going in to dinner in a handsome dining room with a view of the lake, on the other side of the beautiful oval hall which is an unusual feature of the house. The usual dinner menu offers five courses, with the choice limited to one of two main courses, one fish and one meat, although a vegetarian main course - a speciality of of wild mushroom crêpe with parmesan crisp, port reductions & basil pesto, for example - would be available on request. Breakfast is not the event that many people have come o expect of country houses, but it is a pleasant meal. Children welcome. Pets permitted in some areas. Equestrian, fishing, walking, cycling. *Two villas in the courtyard are also available, either for self-catering or fully serviced. The main house can also be rented exclusively for family celebrations and get-togethers, either weekly or for two-night lets. Small conferences (50). Boat trips, hunting/shooting on site; golf and garden visits nearby. Children welcome (under 2s free in parents' room, cots available free of charge, baby sitting arranged, creche). **Rooms 9** (2 shower only, 1 family room, 4 ground floor). B&B from €90-140 pps, ss about €30. 2/5 course residents' dinner , about €35/49 is served between 7 and 9pm. House wine €20. Closed 1 Nov-1 May. Amex, MasterCard, Visa, Laser. **Directions:** N17 to within 7km (4 m) of Tuam, R333 to Caherlistrane.

Inishbofin

The Dolphin Hotel & Restaurant

HOTEL/RESTAURANT

"The Beach" Middle Quarter Inishbofin Co Galway
Tel: 095 45991 Fax: 095 45834
Email: info@dolphinhotel.ie Web: www.dolphinhotel.ie

The Dolphin Restaurant has had a wonderful reputation since 2000 when it was opened by brother and sister, Pat and Catherine Coyne. In 2006 it turned miraculously into a small hotel in beautifully landscaped grounds, and it will be a wonderful addition to this beautiful unspoilt island.

The building is a modern mix of slatted wood and brick and, giving a lead to the island's interest in the environment, solar panels and under floor heating have been installed. There are now eleven large, bright bedrooms, with thick deep blue carpets, walnut furniture, great beds, TV and tea making facilities; all are en suite and some with bath.- the cosy honeymoon suite has a luxurious double bath. Upstairs room have sea and mountain views and three special ground floor rooms have their own private sundeck on to the garden. One bedroom has disabled access and has an interconnecting room next door; dining and lounge areas also have disabled access. Public areas include two dining rooms, which can be joined to accommodate parties of up to 100, with a deck for alfresco dining. There is a lovely resident's lounge, also with access to decking, with great views and a large satellite TV in case you ever tire of the wonders surrounding you! Banqueting (100). Walking, live music (trad.). Boat trips, angling, cycling and scuba diving all nearby. Children welcome (under 3s free in parents' room, cot available at no charge, baby sitting arranged). **Rooms 11** (8 shower only, 1 for disabled, all no smoking); B&B €50-60 pps. **Restaurant:** Menus change throughout the day at Pat and Catherine Coyne's versatile restaurant, which and continues to be a great asset to the island. Catherine, who has just got her culinary arts degree from Galway's Institute of Technology, cooks great food and has started to grow her own organic vegetables and herbs. At lunchtime - which considerately runs all afternoon - there's a range of drinks to comfort or refresh, depending on the weather, then made to order club or open sandwiches, or simple hot meals - home-made pizzas, perhaps, or Thot Inisbofin crab claws in garlic butter, and some with special child appeal. Evening menus are more substantial - rack of lamb with boulangère potatoes & rosemary jus, perhaps, fish of the day or a vegetarian pancake with mushroom, spinach, garlic & ricotta. Lobster is available too, if ordered the day before. **Restaurant seats 100** (outdoor seating, 20). Open daily in summer: L 12-5; D 7-9.30. à la carte; house wine from €17.95. Establishment closed Nov-Mar. MasterCard, Visa, Laser. **Directions:** Travel from Galway to Clifden and on to Cleggan Pier where boat leaves to Inishbofin Island.

Inishbofin

Doonmore Hotel

N HOTEL

Inishbofin Island Co Galway **Tel: 095 45804** / 14 Fax: 095 45804
Email: info@doonmorehotel.com Web: www.doonmorehotel.com

The Doonmore Hotel was built on the site of the Murray family farmhouse in 1968; overlooking the sea and sand dunes, with geraniums along the front lounge, it looks more like a traditional guesthouse than an hotel and offers old fashioned comfort rather than luxury. Traditional music is played regularly and on cold days there are peat fires in the low-ceilinged sitting room and lounge. Margaret, originally from Lusk in north County Dublin, came to teach on the neighbouring island of Inish Shark during the early 1950s, met and married Paddy and started both a family and a guest house some years and seven children later, the Doonmore became the first registered hotel on Inishbofin. Island owned and managed by the Murray family, it still retains some of the original features of the old homestead while a new wing with 20 en suite bedrooms and a function room was added some years ago. It is a very family friendly place and even has a baby listening service in bedrooms, along with the usual direct dial telephone, TV and tea/coffee making facilities. Murray's is well known for wholesome cooking - home baking, local produce like Connemara lamb and fresh seafood. Local fishermen catch lobster on request, and crab claws and a wonderful chowder are served every day in the bar (food served from 12 noon to 9pm). Fine sandy beaches; diving and angling facilities are available. Small conferences/banqueting (40/80); fitness room, cycling, sea angling, boat trips, scuba diving and walking. Children welcome (under 3s free in parents' room, cots available at no charge, baby sitting arranged); toilets wheelchair accessible; broadband Wi/Fi. **Rooms 20** (15 shower only, 5 family rooms, 16 ground floor); B&B €60-65 pps, ss €10. **Restaurant seats 45** and opens daily to residents & non-residents, 12-9pm. Establishment closed Oct-Mar. Heli-pad. Amex, MasterCard, Visa, Laser. **Directions:** Ferry from Cleggan.

Inishbofin

Inishbofin House Days Hotel & Marine Spa

N HOTEL

Inishbofin Island Co Galway **Tel: 095 45809** Fax: 095 45809
Email: info@inishbofinhouse.com Web: www.inishbofinhouse.com

Day's family run hotel on Bofin pier has been transformed to a large luxury hotel and after a long time in the building - opened for the 2006 season. It overlooks the inner harbour and is usually the first port of call for many visitors to the island over the years. Public areas include a large bright high- roofed entrance lobby and lounge with Spanish tiles and cherrywood finish, that has a wonderful John Behan sculpture representing the legend of the white cow 'Bofin' which was in the old house; a long bar with polished wooden floors is smart and stylish, and has large windows looks onto the sea and the dining room, on two levels, has great views to the sea and mountains. On the first floor a truly lovely library/lounge with balconies off it is totally constructed in glass so there is a panoramic view of sea, harbour and mountain. Bedrooms are luxurious and are restful in pale greens and cream, with bucket chairs, flat screen TV and balconies and all have bath and shower. Audio visual equipment and broadband is available. A spa is planned but has not yet been developed. The Day family also operate a bar beside the pier where the ferry comes in (food available in summer). Banqueting (180). Spa, beauty salon. Children welcome (cot available, baby sitting arranged) . No pets. Garden. **Rooms 34** (2 with separate bath & shower, 2 disabled, all no smoking). Lift. Room service (limited hours). Closed Jan-Feb. Visa, Laser. **Directions:** Ferries to the island run regularly from Cleggan, with ticket offices in Clifden (regular buses between Clifden and Cleggan) and also at Kings of Cleggan. For bookings and enquiries, phone: 095 44642 or 095 21520. Credit card bookings are accepted.

Kilcolgan
PUB/RESTAURANT

Moran's Oyster Cottage

The Weir Kilcolgan Co Galway
Tel: 091 796 113 Fax: 091 796 503
Email: moranstheweir@eircom.net Web: www.moransoystercottage.com

This is just the kind of Irish pub that people everywhere dream about. It's as pretty as a picture, with a well-kept thatched roof and a lovely waterside location (with plenty of seats outside where you can while away the time and watch the swans floating by). People from throughout the country beat a path here at every available opportunity for their wonderful local seafood, including lobster, but especially the native oysters (from their own oyster beds) which are in season from September to April (farmed Gigas oysters are on the menu all year). Then there's chowder and smoked salmon and seafood cocktail and mussels, delicious crab salads - and lobster, with boiled potatoes & garlic butter. Private conference room. The wine list is not over-extensive, but carefully selected, informative and fairly priced. Morans was the Guide's Seafood Pub of the Year in 1999. **Seats 100** (private rooms, 8 and 12; outdoor seating, 50/60). Air conditioning. Toilets wheelchair accessible. Meals 12 noon -10pm daily. House wine from €18. Closed 3 days Christmas & Good Fri. Amex, MasterCard, Visa, Laser. **Directions:** Just off the Galway-Limerick road, signed between Clarenbridge and Kilcolgan. ◇

Kinvara
BAR/RESTAURANT

Keogh's Bar & Restaurant

Main Street Kinvara Co Galway **Tel: 091 637 145**
Email: keoghsbar@eircom.net Web: www.kinvara.com/keoghs

Michael Keogh took over this old pub in 1996 and refurbished it to create a cosy bar with an open fire and a more modern restaurant behind it, with wooden floors and benches and oilcloth-covered tables - with character added by a large fireplace with a traditional black stove. The food is modern Irish bar meals, served by charming Filipino and French staff, and there are tables outside in summer. Local seafood is the main speciality - an informal bite of fine, creamy, fishy chowder for example, or steamed mussels (both come with home-made brown bread), or more serious main courses like cod fillet with beurre nantais or pan-fried monkfish Provençal. There are plenty of other choices too, including warm goats cheese salad, made with local St Tola cheese, or rack of Kinvara lamb; homely desserts might include a freshly-baked apple and rhubarb crumble. Children welcome, air conditioning. **Seats 50** (outdoor seating, 18). Weekly music sessions in summer. Food available daily 9.30am-10pm (Sun from 12), B 9.30, L 12.30-5, D 6-10. A la carte. House wine from €15.95. Reservations accepted. Closed 25 Dec, Good Fri. Amex, MasterCard, Visa, Laser. **Directions:** Kinvara village - on the coast road to Doolin, 19km (12 m) from Galway.

Kinvara
RESTAURANT/PUB

The Pier Head Bar & Restaurant

The Quay Kinvara Co Galway **Tel: 091 638 188**

Seafood is, of course, the star at Mike Burke's well-known harbourside establishment in the picturesque village of Kinvara - fat, tasty mussels in moules marinière (about €9), with a milky onion and wine broth; great pan-fried skate (about €17), which is rarely seen on restaurant menus; lobster is a speciality - served in the shell with garlic butter and a side salad it makes a meal for about €35 - and the other thing they take pride in is top of the range steak, using local beef (totally traceable) which is slaughtered and butchered specially. Warm service, from staff with knowledge and skill. A well-balanced wine list includes good value house wines. As well as good food, there's also music, all year: bands on on Friday & Saturday nights, usually also traditional on Sunday afternoon. (Phone ahead to check availability). Children welcome. **Seats 100** (private room 50). D Mon-Sat, 5-9.30pm; a la carte; house wine about €15. Closed 25 Dec & Good Fri. Diners, MasterCard, Visa, Laser. **Directions:** Kinvara harbour front. ◇

LEENANE

There can be few more spectacular locations for a village than Leenane, which is tucked into the shoreline at the head of Ireland's only deepwater fjord, backed by dramatic mountains. In the village you will find the delightful little **Blackberry Café** (see entry) and, just along the shore, is the **Leenane Hotel** (095 42249; www.leenanehotel.com), which is a relatively budget-conscious cousin establishment to **Rosleague Manor** at Letterfrack (see entry). And not far away - an eight mile scenic drive northwest of Leenane, on the Louisbourg road, is the **Delphi Mountain Resort & Spa** (095 42987; www.delphiescape.com); it is closed for major refurbishment at the time of going to press, reopening in 2007 - details will be on their website.

WWW.IRELAND-GUIDE.COM FOR THE BEST PLACES TO EAT, DRINK & STAY

Leenane

Blackberry Café & Coffee Shop

CAFÉ

Leenane Co Galway **Tel: 095 42240**

Sean and Mary Hamilton's lovely little restaurant is just what the weary traveller hopes to happen on when touring or walking in this beautiful area. They're open through the afternoon and evening every day during the summer, serving home-made soups and chowders with home-baked bread, substantial snacks such as fish cakes and mussels, and delicious desserts like rhubarb tart and lemon meringue pie with cream. Extra dishes such as hot smoked trout and a chicken main course might be added to the menu in the evening, but the secret of the Blackberry Café's appeal is that they don't try to do too much at once and everything is freshly made each day. **Seats 40.** Open 12-4.30 and 6-9 daily in high season. A la carte. House wine about €15 (1/4 bottles also available). Closed Tue in shoulder seasons. Closed end Sep-Easter. Visa, Laser, Switch. **Directions:** On main street,opposite car park. ◇

Leenane

Delphi Lodge

COUNTRY HOUSE

Leenane Co Galway **Tel: 095 42222** Fax: 095 42296
Email: stay@delphilodge.ie Web: www.delphilodge.ie

One of Ireland's most famous sporting lodges, Delphi Lodge was built in the early 19th-century by the Marquis of Sligo, and is magnificently located in an unspoilt valley, surrounded by the region's highest mountains (with the high rainfall so dear to fisherfolk). Owned since 1986 by Peter Mantle - who has restored and extended the original building in period style - the lodge is large and impressive in an informal, understated way, with antiques, fishing gear and a catholic collection of reading matter creating a stylish yet relaxed atmosphere. The guest rooms are all quite different, but they have lovely lake and mountain views, good bathrooms (some recently upgraded), and are very comfortably furnished. Dinner, for residents only, is taken house-party style at a long oak table - traditionally presided over by the person lucky enough to catch the day's biggest salmon. The set menu begins with an amuse-bouche ('Tongue Tickler'), of Irish goats cheese beignets with beetroot salad, perhaps, and has earned a reputation that reaches far beyond the valley for good cooking; current house specialities delighting the happy fisherfolk are classic dishes like langoustine bisque, bouillabisse an rib of beef - and there are sometimes unusual ingredients like the nephrops from Killary Bay, which might come with warmed rocket butter. Coffee and home-made chocolates round off the feast in the Piano Room, where, perhaps, the good company of other guests may keep you from your bed. The famous Delphi Fishery is the main attraction, but many people come for other country pursuits, painting, or just peace and quiet. A billiard table, the library and a serious wine list (great bottles at a very modest mark-up) can get visitors through a lot of wet days. * Delphi Lodge was our Country House of the Year in 2006. **Rooms 12** (all executive standard). B&B €100 pps, ss €30. Residents D 8pm; D €50; 8 well-chosen house wines, all €22; SC discretionary. Closed mid Dec 20 - mid Jan. MasterCard, Visa, Laser. **Directions:** 8 miles northwest of Leenane on the Louisburgh road.

Letterfrack

Kylemore Abbey Restaurant & Tea House

RESTAURANT

Kylemore Letterfrack Co Galway **Tel: 095 41155** Fax: 095 41368
Email: info@kylemoreabbey.ie Web: www.kylemoreabbey.ie

Providing you are tolerant of tour buses and high season crowds, this dramatically located Abbey offers a surprising range of things to see: a brief stroll from the abbey along the wooded shore leads to the Gothic church, a fascinating miniature replica of Norwich cathedral, for example, then there's a fine craft shop in a neat modern building beside the carpark and also a daytime self-service restaurant, where everything is made on the premises, including traditional meals like beef & Guinness casserole and Irish stew. Big bowls of the nuns' home-made jams are set up at the till, for visitors to help themselves - beside them are neatly labelled jars to buy and take home. A short distance away, the nuns also run a farm and a restored walled garden, which supplies produce to the Garden Tea House. **Seats 240.** Meals daily 9.30-5.30. Closed Christmas Day & Good Fri. (The Garden Tea House, in the restored walled garden, is open Easter-Hallowe'en, 10.30-5.) Amex, MasterCard, Visa, Laser. **Directions:** 2 miles from Letterfrack, on the N59 from Galway. ◇

Letterfrack
RESTAURANT

Pangur Bán Restaurant

Letterfrack Co Galway **Tel: 095 41243**
Email: pban@indigo.ie Web: www.pangurban.com

John Walsh's pretty, whitewashed roadside cottage has a tiny front garden and a large carpark at the back; you enter into a reception / bar area which is unexpectedly bright and airy, with a raised wooden ceiling and plenty of light from the cottage door as well as windows although, with whitewashed walls and an old fireplace, it retains its natural cottagey character, and table settings in the adjoining dining rooms are appropriately simple. A relaxing meal with John's good home cooking and service to match is the aim, and this is achieved well. Local produce is used whenever possible (mountain lamb is sourced from John's brother) in dishes that vary widely in style from quite traditional specialities, like braised Galway lamb shanks in Guinness with celeriac mash, to those with international influences, such as Thai chicken Chettinad - a Tamil curry with rice & naan bread. But leave some room for a little indulgence from a wide choice of desserts, ranging from home-made ice creams and rhubarb fool through the house variation on treacle tart, and a cheesecake - tangy lime & lemon, perhaps. A nice little wine list, includes a pair of half bottles, a couple of bubblies, wines by the glass and a few beers - including pints of Guinness. *Cookery classes at weekends off-season. **Seats 45.** D Tue-Sun, 6-9.30; closed Mon. (A phone call to check opening times any time except high season is advised.) A la carte. House wine €17.95. Closed Jan & Feb. MasterCard, Visa, Laser. **Directions:** In Letterfrack village.

Letterfrack
COUNTRY HOUSE

Rosleague Manor Hotel

Letterfrack Co Galway **Tel: 095 41101** Fax: 095 41168
Email: info@rosleague.com Web: www.rosleague.com

This lovely, graciously proportioned, pink-washed Regency house looks out over a tidal inlet through gardens planted with rare shrubs and plants. Although the area also offers plenty of energetic pursuits, there is a deep sense of peace at Rosleague and it's hard to imagine anywhere better to recharge the soul. The hotel changed hands within the Foyle family a few years ago and its energetic young owner manager, Mark Foyle, is gradually working his way through a major renovation programme: the conservatory bar, restaurant and a number of bedrooms (and their bathrooms) have now been refurbished (two were actually demolished and re-built) and some have four-poster beds; three bathrooms have been completely re-fitted, and the gardens (already extensive, and listed in the Connemara Garden Trail) were further developed to make new paths and establish a wild flower meadow. This is a very pleasant, peaceful place to stay and, with two lovely drawing rooms with log fires to choose from, as well as the bar, guests have plenty of space. And the restaurant - a lovely classical dining room, with mahogany furniture and a fine collection of plates on the walls - is open to non-residents by reservation. Head chef Pascal Marinot, who has been at Rosleague since 2000, offers a daily-changing dinner menu in a quite traditional style - starters like oysters with shallot vinegar & lemon, or home-made chicken liver paté with cranberry sauce & Melba toast, a soup course, and straightforward main courses such as black sole on the bone. For dessert, Rosleague chocolate mousse is an inherited speciality - going back to Mark's uncle, Paddy Foyle's, time in the kitchen. Children welcome (cot available free of charge, baby sitting arranged) Garden, tennis, fishing, walking. Pets permitted. **Rooms 20** (4 junior suites). B&B €125pps, ss about €85. **Restaurant Seats 50** (Private Room seats 12). D 7.30-9 daily, non-residents welcome by reservation; Set D €45. House wine €21. Closed mid Nov-mid Mar. Amex, MasterCard, Visa, Laser. **Directions:** On N59 main road, 11km (7 miles) north-west of Clifden.

Moycullen
RESTAURANT

White Gables Restaurant

Moycullen Village Moycullen Co Galway
Tel: 091 555 744 Fax: 091 556 004
Email: info@whitegables.com Web: www.whitegables.com

Kevin and Ann Dunne have been running this attractive cottagey restaurant on the main street of Moycullen since 1991 and it's now on many a regular diner's list of favourites. Arriving guests can have an aperitif in the bar before heading into the restaurant, where open stonework, low lighting and candlelight (even at lunch time) create a soothing away-from-it-all atmosphere. Kevin sources ingredients with care and offers weekly-changing dinner and à la carte menus, with daily specials, and a set Sunday lunch which is in great demand and has two sittings. Cooking is consistently good in a refreshingly traditional style and, while there is much else to choose from - roast half duckling with orange sauce is one of their most popular dishes, and local meats always feature, including Connemara lamb and excellent beef from the famous butchers McGeoughs of Oughterard. Fresh fish and seafood is another speciality: lobster from their own sea water tank is fairly priced, and there will be other classics like sole on the bone, scallops mornay, monkfish panfried in garlic butter and poached turbot in martini sauce. Well-cooked seasonal vegetables are always particularly enjoyable at this fine restaurant and their roast rib of beef, as served for Sunday lunch, is like no other. Good desserts, including home-made ices, and friendly, efficient service all help make this one of the area's most popular restaurants. An interesting wine list includes some classics, also well-chosen house wines and a good choice of half bottles. **Seats 45.** Children welcome. Air conditioning. D Tue-Sat, 7-10; L Sun only, 12.30-3. Set D €44.50 (5 course), also à la carte; Set Sun L €26.50. House wine €20; sc discretionary. Closed Mon & 23 Dec-14 Feb. Amex, Diners, MasterCard, Visa, Laser. **Directions:** On N59 in Moycullen village, 11km (8 m) from Galway city.

ORANMORE

Between Galway city and Athenry, first impressions of Oranmore are that it is dominated by the N6 and the **Quality Hotel & Leisure Centre** (091 792244;www.qualityhotelgalway.com) is right on the roundabout, so you can't miss it - has outstanding family facilities and is a popular place for business meetings. But Oranmore itself is a pleasant place - and, shortly before going to press, the beautifully appointed **Asian Fusion / Royal Villa Restaurant** (091-790823) opened in the centre of the village; it replaces the longstanding Royal Villa in Galway city and offers an interesting mix of well-executed Chinese, Thai and Japanese cuisine in lovely surroundings (good wine list; and good puddings too, not usually a strong point in Asian restaurants).

WWW.IRELAND-GUIDE.COM FOR THE BEST PLACES TO EAT, DRINK & STAY

OUGHTERARD

Oughterard is a charming riverside village, famous for various things, depending on your point of view: it is known as the Gateway to Connemara, renowned for its fishing - and for McGeough's butchers, who make the most wonderful air-dried meats, and other specialities well worth seeking out. On the Galway side of the village, **Brigit's Garden** (see entry) at Roscahill is an interesting place to visit, and their tea rooms specialise in home-baking while, in the village itself, **Sweeney's Oughterard House** (091 552 207; www.sweeneys-hotel.com) is a famous old-world hotel that can make a good journey break for a bite in the bar. There is also a restaurant **The Yew Tree** (091 866 986) on the main street, which is open all day, 9am-6pm, Mon-Sat and serves good home-cooked food - also including delicious home baking.

WWW.IRELAND-GUIDE.COM FOR THE BEST PLACES TO EAT, DRINK & STAY

Oughterard

GUESTHOUSE

Corrib Wave Guesthouse

Portcarron Oughterard Co Galway **Tel: 091 552 147** Fax: 091 552 736
Email: cwh@gofree.indigo.ie Web: www.corribwave.com

A fisherman's dream, Michael and Maria Healy's unpretentious waterside guesthouse offers warm family hospitality, comfortable accommodation, an open turf fire to relax by and real home cooking. All rooms have phone, tea/coffee-making, TV, radio and a double and single bed; some are suitable for families. Maria cooks dinner for guests - fresh trout and salmon from the lake, irish stew, bacon & cabbage - just the kind of thing people want. Best of all at Corrib Wave is the location - utter peace and tranquillity. Golf and horseriding nearby and everything to do with fishing organised for you. Children welcome (under 3 free in parents' room). Fishing. Garden; walking. **Rooms 10** (all en-suite, 4 shower only, 2 family rooms, 5 ground floor, all no smoking). B&B €40, ss €15. Breakfast 8-9.30. Residents D 7.30pm. Closed 1 Dec-1 Feb. MasterCard, Visa, **Directions:** From Galway, signed from N59, 1 km before Oughterard.

Oughterard

COUNTRY HOUSE

Currarevagh House

Glann Road Oughterard Co Galway
Tel: 091 552 312 Fax: 091 552 731
Email: mail@currarevagh.com Web: www.currarevagh.com

Tranquillity, trout and tea in the drawing room - these are the things that draw guests back to the Hodgson family's gracious, but not luxurious early Victorian manor overlooking Lough Corrib. Currarevagh, which was built in 1846 as a wedding present for Harry Hodgson's great, great, great grandfather, is set in 150 acres of woodlands and gardens with sporting rights over 5,000 acres. Guests have been welcomed here for nearly half a century; the present owners, Harry and June Hodgson, are founder members of the Irish Country Houses and Restaurants Association ('Ireland's

Blue Book'), and recently joined by their son Henry. Yet, while the emphasis is on old-fashioned service and hospitality, the Hodgsons are adamant that the atmosphere should be more like a private house party than an hotel, and their restful rituals underline the differences: the day begins with a breakfast worthy of its Edwardian origins, laid out on the sideboard in the dining room; lunch may be one of the renowned picnic hampers required by sporting folk. Then there's afternoon tea, followed by a leisurely dinner. Fishing is the ruling passion, of course - notably brown trout, pike, perch and salmon - but there are plenty of other country pursuits to assist in building up an appetite again for Henry's dinners, all based on fresh local produce. His 5-course dinner menus might begin with a salad of air dried lamb (a local speciality from McGeough's butchers in Oughterard), then a crab and watercress soup, followed by medallions of pork rolled in pistachio nuts and finally a dessert such as chocolate truffle, and Irish cheeses; there is no choice but menus are changed daily and there is quite an extensive, fairly priced wine list. Children welcome (u 2s free in parents room, cot available at no charge). Garden, walking, tennis. **Rooms 15** (all en-suite, 2 shower only, 1 family room, 2 ground floor, 13 no smoking). B&B €104pps, ss €35 or single room €90-104. No SC. D €45, at 8pm (non residents welcome by reservation). Wines from €17.50. Closed mid Oct- Apr. MasterCard, Visa, Laser, Switch. **Directions:** Take N59 to Oughterard. Turn right in village square and follow Glann Road for 6.5km (4 m).

Oughterard

HOTEL

Ross Lake House Hotel

Rosscahill Oughterard Co Galway **Tel: 091 550 109** Fax: 091 550 184
Email: rosslake@iol.ie Web: www. rosslakehotel.com

Quietly located in six acres of beautiful gardens, this charming country house was built in 1850 and is now a protected building. The current owners, Henry and Elaine Reid, bought the property in 1981 and have gradually refurbished it, so the hotel now offers luxurious accommodation in spacious rooms and suites individually furnished with antiques - including some with four-poster beds. While graciously-proportioned and impressively furnished, hands-on management and the warm interest of the proprietors and their staff ensure a welcoming and surprisingly homely atmosphere. Weddings are a speciality, especially off season (banqueting, 200). Short breaks offered. Children welcome (under 2s free in parents' room, cot available without charge). No pets. Garden. Tennis. Walking, cycling, fishing. **Rooms 13** (1 suite, 1 junior suite, 3 superior, 1 shower only, 1 family room, 3 ground floor, all no smoking) B&B €85, ss €30. D 7-8.30 daily, L Sun 1.45-5. Closed 1 Nov-15 Mar. Amex, MasterCard, Visa, Laser. **Directions:** Signed off Galway-Oughterard road.

Oughterard

GUESTHOUSE

Waterfall Lodge

Oughterard Co Galway **Tel: 091 552 168**
Email: kdolly@eircom.net Web: www.waterfalllodge.net

Kathleen Dolly's aptly named period residence is on the river side of the road, and set in mature gardens which contain many rare shrubs and trees. It's an appealing place to stay, with private fishing and its own waterfall - and just a short walk to the village. Well-proportioned reception rooms are furnished with antiques, and all of the spacious, comfortably furnished bedrooms have full bathrooms, television and tea/coffee trays. Golfing breaks are a speciality; there are 5 championship golf courses nearby and tee times can be arranged (the proprietor is a keen golfer). **Rooms 6** (all en-suite & no smoking, 3 family rooms). Children welcome (under 5s free in parents' room, cot available without charge, baby sitting arranged). Pets allowed by arrangement. Garden, walking, fishing. B&B €40, ss €10. Closed Christmas. **Directions:** On N59 from Galway; on left after the bridge in Oughterard when heading towards Clifden.

Oughterard Area

€ CAFÉ

Brigit's Garden Café

Pollagh Roscahill Co Galway **Tel: 091 550 905** Fax: 091 550 491
Email: info@galwaygarden.com Web: www.galwaygarden.com

Jenny Beale's beautiful themed garden near Oughterard reflects the Celtic festivals and, in addition to woodland trails, ring fort and stone chamber has a café that is worth a visit in its own right. A pine-ceilinged modern room that also acts as reception/shop has a small kitchen open to view at one end, and is set up with tables covered in old-fashioned oil cloth; everything's very simple, with plain white crockery and stainless cutlery and paper serviettes and, in fine weather, there is seating outside too. A short (vegetarian) blackboard menu offers a daily soup chunky, wholesome vegetable with thyme, perhaps, a meal in itself with brown bread & butter), and a special such as home-grown chard and blue cheese pasta. Lovely toasted sandwiches are generously filled with salad and a choice of fillings (egg mayonnaise, goats cheese & herb, hummus & olive, cheese & scallion), and great home bakes include delicious scones with jam & cream, a luscious, walnut & apricot carrot cake, which is nutty and moist. Good coffee, tea or tisanes, and soft drinks like cranberry or lemon juice - just the kind of place you need to know about when exploring the area, and recent visits suggest it's getting better all the time. Good toilets too, including baby changing facilities. **Seats 40** (+35 outdoors). Toilets wheelchair accessible. Children welcome; children's playground. Open 11-5 daily (Sun 12-5). Closed Oct - mid Apr. MasterCard, Visa, Laser. **Directions:** Just off the N59 between Moycullen and Oughterard.

Portumna

HOTEL

Shannon Oaks Hotel & Country Club

St. Josephs Rd Portumna Co Galway **Tel: 0509 41777** Fax: 0509 41357
Email: sales@shannonoaks.ie Web: www.shannonoaks.ie

Situated near the shores of Lough Derg and adjacent to the 17th century Portumna Castle and estate (with recently restored gardens), this privately-owned hotel is spacious - a large lobby is quite impressive, with polished wooden floor, faux-marble pillaring and ample seating in contemporary style, while other public rooms include a warm-toned restaurant, which can be opened out in summer, and a cosy, pub-like bar with an informal mezzanine restaurant. It's a good choice for business and corporate events - bedrooms have air conditioning and fax/modem lines as standard, and conference and meeting facilities are designed for groups of all sizes, with full back-up services. Off-duty delegates will find plenty to do too, a fine leisure centre on-site has an air-conditioned gymnasium as well as a swimming pool and ancillary services, and nearby activities include river cruising, fishing, golf, horseriding, cycling and clay pigeon shooting. Conference/banqueting (600/350). Children welcome (under 5s free in parents' room). No pets. **Rooms 63** (3 suites, some no smoking, 2 for disabled). B&B from about €90 pps ss about €30. Amex, Diners, MasterCard, Visa, Laser. **Directions:** Situated on St Joseph Road, Portuma. ◇

Recess

HOTEL/RESTAURANT

Ballynahinch Castle Hotel

Recess Co Galway **Tel: 095 31006** Fax: 095 31085
Email: bhinch@iol.ie Web: www.ballynahinch-castle.com

Renowned as a fishing hotel, this crenellated Victorian mansion enjoys a most romantic position in 450 acres of ancient woodland and gardens on the banks of the Ballynahinch River. It is impressive in scale and relaxed in atmosphere - a magic combination which, together with a high level of comfort and friendliness (and an invigorating mixture of residents and locals in the bar at night), all combine to bring people back. The tone is set in the foyer, with its huge stone fireplace and ever-burning log fire (which is a cosy place to enjoy afternoon tea) and the many necessary renovations and extensions through the years have been undertaken with great attention to period detail, a policy also carried through successfully in furnishing both public areas and bedrooms, many of which have lovely views over the river. A stay here is a restorative treat and, after a restful night's sleep, a Ballynahinch breakfast will give you a good start ahead of a day's fishing, wilderness walks on the estate, or simply touring the area. (Ballynahinch was the Connaught winner of our Irish Breakfast Awards in 2002.) **Owenmore Restaurant:** This bright and elegant room has the classic atmosphere of a splendidly old-fashioned dining room, and is carefully organised to allow as many tables as possible to enjoy its uniquely beautiful river setting, where you can watch happy fisherfolk claiming the last of the fading daylight on the rocks below. Daily dinner menus have plenty of fine local produce to call on - wild salmon, of course, also sea fish, Connemara lamb and prime Irish beef (supplied by the renowned butcher, McGeough's of Oughterard) - a great basis for specialities with enduring popularity like poached wild Atlantic salmon, baked Connemara lamb cutlets and lobster. Vegetarians are well looked after too - home-made pasta is a speciality, papardelle served with artichoke hearts, garlic and Parmesan cheese, perhaps. Staff are hospitable and relaxed, and a thoughtfully assembled wine list offers an unusual range of house wines and a good choice of half bottles. *Excellent meals are also served in the hotel's characterful bar - a mighty high-ceilinged room with a huge fireplace, and many mementoes of the pleasures of rod and hunt. An informal alternative to the Owenmore experience - and a great place for non-residents to drop into for a bite when touring Connemara. Fishing: 3 miles of private fly fishing for Atlantic salmon, sea trout and brown trout. Landscaped gardens and wilderness walks on 450 acres; members of Connemara Garden Trail. Small conferences (12). Cycling, walking; Children welcome (under 3s free in parents' room; cots available without charge, baby sitting arranged). No pets. Walking, cycling, tennis. fishing. Golf nearby. **Rooms 40** (3 suites, 40 with separate bath & shower, All no smoking) No lift. 24 hr room service. B&B €105 pps, ss €30, sc 10%. Short/special interest/off season breaks offered - details on application. Owenmore Restaurant open daily, L 12.30-3; D 6.30-9 (Set D €49+10%sc), house wines from €24.70. Bar meals 12.30-3 & 6.30-9 daily. SC 10%. Closed Christmas & Feb. Amex, Diners, MasterCard, Visa, Laser. **Directions:** N59 from Galway - Clifden; left after Recess (Roundstone road), 6 km.

Recess

HOTEL

Lough Inagh Lodge

Recess Connemara Co Galway **Tel: 095 34706** Fax: 095 34708
Email: inagh@iol.ie Web: www.loughinaghlodgehotel.ie

Maire O'Connor's former sporting lodge on the shores of Lough Inagh makes a delightful small hotel, with a country house atmosphere. It has large, well-proportioned rooms, interesting period detail and lovely fireplaces with welcoming log fires, as well as all the modern comforts. Public areas include two drawing rooms, each with an open fire, and a very appealing bar with a big turf fire and its own back door and tiled floor for wet fishing gear. Bedrooms, which include one recently added room and several with four-posters, are all well-appointed and unusually spacious, with views of lake and countryside. Walk-in dressing rooms lead to well-planned bathrooms and tea/coffee-making facilities are available in rooms on request. While it has special appeal to sportsmen, Lough Inagh makes a good base for touring Connemara and is only 42 miles from Galway; in addition to fishing, golf, pony trekking and garden visits are all nearby. Off-season breaks offer especially good value. **Finisglen Room:** This handsome dining room has deep green walls and graceful spoonback Victorian mahogany chairs, and non-residents are welcome for dinner by reservation. Fiona Joyce has been head chef since 2002, and the food in both the restaurant and the bar is excellent; alongside the popular dishes like smoked salmon, pan-fried steaks, wild salmon and lobster (when available) you may find less usual choices including starters of grilled fish sausage, or air-dried Connemara lamb. Desserts, including a wide range of ices, are home made, service is friendly, and portions generous. The wine list includes a fair range of half bottles, some non alcoholic wines and, unusually, a rosé among the house wines. *Tempting bar menus are also offered for lunch, dinner and afternoon tea. Small conferences/banqueting (15/50). Children welcome (under 3s free in parents' room, cots available without charge). Pets permitted. Garden, walking, cycling. **Rooms 13** (5 junior suites, 10 no smoking, 4 ground floor); room service (24 hr). B&B €140 pps, ss €20. Restaurant: L 12.30-4; D daily 6.45-9pm (reservations required), Set D €49; also A la Carte. House wine €21; Bar meals 12.30-4 & 6.30-9pm daily. SC10%. Closed mid Dec-mid Mar. Amex, Diners, MasterCard, Visa, Laser. **Directions:** From Galway city travel on N59 for 64km (40 m).Take rght N344 after Recess; 5km (3 m) on right.

Renvyle

HOTEL

Renvyle House Hotel

Renvyle Co Galway **Tel: 095 43511** Fax: 095 43515
Email: info@renvyle.com Web: www.renvyle.com

In one of the country's most appealingly remote and beautiful areas, this famous Lutyens-esque house has a romantic and fascinating history, having been home to people as diverse as a Gaelic chieftan and Oliver St John Gogarty - and becoming one of Ireland's earliest country house hotels, in 1883. In good weather it is best approached via a stunning scenic drive along a mountain road with views down into a blue-green sea of unparalleled clarity. Once reached, the hotel seems to be snuggling down for shelter and, although it has limited views, there is a shift of emphasis to the comforts within, a feeling reinforced by the cosy atmosphere of the original building, with its dark beams, rug strewn floors and open fires - and a snug conservatory where guests can survey the garden, and the landscape beyond. Photographs and mementoes recording visits from the many famous people who have stayed here - Augustus John, Lady Gregory, Yeats and Churchill among them - keep guests happily occupied for hours, but there is plenty to distract you from this enjoyable activity, including a heated outdoor swimming pool, tennis, trout fishing, golf (9 hole), and croquet - while the surrounding area offers more challenging activities including archaeological expeditions, horse riding, hill walking, scuba diving and sea fishing. Just loafing around is perhaps what guests are best at here, however, and there's little need to do much else. Head chef Tim O'Sullivan looks after the inner man admirably in lovely dinners featuring local seafood and Connemara produce, including Renvyle rack of lamb, local lobster and vegetables in season - and the hotel's bar food is also excellent. All this, plus the scent of a turf fire and a comfortable armchair, can be magic. The grounds and gardens around the hotel are a special point of interest at Renvyle, and come as a delightful contrast to the magnificently rugged surrounding scenery. Special breaks (midweek, weekend and bank holiday) are very good value and Renvyle makes an excellent conference venue (conference/banqueting 200); secretarial services. *Renvyle House was selected for the Féile Bia Award for Creative Use of Vegetables in 2006. Children welcome (under 2s free in parents' room, cots available without charge; crèche (seasonal), playroom, children's playground, children's tea, baby sitting arranged). Pets permitted by arrangement. Archery, all-weather tennis court, clay pigeon shooting, croquet, lawn bowls, fly fishing, sea angling, snooker. **Rooms 68** (4 suites, 40 no smoking, 1 for disabled, 6 family rooms). B&B €119, no ss, no SC. Restaurant open 7-9 daily (Set D €45). Bar meals 11-5 daily (excl 25 Dec, Good Fri). Closed 1-21 Dec & 7 Jan - 8 Feb. Helipad. Amex, Diners, MasterCard, Visa, Laser. **Directions:** 18km (12 miles) north of Clifden.

ROUNDSTONE

This charming village is clustered around its traditional stone-built harbour, so seafood is very much the speciality in every bar and restaurant. The Conneely family's **Eldons Hotel** (095 35933; www.connemara.net) is a comfortable family-run hotel with its own seafood restaurant, Beola, next door, and there is also the Vaughan family's **Roundstone House Hotel** (095 35864; www.irishcountry-hotels.com). Both have a well-earned reputation with locals and visitors alike - and both offer golf and sea angling breaks. **WWW.IRELAND-GUIDE.COM - THE BEST PLACES TO EAT, DRINK & STAY**

Roundstone

O'Dowd's Bar

Roundstone Co Galway **Tel: 095 35809** Fax: 095 35907
Email: odowds@indigo.ie Web: www.odowdsbar.com

The O'Dowd family have been welcoming visitors to this much-loved pub overlooking the harbour for longer than most people care to remember - and, although there are some new developments from time to time, the old bar is always the same. It's one of those simple places, with the comfort of an open fire and good pint, where people congregate in total relaxation - if they can get in (it can be very busy in the summer months). A reasonably priced bar menu majoring in seafood offers sustenance or, for more formal meals, the restaurant next door does the honours: seafood chowder, mussels, crabmeat etc; Connemara lamb; blackberry & apple pie. Meals 12-10 daily (to 9.30 in pub). Reservations required in restaurant. Á la carte. House wine from €17.50. SC 10% on parties of 6+. *Self-catering accommodation available - details on application. Closed 25 Dec. Amex, MasterCard, Visa, Laser. **Directions:** On harbour front in Roundstone village.

Roundstone Area

€ B&B/COUNTRY HOUSE

The Anglers Return

Toombeola Roundstone Co Galway **Tel: 095 31091**
Email: info@anglersreturn.com Web: www.anglersreturn.com

This charming and unusual house near Roundstone was built as a sporting lodge in the eighteenth century and, true to its name, fishing remains a major attraction to this day. But you don't have to be a fisherperson to warm to the special charms of The Anglers Return: peace and tranquillity, the opportunity to slow down in a quiet, caring atmosphere in this most beautiful area - this is its particular appeal. The house is set in three acres of natural gardens (open every day in spring and summer; best in late spring) and makes a good base for the Connemara Garden Trail - and, of course, for painting holidays. Bedrooms are bright and comfortably furnished in a fresh country house style, although only one is en-suite (the other four share two bathrooms between them); this is not a major problem and the overall level of comfort is high. However, bathroom arrangements are gradually being improved - one now features a restored Victorian ball & claw cast-iron bath, and an extra shower is due to be installed soon. As well as fishing, there is golf nearby, and riding and boat trips can be arranged for guests - and there are maps and information for walkers too. No television, but instead there are lots of books to read - and tea or snacks are available at any time during the day or evening, (out in the secluded back garden in fine weather, or beside the fire in the soothing drawing room, perhaps); dinner is available for groups staying several days, otherwise bookings can be made in nearby restaurants. Breakfast will include freshly baked breads, home-made yoghurts, marmalade and jams, and freshly picked herb teas from the garden - and you are even invited to collect your own egg. Not suitable for children. Walking, fishing, garden. **Rooms 5** (1 en-suite, 4 with shared bathrooms; all no smoking). B&B €48, ss by arrangement. *Special interest breaks offered (painting, walking); details on application. Closed 30 Nov-1 Mar. **No Credit Cards. Directions:** Just outside Roundstone.

Tuam

BAR/RESTAURANT

Finns Restaurant

Milltown Tuam Co Galway **Tel: 093 51327**
Fax: 093 51426 Email: johnfinn.indigo.ie

John and Lucy Finn's attractive restaurant is on the river, in a charming little award-winning tidy town a few miles north of Tuam - a welcome sight for hungry travellers between Galway and Sligo. John cooks an eclectic mix of international (cajun chicken, stir-fried beef with pepper sauce) and traditional (smoked salmon chowder, steaks, honey roasted duck) dishes - reasonably priced and served in a relaxed atmosphere. The cooking is sound, it's good value for money and the small village setting - where everyone seems to know someone at another table - makes a welcome change from busy towns. On the down side, bookings are not accepted, which is a major disadvantage when diners may travel specially to eat here and then have the inconvenience of a long wait for a table. Children welcome. **Seats 80** (Private room, 14). No reservations. D Tue-Sun, 5-9pm. A la carte; house wines from about €16. Service discretionary. Closed 3 days Christmas & Easter. Children welcome. MasterCard, Visa, Laser. **Directions:** 8 miles from Tuam, main N17 to Sligo. ◇

COUNTY KERRY

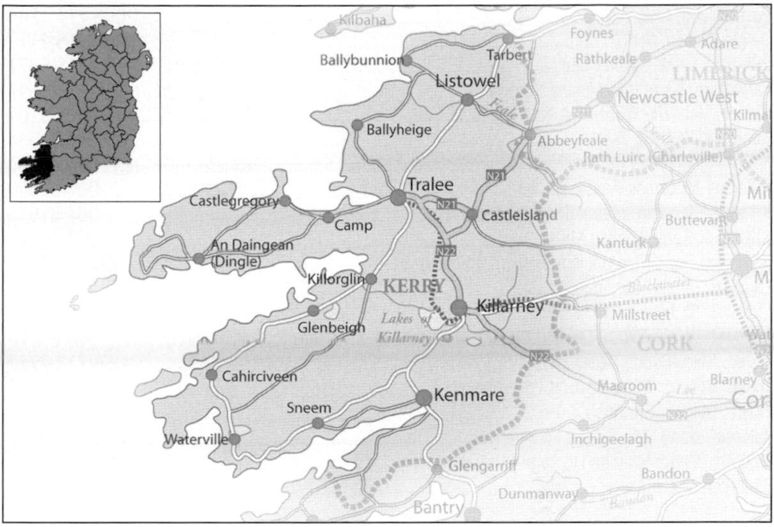

It's something special, being Kerry. This magnificent county in the far southwest has Ireland's highest and most varied mountains, and certain favoured areas also have our longest-lived citizens.

Then, too, it's a region which has long been a global pioneer in the hospitality business. So visitors inevitably arrive with high expectations. Kerry, however, can face the challenge. This magnificent county really is the Kingdom of Kerry. Everything is king size. For not only has Kerry mountains galore - more than anywhere else in Ireland - but there's a rare quality to Carrantuohill, the highest of all.

By international standards, this loftiest peak of MacGillicuddy's Reeks (try pronouncing it "mackil-cuddy") may not seem particularly significant at just 1038 m. But when you sense its mysterious heights in the clouds above a countryside of astonishing beauty, its relative elevation is definitely world league. And all Kerry's mountains sweep oceanwards towards a handsome coastline which rings the changes between sheltered inlets and storm tossed offshore islands.

Visually, Kerry has everything. But these days, spectacular scenery isn't enough on its own. Like other leading visitor destinations, Kerry is well aware of the need to provide accessible entertainment and an increasing choice of places with cultural and historical interest. Here too, the Kingdom can oblige.

The oldest fossil footprints in the Northern Hemisphere are in Kerry, and they're about 350 million years old. You'll find them way down west, on Valentia Island, and they're reckoned one of the seven wonders of Ireland. In much more modern times, the Antarctic explorer Tom Crean was from Kerry. He came from the little village of Annascaul on the majestic Dingle Peninsula, and when he had finished with adventuring, he returned to Annascaul and opened the South Pole Inn.

The town of Killarney among the lakes and mountains has long been a magnet for visitors, but Killarney is determined not simply to rest on its laurels after more than a Quarter Millennium as Ireland's premier tourist destination, for it was in 1754 that its attractions were first internationally promoted.

Then there's Kenmare, across the purple mountains. The lovely little town in South Kerry is both a gourmet focus, and another excellent touring centre. As one of the prettiest places in Ireland, Kenmare puts the emphasis on civic pride,

In the far northeast of this large county, Listowel – famed for its writers – has the restored Lartigue Monorail, another award-winning attraction. It's unique. And so too, in the most spirited way, is the harbour town of Dingle – it's away on the Atlantic edge, yet somehow at the hub of the universe. How so? You'll have to go and see for yourself.

Local Attractions and Information

Beaufort, Hotel Dunloe Castle Gardens	064 44583
Castleisland, Crag Cave	066 714 1244
Dingle, Ocean World	066 915 2111
Dunquin, Great Blasket Centre	066 915 6444 / 915 6371
Farranfore, Kerry International Airport	066 976 4644
Glencar, Into the Wilderness Walking Tours (May-Sep)	066 60104
Kenmare, Walking Festivals	064 41034
Kenmare, Heritage Centre	064 41233
Killarney Muckross House, Gardens & Traditional Farm	064 31440
Killarney, Tourism Information	064 31633
Killorglin, Kerry Woollen Mills	064 44122
Killorglin, Puck Fair (ancient festival), mid-August	066 976 2366
Lauragh, Dereen Gardens	064 83103
Listowel, St John's Art Centre	068 22566
Listowel, Writers' Week (June)	068 21074
Tralee, Kerry County Museum	066 712 7777
Tralee, Rose of Tralee Festival (late August)	066 712 3227
Tralee, Siamsa Tire Arts Centre	066 712 3055
Valentia Island, The Skellig Experience	066 947 6306
Valentia Island, Valentia Heritage (Knightstown)	066 947 6411
Waterville Craft Market	066 947 4212

Annascaul

South Pole Inn

PUB

Annascaul Co Kerry **Tel: 066 915 7388** Web: www.southpoleinn.ie

Annascaul, on the Dingle peninsula, is one of the most-photographed villages in Ireland mainly because of the brilliantly colourful and humorous frontage painted onto his pub by the late Dan Foley (which is still a fine pub). Nearby, The South Pole, which is down at the lower end of the street is equally interesting - named in honour of connections with the great Irish explorer Sir Ernest Shackleton and, more particularly, his second officer, Tom Crean, who was a native of Annascaul and has only recently achieved the recognition he deserved for his own part in Antarctic exploration. On retiring in 1920, he returned to Annascaul, married and ran the South Pole Inn. As well as being a delightful, well-run pub, The South Pole Inn is full of fascinating Shackleton and Crean memorabilia. Bar food available 12-8 daily. Closed 25 Dec & Good Fri. MasterCard, Visa, **Directions:** On the main road between Tralee & Dingle. ◇

Ardfert

Kate Browne's

Ⓝ PUB

Ardfert Co Kerry **Tel: 066 713 4055** / 4030
Email: katebrownepub@eircom.net

féile bia

This attractive old-fashioned pub and restaurant has an old world ambience with its roughly plastered walls, spectacular slate bar, charming use of pinewood and a very old solid fuel stove, which forms the centrepiece of a large bright and airy eating area and there is also another eating area off the main bar, where a great open fire invites guests to make themselves comfortable and feel at home. Whether you stop for morning coffee, lunch or dinner at Kate Browne's the food is good -local seafood is the star, but a wide ranging menu is offered to suit all times of day and tastes, and with generous portions. The restaurant is very popular with families and a special children's menu is offered. Food served daily, 12-10pm. **Directions:** 5 km north of Tralee, on the left as you enter Ardfert. ◇

Ballybunion

Harty-Costello Townhouse Bar & Restaurant

BAR/RESTAURANT/GUESTHOUSE

Main Street Ballybunion Co Kerry
Tel: 068 27129 Fax: 068 27489
Email: hartycostello@eircom.net Web: www.hartycostello.com

Although styled a townhouse, Davnet and Jackie Hourigan's welcoming town centre establishment is really an inn, encompassing all the elements of hospitality within its neatly painted and flower bedecked yellow walls, albeit at different times of day. The spacious bedrooms have television, direct dial phones, tea & coffee-making facilities and hair dryer, and also comfortable chairs and curtains thoughtfully fitted with blackout linings to keep out intrusively early summer light. All bedrooms, and the residents' lounge, were completely refurbished recently; while practical elements of the old rooms were sensibly retained, the style is now more contemporary and uncluttered, with disciplined use of colour and pattern creating a much more spacious atmosphere. There's a choice of no less than three bars in which to unwind and an evening restaurant where seafood is the speciality, complemented by an extensive wine list. It all adds up to a relaxing and hospitable base for a golfing holiday, or for touring the south-west. Golfing breaks and short breaks are offered: details on application. Walking; broadband WI/FI internet access; children welcome (under 12s free in parents' room); no pets. **Rooms 8** (all en-suite). B&B €70 pps, ss €20. Room service (all day). Meals available Mon-Sat, 12-4 (bar); 6.30-9.30 (restaurant). No food on Sun; establishment closed 30 Oct-30 Mar. Amex, MasterCard, Visa, Laser. **Directions:** 50 miles from Limerick N69; 40 miles from Killarney.

Ballybunion

RESTAURANT/COUNTRY HOUSE

Iragh Ti Connor

Main Street Ballybunion Co Kerry
Tel: 068 27112 Fax: 068 27787
Email: iraghticonnor@eircom.net Web: www.golfballybunion.com

The name, which translates as "the inheritance of O'Connor", says it all: what John and Joan O'Connor inherited was a 19th century pub with potential and, thanks to their scrupulous attention to detail when planning and sourcing materials like real slates and wooden windows for its transformation, their inheritance has now been transformed into a fine establishment with exceptionally large, comfortable bedrooms. All rooms have been carefully refurbished and furnished with antiques to complement the convenience of satellite television, direct dial phones and generous bathrooms with cast-iron tubs and power showers - and many rooms even have working fireplaces, where fires can be lit on request. Public areas, which include the original public bar and a lounge bar, are also generous in scale, and furnished with style and individuality. In addition to the good food served in the bar, there's a fine dining restaurant with a well-deserved reputation for its cooking, and a baby grand to add to the atmosphere. Golfing holidays are a serious attraction here and Iragh Tí Connor is fast establishing a reputation as one of the best places to stay on the discerning golfers' circuits. Free broadband; Children welcome (under 3s free in parents' room, cot available without charge). Small conferences (60). Garden. No pets. Meals daily: bar food 9.30-9.30 (1-9.30 Sun); restaurant Mon-Sat 9-9.30; Sun 12-9.30; Set Sun L €23, D à la carte. **Rooms 17** (2 junior suites, 15 superior rooms, all no smoking). B&B €95 pps, ss €60. No SC. *Golf breaks offered, with tee times arranged at Ballybunion Old Course. Closed Dec & Jan. Amex, MasterCard, Visa, Laser. **Directions:** Top of main street, opposite statue of Bill Clinton.

Ballybunion

GUESTHOUSE

Teach de Broc

Links Road Ballybunion Co Kerry
Tel: 068 27581 Fax: 068 27919
Email: info@ballybuniongolf.com Web: www.ballybuniongolf.com

HOSTS OF THE YEAR

You don't have to play golf to appreciate this highly popular guesthouse, but it certainly must help as it is almost within the boundaries of the famous Ballybunion links. Aoife and Seamus Brock offer an extremely high standard of comfort, with satellite television in all rooms, and there is a commitment to constant upgrading and improvement: recent additions include a new guest lounge and a wine/coffee bar, four more fine bedrooms, and the very practical introduction of an electric massage chair for easing golfers' aches and pains after a long day on the links. Yet, however comfortable and well-located this exceptional guesthouse may be, it's the laid-back and genuinely hospitable atmosphere created by this energetic and dedicated couple that really gets them coming back for more. Always keen to provide the best possible service for the discerning golfer, an excellent breakfast is served from 6am, with freshly baked scones and croissants among the good things offered. The wine bar idea, originally intended to offer just a light bite, has developed a little each year; home-made gourmet pizzas are the speciality of the house - a 12" thin crust with olive oil, chorizo, bacon, red onion, goats cheese & herbs for example - and the light evening meals available to residents proved such a popular alternative to going into town to eat that they have developed into 'Strollers Bistro', offering what is effectively an a la carte restaurant menu, with a choice of half a dozen starters and main courses like rack of Kerry lamb and panfried sirloin steak as well as the original pizza menu. Homemade desserts may include a speciality chocolate fondant, and an Irish cheeseboard comes with a glass of port... Wine licence. *Stay & Play golf breaks offered; details on application. Masseuse on call. Laundry service; horse riding nearby; own parking; garden. Not suitable for children; no pets; wine licence. **Rooms 14** (all en-suite, 4 with separate bath & shower, 2 shower only, all no-smoking, 1 for disabled). Lift. Turndown service. B&B €80pps, ss €50. Closed 1 Nov - 15 Mar. MasterCard, Visa, Laser. **Directions:** Directly opposite entrance to Ballybunion Golf Club.

Caherdaniel
HOTEL/RESTAURANT

Derrynane Hotel

Caherdaniel Co Kerry
Tel: 066 947 5136 Fax: 066 947 5160
Email: info@derrynane.com Web: www.derrynane.com

féile bia If only for its superb location on the seaward side of the Ring of Kerry road this unassuming 1960s-style hotel would be well worth a visit, but there is much more to it than the view, or even its waterside position. The accommodation is quite modest but very comfortable, the food is good and, under the excellent management of Mary O'Connor and her well-trained staff, this hospitable, family-friendly place provides a welcome home from home for many a contented guest. Activity holidays are a big draw - there are beautiful beaches, excellent fishing with local fisherman Michael Fenton (who supplies all necessary equipment and has a fully licensed boat), Waterville Golf Course offers special rates at certain times - and the hotel has published its own walking brochure. Don't leave the area without visiting Daniel O'Connell's beautiful house at Derrynane or the amazing Ballinskelligs chocolate factory. *Derrynane Hotel was our Family Hotel of the Year in 2005. Children welcome (under 4s free in parents' room, cots available without charge, baby sitting arranged; playroom) Heated outdoor swimming pool, tennis, pool table. Walking. Garden. **Rooms 70** (all en-suite, 15 family rooms, 32 ground floor, 50 no smoking). Room rate from €95. *Special breaks offered: details on application. Closed Oct-Easter. **Restaurant:** Beautifully located, overlooking the heated outdoor swimming pool and the hotel's gardens (which reach down to the shore), the restaurant enjoys stunning sea views - be sure to ask for a table by the sea, as the view is a major part of the experience; on a warm summer evening the huge plate glass windows slide back to let in purest Atlantic sea air - a rare treat. While not a fine dining experience, good food has always been a feature of the hotel and there is a commitment to high quality ingredients, local where possible (a list of suppliers is given). The 4-course dinner menus offer a good choice of simply presented popular dishes like smoked salmon, duck or chicken liver mousse, Kerry lamb or beef, and duckling - and a very reasonably priced children's menu is offered separately. Attentive staff do everything possible to make a meal here a pleasant experience - and a helpful wine list is clearly presented, with excellent descriptions of each bottle. *A light bar menu is also available every day, 11am-9pm. **Seats 100.** D 7-9 daily, Set D €42. Also a la Carte, sc discretionary. House wine €20. *All day salad bar available for light meals. Hotel closed Oct- Easter. Amex, Diners, MasterCard, Visa, Laser. **Directions:** Midway on Ring of Kerry.

Caherdaniel
COUNTRY HOUSE

Iskeroon

Caherdaniel Co Kerry **Tel: 066 947 5119** Fax: 066 947 5488
Email: info@iskeroon.com Web: www.iskeroon.com

Geraldine Burkitt and David Hare's beautiful old house is in a secluded position overlooking Derrynane Harbour, and the effort taken to get there makes it all the more restful once settled in. All three of the comfortable and interestingly decorated bedrooms overlook the harbour and the islands of Deenish and Scarriff and each has its own private bathroom just across a corridor. The private pier at the bottom of the garden joins an old Mass Path which, by a happy chance, leads not only to the beach but also to Keating's pub (known as Bridie's) where a bit of banter and, perhaps, some good seafood is also to be had in the evenings, although it's wise to check on this beforehand. In keeping with the caring philosophy of this lovely houses, solar panels have recently been installed to heat the water. Free Broadband. Unsuitable for children. No pets. Fishing, walking, garden. *Self-catering studio apartment for two also available. **Rooms 3** (all with private bathrooms, all no smoking). B&B €75 pps, ss €75. Closed Sep-May. MasterCard, Visa, Laser. **Directions:** Between Caherdaniel and Waterville (N70), turn off at the Scariff Inn, signed to Bunavalla Pier. Go to the pier and left through "private" gate; cross beach and enter through white gate posts.

CAHIRCIVEEN

Cahirciveen is a small market town half way round the Ring of Kerry; situated on the River Fealeat, the foot of Benetee mountain, it overlooks Valentia Harbour and is the shopping centre of South Kerry - traditional fairdays are still held on the street. Attractions of interest include the Heritage Centre - situated in the old Royal Irish Constabulary Barracks adjacent to the town centre - which has craft

workshops, an audio-visual display and archaeological remains on view. As well as **QCs**, in the town (see entry), handy places to take a break on the Ring of Kerry include **O'Neills 'The Point Bar'** (066 947 2165) at Renard Point, just beside the car ferry to Valentia island: Michael & Bridie O'Neill's immaculately maintained pub is well-known for its fresh seafood (phone ahead to check times). On the main Ring of Kerry road, it is useful to know about Pat Golden's family-run "one stop shop" the **Quarry Restaurant** (066 947 7601; www.patscraftshop.com): not only will you get good home cooking here, but there's a post office and foodstore, filling station, tourist information point, bureau de change, a fine craft shop, with quality Irish clothing and gift items - and the unique 'Golden Mile Nature Walk'.
WWW.IRELAND-GUIDE.COM FOR THE BEST PLACES TO EAT, DRINK & STAY

Cahirciveen
BAR/RESTAURANT

QC's Seafood Bar & Restaurant

3 Main Street Cahirciveen Co Kerry
Tel: 066 947 2244 Fax: 066 947 2244
Email: info@qcbar.com Web: www.qcbar.com

Kate and Andrew Cooke's sensitively renovated bar and restaurant has some great original features, such as a rugged stone wall and an enormous fireplace, and has great style. The bar counter is also over a century old and there are numerous pictures of local interest and nautical antiques, reflecting Andrew's special love affair with the sea (he runs a yacht charter service* as well as the bar). The sea is fundamental here anyway, as local fish is the main feature, supplied by the family company, Quinlan's Kerry Fish at Renard's Point. Expect delicious chargrills, with lots of olive oil and garlic: fresh crab claws and crabmeat are a speciality for example - cooked with garlic, chilli, Spanish onion & tomato, it's served sizzling in a Spanish cazueala (traditional terracotta dish); sizzling prawns are similar, and pan-seared baby squid is another speciality, served with caramelised onions and salsa verde, while wild Kerry salmon is smoked in the family factory and served simply with caper and red onion salad and home-made brown bread, and also chargrilled fillet steak to balance up all that ultra-fresh seafood. Menus are flexible - any of the starters can be served in a main course size, and, although it undoubtedly helps to like seafood, there are plenty of other choices, especially starters -like baked filo parcel of goats cheese, for example - and main courses that include excellent meats especially rack of Kerry lamb (what else?) and char-grilled fillet steak (supplied by a local butcher). The most pleasing aspect of the food is its immediacy - everything is ultra-fresh, simply prepared and full of zest. Given the quality of the food, it is also good value (average evening starter about €10; main courses from about €17). At the back of the restaurant, there's a charming sheltered outdoor dining area and landscaped garden, carved from the hillside by their own sheer willpower - and, as Andrew is quick to point out, a hired digger. [*For yacht charter information, see www.YachtCharterKerry.com] An interesting wine list leans strongly towards Spain, especially the reds, although house wines are from France & Chile; it is good to see sherry listed as a mainstream wine rather than relegated to aperitif status. €18.50. Children welcome. **Seats 48** (outdoors, 40). Meals: L in Summer (Jun-Aug) only; D 7 days in Summer, shoulder season Tue-Sun only, Winter Thu-Sun) L 12.30-2.30 (closed Sun L) & D 6-9.30; Closed 25 Dec, Good Fri; annual closure 8 Jan - end Feb. Minimum credit card charge, €25. MasterCard, Visa, Laser. **Directions:** In the centre of Caherciveen.

Caragh Lake
RESTAURANT/COUNTRY HOUSE

Carrig House Country House & Restaurant

Caragh Lake Killorglin Co Kerry
Tel: 066 976 9100 Fax: 066 976 9166
Email: info@carrighouse.com Web: www.carrighouse.com

At the heart of Frank and Mary Slattery's sensitively extended Victorian house lies a hunting lodge once owned by Lord Brocket - and he chose well, as it is very attractive and handsomely set in fine gardens with the lake and mountains providing a dramatic backdrop. The house is welcoming and well-maintained, with friendly staff (Frank himself carries the luggage to your room) and a relaxed atmosphere, notably in a series of sitting rooms where you can chat beside the fire or have a drink before dinner. This is a place where you can lose yourself for hours with a book, or playing chess, cards or board games in the games room, or boating out on the lake. Some of the large, airy bedrooms have their own patios, and all are furnished with antiques, and have generous, well-designed bathrooms with bath and shower - an impressive Presidential Suite has a sitting room with panoramic views across the lake to the Magillicuddy Reeks, two separate dressing rooms and jacuzzi bath. The extensive gardens are of great interest - a map is available, and personalised tours can be arranged. Not suitable for children under 8 except small babies (under 1 free of charge, cot available, baby sitting arranged). Dogs allowed in some areas. Swimming (lake), fishing (ghillie & boat available), walking, garden, croquet. **Rooms 16** (1 suite, 1 junior suite, 3 no smoking) B&B about €80 pps, ss €50. Closed Dec-Feb. **Lakeside Restaurant:** Beautifully situated overlooking the lake, the restaurant is a fine room with well-spaced tables and, like the rest of the house, a relaxed atmosphere. Extensive menus offer a balanced choice, with fresh Kerry seafood and Kerry lamb the main specialities; starters like freshly shucked Cromane oysters with cucumber relish and salmon, and potted Valentia Island crab with melba toast are typical and, among the dozen or so main courses offered (and served with home grown vegetables from their own walled kitchen garden) there may be an unusual dish such as a chargrilled loin of lamb with a mini shepherd's pie, several fish dishes, and a vegetarian option. **Seats 55** (private room, 15) Outdoor dining for 20. D daily, 7-9. Extensive à la carte. House wine €25. SC discretionary. Non-residents welcome (booking essential). Establishment closed Dec-Feb. Diners, MasterCard, Visa, Laser. **Directions:** Left after 2.5 miles on Killorglin/Glenbeigh Road N70 (Ring of Kerry), then turn sharp right at Caragh Lake School (1.5 miles), half a mile on the left. ◇

Caragh Lake

HOTEL

Hotel Ard na Sidhe

Caragh Lake Killorglin Co Kerry

Tel: 066 976 9105 Fax: 066 976 9282

Email: hotelsales@liebherr.com Web: www.killarneyhotels.ie

Set in woodland and among award-winning gardens, this peaceful Victorian retreat is in a beautiful mountain location overlooking Caragh Lake. Decorated throughout in a soothing country house style, very comfortable antique-filled day rooms provide plenty of lounging space for quiet indoor relaxation and a terrace for fine weather all with wonderful views. Bedrooms shared between the main house and some with private patios in the garden house are spacious and elegantly furnished in traditional style, with excellent en-suite bathrooms. This is a sister hotel to the Hotel Europe and Dunloe Castle (see entries), whose leisure facilities are also available to guests. Dooks, Waterville, Killeen and Mahony's Point golf courses are all within easy reach. **Rooms 18** (3 suites,1 family room, 5 ground floor, 6 no smoking). Under 2s free in parents' room; cots available free of charge. No pets. B&B €85 pps (ss €50), SC included. Limited room service. **Fairyhill Restaurant:** Like the rest of the hotel, the dining room has intimacy and character and, after a fireside drink and a look through the menu, this is a delightful place to spend an hour or two. There's an emphasis on local ingredients and updated interpretations of traditional Irish themes on menus that may offer aromatic Kerry mountain lamb, and may include several fish dishes, although there is a stronger emphasis on meats than is usual in the area. Finish with imaginative desserts, or the Irish cheese plate. Coffee and petits fours can be served beside the drawing room fire. Non residents are welcome by reservation. Restaurant D only, usually closed on Sun; hotel closed mid Oct- May. Amex, Diners, MasterCard, Visa, Laser. **Directions:** Off N70 Ring of Kerry road, signed 5 km west of Killorglin.

Castlegregory

PUB

Spillanes

Fahamore Maharees Castlegregory Co Kerry **Tel: 066 713 9125**

Fax: 066 713 9538 Email: marilynspillane@tinet.ie

féile bia It's a long way down from the main road to reach the Maharees, but many would make the journey just for a visit to Marilyn and Michael Spillane's great traditional pub - they work hard at both the food and hospitality and have earned loyal following as a result. There's a tempting display of salads and desserts to choose from and seafood stars on the menu - mussels grilled with garlic breadcrumbs, crab claws served in shell with brown bread and a cocktail dipping sauce, fresh and wild salmon in salads and open sandwiches, scampi made from Dingle prawns. And there's plenty for meat-lovers too, such as chargrilled steaks and chicken dishes (in the evening), some vegetarian dishes and some with child-appeal too. The pub is full of character and it can get very busy at times, which can mean a queue to be seated - and this sometimes puts the service under pressure so that tables are not cleared as thoroughly as one might like. *Self-catering accommodation also offered, in two new 2-bedroom apartments opposite the pub (beside beach); each sleeps 5. Meals daily in high season, 1-9.30 (Sun 2-9); early season (Apr-May) and late season (Oct): 1-4 & 6-9pm. Closed Nov-Mar. MasterCard, Visa, Laser. **Directions:** Dingle Peninsula,3.5 miles north of Castlegregory, between Bandon and Tralee bays.

DINGLE AREA

Dingle Town / Ventry / Slea Head Areas: The main town in Kerry's most northerly peninsula, Dingle is a lively all-year destination renowned for its music, crafts, fishing and, for over twenty years, for its most famous inhabitant, Funghi the friendly dolphin. This Gaeltacht (Irish speaking area) is of great historical interest, and there are many ancient remains, especially in the Ventry / Slea Head / Ballyferriter area west of the town. **Dingle Town: Goat Street Café** (066 915 2770), on the main street, does lovely zesty food, including delicious sandwiches (also to take away), and **Global Village** (066 915 2325) on Main Street offers daily-changed menus cooked by proprietor-chef Martin Bealin, and the recently-opened cafe **Cassidys on the Pier** (066 915 2952) serves interesting food all day in summer, beginning with breakfast, and a seriously tempting evening menu at certain times. **West of Dingle: The Stone House** is a restaurant inspired by the Gallarus Oratory, just across the road; this extraordinary grey building even has a stone roof - and fortunately for the hungry visitor, good food too; well-balanced evening menus offer a wide choice, daily lunch menus are on a blackboard. Near Smerwick Harbour, and on the Kerry Way walking route, **Tig Bhric** (066 915 6325; www.tigbhric.com) is beside the early Christian monastic settlement Riasc (7 miles west of Dingle); it's a delightful bar, B&B and shop offering lovely home-made soups and sandwiches in the daytime, and dinner every evening except Friday - when there is traditional music. Nearby, the **Smerwick Harbour Hotel** (066 915 6470; www.smerwickhotel.com) offers all the usual facilities and makes an unusual conference venue.

WWW.IRELAND-GUIDE.COM FOR THE BEST PLACES TO EAT, DRINK & STAY

Dingle

Ashes Bar

N BAR/RESTAURANT WITH ROOMS

Main Street Dingle Co Kerry
Tel: 066 915 0989 Web: www.jamesashes.com

This old pub in the centre of Dingle has a smart traditional frontage, and lots of warm mahogany that makes for a warm and cosy feeling in the friendly bar. The pub goes back to 1849 and is now by a young couple, Thomas Ashe and Sinead Roche, who have put a lot of energy into the business over the last few years, earning a great reputation for both food and hospitality. Menus offer a lot of seafood, as would be expected - lobster and scallops are specialities, although the range is wide - but there are plenty of other choices too, including homely traditional dishes like beef & Guinness stew and pot-roasted lamb shank, plus at least one vegetarian dish. A list of daily specials introduces extra seafood on the day - tempura of pollock, for example, maybe even crayfish (at a price) if you're lucky - and desserts include delicious renditions of old favourites like bread and butter pudding. Good cooking, great staff and a relaxed atmosphere make this an excellent choice for informal dining. **Seats 50;** L&D Mon-Sat, 12-3 & 6-9; Set L €13; Set D €21/30, 2/3 courses; house wine €18. Closed Sun, 25 Dec. *Also have 4 bedrooms (2 family rooms, all shower only, all no smoking); children welcome (under 3s free in parents' room, free cot available, baby sitting arranged); B&B €45 pps, ss €15. MasterCard, Visa, Laser. **Directions:** Lower Main Street, Dingle.

Dingle

Bambury's Guesthouse

GUESTHOUSE

Mail Road Dingle Co Kerry **Tel: 066 915 1244** Fax: 066 915 1786
Email: info@bamburysguesthouse.com Web: www.bamburysguesthouse.com

féile bia Just a couple of minutes walk from the centre of Dingle, Jimmy and Bernie Bambury's well-run, purpose-built guesthouse has spacious modern rooms with tea/coffee trays, phone, satellite TV, hair dryer and complimentary mineral water. Bernie Bambury's breakfasts include griddle cakes with fresh fruit and honey a house speciality and vegetarian breakfasts are offered by arrangement. Not suitable for children under 5; no pets. Own parking. **Rooms 12** (all shower only & no smoking, 3 for disabled) B&B about €55, ss about €20. Open all year. MasterCard, Visa, Laser. **Directions:** On N86, on the left after the Shell garage, on entering Dingle. ◇

Dingle

Captains House

B&B

The Mall Dingle Co Kerry **Tel: 066 915 1531** Fax: 066 915 1079
Email: captigh@eircom.net Web: homepage.eircom.net/ncaptigh/

When Jim, a retired sea captain, and Mary Milhench bought this guesthouse in the late '80s they were renewing a seafaring tradition going back to the original captain, Tom Williams, who first took lodgers here in 1886. Today this charming house is as relaxed and hospitable a place as could be wished for: approached via a little bridge over the Mall River then through a lovely garden, it has been renovated and furnished with the antiques and curios collected by Jim on his voyages. The age and nature of the building - which extends into the next door premises - has created a higgledy-piggledy arrangement of rooms that adds to the charm; rooms vary considerably, as would be expected, but all have comfort (orthopaedic beds, phones, satellite TV, hospitality trays, plenty of hot water) as well as character. A welcoming turf fire in the reception area encourages guests to linger over tea, or with a book, and breakfast - which is a very special feature of a stay here - is served in the conservatory. Don't forget to visit Jim's garden centre, just across the road from the back door. It's a revelation! Not suitable for children. No pets. * Self-catering also available, in a large bungalow with privacy, sea views, terrace, garden, slipway & boat dock; 1 mile from Dingle town. **Rooms 8** (7 shower only, all no smoking). B&B about €50pps, ss about €10. Closed early Nov-mid Mar. MasterCard, Visa, Laser. **Directions:** Turn right at town entrance roundabout; Captains House is 100 metres up on left. ◇

Dingle

Castlewood House

Ⓝ GUESTHOUSE

The Wood Dingle Co Kerry **Tel: 066 915 2788** Fax: 065 915 2110
Email: castlewoodhouse@eircom.net Web: www.castlewooddingle.com

This luxurious new purpose-built guesthouse on the western edge of Dingle town is run by Brian and Helen Heaton - Brian's parents, Nuala and Cameron, run the well-established Heaton's guesthouse next door and a little gate connects the two. Although it is on the land side of the road the house is built on a rise and, from the many rooms with sea views, all you are aware of is the view across Dingle Bay. The scale is generous throughout: public rooms include an impressive dining room where a good breakfast is served, and a drawing room with views across the bay for guests' use. Guest rooms are spacious and individually decorated, with smart bathrooms and a lot of attention to detail. **Rooms 12** (2 Junior Suites, 3 Family Rooms, 1 for disabled) all no smoking. Children under 6 free in parents room, cots available free of charge. Lift. Closed Dec-mid Feb (open few days over New Years day). MasterCard, Visa, Laser. **Directions:** Take Milltown road from Dingle, located around 500m from town centre on the right. ◇

Dingle

The Chart House

☆RESTAURANT

The Mall Dingle Co Kerry
Tel: 066 915 2255 Fax: 066 915 2255
Email: charthse@iol.ie Web: www.charthousedingle.com

féile bia Even in an area so well-endowed with good eating places, Jim McCarthy's attractive stone-built restaurant is outstanding. There's a smart little bar just inside the door - where Jim, the perfect host, always seems to be meeting, seating and seamlessly ensuring that everyone is well looked after and generally having a good time. And head chef Noel Enright leads a talented kitchen team: his menus are based on the best of local ingredients, sometimes in dishes with an international tone - a superb speciality starter of Annascaul black pudding, for example, is wrapped in filo pastry and served with apple and date chutney and hollandaise sauce, while roast breast of Skeaghanore duck comes with crispy polenta, minted yoghurt and chilli garlic oil; other dishes are just gently updated - rack of Kerry mountain lamb, for example, may be accompanied by a butter bean purée and bay leaf jus; accurate, confident cooking lends these traditional foods a new character, and a large selection - perhaps half a dozen or more - of simple, perfectly cooked side vegetables are the ideal complement. Seafood is well represented, of course - three or four seafood choices might include a less usual fish dish like herb crusted skate, and mainstream vegetarian dishes - possibly two or more on each course - have wide appeal. Desserts include classics like a basket of home-made ice creams, or luscious lemon scented pannacotta, with a wild berry compôte and shortbread biscuits: superb! But those with a savoury tooth will still feel that the smart money is on the Irish cheeses (Ardrahan, Gubbeen, Cashel Blue, perhaps, all in perfect condition), which are cannily offered with a glass of vintage port and served with delicious home-made oat biscuits and two varieties of grapes. Terrific hospitality, top class ingredients and gimmick-free creative cooking all add up to a great restaurant, and a recent visit confirms its place among Ireland's finest establishments. Prices are fairly moderate (starters around €9, main courses average about €22). An interesting wine list includes South African wines imported directly, and has helpful tasting notes as well as a clear layout of country of origin and vintages - and, of course, there's always a Chateau MacCarthy in stock. *Jim McCarthy was our Host of the Year in 2003. **Seats 45.** Children welcome. Air conditioning. D 6.30-10, daily in summer (Jun-Sep), restricted opening in winter - please phone ahead to check; set D €35, also à la carte. SC discretionary. House wine €19.50. Closed 6 Jan-13 Feb. MasterCard, Visa, Laser. **Directions:** Left at the roundabout as you enter the town.

Dingle

Dingle Benners Hotel

HOTEL

Main Street Dingle Co Kerry **Tel: 066 915 1638** Fax: 066 915 1412
Email: info@dinglebenners.com Web: www.dinglebenners.com

Major refurbishment and the addition of spacious new rooms at the back have greatly improved this 300 year old centrally-located hotel. Public areas include a streetside bar which has more character than expected of an hotel (food available from 12 noon daily) and a large, bright, dining room towards the back of the building. Bedrooms in the older part of the hotel have more character (some have four-posters), but the newer back bedrooms are quieter and make a very comfortable base within comfortable walking distance of all parts of the town. Golf nearby. Private parking (50). Banqueting (100). Children welcome (under 3 free in parents' room, cot available without charge, baby sitting arranged). No pets. **Rooms 52** (33 superior, 9 no smoking, 4 suitable for less able guests). Lift. B&B €107 pps, ss €25. *Short breaks offer good value - details on application. Closed 18-26 Dec. Amex, Diners, MasterCard, Visa, Laser. **Directions:** Town centre, half way up Main Street on left beside Bank of Ireland.

Dingle
HOTEL

Dingle Skellig Hotel

Dingle Co Kerry **Tel: 066 915 0200** Fax: 066 915 1501
Email: reservations@dingleskellig.com Web: www.dingleskellig.com

FAMILY FRIENDLY HOTEL OF THE YEAR

féile bia It may be modest-looking from the road, but this 1960s hotel enjoys a superb shoreside location on the edge of the town and has won many friends over the years. It is a particularly well-run, family-friendly hotel, with organised entertainment for children - and an especially attractive feature of the hotel is their policy of dedicating floors for family use to avoid disturbing those without children. And, while outdoor activities are a major attraction to the area, it's nice to know there's some kind of insurance for unpredictable weather - in this case an excellent leisure centre, recently joined by a luxurious health and beauty centre, the Peninsula Spa. Public areas in the hotel are roomy and comfortably furnished with a fair degree of style - and good use is made of sea views throughout. Constant improvement and regular refurbishment has always been the policy here and, while there are still some standard bedrooms (fair-sized, with bathrooms that are on the small side but quite well designed), there are now more executive rooms and junior suites. Although best known as a family holiday destination, the Dingle Skellig also has good conference and business meeting facilities. Golf nearby. Conference/banqueting (250/230); video conferencing by arrangement. Children under 3 free in parents' bedrooms; cots available free of charge, baby sitting arranged; crèche, playroom, children's playground. Garden, fishing, leisure centre, swimming pool, spa. [*Dingle Benner's Hotel (see entry) is in the same ownership.] **Rooms 111** (8 suites, 5 junior suites, 28 executive,1 for disabled, 1 shower only, 76 no-smoking). Lift. B&B €120, ss €20. **Restaurant:** Attractively located on the sea side of the hotel, the restaurant is in a large conservatory area and considerately fitted with ant-glare glass. While not a fine dining destination in the sense that some restaurants in this exceptionally well-endowed town may be, you may be sure of a very pleasant dining experience here - there is a commitment to using fresh local ingredients and the cooking is sound; there's always local seafood, of course, but well-balanced menus offer plenty of choice for everyone, and friendly, solicitous staff do everything possible to ensure that all is well. Golf nearby. Conference/banqueting (250/230); video conferencing by arrangement. Children under 3 free in parents' bedrooms; cots available free of charge, baby sitting arranged; crèche, playroom, children's playground. Garden, fishing, leisure centre, swimming pool, spa. [*Dingle Benner's Hotel (see entry) is in the same ownership.] **Rooms 111** (8 suites, 5 junior suites, 28 executive,1 for disabled, 1 shower only, 76 no-smoking). Lift. B&B €120, ss €20. Restaurant: D daily in summer, 7-9; bar meals 12.30-9. *Short breaks (e.g. golf, spa, off-season) offer good value; details on application. Self-catering also available, in the hotel's Dingle Marina Cottages. Hotel open weekends only in winter (Nov-mid Feb); closed 17-27 Dec. Amex, Diners, MasterCard, Visa, Laser. **Directions:** On the sea side of the road as you approach Dingle from Tralee & Killarney.

Dingle
RESTAURANT WITH ROOMS

Doyle's Seafood Restaurant & Townhouse

5 John Street Dingle Co Kerry
Tel: 066 915 1174 Fax: 066 915 1816
Email: cdoyles@iol.ie Web: www.doylesofdingle.com

féile bia Originally a small pub built in 1790, Doyles was established as a restaurant over a quarter of a century ago - and was one of the first in a town which is now renowned for good eating places. Currently in the hospitable hands of Charlotte Cluskey and her son John, it's a cosy, characterful place with an old kitchen range and natural materials - stone floor, kitchen tables and sugan chairs, a real wooden bar and high stools - which all create a relaxed country atmosphere in keeping with its history. Local seafood is the main attraction - nightly specials depend on the day's landings - and lobster, selected from a tank in the bar, is a speciality. Aside from lobster, speciality seafood dishes include hot oysters glazed with a horseradish sabayon, a West Coast platter and baked fish pie 'Doyle's style' (a tasty mixture of fish in a creamy wine sauce with crumb & cheese crust). There are, however, one or two concessions to non-seafood eaters such as Kerry mountain lamb done various ways (roast rack and leg with braised puy lentils, roast garlic & thyme jus is a favourite) or traditional beef & Guinness stew, and vegetarian dishes are available. Puddings are nice and traditional or there's a plated selection of farmhouse cheeses to finish. Accommodation is also offered. **Seats 46;** air conditioning; D only, Mon-Sat 6-10. Early D €25/30 (6-7.15pm), 2/3 course set D €25/30, also à la carte; house wine €19.95; no sc. Restaurant cosed Sun. B&B about €76 pps, ss about €64. Establishment closed 1-26 Dec . Amex, Diners, MasterCard, Visa, Laser. **Directions:** On entering Dingle, take third exit from roundabout into The Mall; turn right into John Street.

Dingle

Emlagh House

COUNTRY HOUSE

Dingle Co Kerry **Tel: 066 915 2345** Fax: 066 915 2369
Email: info@emlaghhouse.com Web: www.emlaghhouse.com

The Kavanagh family's luxurious guesthouse is tucked into a site close to the Dingle Skellig Hotel, on the sea side of the road; it has been built with exceptional attention to detail and is maturing gracefully as the landscaping fills in. The style throughout the house is gracious, in large, well-proportioned rooms furnished in traditional country house style but with a contemporary streak that gives it a welcome lightness of touch. Bedrooms (most of which have harbour views) are elegant and extremely comfortable, with fresh flowers, fruit and chocolates to greet guests on arrival and many features, including individually controlled heating/air conditioning, trouser press with iron, direct dial phone with modem, satellite TV, video, radio & CD - the latter wired to luxurious marbled bathrooms with underfloor heating, separate shower and bath, double basins, heated mirror and towel rails and thick bathrobes. Some interconnecting rooms are available to provide private accommodation for groups. Hosts Marion and Gráinne Kavanagh do everything possible to make guests comfortable, and their attention to detail includes an evening turndown service. Evening meals are not offered, as the restaurants of Dingle are so near, but excellent breakfasts are served in a stylish dining room where contemporary influences in the decor are skilfully blended with antiques. A new conservatory overlooking the harbour is under construction as we go to press, providing another place for guests to read and relax; also a sister property offering self-catering accommodation. Many activities (golf, fishing, sailing, equestrian) available nearby. Not suitable for children under 10 yrs. No pets. Own parking (20). **Rooms 10** (all no smoking, 1 for disabled). Lift. B&B €125pps, ss €40. Residents D Mon-Sat, 6.30-8. No D on Sun. A la carte. House wine from €24. Closed 1 Nov-15 Mar. Amex, MasterCard, Visa, Laser. **Directions:** Upon entering Dingle, take first left after petrol station.

Dingle

Greenmount House

GUESTHOUSE

Upper John Street Dingle Co Kerry
Tel: 066 915 1414 Fax: 066 915 1974
Email: info@greenmount-house.com Web: www.greenmount-house.com

Just five minutes walk from the centre of Dingle, John and Mary Curran have run one of Ireland's finest guesthouses since the mid-70s. It's an exceptionally comfortable place to stay, quietly located on the hillside, with private parking and uninterrupted views across the town and harbour to the mountains across the bay. The spacious, well-appointed bedrooms are mainly junior suites with generous seating areas and particularly good amenities, including fridges as well as tea/coffee-making trays, phone and TV (and, in most cases, also their own entrance and balcony); all bathrooms have recently been upgraded and a hot tub installed. There's a comfortable residents' sitting room with an open fire, and a conservatory overlooking the harbour, where wonderful breakfasts are served. Greenmount won our Irish Breakfast Award for the Munster region, in 2001, and it has always been a point of pride: the aroma of home baking is one of the things that gives this house a special warmth, and all the preserves are home-made too; there's a wonderful buffet - laden down with all kinds of fresh and poached fruits, juices, yogurts, cheeses, freshly baked breads - as well as an extensive choice of hot dishes, including the traditional full Irish breakfast. The wonder is that anyone ever leaves this place of a morning at all. Not suitable for children under 8. No pets. Garden, walking. Parking (15). **Rooms 12** (7 junior suites, 3 shower only, 2 ground floor, all no smoking). B&B €85pps, ss €45, SC discretionary. Closed Dec&Jan. MasterCard, Visa, Laser. **Directions:** Turn right and right again on entering Dingle.

Dingle

The Half Door

RESTAURANT

John Street Dingle Co Kerry **Tel: 066 915 1600**
Fax: 066 915 1883 Web: halfdoor@iol.ie

Denis and Teresa O'Connor's cottagey restaurant is one of the prettiest in town and well-known for great seafood. Menus go with the seasons but whatever is available is perfectly cooked and generously served without over-presentation. An outstanding speciality of the house is the seafood platter, available hot or cold as either a starter or main course with (depending on availability of individual items) lobster, oysters, Dublin Bay prawns, scallops, crab claws and mussels (attractively presented with garlic or lemon butter). Good traditional puddings or Irish farmhouse cheeses to follow. **Seats 50.** Air conditioning. D Mon-Sat, 6-10. Early D 6-6.30 only; later, à la carte. Closed Sun; several days at Christmas. [Times not confirmed at time of going to press.] MasterCard, Visa, **Directions:** On entering Dingle, turn right onto The Mall at roundabout, then right onto John Street. ◇

Dingle
GUESTHOUSE

Heatons House

The Wood Dingle Co Kerry **Tel: 066 915 2288** Fax: 066 915 2324
Email: heatons@iol.ie Web: www.heatonsdingle.com

Cameron and Nuala Heaton's fine purpose-built guesthouse is set in well-maintained gardens just across the road from the water and, although convenient to the town, it's beyond the hustle and bustle of the busy streets. An impressive foyer-lounge area sets the tone on arrival and spacious, regularly refurbished, bedrooms confirm first impressions: all have bathrooms finished to a very high standard and phones, TV and hospitality trays - and the junior suites and superior rooms are not only luxurious, but also very stylish in a refreshingly contemporary idiom. Getting guests off to a good start each day is a point of honour and breakfast includes an extensive buffet (everything from fresh juices to cold meats and Irish cheeses) as well as a full hot breakfast menu. (See also Castlewood House.) Fishing, walking, garden. Not suitable for children under 8. No pets. **Rooms 16** (2 junior suites, 5 superior, 2 family rooms, 5 ground floor, 1 for disabled, all no smoking). B&B €67 pps, ss €32. Room service (limited hours). Closed 7 Jan-2 Feb. MasterCard, Visa, Laser. **Directions:** 600 metres beyond marina, at front of town.

Dingle
BAR/RESTAURANT

Lord Baker's Restaurant & Bar

Dingle Co Kerry **Tel: 066 915 1277** Fax: 066 915 2174
Email: info@lordbakers.ie Web: www.lordbakers.ie

Believed to be the oldest pub in Dingle, this business was established in 1890 by a Tom Baker. A popular businessman in the area, a colourful orator, member of Kerry County Council and a director of the Tralee-Dingle Railway, he was known locally as "Lord Baker" and as such is now immortalised in John Moriarty's excellent bar and restaurant in the centre of Dingle. A welcoming turf fire burns in the front bar, where bar food such as chowder and home-baked bread or crab claws in garlic butter is served. At the back, there's a more sophisticated dining set-up in the restaurant proper (and, beyond it, a walled garden). Seafood (notably lobster from their own tank) stars, of course, and speciality dishes include monkfish wrapped in bacon, with garlic cream sauce, and classic seafood mornay; but there's also a good choice of other dishes using local mountain lamb (roast rack or braised shank, perhaps), also Kerry beef, chicken, and local duckling all well-cooked and served in an atmosphere of great hospitality. In addition to the main menu there are chef's specials each evening - and an unusual house speciality features on the dessert menu: traditional plum pudding with brandy sauce! Sunday lunch in the restaurant is a particularly popular event and very well done (booking strongly advised); on other days, the lunchtime bar menu, plus one or two daily specials such as a roast, can be taken in the restaurant. An informative wine list includes a Connoisseur's Selection of ten wines. John is an excellent host, caring and watchful - no detail escapes his notice, ensuring that every guest in Dingle's largest restaurant will leave contented. **Seats 120.** L Fri-Wed, 12.30-2; D Fri-Wed, 6-10. Set D €24, also à la carte; light lunch, €10. House wine €22. Closed Thurs, 24-26 Dec & Good Friday. Amex, MasterCard, Visa, Laser. **Directions:** Town centre.

Dingle
GUESTHOUSE

Milltown House

Dingle Co Kerry **Tel: 066 915 1372** Fax: 066 915 1095
Email: info@milltownhousedingle.com Web: www.milltownhousedingle.com

The Kerry family's attractive guesthouse on the western side of Dingle, is set in immaculate gardens running down to the water's edge and enjoys beautiful views of the harbour and distant mountains. Day rooms include an informal reception room, a comfortably furnished sitting room and a conservatory breakfast room overlooking the garden - breakfast is quite an event, offering everything from fresh juices and fruit, through cold meats and cheeses, freshly baked breads and an extensive cooked breakfast menu. The bedrooms all very comfortable and thoughtfully furnished with phone, TV with video channel, tea/coffee making facilities and iron/trouser press - include two with private patios. Constant upgrading is the policy here: a number of rooms have recently been increased in size and a new lounge, with sea and mountain views, was added to the front of the house. Not suitable for children under 10. No pets. Garden. **Rooms 10** (6 junior suites, all with full bath en-suite, all no smoking, 3 ground floor). B&B €75 pps, ss €50. Room service (limited hours). Closed 28 Oct-27 Apr. Amex, MasterCard, Visa, Laser. **Directions:** West through Dingle town, 0.75 miles from town centre.

Dingle

B&B

Number Fifty Five

55 John Street Dingle Co Kerry **Tel: 066 915 2378**
Email: stelladoyle@eircom.net Web: www.stella.thewub.com

Stella Doyle's charming B&B in the centre of Dingle offers accommodation with character - and a high level of comfort at a very affordable price. Although the frontage seems small from the road, it is larger than it looks: the two guest bedrooms are on the ground floor and delightfully furnished in a fresh country house style, with television and full bathrooms (bath and power shower). But there is a surprise in store when you go upstairs to the first floor and find a light and spacious open plan living room, which has great style and, like the rest of the house, is furnished with antiques and original art. There's a large seating area at one end and, at the other, a dining area with large windows looking out to fields at the back of the house; here Stella, who spent most of her working life as a chef, serves delicious breakfasts for guests; no menu - 'anything you like, really'. Guests are welcomed to this hospitable haven with a cup of tea on arrival - and breakfast is sure to send them happily on their way. Not suitable for children. No pets. **Rooms 2** (both en-suite with full bath & no smoking). B&B €35-37.50 pps, ss €15. Closed 30 Sep-mid Apr. **No Credit Cards. Directions:** At main road roundabout, turn right up the mall; turn right up John Street - the house is at the top on the left side.

Dingle

RESTAURANT

Out of the Blue

Waterside Dingle Co Kerry **Tel: 066 915 0811**
Email: info@outoftheblue.ie Web: www.outoftheblue.ie

Tim Mason's deli and seafood restaurant is an absolute delight. Discerning locals know how lucky they are to have such an exciting little place on their doorstep and it's just the kind of thing that visitors dream of finding - it is not unusual to find a different language spoken at every table. Although its brightly-painted exterior sends mixed messages from the road, once you get inside it is obvious that this is a highly focused operation, where only the best will do: there's a little wine bar at the front and, in the simple room at the back, seriously delicious seafood cookery is the order of the day for those lucky enough to get a table. Everything depends on the fresh fish supply from the boats that day and if there's no fresh fish, they don't open. Head chef Jean-Marie Vireaux cooks wonderful classics, sometimes with a modern twist - examples might include Glenbeigh mussels 'marinières', traditional French-style soups (with home-made brown bread), Dublin Bay prawns (langoustines) with garlic butter, perhaps, or sweet chilli sauce, and there may be less usual fish like pollock. Lobster is more expensive than it was but still reasonably priced in comparison with some other restaurants, and you may sometimes be offered crayfish, which is a rarity on Irish menus - and this is reflected in the price (€65 per 500g); either might be cooked 'en casserole' with cognac, or chargrilled with thyme & olive oil, then served with garlic butter. A short but skilfully assembled wine list complements the food perfectly - and has a dozen fish named in five languages on the back: this place is a little gem. Toilets wheelchair accessible. **Seats 28** (+ 20 outdoors). L & D Thu-Tue,L 12.30-3, D 6.30-9.30 (Sun 6-8.30). Reservations accepted (required for D). A la carte. House wines from €18. Closed Wed ('usually'), also days when fresh fish is unavailable & mid Nov-early Mar. MasterCard, Visa, Laser, Switch. **Directions:** Opposite the pier on Dingle harbour.

Dingle

GUESTHOUSE

Pax House

Upper John Street Dingle Co Kerry **Tel: 066 915 1518**
Fax: 066 915 2641 Email: paxhouse@iol.ie Web: www.pax-house.com

Just half a mile out of Dingle, this modern house enjoys what may well be the finest view in the area and, thanks to the exceptional hospitality and high standards of the owners, Joan and Ron Brosnan-Wright, is also one of the most comfortable and relaxing places to stay. The furnishing style is daringly bright and fresh, and thoughtfully furnished bedrooms have every amenity (including little fridges as well as phone, TV, tea/coffee making facilities and iron/trouser press) and well-finished bathrooms, most with full bath. Two suites have their own terraces where guests can lounge around and enjoy that stupendous view. Breakfast is a major event with lots of home-made goodies - yogurt, preserves, breads - and some unusual dishes like sardines on toast and home-made white drisheen (also known as white pudding) served on a waffle, with raspberry sauce. Freshly smoked Dingle Bay mackerel (when available), as well as the more usual kippers. Children welcome (u 3s free in parents room, cots available at no charge). Pets permitted by arrangement. Garden, walking. **Rooms 13** (3 superior, 5 shower only, 1 family room, 6 ground floor, all no-smoking). B&B €70 pps, €30 ss. Wine licence. Closed 1 Nov-1Apr. MasterCard, Visa, Laser. **Directions:** Turn off at sign on N86.

Dingle Area

Gorman's Clifftop House & Restaurant

RESTAURANT/GUESTHOUSE

Glaise Bheag Ballydavid Dingle Peninsula Co Kerry
Tel: 066 915 5162 Fax: 066 915 5003
Email: info@gormans-clifftophouse.com Web: www.gormans-clifftophouse.com

féile bia

Beautifully situated near Smerwick Harbour on the Slea Head scenic drive and Dingle Way walking route, Sile and Vincent Gorman's guesthouse is, as they say themselves "just a great place to relax and unwind". It's also a very comfortable place to do this, as the whole premises has recently been virtually rebuilt and upgraded to a high standard. Natural materials and warm colours are a feature throughout the house and open fires, newspapers and books in two generous lounging areas (and a lot of pottery from the nearby Louis Mulcahy workshops) create a welcoming laid-back atmosphere. Bedrooms include some on the ground floor with easy access from the parking area, and four superior rooms with jacuzzi bath, safes suitable for laptops, CD players and ironing facilities; but all rooms are attractively furnished in country style and very comfortable, with beautiful satin cotton sheets, broadband, TV and thoughtfully finished bathrooms with extra large Turkish bath sheets - and most rooms now have king size beds. The Gormans are knowledgeable and helpful hosts too, giving personal advice where it's needed. Breakfast - an excellent buffet with home-baked breads, freshly squeezed juices, fruits, cheeses and cold meats as well as hot dishes cooked to order - is a treat that will set you up for the day. *Gorman's was our Guesthouse of the Year in 2002. Children welcome (under 3s free in parents' room, cot available free of charge). No pets. Garden, cycling, walking. **Rooms 9** (2 junior suites, 2 superior, 1 for less able, 1 shower only, all no smoking). B&B €855 pps, ss €35. Short breaks offered - details on application. **Restaurant:** With large windows commanding superb sea views and, on fine evenings, spectacular sunsets, this is a wonderful place to enjoy Vincent Gorman's good cooking. Begin with a fresh seafood chowder, perhaps - or an attractive speciality of potato cake & Annsacaul black pudding sandwich with mushroom & bacon sauce, which is lighter than it sounds; main courses include several seafood dishes (trio of plaice, John Dory and prawns with carrot & dill sauce, perhaps) and the ever-popular sirloin steak (house style, with scallion mash, mushroom & brandy sauce); vegetarian choices are always given - a main course of grilled aubergine and roasted pepper mille feuille with spinach & goats cheese is a speciality - and copious dishes of delicious vegetables are left on the table for guests to help themselves. Desserts are a strong point too: home-made ice creams, chocolate nemesis, and rhubarb & strawberry crumble are just a few of the temptations on offer, or you can finish with an Irish cheese plate. Sile, who is a warm and solicitous host, supervises front of house. A well thought out wine list includes organic house wines and a good choice of half bottles. **Seats 35.** D Mon-Sat, 7-9pm. Set D €32/38.50. House wine from €18.50. Restaurant closed Sun. House open Oct-Mar by reservation only; Closed 1 Jan-10 Feb. MasterCard, Visa, Laser. **Directions:** 12.5km (8 m) from roundabout west of Dingle Town - sign posted An Fheothanach. Keep left at V.

Dingle Area

The Old Pier

RESTAURANT/GUESTHOUSE

Feothanach Ballydavid Co Kerry **Tel: 066 915 5242**
Email: info@oldpier.com Web: www.oldpier.com

Situated on the edge of the world overlooking the Atlantic and the Blasket Islands, the Old Pier B&B and Restaurant at Ballydavid is so popular with locals that there are two sittings for dinner - and (unusually in this part of the world) the importance of punctuality is stressed: arriving for the first sitting at 6.30, you may well find the restaurant already choc-a-block with people having a good time. Extensive menus are strong on local seafood a choice of about ten fish dishes may include lobster, crayfish, black sole, prawns (langoustine) and squid when available. There's a house chowder (of course), mixed fish dishes based on the available catch, succulent bakes such as fresh cod in breadcrumbs and plenty else besides, including good steaks and other meat dishes such as a delicious fillet of pork in a creamy mushroom sauce. A wide choice of tasty side dishes includes several potato dishes and old favourites like battered onion rings. The cooking is good and this, together with generous portions, moderate prices and efficient, good-humoured service have all earned a following for this big-hearted restaurant. **Accommodation:** The pine-furnished en-suite rooms are offered in various combinations (single, twin, double, family) and have tea/coffee facilities, hair dryer and sea or mountain views. Special offers apply all year round. Children welcome; **Seats 38** (private room, 10, outdoors, 20); reservations required; D served daily, 6.30pm & 8.30 pm; set 5 course D €32.95; house wine from €14.95. Restaurant closed Nov-Mar, accommodation open all year. MasterCard, Visa, Laser. **Directions:** 11.5km (8m) west of Dingle.

Dingle Area

The Phoenix

Ⓝ RESTAURANT/FARMHOUSE

Shanahill East Castlemaine Co Kerry **Tel: 066 976 6284**
Email: phoenixtyther@hotmail.com Web: www.thephoenixorganic.com

This unusual restaurant exudes charm with its rambling gardens you can choose whether to eat outside, beneath trailing honeysuckle and beams adorned with fairy lights, or inside in the relaxed and cheerful little dining area at the gable end of the house. There is a relaxing sense of peace, and the menu promises organic wines and the best of local and organic produce: a delicious salad of artichoke hearts and Castlegregory brie with red pepper salsa, perhaps, or homemade soup that is almost a meal in itself. It may be difficult to choose from the six equally delicious main courses offered: a good choice (provided you like polenta cake, which can seem very bland) might be a dish like goat's cheese on a spinach polenta cake with apricot and red pepper salsa, or perhaps tofu and sweet potato curry with basmati rice and salad, which arrives garnished with herbs and flowers from the garden. Dining at the Phoenix is an earthy experience where there is respect for all that is nature: Lucy the kitten may sleep on a cushioned seat, and there are three dogs which guests sometimes take for a stroll. The Phoenix also offers B&B, hostel accommodation, gypsy caravans, chalet rental, and ample gardens to pitch a tent. Guests are offered an opportunity to explore the natural garden where most of the kitchen produce is picked fresh daily. All in all this is a little gem, where you may find a touch of magic adding an extra dimension to a calm and relaxed evening. Camping, caravans, chalets, packed lunches and airport transfers all available. Rooms from €20-27 pps, ss + 50%; breakfast €8, D from €14.50. Closed Oct-Easter (may open by arrangement). **Directions:** 7km (4 m) west of Castlemaine on the R561 coastal road to Dingle. (N70 from Killarney or Tralee). ◇

Fenit

The Tankard

BAR/RESTAURANT

Kilfenora Fenit Tralee Co Kerry **Tel: 066 713 6164**
Fax: 066 713 6516 Email: tankard@eircom.net

Easily spotted on the seaward side of the road from Tralee, this bright yellow pub and restaurant has built up a great reputation, especially for seafood. An imaginative bar menu, which overlaps to some extent with the restaurant à la carte, is available from lunchtime to late evening, serving a good range of food. Seafood chowder with home-made brown bread, hot snacks such as steamed mussels Tankard-style, warm salads, or cold seafood dishes like fresh crab and apple salad (€9.50) and - a house speciality - The Tankard seafood platter (about €20), for example, and plenty of other dishes too, including warm chicken salad, home-made burgers, pastas sandwiches and wraps. Children's menu. **Seats 130.** D daily 6-10, L daily, 12-4. Set Sun L €20, Set D €35; also à la carte. House wines from €18; sc discretionary *Bar meals daily, 2-10. Closed 25 Dec & Good Fri. Amex, Diners, MasterCard, Visa, Laser. **Directions:** 5 miles from Tralee on Spa/Fenit road.

Fenit

West End Bar & Restaurant

B&B/RESTAURANT/PUB

Fenit Tralee Co Kerry **Tel: 066 713 6246**
Fax: 066 713 6599 Email: westend@hotmail.com

The O'Keeffes have been in business here since 1885, and the present pub - which is exactly seven minutes walk from the marina - was built by chef Bryan O'Keeffe's grandmother, in 1925. Good food is available in both the cosy bar (which has an open fire) and the restaurant, which has earned a sound reputation in the area and includes an attractive conservatory dining area at the harbour end of the building, which has recently been completely refurbished. Bryan is a member of the Panel of Chefs of Ireland and his style is "classic French with Irish popular cuisine", with seafood and meats billed almost equally as specialities. Hand-written menus offer over a dozen starters ranging from Tralee Bay seafood chowder with brown bread, through classic mussels 'Ernie Evans' style, to deep-fried 'Roulet Brie' pieces. Main courses also include old favourites - steaks, half roast duckling - and a very wide range of seafood dishes, leading off with lobster (market price) or grilled black (Dover) sole on the bone, with lemon butter (about €28), through pan-fried Tralee Bay crab claws in garlic butter (about €25.50) to strips of monkfish deep fried in beer batter (about €25). Simple, moderately priced accommodation is offered in ten en-suite rooms (B&B €35, no ss). Bar/restaurant Meals 5.30-10 daily in season. A la carte; house wines from €19.50. Phone ahead to check food service off-season. Closed Jan-Mar. MasterCard, Visa, Laser. **Directions:** 11km (7 miles) from Tralee, well signposted.

KENMARE

Renowned for its fine restaurants and outstanding accommodation (the range and quality is exceptional for a town of its size), The Heritage Town of Kenmare (Neidín/ 'little nest') is pleasingly designed and ideally sized for comfortable browsing of its quality shops and galleries. It also has a full complement of characterful pubs, and makes an excellent base for exploring both south Kerry and the near parts of west Cork. **The Horseshoe** (064 41553; www.neidin.net/horseshoe) is a pleasingly old-fashioned bar and restaurant at the bottom of Main Street is cosy and everyone loves the atmosphere. At **Prego** (Henry Street, 064 42350), Gerry O'Shea's team offer a wide range of tasty dishes throughout the day beginning with a lovely breakfast menu Peter & Amanda Mallinson offer comfortable, moderately priced accommodation at their Killaha East home, **Sheen View Guesthouse** (064 42817; www.sheenview.com), just outside Kenmare on the Castletownbere road. High up at the famous Moll's Gap viewing point on the Ring of Kerry, **Avoca Handweavers** (064 34720; www.avoca.ie) is an outpost of the County Wicklow weaving company, selling its fine range of clothing and crafts - and offering wholesome and appealing home-made fare with that amazing view, to sustain the weary sightseer (10-5 daily mid-Mar-mid-Nov).

WWW.IRELAND-GUIDE.COM FOR THE BEST PLACES TO EAT, DRINK & STAY

Kenmare

N HOTEL

Brook Lane Hotel

Kenmare Co Kerry **Tel: 064 42077** Fax: 064 40869
Email: info@brooklanehotel.com Web: www.brooklanehotel.com

Situated just outside Kenmare on the Ring of Kerry Road (take the turn off for Sneem), this smart boutique hotel looks quite traditional from the outside but the interior is sleek and modern, offering all the flair and comfort of a custom built hotel - but with the service and intimacy of a the very best kind of B&B, and very competitive prices. Public areas include the smart-casual Casey's Bar & Bistro which, with long opening hours (from noon daily), is an ideal place to drop into for a tasty bite in stylish surroundings at any time and a fine dining restaurant, open for dinner and Sunday lunch. The very comfortable bedrooms are decorated in soothing warm neutrals and as elsewhere in the hotel the style is clean and contemporary but definitely not hard-edged minimalism; business guests will find plenty of workspace and broadband access, and everyone will appreciate the emphasis on service, which includes a turndown service (lights on, background music) to make your room welcoming when you go to bed. Bedrooms will have air conditioning for the 2007 season, and there are plans for a spa/ wellness centre. Brook Lane offers just what's wanted, and is great value for money booking well in advance is advised. Conferences/Banqueting (50/100), secretarial services, free Broadband Wi/Fi. Cycling, equestrian, fly fishing, sea angling, garden visits and golf all nearby. Children welcome (under 4s free in parents' room, cots available free of charge, baby sitting arranged). **Rooms 20** (1 junior suite, 8 executive, 2 family rooms, 9 ground floor, 1 for disabled, all no smoking); 24 hr room service; air conditioning Lift; B&B €75 pps, ss €25. Special / off-season offers available. Casey's Bar & Bistro: meals 12.30-9.30 daily; live music in bar at certain times. Restaurant D 6.30-9.30 daily, L Sun only 12.20-3.30. Closed 24-26 Dec. MasterCard, Visa, Laser. **Directions:** A short walk from the centre of town.

Kenmare

N RESTAURANT WITH ROOMS

D'Arcy's Oyster Bar & Grill

Main Street Kenmare Co Kerry
Tel: 064 41589 Fax: 064 41589
Email: keatingrestaurants@ownmail.net Web: www.darcys.ie

Situated at the top of Main Street opposite the Landsdowne Hotel, this well known restaurant was previously a bank and recently came the ownership of John and Georgina Keating, who decided to specialise seafood - including lobster but, especially oysters, which are farmed locally at Cromane, on the Iveragh Peninsula. A bank interior always lends a bit of gravitas and, with timeless jazz and understated décor in white and beige, it provides a pleasingly neutral setting for really good food, including sumptuous desserts. If you think you don't eat oysters, Darcy's will change that and, if you absolutely won't eat raw oysters, try them cooked: the grilled oysters on a bed of dry salt are really scrumptious. To specialise in oysters is courageous, they do it with aplomb. And it seems to have taken off, as they do brisk business in oysters with yummy desserts (a superb raspberry parfait attracted praise on our visit), especially at lunch time - and, if oysters really aren't your cup of tea, there are plenty of other fish and seafood, or meat and vegetarian dishes to choose from instead. Very nice staff will ensure you enjoy your meal, whatever you choose. Restaurant not suitable for children under 7. **Seats 60.** Serving food Tue-Sun 12-10 May-Sept, Thu-Sun 6-10 Oct-Apr; à la carte. House wine €19.50; sc discretionary. Closed Mon in summer, Mon-Wed Oct-Apr & mid Jan 7- mid Feb. *Accommodation also provided in seven pleasant bedrooms. **Rooms 7** (all shower only, 5 no smoking, 2 junior suites), B&B €70 pps (e 20 ss), cots available free of charge. MasterCard, Visa, Laser. **Directions:** Top of Main Street on left. ◇

Kenmare

Jam

€ CAFÉ

6 Henry St Kenmare Co Kerry **Tel: 064 41591**
Fax: 064 40790 Email: info@jam.ie Web: www.jam.ie

James Mulchrone's delightful bakery and café has been a great success since the day it opened, in March 2001 and, unlikely as this may seem in a town that has some of the best eating places in Ireland, it brought something new and very welcome. Affordable prices, friendly service and an in-house bakery have proved a winning combination; everything is made on the premises using the best of local produce and you can pop into the self-service café for a bite at any time all day. To give a flavour of the wide range offered, lovely main course choices include salmon & spinach baked in pastry with horseradish and a selection of quiches (roast vegetable with goats cheese, basil & pinenuts, for example, or bacon, onion & cheddar). If you're planning a day out, they have all you could want for a delicious picnic here, including a wide range of sandwiches and salads, terrines and all sorts of irresistible cakes and biscuits. The café menu changes daily and party platters and celebration cakes are made to order (48 hours notice required for special orders.). The stated aim is "to provide fresh, quality, imaginative food at affordable prices in nice surroundings"; this they are doing very well both here and in their branch on High Street, Killarney. *Also at: 77 High Street, Killarney; Tel: 064 31441. **Seats 55;** air conditioning. Open Mon-Sat, 8am-6pm; house wine €4.75 per glass. Closed Sun, 4 days Christmas. MasterCard, Visa, Laser. **Directions:** Lower Henry Street on the left.

Kenmare

Lime Tree Restaurant Kenmare

☆RESTAURANT

Shelburne Street Kenmare Co Kerry
Tel: 064 41225 Fax: 064 41839
Email: limetree@limetreerestaurant.com Web: www.limetreerestaurant.com

Tony and Alex Daly's restaurant is entering into its fourteenth year and remains one of the most consistently popular dining choices in the area. It's in an attractive cut stone building built in 1832 and set well back from the road: an open log fire, exposed stone walls, original wall panelling and a minstrels' gallery (which provides an upper eating area) all give character to the interior and there is a contemporary art gallery on the first floor, which adds an extra dimension to a visit here - fine original artwork in the restaurant gives a hint of what may be for sale. A la carte menus offer plenty of choice, plus daily specials (including vegetarian options) - a little less emphasis on local seafood than might be expected but that allows for a wider choice and, among several fish dishes, a speciality is fish cooked "en papillotte", which may be a selection or a single fish, such as trout, cooked in parchment paper, with fish stock and wine. Some dishes have a world cuisine tone, and there are plenty of main stream choices too: Kenmare seafood chowder is an enduring favourite, and an imaginatively updated main course of griddled loin of Kerry lamb is served with a cauliflower & goats cheese fondue. Desserts range from the homely (hot vanilla rice pudding with wild berry compote & honeyed mascarpone cream), to tweaked classics (marinated strawberry shortcake with balsamic ice cream). Service, under the direction of restaurant manager Maria O'Sullivan, is professional and relaxed; a user-friendly wine list is organised by style ('light, crisp and appealing', 'soft bodied and fruity'...) and includes some interesting bottles. And remember that it might be wise to budget a little extra for dinner here - you could be taking home a modern masterpiece; gallery open from 4pm. Toilet wheelchair accessible. Air conditioning. Not suitable for children after 7 pm. **Seats 60** (private room, 18). D daily 6.30-10; à la carte (average main course about €23). House wine €20; sc discretionary. Closed-Nov-Mar. MasterCard, Visa, Laser. **Directions:** Top of town, next to Park Hotel.

Kenmare

The Lodge

GUESTHOUSE

Killowen Road Kenmare Co Kerry **Tel: 064 41512** Fax: 064 42724
Email: thelodgekenmare@eircom.net Web: www.thelodgekenmare.com

Rosemarie Quill's large, purpose-built guesthouse is just 3 minutes walk from the centre of town offers hotel-style accommodation in spacious rooms which have everything you could possibly need - including phone, TV, safe, iron/trouser press and tea/coffee facilities, as well as well-finished bathrooms - at guesthouse prices. There is also plenty of comfortable seating and even a bar. Children welcome (under 3 free in parents' room, cot available without charge). 24 hour room service. No pets. Garden. **Rooms 11** (all en-suite & no smoking; 1 disabled with shower). B&B €45-55 pps, ss about €30. Closed mid Nov- mid Mar). MasterCard, Visa, **Directions:** Cork road, 150m from town opposite golf course. ◇

Kenmare
☆RESTAURANT/GUESTHOUSE

Mulcahys Restaurant

36 Henry Street Kenmare Co Kerry
Tel: 064 42383 Fax: 064 42383

If you are ever tired of finding the same old dishes on every menu, just head for Kenmare and refresh your palate at Bruce Mulcahy's original, efficiently run and friendly contemporary restaurant. A light-filled room is spacious and stylish, with smart modern table settings, funky cutlery and delicious breads on a pretty little bamboo tray. Far from being yet another copy-cat chef playing with world cuisines, Bruce has gone to the source to learn his skills - he learned about fusion food in Thailand, for example, and studied the art of sushi making in Japan; but the secret of this restaurant's great success is that, although many dishes are highly unusual, exciting menus cater for conservative tastes as well as the adventurous palate. Bruce's skills are best seen in house specialities such as sushi & sashimi (Japanese nori sheets filled with local seafood and served with wasabi, pickled ginger & mirin dip), and all produce used here is certified organic, and vegetarians get a dish of the day on the black-board. Inspired cooking is backed up by charming and knowledgeable staff, although service can come under pressure at busy times and there may sometimes be a delay before your reserved table becomes available. The early dinner menu is great value - and there's also a magical wine list to match the food. **Virginia's Guesthouse** (**Tel: 064 41021**; email: Virginia's@eircom.net; www.virginias-kenmare.com). The restaurant and guesthouse share an entrance, but are run quite separately. Neil and Noreen Harrington have eight comfortable rooms, all with phone, television, safe and tea/coffee trays - and en-suite power showers. And their breakfasts are a point of honour, offering fresh orange juice and pressed apple juice, porridge (with or without whiskey cream), free range eggs and Kenmare smoked salmon among many other temptations. B&B €40-60 pps, ss about €20. Room service, limited hours. Toilets wheelchair accessible. **Seats 42.** D daily, 6-10. Table D'hote D €22/30 2/3 courses, also à la carte. House wines from €19. SC discretionary. Closed 23-26 Dec. MasterCard, Visa, Laser. **Directions:** Halfway down Henry Street, on the righthand side.

Kenmare
COUNTRY HOUSE

Muxnaw Lodge

Castletownbere Road Kenmare Co Kerry **Tel: 064 41252**
Email: muxnawlodge@eircom.net Web: www.neidin.net

Within walking distance from town (first right past the double-arched bridge towards Bantry), Hannah Boland's wonderfully cosy and homely house was built in 1801 and enjoys spectacular views across Kenmare Bay. This is very much a home where you can relax in the TV lounge or outside in the sloping gardens (you can even play tennis on the all-weather court). A recent building programme has brought a couple of superior new rooms on stream but, while the original ones now seem old-fashioned by comparison, all the bedrooms are tranquil and comfortable, individually furnished with free-standing period pieces and pleasant fabrics - and have cleverly hidden tea/coffee-making facilities. Notice is required by noon if you would like dinner a typical meal cooked in and on the Aga might be carrot soup, oven-baked salmon and apple pie, but guests are always asked beforehand what they like. Not suitable for children. Garden. **Rooms 5** (all en-suite & no-smoking). B&B about €40. Residents D about €20. Closed 24-25 Dec. MasterCard, Visa, **Directions:** 2 minutes drive from Kenmare Town.

Kenmare
BAR/RESTAURANT

P F McCarthys

14 Main Street Kenmare Co Kerry
Tel: 064 41516 Fax: 064 42766

This fine establishment, previously known as the Failte Bar, goes back to 1913 and is now run by Paul and Breda Walsh, who took over in 2006. The recently renovated premises is designed to bring natural light into bright rooms - it has a spacious feeling and a dining area separated from the bar by low partitions, topped by wine bottles for privacy. Everyone loves it, whether for a snack lunch or more leisurely dinner - or just for the craic. Breda - who was head chef in The Horseshoe under the previous management, is known for her wholesome, fresh-tasting food: at lunchtime there's an extensive choice of home-made soups, salads and light international snacks - bruschetta, melts, ciabatta pizza, bagels - and a wide range of regular and hot sandwiches. Evening menus are more selective, offering a full dinner menu, plus daily specials for fresh fish and steak dishes. Ingredients are carefully sourced and there's a home-made flavour to the food, including desserts. There's a great buzz (without over-crowding), a friendly atmosphere and efficient service under Paul's direction. **Seats 60.** Outdoor seating available (garden). Toilets wheelchair accessible. Children welcome before 9pm. Food served Mon-Sat 10.30-3 and 5-9. No food on Sun. A la carte; house wine from €18.95; SC discretionary. Closed 25 Dec, Good Fri. MasterCard, Visa, Laser. **Directions:** First Pub/Restaurant on the right hand side as you travel up Main Street.

Kenmare
☆RESTAURANT

Packie's

Henry Street Kenmare Co Kerry
Tel: 064 41508 Fax: 064 42135

féile bia In a town blessed with an exceptional choice of wonderful eating places, the Foley family's buzzy little restaurant has long been a favourite for returning visitors. The long main room has a little reception bar with a couple of stools shoehorned into it, and a dividing stone feature wall with foliage-filled gaps in it provides both privacy and, along with candlelight, mirrors and framed pictures, makes for a warm, relaxed atmosphere - an impression immediately confirmed by welcoming staff, who are exceptionally friendly and efficient, keeping everyone at the closely packed tables happy throughout the evening. Head chef Martin Hallissey's menus (plus each evening's specials) are based mainly on local ingredients, notably organic produce and fish - and, although there's clear interest in international trends, combinations tend to be based on traditional themes, such as classic Irish stew with fresh herbs, which is a speciality. Close examination of menus will probably reveal more dishes that have stood the test of time than new ones, but what remains impressive is the basic quality of the food, especially local seafood. Finish with Irish farmhouse cheeses or good desserts, including home-made ice creams. An interesting and well-priced wine list offers plenty to choose from, with some available by the glass. Children welcome. **Seats 34.** D Mon-Sat, 6-10; set D €30/45 2/3 courses, also à la carte. House wine from €16.50; sc discretionary. Reservations advised. Closed Sun; mid Jan- end Feb. MasterCard, Visa, Laser. **Directions:** Town centre.

Kenmare
★HOTEL/RESTAURANT

Park Hotel Kenmare

Kenmare Co Kerry
Tel: 064 41200 Fax: 064 41402
Email: info@parkkenmare.com Web: www.parkkenmare.com

This renowned hotel enjoys a magnificent waterside location in the midst of Ireland's most scenic landscape, with views over gardens to the ever-changing mountains across the bay - yet it's only a short stroll to the Heritage Town of Kenmare. Many travellers from all over the world have found a home from home here since the hotel was built in 1897 by the Great Southern and Western Railway Company as an overnight stop for passengers travelling to Parknasilla, 17 miles away. The current proprietor, Francis Brennan, re-opened the hotel in 1985, and has since earned international acclaim for exceptional standards of service, comfort and cuisine; it is a most hospitable and relaxing place, where a warm welcome and the ever-burning fire in the hall set the tone for a stay in which guests are discreetly pampered by outstandingly friendly and professional staff. And since 2004 that pampering has been taken to new heights in the hotel's deluxe destination spa, Sámas, which translates from the Gaelic as 'indulgence of the senses'. Unlike anything else offered in Ireland, Sámas adjoins the hotel on a wooded knoll and is designed to rejuvenate the body, mind and spirit; there are separate male and female areas (also two day suites for couples) and guests can choose from over forty holistic treatments, designed by a team of professionals to meet individual needs. Lifestyle programmes incorporating spa treatments with other activities in the area - walking on the Kerry Way, golf, fishing, horse trekking - offer a unique way to enjoy the deeply peaceful atmosphere of this luxurious hotel. As for the guest accommodation, spacious suites and bedrooms are individually furnished to the highest standards, with personally selected antiques and many special details. And, in line with the excellence which prevails throughout the hotel, the outstanding breakfasts served at the Park start the day in style. [Park Hotel Kenmare was the national winner of our Hotel Breakfast of the Year Award in 2005.] Golf club adjacent (18 hole). Garden, tennis, croquet, cycling, walking, snooker. Reel Room (12-seater cinema). Horse riding, sea and game angling, mountain walks and stunning coastal drives are all nearby.* At the time of going to press another major development is under way, this time The Retreat, a luxurious residential development; it may cause some temporary disruption. **Rooms 46** (9 suites, 24 junior suites, 8 family rooms, 8 ground floor, 1 disabled, 46 no smoking). Lift. 24 hour room service. Children welcome (under 4 free in parents' room, cots available without charge). No pets (but kennels available on grounds). B&B about €173 pps, (single occupancy €215); off season holistic retreats offer very good value. Hotel closed late Nov-mid Feb except Christmas/New Year. **Restaurant:** The more contemporary restaurants become the norm in Ireland, the more precious the elegance of this traditional dining room seems - and the views from window tables are simply lovely. Ensuring that the food will match the surroundings is no light matter but a stylishly restrained classicism has characterised this distinguished kitchen under several famous head chefs, and Mark Johnson - who joined the hotel in 2006 - maintains this tradition admirably. His menus are not over-extensive yet allow plenty of choice and, although there's an understandable leaning towards local seafood, including lobster, at least one imaginative vegetarian dish is offered on each course. Kerry lamb and local Skeaghanore duck are also enduring specialities: a treat of a dish for two people is roast Skeaghanore duck served, perhaps, with sautéed mouli & pomme paille with Kenmare honey & sherry vinegar sauce. Superb attention to detail - from the first trio of nibbles offered with aperitifs in the bar, through an intriguing amuse-bouche served at the table, well-made breads, punctilious wine service and finally the theatrical little Irish coffee ritual and petits fours at the end of the meal - all this contributes to a dining experience that is exceptional. The wine list, although favouring the deep-pocketed guest, offers a fair selection in the €30-40 bracket and includes a wine suitable for diabetics. Service is invariably immaculate. A short à la carte lounge menu is available, 11am-6pm. Not suitable for children after 7 pm. **Seats 80** (private room, 40, outdoor dining 20). D, 7-9 daily; Set D menu €55; gourmet menu €74; also à la carte. House wine from €36; sc discretionary. Amex, MasterCard, Visa. **Directions:** Top of town.

Kenmare

€ BAR/RESTAURANT

The Purple Heather

Henry Street Kenmare Co Kerry **Tel: 064 41016**
Fax: 064 42135 Email: oconnellgrainne@eircom.net

Open since 1964, Grainne O'Connell's informal restaurant/bar was among the first to establish a reputation for good food in Kenmare, and is a daytime sister restaurant to Packie's. It's a traditional darkwood and burgundy bar that gradually develops into an informal restaurant at the rear, as is the way in many of the best Kerry bars - and what they aim for and achieve, with commendable consistency is good, simple, home-cooked food. Start with refreshing freshly squeezed orange juice, well-made soups that come with home-baked breads, or salad made of organic greens with balsamic dressing. Main courses include a number of seafood salads, vegetarian salads (cold and warm), pâtés including a delicious smoked salmon pâté plus a range of omelettes, sandwiches and open sandwiches (Cashel Blue cheese and walnut, perhaps, or crabmeat with salad) or Irish farmhouse cheeses (with a glass of L.B.V Offley port if you like). This is a great place, serving wonderfully wholesome food in a relaxed atmosphere - and it's open almost all year.* Grainne O'Connell also has self-catering accommodation available nearby. **Seats 40.** Meals Mon-Sat, 10.45-7pm. Closed Sun, Christmas, bank hols. Visa, Laser, Switch. **Directions:** Town centre - mid Henry Street (on right following traffic flow). ◇

Kenmare

COUNTRY HOUSE

Sallyport House

Kenmare Co Kerry **Tel: 064 42066** Fax: 064 42067
Email: port@iol.ie Web: www.sallyporthouse.com

The Arthur family's renovated country house on the edge of Kenmare is in a quiet and convenient location overlooking the harbour, with fine garden and mountain views at the rear. It is spacious throughout, from the large entrance hall to bedrooms that are furnished with a mixture of antique and good quality old-style furniture, plus orthopaedic beds, TV, phone and tea/coffee facilities. Practical, fully-tiled bathrooms have powerful over-bath showers and built-in hair dryers. The standard of housekeeping is high - and delicious breakfasts are served in a sunny dining room overlooking the garden. Not suitable for children. garden, walking. No pets. **Rooms 5** (all with full bath & shower, 2 suites, all no-smoking). B&B €85 pps, ss €10. Closed 1 Nov-1 Apr. **No Credit Cards. Directions:** 500m south of town on N71 (Glengarriff road), between town and bridge.

Kenmare

FARMHOUSE/GUESTHOUSE

Sea Shore Farm Guest House

Tubrid Kenmare Co Kerry
Tel: 064 41270 Fax: 064 41270
Email: seashore@eircom.net Web: www.seashorehouse.net

The O'Sullivans' well-named farm guesthouse is beautifully situated overlooking the Beara peninsula, with field walks through farmland down to the shore - and, despite its peace and privacy, it's also exceptionally conveniently located, just a mile from Kenmare town. Mary Patricia O'Sullivan provides old-fashioned Irish hospitality at its best, with friendly, welcoming and efficient reception and spotlessly clean accommodation. A pleasant guest lounge has stunning views and plenty of tourist information and Irish heritage books - and Mary Patricia is herself a veritable mine of local information, who obviously delights in her job of telling guests about it. Spacious, comfortably furnished bedrooms have the considerate small touches that make all the difference to the comfort of a stay: a hairdryer that is placed conveniently in front of a mirror, shelves beside the washbasin for toiletries and a chaise-longue in front of a huge window so you can make the most of those unforgettable views. No dinner, but breakfast is a feast of fruit salads, yoghurt, cereals etc as well as a choice of scrambled eggs draped with locally smoked salmon, pancakes or traditional Irish. Garden, walking. *Glen Inchaquin Park is nearby and should not be missed. Children welcome (under 2s free in parents' room). No pets. **Rooms 6** (all en-suite & no smoking, 4 shower only, 2 family rooms, 2 for disabled). B&B €65 pps, ss €20. Closed 15 Nov-1 Mar. MasterCard, Visa, **Directions:** Off Ring of Kerry N70 Kenmare/Sneem road; signposted at junction with N71.

Kenmare

★ HOTEL/RESTAURANT

Sheen Falls Lodge

Kenmare Co Kerry
Tel: 064 41600 Fax: 064 41386
Email: info@sheenfallslodge.ie Web: www.sheenfallslodge.ie

féile bia Set in a 300-acre estate just across the river from Kenmare town, this stunning hotel made an immediate impact from the day it opened in April 1991; it has continued to develop and mature most impressively since. The waterside location is beautiful, and welcoming fires always burn in the handsome foyer and in several of the spacious, elegantly furnished reception rooms, including a lounge bar area overlooking the tumbling waterfall. Decor throughout is contemporary classic, offering traditional luxury with a modern lightness of touch and a tendency to understatement that adds up to great style; accommodation in spacious bedrooms - and suites, which include an extremely impressive presidential suite - is luxurious: all rooms have superb amenities, including video/DVD and CD players, beautiful marbled bathrooms and views of the cascading river or Kenmare Bay. Outstanding facilities for both corporate and private guests include state-of-the-art conference facilities, a fine library (with computer/internet), an equestrian centre (treks around the 300 acre estate) and The Queen's Walk (named after Queen Victoria), which takes you through lush woodland. A Health & Fitness Spa includes a pretty 15 metre pool (and an extensive range of treatments including seaweed wraps and aromatherapy massages) and, alongside it, there's an informal evening bar and bistro, 'Oscars', which has its own separate entrance as well as direct access from the hotel. But it is, above all, the staff who make this luxurious and stylish international hotel the home from home that it quickly becomes for each new guest. *Two luxuriously appointed self-contained two-bedroomed thatched cottages, Little Hay Cottage and Garden Cottage, and a 5-bedroomed house on the estate, are also available to rent. Conference/banqueting (120/140); business centre, secretarial services, video-conferencing. Health & Fitness Spa (swimming pool, jacuzzi, sauna, steam room, treatments, beauty salon), boutique, snooker, equestrian, walking, fishing, gardens, tennis, cycling. Children welcome (cots available, €25, baby sitting arranged; playground). No pets. **Rooms 66** (1 presidential suites, 11 suites, 8 junior suites, 14 ground floor rooms, 10 no-smoking bedrooms, 1 disabled). Lift. 24 hour room service; turndown service. Room rate €217.50 (max 2 guests). **La Cascade:** This beautifully appointed restaurant is designed in tiers to take full advantage of the waterfalls floodlit at night and providing a dramatic backdrop for an exceptional fine dining experience. Philip Brazil took over as head chef late in 2005, and continues the high standard of cooking which is the hallmark of this lovely restaurant, backed up by faultless service under the supervision of restaurant manager Adrian Fitzgerald. A concise table d'hôte menu offers only three or four choices on each course - of which two of the starters, and one or two main courses may be seafood - crab from Castletownbere and wild salmon from the estate, perhaps - and both pigeon and rabbit are all also popular. Cooking is consistently impressive and the dishes offered often include local ingredients - Kerry lamb is almost de rigeur, of course, and predictably delicious, also duck - although the tone is classic, with only the smallest occasional nod to Irish cuisine and, unsurprisingly, ingredients are often luxurious - a typical speciality dish of Castletownbere lobster with lobster tortellini & lobster cream illustrates the point . Speciality desserts include updated classics like hot soufflés, and farmhouse cheeses are served with scrumptious parmesan biscuits. The atmospheric wine cellar is a particular point of pride - guests can visit it to choose their own bottle, and port may also be served there after dinner - deep-pocketed wine buffs will enjoy the wine list and should make a point of seeing it well ahead of dining if possible, as it details around 950 wines, with particular strengths in the classic European regions, especially Burgundy and Bordeaux, and a fine collection of ports and dessert wines. *Light lunches (smoked salmon, club sandwiches etc) and afternoon tea are available in the sun lounge, 12-6 daily, and the informal Oscar's Bistro offers an extensive à la carte dinner menu, including a children's menu, Wed-Sun, 6-10pm. Restaurant **Seats 120** (private room, 20; outdoor seating, 12). Pianist, evenings. Toilets wheelchair accessible. D daily 7-9. Set D €65, gourmet D €95. House wines from €36.80. SC discretionary. Hotel closed Jan 3 - Feb 1 and midweek Dec. Amex, Diners, MasterCard, Visa, Laser. **Directions:** Take N71 Kenmare (Glengariff road); turn left at Riversdale Hotel.

Kenmare

COUNTRY HOUSE/GUESTHOUSE

Shelburne Lodge

Cork Road Kenmare Co Kerry
Tel: 064 41013 Fax: 064 42135
Email: shelburnekenmare@eircom.net Web: www.shelburnelodge.com

Tom and Maura Foley's fine stone house on the edge of the town is well set back from the road, in its own grounds and lovely gardens. It is the oldest house in Kenmare and has great style and attention to detail; spacious day rooms include an elegant, comfortably furnished drawing room with plenty of seating, an inviting log fire and interesting books for guests to read - it is really lovely, and the feeling is of being a guest in a private country house. Spacious, well-proportioned guest rooms are individually decorated and extremely comfortable; everything (especially beds and bedding) is of the highest quality and, except for the more informal conversion at the back of the house, which is especially suitable for families and has neat shower rooms, the excellent bathrooms have full bath. But perhaps the best is saved until last, in the large, well-appointed dining room where excellent breakfasts are served: tables are prettily laid with linen napkins and the menu offers all kind of treats, beginning with freshly squeezed juices, a choice of fruits (nectarine with strawberries, perhaps) with extras like natural yoghurt, honey and nuts offered too, lovely freshly-baked breads, homemade preserves, leaf tea and strong aromatic coffee, and - as well as various excellent permutations of the full traditional Irish breakfast - there's fresh fish (sole, perhaps, with lemon butter), and Irish farmhouse cheeses too. Simply delicious. [Shelburne Lodge was our Guesthouse of the Year in 2005, and also winner of the Best Guesthouse Breakfast Award.] No evening meals are served, but residents are directed to the family's restaurant, Packie's (see entry). Children welcome (under 2s free in parents' room, cot available without charge). Garden, tennis. Own parking. No pets. **Rooms 10** (3 shower-only, 1 family room). B&B €75, ss €15. Closed Dec 1-mid Mar. MasterCard, Visa, **Directions:** 500 metres from town centre, on the Cork road R569.

Kenmare

RESTAURANT

The Club Restaurant

Market Square Kenmare Co Kerry **Tel: 064 42958**
Fax: 064 42958 Web: www.theclubrestaurant.com

This younger sister restaurant to The Cooperage in Killarney has resulted from the caring renovation of a fine old stone building and is meaningfully named - after a long-established Working Men's Club (who still meet upstairs). Those familiar with Martin McCormack's approach at The Cooperage will have some idea of what to expect - while uncompromisingly contemporary, only the finest quality materials have been used and the decor has great style, which makes for a sympathetic partnership with the original building. Warm tones, sleek shapes and simple table settings provide a classy background for smart modern food offering the same menu as The Cooperage and chefs are interchangeable, a smart idea that reduces the logistical headaches of running two restaurants, and maximises on a tried and tested formula. Children welcome. **Seats 53** (outdoor seating, 6). Air conditioning. Toilets wheelchair accessible. Reservations accepted. D daily, 5-10; L Sun only, 12.30-2.30. Early D €20 (5-7), otherwise à la carte. House wines from €16.45. Closed 25-25 Dec. MasterCard, Visa, Laser, Switch. **Directions:** Opposite the Tourist Information Office. ◇

KILLARNEY

Known all over the world for its romantic beauty (Lakes of Killarney, Killarney National Park, the Ring of Kerry) the Killarney area has long been a source of inspiration for poets, painters and writers and, despite the commercial tone of the town itself which has been a centre of tourism since the days of the Victorian Grand Tour - the surroundings are stunning and, with a number of the country's finest hotels in the town and immediate area, it remains an excellent base for exploring the area, or for leisure activities, notably golf. When visiting Muckross House at the National Park, **The Garden Restaurant** (064 314440; www.muckross-house.ie) is open 9-5 daily, all year except Christmas/NewYear, and offers just the kind of good, wholesome food that's welcome, in attractive surorndings. Nearby, in the Muckross area, **Fuchsia House Guesthouse** (064 33743; www.fuchsiahouse.com) is run by members of the renowned Treacy hotelier family; set in gardens, it offers quietness and a high standard of accommodation. Also nearby, the Huggard family's **Lake Hotel** (064 31035; www.lakehotel.com) is romantically located right on the lakeshore. And, convenient to the Killarney Golf & Fishing Club, Sheehan's **19th Green** family-run guesthouse (064 32868; www.the19thgreen-bb.com) offers a moderately priced haven for golfers.

WWW.IRELAND-GUIDE.COM FOR THE BEST PLACES TO EAT, DRINK & STAY

Killarney

HOTEL/RESTAURANT

Aghadoe Heights Hotel

Killarney Co Kerry **Tel: 064 31766** Fax: 064 31345
Email: info@aghadoeheights.com Web: www.aghadoeheights.com

A few miles out of town, this famous low-rise hotel, dating from the '60s, enjoys stunning views of the lakes and the mountains beyond and also overlooks Killarney's two 18-hole championship golf courses. It is now one of Ireland's most luxurious hotels and, under the caring management of Pat and Marie Chawke and their welcoming staff, it is a very special place. Major developments have recently been completed and, while the controversial exterior remains a subject of debate, the interior - including

24 new junior suites, a palatial glass-fronted two-bedroom penthouse suite and a superb new spa & wellness centre - is superb. Contemporary, stylish public areas are airy and spacious, with lots of marble, original artwork, and a relaxed, open ambience and, from the foyer, hints of the stunning view that invite exploration - perhaps into the chic bar which links up with a new terrace and the swimming pool area (lots of lounging space for sunny days), or up to the first floor open-plan lounge area, where a delicious traditional Afternoon Tea is served (2-5.30pm). Accommodation is seriously luxurious, in spacious rooms with balconies and lake views, large sitting areas, plasma screen televisions, video, DVD (library available) and a host of extras. Bathrooms are equally sumptuous, with separate shower and all the complimentary toiletries you could wish for. The new 10,000 sq ft spa is among Europe's best and offers couples suites, and some unique treatments - including 'Ayervedic Precious Stone therapy' in a custom built Aromatherapy cabin. But at the heart of all this luxury it is the caring hands-on management of Pat and Marie Chawke who, with their outstanding staff, make everyone feel at home. And you will leave on a high too, as breakfast is another especially strong point. [Aghadoe Heights was our Hotel of the Year in 2005.] Conference/banqueting (80/75); business centre, secretarial services, free broadband Wi/Fi. Leisure centre, swimming pool, spa, hair salon. Garden, tennis, walking. Children welcome (Under 2s free in parents' room; cot available, baby sitting arranged). No pets. **Rooms 74** (25 suites, 6 junior suites, 10 family rooms, 10 ground floor rooms, 1 disabled, all non smoking). Lift. Turn down service. 24 hour room service. B&B €185 pps, ss €90. Closed 31 Jan-mid Feb. **The Lake Room:** The restaurant is on an upper floor, integrated into an open plan area, with distant views over the lakes and mountains; it is a bright and elegant space, with beautifully appointed tables and fresh flowers providing an appropriate setting for dining in a hotel of this standard. Robin Suter, who has been Executive Chef since the hotel opened and established the classic French style of food and service for which it is famous, was joined in 2004 by chef de cuisine, Gavin Gleeson, who brought experience at a number of top kitchens, including Dromoland Castle. Together they have developed new menus which continue in the classical tradition but with a lighter, more contemporary tone which is more in keeping with the atmosphere of the hotel. Gone, at least for the time being, are the great classics, like grilled chateaubriand sauce béarnaise and sole meunière, now replaced by news specialities like trellis of sea trout with rock salt beans & sauce vierge, and fashionable confit belly of pork & milk fed veal, with peach sauce. A pianist sets the scene each evening, and service is solicitous, as ever. An extensive and informative wine list includes a good range of classics, several magnums and plenty of half bottles. **Seats 120** (private room, 75). Reservations accepted. Children welcome. D daily, 6.30-10.30. Set D €65, also à la carte. House wines from €28. 12.5% SC on groups of 12+. *Informal menus also offered in The Heights Lounge and The Terrace Bar & Bistro (from noon daily in summer). Restaurant closed end Dec-mid Feb. Helipad Amex, Diners, MasterCard, Visa, Laser. **Directions:** 3.2km (2 m) north of Killarney; signposted off N22.

The Brehon

Killarney

N HOTEL

Killarney Co Kerry **Tel: 064 30700** Fax: 064 30701
Email: info@thebrehon.com Web: www.thebrehon.com

Appropriately enough, as is so close to Irish National Entertainment Centre (INEC), everything at this new hotel, conference centre and spa is on a grand scale - and, while the exterior of the vast five-storey building may be overpowering, most would agree that the contemporary interior matches the official description of 'tasteful splendour'. Everything seems larger than life, and the style is contemporary - the design, decor and furnishings of the public spaces are striking and feature some interesting modern art and sculpture. This house style continues through bedrooms and suites, which are extremely comfortable, with air-conditioning as well as more usual features, and luxurious marble bathrooms with separate shower and bath. The restaurant is airy and bright, and a wide ranging breakfast menu is offered. The hotel takes pride in its spa: developed by the Banyan Tree Spa, it is Europe's first Angsana spa and based on holistic Asian healing customs. Conference facilities include four meeting rooms and a large function space, which is also available for weddings. Conferences/Banqueting (250/180); Spa, walking; Golf and equestrian nearby. **Rooms 125** (1 Presidential suite, 4 suites, 30 superior, 85 deluxe). B&B from €90 pps, ss€25. *Special interest breaks each Spring & Autumn, contact for details. ◇

Bricín

Killarney

RESTAURANT

26 High Street Killarney Co Kerry
Tel: 064 34902 Fax: 064 39030

Upstairs, over a craft shop (which you will find especially interesting if you like Irish pottery, of which there is a very wide range), Paddy & Johnny McGuire's country-style first-floor restaurant has been delighting visitors with its warm atmosphere and down to earth food since 1990. It's a large area, but broken up into "rooms", which creates intimate spaces - and the country mood suits wholesome cooking, in menus offering a good range of popular dishes. Salmon & crab bake is an enduring favourite, for example, and there are traditional dishes like boxty (potato pancakes) which are not seen as often as they should be in Irish restaurants, and are the house speciality here - you can have them with various fillings - chicken, lamb vegetables - and salad. An interesting range of desserts includes good home-made ice creams. This is a welcoming restaurant, and it has an old-fashioned character which is becoming especially attractive as so many others are adopting a contemporary style. **Seats 29.** Air conditioning. Children welcome. D Mon-Sat, 6-9. Value D €19 daily 6-7; Set D from €25; also 'specials'. House wine from €19. Closed Sun and Feb. Amex, Diners, MasterCard, Visa, Laser. **Directions:** On the High Street, Killarney.

Killarney

HOTEL

Cahernane House Hotel

Muckross Road Killarney Co Kerry **Tel: 064 31895** Fax: 064 34340
Email: info@cahernane.com Web: www.cahernane.com

This family-owned and managed hotel is in a lovely quiet location, convenient to Killarney town yet - thanks to a long tree-lined avenue and parkland which stretches down to the water - with a charmingly other-worldly atmosphere. The original house was built by the Herbert family, Earls of Pembroke, in the 17th century, and accommodation is divided between fine old rooms (including some suites and junior suites) in the main house, and more contemporary rooms in a recent extension. The hotel has many attractive features, not least its classically elegant dining room (The Herbert Room Restaurant), and a characterful cellar bar - complete with a real old-fashioned wine cellar. At the time of going to press a major development programme - the construction of a spa, meeting facilities and 30 additional bedrooms - is under way, due for completion in summer 2007. Banqueting (80). Free Broadband Wi/Fi. Children welcome (under 3s free in parents' room, cot available without charge, baby sitting arranged.) No pets. Garden, walking, fishing, tennis. Golf nearby. **Rooms 38** (28 with separate bath & shower, 15 no smoking). B&B €132 pps, Single from €150. Restaurant: L & D daily, 12.30-3 & 7-9.30; set L €35, set 5 course D €55; also bar food, noon-9.30pm; house wine €24.* Off-season breaks offered. Closed mid Dec-mid Jan. Amex, Diners, MasterCard, Visa, Laser. **Directions:** Ouskirts of Killarney, off the N71 near Muckross Park.

Killarney

Ⓝ RESTAURANT

Chapter 40

New Street Killarney Co Kerry **Tel: 064 71833**
Email: info@chapter40.ie Web: www.chapter40.ie

A recent arrival on the Killarney dining scene, this smart high-ceilinged restaurant feels spacious and is attractively set up with simple darkwood tables ,echoing the polished wooden floor, and contrasting cream leather used on high-backed chairs and bar stools. Menus offered are international in style and include an early dinner which is very good value, a wide ranging a la carte and a daily specials for all courses - typically Thai style beef salad, duo of lemon sole and scallops with wilted spinach, and pavlova with warm caramelised plums. Sharing dishes like an antipasto platter and duck confit pancakes get a meal off to a sociable start which, along with friendly service, may be one of the reasons for this restaurant's success, as it always busy and reservations are essential, especially at weekends. D Mon-Sat, 5-10pm; early D, 5-6.30pm €20/25 2/3 courses, also a la carte; house wine €18. Closed Sun. **Directions:** A few minutes' walk from car park beside the Tourist Office, near Dunnes Stores.

Killarney

COUNTRY HOUSE

Coolclogher House

Mill Road Killarney Co Kerry
Tel: 064 35996 Fax: 064 30933
Email: info@coolclogherhouse.com Web: www.coolclogherhouse.com

Mary and Maurice Harnett's beautiful early Victorian house is just on the edge of Killarney town and yet, tucked away on its 68 acre walled estate, it is an oasis of peace and tranquillity. The house has been extensively restored in recent years and has many interesting features, including an original conservatory built around a 170 year-old specimen camellia - when camellias were first introduced to Europe, they were mistakenly thought to be tender plants; it is now quite remarkable to see this large tree growing under glass. It is an impressive yet relaxed house, with well-proportioned, spacious reception rooms stylishly furnished and comfortable for guests, with newspapers, books, fresh flowers - and open fires in inclement weather - while the four large bedrooms have scenic views over gardens, parkland and mountains. Gazing out from this peaceful place, it is easy to forget that the hustle and bustle of Killarney town is just a few minutes' drive away; it could just as well be in another world. Mary and Maurice enjoy sharing their local knowledge with guests to help them get the most of their stay at what they quite reasonably call 'perhaps the most exclusive accommodation available in Killarney'. Children over 8 welcome. No pets. Garden, walking. Golf, fishing, garden visits nearby. **Rooms 4** (all en-suite, all no smoking). B&B €120, ss about €50. *Coolclogher House is also offered as a weekly rental (from €4,500) for special occasions; suits groups of 10-12; staff can be arranged if required. *Golf breaks offered (B&B or rental). MasterCard, Visa, Laser. **Directions:** Leaving Killarney town, take (Muckross Road) onto Mill Road; take first left turn into Mill Road (after metal bridge); gates on right after 1km (0.5 m).

Killarney
RESTAURANT

The Cooperage Restaurant

Old Market Lane Killarney Co Kerry **Tel: 064 37716**
Fax: 064 37716 Email: info@cooperage restaurant.com

This striking contemporary restaurant is well-located, in a pedestrianised laneway between Main Street and the Glebe public carpark, and its smartly painted frontage gives a good impression on arrival. There's an attractive lounge area, where you can have a relaxing aperitif (and an after dinner drink), the decor is minimalist yet also comfortable, with effective lighting - and the pleasing surroundings, together with gentle background jazz, create an atmospheric setting. And, in the Guide's experience, the food and service live up to the surroundings: fairly priced menus based on quality ingredients show a respect for seasonality and provenance of ingredients, as well as eye appeal. Menus offer plenty of choice, including game in season, and there's always a list of specials, including at least one imaginative vegetarian choice and several fish dishes - possibly something unusual like grilled butterfish with Café de Paris butter with tomato fondue, basil pesto & cracked pepper. Home-made desserts range from wholesome (apple & mixed berry crumble) to indulgent (rich dark chocolate cake). With a lively atmosphere, stylish, flavoursome food, and a concise, well priced wine list this popular restaurant offers good value, and reservations are advised, especially at weekends. **Seats 80.** Air conditioning. Children welcome (under parental control). D 6-9.30 daily in summer. Early D €20 (6-7.30), otherwise à la carte. House wine about €16.45. Closed Mon off-season; 25 Dec. MasterCard, Visa, Laser. **Directions:** Under the arch at the Old Town Hall, just off Main Street. ◇

Killarney
GUESTHOUSE

Earls Court House

Woodlawn Junction Muckross Road Killarney Co Kerry
Tel: 064 34009 Fax: 064 34366
Email: info@killarney-earlscourt.ie Web: www.killarney-earlscourt.ie

A neat, functional exterior does little to prepare first-time visitors for the comfort and character to be found at this purpose-built guesthouse quite near the town centre, which offers exceptionally comfortable accommodation at moderate prices and is run with warmth and professionalism by Roy and Emer Moynihan. A welcoming open fire burns in the large beautifully furnished foyer which, together with an adjoining guest sitting room, has plenty of comfortable seating for guests - an ideal rendez-vous, or simply a place to relax - and, as elsewhere in the house, antiques, books, paintings and family photographs are a point of interest and emphasise the personality of this spacious home from home. Emer's personal attention to the details that make for real comfort - and the ever-growing collection of antiques that guarantees individuality for each room - are the hallmarks of the outstanding accommodation offered, which includes four rooms with canopy beds. All the bedrooms are well-planned and generously-sized, with double and single beds, well finished bathrooms, phone and satellite TV; tea/coffee-making facilities are available on request. Guests are directed to restaurants in the town for evening meals, but superb breakfasts are served in a large, antique-furnished dining room, where guests are looked after with charm and efficiency. Earls Court was our Guesthouse of the Year for 2004. Fully certified for disadvantaged access. Children welcome (under 3s free, cot available without charge, baby sitting arranged). Pets allowed in some areas. Garden. Parking. **Rooms 24** (4 suites (to be completed bt March 2007), 4 family rooms, 2 for disabled, all no smoking). Lift. Room service (limited hours). B&B €60 pps, ss €40. Closed mid Nov-mid Feb. Amex, MasterCard, Visa, **Directions:** Take the first left at the traffic lights on Muckross road (signed), then 3rd premises.

Killarney
RESTAURANT

Gaby's Seafood Restaurant

27 High Street Killarney Co Kerry
Tel: 064 32519 Fax: 064 32747

One of Ireland's longest established seafood restaurants, Gaby's has a cosy little bar beside an open fire just inside the door, then several steps lead up to the main dining area, which is cleverly broken up into several sections and - although this is an expensive restaurant - it has a pleasantly informal atmosphere. Chef-proprietor Gert Maes offers well structured seasonal à la carte menus in classic French style and in three languages. Absolute freshness is clearly the priority a note on the menu reminds that availability depends on daily landings but there's always plenty else to choose from, with steaks and local lamb as back-up. Specialities include wild Atlantic salmon, with chive & lemon cream and red onion marmalade, Atlantic prawns on a bed of tagliatelle in a light garlic sauce and lobster "Gaby" (€48): fresh lobster, cognac, wine, cream and spices - cooked to a secret recipe! Lovely desserts include "my mother's recipe" - an old-fashioned apple & raspberry crumble with warm wild honey scented berries, sauce anglaise and caramel ice cream - or you can finish with an Irish cheese selection and freshly brewed coffee. Toilets wheelchair accessible. Air conditioning. Children welcome. **Seats 75.** D only, Mon-Sat 6-10; à la carte; house wine €25; sc discretionary. Closed Sun, Christmas week. last 2 weeks Feb. Amex, MasterCard, Visa, Laser. **Directions:** On the main street. ◇

Killarney
HOTEL

Great Southern Hotel Killarney

East Avenue Road Killarney Co Kerry **Tel: 064 31262** Fax: 064 31642
Email: res@killarney-gsh.com Web: www.greatsouthernhotels.com

féile bia The pillared entrance and ivy-clad facade of this classic Victorian railway hotel still convey a sense of occasion and recent refurbishment has restored the sparkle to the interior. A welcoming open fire at the entrance draws guests through to a spacious grandly-pillared foyer (where afternoon tea is served), and there's a soothing atmosphere which makes a refreshing contrast to the bustle of Killarney town. Fine bedroom corridors (originally built wide enough 'to allow two ladies in hooped dresses to pass comfortably'), set the tone for generously-proportioned suites and executive rooms, furnished to individual designs.There are two restaurants: the great gilt-domed Garden Room Restaurant is a prime example of Victorian opulence - contrasting with the smaller contemporary restaurant, Peppers. Extensive facilities include a leisure centre, spa and tennis - and, belying its central position, the hotel is set in 20 acres of landscaped gardens. *Hotels in the Great Southern group were sold shortly before going to press - and this hotel, along with Great Southern hotels in Galway, will now be in common ownership with the 'g' and the 'd' hotels; however, there have been no immediate changes. **Rooms 172** (2 suites, 34 junior suites, 70 superior rooms, 120 no smoking, 4 disabled). Lift. 24 hour room service. B&B about €140 pps, ss about €30; no SC. Open all year. **Peppers:** While the newly restored Garden Room Restaurant is very grand, Peppers is the hotel's newer bistro-style restaurant - and very much in demand. Situated quietly in a corner position behind the bar and overlooking the gardens, it is dashingly decorated in contemporary style, with high-back chairs, an elegant black, brown and beige/gold colour scheme and (in common with other areas of the hotel) fine paintings. The ambience, professional service, imaginative Mediterranean menus and consistently sound cooking make an appealing combination and - unusually for an hotel restaurant - it is well established as one of Killarney's leading eating places. **Seats 60.** D Tue-Sat, 6.30-9.30; advance reservations advised. Amex, Diners, MasterCard, Visa, Laser. **Directions:** In the heart of Killarney town beside Railway Station. ◇

Killarney
CAFÉ

Jam

77 High Street Killarney Co Kerry
Tel: 064 31441 Email: info@jam.ie Web: www.jam.ie

James Mulchrone's delightful bakery and café in Kenmare was such a success that he opened a second one in Killarney, bringing the same principles of affordable prices, friendly service and real home-made food using the best of local produce (see entry under Kenmare for details). Children welcome. **Seats 24.** Air conditioning. Open Mon-Sat, 8am-5pm. menu changes daily. Closed Sun, 4 days Christmas. MasterCard, Visa, Laser. **Directions:** Town centre.

Killarney
GUESTHOUSE

Kathleen's Country House

Madams Height Tralee Road Killarney Co Kerry
Tel: 064 32810 Fax: 064 32340
Email: info@kathleens.net Web: www.kathleens.net

féile bia Kathleen O'Regan Sheppard has been offering hotel standard accommodation at guesthouse prices since 1980, and this family-run business - which is off the main Tralee road, just a mile from the town centre - continues to offer good value, hospitality and comfort. Individually decorated rooms are furnished to a high standard, with orthopaedic beds, phone, TV, and tea/coffee-making facilities, and the fully tiled bathrooms all have bath and shower. An ongoing programme of maintenance and refurbishment ensures that everything is immaculate, including spacious public areas that provide plenty of room for relaxing - there are several sitting areas and even a library. Excellent breakfasts are served in a spacious dining room overlooking the garden, setting you up for a day that's as energetic or as relaxing as you choose to make it: Kathleen's is well situated for a wide range of outdoor pursuits (golf, fishing, pony-trekking, horse riding, walking, cycling and tennis are all nearby) and for some of the country's most beautiful scenic drives. Everything served at breakfast is based on the finest produce, local where possible, and beautifully presented - a speciality fresh fruit plate, for example, is as pretty as a picture and, like many other things around the house, reflects Kathleen's love of art. Special rates are offered off-season. Wheelchair access ground floor only. Children welcome (baby sitting arranged). Garden, walking. **Rooms 17** (all no smoking, 2 ground floor). B&B €65 pps, ss €15. Turndown service offered. Closed 20 Oct-15 Mar. Amex, MasterCard, Visa, Laser. **Directions:** 1.6km (1mile) north of Killarney Town off N22 (Tralee road).

Killarney

Killarney Lodge

GUESTHOUSE

Countess Road Killarney Co Kerry **Tel: 064 36499** Fax: 064 31070
Email: klylodge@iol.ie Web: www.killarneylodge.net

Catherine Treacy's fine purpose-built guesthouse is set in private walled gardens just a couple of minutes walk from the town centre and offers a high standard of accommodation at a fairly moderate rate. Large en-suite air-conditioned bedrooms have all the amenities expected of an hotel room and there are spacious, comfortably furnished public rooms to relax in. Run by a member of one of Killarney's most respected hotelier families, this is a very comfortable place to stay; you will be greeted with complimentary tea and coffees on arrival - and sent off in the morning with a good Irish breakfast, including home-baked breads and scones. A good choice for the business traveller, and short breaks are available in conjunction with Killarney Golf & Fishing Club - accommodation and green fees are offered at preferential rates. Children welcome (under 12 free in parents room; cot available without charge). Wheelchair accessible. No pets. Garden. Own secure parking. **Rooms 16** (2 junior suites, 13 superior, 1 shower only, 6 ground floor, all no smoking). Room service (all day). B&B €70 pps, ss €30; no sc. Closed 1 Nov-15 Feb. Amex, Diners, MasterCard, Visa, Laser. **Directions:** 2 minutes walk from town centre off Muckross Road.

Killarney

Killarney Park Hotel

★HOTEL/RESTAURANT

Kenmare Place Killarney Co Kerry
Tel: 064 35555 Fax: 064 35266
Email: info@killarneyparkhotel.ie Web: www.killarneyparkhotel.ie

féile bia

Situated in its own grounds, a short stroll from the town centre, the Treacy family's luxurious, well run hotel is deceptively modern - despite its classical good looks, it is barely fifteen years old. However it has already undergone more than one transformation, indeed, constant improvement is so much a theme here that it is hard to keep up with developments as they occur. The exceptionally welcoming atmosphere strikes you from the moment the doorman first greets you, as you pass through to a series of stylish seating areas, with fires and invitingly grouped sofas and armchairs; the same sense of comfort characterises the Garden Bar (which has a sheltered terrace for fine days) and also the quiet Library, which provides a relaxing haven. Elegant public areas are punctuated by a sweeping staircase that leads to bedrooms luxuriously furnished in a choice of two strongly contrasting styles, with great attention to detail in each case. Spacious traditional suites have a private entrance hall and an elegant sitting area with a fireplace creating a real home from home feeling; all the older rooms are also furnished in a similar warm country house style, with judiciously selected antiques. However, the junior suites offer a dramatically contemporary style - and a new wow factor; thoughtfully and individually designed, they have air conditioning, well-planned bathrooms and the many small details that make a hotel room really comfortable. Housekeeping is impeccable and the staff at this wonderful hotel are committed to looking after guests with warmth and discretion, making it an ideal choice for both business and pleasure. A stunning health spa offers eight treatment rooms, outdoor hot tub, plunge pool and jacuzzi; the menu of treatments offered is seriously seductive and it may well happen that some guests never feel the need to leave the hotel at all during their stay. [Park Hotel Killarney was our Hotel of the Year in 2002.] *The much older sister hotel, **The Ross** (064 31855; www.theross.ie), nearby, has been under reconstruction and is about to re-open at the time of going to press. Conference/banqueting (150/150); business centre. In-room safe. Spa, hot tub, jacuzzi. Leisure centre, swimming pool (20m), sauna, plunge pool, jacuzzi pool. Library; billiard room. Garden, walking, cycling. Children welcome (under 2 free in parents room; cots available without charge, playroom, baby sitting arranged). No Pets. **Rooms 72** (3 suites, 30 junior suites, 3 family rooms, 1 for disabled, all no-smoking). Lift. 24 hour room service. Turndown service. B&B €200 pps, ss €200; no sc. Closed 24-27 Dec. **The Park Restaurant:** This large and opulent room has the essential elements of grandeur - the ornate ceiling, glittering chandeliers - but has recently been lightened by a contemporary tone in the furnishings. Odran Lucey, who has been head chef since 1999, has earned a reputation for this restaurant as a dining destination in its own right, making it a great asset to this fine hotel. Although they are not overlong or unnecessarily wordy, plenty of choice is offered on appealing menus which make up a five course dinner or, as dishes are priced individually, also allow à la carte choices. The underlying style is classical but this is creative food, cooked with panache. An enduring house speciality that illustrates the style is a starter of pan-seared foie gras served with Clonakilty black pudding, with peach chutney which is a nicely judged combination of classical and modern influences - and a main course of roast breast of Skeghanore duck with colcannon cake & poached kumquats shows the same skilful blending of traditional partnerships and innovative additions. But when it comes to a real classic - Dover sole - it is cooked classically, 'meunière' and served with parsley potatoes - and what a joy to find lobster offered simply, with butter and lemon juice. Courteous service and the presence of a pianist, who plays throughout dinner, add to the sense of occasion. A wide-ranging wine list includes many of the classics and, not only a fair choice of half bottles, but also a sommelier's choice of the week, offering half a dozen good wines by the glass. An interesting feature of the restaurant is an open wine cellar, which guests are free to browse.* Odran Lucey is also responsible for the excellent bistro style food served The Garden Bar where - as elsewhere in the hotel - children are made very welcome. Restaurant **seats 150** (private room,40). Reservations required. Air conditioning. Toilets wheelchair accessible. D daily 7-9.30; Set D €62.50; also à la carte. House wines from €28. SC discretionary. *Food is also served in the bar, 12 noon-9pm daily. Hotel closed 24-27 Dec. Amex, MasterCard, Visa, Laser. **Directions:** Located in Killarney town - all access routes lead to town centre.

Killarney
HOTEL

Killarney Plaza Hotel

Kenmare Place Killarney Co Kerry **Tel: 064 21100** Fax: 064 31755
Email: info@killarneyplaza.com Web: www.killarneyplaza.com

féile bia In seeking to regain the glamour of the grand hotels, this new hotel offers an alternative to the ubiquitous minimalist good taste that has taken over in Irish hotels of late. The scale is large, but the proportions are pleasing and, although undoubtedly glitzy - miles of polished marbled and a great deal of gold - quality materials have been used and the building should age well. Meanwhile, it has a lot to offer: central location with underground parking; luxurious accommodation at prices which are relatively reasonable; a choice of three very different dining experiences (see separate entry for Mentons); good leisure and relaxation facilities, including a Molton Brown Spa. *Short / off-season breaks are available - details on application. Children welcome (under 3s free in parents' room, cot available free of charge, baby sitting arranged). Pets permitted by arrangement. Leisure centre (swimming pool, sauna, steam room, jacuzzi; spa). Secure parking (125); valet parking. **Rooms 198** (5 suites, 28 executive, 12 disabled, 114 no smoking). Lift. 24 hour room service. Turndown service. B&B €130 pps, ss €40. Restaurant Grand Pey (250), B'fst 7-10.30; D daily 6-9.30. Restaurant Petrus (50), D daily 6-9.30. Open all year. Amex, Diners, MasterCard, Visa, Laser. **Directions:** Town centre. ◇

Killarney
HOTEL

Killarney Royal Hotel

College Street Killarney Co Kerry **Tel: 064 31853** Fax: 064 34001
Email: info@killarneyroyal.ie Web: www.killarneyroyal.ie

féile bia Another of Killarney's unrivalled collection of fine hotels, this family-owned establishment is a charming older sister to the luxurious Hayfield Manor Hotel in Cork city (see entry). Proprietors Joe and Margaret Scally have recently lavished care and investment on it, resulting in a beautifully furnished hotel in an elegant period style that is totally appropriate to the age and design of the building. No expense was spared on the highest quality of materials and workmanship, air conditioning was installed throughout the hotel and individually designed rooms all have sitting areas and marble bathrooms. But what is most remarkable, perhaps, is the warm and friendly atmosphere that prevails throughout the hotel, conveyed partly through the soft warm tones chosen for furnishing schemes, but also through the attentive attitude of friendly, caring staff. Modern food is served every day in the bar, which is popular meeting place, while the main dining room - also recently refurbished - is more traditional and reservations are required. Conference/banqueting (50/100); secretarial services. Wheelchair accessible. Children welcome (under 7s free in parents room, cots available without charge, baby sitting arranged). Pets permitted by arrangement. No on-site parking (arrangement with nearby car park). **Rooms 29** (5 junior suites, 3 family rooms, 15 no-smoking, 1 disabled). Lift. 24 hour room service. B&B €100 pps, ss €40. Restaurant **Seats 100** (reservations advised): L daily, 12.30-2.30; D daily, 6.30-9.30. Early D €25 (6.30-7.30), Set D €25/35; Set L €25. Also à la carte. Closed 23-26 Dec. Amex, Diners, MasterCard, Visa, Laser. **Directions:** In Killarney town centre on College Street, off the N22.

Killarney
HOTEL/RESTAURANT

Killeen House Hotel

Aghadoe Killarney Co Kerry **Tel: 064 31711** Fax: 064 31811
Email: charming@indigo.ie Web: www.killeenhousehotel.com

Just 10 minutes drive from Killarney town centre and 5 minutes from Killeen and Mahoney's Point golf courses, this early nineteenth century rectory has become Michael and Geraldine Rosney's "charming little hotel". You don't have to be a golfer to stay here but it must help, especially in the pubby little bar, which is run as an "honour" bar with guests' golf balls accepted as tender; most visitors clearly relish the bonhomie, which includes addressing guests by first names. Rooms vary in size but all have full bathrooms (one with jacuzzi) and are freshly-decorated, with phone and satellite TV. There's a comfortable traditional drawing room with an open fire for guests, furnished with a mixture of antiques and newer furniture. The hotel is popular with business guests as well as golfers; secretarial services are available, also all day room service. **Rooms 23** (all en-suite). B&B €80 pps, ss €20; sc 10%. **Rozzers**: Resident guests see no need to go out when a good dinner is offered under the same roof as their (very comfortable) beds, and this charming restaurant is also very popular locally. You can have an aperitif in the friendly little bar while browsing 5-course dinner menus that offer a wide choice on each course, plus specials each evening which include a daily pasta dish and a vegetarian dish. The range offered is well-balanced, allowing for conservative and slightly more adventurous tastes, and some of the more luxurious dishes attract a supplement (oysters cost an extra €6 and chateaubriand steak, for a minimum of two guests, is an extra €8 per person, for example, and lobster is charged at market price). Although the style is quite hearty - perfect for hungry golfers- some lighter choices on each course will appeal to smaller appetites. Like the rest of the hotel, the dining has a cosy charm and the owners' hospitality is outstanding. Restaurant is open to non-residents; **Seats 50** (private room, 28); D daily, 6-9.30pm; Set D €52, house wines from €22, restaurant sc discretionary. Closed mid Oct-mid April. Amex, Diners, MasterCard, Visa, Laser. **Directions:** 6.5km (4 m) from Killarney town centre - just off Dingle Road.

Killarney
RESTAURANT

Mentons @ The Plaza

Killarney Plaza Hotel Kenmare Place Killarney Co Kerry
Tel: 064 21150 Fax: 064 41839
Email: info@mentons.com Web: www.mentons.com

This first-floor restaurant in bustling downtown Killarney has two entrances - one up a rather grand flight of steps from the street (asserting its independence), the other through the hotel (up stairs or on the lift). It's a bright contemporary space on two levels and several areas, with classy modern table settings and quite a luxurious atmosphere - aided by welcoming staff. It's a popular lunch spot, when informal menus offer a range of light dishes such as Mentons chicken and bacon Caesar salad, hot panini with salad, house fries and a choice of fillings, and more substantial choices like Cronin's jumbo spicy sausages with rosemary mash and thyme jus. An early dinner offers good value, and more structured evening menus are sprinkled with house dishes - a layered starter salad, with Parma ham, grapes, red onion, cherry tomatoes, maple vinaigrette and shaved parmesan, for example, and Mentons paté, with summer leaves & cherry jam - and include local ingredients such as Cromane mussels and Spillanes smoked salmon. A new head chef took over the kitchen shortly after our most recent visit but, in the Guide's experience, the cooking at Mentons has always been good. **Seats 65.** Air conditioning. Children welcome. L daily 12.30-4.30, D daily 6-9. Early D 6-7 €24.95. ALso A la C L&D. Closed last 3 weeks Jan. MasterCard, Visa, **Directions:** Killarney town centre - up steps beside main entrance to Plaza Hotel.

Killarney
HOTEL

Randles Court Hotel

Muckross Road Killarney Co Kerry **Tel: 064 35333** Fax: 064 35206/39301
Email: info@randlescourt.com Web: www.randlescourt.com

Within easy walking distance of the town centre, but also convenient to attractions such as Muckross House and Killarney National Park, this family-owned and managed hotel has been developed around an attractive house originally built in 1906 as a family residence, and extensively refurbished before opening as an hotel in 1992. Although it has grown since then, it still has some of the domesticity and warmth of the family home - period features, including fireplaces and stained glass windows, have been retained and comfortably furnished public rooms include a small bar, a large drawing room with log fire, tapestries and antiques and an elegant restaurant, Checkers, which opens onto a sheltered patio. Spacious bedrooms are furnished to a high standard, with direct dial telephones, satellite television, radio, hair dryers and well-appointed bathrooms - less "country house" than the public areas, perhaps, but very comfortable. *An additional 23 rooms, underground parking and a mountain view garden were nearing completion at the time of going to press. The neighbouring **Dromhall Hotel** (064 39300; www.dromhall.com) is a sister establishment and shared leisure facilities, including a 17 metre pool, sauna, steam room, gym and spa/treatment rooms (including a new Zen Day Spa) are accessible from both hotels. Conference/banqueting (80/30); business centre, secretarial service. Children welcome (under 5 free in parents' room, cot available without charge, baby sitting arranged). Own parking. Pets permitted by arrangement. **Rooms 55** (3 junior suites, 10 superior, 3 shower only, 15 no smoking). Lift. 24 hour room service. Turndown service. B&B €100 pps, ss €45, SC inc. **Checkers Restaurant:** D daily, 7-9.30; bar meals 12-6. Special breaks offered - details on application. Closed 23-27 Dec. Amex, Diners, MasterCard, Visa, Laser. **Directions:** 5 mins walk out of Killarney centre on Muckross Road.

Killarney
RESTAURANT

Treyvaud's Restaurant

62 High Street Killarney Co Kerry **Tel: 064 33062** Fax: 064 22793
Email: info@treyvaudsrestaurant.com Web: www.treyvaudsrestaurant.com

Brothers Paul and Mark Treyvaud opened this attractive and friendly town-centre restaurant in 2003 and it has earned a well-deserved local following. The decor is gently contemporary, daytime menus are carefully constructed to allow anything from a tasty little bite to a full blown meal. You could start with a delicious bowl of minestrone soup, perhaps, or seafood chowder, which come with excellent home-made bread, and then something from the 'Nibbles' section of the menu, such as tasty Treyvaud's fish cakes, served with wholegrain mustard & garlic aioli, or one of their speciality Sambo's (the Famous Club Sambo, perhaps, with toasted focaccia & rosemary bread, with house fries). For larger appetites, hot main courses include warm salads and Mark's Specials - the beef & Guinness pie with mashed potatoes is one of the best you'll find anywhere. The dinner menu takes over at 5 o'clock, and includes some items from the day menu - the soups and the speciality fish cakes, for example - plus a wide range of appealing and fairly priced dishes including favourites like roast rack of Kerry lamb, slow cooked pork belly with mash, some less usual (ostrich, for example, which is farmed in Ireland), several seafood choices and at least two for vegetarians (one of which is likely to be a pasta dish). A short mid-range wine list offers a couple of half carafes and half a dozen fine wines. Good cooking, moderate pricing, long opening hours and a clear desire to send customers away happy with their meal have proved a winning formula for this deservedly popular restaurant. **Seats 80** (private room, 50). Reservations required. Air conditioning. Daily L12-5; D 5-10.30 (Sun to 10). D à la carte (early D 10% discount on food & drink, 5-6.45pm). Set Sun L €19.95. House wine €17.50. Closed Mon & Tue off season. MasterCard, Visa, Laser. **Directions:** 500 yards up main street, on the left.

Killarney
RESTAURANT

West End House

Lower New Street Killarney Co Kerry
Tel: 064 32271 Fax: 064 35979

The Fassbenders' unusual restaurant has a somewhat Tyrolean atmosphere and a most unusual history, having once been (most appropriately) one of Ireland's oldest schools of housewifery. Today it ranks as one of the "old guard" in Killarney hospitality terms as it has been serving wholesome, hearty fare at lunch and dinner without fuss or ostentation for many years and has retained an enviable reputation for reliability and good value. The surroundings are simple but comfortable - a fireplace set at a attractively high level in the wall at the end of the bar casts warmth across the room, which can be very welcome on chilly evenings - and the cooking is comfortingly traditional in a strong house style untroubled by fashion. Local produce is used to advantage, typically in good home-made soups that come with freshly-baked bread, main courses such as rack of Kerry lamb. (B&B accommodation is also available.) D Tue-Sun, 6-9.30pm. Closed Mon. MasterCard, Visa, **Directions:** Opposite St Mary's Church. ◇

Killarney Area
BAR/RESTAURANT

The Beaufort Bar & Restaurant

Beaufort Killarney Co Kerry **Tel: 064 44032** Fax: 064 44390
Email: beaurest@eircom.net Web: www.beaufortbar.com

féile bia In the fourth generation of family ownership, Padraig O'Sullivan's immaculate establishment near the Gap of Dunloe is a pleasure to visit. The old tree at the front was left safely in place during renovations which, together with features like the stonework and an open fire in the bar for winter, all contribute to the genuine character that can easily be lost in refurbishments. The pride taken by the family in running this fine pub is palpable and the upstairs restaurant (which can be reached through the bar or by a separate entrance from the carpark) is a logical extension of the bar business. Head chef Tim Brosnan, who joined the team in 1999, presents quite extensive, well-balanced à la carte and set dinner menus with a generous, traditional tone: seafood cocktail, chilled ogen melon with a seasonal fruits & strawberry sorbet, chicken liver paté; roast rack of Kerry lamb or duckling, sole meunière) plus a few more international dishes; finish with classic desserts (pavlova with strawberries & cream, warm apple crumble with custard sauce) or farmhouse cheeses. The set menu is well-priced and the carte is also fairly moderate (main courses from about €16), and Sunday lunch, which is very popular, is especially good value. Children welcome. Restaurant **Seats 80** (private room, The Kalem Room, seats 20). D Tue-Sat, 6.30-9.30, à la carte; L Sun only, 1-3; Set Sun L €22. House wine €18. SC discretionary. Restaurant closed D Sun, all Mon. Establishment closed Nov. MasterCard, Visa, Laser. **Directions:** Follow the N72 to Killorglin. Turn left at Beaufort bridge, first stone building on left in village.

Killarney Area
HOTEL

Hotel Dunloe Castle

Beaufort Killarney Co Kerry **Tel: 064 44111** Fax: 064 44583
Email: hotelsales@liebherr.com Web: www.killarneyhotels.ie

féile bia Sister hotel to the Hotel Europe (Fossa) and Ard-na-Sidhe (Caragh Lake), this beautifully located hotel is mainly modern (although the original castle is part of the development) and has much in common with the larger Europe: the style is similar, the scale is generous throughout, and standards of maintenance and housekeeping are exemplary. Like the Europe, the atmosphere is distinctly continental; some of the exceptionally spacious guest rooms have dining areas, and all have magnificent views, air conditioning and many extras. The surrounding park is renowned for its unique botanical collection, which includes many rare plants. Golf is, of course, a major attraction here and there is an equestrian centre on site, also fishing on the River Laune, which is free of charge to residents. Conference/banqueting (250/200). Leisure centre, swimming pool. Snooker, pool table. Garden, fishing, walking, tennis, equestrian. Children welcome (under 2s free in parents' room, cot available without charge, baby sitting arranged; playroom, playground). No pets. **Rooms 110** (2 suites, 29 executive, 10 family rooms, 1 for disabled, 18 ground floor, 40 no smoking). Lift; 24 hr room service. B&B from €105, ss €75 (weekend specials from about €210). Closed 1 Nov- 6 April. Amex, Diners, MasterCard, Visa, Laser. **Directions:** Off main Ring of Kerry road.

Killarney Area
HOTEL

Hotel Europe

Fossa Killarney Co Kerry **Tel: 064 71350** Fax: 064 37900
Email: sales@kih.liebherr.com Web: www.killarneyhotels.ie

féile bia Although now around thirty five years old, this impressive hotel was exceptionally well built and has been so well maintained through the years that it still outshines many a new top level hotel. Public areas are very large and impressive, comfortably furnished and make full use of the hotel's wonderful location, and bedrooms follow a similar pattern, with lots of space, quality furnishings, beautiful views and balconies all along the lake side of the hotel. Leisure facilities include a 25-metre swimming pool, fitness suite and sauna; the hotel adjoins the three Killarney golf courses - Killeen, Mahony's Point and Lackabane - and the two nine hole courses, Dunloe and Ross, are nearby. The hotel's continental connections show clearly in the style throughout but especially, perhaps, when it comes to food - breakfast, for example, is an impressive hot and cold buffet. Housekeeping is exemplary and, perhaps unexpectedly, this is a very family-friendly hotel. *At the time of going to press the hotel has closed and a major development project is under way: by the time of re-opening, just after Easter 2007, this will include new state of the art conference and business facilities, and the complete refurbishment of the ground floor. A later phase (due early September 2007) will add a 50,000 square foot spa, new swimming pool and a lifestyle restaurant. Equestrian, fishing, (indoor) tennis, snooker. Children welcome (under 12s free in parents room, cot available without charge; playroom, playground). No pets. Lift. **Rooms 204** (8 suites, 60 no smoking, 154 twin rooms). B&B from €105, ss €75. No sc. Closed Oct -Easter. Equestrian, fishing, (indoor) tennis, snooker. Children welcome (under 12s free in parents room, cot available without charge; playroom, playground). No pets. Lift. **Rooms 204** (8 suites, 60 no smoking, 154 twin rooms). B&B from €105, ss €75. No sc. Closed Oct -Easter. Amex, Diners, MasterCard, Visa, Laser. **Directions:** On main Ring of Kerry road, N72.

Killarney Area
N HOTEL/RESTAURANT

Muckross Park Hotel

Muckross Village Lakes of Killarney Co Kerry
Tel: 064 23400 Fax: 064 31965
Email: info@muckrosspark.com Web: www.muckrosspark.com

At the heart of this large, well-executed development lies a fine Victorian house and, although the newer areas have an elegant contemporary style, an atmosphere of timeless quality pervades throughout. With a large conference centre, break out meeting rooms and mediaeval-style banqueting suite, it is a popular choice for business and weddings, but it also makes a convenient and luxurious base for the independent traveller it is located within the Killarney National Park, near Muckross House and Garden, handy to all the championship golf courses in the area, and ideally situated for exploring south Kerry. Beautifully furnished accommodation offers all that would be expected of an hotel of this calibre - ranging from romantic four-poster suites to spacious contemporary rooms, all featuring luxurious fabrics and many extras - and food and service to match. A good breakfast here will set you up for the day, and a particularly attractive feature of the hotel is the warm 'Irishness' of the staff. The adjacent Molly Darcy's pub is in common ownership with the hotel. **Restaurants:** Dining options are between the Blue Pool restaurant (named after the nearby Cloghreen Blue Pool Nature Trail), and the newer GB Shaw's, which is earning a following for fine food and service (the fillet of beef and sizzling duck attracted special praise on a recent visit). Conferences/Banqueting (300/160); Spa, walking, hillwalking, cycling, holistic healing, yoga, tai-chi; Championship golf and equestrian nearby. Rooms include 6 suites, and 42 double/twin bedrooms with separate seating areas that can be combined to create family rooms. B&B from €80-100 pps in Garden Wing. **Directions:** in Killarney National Park.

Killorglin

Nick's Seafood Restaurant & Piano Bar

E RESTAURANT

Lr Bridge Street Killorglin Co Kerry **Tel: 066 976 1219**
Fax: 066 976 1233 Email: info@nicks.ie

This is one of the famous old restaurants of Ireland and Nick Foley's is clearly thriving. It consists of two attractive stone-faced townhouses - one a traditional bar with a piano and some dining tables, where arriving guests can linger over a drink and place their orders, the other the main dining area. With quarry tiles, darkwood furniture, heavily timbered ceiling, wine bottles lining a high shelf around the walls - and piano playing drifting through from the bar - the diningroom has great atmosphere. Nick's cooking of classic French with an Irish accent has earned a special reputation for his way with local seafood and - although there are always other choices, notably prime Kerry beef and lamb - it is for classic seafood dishes like grilled Cromane mussels, home cured gravadlax, lobster thermidor, and Valentia scallops mornay that his name is synonymous throughout Ireland. And, if you want to see what that much-maligned item the speciality seafood plate is like at its best, make the journey to Nick's - for sheer quality, variety and attention to detail), it's unbeatable:Irish seafood at its best, and very good value for money. Desserts, all home-made and changed weekly, may well be little more than an afterthought after such savoury delights - perhaps a shared tasting plate is the best solution - and there's a good cheeseboard too. Although it would be a shame to come here without enjoying such exceptional seafood, vegetarians aren't forgotten either and the service is outstanding, and the music and great atmosphere as beguiling as ever. An extensive wine list, hand-picked by Nick and with many bottles imported directly, includes interesting house wines and an unusual choice of half bottles. *At the time of going to press, the Foley family has plans to develop a second establishment at a nearby church. Children welcome. **Seats 90** (private room, 40). Air conditioning. Live Piano nightly. D Wed-Sun 6.30-9.45 in winter, daily in summer (to 9.30 Sun); 2 sittings at 6.45 and 9.15. Set D €48/52. Extensive wine list; house wine from €19.20; sc discretionary. Closed all Nov and 2 weeks Feb, Mon-Tue in Dec-Mar & Christmas. MasterCard, Visa, Laser. **Directions:** On the Ring of Kerry road, 20 km from Killarney.

Listowel

Allo's Restaurant, Bar & Bistro

€ BAR/RESTAURANT WITH ROOMS

41/43 Church Street Listowel Co Kerry
Tel: 068 22880 Fax: 068 22803 Email: allos@eircom.net

Named after the previous owner ("Alphonsus, aka Allo"), Helen Mullane's café-bar seems much older than it is, as the whole interior was reconstructed with salvaged materials (the flooring was once in the London Stock Exchange). It is brilliantly done with the long, narrow bar divided up in the traditional way, with oilcloth-covered tables along the side and at the back, now extending into a restaurant in the house next door which can have great atmosphere on a busy evening. A team of six chefs cook tasty bistro food at lunch and dinner, and a meal here should be fun - expect lively combinations of traditional and new Irish cooking with some international influences, based on carefully sourced ingredients. Theme nights are often held. **Seats 50** (private room, 20, outdoor, 20). Open Tue-Sat, 12-9, L12-7, D 7-9 L & D à la carte; also Early D €27.50 7-9 Tue-Thurs; House wine €22. Closed Sun & Mon, 25 Dec & Good Fri. D reservations required. **Accommodation:** There are three beautiful guest bedrooms. Spacious and stylishly furnished with antiques, they have four-poster beds, luxurious Connemara marbled bathrooms and tea/coffee making facilities. **Rooms 3** (1 shower only). Accommodation €50 pps, ss€10; breakfast available at local café/hotel. Amex, MasterCard, Visa, Laser. **Directions:** Coming into Listowel on the N69, located half way down Church Street on the right hand side (almost opposite Garda Station).

Listowel
HOTEL

Listowel Arms Hotel

Listowel Co Kerry **Tel: 068 21500** Fax: 068 22524
Email: info@listowelarms.com Web: www.listowelarms.com

féile bia This much-loved old hotel is rich in history and especially famous as the main venue for the annual Listowel Writers Week. Since 1996 the hotel has been in the energetic and discerning ownership of Kevin O'Callaghan, who has overseen a major extension and overhaul of the whole premises during the last few years. A new restaurant, kitchen, banqueting area and bedrooms all overlook the River Feale; improvements have all been done with great sensitivity, so greater comfort has been gained throughout the hotel without loss of character. Non-residents find this a handy place to drop into for a bite in the bar where they serve traditional dishes like braised beef & stout casserole (L12-3, D 5.30-9.30) and you can have tea or coffee in the lounge at other times. Conference/banqueting (500/400); video-conferencing, ISDN lines. Wheelchair accessible. Lift. Children welcome (under 5s free in parents' room, cots available without charge). Pets permitted by arrangement. **Rooms 37** (all en-suite). B&B from about €55 pps, ss about €20. (Higher rates apply to Festival weeks, incl Irish Open & Listowel Race Week.) Closed 24-26 Dec. **Directions:** In the corner of the historic old square in Listowel town centre. ◇

Portmagee
RESTAURANT/PUB/GUESTHOUSE

The Moorings

Portmagee Co Kerry **Tel: 066 947 7108**
Fax: 066 947 7220 Email: moorings@iol.ie Web: www.moorings.ie

Gerard & Patricia Kennedy's guesthouse overlooks the harbour and many bedrooms - which are comfortably furnished with phone, TV, tea/coffee making facilities and full bathrooms - have a sea view. Children welcome (under 3 free in parents' room, cot available without charge, baby sitting arranged). No pets. Traditional Irish music. **Rooms 14** (all en-suite, 5 shower only, all no smoking). B&B from €40 pps, ss about €15. The adjacent **Bridge Bar** is a good place to drop in for a bite to eat, especially seafood, when touring this beautiful area - meals are usually available all day, but a phone call to check times is advised. There is also a restaurant, which is open for evening meals and Sunday lunch. Establishment closed Nov-Feb. Amex, MasterCard, Visa, Laser. **Directions:** Turn right for Portmagee 3 miles outside Caherciveen on the Waterville Road. ◇

SNEEM

Situated on the Ring of Kerry between Kenmare and Waterville, Sneem is "a knot" in Irish, and this colourful, immaculately kept village is divided in two by the River Sneem, creating an unusual "hour-glass" shape ("The Knot in the Ring"). The first week of August sees Sneem at its busiest with the "Welcome Home Festival", in honour of those who emigrated from Ireland. Moderately priced accommodation and stunning views make a good combination at the O'Sullivan family's hospitable **Old Convent House B&B** (064 45181), and **Sacre Coeur** (064 45186), in the village, is the place where locals and holiday home owners dine: good plentiful food and value for money.
WWW.IRELAND-GUIDE.COM FOR THE BEST PLACES TO EAT, DRINK & STAY

Sneem
HOTEL

Great Southern Hotel, Parknasilla

Parknasilla Sneem Co Kerry **Tel: 064 45122** Fax: 064 45323
Email: res@parknasilla-gsh.com Web: www.gshotels.com

féile bia Set in 300 acres of sub-tropical parkland, overlooking Kenmare Bay, this classic Victorian hotel is blessed with one of the most beautiful locations in Ireland The spacious foyer with its antiques and fresh flowers sets a tone of quiet luxury, enhanced by the hotel's impressive collection of original art (currently being catalogued). Whether activity or relaxation is required there are excellent amenities at hand including an outdoor swimming pool and Canadian hot tub - and an abundance of comfortable places for a quiet read or afternoon tea. Public rooms include the impressive Pygmalion Restaurant and a library (added in 1995 to mark the hotel's centenary and available for the use of all guests, although also ideal for meetings and small conferences). Bedrooms vary in size and outlook but most have been upgraded recently and all have en-suite bathrooms with bath and shower, tea/coffee making facilities, direct-dial telephone, radio, TV with in-house movie channel, trouser press and hair dryer. Afternoon tea at Parknasilla is a relaxing affair, served in the spacious interconnecting lounges along the front of the hotel. An impressive range of outdoor activities available on-site includes walking (routes marked, map available), golf (12 hole), horseriding, inshore and deep sea fishing and cruises on the hotel's own boat, Parknasilla Princess - this is a place to slow down and take time for yourself. *At the time of press, the property has been sold; however, although its future is uncertain, it is still operating as an hotel. Conference/banqueting (20/60). Children welcome (under 2 free in parents room; cots available without charge; children's tea 5.30-6, baby sitting arranged) Leisure centre, swimming pool. Golf (12 hole), tennis, fishing, equestrian, walking. Snooker, pool table, games room. No pets. **Rooms 83** (2 suites, 8 junior suites, 73 superior rooms, 2 for disabled). Lift. 24 hour room service. Turndown service. Room rate from about €150. No SC. Short breaks/special interest breaks offered. Open all year. Amex, Diners, MasterCard, Visa, Laser. **Directions:** 25 km west of Kenmare, on Ring of Kerry. ◇

Sneem

COUNTRY HOUSE/GUESTHOUSE

Tahilla Cove Country House

Tahilla Cove Sneem Co Kerry
Tel: 064 45204 Fax: 064 45104
Email: tahillacove@eircom.net Web: www.tahillacove.com

Although it has been much added to over the years and has a blocky annexe in the garden, this family-run guesthouse has an old house in there somewhere. There's a proper bar, with its own entrance (which is used by locals as well as residents) and this, together with quite an official looking reception desk just inside the front door, makes it feel more like an hotel than a guesthouse Yet this is a refreshingly low-key place, and it has two very special features: the location, which is genuinely waterside, is really lovely and away-from-it-all; and the owners, James and Deirdre Waterhouse. Tahilla Cove has been in the family since 1948, and run since 1987 by James and Deirdre who have the wisdom to understand why their many regulars love it just the way it is and, apart from regular maintenance (and some recent major refurbishment) little is allowed to change. Comfort and quiet relaxation are the priorities. All the public rooms have sea views, including the dining room and also a large sitting room, with plenty of armchairs and sofas, which opens onto a terrace (where there are patio tables and chairs overlooking the garden and the cove with its little stone jetty). Accommodation is divided between the main house and the annexe, which is very close by; rooms vary considerably but all except two have sea views, many have private balconies, and all are en-suite, with bathrooms of varying sizes and appointments (only one single is shower-only). All rooms have phone, TV, hair-dryer and individually controlled heating. Food is prepared personally by James and Deirdre and, although the dining room (20) is mainly intended for residents, others are welcome to share their Irish home cooking when there is room; simple 5-course menus change daily. It's also a lovely place to drop into for a cup of tea overlooking the little harbour. Garden; walking; fishing. Children welcome (under 2s free in parents' room, cot available without charge). Pets allowed in some areas by prior arrangement. **Rooms 9** (1 shower only, 3 family rooms, 3 ground floor, all no smoking). B&B €70 pps, ss €30. D at 7.45; Set D about €30; house wine €19. Non-residents' welcome by reservation. Closed for D Tue-Wed; house closed mid Oct-Easter. Amex, MasterCard, Visa, Laser. **Directions:** 16km (11 miles) west of Kenmare and 8km (5 m) east of Sneem (N70).

Tralee

HOTEL/RESTAURANT

Ballygarry House Hotel

Killarney Road Tralee Co Kerry
Tel: 066 712 3322 Fax: 066 712 7630
Email: info@ballygarryhouse.com Web: www.ballygarryhouse.com

Recently renovated and upgraded to a high standard, this pleasant roadside hotel presents a neat face to arriving guests and also has extensive landscaped gardens at the back. The furnishing style is traditional with occasional contemporary twists; warm colours, notably in oriental rugs used on wooden floors, create a welcoming atmosphere in public areas and darkwood furniture in bedrooms is used to effect against contrasting furnishings and pale walls. Accommodation Is very pleasing, with many thoughtful details adding to the comfort of a stay - rooms at the back should be quieter. This is an appealing hotel, with exceptionally friendly and helpful staff, and it is moderately priced for the standard offered. It is understandably popular for weddings (conference/banqueting 250/400). Spa. Children welcome (free in parents' room up to 12; cot available without charge, baby sitting arranged). Golf nearby. Walking, garden. No pets. **Rooms 61** (1 suite, 5 junior suites, 1 for disabled) Lift. 24 hour room service. Turndown service. B&B €95 pps, ss €35, no sc. Closed 20-26 Dec. **Brooks:** This well appointed restaurant is pleasingly set up towards the back of the hotel and the modern classical food has great appeal. Quite an extensive a la carte menu is offered, based largely on local produce, and its strength is in the presentation of traditional dishes with a successful modern twist. Cooking is sound, presentation attractive - and, best of all, staff are attentive and hospitable.
Seats 80. D daily 6.30-9.30; L Sun only 12.30-2.30. D à la carte; Set Sun L €22.50. House wine from €20. SC discretionary. Bar meals also available 12-9 daily). Amex, MasterCard, Visa, Laser.
Directions: 1 mile fromTralee, on the Killarney road. ◇

Tralee
HOTEL

The Brandon Hotel

Princes Street Tralee Co Kerry
Tel: 066 712 3333 Fax: 066 712 5019

féile bia Overlooking a park and the famous Siamsa Tire folk theatre, and close to the Aquadome, Tralee's largest hotel is at the heart of activities throughout the area. Spacious public areas are impressive, and while there are suites and superior rooms available, some of the standard bedrooms are on the small side; however, all have been refurbished or are due for refurbishment and have direct-dial phone, radio and TV (no tea/coffee-making facilities) and tiled bathrooms. There's a well-equipped leisure centre and good banqueting/conference facilities. Private parking. **Rooms 183.** B&B from about €60 pps. Closed 21-29 Dec. Amex, Diners, MasterCard, Visa, **Directions:** Town centre. ◇

Tralee
GUESTHOUSE

Brook Manor Lodge

Fenit Road Tralee Co Kerry **Tel: 066 712 0406** Fax: 066 712 7552
Email: brookmanor@eircom.net Web: www.brookmanorlodge.com

Set back from the road, in 3.5 acres of grounds, Sandra Lordan's large purpose-built guesthouse offers immaculate and particularly spacious accommodation. Public rooms and bedrooms are large and very comfortably furnished - bedrooms have generous beds and all the usual modern facilities - TV, phone, trouser press, tea/coffee making, hair dryer and radio/alarm - everything, in short, that the traveller (and, specifically, the golfing traveller) could need. Breakfast is cooked to order from an extensive menu. Children welcome (under 8s free in parents' room, cot available free of charge). Free broad-band WI/Fi; No pets. **Rooms 8** (1 suite, 1 junior suite, 2 superior rooms, 2 shower only, 2 family rooms, all no smoking.) B&B €70 pps; (single supplement applies). Closed 1 Nov - 1 Feb. MasterCard, Visa, Laser. **Directions:** 2 km from town centre on Fenit road.

Tralee
GUESTHOUSE

Castlemorris House

Ballymullen Tralee Co Kerry
Tel: 066 718 0060 Email: castlemorris@eircom.net

Tony and Ciara Fields have recently taken over this attractive creeper-clad Georgian house, the story will be updated when the guide next stays there but it makes a lovely place to stay and we hope that they will continue with the good home baking (complimentary afternoon tea in front of the drawing room fire on arrival) and the friendly atmosphere of a family home. Bedrooms are spacious and well-furnished for comfort with style. Breakfast is a speciality and there are good restaurants nearby for dinner. Garden. Children welcome (under 10s free in parents room, cot available at no charge, baby sitting arranged). No pets. **Rooms 7** (4 shower only, 2 family rooms, all no smoking). B&B €45 pps, ss €10. Closed Christmas. Amex, MasterCard, Visa, Laser. **Directions:** on south Ring Road /Killorglin road (Ring of Kerry) leaving Tralee.

Tralee
Ⓝ CAFÉ/RESTAURANT

Dawson's Restaurant & Café

19-20 The Mall Tralee Co Kerry
Tel: 066 712 7745

Nuala Dawson's first floor daytime restaurant is a popular place for discerning locals in the know. It's a bit old-fashioned but bright and airy, and there's such a strong emphasis on freshness and flavour that the choice becomes limited in the afternoon, as lunch is the main business and only food freshly cooked each day is served. The menu changes daily and offers lovely hot lunches, a huge selection of wonderful salads, quiches, home-made soups, breads (including breads suitable for special diets, eg gluten free), cold meats and salmon cooked on the premises and - best of all - the most beautiful home-made confectionery. Staff are friendly and efficient and Nuala, who is from Northern Ireland, keeps a close eye on everything. Food to go is also offered perfect at Christmas, when delicious Christmas puddings and mince pies are available. **Directions:** Upstairs above Heaton's retail store. ◇

Tralee
HOTEL

Meadowlands Hotel

Oakpark Rd Tralee Co Kerry
Tel: 066 718 0444 Fax: 066 718 0964
Email: info@meadowlandshotel.com Web: www.meadowlandshotel.com

féile bia This hotel in a peaceful part of the town is set in 3 acres of grounds and landscaped gardens, yet within walking distance of the town centre. Open since 1998, the high quality of materials and workmanship is now paying off as the building mellows and takes on its own person-ality - and this, together with caring service from well-trained staff, is ensuring its position as one of the area's leading hotels. The interior layout and design of the hotel are impressive; notably the whole hotel is wheelchair friendly and furniture, commissioned from Irish craft manufacturers, is interesting, well-made and practical. Stylish, well-designed bedrooms are spacious and comfortable, with striking decor - and the suites have jacuzzis. The main restaurant, An Pota Stóir, is open for dinner only (except Sunday - lunch only) and booking is advised as it is popular with locals as well as residents. Informal meals, including seafood from the proprietor's fishing boats, are available in Johnny Franks bar, (12-9 daily). Conference/banqueting (200/180). Golf nearby. Garden. Children welcome (under 3s free in parents' room, cots available free of charge, baby sitting arranged). Wheelchair accessible. No pets. **Rooms 58** (2 suites, 10 superior rooms, 25 no smoking, 2 for disabled). Lift. 24 hour room service. B&B €105 pps, ss €20. Off-season value breaks available. Closed 24-25 Dec. Amex, MasterCard, Visa, Laser. **Directions:** 1km from Tralee town centre on the N69, but usually accessed by N21/N22: go straight through the last two roundabouts and turn right at each of the next two traffic lights; the hotel is on the right.

Tralee

Oyster Tavern

RESTAURANT/PUB

The Spa Tralee Co Kerry **Tel: 066 713 6102** Fax: 066 713 6047

féile bia

This well-maintained roadside bar and restaurant has a loyal local following. Wide-ranging menus are moderately priced, and seafood is a strength. Although the style is largely traditional, there may be some unusual dishes; a balanced choice of non-seafood dishes offers prime meat and poultry and a couple of vegetarian dishes. Sunday lunch is especially good value and very popular. Bar open usual hours (no food served in the bar). Restaurant **Seats 140.** D daily, Summer hours 5-10.15pm (Sun from 6), Winter hours 6-9.45pm (Sun to 8.45pm), L Sun only all year, 12.30-2.30. Set Sun L about €16, D à la carte. House wine from about €15. *Times not confirmed at time of going to press - a phone call to check is advised. Closed 25 Dec, Good Fri. Diners, MasterCard, Visa, Laser. **Directions:** 4 miles outside Tralee, on the Fenit road. ◇

Tralee

Restaurant David Norris

☆RESTAURANT

Ivy House Ivy Terrace Tralee Co Kerry
Tel: 066 718 5654 Email: restaurantdavidnorris@eircom.net

féile bia

Restaurant David Norris has earned wide recognition as Tralee's leading fine dining restaurant. Although located on the first floor of an unprepossessing modern building, it has a nice little reception area with a sofa and stools at a small bar and well-spaced tables are dressed with quality linen, plain glasses and white china, relieved by fresh flowers. A Euro-Toques chef, David Norris sources food with care; the ingredients used are organic wherever possible and everything served is hand-made on the premises (breads, pasta, ice creams). The emphasis is on taste, and presentation that is beautiful yet not over-elaborate - and the aim is to offer the best of food at reasonable prices. This he is achieving well: seasonal menus are simply written and, while very promising, are not over-ambitious in extent. About seven choices are offered on each course of an à la carte menu: seafood is well-represented, as would be expected in this area, but the range of foods offered is wide - Kerry beef may top the bill, for example (a sirloin steak, perhaps, with a mushrooms & shallot 'lasagne' and a bay leaf jus), also local lamb - and imaginative vegetarian dishes, like handmade potato & parmesan ravioli, with chargrilled leeks, wild mushrooms and a leek cream, have mainstream appeal. Classic desserts, which include speciality hand-made ice creams, round off the meal in style, or there are Irish farmhouse cheeses, served with fresh fruit, home-made preserves and biscuits. Thoughtful detail is evident throughout, from the complimentary amuse-bouche that arrives with your aperitif to the home-made fudge served with your tea or coffee. Good cooking, professional service, an informative but sensibly limited wine list and good value for money have all won this fine restaurant many friends - and recent visits by the guide confirm David Norris's position as the premier restaurant in the area. **Seats 45.** D Tue-Sat 5.30-9.30 (Sat 7-9.30); early D €25.95, Tue-Fri 5.30-7; also à la carte. House wine €19.95; sc discretionary, except 10% (charged on food only) on parties of 10+. Closed Sun, Mon, all bank hols, 1 week Oct, 2 weeks Feb. Amex, MasterCard, Visa, Laser. **Directions:** Facing Siamsa Tire, across the road from the Brandon Hotel.

Tralee

Val O'Shea's Bar & Bistro

BAR/RESTAURANT

Bridge Street Tralee Co Kerry **Tel: 066 712 1559**
Fax: 066 712 5495 Email: vals@ohallorangroup.com

féile bia

This is the happening place in Tralee for informal dining and music. Very stylish, designer-driven, it's all of a piece with tinted windows, very dark woods and very dark leather on seats and bar stools - and traditional music most week nights (phone for details). Differing floor heights are cleverly exploited, and there's a mammoth feature area at the bottom of the stairs up to the bistro, which looks like an enormous three-sided sofa seating about 10 people. Although gloomy if you come in out of bright sunlight, the lighting is subtle and effective once your eyes adjust. Consistent standards, of both bar and the upstairs bistro food, have been maintained even when there have been changes of personnel, so the policy of providing quality and good value is likely to continue. Menus are well-balanced and have youth appeal - expect popular international dishes like chicken kebabs with onion, peppers and mushrooms, with sweet & sour sauce and pitta bread, served with some style - and prices are reasonable: you could have a 3-course meal from about €25. The bar menus is also attractive - and the wine list includes eight well-chosen house wines. Bistro **Seats 60** (outdoor seating, 20). Reservations required. Air conditioning. Toilets wheelchair accessible. L Mon-Sat,12.30-2.30; D daily 6.30-9.30 (Sun to 9). Bar meals 5.30-9 daily. [Times not confirmed at time of going to press, a phone call to check is advised.] Closed L Sun, 25 Dec, Good Fri. MasterCard, Visa, Laser. **Directions:** Town centre, beside Abbey carpark.

Valentia Island
CAFÉ

Sea Breeze - Knightstown's Coffee Shop

Knightstown Valentia Island Co Kerry **Tel: 087 783 7544**

Grainne Houlihan's bright and funky coffee shop is a great place to break a journey when touring the area. There's outdoor seating at the front for fine days and, inside, there's a pleasingly old-fashioned café with oilcloth-covered tables; aside from terrific coffees, good home cooking is the great strength, especially baking (warm scone with jam, butter & fresh cream, chocolate fudge cake...). You can have something as simple as a mug of soup and some home-made bread, a speciality sandwich, or one of half a dozen substantial savoury platters, including a vegetarian one. At the back, a long corridor down to the loos is decorated with an eclectic collection of old mirrors - an inspired way to brighten up a long corridor. Open weekends from Easter, 12noon-6.30pm; open daily in high season (June-end Sep). Closed Oct-Easter. **Directions:** On right in main street of village, coming from ferry.

Waterville
N GUESTHOUSE

Brookhaven House

New Line Road Waterville Co Kerry
Tel: 066 947 4431 Fax: 066 947 4724
Email: brookhaven@esatclear.ie Web: www.brookhavenhouse.com

Overlooking the Atlantic Ocean and Waterville Championship Golf Course, Mary Clifford's family-run custom built guesthouse lays the emphasis on comfort and personal service and, although it may seem a little stark from the road, it is set in an attractive garden, which is peaceful and colourful. The spacious en-suite bedrooms have all the necessary amenities, twin, double and triple rooms are all available some with seating areas, all with direct dial phone, TV, hairdryer and tea & coffee making facilities and most with lovely views over the bay- so book a room with a view of the sea if possible. And, as Mary is keen to point out, there's more to Waterville than golf - hill walking, watersports, angling and horse riding are all nearby. Free Broadband. Drying room. Children welcome (under 5s free in parents room, cot available at no charge). **Rooms 6** (2 junior suites, 1 shower only, 1 family room, 1 ground floor, all no smoking); B&B €50 pps, ss €40. MasterCard, Visa, Laser. **Directions:** Less than 1km from Waterville on the north side.

Waterville
HOTEL/RESTAURANT

Butler Arms Hotel

Waterville Co Kerry **Tel: 066 947 4144** Fax: 066 947 4520
Email: reservations@butlerarms.com Web: www.butlerarms.com

One of Ireland's best-known hotels it is one of several to have strong links with Charlie Chaplin Peter and Mary Huggard's hotel dominates the seafront at Waterville. Like many hotels which have been owner-run for several generations, it has established a special reputation for its homely atmosphere and good service. Improvements are constantly being made and public areas, including two sitting rooms, a sun lounge and a cocktail bar, are spacious and comfortably furnished, while the beamed Fisherman's Bar (which also has a separate entrance from the street) has a livelier atmosphere and can be a useful place for a break on the Ring of Kerry route. Bedrooms vary from distinctly non-standard rooms in the old part of the hotel (which many regular guests request) to smartly decorated, spacious rooms with neat en-suite bathrooms and uninterrupted sea views in a newer wing. Off season value breaks; shooting (woodcock, snipe) Nov-Jan. Golf nearby. Garden; fishing; tennis. Snooker. Wheelchair accessible. Own parking. Children welcome (free cot, baby sitting arranged). No pets. **Rooms 40** (12 junior suites, 34 no-smoking rooms, 1 disabled). Lift. Room service (limited hours). Turndown service. B&B €120 pps, ss €30. SC discretionary. **Fishermen's Restaurant:** On the sea side of the old building, the restaurant is relaxing, with a pleasant ambience, well-appointed linen-clad tables and friendly staff. The menu is flexible, priced as a full 5-course meal or à la carte, and offers a wide-ranging selection of dishes - main courses have an understandable leaning towards local seafood, including lobster, but Kerry mountain lamb (a classic roast rack, with garlic & rosemary jus perhaps) beef, and duckling are also likely choices and there will be at least one for vegetarians - a sumptuous, richly-flavoured dish of fresh tagliatelle with wild mushroom & parmesan cream, for example. The house style is quite traditional and will please those who rate good, well-cooked food (with lots of flavour) above trendy international menus: good breads, faithfully rendered classics like roast duckling with orange sauce and excellent fish cooking are all strong points. And do save a little room for delicious homemade desserts - or a trio of Irish cheeses (Cooleeny, Cashel Blue & smoked Gubeen, perhaps), served with homemade tomato chutney. **Fisherman's Bar:** bar food available daily 12-3 & 6.30-9. Closed Oct-Mar. **Restaurant Seats 70.** Reservations accepted (non residents welcome). Children welcome. Toilets wheelchair accessible. D daily, 7-9.30. Set D €45, also à la carte. Hotel closed mid Oct-Easter except for special bookings. Amex, MasterCard, Visa, Laser. **Directions:** On Ring of Kerry road.

Waterville
N B&B/RESTAURANT

The Old Cable House

Milestone Heritage Site Old Cable Station Waterville Co Kerry
Tel: 066 947 4233 Fax: 066 947 4869
Email: interestingstay@iol.ie Web: www.oldcablehistorichouse.com

For those seeking something different from the double-glazed comforts of modern accommodation, Alan and Margaret Brown's Old Cable House has real Victorian character and the added interest of its transatlantic cable history. It is set high above the town to give clear Atlantic views and simply furnished rooms have everything necessary (including en-suite facilities) but with the emphasis on home comfort, Victorian atmosphere and personal warmth; the pine floors, original sash windows and the feeling of spending time in someone's treasured home are the real plus for those who appreciate vernacular architecture. The restaurant an informal dining room, with an open fire - is open to non-residents, and offers what the Browns correctly describe as unpretentious good food: this is not a high-flying restaurant but, like the rest of the house, it has character - and Alan, who is the chef, lays the emphasis on seafood and locally sourced meats served in an hospitable atmosphere. Waterville Golf Club is on the doorstep, of course, the whole of the Ring of Kerry is very close by, and there are many interesting things to do when staying here. Cycling, fishing, equestrian, golf and walking all nearby. B&B €30-35 pps. Restaurant **seats 32**; D daily in summer. Closed 22 Dec-1 Jan. **Directions:** In Waterville town. ◇

Waterville
RESTAURANT

Paddyfrogs Restaurant

The New Line Waterville Co Kerry
Tel: 066 947 8766 Email: paddyfrogs@eircom.net

Sandra Foster and chef Max Lequet has a following with locals, golfers and holidaymakers alike, for its upbeat atmosphere and cooking by a chef who respects good ingredients and obviously loves what he is doing. The restaurant was designed by local architect Albert Walsh and is in a lovely situation, right on the shoreline; bright and open with eye-catching modern decor - perfectly suited to the style of food. Menus offer about half a dozen unusually varied choices on each course, with seafood a strength and a short separate vegetarian menu also offered; dishes which illustrate the style include a moreish starter of pan seared baby squid served with marinated sautéed courgettes, fresh coriander and caper salad (€11.95) and, from a range of main courses that include variations on the ever-popular fillets steak and excellent roast rack of lamb (with crushed carrot & parsnip purée and red wine & garlic reduction, perhaps), a dish of grilled cod fillet on potato & spinach mousseline with lime butter sauce (€23.95) works really well. Excellent desserts tend toward the classics - a gorgeous dark Belgian chocolate & brandy mousse on an orange & vanilla sauce perhaps (€6.95), or there's a Paddyfrogs Irish cheese platter, served with delicious accompaniments - including a shot of home-made spicy white wine. A well-balanced wine list includes interesting house wines and at least six half bottles. Wheelchair Accessible. Ample parking. **Seats 60** (private room, 12, outdoors, 20); D daily 6.30-10.; Set D €39.50, also à la carte or Vegetarian Menu; house wine €18-20. Closed Nov-mid Mar. MasterCard, Visa, Laser, Switch. **Directions:** Ring of Kerry - right on the waterfront in Waterville.

Waterville

BAR/B&B/RESTAURANT

The Smugglers Inn

Cliff Road Waterville Co Kerry
Tel: 066 947 4330 Fax: 066 947 4422
Email: thesmugglersinn@eircom.net Web: www.the-smugglers-inn.com

Harry and Lucille Hunt's famous clifftop inn enjoys a remarkable location right beside the world famous championship Waterville Golf Links - and it's a real inn, providing food, drink and shelter. Colourful window boxes make a welcoming first impression and, whether you are dropping in for a meal in the comfortable bar or, in fine sunny weather, at garden tables that overlook a mile of sandy beach to the sea and mountains beyond or dining in the restaurant, it's a good place to be. The restaurant, which is very popular, is in a large conservatory dining area with uninterrupted views of the clubhouse, Ballinskelligs Bay and the McGillycuddyreeks. Although shaded to avoid glare, it's a bright place to be on even the darkest day, and the views are magnificent. Refurbishment of the premises generally has seen big improvements recently although table settings with plastic water jugs and well-worn cutlery give no hint of a special dining experience in the making. However, Harry runs the kitchen with his son Henry, who is also a talented and dedicated chef, and local ingredients star in cooking which has a classical foundation (Cromane moules marinière, crab au gratin, lobster mayonnaise - lobster from their own tank) but includes modern dishes too, most noticeably on the bar menu. Seafood is the speciality, but non seafood-lovers have plenty of other choices, including Kerry lamb and beef, of course; there area also really good vegetarian dishes and some less usual choices such as saddle of rabbit (with puy lentils with an oatmeal froth and crispy pancetta), an imaginative dish that was much enjoyed on a recent visit. Lunch is served every day (the set lunch menu is good value, as is the early dinner), and bar snacks are available throughout the day, making this a good place to take a break when on the Ring of Kerry - although a phone call to check availability of food is always wise. Restaurant/Bar **Seats 90.** Air conditioning. Restaurant: L12-3 (to 4 Sun), D 6-9.30; bar food 12-8.30, (snack menu only 3-6 pm). Set Sun L €30. Early D €25 (6.45-7.30). Set D €42, also à la carte. House wine about €17.50 NB: NB - Minimum credit card transaction is €50. **Accommodation** is also offered, in modest but pleasantly decorated rooms which vary in size, outlook and facilities (one has a balcony) and price, but all are comfortably furnished in a homely style. There's a first-floor residents' sitting room with sofas and armchairs, books, television and magnificent sea views. Children welcome (under 6 free in parents' room, cots available without charge). Pets by arrangement. Garden, walking, fishing. **Rooms 14** (7 shower only). B&B €45, ss €30. Closed Nov-Mar. Amex, Diners, MasterCard, Visa, Laser. **Directions:** Before village of Waterville, on coast road next to Golf Club.

COUNTY KILDARE

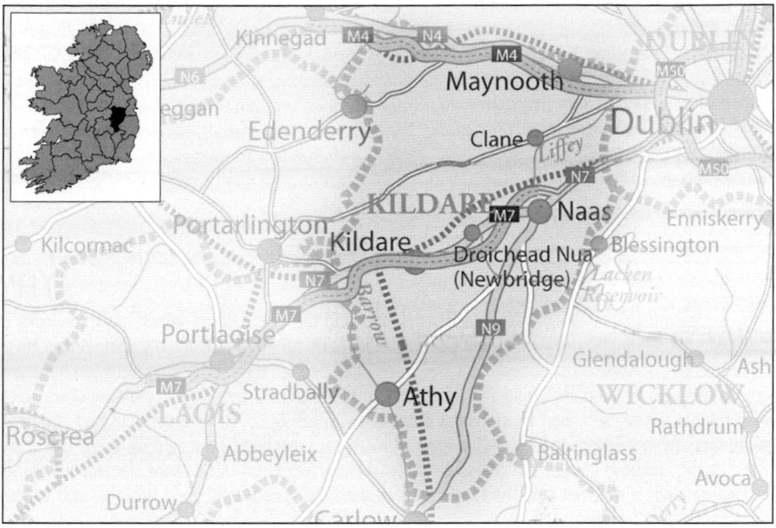

As would be expected of an area which includes the famed racecourses of The Curragh, Punchestown and Naas among its many amenities, Kildare is the horse county par excellence. The horse is so central and natural a part of Irish life that you'll find significant stud farms in a surprisingly large number of counties. But it is in Kildare that they reach their greatest concentration in the ultimate equine county. Thus it's ironic that, a mere 400 million years ago, Kildare was just a salty ocean where the only creatures remotely equine were the extremely primitive ancestors of sea horses.

But things have been looking up for the horse in County Kildare ever since, and today the lush pastures of the gently sloping Liffey and Barrow valleys provide ideal country for nurturing and training champions. Apart from many famous private farms, the Irish National Stud in Kildare town just beyond the legendary gallops of The Curragh is open for visitors, and it also includes a remarkable Japanese garden, reckoned the best Japanese rock garden in Europe, as well as the Museum of the Horse.

The development of Ireland's motorway network has been particularly beneficial to Kildare, as it has lightened the traffic load through the county's towns. In fact, getting off the main roads is what enjoyment of life in Kildare is all about. It is surprisingly easy to get away from the traffic, and you'll quickly find areas of rural enchantment and unexpected swathes of relatively untamed nature.

In the northwest of the county is the mystical Bog of Allen, the largest in Ireland, across whose wide open spaces the early engineers struggled to progress the Grand Canal on its route from the east coast towards the Shannon. Such needs of national transport are intertwined through the county's history. But between the arterial routes, railroads and canals, there is an easier pace of life, and gentle country with it.

A southern leg of the Grand Canal – originally the main waterway - curves away to become the Barrow Navigation, windings it way to Waterford. Beyond Athy, it goes near Kilkea, birthplace of Antarctic explorer Ernest Shackleton, whose growing fame is increasingly celebrated in his native county where his ancestors were involved in building the meeting -house which is now the Quaker Museum in Ballitore.

Local Attractions and Information

Athy, Heritage Centre 059 863 3075
Ballitore, Quaker Museum & Library 059 862 3344
Carbury, Ballindoolin House & Garden 046 953 1430
Celbridge, Castletown House 01 628 8252
Curragh, The Curragh Racecourse 045 441 205
Edenderry, Grange Castle & Gardens 046 973 3316
Kilcock, Larchill Arcadian Gardens (follies) 01 628 7354
Kildare (Tully), Irish National Stud 045 521 617

Kildare (Tully), Japanese Gardens 045 521 251
Kildare, Tourism Information 045 522 696
Kill, Goff's Bloodstock Sales (frequent) 045 886 600
Naas, Kildare Failte 045 898 888
Naas, Naas Racecourse 045 897 391
Newbridge, Riverbank Arts Centre 045 433 480
Punchestown, Punchestown Racecourse 045 897 704
Straffan, Lodge Park Walled Garden 01 628 8412
Straffan, Steam Museum 01 627 3155
Timolin-Moone, Irish Pewtermill 059 862 4164

ATHY

Athy is pleasantly situated alongside the River Barrow and the Grand Canal, which has three locks in the town, descending to the river. Three hotels have recently opened in the area: **Carlton Abbey Hotel** (059 863 0100; www.carltonabbeyhotel.com) is the most central; it was once a convent and has many original features retained, including an impressive high-ceilinged bar with stained glass windows which is in the old abbey itself. **Bert House Hotel & Leisure** (059 863 2578; www.berthouse.ie) is a renovated property in a waterside location nearby at Kilberry; approached by a long drive it has lots of old world charm and good leisure facilities. **Clanard Court Hotel** (059 864 0666; www.clanardcourt.ie) set in large grounds a mile out side the town, is a popular hotel locally with good business and conference/banqueting facilities.

WWW.IRELAND-GUIDE.COM FOR THE BEST PLACES TO EAT, DRINK & STAY

Athy
COUNTRY HOUSE

Coursetown Country House

Stradbally Road Athy Co Kildare **Tel: 059 863 1101**
Fax: 059 863 2740 Web: www.coursetown.com

Jim and Iris Fox's fine 200 year old house just off the Stradbally road is attached to a large arable farm. The house is welcoming, immaculately maintained and very comfortable, with some unusual attributes, including Jim's natural history library (where guests are welcome to browse) and extensive, well-tended gardens stocked with many interesting plants, including rare herbaceous plants, and old roses and apple trees. Bedrooms vary according to their position in the house, but all are thoughtfully furnished in a pleasantly homely country house style and have direct dial phones, tea/coffee facilities and hair dryers. Iris takes pride in ensuring that her guests have the comfort of the very best beds and bedding - and the attention to detail in the pristine shower rooms is equally high, with lots of lovely towels and quality toiletries. (A bathroom is also available for anyone who prefers to have a good soak in a tub.) Another special feature is a ground floor room near the front door which has been specially designed for wheelchair users, with everything completed to the same high standard as the rest of the house. Then there is breakfast - again, nothing is too much trouble and the emphasis is on delicious healthy eating. The wide selection offered includes fresh juices and fruit salad, poached seasonal fruit (plums from the garden, perhaps) pancakes, French toast with banana & maple syrup, Irish farmhouse cheeses, home-made bread and preserves - and the traditional cooked breakfast includes lovely rashers specially vacuum-packed for Iris by Shiel's butchers, in Abbeyleix. Small weddings catered for (20). Not suitable for children under 8 and older children must have their own room. No smoking house. Pets allowed in some areas by arrangement. Garden. **Rooms 4** (all with en-suite shower, all no smoking, 1 for disabled). B&B €55pps ss €20. 10% discount on breaks of 2 nights or more. Closed 3 Nov- 12 Mar. MasterCard, Visa, Laser. **Directions:** Just outside Athy, on R428. Turn off N78 at Athy, or N80 at Stradbally; well signposted.

Ballymore Eustace
RESTAURANT/PUB

The Ballymore Inn

Ballymore Eustace Co Kildare
Tel: 045 864 585 Fax: 045 864 747
Email: theballymoreinn@eircom.net Web: www.ballymoreinn.com

FEILE BIA AWARD

féile bia It's the fantastic food that draws people to the O'Sullivan family's pub and it's wise to book well ahead to get a taste of the wonderful things this fine country kitchen has to offer, especially at weekends. The building gives out a few hints about what's in store as you approach - the neatly painted cream and navy exterior, the clipped trees in tubs flanking the front door, the Féile Bia plaque

- all bring a sense of anticipation. Major renovations and extensions have changed the interior recently, and this has made it possible to feed a lot more happy diners, without in any way detracting from the atmosphere, food or service. Aside from great food, hospitality is a strong point at this stylish bar - arriving guests are greeted at a reception area at the door, which makes you feel at home from the minute you walk in the door, and you will either be given a table in the front Café Bar area, which is set up in restaurant style with booths, or you can go through to the 'Back Bar' a big open plan bar with a vibrant atmosphere where, again, arriving guests are swiftly seated and drinks orders taken. There's a bar specials board and a 'pizza & snack' menu offering homemade soup, delicious salads, warm panetella with various fillings and the famous Ballymore Inn speciality pizzas, which are based on artisan products and baked in a special pizza oven - Greek lamb with yoghurt for example, or a gorgeous vegetarian combination of tomato, goat's cheese, roasted pepper, grilled courgette and basil... Varying menus meet the requirements of different times of day - an Express Lunch Menu, for example, offers real food for customers in a hurry: a delicious home-made soup with home-made granary bread (baked twice daily), perhaps, and their renowned Kildare sandwich, with baked ham, vintage cheddar & apricot chutney, or a simple hot dish like lamb chilli con carne, and a fish dish of the day.(Just keep off the Ballymore Inn home fries: they're addictive.) Evening Café Bar menus are more formal, offering a range of around eight dishes on each course - a well-balanced choice, but this is beef country and the inn is renowned for its steaks - aged sirloin, perhaps, chargrilled and served with Crozier Blue & bacon sauce, and crispy onions, or a tender fillet with organic mushrooms, shallot & red wine butter. And lamb is almost equally popular - a juicy rack of Slaney lamb may be served with creamed spinach, puy lentils & Wexford honey jus. Georgina O'Sullivan will be remembered by many for her days with Bord Bia, when she was a source of encouragement and inspiration for everyone interested in good food in Ireland - nobody understands the importance of careful sourcing better than she does and, as a matter of course, membership of the Feile Bia programme is highlighted on menus ("beef, lamb, bacon, chicken and eggs come only from recognised quality assured Irish farms"), and producers and suppliers are credited on dishes. So you will find mention through the menu of, for example, Penny Lange's local organic vegetables, Margaret McDonnells free range organic chicken, organic salmon from Clare Island, and Irish farmhouse cheese from Sheridans Cheesemongers in Dublin, who ensure that every cheese is correctly ripened before delivery. And the policy of Immaculate sourcing, careful cooking and a relaxed ambience have proved a winning formula, as this delightful place has become a must-visit destination for food lovers throughout the country, and beyond. And a concise, customer-friendly wine list includes house wines by the bottle, carafe (50cl) and glass, half a dozen bubblies and ten half bottles. Children welcome to 10pm. **Seats 120** (+16 outside). Air conditioning. Food served daily, L 12.30-3, D 6-9. House wines from €19.50; sc discretionary. Bar food also served daily 3-9 (Sat/Sun 12.30-9). Closed 25 Dec & Good Fri. Amex, MasterCard, Visa, Laser. **Directions:** From Blessington, take Baltinglass road. After 1.5.miles, turn right to Ballymore Eustace.

Castledermot

HOTEL/RESTAURANT

Kilkea Castle Hotel

Castledermot Co Kildare **Tel: 059 914 5156** Fax: 059 914 5187
Email: kilkea@iol.ie Web: www.kilkeacastle.ie

féile bia The oldest inhabited castle in Ireland, Kilkea dates back to the twelfth century and, as an hotel, has lost none of its elegance and grandeur. Many of the guest rooms have lovely views over the formal gardens and surrounding countryside, and some are splendidly furnished while incorporating modern comforts. Public areas include a hall complete with knights in armour and two pleasant ground floor bars - a cosy back one and a larger one that opens onto a terrace overlooking gardens and a golf course. Some of the bedrooms in the main castle are very romantic - as indeed is the whole setting - making it understandably popular for weddings. The adjoining (architecturally discreet) leisure centre has an indoor swimming pool, saunas, jacuzzi, steam room, well-equipped exercise room and sun bed. Outdoor sports include clay pigeon shooting, archery, tennis and fishing. An 18-hole championship golf course, which has views of the castle from every fairway, uses the River Greese flowing through the grounds as a natural hazard and a couple of extra lakes were added to increase the challenge still further; informal meals are served in the golf club. Special weekend breaks at the castle are good value. Conferences/banqueting (300/200). Leisure Centre, swimming pool. Garden. Tennis, Golf (18). Children welcome. No pets. **Rooms 36** (1 suite, 3 junior suites, 8 executive, 2 shower only). 24 hour room service. B&B from about €120 pps, ss about €40. SC 12.5%. Open all year. **De Lacy's**: Named after Hugh de Lacy, who built Kilkea Castle in 1180, this beautiful first-floor restaurant has a real 'castle' atmosphere and magnificent views over the countryside. Large tables sport crisp white linen, and there fresh flowers and candles on every table. The restaurant overlooks the delightful formal kitchen garden (source of much that appears on the table in summer) and has a bright, airy atmosphere: there is a sense of occasion here. Menus offer a wide choice, with carefully sourced ingredients providing a sound base for enjoyable meals. Dishes enjoyed on a recent visit included a well-made goats cheese risotto with chorizo, and an exceptionally good steak - beef is a speciality here, and aged for four weeks; an updated classic of ever-popular (perfectly cooked) fillet steak is usually on the menu, typically served with wilted garlic-flavoured spinach and a delicious red wine jus, accompanied by pleasingly simple side dishes. A middle course offers soup or sorbet (refreshing apple, perhaps), and desserts may include old favourites like apple and raisin crumble with ice cream. Afterwards, it is pleasant to take coffee on the terrace in summer and wander around to see the old fruit trees, vegetables and herbs. Restaurant **Seats 60** (private room 40). L (daily by reservation) 12.30-2, D 7-9.30. Set L about €26. Set D about €50. House wine about €21; sc 12.5%. Toilets wheelchair accessible. Closed 3 days at Christmas. Amex, Diners, MasterCard, Visa, Laser. **Directions:** 3 miles from Castledermot (off M9); signed from village. ◇

Celbridge

N E RESTAURANT

The Village at Lyons Demesne - The Mill & Café la Serre

The Village Lyon's Demesne Celbridge Co Kildare
Tel: 01 630 3500 Fax: 01 630 3505
Email: snolan@villageatlyons.com Web: www.villageatlyons.com

In an exciting year in terms of new openings, the most eagerly awaited was undoubtedly the pair of restaurants at the Lyons Demesne overseen by Irish celebrity chef Richard Corrigan, which opened just in time for the Ryder Cup. Richard Corrigan is renowned for his dedication to local and artisan foods, and the styles of the fine dining Mill Restaurant here, and informal Café La Serre are based on his London success stories, Lindsay House and Bentleys, respectively. These restaurants are the first stage of an unusual project, The Village at Lyons, which will take about two years to complete, and will include some small specialist shops, a cookery school and accommodation. It is beautifully situated alongside the Grand Canal the entrance, guarded by stone lions and a new lodge which sports the trademark soft Lyons green, is just beside the 14th lock; approaching along the new driveway you will glimpse proprietor Tony Ryan's beautifully proportioned 1797 Lyons House on a rise to your left, shortly before the restored stone mill buildings appear ahead. The most striking first impression is how well finished the completed sections are, and how well they sit in their imaginatively landscaped setting with delightful little gardens and ever-present water establishing a caring tone that is evident throughout. There's a welcoming scent of woodsmoke on the air as you approach past stone statuary (softened by a scented pink rose) and a bed of box balls, over the little bridge (pausing to admire the mill race below) and in through a massive front door which leads straight into the bar. Known as The Lyons Den (proclaimed in 'antique' stone over the bar one of the few off-key notes in this theatrical and usually well-judged setting), it's a welcoming room with a huge fireplace, plenty of comfortable well worn leather furniture and a full figure portrait of a lady to welcome arriving guests something that seems to be de rigeur in these parts. The fine dining restaurant, **The Mill,** is on the lower ground floor and, approached from the bar, first sight of the room from the top of a steep steps is dramatic: a fine (very) high-ceilinged dining room, it is classically appointed with crisp white linen and gleaming glasses - and has a range of stunning features including a screen of thinly sliced agate, backlit to show off its complex structure and rich colouring to full advantage and, of course, the mill race itself, which is a sight to behold and thunders magnificently when the windows are opened. Although only just open at the time of our visit, the food and service are matching up to the setting, and a meal here is a very special experience **Café La Serre,** on the other hand is a place where guests wandering in can feel at home in a genuinely dressed own sense; this very relaxed and informal space includes a covered courtyard area for the betwixt & betweeners (neither inside nor out), an oyster bar (where superb plump native oysters, natural or Rockefeller, are offered, along with the main café menu) and a high-windowed Turner style conservatory that offers tables in a bright space alongside the nascient gardens. The menu here is a delightful mix of brunch treats (Richard's black pudding; risotto with poached free range eggs and the like) and heartier stuff like fish pie or a superb Tipperary Hereford sirloin steak with béarnaise sauce, hand cut chips, the most scrumptious light & crispy onion rings you've ever tasted and a simple green salad. Simply heaven. This also promises to be a delightful venue for private gatherings, including exclusive small weddings there is a tiny chapel (it has to be seen to be believed), and the accommodation, in luxurious 2-bedroom 'cottages' (complete with Aga in their bespoke kitchens, amongst many other un expected features), will delight all who stay here. **Seats 80** (ooutdoors, 20); open all day Wed-Sun; reservations not necessary; housewine €26. Closed Mon & Tues, 25-26 Dec, Good Fri. Heli-pad. Amex, MasterCard, Visa, Laser. **Directions:** Left turn just before bridge in Celbridge village for Ardclough. Follow road for a couple of miles, you will come to a part in the road that has some really tight bends with warning signs. Shortly after that there is a left turn (as signed by a small pale green sign opposite turn). Drive over the hump back bridge and it is immediately on the right with 2 big lions on pillars flanking a gate.

Clane

Zest Café

N CAFÉ/RESTAURANT

Unit 6/7 Clane Shopping Centre Clane Co Kildare
Tel: 045 893 222

Mark Condron's well-named lunch time café and evening restaurant has earned a following for its relaxed atmosphere, friendly staff and fresh home cooked food. Menus change constantly, but delicious starters might include unusual home made soups - pea & mint with creme fraiche & garlic bread, for example, and quite classic options like chicken liver terrine with apple & onion compôte, or crab & gruyere tartlets. But, for the most part, the style of food is informal, offering a range of interesting pasta dishes, for example, and gourmet pizzas - Morrocan spiced lamb with red onion, chick pea, coriander & tzatziki, perhaps, or a tempting 'Greek' vegetarian one with spinach, feta cheese, black olives tomato & mozzarella. More serious main courses include good steaks - a 10 oz sirloin, for example, with pink peppercorn & thyme butter, served with stir-fried vegetables and potatoes, or a chargrilled fillet with bacon & spring onion potato and Madeira jus - several good fish dishes, and an imaginative chicken dish such as chargrilled chicken breast marinated in lime, ginger & coriander and served with roast tomatoes, pistachios, mixed leaves and citrus dressing. Lunch menus are much simpler than dinner - vegetable soup and home made quiche topped with goats cheese and salad, perhaps, or a succulent chicken wrap, but everything is done well here and even the simplest meal is sure to be enjoyable. The wine list is not extensive but offers a surprising range; four wines are available by the glass and there are a couple of half bottles. Children welcome; Toilets wheelchair accessible; **Seats 54;** air conditioning; L & D Mon-Sat, 12-3.30pm and 5.45-10pm, Sun 1pm-9pm; L&D a la carte; house wine from €18. Amex, MasterCard, Visa, Laser. **Directions:** Off Main Street - turn at AIB, left hand side.

Curragh

Martinstown House

E COUNTRY HOUSE

Curragh Co Kildare **Tel: 045 441 269** Fax: 045 441 208
Email: info@martinstownhouse.com Web: www.martinstownhouse.com

Just on the edge of the Curragh, near Punchestown, Naas and The Curragh race courses, this delightful 200 year old house was built by the famous architect Decimus Burton who also designed the lodges in the Phoenix Park, Dublin, and is the only known domestic example of this 'Strawberry Hill' gothic architectural style in Ireland. It is on a farm, set in 170 acres of beautifully wooded land, with free range hens, sheep, cattle and horses, an old icehouse and a well-maintained walled kitchen garden that provides vegetables, fruit and flowers for the house in season. Meryl Long welcomes guests to this idyllic setting, aiming to offer them 'a way of life which I knew as a child (but with better bathrooms!), a warm welcome, real fires and good food.' It is a lovely family house, with very nicely proportioned rooms - gracious but not too grand - open fires downstairs, and bedrooms that are all different, each with its own special character and very comfortably furnished, with fresh flowers. A stay here is sure to be enjoyable, with the help of a truly hospitable hostess who offers a delicious afternoon tea on arrival - and believes that holidays should be fun, full of interest and with an easy-going atmosphere. Croquet lawn. Golf and equestrian activities nearby. Not suitable for children under 12. No pets. **Rooms 4** (3 en-suite, 1 with private bathrooms, all no smoking) B&B €110 pps, ss €35. Residents D €55 (by arrangement - book the previous day). House wine about €22.50. Closed Dec & Jan. Amex, MasterCard, Visa. **Directions:** Kilcullen exit off M9 then N78 towards Athy. Sign at 1st crossroads.

Leixlip

The Courtyard Hotel

N HOTEL

Main Street Leixlip Co Kildare **Tel: 01 629 5100** Fax: 01 629 5111
Email: info@courtyard.ie Web: www.courtyard.ie

Although the restored stone walls of the original 18th century building are impressive, the street entrance of this attractive new hotel does not do it justice first impressions will be far better if you arrive through an arch from the car park at the back, beside the River Liffey. The reception area is comfortably set up with comfy armchairs and a fire place and, off it, the Piano Bar and the Riverbank Restaurant attractive rooms with high arched ceilings and big wooden beams - have views out over the Liffey, and views from a roof garden restaurant above are even more impressive. Accommodation is warmly furnished in a simple contemporary style and will appeal to business guests, with air conditioning, desk with data/fax lines and Wi-Fi internet; suites have balconies overlooking the gardens and river (one has a hot tub on a private balcony). Arthur Guinness established his first brewery here in 1759, four years before the world famous St. James' Gate Guinness Brewery, and it seems appropriate that the 'black stuff' should now be served here in 'Arthur's Bar', a simple, warmly decorated and friendly bar (with large flat screen for those all-important matches). And smokers, especially, will enjoy the large stone-paved courtyard which is on several levels, with a waterfall feature and well spaced tables and chairs (some with canopies) surrounded by manicured plant beds, and hanging baskets;

weekend entertainment here is aimed to please all age groups. **Rooms 40;** broadband Wi/Fi, garden; golf, equestrian, fishing and walking nearby. Room rate from €99. MasterCard, Visa, Laser. **Directions:** Centre of Leixlip. ◇

Leixlip
HOTEL/RESTAURANT

Leixlip House Hotel

Captains Hill Leixlip Co Kildare
Tel: 01 624 2268 Fax: 01 624 4177
Email: info@leixliphouse.com Web: www.leixliphouse.com

féile bia Up on a hill overlooking Leixlip village, just eight miles from Dublin city centre, this fine Georgian house was built in 1722 and is furnished and decorated to a high standard in period style and, with gleaming antique furniture and gilt-framed mirrors in thick carpeted public rooms decorated in soft country colours, the atmosphere is one of discreet opulence. Bedrooms include two suites furnished with traditional mahogany furniture; the strong, simple decor particularly pleases the many business guests who stay here and there is a welcome emphasis on service - all day room service, nightly turndown service with complimentary mineral water and chocolates - and a shoe valet service. Hotel guests have complimentary use of a nearby gym. Conference/banqueting (100/140). Secretarial services. Children welcome. No pets. **Rooms 19** (5 executive, 6 with bath & shower, 14 shower only). All day room service. B&B from about €80 pps, ss about €40. **The Bradaun Restaurant:** The commitment to quality evident in the hotel as a whole is continued in the restaurant, a bright, high-ceilinged, formally appointed dining room. Consistently good modern Irish cooking is offered through wide-ranging menus, based on fresh seasonal produce and well executed with pleasing attention to detail. Set menus offer particularly good value for money and there's an attractive lounge menu for those who prefer an informal meal. An extensive, informative and carefully chosen wine list would make good bedtime reading. Children welcome. **Seats 46.** Food served daily 12-9. D Tue-Sun, 6.30-10 (Sun to 8); Earlybird D €27.95 Tue-Fri 6.30-7.30. Restaurant closed Mon (except for group bookings). Hotel closed 25-26 Dec. Amex, Diners, MasterCard, Visa, Laser. **Directions:** Leixlip exit off M4 motorway. Take right in Leixlip village at traffic lights.

MAYNOOTH

Attractively situated beside the Royal Canal, Maynooth is a university town and the centre for the training of Catholic diocesan clergy in Ireland. The ever-expanding **Glenroyal Hotel** (01 629 0909; www.glenroyal.ie) has outstanding conference/business and leisure facilities, and - a novel idea that came to our attention shortly before going to press (and not yet viewed by the Guide) - **Maynooth Campus** can offer accommodation, in Georgian and Neo-Gothic en-suite rooms; Tel: 01 708 3726 for further details. Reflecting its youthful population, there are plenty of places to eat in Maynooth, including a good Indian restaurant, **Meghna** (01 505 4868), above Caulfield's pub on the main street.
WWW.IRELAND-GUIDE.COM FOR THE BEST PLACES TO EAT, DRINK & STAY

Maynooth
N HOTEL

Carton House Hotel

Maynooth Co Kildare **Tel: 01 505 2000**
Email: reservations@carton.ie Web: www.carton.ie

Previously the residence of the dukes of Leinster, Carton House is an imposing mansion designed in classic style by the renowned architect Richard Castles, and built around 1740. It is set in one of Ireland's finest country estates - now home to two championship golf courses - and opened as an hotel shortly before the guide went to press. Nobody could fail to be impressed by the building itself, which is vast yet very elegant - and it has now been skilfully adapted to its new use through a stimulating combination of old and new. It is a natural choice for major corporate events and meetings, and would make a wonderful venue for special occasions of all kinds - these are, after all, uses that are not so very far from its previous life of entertainment on a grand scale. Public areas include a whole series of grand rooms, including The Duke's Study and The Gold Salon, each more impressive than the last, and the old kitchen - with its vast cast-iron stoves still in place - is now a bar, furnished rather surprisingly (but comfortably) in a very modern style. The restaurant, The Linden Tree, is a famous room overlooking the golf course and gardens, and has been allowed a more classical style, with pristine white linen and simple, elegant table settings; an informal dining option is available (to members and visitors) in the Clubhouse, which is some distance from the house in renovated stables. The accommodation has been designed and built in sympathy with the main house; the style is luxurious and contemporary, pleasingly bold in scale and with some appropriately regal colours - and, of course, rooms have all the little luxuries including robes and slippers and a minibar, as well as king size beds, LCD screen television, DVD and CD player. Sporting activities are central to Carton House, and are certain to be a major attraction at a stylish destination so close to the capital - as will the hotel's spa, which is due to open shortly after we go to press. Prices are not unreasonable for a hotel of this calibre, and promotional opening offers are very attractive. Conferences/Banqueting (multiple rooms available to max. 480), broadband Wi/Fi; Spa, golf (36); **Rooms 165;** B&B from €100 pps. **Directions:** 20 km west of Dublin's city centre (about 30 minutes from Dublin airport), Carton House is just east of Maynooth and signed from the town. ◇

Maynooth

HOTEL/RESTAURANT

Moyglare Manor

Maynooth Co Kildare

Tel: 01 628 6351 Fax: 01 628 5405

Email: info@moyglaremanor.ie Web: www.moyglaremanor.ie

Norah Devlin's classical Georgian manor is approached by a tree-lined avenue, allowing the arriving guest to appreciate this imposing stone built house to the full. Mrs Devlin's love of antiques is famous - gilt-framed mirrors and portraits are everywhere, shown to advantage against deep-shaded damask walls, and chairs and sofas of every pedigree ensure comfortable seating, even at the busiest times; no wonder a visit here is sometimes described it as 'like being in an antique shop'. Spacious bedrooms and suites are also lavishly furnished in period style, some with four-poster or half tester beds, and all have well-appointed bathrooms. Golf nearby (four courses within 10 miles), also tennis and horse riding locally. Small conferences/banqueting (30); secretarial services. Not suitable for children under 12. No pets. Garden; Walking. **Rooms 16** (1 suite, 4 exec., 2 disabled). B&B from €125 pps, ss €25. **Restaurant:** Dining in the traditionally appointed Restaurant is always a treat: grand and romantic, it's just the place for a special occasion. Edward Cullen, who has been head chef since 2002, maintains the house style of country house cooking, and both lunch and dinner menus offer a nicely balanced combination of traditional favourites and sophisticated fare, with an emphasis on seafood and game in season - and a fine wine list to match. Not suitable for children under 12. Restaurant **seats 60** (private room, 25). D Mon-Sat 7-9. Set D €60, also à la carte. House wine from €21. Pianist 4 evenings a week. House closed 24-26 Dec. Amex, MasterCard, Visa, Laser. **Directions:** From Dublin, N4 west; exit for Maynooth, keep right at church; after 4km (2 .5 m), turn left at Moyglare crossroads, then next right.

Moyvalley

Ⓝ PUB

Fureys Bar

Moyvalley Co Kildare **Tel: 046 955 1185**

Down a slip road off the N4 and insulated by thick hedges, this charming and immaculately maintained bar and informal restaurant has something of the best kind of Victorian country railway station about it, with its neat brickwork, jaunty flowers and wooden floors. Although by no means huge, a welcoming bar divides informally into cosy sections, and an area towards the back has a stove and views over the Royal Canal giving it the best of every world. Menus posted beside the front doors don't give too much away - soups, sandwiches, steaks, burgers, salads - but references to home-made 'house paté' and 'home cut chips' hint at the good home cooking for which they are renowned, and one of their famous steaks, with 'all the trimmings' should be just the ticket for whether you're breaking a journey or coming up off a boat. Do call ahead, though, especially if numbers in your party are large, as 'groups can only be fed by arrangement'. Meals Mon-Sat, 12-7.30pm (to 8pm Sat); no food Sun. MasterCard, Visa, Laser. **Directions:** Where the road, railway & canal meet between Enfield & Moyvalley. ◇

NAAS

Naas is well located for many of the county's sporting activities including horse racing (four courses nearby), golf (five clubs nearby), car racing (Mondello Park) and attractions such as the Wicklow Mountains, The Japanese Gardens and The National Irish Stud. Although the casual visitor may not be especially aware of it, as this bustling town turns its back to its most attractive amenity, Naas is attractively situated on a branch of the Grand Canal and has a proper little harbour. It's a fast-growing place and the youthful new **Osprey House Hotel & Spa** (045 881111; www.osprey.ie), in the Devoy Quarter, provides conference/business and leisure facilities. A wide choice of eating places includes a branch of the popular Dublin restaurant **Pasta Fresca** (045 901542), which is very close to the harbour and, in the town centre, **Lemongrass** (045 482446/871544; www.lemongrass.ie) is behind the Town Hall (just off the main street); this smart modern place is the parent restaurant of a growing chain that now has franchises offering reliable Asian food in many other places and, like Pasta Fresca, has the great advantage of long opening hours (about 12.30/1pm-10pm, daily). At the other end of the main street (behind the former Lawlors Hotel, which is under renovation at the time of going to press), **The Storehouse** (045 889333) restaurant has character - and if you want real place of character, make a point of dropping into one of Ireland's finest unspoilt old pubs, **Thomas Fletcher** (045 897 328) on the main street, if they are open - it's not a morning place.

WWW.IRELAND-GUIDE.COM FOR THE BEST PLACES TO EAT, DRINK & STAY

Naas

HOTEL

Killashee House Hotel & Villa Spa

Old Killcullen Road Naas Co Kildare

Tel: 045 879 277 Fax: 045 879 266

Email: reservations@killasheehouse.com Web: www.killasheehouse.com

Set in 80 acres of gardens and woodland just outside Naas town, this hotel is approached along an attractive driveway through gardens and the setting is impressive, although spoilt a little by the car parking arrangements in front of the building. The entrance and lobby areas are striking and a fine inner courtyard is planted with Virginia creeper, which is becoming an attractive feature. A rather grand staircase leads to a large traditionally furnished lounge area on the first floor, with views of the grounds and courtyard and well-grouped seating areas; it's a pleasant place for afternoon tea and informal socialising - there is a pianist at certain times - and resident guests now have the quieter option of a new residents' lounge. Conference and business events are well catered for, with conference and meeting rooms of various sizes available, and it is a deservedly popular venue for weddings. Bedrooms, which have everything required for business guests, include a number of suites and some with four-poster beds; all rooms have multi-line phones, data ports, voicemail, fax (on request), and safe as well as the more usual amenities. Formal dining is offered at the beautifully appointed main restaurant, Turners (where a harpist plays at weekends), and informal food is available in other areas. On site facilities include the new Villa spa (18 treatment rooms), also leisure centre with 25m pool; games room; archery, cycling, woodland walks. Conference/banqueting (750/720). Business centre; video conferencing. Children welcome (cot available without charge, baby sitting arranged), but not in restaurant after 7pm. Pets allowed in some areas. Garden, walking, cycling. **Rooms 142** (27 suites, 11 junior suites, 9 shower only, 4 family rooms, 70 no smoking, 6 for disabled). Lift. Room service (24 hrs). B&B from €99 pps, ss €45. Closed 24-25 Dec. MasterCard, Visa, Laser. **Directions:** 30 minutes from Dublin on N7 to Naas, then 2km (1.5m) on R448, Kilcullen road.

Naas

RESTAURANT

La Primavera

27 South Main Street Naas Co Kildare **Tel: 045 897 926**

Fax: 045 883 897 Email: info@lap.ie Web: www.laprimavera.ie

An attractive frontage, with well-maintained hanging baskets in summer, make this town centre restaurant easy to spot - and good first impressions are carried through into a pleasant split-level dining room, and a warm welcome from friendly staff who show arriving guests to appealing, simply-laid tables. Then comes a surprise for first-time visitors, as the menu is not mainly Italian as might be expected, but offers a wide-ranging, fairly contemporary, collection of dishes (many of which are broadly 'Mediterranean'), including some seafood but mainly showcasing Irish meats - beef, in particular. There are some interesting and unusual dishes offered, and a welcome emphasis on house specialities including starters like a good beef carpaccio, and also tasty crab & prawn cakes; an unusual main course of house-smoked loin of pork comes with apple chutney & a ginger-infused demi-glaze, and home-made spicy sausages feature in a pasta dish with a wild mushroom pomodoro. A speciality 'Charcoal Combo' - fillet steak, smoked pork & rosemary-skewered prawns, each with its own sauce or accompaniment - demonstrates originality and skill, each item perfectly cooked and skilfully sauced; side orders like crème fraîche mash, and fresh tossed vegetable strips in herbs and olive oil are also a little unusual and work well. Well-made desserts - a rich chocolate tart, or a blueberry crème brulée perhaps - and good coffee to finish. Well-balanced wine list, although otherwise well-trained staff seem less knowledgeable in this area. All round: imaginative food, good cooking and caring service - and, as experienced on a recent visit that confirmed this recommendation, good value too. **Seats 60.** Reservations accepted. Air conditioning. D daily, 5-10 (Sun to 9.30). Early D €14 (5-7), otherwise à la carte. House wine €16. Amex, Diners, Visa, Laser, Switch. **Directions:** At traffic lights on Limerick/Kilcullen junction. ◇

Naas

RESTAURANT

Les Olives

10 South Main Street Naas Co Kildare **Tel: 045 894 788**

Email: lesolives@eircom.net Web: www.lesolivesrestaurant.com

Olivier and Maeve Pauloin-Valory's first floor restaurant has earned a loyal following from a wide area around the town. It's an attractive room (recently refurbished), with comfortable seating, formal white-clothed tables and a lobster tank all paving the way for a seriously good dining experience. Seafood is a particular attraction, especially oysters and lobsters which you can choose from the tank yourself; in addition to dishes on the main menu - which is in French and English and may include some unusual items, such as roasted rabbit cassolette - daily fish specials (prawn kebab, lobster salad) are shown on a blackboard, where you may also find some less likely choices, such as ostrich (which is farmed nearby) and, of course, local meats like Kildare beef and lamb. Olivier's good cooking, and friendly, efficient service under Maeve's direction promise a good night out - and the wine list offers a wide range of wines by the glass. Beer garden area for smokers. Not suitable for children. **Seats 50.** Reservations required. D Tue-Sat, 7-10; D Gourmet Menu €70, also à la carte. House wines from €19.50; sc discretionary (but10% added for parties of 6+). Closed Sun, Mon (& Tue after bank hol weekends); Christmas, Good Fri. MasterCard, Visa, Laser. **Directions:** Over Kavanagh's pub, in the centre of Naas.

Newbridge

Keadeen Hotel

HOTEL

Newbridge Co Kildare **Tel: 045 431 666** Fax: 045 434 402
Email: info@keadeenhotel.ie Web: www.keadeenhotel.ie

Centrally located and easily accessible from the M7 motorway, the O'Loughlin family's popular owner-managed hotel is set in ten acres of fine landscaped gardens just south of the town (and quite near the Curragh racecourse). The hotel has recently been refurbished and generously spacious accommodation is furnished to a high standard. A fine romanesque Health & Fitness Club has an 18-metre swimming pool and aromatherapy room among its attractions, plus a staffed gymnasium. Extensive conference and banqueting facilities (1,000); secretarial services. Video conferencing can be arranged. Leisure centre, swimming pool. Garden. Parking. No Pets. Children welcome (under 3s free in parents rooms; cots available). Weekend specials available. **Rooms 75** (1 suite, 3 junior suites, 20 executive, 1 for disabled) B&B from about €101. Weekend specials offered. Closed 24-27 Dec . Amex, Diners, MasterCard, Visa. **Directions:** From Dublin take N7 off M50, take sliproad sign posted Curragh race course & follow signs for Newbridge. ◇

Straffan

Barberstown Castle

HOTEL/RESTAURANT

Straffan Co Kildare
Tel: 01 628 8157 Fax: 01 627 7027
Email: barberstowncastle@ireland.com Web: www.barberstowncastle.ie

Steeped in history through three very different historical periods, Barberstown Castle has been occupied continuously for over 400 years. It now includes the original keep in the middle section of the building, a more domestic Elizabethan house (16th century), a 'new' Victorian wing added in the 1830s by Hugh Barton (also associated with nearby Straffan House, now The K Club, with whom it shares golf and leisure facilities) and, most recently, a large new wing added by the current owner, Kenneth Healy, which is built in keeping with its age and style. Some of the individually decorated rooms and suites are in the oldest section, the Castle Keep, others are more recent, but most are stylish and spacious, and some have four-posters. Public areas include two drawing rooms and an elegant bar, and there are big log fires everywhere. Conference/banqueting 200. Garden, walking. Golf. Children welcome (cot available, €20.) No pets. **Rooms 59** (16 junior suites, 17 premier rooms, 21 ground floor, 1 shower only, 3 disabled, all no smoking.) Lift. B&B €115 pps, ss €35. Closed 24-26 Dec. **Restaurant:** Fine dining of character is offered in The Castle Restaurant, where head chef Bertrand Malabat, who joined the castle in 1999, presents a number of menus including a six-course Tasting Menu (served to complete parties only) and a seasonal à la carte with about seven choices on each course. The style is classic French with the occasional nod to international fashions; local beef or lamb usually feature, also game in season, and there will be several appealing fish dishes and at least one imaginative vegetarian dish. Finish with a classic sweet like vanilla crème brulée with an almond tuile - or a selection of Irish farmhouse cheeses and home-baked breads. Very professional service. Not suitable for children after 7pm. **Seats 100** (private room 32). Reservations advised. D 7-9.30 (Sun, 6-8); L Sun only 12-2.30. Set Sun L €35. Set D €65 (6-course Tasting Menu); à la carte D also available. House wine €23.50; sc discretionary (but 10% on parties of 7+). Fine dining restaurant closed Mon. Light meals are available in the Tea Rooms, 10-7 daily. Closed 24-26 Dec and Jan. MasterCard, Visa, Laser. **Directions:** West M4 - turn for Straffan exit at Maynooth - follow signs for Naas/Clane.

Straffan

K Club - Kildare Hotel & Golf Club

HOTEL/RESTAURANT

Straffan Co Kildare
Tel: 01 601 7200 Fax: 01 601 7298
Email: hotel@kclub.ie Web: www.kclub.ie

The origins of Straffan House go back a long way - the history is known as far back as 550 AD - but it was the arrival of the Barton wine family in 1831 that established the tone of today's magnificent building, by giving it a distinctively French elegance. It was bought by the Smurfit Group in 1988 and, after extensive renovations, opened as an hotel in 1991. Set in lush countryside, and overlooking formal gardens and its own pair of championship golf courses, the hotel boasts unrivalled opulence. The interior is magnificent, with superb furnishings and a wonderful collection of original paintings by famous artists, including Jack B.Yeats, who has a room devoted to his work. All suites and guest rooms are individually designed in the grand style, with sumptuous bathrooms, superb amenities and great attention to detail. Ahead of the 2006 Ryder Cup, major developments were undertaken by the hotel, including a new bedroom extension, an extension to the Byerley Turk Restaurant, and a spa. Although most famous for its golf, the hotel also offers river fishing for salmon and trout and coarse fishing with a choice of five stocked lakes (equipment bait and tackle provided; tuition available). For guests interested in horticulture there is a mapped garden walk, with planting details. On site amenities include: swimming pool; specialist therapies; beauty salon. Tennis; walking; fishing; cycling; equestrian. Snooker; pool table. 24 hour concierge; 24 hour room service; twice daily housekeeping. **Rooms 92.** Lift. Room rate from €265. **The Byerly Turk:** Beside the K Club's premier restaurant, a pleasantly clubby bar opens onto an elegant terrace with a distinctly French tone - here, on fine summer evenings, guests can consider menus over an aperitif and admire the new golf course across the river before heading in to the restaurant, where tall, dramatically draped windows, marble columns, paintings of racehorses, tables laden with crested china, monogrammed white linen, gleaming crystal and silver all create an impressive background for the hotel's fine food, using the best of local and estate-grown produce. The Menu du Jour is concise, but all the little touches - a complimentary amuse-bouche, home-made petits fours with the coffee - that make a special dining experience memorable will be in place. A seasonal à la carte menu is also offered, and a surprise "Tasting Menu" (on request), for complete parties. Service is friendly as well as professional - and, given the intertwined history of Straffan House and the Barton family, it is appropriate that the Bordeaux Reserve from Barton and Guestier should be the label chosen for the hotel's house wine. Children welcome. **Seats 115** (private room 14). Air conditioning. Pianist in the evening. D 7-9.30 (Tue-Sat). Set D about €70; also à la carte. House Wine from about €26; sc discretionary. ***Legends Restaurant** (stylish European cuisine at the clubhouse of the Arnold Palmer Course): 12.30-9.30 daily; **Monza Restaurant** (casual Irish/Italian fare at the clubhouse of the new Michael Smurfit course): open 7am-10.30, meals from noon daily. Amex, Diners, MasterCard, Visa, Laser. **Directions:** 30 mins south west of Dublin airport and city (M50 - N4). ◇

COUNTY KILKENNY

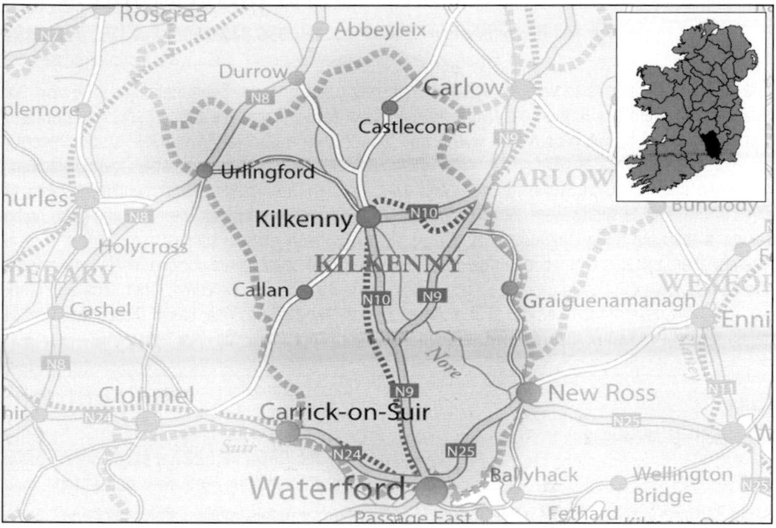

Kilkenny is a land of achingly beautiful valleys where elegant rivers weave their way through a rich countryside spiced by handsome hills. So naturally it's a place whose people care passionately about their county, and the miniature city at its heart. For Kilkenny - the Marble City - is one of Ireland's oldest cities, and proud of it. Its array of ancient buildings is unrivalled. By today's numerical standards of population, this gem of a place is scarcely a city at all. Yet it's a city in every other way, with great and justified pride in its corporate status.

Civic pride is at the heart of it, and the city benefits from the refurbishment of its ancient quay walls along the River Nore, and the increase in pedestrian zones. Enjoying its reputation as a major centre for civilisation and culture for well over 1500 years, Kilkenny city thrives on a diverse mixture of public debates about conservation, arts festivals, and a comedy festival of international standing.

Rivers define the county. Almost the entire eastern border is marked by the Barrow, which becomes ever more spectacularly lovely as it rolls gently through beautiful Graiguenamanagh, then thrusts towards the sea at the tiny river port of St Mullins. The southern border is marked by the broad tidal sweep of the Suir, and this fine county is divided diagonally by the meandering of perhaps the most beautiful river of all, the Nore.

Invaders inevitably progressed up its tree-lined course past what is now the lovely river village of Inistioge, towards the ancient site of Kilkenny city itself. They quickly became Kilkenny folk in the process, for this is a land to call home.

Local Attractions and Information

Callan, Edmund Rice House 056 772 5993
Gowran, Gowran Park Racecourse 056 772 6225
Inistioge, Woodstock Gardens 056 52699
Graiguenamanagh, Cushendale Woollen Mills 059 972 4118
Kilkenny, Kilkenny Castle 056 772 1450
Kilkenny, Cat Laughs Comedy Festival (May) 056 776 3416
Kilkenny, Rothe House (16c house, exhibitions) 056 772 2893
Kilkenny, City Tourist Information 056 775 1500
Thomastown, Jerpoint Abbey 056 772 4623
Thomastown, Kilfane Glen & Waterfall 056 772 4558
Thomastown, Mount Juliet Gardens 056 777 3000
Tullaroan, Kilkenny GAA Museum 056 69202

Bennettsbridge

CAFÉ

Nicholas Mosse Pottery Irish Country Shop

The Mill Bennettsbridge Co Kilkenny **Tel: 056 772 7505** Fax: 056 772 7491
Email: sales@nicholasmosse.com Web: www.nicholasmosse.com

One of the best reasons to venture out from Kilkenny city to nearby Bennettsbridge is to visit the Nicholas Mosse Pottery in their old riverside mill. Major renovations have created spacious premises that allow visitors to watch potters at work - and there's even a 'decorate-it-yourself' studio, recently opened. The full range of products is wide, including hand blown glass and table linens, blankets, quilts and knitwear, Clive Nunn furniture and even jewellery from leading craftspeople - as well as acres of the famous spongeware. Their café is on the first floor, overlooking the river, and good home baking is their big thing - including, of course, delicious freshly-baked scones made with the local Mosse's flour, and sold with good coffee or tea. But the range of reasonably priced wholesome snacks offered has now extended to include light lunches. **Seats 40.** Children welcome. Open Mon-Sat 11-5, Sun 1.30-4. Closed 24-26 Dec & 1-2 Jan. Amex, Diners, MasterCard, Visa, Laser. **Directions:** 7km (4 miles) south of Kilkenny, just before bridge turn off.

Callan

COUNTRY HOUSE

Ballaghtobin

Ballaghtobin Callan Co Kilkenny
Tel: 056 772 5227 Fax: 056 772 5712
Email: catherine@ballaghtobin.com Web: www.ballaghtobin.com

Set in parkland in the middle of a five hundred acre working farm, this immaculately maintained house has been in the Gabbett family for three hundred and fifty years. Graciously proportioned rooms are beautifully furnished and the spacious bedrooms - which Catherine Gabbett has decorated stylishly - all have antique furniture and every comfort, including lovely bathrooms with bath and overbath shower, and tea/coffee trays. The house is surrounded by large gardens, with a hard tennis court, croquet lawn - and even a ruined Norman church - for guests' use. No dinners, but Catherine will direct you to one of the good restaurants within a short drive. Children welcome (under 3s free in parents' room; cot available without charge). Pets allowed by arrangement. Garden, walking, tennis, croquet. **Rooms 3** (all en suite & no smoking, 2 family rooms). B&B €45 pps, ss €10. Closed Dec-Jan. MasterCard, Visa. MasterCard, Visa. **Directions:** Past Golf Club on left, 4km (2.3 m), bear left; bear left at junction, entrance on left opposite Gate Lodge.

Graiguenamanagh

€ RESTAURANT/GUESTHOUSE

Waterside

The Quay Graiguenamanagh Co Kilkenny
Tel: 059 97 24246 Fax: 059 97 24733
Email: info@watersideguesthouse.com Web: www.watersideguesthouse.com

An attractive old stone warehouse on the quayside of this charming village on the River Barrow makes a characterful setting for Brian and Brigid Roberts' well-run restaurant and guesthouse. On fine summer days there are tables outside, then a comfortable reception area leads into the restaurant, where Brigid offers modern European food on varied and enticing menus - in very pleasant waterside surroundings. She uses fresh local produce wherever possible, sometimes including a speciality starter of Graiguenamanagh smoked eel with side salad & horseradish sauce - the eel fishery at Graiguenamanagh dates back to the Cistercian monks who built the town and weirs on the river, and is now active again. Aside from a range of mainstream choices (salmon, pork steak, striploin beef steaks) game might be offered in season (venison fillet with caramelised apple rings & wild berry sauce, perhaps) and interesting vegetarian choices, such as puff pastry parcel with seasonal vegetables, Knockdrinna goat cheese, marjoram and white wine sauce, are always included. Finish with a nice homely dessert such as brandy soaked bread & butter pudding, served with fresh cream. There's always an an Irish cheese plate too, with a choice of half a dozen ports to accompany, if you wish. Sunday lunch menus are more extensive, cleverly integrating casual choices like panini and sandwiches alongside more substantial dishes. Service is friendly and willing under Brian's supervision - and the wine list, which is extensive for a country restaurant, is interesting and fairly priced. An early dinner menu offers outstanding value for money. **Seats 50.** Outdoor Dining available in the Summer. D 6.30-9.30 daily; L Sun only 12.30-3. Set Sun L €20, Early D €20 (6.30-7.45). Set D €36, also à la carte. House wine, €19.75. No SC. *In summer there's also a light Daytime Menu available, 11-4. Restaurant open weekends only in winter. **Accommodation:** Ongoing renovations are gradually upgrading the accommodation, which is quite simple but comfortable, with direct dial phones, tea/coffee making facilities and TV in all rooms. Some rooms at the top of the building are especially spacious and all overlook the river. Book lovers may be interested in weekend book sales at Waterside, which is the home of the Graiguenamangh Book Festival and booktown project (details from Brian). Hillwalking holidays for small groups are offered (guide, maps, packed lunch, transport etc all arranged). Children welcome (under 3s free in parents' room, cot available without charge, baby sitting arranged). No pets. **Rooms 10** (all shower only & no smoking, 4 family rooms) B&B €49pps, ss €13.50. *Weekend packages/ short breaks from €79 pps. No lift. Closed Jan. Amex, MasterCard, Visa, Laser. **Directions:** 27km (17 m) south east of Kilkenny on Carlow/Kilkenny border.

Inistioge
N RESTAURANT

Bassett's at Woodstock

Woodstock Gardens Inistioge Co Kilkenny **Tel: 056 775 8820**
Email: info@bassetts.ie Web: www.bassetts.ie

John Bassett grew up in Inistioge and returned recently with his partner Mijke Jansen to run this scenically located contemporary restaurant at the historic and beautifully restored Woodstock Gardens & Arboretum. In a modern building overlooking the Nore valley, and conveniently situated beside the visitors' carpark, this is not just a 'garden visits café' but a fully fledged restaurant which has become a destination in itself and must now be a great asset to the Woodstock Gardens. Recognising the strengthening trend towards informal dining, head chef Emilio Martin Castilla (previously at Kilkenny city's premier fine dining restaurant, Lacken House), offers a range of starter size dishes on frequently changed menus that are based on seasonal and mainly local produce (including their own home reared suckling pig some luxurious choices such as foie gras and pheasant, in season), but bypass the usual 'three course meal' format in favour of a series of smaller dishes - more akin to the oriental style of eating, perhaps, except that dishes you order arrive in progression rather than as a shared 'banquet', and there is a suggested wine (by the glass) to accompany each one. The beautiful location, warm atmosphere and good food are enhanced by good service and a short but well chosen wine list - what more could any visitor wish for? Children welcome. **Seats 34** (outdoors, 40); L wed-sun, 12-4 (to 6 on Sun); D Wed-Sat from 7. Closed Mon & Tue. MasterCard, Visa, Laser.

Inistioge
RESTAURANT

The Motte Restaurant

Plas Newydd Lodge Inistioge Co Kilkenny
Tel: 056 775 8655 Email: rodneydoyle@eircom.net

féile bia On the edge of the picturesque village of Inistioge, with views of extensive parklands and the River Nore, Rodney & Deirdre Doyle's restaurant is situated in the classically proportioned Plas Newydd Lodge, named in honour of the ladies of Llangollen, who eloped from Inistioge in the late 18th century. Although small in size, this unique country restaurant has great charm. An L-shaped room with a Kilkenny marble fireplace and simple, effective decor - deep carmine walls and linen clad tables - makes a good setting for Rodney Doyle's accomplished cooking, which features many specialities which some guests will remember from their previous restaurant Rodney's Bistro in Cabinteely, Dublin: delicious home-made breads, starters like baked goats cheese in puff pastry, warm duck salad, or a superb warm terrine of monkfish, salmon and sole wrapped in spinach, and main courses such as Thai chicken curry, baked cod with a chorizo mash, or fillet of beef with the (excellent) trademark pepper & brandy cream. Menus are sensibly limited, but always include an imaginative vegetarian dish, and desserts are delicious - don't miss the crème brulée. Small weddings or private parties can be catered for. **Seats 40** (private room 16). Reservations required. Toilets wheelchair accessible. D Wed-Sat 7-9.30 (also Sun of bank hol weekends). Set D €35. House wine €18. SC discretionary (except 12.5% on groups of 6+). Closed Mon, Tue (also Sun, except bank hol weekends); 1 week autumn, 1 week Christmas. Amex, MasterCard, Visa, Laser. **Directions:** Opposite village "name sign" on Kilkenny side of village. ◇

Kilkenny
GUESTHOUSE

Butler House

16 Patrick Street Kilkenny Co Kilkenny **Tel: 056 776 5707**
Fax: 056 776 5626 Email: res@butler.ie Web: www.butler.ie

Located close to Kilkenny Castle, this elegant Georgian townhouse was restored by the Irish State Design Agency in the 1970s - and the resulting combination of what was at the time contemporary design and period architecture leads to some interesting discussions. However bedrooms are unusually spacious - some have bow windows overlooking the gardens and Kilkenny Castle - and the accommodation is very adequate, with all the amenities now expected of good guesthouse accommodation. Bathrooms - which, for many years, let down an otherwise high level of comfort - are at last being refurbished; all will be upgraded and most rooms will now have full bath. Three magnificent bow-windowed reception rooms are available for receptions and dinners. An excellent breakfast is served at the Kilkenny Design Centre, which is just across the gardens in the refurbished castle stables. Conferences/banqueting (120/70).

Children welcome (under 2 free in parents' room; cot available without charge, baby sitting arranged). Parking (20). Walking, garden. No pets. **Rooms 13** (1 suite, 3 exeecutive,12 shower only). B&B €85 pps, ss €40, sc discretionary. Off-season breaks offered. Closed 23-29 Dec. Amex, Diners, MasterCard, Visa, Laser. **Directions:** City centre, close to Kilkenny Castle.

Kilkenny
RESTAURANT

Fléva

84 High Street Kilkenny Co Kilkenny **Tel: 056 777 0021**
Fax: 056 777 0021 Email: flevarestaurant@eircom.net

féile bia Bright paintwork will attract you to this colourful and spacious first floor restaurant - and it is just the kind of place that visitors enjoy finding. Well-appointed, with white-clothed tables a slightly funky style and exhibitions by local artists, its most obvious asset is friendly and welcoming staff, who go out of their way to make arriving guests feel at home. The food style is eclectic - they describe it quite accurately as international food with a contemporary Irish twist - and local produce such as Kilkenny beef is always on the menu of course, but you will also find less likely choices such as ostrich (which is farmed in Ireland); a more predictable house speciality is roast rack of lamb with garlic, mint cream & boulangère potatoes; colourful, refreshing salads are appealing, vegetarian dishes are imaginative and and pride is also taken in fish and game cookery. Open Tue-Sat, L 12.30-2.30 & D 5.30-10 (to 10.30 Sat), food served all day Sun (12.30-9.30); Set Sun L €21.50, early D €21.50, 5.30-7. Closed Mon. Amex, Diners, MasterCard, Visa, Laser. **Directions:** Near Town Hall - first floor, over Bennetton.

Kilkenny
N HOTEL

Hotel Kilkenny

College Road Kilkenny Co Kilkenny
Tel: 056 776 2000 Fax: 056 776 5984
Email: kilkenny@griffingroup.ie Web: www.griffingroup.ie

féile bia Having undergone a multi-million euro redevelopment to upgrade all its facilities, the Hotel Kilkenny has recently re-opened; dubbed 'the four star with flair', this is a sister hotel to the very successful and well-run Ferrycarrig Hotel and the stunning new Monart destination spa, both in County Wexford. The tone of the new Hotel Kilkenny is set in the spacious contemporary foyer, which has a very large modern reception desk and relaxed seating areas; accommodation includes the original hundred or so rooms which have all now been refurbished in a contemporary that is not too hard edged, and a further 36 new deluxe rooms (not yet open at the time of going to press). Public areas include a new bar 'Pure' which is very modern and has an exceptional speciality drinks menu with 15 cocktails, 6 premium beers and 20 premium spirits listed, also a description of each which you are not likely to see elsewhere; it makes very interesting reading and the barman is clearly enthusiastic about it too. There is also a new restaurant, 'Taste': a large room on two levels, it is decorated in a very understated colour palate, and has a 'hotel ding room' atmosphere. The hotel had only recently re-opened after its major upgrade at the time of the Guide's visit and the food was a little uneven, as was the bar service. In addition to the new bedrooms, areas still due for completion at the time of going to press include 'City', a state-of-the-art conference centre, and new syndicate rooms for smaller meetings, and 'Skyline', a large venue for weddings and larger conferences. The hotel is set in award winning gardens and has ample complimentary car parking, and a 5 star Active Health and Fitness club with extensive facilities including hairdressing. Conference/banqueting 400/380. Children welcome (under 2s free in parents' room; cots available without charge). No pets. **Rooms 103** (24 executive rooms, 5 no smoking, 2 disabled). B&B €100. Open all year. Amex, Diners, MasterCard, Visa, Laser. **Directions:** On ring road at Clonmel roundabout exit. ◇

Kilkenny
€ RESTAURANT

Kilkenny Design Centre

Castle Yard Kilkenny Co Kilkenny
Tel: 056 772 2118 Fax: 056 776 5905
Email: info@kilkennydesign.com Web: www.kilkennydesign.com

féile bia Situated in what was once the stables and dairy of Kilkenny Castle - and overlooking the craft courtyard - this deservedly popular first floor self-service restaurant is situated above temptations of a different sort, on display in the famous craft shop. Wholesome and consistently delicious fare begins with breakfast for guests staying at Butler House, as well as non-resident visitors. The room is well-designed to allow attractive and accessible display of wonderful food, all freshly prepared every day: home baking is a strong point and, although there is plenty of hot food to choose from as well, salads, are a particular strength, always colourful and full of life - fresh beetroot, asparagus, spinach, red onion, coriander & crumbly Lavistown local cheese makes a salad worth travelling for, for example, and the selection changes all the time. Wines and beers are available, also gourmet coffees and herbal teas. Very reasonably priced too - well worth a visit. Toilets wheelchair accessible. Lift. **Seats 150.** Meals daily 11-7. Self service. Closed Sun & banks hols off-season (Jan-Mar). Amex, Diners, MasterCard, Visa, Laser. **Directions:** Opposite Kilkenny Castle.

Kilkenny
HOTEL/RESTAURANT

Kilkenny Ormonde Hotel

Ormonde Street Kilkenny Co Kilkenny
Tel: 056 772 3900 Fax: 056 772 3977
Email: info@kilkennyormonde.com Web: www.kilkennyormonde.com

Kilkenny city's leading hotel enjoys an outstandingly convenient central location for both business and leisure guests, beside (but not adjacent to) a multi-storey carpark and within walking distance of the whole city. Spacious public areas include an impressive foyer, the informal Earls Bar & Bistro - where appealing international cooking is available at lunch and dinner daily - and an elegant restaurant, Fredricks. Generously large bedrooms are furnished to a high standard in a pleasing contemporary style, with ISDN lines and safes in addition to the more usual amenities, and both business/conference and on-site leisure facilities are excellent. Friendly, professional staff provide outstanding service, ensuring a pleasant stay or well-run business event - the hotel's excellent conference centre and 10 fully equipped meeting rooms offer the region's premier conference and business venue and well-trained staff to match. Conference/banqueting (500/400). Business centre, video conferencing. Leisure centre, 21m swimming pool, crèche. **Rooms 118** (6 suites, 6 executive rooms, 59 no smoking, 4 disabled). Lift. 24 hour room service. B&B from about €68 pps, ss €31. Children welcome (under12s free in parents' room, cots available without charge, bay sitting arranged). Earls Bistro: 11.30am-11.30pm. Closed 24-26 Dec. **Fredricks:** This very comfortable, rather clubby, room has well-spaced, elegantly appointed tables and a pleasing ambience. International menus are based mainly on carefully sourced produce - some, such as Lavistown cheese, is clearly local; cooking is quite ambitious and service, as in other areas of the hotel, is a strong point. The restaurant is also used for breakfast. **Seats 75.** Toilets wheelchair accessible. Open D daily 6.30-9, L Sun only 12.30-2.30. Set D from €38/42. House wine about €25. sc discretionary. Amex, MasterCard, Visa, Laser. **Directions:** Kilkenny city centre off the parade opposite castle.

Kilkenny
HOTEL

Kilkenny River Court Hotel

The Bridge John Street Kilkenny Co Kilkenny
Tel: 056 772 3388 Fax: 056 772 3389
Email: reservations@kilrivercourt.com Web: www.kilrivercourt.com

Beautifully situated in a courtyard just off the narrow, bustling streets of the city centre, with only the River Nore separating it from Kilkenny Castle, this fine hotel enjoys the city's premier location, and has a beautiful riverside terrace area at the front. While equally attractive for business or leisure - bedrooms and public areas are all finished to a high standard and the Health & Leisure Club provides excellent facilities for health, fitness and beauty treatments - the hotel has established a special reputation for conferences and incentive programmes, with state-of-the-art facilities for groups of varying numbers and plenty to do when off duty in the city, as well as outdoor pursuits - golf, fishing, equestrian - nearby. Conference/Banqueting (220/190). Leisure centre, indoor swimming pool. Children welcome (under 3 free in parents' room, cot available without charge). Limited private parking (access can be a little difficult). Short breaks/ special interest breaks offered. **Rooms 90** (2 suites, 45 executive, 60 no smoking, 4 for disabled). Lift. All day room service; turndown service. B&B about €105pps, ss about €50. Closed 25-26 Dec. **Restaurant:** The restaurant, which is well-located within the hotel to take full advantage of the riverside setting, is an elegant room, with beautifully appointed tables, silver candle sticks and a grand piano conveying a sense of occasion. The atmosphere is that of a restaurant rather than a hotel dining room and both menus and cooking style reinforce that impression. The à la carte offers 8-10 choices on each course and cooking is generally good; although there are plenty of more unusual dishes to choose from, a popular house speciality is a classic pan-fried tournedos of beef fillet, with a chunky wild mushroom duxelle, a red wine & thyme jus and caramelised pear onions. The early dinner and Sunday lunch menus are particularly good value, and charming service adds to the occasion. **Seats 80** (private room 40). D daily 6-9.15, L Sun only 12.30-3. Early D €24 (6-7.30); Set D €40, also à la carte. Set Sun L €24. [Food is also served in the Riverview Bar, 12-6 daily.] Amex, Diners, MasterCard, Visa. **Directions:** Follow city centre signs, directly opposite Kilkenny Castle. Two archways on Dublin side of bridge - use the castle as a landmark. ◇

Kilkenny
RESTAURANT WITH ROOMS/GUESTHOUSE

Lacken House

Dublin Road Kilkenny Co Kilkenny
Tel: 056 776 1085 Fax: 056 776 2435
Email: info@lackenhouse.ie Web: www.lackenhouse.ie

féile bia Jackie and Trevor Toner's period house on the edge of Kilkenny city is best known as a restaurant, but also appeals to those who want the comfort of an hotel with the hospitality of a smaller establishment. The restaurant offers a combination of traditional and modern fine dining - most importantly the head chef, Michael Thomas's philsosophy is to use only the best local produce and mainly organic vegetables and fruit: there's a formal commitment to the Féile Bia Charter on menus, and some suppliers are credited: lamb comes from Dick Dooley's family butches in Callan, for example. The cooking style is a combination of traditional and modern fine dining, and menus offered include an à la carte which includes specialities, some of them luxurious - foie gras terrine, roast suckling pig, roast crispoy duckling all feature. Menus are well-balanced, with more seafood than might be expected in a midlands restaurant and one or two unexpected ingredients, such as ostrich fillet, but local meats are exceptional: Kilkenny beef is renowned and there will always be at least one dish amongst the specialities - a fillet, perhaps, served with with parsnip & truffle purée, spiced onion rings and Madeira jus. And then of course there are desserts or cheese plates too - the farmhouse cheese selection includes the lovely local cheese, Lavistown, and comes with scrumptious home-baked biscuits. An interesting wine list includes ten house wines, a page dedicated to half bottles and an unusually extensive choice of dessert wines. Private parties and functions are also catered for (conference/banqueting 25/50). Children welcome. **Seats 50.** (Private room, 25). D Tue-Sat, 6.30-9.30; also Sun of bank hol weekends & in summer (1 Jun-30 Sep); Earlybird D €35 (6-7.30). Set D €59; house wine from €21. Closed Mon (also Sun during winter except bank hol weekends); 24-27 Dec. **Accommodation:** Guest bedrooms vary in size and outlook but all have been extensively refurbished recently, effectively recreating Lacken House as a boutique hotel, with appeal to those who want the comfort of an hotel with the hospitality of a smaller establishment. Excellent breakfasts are served in the restaurant. Room service (limited hours); in-room treatments and massage. Children welcome (under 4 free in parents' room, cot available free of charge, baby sitting arranged). No pets. Garden. **Rooms 10** (2 junior suites, 5 power shower only, 2 family rooms, 4 ground floor, all no smoking). B&B €75 pps, ss €25. Amex, MasterCard, Visa, Laser. **Directions:** On N10 Carlow/Dublin Road into Kilkenny City.

Kilkenny
HOTEL

Langton House Hotel

69 John Street Kilkenny Co Kilkenny **Tel: 056 776 5133** Fax: 056 776 3693
Email: reservations@langtons.ie Web: www.langtons.ie

féile bia Langton's is mainly famous for its maze of bars, with seating areas and restaurants that stretch right through this substantial building to a garden and secure private car park at the back. Until quite recently there was a lovely old traditional bar at the front but this, alas, has been modernised, although the fine classic frontage remains; an outdoor bar and dining area has recently been added, and the big Langton Ballroom, beyond the bar, is to be renovated shortly after we go to press. The hotel reception area has an entrance from the front bar and, given the size of the premises, it is surprisingly small - although graced with a dramatic flower arrangement. Efficient reception, good-sized rooms furnished to a high standard, and unusually well-appointed bathrooms all make this a good place to stay if you want to be in the city centre and, although there may be some small annoyances (residents have to go through the bar in the morning for breakfast), this is a slightly wacky hotel of some character and people generally take to it. Langton's also offers a lively middle of the road dining experience - good food without frills, friendly service and good value for money. Conferences/Banqueting (200/250). Private car park. Children welcome (under 5s free in parents room, cot available at no charge, babysitting arranged). **Rooms 30** (2 suites, 4 family rooms, 8 ground floor, 22 no smoking). B&B from €100 pps, ss €25. L & D daily, 12-5.30 & 5.30-10.30.Closed 25 Dec. Amex, MasterCard, Visa, Laser. **Directions:** Town centre.

Kilkenny
N B&B

Laragh House

Waterford Road Kilkenny Co Kilkenny
Tel: 056 776 4674 Fax: 056 770 3605
Email: info@laraghhouse.com Web: www.laraghhouse.com

Helen Cooney's modern two-storey white plastered guesthouse was only built in 2005, but is already one of the most popular in the area as it is within walking distance of Kilkenny city centre in fine weather (15 minutes), has off-street parking and, with all the modern amenities, offers a very reasonably priced alternative to an hotel. The eight bedrooms are individually styled, with multi channel TV, direct dial telephone and internet access and all have whirlpool bath or power showers. There's also a comfortably furnished lounge for guests to relax in, and a smoking area is provided. Rates, Season.. week end €45.00 pp, week day €35.00 pp. off season €30.00pp including breakfast. **Rooms 8** (all en-suite); B&B €30-35 pp weekdays, €45 pp weekends (off season 30 pp including breakfast). MasterCard, Visa, Laser. **Directions:** Easily reached from any direction via the city by-pass. ◇

Kilkenny

HOTEL

Lyrath Estate Hotel - Spa & Convention Centre

Dublin Road Kilkenny Co Kilkenny **Tel: 056 776 0088**
Fax: 056 776 0089 Email: info@lyrath.com Web: www.lyrath.com

This new hotel, spa and convention centre is set in 170 acres of mature parklands on the outskirts of Kilkenny city. At its centre is a 17th century house which has been extended to become a large modern hotel with a state of the art conference centre (capable of seating 1500 delegates) and a spa. Accommodation is well appointed in a modern classic style but, although open about six months at the time of the Guide's visit, parts of the hotel were not fully operational. Bar service was less than perfect (how many tries are necessary to get a dry sherry?) and, although Tuppers Bar serves good food as does the main restaurant - where service is also likely to meet expectations - the restaurant experience overall may not represent good value for the price. A wine cellar for pre dinner drinks or for tasting events is planned, and a Thai restaurant is also due to open at the time of going to press. This is an hotel with great potential and, despite an uneven start, it could offer a very enjoyable experience when it settles down. Conferences/Banqueting (1,500/950), 7 board rooms, 3 business centres; Spa; Private club floor. **Rooms 137** (1 penthouse suite, 9 suites, 28 executive). Room rate from €200. **Directions:** Just before Kilkenny on the Dublin/Carlow road. ◇

Kilkenny

PUB

Marble City Bar

66 High Street Kilkenny Co Kilkenny **Tel: 056 776 1143**
Fax: 056 776 3693 Web: www.langtons.ie

féile bia The Langton family's historic bar was redesigned by the internationally acclaimed designer, David Collins, a few years ago. Although initially controversial (especially the ultra-modern stained glass window which now graces an otherwise traditional frontage), it is a wonderful space to be in and attracts a varied clientèle. Everyone enjoys the vibrant atmosphere, and the excellent ingredients-led contemporary European bar food: a dish like confit of pork sausages with creamy potatoes and red wine onion gravy, for example, will probably be based on the superb lean sausages hand-made nearby by Olivia Goodwillie (who also makes Lavistown cheese), and the fresh cod'n'chips in a crispy beer batter will be just in from Dunmore East. More recently the bar has reinvented itself again and they have now introduced the Marble City Tea Rooms, below the main restaurant area, where lighter food like coffees, teas and pastry are available, 9-7 daily - and there's outdoor seating for a couple of dozen people. Good service, even at busy times; well chosen small wine list. Bar food served from 10 am, daily. Food service begins with breakfast, from 10am daily; main menus from 12 noon-9.15 pm (Sun: L 12-3; D 3-9). A la carte. House wine about €20 (€5 per glass). Closed 25 Dec & Good Fri. Amex, Diners, MasterCard, Visa, Laser. **Directions:** Ample car parking at rear. Main Street, city centre. ◇

Kilkenny

CAFÉ/RESTAURANT

Restaurant Café Sol

William Street Kilkenny Co Kilkenny
Tel: 056 776 4987 Fax: 056 775 6720
Email: info@cafesolkilkenny.com Web: www.cafesolkilkenny.com

Noel McCarron's popular daytime café and evening restaurant is easy to find, just off the High Street. A small interior porch leads in to a large room warmly decorated in yellow and terracotta with large paintings by local artist Catherine Barron, giving it a sunny, Mediterranean feeling; daytime is very casual with oilcloths or plain wooden table tops, and in the evening - when the building is floodlit and heavy white paper cloths and candles are used - there's a distinct change of atmosphere. Liam O'Hanlon took over as head chef in 2004, and the house style remains colourful and punchy, showing international influences but based on the best local produce like delicious Lavistown sausages, beef and lamb from Mullins butchers, and fish from Dunmore East, Co Waterford; suppliers are credited on the menu, together with the offer to prepare gluten free or dairy free dishes on request. Daytime menus offer informal dishes like open sandwiches, panini and salads, and perhaps ten hot dishes including comfort food like grilled Lavistown sausages with colcannon, and spicier dishes such as an oriental stirfry. Evening menus move up a gear or two, and as well as the more predictable dishes (local beef, of course) include some unusual choices - a tasting plate of cured meats, Lavistown cheese, aged balsamic and rocket leaves, for example. Vegetarians always do well here, too - and lovely desserts might include homely treats like warm mixed berry and apple crumble, with whipped cream - simply delicious. Stylish plain white plates do a lot for the food, which is attractively presented but not overworked. This is an interesting restaurant, offering something different from the 'sameness' of so many menus, and at reasonable prices. *At the time of going to press the restaurant is about to undergo refurbishment, and possibly also a change of name. **Seats 45.** Air conditioning. Open all day Mon-Sat, 12-10, Sun 12-9. Set D €23; Set D for 2 & bottle wine €60. also á la carte. Wines from €18. SC 10% on parties 6+. Closed 25 Dec, 1 Jan. *Free Broadband/WIFI Amex, MasterCard, Visa, Laser. **Directions:** Coming from castle - up High St. - 2nd turn left opposite Town Hall.

Kilkenny

RESTAURANT WITH ROOMS

Rinuccini Restaurant

1 The Parade Kilkenny Co Kilkenny
Tel: 056 776 1575 Fax: 056 775 1288
Email: info@rinuccini.com Web: www.rinuccini.com

Antonio and Marion Cavaliere's well-known Italian restaurant is in a semi-basement in the impressive terrace opposite Kilkenny Castle and the closely packed tables are an indication of its popularity. When empty it looks a little bleak, but the room quickly fills up with a healthy mixture of locals (who clearly have their preferred tables) and tourists. The cooking style is mainly classic Italian, with quite an extensive à la carte evening menu plus a shorter one available as an option at lunchtime. Service is prompt, from the time fresh bread and butter is delivered speedily with the menu. Food is characterised by freshness of ingredients and a high standard of cooking: excellent minestrone (a classic test), a superb plate of house antipasti (Parma ham, smoked pork, two different salami, barbecue-seared aubergine slices, pungent roast peppers, black olives & garlic toasted foccacia) delicious seafood and memorable pasta. The simple things are right, which is always a good sign - but that doesn't necessarily preclude luxury: spaghetti with fresh lobster is one of the house specialities. While regular guests might like to see changes to the menu more often (some daily specials, perhaps), visitors will find great service and outstanding value for money too; the only downside to this popularity is that there is sometimes pressure to fit in an extra sitting, which can make for a less than relaxed meal. Not suitable for children after 8pm. **Seats 60.** L daily 12-2.30, D daily 5.30-10.30. Reservations accepted. Early D €25 (5.30-7), otherwise à la carte. House wines from €19.95 **Accommodation:** Seven large, en-suite rooms are offered with air conditioning, TV, tea/coffee facilities and trouser press with iron. A breakfast tray is supplied, for you to make up your own continental breakfast in the room. **Rooms 7** (1 junior suite, all shower-only & no-smoking) B&B €60 pps. Amex, Diners, MasterCard, Visa, Laser. **Directions:** Opposite Kilkenny Castle. ◇

Kilkenny

Ⓝ RESTAURANT

Swans Chinese

101 High Street The Parade Kilkenny Co Kilkenny
Tel: 056 772 3088 Email: info@swans.ie
Web: www.swansrestaurant.com

Situated on the corner of High Street and Rose Inn street over Ladbrokes bookie office, with the entrance from High Street, Swans is a very pleasant venue for enjoying well prepared and presented Oriental Cuisine. The room is bright and very relaxing, with red alcoves, comfortable dark brown leather chairs and Chinese wall hangings; charming Chinese waitresses contribute to the ambience and the food has great flavour, bringing nicely served classics like crispy spring rolls, chicken chow mein and szechuan style dishes to life. With good espressos to finish, this is a useful place to know. Children welcome. **Seats 56;** air conditioning; L Mon-Sat, 12-2.30; L Sun 12.30-5, D daily 5pm-11.30pm; set Sun L €16.50; value D avail 7 days €18.50, also a la carte; house wine €16. Closed 25 Dec, Good Fri. MasterCard, Visa, Laser. **Directions:** Kilkenny centre, 2 mins walk from Kilkenny Castle.

Kilkenny

Ⓔ HOTEL/RESTAURANT

Zuni Restaurant & Townhouse

26 Patrick Street Kilkenny Co Kilkenny
Tel: 056 772 3999 Fax: 056 775 6400
Email: info@zuni.ie Web: www.zuni.ie

Although Zuni is an hotel ('boutique' style, and offering a more youthful style of accommodation than other comparable establishments), the atmosphere is more restaurant with rooms: an oasis of contemporary chic in this bustling city, it is well established as an in-place for discerning Kilkenny diners. The room is large and airy, overlooking a courtyard (alfresco dining in fine weather) and there's a separate restaurant entrance so you don't have to go through the hotel. Maria Raftery's menus are based on local ingredients but international in tone, with a dish like mixed seafood in saffron broth with seasonal vegetables offered alongside chargrilled Irish sirloin with fresh chips, sautéed mushrooms, onion & grilled tomato. Attractively presented food is always full of flavour: smart salads make tasty starters and Maria, who cooks with panache in view of diners, is a cool and accomplished chef. Menus to note include an early dinner menu which offers a good choice and gives great value for money - and an upbeat contemporary variation on the traditional lunch which packs them in on Sundays. ***Zuni Espress,** a café nearby, offers coffees and gourmet sandwiches with a global flavour; you can pre-order on 056 779 5899 - just the thing for a picnic lunch, perhaps. Toilets wheelchair accessible. Children Welcome. **Seats 70** (Outdoor seating, 24). (Breakfast); L Tue-Sun 12.30-2.30 (Sun 1-3), D daily 6.30-10 (Sun 6-9). Early D €25 (6.30-7.30). Otherwise à la carte. House wine from €22. SC 12.5% added to parties 6+. **Accommodation:** This boutique hotel offers a more youthful style of accommodation than other comparable establishments; the minimalist decor is difficult to keep immaculate, but a new round of refurbishment (painting, replacement of bathroom fittings, carpets and soft furnishings) is about to begin shortly after we go to press. Rooms have direct dial phones, AC, Iron/trouser press, TV, tea/coffee-making facilities. Breakfast is served in the restaurant. Children welcome (under 12s free in parents' room; cot available without charge, baby sitting arranged). No pets. Private parking, but guests must get the receptionist to open the security bar (best to use the mobile phone, perhaps). **Rooms 13** (8 shower only, 5 no smoking, 1 family room, 1 for disabled, all no smoking). Lift. B&B €50ps, ss €20. Hotel closed 23-27 Dec. Amex, MasterCard, Visa, Laser. **Directions:** On Patrck Street - leads to Waterford road; 200 yards from Kilkenny Castle.

KILKENNY

A rich vein of hospitality runs throughout Kilkenny city and county and, in addition to those selected here, there are numerous places that may be of interest to visitors. **The Newpark Hotel** (056 776 0500; www.newparkhotel.com), for example, is very much at the heart of local activities, and is a popular venue for conferences and meetings; and, in the city centre, **The Hibernian Hotel** (056 777 1888; www.kilkennyhibernianhotel.com)is in an old banking building and has character as well as a degree of luxury. Also in the city, Café Pierre's on Parliament Street is popular for its reliable fare and good atmosphere; for details of a variety of other eating places for every budget and occasion, including daytime snacks, the **Kilkenny Good Food Circle Guide** (www.kilkenny tourism.ie) is available from Tourist Information Offices. Outside the city, should your travels take you to the Callan area, you might be glad to find the **Old Charter House** (056 775 5902), a village pub offering reliable bar meals and moderately priced accommodation.

WWW.IRELAND-GUIDE.COM FOR THE BEST PLACES TO EAT, DRINK & STAY

Maddoxtown

COUNTRY HOUSE

Blanchville House

Dunbell Maddoxtown Co Kilkenny

Tel: 056 772 7197 Fax: 056 772 7636

Email: mail@blanchville.ie Web: www.blanchville.ie

Monica Phelan's elegant Georgian house is just 5 miles out of Kilkenny city, surrounded by its own farmland and gardens. It's easy to spot - there's a folly in its grounds. It's a very friendly, welcoming place and the house has an airy atmosphere, with matching well-proportioned dining and drawing rooms on either side of the hall, and the pleasant, comfortably furnished bedrooms in period style all overlook attractive countryside. Dinner is available to residents, if pre-arranged, and, like the next morning's excellent breakfast, is taken at the communal mahogany dining table. The Coach Yard has been renovated to make four self-catering coach houses, and the house can also be rented - an ideal arrangement for groups of 12-20 people, for family get-togethers or other special occasions, where guests may have exclusive use of the house and coach yard. More recently, a small spa and holistic centre has been added in the coach yard, with a resident therapist. Blanchville is well-situated for golfers (5 great courses within half an hour's drive, including Mount Juliet). Special breaks offered include art workshop weekends, and bridge breaks. Horseriding, hunting, fishing, shooting and garden visits nearby. Walking, garden, cycling. Small conferences/private parties (25). Children welcome, under 5s free in parents' room; cot available without charge; baby sitting can be arranged. Pets permitted by arrangement. **Rooms 6** (5 en-suite, 1 with private bathroom, 2 shower only, all non-smoking, 1 family room). B&B €55-60 pps, ss €10. No SC. Turndown service offered. Residents D €50 by prior arrangement only. Closed 1 Nov-1 Mar. Amex, MasterCard, Visa, Laser, Switch. **Directions:** From Kilkenny take N10 (Carlow-Dublin road), 1st right 1/2 mile after 'ThePike'. Continue 2 miles to crossroads (Connolly's pub). Take left, large stone entrance 1 mile on left.

Thomastown
COUNTRY HOUSE

Ballyduff House

Thomastown Co Kilkenny
Tel: 056 775 8488 Email: ballydhouse@eircom.net

Set in fine rolling countryside in its own farmland and grounds, Breda Thomas's lovely 18th century house overlooking the River Nore is blessed with an utterly restful location. Breda is a relaxed and welcoming host, and offers exceptionally spacious and comfortable accommodation in large period bedrooms with generous bathrooms and beautiful views over the river or gardens. Guests also have the use of large well-proportioned day rooms furnished with family antiques - and many return often, finding this rural retreat a warm and welcoming home from home. Beautiful walks on the estate. Fishing (salmon, trout). Riding, hunting and other country pursuits can be arranged. Garden visits nearby. Children welcome. Pets permitted by arrangement. *Self-catering accommodation also offered at Ballyduff Castle, adjoining Ballyduff House (2-4 bedrooms). **Rooms 3.** B&B about €40, ss about €10. Cpen all year. **No Credit Cards. Directions:** 5km (3 m) south of Thomastown.

Thomastown
(N) CAFÉ/RESTAURANT

Ethos

Low Street Thomastown Co Kilkenny **Tel: 056 775 4945** Email: cathal@ethosbistro.com Web: www.ethosbistro.com

Cathal O'Sullivan and (chef) Paul Cullen opened this new venture just shortly before we went to press; it is already earning a local following, and its situation on the main street means that new business will find it very quickly. It's an inviting spot and the setup - café by day and bistro by night - is very customer friendly. Paul's lunch menus are casual - soup, salads, sambos, panini, bagels - and a more structured evening menu in a French/Asian style offers half a dozen starters, and about eight main courses, ranging from around €8 to €21.00, a good mid-range that will go down very well in the area. Specialities include seafood dishes like mussels with Thai green curry, pak choi & coriander, or sea bass with chorizo & red pepper - and there will always be good local meats, including Kilkenny beef, of course, but also pork - homely roast stuffed pork, perhaps, with apple, champ and buttered cabbage. Duck also features, and vegetarian dishes too - and there's a lovely choice of desserts. Cooking and service are good - this is a place that should do well. Children welcome; toilets wheelchair accessible; **Seats 40** (outdoors, 16); L Mon-Sat, 12-3.30pm, D daily 6.30-9.30pm except Sun & Tue; Sun L only, 12-5pm; house wine €18; SC 10% on parties 10+. Closed D Sun & Tue, 25 Dec. Amex, MasterCard, Visa, Laser. **Directions:** N9 from Dublin/Waterford - just off Main St.

Thomastown
RESTAURANT

Hudsons

Station Road Thomastown Co Kilkenny
Tel: 056 779 3900 Email: hudsonsrestaurant@eircom.net

Richard and Kyra Hudson's stylish restaurant overlooks a charming old stone-walled garden at the back, with a romantic arch and trailing climbers: a delightful contrast to the modern interior. Menus are contemporary, offering modern classics (Caesar salad, beef carpaccio, seared salmon) and a range of char-grills (which should please golfers down from nearby Mount Juliet, especially). There may also be some less usual dishes - pot roast duck, on a bed of mixed greens, with puy lentils & hoi sin jus, for example. Service, under the management of the proprietors, is friendly and attentive. *NB Please phone to check opening times well ahead of a visit, as they have not been confirmed at the time of going to press. Children welcome. **Seats 70.** D Wed-Sun; à la carte. House wine about €24. Mastercard, Visa, Laser. **Directions:** On road to Mount Juliet from Dublin to Waterford.

Thomastown

HOTEL/RESTAURANT

Mount Juliet Conrad

Thomastown Co Kilkenny
Tel: 056 77 73000 Fax: 056 77 73019
Email: mountjulietinfo@conradhotels.com Web: www.mountjuliet.com

HOTEL OF THE YEAR

féile bia Lying amidst 1500 acres of unspoilt woodland, pasture and formal gardens beside the River Nore, Mount Juliet House is one of Ireland's finest Georgian houses, and one of Europe's greatest country estates. Even today it retains an aura of eighteenth century grandeur, as the elegance of the old house has been painstakingly preserved - and it has a uniquely serene and restful atmosphere. Suites and bedrooms in the main house have period decor with all the comfort of modern facilities and there's additional accommodation in the Club Rooms at Hunters Yard, which is very close to the main house, and where most of the day-to-day activities of the estate take place. There is also self-catering accommodation offered, at the Rose Garden Lodges (close to Hunters Yard) and The Paddocks (at the tenth tee). Although the K Club was the focus of attention leading up to the Ryder Cup, Mount Juliet is equally respected as a golfing destination, and considerable investment has recently gone into upgrading the golf course, which now offers an 18-hole putting course in addition to the Jack Nicklaus designed championship course. But there is much more to this wonderfully relaxing hotel than golf: it is well located for exploring one of Ireland's most beautiful areas and there is no shortage of things to do on the estate: gardens and woodlands to wander, new sports to try, the Spa & Health Club for pampering. In order to build on the hotel's growing reputation as a destination for activity breaks, a new equestrian centre is under way as we go to press, and also a new spa; Mount Juliet has also recently launched a range of Master Classes in a number of disciplines, including fishing, painting, salsa and wellness. And, with all that fresh air and exercise to build up a healthy appetite, dining is another of the great pleasures that Mount Juliet has to offer, with a choice of fine dining in the Lady Helen Dining Room (see below), or an equally attractive contemporary option in the stylish Kendals restaurant at Hunters Yard. Eugene McSweeney, well known as the previous proprietor-chef at Lacken House in Kilkenny city, has been acting Executive Head Chef at Mount Juliet since the autumn of 2005 - first working in Kendals, where he trained two head chefs to take over from him, and then in the Lady Helen Dining Room, where he has also trained a promising young successor, Richard Stratton. Mr McSweeney remains at Mount Juliet for the foreseeable future, but the hotel is fortunate to have a teaching chef/consultant of his calibre to ensure the future standards of this respected kitchen. Conference/banqueting (140/140). Children welcome (under 12 free sharing with 2 adults, but with extra bed is about €65; cot available €50, baby sitting arranged; children's play area). No pets. Gardens. Equestrian; Angling. Clay pigeon shooting, Archery, Tennis, Croquet, Cycling, Walking, Trails. Spa and Health Club (15m Swimming Pool; Treatments; Hair Dressing). Banqueting (romantic wedding venue, in large marquees set up outside the front of the house, overlooking the river...) **Rooms 58** (2 suites, 8 junior suites, 8 superior, 1 disabled; all no smoking). No Lift. B&B from about €117 sc discretionary. Open all year. **Lady Helen Dining Room:** Although grand, this graceful high-ceilinged room, softly decorated in pastel shades and with sweeping views over the grounds, is not forbidding and has a pleasant atmosphere. To match these beautiful surroundings, classic daily dinner menus based on local ingredients are served, including wild salmon from the River Nore, vegetables and herbs from the Mount Juliet garden, and regional Irish farmhouse cheese. Service is efficient and friendly, and there is an extensive international wine list. **Seats 60** (private room 25). Toilets wheelchair accessible. D daily 7-9.30. A la carte. House wine from €28. *It can be difficult to get a reservation at the Lady Helen Dining Room, especially for non-residents, so booking well ahead is advised. A very attractive alternative dining option is offered at the newer contemporary restaurant, Kendals, which is open for breakfast, & also for dinner (6-10) daily, *Informal dining is available in The Club, Presidents Bar (12am-9pm). Amex, Diners, MasterCard, Visa, Laser. **Directions:** M7 from Dublin, then M9 towards Waterford, arriving at Thomastown on the N9 via Carlow and Gowran. (75 miles south of Dublin, 60 miles north of Rosslare). ◇

COUNTY LAOIS

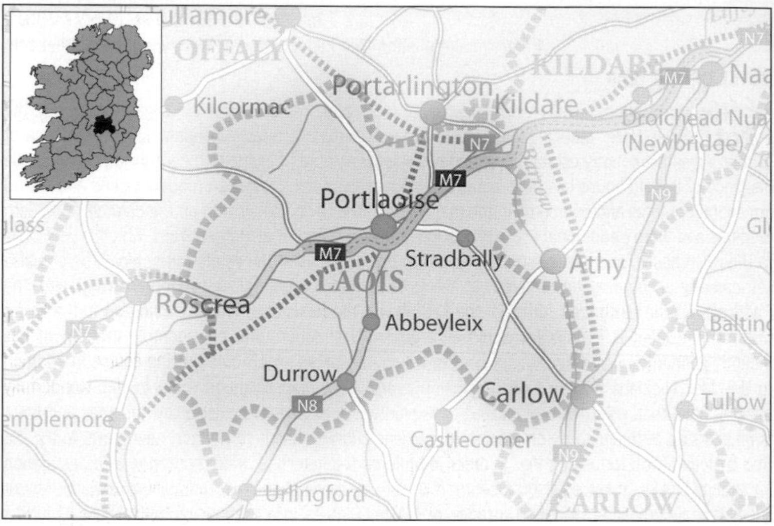

With its territory traversed by the rail and road links from Dublin to Cork and Limerick, Laois is often glimpsed only fleetingly by inter-city travellers. But as with any Irish county, it is a wonderfully rewarding place to visit as soon as you move off the main roads. For Laois is the setting for Emo Court and Heywood, two of the great gardens of Ireland at their most impressive.

And it's a salutary place to visit, too. In the eastern part, between Stradbally and Portlaois, there's the Rock of Dunamase, that fabulous natural fortress which many occupiers inevitably assumed to be impregnable. Dunamase's remarkably long history of fortifications and defences and sieges and eventual captures has a relevance and a resonance for all times and all peoples and all places.

But there's much more to Laois than mournful musings on the ultimate vanity of human ambitions. With its border shared with Carlow along the River Barrow, eastern Laois comfortably reflects Carlow's quiet beauty. To the northwest, we find that Offaly bids strongly to have the Slieve Bloom Mountains thought of as an Offaly hill range, but in fact there's more of the Slieve Blooms in Laois than Offaly, and lovely hills they are too. And though the River Nore may be thought of as quintessential Kilkenny, long before it gets anywhere near Kilkenny it is quietly building as it meanders across much of Laois, gathering strength from the weirdly-named Delour, Tonet, Gully, Erskina and Goul rivers on the way.

Along the upper reaches of the Nore in west Laois, the neat little village of Castletown has long been a tidy place. Castletown has for many years been in the top rankings in the annual Tidy Towns contest, a byword for civic pride.

Local Attractions and Information

Abbeyleix, Abbeyleix Heritage House 057 863 1653
Abbeyleix, Sensory Gardens 057 863 1325
Ballinakill, Heywood (Lutyens gardens) 057 863 3563
Donaghmore, Castletown House Open Farm 0505 46415
Donaghmore, Donaghmore Workhouse Museum 0505 46212
Emo, Emo Court (Gandon house & gardens) 057 862 6573
Portlaois, Dunamaise Theatre & Arts Centre 057 866 3356
Portlaois, Tourist Information 057 862 1178
Slieve Bloom, Slieve Bloom Rural Dev. Assoc. 057 913 7299
Stradbally, National Steam Traction Rally (August) 057 862 5444

ABBEYLEIX

Abbeyleix takes its name from a 12th century Cistercian abbey and today it is an attractive town with tree-lined streets. One of Ireland's best-loved old pubs, **Morrissey's** (0502 31281) is on the main street; it first opened as a grocery in 1775 and, true to the old tradition, 'television, cards and singing are not allowed'. A little down the street, the Dowlings' **Preston House** (0502 31432) has offered wholesome fare for travellers for many a year; although on the market at the time of going to press, its many devotees hope it might still be there for a little while longer. Across the road, **Abbeyleix Manor** Hotel (057 873 0111; www.abbeyleixmanorhotel.com) offers practical modern facilities.
WWW.IRELAND-GUIDE.COM FOR THE BEST PLACES TO EAT, DRINK & STAY

Durrow

Castle Durrow

HOTEL/RESTAURANT

Durrow Co Laois **Tel: 057 873 6555** Fax: 057 873 6559
Email: info@castledurrow.com Web: www.castledurrow.com

féile bia

Peter and Shelley Stokes' substantial 18th century country house midway between Dublin and Cork is an impressive building with some magnificent period features, and offers comfort and relaxation with style. A large marbled reception area with fresh flowers gives a welcoming impression on arrival, and public rooms include a large drawing room/bar, where informal meals are served, and a lovely dining room with a gently pastoral outlook at the back of the house (see below). Very spacious, luxurious accommodation is in high-ceilinged, individually decorated rooms and suites in the main house (some with four posters), with views over the surrounding parkland and countryside; some more contemporary but equally luxurious ground floor rooms are in a wing - particularly suitable for guests attending the weddings which have become a speciality, as they are convenient to the banqueting suite and avoid disturbing other guests. Conference/banqueting (160/170). Children welcome (under 5s free in parents' room, cot available without charge, baby sitting arranged, children's playground). Pets allowed by arrangement. Garden, walking, tennis (all weather, floodlit), cycling, snooker. Golf, fishing, equestrian all nearby. Hairdressing, beauty salon. **Rooms 24** (3 ground floor, 4 family rooms, all no smoking). B&B €100 pps, ss €40. 24 hr room service. Turn down service. Closed 31 Dec-15 Jan. **Castle Restaurant:** Candles are lit in the foyer and restaurant at dusk, giving the whole area a lovely romantic feeling. Head chef David Rouse's policy is for careful sourcing of all food, and the quality shows. Fish dishes, especially, have come in for praise on recent visits; wild Irish venison is a speciality in season, and a well-balanced cheese plate, might include the delicious local Lavistown cheese, from Kilkenny. Staff are very pleasant and helpful. **Seats 60** (private room, 18). Reservations accepted. Toilets wheelchair accessible. Breakfast 8-10, D daily, 7-8.45. Bar meals also available, 12-7 daily. Set D €50; Bar L à la carte. SC discretionary. House wines €20. Closed 31 Dec-15 Jan. Amex, MasterCard, Visa, Laser. **Directions:** On main Dublin-Cork road, N8.

Killenard

The Heritage at Killenard

N HOTEL

Killenard Co Laois **Tel: 057 864 5500** Fax: 057 864 2350
Email: info@theheritage.com Web: www.theheritage.com

This new luxury hotel and golf resort is set in the Laois countryside, just off the main Dublin-Cork road (N7). It is a very large development and needs some time for landscaping to soften the hard edges. An impressive atrium sets the tone as you enter the hotel, and this touch of grandeur is underlined by the lines of a bifurcated staircase, crystal chandeliers and marbled floors - all a little OTT perhaps, but carried through with confidence; other public areas are spacious and furnished in a similar style. Generous accommodation is in sumptuously furnished suites and guest rooms, which are extremely comfortable - and have beautiful bathrooms with separate shower and free-standing bath - although, surprisingly, some rooms do not have a view. But exceptional leisure facilities are the trump card at this hotel - as well as golf, there is a health club & spa (linked to the hotel by a tunnel), indoor and outdoor bowls, tennis, a 4 mile floodlit walking and jogging track around the golf course - and much more; new facilities are being added all the time. Dinner in the comfortable and well-appointed Arlington Room restaurant is a relaxing experience, with excellent home-baked breads and attentive service among the highlights. Although perhaps still not fully settled at the time of going to press, the restaurant seems set to become a fine dining destination of note. **Rooms 98** (3 suites, 10 junior suites, 5 family rooms, 5 disabled, 88 no smoking). B&B €162.50 pps, ss €100. Wheelchair Accessible. **Restaurant: Seats 80** (Private room available seats 45), Piano Sat 8-11, Air Con; House Wine €23. Children welcome but not after 8. Hotel closed 24-26 Dec. *Food also available in: Greens golf club restaurant (High season 7 days 7-9.30); Sol O'Briens Italian restaurant and steakhouse (Wed-Sun 6.30-10) and The Hotel Bar 12-7 daily, includes outdoor seating on patio for 40. 12 Self Catering houses available on the resort.* The 110-room **Heritage Hotel Portlaoise** (057 867 8588;

www.theheritagehotel.com) is an older sister to the Killenard hotel in Portlaoise town centre, and offers the same high standard of accommodation and excellent facilities, including a health & fitness centre, spa and conference facilities (500). Amex, MasterCard, Visa, Laser. **Directions:** M7 exit for Mountmellick, on to Killenard.

Mountrath

COUNTRY HOUSE

Roundwood House

Mountrath Co Laois **Tel: 057 873 2120** Fax: 057 873 2711
Email: roundwood@eircom.net Web: www.roundwoodhouse.com

It is hard to see how anyone could fail to love this unspoilt early Georgian house, which lies secluded in mature woods of lime, beech and chestnut, at the foot of the Slieve Bloom mountains. A sense of history and an appreciation of genuine hospitality are all that is needed to make the most of a stay here. Forget about co-ordinated decor and immaculate maintenance, just relax and share the immense pleasure and satisfaction that Frank and Rosemarie Kennan derive from the years of renovation work they have put into this wonderful property. Although unconventional in some ways, the house is extremely comfortable and well-heated (with central heating as well as log fires) and all the bathrooms have been recently renovated (all have full bath, some also with over-bath shower). Each bedroom has its particular charm, although it might be wise to check if there is a large group staying, in which case the bedroom above the drawing room may not be the best option. Restoration is an ongoing process and an extraordinary (and historically unique) barn is possibly the next stage; this enterprise defies description, but don't leave Roundwood without seeing it. Children, who always love the unusual animals and their young in the back yard, are very welcome and Rosemarie does a separate tea for them. Dinner is served at 8 o'clock, at a communal table, and based on the best local and seasonal ingredients (notably locally reared beef and lamb); Rosemarie's food suits the house - good home cooking without unnecessary frills, and Frank is an excellent host. A relatively extensive wine list includes a generous choice of half bottles. Children welcome (under 3 free in parents' room, cot available without charge; playroom). Garden, croquet, boules, walking - there is a mile long walk in the grounds and garden renovation is ongoing. Stabling available at the house; horse riding nearby. Golf nearby. Pets permitted in certain areas. **Rooms 10** (all en-suite, 6 no-smoking, 2 ground floor). B&B €75 pps, ss €20. No sc. D at 8pm; 5-course set D, €50 (non-residents welcome by reservation if there is room); please book by noon. House wine €15.50. Dining room closed Sun except for resident guests. Establishment closed 25 Dec & month of Jan. Amex, Diners, MasterCard, Visa, Laser, Switch. **Directions:** On the left, 5km (3 miles) from Mountrath, on R440.

Portlaoise

GUESTHOUSE

Ivyleigh House

Bank Place Church Street Portlaoise Co Laois
Tel: 057 862 2081 Fax: 057 863 343
Email: info@ivyleigh.com Web: www.ivyleigh.com

This lovely early Georgian house is set back from the road only by a tiny neatly box-hedged formal garden, but has a coachyard (with parking), outhouses and a substantial lawned garden at the back. It is a listed building and the present owners, Dinah and Jerry Campion, have restored it immaculately and furnished it beautifully in a style that successfully blends period elements with bold contemporary strokes, giving it great life. Two sitting rooms (one with television) are always available to guests and there's a fine dining room with a large communal table and a smaller one at the window for anyone who prefers to eat separately. Bedrooms are the essence of comfort, spacious, elegant, with working sash windows and everything absolutely top of the range including real linen. Large shower rooms have power showers and many excellent details, although those who would give anything for a bath to soak in will be disappointed. But it is perhaps at breakfast that this superb guesthouse is at its best. An extensive menu shows a commitment to using quality local produce that turns out to be even better than anticipated: imaginative, perfectly cooked and beautifully presented. As well as a full range of fresh juices, fruits, yogurts, cereals and porridge, speciality hot dishes include Cashel Blue cheesecakes - light and delicious, like fritters - served with mushrooms and tomatoes. And through it all Dinah Campion (who must rise at dawn to bake the bread) is charming, efficient and hospitable. This is one of Ireland's best guesthouses, and was Leinster winner of our Irish Breakfast Awards in 2002. No evening meals, but the Campions direct guests to good restaurants nearby. Not suitable for children under 8. No pets. Garden. Golf & garden visits nearby. **Rooms 6** (all shower only & no smoking). B&B €60, ss €20. Closed Christmas period. MasterCard, Visa. **Directions:** Centre of town follow signs for multi storey car park, 30 metres from carpark.

Portlaoise
RESTAURANT

Kingfisher Restaurant

Old AIB Bank Main Street Portlaoise Co Laois **Tel: 057 866 2500**
Fax: 057 866 2700 Web: www.kingfisherrestaurant.com

féile bia Situated in the centre of Portlaoise in the old AIB bank, this atmospheric and highly regarded Indian restaurant specialises in Punjabi cuisine. You enter into a very large, high-ceilinged room (the former banking hall), with a reception area off it where you are greeted by immaculately attired and genuinely friendly staff. The decor is unusual, using pale washes to portray the crumbling sandstone walls of an ancient Indian temple, including disintegrating murals with some entertainingly mischievous details. The relaxed ambience and people of all ages enjoying themselves makes for a very attractive room. Simple table presentation and enormously long menus may send out warning signals, but there are poppadums with dipping sauces to see you through the decision-making phases and, once food appears, it is clearly accomplished cooking, without recourse to elaborate presentation but well-flavoured with the fresh flavours of individual ingredients and authentic spicing creating satisfying combinations - in dishes that vary from creamy styles with almonds, to very spicy dishes with 'angry' green peppers. Tandoori, balti, biryani, 'exquisite' dishes and 'old favourite' dishes like korma, rogan josh, do piaza are all there, but they are skilfully executed, served with professionalism and charm, and reasonably priced. Reasonably priced. **Seats 75.** L Wed-Fri 12-2.30, à la carte; D daily, 5.30-11.30; Set L menus from €13 per person; set D menus from €29 pp; also à la carte. House wine €15.95. Parking (15). Closed L Sat-Tue; 25 & 26 Dec, Good Fri. Amex, MasterCard, Visa, Laser, Switch. **Directions:** Town Centre.

Portlaoise
€ RESTAURANT

The Kitchen & Foodhall

Hynds Square Portlaoise Co Laois **Tel: 057 866 2061**
Fax: 057 866 2075 Email: jimkitchen@eircom.net

féile bia Jim Tynan's excellent restaurant and food shop is definitely worth a little detour. Delicious home-made food, an open fire, relaxed atmosphere - a perfect place to break a journey or for a special visit. The food hall stocks a wide range of Irish speciality food products (and many good imported ones as well) and also sells products made on the premises: home-made terrines and breads for example (including gluten-free breads - which are also available in the restaurant) lovely home-bakes like Victoria sponges, crumbles and bread & butter pudding, and home-made chutneys and jams. You can buy home-made ready meals too and any of the extensive range of wines from the shop can be bought for the restaurant without a corkage charge. The restaurant offers a great choice of wholesome fare, including at least three vegetarian dishes each day - old favourites like nut roast, perhaps and others like feta cheese tart and broccoli roulade. Hereford premium beef is typical of the Irish produce in which such pride is taken - and self-service lunches come with a wholesome selection of vegetables or salads. It's well worth making a special visit here in the autumn, to stock up their home-made and speciality Christmas food. *The restaurant - always notable for its original art - is now officially home to 'The Tynan Gallery' , with regular art exhibitions featuring both local and national artists. **Seats 200** (also outdoor 50+). Open all day Mon-Sat, 9-5.30; L12-2.30. Value L €10.50. A la carte & Vegetarian Menu. House wine from €10.99. Wheelchair access. Closed Sun, 25 Dec-1 Jan. Amex, MasterCard, Visa, Laser. **Directions:** In the centre of Portlaoise, beside the Courthouse.

COUNTY LEITRIM

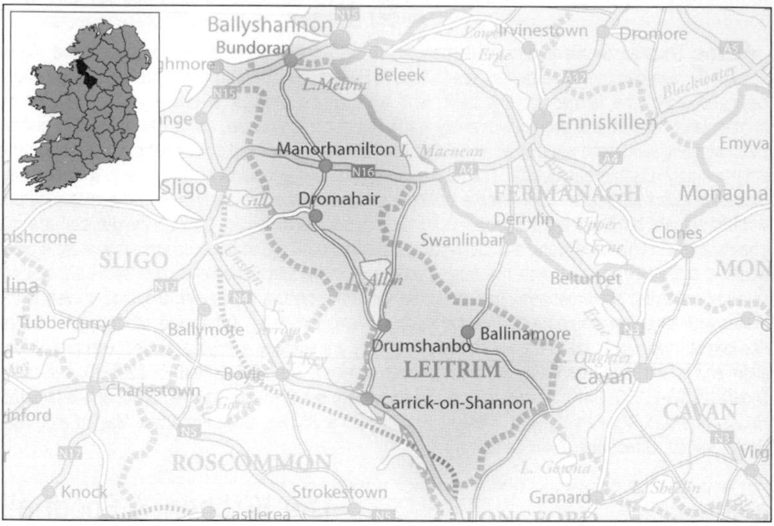

If you seek a county which best symbolises the resurgence of Ireland, you need look no further than Leitrim. In times past, it was known as the Cinderella County. Official statistics admitted that Leitrim did indeed have the poorest soil in all Ireland, in places barely a covering of low fertility. Back in the sad old days of the 1950s, the county's population had fallen to 30,000. It was doubted that it was still a viable administrative entity.

You'd be hard put to visualise those gloomy times today. Leitrim prospers. The county town, Carrick-on-Shannon, is one of Ireland's brightest and best, a bustling river port. Admittedly, there are drawbacks. The town's very first traffic lights have come into action. Formerly, there were no traffic lights in all Leitrim county. Or at least, not on the roads. The modern automated locks on the restored Shannon-Erne Waterway – whose vitality has contributed significantly to Leitrim's new prosperity – may have had their own boat traffic lights since the waterway was reopened in 1994. But it took another ten years before the roads followed suit.

Yet despite the new energy, Leitrim is rightly seen as a pleasantly away-from-it-all sort of place which has many attractions for the determined connoisseur. So with some of Ireland's better known holiday areas suffering if anything from an excess of popularity, the true trail-blazers may still be able to find the relaxation they seek in Leitrim.

But is it really so remote? Popular perceptions may be at variance with reality. For instance, Leitrim shares the shores of Lough Gill with Sligo, so much so that Yeat's legendary Lake Isle of Innisfree is within an ace of being in Leitrim rather than Sligo of Yeatsian fame. To the northward, we find that more than half of lovely Glencar, popularly perceived as being one of Sligo's finest jewels, is in fact in Leitrim. As for the notion of Leitrim being the ultimate inland and rural county - not so. Leitrim has an Atlantic coastline, albeit of only four kilometres, around Tullaghan.

It's said this administrative quirk is a throwback to the time when the all-powerful bishops of the early church aspired to have ways of travelling to Rome without having to cross the territory of neighbouring clerics. Whatever the reason, it's one of Leitrim's many surprises, which are such that it often happens that when you're touring in the area and find yourself in a beautiful bit of country, a reference to the map produces the information that, yes indeed, you're in Leitrim, a county which also provides most of the land area for Ireland's first Ecotourism 'Green Box'.

Local Attractions and Information

Ballinamore, Shannon-Erne Waterway 071 964 4855
Ballinamore, Slieve an Arain Riverbus Cruises 071 964 4079
Carrick-on-Shannon, Moonriver Cruises 071 962 1777
Carrick-on-Shannon, Tourism Information 071 962 0170
Carrick-on-Shannon, Waterways Ireland 071 965 0898

Dromahair, Parke's Cas. (restored 17c fortified hse) 071 916 4149
Drumshanbo, Sliabh an Iarainn Visitor Centre 071 964 1522
Manorhamilton, Glens Arts Centre 071 985 5833
Mohill, Lough Rynn House and Gardens 071 963 1427
Rossinver, The Organic Centre (Ecotourism) 071 985 4338

BALLINAMORE

Ballinamore is a small town beside the Shannon-Erne Waterway, and this area is a great place for a family holiday as there's lots to do. Teresa Kennedy's farm guesthouse **Glenview House** (071 9644157), for example, is attractively situated overlooking the waterway, and has a tennis court and an outdoor play area as well as an indoor games room; there's even a little agricultural museum in the outbuildings, and Teresa runs a populars a popular restaurant too. Nearby, also overlooking the canal, **Riversdale Farm Guesthouse** (071 964 4122; www.riversdaleguesthouse.biz) is another homely place to stay, also with lots to do on site - no restaurant, but there's a small leisure complex, with swimming pool and squash - and barges at the bottom of the garden, available for holidays afloat.
WWW.IRELAND-GUIDE.COM FOR THE BEST PLACES TO EAT, DRINK & STAY

CARRICK ON SHANNON

This thriving town is cosmopolitan in its outlook, with a growing range of restaurants and some fascinating shops: the Market Yard is a good browsing spot, with an interesting range of little shops and eating places around the central yard: **Vitto's** (071 96 27000) is a bright and airy Italian, casual in style and (with the execption of bought-in desserts, perhaps), serving tasty casual food; nearby, **The Larder** (071 96 50525; www.thelarder.ie) is run by Lorcan Fagan, formerly of The Oarsman Bar around the corner - this little café serves gourmet sandwiches and home made soup; deli items are the mainstay and you'll find tasty, healthy food on the go here (closed Sun). Beside the bridge, **Cryan's Bar & Restaurant** (Tel: 071-962 0409) is well known for steaks and music. For accommodation, don't overlook **Glencarne Country House** (071-966 7013) which is across the bridge on the Boyle road, with a Co Roscommon postal address, and **Caldra House** (071 962 3040; www.caldrahouse.ie), which is about 2 miles out of town off the R280. **The Dock** (071 9650828; www.thedock.ie) is Carrick's cultural centre - housed in the beautiful 19th Century former Courthouse building, overlooking the River Shannon, it has been wonderfully restored into Leitrim's first integrated centre for the arts, with a 100+ seat performance space, three art galleries, artists studios, an arts education room, it is also home to The Leitrim Design House.
WWW.IRELAND-GUIDE.COM FOR THE BEST PLACES TO EAT, DRINK & STAY

Carrick-on-Shannon

Bush Hotel

HOTEL

Carrick-on-Shannon Co Leitrim **Tel: 071 967 1000** Fax: 071 962 1180
Email: info@bushhotel.com Web: www.bushhotel.com

féile bia One of Ireland's oldest hotels, the Bush has undergone considerable refurbishment in recent years and, while rooms will vary in size and comfort, this is an hotel that has always made up in personality anything it may have lacked in contemporary style and finish; however the 40 new rooms added to the rear of the building in 2004 have brought a new and more luxurious dimension to the accommodation options in the hotel, and the older ones have now all been refurbished. A new conference room has also been added, and the hotel now offers a full range of business and conference facilities, with air conditioning, broadband, and full secretarial support among the features offered. The Orchard Ballroom has also been rebuilt, and now provides a bright and inviting venue for corporate events and other large get-togethers. Public areas, including a very pleasant restaurant and two bars, have character and a pleasing sense of history, and staff are exceptionally pleasant and helpful. The restaurant - notable for its traditional style and courteous service - has been extended and remains a popular destination for locals as well as resident guests. There is also evening bar food, and informal meals are available all day at the self-service coffee shop/carvery. The carpark at the back of the hotel has direct access to the hotel. Conference/Banqueting (120/400). Children welcome (cot available without charge). The hotel has a gift shop, tourist information point and bureau de change and can arrange car, bicycle and boat hire and supply fishing tackle and golf clubs. Golf nearby. Tennis; garden. Parking (180). **Rooms 60** (2 suites, 3 family rooms) B&B € 79.50pps, single €89. *Short breaks offered - details on application. Closed 24-31 Dec. MasterCard, Visa, Laser. **Directions:** Town centre - signed off the N4 bypass.

Carrick-on-Shannon
COUNTRY HOUSE

Hollywell Country House

Liberty Hill Cortober Carrick-on-Shannon Co Leitrim
Tel: 071 962 1124 Fax: 071 962 1124
Email: hollywell@esatbiz.com Web: www.hidden-ireland.com/hollywell

After many years as hoteliers in the town (and a family tradition of inn-keeping that goes back 200 years), Tom and Rosaleen Maher moved some years ago to this delightful period house on a rise across the bridge, with its own river frontage and beautiful views over the Shannon. It's a lovely, graciously proportioned house, with a relaxed family atmosphere. Tom and Rosaleen have an easy hospitality (not surprisingly, perhaps, as their name derives from the Gaelic "Meachar" meaning hospitable), making guests feel at home very quickly and this, as much as the comfort of the house and its tranquil surroundings, is what makes Hollywell special. Bedrooms are all individually furnished in period style, with tea and coffee making facilities, and delicious breakfasts are worth getting up in good time for: fresh juice, fruits and choice of teas, coffees and herbal teas, freshly-baked bread, home-made preserves, lovely choice of hot dishes - anything from the "full Irish" to Irish pancakes with maple syrup or grilled cheese & tomato with black olive pesto on toast. No evening meals, but Tom and Rosaleen advise guests on the best local choices and there's a comfortable guests' sitting room with an open fire to gather around on your return. A pathway through lovely gardens leads down to the river; fishing (coarse) on site. Lots to do in the area - and advice a-plenty from Tom and Rosaleen on the best places to visit. Not suitable for children under 12. Pets allowed by arrangement. **Rooms 4** (2 junior suites, 2 shower only). B&B about €60 pps, ss about €30. Closed early early Nov- early Feb. Amex, MasterCard, Visa, Laser. **Directions:** From Dublin, cross bridge on N4, keep left at Gings pub. Hollywell entrance is on left up the hill. ◇

Carrick-on-Shannon
HOTEL/RESTAURANT

The Landmark Hotel

Dublin Road Carrick-on-Shannon Co Leitrim
Tel: 071 962 2222 Fax: 071 962 2233
Email: landmarkhotel@eircom.net Web: www.thelandmarkhotel.com

féile bia This aptly named almost-riverside hotel has a dramatic lobby with a large marble and granite fountain feature, and an imposing cast iron staircase creates a certain expectation. Bedrooms, many of which have views over the Shannon, are spacious and comfortable, with individual temperature control as well as the more usual amenities (direct dial phone, TV, tea/coffee facilities, trouser press) and well-finished bathrooms. Informal daytime meals are offered in Aromas Café, and the balcony dining area previously known as Ferrari's (the reason for the name is obvious when you get there) is now more suitably used as a bar. Conference/banqueting (500/350); secretarial services; Broadband WI/FI. Cycling. Golf nearby. Off-season breaks. Children welcome (under 4 free in parents' room; cots available without charge, baby sitting arranged). No pets. Parking. **Rooms 60** (2 suites, 6 family rooms, 2 for disabled, 3 no smoking). Lift. B&B €104 pps, ss €30. **CJ's Restaurant:** The hotel's fine dining restaurant, CJ's, has really come into its own recently, earning a place with discerning locals who enjoy the setting - it is a very elegant room - the welcoming ambience, comfortable surrounds and good cooking. Menus offer a wide selection to choose from - a seafood dish of pan fried sea bream infused with lemongrass and served with chive mash, roasted cherry tomato and a ragoût of fennel, red onion & chorizo is a speciality, but the range is very wide. A meal here has lots of extra little touches, including an amuse-bouche of paté on toasted brioche before your meal, perhaps, and a complimentary liqueur afterwards, and professional service and waitressing that makes your night feel special. This not an inexpensive restaurant, but it does give good value - and diners now have the choice of moving out to the conservatory, to dine there if liked, and it can be a lovely experience on a fine summer evening. CJ's Restaurant, D 6-10 daily. SC discretionary; Aromas Café, 9-5; Bar food served daily. Hotel closed 25 Dec. Amex, MasterCard, Visa, Laser. **Directions:** On N4, 2 hours from Dublin.

Carrick-on-Shannon
PUB

The Oarsman Bar & Café

Bridge Street Carrick-on-Shannon Co Leitrim
Tel: 071 962 1733 Fax: 071 962 1734
Email: info@theoarsman.com Web: www.theoarsman.com

féile bia This attractive and characterful pub moved into a new era when Conor and Ronan Maher took it over in 2002. The brothers are sons of Tom and Rosaleen Maher (see entry for Hollywell), and clearly have what's known as "the hotelier's gene": numerous visits by the Guide at different times of day and days of the week have invariably found everything spick-and-span, very welcoming and efficiently run, even at busy times. The bar - which is very pleasantly set up in a solidly traditional style with two fires, comfortable seating arrangements for eating the excellent bar meals, and an occasional gesture towards contemporary tastes in the decor - leads off towards a sheltered patio at the back, which makes a spot for a sunny day and gives the bar an open atmosphere; just the place for one of their delicious Illy coffees with a complimentary house chocolate. Conor and Ronan's sister, Claire re-joined the team in 2006, and there are various plans afoot, mainly with a view to becoming more of a gastro-pub (ie moving away from the idea of having a dedicated restaurant, towards informal dining throughout the premises). Meanwhile, a strong kitchen team led jointly by Sheila Sharpe and James Burbridge produce consistently excellent food, offered on sassy lunchtime bar menus (warm wraps and pittas, great main course salads with homemade brown bread, enticing organic pastas - Noodle House, made locally) and exciting à la carte evening menus offered upstairs. Here you might have a great meal beginning with filo parcel of confit of duck leg & foie gras with creamed lentils & barley and apple jus, or seared scallops with celeriac purée, mango & lime salsa, followed by any one of half a dozen terrific main courses, say house speciality slow cooked belly of tom beirne's pork with sticky honey & mustard glaze, and lyonnaise potateos. And, as one of Ireland's best pastry chefs, Sheila Sharpe, is in the kitchen don't forget to save a space for a wonderful ending - such as pear & pineapple dim sum with passion fruit parfait & plum sauce. This is one of the country's pleasantest pubs and it just goes on getting better - definitely worth a detour. Free Broadband/WIFI. L & D Tue-Sat 12-3.30 and 6.45-9.45 (Opening hours are under review at the time of going to press). A la carte. House wine from €17. Not suitable for children after 9pm. Bar closed 25 Dec, Good Fri. MasterCard, Visa, Laser. **Directions:** Town centre: coming from Dublin direction, turn right just before the bridge.

Carrick-on-Shannon

RESTAURANT

Shamrat Restaurant

Bridge Street Carrick-on-Shannon Co Leitrim
Tel: 071 965 0934 Fax: 071 965 0935

This appealing Indian restaurant has earned a loyal following since it opened in 2001. Although the entrance is small from the street, first-time visitors will be surprised to find a spacious L-shaped first floor dining area and enough room for a comfortable reception area at the top of the stairs. Uncluttered contemporary decor and well-spaced tables with comfortable high-back chairs add to the sense of thoughtful design that prevails - all of which, together with attentive service from friendly and helpful staff, add to the enjoyment of interesting, authentic and well-cooked food. Menus are wide-ranging, offering a varied selection of Indian and Bangladeshi dishes; the familiar ones are all there - onion bahjee, chicken tikka or pakora, biryani dishes and perhaps a dozen tandoori specialities - but there are also less usual choices such as murgi makanwala, a special delicately spiced dish from the south-west of India: half a spring chicken is stuffed with diced lamb, egg and tomato, then covered with a thick sauce of lightly spiced yogurt and brandy, in which it is cooked. Children welcome. L&D daily; Mon-Sat: D 6-11.30; Sun, special family lunch 1-4, à la carte 4-11.30. Set L from €12.50; D €25.95, D also à la carte; Vegetarian Menu €20.95. House wine €17.50. Closed 25 Dec. Amex, MasterCard, Visa, Laser. **Directions:** Near the bridge, on right-hand side walking into town.

Carrick-on-Shannon

RESTAURANT

Victoria Hall

Quay Road Carrick-on-Shannon Co Leitrim
Tel: 071 962 0320 Fax: 071 962 0320
Email: info@victoriahall.ie Web: www.victoriahall.ie

féile bia

This stylish contemporary restaurant is in an imaginatively restored and converted, almost-waterside Victorian building beside the Rowing Club. Bright, colourful and classy, it has great appeal (chic minimalist table settings, well-spaced tables, good lighting) with a first floor dining space that is especially attractive. The menu offers a wide range of broadly Asian and European dishes, translating into meals that are well-executed and good value - and served by smart, attentive staff. * Associated accommodation is offered at **Caldra House,** quietly located 2 miles outside the town (096 23040). Children welcome. **Seats 75.** Reservations accepted. Air conditioning. Toilets wheelchair accessible. Braille menu available. Bento box L available. Open daily, 12.30-10. L, 12.30-5, D 5-10. Set D from about €25, also à la carte. Gluten free menu available. House wine from about €16. Closed 25 Dec, Good Fri. MasterCard, Visa, Laser, Switch. **Directions:** On Boathouse Quay, behind the Rowing Club.

Carrick-on-Shannon Area

PUB

Lynch's Bar/The Sheermore

Kilclare Carrick-on-Shannon Co Leitrim **Tel: 071 964 1029**

Well away from the bustle of nearby Carrick-on-Shannon, Padraig and Christina Lynch's friendly traditional bar, grocery and hardware shop on the Shannon-Erne Waterway is known from the road as "The Sheermore" - but presents its much more attractive side to the water. You can sit outside at the back in fine weather and watch the boats going by, or choose between a conservatory overlooking the bridge or a move right into the bar if the weather dictates. This isn't really a food place, but Christina Lynch makes home-made soup every day and cuts sandwiches freshly to order - which can be just the right thing, in the right place. Children welcome. Pets allowed in some areas. Bar food available 12.30-9.30 daily. Wheelchair accessible. Closed 25 Dec, Good Fri. MasterCard, Visa, Laser. **Directions:** 6 miles from Carrick-on-Shannon towards Ballinamore, on the Shannon-Erne Waterway.

Drumshanbo
HOTEL

Ramada Lough Allen Hotel & Spa

Drumshanbo Co Leitrim **Tel: 071 964 0044** Fax: 071 964 0101
Email: info@loughallenhotel.com Web: www.loughallenhotel.com

Although it is not especially impressive from the outside, the interior of this bright and interesting contemporary hotel begins to win you over from the moment you step into the foyer - an attractive area with appealing modern sofas and armchairs grouped along the fireplace wall and a collection of striking modern paintings high up over the long reception desk. Glazed doors at the far end allow a tantalising glimpse into a high-ceilinged bar which features more contemporary artworks; an interesting room, which demands an initial prowl - it does well to distract the arriving guest from the clear lake view seen through what is pretty much a wall of glass, with a deck and trendy little tables an chairs outside for fine weather. But there is also an open fire in the bar, a reminder that this, the area's first destination hotel, has no intention of closing shop when "the season" ends; what a fine place for a winter trip, when the turf-brown lough is whipped up in creamy heads and, after long walks or a cycle to explore this little-known area, you can return to the warmth of the fire, or perhaps spend some time in the pool or spa before dinner... Rushes Restaurant (which, oddly, does not overlook the lough) offers pleasing food with appeal to local diners as well as residents, and pleasing meals are also served in the bar. Accommodation - in spacious and very comfortable rooms, furnished in an understated, disciplined modern style that allows views of the lough (or Sliabh an Iiarann mountain) to take pride of place - includes some suites and family rooms, and also self-catering apartments. Conference/banqueting (220/160). Leisure centre (lakeview swimming pool, hot tub, gym), spa. Children welcome (under 2s free in parents' room, cot available without charge, baby sitting arranged). Garden, walking, cycling, equestrian. No pets. **Rooms 64** (5 junior suites, some family rooms, 4 shower only, 4 for disabled, all no smoking). Lift. 24 hr room service. B&B about €83, ss about €23. Amex, Diners, MasterCard, Visa, Laser. **Directions:** 15 km from Carrick-on-Shannon, on Drumshanbo-Sligo road. ◇

Jamestown
RESTAURANT

Al Mezza

Jamestown Carrick on Shannon Co Leitrim
Tel: 071 962 5050 Email: almezza@hotmail.com

This colourful little Lebanese/Mediterranean restaurant on the edge of the pretty village of Jamestown is run by proprietor-chef Milad Serhan and Dorothy Serhan, who is front of house. It's an unusual little place for a country area, with friendly service as well as good food. For those arriving in Jamestown by boat, it's about half a mile from the quay, but it's a pleasant walk through the village - pavement all the way and past two particularly enticing pubs for a visit in each direction, perhaps. Milad's authentic middle eastern menus are quite extensive and it is a good idea, especially on a first visit, to order one of the mezza selections (some of them vegetarian) either as a shared starter, or for a whole meal - this sociable dining style saves a lot of anxious trawling through the menu. Reservations are not essential, but this is an understandably popular little restaurant and it can be very busy, especially at weekends. Children welcome until 8.30. **Seats 30** (private room, 20, outdoor +8). Open Wed-Sun 6-10 (to 9.30 Sun). House wine from €16. Closed Tue. Closed Christmas and New Year. MasterCard, Visa, Laser. **Directions:** On right just before entering Jamestown village.

Keshcarrigan
RESTAURANT/GUESTHOUSE

Canal View House & Restaurant

Keshcarrigan Carrick on Shannon Co Leitrim
Tel: 071 964 2404

Michael and Cathy Flaherty have run the restaurant here for some years and it has both a local following and particular appeal for boating guests who may use the private mooring facilities overnight when dining here. Michael offers traditional cooking in a mainly classical style with some international influences - and many house specialities feature on menus that could include home-made pâté with Cumberland sauce, steaks various ways, poached salmon in filo and a good choice of vegetarian dishes vegetable fettucini, perhaps, or a spicy vegetable stir-fry. There might be game in season - venison & mushroom pie is a speciality. There's a very hospitable atmosphere here,and people feel very comfortable. Children welcome. Seats 45. Air conditioning. Reservations accepted but not necessary. D daily, 6-9.30; L Sun 12-3 (possibly also other days in summer - phone to inquire); Set Sun L €25; Set D €40, also à la carte. House wine €16; sc discretionary. Wheelchair accessible. Open all year except Christmas. **Accommodation:** Six comfortably furnished rooms, with direct-dial telephones and neat en-suite shower rooms are available for guests, also a comfortable residents' lounge (with views of the cruisers passing). Peace and quiet are an attraction here, but television is available in bedrooms on request. Families are welcome and well looked after. **Rooms 6.** B&B about €35 pps, ss about €5. Open all year. Visa, Laser. **Directions:** R209 from Carrick-on-Shannon.

Kinlough

B&B/RESTAURANT

The Courthouse Restaurant

Main Street Kinlough Co Leitrim
Tel: 071 984 2391 Fax: 071 984 2824
Email: thecourthouserest@eircom.net Web: www.thecourthouserest.com

In the old courthouse of the attractive village of Kinlough, Piero Melis's little restaurant is a welcoming place and offers good contemporary cooking in the Mediterranean style with some more down to earth local influences - especially at lunchtime. A wide ranging menu includes specialities like the perennially popular Linguini di Mare, flat spaghetti with clams and crab in a spicy tomato and garlic sauce. and there are always daily specials; other house specialities include starters like seafood risotto (with smoked salmon, smoked tuna & prawns, perhaps) and pasta dishes, which may include homemade lobster ravioli and a wide range of main course specialities includes Thornhill duck with spinach & wild mushroom sauce, amongst many more traditional Mediterranean dishes. Traditional desserts can be selected from a choice of good home made ice-creams and cakes - everything is freshly made on the premises. Good food and the service from professional and helpful staff all encourage return visits. Not suitable for children after 8 pm. **Seats 40** (private room 12). D Wed-Mon, 6.30-9.30, Sun L only 12.30-2.30. D à la carte; Set Sun L €21.50. House wines from €16.50; sc discretionary except 10% on parties of 6+. Closed - Tue, 2 weeks after Feb 14, Christmas. **Accommodation:** Neat, freshly decorated bedrooms offer comfortable accommodation at a very reasonable price. **Rooms 4** (all shower only, 1 family room, all no smoking). B&B €40 pps, ss €10. MasterCard, Visa, Laser. **Directions:** Off main Donegal-Sligo road (N15), 5 km towards Sligo from Bundoran. Take turning directly opposite Tullaghan House.

Leitrim

BAR/RESTAURANT

The Barge Steakhouse

Leitrim Village Carrick-on-Shannon Co Leitrim
Tel: 071 962 0807 Fax: 071 962 2957

This inviting stone building on the main street has been extensively renovated and gradually developed under the current ownership of John and Rose Pierce. It began with the characterful bar, which they opened in 2001, and has since developed to include a spacious restaurant and conservatory - and, more recently, a beer garden at the back, which is very popular for barbecues when weather permits and, like everything else in this immaculate maintained establishment, kept scrupulously clean and tidy. Head chef Martin Purdue provides a daytime bar menu as well as an à la carte for the restaurant; while there's the occasional nod to fashion, the style is quite traditional - typical starters include garlic mushrooms, prawn cocktail and egg mayonnaise and, as the name implies, steaks are the speciality of the house, served with all the traditional trimmings: mushrooms, onions, salad, fries and pepper sauce or herb butter. Crispy duckling is another speciality, and there are always several fish dishes and at least one for vegetarians; there may sometimes be really traditional dishes like beef & Guinness casserole or bacon & cabbage too. Although not a gourmet destination, pleasing surroundings, freshly prepared food and good value should ensure an enjoyable visit. There's a little children's menu too, and a short list of popular wines. *Marquee available for private functions. Not suitable for children after 9pm. Toilets wheelchair accessible. **Seats 90** (32 in conservatory; private room 21). Open 12.30-9.30 daily, L 12.30-6, D 6-9.30 (Sun to 9). A la carte. House wines from €14.50. Closed 25 Dec & Good Fri. MasterCard, Visa, Laser. **Directions:** In Leitrim village: take Drumshambo road out of Carrick-on-Shannon.

Mohill

Lough Rynn Castle Hotel & Estate

HOTEL/CASTLE/HISTORIC HOUSE

Lough Rynn Mohill Co Leitrim
Tel: 071 963 2700 Fax: 071 963 2710
Email: slong@hbl.ie Web: www.loughrynn.ie

Set amongst 300 acres of rolling countryside, historic Lough Rynn Castle has recently seen major investment and a great deal of TLC restore it to its former glory for its new use as an hotel. Aside from structural restoration, original furnishings were located and refurbished before being reinstated in their original home, and many other luxurious items, including hand painted silk wallpaper from Paris, were carefully sourced to complement the property. Approached via a winding wooded road and now entered through an impressive manned black and gold wrought iron gate - there are opulently appointed lounges, drawing rooms and a library that are remarkably private and intimate for public rooms in an hotel and have views out over the lawns and lake: a peaceful and comfortable place to read, or to take afternoon tea. Bedrooms - ten at present - include luxurious castle rooms offering unique accommodation, with wonderful views of the estate and surrounding countryside. The aim is to make Lough Rynn a perfect country haven, and no expense or effort has been spared; there is over a square mile of lake, with a marina, and the gardens -which are also of significant historical interest - are under restoration too, together with the nature trails and lakeside walks. A leisure centre and spa, and the Nick Faldo designed golf course, are to follow in 2007 and 2008 respectively, but there is plenty to keep visitors occupied here already, including walking, fishing and horse riding. The hotel is managed by Adrian Harkins, formerly Assistant Manager at Adare Manor, and he has set out to achieve similar status at Lough Rynn. Banqueting (75). Fishing, walking, garden; equestrian nearby. Children welcome. **Rooms 58** (including suites and standard & deluxe lake view rooms); B&B (*introductory rate) from about €100 pps. ◇

Rooskey

Shannon Key West Hotel

HOTEL

The Waters Edge Rooskey Co Leitrim
Tel: 071 963 8800 Fax: 071 963 8811
Email: info@shannonkeywest.com Web: www.shannonkeywest.com

This well-run riverside hotel on the Leitrim/Roscommon border brings valuable facilities to the area and is open all year (except Christmas), making it a particularly good venue for off-season short breaks, meetings and conferences. Comfortably furnished bedrooms have all the usual amenities - direct dial phones, TV with video channel, tea & coffee-making facilities and trouser press; two rooms also have fax machines and there is a safe available on request. A planned extension will add 25 new bedrooms, including a bridal suite, with expected completion sometime in 2007. On-site amenities include a gym, jacuzzi, solarium and steam room (but no swimming pool) and there is plenty to do and see in the area. Reliable bar food also makes this a useful place to bear in mind for breaking a journey. Conference/banqueting (500/360), broadband, secretarial services available; Fitness room, tennis, walking. Children welcome (cots available without charge, baby sitting arranged). **Rooms 40** (17 shower only, 5 family rooms, 15 no smoking, 13 ground floor, 1 for disabled). B&B €75 pps, no ss. Amex, MasterCard, Visa, Laser. **Directions:** On N4, main Dublin-Sligo route, midway between Longford and Carrick-on-Shannon.

COUNTY LIMERICK

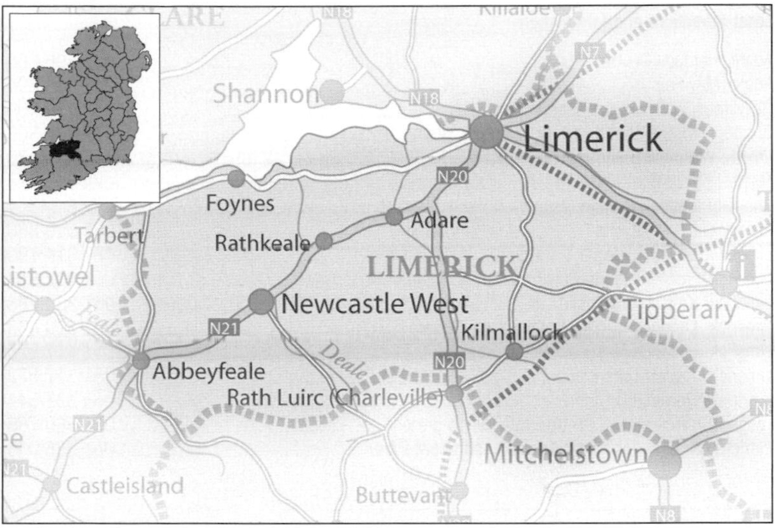

The story of Limerick city and county is in many ways the story of the Shannon Estuary, for in times past it was the convenient access provided by Ireland's largest estuary - it is 80 kilometres in length - which encouraged the development of life along the estuary's sea shores, and into the fresh water of the River Shannon itself.

Today, the area's national and global transport is served by air, sea and land through Shannon International Airport, the increased use of the Estuary through the development of Foynes Port and other deepwater facilities, and a rapidly improving but inevitably busy road network.

In Limerick city in recent years, the opening of improved waterway links through the heart of town has seen the welcome regeneration of older urban areas continuing in tandem with the attractive new developments. But significant and all as this is, there's much more to the totality of Limerick county than the city and its waterways.

Inland from the river, the very richness of the countryside soon begins to develop its own dynamic. Eastern Limerick verges into Tipperary's Golden Vale, and the eastern county's Slieve Felim hills, rising to Cullaun at 462 m, reflect the nearby style of Tipperary's Silvermine Mountains.

Southwest of Limerick city, the splendid hunting country and utterly rural atmosphere of the area around the beautiful village of Adare makes it a real effort of imagination to visualise the muddy salt waters of the Shannon Estuary just a few miles away down the meandering River Maigue, yet the Estuary is there nevertheless. Equally, although the former flying boat port of Foynes and the nearby jetty at Aughinish may be expanding to accommodate the most modern large ships, just a few miles inland we find ourselves in areas totally remote from the sea in countryside which lent itself so well to mixed farming that the price of pigs in Dromcolliher (a.k.a. Drumcolligher) on the edge of the Mullaghareirk Mountains reputedly used to set the price of pigs throughout Ireland.

The growth of the computer industry in concert with the development of the remarkably vibrant University have given Limerick a completely new place in Irish life, and the city's energy and urban renewal makes it an entertaining place to visit, while the eclectic collection on stunning display in the unique Hunt Museum in its handsome waterside setting has a style which other areas of Limerick life are keen to match.

With newfound confidence, Limerick has been paying greater attention to its remarkable heritage of Georgian architecture, with Limerick Civic Trust restoring the Georgian house and garden at 2 Pery Square. It acts as the focal point for an area of classic urban architecture which deserves to be better known.

That said, Limerick still keeps its feet firmly on the ground, and connoisseurs are firmly of the opinion that the best pint of Guinness in all Ireland is to be had in this no-nonsense city, where they insist on being able to choose the temperature of their drink, and refuse to have any truck with modern fads which would attempt to chill the rich multi-flavoured black pint into a state of near-freezing tastelessness aimed at immature palates.

Local Attractions and Information

Adare, Heritage Centre	061 396 666
Adare, May Fair	061 396 894
Ballysteen, Ballynacourty Gardens	061 396 409
Bruree, Heritage Centre and de Valera Museum	063 91300
Croom, Waterwheel and Heritage Centre	061 397130
Foynes, Flying Boat Museum	069 65416
Glin, Glin Castle Pleasure Grounds & Walled Garden	068 34364
Limerick, Belltable Arts Centre, 69 O'Connell St	061 319 866
Limerick, Georgian House & Garden, 2 Pery Square	061 314 130
Limerick, Hunt Museum, Customs House, Rutland St	061 312 833
Limerick, King John's Castle	061 360 788
Limerick, Limerick City Art Gallery, Pery Square	061 310 633
Limerick, Limerick Museum, John's Square	061 417 826
Limerick, Tourism Information	061 317 522
Limerick, University of Limerick	061 333 644
Lough Gur, Interpretive centre, 3000BC to present	061 360 788
Patrickswell Limerick Racecourse (Greenmount Park)	061 355 055

LIMERICK

Of great historical and strategic importance, Ireland's fourth city is also renowned for its rich cultural tradition, with many excellent museums, galleries and theatres to visit - and Ireland's first purpose-built concert hall. The city also offers a wide range of accommodation, restaurants and pubs, many of them in attractive waterside locations. The famous old restaurant & bar **Moll Darby's** (Tel 061 411522; www.mhm.ie), is on George's Quay, for example, and the wholesome good food served there is pleasing many a visitor these days. Just along the quay (and easily recognised by its bright red awning) the **River Bar & Restaurant** (061 401 883) offers informal dining with a French accent -and across the bridge, you'll find an agreeable modern café/restaurant, **DuCartes** (061 312662, on the river side of the Hunt Museum. Just across the road, the funky **Green Onion** (061 400 710) is a long-established and somewhat theatrical café-restaurant, serving inexpensive informal meals. For good, inexpensive accommodation try the reliable **Jurys Inn** (061 207000; www.jurysdoyle.com), on Lower Mallow Street; this no-frills hotel is comfortable and gives a lot for a little - some rooms even have views across the Shannon.
WWW.IRELAND-GUIDE.COM FOR THE BEST PLACES TO EAT, DRINK & STAY

Limerick
BAR/RESTAURANT

Aubars Bar & Restaurant

49-50 Thomas Street Limerick Co Limerick
Tel: 061 317799 Fax: 061 317572
Email: linda@aubars.com Web: www.aubars.com

Padraic Frawley's modern city centre bar and restaurant typifies the renewal of Limerick itself - a university city with a youthful population and, it is said, with more cafés, pubs and restaurants than any other in Ireland. Padraic, a hotel management graduate who trained at the highly respected catering college nearby in Shannon, returned to his home city at the grand old age of 27 bursting with ideas collected during experience abroad and proceeded to transform an old pub into this dashing contemporary bar and restaurant. The layout is on several levels with no hard divisions and a mixture of seating in various areas, which can lead to confusion between customers coming in to eat rather than have a drink, although watchful staff soon have new arrivals sorted. While the style is uncompromisingly modern, down to the designer crockery, chef Mike Ryan's values are quite traditional and sound cooking is inspired by the admirable Gary Rhodes' style: 'dishes that are simple to make, tasty and look great'. Appealing, well-balanced menus change frequently and offer a number of different options for bar food (AuBars) and more structured meals in the casual value dining café/bar (The Grill @ Aubars); rib eye steak with béarnaise sauce, rocket salad & chunky chips is a sound specialty - presentation is stylish but there is a welcome down-to-earth feeling about the food here, and you'll find upbeat versions of traditional dishes like bacon & cabbage too; vegetarians are well looked after, with appealing dishes marked clearly on menus and, all round, a visit here should be an enjoyable experience - and, with main courses all under €15, good value too. **Seats 45.** Reservations required for restaurant. Open from 8 am; all day brunch menu. L 12-5.30 daily (Sun from 11). Set L €15 (12-

3); D Tue-Sat 5.30-9.30; early D €19 (5.30-7.30); Set D €30. A la carte L & D also offered. House wines €18.95. SC discretionary. Bar meals: 12-8.30 daily. Restaurant closed D Sun & Mon. Establishment closed 25 Dec & Good Fri. Amex, MasterCard, Visa, Laser. **Directions:** Off O'Connell Street, second on the left, opposite Brown Thomas.

Limerick

Brûlées Restaurant

Ⓔ RESTAURANT

Corner of Henry St & Mallow St Limerick Co Limerick
Tel: 061 319 931 Email: brulees@eircom.net

féile bia Donal and Teresa Cooper's restaurant is on a busy corner, with window tables catching a glimpse of the River Shannon and County Clare across the bridge. The interior is well-appointed, with little dining areas on several levels that break groups up nicely, and are elegantly furnished in a simple classic style that makes the most of limited space. For some years this has been the first choice in the city, for discerning local diners and visitors alike. A soothing ambience and nice details - real linen napkins, olives and freshly baked breads to nibble - make a good start while you read appealing menus which show pride in using the finest of ingredients, both local and imported in imaginative, colourful modern Irish cooking, which is as good as it sounds - a speciality starter of pan-fried goats cheese & pancetta parcels with mixed leaves and pecan oil makes a good beginning, or a vegetarian dish like a tartlet of cherry tomato, buffalo mozzarella, pine nut & basil drizzled with truffle oil might be a tempting option. Main courses offer a balanced combination of ingredients in sound modern Irish cooking, such as a speciality dish of pan-fried escalope of pork in a herb crumb, with caramelised apples, baby spinach and a mustard & caper fruit sauce. Menus are consistently appealing - vegetarian dishes are invariably imaginative, also fish and seafood, which will always include daily specials, which Donal describes to guests very accurately, with prices - Donal's hospitality and thoughtful, professional service are an important part of the experience here. Teresa's cooking is accurate, the presentation attractive without being fussy and, with main courses averaging around €24, this is good value for the high quality of food served. Side dishes are simple, there's a good cheese selection - and puddings always include, of course, a classic crème brûlée, served with a crunchy brandysnap. Lunch menus offer especially good value. Interesting, fairly priced wine list. **Seats 30.** L 12.30-2.15 (Thu-Fri only); D 5-9.15. Early Bird D €30 (5-7), also à la carte. House wine €20; SC discretionary (12.5% on groups of 6+). Closed Sun, Mon; 25 Dec-1 Jan. Amex, Diners, MasterCard, Visa, Laser. **Directions:** On the corner of Henry Street and Lower Mallow Street, near Jurys Inn roundabout. ◇

Limerick

Castletroy Park Hotel

HOTEL

Dublin Road Limerick Co Limerick **Tel: 061 335 566** Fax: 061 331 117
Email: sales@castletroy-park.ie Web: www.castletroy-park.ie

féile bia This blocky redbrick hotel is not especially architecturally pleasing, but it has mellowed a little with time - and the surroundings gardens are maturing well and (like the rest of the hotel) always immaculately well-maintained. Generous car parking is kept at a discreet distance from the building and the walkway, through trellises clothed in honeysuckle and vines (and past a window that affords a glimpse into the recently refurbished leisure suite and deck level pool), creates a good impression, immediately reinforced by a warm and welcoming atmosphere in the large foyer. Staff are welcoming and helpful and, while not individually decorated, spacious bedrooms are regularly refurbished and thoughtfully furnished with special attention to the needs of the business traveller (good desk space, second phone, fax and computer points). The hotel is much sought after as a conference venue and, after work, excellent leisure facilities (which include a 1 km jogging track) and The Merry Pedlar pub offer a change of scene. Conferences / Banqueting (450-260). Video conferencing. Leisure/fitness centre, swimming pool; beauty salon - Celia Larkin 'Beauty at Blue Door'. Children welcome (under 6 free in parents room, cot available without charge, baby sitting arranged). Conservatory. Garden. **Rooms 107** (7 suites, 5 junior suites, 11 executive, 2 shower only, 1 disabled, 72 no-smoking). Lift. 24 hour room service. Turndown service. B&B from €85 PPS, ss €55. No SC. Hotel closed 24-26 Dec. **McLaughlins Restaurant:** The hotel's fine dining restaurant is an airy room with an attractive outlook (making it more appealing at breakfast time) and provides an impressive and comfortable setting for international cuisine. In addition to the table d'hôte menus, a wide-ranging à la carte ensures that guests staying in the hotel for several days have plenty of choice. Specialities include a starter platter of duck confit, foie gras and rillette - and, among the main courses, there will always be old favourites like chargrilled fillet of Irish beef with foie gras ravioli, spinach and wild mushroom sauce. An informative wine list offers a fair selection of half bottles. **Seats 70.** Air conditioning. L Sun only 12.30-5.30, D daily 6-10. Early D €35, 5.30-7; Gourmet D €100 pp inc wine; D also à la carte. Pianist Fri/Sat night. Amex, Diners, MasterCard, Visa, Laser. **Directions:** Dublin road, directly opposite the University of Limerick.

Limerick
HOTEL

Clarion Hotel Limerick

Steamboat Quay Limerick Co Limerick
Tel: 061 444 100 Fax: 061 444 101
Email: info@clarionhotellimerick.com Web: www.clarionhotelsireland.com

This dramatic cigar-shaped 17-storey hotel right on the River Shannon waterfront in the centre of Limerick enjoys panoramic views over the city and the Shannon region. Like other recently built sister hotels, clean-lined contemporary elegance is the theme throughout and there is a semi-open plan arrangement of foyer, bars and dining spaces, which take full advantage of the location. Business facilities are excellent and bedrooms - which vary more than usual in hotels due to the unusual shape of the building - are offered in several pleasingly simple, modern colour schemes (although a high-silled window design means you must stand to enjoy the view). All rooms have striking maple furniture, air conditioning, and everything that makes an hotel room the perfect retreat, including many nice little extras, and the top two floors have suites and penthouses available for long lets. Residents have unlimited use of leisure facilities - there is a health and fitness club on the first floor - and several decked balconies and terraces at different levels encourage guests to take full advantage of fine weather. Apart from the Malaysian/Thai all-day menu offered in the hotel's Kudos Bar, all meals are served in the well-appointed Sinergie Restaurant, a very attractive contemporary room with river views. Menus are lively and generally well-executed; at its best, a meal here can be a most enjoyable experience. Although this landmark building is easily located, gaining access to the hotel can be tricky for those unfamiliar with the city's one-way system; a nearby car park is used by the hotel and it is advisable to get clear instructions before arrival. (There is a moderate charge for parking.) Conference/banqueting (180/150). Secretarial services. Golf nearby. Video-conferencing. Leisure centre; swimming pool. **Rooms 158.** (3 suites, 80 no smoking, 6 disabled, 5 family rooms). Lift. Room service, limited hours. Children welcome (under 12 free in parents' room; cot available without charge). B&B €110pps, ss €110. **Sinergie Restaurant:** L Sun-Fri,12.30-2.30; D daily, 7-9.45; (closed L Sat). Set Sun L €25; Set D €25; also à la carte. Kudos Bar serves Asian food, 12-9 daily. Short breaks (inc golfing breaks) offered; details on application. Closed 24-26 Dec Amex, Diners, MasterCard, Visa, Laser, Switch. **Directions:** Take Dock Road exit off the Shannon Bridge Roundabout, then first right.

Limerick
RESTAURANT

Copper & Spice

2 Cornmarket Row Limerick Co Limerick
Tel: 061 313 620 Fax: 061 313 922
Email: brian@copperandspice.com Web: www.copperandspice.com

Well situated near the recently restored Milk Market buildings, this attractively named restaurant is bright orange and would be hard to miss. You have to ring a bell to get in, so you are assured of immediate attention from agreeable staff (all decked out in black, still in Indian Kurta Pajama style), who show arriving guests directly to tables. Indian background music creates atmosphere and the orange theme is continued in stylish modern (distinctly Indian) decor and on promptly presented, clearly laid out menus, which offer an unusual combination of Indian and Thai cuisine. Each dish on the menu is explained and dishes suitable for vegetarians - and also wheat-free dishes - indicated. There is a stronger leaning towards authentic Indian food, than the Thai dishes offered; mango chutney, lime pickle and minted yoghurt are provided on tables and food is presented on steel plates as you would find if ordering a thali in India. Some combination platters are offered, and also some less usual dishes - an Indian starter of paneer rolls, for example, is made of home-made Indian cheese mixed with potatoes, bread-crumbed and fried, while pudina chicken is flavoured with mint and coriander. Saag meat - which one might expect to be beef, but here it is lamb - comes with a tasty, sharply flavoured spinach sauce and an unusual type of naan bread, rather thin to mop up juices. This stylish restaurant offers a different experience from other ethnic restaurants in the city, and gives value for money. It would be a particularly good choice for anyone with a preference for a meat-free meal as the range of vegetarian dishes offered is wide - and the dessert menu contains many homemade ethnic Asian desserts, a nice touch at the end of your meal. A fairly priced wine list offers a balanced selection of world wines, and a good choice of Asian beers. *A sister restaurant is located just off the main Limerick-Dublin road above the Mill Bar in Annacotty Village. It is in a restored mill overlooking the Mulcair River (Tel. 061 338791). Children welcome; toilets wheelchair accessible. **Seats 75;** air conditioning; D daily, 5-10.30. (L Sun, Annacotty branch only, 12.30-4.30). Value D inc. drink €24.50 (5-7); house wine €18.50; sc 10% on groups 10+. Closed Mon (except Bank Hols), 24-25 Dec, 1 Jan, Good Fri. Amex, MasterCard, Visa, Laser. **Directions:** Near Milk Market buildings.

Limerick
HOTEL

Lynch South Court Hotel

Raheen Roundabout Adare Road Limerick Co Limerick
Tel: 061 487 487 Fax: 061 487 499
Email: southcourt@lynchotels.com Web: www.lynchotels.com

féile bia Ideally located for Shannon Airport and the Raheen Industrial Estate, the South Court Hotel presents a somewhat daunting exterior, but once inside visitors soon discover that it caters especially well for business guests, both on and off-duty. In addition to excellent conference and meeting facilities, comfortable bedrooms are impressively spacious and well equipped, with generous desk areas and the latest technology, including fax/computer points, in every room. Executive bedrooms have a separate work area providing a 'mini-office' - and 'lifestyle suites' have an in-room gym, designed by Irish designer Paul Costelloe. Leisure facilities include the 'Polo Lifestyle Club', designed with international rugby player (and local hero) Keith Wood and, continuing the hotel's policy of working with internationally recognised specialists in their field, Paul Costelloe was again involved in a new design, this time of a stylish café bar, The Cream Room, which quickly became a popular meeting place for coffee or speciality sandwiches. Bar lunches are available every day and the 100-seater Boru's Bistro is open for dinner every evening. Conference/banqueting (1250/1000); business centre; video conferencing. Gym, sauna, solarium. Hairdressing. Shop. Children welcome (under 2s free in parents' room, cot available without charge, baby sitting arranged). No Pets. **Rooms 127** (1 suite, 15 junior suites, 55 executive, 14 no-smoking). Lift. 24 hour room service. B&B €79 pps, ss €26; room-only rate also available, €135 (max 3 guests). Amex, Diners, MasterCard, Visa, Laser. **Directions:** Located onthe main N20 Cork/Killarney road, 20 minutes from Shannon Airport. ◇

Limerick
HOTEL

Radisson SAS Hotel Limerick

Ennis Road Limerick Co Limerick **Tel: 061 456 200** Fax: 061 327 418
Email: sales.limerick@radissonsas.com Web: www.radissonsas.com

féile bia This low rise hotel is set well back from the road in its own grounds and, although just a short drive from the city centre, enjoys an almost rural setting and views of the Clare Mountains. The original building dates back to the 1970s but was completely revamped recently, when taken over by Radisson SAS, and re-opened with an elegant new interior. The size and layout of the building suits the Radisson style well - public areas, notably the large open-plan foyer/lounge, have a great a great sense of space and style, with seating groups arranged around glass-topped tables on marbled floors softened by specially commissioned rugs and a few dramatic pieces of art. Accommodation is also notable for its spaciousness: all rooms are styled deluxe, with the comfort and amenities that implies (air conditioning, TV with video, broadband/ISDN line, personal safe, bathroom with full bath and shower) but, for people who like a bit of room around them, the sense of space is the main attraction of this hotel over its city centre rivals. Fine conference and business facilities have ample free parking. Conference/banqueting (500/336); business centre. Leisure centre (indoor swimming pool, steam room, sauna, fitness room, treatment rooms). Tennis courts. Children welcome (cots available without charge; baby sitting arranged). Children's adventure playground. Gardens. Parking. Helipad. **Rooms 154** (2 suites, 4 junior suites, 14 executive, 3 disabled, 116 no smoking). Lift. 24 hour room service. Turndown service. B&B €72.50 PPS, ss €52.50. * Short breaks offered - details on application. **Porters Restaurant:** L 12.30-2.30 daily (to 3 Sun), D 5.45-9 daily. A la carte. Bar food also available daily, 2-8.30. Amex, MasterCard, Visa, Laser. **Directions:** On N18, 5 km from Limerick city centre, 20 minutes from Shannon.

ADARE

The chocolate-box village of Adare is not only an interesting and well-located destination in it s own right, but also an excellent place to break a long journey. Useful places to know about in the pretty row of cottages along the main street include **The Inn Between** (061 396633), an informal restaurant belonging to The Dunraven Arms across the road, is a good choice but only open in summer, while **Lloyds of Adare** (061 395796) is a restaurant, coffee shop, deli and wine bar that is open for long hours everyday - and all year except Christmas. **Fitzgeralds Woodlands House Hotel** (Tel 061 605100; www.woodland-hotel.ie) is a little way out of the village on the Limerick side; especially popular for weddings and large gatherings, they offer special breaks and have excellent leisure/health facilities including a wide range of therapies and treatments.

WWW.IRELAND-GUIDE.COM FOR THE BEST PLACES TO EAT, DRINK & STAY

Adare

HOTEL/RESTAURANT

Adare Manor Hotel & Golf Resort

Adare Co Limerick

Tel: 061 396 566 Fax: 061 396 124

Email: reservations@adaremanor.com Web: www.adaremanor.com

The former home of the Earls of Dunraven, this magnificent neo-Gothic mansion is set in 900 acres on the banks of the River Maigue. Its splendid chandelier drawing room and the glazed cloister of the dining room look over formal box-hedged gardens towards the Robert Trent Jones golf course. Other grand public areas include the Gallery, named after the Palace of Versailles, with its unique 15th century choir stalls and fine stained glass windows. Luxurious bedrooms (21 of them recently refurbished) have individual hand carved fireplaces, fine locally-made mahogany furniture, cut-glass table lamps and impressive marble bathrooms with powerful showers over huge bathtubs. Quite recent additions include a new clubhouse in the grounds (complete with full conference facilities) and a "golf village" of two and four bedroom townhouses which provides a comfortable accommodation option for longer stays, large groups and families. In 2006 this concept was developed further with the introduction of the Villas, 46 deluxe serviced residences sleeping up to eight guests. Conference/banqueting (220/150). Leisure centre, swimming pool, spa treatments; beauty salon; hairdressing. Shop. Golf (18), equestrian; fishing; walking; cycling. Garden. Children welcome (cots available without charge, baby sitting arranged). No pets. **Rooms 63** (1 state room, 5 suites, 8 junior suites, 15 ground floor rooms); also townhouses, carriage house & villas (total 246). Lift. 24 hour room service. Room rate from €434. No SC. Open all year. **Restaurant:** The beautifully appointed Oak Room Restaurant provides a fine setting for Mark Donohue's modern classical cuisine, which is cooking based on seasonal produce, including vegetables from the estate's own gardens. Local ingredients feature - roast fillet of local beef with horseradish mash and onion sauce is a popular example, and a newer dish attracting praise is medallions of rabbit saddle and bacon with black pudding & whole grain mustard sauce; vegetarian dishes such as spinach and blue cheese lasagne with roast baby beetroot and sweet potato wedges are offered on the main menu. An 8-course Tasting Menu has also been recently introduced, featuring favourites from the a la carte and some surprises. A predictably high end wine list includes some unusual wines (a Pomerol Pétrus 1970, at €4,450, for example) but there's a sprinkling of affordable bottles, and quite a few by the glass and half bottle. **Seats 60** D (6.30-9.30) daily; Set D €58.50; 8-course Tasting Menu €70.house wine from €25; SC discretionary. *More informal bistro style dining is offered all day at the Carriage House Restaurant, daily, 7am -10 pm (to 9.30 off season). Open all year. Amex, Diners, MasterCard, Visa, Laser. **Directions:** On N21 in Limerick.

Adare

GUESTHOUSE

Carrabawn Guesthouse

Killarney Road Adare Co Limerick **Tel: 061 396067**

Email: bridget@carrabawnhouseadare.com Web: www.carrabawnhouseadare.com

In an area known for high standards, with prices to match, this immaculate owner-run establishment set in large mature gardens provides a moderately-priced alternative to the luxury accommodation nearby. Bedrooms are very well maintained with all the amenities required and Bernard and Bridget Lohan have been welcoming guests here since 1984 - many of them return on an annual basis because of the high level of comfort and friendly service provided. A good Irish breakfast is served in a conservatory dining room overlooking lovely gardens, and light evening meals can be provided by arrangement. Children welcome (cot available without charge). No pets. **Rooms 8** (all shower only & no smoking, 2 family rooms, 3 ground floor). Room service (limited hours). B&B €50 PPS, ss €20. Open all year except Christmas. MasterCard, Visa, Laser. **Directions:** On N21, 11km (8 m) south of Limerick.

Adare

HOTEL/RESTAURANT

Dunraven Arms Hotel

Adare Co Limerick

Tel: 061 396 633 Fax: 061 396 541

Email: reservations@dunravenhotel.com Web: www.dunravenhotel.com

Established in 1792, the Murphy family's large hotel has somehow retained the comfortable ambience of a country inn. A very luxurious inn nevertheless, especially since the recent completion of 12 new junior suites: under the personal management of Bryan and Louis Murphy, the furnishing standard is superb throughout, with antiques, private dressing rooms and luxurious bathrooms, plus excellent amenities for private and business guests, all complemented by an outstanding standard of housekeeping. It's a great base for sporting activities - equestrian holidays are a speciality and both golf and fishing are available nearby - and also ideal for conferences and private functions, including weddings (which are held beside the main hotel, with separate catering facilities). In recent times the hotel has earned an unrivalled reputation for the quality and value of short breaks offered, and there is an ongoing determination to provide personal service and quality in all aspects of its operation which makes Dunraven Arms an outstanding example of contemporary Irish hospitality at its best. *Dunraven Arms was the our Hotel of the Year in 2004. Free WIFI throughout the hotel. Equestrian; hunting; fishing; shooting; archery. Bike hire; walking. Leisure centre, indoor swimming pool, beauty salon. Garden. No pets. **Rooms 86** (6 suites, 24 junior suites, 56 executive, 30 ground floor, 1 family room, all no smoking). Lift. 24 hour room service. Turndown service. B&B €132.50 PPS, no ss. Room-only rate €195. SC12.5%. Open all year. **Maigue Restaurant:** Named after the River Maigue, which flows through the village of Adare, the restaurant is delightfully old fashioned - more akin to eating in a large country house than in an hotel. Joint head chefs, Colin Greensmith and Shane McGrath, continue the tradition of pride in using the best of local produce. Menus offer a balanced selection of about half a dozen dishes on each course and, although particularly renowned for their roast rib of beef (carved at your table from a magnificent trolley), other specialities like River Maigue salmon and local game in season, especially pheasant, are very popular. Menus are not overlong but may offer some dishes not found elsewhere - a main course of pan-fried calves liver on a bed of colcannon with shallots and lardons of bacon, perhaps - and little home-made touches add an extra dimension - farmhouse cheeses are served with home-made biscuits as well as grapes and an apple And date dressing, for example. Service, under the direction of John Shovlin, who has been restaurant manager since 1980, is exemplary - as elsewhere in the hotel. A wide-ranging wine list offers some treats for the connoisseur as well as plenty of more accessible wines. Restaurant not suitable for children under 12 after 7pm. **Seats 70** (private room 40). Reservations required. D daily 7-9.30, L Sun only 12.30-1.30. Set Sun L about €27, also á la carte; D à la carte. House wine €22, SC 12.5%. [*The Inn Between, across the road in one of the traditional thatched cottages, is an informal brasserie style restaurant in common ownership with the Dunraven Arms; D Tue-Sat, 6.30-9.30 in summer. *Light bar food (soup and sandwiches) available daily, 12-7.] Amex, MasterCard, Visa, Laser. **Directions:** First building on right as you enter the village coming from Limerick (11 miles).

Adare
RESTAURANT

The Wild Geese Restaurant

Rose Cottage Main Street Adare Co Limerick
Tel: 061 396451 Fax: 061 396451
Email: wildgeese@indigo.ie Web: www.thewildgeese.ie

David Foley and Julie Randles' restaurant is in one of the prettiest cottages in the prettiest village in Ireland - and, with consistently good modern Irish cooking and caring service, it's an irresistible package. David Foley is a fine chef who sources ingredients with care - seafood comes from west Cork, there are local meats, poultry and game in season; everything comes from a network of small suppliers built up over the years. Menus offered include a shortish 'Value' menu (no time restriction), a semi à la carte which is considerately priced by course, and a separate vegetarian menu, on request. All the niceties of a special meal are observed - delicious home-baked bread (mustard seed, perhaps) is delivered with an amuse-bouche, such as a shot glass of asparagus soup. The cooking style is sophisticated - a luxurious main course example is pan-fried Castletownbere scallops on potato & chive pancakes, with champagne cream sauce, although a more homely rack of Adare lamb with traditional accompaniments such as potato & garlic gratin and rosemary jus is an enduring favourite. Like everything else in your meal, desserts (including ice creams) are freshly made on the premises. Friendly staff and a carefully selected, informative wine list add greatly to the dining experience. **Seats 50** (private room, 30, +Outdoor, 10). D Mon-Sat 6.30-10, Sun 5.30-10 summer only. Earlybird D €30 Sun-Fri 6.30-7.45; Set D €32/38 (2/3 course), also à la carte & vegetarian menu. House wines €22. Closed Mon, Sun & Mon off season (Oct-Apr). Closed 24 Dec - 2 Jan. Amex, Diners, MasterCard, Visa, Laser, Switch. **Directions:** From Limerick, at top of Adare village, opposite Dunraven Arms Hotel.

Ballingarry
☆RESTAURANT/COUNTRY HOUSE

The Mustard Seed at Echo Lodge

Ballingarry Co Limerick
Tel: 069 68508 Fax: 069 68511
Email: mustard@indigo.ie Web: www.mustardseed.ie

Dan Mullane's famous restaurant The Mustard Seed started life in Adare in 1985, then moved just ten minutes drive away to Echo Lodge, a spacious Victorian country residence set on seven acres of lovely gardens, with mature trees, shrubberies, kitchen garden and orchard - and very luxurious accommodation. Elegance, comfort and generosity are the hallmarks - seen through decor and furnishings which bear the mark of a seasoned traveller whose eye has found much to delight in while wandering the world. As well as offering accommodation in the main house, the conversion of an old schoolhouse in the garden now provides three newer superior suites, a residents' lounge and a small leisure centre with sauna and massage room - this stylish development offers something quite different from the older accommodation and is in great demand from regular guests who make Echo Lodge their base for golf and fishing holidays. Small conferences (20); banqueting (65). Children welcome (under 2s free in parents' room, cots available without charge, baby sitting arranged). Pets allowed by arrangement. Garden, walking. Sauna, massage room. **Rooms 16** (2 suites, 8 shower only, 1 family room, 2 ground floor, 1 for disabled, 8 no smoking,). Turndown service. B&B about €90 PPS, ss about €20. Special winter breaks offered, depending on availability. Closed Christmas week, 2 wks Feb. **Restaurant:** Food and hospitality are at the heart of Echo Lodge and it is in ensuring a memorable dining experience, most of all, that Dan Mullane's great qualities as a host emerge (he was our Host of the Year in 2001). The evening begins with aperitifs in the Library, prettily served with a tasty amuse-bouche - and this attention to detail is confirmed in the beautiful dining room, where fresh flowers on each table are carefully selected to complement the decor. Head chef Tony Schwartz cooks in a modern Irish style, and the wonderful organic kitchen gardens supply him with much of the produce for the restaurant - do allow time to see them before dinner and, perhaps, hazard a guess as to what will be on the menu - while other ingredients are carefully sourced from organic farms and artisan food producers. Menus are wide-ranging and very seasonal - the components of a delicious salad will be dictated by the leaves and herbs in season. Plum tomatoes and asparagus, in mid summer perhaps, accompanied by a Parmesan, basil and a balsamic reduction, and the soup course - typically of roast vegetable - is also likely to be influenced by garden produce. Main courses such as pan seared salmon with crushed new potatoes are based on the best local meats, seafood just up from the south-western fishing ports and seasonal game. With such an abundance of garden produce, vegetarians need have no fear of being overlooked - every course features an unusual vegetarian offering. Finish with Irish farmhouse cheeses at their peak of perfection, or gorgeous puddings, which are also likely to be inspired by garden produce. Finally, irresistible home-made petits fours are served with tea or coffee, at the table or in the Library. All absolutely delicious - and, with service that is professional and efficient, yet always relaxed and warm, the hospitality here is truly exceptional. After dinner, take a stroll through the lushly planted pleasure garden; there is even a special route - of just the right length - marked out for smokers. *(The Mustard Seed was selected for our Natural Food Award in 2005, presented in association with Euro-Toques.) An interesting wine list includes an unusually wide range of half bottles, a couple of magnums and a wine of the month. Not suitable for children. **Seats 55.** Reservations required; non residents welcome. D 7-9.30. Earlybird D €38 (Mon-Thurs,7-8); 4-course D, €57. House wine €26. Closed 24-26 Dec, 20 Jan - 9 Feb. Amex, MasterCard, Visa, Laser. **Directions:** From top of Adare village take first turn to left, follow signs to Ballingarry - 11km (8 miles); in village.

Glin

CASTLE/HISTORIC HOUSE

Glin Castle

Glin Co Limerick
Tel: 068 34173 Fax: 068 34364
Email: knight@iol.ie Web: www.glincastle.com

Surrounded by formal gardens and parkland, Glin Castle stands proudly on the south bank of the Shannon; the FitzGeralds, hereditary Knights of Glin, have lived here for 700 years and it is now the home of the 29th Knight and his wife Madame Fitzgerald. The interior is stunning, with beautiful rooms enhanced by decorative plasterwork and magnificent collections of Irish furniture and paintings. But its most attractive feature is that everything is kept just the same as usual for guests, who are magnificently looked after by manager Bob Duff. Guest rooms and suites are decorated in style, with all the modern comforts, plus that indefinable atmosphere created by beautiful old things; accommodation was originally all in suites - huge and luxurious, but not at all intimidating because of the lived-in atmosphere that characterises the whole castle - but additional rooms -"smaller, friendly, with a family atmosphere"- were more recently opened (no need for this family to haunt the auctions in order to furnish the extra rooms!). And there are many small thoughtfulnesses - the guests' information pack, for example, lists possible outings and itineraries under different interests (gardens, historical etc) and how much time you should allow. When the Knight is at home he will take visitors on a tour of the house and show them all his pictures, furniture and other treasures; interested guests will also relish the opportunity to enjoy the famous gardens, including the 2 acre walled kitchen garden which provide an abundance of seasonal produce for the castle kitchens. There is tennis on site, also an interesting shop - and make sure you fit in a visit to **O'Shaughnessy's** lovely old pub, just outside the castle walls. Head chef Seamus Hogan's menus change daily with the seasons, but a favourite dish is roast rack of lamb with puy lentils, wilted spinach & rosemary jus. *Glin Castle was our Country House of the Year in 2005. The garden and house are open to the public at certain times. Small conferences/private parties (20/30). Not suitable for children under 10 except babies (cot available without charge, baby sitting arranged). Pets permitted by arrangement in certain areas. Gardens, walking, tennis. **Rooms 15** (3 suites; all no-smoking). B&B €147.50 PPS. Dinner is available by reservation; an attractive menu with about four choices on each course is offered. Dining Room Seats 30. D 7-9.30, Set D €52. House wine from about e€231; sc discretionary. Closed Nov 30-Mar 1 Amex, Diners, MasterCard, Visa, Laser. **Directions:** 32 miles west of Limerick on N69, 4 miles east Tarbert Car Ferry; drive up main street of Glin village, turn right at the top of the square.

Glin

O'Shaughnessy's

PUB

Glin Co Limerick **Tel: 068 34115**

Not to be missed while in Glin is O'Shaughnessy's pub, just outside the castle walls; one of the finest pubs in Ireland, it is now in its sixth generation of family ownership and precious little has changed in the last hundred years. Open Thu-Tue: Thu & Fri, 10.30-2.30 7 5.30-10.30/11pm; Sat 10.30am-11pm, Sun, 12-3, Mon & Tue10.30-2.30. Closed Wed. **Directions:** Up into village, take right turn; pub is on your left before the gates to Glin Castle.

Kilmallock

Flemingstown House

Ⓔ FARMHOUSE

Kilmallock Co Limerick **Tel: 063 98093** Fax: 063 98546
Email: info@flemingstown.com Web: www.flemingstown.com

Imelda Sheedy King's welcoming farmhouse is on the family's dairy farm just two miles from the medieval village of Kilmallock; well-signed at the entrance, it sits well back from the road up a long drive flanked by fields of grazing cattle, and leading to an immaculately maintained garden in front of the house. The original house dates back to the 18th century and has been sympathetically extended down through the years, to make a large and well-proportioned family home with pleasingly spacious, comfortably furnished reception rooms - and huge bedrooms, furnished with antique furniture and unfussy neutral decor that contrasts well with the dark furniture. En-suite facilities don't include baths, but have power showers - and, like the rest of the house, everything is well maintained and immaculate. Imelda is a great host, offering genuinely warm and welcoming hospitality - and she's also a great cook, as guests discover at a wonderful breakfast spread that includes a selection of her sister's Bay Lough farmhouse cheeses, home-baked bread and scones, home-made preserves and even their own farm butter. The menu also offers several choices of prepared fresh seasonal fruit (much of it home-grown, of course), a choice of cereals and, in addition to the "full Irish", you may choose from kippers, smoked salmon with scrambled eggs, pancakes with fruit, or a platter of cheese. Dinner is also available, by prior arrangement - there's a choice of two or three dishes on each course, including treats like chicken liver paté with Cumberland sauce, or cucumber soup garnished with smoked Irish salmon, Slaney Valley leg of lamb (carved at the table) with timbales of garlic & herb potato, and apple tart with crème anglaise. This is a lovely place to stay and, aside from the many things to do and see nearby, is well placed to break a journey to or from the south-west. Pets permitted by arrangement. Children over 2 years welcome (2-4 yrs free in parents' room). **Rooms 5** (all shower only & no smoking, 1 family room). B&B €60 pps. ss €10. D €40 (residents only). Packed L on request. Likely to be closed Nov-Mar. MasterCard, Visa. **Directions:** R512 to Kilmallock from Limerick; then towards Fermoy for 3.5km (2 m). House set back from road, on left.

COUNTY LONGFORD

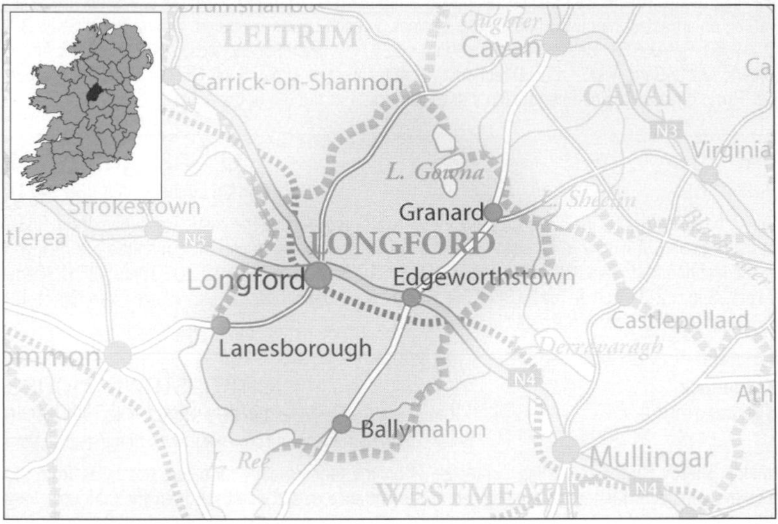

Longford is mostly either gently undulating farming country, or bogland. The higher ground in the north of the county up towards the intricate Lough Gowna rises to no more than 276m in an eminence which romantics might call Carn Clonhugh, but usually it's prosaically known as Corn Hill. The more entertainingly named Molly Hill to the east provides the best views of the lake in an area which arouses passionate patriotism. A few miles to the north is Ballinamuck, scene of the last battle in the Rising of 1798 in a part of Longford renowned for its rebellions against foreign rule.

To the southeast, there is even less pulling of the punches in the name of the little market town in its midst, for Granard - which sounds rather elegant - may be translated as "Ugly Height". Yet this suggests a pleasure in words for their own sake, which is appropriate, for Longford produced the novelist Maria Edgeworth from Edgeworthstown, a.k.a Mostrim, while along towards that fine place Ballymahon and the south of its territory on the Westmeath border, Longford takes in part of the Goldsmith country.

Goldsmith himself would be charmed to know that, six kilometres south of the road between Longford and Edgeworthstown, there's the tiny village of Ardagh, a place of just 75 citizens which is so immaculately maintained that it has been the winner of the Tidiest Village in the Tidy Towns awards. Another award-winner is Newtowncashel in the southwest of the county, atop a hill immediately eastward of Elfeet Bay on northern Lough Ree, where the scenery becomes more varied as County Longford has a lengthy shoreline along the Shannon's middle lake.

West of Longford town at Clondra, the attractive Richmond Harbour is where the Royal Canal - gradually being restored along its meandering track from Dublin - finally gets to the Shannon. And as for Longford town itself, they're working on it, with an urban regeneration landmark in the restoration of a watermill on the Camlin River, providing the power for the ornamental lamps along the riverside walkway.

Local Attractions and Information

Ardagh, Heritage Centre	043 75277
Ballinamuck, 1798 Memorial & Visitor Centre	043 24848
Ballymahon, Bog Lane Theatre	0902 32252
Kenagh, Corlea Trackway (Bog Road) Visitor Centre	043 22386
Longford, Backstage Theatre & Arts Centre	043 47885
Longford, Carrigglas Manor (Gandon stableyard, lace museum)	043 41026
Longford, Tourism Information	043 46566
Newtowncashel, Heritage Centre	043 25021

Granard

FARMHOUSE

Toberphelim House

Granard Co Longford **Tel: 043 86568**

Email: tober3@eircom.net Web: www.toberphelimhouse.com

Dan and Mary Smyth's Georgian farmhouse is about half a mile off the road, on a rise that provides a lovely view of the surrounding countryside. Very much a working farm cows, beef cattle and sheep plus an assortment of domestic animals, (but no more hens "they're gone with the fox") it is an hospitable, easy-going place. Guests are welcome to wander around and walk the fields. ("Rubber boots are a must"). There's a guests' sitting room with television and three bedrooms: two en-suite (shower) with a single and double bed in each and one twin room with a separate private bathroom. All are comfortably furnished and well-maintained - the front bedroom, overlooking the garden, has a lovely old wooden floor and TV - but don't expect too much in the way of amenities. Always improving, the Smyths gave the house a facelift for their 25th wedding anniversary - solid mahogany interior doors, re-tiling the bath and shower-rooms, re-painting the hall, stairs and landing - and an ongoing programme of maintenance continues. Families are welcome and light meals and snacks can usually be arranged. Children welcome. Garden, walking. No pets. **Rooms 3** (2 en-suite shower only, 1 private bathroom, all no smoking). B&B €45 pps, ss €5. Minimum stay 2 nights; prior booking advisable. Closed 20 Sep-1 May. MasterCard, Visa. **Directions:** Take the N55 at the Cavan end of Granard, turn off at the Statoil station taking a right at the next junction. The house is situated about a km towards Abbeylara, to the left.

Longford

RESTAURANT

Aubergine Gallery Café

1st Floor The White House 17 Ballymahon Street Longford Co Longford

Tel: 043 48633

The Devlin siblings - who did so much to put Longford town on the diners map with their original Aubergine Gallery Café - moved the restaurant a few years ago, just a hundred yards down Ballymahon Street at The White House pub. Up steep stairs in a smart, light-filled room, it has a lovely curved bar as the focal point as you arrive, which breaks up what might otherwise seem like a long narrow room; informal seating arranged around the bar allows extra serving space at lunchtime, and is transformed into a reception area for aperitifs in the evening. Lightwood tables and a variety of coloured banquettes and comfortable high-back chairs allow flexible seating arrangements and, together with some interesting artwork, create a vibrant, youthful atmosphere. Something that hasn't changed, however is Stephen's sassy food - his menus are Irish/Mediterranean and he creates delicious, fresh-flavoured dishes with more emphasis on vegetables than in most restaurants; vegetarians do very well here - several first courses and at least one main course will be vegetarian and quite a few of the other dishes are potentially adaptable. Seafood is well represented too and some things never change, so a good steak is de rigeur in these parts - here it may be a 10 oz aged sirloin steak with garlic and pepper cream sauce - and there will always be delicious poultry (crispy duck leg confit perhaps). Service, under the direction of Linda Devlin, is charming and efficient, and another brother, Karl, is the sommelier. Friendly staff, a warm relaxed atmosphere, stylish crative cooking and good value too - lucky Longford. **Seats 45** (+ 20 in lounge area). L Tue-Thu, 12-5, Fri-Sat, 12-4 (Sun open 2-8); D Wed & Thu, 6-8; Fri & Sat, 6-9.30. Set D €32, also à la carte. House wine €16. No reservations. Closed all Mon & Tue D. MasterCard, Visa, Laser. **Directions:** On main street (left as you're heading west), over the old White House pub (entrance on right of ground floor shop).

Longford

RESTAURANT/COUNTRY HOUSE

Viewmount House

Dublin Road Longford Co Longford

Tel: 043 41919 Fax: 043 42906

Email: info@viewmounthouse.com Web: www.viewmounthouse.com

James and Beryl Kearney's lovely 1750s Georgian house just on the edge of Longford town was once owned by Lord Longford, and is set in four acres of beautiful wooded gardens. It really is a delightful house and has been sensitively restored with style, combining elements of grandeur with a human scale that makes guests feel very comfortable. Its warmth strikes the first-time visitor immediately on arrival in the hall, which has a welcoming open fire and a graceful white-painted staircase seen against warm red walls. An elegant period drawing room and the six guest bedrooms all have their particular charm (one is especially large, but all are delightful); but perhaps the handsomest room of all is the unusual vaulted dining room, where an extensive breakfast menu is served. This is a most appealing house, with old wooden floors, rugs, antique furniture - and, most importantly, a great sense of hospitality. The original intention was to operate a restaurant here and that is now expected to come to fruition in spring 2007, not in the main house but in one of the classic stone outbuildings, which have been under restoration for some time, and already include self-catering accommodation. The restaurant was nearing completion on the Guide's last visit - a fine room of great character overlooking a Japanese garden with water features - and the lovely gardens, which are of great interest and designed as a series of rooms, are also nearing completion. Golf nearby. Children welcome (under 4 free in parents' room). Gardens. No pets. **Rooms 6** (1 suite, 3 bath & shower, 3 shower only, all no smoking). B&B €55, ss €10. *Self-catering also available - details on application. Amex, MasterCard, Visa. **Directions:** From Longford R393 to Ardagh. 11km (7 m), up sliproad to right following signs. Entrance 200m on right.

COUNTY LOUTH

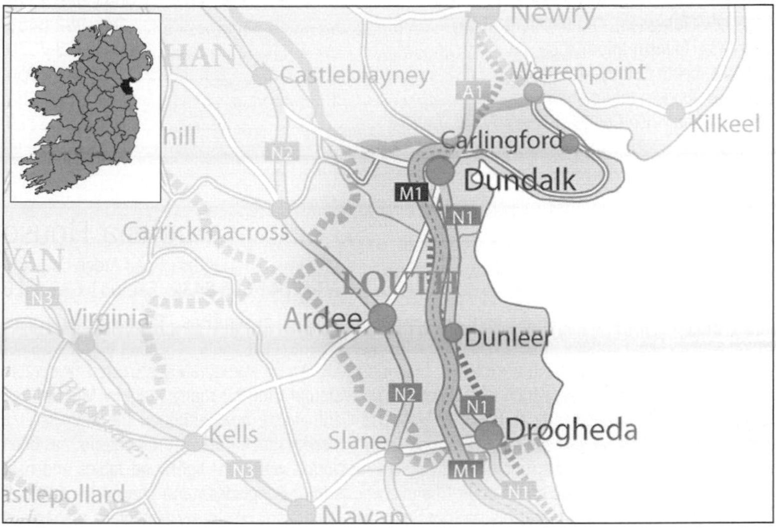

Strategically located in the middle of the main East Coast corridor between Dublin and Belfast, Louth is enjoying the opportunities provided by the continuing development of the M1 as it extends west of Dundalk to provide a clear link northwards. To the south, the motorway crosses to Meath over the River Boyne near Drogheda on a handsome modern structure which is the largest cable-stayed bridge of its type in Ireland, a much admired piece of work designed by Joe O'Donovan. With traffic pressure removed from its other roads, Louth finds itself anew. And though it may be Ireland's smallest county at only 317 square miles (it's just an eighth the size of Cork, the largest) Louth still seems to be two or even three counties in one.

Much of it is fine farmland, at its best in the area west of the extensive wildfowl paradise of Dundalk Bay, on whose shores we find the attractive village of Blackrock, one of Ireland's better kept secrets. But as well there are the distinctive uplands in the southwest, whose name of Oriel recalls an ancient princedom which is also commemorated in Port Oriel, Louth's main fishing port at Clogherhead. And in the north of the county, the Cooley Mountains sweep upwards in a style which well matches their better-known neighbours, the Mountains of Mourne on the other side of the handsome inlet of Carlingford Lough.

Its name might suggest that this is a genuine fjord as defined by geologists, but it isn't, though the Vikings named it so. However, its beauty is such that there's more than enough to be going along with, and on its Louth shore the ancient little port of Carlingford town used to be a best-kept secret. It was a quiet little place imbued with history, but today it is happily prospering both as a recreational harbour for the Dundalk and Newry area, and as a bustling visitor attraction in its own right.

The county's three main townships of Ardee, Dundalk and Drogheda each have their own distinctive style, and all three have been coming vibrantly to life in recent years. The historic borough of Drogheda is the main commercial port, its river valley crossed by the Boyne Viaduct of 1855 vintage, such a remarkable piece of engineering work that it is reckoned one of the seven wonders of Ireland, while Dundalk - the county town - is home to the Louth Museum, whose exhibits include the riding jacket worn by William of Orange at the Battle of the Boyne in 1690.

Local Attractions and Information

Ardee (Tallanstown), Knockabbey Castle & Gardens	042 937 4690
Carlingford, Carlingford Adventure Centre	042 937 3100
Carlingford, Carlingford Sea School	042 937 3879
Carlingford, Heritage Trust	042 937 3888
Carlingford, Tourism Information	042 937 3033
Castlebellingham, Farm Market	0404 43885
Drogheda, Beaulieu House and garden	041 983 8557

Drogheda, Droichead Arts Centre	041 983 3946
Drogheda, Millmount Museum	041 983 3097
Drogheda, Highlanes Art Gallery	041 980 3311
Drogheda (Tullyallen), Old Mellifont Abbey	041 982 6459
Drogheda, Tourism Information	041 983 7070
Dundalk, Louth County Museum	042 932 7056
Dundalk, Tourism Information	042 933 5484
Termonfeckin, Irish Countrywomens Assoc. College	041 982 2119

Ardee

Fuchsia House

N RESTAURANT

Dundalk Road Ardee Co Louth
Tel: 041 685 8432 Fax: 041 685 8428

This new restaurant and bar on the northern edge of Ardee is full of surprises - the name, for a start, which sounds like a cottage in west Cork and (although there is much more to it than ethnic cuisine) it would certainly not suggest the excellent Indian cooking which immediately attracted favourable attention. It's at The Gables, which was a well known restaurant run for many years by Michael and Glynis Caine (who are curently at Beaufort House in Carlingford); now, although the premises - a nondescript building set well back from the road - may not seem much different, the interior has been transformed to create a smart, uncluttered modern restaurant with bare lightwood tables and neat highbacked chairs. Proprietor chef Sarajit Chanda, who is from Bangladesh and previously cooked at TriBeca restaurant in Dublin, and his partner Sarah Nic Lochlainn, previously restaurant manager at Mint in Ranelagh, set up here early in 2006 and it was not long before word of their fine food and hospitality got around the locality and discerning diners began to beat a path to their door. The menu, which is international and offers European food and several types of Asian and European cuisine, has struck a special note with lovers of Indian food. Many of the familiar Indian dishes - curries, tandoori dishes and so on - are offered but everything is made freshly on the premises, including all the sauces, so there is none of the 'sameness' which you so often find in ethnic restaurants. The lamb rogan josh attracted especially high praise on a recent visit, and vegetarians will do very well here too. Skilful cooking across a range of cuisines, warm hospitality and good value make this a great addition to dining choices in an area where people are prepared to travel for a good meal, and it deserves to succeed. The wine list includes Cobra, among a range of beers. Plenty of parking; Fully wheelchair accessible; children welcome, kids menu. Special dietary needs catered for; full bar; take away available. L & D, Tue - Sat, 12-3 & 6-11pm, Sun& Bank Hol Mon, 12-9pm. Set D € 24.50, quick L menu €9, also a la carte L & D. Traditional Sun L €10.50, mid-week special D menu Tue-Thu, 3 courses & 1/2 bottle wine €24 pp. Closed Mon (apart from Bank Hols), 25-26 Dec. **Directions:** On the northern edge of Ardee, on the right heading towards Dundalk. 5 minutes from M1. ◇

Ardee

Rolf's Bistro

RESTAURANT

52 Market Street Ardee Co Louth
Tel: 041 685 7949 Fax: 041 685 7949
Email: rolfsbistro@eircom.net Web: www.rolfsbistro.com

Paul and Bernadette Svender's attractive restaurant in the centre of Ardee is a favourite in the town for its pleasing informality, relaxed atmosphere and a refreshing determination to provide quality food and attentive service at affordable prices. The menu, which changes daily, is well-balanced and well-judged - not over-long yet allowing plenty of choice for regulars, with about ten dishes on each course. Paul is the chef and his speciality dishes reflect his background - Scandinavian prawn toast with Swedish caviar, gravad lax and Swedish beef Lindstrom (a main course based on minced meat, capers and beetroot), for example - but he uses local produce a lot and there really is something for everyone here, including popular starters like steamed mussels (with a sparky tomato & chilli sauce and aoïli bread) and a first course vegetarian tartlette with mushrooms, onions and gratinated Bellingham Blue cheese. There will always be at least a couple of fish dishes, some kind of pasta (perhaps for vegetarians, with goats cheese and sweet peppers) and old favourites like fillet steak (with Stilton gratinated tomato & brandy & black pepper sauce). Deft cooking, professional service, a relaxed ambience and fair prices add up to a successful formula and, with a reception area with squashy sofas recently added, there's now more emphasis on comfort - and a smoking terrace at the back too. An early dinner menu is particularly good value. **Seats 36.** Toilets wheelchair accessible. Children welcome, but not after 9pm. D Mon-Sat, 5.30-10 (Sat 6-10). Early D €17.50/21.50 (5.30-7). House wine from €18. SC discretionary. Closed: Sun; 24-26 Dec. MasterCard, Visa, Laser, Switch. **Directions:** Centre of Ardee, opposite SuperValu & Wogan Interiors. Beside Hatch Castle. ◇

Blackrock

The Brake

RESTAURANT/PUB

Main Street Blackrock Co Louth **Tel: 042 932 1393**

There is little about the neat but plain exterior to prepare first-time visitors for the warmth and country charm of The Brake all old pine and rural bric-à-brac, it has open fires and friendly staff. It's a great place to stop just for a late afternoon cup of tea, but even better if you're hungry it has a well-deserved reputation for good bar meals, and not just the usual pub staples, but a very wide choice including proper home-made chicken kiev, for example and all kinds of seafood including prawn or crab cocktail, wild smoked salmon, smoked mussels and prawns or crab claws in garlic butter - and that's just for starters. Main course seafood includes a seafood platter (hot or cold), poached wild salmon in season, jumbo prawns and maybe even lobster. There are plenty of meat dishes, too, especially steaks (beef and gammon), and. salads and accompaniments are particularly good, all arranged buffet style. Prices are fairly moderate - hot main courses range from about €15 (chicken curry or vegetarian platter) to about €23 for scallops or €27 for fillet steak, but many of the lighter dishes and salads are much less. Beware of the unusual opening hours though this is a late afternoon into evening place. Not suitable for children under 12. **Seats 120.** Air conditioning. Toilets wheelchair accessible. Bar open 5-11.30. D daily 6-10 (Sun 6-9.30). A la carte; house wine €18; sc discretionary. *The Clermont Arms, a few doors along the front, is in the same family ownership. Closed 25 Dec, Good Fri. MasterCard, Visa, Laser. **Directions:** Turn off the main Dublin-Belfast road 5km (3 m) south of Dundalk.

CARLINGFORD

This delightful medieval village is set amongst spectacular scenery with views across Carlingford Lough to the Mountains of Mourne in County Down. It is a small place and, although off the beaten track, is gradually being 'discovered' so it is best to avoid busy times like festivals, if you want to see it at its best. In the village, the 59-room **Four Seasons Hotel** (042 93 73530; www.4seasonshotel.ie) has good leisure and business facilities, including a leisure centre and function room; it is unconnected with the international brand. The village is very compact and visitors looking around can easily compare the prices, menus and style of the various restaurants and bars: **O'Hares** (042 937 3106) in the centre of the village is a renowned tradition pub/grocery shop and, although it has expanded in recent years (and serves a lot more food than the speciality Carlingford oysters and brown bread of old), the old back bar and open fire remain intact. Just across the road you will find **Magees** (042 937 3751), a lively informal restaurant with great staff that is currently serving some of the best food in the town. Around the corner, opposite the old-fashioned **McKevitt's Village Hotel** (042 937 3116; www.mckevittshotel.com), **The Oystercatcher Lodge & Bistro** (042 937 3989; www.theoystercatcher.com) offers spacious, clean-lined accommodation; the bistro is run separately and offers a mid-range menu with daily specials emphasising local seafood, notably oysters. Around the corner at the heritage centre the small restaurant **Kingfisher Bistro** (042 937 3716) has a loyal local following, and, further out on the same road on the outskirts of the village, the new commmunity development The Foy Centre includes a fine contemporary restaurant **Fusion** (042 938 3627). Back in the village, on Newry Street, **Capitano Correlli Restaurant** (042 938 3848; www.belvederehouse.ie) offers authentic Italian food - and B&B at the adjacent Belvedere House. It might also be of interest to know that bar and restaurant at **Carlingford Marina** (042 937 3073; www.carlingfordmarina.ie) are open to the public. A little way outside Carlingford - signed off the Dundalk road - **Lilly Finnegans** (042 937 3730) is a pretty, traditional pub (open evenings only.

WWW.IRELAND-GUIDE.COM FOR THE BEST PLACES TO EAT, DRINK & STAY

Carlingford

Beaufort House

GUESTHOUSE

Ghan Road Carlingford Co Louth **Tel: 042 937 3879** Fax: 042 937 3878
Email: michaelcaine@beauforthouse.net Web: www.beauforthouse.net

Michael and Glynnis Caine's immaculate property is well-placed to maximise on the attractions of a quiet and beautiful waterside position with wonderful sea and mountain views, while also being just a few minutes walk from Carlingford village. All areas are spacious and furnished to high specifications: hotel standard bedrooms have phone, TV with video channel and tea/coffee making facilities. The Caines were previously restaurateurs, and dinner is available by arrangement for parties of eight or more. (Set D about €35). Associated activities include a sailing school and yacht charter - corporate sailing events (team building and corporate hospitality), including match racing in Carlingford Lough, are a speciality. Golfing can be arranged at any of the five golf courses within 20 minutes' drive. Golf nearby. Ample car parking. Small conference/banqueting (20). Children welcome (under 2s free in parents' room). Fishing, cycling, hill walking, bird watching, walking, garden. No pets. **Rooms 5** (2 shower only, 2 family rooms, 1 ground floor, all no smoking). B&B €50 pps, ss €25. D by arrangement only. Closed 25 Dec. MasterCard, Visa, Laser. **Directions:** Approaching from Dundalk, turn right just before the village and harbour; house on shore.

Carlingford

CAFÉ

Georgina's Bakehouse Tearooms

Castle Hill Carlingford Co Louth

Tel: 042 937 3346 Email: georginastearooms@eircom.net

Georgina Finegan's little daytime restaurant high up in the web of small roads above King John's Castle is well worth seeking out. The bakery has been going for over twenty years now, specialising in meringues and desserts and, since opening the tea rooms in 1997, Georgina has built up a loyal customer base including "people who return on a daily, weekly or even annual basis for the good food and friendly tea room setting." They come from Belfast, Dublin and "places in between", they're local, and they're visitors from all over the world - the fact is that there is something for everyone at this friendly and unpretentious café. A conservatory and other extra seating has brought some extra space recently, but the original café is really quite small; but it's cosy and seems just right for simple wholesome fare like soup of the day (Italian Peasant, perhaps, made with carrots, parsnips, fennel, basil & sun-dried tomatoes) with a traditional sandwich like egg, tomato & parsley, or open sandwiches like ham & apple salad or ploughman's cheese platter, made with home-made wholemeal or white soda bread, while summer menus offer some colourful seasonal dishes like Greek salad, feta cheese & tomato tart, and tomato, basil & mozzarella salad. Then there are toasted sandwiches - pastrami and gouda, perhaps, with sweet beetroot - and contemporary snacks like tortilla wraps, with smoked salmon & cream cheese, for example. But many people just drop in for a wedge of old-fashioned lemon meringue pie, or Austrian apple pie, or maybe a slice of carrot cake and a cup of tea - after all, that's where it all started. **Seats 34.** Children welcome. Open daily, 10-5.45 (to 6 Sun). Closed 1 week Sep, Christmas, 1 week Jan. **No Credit Cards. Directions:** Opposite King John's Castle.

Carlingford

RESTAURANT/COUNTRY HOUSE

Ghan House

Carlingford Co Louth

Tel: 042 937 3682 Fax: 042 937 3772

Email: ghanhouse@eircom.net Web: www.ghanhouse.com

Conveniently located just an hour from Dublin or Belfast airports, the Carroll family's 18th century house is attractively situated in its own walled grounds on the edge of Carlingford village, with views across the lough to the Mountains of Mourne. A proper little bar offers a relaxing space where guests can mingle - in a more convivial atmosphere, perhaps, than beside the drawing room fire, although that too has its moments; it's very pleasant for residents to return to, and especially welcoming for non-residents just coming in for dinner. Accommodation is in four rooms of character in the main house, each with sea or mountain views, and eight newer bedrooms in a separate building, which have been finished to a fairly high standard. And there's even more to it than comfortable accommodation and the delicious meals you will enjoy for dinner or breakfast, as the Carrolls also run a cookery school - just upgraded, with a new hands-on kitchen installed - on the premises. Conference/banqueting (55/85); house available for exclusive use. Garden; walking. Children welcome (under 5s free in parents' room; cots available without charge; baby sitting arranged). No pets. **Rooms 12** (1 shower only, 3 superior, 2 family). B&B Double Room €95 pps, single €75. (Discounts applied on stays of 2 or more nights.) Open all year except Christmas & New Year. **Restaurant:** Dinner is, of course, a high priority at Ghan House. The style is contemporary, based mainly on quality home-grown (vegetable, fruit and herbs), home-made (breads, ice creams, everything that can be made on the premises) and local produce, notably Cooley lamb and beef, dry cured bacon, free range eggs - and seafood: oysters are synonymous with Carlingford (there are also mussels from the lough and lobster from Ballagan, while smoked salmon and crab come from nearby Annagassan). A user-friendly set dinner menu with about five choices on each course is also priced by course, allowing considerable flexibility without having a separate à la carte: typical dishes on a late summer menu might include Carlingford Lough seafood chowder with saffron & herbs, char-seared sirloin of Cooley beef on creamed cabbage with roast potatoes, fondant carrots, button onions & red wine sauce, then Irish farmhouse cheese or a classic dessert - hot chocolate fondant, perhaps, with home-made pistachio ice cream. Interesting, fairly priced wine list. Non-residents are welcome by reservation. **Seats 55** (private room 55). D only, "most days" 7-9.30; Set D €42.50; L Sun only 12.30-3.30, €49.50 (5 course). House wine €18.50; sc discretionary. Children welcome. House closed 24-26 Dec and 31 Dec & 1 Jan. Amex, MasterCard, Visa, Laser. **Directions:** 15 minutes from main Dublin - Belfast Road N1.10 metres after 30 mph sign on left hand side after entering Carlingford from Dundalk direction.

Clogherhead
RESTAURANT

Little Strand Restaurant

Strand Street Clogherhead Co Louth
Tel: 041 988 1061 Fax: 041 988 1062
Email: food@littlestrand.com Web: www.littlestrand.com

Catherine Whelahan's popular restaurant is in a neat modern building, on the right hand side as you go through the village of Clogherhead to the beach, set back a little from the road, with steps up to the front door. The fairly large ground floor restaurant is surprisingly formally appointed for the location and, upstairs, there's an impressive lounge area, used for aperitifs and coffee at busy times. You don't have to be a fish-lover to enjoy a meal here - menus offer a range of meat and vegetarian dishes including, intriguingly, Skipper's Choice (a 12 oz sirloin steak topped with Clogherhead prawns) but local seafood, brought in to the nearby fishing harbour of Port Oriel, is of course the speciality and very good it is too. House specialities include crab claws in garlic/lemon butter, lobster thermidor and sole on the bone with lemon, lime and dill butter; an exceptional dish is Clogherhead scampi, cooked and served the traditional way with sauce tartare. **Seats 60** (Private room 12-16). Air conditioning. D Wed-Sun and Bank Holidays, 7-"late" (Sun from 5); à la carte; special value menus offered; house wine about €18, sc discretionary. Closed Mon, Tue. MasterCard, Visa. **Directions:** 7 miles from Drogheda, 3 miles from Termonfeckin village. ◇

Collon
RESTAURANT WITH ROOMS

Forge Gallery Restaurant

Church Street Collon Co Louth
Tel: 041 982 6272 Fax: 041 982 6584
Email: info@forgegallery.ie Web: www.forgegallery.ie

This charming two-storey restaurant has been providing good food, hospitality and service for over twenty years now - and still retains a well-earned reputation as the best eating place for miles around. It's a most attractive place; the exterior is invariably immaculate when seen from the road and, as you enter under a fine old arch, an equally impeccably landscaped parking area is revealed - and also a pretty garden area outside the attached accommodation, and a neat smokers' area outside the entrance. The building itself has loads of character, and has been furnished and decorated with flair, providing a fine setting for food that combines country French and New Irish styles, with a few other influences along the way. Seasonal produce stars, much of it local especially seafood, but also game in season, vegetables and fruit - and this quality produce, plus sound cooking, excellent service and an interesting ambience make for an enjoyable dining experience. Favourite starters include a delicious warm salad of Dublin Bay prawns with salad leaves and fresh herbs - followed, perhaps, by main courses of roast duckling (a great house speciality, served on a bed of pak choi or spinach, with spring onion, soy and ginger sauce) or a combination dish of beef fillet with Boyne salmon, with a tarragon sauce. Although menus - which are quite extensive - seem quite conservative, there's also some contemporary flair in the kitchen, and presentation is stylish. A short vegetarian menu is also offered, and a tempting dessert menu might include Kath's bread and butter pudding, and a seasonal crème brulée - and, of course, Irish cheeses. This not an inexpensive restaurant although not as alarming as it seems at first: starters are costly, beginning at €7 for soup rising to €25 for a combination dish of prawns, crab claws and smoked salmon, but they are very good; main courses (€25-35) are on a par with other comparable restaurants and there is a shorter, more moderately priced daily menu in addition to the main carte. Sunday lunch offers very good value. An interesting wine list, strong on clarets, includes a dozen house wines and an unusually wide choice of half bottles. Private parking (9). **Seats 60.** Air conditioning. Bar. L Sun only, 12.30-2.30. D Tue-Sun, 7-9.30 (Sun 6-8). D à la carte. Set Sun L €30. House wine from €24; sc discretionary (except 10% on parties of 6+). Accommodation details on application. Closed Mon; Christmas & 2nd week Jan. Amex, Diners, MasterCard, Visa, Laser. **Directions:** On N2, 56km (35 m) from Dublin due north, midway between Slane and Ardee, in centre of village.

Drogheda
HOTEL

Boyne Valley Hotel & Country Club

Drogheda Co Louth **Tel: 041 983 7737** Fax: 041 983 9188
Email: reservations@boyne-valley-hotel.ie Web: www.boyne-valley-hotel.ie

Set in large gardens just on the Dublin side of Drogheda town - and handy to the motorway - this substantial hotel has an 18th century mansion at its heart. It is not as obvious as it used to be since developments created a completely new entrance, but it is still there and provides some unspoilt, graciously proportioned rooms that contrast well with the later additions, including 34 new rooms added several years ago. Owner-run by Michael and Rosemary McNamara since 1992, it has the personal touch unique to hands-on personal management and is popular with locals, for business and pleasure, as well as a base for visitors touring the historic sites of the area. While rooms in the old building have more character, the new ones are finished to the high standard demanded by today's travellers. Fine conference facilities and excellent leisure centre add greatly to the hotel's attraction. Conference/banqueting (450/450); secretarial services. Leisure centre, indoor swimming pool; beauty salon. All weather tennis; pitch & putt. Garden. Pets allowed by arrangement. **Rooms 72** (1 suite, 13 shower only, 35 no-smoking, 1 disabled). B&B from about €85 pps. Open all year. Amex, Diners, MasterCard, Visa, Laser. **Directions:** On southern edge of Drogheda town. From Dublin turn off M1 to N1 at Julianstown; from Belfast turn off M1 to N1 at Drogheda north. ◇

Drogheda
N HOTEL

D Hotel

Scotch Hall Drogheda Co Louth
Tel: 041 987 7700 Fax: 041 987 7702
Email: reservethed@monogramhotels.ie Web: www.thed.ie

This cool new hotel - a sister to the celebrated 'g' hotel in Galway - is part of an impressive waterfront development on the south bank of the River Boyne in Drogheda, about 30 minutes from Dublin Airport, and is now setting the benchmark for high standards of rejuvenation in the centre of Drogheda, a 12th century town built by the Normans. The development includes a shopping centre and multi-storey parking (mundane, perhaps, but very handy, and appealingly designed) as well as a riverside walkway and spacious café/dining areas for fine weather - and, when complete, it will also offer state of the art leisure facilities for 'the d'. The hotel's contemporary lines contrast pleasingly with the old town, and the interior is bright, clean-lined, spacious and easy on the eye - unlike many style-conscious new buildings, however, it has a friendly atmosphere and staff are keen to do everything possible to make guests feel comfortable. A huge foyer with some very modern seating divides into the reception/lounge area, and a smart bar and restaurant overlooking the river. Bedrooms designed with the comfort of the guest in mind, many with superb views over the river and Drogheda's town centre, all have comfortable chairs and standard features such as direct dial telephone, internet connection, safe, tea/coffee making facilities, tv and trouser press, and two superior rooms are particularly appealing. With seven meeting and event suites this is an ideal place host business meetings, or for private gatherings. Wheelchair accessible; Children welcome (under 12s free in parents room, cots avail at no charge, baby sitting arranged); pets permitted in some areas. **Rooms 104** (2 superior, 6 for disabled), 24hr room service; lift. complimentary guest parking. B&B €110. Open all year except Christmas. Amex, MasterCard, Visa, Laser. **Directions:** The entrance to the hotel is c. 300 metres on the left adjacent to the Scotch Hall Shopping Complex.

DUNDALK

The county town of Louth (Ireland's smallest county), Dundalk is in an area rich with historical folklore, and is convenient to the Cooley Peninsula and the charming medieval town of Carlingford on the southern shore of Carlingford Lough. Architecturally, Dundalk town is dominated by a massive seven-storey windmill, which begs restoration. Good reasonably priced accomodation is avauloable at **Park Inn Dundalk** (042 939 5700; www.dundalkparkinn.ie), which is just north of the town on the Armagh road and has leisure and conference facilities. And, on the Dublin road, a colourful garden ablaze with masses of home-raised flowers will lead you to the Meehan family's spick and span B&B, **Rosemount** (042 933 5878).
WWW.IRELAND-GUIDE.COM FOR THE BEST PLACES TO EAT, DRINK & STAY

Dundalk
HOTEL

Ballymascanlon House Hotel

Dundalk Co Louth **Tel: 042 935 8200** Fax: 042 937 1598
Email: info@ballymascanlon.com Web: www.ballymascanlon.com

féile bia Set in 130 acres of parkland, this hotel just north of Dundalk has developed around a large Victorian house. It has been in the Quinn family ownership since 1948 and major improvements made over the last few of years have been done with panache, lifting the hotel into a different class; bright and spacious public areas are furnished and decorated in a warm, comfortably contemporary style with plenty of table lamps, good paintings and a variety of seating - comfy sofas and armchairs, Lloyd loom chairs - all of which combines to create a stylishly homely atmosphere. Spacious and very attractive new bedrooms share the same qualities, with specially commissioned furniture adding interest - and, in many cases, views over lovely gardens, the golf course or the attractive old stable yard, which is under restoration. Corporate facilities include three versatile meeting rooms, with back-up business services available. Impressive new leisure facilities include a 20 metre deck level pool and tennis courts. With so much to do on the premises and easy access to areas of great natural beauty and historical interest, this hotel makes a good base for a break (special interest and off-season deals available). Conference/banqueting (300/250). Leisure centre, swimming pool, Canadian hot tub; golf (18); garden, walking. Children welcome (under 3s free in parents' room; cots available without charge, baby sitting arranged). **Rooms 90** (3 suites, 87 executive rooms, 51 no smoking, 1 for disabled). Lift. Room service (limited hours). B&B €85 pps, ss €30. Open all year. Amex, Diners, MasterCard, Visa, Laser. **Directions:** M1 from Dublin; on the Carlingford road, 5km (3 miles) north of Dundalk.

Dundalk
PUB

McKeown's Bar & Lounge

16 Clanbrassil Street Dundalk Co Louth
Tel: 042 933 7931

This well-run pub of character has a great atmosphere and friendly staff - just the place for a pint and welcome reassurance that the great Irish pub is alive and well in Dundalk. Open Mon-Wed, 10.20-11.30; Thu-Sat, 10.30-12.30. Food (soup & freshly made sandwiches) served daily, 10.30-6.30. Closed 25 Dec, Good Fri. **No Credit Cards. Directions:** Town centre - middle of the main street.

Dundalk
BAR/RESTAURANT

Quaglinos at The Century

The Century Bar 19 Roden Place Dundalk Co Louth
Tel: 042 933 8567 Fax: 042 933 4147

Well known restaurateurs Pat and Eileen Kerley now run The Century Bar, which is a listed building on a corner site opposite St Patrick's Cathedral. It's a romantic building dating back to 1902, with an ornamental turret on the corner, above the front door - and it has retained many features of historical interest, including the original bar counter and hand-carved bar backdrop. The restaurant is above the bar and here Pat Kerley - a committed Euro-Toques chef - takes great pride in the active promotion of Irish cuisine and uses as much local produce as possible: Carlingford oysters, Annagassan salmon, lobster and, of course, Cooley lamb all make their mark on menus that offer an appealing blend of traditional and modern Irish cooking. As in most Louth restaurants, generosity remains the keynote and providing good service with good value is a priority. Quaglino's has always had a strong following and loyal customers (plus many new ones) like this restaurant very much, so reservations are essential. The early dinner menu offers outstanding value. Children welcome. **Seats 30.** D daily, 5-10.30. Early D €24 (5-7); Gourmet Menu about €45. also à la carte; no SC. House wine €17.50. Bar meals Mon-Sat, 12-2.30. Closed 25 Dec, Good Fri. Amex, Diners, MasterCard, Visa, Laser, Switch. **Directions:** Just off town centre almost opposite St. Patrick's Cathedral. ◇

Dundalk
RESTAURANT

Restaurant Number Thirty Two

32 Chapel Street Dundalk Co Louth
Tel: 042 933 1113 Email: no.32@ireland.com Web: www.no32.ie

Attractively situated in a leafy corner of town near the museum, Susan Heraghty's great little place is the neighbourhood restaurant par excellence and a great asset to Dundalk. It occupies a corner site, with windows all along one side giving it a sense of space - and more real space is available too, now that the first floor is also available for dining. The smart simplicity of the decor and table settings is very appealing, and menus are written in an admirably down-to-earth style - and the same can be said of the prices, notably an exceptional early evening menu (the 'Express') which allows you two courses (from a generous selection of about half a dozen starters and main courses, plus several daily fish and vegetarian specials) and includes coffee with a mini-dessert - and the later set menu is not far behind. On whichever, you might get such delicious starter combinations as deep-fried tempura aubergine & courgette with red onion jam & curry oil, or a lovely tin of crab & celeriac with confit tomato & sweet mustard dressing - and main courses like grilled lamb burger with cucumber & mint raita, roast tomatoes & chips, or pan-fried chicken in a wholegrain mustard cream sauce, with mash & root vegetables. There has always been a terrific generosity of spirit here - not in overladen plates, but in quality of food and service; the later menu is like the Express but with a little more choice and slightly more sophisticated dishes - but prices are still very reasonable. Everything is just as delicious as it sounds (or even more so), service is good-humoured and efficient. Would that every town in Ireland had a place like this. **Seats 60.** Reservations required. Children welcome. D Mon-Sat, 5.30-10. Early 'Express' D €17 (Mon-Thu 5.30-6.30), Set D €26. House wine from €18.95. SC 12.5% on parties 6+. Closed Sun, bank hols. Amex, MasterCard, Visa, Laser. **Directions:** First left turn after courthouse at "home bakery".

Dundalk

Ⓝ RESTAURANT

Rosso Restaurant

5 Roden Place Dundalk Co Louth
Tel: 042 935 6502 Fax: 042 935 6503
Email: enquiries@rossorestaurant.com Web: www.rossorestaurant.com

Just opposite St Patrick's Cathedral, in Dundalk's new 'dining quarter', this smart contemporary restaurant has recently opened under the direction of Raymond McArdle, acclaimed executive chef of the Gilhooley family's Nuremore Hotel in Co Monaghan, and Louisa Gilhooley. The proprietors have assembled a fine team led by head chef Conor Mee, who brings a new dimension to dining options in the area with his predictably high standard of cutting edge cuisine and a stylish setting. A spacious reception area - very comfortably furnished with low sofas and chairs - leads into two dining areas one square and the other larger, long and narrow: a cool coffee and cream colour scheme with polished wood tables is enhanced by clever use of light-reflecting mirrors; the design and stylish contemporary décor make the most of this period town house and like the menus, which offer a combination of traditional and unexpected interpretations of classic dishes as well as modern ones, often offered as a starter or in main course portions - the ambience is reminiscent of the sister establishment, Restaurant 23 in Warrenpoint (see entry). Tables are set up in plain contemporary style with crockery in various shapes (some rather fun, others a little too oversized for rather small tables). A summer lunch menu - clearly based on top quality ingredients although, unexpectedly, with little indication of provenance - might offer versatile light dishes like Caesar salad & seared tuna, crisp duck pastilla or smoked salmon with pickled shallots and capers, alongside more substantial choices like chicken with green vegetable chilli & spiced basmati rice, local fish cake with poached egg and bacon salad, or braised beef with champignon mushrooms. Delicious desserts (coconut parfait with blood orange sorbet, toffee apple caramelised ice cream, hot Valhrona chocolate pudding) are worth saving a little room for, or there's a cheese selection with white and walnut bread (unusually, no bread is otherwise offered); finish off with tea or coffee from a wide range of herbal teas, teas and coffees. Dinner menus are rather grander and offer more choice than lunch, but the high standard of the cooking and artistic presentation of dishes is a constant factor. A well chosen wine list includes a short choice of wines by the glass, and service is friendly and willing. All round, a very welcome newcomer to Dundalk. Children welcome. **Seats 75** (private room, 60); air conditioning; L Tue-Fri, 12.30-2.45; D Tue-Sat, 6-9.45; L&D a la carte; Sun, 12.30-7.30; Value meal Sun all day, 3 courses €26.50; house wine about €20. Closed Sat L, Mon, 25 Dec, 1 Jan. MasterCard, Visa, Laser. **Directions:** Opposite St. Patrick's Cathedral.

Dundalk

BAR

The Spirit Store

George's Quay The Harbour Dundalk Co Louth **Tel: 042 935 2097**
Email: info@spiritstore.ie Web: www.spiritstore.ie

This pub of great character and friendliness is right on the quay, where coasters dock, so you never know what country visiting sailors may come from. But everyone mixes well in the wackily-furnished bars downstairs and - although a youthful place best known for its music (regular events are held in the upstairs bar, often famous names) - people of all ages and backgrounds are welcomed here, even if only for a cup of tea to break a journey. Closed 25 Dec, Good Fri. MasterCard, Visa, Laser. **Directions:** On the quayside, beside the bridge.

Dundalk Area

BAR/RESTAURANT

Fitzpatrick's Bar & Restaurant

Jenkinstown Rockmarshal Dundalk Co Louth
Tel: 042 937 6193 Fax: 042 937 6274
Email: admin@fitzpatricks-restaurant.com Web: www.fitzpatricks-restaurant.com

Masses of well-maintained flowers and a neat frontage with fresh paintwork always draw attention to this attractive and well-run establishment. It has plenty of parking and is well organised for the informal but comfortable consumption of food in a series of bar/dining rooms, all with character and much of local interest in pictures and artefacts. Prompt reception, friendly service and traditional home-cooked food (sometimes with a modern twist) at reasonable prices all add up to an appealing package - and its obvious popularity with locals and visitors alike is well deserved. Well-balanced menus always include a good selection of fresh seafood - a tian of fresh crabmeat to start perhaps, with a purée of apple, avocado & lambs lettuce, main courses like fillet of turbot with chorizo, confit aubergine & roast peppers - and delicious informal meals from the Grill Menu including proper scampi, made with fresh Dublin Bay prawns (langoustine), coated in home-made breadcrumbs and served with tartare sauce. This is not inexpensive food (some main courses may be over €25), but it is real food, and the quantities are generous. It's also a pleasant place to drop into for a cup of tea or coffee - and, a very nice touch, they have a 'Very Important Pet' compound where you can leave your dog while having a meal. *At the time of going to press there are plans to build 28 bedrooms, and a function room. Children welcome before 9pm. Seats 65 (private room 35). Air conditioning. Open daily in summer, otherwise Tue-Sun 12.30 -10pm (Sun 12.30-3.30, 5.30-9pm), L from 12.30, D 6-10. A la carte menus. Closed Mon off-season (Sep-June), open bank hols, Good Fri, 25 Dec. MasterCard, Visa, Laser. **Directions:** Just north of Dundalk town, take Carlingford road off main Dublin-Belfast road. About 8km (5 m) on left.

Dunleer

Carlito's

RESTAURANT — Main Street Dunleer Co Louth **Tel: 041 686 1366**

People come from miles around to eat at this unassuming Italian restaurant, so it is wise to book well ahead, especially at weekends. Although quite unremarkable from the street, the interior is welcoming, with a comfortable seating area just inside the door where groups can assemble over an aperitif before heading for their table. Tables are simply set (night light, cutlery and a paper napkin) but the welcome is very friendly and you'll quickly be settled into a menu that is well planned to please everyone, regardless of age or the occasion. Expect lovely home-baked bread, real minestrone soup with heaps of flavour, mixed leaf salads with creamy home-made dressing, deliciously crisp thin-based pizzas, a range of pastas and daily specials - such as herb-crusted cod, perfectly cooked and served with local vegetables (choice of boiled or chipped potatoes). Desserts are equally good: real tiramisu, crème brulée with fresh strawberries perhaps, and freshly brewed coffee to finish. Great value too. D Tue-Sat, 6pm -"late", Sun 5-9pm. MasterCard, Visa. **Directions:** On main street. ◇

Termonfeckin

Triple House Restaurant

RESTAURANT — Termonfeckin Co Louth

Tel: 041 982 2616 Fax: 041 982 2616

The pretty village of Termonfeckin provides a fine setting for Pat Fox's popular restaurant, which is in a 200-year-old converted farmhouse in landscaped gardens surrounded by mature trees. In winter you can settle in front of a log fire in the reception area on cold evenings while pondering the menu over a glass of wine (there's also a conservatory, used for aperitifs in summer). Committed to using the best of local produce, Pat offers wide-ranging menus and daily blackboard seafood extras from nearby Clogherhead fresh Clogherhead prawns, Annagassan crab, and a dish he entitles, intriguingly, Port Oriel Pot-Pourri. But locally-reared meats feature too, in roast Drogheda smoked loin of pork with a nectarine & Calvados sauce, for example. Specialities include lovely spinach-filled crêpes (baked with cream sauce, tomato sauce and Parmesan) and, for dessert, a chewy meringue dacquoise that varies with the season's fruits. Plated farmhouse cheeses typically include Cashel Blue, Cooleeney and Wexford Cheddar. The wine list reflects Pat's particular interests and special evenings are sometimes held for enthusiasts off-season. Children welcome. **Seats 40.** D Tue-Sat 6.30-9.30, L Sun only 1-3; Set D about €30, à la carte available; early D about €22, 6.30-7.30 only; Set Sun L about €22. House wines about €17-20; sc discretionary. Toilets wheelchair accessible. Closed Mon, Christmas. MasterCard, Visa. **Directions:** 5 miles north east of Drogheda. ◇

COUNTY MAYO

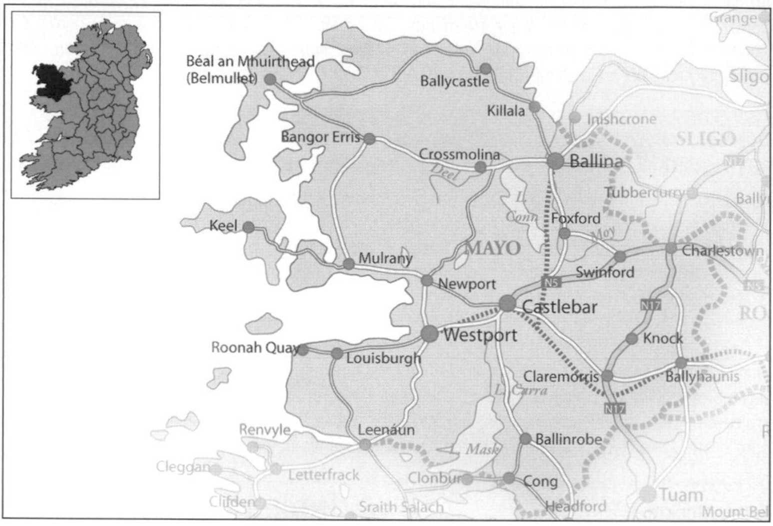

Mayo - far Mayo - might have been a byword for remoteness and declining population in times past. But now it is thriving, with the recent Census showing a population increase of 5.3% (to 118,000). However, Mayo is so spacious that it still seems totally uncrowded. And they are a people who enjoy the present as much as savouring the past. No more so than at Westport on Clew Bay, near the famed Holy Mountain of Croagh Patrick. Westport is a neatly planned town which has deservedly collected national and international civic awards.

Five kilometres east of Mayo's bustling county town of Castlebar, the Museum of Country Life at Turlough Park House, the first fully-fledged department of the National Museum to be located anywhere outside Dublin, celebrates Irish country life as it was lived between 1850 and 1960 with a remarkable display of artefacts which were in regular everyday use, yet now seem almost exotic.

As often, indeed, does Mayo itself - for Mayo is magnificent. All Ireland's counties have their devotees, but enthusiasts for Mayo have a devotion which is pure passion. In their heart of hearts, they feel that this austerely majestic Atlantic-battered territory is somehow more truly Irish than anywhere else. And who could argue with them after experiencing the glories of scenery, sea and sky which this western rampart of Ireland puts on ever-changing display?

Yet among Mayo's many splendid mountain ranges we find substantial pockets of fertile land, through which there tumble fish-filled streams and rivers. And in the west of the county, the rolling hills of the drumlin country, which run in a virtually continuous band right across Ireland from Strangford Lough, meet the sea again in the island-studded wonder of Clew Bay.

Along Mayo's rugged north coast, turf cutting at Ceide Fields near Ballycastle has revealed the oldest intact field and farm system in existence, preserved through being covered in blanket bog 5,000 years ago. An award-winning interpretive centre has been created at the site, and even the most jaded visitor will find fascination and inspiration in the clear view which it provides into Ireland's distant past. A few miles eastward, the charming village of Ballycastle is home to the internationally-respected Ballinglen Arts Foundation, creative home-from-home for artists worldwide.

Nearby, the lively town of Ballina is where the salmon-rich River Moy meets the sea in the broad sweep of Killala Bay. It takes a leap of the imagination to appreciate that the sheltered Moy Valley is in the same county as the spectacularly rugged cliffs of Achill Island. But leaps of the imagination is what Mayo inspires.

Local Attractions and Information

Ballina, Street Festival/Arts Week (July) 096 70905
Ballina, Tourism Information 096 70848
Ballycastle, Ballinglen Arts Foundation .... 096 43184 / 43366

Castlebar, Linenhall Arts Centre 094 902 3733
Castlebar, Tourism Information 094 902 1207
Ceide Fields, Interpretive Centre 0996 43325
Clare Island Ferries 098 27685
Foxford, Woollen Mills Visitor Centre 094 925 6756
Inishkea Island Tours, Belmullet 097 85741
Inishturk Island Ferries .... 098 45520 / 45541
Killasser (Swinford) Traditional Farm Heritage Centre 094 925 2505
Kiltimagh, Glore Mill Follain Arts Centre 094 82184
Knock Interational Airport 094 936 7222
Moy Valley Holidays 096 70905
Turlough, Turlough Park House. Museum of Country Life. Open Tuesday to Saturday 10am to 5pm, Sundays 2pm to 5pm, closed Mondays 094 903 1589
Westport, Clew Bay Archaeological Trail 087 293 5207
Westport, Westport House & Children's Zoo .... 098 25430 / 27766
Westport, Tourism Information 098 25711

ACHILL ISLAND

Don't forget to top up with fuel as you're driving onto Achill Island; there's a large service station, Lavelle's Esso Garage, on the right - and it is open on Sundays. An interesting place that is also useful to know about is Seasamh O'Dalaigh's workshop and gallery, **Dánlann Yawl** (098 36137), at Owenduff (on the right coming from the mainland); it has a teashop during gallery hours, making a pleasant place for a break - and also a 2-bedroom apartment with magnificent views. On the island, the McNamara's family-run **Achill Cliff House Hotel** (098 43400; www.achillcliff.com); quiet, purpose-built, it is especially useful to know about as it is open all year except Christmas.

WWW.IRELAND-GUIDE.COM FOR THE BEST PLACES TO EAT, DRINK & STAY

Achill Dugort

GUESTHOUSE

Gray's Guest House

Dugort Achill Island Co Mayo **Tel: 098 43244**

Vi McDowell has been running this legendary guesthouse in the attractive village of Dugort since 1970, and nobody understands better the qualities of peace, quiet and gentle hospitality that have been bringing guests - especially artists and writers - here for the last hundred years. Mrs McDowell is very involved with the cultural life of the island - especially the Desmond Turner Achill Island School of Painting, and the cottage where Nobel prize-winning author Heinrich Böll once lived, which now offers a haven for artists and writers - and is an extraordinarily interested and hospitable hostess. This is an unusual establishment, occupying a series of houses, and each area has a slightly different appeal: there's a large, traditionally furnished sitting room with an open fire, comfortable leather lounge furniture, and several conservatories for quiet reading. Bedrooms and bathrooms vary considerably due to the age and nature of the premises, but the emphasis is on old-fashioned comfort; each of the three houses now has a fitted kitchen with everything you need to rustle up a light lunch, also a washing machine and tumble dryer, and the rooms all have tea & coffee-making trays; phones for incoming calls were introduced quite recently and there are extra shared bathrooms in addition to en-suite shower facilities. Children are welcome and have an indoor playroom and safe outdoor play area, plus pool and table tennis for older children. Dinner for residents is served in a large, quite formally appointed dining room, where lovely old-fashioned menus are offered - dishes like smoked mackerel with apple sauce or lemon wedge, homemade carrot & orange soup, roast lamb or beef, poached Keem Bay salmon with hollandaise sauce, Eve's pudding with whiskey sauce or fresh strawberry meringue. Packed lunches are also available on request. Pets permitted in some areas by arrangement. Children welcome (under 3s free in parents' room). Garden, fishing, walking. Pool table. Wheelchair accessible. Stair lift. Rooms 14 (13 en-suite, 1 with private bathroom, 1 with bath & shower, 13 shower only, 1 family room). B&B €55 pps, ss €6, SC discretionary. D 7pm. Set D €32, house wine €18. Closed 24-26 Dec. Personal cheques accepted. **No Credit Cards. Directions:** Castlebar, Westport, Newport, Achill Sound - Dugort!

Achill Keel

Bervie

B&B

Keel Achill Island Co Mayo **Tel: 098 43114** Fax: 098 43407
Email: bervie@esatclear.ie Web: www.bervieachill.com

John and Elizabeth Barrett's magical beachside house was once a coast guard station and, since 1932, has been the ultimate escape for the many guests who have stayed here. It's a low, tucked-in kind of a place with a little wicket gate giving direct access to the beach, and an other-worldliness which is very rare these days. Elizabeth was born here and, aside from the location and the charm of the house itself - which has style without being at all 'decorated' - it is the sense of continuity that makes it special; and, of course, she has the 'hotelier's gene' which makes hospitality come naturally. Bedrooms, while not especially large, are comfortably furnished with everything you need to feel at home, there is a large dining room, where Elizabeth serves a home-cooked dinner with several choices on each course, and plenty of room for sitting around the turf fire; while meals are primarily for residents, there's a natural hospitality here - beginning with the hot-buttered scones and home-made jam Elizabeth makes for afternoon tea - and a willingness to fit in extra guests if there is room. Children welcome (cot available without charge). Pets allowed in some areas. Pool table, playroom, garden. **Rooms 14** (all en-suite & no smoking, 11 shower only). Room service (limited hours). B&B €45-60 pps. ss €15-25. Weekend Dining Room seats 32. D €30-40 (reservations required; non-residents welcome if there is room). Closed Nov-Mar. MasterCard, Visa. **Directions:** Follow signs to Keel from bridge onto island; turn left in village, towards beach.◇

Achill Keel

Ferndale Restaurant

RESTAURANT

Crumpaun Keel Achill Island Co Mayo **Tel: 098 43908/9**
Email: achillfinedining@eircom.net Web: www.ferndale-achill.com

Stunning views and all-year opening are among the many attractions of Jon Fratschol's unusual restaurant: high over Keel village, it has huge picture windows to make the most of the view and there is, by his own admission, an air of fantasy about the whole place. You would have to look through the menu very carefully to find influences from Jon's Swiss roots, as the Ferndale specialities - a whole page of special dishes - lead off with Mongolian barbeque (a mixture of marinated meats, served with mashed sweet potato & honeyed onions) and Bora Bora Tahiti Dream (skewered fillets of ostrich & chicken, with a pineapple dip). A matching page of fish and seafood dishes includes equally unusual creations - but traditionalists will be pleased to know that there are a few more familiar items in there, including fillet steak Ferndale, which peppercorn sauce, or a mushroom cognac jus. Accommodation is also offered in three rooms (two with four-posters, one with a waterbed). **Seats 40.** Reservations required. Toilets wheelchair accessible. D daily in summer, 6-10.30; after Hallowe'en open weekends only (Thu-Sun) except fully open over Christmas. A la carte (main courses about €15-25). House wine from about €16. Amex, MasterCard, Visa, Laser. **Directions:** Signed up the hill from Keel village.

Achill Keel

The Beehive

CAFÉ/RESTAURANT

Keel Achill Island Co Mayo
Tel: 098 43134/43018 Fax: 098 43018

At their informal restaurant and attractive craft shop in Keel, husband and wife team Michael and Patricia Joyce take pride in the careful preparation and presentation of the best of Achill produce, especially local seafood such as fresh and smoked salmon, mussels, oysters and crab. Since opening, in 1991, they have extended both the menu and the premises more than once and now offer great all-day self-service food, which you can have indoors, or take out to a patio overlooking Keel beach in fine weather Everything is homemade, and they make delicious soups such as cheddar & onion, courgette & onion, leek & mussel, seafood chowder and traditional nettle soup (brotchán neantóg) all served with homemade brown scones. As baking is a speciality, there's always a tempting selection of cakes, bracks, teabreads, fruit tarts, baked desserts and scones with home-made preserves or you can simply have a toasted sandwich, or an Irish farmhouse cheese plate (with a glass of wine perhaps). * The family also has accommodation on the island; details from the restaurant. **Seats 100** (outdoor seating, 60; private room, 50). Toilet wheelchair accessible; children welcome, baby changing facility. Meals 9.30-6pm daily, Easter-early Nov. A la carte; wine licence: 1/4 bottle wine from €4.75. No sc. Closed Nov-Easter Amex, Diners, MasterCard, Visa, Laser. **Directions:** Situated in the centre of Keel village overlooking beach and Minuan cliffs.

Ballina

Belleek Castle

HOTEL

Ballina Co Mayo **Tel: 096 22400** Fax: 096 71750
Email: belleekcastlehotel@eircom.net Web: www.belleekcastle.com

Situated just outside Ballina amidst 1,000 acres of woodland and forestry, on the banks of the River Moy - and entered via an ancient gateway and woodland drive - Belleek Castle was the ancestral home of the Earl of Arran and, despite extensive recent refurbishment, it retains its quirky character with antiquities such as suits of armour, heavy tables and chandeliers along the corridors and ceilings. The "Armada Bar" is a recreation of the Captains Ward Room from a galleon in the Spanish Armada - partly constructed from oak balks salvaged from the galleons of the ill fated "Castile Squadron" wrecked on the Atlantic Coast of Co. Mayo four centuries ago, it should provide plenty of talking points to pep up your drink - a superb collection of artefacts is exhibited and a classic "figurehead" of a Spanish Conquistador (Hernando Cortez) surveys all. But, far from feeling like a theme park, this impressive hotel manages to combine old world elegance and all the necessary modern comforts in bright and spacious bedrooms, many with four-poster beds and views out over the grounds, where guests can enjoy lakeside and woodland walks. It makes a romantic wedding venue (the banqueting room is in medieval castle style and has a real castle feel and its own bar). The many activities to choose from nearby include championship golf, walking, surfing and there's salmon and trout fishing on site; or, with its informal and friendly ambience, the castle simply makes a comfortable base to explore this beautiful area. Rooms: B&B €70 pps, ss €20. **Directions:** Follow signs on way into Ballina for Belleek. ◇

Ballina

Crockets on the Quay

BAR/RESTAURANT/GUESTHOUSE

Ballina Co Mayo
Tel: 096 75930 Fax: 096 70069
Email: info@crocketsonthequay.ie Web: www.crocketsonthequay.ie

This well-known hostelry is attractively situated on the quay in Ballina, overlooking the River Moy (which may well provide some of the wild salmon on the menu), and it's a surprisingly large premises once you start exploring. It's inviting from the road, with seating outside for fine weather and a very pleasant old-style bar with an open fire (gas, alas) and plenty of pictures and artefacts of local interest giving it a sense of history. Extending behind the traditional bar is a series of contemporary bar areas with trendy low seating and big tables, finishing up with a stylish big bar right at the back, with lots of low seating and access to a car park behind the building. Interesting bar meals are served all day by exceptionally friendly, helpful staff and, although the dim lighting seems quite surreal when coming in from the sunshine on a bright summer's day, it's a hospitable place - and it leaps into life at night. The restaurant is at the front of the building, overlooking the river, and has recently been refurbished in quiet warm browns and soft beiges, giving it a stylish, gently modern feel. Well-balanced, interesting menus show pride in local produce and include some unusual ideas alongside well-known dishes. Quality ingredients, sound cooking and some welcome originality make this a great place to eat - enhanced by the riverside location, and excellent service by friendly and very professional staff. The wine list is interesting although, after the house wines, prices rise quite steeply; fair choice of half bottles. *Moderately-priced accommodation is offered in eight en-suite rooms; while not luxurious, they are very adequate - and a comforting breakfast is served with a smile. Pool table, free broadband Wi/Fi. Not suitable for children after 7.30pm. Parking (30). **Seats 50** (outdoor seating, 40). Toilets wheelchair accessible. D daily, 5.30-9.30; L daily, 12.30-3. Set D €22.95; also à la carte. House wine €18. Bar menu available daily, 12.30-9. **Accommodation: Rooms 8** (7 shower only. 4 no smoking). B&B about €35pps, ss €5. Closed 25 Dec, Good Fri. Amex, MasterCard, Visa, Laser. **Directions:** On the edge of Ballina; from town, take main Sligo road, turn left at first traffic lights.

Ballina

Gaughans

PUB

O'Rahilly Street Ballina Co Mayo
Tel: 096 70096 Email: edgaug@eircom.net

féile bia

This is one of the great old pubs of Ireland and has a gentle way of drawing you in, with the menu up in the window and a display of local pottery to arouse the curiosity. It's a fine old-fashioned bar, with everything gleaming and a great sense of the pride taken in its care. Michael Gaughan opened the pub in November 1936 and his son, Edward, took over in 1972. Edward's wife Mary is a great cook and, once they started doing food in 1983 they never looked back; everybody loves the way they run the place and Mary still does all the cooking. Her specialities (all good home cooking) include home-made quiche Lorraine with salad, lovely old-fashioned roasts - roast stuffed chicken with vegetables and potatoes, perhaps, or baked gammon, and local seafood, when available:

fresh crab is served from May to the end of August, wild sea salmon from 1st June to the second week in July, and smoked salmon all year round - such respect for seasonality is rare enough these days, and it is good to see it. There's always a daily special (€9.50) and old favourites like lemon meringue pie and pineapple upside down pudding for dessert. Lighter options on the menu include open smoked salmon or crab sandwich (in season), smoked salmon salad, ploughman's lunch, and it's all great wholesome fare. And, charmingly listed along with the Bewley's tea and coffee, the wine and Irish coffee "Glass of spring water: Free." Now that's style. Children welcome. Opening hours: Mon-Sat from 11 am (Mon-Thu to 11.30; Fri & Sat to 12.30). Bar food served Mon-Sat, 11am-5pm. Closed Sun, 25 Dec & Good Fri. Amex, Diners, MasterCard, Visa, Laser. **Directions:** Up to the post office, on the left.

Ballina

Mount Falcon Country House Hotel & Estate

HOTEL

Foxford Road Ballina Co Mayo **Tel: 096 74472** Fax: 096 74473
Email: info@mountfalcon.com Web: www.mountfalcon.com

Mount Falcon will be fondly remembered by many for its lovable eccentricity under the previous owner, Connie Aldridge (whose late husband Major Robert Aldridge, a keen archaeologist, helped discover the Ceidhe Fields) and it is now owned by the locally based Maloney brothers, who fell in love with it when visiting in 2002 and bought the estate when she retired. They have since been working on a sensitively executed multi-million euro building and refurbishment plan that included extending the original house and erecting a selection of luxurious courtyard houses and woodland lodges. Mount Falcon has now re-opened as a 32 bedroom luxury hotel and it is a welcoming place, first seen in a series of ground floor drawing rooms and lounges with comfy sofas, open fires and coffee tables scattered with books and magazines about fishing, hunting and country life in general. Accommodation includes six deluxe rooms (including two suites the Wallpool and Connor's Gap, which are named after famous pools on the Mount Falcon Fishery) on the upper floors of the original house, carefully restored with pitch-pine shutters and floors original cornices, marble fireplaces and, of course, all the modern comforts. The other rooms are new, spacious and furnished to a high standard with custom designed furniture, television and radio, direct dial phone, personal safe and hairdryer as standard. The estate enjoys more than 2 miles of double bank salmon fishing on the River Moy, and the 100 acres of grounds have been redeveloped and landscaped to incorporate lakeside and woodland walks. Other local activities include championship golf, at nearby Enniscrone Golf Club, and horse riding - and there are many beaches nearby. Conferences/Banqueting (250/180), broadband WI/Fi, video conferencing. Salmon fishing and walking on site. Spa, leisure centre with indoor 'Pool, steam room, sauna, jacuzzi and gym. Conferences/Banqueting (180). **Rooms 32** (6 de-luxe suites, 26 superior); Children welcome (cots available, baby sitting arranged); Lift; 24 hr room service. Self catering also available. Helipad. Amex, MasterCard, Visa, Laser. **Directions:** Just outside Ballina on the N26.

Ballina Area

Enniscoe House

COUNTRY HOUSE

Castlehiill Crossmolina Ballina Co Mayo
Tel: 096 31112 Fax: 096 31773
Email: mail@enniscoe.com Web: www.enniscoe.com

In parkland and mature woods on the shores of Lough Conn, Enniscoe can sometimes seem stern and gaunt, as Georgian mansions in the north-west of Ireland tend to be, but this hospitable house has great charm: with family portraits, antique furniture, crackling log fires, warm hospitality and good home cooking, it makes a lovely place to come back to after a day in the rugged countryside. It was built by ancestors of the present owner, Susan Kellett, who settled here in the 1660s, and is a very special place for anglers and other visitors with a natural empathy for the untamed wildness of the area. Large public rooms include a fine drawing room, with a big log fire and plenty of seating, and a more intimate dining room (which can accommodate some extra non-resident guests nevertheless). Susan's wholesome 5-course dinners change daily and make good use of local produce in dishes like timbales of smoked salmon (from Clarkes of Ballina) with cucumber salad, curried courgette soup and - a delicious house speciality - roast free-range pork with apricot and walnut sauce. Homely desserts to finish (rhubarb and orange crumble, perhaps) and cheeses laid out on the sideboard as they are again next morning, as part of an excellent breakfast. Traditionally furnished bedrooms are large, very comfortable and, like their en-suite bathrooms, regularly refurbished. And there is also much of interest around converted outbuildings at the back of the house, including a genealogy centre (The Mayo North Family History Research Centre, Tel: 096 31809), a small but expanding agricultural museum with working blacksmith, and conference facilities. The house is surrounded by woodlands, where Susan has built a network of paths, and major renovations have recently taken place in the walled gardens, which are open to the public and have tea-rooms and a shop stocking quality "non-tourist" items, collectables, and garden plants. There is brown trout fishing on Lough Conn and other trout and salmon fishing nearby; boats, ghillies, tuition and hire of equipment can be arranged. Golf (three courses within easy reach) and equestrian nearby. Children welcome (under 2s free in parents' room, cot available without charge, baby sitting arranged), and dogs are also allowed by arrangement. Gardens open at all times for residents (without charge). *Self-catering units also available. Small conferences (50). **Rooms 6** (all en-suite & no smoking, 2 family rooms) B&B €98 pps, ss €20. Turndown service. Restaurant: Seats 20. D daily, 7.30-8.30pm; reservations accepted; non residents welcome by reservation. 3-course Set D €48; house wines €18-24. Closed 1 Nov-1 Apr. MasterCard, Visa, Laser. **Directions:** 3km (2 m) south of Crossmolina on R315.

Ballinrobe

JJ Gannons Hotel

Ⓝ HOTEL

Main St Ballinrobe Co Mayo **Tel: 094 954 1008** Fax: 094 952 0018
Email: info@jjgannons.com Web: www.jjgannons.com

Right in the heart of the thriving town of Ballinrobe, JJ Gannons goes back to 1838 but it's now in the third generation and rather funky from the outside preparing first time visitors for a mainly modern style, which is unusual for the area and reflects the taste of an energetic and very committed young couple, Niki and Jay Gannon, who are developing it as a 'green' hotel. (Mayo County Council are using the hotel as a prototype: a geo thermal heating system converts energy from the river, and a wood pellet burner provides back up.) On entering, there's a contemporary bar - chrome bar stools, cream leather chairs and cubes and, connected to it, a more traditional room; between them they cater for all age groups and, impressively, a blackboard offers some twenty wines available by the glass (including Deutz champagne at €9 a glass, which is pretty good by any standards). Although open and functioning well, the hotel was very much a work in progress at the time of our visit, and many changes and improvements, both big and small, are in the pipeline. The original eleven bright bedrooms offer a range of standards including a junior suite, and a further 12 bedrooms are under construction (as cottage style suites at the river end of the garden); and, in a move towards a more luxurious style, new tailor-made linen and goose down duvets have been purchased to fit the huge (6'6") beds, also velour bathrobes and slippers. On the food front things have got off to a good start and the restaurant, which is a bright and airy room with wooden floors and lots of windows, is earning a local following and improvements are afoot here too as we go to press, with the introduction of new seasonal menus and a new wine list. With such committed owners, lovely friendly staff and a good buzz, this is a place to watch. Conferences/Banqueting (50/80), business centre, secretarial services, free broadband WI/Fi. Fishing, golf nearby, equestrian nearby, walking, massage, short breaks. Children welcome (under 2s free in parents' room, cot available at no charge, baby sitting arranged). **Rooms 11** (1 suite, 4 junior suites, 1 shower only, 4 family rooms, 1 for disabled, all no smoking); lift; limited room service; B&B €60 pps, ss €15. **"Red" Restaurant:** seats 50 (private room, 50, outdoor, 20); air conditioning; reservations recommended; children welcome before 7pm; L Mon-Sat, 12.30-3.30; D Mon-Sat 6-9.30; Sun, 12.30-8.30; Early D €30, 5-7pm; gourmet D €80 (food & wine); also a la carte L&D; house wine €16.50. *Bar food served daily 8am - 9.30pm. Open all year. MasterCard, Visa, Laser. **Directions:** Southern Mayo, off N84.

Ballycastle

Mary's Bakery & Tea Rooms

€ RESTAURANT

Main Street Ballycastle Co Mayo
Tel: 096 43361

Mary Munnelly's homely little restaurant is the perfect place to stop for some tasty home cooking. Baking is the speciality but she does "real meals" as well - a full Irish breakfast, which is just the thing for walkers, home-made soups like mushroom or smoked bacon & potato, wild salmon various ways (in season) and free range chicken dishes. And, if you strike a chilly day, it's very pleasant to get tucked in beside a real fire too. There's also a garden with sea views for fine weather - and home-made chutneys and jams on sale to take home. **Seats 30** (also outdoor seating for 12). Toilets wheelchair accessible. Open 10am-6pm daily in summer (may open later - to 8-ish - in high season; shorter hours off season); Closed Sun off-season (Oct-Easter), & first 3 weeks Jan. **No Credit Cards. Directions:** From Ballina - Killala - main road to Ballycastle, on way to Ceide Fields. ◇

Ballycastle

Polke's

PUB

Main Street Ballycastle Co Mayo **Tel: 096 43016**

This lovely old general merchants and traditional pub is just across the road from Mary's Bakery, and well worth a visit. It was established in 1820 and has remained in the family since then - the present proprietor, Brian Polke, has had responsibility for this national treasure since 1962. Not much has changed it seems: the long, narrow bar behind the shop is completely unspoilt, friendly and a joy to find yourself in. The whole place is immaculate too (including the outside loo in a whitewashed yard at the back), giving the lie to the widely-held view that "character" pubs are, by definition, scruffy. A nice touch of modernity which reflects the close-knit nature of the local community is the collection of pictures donated by artists from the nearby Ballinglen Arts Centre, which are exhibited in the bar and make a fascinating talking point for new arrivals. Open 10am-11.30pm. Closed 25 Dec & Good Fri. **Directions:** On main street.

Ballycastle

HOTEL/RESTAURANT

Stella Maris Hotel

Ballycastle Co Mayo
Tel: 096 43322 Fax: 096 43965
Email: info@stellamarisireland.com Web: www.stellamarisireland.com

Built in 1853 as a coast guard regional headquarters, this fine property on the edge of the wonderfully away-from-it-all village of Ballycastle was later acquired by the Sisters of Mercy, who named it Stella Maris, and it now makes a very special small hotel, restored by proprietors Terence McSweeney and Frances Kelly, who have created a warm and stylish interior where antiques rub shoulders with contemporary pieces. There's a welcome emphasis on comfort throughout public areas, including a cosy bar - but the location is this hotel's major asset and a conservatory built all along the front takes full advantage of it, allowing guests to relax in comfort and warmth while drinking in the majestic views of the surrounding coastline and sea. Accommodation blends understated elegance with comfort in uncluttered rooms that have magnificent views and are furnished with antiques but - with complimentary broadband, modern bathrooms and power showers - offer the best of both worlds. Children welcome (under 3s free in parents' room; baby sitting arranged). Walking; fishing. Garden. No pets. **Rooms 12** (1 suites, 6 shower only, 1 ground floor, 1 disabled, all no smoking). B&B €102.50 pps, ss €42.50. **Restaurant:** Dinner - cooked under Frances' direct supervision - is a very enjoyable experience, based on local ingredients as far as possible, including organic produce from nearby Enniscoe (see entry) and also from the hotel's own new gardens. Menus are well-balanced and imaginative, without being over-influenced by fashion: sautéed lambs kidneys (in season), carrot & orange soup, rack of Mayo lamb with puy lentils and sage-flavoured jus are all typical and there is usually a choice of two fish dishes (vegetarian option on request). Classic desserts include refreshing seasonal fruits - poached plums with vanilla ice cream, glazed Italian meringue & mango coulis, perhaps - and there will always be an Irish farmhouse cheese plate - then it's back to the conservatory for a digestif... The wine list, while relatively short, has been chosen with care. Residents also have a treat in store each morning, as the Stella Maris breakfast is worth lingering over: lashings of freshly squeezed juice, a beautiful fruit plate, gorgeous freshly-baked brown bread, hand-made preserves and perfect hot food cooked to order, be it a traditional Irish or a special like creamy scrambled eggs with smoked salmon; not a grand display, but exceptionally delicious. Stella Maris was selected as Connaught winner of our Irish Breakfast Awards in 2004. This is indeed a wonderful retreat. Short breaks offered - details on application. Banqueting (40). **Restaurant seats 28.** Reservations required; non-residents welcome. D 7-9 (Mon residents' only), D à la carte, house wine €22. Restaurant closed Mon (to non-residents); hotel closed Oct-Mar. *Complimentary broadband access. MasterCard, Visa, Laser. **Directions:** West of Ballina on R314; 2km (1.5 m) west of Ballycastle.

Bangor Erris

HOTEL

Teach Iorrais Hotel

Geesala Bangor Erris Ballina Co Mayo **Tel: 097 86888** Fax: 097 86855
Email: teachlor@iol.ie Web: www.teachiorrais.com

Facilities in this remote and fascinating Gaeltacht area were pretty thin on the ground before this friendly hotel opened in 1998 and it has proved a tremendous success. It's a great place to drop into during the day for a bite to eat or just a cup of tea - there's always a welcoming fire in the bar (which has character, although the hotel is modern), and staff are invariably friendly and helpful. While not luxurious, the accommodation is very acceptable for the price charged, and pleasant, comfortably furnished bedrooms have neat en-suite bathrooms, direct dial phone, tea/coffee facilities and television with video channel. Off-season breaks offer especially good value and there are many activities nearby, including golf (Carne), horse riding, walking, boating and fishing (there's a drying room for tackle and bait). Teach Iorrais is a popular place for weddings and would also be an interesting choice for conferences and corporate events - or for a very different Christmas or New Year break. It has a wonderfully away-from-it- all atmosphere. Conference/banqueting (300); secretarial services. No pets. Children welcome (under 5s free in parents' room; cots available without charge, baby sitting arranged). Garden, fishing, walking, cycling. **Rooms 30** (all en-suite,1 suite, 10 no-smoking, 1 for disabled). B&B about €50 pps, ss €10. Light bar food 12.30-4pm daily. D offered daily, 7-9.30; L Sun 1-4), 7-9.30. Short breaks offered; details on application. Open all year. Amex, MasterCard, Visa, Laser. **Directions:** 40 minutes drive west from Ballina. ◇

Belmullet

An Chéibh

Ⓝ PUB

Barrack Street Belmullet Co Mayo **Tel: 097 81007**

Situated in the heart of one of Ireland's most far flung towns, and one almost surrounded by the sea, the Talbot family's friendly An Chéibh ("the anchor") is a very fitting place to find a seafood bar with a comfortable bar and lounge adorned with nautical memoribilia and local photos of bygone times. Although there's plenty of choice for non fish eaters, menus are weighted heavily in favour of local seafood as is the Specials Board, offering seasonal fish such as mackerel or wild salmon and their Fishermans Platter is legendary, guaranteeing to satisfy the hungriest traveller. **Seats about 40;** air conditioning; children welcome; food served Mon-Sat, 12.30-9.30 in summer, to 8pm in winter, Sun 1pm-7.30pm; à la carte; house wine €17.50. Closed Good Fri, 25 Dec. MasterCard, Visa, Laser. **Directions:** Blue pub on the left on main entrance into Belmullet.

Belmullet

Broadhaven Bay Hotel

Ⓝ HOTEL

Ballina Road Belmullet Co Mayo **Tel: 097 20600** Fax: 097 20610
Email: info@broadhavenbay.com Web: www.broadhavenbay.com

This large new hotel enjoys commanding views over Broadhaven Bay and offers not only accommodation but also extensive bar, restaurant and banqueting facilities - all much needed services in the area. Comfortably appointed bedrooms look over the bay to the front and a courtyard to the rear, and all have a safe, tea/coffee making facilities, direct dial phone, iron and plasma tv as standard. Friendly, helpful staff are more than happy to help guests arrange any of the many activities in the area, including championship golf at the world famous Carne Golf Links, canoeing, walking, fishing, diving, cycling and horse riding and, with a leisure centre and spa due to be completed by 2007, this is a comfortable place to be based when visiting one of the most beautiful parts of Ireland. Conferences/Banqueting (600/500); leisure centre; golf, walking, diving, golf and canoeing available locally. **Rooms 70,** B&B around €75 pps, ss around €10. **Directions:** On the road into Belmullet. ◇

Castlebar

An Carraig

RESTAURANT

Chapel Street Castlebar Co Mayo
Tel: 094 902 6159 Fax: 094 902 7422

Eimar Horan's family-run restaurant in a quiet street just off the town centre has earned a loyal local following. It's an attractive, quite traditional restaurant with cut stone walls and a nautical theme with lots of wood, portholes and an arch that links smaller dining areas and also provides visual interest, and a cosier more intimate atmosphere - a feeling enhanced by gentle lighting and candles. Menus are updated traditional, with steaks and seafood taking the starring roles in dishes like char-grilled steaks various ways, seafood chowder, steamed mussels, lobster - many of the old favourites are there; also home-made paté, honey roast duckling, chargrilled chicken breast - but most will have some kind of twist in the presentation, bringing them up to date. Finish with the shared dessert platter for two. Healthy options are offered and there's willingness to provide for special diets and allergies (advance notice preferred). Good customer care and home cooking is the aim, achieved very successfully - and they give good value too. Guests are even urged to take home a loaf of the home-made bread. **Seats 55.** D Tue-Sun, 6-10pm (Sun 5.30-9.30). Early D €22 (6-7.15); Set D about €28. House wine, about €18. Closed Mon, last 2 weeks Jan. MasterCard, Visa, Switch. **Directions:** Town centre, opposite Church of the Holy Rosary. ◇

Castlebar

Café Rua

€ RESTAURANT

New Antrim Street Castlebar Co Mayo
Tel: 094 902 3376 Email: aran@iol.ie

Well located near the Linenhall Arts & Exhibition Centre, you can't miss this attractive little restaurant, with its cheerful red frontage. Ann McMahon set up here over 10 years ago and is still very involved although Aran and Colleen McMahon now look after the day to day running. Although they are very serious about the food they serve, the tone is light-hearted - it's not a very large room but pine tables (some covered in red oilcloths) are quite well-spaced and most have a good view of the large blackboard menu that lists all kinds of good things to raise the spirits of weary shoppers and culture vultures. Wholesome, home-made fresh food is the order of the day here, and careful sourcing of ingredients is a point of pride - so pasta dishes are based on the excellent Noodle House pastas from Sligo, Irish farmhouse cheeses and other speciality ingredients are supplied by Sheridans cheesemongers, fish comes from Clarkes of Ballina and pork from Ketterich's of Castlebar. Organic vegetables are supplied by a nearby organic scheme in summer, Macroom stoneground oats go into the porridge that is served with home-made apple compôte in winter - and ingredients for the full Irish (sausages, puddings) come from the renowned butchers, Kellys of Newport. Regular dishes like home made chicken liver paté, warm chicken salad with chilli mayonnaise and ratatouille crostini are announced on one blackboard, while another gives hot specials like potato & lovage soup, grilled pork chops with carrots, new season potatoes & mushroom à la crème and organic spinach & Crozier Blue cheese tart with tomato & basil salad. There's an interesting drinks menu (wines, juices, hot chocolate with marshmallows) and 'because we know that they love food too', there's also a special children's menu, one of many thoughtful touches. Luscious desserts (rhubarb trifle, for example) and good home bakes too: great little place. Children welcome. Wheelchair accessible. **Seats 35.** Open all day Mon-Sat, 9.30-5.30. Closed Sun; Bank Hols, 1 week at Christmas. MasterCard, Visa, Laser. **Directions:** Opposite Tourist Information Office.

Castlebar
HOTEL

Lynch Breaffy House Hotel & Spa

Castlebar Co Mayo
Tel: 094 902 2033 Fax: 904 902 2276

This handsome hotel set in its own grounds just outside Castlebar town dates back to 1890 and retains some of its original country house atmosphere, although it can now be very busy at times. It has undergone major renovation in recent years, and considerable refurbishment has been undertaken in public areas (including the restaurant) and bedrooms; sixty five new deluxe bedrooms (including two presidential suites and 20 interconnecting family rooms) have been added. An impressive leisure complex and health spa, Life-Spa and Ku'dos Aqua & Fitness Club, has also been added to the hotel, making this an all-year destination for short breaks. New facilities include a gymnasium, 20 metre pool, Café West (for refreshments at the leisure complex), also an exhaustive range of treatments, some of which are unique in Ireland. Conference/banqueting (500); business centre. Preferential local golf rates. Leisure centre, swimming pool; spa. Off season value breaks. Children welcome (under 2 free in parents' room, cots available without charge, baby sitting arranged). No pets. Garden, walking. **Rooms 125** (10 suites, 40 executive, 10 no smoking, 2 disabled). Lift. 24 hr room service. B&B about €80pps, ss about €26. SC incl. Open all year. Amex, Diners, MasterCard, Visa, Laser. **Directions:** 4km outside Castlebar on the Claremoris Road. ◇

Castlebar area
Ⓝ CAFÉ

An Grianán Museum Café

National Museum of Ireland for Country Life Turlough Castlebar Co Mayo
Tel: 094 928 9972 Fax: 096 29989
Email: info@leonardcatering.com Web: www.leonardcatering.com

The National Museum of Ireland's Museum of Country Life is a great place to spend an afternoon with the family and, although the grounds would be best enjoyed in the sunshine, it's a useful haven if you happen to strike a bad spell of weather. The old house has some rooms restored to their 19th century glory and a rolling lawn leads down to a large tree-lined lake where, by contrast, the eye is drawn to the straight lines of the large, modern museum; here three floors of photos and exhibits which have been gathered by the government over the last two centuries. After building up a healthy appetite mooching around the museum, a visit to the courtyard Café in the old house is called for, and it should not disappoint: a short but appealing menu offers a limited choice of wholesome dishes including home bakes such as a freshly made quiche with an Irish farmhouse cheese such as Gubbeen, perhaps, served with a selection from an excellent salad bar that offers a range such as roasted spiced chick peas, new potatoes in a creamed mustard sauce, feta, mixed salad leaves, and cous cous all enhanced by a well-flavoured home made salad dressing. Children welcome; Toilets wheelchair accessible. **Seats 85** (private room, 40, outdoors, 20); air conditioning; food served during museum opening hours, Tue-Sun, 12-5, L 12-4. Closed Mon and Bank Hols. MasterCard, Visa, Laser. **Directions:** In National Museum of Ireland for Country Life in Turlough, off N5 Castlebar road.

Claremorris
BAR/RESTAURANT

Old Arch Bar & Bistro

James Street Claremorris Co Mayo **Tel: 094 936 2777**
Fax: 094 936 2888 Web: www.theoldarchbistro.com

Fergus and Anne Maxwell's bar and informal restaurant in this recently by-passed town, has an inviting black and white frontage with well-maintained window boxes, and there's a welcoming atmosphere in the comfortable, low-ceilinged reception area and bar. The restaurant is informal (darkwood tables with linen napkins, but no table mats or flowers) and friendly staff neatly dressed in black trousers and wine aprons, present large, cheerful dinner menus offering a wide selection of popular dishes, arranged by section offering light dishes, soups & salads, fish & poultry, meat and vegetarian, and there is a separate children's menu - something for everyone, whether you want a full meal or something lighter. Typically, starters might include mussels in a coconut, cream & coriander sauce, or baked goats cheese in filo, with a pesto dressing, and main course specialities like Old Arch chicken supreme (chicken breast stuffed with black pudding then wrapped in bacon, served with mushroom & brandy sauce), and also roast five spice boneless half duck, stuffed with potato & herbs and served with red onion confit and a Madeira jus. Portions are generous, the cooking is generally good and prices are moderate: ideal for a family-friendly restaurant in a growing town. At lunchtime, sandwiches get a menu of their own, and the main lunch menu changes daily. There's a large garden area too, with gas heaters, barbecue and plenty of seating. Children welcome before 9pm. L &D daily: L12-4, D6-9 (10 Fri/Sat). Private room (55), Outdoor dining (30). MasterCard, Visa, Laser. **Directions:** 10km fron Knock, on Galway-Sligo/Derry road. Beside railway bridge, on the main street.

Cong

★ HOTEL/RESTAURANT

Ashford Castle

Cong Co Mayo

Tel: 094 954 6003 Fax: 094 954 6260

Email: ashford@ashford.ie Web: www.ashford.ie

CHEF OF THE YEAR

Ireland's grandest castle hotel, with a history going back to the early 13th century, Ashford is set in 350 acres of beautiful parkland. Grandeur, formality and tranquillity are the essential characteristics, first seen in immaculately maintained grounds and, once inside, in a succession of impressive public rooms that illustrate a long and proud history - panelled walls, oil paintings, suits of armour and magnificent fireplaces. Accommodation varies considerably due to the size and age of the building, and each room in some way reflects the special qualities of the hotel. The best guest rooms, and the luxurious suites at the top of the castle - many with magnificent views of Lough Corrib, the River Cong and wooded parkland - are elegantly furnished with period furniture, some with enormous and beautifully appointed bathrooms, others with remarkable architectural features, such as a panelled wooden ceiling recently discovered behind plasterwork in one of the suites (and now fully restored). The hotel's exceptional amenities include a neo-classical fitness centre, and sporting activities are detailed in a very handy little pocket book. The castle has three restaurants: The Connaught Room, which is mainly for residents, is the jewel in Ashford Castle's culinary crown and one of Ireland's most impressive restaurants; the George V Dining Room offers fine dining for larger numbers; the new Cullen's Cottage, in the grounds, offers accessible all-day informal dining. Executive Head Chef, Stefan Matz oversees the cooking for both restaurants in the castle, and Cullen's Cottage, in the grounds; since joining the team in 2003, this highly skilled and likeable chef has worked wonders to introduce some gentle modernisation of menus, bring the varying dining operations together, and ensure high standards in each. Conference/banqueting (110/65); business centre; secretarial services; video conferencing. Fitness centre, beauty salon, hairdressing. Children welcome: under 12 free in parents' room (deluxe rooms only), cot available without charge, baby sitting arranged. No pets. **Rooms 83** (6 suites, 5 junior suites, 32 executive, some no smoking). Lift. 24 hour room service. Turn down service. Room rate about €485 (max 2 guests, with breakfast), room only €430; SC 15%. Short/off-season breaks offered - details on application. **The Connaught Room:** This small room is one of Ireland's most impressive restaurants. The style is broadly classical French, using the best of local ingredients - Atlantic prawns, Galway Bay sole, Cleggan lobster, Connemara lamb, and speciality produce like James McGeough's wonderful cured Connemara lamb from Oughterard, in sophisticated dishes that will please the most discerning diner. If at least two people (preferably a whole party) are agreed, a seasonal 7-course Menu Dégustation tasting menu is available - and after dinner you will be presented with a souvenir copy of the menu: a wonderful way to commemorate a special occasion. Dishes attracting special praise on a recent visit include fillet of turbot, with smoked oyster & sautéed chard (sublimely fresh fish set off by the delicately smoked oyster and earthy chard); roast loin of veal, with wild mushrooms & creamed potato (a welcome change from the usual imported milk-fed variety - young Irish beef at its best, cooked as ordered), and cardamom roasted yellow peaches, with honey yogurt & lime ice cream (a beautiful balance of flavours, artfully presented) - and a trolley of 13 outstanding Irish farmhouse cheeses in prime condition with their own explanatory menu, is very impressive. Attention to detail is superb throughout, and the experience benefits greatly from the personal attendance of Martin Gibbons whose constant, caring presence is at the heart of this theatrical experience, complete with perfectly groomed staff and his own unobtrusive commentary on the various dishes as they are served with perfect, silver-domed timing. **Seats 36** (max table size 14). D only, 7-9.30; reservations essential (usually residents only); Menu Dégustation 5/7 courses €75/85, also à la carte. The wine list is a stunning example of an old-fashioned, grand hotel list. **George V Dining Room:** Dinner and off-season Sunday lunch are served in this much larger but almost equally opulent dining room, where a combination of fine food and attentive service, under the direction of

Maitre d'Hôtel Seamus Judge, promise an outstanding dining experience. A five-course dinner menu offers a choice of about five dishes on the first and main courses, including some tempting vegetarian suggestions. The choice is wide, offering about eight dishes on each course, with a suggested wine (all offered by the glass or bottle) with each starter and main course. You might begin with the Ashford Castle version of Caesar Salad, which is made with crisp dried Connemara ham, or a speciality of potato wrapped prawn tails, with char grillled asparagus; of the main courses, there's a slight leaning towards seafood - fillet of turbot with black and white seafood pudding, for example - game will be offered in season, and a speciality that may surprise is the daily roast, which is served in fine old style from a carving trolley. Irresistible desserts - apple beignet with hazelnut chocolate parfait and toffeee & apple sauce, perhaps - or that superb cheese trolley (see Connaught Room). All the little niceties of a special meal are observed including appetisers, a range of excellent home-made breads and wonderful petits fours (by pastry chef Bernd Strauss). Although unarguably expensive, the dining experience at Ashford castle gives value for money - and the Sunday lunch menu is very reasonable for the quality of food, service and surroundings; it offers a shortened and somewhat simplified version of the dinner menu, but the same high standards apply: every meal bears the hallmarks of confident cooking and a light touch that, while classically correct, is thoroughly modern as well. *All meals in the castle are by reservation. *A light daytime menu is available in The Gallery. **Seats 140.** D daily 7-9.30, L Sun only (Oct-May), 1-2pm Set Sun L €39, Set 5 course D €67. A la carte D also available; house wines from €26. SC.15% **Cullen's at The Cottage:** A stone's throw from the Corrib and within sight of the castle, on Ashford's manicured lawns, Cullen's at The Cottage, named after the late Peter Cullen, a much-loved former Maitre D', offers a completely new experience: mid-priced dining, open to the public, with none of the pomp and ceremony associated with the grandeur of meals served in the castle itself. The kitchen is operated under Stefan Matz's direction, but functions independently from the main castle kitchen. Internally the cottage has been transformed, with burgundy coloured banquette seating, plain wood tables, tiled floors, and white walls. The menu, while leaning towards seafood, offers a varied selection of meat and vegetarian dishes, salads and side orders, also a daytime sandwich, pitta and panini section, and coffees, teas and desserts. On a fine summer's day dining al fresco here has a continental air. Dishes enjoyed with relish on a recent visit included lobster pie (€25), halibut in olive oil & vinegar (€19) and cold seafood platter (salmon, prawns and crabmeat), €19, all excellent dishes and, like the selection of homemade ice creams and coffees that followed, good value - and, from a short list of 18 wines ranging fom €16-55, a Pinot Grigio, Corte Giara 2005 is fairly priced @ €22. Well-trained staff give good service, while appearing to have all the time in the world to chat. **Cullen's Cottage: Seats 65** (private room 48, outdoor seating 48). Open 12-9.30 daily (a phone call to check is advised, especially off season). Reservations accepted. A la carte. Wines from €16. Amex, Diners, MasterCard, Visa, Laser. **Directions:** 48km (30 m) north of Galway on Lough Corrib.

Cong

Ⓝ COUNTRY HOUSE

Ballywarren Country House

Cross Cong Co Mayo

Tel: 094 954 6989 Fax: 094 954 6989

Email: ballywarrenhouse@eircom.net Web: www.ballywarrenhouse.net

Diane and David Skelton's hospitable country house is in a pleasant rural area of gentle farming countryside just a few minutes' drives east of Cong and Ashford Castle. Large and well-proportioned, it has a welcoming feeling from the minute you arrive through the door into the classic back and white tiled hall - and, no doubt, you will find a very warm welcome, as Diane and David are natural hosts who take genuine pleasure in sharing their home with guests, and introducing them to all the things this lovely area has to offer. It is perfectly placed for fishing holidays, for example, and the Connemara National Park is easily accessible. Public rooms, furnished stylishly with antiques set off against boldly coloured walls, include a spacious drawing room with a cosy open fire, and the lovely Garden Room dining room, where dinner is available to guests by arrangement. An oak staircase leads up to a galleried landing, and the three charming bedrooms: all are very nicely set up, and have lots of little extras (chocolates, plenty to read, even playing cards...). One especially romantic room has a four-poster bed, and all have luxurious, well-finished bathrooms, complete with Crabtree & Evelyn toiletries. This would make a very comfortable base for a few days spent in the area, and is a good alternative for guests attending weddings nearby at Ashford Castle. The only slight downside (unexpected in a country house) is that the road is quite close; however, it is not a busy road (especially at night) and traffic noise should not be a problem. Fishing, golf, lake cruising, horse riding, hill walking all nearby. Garden. Pets permitted in certain areas by prior arrangement. **Rooms 3** (all non-smoking, cot available free of charge, turndown service; TV/video, iron/trouser press). Residents' D at 8pm in the Garden Room; dining room seats 8; Set D about €38 (4 course); reservation required and should be ordered earlier in the day. House wine about €16; No SC. Amex, MasterCard, Visa. **Directions:** East of Cong, on the Headford road. ◇

Cong

Hungry Monk Café

CAFÉ

Abbey Street Cong Co Mayo **Tel: 094 954 6866**
Email: robertdevereux@gmail.com Web: www.cong-ireland.com

Poised scenically on the border between Galway and Mayo, Cong is a delightful village in its own right but thanks to its connections with The Quiet Man - and the interest of Ashford Castle and it surroundings - it is a place where most visitors choose to take a break when exploring the area. And this is where the Hungry Monk comes in - Robert Devereux's attractive all-day café is just the place to drop in for a wholesome meal or snack, at any time of day. Open Mar-Nov, Tue-Sun, 10 - 6pm. Closed Mon; Dec-Feb. **Directions:** Centre of Cong village. ◇

Foxford

Healys Hotel

HOTEL

Pontoon Foxford Co Mayo **Tel: 094 925 6443** Fax: 094 925 6572
Email: info@healyspontoon.com Web: www.healyspontoon.com

féile bia This famous old hotel, loved by fisherfolk, landscape artists and many others who seek peace and tranquillity, changed hands in 1998, and there has since been a flurry of renovation and refurbishment, without spoiling the old-fashioned qualities that have earned this hotel its special reputation: just a good bit of painting and decorating, some overdue refurbishment in the bar and a general tidy up around the front while, at the back, old gardens have been re-established (500 new roses have been planted), and a beer garden has been created. Accommodation is modest but comfortable - and also fairly moderately priced. There's a great feeling of people happy in what they're doing around here (notably the fisherfolk); it's all very relaxed and the hotel has lots of information on things to do in the area - including golf at around a dozen courses within an hour's drive. Aside from fishing, other country pursuits available nearby include shooting, horse racing, mountain climbing and golf (links and parkland courses nearby). Both bar and restaurant food is above average for a country hotel, but it should be noted that this is not a gourmet dining destination; however, although can get very busy in summer, this can be a pleasant spot for a meal to break a journey, or for a quiet off-season sporting break. Small banqueting facilities (70); garden, fishing. Packed lunches available. Children welcome (under 3s free in parents' room; cots available at no charge). No pets. The restaurant is open for lunch & dinner daily - 12.30-5.30 (to 4.30 Sun) & 6.30-9.30. Early D 10% disc 6.30-7.30; Set Sun L €30; Set D €35. **Rooms 14** (all shower only). B&B €45pps, ss €20.* Bar food available 12.30-9.30 daily. Closed 25 Dec. Amex, Diners, MasterCard, Visa, Laser. **Directions:** R310 from Castlebar - 10 min drive; R318 from Foxford to junction R310; R310 from Ballina - 10 min drive.

Lahardane

Leonard's

PUB

Lahardane Ballina Co Mayo **Tel: 096 51003**

This unspoilt roadside traditional pub & grocery shop was established in 1897 and the original owners would be proud of it today. If you get hungry, there's always the makings of a picnic on the shelves. Closed 25 Dec & Good Fri.

Lecanvey

T.Staunton

BAR

Lecanvey Westport Co Mayo **Tel: 098 64850/64891**

Thérèse Staunton runs this great little pub near the beginning of the ascent to Croagh Patrick - genuinely traditional, with an open fire it has the feeling of a real 'local'. Not really a food place, but home-made soup and sandwiches or plated salads are available every day until 9pm. Occasional traditional music sessions - and frequent impromptu sing-songs. Closed 25 Dec & Good Fri. **No Credit Cards. Directions:** 12.5km (8 m) from Westport on Louisburgh Road.

Mulranny

Park Inn Mulranny

☆HOTEL

Mulranny Westport Co Mayo **Tel: 098 36000** Fax: 098 36899
Email: info@parkinnmulranny.ie Web: www.parkinnmulranny.ie

This landmark hotel, originally built by the Midland Great Western Railways, first opened for business in March 1897 and it became a famous destination during the lifetime of the railway between Westport and Achill Island. Situated on a 42 acre woodland estate the hotel is now owned by Tom and Kathleen O'Keeffe, who have has retained much of its original character and charm while developing a contemporary style. It now has 60 guest bedrooms, and an elegant dining room, modern bar, relaxing lounges and luxurious leisure centre with 20 metre pool - all of which make this an attractive destination for a day out or a holiday. The local blue flag beach, a local golf course and wonderful walks will make this a haven for both Irish guests and visitors from other countries. Conference/banqueting 500/300; business centre. Children welcome (free cot available, baby sitting arranged). No pets. **Rooms 60** (3 superior, 7 shower only, 23 family, 3 disabled, 56 no smoking). B&B €105 pps ss€25. **Nephin Restaurant:** The restaurant is the most elegant room in the hotel and it has the best view, overlooking the great Atlantic. It is a formal room, as befits the dining experience offered here, and is set up comfortably but in no way ostentatiously, with good-sized square and round tables, traditional mahogany dining chairs and crisp white linen. Head chef Seamus Commons, who is from Bohola in east Mayo, is well known in Ireland and has worked in some leading restaurants including L'Ecrivain, in Dublin, where he was head chef - now he is back, making his mark in this 'oasis in the west', where he has attracted a strong following from a wide area and established the hotel as a destination for food lovers. Menus are a pleasure to read - not over-extensive, but clearly ambitious and offering many unusual ingredients and creative combinations. And they deliver on the promise. At €39 the Table d'Hôte menu offers three choices on each course and is extremely good value - and, for a mere €15 supplement, residents have freedom of the à la carte. Dishes greatly enjoyed on a recent visit included a starter of seared red tuna & star anise terrine, yellow pepper ice cream, tomato & lime salsa, which could be over-complicated but the flavours were superb individually and fused together brilliantly; also a main course of perfectly cooked Irish beef fillet, with a celeriac & truffle cream, rich red wine jus, rocket salad & blue cheese crust. The Irish love their steaks and a dish like this lifts the nation's favourite food very firmly into the celebratory class. Served on wave shape, oval and square plates, presentation is classic but also funky, and all the little niceties of a special meal are observed. Service is excellent and friendly, under the direction of restaurant manager Nick Faujour, and sommelier Nicolas Bonnet's wine list is interesting - and he is manner in assisting guests to make the best choice is impressive. For more stylish cooking showcasing local foods and seafoods, great service and value, you would have to travel a long way. Nephin Restaurant: private room, 50; D daily, 7-9.30pm; set 3 course D, €39; Tastiing Menu, €75, Tasting Menu with wines, €105. Vegetarian menu, also a la carte. Bar food also available, 12.30-9pm. Establishment closed 18-26 Dec. MasterCard, Visa, Laser. **Directions:** In Mulranny village on the N59.

Mulranny

B&B

Rosturk Woods

Mulranny Westport Co Mayo **Tel: 098 36264** Fax: 098 36264
Email: stoney@iol.ie Web: www.rosturk-woods.com

Beautifully located in secluded mature woodland and gardens, with direct access to the sandy seashore of Clew Bay, Louisa and Alan Stoney's delightful family home is between Westport and Achill Island, with fishing, swimming, sailing, walking, riding and golf all nearby. It is a lovely, informal house; the three charming guest bedrooms are all en-suite with pretty, individualistic bathrooms, and very comfortably furnished. There is also an elegantly relaxed sitting room for guests' use, and an abundance of local low-down from the Stoneys, who will direct you to all the best places to eat nearby and make sure you get the most from a visit to this beautiful area. Self-catering accommodation is also offered - details on inquiry. Children welcome (under 4 free in parents' room, cot available without charge, baby sitting arranged). Garden. Pets allowed by arrangement. **Rooms 3** (all en-suite & no-smoking, 1 shower only). B&B about €50 pps, ss about €20. Self-catering cottages also available. Closed Nov-Mar. No Credit Cards. **No Credit Cards**. **Directions:** 7 miles from Newport on Achill Road. ◇

Newport

RESTAURANT/COUNTRY HOUSE

Newport House

Newport Co Mayo
Tel: 098 41222 Fax: 098 41613
Email: info@newporthouse.ie Web: www.newporthouse.ie

For two hundred years this distinctively creeper-clad Georgian House overlooking the river and quay, was the home of the O'Donnells, once the Earls of Tir Connell. Today it symbolises all that is best about the Irish country house, and has been especially close to the hearts of fishing people for many years. But, in the caring hands of the current owners, Kieran and Thelma Thompson, and their outstanding staff, the warm hospitality of this wonderful house is accessible to all its guests not least in shared enjoyment of the club-fender cosiness of the little back bar. And, predating the current fashion by several centuries, pure spring water has always been piped into the house for drinking and ice-making The house has a beautiful central hall, sweeping staircase and gracious drawing room, while bedrooms, like the rest of the house, are furnished in style with antiques and fine paintings. The day's catch is weighed and displayed in the hall - and the fisherman's bar provides the perfect venue for a reconstruction of the day's sport. Newport was our Country House of the Year in 1999, and also selected for our annual Wine Award in 2004. Fishing, garden, walking, snooker. **Rooms 18** (2 with private (non connecting) bathrooms, 2 with bath & separate shower, 4 ground floor, 1 disabled). Children welcome (under 2s free in parents' room; cots available, baby sitting arranged). Limited wheelchair access. Pets allowed in some areas. B&B €151, ss €26, no S.C. Closed mid Oct-mid Mar. **Restaurant:** High-ceilinged and elegant, this lovely dining room makes the perfect backdrop for "cooking which reflects the hospitable nature of the house" in fine meals made with home-produced and local foods. Home smoked salmon is a speciality and fruit, vegetables and herbs come from a walled kitchen garden that has been worked since 1720 and was established before the house was built, so that fresh produce would be on stream for the owners when they moved in. John Gavin has been head chef since 1983 and his 5-course menus feature fresh fish, of course freshwater fish caught on local lakes and rivers, and also several varieties of fish delivered daily from nearby Achill island; wild salmon is from the house smoking room (prepared to a secret recipe...), but carnivores will be equally delighted by charcoal grilled local beef or roast spring lamb, and perhaps game in season. To finish, there are Irish farmhouses cheeses with fresh fruit, and classic desserts, often using fruit from the garden. And then there is Kieran's renowned wine list that, for many, adds an extra magic to a meal at Newport. It includes classic French wines about 150 clarets from 1961-1996 vintages, a great collection of white and red burgundies, excellent Rhônes and a good New World collection too. The foundations of this cellar go back many decades to a time when Kieran was himself a guest at Newport; great wines are a passion for him and, while acknowledging that they are irreplaceable, he offers them to guests at far less than their current retail value. Great lists of this scale and quality are almost a thing of the past, so is a matter of celebration that such a collection should belong to a generous spirit like Kieran, who takes pleasure in allowing others to share his passion. **Seats 38.** L daily, 12-2pm; D daily, 7-9. Set 6 course D €63; house wine from €24. Toilets wheelchair accessible. Non-residents welcome by reservation. House closed 10 Oct-18 Mar. Amex, Diners, MasterCard, Visa, Laser. **Directions:** In village of Newport.

WESTPORT

A great example of good town planning - Westport was designed by the Georgian architect James Wyatt - this charming town has high standards of accommodation and restaurants, making it a very agreeable base. It is a delightful place to spend some time: The Mall, with its lime trees flanking the Carrowbeg River, is especially pleasing to the eye, and nearby Westport House is open to the public in summer and well worth a visit. Along the harbour front there are several; pubs and cafes, including **The Creel** (098 26174) a relaxed restaurant that is a good choice for for a daytime bite, and - out of town in the same direction, at Rosbeg - **The Shebeen** (098 26528) is an attractive waterside pub with restaurant attached.

WWW.IRELAND-GUIDE.COM FOR THE BEST PLACES TO EAT, DRINK & STAY

Westport

HOTEL/RESTAURANT

Ardmore Country House Hotel

The Quay Westport Co Mayo

Tel: 098 25994 Fax: 098 27795

Email: ardmorehotel@eircom.net Web: www.ardmorecountryhouse.com

Pat and Noreen Hoban's small family-run hotel is quietly located in immaculately maintained gardens near Westport harbour, with views over Clew Bay, and it offers warm hospitality, very comfortable accommodation and good food. Spacious, individually decorated guest rooms are all furnished to a very high standard; the style is luxurious and the range of facilities - which includes an iron and ironing board and, in many rooms, a separate bath and shower - is impressive. Guests are given the choice of seaview or back of house rooms, allowing for a less expensive option; this also applies to short breaks offered. An outstandingly good breakfast includes (amongst other equally tempting items) a choice of freshly squeezed juices in generous glasses, fresh fruit (correctly prepared according to type, eg skinned grapefruit segments), delicious cafetière coffee, a perfectly-cooked, simple version of 'the full Irish', and a superb fish plate (perhaps a combination of monkfish and seabass fillets, and 'a few scallops' if you are lucky). Great details too - freshly baked breads, home-made preserves and prompt service. [Ardmore was selected for our Best Hotel Breakfast Award in 2005.] Not suitable for children. No pets. Garden. **Rooms 13** (all superior; 2 ground floor; all no smoking). Room service (limited hours); turndown service. B&B €95 pps, ss €35. Closed Jan & Feb. **Restaurant:** The restaurant - a well-appointed irregularly shaped room with a sea view over the front gardens, and some useful corners for têtes-à-tête conversations - is the heart of this house, and owner-chef Pat Hoban presents pleasingly classic menus which make good reading over an aperitif in the comfortable bar and include a wide range of meat and poultry but have a strong emphasis on local seafood, including shellfish such as scallops and lobster when available. From a strong selection of starters, chicken liver terrine served with Cumberland sauce and toasted brioche attracted praise on a recent visit - dramatically presented with big pieces of brioche used like bookends, this was an imaginative (and tasty) re-interpretation of an old classic. Staff, some of whom may recently have arrived from abroad, employ charm and determination to ensure that an enjoyable evening is had by all. **Seats 50.** D 7-9 (daily in summer, Tue-Sat low season); set D €45, also A la carte. House wine €19.50. Closed Sun & Mon in low season, all Jan & Feb. Amex, MasterCard, Visa, Laser. **Directions:** 1.5 kms from Westport town centre, on the coast road.

Westport
HOTEL/RESTAURANT

Carlton Atlantic Coast Hotel

The Quay Westport Co Mayo **Tel: 098 29000** Fax: 098 29111
Email: info@atlanticcoasthotel.com Web: www.atlanticcoasthotel.com

Behind the traditional stone façade of an old mill on Westport harbour, this bright modern hotel has spacious public areas designed and furnished in a pleasing combination of traditional and contemporary themes and materials,. This smart youthful tone is continued through to good-sized bedrooms, with good facilities and stylish Italian bathrooms. Although it may seem like an impersonal city hotel in some ways, staff (including those in the excellent leisure centre, and recently opened spa) are exceptionally friendly and efficient. Conferences/banqueting (160/140). Business centre; secretarial services; video-conferencing. Children welcome (under 4s free in parents' room, cots available without charge, baby sitting arranged). Leisure centre, swimming pool; spa; fishing; discount at local golf club. Golf breaks; details on application. Although slightly reduced from last year, prices remain high, making it worthwhile to shop around; however better value off-season/special interest breaks are often available. **Rooms 85** (1 suite, 2 junior suites, 10 superior, 55 no smoking, 3 for disabled). Lift. 24 hr room service. B&B €135, ss €25; SC incl. Closed 22-27 Dec. **Blue Wave Restaurant:** The restaurant is situated right up at the top of the building, which is a good idea, although the view is somewhat restricted by sloping roof windows and the room can be very warm in summer. Frank Walsh, who took over as head chef in 2003, presents interesting and well-balanced contemporary menus offering about half a dozen imaginative dishes on each course, with a natural leaning towards seafood. Accurately cooked food is presented with flair and, as elsewhere in the hotel, friendly and helpful service adds to the occasion. Breakfast is also served in the Blue Wave Restaurant - and a very good start to the day it is: a cold buffet selection includes (in addition to the usual fruits and cereals), fresh fruit salad, Greek yoghurt and fruit coulis, a fine continental style choice of cooked meats and cheese, Irish smoked salmon and home-baked breads and pastries - and hot cooked-to-order dishes run to grilled kippers, fresh fish of the day (very nicely cooked) and less hot dishes like pan fried lambs livers and toasted bagel with cream cheese and Ballina smoked salmon. Children welcome. **Seats 90.** Reservations required. Air conditioning. Lift. Toilets wheelchair accessible. D daily, 6.30-9.15. Set D €36. House wine €17.50. SC discretionary. Informal bar menu also offered, 12.30-9 daily. Amex, MasterCard, Visa, Laser. **Directions:** Located at Westport harbour, 1 mile from town centre on main Louisburgh and coast road.

Westport
HOTEL

Hotel Westport

Newport Rd Westport Co Mayo **Tel: 098 25122** Fax: 098 26739
Email: reservations@hotelwestport.ie Web: www.hotelwestport.ie

Just a short stroll from Westport town centre this large modern hotel is set in its own grounds and offers excellent facilities for both leisure and business guests. It makes a good base for a holiday in this lovely area and numerous short breaks are offered, including family breaks at times when special children's entertainment is available (June-August), golf and other special interest breaks. The conference and business centre provide a fine venue for corporate events of all kinds, including incentive breaks, and the hotel and surrounding area provide all the activities and amenities necessary for off-duty delegates. Bedrooms, which include some with four-poster beds, are well-appointed, with phone/ISDN lines, TV/video, tea/coffee facilities and trouser press; constant refurbishment and upgrading is an ongoing feature of this well-managed hotel, and a further 48 bedrooms are to be added in 2007/8/. Recent additions to the hotel's extensive leisure facilities include the White Flag Ocean Spirit Spa which is now linked directly to the hotel. The hotel also provides a year round Cub's Corner for junior guests (0-3). The whole hotel is unusually wheelchair-friendly, without steps or obstacles, and staff are invariably helpful and friendly. Conference/banqueting (500/350); video conferencing; business centre; secretarial services. Leisure centre, swimming pool; spa, treatment rooms. Garden. Children welcome (under 3s free in parents' room; cots available without charge, baby sitting arranged; children's playground & playroom). **Rooms 129** (6 suites, 7 for disabled, 86 no smoking). Lift. 24 hr room service. B&B €130 pps, ss €20. No SC. Open all year. Amex, Diners, MasterCard, Visa, Laser. **Directions:** From Castlebar Street, turn right onto north mall (do not go over the hump back bridge), then turn onto Newport Road, 1st left and at the end of the road.

Westport

HOTEL/RESTAURANT

Knockranny House Hotel & Spa

Knockranny Westport Co Mayo
Tel: 098 28600 Fax: 098 28611
Email: info@khh.ie Web: www.khh.ie

féile bia Set in landscaped grounds on an elevated site overlooking the town, this privately owned Victorian-style hotel opened in 1997. A welcoming open fire and friendly staff at reception create an agreeably warm atmosphere: the foyer sets the tone for a hotel which has been built on a generous scale and is full of contrasts, with spacious public areas balanced by smaller ones - notably the library and drawing room - where guests can relax in more homely surroundings. Bedrooms are also large - the suites have four poster beds and sunken seating areas with views - and most are very comfortable (some with jacuzzi baths). 'Spa Salveo', a new health spa with nine treatment rooms, swimming pool, gym, and hair salon opened in 2005 and, since then, development has continued with a new conference and meeting area, and 43 new rooms. Snooker room. **Rooms 54** (3 suites, 9 deluxe, 3 executive, 3 shower only, some no smoking, 2 for disabled.) Lift. Room service. B&B about €125, ss €50. Closed 22-27 Dec. **La Fougère:** Contemporary Irish cooking is offered in the hotel dining room, La Fougère ("the fern"), which is at the front of the hotel, with views across the town to Clew Bay and Croagh Patrick. Menus are wide-ranging, in a classic/modern style; there is pride in local produce, including the renowned organic Clare Island salmon and Mayo lamb - specialities include home-smoked salmon (on a herb & potato pikelet with wasabi vinaigrette, for example). Even in a town with plenty of good restaurants to choose from, this is a pleasant place for an outing - there is a sense of the restaurant being well-run, with friendly interaction between staff and guests which adds greatly to the enjoyment of a good meal. A user-friendly wine list blends entertainment and information in various ways; there's a good choice of mid-range wines, and plenty available by the glass. **Seats 140.** D 6.30-9.30. L 1-2.30. Set D €45; Set Sun L €24.95. House wines from €20. SC discretionary. Hotel closed 22-27 Dec. Amex, MasterCard, Visa, Laser. **Directions:** Take N5/N60 from Castlebar. Hotel is on the left just before entering Westport.

Westport

RESTAURANT

The Lemon Peel

The Octagon Westport Co Mayo **Tel: 098 26929** Fax: 098 26965
Email: info@lemonpeel.ie Web: www.lemonpeel.ie

Proprietor-chef Robbie McMenamin's simply-furnished little town centre restaurant just off The Octagon has been a favourite with locals and visitors alike ever since it opened in 1997 - and, despite the arrival of more restaurants in the area, it remains the most popular restaurant in town. The atmosphere is buzzy and friendly and the food interesting. Robbie sources ingredients with care - local seafood features but there's also a wide choice of other local produce, including organic vegetables - and his cooking is creative and accurate. Menus are considerately sprinkled with symbols to help your selection meet the mood; specials change on a weekly basis and everything comes with a choice of mashed potatoes - plain, basil, champ, garlic, or olive olive - in addition to the vegetables of the day. Lovely homely puddings like fruit crumble, and freshly brewed coffee to finish. The early dinner menu is outstanding for value and friendly, helpful staff create a relaxed atmosphere. Not suitable for children under 12. **Seats 32.** Air conditioning. D only 6-9.30 (Sun 6-9). Early menu about €22 (6-7pm), Also à la carte. House wines about €17-20; SC discretionary. Closed Mon (Sun & Mon Nov-Feb) & all Feb. (Telephone off season to check opening times.) Amex, MasterCard, Visa, Laser. **Directions:** Westport Town Centre. ◇

Westport

PUB

Matt Molloy's Bar

Bridge Street Westport Co Mayo **Tel: 098 26655**

If you had to pick one pub in this pretty town, this soothingly dark atmospheric one would do very nicely not least because it is owned by Matt Molloy of The Chieftains, a man who clearly has respect for the real pub: no TV (and no children after 9 pm). Musical memorabilia add to the interest, but there's also the real thing as traditional music is a major feature in the back room or out at the back in fine weather. Matt is often away on tour, but he's a real local when he's back and takes great pride in this smashing town. It's worth noting that normal pub hours don't apply, this is an afternoon into evening place, not somewhere for morning coffee. Closed 25 Dec & Good Fri. **No Credit Cards. Directions:** Town centre.

Westport

McCormack's at The Andrew Stone Gallery

CAFÉ/RESTAURANT

Bridge Street Westport Co Mayo
Tel: 098 25619 Fax: 098 25619

Go under the archway beside Kate McCormack's sixth generation butcher's shop and up the stairs, where you will find an art gallery on your right and, on your left, this small, unpretentious restaurant with an open counter displaying an array of good things, including home-baked cakes, quiches and patés - the product of generations of family recipes and particularly of Annette McCormack's table, where family and friends have tasted great dishes. Here, her two daughters, Katrina and Mary Claire, carry on the tradition - and the welcome. Treats especially worth trying include seafood chowder with home-baked bread, leek and bacon quiche and, in season, fresh crab on home-made baps. Locally reared meats - obtained, of course, from their butchers shop next door - go into specialities like bacon and cabbage, and a casserole of spring lamb with julienne vegetables (a kind of modernised version of Irish stew). And don't leave without one of the gloriously home-made desserts like almond Madeira pie with seasonal fruits like rhubarb or blackcurrants, or traditional apple tart. Many of the deli dishes from the shop are on the menu, as well as farmhouse cheeses including the local Carrowholly cheese. Works by local artists like John Brady, Michael McCarthy and Henry Blackmoor hang in the restaurant and adjacent rooms: well worth a visit. **Seats 34.** Children welcome. Open all day Thu-Sat and Mon. Closed Sun & Wed. MasterCard, Visa. **Directions:** Westport town centre - on the main street (the one with the clock tower at the top). ◇

Westport

The Olde Railway Hotel

HOTEL

The Mall Westport Co Mayo **Tel: 098 25166** Fax: 098 25090
Email: railway@anu.ie Web: www.theolderailwayhotel.com

féile bia Once described by William Thackeray as 'one of the prettiest, comfortablist hotels in Ireland', The Olde Railway Hotel was built in 1780 as a coaching inn for guests of Lord Sligo. Attractively situated along the tree-lined Carrowbeg River, on the Mall in the centre of Westport, it remains a hotel of character, well known for its antique furniture and a slightly eccentric atmosphere. Warm, friendly reception and a complimentary cup of tea on arrival (and served to your bedroom without charge at any other time during your stay) immediately makes guests feel welcome - and certain concessions have been made to the demands of modern travellers, including en-suite bathrooms, satellite television and private car parking. Several very spacious ground floor rooms with smart en-suite shower rooms were recently added. There's a conservatory dining room quietly situated at the back of the hotel, and the large bar, which is the public face of an otherwise quite private hotel, also serves very acceptable bar food - an organic garden supplies herbs, vegetables and fruit for the hotel. Own parking (20). Preferential rates at adjacent leisure centre (swimming pool, fitness suite, health spa). Garden, fishing, cycling (bicycles provided without charge). Horseriding & golf nearby. Shooting arranged in season. Banqueting (70). Secretarial services Children welcome (cots available at no charge). No pets. **Rooms 26** (12 superior, 16 shower only, 2 family rooms, 2 ground floor, all no-smoking). 24 hour room service. B&B €85 pps, ss €75. Bar L & D, 12.30-2.30 & 6-9.30 daily. Closed Nov-Mar. Amex, MasterCard, Visa, Laser. **Directions:** Entering Westport from N5 (Dublin-Westport) road, turn right just before bridge. Hotel is on the mall overlooking the river.

Westport

Quay Cottage Restaurant

E RESTAURANT

The Harbour Westport Co Mayo **Tel: 098 26412** Fax: 098 28120
Email: quaycottage@eircom.net Web: www.quaycottage.com

Kirstin and Peter MacDonagh have been running this charming stone quayside restaurant just outside Westport since 1984, and it never fails to delight. It's cosy and informal, with scrubbed pine tables and an appropriate maritime decor, which is also reflected in the menu (although there is also much else of interest, including steaks, honey roast duckling and imaginative vegetarian options). But seafood really stars, typically in starters of chowder or garlic grilled oysters and main courses like cajun spiced monkfish tail, served with raita dressing - or baked fillet of salmon with classic hollandaise. Daily specials are often especially interesting (langoustine, halibut, scallops, lobster for example) and there are nice homely desserts, like rhubarb pie with real custard or a plated farmhouse cheese selection such as Cashel Blue, smoked Gubbeen and an Irish brie, with fresh fruit and biscuits. Freshly-brewed coffee by the cup to finish. There's a great atmosphere in this immaculately maintained restaurant, and Kirstin supervises a friendly front of house team. The compact, reasonably priced wine list is well-chosen. Children welcome. **Seats 80** (private room, 40/15; outdoor seating, 8). Toilets wheelchair accessible. D 6-10 (daily in summer, Tue-Sat in winter). Set D €35, also à la carte; house wine €17.50; SC discretionary (except 10% on parties of 6+). Closed Sun &

Mon in winter, Christmas, all Jan. Amex, MasterCard, Visa, Laser. **Directions:** On the harbour front, at gates to Westport House.

Westport area

Ⓝ BAR/RESTAURANT

The Tavern Bar & Restaurant

Murrisk Westport Co Mayo **Tel: 098 64060** Fax: 098 64790
Email: info@tavernmurrisk.com Web: www.tavernmurrisk.com

Myles and Ruth O'Brien have been running this fine bar and restaurant just outside Westport, at the foot of Croagh Patrick, since 1999 - and, during that time, they have built up an enviable reputation for the quality of both food and hospitality. Although both bar and restaurant menus offer a wide range of dishes to suit all tastes, local seafood is very much the speciality here, and menus sprinkled with references to local ingredients are a delight. Clew Bay is the source for much of the seafood - mussels, oysters, lanagoustines, and a wide range of fish listed on the daily specials board - and other named local and artisan foods include McGeough's air-dried Connemara lamb, from Oughterard, and also fresh lamb and beef from the same source. Bar menus are quite extensive, with a children's menu as well as an unusually well-judged choice of starters/main dishes for full meals, and a range of sandwiches - including fresh crabmeat with homemade brown bread with lemon & dill mayonnaise and salad, which is always a popular choice in summer. The fine dining restaurant, Upstairs At The Tavern, offers several very attractive menus, including an early dinner which is exceptionally good value, a midweek special priced to include a bottle of wine, and an a la carte. Traditional Irish music on Wed. Children welcome (playground, playroom); beer garden; air conditioning; free broadband Wi/Fi; **Seats 60;** reservations required; D served daily in summer, 6-10pm (D weekends only off season, although bar food is served daily all year, 12-9.30pm), set D €20/25 2/3 courses, value D €25 pp on Wed, also a la carte; house wine €15.50. Restaurant closed during the week off season. Establishment closed Good Fri, 25 Dec. Amex, MasterCard, Visa, Laser. **Directions:** At the foot of Coragh Patrick, 5 mins from Westport.

COUNTY MEATH

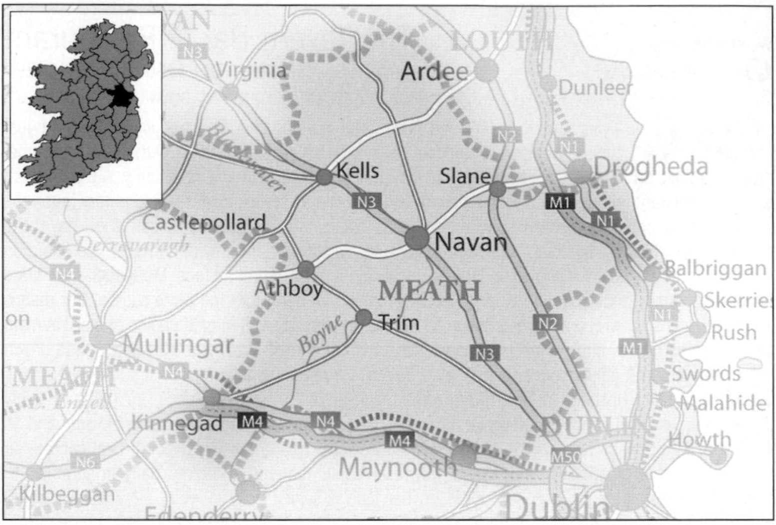

Royal Meath. Meath of the pastures. Meath of the people. Meath of many people... The most recent Census confirmed what had been expected. The population of Ireland may have increased by 8%, but Meath is one of the fastest-growing places of all, its increase clocking in at 22.1% to bring the county total to 134,000 and counting.

Not a huge number in today's overcrowded world, perhaps, but nevertheless Meath is a county which finds itself living in interesting times. The proximity of Dublin - with the inevitable pressures of prosperity and population – can be challenging. But it also brings benefits. With an increasingly affluent and discerning population, Meath is able to support an expanding and impressive range of hospitality options.

For this is a county which is comfortable and confident with itself, and rightly so. The evidence of a rich history is everywhere in Meath. But it's a history which sits gently on a county which is enjoying its own contemporary prosperity at a pace which belies the bustle of Dublin just down the road.

And anyone with an interest in the past will find paradise in Meath, for along the Boyne Valley the neolithic tumuli at Knowth, Newgrange and Dowth are awe-inspiring, Newgrange in particular having its remarkable central chamber which is reached by the rays of sun at dawn at the winter solstice.

Just 16 kilometres to the southwest is another place of fascination, the Hill of Tara. Royal Tara was for centuries the cultural and religious capital of pre-Christian Ireland. Its fortunes began to wane with the coming of Christianity, which gradually moved the religious focal point to Armagh, though Tara was a place of national significance until it was finally abandoned in 1022 AD.

Little now remains of the ancient structures, but it is a magical place, for the approach on its eastern flank gives little indication of the wonderful view of the central plain which the hill suddenly provides to the westward. It is truly inspiring, and many Irish people reckon the year is incomplete without a visit to Tara, where the view is to eternity and infinity, and the imagination takes flight.

Local Attractions and Information

Donore, Bru na Boinne Visitor Centre	041 988 0300
Dunboyne, Hamwood House & Gardens	01 825 5210
Good Food Circle (Meath)	c/o 046 907 3426
Kells, Grove Gardens & Tropical Bird Sanctuary	046 923 4276
Laytown, Sonairte (National Ecology Centre)	041 982 7572
Navan, Tourism Information	046 907 3426
Navan, Navan Racecourse	046 902 1350
Newgrange (inc Dowth & Knowth)	041 988 0300 / 982 4488
Oldcastle, Loughcrew Historic Gardens	049 854 1922

Oldcastle, Loughcrew Passage Tombs (3000BC) 049 854 2009
Ratoath, Fairyhouse Racecourse 01 825 6167
Summerhill, Larchill Arcadian Gardens 01 628 7354
Tara, Interpretive Centre 046 25903
Trim, Butterstream Garden 046 943 6017
Trim, Tourism Information 046 943 7111
Trim, Trim Castle (restored Norman stronghold) 046 943 8619

Ashbourne
GUESTHOUSE

Broadmeadow Country House & Equestrian Centre

Bullstown Ashbourne Co Meath
Tel: 01 835 2823 Fax: 01 835 2819
Email: info@irishcountryhouse.com Web: www.irishcountryhouse.com

The Duff family's country guesthouse is also home to a fine equestrian centre; an interest in horses is certainly an advantage here, although by no means essential as this well-located house also makes a good base for other activity holidays, or visiting the many places of interest in the area. Very much a family business, the house is set well back from the road and surrounded by landscaped gardens. The spacious bedrooms are all en-suite and furnished to hotel standards with TV, phone (ISDN), tea/coffee facilities and trouser press. Residential riding holidays are a speciality but, as there are 20 golf courses within easy reach (two of them championship courses), golfing breaks are almost equally popular; tee times can be arranged. The location - close to Dublin airport and a fairly short distance from the city centre - also makes this a convenient venue for meetings and seminars, perhaps with some equestrian activity thrown in for team building. A supper menu is available to residents. Small conferences (20). Children welcome (under 5s free in parents' room, cot available without charge, baby sitting arranged). No pets. Garden, tennis, cycling, equestrian. **Rooms 8** (all en-suite, 1 executive with separate bath & shower, 5 with over-bath shower, 2 shower only, 3 family rooms; all no smoking). Room service (all day). B&B €60 pps, ss €20. No SC. *Short breaks offered (equestrian & golf). Closed 23-2 Jan. MasterCard, Visa, Laser. **Directions:** Off N2 at R125 towards Swords village.

Ashbourne
Ⓝ RESTAURANT

Eatzen Chinese Restaurant

Unit 4 Building 3b Ashbourne Town Centre Ashbourne Co Meath
Tel: 01 835 2110 Fax: 01 835 2977 Web: www.eatzen.ie

Airy and bright, with design by well-known Hong Kong interior designer, Cindy Lee, this restaurant has lots of windows, and is arranged stylishly with tables in the centre and booths around the sides. Cantonese cuisine with a twist is the speciality, and this restaurant - which is highly regarded by the Chinese community - gets top marks for imaginative presentation and excellent courteous service. Head chef Simon Tsang has wide experience in Asian cooking and, from the wide-ranging menu, dishes singled out for special praise on a recent visit include seabass in salt and chilli with egg white fried rice, and lack cod in champagne sauce. Other specialities include stir fried Chinese vegetables with lily bulbs, deep fried soft shell crabs and - their pride and joy - Mango Duck. Private room for special functions for twelve, complete with karaoke. **Seats 100.** Open Mon-Sat 5.30-11.30; Sun 1-10. *There is a branch of Eatzen at Clonee, Co Meath. MasterCard, Visa. **Directions:** ◇

Athboy
Ⓝ B&B

The Blue Door

Frankville House 9 Park View O'Growney St Athboy Co Meath
Tel: 046 943 0028

The Geraghty family's charming guesthouse is located on the edge of the pretty town of Athboy opposite the church. There is a comfortable lounge for the use of guests, and a bright dining area, both filled with interesting and carefully-chosen antique furniture. Of the five individually-decorated bedrooms four are en-suite - including a master bedroom - and one has a private bathroom. In addition, an unusual dormitory room downstairs has four bunk beds and access to a showering area with under-floor heating a boon for families. Small conference/meeting facilities for approximately 10 are available in a small room off the dining room which also has a projector and an organ. The Geraghtys enjoy catering for private functions as well as their regular guests, and they are currently constructing a hot-tub outside. Meetings/small conferences (10). **Rooms 5** (4 en suite, 1 with private bathroom). **Directions:** North-west of Trim; on edge of town, opposite the church. ◇

CLONEE

The Clonee/Dunboyne area has attracted a lot of young families to settle here lately, and acts like a magnet for the growing number of new gardeners - and a good few experienced ones too - who head here to visit the famous **Gardenworks Garden Centre** (01 825 5375); they're also well-known for the wholesome meals served in their Café, which is open all day (Mon-Sat, 9.30-5; Sun & bank hols, 12-5). In fact, many people come for a bite to eat and only think about buying things for the garden afterwards. [Also at: Malahide Garden Centre. Tel 01 8450110.]

WWW.IRELAND-GUIDE.COM FOR THE BEST PLACES TO EAT, DRINK & STAY

Duleek
E RESTAURANT

The Spire Restaurant

Church Lane Duleek Co Meath **Tel: 041 982 3000**
Email: info@spirerestaurant.ie Web: www.spirerestaurant.ie

Shay and Deborah Kendrick's converted church in the historic village of Duleek - which is the site of many an interesting item including Ireland's oldest and largest lime tree - was formerly St Kienan's Church of Ireland and, together with the adjacent St Mary's Abbey, it makes a specular sight when lit up at light. From a virtual ruin, the church has been given a clean-lined contemporary look, with clear glass windows, uncluttered pale walls lit by big torchon style sconce lamps, some modern paintings, large plants that break up the space, and a mezzanine floor that virtually doubles the dining space and makes a perfect venue for private functions. Darkwood tables are set up simply in quality modern style, and Shay's well-balanced menus offer plenty of treats, including a strong vegetarian option and delicious starters, which might include a sophisticated chicken and smoked duck terrine. Menus are admirably seasonal so, for example, comforting cuisine gran'mère dishes like pot-roasted lamb and delicious beef cassoulet with root vegetables are offered in the colder months. Accomplished cooking, caring staff, great atmosphere and fair prices keep this restaurant busy. MasterCard, Visa, Laser. **Directions:** Situated near the M1 south of Drogheda. ◇

Dunboyme
RESTAURANT

Caldwell's Restaurant

Summerhill Road Dunboyne Co Meath
Tel: 01 801 3866

In a neat modern building in the centre of Dunboyne, this smart two-storey restaurant is simple and modern in style - clean lines, unfussy table settings, comfortable high-back chairs; the high-ceilinged ground floor area overlooks a large patio, which gives it a light, bright atmosphere, while tables on the balcony area above have a cosier ambience. Guests are shown straight to their tables to look over the menu and order aperitifs; home-made breads are offered (probably more than once before food is served). Promising menus are refreshingly simply worded and sources highlighted - suppliers named, vegetables from the family garden - along with membership of Féile Bia, which is all interesting and confidence-inspiring. Set menus offer a choice of three on each course, while the à la carte is wider ranging and dishes sound more luxurious. There will always be several seafood specialities but, unusually, the leaning is towards red meats - and, like the vegetables, very tasty they are too. Desserts tend to be enjoyable variations on classics, with a welcome emphasis on fruits in season. Caldwell's has its heart in the right place - it's great to see the provenance of ingredients given due recognition on a menu - and offers good cooking and a pleasant ambience at fair prices. **Seats 60** (private balcony area 22). Children welcome for Sun L (not after 7.45pm). D Wed-Sat, 5.30-'late'; L Sun only, all day: 1.30-9.30. Early D about €20 (5.30-7); 2-4 course Set D about €20-35. House wine about €19. Closed Mon. Amex, MasterCard, Visa, Laser. **Directions:** Dunboyne village, through lights, 2nd building on left. ◇

Dunboyne
N HOTEL

Dunboyne Castle Hotel & Spa

Dunboyne Co Meath **Tel: 01 801 3500** Fax: 01 487 5192
Email: info@dunboynecastlehotel.com Web: www.dunboynecastlehotel.com

Set in 21 acres of woodland and gardens on the the Meath-Dublin border, this 18th century mansion - a sister of the new boutique hotel, Dylan, in Dublin 4 - opened to widespread acclaim in 2006. It is a stylish development in which the original building, a large 3-storey over basement country house, remains very much the dominant feature in the overall design. The fine interior has been beautifully restored and the two main reception rooms, especially, are very impressive in scale and have many original features including intricate plasterwork, original doors and fireplaces; a beautiful original staircase leads to a romantic bridal suite, with an antique four-posted bed. Most of the accommodation is in the new development, which is sensitively set back a little from the old house; spacious, luxuriously furnished high-ceilinged rooms reflect the proportions of the old house, but have a lot of glass to make the most of the parkland setting. The development as a whole is extensive, including a choice of restaurants and bars, conference and meeting facilities, a dedicated exhibition complex and spa. The spa, Seoid - which has 18 treatment rooms and offers a wide range of therapies, including some not available elsewhere - was an immediate success, and is a natural companion to the wedding business the hotel attracts. Conferences/Banqueting (400/300), business centre, video conferencing, Broadband Wi/Fi; equestrian and golf nearby, fitness room. Children welcome (under 12s free in parents' room, cot available at no charge, baby sitting arranged); **Rooms 145** (2 suites, 2 junior suites, 8 executive, 6 shower only, 106 no smoking, 39 ground floor, 8 for disabled); 24 hr room service, Lift; B&B €85 pps, ss €60. Open all year. Amex, MasterCard, Visa, Laser. **Directions:** N3 into Dunboyne village, left at Slenns pub, few hundred metres down the road on the left.

Enfield
HOTEL/RESTAURANT

Marriott Johnstown House Hotel & Spa

Enfield Co Meath
Tel: 046 954 0000 Fax: 046 954 0029

Although close to the motorway, this mainly modern hotel has a carefully restored mid-18th century house at its heart and something of its country house atmosphere lives on. The original house is only a small part of the hotel, but it is the focal point and an unusually fine feature is a drawing room with a ceiling by the renowned Francini brothers, who were responsible for some of Ireland's finest plasterwork in great houses of the time. The hotel has been open for some years but development continues - a long-awaited spa and leisure club opened late in 2005, and 40 new executive suites are due to come on stream at around the time of going to press. The hotel is very attractive for corporate events and business meetings, and has a dedicated outdoor events and corporate activity centre on site (Quest Corporate Events). It is also a pleasing and well-appointed hotel for private guests to stay, and its location well west of Dublin makes it a useful place to break a journey. **Pavilion Restaurant:** D daily 6-11; Sun L 1-4. Atrium Brasserie: B'fst 6.30-11, L 12.30-3.30. Bar meals all day, 12-11. Set D from €32, Set Sun L €25. Otherwise à la carte. House wine €23. SC discretionary. Amex, Diners, MasterCard, Visa, Laser. **Directions:** Take M4 from Dublin - exit at Enfield.

Kells
RESTAURANT

The Ground Floor Restaurant

Bective Square Kells Co Meath **Tel: 046 924 9688**
Fax: 046 922 8347 Email: debbie@chuig.com

A bright and attractive contemporary restaurant in the centre of Kells, The Ground Floor is a sister of The Loft in Navan and has much in common with it: wacky paintings and a youthful buzzy atmosphere, plus interesting, colourful food at accessible prices - the most expensive dish on the regular menu is a fillet steak at about €22, but most main courses are much less. Popular dishes from around the world abound in starters like saté Ayam (strips of chicken breast with a peanut sauce), Mexican quesadilla (a vegetarian version with avocado) and the Ground Floor Combination, a selection of potato skins, buffalo wings and crostini, with home-made dips (about €12 for two). Equally cosmopolitan main courses range from Caesar salads (several variations), through sizzling fajitas and home-made burgers to steaks, pastas and pizzas. Interesting daily blackboard specials are often a good bet - and there are weight-watching options are available for some dishes, marked up on the menu. Consistent quality and exceptionally pleasant and helpful staff add greatly to the relaxed ambience. The early dinner menu is particularly good value. Children welcome (baby changing facility available). Toilets wheelchair accessible. **Seats 65.** Air conditioning. D Mon-Sat, 5.30-10.30 (to 11 Fri/Sat), Sun 4-9. Early D €17.50 (Mon-Sat 5.30-7.30 & all day Sun); otherwise à la carte. House wine about €18. Discretionary except 10% SC on parties of 4+. Closed 25-26 Dec. MasterCard, Visa, Laser. **Directions:** Centre of Kells on the Athboy/Mullingar Road, in Bective Square.

Kells
RESTAURANT

Vanilla Pod Restaurant

Headfort Arms Hotel Kells Co Meath
Tel: 0818 222 800 Fax: 046 9240587
Email: info@headfortarms.ie Web: www.headfortarms.ie

Although reached through an entrance just inside the foyer of the Headfort Arms Hotel and in common ownership, The Vanilla Pod is an attractive bistro style restaurant run as an independent entity. In contrast to the hotel, it is very modern, with lots of pale wood, recessed lighting and sleek informal table settings. Efficient staff show you straight to your table to choose from a well-structured contemporary menu, which offers a significant number of dishes (including some vegetarian) which can be chosen as a starter or main course. Good quality, carefully sourced ingredients are used, the cooking is sound and service is friendly and knowledgeable. There is an interest in wine - specials are offered from time to time, and there are sometimes wine evenings. **Seats 70.** Air conditioning. D 5.30-9.45, L Sun only, 12-3. Early D about €18 (5.30-7.30), also à la carte; Set Sun L about €22. SC10%. House wine about €18. Closed 25 Dec, Good Fri. Amex, MasterCard, Visa, Laser. **Directions:** On main Dublin-Cavan road, left section of black &white building on right. ◇

Kilmessan

HOTEL/RESTAURANT

The Station House Hotel

Kilmessan Co Meath **Tel: 046 902 5239**
Fax: 046 902 5588 Email: info@thestationhousehotel.com
Web: www.thestationhousehotel.com

The Slattery family's unique establishment is an old railway junction, which was closed in 1963, and all the various buildings were converted to a make an hotel of character. It is an interesting and unusual place to visit, with lovely gardens, and makes a good base for business, or for exploring this fascinating county. The restaurant attracts diners from a wide area - their traditional Sunday lunch is especially renowned. **Seats 90.** (Private rooms; outdoor seating, 50). Reservations advised. Children welcome. Toilets wheelchair accessible. L daily 12.30-3 (Sun to 5.30); D daily 7-10.30 (Sun to 9.30). Set D: Mon-Fri about €25.95; Sat €49.95; Sun about €29.95. A la carte L & D also available, except Sat D. Bar Menu Mon-Sat, 11-6. House wine from about €18. Amex, Diners, MasterCard, Visa, Laser. **Directions:** From Dublin N3 to Dunshaughlin and follow signposts. ◇

Navan

Best B&B

Killyon House

Dublin Road Navan Co Meath **Tel: 046 907 1224** Fax: 046 907 2766
Email: info@killyonguesthouse.ie Web: www.killyonguesthouse.ie

B&B OF THE YEAR

B&B BREAKFAST AWARD WINNER

You couldn't miss Michael and Sheila Fogarty's modern guesthouse, with its striking array of colourful flowers and hanging baskets. it has gardens leading down to the banks of the Boyne, making the back of the house unexpectedly tranquil, and the dining room overlooks the river, which gives guests the added interest of spotting wildlife, sometimes including otters and stoats, along the bank from the window. The rooms (double-glazing to reduce the noise of traffic) are spacious and comfortable, complete with Sheila's handmade blankets and antiques, which are a point of interest in all guest areas. Bathrooms have powerful showers, and housekeeping is immaculate. There's also a separate guests' sitting room and, although they are too close to the restaurants of Navan to make evening meals a viable option, they do a particularly good breakfast - and, of course, the Fogartys will direct you to the best local restaurant for your needs. Their wholesome breakfast really is a high point, served in a bright room which leads onto a balcony full of colourful flowers; sitting at the long table with the other guests while overlooking the Boyne is a pleasurable experience, and their delicious food is a treat: firstly, there is an array of fresh and marinated fruit, handpicked blackberries, homemade cereals and breads on offer, then you can choose from hot dishes like free range eggs mixed with feta cheese, or full Irish as you like it, all cooked to order. It is a sociable affair, leaving guests with a good last impression. The Fogartys are extremely hospitable hosts, rooms are very comfortable and nothing (even preparing a very early breakfast) is too much trouble - this is a lovely place to stay. Children welcome (under 5 free in parents' room; cots available without charge, baby sitting arranged). Pets permitted. Garden, walking; fishing. Parking. **Rooms 6** (5 shower only, 2 family rooms, 1 ground floor, all no smoking). Room service (limited hours). B&B €40 pps, ss €5. Closed 24-26 Dec. MasterCard, Visa, Laser. **Directions:** On N3, opposite Ardboyne Hotel on River Boyne.

Navan

RESTAURANT

The Loft Restaurant

26 Trimgate Street Navan Co Meath **Tel: 046 907 1755**
Fax: 046 906 6197 Email: debbie@chuig.com

Older sister to The Ground Floor in Kells, and the newer Side Door in Cavan (see entries), this thriving two-storey restaurant has much in common with them, notably strong modern decor (including some interesting original paintings by the Northern Ireland artist Terry Bradley), exceptionally pleasant, helpful staff and a lively global menu at reasonable prices that lays the emphasis on accessibility: this is a place for all ages and every (or no particular) occasion. The main menu is similar to The Ground Floor, also with daily blackboard specials - typically a main course of poached supreme of Boyne salmon with a light yogurt & prawn sauce and desserts like bread & butter pudding, served prettily presented, surrounded by strawberry coulis. Downstairs the "Tapas Bar" serves a range of cold and hot tapas, with wine available by the glass and by the bottle. Children welcome. **Seats 90.** Air conditioning. D daily, 5.30-10.30 (Fri/Sat to 11). Early D €16.50 (Mon-Sat 5.30-7.30, all Sun), otherwise à la carte. House wine about €17.95. 10% sc added to tables of 4+. Closed 25-26 Dec. MasterCard, Visa, Laser. **Directions:** Centre of Navan,corner of Trimgate Street and Railway Street.

Navan

PUB

Ryan's Bar

22 Trimgate Street Navan Co Meath
Tel: 046 902 1154 Fax: 046 907 8333

This pleasant, well-run and very popular pub makes a good meeting place for a drink or at lunch-time, when contemporary light meals are offered: soups, hot panini bread (stuffed with smoked salmon, cream cheese & tomato perhaps, or chicken with a satay sauce), wraps (including a vegetarian one filled with grated cheese, apple, carrot and a chive mayonnaise) and toasties (honey baked ham, perhaps, with a salad garnish). Apple pie and cream may be predictable but it's enjoyable nonetheless - and there's always a dessert among the daily specials. It's good value, the airy bar makes for a comfortable atmosphere and staff are friendly and efficient. Disc parking. Open from 11.30 am; L Mon-Fri. 12.30-2.30. Closed 25 Dec & Good Fri. MasterCard, Visa, Laser. **Directions:** Main Street Navan. ◇

Navan area

Ⓝ HOTEL/COUNTRY HOUSE

Bellinter House

Navan Co Meath **Tel: 046 903 0900**
Email: info@bellinterhouse.com Web: www.bellinterhouse.com

This elegant Palladian mansion on the banks of the River Boyne was designed by Richard Castle (Carton, Russborough, Powerscourt, Leinster Houses). Now owned by Jay Bourke, Eoin Foyle and John Reynolds, the team who own many of Dublin's most successful informal restaurants - Eden, Odessa, Mackerel, The Market Bar and the Cafe-Bar-Deli chain among them - it has been the most talked about development in County Meath for many years, and is due to open shortly after we go to press. Set in 12 acres of beautiful parkland, it is only about 45 minutes from both Dublin and Dublin Airport and promises to be the first of a new generation of cool country house hotels. The interior has been restored with meticulous attention to the architectural integrity of the building, but with a youthful, contemporary twist; public rooms include the Drawing Room on the main floor (all day dining is available there), the Bellinter Bar (ground floor, perfect for 'pints and cocktails'; bar food available any time) and The Wine Bar in the basement, which is adjacent to the restaurant and offers an interesting competitively priced wine-list. Outdoors, when the weather permits, the terraces and lawns are ideal for dining al fresco, for barbecues and for picnics. Accommodation, in 37 individually styled rooms and suites, is divided between the Main House, the West Wing, the East Wing and several restored outbuildings, known as the Stables, the Lean-To, the Ruin and St. Pauls. There are two grades (deluxe and standard) but all rooms are luxuriously furnished in a fun way with hand made and old furniture, and have extra large beds (with goose down pillows wrapped in Egyptian cotton), centrally controlled mood lighting, drinks cabinet, custom made Italian multi-media 40 "plasma screens, Bose Sound systems, DVD players WIFI, and the beautiful bathrooms have full bath and/or power showers and pampering details including a full range of certified organic seaweed toiletries. The gardens are worth a special mention as the amazing, colourful and fun 'pavilion pod' that won Diarmuid Gavin a silver medal at the Chelsea Flower Show has found a new home in the gardens here - a great decision that neatly sums up the philosophy behind Bellinter. Fishing on adjoining Boyne; overlooks Royal Tara Golf Club grounds Spa, massage, indoor & outdoor 'pool, leisure centre, walking, cycling, fly fishing, pool table. Small Conferences/Banqueting (30/70), secretarial services, free broadband Wi/Fi. Wheelchair friendly, children welcome (cots available, baby sitting arranged, crèche). **Rooms 37** (22 deluxe, 15 standard, 13 shower only, 1 family room, 10 ground floor, 2 for disabled); 24 hr room service. B&B room rate €270. **Eden Restaurant:** Eleanor Walsh, who has been the driving force behind all of the impressive food operations in the group and is particularly closely associated with the flagship restaurant Eden in Temple Bar, is now responsible for Eden at Bellinter. She is known for her commitment to fresh seasonal food with a distinctive contemporary Irish flavour, and the arrival of Eden is very good news for diners in the area - and will certainly be a big attraction for anyone considering a stay here. The elegant restaurant is in a vaulted basement with natural daylight, and Eleanor's modern food will contrast nicely with it; non-residents are welcome, there is no formal dress code and, with relaxed and friendly service, it promises to be a very enjoyable experience. Eden Restaurant: Not suitable for children after 7pm; Seats 90 (private room, 28, outdoors, 30); reservations required; food served all day,

11am-11pm; L 12-4pm, D 5-10.30pm (to 10pm Sun); set 3 course L €25; set Sun L €25; early D €25, 5-7pm; also a la carte L&D; house wine from €24. Restaurant closed 24-26 Dec Amex, MasterCard, Visa, Laser. **Directions:** Off N3 near the Hill of Tara.

Navan area
O'Brien's Good Food and Drink House
Ⓝ RESTAURANT/PUB

The Village Johnstown Navan Co Meath
Tel: 046 902 0555 Fax: 046 902 0558

Located in a new development in the centre of Johnstown village, just five minutes' drive from Navan, this popular and fashionable gastro-pub is in the same ownership as Franzini O'Briens Restaurant in Trim, and worth a visit. Wood-panelling, red brick walls and candles on the tables combine to create a modern rustic feel, and the international-style menu has broad appeal, with starters like duck spring rolls, pan-fried black pudding and prawn wontons all well under €10, and main dishes including pizzas, pastas burgers and chicken dishes under €20, although fresh fish may rise a little above this level. There are tasty vegetarian choices too, including good salads, also appealing side dishes (eg stringy onions, spring onion mash and homemade fries) and a nice dessert menu a light tangy ginger and honeycomb pudding, for example, with crème anglaise. Service is friendly and efficient, and a well-priced wine list offers a balanced range including a house champagne, two dessert wines and some decent wines by the glass. The weekday Early Bird dinner offers particularly good value. Children welcome until 9pm; Toilets wheelchair accessible. **Seats 110** (private room, 60); reservations not necessary; D Mon-Sat 5-10pm; Sun 1-9; Early D € 19.95, 5.30-7.30; also a la carte and vegetarian menu; SC 10%. Closed Good Fri, 25 Dec. Amex, Diners, MasterCard, Visa, Laser. **Directions:** 1km from Navan on Dublin road.

SLANE

This appealing village is well placed for visiting the historic sites of the area and has a traditional stone-faced 19th century hotel, **The Conyngham Arms** (041 988 4444; www.conynghamarms.com), named after the Conyngham family of Slane Castle, and a remarkable old-world bar, **Boyles Licensed Tea Rooms** (041 982 4195). More recent arrivals include **George's Patisserie,** a neat little deli-café in the centre of the village where chef/proprieter Georg Heise offers a delicious range of desserts and pastries, home-made breads, preserves, jams, chutneys and locally-grown organic fruit and veg - and also a small, interesting selection of wines including organic wines; currently a good place for a snack (Tue-Sat), a bigger café/restaurant is planned. And a boutique hotel, **The Mill House** (contact: Janey Quigley, 086 382 8979), scenically located right on the River Boyne, is due to open shortly after the guide goes to press - dramatic contemporary décor contrasts with the old building and the eleven bedrooms are individually designed; a restaurant/ bar is also planned.
WWW.IRELAND-GUIDE.COM FOR THE BEST PLACES TO EAT, DRINK & STAY

Tara Area
O'Connell's
PUB

Skryne Nr. Tara Co Meath **Tel: 046 902 5122**

Three generations of O'Connells have been caretakers of this wonderfully unspoilt country pub. The present owner, Mary O'Connell, has been delighting customers old and new for over ten years now. It's all beautifully simple two little bars with no fancy bits, lots of items of local interest, and a welcoming fire in the grate. What more could anyone want? As for directions: just head for the tower beside the pub, which is visible for miles around. Closed 25 Dec & Good Fri. **No Credit Cards.** ◇

TRIM

Most famous for its enormous Anglo-Norman castle (restored and open to the public) and other medieval monuments, Trim is a small but - thanks to its location only 45km north-west of Dublin - fast-growing town. Well located for visitors interested in the history of the area, it is also becoming a popular short break destination and has recently acquired two new hotels: **Trim Castle Hotel** (046 9483000; www.trimcastle.com) is located shockingly near the castle and its dull, concrete exterior is at odds with the castle walls across the road; however, once inside, it is an exciting new establishment furnished in a contemporary, minimalist style and, in the Guide's (early) experience, with friendly staff serving tasty food. A short distance away and well-signed in the area, **Knightsbrook Hotel and Golf Resort** (046 948 2100; www.knightsbrook.com) is palatial, both externally and internally, although many details remained to be completed at the time of going to press.

Trim

RESTAURANT

Franzini O'Briens

French's Lane Trim Co Meath
Tel: 046 943 1002 Fax: 046 943 1118

Modern and spacious, this smart and very popular restaurant beside Trim Castle has well-trained staff who greet and seat arriving guests promptly, immediately presenting menus, taking drink orders and - by ensuring that everyone settles in comfortably from the start - setting a tone of relaxed efficiency that ensures an enjoyable outing. Space is attractively broken up around a central carpeted square with leather sofas to provide a variety of seating areas (the more intimate ones, with banquette seating, are towards the back) and simple, uncluttered table settings are modern and elegantly functional - tall water carafes, finger bowls for nachos and paper napkins (replaced with each course). Light-hearted menus offer an excellent range of choices in the International style and, together with an informal, buzzy atmosphere, indicate that this is a place for a good night out. And attractively served food should not disappoint - typically, a tomato-based seafood chowder is served with delicious dark treacle bread, and skilfully prepared fajitas come with a generous amount of tasty nachos and well-made accompaniments. Service is excellent, even at very busy times. Interesting wine list (supplied by Jim Nicholson). *See also O'Briens Good Food & Drink House, Navan. **Seats 110.** Reservations accepted. Children welcome before 8.30. Toilets wheelchair accessible. Air conditioning. D Mon-Sat, 6.30-10, Sun L 1-4, D 4-8.30. Early bird D Mon-Fri 6.30-7.30 €19.95. Also A la carte. House wines from €16.50. Closed Mon off season (Sept-May), 24-26 Dec, Good Fri. MasterCard, Visa, Laser, Switch. **Directions:** Beside Trim Castle.

COUNTY MONAGHAN

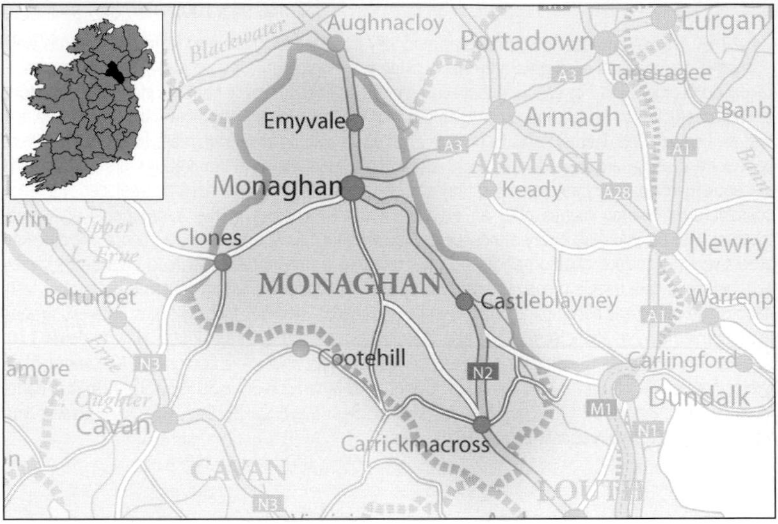

Of all Ireland's counties, it is Monaghan which is most centrally placed in the drumlin belt, that strip of rounded glacial hills which runs right across the country from Strangford Lough in County Down to Clew Bay in Mayo. Monaghan, in fact, is all hills. But as very few of them are over 300 metres above sea level, the county takes its name from Muineachain - "Little Hills". Inevitably, the actively farmed undulating country of the little hills encloses many lakes, and Monaghan in its quiet way is a coarse angler's paradise.

Much of the old Ulster Canal is in Monaghan, while the rest is in Armagh and Tyrone. Once upon a time, it connected Lough Erne to Lough Neagh. It has been derelict for a very long time, but with the success of the restored Shannon-Erne Waterway along the line of the old Ballinamore-Ballyconnell Canal bringing added vitality to Leitrim, Cavan and Fermanagh, the even more ambitious vision of restoring the Ulster Canal is being given serious consideration, and local enthusiasts have been restoring some of the old canal's basic structures.

Vision of a different sort is the theme at Annaghmakerrig House near the Quaker-named village of Newbliss in west Monaghan. The former home of theatrical producer Tyrone Guthrie, since 1981 it has been a sanctuary for writers and artists who can stay there to complete 'work in progress'.

In the east of the county at Castleblayney, there's a particularly attractive lake district with forest park and adventure centre around Lough Mucko. Southwards of Castleblayney, we come to the bustling town of Carrickmacross, still famous for its lace, and a Tidy Towns award winner.

And at Clontibret in northeast Monaghan, there's gold in them thar little hills. Whether or not it's in sufficient quantities to merit mining is a continuing matter of commercial debate, but the fact that it's there at all is another of Monaghan's more intriguing secrets. Another is the county's uncrowded character. The recent Census revealed that Monaghan's population has risen by only 2.8%, the smallest increase of any county, bringing Monaghan's total population to a modest 52,772. In an over-crowded world, this is surely interesting news.

Local Attractions and Information

Carrickmacross, Carrickmacross Lace Gallery	042 966 2506
Carrickmacross (Kingscourt Rd) Dun a Ri Forest Park	042 966 7320
Castleblayney, Lough Muckno Leisure Park	042 974 6356
Clones, Clones Lace Exhibits	047 51051
Glaslough, Castle Leslie Gardens	047 88109
Inniskeen, Patrick Kavanagh Centre	042 937 8560
Monaghan town, Tourism Information	047 81122
Monaghan town, Monaghan County Museum	047 82928
Monaghan town (Newbliss Rd.), Rossmore Forest Park	047 81968
Newbliss, Annaghmakerrig (Tyrone Guthrie Centre)	047 54003

Carrickmacross
☆HOTEL/RESTAURANT

Nuremore Hotel & Country Club

Carrickmacross Co Monaghan
Tel: 042 966 1438 Fax: 042 966 1853
Email: info@nuremore.com Web: www.nuremore.com

féile bia This fine owner-managed country hotel just south of Carrickmacross is set in a parkland estate, with its own 18-hole golf course, and serves the sporting, leisure and business requirements of a wide area very well. As you go over the little bridge ("Beware - ducks crossing") and the immaculately maintained hotel and golf club open up before you, worldly cares seem to recede - this is a place you can get fond of. The hotel invariably gives a good impression on arrival and this sense of care and maintenance is continued throughout. Spacious, comfortably arranged public areas and generous bedrooms with views over the gardens and lakes are regularly refurbished. It would make an excellent base to explore this little known area - and there is plenty to do on site. The superb country club has a full leisure centre and a wide range of related facilities - including a gymnasium and spa - and there are conference and meeting rooms for every size of gathering, with state-of-the-art audio-visual equipment available. Conference/banqueting (600/400); business centre, secretarial services on request, video conferencing. Leisure centre, swimming pool, spa; beauty salon; golf (18), fishing, walking, tennis, garden; snooker. Children welcome (cots available, €13; baby sitting arranged). No pets. **Rooms 72** (7 junior suites, 11 executive, 5 family, 42 no smoking). 24 hr room service. B&B €130 pps, ss €50. *Short breaks offered, including spa and golf breaks; details on application. Open all year. **Restaurant:** Although not aspiring to fashionable decor, the restaurant is well-appointed in a fairly formal country house style, with generous white-clothed tables and a couple of steps dividing the window area and inner tables, allowing everybody to enjoy the view over golf course and woodland. Not only is The Restaurant at Nuremore well established as the leading restaurant in the area, but the head chef, Raymond McArdle, has earned a national reputation for the hotel, which is now on the must-visit destination list for discerning travellers in Ireland. Proprietress Julie Gilhooly has lent every possible support to this talented protegé since his arrival here in 2000, and his spacious, state-of-the art kitchen is the envy of chefs throughout the country. Raymond sources ingredients meticulously, using local produce as much as possible in top rank daily set lunch and dinner menus, a separate vegetarian menu, a 'grown-up' children's menu, and an evening à la carte. Recent visits confirm the consistent excellence and innovativeness of the cooking, seen in perfectly executed and well-flavoured dishes like a summer starter, a tian of Annagassan white crab & Dublin Bay prawns, with avocado, crème fraîche and tomato compôte and a glorious main course, 'celebration of Old Spot Pig', with choucroûte, caramelised apple chutney & Calvados jus. Everything, it seems, is similarly impressive - and, on the dessert menu, difficult choices must be made between half a dozen equally desirable and beautifully presented dishes; toss a coin, perhaps, and hope it comes down in favour of Valhrona coulant, with white chocolate fudge & pistachio ice cream.... A selection of French and Irish cheeses comes with a walnut and apricot brioche - and wonderful petits fours are served with cappuccino or espresso. This is exceptional cooking and, under the supervision of restaurant manager Frank Trutet, service is in line with the high standard of food. There's many a treat in store on the extensive and well-organised wine list, which includes a good house wine selection and a further Sommelier Recommendation in the €30-60 bracket, an unusually wide choice of dessert wines and half bottles, a fair number of magnums and a menu of Caterède armagnacs going back to 1920. This is a restaurant offering outstanding value for money, especially at lunch time. *Raymond McArdle was our Chef of the Year in 2005. **Seats 100** (private room, 50). Air conditioning. L Sun-Fri, 12.30-2.30; D daily 6.30-9.30 (Sun to 9). Set L €25 (Set Sun L, €30); Set D €52 (Vegetarian Menu about €25, Children's Menu €17.50); Prestige Menu €80. House wine from €26; sc discretionary. Closed L Sat. Open all year. Amex, Diners, MasterCard, Visa, Laser. **Directions:** Just south of Carrickmacross, 88km (55 m) from Dublin on N2 ot take M1 from Dublin and turn off at Ardee/Derry exit.

Clones
COUNTRY HOUSE

Hilton Park

Clones Co Monaghan **Tel: 047 56007** Fax: 047 56033
Email: mail@hiltonpark.ie Web: www.hiltonpark.ie

Once described as a "capsule of social history" because of their collection of family portraits and memorabilia going back 250 years or more, Johnny and Lucy Madden's wonderful 18th century mansion is set in beautiful countryside, amidst 200 acres of woodland and farmland. With lakes, Pleasure Grounds and a Lovers' Walk to set the right tone, the house is magnificent in every sense and the experience of visiting it a rare treat. Johnny and Lucy are natural hosts and, as the house and its contents go back for so many generations, there is a strong feeling of being a privileged family guest as you wander through grandly-proportioned, beautifully furnished rooms. Four-posters and all the unselfconscious comforts that make for a very special country house stay are part of the charm, but as visitors from all over the world have found, it's the warmth of Johnny and Lucy's welcome that lends that extra magic. The gardens are also of particular interest - formal gardens have recently been restored to their former glory and Lucy, an enthusiastic organic gardener and excellent cook, supplies freshly harvested produce for meals in the house, while other ingredients are carefully sourced from trusted suppliers of organic and free-range products. Dinner for residents is served in a beautiful dining room overlooking the gardens and lake - and memorable breakfasts are taken downstairs in the Green Room next morning. This is exceptional hospitality, with an Irish flavour and, in recognition, Hilton Park was selected for our International Hospitality Award in 1999. Not suitable for children under 8 (except babies under 1 year, free in parents' room, cot available), playroom for older children. Pets allowed in some areas by arrangement. Gardens, boating, fishing (own lake), walking, cycling. Golf nearby. *Self catering accommodation also available - details on inquiry. *Hilton Park is available for group bookings - family celebrations, small weddings and small conferences. **Rooms 6** (all en-suite & no smoking). B&B €125 pps, ss €40. Not suitable for children under 8 yrs (8-14, 50% disc). Residents D Tue-Sat, €55 at 8 pm (Fri, 8.30); please give 24 hours notice. Interesting short wine list; house wine €20/22. SC discretionary. Closed - none specifically, groups only off-season. MasterCard, Visa, Laser. **Directions:** 5km (3 m) south of Clones on Scotshouse Road.

Glaslough

Castle Leslie

RESTAURANT/CASTLE/HISTORIC HOUSE

Glaslough Co Monaghan
Tel: 047 88100 Fax: 047 88256
Email: info@castleleslie.com Web: www.castleleslie.com

féile bia During the three centuries that this extraordinary place has been in the Leslie family it has changed remarkably little - and its fascinating history intrigues guests as much as the eccentricity of Castle Leslie as they find it today. Once inside the massive front door (guarded by family dogs who snooze in beds flanking the stone steps) there is no reception desk, just a welcoming oak-panelled hall (and afternoon tea in the drawing room), and there are no phones, television sets or clocks in the rooms, although concessions to the 20th century have been made in the form of generous heating and plentiful hot water. The bedrooms are all different, furnished and decorated around a particular era, with en-suite bathrooms a feature in their own right with huge baths, wacky showers and outrageous toilets, all done in a tongue-in-cheek style, reflecting the family's eccentric history and the wonders of Victorian plumbing. In a charming reverse of circumstances, the family lives in the servants' wing, so guests can enjoy the magnificence of the castle to the full it has all the original furniture and family portraits. The estate has wonderful walks, and pike fishing; boating and picnic lunches on the estate are available by arrangement. Due to the nature of the castle (and the fact that the Leslies see it as a wonderful refuge from the outside world for adults) this is not a suitable place to bring children. However, children are very welcome at the Hunting Lodge & Castle Leslie Equestrian Centre, which is just inside the castle gates; various equestrian programmes are offered and accommodation is more reasonably priced. There is also an informal restaurant at the Hunting Lodge, which is open to non-residents. Despite the extreme eccentricity suggested by details such as the answering machine ("please leave your message after the (scream)", this is actually a professionally run business and a little more 'hotel-like' than the publicity suggests. Cookery School. Conferences/banqueting (60/98). Spa, boat trips, equestrian, gardens, walking, fishing, tennis. No children (except at Hunting Lodge). Pets allowed by arrangement. **Rooms 20** (3 suites; 5 ground floor, all no smoking). Turndown service; no room service; no lift. B&B from about €145pps, ss €35; 2-night bookings only at weekends. [Hunting Lodge: B&B about €75 pps, ss €25]. Short breaks offered, including Christmas at the castle, or equestrian Christmas breaks, at the Hunting Lodge. Open all year. **Restaurant:** The dining experience is a high point of any visit to Castle Leslie and non-residents are welcome to come for dinner, by reservation. It is all done in fine old style with pre-dinner drinks in the drawing room (or the Fountain Garden in summer) and dinner, which is served in rooms including the original dining room, unchanged for over a century, by waitresses wearing Victorian uniforms. However, despite the obvious oddities of faded grandeur - tables with a slight list, chairs and sofas which have long since lost their stuffing - Noel McMeel, executive head chef since 2000, is essentially offering a restaurant dining experience rather than a country house dinner; the list of signature dishes is quite extensive and includes freshly smoked Irish salmon, with black pepper, sea salt, lavender honey, mustard, chive cream and basil oil - served with a glass of Madfish unwooded Chardonnay - and roasted shank of sprig lamb with traditional Irish champ, roasted vegetables & rosemary jus. Separate vegetarian menu available. Many entertaining wine and food events are held during the year - contact the Castle for details - and the Castle Leslie range of preserves and speciality foods is available from the castle and Brown Thomas, in Dublin. **Seats 70.** Reservations required; Residents only. D daily at 8pm; Set D €52 (Gourmet Menu €57, 5 course Eclectic Menu €60), Vegetarian Menu also available. House wine from €20.50 Amex, MasterCard, Visa, Laser. **Directions:** 10 mins from Monaghan Town: Monaghan-Armagh road-Glaslough.

Monaghan
BAR/RESTAURANT

Andy's Bar and Restaurant

12 Market Street Monaghan Co Monaghan **Tel: 047 82277**
Fax: 047 84195 Web: www.andysmonaghan.com

Right in the centre of Monaghan, opposite the old market house, the Redmond family's bar is furnished and decorated in traditional Victorian style, with a lot of fine mahogany, stained glass and mirrors. It has earned a strong local following, and it is easy to see why: everything is gleaming clean and arranged well for comfort, with high-backed bar seats and plenty of alcoves set up with tables for the comfortable consumption of their good bar food. Substantial bar meals include a range of specials on a blackboard as well as a concise written menu. The restaurant upstairs, which has a pleasingly old-fashioned ambience, offers a much more extensive range of popular and classic dishes, including a good choice of prime fish and steaks various ways - specialities include garlic Monaghan mushrooms and crispy breast of duckling (with orange & brandy sauce) and more contemporary dishes like halibut steak with sundried tomatoes, roasted peppers & shrimps, with herb-flavoured olive oil; while not especially adventurous, this is good cooking based on quality ingredients and the results are extremely tasty, satisfying - and good value too. Traditional desserts like pavlova, lemon cheesecake, fresh fruit salad and home-made Ices are served from a trolley, and there might be something comforting like a hot treacle sponge pudding in cold weather. Members of the Redmond family are everywhere, keeping an eye on things, and service is charming and efficient. Bar meals Tue-Sun, 4-10.15. Restaurant D only, Tue-Sun, 4-10.15 (Sun 3.30-10). à la carte; house wine €15.60. Closed Mon, 25 Dec, Good Fri, bank hols & 23 Jun - 11 Jul. MasterCard, Visa, Laser. **Directions:** Town centre, opposite the Market House.

Monaghan
Ⓝ HOTEL

Hillgrove Hotel

Old Armagh Rd Monaghan Co Monaghan
Tel: 047 81288 Fax: 047 84951
Email: info@hillgrovehotel.com Web: www.hillgrovehotel.com

Overlooking the town from a fine hillside location, the well-named Hillgrove is the leading hotel in the area. After many years in the Quinn Group, it was purchased by Colm and Audri Herron in 2004 and is flourishing under this energetic new ownership. The whole hotel has been smartly refurbished in pleasing a classic contemporary style and there have been significant new developments, including the addition of a state of the art conference centre and syndicate meeting rooms, new bedrooms and, most recently, a leisure club and health spa & wellness centre opened shortly before the guide went to press. An impressive foyer sets the tone and the public areas around it are spacious and inviting. The main bar, PK's, is the place everyone drops into for a drink or a casual bite to eat at any time, and there's a second one, the Toulouse-Lautrec lounge where residents, especially, can sit in comfort and enjoy the view or read one of the complimentary newspapers. The restaurant, Vettriano, offers stylish informality with a view, and is open for lunch and dinner every day. Accommodation is offered in the 44 original rooms, now completely refurbished, and 43 new rooms which came on stream in 2006; all are spacious and contemporary, with a full range of facilities (multichannel tv and radio, hairdryer, trouser press, direct dial phone and tea/coffee making) and smart en-suite bathrooms about half of the rooms now have separate bath and shower, and some have jacuzzi baths. The range of rooms offered is comprehensive (twins, doubles, family, deluxe, executive and romantic bridal suites, with four-posters); some are wheelchair friendly and/or non-smoking. and all have pleasant town or garden views. Although so familiar to many, the Hillgrove is effectively a new hotel and the staff are as friendly and helpful as ever. Conference/banqueting (1,500/900), business centre, secretarial services, free broadband WI/FI. Leisure centre with 'pool, fitness room, Spa (including beauty salon, massage, hair dressing), garden, fly fishing. **Rooms 87** (2 suites, 2 junior suites, 8 family rooms, 4 for disabled, 18 ground floor, 16 no smoking); Children welcome (under 4s free in parents' room, cot available at no charge, baby sitting arranged, creche, play room); Lift, 24 hr room service, pets permitted in some areas by arrangement. B&B from €60 pps, ss €30. Bar meals 10-9 daily; restaurant L daily, 12.30-2.30 9 (Sun to 3); D daily 6-9 (Sun from 5.30). Closed 25 Dec. Helipad. Amex, MasterCard, Visa, Laser. **Directions:** Take N2 from Dublin to Monaghan town.

COUNTY OFFALY

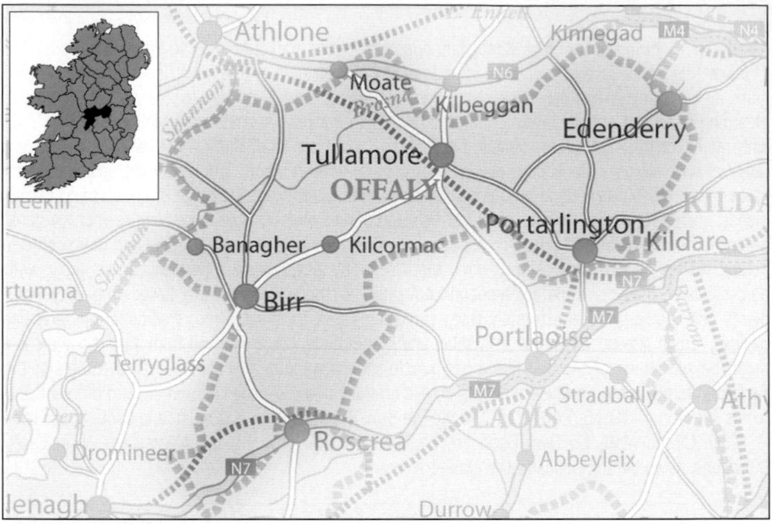

At the heart of the old Ely O'Carroll territory, Offaly is Ireland's most sky-minded county. In the grounds of Birr Castle, there's the Parsons family's famous restored 1845-vintage 1.83m astronomical telescope – rated one of the Seven Wonders of Ireland - through which the 3rd Earl of Rosse observed his discovery of the spiral nebulae. And in Tullamore, there's a thriving amateur Astronomical Society whose members point out that the wide clear skies of Offaly have encouraged the regular observation of heavenly bodies since at least 1057 AD, when astronomy was the province of moon-minded monks.

On a more modern note, the Tullamore Dew Heritage Centre is housed in the restored 1897 canal-side bonded warehouse, which formerly stored the famous local whiskey. The Centre explores Tullamore's distilling, canal and urban history with entertaining style.

Back in Birr meanwhile, the restored gardens of Birr Castle are an added attraction. And it's also in the heart of historic hunting country. Offaly is home to the Ormonde, which may not be Ireland's largest or richest hunt, "but it's the oldest and undoubtedly the best." Once upon a time, they invited the neighbouring County Galway Hunt for a shared meet, and afterwards the carousing in Dooly's Hotel in Birr reached such a hectic pitch that the hotel was joyously torched by the visitors. Dooley's was rebuilt to fulfill its central role in Birr, and the hunt from across the Shannon has been known as the Galway Blazers ever since.

The Grand Canal finally reaches the great river at Shannon Harbour in Offaly, after crossing Ireland from Dublin through Tullamore, and on the river itself, waterborne travellers find that Offaly affords the opportunity of visiting Clonmacnoise, where the remains of an ancient monastic university city give pause for thought.

In the south of the county, the Slieve Bloom Mountains rise attractively above Offaly's farmland and bogs. These are modest heights, as they attain just 526 m on the peak of Arderin – it has been observed that the Slieve Bloom are gallant hills which think they're mountains. However, it is their understated charms which particularly appeal - nestling in a valley of the Slieve Blooms is the unspoilt village of Kinnitty, where Offaly's quality of life is most in evidence.

Local Attractions and Information

Banagher Cloghan Castle (15C Tower House)	0509 51650
Birr, Castle Demesne & Historic Science Centre	0509 20336 / 22154
Birr, Tourism Information	0509 20110
Clonmacnoise Visitor & Interpretive Centre	090 967 4195
Edenderry, Canal Festival (June)	046 973 2071
Shannonbridge, Clonmacnoise & West Offaly Railway	090 967 4114
Slieve Bloom, Rural Development Society	0509 37299
Tullamore, Offaly Historical Society	0506 21421

Tullamore, Offaly Tourist Council 0506 52566
Tullamore, Tullamore Dew Heritage Centre 0506 25015
Tullamore, Tourism Information 0506 52617

Banagher

PUB

J.J.Hough

Main Street Banagher Co Offaly
Tel: 0509 51893 Email: johnhough@eircom.net

Hidden behind a thriving vine, which threatens to take over in summer, this charming 250-year old pub is soothingly dark inside making a fine contrast to the cheerful eccentricity of the current owner, Michael Hough. A world famous music pub, it's authentic and unique, family-run and with a wealth of Irish art on the walls. It's a great local and also popular with people from the river cruisers, who come up from the harbour for pints, music and craic - for the last thirty years there's been traditional Irish music here every night from March to November, and on Friday, Saturday & Sunday in winter. Nothing ever changes much here, although they did add a beer garden when the no-smoking law came in. Children and pets welcome. Open 10.30 am - 1 am. No food. Closed 25 Dec & Good Fri. **Directions:** Lower Main Street.

Birr

PUB

The Chestnut

Green Street Birr Co Offaly
Tel: 057 91 22011 Email: clodaghfay@hotmail.com

Clodagh Fay, sister of Caroline Boyd of The Stables, operates the old Chestnut pub in Birr town, which poured its first pint back in 1823. She refurbished the place beautifully a couple of years ago, with no expense spared on the stylish dark wood interior, slick bar and comfy layout. It is a great place to while away a Sunday afternoon reading the papers by the fire. They serve great cappuccinos and mochacinos along with some of the best Guinness you are likely to find anywhere in the country. Look out for the mouthwatering BBQs they host in the summer - and the full moon market, which takes place on the third Saturday of each month in the courtyard of the pub, stocking everything from organic vegetables to American Indian pottery. (The courtyard is also adjacent to a beautiful secret garden - perfect for long summer evenings.) Open: Mon-Fri 5pm-closing; Sat & Sun 12 noon-closing. Closed 25 Dec, Good Fri.

Birr

N CAFÉ/GUESTHOUSE

The Stables Emporium, Tea Rooms & Guesthouse

6 Oxmantown Mall Birr Co Offaly
Tel: 057 912 0263 Fax: 057 912 1677
Email: cboyd@indigo.ie Web: www.thestablesrestaurant.com

féile bia The Boyd family's characterful establishment is in a lovely old Georgian house overlooking the tree-lined mall. It was renowned for many years as one of the area's favourite restaurants - now it is run by Caroline Boyd, who has transformed it into a high quality furniture and gift shop, Emporium at the Stables. The store, which is located in the atmospheric old coach house, stocks crystal and glassware, fine furniture, lighting, garden accessories, jewellery and giftware. (Worldwide delivery can be arranged). Better still, in the main house, light lunches, snacks, wine, tea, coffee and delicious desserts are served in the elegant drawing room, complete with open fire and comfortable armchairs - and there are six delightful guest rooms upstairs too. Children welcome. Open Tue-Sat, 10.30-6 and Sun 1-5.30 (Nov, Dec, Jun, Jul & Aug). Air conditioning. Toilets wheelchair accessible. Closed Dec 25-29. **Accommodation:** Charming old world en-suite bedrooms overlooking the mall or the courtyard include two large newer rooms. **Rooms 6.** B&B about €45 pps, ss €5. Amex, Diners, MasterCard, Visa, Laser. **Directions:** Town centre, between St Brendan's church & private gates of Birr castle.

Birr

RESTAURANT/PUB

The Thatch Bar & Restaurant

Crinkle Birr Co Offaly
Tel: 0509 20682 Fax: 0509 21847

This characterful little thatched pub and restaurant just outside Birr shows just how pleasing a genuine, well-run country pub can be. Des Connole, proprietor since 1991, has achieved a well-earned reputation for the immaculate maintenance and atmosphere of the pub, and both bar food and restaurant meals are usually above average. Children welcome. Parking. **Seats 50** (private room, 15-20). D 6.30-9.30 daily, Set D about e37, also à la carte; L Sun-12.30 & 2.30; Set Sun L about e20; early evening bar menu Mon-Sat 5-7.30 (except Jul-Aug), à la carte; house wine about e18; SC discretionary. Bar meals Mon-Sat, 12.30-3.30 & 5-7.30. Toilets wheelchair accessible. Restaurant closed D Sun, establishment closed 25 Dec, Good Fri. Diners, MasterCard, Visa, Laser. **Directions:** 1 mile from Birr (Roscrea side). ◇

Kinnitty
COUNTRY HOUSE

Ardmore Country House

The Walk Kinnitty Co Offaly **Tel: 057 91 37009**
Email:info@kinnitty.com Web: www.kinnitty.com

Set back from the road in its own garden, Christina Byrne's stone-built Victorian house offers old-fashioned comforts: brass beds, turf fires and home-made bread and preserves for breakfast. Bedrooms are deliberately left without amenities, in order to make a visit to Ardmore a real country house experience and encourage guests to spend less time in their rooms and mix with each other - tea is available downstairs at any time. All bedrooms are decorated to a high standard - one with jacuzzi bath - and a ground floor room is wheelchair friendly. Christina now runs 1-7 day guided walking breaks, with dinner in local restaurants, including Kinnitty Castle and Leap castle - Ireland's most haunted castle (brochure available on request). There's a traditional Irish night on Friday nights, at nearby Kinnitty Castle. Children welcome (under 2s free in parents' room, cot available at no charge, baby sitting arranged); pets allowed in certain areas. **Rooms 5** (4 en-suite, 3 shower only, 1 with private bathroom, 1 family room, 1 ground floor, 1 for disabled, all no smoking). B&B €38 pps, ss €12. Closed 23-27 Dec. **No Credit Cards**. **Directions:** In village of Kinnitty, 9 miles from Birr (R440).

Kinnitty
B&B/RESTAURANT

The Glendine Bistro

Kinnitty Co Offaly
Tel: 0509 37973 Fax: 0509 37975

Situated in a charming village at the foot of the Slieve Bloom mountains, the clean-lined simplicity of Percy and Phil Clendennan's attractive contemporary restaurant provides a welcome contrast to other, more traditional, dining options nearby, giving visitors to this unspoilt area a choice of styles. Wide-ranging menus suit the surroundings: this is steak country and prime Hereford beef is sure to feature in steaks various ways, but there are also many more international dishes - barbecued tiger prawns & king scallops with chargrilled peppers, perhaps, or Irish ostrich on a bed of pesto courgettes, with balsamic dressing - and sound cooking is backed up by friendly service. Vegetarian options, typically stir-fries and fresh pasta dishes, are always available. Children welcome. **Seats 60** (private room 15). Air conditioning. D Thu- Sun, 6.30-9. L Sun only, 12.30-2.30. D à la carte. Set Sun L about €20. House wine €18. Closed Mon-Wed; all Jan. **Accommodation:** Bright, comfortably furnished en-suite bedrooms are offered, all with direct dial phones, TV and tea/coffee-making facilities. Children under 8 free in parents' room (cot available without charge). Rooms 5 (all shower-only & no smoking). Closed Jan. B&B about €32 pps, ss €7. MasterCard, Visa, Laser. **Directions:** 7 miles from Birr, in centre of Kinnitty Village. ◇

Kinnitty
HOTEL

Kinnitty Castle

Kinnitty Co Offaly **Tel: 057 913 7318** Fax: 057 913 7284
Email: kinnittycastle@eircom.net Web: www.kinnittycastle.com

Furnished in keeping with its dramatic history and theatrical character, this luxurious Gothic Revival castle in the foothills of the Slieve Bloom Mountains is at the centre of a very large estate (accessible for horse-riding and walking) with 650 acres of parkland and formal gardens. Public areas a library bar, Georgian style dining room, Louis XV drawing room and an atmospheric Dungeon Bar where there is traditional music on Friday nights all year are mainly furnished in the style expected of a castle hotel. The accommodation, however, is slightly different: bedrooms are all interesting and comfortable but vary considerably according to their position in the castle: the best are big and romantic, with stunning views over the estate (and sumptuous, dramatically styled bathrooms). There are new, but atmospheric, medieval-style banqueting/conference facilities for up to 180/200 in a courtyard at the back of the castle, which are understandably popular for weddings, also a small leisure centre (no swimming pool as yet). Apart from its olde-worlde character, what makes this hotel special is the staff, for whom nothing is too much trouble and who contribute greatly to the overall sense of fun. The restaurant - which is elegantly set up in one of the large, well-proportioned front rooms, offers an unusual and enjoyable dining experience. * Kinnitty Castle has just changed ownership at the time of going to press so information given is liable to change during 2007. Tennis, fishing, equestrian, garden. Children welcome (Under 12s free in parents' room; cots available without charge). No pets. **Rooms 37** (10 suites, 11 junior suites). No lift (long corridors and a lot of stairs). B&B about €120 pps, s.c.12.5%. Restaurant: D daily & L Sun. Open all year. Amex, Diners, MasterCard, Visa, Laser, Switch. **Directions:** On the R422- Emo to Birr Road,off main N7 Limerick Road. ◇

Shannonbridge
PUB

The Village Tavern

Main Street Shannonbridge Co Offaly
Tel: 0905 74112

At J.J. Killeen's wonderful pub and shop weary travellers can be restored, particularly by the house special of hot rum and chocolate - perfect after a damp day on the river. Meanwhile you can also top up on groceries, fishing bait and gas. Music nightly May-September; weekends only off-season. **Directions:** On the main street of Shannonbridge, between Ballinasloe and Cloghan.

TULLAMORE

This thriving canalside town is perhaps best known for its most famous product, Tullamore Dew, and, while it may no longer be made here, there is plenty of other hospitality-related activity going on today. Well-established restaurants in the town to check out include **Anatolia**, on Harbour Street (0506 23669; www.anatolia.ie) which is open for lunch and dinner, and the evening Italian restaurant, **Senor Rico** (0506 52839), which is nearby. Several popular ethnic restaurants include **Shisar** (057 935 1439) on High Street, specialising in in Thai/Indian cuisine. Also, there is an exciting bar and restaurant on William Street, **The Wolftrap** (see entry). The main hotel in the area is the Tullamore Court (see entry), but the recently opened **Days Hotel** (057 932 0350; www.dayshoteltullamore.com) offers a moderately priced alternative likely to be of particular interest to business guests.
WWW.IRELAND-GUIDE.COM FOR THE BEST PLACES TO EAT, DRINK & STAY

Tullamore
HOTEL

Tullamore Court Hotel

O'Moore Street Tullamore Co Offaly **Tel: 057 934 6666** Fax: 057 934 6677
Email: info@tullamorecourthotel.ie Web: www.tullamorecourthotel.ie

féile bia An attractive building, set back from the road a little and softened by trees, this large modern hotel is welcoming, with an extensive foyer, and bright and cheerful public areas. It serves the local community very well, with an excellent leisure centre and fine banqueting facilities. Bedrooms are very pleasantly decorated in an easy modern style, using warm colours and unfussy fabrics - and the staff are exceptionally friendly and helpful. It makes an ideal base for visiting the area and, as the food is generally above the standard expected in hotels, this can be a refreshing place to break a journey. However, the hotel's greatest strength has always been its business and conference facilities and now, a decade after opening with what were state of the art facilities at the time, a major development is just opening as the guide goes to press. This includes nine conference rooms, a business centre, 33 new executive bedrooms (including four suites) and a business centre. Free Broadband, leisure centre, swimming pool, garden. Children welcome (under 4s free in parents room, cot available with no charge, baby sitting arranged). **Rooms 105** (1 suite, 4 junior suites, 8 family rooms, 90 no smoking, 6 for disabled). Lift. B&B €105 pps, ss €20. Closed 24-26 Dec. Amex, MasterCard, Visa, Laser. **Directions:** South end of town.

Tullamore
BAR/RESTAURANT

The Wolftrap

William Street Tullamore Co Offaly
Tel: 057 932 3374 Fax: 057 932 3376
Email: info@thewolftrap.ie Web: www.thewolftrap.ie

The brainchild of Gina Murphy and her husband Padraig McLoughlin (previously of the well-known bar and restaurant, Crockets on the Quay, in Ballina, Co Mayo, which is still run by members of the family), this large bar and 'informal fine dining' restaurant is named after a mountain in the nearby Slieve Blooms (the border between Laois and Offaly is at its peak), and occupies a large town centre building near the harbour, which they have renovated and furnished with flair. With its warm atmosphere, long opening hours, imaginative menus and great service, it's the in place - and consistently good cooking (a judicious mixture of traditional and contemporary) invariably hits the spot. The stylish first floor restaurant offers an informal but sophisticated experience; menus change every 5-6 weeks, but is renowned for its excellent steaks, a good range of seafood and delicious desserts, including a yummy chocolate soufflé. All dishes are cooked to order and everything, including breads and ice creams, is homemade on the premises. A new chef, Stephen Johnston, joined the team just before we went to press and, with experience at Dublin's Chapter One under his belt, the future of this delightful restaurant looks very promising. Traditional music every Tuesday (Padraig is a musician). Late bar with DJ Fri & Sat to 2am. Bar food 7 days, 12-8.30pm (to 8pm Sat). Restaurant D 6.30-10.30 Tue-Sat. House wine €18. Closed Good Fri, 25 Dec. MasterCard, Visa, Laser. **Directions:** In the centre of Tullamore @ the junction of William and Harbour Streets.

Tullamore Area
GUESTHOUSE

Annaharvey Farm

Tullamore Co Offaly **Tel: 0506 43544** Fax: 0506 43766
Email: info@annaharveyfarm.ie Web: www.annaharveyfarm.ie

Henry and Lynda Deverell's restored grain barn, with pitch pine floors and beams, open fires and comfortable accommodation, provides a good base for a holiday offering all the pleasures of the outdoor life. Equestrian activities are the main attraction (including tuition in indoor and outdoor arenas), but walking, cycling and golfing also lay their claims - and, for the rest days, major sights including Clonmacnoise and Birr Castle are nearby. Good home cooking has always been a central feature here, and it has developed dramatically recently as Annaharvey Farm Foods is now part of the 'Offaly Delicious' local food producers network and the kitchen, with Rachael Deverell now overseeing the operation, produces even more delicious home-baking and preserves on sale at their Saturday markets. Small conference/banqueting (40/20). Cookery school. Children welcome (under 2 free in parents' room; cot available without charge). No pets. **Rooms 7** (6 shower only, 1 with bath; all no-smoking). B&B €36 pps, ss €10. Meals available - details on application. Closed Dec & Jan. MasterCard, Visa, Laser. **Directions:** R420 Tullamore - Portarlington. ◇

COUNTY ROSCOMMON

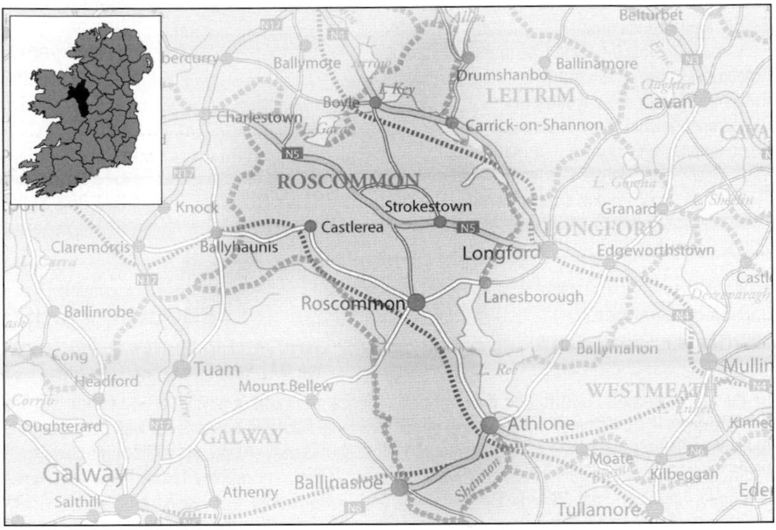

It could be said that in times past, Roscommon was a county much put upon by the counties about it. Or, put another way, to the casual visitor it seemed that just as Roscommon was on the verge of becoming significant, it became somewhere else. In one notable example - the hotel complex at Hodson's Bay on the western shores of Lough Ree - the location is actually in Roscommon, yet the exigencies of the postal service have given it to Athlone and thereby Westmeath.

But Roscommon is a giving sort of county, for it gave Ireland her first President, Gaelic scholar Douglas Hyde (1860-1949), it was also the birthplace of Oscar Wilde's father, and as well the inimitable songwriter Percy French was a Roscommon man. Like everywhere else in the western half of Ireland, Roscommon suffered grieviously from the Great Famine of the late 1840s, and at Strokestown, the handsome market town serving the eastern part of the county, Strokestown Park House has been sympathetically restored to include a Famine Museum. A visit to it will certainly add a thoughtful element to your meal in the restaurant.

Roscommon town itself has a population of 1,500, but it's growing, though the presence of extensive castle ruins and a former gaol tell of a more important past. The gaol was once noted for having a female hangman, today it has shops and a restaurant. Northwestward at Castlerea - headquarters for the County Council - we find Clonalis House, ancestral home of the O'Conor Don, and final resting place of O'Carolan's Harp.

In the north of the county, the town of Boyle near lovely Lough Key with its outstanding Forest Park is a substantial centre, with a population nearing the 2,000 mark. Boyle is thriving, and symbolic of this is the restored King House, a masterpiece from 1730. Reckoned to have been the most important provincial town house in Ireland, it is today filled with exhibits which eloquently evoke the past. Nearby, the impressive riverbank remains of Boyle Abbey, the largest Cistercian foundation in Ireland, date from 1148.

Lough Key is of course on one of the upper reaches of the inland waterways system, and a beautiful part it is too. In fact, all of Roscommon's eastern boundary is defined by the Shannon and its lakes, but as the towns along it tend to identify themselves with the counties on the other side of the river, Roscommon is left looking very thin on facilities. But it has much to intrigue the enquiring visitor. For instance, along the Roscommon shore of Lough Ree near the tiny village of Lecarrow, the remains of a miniature city going back to mediaeval times and beyond can be dimly discerned among the trees down towards Rindown Point. These hints of of an active past serve to emphasise the fact that today, Roscommon moves at a gentler pace than the rest of Ireland.

Local Attractions and Information

Boyle, Boyle Abbey (12th C Monastery) 071 966 2604
Boyle, Frybrook House (18thC town hse) 071 966 2513
Boyle, King House (500 years of Irish life) 071 966 3242

Boyle, Lough Key Forest Park 071 966 2363
Boyle, Tourism Information 071 966 2145
Castlerea, Clonalis House 094 962 0014
Elphin, Restored windmill 071 963 5181
Frenchpark Dr Douglas Hyde Interpretive Centre 0907 70016
Roscommon town, Arts Centre 090 662 5824
Roscommon town, County Museum 090 662 5613
Roscommon townm Race Course 090 662 6231
Roscommon town, Tourism Information 090 662 6342
Strokestown, Park House, Garden & Famine Museum 071 963 3013
Strokestown, Roscommon County Heritage Centre 071 963 3380

Carrick-on-Shannon
COUNTRY HOUSE/FARMHOUSE

Glencarne House

Ardcarne Carrick-on-Shannon Co Roscommon
Tel: 071 966 7013 Fax: 071 966 7013

On the border between Leitrim and Roscommon - Glencarne House is physically in Leitrim, but the postal address is Roscommon - the Harrington family's large Georgian house is set well back from the road, with a large garden in front and farmland behind, so it is easy to find, yet without intrusion from traffic. Spacious and elegantly furnished with antiques, this is very much a family home and Agnes Harrington has won many awards for hospitality and home-cooked food based on their own farm produce. Good-sized bedrooms all have en-suite bathrooms, and a fine breakfast, cooked to order, will set you up for the day. Garden. Children welcome; pets permitted by arrangement. **Rooms 4** (all en-suite & no smoking). B&B about €35 pps, ss about €5. Set D about €25.50, 7.30pm (book by 6pm); wine licence. Closed Oct-Mar. **No Credit Cards. Directions:** On the N4,halfway between Carrick-on-Shannon and Boyle. ◇

Castlecoote
Ⓝ COUNTRY HOUSE

Castlecoote House

Castlecoote Co Roscommon
Tel: 0906 663794 Fax: 0906 663795
Email: info@castlecootehouse.com Web: www.castlecootehouse.com

This fine Georgian residence overlooking the beautiful River Suck was built in the enclosure of a medieval castle between 1690 and 1720, and is of historic interest - not least as the birthplace of the Gunning sisters, who became the Duchess of Hamilton (and later, of Argyll) and Countess of Coventry; celebrated for their beauty; their portraits by Sir Joshua Reynolds hang in the main hall. Having restored the house to its former glory, the present owners, Sarah Lane and Kevin Finnerty, now offer magnificent country house accommodation and they are members of the Ireland West Garden Trail - guided tours of the gardens, which include an orchard of rare apple trees, the towers of the ruined castle, a medieval bridge and even an ice house, are offered by appointment. Snooker, walking, garden, croquet, tennis, trout and coarse fishing on site; equestrian and golf nearby. **Rooms 5,** not suitable for children or wheelchairs. **Directions:** Castlecoote is about 5km southwest of Roscommon, into village, cross bridge, bear right, gates are directly ahead. ◇

Castlerea
COUNTRY HOUSE

Clonalis House

Castlerea Co Roscommon
Tel: 094 962 0014 Fax: 094 962 0014
Email: clonalis@iol.ie Web: www.clonalis.com

Standing on the land that has been the home of the O'Conors of Connacht for 1,500 years, this 45-roomed Victorian Italianate mansion may seem a little daunting on arrival, but it's magic - and the hospitable owners, Pyers and Marguerite O'Conor-Nash, enjoy sharing their rich and varied history with guests, who are welcome to browse through their fascinating archive. Amazing heirlooms include a copy of the last Brehon Law judgment (handed down about 1580) and also Carolan's Harp. Everything is on a huge scale: reception rooms are all very spacious, with lovely old furnishings and many interesting historic details, bedrooms have massive four poster and half tester beds and bathrooms to match and the dining room is particularly impressive, with a richly decorated table to enhance Marguerite's home cooking. Clonalis House is set amid peaceful parklands and is a good base from which to explore counties Roscommon, Galway, Mayo and Sligo. *Two attractive self-catering cottages are also offered, in the courtyard; details on application. A 10% reduction is offered for stays of three or more nights. Horse riding, fishing, shooting and golf (9) are all nearby. Unsuitable for children under 12 years. No pets. **Rooms 4** (3 en-suite, 1 with private bathroom; all no smoking). Garden, walking. Golf nearby. B&B €95-110 pps, ss €20. Residents D Tue-Sat, 8pm, €44 (24 hrs notice required); wines about €20. (D not available Sun or Mon.) Closed Oct-Apr. MasterCard, Visa, Laser. **Directions:** N60, west of Castlerea.

Cootehall
RESTAURANT

Cootehall Bridge Riverside Restaurant

Cootehall Boyle Co Roscommon
Tel: 071 966 7173

Cootehall is one of those places which can't decide which county it is in but, whether it is in Roscommon or Leitrim, this waterside restaurant provides a very complete service. After many years under the stewardship of Manfred Khan, the restaurant changed hands in 2006 and the style is now rustic French/Italian food with Irish influences, although new owner Eric Cahill and his kitchen team have kept some of the old favourites like French onion soup and wiener schnitzel on new menus, which are based mainly on local and organic produce. And Manfred often drops in, as a customer, just to make sure everything is being done right. Good food and value for money send many a customer happy into the night. L served Wed-Sat 1-4, Sun L 12.30-5.30; D Wed-Sat 6-9.30. 3 course meal €30-40. Dinner reservations recommended, especially at weekends. A phone call to check opening times is recommended, especially off season. Closed Sun D, Mon, Tues and Nov & Jan. MasterCard, Visa, Laser. **Directions:** Right of the bridge as you approach the village.

Cootehall
PUB

M. J. Henry

Cootehall Boyle Co Roscommon
Tel: 071 966 7030

The more theme pubs and superpubs there are, the better everyone likes M J Henry's bar, which hasn't changed in at least 30 years and, in true country Irish fashion, is also a food store 'that caters for all your grocery needs'. A visit to Cootehall (the village of well-known writer John McGahern) would be unthinkable without checking on this little gem They don't make them like this any more, alas, but this delightful old pub - complete with formica from the most recent renovation - is a gem. Get in beside the fire with a hot whiskey and the world will do you no harm. No bar food. Closed 25 Dec & Good Fri. **No Credit Cards. Directions:** 2 miles off N4 Sligo - Dublin road, between Boyle & Carrick-on-Shannon.

Knockvicar
(N) B&B/RESTAURANT/PUB

Clarendon House Restaurant

Knockvicar Boyle Co Roscommon
Tel: 071 966 7016 Fax: 071 966 7016
Email: greg.bird@gmail.com Web: www.clarendonhouse.com

Half way between Carrick on Shannon and Boyle, you take the road towards Keadue, one of Ireland's tidiest towns. Two miles on, past the post office, veer on to your right and you will see Donnellan's on your right. Ask. The Leitrim people are friendly and they all know it. This out of the way ordinary looking pub and restaurant is worth getting to, if only for the courgette and brie soup prepared by head chef, Stephen Coley, the home made pasta dish of the day by Italian, Enrico or simply the great Sunday lunch for €19. In winter the turf stove which divides the bar from the small lounge will have extra attraction for locals and visitors alike. Greg Bird and Enrico Pastorelli bought this pub two years ago and their mission is to serve honest to goodness locally sourced food like home made soups, good salads, great steaks and interesting vegetarian dishes like roast sweet red peppers stuffed with rice, sun dried tomatoes and goat's cheese. Cooking is seriously good here and it is created with passion. There is a children's menu and a bar food menu with Thai beef wrap which has marinated beef, spring onion, fresh coriander, cashew nuts in a chilli dressing. Glazed plum pastry flan, jelly and ice cream and great coffee make this both sophisticated and friendly which befits lovely Leitrim. There are plans to extend the dining room to give a view of the fine garden and already there is a lovely summer gazebo set up there for small weddings and parties. **Accommodation:** At the time of going to press there are four guest rooms available, and another five in an adjoining house; this may well be increased. Banqueting (50); Children welcome; **Seats 38** (private room, 8); D Wed-Mon 5-10pm; set D €23.50/27.50, also a la carte; L Sun only, 12.30-4; set Sun L €19.50; house wine €18. Closed Tues. *Restaurant due to be demolished and rebuilt Jan 07 to include toilet facilities for wheelchairs. B&B; €29 pps. MasterCard, Visa, Laser. **Directions:** Take a right off N4 Carrick on Shannon - Sligo road after 7km (4m) for Knockvicar.

Knockvicar
RESTAURANT

Italia

Knockvicar Boyle Co Roscommon
Tel: 071 96 67788 Email: brunoboe@eircom.net

Bruno Boe's beautifully located contemporary restaurant is a hit with discerning diners in the area - and boating visitors to the marina. The interior is well-designed on two levels to take full advantage of views over the river and Knockvicar marina, and enhanced by decor which is colourful, comfortable and stylishly appointed - fashionable high-back chairs, classy tableware, fine glasses - an unusually cosmopolitan approach for a rural restaurant. Expect a real Italian welcome, authentic Italian cooking - and very fair prices. Service can be slow, but the overall package is so attractive that everybody keeps coming back. **Seats 56.** D 6-"late", L Sun only 1-4. A la carte. House wine about €17. No SC. (reservations required; advisable to ring and check opening hours, especially off season.) Closed Mon & a few weeks Oct-Nov & Feb. Amex, MasterCard, Visa, Laser. **Directions:** Near Carrick-on-Shannon, on the Knockvicar-Cootehall road. ◇

Roscommon
HOTEL

Abbey Hotel & Leisure Centre

Abbeytown Galway Road Roscommon Co Roscommon
Tel: 090 662 6240 Fax: 090 662 6021
Email: info@abbeyhotel.ie Web: www.abbeyhotel.ie

féile bia The heart of this pleasing hotel is an old manor house and, despite major developments, the atmosphere of the original building prevails and there's a romantic honeymoon suite with a four-poster in the old house. Big changes taking place recently include the addition of a contemporary wing with spacious new bedrooms, all designed and decorated to a high standard and with pleasant views. A high level of comfort, together with excellent leisure facilities and good value offered, adds greatly to the hotel's appeal for short breaks - and it would make an excellent base for exploring an area that deserves to be better known. *Short/golfing breaks offered; details on application. Conference/banqueting (250/280); video-conferencing. Leisure centre (20m swimming pool, sauna, steam room, gym, jacuzzi). Children welcome (under 12s free in parents' room; cots available without charge, baby sitting arranged). Garden. No pets. **Rooms 50** (36 no smoking, 4 disabled, 1 shower only). Lift. Room service (limited hours). B&B €85 pps, ss €10. Short breaks offered. Restaurant L 12.45-2.45, D 7-9.30 (Sun to 9). Set L €25, Set Sun L €30; D à la carte. House wines from €16.50, no SC. Hotel closed 24-26 Dec. Amex, Diners, MasterCard, Visa, Laser. **Directions:** N4 to Roscommon, Galway Road; next to the library, on the left. ◇

Shannonbridge
RESTAURANT

The Old Fort

Shannonbridge Co Roscommon **Tel: 090 967 4973**
Email: info@theoldfortrestaurant.com Web: www.theoldfortrestaurant.com

In a very pleasant site right beside the Shannon, this restaurant is in a restored fort and has oodles of character. The proprietor, Fergal Moran, grew up here and started restoration of the fort about eight years ago, working with Dúchas to ensure it was done correctly. Initial impressions on arrival are confirmed in the large reception area, which has lovely old timbers, fresh flowers, good lighting and comfortable sofas beside an open fire - a great start by any standards, and a useful extra dining space for elderly guests, or anyone in a wheelchair, who may not be comfortable with stairs. The main dining room is upstairs (also a second room used for busy times or for private functions) and the ambience is lovely, with old wooden floors, well-spaced polished wood tables smartly laid with starched linen napkins and candles, which are also everywhere in sconces. The head chef, Brian Maher, offers several attractive evening menus - an early evening à la carte, a more extensive set dinner and a special Thursday and Friday menu, which is very good value. The simplest dishes are often best - an excellent steak, cooked as ordered, comes with a creamy mushroom sauce and perfectly cooked, very good quality vegetables; most people will go home happy after such a dish. This is very good food, enhanced by attentive service and lovely surroundings. This restaurant is a great asset to the area, and is enjoyed enormously by discerning visitors, whether arriving by river or road. Small weddings. Children welcome. Toilets wheelchair accessible. **Seats 80** (private room, 30). Reservations advised. D Wed-Sun, from 5-9.30 (Sun, in summer only, 5-8); L Sun only 12.30-3. Value D €25 (Wed-Fri, 5-9.30 & sat 5-7), Set D €37.50, also à la carte. Set Sun L, €22. House wine €17.50. Closed 3 weeks Jan. 1 week Nov. MasterCard, Visa, Laser. **Directions:** Beside the bridge in Shannonbridge.

Tarmonbarry
BAR/RESTAURANT

Keenans Bar & Restaurant

Tarmonbarry (via Clondra) Co Roscommon
Tel: 043 26052 / 26098 Fax: 043 26198
Email: info@keenans.ie Web: www.keenans.ie

féile bia Just beside the bridge over the Shannon in Tarmonbarry, this well-run bar and restaurant is a favourite watering hole for river folk and makes a great place to break a journey between Dublin and the north-west. The bar is comfortably set up for food and informal meals - mostly quite traditional, but with more international influences in the more expensive evening dishes - are served all day; open sandwiches on home-made wholemeal or soda bread, toasted sandwiches, salads and scones with jam & cream are typical, plus half a dozen daily specials (including specialities such as smoked fish casserole and bacon & cabbage at lunch, perhaps, and more elaborate dishes like roast half duckling on an orange & redcurrant stuffing with a plum & sherry sauce in the evening). A la carte menus are similar in tone but more extensive - wholesome, hearty fare that pleases all age groups; the steak sandwich (served with onions, chips, garlic butter & home-made horseradish sauce) is not to be missed - while the set dinner menu is a little more formal. Good unpretentious food and cheerful, efficient service keep happy customers coming back. **Restaurant seats 30.** Food served daily 12.30-8.30; L 12.30-2.30, D 6.30-8.30. D A la C, Set Sun L €23.95. House wine €18.95. Restaurant closed D Sun. Establishment closed 25 Dec, Good Fri. Amex, MasterCard, Visa, Laser. **Directions:** On N5, west of Longford town.

COUNTY SLIGO

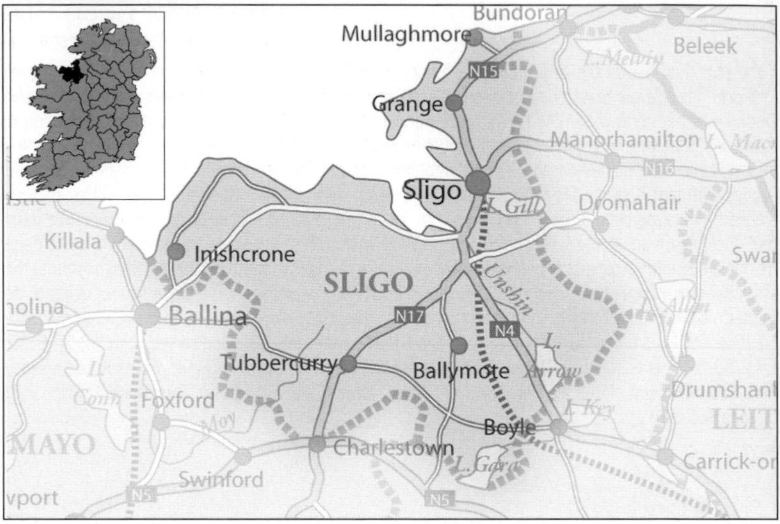

There's a stylish confidence to Sligo which belies its compact area as one of Ireland's smallest counties. Perhaps it's because they know that their place and their way of life have been immortalised through association with two of the outstanding creative talents of modern Ireland, W.B.Yeats and his painter brother Jack. The former's fame seems beyond question, while the latter's star was never higher than it is today.

The town and the county have many associations with Yeats, but few are more remarkable than Lissadell House, the former home of the Gore-Booths. Best known as the family of Constance Gore-Booth - who as Countess Markievicz was much involved with the Easter Rising of 1916 – the Gore-Booths were extraordinary people in several generations, and Lissadell – which is open to the public – is a timely reminder of this, and of Sligo's unique qualities.

But whatever the reason for Sligo's special quality, there's certainly something about it that encourages repeat visits. The town itself is big enough to be reassuring, yet small enough to be comfortable. And the countryside about Sligo town also has lasting appeal. Mankind has been living here with enthusiasm for a very long time indeed, for in recent years it has been demonstrated that some of County Sligo's ancient monuments are amongst the oldest in northwest Europe. Lakes abound, the mountains are magnificent, and there are tumbling rivers a-plenty.

Yet if you wish to get away from the bustle of the regular tourist haunts, Sligo can look after your needs in this as well, for the western part of the county down through the Ox Mountains towards Mayo is an uncrowded region of wide vistas and clear roads.

Local Attractions and Information

Carrowmore, Largest Megalithic Cemetry in Ireland	071 916 1534
Drumcliff, Drumcliffe Church & Visitor Centre (Yeats)	071 914 4956
Drumcliff, Lissadell House	071 916 3150
Inniscrone, Seaweed Bath House	096 36238
Lough Gill, Waterbus Cruises	071 916 4266
Sligo, Discover Sligo Tours	071 914 7488
Sligo, Model Arts & Niland Gallery	071 914 1405
Sligo Abbey, (13thC Dominican Friary)	071 914 6406
Sligo, Sligo Airport, Strandhill	071 916 8280
Sligo, Sligo Art Gallery	071 914 5847
Sligo, Tourism Information	071 916 1201
Sligo Yeats Memorial Building, Hyde Bridge	071 914 2693
Strandhill, Seaweed Baths, Maritime House	071 916 8686

Aughris Head

B&B/PUB

Beach Bar/Aughris House

Aughris Head Templeboy Co Sligo
Tel: 071 916 6703 / 071 917 6465

The McDermott family's picturesque and beautifully located thatched pub seems too good to be true when you first find it in this quiet and unspoilt place, but there it has been since the 18th century when, apparently, it was a shibín known as Maggie Maye's. Today, after sensitive restoration, it has retained some of the best characteristics of the past and makes a lovely stopping place, with food served in the flag-stoned bar - and access to a beach just a hop across the wall from the car park. Wholesome, home-cooked meals are served here - creamy Atlantic seafood chowder, for example, great steaks with all the traditional trimmings, honey roast pork, bangers and mash - and much more. Delicious home-made desserts too- 'Brambly' apple crumble, perhaps, or lemon cheesecake. **Accommodation:** In a neat bungalow just beside the pub and overlooking the Atlantic Ocean, the McDermotts also offer comfortable, inexpensive, family-friendly B&B accommodation, with neat shower rooms and TV. Complimentary tea and biscuits on arrival. Children welcome (under 2 free in parents' room, cot available, baby sitting arranged); pets allowed in some areas. Garden, scenic walks, sandy beach, boat trips and sea angling arranged. B&B €30-33, single €35-38. (Short breaks & family rates available). Open all year. MasterCard, Visa. **Directions:** Off N59 Sligo/Ballina Road, Coast road to Aughris Head/Pier. ◇

Ballygawley

Ⓝ HOTEL

Castle Dargan Estate - Hotel & Golf Resort

Castle Dargan Estate Ballygawley Co Sligo **Tel: 071 911 8080**
Fax: 071 911 8090 Email: info@castledargan.com Web: www.castledargan.com

Named after the ruins of the ancient castle which remain within its Darren Clarke designed championship golf course, Castle Dargan Estate is set amongst dramatic scenery on 170 acres of mature woodlands. Castle Dargan House - which replaced the castle has uninterrupted views over the countryside and golf course and makes a fine centrepiece for this new contemporary hotel. A lovely period drawing room and meeting room within the original house sets the tone for the well-designed new section across a courtyard to the rear of the old house, which is larger than it seems and makes the most of the scenic views. A large reception area with high ceilings, warm colour schemes and log fires establish the warm, contemporary tone that prevails throughout the new areas and acts as a hub, with the bedrooms to one side and restaurant, bar and residents' lounge to the other. The bar is stunning, featuring a mezzanine level with floor to ceiling windows overlooking a large decking area and the golf course - a bright and airy place to enjoy a cup of coffee and read the papers. Alongside is an intimate restaurant, which shares the same views. Accommodation is mainly in the new area - all bedrooms are finished to a high standard, with plasma TV, tea-coffee making facilities and iron/trouser press as standard, and have views of the golf course but the suites are in the old house and enjoy a special atmosphere. Apartments separately located at the gate of the hotel are also available, each sleeping up to four people. The hotel would make a magnificent wedding venue the function room, an L shaped room with floor to ceiling windows on two sides and a private bar, is in a prime location on the first floor. Wheelchair friendly. Conferences/Banqueting (400/300), free broadband Wi/Fi, video conferencing. Championship golf (18), Spa, beauty salon, walking; Hunting/shooting and equestrian nearby. **Rooms 54** (16 junior suites, 4 executive, 14 ground floor, 1 for disabled); Children welcome (under 4s free in parents' room, cot available at no charge, baby sitting arranged); 24 hr rooms service, Lift. Restaurant: seats 60, D daily 6.30-9pm; L Sun only, 12-4pm. Bar food available all day, 10am-9pm. Open all year. Heli-pad. Amex, MasterCard, Visa, Laser. **Directions:** 10 minutes from Sligo town- take the R284 to Ballygawley. There is an alternative access from the Collooney By Pass roundabout via the Dromahair Road.

Ballymote

COUNTRY HOUSE

Temple House

Ballinacarrow Ballymote Co Sligo
Tel: 071 918 3329 Fax: 071 918 3808
Email: enquiry@templehouse.ie Web: www.templehouse.ie

One of Ireland's most unspoilt old houses, this is a unique place - a Georgian mansion situated in 1,000 acres of farm and woodland, overlooking the original lakeside castle which was built by the Knights Templar in 1200 A.D. The Percevals have lived here since 1665 and the house was redesigned and refurbished in 1864 - some of the furnishings date back to that major revamp. Sandy and Deb Perceval first opened the doors of their home to guests in 1981 and it is now managed by their son Roderick and his wife Helena, who are bringing their own brand of youthful energy and enthusiasm to running this amazing house. The whole of the house has retained its old atmosphere and, in addition to central heating, has log fires to cheer the enormous rooms. Spacious bedrooms are furnished with old family furniture (some also have some modern additions) and bathrooms are gradually being upgraded - not an easy task in a house of this age, but a high pressure water system has now been installed in most of them. Guests have the use of an elegant sitting room with open fires, and evening meals are served (every day except Sunday or Wednesday) in the very beautiful dining room and are a treat to look forward to, based on seasonal produce from the estate and other local suppliers. Floriane Beguin, previously at Cromleach Lodge is currently cooking at Temple House and a typically delicious menu might include: walnut & apricot tartlet with Cashel Blue cheese, panfried wild salmon, and rhubarb fool; there's always an Irish cheeseboard too - and home-made fudge with coffee in the Morning Room. Traditional Irish music and dancing sessions are often held nearby. Children welcome (under 12s 60% discount, babies free in parents' room; cots available at no charge, baby sitting arranged). Pets permitted in some areas. **Rooms 6** (5 en-suite, 2 shower only, 1 with private bathroom, all no smoking). B&B €90 pps, ss €25. Residents 4-course D €42, 7.30pm (book by 1pm, not available Sun); house wine about €17. Children's tea 6.30pm; SC discretionary. *Golf nearby, at Rosses Point, Strandhill and Enniscrone - short breaks available. Closed Dec-Mar. MasterCard, Visa, Laser. **Directions:** Signposted on N17, 11km (7 m) south of N4 junction.

Castlebaldwin
RESTAURANT WITH ROOMS/WINE BAR

Clevery Mill

Castlebaldwin Co Sligo
Tel: 071 912 7424
Email: cleverymill@eircom.net Web: www.cleverymill.com

This charmingly converted old mill, complete with millwheel, is located in the countryside about 20 minutes' drive from Sligo. From the moment you push open the door of the old stone building, you get a sense of warmth and relaxation - although the kitchen is obviously not too relaxed, as the quality of the food coming out of it is of a high calibre. Most diners enjoy an aperitif in the bar area with its open fire or perhaps in the smaller snug room adjacent, and make put in their orders, before going through to the main dining room, which is classically appointed with white linen and full of character: artfully broken up into different levels, so as to make little intimate corners in what is essentially one big space, it is a lovely room overlooking the old waterwheel. The menu tempts with a wide selection of dishes and always a good sign - lists sources, which are mostly local and organic. Typical dishes include starters such as pan seared scallops with a salsa verde, crab parcel, young spinach, marinated sultanas and a red pepper puree, or breast of squab with a roasted green pepper polenta, grilled fig & balsamic pan juices. Main courses might be pan-fried breast of duck from Thornhill, Blacklion, served with plum chutney, celeriac and swede gratin and a red wine jus infused with couverture chocolate, or fillet of sea bass with sauté pak choy, crab ravioli and cep velouté. Puddings won special praise on a recent visit - notably a rhubarb and ginger custard tart served with Chantilly cream and raspberries -and great attention is paid to presentation throughout. Recommended for a cosy stay and high-class food. **Accommodation:** There are six comfortable bedrooms furnished in a country style with old stripped pine, have modern en suite shower rooms, and some rooms have four-poster beds. Breakfasts are generous and the service is good. **Restaurant seats 54;** L Sat-Sun, 12.30-4, set L €27; D Tue-Sat, 6.30-10, set D €40. Rooms 6; B&B from €50 pps; midweek specials available on request. Closed D Sun, Mon; house closed Christmas & New Year. MasterCard, Visa, Laser. **Directions:** 14 miles from Sligo, N4 towards Dublin.

Castlebaldwin
★ HOTEL/RESTAURANT

Cromleach Lodge

Castlebaldwin via Boyle Co Sligo
Tel: 071 916 5155 Fax: 071 916 5455
Email: info@cromleach.com Web: www.cromleach.com

Quietly situated in the hills just above Lough Arrow, Christy and Moira Tighe's small hotel enjoys one of the finest views in Ireland - and it makes a luxurious retreat for the most discerning of guests. Cromleach is rightly renowned for exceptionally high standards of both food and accommodation - and, most importantly, the Tighe family and their staff have the magic ingredient of genuine hospitality, doing everything possible to ensure comfort and relaxation for their guests. Spacious bedrooms have an emphasis on comfort rather than fashion, and are thoughtfully furnished, with king-size and single beds, seating areas overlooking the lough with easy chairs to relax in, and well-planned bathrooms with lots of luxurious little extras and hospitality, housekeeping and attention to detail are all outstanding. The area around Cromleach is beautiful and unspoilt, and the Tighes like nothing better than to introduce guests to the many places of interest and activities nearby but, for many, just being here is more than enough. Major development has taken place here during 2005/6 and additions include the 'Diarmaid & Grainne' banqueting suite, where weddings for up to 160 can be held; also a smart little bar, Nuada's, where a light snack menu is available all day. Small conferences (20). Children welcome (under 3 free in parents' room, cot available without charge, baby sitting arranged). Pets permitted by arrangement. Garden; walking; fishing. Golf nearby. **Rooms 10** (2 junior suites, 6 no-smoking). Room service (limited hours). Turndown service. B&B €146 pps, ss €50. Short breaks and off-season value breaks available. **Moira's:** Re-named and completely re-styled, the restaurant is now contemporary, elegant and calm as you dine. Arranged to allow every table to take full advantage of the view, it is decorated in shades of cream and coffee, with black leather high backed chairs and long stylish seating at each end of dining room - stripes of lime green, pale mauve, moss green and grey fit beautifully with the voile curtains embroidered in golds and lined in silk. Although Moira Tighe (who was our Chef of the Year in 2000) is still very involved with the kitchen, Alan Kinsella, previously at Locks in Dublin, is now head chef; they work closely as a team and both the menus - based on meticulously sourced ingredients - and the modern Irish cooking style are still very much 'Cromleach', with Alan now adding his own touch. The many regular guests who have grown attached to Cromleach will be glad to know that the specialities created by Moira over the years will still feature, along with new dishes, as has always been the case. Dishes enjoyed on recent visit include the house seafood chowder, a main course loin of lamb with a black sweet pepper crust, parsnip purée, cinnamon & vanilla jus, and a delicious hot chocolate fondant, with mascarpone ice cream, cinnamon anglaise & chocolate macaroons. Everything, from the first little amuse-bouche to the last petit four with coffee is a treat - and, as in all aspects of this wonderful place, service is flawless. Children welcome; toilets wheelchair accessible; reservations required. **Seats 60** (private rooms, 4-24). Food served daily, 11-7pm; L 12.30-3.30pm, D 6.30-9.30pm; Set L €29.75, Set D €50, Residents' Tasting Menu, €65, also a la carte L&D; house wines from €19.95; sc discretionary. Establishment closed 2 weeks Nov, 4 days at Christmas. Amex, MasterCard, Visa, Laser. **Directions:** Signposted from Castlebaldwin on the N4.

Cliffoney
Ⓝ RESTAURANT

The Old Post House

Cliffoney Co Sligo **Tel: 071 917 6777**
Fax: 071 917 7688 Email: theoldposthouse@eircom.net

This attractive stone-faced former post office - which has views of Donegal Bay, Classiebawn Castle and Mullaghmore headland in the distance - was taken over in 2006 by Shane McGonigle (previously with Conrad Gallagher at Peacock Alley in Dublin) and his partner Kay Ryan. Have an aperitif in a small but pleasant reception area, or at your table in a large high-ceilinged dining room with understated modern décor and uncurtained windows that make the most of the sweeping coastal views; promptly presented menus reveal an emphasis on fish and seafood - often contemporary in style, perhaps with an Asian spin (scallops with bacon and Asian greens for example), although you will also find classics like mussels in white wine and local oysters au naturel. Main course fish could include brill with a fennel compôte & deep fried salsify, and John Dory with chorizo, potatoes & a balsamic reduction, while meat dishes from an early season menu tended towards classic, slow cooked French dishes such as a wonderfully rich daube of tender beef with mash and carrots or lamb shank slow cooked in port. Stylish presentation adds to the sense of occasion and rather high-end prices are justified by the quality of ingredients and cooking and warm and friendly service. Sunday lunch is good value and, while featuring traditional options such as roasts and homely desserts, also includes luxurious starters such as a dozen oysters, and fish main courses. Children welcome. Toilets wheelchair accessible. **Seats 80.** L Wed-Sat, 12-3 (Sun, 12-6); D Wed-Sat, 6-10 and Sun, 6.30-8.30, L&D à la carte. House wine €19; SC 10% on parties 6+. Closed Mon (open Bank Hols), Tue, 25 Dec and all of Oct, Nov, Jan. MasterCard, Visa, Laser. **Directions:** On side of main Sligo/Bundoran/Donegal road in the village of Cliffoney.

Collooney
HOTEL/RESTAURANT

Markree Castle

Collooney Co Sligo **Tel: 071 9167800** Fax: 071 916 7840
Email: markree@iol.ie Web: markreecastle.ie

Sligo's oldest inhabited house has been home to the Cooper family for 350 years. Set in magnificent park and farmland, this is a proper castle, with a huge portico leading to a covered stone stairway that sweeps up to an impressive hall, where an enormous log fire always burns. Everything is on a very large scale, and it is greatly to the credit of the present owners, Charles and Mary Cooper, that they have achieved the present level of renovation and comfort since they took it on in a sad state of disrepair in 1989 - and they have always been generous with the heating. Ground floor reception areas include a comfortably furnished double drawing room with two fireplaces (where light food including afternoon tea is served). There is a lift and also disabled toilets, but the layout of the castle makes it difficult for elderly people or wheelchair users to get around; a phone call ahead to ensure the (very willing) staff are available to help would be wise. The dining room is a very beautiful room and open to non-residents for dinner, and lunch on Sunday. While by no means perfect - investment is clearly needed to bring it up to the standard that guests may expect of a castle, and there are many idiosyncrasies, in bedrooms, for example - this slightly eccentric place has got real heart; do, however, beware of times when very inexpensive offers are available, as it can be noisy and children are not always kept under control. Horse riding. Conferences/banqueting (50/150). Children welcome (under 4s free in parents' room; cots available). Pets permitted. **Rooms 30** (all en-suite, 5 executive rooms, 1 for disabled). Lift. B&B from about €92 pps, ss about €10. Non-residents are welcome. (Reservations recommended). **Seats 80** (private room, 40) D 7.30-9.30 daily; L 1-2.30 Sun only. Set D about €30, Set Sun L about €18; house wine about €14; no sc. No smoking restaurant. Hotel closed 24-27 Dec. Amex, Diners, MasterCard, Visa. **Directions:** Just off the N4, take the Dromohair exit at Collooney roundabout. ◇

Mullaghmore

Eithna's Seafood Restaurant

RESTAURANT

The Harbour Mullaghmore Co Sligo **Tel: 071 916 6407**
Email: eithnasrestaurant@eircom.net Web: www.eithnasseafoodrestaurant.com

Situated right on the harbour at Mullaghmore, Eithna O'Sullivan Huel's atmospheric seafood restaurant specialises in fish and shellfish caught by local fishermen in Donegal Bay. Since opening in 1990 she has gradually built up a reputation that extends far beyond the local population - those in the know now travel specially for Eithna's cooking, particularly lobster (served various ways) and the seafood platter which, even at €48, is better value than the various lobster dishes served separately. For this you get a cold half lobster, prawns, crab, crab claws, razor fish, mussels and clams; all served in the shell - the exact ingredients may vary a little according to availability but it will balance out. The platter is attractively served and comes with tossed organic salad greens, mayonnaise, fresh lemon, a bread basket and a dish of potatoes (quite probably from Normandy). There are fish specials too, offering two or three varieties daily, and some options other than seafood, including starters like smoked chicken salad, and main course rack of Cliffoney lamb; vegetarian dishes change daily - and tempting desserts might include a classic crème brulée or chocolate & pear tart. Children welcome. **Seats 60** (private room, 30, outdoor terrace seating, 20). D daily in high season, 6.30-9.30. A la carte (main courses from around €20-€50). House wine €19. Often closed during Nov-Feb, as seasonal variations apply so it is better to phone ahead off season. Diners, MasterCard, Visa, Laser. **Directions:** 26km (16 m) from Sligo on N15 (Donegal road); turn right at Cliffoney village.

Riverstown

Coopershill House

COUNTRY HOUSE

Riverstown Co Sligo **Tel: 071 916 5108** Fax: 071 916 5108
Email: ohara@coopershill.com Web: www.coopershill.com

Undoubtedly one of the most delightful and superbly comfortable Georgian houses in Ireland, this sturdy granite mansion was built to withstand the rigours of a Sligo winter but its numerous chimneys suggest there is warmth to be found within the stern grey walls. Peacocks wander elegantly on the croquet lawns (and roost in the splendid trees around the house at night) making this lovely place, home of the O'Hara family since it was built in 1774, a particularly perfect country house. Nothing escapes Brian O'Hara's disciplined eye: in immaculate order from top to bottom, the house not only has the original 18th century furniture but also some fascinating features, notably an unusual Victorian free-standing rolltop bath complete with fully integrated cast-iron shower 'cubicle' and original brass rail and fittings, all in full working order. Luxurious rooms are wonderfully comfortable and have phones and tea/coffee making facilities. Lindy runs the house and kitchen with the seamless hospitality born of long experience, and creates deliciously wholesome, country house home cooking which is served in their lovely dining room (where the family silver is used with magnificent insouciance even at breakfast). As well as their own neatly maintained vegetable garden, the O'Hara's have a deer farm: pot roast leg of venison with red wine is a house speciality. A surprisingly extensive wine list offers no less than six house wines - and has many treats in store. Coopershill is well placed for exploring this unspoilt area - and makes a good base for golfers too, with several championship courses, including Rosses Point within easy range. Tennis, cycling, boating, fishing, garden, croquet; snooker room. Children welcome (under 2 free in parents' room; cots available without charge, baby sitting arranged). No pets. **Rooms 8** (7 en-suite, 1 shower only, 1 private bathroom, 1 family room, all no smoking). Turndown service. B&B about €111 pps, ss €30. Dining Room Seats 16-20. D 8.15 daily (non-residents welcome by reservation); Set D €55, house wines from €16.55; sc discretionary.* 10% discount on stays of 3+ days. Closed end Oct-1 Apr. (Off season house parties of 12-16 people welcome.) Amex, Diners, MasterCard, Visa, Laser. **Directions:** Signposted from N4 at Drumfin crossroads.

Rosses Point
PUB

Austie's

Rosses Point Co Sligo
Tel: 071 917 7020 / 917 7111

This 200 year-old pub overlooking Sligo Bay has always been associated with a seafaring family and the old bar is full of fascinating nautical memorabilia. It has a very appealing ship-shape feeling about it and friendly people behind the bar, which was extended through to a very agreeable adjoining room recently, adding to the existing conservatory style dining room for the service of food - which is well above the usual bar food standard. Naturally enough, local seafood stars on menus, in starters like poached mussels in cream & garlic, for example, or delicious battered squid rings with sweet chilli sauce, and main courses like updated battered cod, or pan-fried John Dory in white wine sauce. There are lots of other choices, too including ever-popular steaks - expect wholesome food, with traditional appeal and a little gentle updating. A deck area looking across to Oyster Island was added quite recently - a pleasant spot for a sunny day. Traditional music at weekends. **Seats 60.** Children welcome to 9pm. Food served daily 5.30-9.30 in summer (also L Sun, 12.30-3.30). Bar Menu from 3pm. Times may vary off-season (Sept-Mar). A la carte menu; house wine from about €15; sc discretionary. Phone ahead to check opening off season. Closed 25 Dec & Good Fri. MasterCard, Visa, Laser. **Directions:** On the seafront. ◇

Rosses Point
BAR/RESTAURANT

The Waterfront

Rosses Point Co Sligo **Tel: 071 917 7122**
Fax: 071 9177040 Email: waterfrontbar@eircom.net

Joe Grogan's busy bar and restaurant on the front at at Rosses Point offers a choice between light bar bites like oysters, local mussels, garlic mushrooms, a range of gourmet pizzas, and a tempting à la carte. There could be a choice of about ten starters (mussels with papardelle, perhaps) and equally interesting, sometimes luxurious mains, like whole lobster with lemon butter sauce or brandy mustard. Desserts can be delicious (tangy lemon soufflé with sponge finger and a pink grapefruit salad...) or you can finish with Irish cheeses. There's a courtyard and smoking area - and also an art gallery, with access to the restaurant. Children welcome. *Self-catering accommodation also offered - details on application. **Seats 100** (outdoor seating, 20). Toilets wheelchair accessible. D daily 5-10. L Sun only 12-3. A la carte. Wines from about €17.50. Closed 25 Dec, Good Fri. Amex, MasterCard, Visa, Laser. **Directions:** In Rosses Point village, looking out on the bay. ◇

SLIGO

A fascinating town, with a rich heritage, Sligo has several hotels: if business and leisure facilities convenient to the town are important, the **Sligo Park Hotel** (Tel 071 916 0291; www.leehotels.com) is on the edge of the town and has ample parking. There are plenty of popular little coffee shops and cafés to sustain a day around the town: informal food, people-watching and entertainment are to be found at **Garavogue & Café Bar Deli** (Tel 071 40100) - a brilliantly located contemporary riverside bar and café with outside seating for fine weather. **Bistro Bianconi** (Tel 071 41744) continues to meet the informal dining ' family market well, and, for lovers of ethnic food, there's a fine Indian restaurant, **Sher-E-Punjab** (Tel 071 9147700) on Market Street. Rosses Point, a few minutes' drive from Sligo town has views across to Oyster Island and Coney Island (after which the island off New York was named), golf and a lovely beach; the restaurant and bar with the best view is **The Moorings** (Tel: 071 917 7112) which looks across to the islands and the famous Metal Man navigation mark; well-regarded locally, they do the best gourmet pizzas in Sligo (or, to me more precise "the second best in the world").
WWW.IRELAND-GUIDE.COM FOR THE BEST PLACES TO EAT, DRINK & STAY

Sligo
CAFÉ

The Atrium Café

The Niland Model Arts Centre The Mall Sligo Co Sligo
Tel: 071 914 1418 Email: info@modelart.ie Web: www.modelart.ie

If you are planning a visit to Sligo town, the Model Arts Centre is well worth a visit and it could make sense to arrange your day around a break here. Well-known chef Brid Torrades runs the delightful daytime restaurant, an open-plan café that spills out into the bright atrium area of the gallery - stylish, yet accessible, the perfect spot for seriously tempting simple, food with an emphasis on good quality and flavour: superb soups, for example, delicious omelettes or tuna & black olive bruschetta (both prettily presented with herbs and leaves from Rod Alston's Organic Centre, nearby) and hot daily blackboard specials. Pretty compôtes topped with cream - rhubarb, blackberry - are simply delicious, and there's good coffee too. *Just before the guide went to press Brid Torrades opened another Sligo venue, **Ósta Café Wine Bar** (071 9144639) at Weirview House, Stephen Street (beside Hyde Bridge); open 8.30-10 Mon-Fri and from noon at weekends, breads and pastries from Brid's bakery at Ballinafad are a speciality, also Irish cheeses and charcuterie, Java Republic coffee and a small selection of wines. Parking (up the steep hill, behind the gallery). Meals: Tue-Sat 12-3 (Sun Brunch 11-3), Veg menu avail. Closed Mon, 23 Dec-4 Jan, Easter weekend, 17 Mar. **No Credit Cards. Directions:** Sligo town centre; prominent building on The Mall.

Sligo
HOTEL

Clarion Hotel Sligo

Clarion Road Sligo Co Sligo **Tel: 071 911 9000** Fax: 071 911 9001
Email: info@clarionhotelsligo.com Web: www.clarionhotelsireland.com

This new hotel in Sligo actually dates back to 1848 but , since being given 'the works' , it has emerged as a modern classic with the contemporary style that is associated with the new Clarion hotels. The warm-toned reception area has a welcoming atmosphere and accommodation is well up to the expected standard, with a high proportion of suites (including a penthouse suite) and good-sized rooms, high quality bedding, smart bathrooms, broadband, and irons & ironing board as standard. Dining options offer the now familiar choice between the well-appointed Sinergie restaurant (crisp white linen, international menu, attentive service) and casual dining Asian style in the Kudos Bar. Leisure and pampering facilities include a 20m pool, gym and spa treatments. Business and conference facilities offer meeting rooms for groups of 4 to 400, and a business team to co-ordinate events if necessary. **Rooms 167** (91 suites). Sinergie seats 160 (private room, 35); D daily 6-10; Sun: L 1-3, D 6-9.30; Set Sun L €28; Set D €35. House wine €24. Food served in Kudos Bar & Rest 12.30-10 daily. Amex, Diners, MasterCard, Visa, Laser. **Directions:** Follow N16 signs for Enniskillen.

Sligo
RESTAURANT/PUB

Coach Lane Restaurant @ Donaghy's Bar

1-2 Lord Edward Street Sligo Co Sligo
Tel: 071 916 2417 Fax: 071 917 1935

The restaurant over Orla and Andy Donaghy's pub is approached by an attractive side alley, with a menu board displayed on the street. It's a long narrow room, furnished in a comfortable mixture of traditional and contemporary styles, with well-appointed white-clothed tables, soft lighting and neatly uniformed waitresses in black polo shirts and trousers with white aprons all creating a good impression. Andy's menus are lively and attractive, the cooking is confident and his specialities include some less usual dishes such as ostrich with marsala; an active supporter of local produce, he does a great line in well-aged steaks, and seafood such as fresh whole lobster and Sligo Bay salmon. There's also a wide choice of salads, pasta dishes and chicken - and the cooking style ranges from traditional (steak with home-made fries, crispy onion rings & HP sauce) to spicy (cajun chicken with a fresh fruit salsa). **Seats 120** (plus 40 on an outside terrace, weather permitting). Air conditioning. Toilets wheelchair accessible. D daily 3-10, à la carte. House wine from €20.50; service discretionary except 10% on parties of 8+.Closed 25 Dec, Good Fri, 2nd week Feb. Amex, MasterCard, Visa, Laser. **Directions:** N4 to Sligo, left at Adelaide Street, right into Lord Edward Street.

Sligo
RESTAURANT

Montmartre

1 Market Yard Sligo Co Sligo **Tel: 071 916 9901**
Fax: 071 919 2232 Email: edelmckeon@eircom.net

French run and staffed, this is the area's leading restaurant and has a strong local following, so reservations are strongly advised, especially at weekends. Although not big, there is a little bar area that doubles as reception and a bright and airy feeling, with potted palms, white crockery and smartly uniformed staff all emphasising the French style. Proprietor-chef Stéphane Magaud's varied menus offer imaginative French cuisine in a light, colourful style with local produce featuring in some dishes, especially seafood - Lissadell oysters and mussels, for instance, also lobster which is great value (€29.50 per lb) and served with an unusual saffron hollandaise; there may also be game in season, and there will always be imaginative vegetarian dishes . Sound cooking, attractive presentation and reasonable prices have brought this restaurant many friends. The wine list, which is mostly French with a token gesture to the New World, includes an unusually good selection of half bottles and wines by the glass. An early dinner menu offers exceptional value. **Seats 50.** Children welcome. Air conditioning. Toilets wheelchair accessible. D Tue-Sun, 5-11pm. Early D €16 (5-7pm), D a la carte. House wines from €18. Closed Mon, 24-26 Dec. Amex, Diners, MasterCard, Visa, Laser. **Directions:** 200 yards from Hawks Well Theatre & Tourist Office.

Sligo
HOTEL

Radisson SAS Hotel Sligo

Ballincar Rosses Point Sligo Co Sligo
Tel: 071 914 0008 Fax: 071 914 0006
Email: info.sligo@RadissonSAS.com Web: www.radissonsas.com

This fine contemporary hotel is out of town, towards Rosses Point; it is not especially attractive from the road but, once inside the door it's a different story as it has that lovely light and appealing atmosphere that the new Radisson hotels seem to achieve especially well, and a huge welcoming flower arrangement in the large foyer to win over any waiverers. Staff are keen to make guests feel at home, and clearly take pride in the hotel - and it's easy to see why. Simple lines and classy contemporary decor in quality materials and warm tones create a pleasing ambience, without distracting from the hotel's great attraction - the views over Sligo Bay. Bedrooms are well-sized and very comfortable, with all the facilities now expected of new hotels (TV options, voicemail, safe, mini bar, iron/ironing boar as well as trouser press, and so on), and there are various room combinations offered, including family rooms. **The Classiebawn Restaurant,** which is an open-plan dining area along the front of the hotel (and gains in smart design and, especially, views are greater than anything it loses in lack of privacy) is an especially pleasant place for a weekend lunch, or dinner on a long summer evening, when the views can be enjoyed to the full. Conference/banqueting (900/590); business centre, video-conferencing on request. Leisure centre, swimming pool, spa. Golf nearby. **Rooms 132** (3 suites, 7 junior suites, 18 executive rooms, 6 disabled). 24 hr room service. Turndown service offered, Children welcome (under 17 free in parents' room; cots available without charge, baby sitting arranged). B&B about €75pps, ss €20. **Classiebawn Restaurant:** D daily 7-10.30, L sat & Sun 12.30-2.30. Set 2/3 course about D €32/40; set L from about €15.50. Set Sun L about €23.50. House wine, about €20. Bar meals also available, 12-7 daily. No SC. *Short breaks offered; golf breaks are a speciality (3 championship courses nearby). Open all year. Amex, MasterCard, Visa. **Directions:** From Sligo town, follow signs for Rosses Point; the hotel is on the right after 3km (2 m).◇

Strandhill
PUB

Strand House Bar

Strandhill Co Sligo
Tel: 071 916 8140 Fax: 071 916 8593

Just ten minutes drive from Sligo, close to the airport and one of Europe's most magnificent surfing beaches, this well-known bar has a big welcoming turf fire, cosy snugs and friendly staff. No children after 9pm. Bar meals served all day (12-3pm). Toilets wheelchair accessible. Air conditioning. Closed 25 Dec & Good Fri. **No Credit Cards. Directions:** Follow signs to Sligo airport (Strandhill). Strand House is situated at the end near the beach.◇

COUNTY TIPPERARY

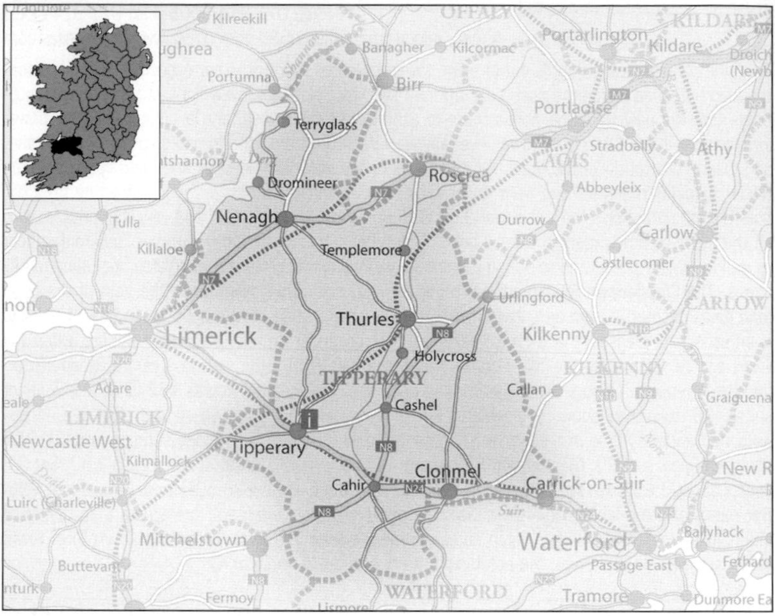

The cup of life is overflowing in Tipperary. In this extensive and wondrously fertile region, there's an air of fulfillment, a comfortable awareness of the world in harmony. And the placenames reinforce this sense of natural bounty.

Across the middle of the county, there's the evocatively-named Golden Vale, with prosperous lands along the wide valley of the River Suir and its many tributaries, and westwards towards County Limerick across a watershed around Donohill.

The county's largest town, down in the far south under the Comeragh Mountains, is the handsome borough of Clonmel - its name translates as "Honey Meadow". Yet although there are many meadows of all kinds in Tipperary, there's much more to this largest inland county in Ireland than farmland, for it is graced with some of the most elegant mountains in the country.

North of the Golden Vale, the Silvermine Mountains rise to 694 m on Keeper Hill, and beyond them the farming countryside rolls on in glorious profusion to Nenagh - a town much improved by by-passes on either side - and Tipperary's own "sea coast", the beautiful eastern shore of Lough Derg. Inevitably, history and historic monuments abound in such country, with the fabulous Rock of Cashel and its dramatic remains of ancient ecclesiastical buildings setting a very high standard for evoking the past.

But Tipperary lends itself every bit as well to enjoyment of the here and now. Tipperary is all about living life to the full, and they do it with style in a place of abundance.

Local Attractions and Information

Aherlow, Glen of Glenbrook Trout Farm	062 56214
Birdhill, Tipperary Crystal Visitor Centre	061 379066
Cahir, Cahir Castle	052 41011
Cahir Farmers Market Sats 9am-1pm	086 648 2044
Carrick-on-Suir, Ormond Castle	051 640787
Carrick-on-Suir, Tipperary Crystal Visitor Centre	051 641188
Cashel, Bru Boru Culture Centre	062 61122
Cashel, Rock of Cashel	062 61437
Cashel, Tourism Information	062 61333
Clonmel, Clonmel Racecourse	052 23422
Clonmel Theatre & Arts Festival (July)	052 29339
Clonmel, Tourism Information	052 22960

Nenagh, Heritage Centre 067 32633
Nenagh, Tourism Information 067 31610
Roscrea, Roscrea Heritage - Castle & Damer House 0505 21850
Thurles, Holy Cross Abbey 0504 43241
Thurles, Race Course 0504 21040
Tipperary Race Course (Limerick Junction) 062 51357
Tipperary town, Tourism Information 062 51457

Ballinderry
Ⓔ RESTAURANT

Brocka-on-the-Water Restaurant

Kilgarvan Quay Ballinderry Nenagh Co Tipperary
Tel: 067 22038 Fax: 067 22995

Anthony and Anne Gernon's almost-waterside restaurant has attracted a following disproportionate to its size over the years and, although it has been extended at the back to include a high-ceilinged conservatory style room which opens onto a garden patio, it is still basically carved out of the lower half of a family home that is by no means huge. The atmosphere is very much a "proper restaurant" - yet with all the warmth of welcome that the family situation implies. There's a reception room with an open fire, comfy chairs, interesting things to read and look at (Anthony's a dab hand at wood carving) - and aperitifs served in generous wine glasses, while you read a menu that promises good things to come in the adjoining dining room and conservatory. Guests arriving in daylight will notice hens clucking around a garden well-stocked with fruit and vegetables - promising the best of all possible beginnings for your dinner. Seasonal menus depend on availability of course - if you are here in late spring, for example, you might be offered avocado pear with local goats cheese, yoghurt, capers & wild garlic - but there are always some specialities retained by popular demand, including Cooleeney cheese croquettes with home-made chutney (Cooleeney is one of Ireland's finest cheeses, made by Breda Maher on the family farm near Thurles). A late summer menu might include pork medallion in a herb crust with plum & cranberry - and there will always be home-grown vegetables in season. **Seats 30** (private room, 30). Air conditioning. Toilets wheelchair accessible. Reservations strongly advised. D 6.30-9 Mon-Sat in summer (call to check opening times off season). Set D about €40, also à la carte and a Vegetarian Menu. SC discretionary. House wine about €22. Closed Sun. **No Credit Cards. Directions:** Lough Derg drive, half way between Nenagh and Portumna. ◇

Borrisokane
COUNTRY HOUSE

Ballycormac House

Aglish Borrisokane Roscrea Co Tipperary
Tel: 067 21129 Email: ballyc@indigo.ie Web: www.ballyc.com

John and Cherylynn Lang's farmhouse is a charming, cottagey place, delightfully furnished and very comfortable in a laid-back way a new bedroom extension was recently added, but one of the five original bedrooms is a romantic suite with a four-poster bed and its own fireplace. Country pursuits are the big attraction here, especially equestrian activities - the Langs have up to 30 horses and ponies on site so there's something to suit everyone, from the novice to the experienced rider. They are approved by A.I.R.E. (Irish Association of Riding Establishments) and offer trail riding and cross country riding in spring and summer, also fox hunting breaks in winter. Golf, fishing, watersports and rough shooting can also be arranged. Children and well-behaved pets welcome (children under 2 free in parents' room; cot available, baby sitting arranged). A hot tub is available for guests' use (€8 per person). **Rooms 12** (1 suite, 8 shower only, all no smoking). B&B €45-60, no ss. * Short breaks offered: various country pursuits, including fishing, shooting, golf, walking and cycling as well as equestrian activities. Open all year. MasterCard, Visa. **Directions:** N54 through Borrisokane towards Portumna. Right out of Borrisokane at sign. ◇

Borrisokane
B&B

Dancer Cottage

Curraghmore Borrisokane Co Tipperary **Tel: 067 27414** Fax: 067 27414
Email: dcr@eircom.net Web: www.dancercottage.cjb.net

A neat well planned garden and plenty of parking make a good impression at Carmen and Wolfgang Roedder's modern Tudor style house near Borrisokane - which is just 20 km from Birr castle, with its magnificent park and gardens. An extensive array of tourist literature in the big hall guarantees that no guest here will ever be short of things to do in the area and there's a comfortable L shaped sitting/dining room to relax in when you get back, with a wood-burning stove and lots of books. The bedrooms, with large beds, include two for less mobile guests and a family room with an extra bed; all are comfortably furnished with some lovely pieces of antique furniture, immaculate bathrooms and tea/coffee facilities. Carmen and Wolfgang do everything possible to ensure that their guests enjoy a stay here and extensive breakfast menus include several home-baked breads, speciality porridge, stuffed pancakes and French toast as well as the traditional Irish fry - and, like the evening meals, breakfast is served at a communal table overlooking the lovely back garden, which has seating for guests' use. A small sauna is available by arrangement - ask for details. Children welcome (under 2s free in parents' room, cot available without charge). Pets allowed by arrangement. Garden, cycling. **Rooms 4** (all with shower & no smoking, 2 for less mobile guests). Residents Set D €24 (when booked in advance). B&B from €33 pps, ss €7. Closed 1 Dec-5 Jan Amex, MasterCard, Visa. **Directions:** N 52 from Nenagh or Birr to Borrisokane; road signs in town (2km).

Cashel

Bailey's Cashel

(N) BAR/RESTAURANT/GUESTHOUSE

Main Street Cashel Co Tipperary
Tel: 062 61937 Fax: 062 62038
Email: info@baileys-ireland.com Web: www.baileys-ireland.com

Set back from the road this fine early 18th Century building in the heart of Cashel was previously a seven-bedroom guesthouse but a cleverly-concealed, recently-built extension has allowed it to grow, gracefully, into a fully-fledged family-run hotel (with 14 new bedrooms, a well-designed, spacious restaurant, a cosy cellar bar, and a lovely swimming pool and leisure centre). There's a comfortable and spacious residents' drawing room, and attractive contemporary bedrooms have no tea/coffee facilities but otherwise tick all the right boxes: good lighting, quality furnishing, air conditioning (that works), windows that open. comfortable chairs, flat screen TV, irons and boards, hair-dryers, safes and plenty of connection points for laptops, chargers and so on - and well laid out, if compact, bathrooms. Banqueting (80). Children welcome (under 3s free in parents' room, cot available free of charge); **Rooms 19** (1 suite, 1 for disabled, all no smoking); lift, room service (limited hours); B&B €80 pps, ss €15. **Restaurant Number 42** offers a balanced menu combining modern Irish and European cuisine, with some local ingredients featured. High quality food, professional culinary skills and enticing presentation make this a pleasant place to relax and enjoy a good dinner in gently contemporary surroundings. Begin, perhaps, with a crisp baby leaf salad, Cashel Blue cheese, crisp bacon & roast tomatoes, or tiger prawn in a crisp tempura batter with a sweet chilli & soy dipping sauce and follow with main dishes that include excellent beef (fillet with shallot tartine, creamy potato gratin & red wine juice, perhaps) or a tender rack of lamb with champ & spiced carrot purée. The bar menu, which is similar in style, provides a casual option and particularly good value. This is a well-run place that delivers the goods in friendly Irish style... Free private parking in an underground car park makes this a particularly attractive all-purpose stop for business people and visitors alike. An all-day café opening out onto well-planted plaza will shortly open. "No 42": **Seats 80** (outdoors, 15); air conditioning; children welcome until 7pm; food served daily 12.30-9.30; Sun L 12.30-4, Sun D 6-9.30; set Sun L €25; also a la carte L&D; house wine €19. Establishment closed 23-27 Dec. Amex, MasterCard, Visa, Laser. **Directions:** Centre of town, on Main Street.

Cashel

Café Hans

CAFÉ

Moor Lane Cashel Co Tipperary **Tel: 062 63660**

Hans and Stefan Matthia' smashing little contemporary café is the perfect complement to the parent establishment, Chez Hans, next door. A neat renovation job has been done with clean-lined style, creating a bright and airy space out of very little; bare-topped tables are laid café-style and a canny little menu offers just the kind of food that's needed during the day: colourful, sassy dishes including lots of salads - several versions of Caesar salad include a vegetarian one, and there's an irresistible house salad with pear Cashel Blue cheese (what else?) and Parma ham; open sandwiches come with home-made French fries and there are half a dozen hot dishes - grilled lamb cutlets with mushroom sauce, poached salmon with new potatoes, green beans and salsa verde. Good desserts and afternoon tea (2-5.30), lovely coffee; wine list. Well worth planning a journey around a break here - everyone travelling the Dublin-Cork route should make a note of this place and its hours. There is some menu overlap with Chez Hans, where, together with Jason Matthia, Stefan is also responsible for the early dinner. Children welcome. **Seats 30.** Open Tue-Sat, 12-5.30 (advisable to check off-season). Closed Sun & Mon. No reservations. **No Credit Cards. Directions:** Off N8 in Cashel, 50m in Rock of Cashel direction. ◇

Cashel
HOTEL

Cashel Palace Hotel

Main Street Cashel Co Tipperary **Tel: 062 62707** Fax: 062 61521
Email: reception@cashel-palace.ie Web: www.cashel-palace.ie

One of Ireland's most famous hotels, and originally a bishop's residence, Cashel Palace is a large, graciously proportioned Queen Anne style house (dating from 1730), set well back from the road in the centre of Cashel town. The beautiful reception rooms and some of the spacious, elegantly furnished bedrooms overlook the gardens and the Rock of Cashel at the rear. The present owners, Patrick and Susan Murphy, took over the hotel in 1998 and, since then, have been gradually renovating and refurbishing both public areas and bedrooms; the whole hotel has been redecorated recently, and a new function room opened. Conference/banqueting (85/94). Children welcome (Under 3 free in parents' room, cot available without charge, baby sitting arranged). No pets. Garden. **Rooms 23** (5 suites). Lift. Room service (limited hours). B&B about €111, €35. Closed 24-26 Dec. **Meals:** Lunch and dinner are served every day in the vaulted basement restaurant, The Bishops Buttery, and there is also a formal ground floor restaurant, the Dining Room, overlooking the gardens, which successfully juggles the various demands of a mixed clientele ranging from passing trade to local business people, corporate guests, families out for a treat - and, of course, residents. Menus are well-balanced, offering the traditional choices like steak and chicken breast alongside more adventurous ones (ostrich, perhaps); cooking is sound and quite modern, with the generosity expected in country areas. In the Guide's experience, the food has been consistently enjoyable - interesting, well-cooked and attractively presented - although sometimes a little let down by off-hand service. **Seats 60.** L 12.30-2.30 (Sun to 3.30); D 6-9.30. Set D €35, Set L (1-3 courses) €11.50-22.50, D also à la carte. House wines €20.50 *Food is also available in the Guinness Bar, 10.30am-8pm (Fri & Sat to 6pm). Amex, Diners, MasterCard, Visa, Laser. **Directions:** On N8 which runs through Cashel; hotel is just off main road. ◇

Cashel
Ⓔ RESTAURANT

Chez Hans

Moore Lane Cashel Co Tipperary
Tel: 062 61177 Fax: 062 61177

Although many others have since followed suit, the idea of opening a restaurant in a church was highly original when Hans-Peter Matthia did so in 1968. The atmosphere and scale - indeed the whole style of the place - is superb and provides an excellent setting for the fine food which people travel great distances to sample. Hans-Peter's son, Jason (who brought experience in great kitchens like Le Gavroche, La Tante Claire, and Restaurant Marco Pierre White) joined him in the business several years ago and this - together with the more recent opening of their excellent daytime restaurant, Café Hans, next door - has brought renewed energy, confirming its status as the leading restaurant in a wide area. Ably assisted by restaurant manager Louise Horgan and a strong kitchen brigade, Jason offers menus that include an early dinner menu which is definitely worth travelling for - with an outstanding choice of about ten excellent dishes on each course, it offers some of the best value to be found in Ireland. The à la carte offers an even wider range including many specialities - their famous cassoulet of seafood (half a dozen varieties of fish and shellfish with a delicate chive velouté sauce), for example, and classics like sole on the bone, imaginative vegetarian dishes - and, of course, the great lamb and beef for which the area is renowned. Finish perhaps with lemon tart and orange curd ice cream, and coffee with home-made chocolates. A wine list strong on classic old world wines offers some treats for the deep-pocketed as well as half a dozen special recommendations under about €25. Booking ahead is essential. **Seats 70.** D Tue-Sat, 6-10. Early D 2/3 courses, €27.50/33 (6-7.15); also à la carte. House wines from €23.50. Closed Sun, Mon.1st week Sep, last 2 weeks Jan. MasterCard, Visa, Laser. **Directions:** First right from N8, 50m on left; at foot of Rock of Cashel.

Cashel
GUESTHOUSE

Hill House

Palmer Hill Cashel Co Tipperary **Tel: 062 61277**
Email: hillhouse1@eircom.net Web: www.hillhousecashel.com

Carmel Purcell's lovely Georgian house was built in 1710 and has great character. It is set well back from the road in large gardens, with plenty of parking and a magnificent view of the Rock of Cashel and a welcoming hospitable atmosphere, noticeable immediately on arrival in the spacious entrance hall, which has fine Georgian features and fresh flowers. While Carmel shows guests to one of the large rooms (some with four posters), she gives all the lowdown on local attractions and settles you in; rooms are very comfortable, with television, radio and tea/coffee facilities and good bathrooms, with plenty of towels. Breakfast is a high point, served at a large communal table very nicely set up with good linen, baskets of freshly-baked breads and scones and homemade preserves; a side table offers fruits and cereals and the cooked breakfasts are delicious. Porridge is made with local Tipperary stoneground oatmeal and, in addition to the traditional Irish breakfast, choices include pancakes and smoked salmon with scrambled eggs. Not suitable for children under 8 years. No pets. Garden. **Rooms 5** (all shower only & no smoking, 1 family room). B&B €50, ss €25. MasterCard, Visa, Laser. **Directions:** 2 minutes from cashel town centre; from Dublin, bear left after the turn signed Rock of Cashel - Hill House is opposite the next juntion.

Cashel Area

Carron House

FARMHOUSE

Carron Cashel Co Tipperary **Tel: 052 62142** Fax: 052 62168
Email: hallyfamily@eircom.net Web: www.carronhouse.com

Mary Hally's country home is on an award-winning farm, in a peaceful location in the heart of the Golden Vale, yet only minutes from Cashel and just an hour from Kilkenny. Approached up a long, well-maintained drive, first impressions are very encouraging, as there's a lovely front garden in front of the large, modern house - and separate entrances for the house and farm. Large individually decorated bedrooms include one triple room (with double and twin beds) and are very comfortably furnished, with generous beds, television, tea/coffee facilities, hair dryers and neat en-suite shower rooms. Housekeeping throughout is immaculate and there's a guest sitting room with antique furniture and interesting books, which is always available to guests. Mary, who is a friendly, attentive and informative hostess, gives guests a good send-off in the morning, with a generous, well-cooked and nicely presented breakfast in a large sun room overlooking the garden. Not suitable for children. **Rooms 4** (all with en-suite shower & all no smoking). B&B €35pps, ss €20. Closed 1 Oct-1 Apr. MasterCard, Visa. **Directions:** Take N8 south bound from Cashel for 2.5 miles. Signposted left atcrossroads; follow signs.

Cashel Area

Dualla House

COUNTRY HOUSE/FARMHOUSE

Dualla Cashel Co Tipperary
Tel: 062 61487 Fax: 062 61487
Email: duallahse@eircom.net Web: www.tipp.ie/dualla-house.htm

Set in 300 acres of of rolling Tipperary farmland in the "Golden Vale", Martin and Mairead Power's fine Georgian manor house faces south towards the Slievenamon, Comeragh, Knockmealdown and Galtee Mountains. Just 3 miles from the Rock of Cashel, this is a convenient base for exploring the area but its special appeal is peace and tranquillity which, together with comfortable accommodation in large airy bedrooms (with tea/coffee trays), great hospitality and Mairead's home cooking, keep guests coming back time and again. An extensive breakfast menu includes local apple juice as well as other fresh fruits and juices, farmhouse cheeses, porridge with local honey, also free-range eggs and sausages from the local butcher in the traditional cooked breakfast - and home-made bread and preserves. Children welcome (under 3s free in parents' room, cot available without charge). **Rooms 4** (3 with en-suite shower, 1 with private bathroom, all no smoking). B&B about €50 pps, ss €10/15. Closed mid Oct - mid Apr. MasterCard, Visa. **Directions:** 3 miles from Cashel on R691. Coming from Dublin signed from N8, 5 miles after Horse & Jockey. Sign on left. 2.5 miles to house. ◇

Clogheen

The Old Convent Gourmet Hideaway

Ⓝ☆RESTAURANT

Mount Anglesby Clogheen Co Tipperary **Tel: 052 65565**
Email: info@theoldconvent.ie Web: www.theoldconvent.ie

Dermot and Christine Gannon, formerly of the highly regarded Cahir restaurant Gannons Above The Bell, have relocated to one of the most stunning parts of the country where they have opened a restaurant with rooms, styled a 'gourmet hideaway'. Designed to cater for couples 'seeking a short getaway from it all experience' it's an unusual, very comfortable, beautifully designed, and decorated country guesthouse with some stunning mountain views across the famously scenic 'Vee' emphatically not for 'family weekends', bookings are not accepted for children under 12. Although recently open at the time of going to press, there are several major golf courses nearby and their culinary reputation preceded them so the Gannons have already earned a following. A lofty double drawing room with large windows and a mixture of antiques and good modern furnishings makes a comfortable reception area, and the spacious, airy restaurant is in what was once the convent refectory and adjoining sacristy - now one large area, but still complete with stained glass windows. An unusual setting, for an exceptional. meal - only a 9-course Tasting Menu is offered, plus an optional cheese platter of seven Irish cheeses with Trass Farm fruit and plum jam (€10 supplement). Ingredients are sourced locally (and organic) when possible and, as anyone who has experienced a meal cooked by this talented chef will testify, the cooking is stunningly accurate: the discernible difference between beautiful pieces of Irish beef cooked 'rare' and 'very rare' a joy to behold, for example. Many diners might be wary of the Tasting Menu, but servings are well-judged and could never be described as 'grudging' or 'mean'; furthermore, in deference to Irish taste, the meat course is very generous indeed. And at €50 it is very good value for a skilfully cooked, generous and beautifully presented meal. **Accommodation:** The bedrooms, all individually styled, are sumptuously appointed and have wonderful views although no tea and coffee making facilities; bathrooms are also stylishly appointed, and have separate bath and shower. There was still a little finishing to be done at the time of our visit (a few more shelves for personal belongings would not have gone amiss, for example, especially in the bathroom), but this is a lovely place that is definitely 'itself' - and you could very quickly become fond of it. Free Broadband Wi/Fi. **Seats 50;** children over 12 years welcome; D Thu-Sun, 7-9; Set 8 course gourmet D €50. House wine from €20. Closed Mon-Wed and 2 weeks Nov / 2 weeks Spring. **Rooms 7** (4 suites, 1 shower only, all no smoking); B&B from €60 pps, ss €25. House avail for private rental for conferences, weddings etc. MasterCard, Visa, Laser. **Directions:** From Clogheen take the Vee/Lismore road, 0.5km on right.

Clonmel

RESTAURANT

Angela's Restaurant

14 Abbey Street Clonmel Co Tipperary
Tel: 052 26899

féile bia A great little daytime restaurant in the centre of town, Angela's is renowned for delicious, wholesome food - and wholefoods. Baking is a speciality and seasonal and organic produce goes into an imaginative range of dishes with both traditional and contemporary influences. There will always be savoury flans - potato, leek & Cooleeney, perhaps and special sandwiches include bruschetta (typically with goat's cheese, rocket, sundried tomato & tossed salad - vegetarians do well here) and warm croissants like grilled chicken with cheese, bacon and relish. Hot specials might include country pork casserole, and desserts tend to towards the comforting - bread & butter pudding, plum & almond tart. They're open all day for tea, coffee and sandwiches - La Scala coffee is served ("skinny" and decaff available) - and a cuppa with one of their special oaten Anzac biscuits is just ace. Takeaway and outside catering service also available. *At the time of going to press an extension and renovations are planned - please phone to check opening. Children welcome. **Seats 60** (outdoor seating, 10). Open all day; L Mon-Sat, 12-3. All à la carte. Wine licence. Closed Sun, Christmas, Good Fri. **No Credit Cards. Directions:** Near Friary Church on River Suir. ◇

Clonmel

Ⓝ RESTAURANT

Befani's Mediterranean & Tapas Restaurant

6 Sarsfield Street Clonmel Co Tipperary
Tel: 052 77893 Fax: 052 77893
Email: info@befani.com Web: www.befani.com

This stylish new Mediterranean and tapas restaurant is in a recently restored listed building just up from the quays, and it's a very welcome arrival in Clonmel. Co-owner and chef, Adrian Ryan, and his business partner and restaurant manager, Fulvio Bonfiglio, are thorough professionals with a long history in hospitality and have quickly won the hearts of discerning diners in the town. Spacious and simply furnished the restaurant has a small bar, tiled floor, and darkwood tables and a pleasant ambience; appealing menus (for breakfast, lunch and dinner) are deliberately (but not too) restricted and include an unusual 'after lunch to closing time' tapas menu which, together with the high quality of ingredients, cooking and service, and the real value for money offered, has won them a lot of friends. Typical tapas/starters might include smoked salmon with salsa verde & red onion calamari fritos or Manchego cheese with garlic & lime and there are main courses like hot ciabatta with roast beef & rocket with pesto mayonnaise and maybe seafood tagliatelle with lobster and cream sauce or chargrilled chicken breast, chorizo & goat cheese with an apricot salsa, homemade fries and side salad. Local organic ingredients are sourced where possible and vegetarians are extremely well catered for. Look out for the 'fish of the day' and also a monthly special offer on the carefully chosen wine list. Befani's is a delightful experience with a southern European atmosphere and the long opening hours (seven days a week from breakfast through to dinner) are a great bonus. **Seats 55** (outdoors, 15); children welcome; wheelchair access to courtyard only; air conditioning. Food served daily, 9am-9.30pm; L 12.30-3. D 6-9.30; set D €31.50, set Sun L €21.50, also a la carte L&D; house wine €16.95. Closed 25 Dec, 1 Jan. MasterCard, Visa, Laser. **Directions:** Town centre.

Clonmel

Hotel Minella

HOTEL

Coleville Road Clonmel Co Tipperary **Tel: 052 22388** Fax: 052 24381
Email: hotelminella@eircom.net Web: www.hotelminella.ie

féile bia Sparky, the Old English sheepdog, establishes a friendly tone from the outset as he welcomes arriving guests to this pleasant hotel, which is attractively located in its own grounds, overlooking the River Suir. The original house was built in 1863 as a private residence and was purchased in 1961 by the current owners, the Nallen family. They are great racing enthusiasts and have stables nearby, where their Minella horses are trained and the racing theme is carried throughout the hotel. They've extended the hotel several times over the years, most recently to add a further 22 rooms (penthouse, including four suites), and the existing rooms have been refurbished and upgraded; there are suites with four-posters and steam rooms, and junior suites with jacuzzis; all are furnished to a high standard with smart bathrooms - and housekeeping is exemplary. This is the main hotel in the area, and has extensive banqueting and conference facilities and a fine leisure centre. The old house now looks small beside the newer areas, but it is still intact and the public areas - including a cocktail bar, restaurant (where reliable traditional food is served) and lounge areas - have a lovely view over well-kept lawns and the river. Excellent facilities and the romantic situation make the hotel especially popular for weddings. Leisure centre with 20 metre swimming pool and outdoor Canadian hot tub, jacuzzi, steam room and gym; Broadband. Children welcome (under 16 free in parents' room, cot available without charge, baby sitting arranged). Tennis, fishing. Garden. **Rooms 90** (4 suites, 5 junior suites, 80 no smoking, 3 for disabled, 13 ground floor, 10 family rooms). B&B €80 pps, ss €30. Closed 23-27 Dec. Amex, MasterCard, Visa, Laser. **Directions:** Edge of Clonmel town.

Clonmel

Sean Tierney

PUB

13 O'Connell Street Clonmel Co Tipperary **Tel: 052 24467**

This tall, narrow pub is packed with "artefacts of bygone days" in short a mini-museum. A giant screen is discreetly hidden around the corner, for watching matches. Upstairs (and there are a lot of them this is a four storey building) there's a relaxed traditional family-style restaurant. Expect popular, good value food like potato wedges, mushrooms with garlic, steaks and grills rather than gourmet fare, although the evening restaurant menus are more ambitious. Toilets are at the very top, but grand when you get there. Housekeeping can slip a little sometimes, but this is a pub of character. Children welcome before 8.30 pm. Food served daily, 12.30-9. Air conditioning. Closed 25 Dec, Good Fri. MasterCard, Visa, Laser. **Directions:** Situated 1/2 way down O'Connell St. on the left opposite Dunnes Stores. ◇

Clonmel Area

Kilmaneen Farmhouse

€ FARMHOUSE

Ardfinnan Newcastle Clonmel Co Tipperary
Tel: 052 36231 Fax: 052 36231
Email: kilmaneen@eircom.net Web: www.kilmaneen.com

As neat as a new pin, Kevin & Ber O'Donnell's delightfully situated farmhouse is on a working dairy farm, surrounded by three mountain ranges - the Comeraghs, the Knockmealdowns and the Galtees - and close to the river Suir and the Tar, making it an ideal base for walking and fishing holidays. Kevin is trained in mountain skills and leads walking groups, and trout fishing in the Suir and Tar on the farm is free (hut provided for tying flies, storing equipment and drying waders). It's an old house, but well restored to combine old furniture with modern comforts. Bedrooms are not especially big, but they are thoughtfully furnished (including tea/coffee facilities and iron/trouser press) and, like the rest of the house, immaculate. There's a great welcome and guests feel at home immediately - especially once they get tucked into Ber's delicious dinners. Don't expect any fancy menus or a wine list (you are welcome to bring your own wine), what you'll get here is real home cooking, based on fresh farm produce: home-produced beef, perhaps, or chicken stuffed with ricotta, spinach & parmesan and wrapped in cured ham, then apple pie for afters, perhaps - and breakfast are equally delicious, with stewed fruits from the garden and home-made breads and preserves as well as lovely porridge or the 'full Irish'. Genuinely hospitable hosts, homely comforts - including a log fire to relax beside after dinner and a large, well-maintained garden, where guests can enjoy the peaceful setting - all add up to a real country break. Kilmaneen was our Farmhouse of the Year in 2005. Fishing, walking. *Self catering accommodation also available (with option of dinner at the farmhouse). **Rooms 3** (2 shower only, all en-suite & no smoking). B&B €40 pps, ss €10. Children welcome (under 2s free in parents' room, cots available without charge). Pets may be permitted by prior arrangement. Dining room seats 12. Residents' D 7pm except on Sun (must book in advance); Set D €25.00. No SC. Closed 31 Oct - 16 Mar. MasterCard, Visa. **Directions:** In Ardfinnan, follow signs at the Hill Bar.

DROMINEER

Dromineer is an appealing little place on Lough Derg, with a pretty harbour and lovely woodland walks. It's a popular destination for Shannon cruisers, sailing folk and families out for the day at weekends. **The Dromineer Bay Hotel** (067 24114) offers simple accommodation right beside the harbour and is now run by Declan Collison and Fiona Neilan, previously well known for their food at the Whiskey Still, so you should be sure of a good meal here. **The Whiskey Still** (067 24129), an attractive pub with a deck overlooking the harbour, is now in new ownership.
WWW.IRELAND-GUIDE.COM FOR THE BEST PLACES TO EAT, DRINK & STAY

Fethard

Mobarnane House

COUNTRY HOUSE

Fethard Co Tipperary **Tel: 052 31962** Fax: 052 31962
Email: info@mobarnanehouse.com Web: www.mobarnanehouse.com

Approached up a stylish gravel drive with well-maintained grass verges, Richard and Sandra Craik-White's lovely 18th century home has recently been restored to its former glory and makes a wonderfully spacious retreat for guests; the aim is to provide peace and quiet in great comfort, with very personal attention to detail. A large, beautifully furnished drawing room has plenty of comfortable seating for everyone when there's a full house - and the dining room, where Richard's good country cooking is served (usually at a communal table, although separate tables can be arranged on request), is a lovely room; everything served for dinner is freshly prepared on the day, allowing for any preferences mentioned at the time of booking. Accommodation is of the same high standard: all rooms have lovely views and comfortable seating (two have separate sitting rooms), quality bedding and everything needed for a relaxing stay, including tea/coffee making facilities, phones and television - and fresh flowers from the garden. Bathrooms vary somewhat (bedrooms without sitting rooms have bigger bathrooms), but all have quality towels and toiletries. An excellent breakfast gets the day off to a good start - and, as well as being well-placed to explore a large and interesting area blessed with beautiful scenery, an interesting history, local crafts and sports, there is tennis and croquet on site, and lovely lake and woodland walks in the grounds. Not suitable for children under 5 except babies (cot available without charge, baby sitting arranged), children aged 5-10 stay free in parents room. Pets by arrangement. **Rooms 4** (2 junior suites, 2 executive, all no smoking). B&B €90 pps, ss €30. Residents' 4-course D 8pm, €45; advance reservation essential. House wine €15. SC discretionary. Closed Nov-Mar. MasterCard, Visa. **Directions:** From Fethard, take Cashel road for 3.5 miles; turn right, signed Ballinure and Thurles; 1.5 miles on left.

Garrykennedy

Larkins

RESTAURANT/PUB

Garrykennedy Portroe Nenagh Co Tipperary
Tel: 067 23232 Fax: 067 23264
Email: infoatlarkins@eircom.net Web: www.larkinspub.com

You can't miss this pretty white cottage pub with its cheerful red paintwork, and it's a great asset to the charming little harbour at Garrykennedy. Good food includes an excellent house chowder, and traditional daytime bar menus move up a notch or two for dinner, when you can look forward to dishes like succulent duckling and great steaks, with lovely fresh vegetables - good service too. New owners, Maura and Cormac Boyle, took over Larkins in 2006 but, thankfully, all is just the same as it was. Food available 10.30 am- 9.45 pm daily (12.30-9.30 Sun). Closed Good Fri, 25 Dec. MasterCard, Visa, Laser. **Directions:** 12km (7 m) from Nenagh.

NENAGH

This thriving town in the heart of Ireland's best farmland can provide a convenient base within easy reach of many attractions in the mid-west, including Lough Derg, or makes a handy place to break a journey - the modern **Abbey Court Hotel** (Tel: 067 41111; www.abbeycourt.ie) is located on the edge of town, with ample parking and good facilities. Little places in the town that might be handy to know about include **Roots** (19a Pearse Street 067 42444) a quirky casual restaurant with a chess set for customers, newspapers and a selection of books on alternative healing and therapy to browse through, and the nice old-fashioned Gleeson's Tearooms on Sraid Misteil. **Gaffney's Wine Bar** (067 42450) on Silver Street had just opened on a recent visit - one to watch. An unusual and hospitable farm B&B with 'cows, trees and total quiet' is **Bayly Farm** 067 31499; www.baylyfarm.ie) at Ballnaclough.
WWW.IRELAND-GUIDE.COM FOR THE BEST PLACES TO EAT, DRINK & STAY

Nenagh

Country Choice Delicatessen & Coffee Bar

€ CAFÉ/RESTAURANT

25 Kenyon Street Nenagh Co Tipperary
Tel: 067 32596 Fax: 067 32736
Email: info@countrychoice.ie Web: www.countrychoice.ie

Food-lovers from all over the country plan journeys around a visit to Peter and Mary Ward's unique shop. Old hands head for the little café at the back first, fortifying themselves with simple home-cooked food that reflects a policy of seasonality if the range is small at a particular time of year, so be it. Meats, milk, cream, eggs, butter and flour: "The economy of Tipperary is agricultural and we intend to demonstrate this with a finished product of tantalising smells and tastes." Specialities developed over the years include Cashel Blue and broccoli soup served with their magnificent breads (made with local flours - try the speciality yeast breads) savoury and sweet pastry dishes (quiches, fruit tarts) and tender, gently-cooked meat dishes like Irish stew and Hereford beef (from their own farm) and Guinness casserole. The shop carries a very wide range of the finest Irish artisan produce, plus a smaller selection of specialist products from further afield, such as olive oil and a range of superb dried and glacé fruits that are in great demand for Christmas baking (they make outstanding Christmas puddings too, for sale in the shop). Specialities that make this place so special include a great terrine, made from the family's saddleback pigs; the preserves - jam (Mary Ward makes 12,000 pots a year!) and home-made marmalade, based on oranges left to caramelise in the Aga overnight, producing a runny but richly flavoured preserve; then there is Peter's passion for cheese. He is one of the country's best suppliers of Irish farmhouse cheeses, which he minds like babies as they ripen and, unlike most shops, only puts on display when they are mature: do not leave without buying cheese. As well as all this, they run regular art exhibitions in the shop, wine courses and poetry readings. Definitely worth a detour. [Country Choice was the winner of our Natural food Award in 2004]. **Seats 35.** Picnic service available. Open all day (9-5.30); L 12-3 daily, à la carte; house wine - any bottle in the shop + €5 corkage; Vegetarian Menu available. Children welcome. Closed Sun. MasterCard, Visa, Laser. **Directions:** Centre of town,on left half way down Kenyon Street.

Nenagh

The Pepper Mill

RESTAURANT

26 Kenyon Street Nenagh Co Tipperary
Tel: 067 34598 Fax: 067 34597

A smartly painted black frontage and colourful geraniums spilling over a well-maintained container beside the door give out good signals on arrival at Mairead and Robert Gill's pleasant town-centre restaurant. A longish room, painted in burgundy and cream, has large framed pictures, sympathetic lighting and a big vase of fresh flowers at the reception bar; Robert is a good host and makes guests very welcome, settling people into well-spaced, simply laid tables and immediately offering printed menus which give clear descriptions - and yet give away very little about the treats in store. A blue cheese tartlet for example, is made with very crisp, light pastry , is full of flavour - and is served with a lovely salad, and a simple dish like deep-fried garlic mushrooms is crisp and flavoursome - a reminder of why this dish is so popular. Although it is, on the whole quite predictable - house specials (all €23) offer a top-of-the-range choice of popular main courses - rack of lamb, roast stuffed duck, medallions of beef, fresh prawns - the menu offers a well-balanced choice, notably steaks (this is beef country after all), also poultry and vegetarian dishes; but the surprise in this midland town is the fish dishes, which are well-priced and, in the Guide's experience, outstanding: a Moroccan salmon couscous with lime dressing attracted special praise on a recent visit, for example, for its intriguing spicing and accurate cooking. delicious desserts too - an exemplary strawberry meringue roulade, perhaps, and wonderfully gooey pecan brownies with butterscotch sauce, packed nuts and fruit. Efficient, pleasant service, good value - and a well-organised and fairly priced wine list too. **Seats 40.** Reservations required. Air conditioning. Toielts wheelchair accessible. D Tue-Fri, 5-10 (Sat 4-10, Sun 4-9). House wine €14.95. Closed Mon, 25 Dec & Good Fri, all bank hols. Amex, Diners, MasterCard, Visa, Laser, Switch. **Directions:** Nenagh town centre. ◇

Nenagh Area

Ashley Park House

COUNTRY HOUSE

Ardcronney Nenagh Co Tipperary **Tel: 067 38223** Fax: 067 38013
Email: margaret@ashleypark.com Web: www.ashleypark.com

From the moment you turn off the busy Nenagh-Borrisokane road, you enter a time warp. Margaret and P J Mounsey's home, Ashley Park, is one of those beautiful 18th century houses where all is elegance and comfort. It has the necessary mod cons (all the main bedrooms have en suite bathrooms) but this is a place which breathes an old-fashioned order, comfort and charm. The views of Lough Ourna, right in front of the house, with the distant Slieve Bloom Mountains looming up on the horizon, are stunningly lovely, and you can walk down to the lakeshore or through the walled garden, which - together with the gardener's cottage -is under restoration; the house is surrounded by 76 acres of woodland and walks are being created through it to make it accessible for guests. Whether you stay in the President's Room, (Mary MacAleese once stayed here), the Bishop's Room or any of the other rooms, you are guaranteed a fine view, a good night's rest in one of the old brass or mahogany beds, and a hearty breakfast the next morning in the splendour of the double dining room. Dinner can be booked by arrangement in advance, but Nenagh is just down the road, with Limerick not so far away, so dining in the area is no problem. Do not come expecting satellite television or ISDN points in the rooms, for you will be disappointed, but if you want peace and comfort in really splendid surroundings, this is recommended. **Rooms 5** (all with private bathrooms, 2 shower only, 4 no smoking, 1 for disabled). B&B €50, ss €10. Residents L&D available by prior arrangement only, €30-38. Open all year. **No Credit Cards. Directions:** On the N52, 7km (4 miles) north of Nenagh. Heading north, look for the lake on the left and go through the stone archway, past the gatehouse.

Nenagh Area

Coolbawn Quay Lakeshore Spa

HOTEL

Coolbawn Nenagh Co Tipperary **Tel: 067 28158** Fax: 067 28162
Email: info@coolbawnquay.com Web: www.coolbawnquay.com

Spas and retreats are appearing all over Ireland at the moment, but few could rival the beauty of this magic place. This unique resort on the eastern shores of Lough Derg is modelled on the lines of a 19th century Irish village with quietly understated luxurious accommodation in suites and rooms scattered throughout the cottages in the village - with hotel style service throughout, should you require it. The shoreside situation is truly lovely and there is a sense of being very close to the changing moods of nature, partly because the main building - which has a small traditional bar and a country style dining room - is only a few feet from the water, and partly because guests move around from building to building much more than in an ordinary hotel. Rooms are simple in style but furnished with everything you could wish for, including sound systems and - a very nice touch this - a turf-burning stove which is set up in advance, with matches at the ready, so you can have your own real fire whenever you like. The contrasts are wonderful here: whether you want to pamper yourself at the spa, hold a small conference or board meeting - or simply to unwind with style - this unusual village could be the ideal destination. And the inner man will be well looked after too, with excellent cooking by well known chef, Rob von Oosterbaan. This is a romantic location for weddings, which can be held in a luxury banqueting marquee set by the water's edge. [*Coolbawn Quay was our Hideaway of the Year in 2005.] (Small conference/banqueting (40/200); lakeside marquee available for weddings or events. Spa; beauty treatments. Walking, fishing. Pool table. Children welcome (baby sitting arranged). Garden. No pets. Wheelchair accessible. **Rooms 48** (9 suites, 7 shower only, 1 family room, 1 for disabled, all no smoking). Room service (all day). B&B €110 pps, ss € 30. *Short / off season breaks offered. **Restaurant Seats 35.** Non residents welcome by reservation if there is room (not suitable for children after 7pm). D Tue-Sat, 7-9; Set D €45, also small à la carte menu. Sun L 12.30-2.30. Bar food daily in high season, 12.30-2,30 (residents & members only); also barbecues. House Wine from €18.95. *Luxury 3 & 4 bed cottages available with hotel-style service Amex, Diners, MasterCard, Visa, Laser. **Directions:** On eastern side of Lough Derg; access from N7.

Roscrea

The Tower

BAR/RESTAURANT

Church Street Roscrea Co Tipperary **Tel: 0505 21774** Fax: 0505 22425
Email: info@thetower.ie Web: www.thetower.ie

féile bia

Gerard and Bridie Coughlan's reassuringly olde-worlde bar and restaurant has dark furniture, beams, dim lighting from shaded wall sconces- and a welcome emphasis on warm hospitality and good down to earth food. Round oak tables are unpretentiously laid with table mats, stainless steel cutlery and paper napkins - and menus, which offer plenty of choice, are generally fairy predictable with an emphasis on steaks, grills and traditional favourites such as boiled bacon and parsley sauce, although more adventurous choices are also offered. But this is good quality food, competently handled and very enjoyable for its simplicity and flavour - and there's a sense that the kitchen, while happy to provide popular dishes, is also very capable of more if the demand is there. Known by regulars as a reliable place where consistently good food is served at a reasonable price, the atmosphere is unashamedly old-fashioned and service is attentive and friendly - somewhere you would be happy to bring a guest of any age, whether a business associate or a friend or relative for a night out. Also useful to know about for a journey break. [Accommodation is also offered in 10 en-suite rooms, €38pps, ss€7; not viewed by the Guide.] Parking (50). Restaurant: Seats 44 (reservations advised). Open all day, 7.30-9; bar meals 11-9. L daily 12.30-3; D daily 6-9 (live music Fri). L Mon-Sat (Rest & Bar) à la carte; Set Sun L €23. D à la carte. House wine around €16.50. SC discretionary. Closed 25-27 Dec. Amex, Diners, MasterCard, Visa, Laser. **Directions:** Town centre - beside Round Tower.

Roscrea Area
RESTAURANT

Fiacrí Country House Restaurant & Cookery School

Boulerea Knock Roscrea Co Tipperary **Tel: 0505 43017** Fax: 0505 43018
Email: fiacrihouse@eircom.net Web: www.fiacrihouse.com

féile bia Enda & Ailish Hennessy's lovely country house style restaurant and cookery school is not the easiest place to find (it is sensible to get directions when booking) but, once discovered, what a welcome sight their neat pink-painted farmhouse presents. Enda will be at hand to welcome guests, offering an aperitif beside the fire in the comfortably furnished bar, where you can look over Ailish's five-course menus, which are based on carefully sourced local and Quality Assured ingredients and credit suppliers on the first page. Menus are balanced, to include fish, poultry and vegetarian choices, but local meats are especially good, and generous portions of seasonal vegetables are served separately. House specialities include a delicious starter salad of baked Clonakilty black pudding & caramelised apple, and fairly traditional main courses like rack of Tipperary lamb with parsnip purée, homemade mint sauce & rosemary jus, or the ever-popular grilled sirloin steak Diane, with roasted garlic mash. Like the bar, the restaurant has an open fire, and the style is pleasingly traditional - white linen, mahogany chairs, a warm green and red colour scheme - making a special yet a relaxed setting to enjoy a good meal. From a long list of desserts, you could try the excellent Assorted Dessert Plate - miniature servings of the day's desserts such as hazelnut meringue roulade, apple & summer fruit crumble, strawberry shortcake - or farmhouse cheeses. Caring service enhances the experience, and a compact, informative wine list offers good value and includes some half bottles. Ailish also offers cookery classes throughout the year - a new demonstration kitchen is under construction at the time of going to press. This is a very popular restaurant and advance booking is essential. *Fiacri was selected for our Féile Bia Award in 2004. Toilets wheelchair accessible. **Seats 80.** Reservations required. Not suitable for children under 12. D Wed-Sat, 7-9.15. Set D €50. House wine €18. Full bar licence. Closed Sun, Mon, Tue and 25 Dec, Good Fri. *Cookery classes held Tue night. over a 5 week period (€140pp). In addition 1 day courses (€100) are held at such culinary demanding times as Christmas and Easter. Also BBQ evenings in the summer with Q&A. Classes are intimate and interactive and you get to eat it all after! Accommodation is available locally for the cookery classes. MasterCard, Visa, Laser. **Directions:** Roscrea 6.5 miles, Erril 4.5, Templemore 8.

Templemore Area
B&B/COUNTRY HOUSE

Saratoga Lodge

Barnane Templemore Co Tipperary **Tel: 0504 31886**
Fax: 0504 31491 Email: saratogalodge@eircom.net

In a particularly unspoilt and peaceful part of the country, just below the famous Devil's Bit in the Silvermine mountain range, Valerie Beamish's lovely classically proportioned house on a working stud farm is well-situated on an open, sunny site looking out over the hills. Good equestrian paintings enhance the large, traditionally furnished reception rooms opening off a spacious hall and there is also a little TV room for children. Bedrooms are very comfortably furnished, and two new bathrooms are planned at the time of going to press. (A drying room, sports equipment room, indoor sports room and hard tennis court are also to be added.) Valerie takes great pride in giving guests a good breakfast, and she's also willing to cook 4-course dinners on request (using home-produced vegetables, herbs and honey), and make picnics - this is extremely hospitable house all round. Children welcome (under 3s free in parents' room, cots available free of charge, baby-sitting arranged). Pets by arrangement. Garden, walking, cycling, tennis. Golf, fishing, horse riding, hiking, racing (horses, greyhounds), cheesemakers and garden visits all nearby. **Rooms 3** (2 en-suite but shared, 1 shower only, 1 family room, 1 with private bathroom, all no smoking). B&B €55-60 pps, no ss. Residents' D €30, on request. House wine €12-18. Closed 23 Dec-3 Jan. MasterCard, Visa, Laser. **Directions:** From Templemore, take the Nenagh road for 2 miles; take 2nd turn on right. 2.5km (1.5 m), left at junction; house is on the left.

Terryglass Area
COUNTRY HOUSE

Kylenoe House

Balinderry Terryglass Nenagh Co Tipperary **Tel: 067 22015**
Fax: 067 22275 Email: ginia@eircom.net

Virginia Moeran's lovely old stone house on 150 acres of farm and woodland offers homely comfort and real country pleasures close to Lough Derg. The farm is home to an international stud and the woodlands are a haven for wildlife, including deer, stoats, red squirrels, badgers, rabbits and foxes as well as many varieties of birds and flowers. With beautiful walks, riding (with or without tuition), golf and water sports available on the premises or close by, this is a real rural retreat. Spacious, airy bedrooms are furnished in gentle country house style, with antiques and family belongings, and overlook beautiful rolling countryside; recent refurbishment has included new super-comfortable beds. Downstairs there's a delightful guests' sitting room and plenty of interesting reading. Virginia enjoys cooking, her breakfasts are a speciality and dinner is available to residents by arrangement. Importantly for people who like to travel with their dogs, this is a place where man's best friend is also made welcome and Kylenoe was our Pet Friendly Establishment of the Year in 1999. Children welcome (under 8 free in parents' room; cot available, baby sitting arranged). Pets welcome. Garden, walking. **Rooms 4** (3 en-suite, 1 with private bathroom, all no-smoking) B&B €60 pps, ss €10. Residents D 7-8pm, €38 (book by noon). Wines from €16. Closed 18-30 Dec. MasterCard, Visa. **Directions:** N7 to Moneygall, Cloughjordan, Borrisokane, leave Egans shop on right and straigt 10km (6.5m) on right.

Thurles Area

Inch House Country House & Restaurant

RESTAURANT/COUNTRY HOUSE

Bouladuff Thurles Co Tipperary
Tel: 0504 51348 Fax: 0504 51754
Email: inchhse@iol.ie Web: www.inchhouse.ie

féile bia Built in 1720 by John Ryan, one of the few landed Catholic gentlemen in Tipperary, this magnificent Georgian house managed to survive some of the most turbulent periods in Irish history and to remain in the Ryan family for almost 300 years. John and Norah Egan, who farm the surrounding 250 acres, took it over in a state of dereliction in 1985 and began the major restoration work which has resulted in the handsome, comfortably furnished period house which guests enjoy today. Reception rooms on either side of a welcoming hallway include an unusual William Morris-style drawing room with a tall stained glass window, a magnificent plasterwork ceiling (and adjoining library bar) and a fine dining room which is used for residents' breakfasts and is transformed into a restaurant at night. Both rooms have period fireplaces with big log fires. The five bedrooms are quite individual and are furnished with antiques. Small weddings. Children welcome (under 6 free in parents' room; cot available without charge, baby sitting arranged). No Pets. **Rooms 5** (all en-suite, 1 shower only). B&B €60 pps, ss €10. Closed Christmas & New Year. **Restaurant:** The restaurant, which is open to non-residents by reservation, has polished wood floors, classic country house decor and tables laid with crisp white linen and fresh flowers, which provide a pleasing setting for dinner, especially when the atmosphere is softened by firelight and candles. Dinner menus offer a well-balanced choice of about six dishes on each course, in a fairly traditional style that combines French country cooking and Irish influences, and makes good use of local produce. Dishes like smoked salmon terrine, for example, and the ever-popular entrecôte steak with mushroom & whiskey sauce illustrate the style. Anyone with special dietary needs, including vegetarians, should mention this on booking to allow for preparation of extra dishes. Not suitable for children after 7 pm. **Seats 50.** D Tue-Sat 7-9; Set D from €48; house wine €17; sc discretionary. Closed Sun & Mon, Christmas week. MasterCard, Visa, Laser. **Directions:** Four miles from Thurles on Nenagh Road.

COUNTY WATERFORD

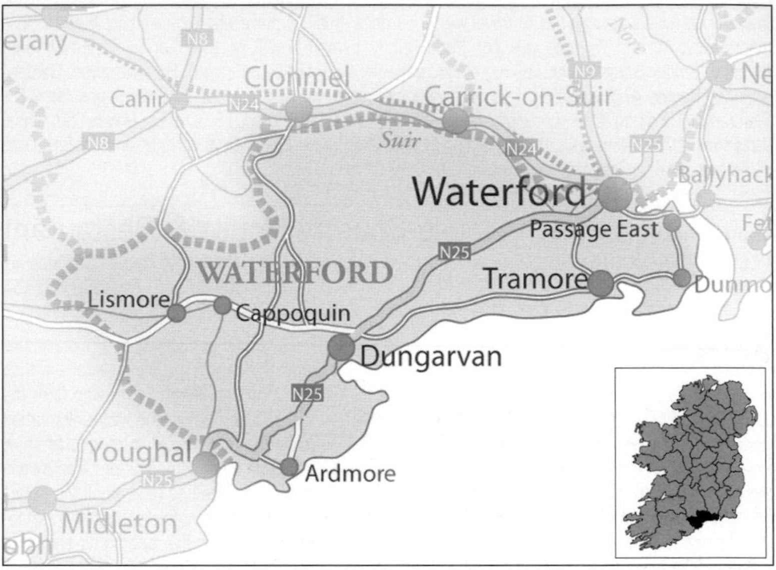

On the quays of Waterford city, we are witness to a trading and seafaring tradition which goes back at least 1,150 years. Today's larger commercial ships may be berthed downstream on the other side of the river at Belview, but the old cityside quays on the south bank retain a nautical flavour which is accentuated by very useful marina berthing facilities in the heart of town.

This fine port was founded in 853 AD when the Vikings - Danes for the most part - established the trading settlement of Vadrefjord. Its strategic location in a sheltered spot at the head of the estuary near the confluence of the Suir and Barrow rivers guaranteed its continuing success under different administrators, particularly the Normans, so much so that it tended to overshadow the county of Waterford, almost all of which is actually to the west of the port.

But for many years now, the county town has been Dungarvan, which is two-thirds of the way westward along Waterford's extensive south coast, which includes the attractive Copper Coast - between Fenor and Stradbally - in its midst. This spreading of the administrative centres of gravity has to some extent balanced the life of the Waterford region. But even so, the extreme west of the county is still one of Ireland's best kept secrets, a place of remarkable beauty between the Knockmealdown, Comeragh and Monavullagh mountains, where fish-filled rivers such as the Bride, the Blackwater, and the Nire make their way seawards at different speeds through valleys of remarkable variety and beauty, past pretty towns and villages such as romantic, castle-bedecked Lismore.

West Waterford is a place of surprises. For instance, around the delightful coastal village of Ardmore, ancient monuments suggest that the local holy man, St Declan, introduced Christianity to the area quite a few years before St Patrick went to work in the rest of Ireland. And across the bay from Ardmore, the Ring neighbourhood is a Gaeltacht (Irish-speaking) area with its own bustling fishing port at Helvick.

Dungarvan itself is enjoying the fruits of an attractive revival. It has relinquished its role as a commercial port, but is enthusiastically taking to recreational boating and harbourside regeneration instead. Along the bluff south coast, secret coves gave smugglers and others access to charming villages like Stradbally and Bunmahon. Further east, the increased tempo of the presence of Waterford city is felt both at the traditional resort of Tramore, and around the fishing/sailing harbour of Dunmore East.

Local Attractions and Information

Ballymacarbry, Nire Valley & Comeraghs on Horseback 052 36147
Cappoquin, Mount Melleray Activity Centre 058 54322
Cappoquin, Tourism Information 058 53333
Dungarvan, Tourism Information 058 41741

Kilmeaden, Old School House Craft Centre	051 853 567
Lismore, Lismore Castle & Gardens	058 54424
Passage East, Car Ferry (to Ballyhack, Co Wexford)	051 382 480
Tramore, Tramore House Gardens	051 386 303
Waterford Airport	051 875 589
Waterford, Christ Church Cathedral (18c Neoclassical)	051 858 958
Waterford, Waterford Crystal Glass Centre	051 332 500
Waterford, Heritage Museum	051 871 227
Waterford, Int. Festival of Light Opera (Sept)	051 375 437
Waterford, Reginald's Tower 13th C Circular Tower	051 304 220
Waterford, Theatre Royal	051 874 402
Waterford, Tourism Information	051 875 823
Waterford, Waterford Treasures at the Granary	051 304 500

Ardmore

White Horses Restaurant

RESTAURANT

Ardmore Co Waterford **Tel: 024 94040**
Fax: 024 94040 Email: whitehorses@eircom.net

Christine Power and Geraldine Flavin's delightfully bright and breezy café-restaurant on the main street of this famous seaside village is one of those places that changes its character through the day but always has style. They're open for all the little lifts that visitors need through the day - morning coffee, afternoon tea - as well as imaginative lunches (plus their traditional Sunday lunch, which runs all afternoon) and a more ambitious à la carte evening menu. Vegetarian dishes feature on both menus - a pasta dish during the day perhaps, and spinach & mushroom crêpe with toasted brie in the evening - and there's a good balance between traditional favourites like steaks and more adventurous fare: a daytime fish dish could be deep-fried plaice with tartare sauce, for example, while its evening counterpart might be grilled darne Helvick salmon on asparagus, with a wine & cream sauce. Attractive and pleasant to be in - the use of local Ardmore pottery is a big plus on the presentation side, and emphasises the sense of place - this is a friendly, well-run restaurant and equally good for a reviving cuppa and a gateau or pastry from the luscious home-made selection on display, or a full meal. Even when very busy, service is well-organised and efficient. **Seats 50.** Air conditioning. In summer (May-Sep) open: Tue-Sun 11-'late'; L 12.30-3.30, D 6-10. In winter (Oct-Apr) open weekends only: Fri from 6 pm, Sat 11-11 & Sun 12-6. A la carte except Sun - Set L €25. Licensed; House Wine €17.50; sc discretionary. Closed Mon all year, except bank hols (bank hol opening as Sun), 1 Jan-13 Feb. MasterCard, Visa, Laser. **Directions:** Centre of village. ◇

Ballymacarbry

Glasha

FARMHOUSE

Glasha Ballymacarbry Co Waterford **Tel: 052 36108** Fax: 052 36108
Email: glasha@eircom.net Web: www.glashafarmhouse.com

FARMHOUSE OF THE YEAR

Paddy and Olive O'Gorman's spacious farmhouse is set in its own gardens high up in the hills and makes a very comfortable and hospitable base for a relaxed rural break. Fishing is a major attraction (the Nire runs beside the farmhouse and permits are available locally), also walking (Glasha links the Comeragh and Knockmealdown sections of the famous Munster Way), pony trekking, golf (available locally), and painting this beautiful area. Olive thinks of everything that will help guests feel at home and bedrooms - which are extremely luxurious for a farm stay - have lots of little extras including TV/radio, hair dryers, electric blankets, tea/coffee-making, spring water and magazines; most rooms have king size beds, all are en-suite, and the newer ones have lovely bathrooms with jacuzzi baths. There's plenty of comfortable lounging room for guests' use, too, including a conservatory - and the nearest pub is just 3 minutes' walk from the house. Olive makes a delicious home-cooked dinner for guests, by arrangement, and it is served in a comfortable big dining room; her 3-course menus change daily and you might begin with something that showcases local seafood, like Dungarvan mussels in a creamy basil sauce, then a main course of Comeragh lamb - a rack, perhaps, stuffed with apricots and served with a rosemary sauce - and finish with apple & blueberry crumble, or whiskey & coffee gateau, then tea or coffee and chocolates in the conservatory, or in beside the fire on chilly evenings. The food is gorgeous with its farmhouse simplicity, and you'll get a good breakfast to set you up for the day too. This is a lovely place to stay, and a perfect antidote to the stresses of urban life. Children welcome, cots available. **Rooms 6** (4 with jacuzzi, 2 shower only, 1 family room, 2 ground floor, all no-smoking). B&B €50 pps, ss €10. Residents' D, 7.30 by arrangement (short à la carte), €25-35. Closed 20-27 Dec. MasterCard, Visa. **Directions:** Off 671 road between Clonmel and Dungarvan, 3.5km (2 m) from Ballymacarbry; signed on 671.

Ballymacarbry

Hanora's Cottage

RESTAURANT/GUESTHOUSE

Nire Valley Ballymacarbry Co Waterford
Tel: 052 36134 Fax: 052 36540
Email: hanorascottage@eircom.net Web: www.hanorascottage.com

The Wall family's gloriously remote country guesthouse is now a very substantial building, yet they still actively nurture the spirit of the ancestral home around which Hanora's is built. This a very special place - equally wonderful for foot-weary walkers, or desk-weary city folk in need of some clear country air and real comfort - and the genuine hospitality of the Wall family is matched by the luxurious accommodation and good food they provide. Comfortably furnished seating areas with sofas and big armchairs provide plenty of room to relax, and the spacious thoughtfully furnished bedrooms all have jacuzzi baths (one especially romantic room is perfect for honeymooners); there's also a spa tub in a conservatory overlooking the garden, with views of the mountains. Overnight guests begin the day with Hanora's legendary breakfast buffet, which was the National Winner of our Irish Breakfast Awards in 2002; it takes some time to get the measure of this feast, so make sure you get up in time to make the most of it. Local produce and exotics (some of which you may not previously have encountered) jostle for space on the beautifully arranged buffet: fruits and freshly squeezed juices (including luscious Crinnaghtaun Apple Juice from Lismore), homemade muesli and porridge... a whole range of freshly-baked breads, including organic and gluten free varieties... local farmhouse cheeses, smoked salmon, home made jams - and all the cooked breakfast options you could wish for. This is truly a gargantuan feast, designed to see you many miles along the hills before you stop for a little packed lunch (prepared that morning) and ultimately return for dinner... Small weddings (40). **Rooms 10** (1 suite, 3 junior suites, all no smoking). Not suitable for children. No pets. B&B from €75 pps. Closed Christmas week. **Restaurant:** One of the best things about Hanora's is that people travel from far and wide to dine here, which adds to the atmosphere. How pleasant to mingle with residents at the fireside, have an aperitif and ponder on Eoin and Judith Wall's imaginative, well-balanced menus - then, difficult choices made, you move through to the restaurant, which overlooks a secluded garden and riverside woodland. Enthusiastic supporters of small suppliers, Eoin and Judith use local produce whenever possible and credit them on the menu - fresh fish from Dunmore East, free range chickens from Stradbally and local cheeses, for example. There's a separate vegetarian dinner menu on request as well as an à la carte which offers about seven dishes on each course, usually including some vegetarian options. Popular dishes include starters of sautéed lambs kidneys on a croustade with mushroom cream and stuffed mushrooms with walnuts, blue cheese & garlic mayonnaise, and main courses including beautifully fresh and accurately cooked fish or, as lamb is so abundant locally, the all-time favourite is roast rack of lamb (served, perhaps, with a delicious mint hollandaise). Desserts include classics like lemon tart with crème anglaise and good home-made ice creams - and, of course, there's always an Irish cheese selection. Not suitable for children under 12. Not suitable for children under 12. Seats 30/40 D Mon-Sat, 7-9, Set D about €40, also à la carte. House wine about €14.50. Closed Sun, bank hols. MasterCard, Visa, Laser. **Directions:** Take Clonmel/Dungarvan (R671) road, turn off at Ballymacarbry.

Cappoquin

Richmond House

RESTAURANT/COUNTRY HOUSE

Cappoquin Co Waterford
Tel: 058 54278 Fax: 058 54988
Email: info@richmondhouse.net Web: www.richmondhouse.net

féile bia Genuine hospitality, high standards of comfort, caring service and excellent food are all to be found in the Deevy family's fine 18th century country house and restaurant just outside Cappoquin - no wonder this is a place so many people like to keep as a closely guarded secret. For returning guests, there's always a sense of pleasurable anticipation that builds up as you approach through parkland along a well-maintained driveway, which is lit up at night; after a brief pause to admire the climbing plants beside the door, you're into the fine high-ceilinged hall with its warming wood-burning stove and catch the scent of fires burning in the well-proportioned, elegantly furnished drawing room and restaurant opening off it. Claire or Jean Deevy will usually be there to welcome arriving guests, and show you to one of the nine individually decorated bedrooms; they vary in size and appointments, as is the way with old houses - some guests love the smallest cottagey bedroom, while others may prefer the larger ones - but all are comfortably furnished in country house style with full bathrooms. As well as serving wonderful dinners in the restaurant (see below), the Deevys make sure that you will have a memorable breakfast to see you on your way - it is a wonderful area to explore, and Richmond House makes an excellent base. Children welcome (under 3 free in parents' room, cot available without charge, baby sitting arranged). No pets. Garden; walking. Golf, garden visits nearby. **Rooms 9** (1 junior suite, all with full bathrooms & no smoking). B&B €75 pps, ss €20. Closed 22 Dec-10 Jan. **Restaurant:** The restaurant is the heart of Richmond House and non-residents usually make up a high proportion of the guests, which makes for a lively atmosphere. Warm and friendly service begins from the moment menus are presented over aperitifs - in front of the drawing room fire, or in a conservatory overlooking the garden. Paul is an ardent supporter of local produce and sources everything with tremendous care: Quality Assured meats (beef, lamb, bacon and sausages) come from his trusted local butcher, fresh seafood is from Dunmore East and Dungarvan herbs, fruit and vegetables are home grown where possible, and extra organic produce is grown nearby. There is a sureness of touch in Paul's kitchen, seen in stimulating menus that offer a balance between traditional country house cooking and more adventurous dishes inspired by international trends; dinner menus offering about five choices on each course are changed daily, and a slightly shorter separate vegetarian menu is also offered. House specialities include Helvick prawns (tempura, perhaps) and - a dish it would be hard to resist at Richmond House - roast rack of delicious West Waterford lamb, a memorable dish presented on braised puy lentils and buttered green beans, with home-made mint jelly and rosemary & garlic jus; vegetables, served separately, are invariably imaginative and cooked 'au point'. Classic desserts are always a treat too, including plenty of imaginative and beautifully executed fruit-based choices to balance the richness of a fine meal here - orange pannacotta with orange segments, perhaps - and, of course, there will always be Irish farmhouse cheeses with home-made biscuits. Service, under Claire's direction, is attentive and discreet. A carefully selected and fairly priced wine list includes about twenty offered by the glass, several wines of the month, and a good choice of half bottles. The early dinner menu offers particularly good value. *Richmond House received the Féile Bia Award in 2006. Children welcome. **Seats 45** (private room, 14). D 6.30-9.30 daily; Set D €50, Early Bird €35 (Vegetarian Menu also avail); house wine €20; sc discretionary. Closed 22 Dec-10 Jan. Amex, Diners, MasterCard, Visa, Laser. **Directions:** 1km (0.5 mile) outside Cappoquin on N72.

Cheekpoint
RESTAURANT

The Cottage Bistro

Cheekpoint Village Co Waterford **Tel: 051 380 854**
Email: cottagebistro@eircom.net Web: www.cottagebistro.com

féile bia Aidan and Marian McAlpin's neat cottagey restaurant is spick and span and the style is pleasingly simple, with a small bar area and plain, handsomely-laid tables softened by warm lighting and fresh flowers. Good home-made brown bread and iced water are served promptly, along with hand written menus that offer plenty of choice, although local seafood is a speciality and starters, in particular, offer mainly seafood dishes - prawn & shrimp cocktail, mussels or crab claws in garlic butter, smoked salmon salad, plus perhaps a soup and a vegetarian alternative such as fried camembert with tomato chilli chutney. Main courses offer a wider choice - including a very tempting speciality vegetarian shepherd's pie, no less (cheese topping optional), as well as steaks and chicken - but seafood remains dominant in dishes like fresh salmon mayonnaise, fillets of sole baked in chive sauce with (perhaps a little too much) creamed potato topping and seafood gratin, which is a house speciality. A side salad is served after the main course, and desserts are home-made. What you get here is Marian McAlpin's sound home cooking, simply presented - and prices are reasonable, especially for seafood; there's still nothing over €22 on the menu, and that is for the Seafood Platter which could include none or ten different fish and shellfish. An interesting, informative and well-priced wine list includes unusual house wines and an equally carefully selected choice of half bottles. Children welcome before 7pm. **Seats 45** (+10 outside). Reservations required. Toilets wheelchair accessible. D Tue-Sat, 6-9.30 (Sun, June-Aug only, 5.30-8.30). A la carte. House wine €18. SC discretionary. Closed Mon (also Sun off season), last week Sept, all Jan. Amex, MasterCard, Visa, Laser, Switch. **Directions:** 7 miles east of Waterford city; in village, above the harbour.

Cheekpoint
RESTAURANT

The Suir Inn

Cheekpoint Co Waterford **Tel: 051 382 220**
Email:frances@mcalpins.com Web: www.mcalpins.com

féile bia This immaculately maintained black-and-white painted inn is 300 years old and has been run by the McAlpin family since 1972. It's a characterful, country style place with rustic furniture, cottagey plates and old prints decorating the walls - more like a traditional bar than a restaurant. Seasonal menus offer a choice of about six starters (mostly seafood and not more than about €8) and ten main courses, including several cold dishes and two vegetarian ones, again all moderately priced - specialities include a generous and reasonably priced seafood platter (about €20) and home-made seafood pie. All meals come with brown soda bread and butter, and a side salad and a nice little wine list includes a choice of eight moderately priced wines. No children after 9pm. **Seats 62.** D Tue-Sat, 5.30-9.30; à la carte; sc discretionary. House wine from €13.50. SC discretionary. Closed Sun, Mon. MasterCard, Visa, Laser. **Directions:** 7 miles east of Waterford, on harbour front. ◇

DUNGARVAN

DUNGARVAN is the county's main town outside Waterford city and is beautifully located on Dungarvan Harbour (renowned for its wildlife), with much of interest nearby: the Gaeltacht of Ring is just a few miles away, for example, and the lovely Nire Valley (walking, pony trekking) runs deep into the Comeragh Mountains north of the town. West of Dungarvan, the Heritage Town of Lismore, with its fairytale castle and gardens, is just a short drive. The main hotel in Dungarvan is the Flynn family's Park Hotel (058 42899; www.flynnhotels.com), which is just on the edge of town overlooking the Colligan River esturay; spacious and comfortable, with leisure centre/swimming pool. For informal dining in the town, try the popular Restaurant Q82 (058 24555).

WWW.IRELAND-GUIDE.COM FOR THE BEST PLACES TO EAT, DRINK & STAY

Dungarvan

N B&B/COUNTRY HOUSE

Cairbre House

Strandside North Abbeyside Dungarvan Co Waterford
Tel: 058 42338
Email:cairbrehouse@eircom.net Web: www.cairbrehouse.com

A reader recommendation led us Brian Wickham's fine old house just across the bridge from Dungarvan town centre, and it is indeed a delightful place - right on the water, it is of great historical interest and set in wonderful gardens, which are his pride and joy. The house has a very homely feel to it and there's a lounge and fire for guests, and lots of information about everything locally, including the bird watching that is such an attraction in the area for nature lovers. Bedrooms are a little old-fashioned but spacious and comfortable, with hair dryers, electric blankets and beautiful views out over the water, the birds on it and the hills or town in the background yet it's just a 10-15 minute walk to the restaurants in town. Various combinations are available, including rooms for families or groups travelling together and, as well as en-suite facilities, there's an extra communal bathroom on the landing. There are some wooden tables and benches in the back garden, where Brian is happy to serve breakfast in fine weather - it's very different from staying in an hotel, and much appreciated by his many regular guests. Brian loves everything about his house, its history and the hospitality business but the gardens, which are in the South East Garden Trail and enjoy a micro-climate that allows many 'impossible' plants to survive here, are his greatest love and a source of great pleasure to guests. A conservatory is planned too, which will have views of the hills and water, and, as he says, "it will be a perfect place for a G&T". Walking, garden. Garden visits, golf and sea angling nearby. Free broadband WI/Fi. Children welcome (under 3s free in parents' room, cot available free of charge). **Rooms 4** (all shower only, 1 family room, 3 no smoking, 1 ground floor); B&B €45 pps, ss €7. Closed Nov-mid Feb. Amex, Diners, MasterCard, Visa. **Directions:** From Waterford take right exit off N25 at Strandside roundabout, house 200m up on the left.

Dungarvan

GUESTHOUSE

Powersfield House

Ballinamuck West Dungarvan Co Waterford **Tel: 058 45594**
Email: powersfieldhouse@cablesurf.com Web: www.powersfield.com

féile bia

You could be forgiven for thinking that Edmund and Eunice Power's fine guesthouse has been here for a long time - although new, the garden has matured well and this, together with traditional country house style furnishing, gives it an unexpected sense of age. Antiques and interesting fabrics creating a soothing and relaxing atmosphere throughout the house, including a comfortable, homely sitting room as well as bedrooms which have been individually decorated and finished to a high standard, with smart bathrooms and all the necessary comforts: phones (with ISDN & fax facilities)TV and tea/coffee trays). Eunice is an enthusiastic cook and offers dinner to residents by arrangement; her menus are based on local produce such as Helvic seafood (typically, in a speciality of lemon sole en papillotte with Thai herbs & lemon butter), local organic vegetables and Ardsallagh goat cheese. This is a lovely, friendly place to stay and would make a good base for exploring the area. Children welcome (under 4 free in parents' room; cot available without charge; children's playground, baby sitting arranged). **Rooms 5** (all en-suite and no smoking, 4 shower only, 1 for disabled). Room service (limited hours). B&B €65 pps, ss €10. Residents' D by arrangement €25-35; house wine €20; sc discretionary. *Cookery Courses available, details on application. Amex, MasterCard, Visa, Laser. **Directions:** R672 from Dungarvan at Kilrush roundabout; second turn left, first house on right.

Dungarvan

★RESTAURANT WITH ROOMS

The Tannery

10 Quay Street Dungarvan Co Waterford
Tel: 058 45420 Fax: 058 45814
Email: tannery@cablesurf.com Web: www.tannery.ie

Discerning diners from all over Ireland (and beyond) make a beeline for Paul and Maire Flynn's stylish contemporary restaurant, which is in an old leather warehouse - the tannery theme is imaginatively echoed throughout the light, clean-lined interior, creating a sense of history that adds greatly to the atmosphere. Pausing, perhaps, to have an aperitif in the little bar/reception area, arriving guests can see Paul and his team at work in the open kitchen on their way upstairs to the first-floor dining area, which is bright and welcoming, with dramatic paintings and fresh flowers. Menus are wonderfully simple, written with a confidence that transfers to the hungry guest: you just know that every dish will be an experience. While inspired to some extent by global trends and regional cooking - particularly of the Mediterranean countries - menus are based mainly on local ingredients, which Paul supports avidly and sources with care: local seafood stars in irresistible dishes like an unusual starter of crab crème brulée, and a main course of pan fried scallops with a casserole of wild mushrooms, butter beans and leeks. Pork and bacon supplied by local butcher JD Power are rightly another source of pride, as of course, is local lamb - a delicious starter of seared lambs kidneys with bacon & spiced red cabbage neatly combines the two. Dashing desserts are invariably tempting, and often appealingly simple too - blackcurrant meringue fool, or apple & treacle steamed pudding, for example... or an Irish farmhouse cheese platter, in perfect condition, which makes a fine finale to the meal. The à la carte is very fairly priced for food of this quality, but the lunch and early evening menus (both changed daily) are outstandingly good value. Attentive and efficient service under Maire's direction, an interesting and kindly-priced wine list (with wines by the glass changed every week) and, above all, Paul's exceptional cooking, make for memorable meals. *The Tannery was our Restaurant of the Year in 2004. Toilets wheelchair accessible. Children welcome. **Seats 60** (private room up to 28). L Tue-Sun, 12.30-2.15 (Sun to 2.30); D Tue-Sat, 6.30-9.30. Early D €27 (Tue-Fri, 6.30-7.15); Set Sun L €27; house wine €22; sc discretionary (10% on parties of 6+). Closed Mon, also D Sun; annual closure 2 weeks end Jan, 1 week Sept. **Rooms:** Accommodation is offered in a boutique guesthouse just around the corner, in Church Street. Public areas of the house are very bright and funky but, while also contemporary, the seven double rooms and a self-catering apartment are furnished more elegantly and to a very high standard. Ingenious breakfast arrangements provide the best of all possible worlds for the guest, without giving late night restaurant staff the problems of an early morning start - try it and see. **Rooms 7** (all en-suite, 2 shower only), children welcome (under 4s free in parents' room, cots available at no charge); B&B €60 pps, ss€10. Amex, Diners, MasterCard, Visa, Laser. **Directions:** End of lower main street beside old market house.

Dungarvan Area

Gortnadiha Lodge

B&B/FARMHOUSE

Ring Dungarvan Co Waterford **Tel: 058 46142**

Eileen and Thomas Harty's house is west of Dungarvan in the Ring Gaeltacht (Irish speaking) area, and it is in a lovely setting, with woodland gardens and sea views. Accommodation in the family home is comfortable, hospitality is warm and breakfasts offer a very wide selection of local and home produce, including fresh fish in season. Children welcome (under 5 free in parents' room, cot available without charge, baby sitting arranged). Pets permitted. **Rooms 3** (2 shower only, 1 ground floor). B&B room rate €90. Closed 21 Dec - 21 Jan. Visa. **Directions:** N25 Rosslare to Cork, 3 km from Dungarvan: follow the sea.

Dunmore East

Beach Guesthouse

GUESTHOUSE

1 Lower Village Dunmore East Co Waterford
Tel: 051 383316 Fax: 051 383319
Email: beachouse@eircom.net Web: www.dunmorebeachguesthouse.com

Breda Battles' smart modern guesthouse has outstanding views and easy accessibility to the beach, and offers good value. Rooms to the front - including the pleasant breakfast room and lounge, as well as some of the bedrooms - have a sea view, and this would make a good, moderately priced base for exploring the area. Everything is very clean and well-maintained and, although hard flooring throughout can be noisy, bedrooms have plenty of hanging space and a writing desk as well as TV/radio and tea/coffee making. Tasty breakfasts include lovely scones and preserves, well-made traditional Irish and some other options, such as scrambled egg with smoked salmon. Not suitable for children under 6. No pets. **Rooms 7** (1 suite, 2 shower only, 1 family room, 1 ground floor, 1 for disabled, all no smoking). B&B €45, ss 10. Closed 1 Nov - 1 Mar. Amex, MasterCard, Visa, Laser. **Directions:** Left after pertol station in village; house facing sea wall.

Dunmore East

Strand Inn

N PUB/RESTAURANT WITH ROOMS

Dunmore East Co Waterford
Tel: 051 383 174 Fax: 051 383 161
Email: strandin@iol.ie Web: www.dunmoreeast.com

Right on the beach, and with sea views out towards the Hook Lighthouse, The Strand goes back a good few hundred years but today it is the first choice for discerning locals when it comes to seafood. 'Fish, fish, fish' is how they describe their menu, and so it is - up to a point: non seafood eaters will be glad to know that there are some concessions, including a roast perhaps, or poultry such as traditional duck with orange sauce. But it is mainly for the seafood that people head for the Strand - and it couldn't be fresher as much of it comes from the nearby harbour, which is one of Ireland's main fishing ports. Toilets wheelchair accessible. **Seats 70** (outdoor, 40); children welcome before 8pm; L daily in summer, 12.30-4.30 (to 2.30 Sun), set L €22.50; D daily all year, 6.30-10; early D €22.50, 6.30-7.30; House wine €17; SC 10% on parties 8+. Restaurant closed all of Jan and Mon-Tue in Nov-Mar. Amex, Diners, MasterCard, Visa, Laser.

Lismore
HOTEL

Ballyrafter Country House Hotel

Lismore Co Waterford **Tel: 058 54002** Fax: 058 53050
Email: info@waterfordhotel.com Web: ballyrafter@waterfordhotel.com

Fishing is a big draw to Joe & Noreen Willoughby's welcoming country house hotel, but a relaxing laid-back atmosphere, log fires and good home cooking also appeal to a growing number of people who simply enjoy the area and have come to see the unpretentious comforts of Ballyrafter as a home from home. The bar, where informal meals are served, is lined with photographs of happy fisherfolk - if you are dining in the restaurant, you can have an aperitif here while looking at the menu, or beside the fire in the drawing room next door. Bedrooms in the main house are simple and comfortable and one side of the the courtyard area at the back of the hotel has been thoughtfully developed to provide five new executive bedrooms, all carefully designed to replicate the older ones. On the ground floor, an attractive conservatory area is available for small functions. **Rooms 14** (5 shower only). B&B about €60 pps, ss about €20. Closed Dec-Feb. **Restaurant**: An open fire, family antiques and flowers from the garden create a caring atmosphere in the restaurant and the Duke of Devonshire's fairytale castle looks magical from window tables when floodlit at night. Appetising home-cooked meals are based on local ingredients including, of course, fresh and smoked Blackwater salmon, along with home-produced honey and local cheeses like Knockanore, and service is friendly and helpful. **Seats 30.** D daily, L Sun only 1-3 pm. SC 10% sc. Bar Meals: 12-6.30 daily (L 1-2.30). Closed Dec-Mar. Amex, Diners, MasterCard, Visa. **Directions:** On the edge of Lismore town, from Cappoquin direction. ◇

Lismore
CAFÉ/RESTAURANT/WINE BAR

Barça Wine Bar & Restaurant

Main Street Lismore Co Waterford **Tel: 058 53810**
Fax: 058 53806 Email: barcawine@eircom.net

The spirit of a wonderful old bar in Lismore lives on in the chic tapas bar and restaurant, Barça. The frontage has been discreetly changed but, once inside the door, it's wonderful to find that - while clearly contemporary, with wine bottles lining the walls and the mandatory leather high stools - the essentials are still there, and the soft pastel tones are gently reminiscent of the way things were. The front area offers tapas based on seasonal organic produce, preferably Irish; an 'in between area' behind the bar has armchairs and an open fire, and the restaurant is in two rooms towards the back of the building - opening onto a walled garden, with a deck and seating for fine weather. Simply decorated with some style, the restaurant has classy bare-topped tables, high-backed leather chairs and white walls hung with black and white photographs recording the changes to this fine old building. Tapas can be ordered here as a larger appetiser portion, overlapping with a restaurant menu that offers a concise choice of main courses, usually including at least one tempting vegetarian option. There have been changes of personnel recently, but Barça is an attractive spot with friendly service and well worth a visit when you're in Lismore. Not suitable for children after 7pm. **Seats 40** (outdoor seating, 20). Restaurant reservations required. Toilets wheelchair accessible. L Thu-Sat, 12.30-2.30 (Set L €10). D Thu-Sat, 6-10 (Set D €30), Open all day Sun (12.30-8); also A la carte. Closed Mon, Tue, Wed; Jan. MasterCard, Visa, Laser. **Directions:** At the east end of the main street in Lismore. ◇

Lismore
PUB

Eamonn's Place

Lismore Co Waterford
Tel: 058 54025

Friendly and obliging staff, attractive surroundings with lots of polished wood panelling and plenty of tables with comfortable seating for the enjoyment of well-cooked and reasonably-priced bar food - there are the qualities that draw people to Eamonn Walshe's hospitable and family-friendly pub in the centre of Lismore. menus offer a range of popular dishes - deep-fried mushrooms in garlic butter, steaks, scampi and desserts like home-made lemon meringue pie and apple pie with cream - and there are daily specials on a board. It is well-cooked, substantial food and, with little on the menu much over €15, very good value too. A lovely well-planted walled garden at the back adds an unexpected dimension, providing a sheltered place to eat out or enjoy a drink in fine weather. L daily, 12.30-3; bar snacks until 5/6pm. Closed on Wed. **Directions:** Centre of Lismore.

Lismore Area

The Glencairn Inn & Pastis Bistro

RESTAURANT WITH ROOMS

Glencairn Lismore Co Waterford
Tel: 058 56232 Fax: 058 56232
Email: info@glencairninn.com Web: www.glencairninn.com

Husband-and-wife team Stéphane and Fiona Tricot, previously of Barça in Lismore, have now fulfilled a dream by buying the nearby Glencairn Inn, and the restaurant which has been renamed Pastis French Bistro has quickly earned a following. Three delightful old-world dining rooms ooze charm and cosiness and, just off the small bar, there is an alcove for intimate dining for four. Fiona manages front-of-house while Stéphane continues to produce wonderful food, offering menus with six choices on each course and a daily special on the board and using plenty of local produce: crabmeat salad with cumin avocado emulsion makes an unusual starter, Ardsallagh goat's cheese fritters have crunchy pine nuts added to give a rich texture and scallops with asparagus & sun-dried tomatoes are popular as a starter, and also available as a main course when they're plentiful. Typical main course might include grilled swordfish with carmelised onions (setting off the meaty fish to perfection) or pan-fried hake with lavender sauce, asparagus and sundried tomato. Meat lovers, on the other hand, will find that slow-roasted shank of lamb with star anise and thyme is rich and satisfying. To finish, a classic crème brulee might be flavoured with lavender in summer, and other choices may include mango sorbet with fresh fruit, caramelised lemon tart with fresh raspberries or summer berries in red wine and vanilla jus and Irish farmhouse cheeses like Cashel Blue, Ardrahan and Smoked Gubeen, offered with vintage port. On a sensibly limited wine list, the old world is represented by France, Spain and Italy and the new by Chile and Australia; wines by the glass include a delicious Italian Prosecco. Service is excellent, with friendly and knowledgeable staff - a rare treat. **Accommodation:** Upstairs there are four delightful en-suite rooms, all no smoking (€60 pps, ss €20). Not suitable for children under 12. **Seats 40.** D Tue-Sun 6.30-8.30 (to 9.30 Fri/Sat), à la carte; house wine about €18; SC disc. Closed Mon, Tue off season (Oct-Apr), Christmas period & Jan. MasterCard, Visa, Laser, Switch. **Directions:** 3.5km (2 m) from Lismore off N72 Lismore/Tallow Road.

Millstreet

The Castle Country House

FARMHOUSE/CASTLE/HISTORIC HOUSE

Millstreet Dungarvan Co Waterford
Tel: 058 68049
Email: castlefm@iol.ie Web: www.castlecountryhouse.com

Set in 1.5 acres of recently landscaped gardens overlooking the River Finisk, the Nugent family's unusual and wonderfully hospitable farmhouse is in the 18th century wing of a 16th century castle. Although most of the house seems quite normal inside, it blends into the original building in places - so, for example, the dining room has walls five feet deep and an original castle archway. Spacious, comfortably appointed rooms have king size beds, television, tea/coffee facilities and neat shower rooms; (there is also a full bathroom available for any guest who prefers a bath). Meticulous housekeeping, a very pleasant guests' sitting room and fresh flowers everywhere all add up to a very appealing farmhouse indeed, and Joan uses their own produce - fruit, vegetables, meats and herbs - in her cooking. Excellent breakfasts, also dinner by arrangement: menus change daily and offer a choice; typical dishes might include blue cheese & onion tart with mixed leaves & soured cream; baked fillet of Helvick salmon with hollandaise sauce and home-grown apple tart with vanilla ice cream; there's also a choice of half a dozen wines. Children welcome (under 5 free in parents' room, cot available without charge). Pets permitted by arrangement. Garden, walking, fishing. **Rooms 5** (all en-suite, shower only and no smoking). B&B €50pps, ss €20. Dining Room Seats 20 (+5 outside); Residents D 7pm €30, House wine €16. Closed 1 Nov-31 Mar. MasterCard, Visa. **Directions:** Off N25 on R671.

Tallowbridge

The Brideview Bar & Restaurant

RESTAURANT/PUB

Tallowbridge Tallow Co Waterford
Tel: 058 56522 Fax: 058 56729

This attractive roadside bar and restaurant is beautifully located just outside Tallow, beside an old stone bridge over the River Bride and with parking space in a yard beside the pub. Recent extensions and renovations have kept some character in the older bar - which is along the road side of the building and has an open fire - while creating a fine informal dining space with large windows overlooking the river and a large garden and apple orchard (which is well away from the road, with picnic tables set up for sunny days. Menus are interesting and change monthly (plus daily blackboard specials); the emphasis is on providing home-cooked food and good value. A good range of home-cooked bar food is available all day - home-made soups with freshly-baked bread, marinated warm chicken salad, and crispy fried lemon sole are typical. Evening menus offer a wider choice and some 'grander' dishes (the steaks have a great reputation), and a rather unexpected speciality is lobster, which is very keenly priced (€29.95 for a lobster 11/4-11/2lb in weight);oysters are also offered, and other fresh fish daily according to availability. Other less usual local foods that you might find here are pigeon and venison, in season. A new after dinner lounge with an open fire has recently been added, allowing a more comfortable dining experience. This a useful place to know about, especially if you are touring or walking in the area. Children welcome. Food available Mon-Sat, 12.30-9. (restaurant more limited hours), Sun L&D, 12.30-2.30pm and 5.30-8.30pm Closed 25-28 Dec & Good Fri. Amex, MasterCard, Visa, Laser. **Directions:** Near Tallow on N72; 12 miles east of Fermoy - 3 from Lismore.

Touraneena
FARMHOUSE

Sliabh gCua Farmhouse

Touraneena Ballinamult Dungarvan Co Waterford
Tel: 058 47120 Email: breedacullinan@sliabhgcua.com
Web: www.sliabhgcua.com

Breeda Cullinan's lovely creeper-clad farmhouse is in a beautiful area for lovers of the rural life; it is not as old or as large as it looks, but it was built with the classical proportions that create handsome, light-filled rooms, and has a happy atmosphere. Bedrooms, individually furnished and decorated with great care by Breeda, are very comfortable and have tea/coffee making facilities - and wholesome food, based on fresh farm produce, is served in a lovely dining room overlooking the garden: there are home-made cereals, fruit salads, freshly baked breads, local cheeses and hot cooked dishes to set guests up for the day. Children welcome (under 3 free in parents' room, cot available without charge, baby sitting arranged, playground). Walking; garden. **Rooms 4** (all en-suite, shower-only & no smoking). B&B €40 pps, ss €5. Closed Nov-Mar. **Directions:** 16km off the N25, signposted on main Dungarvan- Clonmel Road(R672).

Tramore
RESTAURANT WITH ROOMS

Coast Restaurant & Townhouse

Upper Branch Road Tramore Co Waterford
Tel: 051 393646 Fax: 051 393647
Email: coastrestaurant@eircom.net Web: www.coast.ie

Turlough McNamaras fine contemporary restaurant has a lovely bar area for pre-dinner drinks and the chic, smartly appointed dining room overlooking Tramore also has a fine terrace for outside dining. A la carte menus offer a well-balanced choice, with a strong emphasis on seafood; the cooking style is modern international - seen in starters like chorizo with buffalo mozzarella & sundried tomato risotto, for example; Angus beef fillet comes in an updated classic style, with béarnaise sauce and shoe string potatoes, and vegetarian choices are persuasive. Finish with a luscious dessert - another retro inspiration like baked Alaska, perhaps - and a delicious Illy coffee. Cooking is accomplished, flavours well-judged and presentation appealing - small wonder that this gem of a restaurant has earned a loyal following. An interesting if rather pricey wine list includes a house selection of half a dozen wines around €20. Early dinner and Sunday lunch offer outstanding value. **Seats 45** (private room 15, outdoor seating 30). Children welcome. Toilets wheelchair accessible). D Tue-Sat 6.30-10, L Sun only, 1-3. Early D €30 (Tue-Fri, 6.30-7), Sun L €28, otherwise à la carte. Closed Mon & D Sun, all Jan, 2 weeks Feb. **Accommodation:** Four stylish and beautifully appointed rooms are offered - as elsewhere at Coast, a judicious mixture of ultra modern and antique furnishings all add up to a very special atmosphere. **Rooms 4** (2 junior suites, 2 executive, 2 shower only, all no smoking). Children welcome (cots available at no charge, baby sitting arranged). No pets. B&B €65 pps, ss €25. Closed Jan, 2 weeks Feb. Amex, MasterCard, Visa, Laser. **Directions:** From Waterford direction: right up a hill after main roundabout, first right, restaurant is on the left.

Tramore
RESTAURANT/PUB

Rockett's of The Metal Man

Heathfield House Newtown Tramore Co Waterford
Tel: 051 381496 Fax: 051 390263
Email: rockettsofthemetalman@eircom.net

Open fires and a friendly, welcoming atmosphere will always draw you into this unusual pub but it's the speciality of the house, Crubeens (pig's trotters) which has earned it fame throughout the land. Crubeens (cruibíns) were once the staple bar food in pubs everywhere in Ireland but, as they've been supplanted by crisps, peanuts and lasagne & chips, Rockett's is one of the few places to keep up the old tradition. Two bars are set up with tables for the comfortable consumption of these porcine treats, served with cabbage and colcannon. Other traditional foods like boiled bacon & cabbage, spare ribs, colcannon and apple pie are also very much on the menu at Rockett's - and all prepared freshly. **Seats 100.** Air conditioning. Food served daily 12-8.30 (Sun to 9). A phone call is advised to check times off-season. Closed 25 Dec & Good Fri. MasterCard, Visa, Laser. **Directions:** From Waterford, straight through Tramore, 1.5km (one mile) far side.

Tramore area

Kiely's Restaurant

Ⓝ RESTAURANT

above Mother MacHugh's Pub Fenor Nr Tramore Co Waterford
Tel: 051 391 562

On the scenic Youghal-Waterford coastal route just west of Tramore, you'll find Kiely's Restaurant on the first floor, over Mother MacHughes pub in Fenor village. There's a spacious reception area with an open fireplace featuring a local artist's mosaic depiction of the unfinished Gaudi Cathedral in Barcelona - a talking point amongst guests, who like to take their coffee here beside the fire. The lofty restaurant has dark beams, divisions made of railings from old church pews and work by local artists on the walls it's a pleasing space with a tranquil coffee and cream colour scheme and plenty of fresh air and natural light from skylight windows. Welcoming staff bring guests to tables smartly set up with crisp white linen and promptly present menus offering a well-balanced choice of about 10 dishes on each course. You could start with a wholesome chowder and good homemade brown bread, perhaps, or delicious baked mushrooms stuffed with truffle and served with a crisp side salad, followed typically by chicken filled with mozzarella in a light and creamy sauce, or a perfectly cooked sirloin steak with a good peppery sauce, both served with lovely crisp side vegetables. Desserts match up to all the rest, and service is a highlight - friendly and efficient, with staff taking time to smile and enjoy the banter with guests. **Seats 45.** Open D, Tue-Sun. ◇

Waterford

33 The Mall

Ⓝ RESTAURANT

33 The Mall Waterford Co Waterford
Tel: 051 859 823

This four storey restaurant in the centre of Waterford is in a stunning restored Georgian bow-front building, with the ground floor given over to a bar/reception area and - like the restaurant floors - decorated with an interesting mixture of antiques and modern furnishings and artwork. Unadorned bow windows lend great style to the beautiful plain Georgian rooms, a fitting setting for food which is unfussily presented and depends on the excellence of raw materials and culinary skills for its success: choices lean towards the familiar - tomato & basil soup, Caesar salad, dressed crab, wild mushroom risotto, confit of duck with roast garlic mash, grilled sole on the bone are all typical - and are none the worse for that. On the down side, bread and side dishes all have to be ordered separately - and no reservations are accepted, so get there early to be sure of a table. **Seats 70** (private room, 20); Children welcome; D daily 5.30-11, L Sun only 12-6. House wine from €16. MasterCard, Visa, Laser. ◇

Waterford

Athenaeum House Hotel

Ⓝ HOTEL/RESTAURANT

Christendom Waterford Co Waterford
Tel: 051 833 999 Fax: 051 833 977
Email: info@athenaeumhousehotel.com Web: www.athenaeumhousehotel.com

Guests feel very much at home in this recently opened boutique hotel, which is set amidst 10 acres of parkland overlooking the River Suir, just outside Waterford city - and owner-managed by Stan Power, a previous General Manager of Mount Juliet House in County Kilkenny, and his wife Mailo. Chic contemporary decor, luxurious suites and deluxe rooms and a welcome emphasis on service are the characteristics that will appeal most to discerning travellers. The restaurants of Waterford city are just a short taxi ride away, or you can dine in-house at the hotel's Zaks Restaurant. **Rooms 28.** B&B from €90. **Seats 65** (private room, 40; also outdoor area, 20). Toilets accessible by wheelchair; Live Music Sat pm. Food served all day 7.30-9.30; D Tue-Sun (7- 9 on Sun), Early Bird D €23 (5.30-7.30), also a la carte; L Sun, 12.30-3; Set Sun L €21. House Wine from €22. Rest closed Mon, House closed 25-27 Dec. **Directions:** Leaving railway station on N25 in the direction of Wexford, take the first right after the traffic lights on to Abbey Road, half a mile later take the first right. ◇

Waterford

Bodéga!

RESTAURANT

54 John St. Waterford Co Waterford **Tel: 051 844 177**
Fax: 051 384 868 Email: cormac_cronin@hotmail.com

With its warm Mediterranean colours, this place would bring the sun out on the darkest of days: interesting artwork, pine tables, covered with the occasional oilcloth, a mix'n'match collection of seating. A written menu offers everything from lunchtime dishes like soup of the day and real croque monsieur (toasted ham sandwich with Conté cheese & béchamel sauce, and salad) to Bodega fish pie and steaks (sirloin with sautéed potatoes) to dinner specialities such as roast guinea fowl stuffed with venison and wild mushrooms, and lapin à la bière, with paysanne potatoes ...There are also blackboard specials, which are likely to be the best bet - and friendly staff are well-informed to advise. At lunch time the place fills up with young people, some with children - who are made especially welcome - and there are lots of regulars. Dinner is a little more structured - and the prices heat up a bit too, with main courses like steaks (fillet/sirloin) clocking in at over EUR20, whereas a lunchtime dish is half that, but it's still good value. Seats 55 (private room 20). L & D Mon-Sat, 12-5pm & 5-10.30pm, D Mon-Sat. A la carte. House wines about EUR19. SC discretionary. Closed Sun (except bank hol w/ends), bank hol Mons. Amex, MasterCard, Visa, Laser. Directions: A few doors down from the Applemarket, in city centre.

Waterford
GUESTHOUSE

Diamond Hill Country House

Slieverue Waterford Co Waterford
Tel: 051 832 855 Fax: 051 832 254
Email: info@stayatdiamondhill.com Web: www.stayatdiamondhill.com

The Smith-Lehane family's long-established and moderately-priced guesthouse just outside Waterford city is set in one and a half acres of landscaped gardens; it would make a good base for exploring the area, and will appeal to anyone who wants to be quietly located yet handy to the city. The house has recently been completely refurbished and most of the well-equipped bedrooms have king-size beds as well as power showers and all the other usual amenities (phone, TV, tea/coffee facilities etc). With ten courses, including Mount Juliet, within half an hour's drive it's ideal for golfing breaks; other sporting activities nearby include fishing and horse riding. **Rooms 17** (14 shower only, all no smoking). Children welcome (under 5s free in parents' room, cot available without charge). No pets. Gardens. B&B about €40, ss €5. Closed Dec. MasterCard, Visa, Laser. **Directions:** Off N25 - 0.5 miles outside Waterford.

Waterford
FARMHOUSE

Foxmount Country House

Passage East Road Waterford Co Waterford
Tel: 051 874 308 Fax: 051 854 906
Email: Info@foxmountcountryhouse.com Web: www.foxmountcountryhouse.com

For those who prefer a country house atmosphere, rather than an hotel, the Kent family's 17th century home on the edge of Waterford city is a haven of peace and tranquillity. The house is lovely, with classically proportioned reception rooms, and accommodation in five very different rooms which are all thoughtfully, and very comfortably, furnished - but, as peace and relaxation are the aim at Foxmount, don't expect phones or TVs in bedrooms, or a very early breakfast. However, Margaret Kent is a great cook and she loves baking, as guests quickly discover when offered afternoon tea in the drawing room - or in the morning, when freshly-baked breads are presented at breakfast. No evening meals are offered, but the restaurants of Waterford and Cheekpoint are quite close - and guests are welcome to bring their own wine and enjoy a glass at the log fire before going out for dinner. Children welcome (under 2s free in parent' room, cot available without charge). No pets. Garden. **Rooms 5** (all with en-suite or private bathrooms, all no-smoking, 1 family room). B&B €55 pps, ss€10. Closed Nov-mid Mar. No Credit Cards. **No Credit Cards. Directions:** From Waterford city, take Dunmore Road - after 4 km, take Passage East road for 1 mile.

Waterford
PUB

The Gingerman

6/7 Arundel Lane Waterford Co Waterford
Tel: 051 879 522 Fax: 051 879 522

In the old Norman area of the city, this hospitable pub is in a pedestrianised lane just off Broad Street. It can be very busy but, at quieter times it's a pleasant place, with welcoming open fires in several bars - and this lovely ambience together with pleasant staff, a good-humoured hands-on owner and a commitment to serving wholesome food has earned The Gingerman a loyal local following. A useful place to drop into for a drink, a cuppa, or a casual bite to eat. Parking in nearby multi-storey carpark. Open 10am-11.30pm. Food served Mon-Sat, 12-6. No food on Sun. Closed 25 Dec, Good Fri. Amex, Diners, MasterCard, Visa, Laser. **Directions:** Off John Roberts Square.

Waterford
HOTEL

Granville Hotel

The Quay Waterford Co Waterford **Tel: 051 305 555** Fax: 051 305 566
Email: stay@granville-hotel.ie Web: www.granville-hotel.ie

One of the country's oldest hotels, this much-loved quayside establishment in the centre of Waterford has many historical connections with Bianconi, for example, who established Ireland's earliest transport system, and also Charles Stuart Parnell, who made many a rousing speech here. Since 1979, it's been owner-run by the Cusack family, who have overseen significant restoration and major refurbishment. It's a large hotel bigger than it looks perhaps with fine public areas and well-appointed bedrooms (all with well-designed bathrooms, with both bath and shower). This is a good choice for business guests and would also make a comfortable base for touring the area or participating in the many activities available locally, including boating, fishing, golf, walking and horse riding. Off season value breaks available. Conference/banqueting (200). Parking nearby. Children welcome (under 3s free in parents' room; cots available without charge). No pets. **Rooms 98** (3 junior suites, 60 executive rooms, 90 no-smoking). Lift. B&B about €80 pps, ss €35 (winter rate from about €55pps, ss €20). Meals: D daily, L Sun-Fri (except bank hol Mons); bar meals 10.30-6 daily. Closed 25-27 Dec. Amex, Diners, MasterCard, Visa. **Directions:** In city centre, on the quays opposite Clock Tower. ◇

Waterford

Henry Downes

PUB

8-10 Thomas St. Waterford Co Waterford **Tel: 051 874 118**

Established in 1759, and in the same (eccentric) family for six generations, John de Bromhead's unusual pub is one of the few remaining houses to bottle its own whiskey. Although not the easiest of places to find, once visited it certainly will not be forgotten. Large, dark and cavernous with a squash court on the premises as well as the more predictable billiards and snooker it consists of a series of bars of differing character, each with its own particular following. It achieves with natural grace what so-called Irish theme pubs would dearly love to capture, and friendly, humorous bar staff enjoy filling customers in on the pub's proud history and will gladly sell you a bottle of Henry Downes No.9 to take away. Wine about €10 (to drink in pub). Not suitable for children. Open from 4.30pm to normal closing time. No food. Closed 25 Dec & Good Fri. **No Credit Cards. Directions:** Second right after Bridge Hotel, halfway up Thomas Street on right.

Waterford

L'Atmosphère

Ⓝ RESTAURANT

19 Henrietta Street Waterford Co Waterford **Tel: 051 858 426**
Email: latmosphererestaurant@hotmail.com
Web: www.restaurant-latmosphere.com

The closely packed tables in Arnaud Mary and Patrice Garreau's informal French restaurant (in the former Goose's Barbecue premises) don't matter too much - the décor is basic, with pine tables, paper napkins, and menus that double as paper mats, and it all adds up to a cheerful bistro atmosphere. Three menus are offered, an early bird, the day's specials and an à la carte. The early dinner menu (5.30 to 7) is very good value at €20 this even includes a glass of house wine, which is unusually generous. Expect typical French cooking: for starters there are good soups (fish, perhaps) and excellent breads (Arnaud has a French Bakery in the town), then maybe chicken liver terrine or a good hearty salad (warm potato, beet root and cheese, wrapped in Serrano ham and well dressed). Main courses could include a classic beef bourguignon - the meat tender but still juicy, the vegetables with a little bite - and, perhaps, a fish such as red mullet, perfectly cooked and served with a good risotto and provençal vegetables, and a shared side dish of boulangère potatoes. Finish, perhaps with a classic apple flan. Menus also offer luxurious items like foie gras, or lobster, but the same philsophy applies. With delicious, keenly priced, food and friendly service from French and Irish waiting staff, the whole impression is of eating in a good French bistro, rare today even in France. **Seats 48;** air conditioning; children welcome; Open for L&D Mon-Fri; D only Sat; early D €20, 5.30-7; set D €25/33, 2/3 course; House wine €18, Closed Sat L, Sun and Bank Hol Mons. MasterCard, Visa, Laser.

Waterford

La Bohème

Ⓝ RESTAURANT

2 George St Waterford Co Waterford
Tel: 051 875 645 Fax: 051 875 645

Eric Thèze, previously head chef at Faithlegg House Hotel, and his wife Christine opened their new restaurant in 2006, in the basement of one of Waterford's most prestigious buildings, the Chamber of Commerce. The cellar has been beautifully converted, with the original high arched ceilings retained but all painted white; it seems very bright and there are plenty of flowers and some nicely restrained art on the walls. It is a very French restaurant - nearly all of the staff are French, and the welcome is friendly but formal as you are shown to the bar for your aperitif - a perfect, extremely pale and chilled Kir, perhaps, served with amuse gueules such as a tiny glass of carrot mousse with parmesan and crunchy nuts, or a tiny square of goats cheese and broccoli roulade. The menu, which is not overlong but offers plenty of choice, changes seasonally and is modern classic French: good fish choices, lamb and beef, with daily specials and the soup pinned on the menu. Rather small white-clothed tables set with good glasses, heavy silver and a flower on each, are well separated to give a nice sense of privacy. The house speciality is lobster (per 100g; grilled, flamed in Pastis and served with a beurre blanc sauce), so if that is your choice you might start lightly, with a delicately flavoured broccoli & blue cheese soup (€8.50), along with a fine selection of home made breads. Or, if your main course selection is lighter - monkfish with a poelle of forest mushrooms and sweet potatoes, for example, you might begin with luxurious, perfectly pink foie gras of duck (€13), served with caramel apples and raspberries. The lobster, average weight 500g, is priced at €8 per 100g (ie about €40, but it is a real treat: the tail is grilled and smothered in beurre blanc, the claws are not grilled but served separately with a little salad a clever idea, as the delicate claws are not improved by strong grilling. Pleasingly, for Irish tastes, main courses are accompanied by some good mashed potatoes and vegetables. Finish with classic desserts - a dark, rich chocolate & lemon tart in crisp pastry with a mango sorbet, perhaps - or an excellent all French cheese board, served with plenty of crackers. Good wines, a little on the pricey side, and very good service. This is a restaurant that is serious about its food something Waterford city has needed badly since the excellent Dwyers closed a couple of years ago and, although expensive, it is worth it. Stair lift. Not suitable for children under 10 years. **Seats 70** (private room, 10 & 20); air conditioning; reservations required; D Mon-Sat (& Bank Hol Sun), 5.30-10pm; Early D €28, 5.30-7 Mon-Fri; gourmet menu €70; house wine from €26; SC 10% on groups 6+. Closed Sun (except Bank Hols). MasterCard, Visa, Laser. **Directions:** Across from Bank Bar on O'Connell Street.

Waterford

La Palma on the Mall

N RESTAURANT

20 The Mall Waterford Co Waterford **Tel: 051 879 823**
Fax: 051 850 877 Email: info@lapalma.ie Web: www.lapalma.ie

Claudio, Rachel and Dario Cavilieri's popular Italian restaurant is in a graceful Georgian building on Waterford's Mall. The reception is upstairs in a tall navy and beige drawing room, now working as a cocktail bar, where guests are greeted and seated, and offered a drink while you look at the menu. As well as an A La Carte, there's a very good value mid week "Treat" menu available. The restaurant is downstairs in a series of pleasant high-ceilinged Georgian rooms- the décor is neutral beiges and olives but a good marble fireplace has a bust of Verdi, a reminder that you are in an Italian restaurant across the road from Theatre Royal. Meals begin with a little amuse bouche (roast vegetables in a roll of pancake, perhaps) and a choice of breads including an excellent Italian country loaf, baked by the house. Service is very pleasant and attentive, and the wine waiter happy to give a good recommendation for the perfect bottle to accompany your meal. Starters might include a rustic, hearty bruschetta of garlic tomatoes and mozzerella, or perhaps a delicious dish of mushrooms in a creamy garlic and Gorgonzola sauce. A main course of confit of Duck on black olive mash works very well, and vegetarian dishes may include a main course of a spinach and tomato tagliatelle. For dessert you might try a Guinness & orange Ice cream in a brandy snap basket (home made and good), or a classic a Tiramisu. Good coffee and espresso to finish, and an agreeably reasonable bill. [The Old Palma further down the street is now called the Espresso and serves pizzas and pasta to families and the younger crowd.] Children welcome; toilets wheelchair accessible. **Seats 75** (private room, 35, outdoors, 10); L & D Mon-Sat, 12.30-2.30pm & 5.30-10.30pm; early D €25 5.30-7pm Mon-Sat; house wine from €19. Closed Sun and 25-26 Dec. Amex, Diners, MasterCard, Visa, Laser. **Directions:** In city centre opposite Bishop's palace & Theatre Royal.

Waterford

Tower Hotel Waterford

HOTEL

The Mall Waterford Co Waterford **Tel: 051 875 801** Fax: 051 870 129
Email: reservations@thw.ie Web: www.towerhotelwaterford.com

féile bia A central location, within easy walking distance of everything in the city, ample secure private parking, large conference/banqueting capacity and excellent on-site leisure facilities are major attractions at this big hotel. Considerable investment over the last few years has seen an improvement in standards throughout the hotel: a smart bistro, a carvery restaurant and a state of the art conference centre are all quite recent additions and the lobby and reception area have been renovated. Major refurbishment of bedrooms has also taken place but some bedrooms may not yet have been completed, so it is worth checking on this when making a reservation; there would be a big difference between old and new rooms. Conference/banqueting facilities (450/350). Leisure Centre, indoor swimming pool. Children welcome (cots available free of charge). Own parking. No pets. **Rooms 136** (3 suites, 6 junior suites, 15 executive, 38 no smoking, 3 for disabled). Lift. B&B from €66 pps, ss €20. Closed 24-26 Dec. Amex, Diners, MasterCard, Visa, Laser, Switch. **Directions:** Waterford city centre.

Waterford

Waterford Castle Hotel & Golf Club

HOTEL/RESTAURANT

The Island Ballinakill Waterford Co Waterford
Tel: 051 878 203 Fax: 051 879 316
Email: info@waterfordcastle.com Web: www.waterfordcastle.com

féile bia This beautiful hotel dates back to the 15th century, and is uniquely situated on its own 310 acre wooded island (complete with 18-hole golf course), reached by a private ferry. The hotel combines the elegance of earlier times with modern comfort, service and convenience - and the location is uniquely serene - its quietness (and the golf facility for off-duty relaxation) makes the castle a good venue for small conferences and business meetings, but it is also a highly romantic location and perfect for small weddings. All guest rooms have recently been refurbished and, although they inevitably vary in size and outlook, all are very comfortably furnished in a luxurious country house style. There are plans to extend the accommodation and add a health spa but, at the time of going to press, permissions have not yet been granted. Conference/banqueting (30/80). Golf, archery, clay pigeon shooting, fishing, tennis, walking, gardens. Pool table. Children welcome (under 4 free in parents' room; cots available; bay sitting arranged). **Rooms 19** (5 suites, 3 junior suites, 2 family, 4 ground floor, all no smoking). Lift. 24 hr room service. Turndown service. B&B €187.50pps, ss €107.50. Closed Jan. **Munster Room:** This beautiful dining room is appointed to the highest standard and head chef Michael Quinn and a fine kitchen brigade can be relied on to provide the food to match: menus are peppered with luxurious ingredients like lobster, foie gras, scallops, prawns, black sole, aged Irish beef and game, such as wild Irish venison; local produce is used as much as possible, including organic vegetables, and the cooking, in a modern classical style, is excellent. A set dinner menu is offered, but considerately priced by course, allowing for a semi à la carte selection. Children welcome. **Seats 60.** D daily, 7-9 (to 8.30 Sun), L Sun only (12.30-2); Set D €58, à la carte and vegetarian menu also available; Set Sun L €30. House wines €28. SC 10%. Pianist at dinner. Amex, Diners, MasterCard, Visa, Laser. **Directions:** Outskirts of Waterford City just off Dunmore East road.

Waterford
RESTAURANT

The Wine Vault

High Street Waterford Co Waterford
Tel: 051 853 444 Fax: 051 853 784
Email: ddfw@eircom.net Web: www.waterfordwinevault.com

féile bia Situated in the medieval part of the city, in an 18th century bonded warehouse with the remains of a 15th century tower house, David Dennison's informal little wine bar and restaurant includes a vaulted wine merchant's premises, and has great atmosphere. There have been some changes over the last year or two - a cheerful laminated menu was introduced at one stage, offering 'popular' dishes with pizzas and grills taking centre stage but those who had come to love the fresh 'daily' feel of the old menus were less than delighted. However, things have come more or less full circle now, as a new range of menus now offers a combination of the simple classic dishes enjoyed by the original clientele (West Cork mussels in white wine, garlic & cream sauce, chicken liver parfait with Melba toast...) and modern dishes like chicken satay with basmati rice, red onion salad and peanut sauce - and a list of daily specials probably offers the best choices.. Sadly the previous policy of naming artisan products and suppliers does not seem to have been revived, but at least menus are generally moving back on course. And, of course, you can rely on wine-man David to ensure a great choice of bottles for every conceivable occasion; informative and readable, this extensive list is outstanding by any standards. Toilets wheelchair accessible. Children welcome. **Seats 50** (private room 20). L& D Mon-Sat, 12.30-2.30 & 5-10.30. Early D €22 (5-7.30 only), otherwise a la carte. House wines (26) €18-€22. sc discretionary. Closed Sun (except bank hol weekends), 25 Dec, Good Fri. Amex, MasterCard, Visa, Laser. **Directions:** Left to High Street, after City Square car park.

Waterford Area
HOTEL

Faithlegg House Hotel

Faithlegg Co Waterford **Tel: 051 382 000** Fax: 051 382 010
Email: reservations@fhh.ie Web: www.faithlegg.com

féile bia Set in wooded landscape with magnificent views over its own golf course and the Suir estuary, this lovely 18th century house has a splendid Waterford Crystal chandelier to set the tone in the foyer, and public areas are elegant throughout. Accommodation, in the old house and a discreetly positioned new wing, is furnished to a high standard; the large, graciously proportioned rooms and suites in the old house are really lovely, while those in the new wing are more practical. (Self-catering accommodation is also offered in the grounds.) Aside from golf, the range of activities available on site includes a swimming pool, and numerous health and beauty treatments. There is a choice of restaurants nearby (Waterford city, or Cheekpoint, are each only a few minutes' drive), and the hotel's fine dining restaurant, The Roseville Rooms, offers classical cuisine. **Rooms 82.** B&B from €95 pps. **Roseville Rooms:** The bar is comfortably furnished in a clubby style - a good place to have an aperitif and look at the menu; orders may be taken here and you will be called through when your table is ready. Menus change daily, which is ideal for residents staying for several nights, and offers a balanced choice of about four on each course. The restaurant is shared between two lovely classical, formally appointed dining rooms and it is a very pleasant place to enjoy an evening meal. **Seats 90** (private room 40). Not suitable for children after 8.30pm. D daily, 6.30-9.30; L Sun only, 12.30-2.30. Set D €48, Set Sun L €28. House wines from €18. Amex, MasterCard, Visa, Laser. **Directions:** Off Dunmore East Road 6 miles outside Waterford city.

COUNTY WESTMEATH

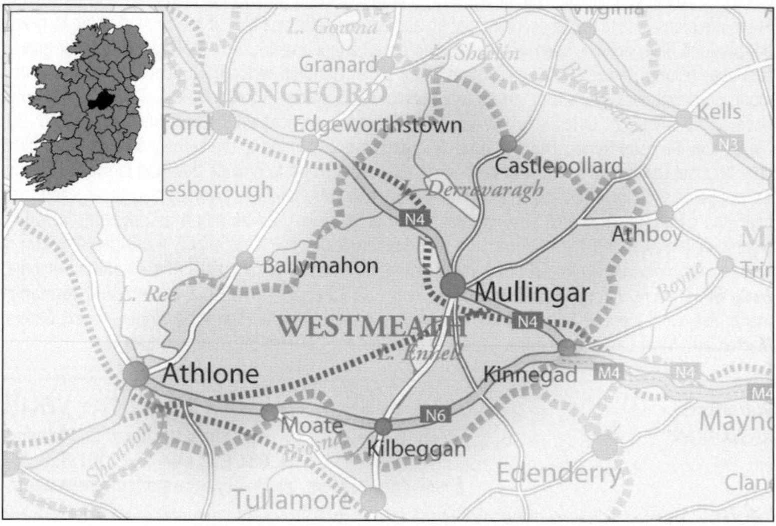

As its name suggests, in the distant past Westmeath tended to be ruled by whoever held Meath, though at times it was the other way around. Be that as it may, Westmeath today is a county so cheerfully and successfully developing its own identity that perhaps they should find a completely new name for the place. For this is somewhere that makes the very best of what it has to hand.

Its highest "peak" is only the modest Mullaghmeen of 258 m, 10 kilometres north of Castlepollard. But this is in an area where hills of ordinary height have impressive shapes which make them appear like miniature mountains around the spectacularly beautiful Lough Derravaragh, famed for its association with the legend of the Children of Lir, who were turned into swans by their wicked step-mother Aoife, and remained as swans for 900 years until saved by the coming of Christianity.

Westmeath abounds in lakes to complement Derravaragh, such as the handsome expanses of Lough Owel and Lough Ennell on either side of the fine county town of Mullingar, where life has been made even more watery in recent years with continuing work to restore the Royal Canal, which loops through town on its way from Dublin to the north Shannon.

Meanwhile, Athlone to the west is confidently developing as one of Ireland's liveliest river towns, its Shannonside prosperity based on its riverside location, and a useful manufacturing mixture of electronics, pharmaceuticals and the healthcare industry. Following a period of riverside development, Athlone's waterfront in 2005 is an entertaining mixture of old and new, with the traditional quayside area below the bridge on the west bank now complemented by impressive modern facilities above the bridge along the eastern shore.

Despite such modern trends, this remains a very rural place - immediately south of the town, you can hear the haunting call of the corncrake coming across the callows (water meadows). Yet Athlone itself has a real buzz, particularly in the compact left bank area around the old castle. And north of it, there's Lough Ree in all its glory, wonderful for boating in an area where, near the delightful village of Glasson, the Goldsmith country verges towards County Longford, and they have a monument to mark what some enthusiasts reckon to be the true geographical centre of all Ireland. You really can't get more utterly rural than that.

Local Attractions and Information

Athlone, All Ireland Amateur Drama Festival (May)	090 647 3358
Athlone, Athlone Castle Visitor Centre	090 649 2912
Athlone, River Festivals	090 649 4981
Athlone, Tourism Information	090 649 4630
Ballykeeran, MV Goldsmith Lake & River Cruises	090 648 5163
Castlepollard, Tullynally Castle & Gardens	044 49060
Clonmellon, Ballinlough Castle Gardens	046 943 3135

Glasson, Glasson Rose Festival (August) 090 648 5677
Kilbegggan, Locke's Distillery Museum 057 933 2134
Kilbeggan, Race Course 057 933 2176
Moate, Dun na Si Folk Park 090 648 1183
Mullingar, Belvedere House, Gardens & Park 044 49060
Mullingar, Tourism Information 044 48761
Mullingar, Westmeath Tourism Council 044 48571

ATHLONE

This bustling, youthful centre town of Ireland has much of historical interest - and, although other towns along the mighty Shannon will no doubt be keen to mount a challenge, Athlone is presently the culinary capital of the inland waterways, with a cluster of good eating places in the town itself and surrounding area. Quality accommodation has been in shorter supply in the town than good restaurants in recent years, but that is all changing; **The Prince of Wales Hotel** (090 647 7246; www.theprinceofwales.ie) re-opened in the centre of the town, after a complete re-build; just out of town on the Roscommon side, the large beautifully located waterside **Hodson Bay Hotel** (090 644 2000)serves the area well by offering extensive conference and leisure facilities - and it gets bigger all the time. The town is gaining a reputation for good ethnic restaurants too: lovers of spicy foods should check out the authentic **Kin Khao Thai Restaurant** (090 649 8805) in Abbey Lane, and **Saagar Indian Restaurant** (090 647 0011) in Lloyds Street.

WWW.IRELAND-GUIDE.COM FOR THE BEST PLACES TO EAT, DRINK & STAY

The Left Bank Bistro

Athlone
☆RESTAURANT

Fry Place Athlone Co Westmeath
Tel: 090 649 4446 Fax: 090 649 4509
Email: info@leftbankbistro.com Web: www.leftbankbistro.com

Athlone makes a perfect break for anyone crossing the country, but it's much more than a handy stopover: it is now a destination town for discerning travellers. And, for many, it would be unthinkable to go through the area without a visit to Annie McNamara and Mary McCullough's elegant and spacious restaurant, where architectural salvage materials and interesting, subtle colours combine well with bare tables and paper napkins to convey an informal atmosphere that suits their lively food. Short, keenly-priced menus - plus specials chalked up on a blackboard - offer a wide range of delicious-sounding dishes with a multi-cultural stamp which, together with carefully sourced ingredients and snappy cooking, make this the number one choice for an informal meal in Athlone. Wraps, bruschetta, focaccia and pasta are typical lunch time dishes - try the tandoori chicken on focaccia - and vegetables are always colourful and full of zing. Fresh fish has its own menu (oysters baked with sweet chilli & coriander butter, and chargrilled citrus marinated tuna steak with cherry tomato & basil salsa are typical), and vegetarians can choose between blackboard specials and dishes from the regular menu, including favourites like Left Bank Salad (a gorgeous mixture of good things, with a wedge of foccacia) and vegetable spring rolls. Dinner menus are more extensive and tend to be based on more expensive ingredients, but the style is similar and they also include attractive vegetarian choices; delicious desserts are all home made and, of course, there's a farmhouse cheese plate too. A concise, well-chosen wine list offers a fair choice half bottles and several champagnes. For the quality of food and cooking, not to mention the sheer style of the place, a meal here is always good value - especially the early dinner menu. * A range of speciality products is now sold at the Left Bank: salamis, pestos, house dressing, oils, olives, pastas, and coffee are just a few examples - and breads, dressings, chutneys and desserts from the restaurant too. **Seats 60.** Air conditioning. Toilets wheelchair accessible. Open Tue-Sat L 12-5 & D 5.30-9.30; Early bird D €25 (5.30-7.30), also à la carte; house wine €19. Closed Sun & Mon, bank hols & 10 days Christmas/New Year. Amex, MasterCard, Visa, Laser. **Directions:** Behind Athlone Castle, west side of the Shannon.

The Olive Grove Restaurant

Athlone
RESTAURANT

Bridge Street Custume Place Athlone Co Westmeath **Tel: 0902 76946**
Email: info@theolivegrove.ie Web: www.theolivegrove.ie

Garry Hughes and Gael Bradbury celebrate a decade in their charming restaurant in 2007, and it is very much a part of the Athlone dining scene - popular for its pleasant, informal atmosphere (seasoned with a good dash of style), excellent home-cooked food from noon until late (light food in the afternoon), good value and a great willingness to do anything which will ensure a good time being had by all. The cooking style is Mediterranean-influenced international and youthful as seen in starters such as traditional Greek salad and lunchtime pastas like prosciutto & ricotta tortellini; vegetarians have particularly good choice here on both lunch and the more ambitious evening menus although this is beef country and the speciality of the house has always been chargrilled steaks. The entire restaurant was refurbished recently, and more extensive new menus introduced - a kind of coming of age. Children welcome. Parking nearby. **Seats 50.** L &D Tue-Sun,12-4 & 5.30-10); à la carte (average main course about €10 (L); €18-20 (D); house wine €16.95, sc discretionary. Closed Mon, 24-28 Dec. Amex, MasterCard, Visa, Laser. **Directions:** Travelling from Dublin, take the left before the bridge in Athlone town centre.◇

Athlone
HOTEL

Radisson SAS Hotel Athlone

Northgate Street Athlone Co Westmeath
Tel: 090 644 2600 Fax: 090 644 2655
Email: Info.Athlone@RadissonSAS.com Web: www.athlone.radissonsas.com

féile bia Magnificently located right on the river and bang in the middle of town, this hotel has impressive public areas and great style: an expansive foyer leads off to an informal split-level restaurant one side, conference and meeting rooms on the other - and opens out onto a huge riverside deck overlooking the marina and set up with teak furniture, umbrellas and patio heaters, which is a great asset to a town centre hotel. The usual Radisson attributes of contemporary chic apply throughout the hotel, and also a choice of room styles - Urban of you like warm tones, Ocean if you prefer a cooler, watery theme; all rooms have excellent facilities, including mini-bar, hospitality tray and broadband internet access - and some have great views of the River Shannon and the town. Athlone has character and is well-placed to explore an area of great interest. Golf nearby (golf breaks offered). Conference/banqueting (700/500). Children welcome (under 17 free in parents' room, cots available). No pets. **Rooms 124** (1 suite, 4 junior suites, 4 executive, 7 disabled). Lift. 24 hr room service. Turndown service offered. Conference/banqueting 750; business centre; video conferencing. Room rate about €175 (various packages and offers available). Meals available all day. Open all year. **Directions:** Town centre, east side of the bridge.◇

Athlone
RESTAURANT

Restaurant Le Chateau

St. Peter's Port The Docks Athlone Co Westmeath
Tel: 090 649 4517 Fax: 090 649 3040
Email: lechateau@eircom.net Web: www.lechateau.ie

féile bia Steven and Martina Linehan's quayside restaurant is in a converted Presbyterian Church, just west of the bridge, and it makes a two-storey restaurant of character which complements a well-earned reputation for good food and hospitality. Designed around the joint themes of church and river, the upstairs section has raised floors at each end, like the deck of a galleon, while the church theme is reflected in the windows notably an original "Star of David" at the back of the restaurant. Steven Linehan is a talented chef and, backed up by a well-trained staff, is providing a fine dining experience at formal meal times, notably their renowned Candlelight Dinners, when candles are used generously to create a relaxed, romantic atmosphere. Opening hours have been extensive in recent years, but the team works hard to maintain standards, and local produce is very much in evidence - notably Angus beef and rack of lamb; at its best, a meal at Le Chateau will be remembered for real flavour, attention to detail and professional service. The cooking style is modern, with some international influences - but there is a welcome sense that the chef is in control rather than the fashion. The early dinner and Sunday lunch menus are popular locally, and very good value. Children welcome. **Seats 100** (private room, 25, outdoor, 8) Air conditioning. Open 12.30-10 daily: L 12.30-3 (Sun to 5.30), D 5.30-10; Set 2/3 course L €13.50/17.50, Set Sun L €26.50, Early D €26.50 (5.30-6.30 only); also à la carte; house wines from €22.50; SC10%. Full bar. Closed Christmas. Amex, MasterCard, Visa, Laser. **Directions:** Heading west through Athlone,over Shannon and left at castle, left again and onto bank of Shannon.

Athlone
PUB

Sean's Bar

13 Main Street Athlone Co Westmeath **Tel: 090 6492358**

West of the river, in the interesting old town near the Norman castle (which has a particularly good visitors' centre for history and information on the area, including flora and fauna of the Shannon), Sean Fitzsimons' seriously historic bar lays claim to being the pub with the longest continuous use in Ireland all owners since 900 AD are on record. (It has actually been certified by the National Museum as the oldest pub in Britain and Ireland - and the all-Europe title is under investigation.) Dimly-lit, with a fine mahogany bar, mirrored shelving, open fire and an enormous settle bed, the bar has become popular with the local student population and is very handy for visitors cruising the Shannon (who have direct access to the river through the back bar and beer garden). The sloping floor is a particularly interesting feature, cleverly constructed to ensure that flood water drained back down to the river as the waters subsided (it still works). A glass case containing a section of old wattle wall original to the building highlights the age of the bar, but it's far from being a museum piece. Food is restricted to sandwiches (Mon-Sat), but the proper priorities are observed and they serve a good pint. Closed 25 Dec & Good Fri. **Directions:** On the west quayside, just in front of the castle. ◇

Glasson

Glasson Golf Hotel

HOTEL

Glasson Athlone Co Westmeath **Tel: 090 648 5120** Fax: 090 648 5444
Email: info@glassongolf.ie Web: www.glassongolf.ie

Beautifully situated in an elevated position overlooking Lough Ree, the Reid family's impressive hotel has been developed around their fine old family home (now the clubhouse) and, despite the name, it will delight all discerning visitors to this lovely area equally. The golfing dimension pre-dated the hotel (Christy O'Connor Junior course) and has earned an international reputation as one of Ireland's premier inland courses - the views are spectacular from every hole and the golf is challenging and rewarding - but the hotel is equally geared to business guests and those looking for peace and relaxation in beautiful surroundings. It is a bright, contemporary place, with the welcoming atmosphere that comes from hands-on family ownership; guest rooms are spacious, thoughtfully furnished, and decorated in an attractive modern style which is not over-designed - allowing views over the lough and golf course to take centre stage. The bar and restaurant are in the clubhouse section of the hotel, and both have been refurbished in a more traditional style appropriate to the older building. There's also a private jetty between the 15th and 17th greens, where visiting cruisers coming to the hotel may berth, or residents can arrange a private cruise. The hotel has proved a welcome addition to the accommodation choices around Athlone and is a great asset to the area. New conference rooms have recently been added, also 34 new bedrooms; a leisure centre and hot tub are planned. Conference/banqueting (100/130). Children welcome (under 5 free in parents' room, cots available without charge, baby sitting arranged). Walking, fishing. Garden. Pets by arrangement. **Rooms 65** (3 suites, 6 junior suites, 13 executive, 3 disabled, 15 family rooms, all no smoking). Lift. Room service (all day). B&B €100pps, ss€40. Special breaks offered. Food available to non-residents all day in the Killinure Bar & Cafe (7.30am-9.30pm); Lakeside Restaurant open 12.30-9.30 daily - L 12.30-5, D 5.30-9.30. Set L €25, set Sun L €27, set D €38. *Golf breaks are offered - details on application. Closed 25 Dec. Amex, Diners, MasterCard, Visa, Laser. **Directions:** 10km (6 miles) north of Athlone, off the N55 Cavan-Longford road.

Glasson

Glasson Village Restaurant

RESTAURANT

Glasson Co Westmeath **Tel: 090 648 5001**
Email: michaelrosebrooks@gmail.com Web: www.glassonvillagerestaurant.com

féile bia

In an attractive stone building which formerly served as an RIC barracks, chef-proprietor Michael Brooks opened the Village Restaurant in 1986, making his mark as a culinary pioneer in the area - and consistent standards and good value remain the hallmarks of this restaurant today. On the edge of the village, there's a real country atmosphere about the place, enhanced by old pine furniture and a conservatory which is particularly pleasant for Sunday lunch, or on long summer evenings. The style is imaginative and fairly traditional country French meets modern Irish perhaps; à la carte menus change with the seasons, set menus weekly and there are always a couple of interesting vegetarian dishes. As has been the case since they opened, fresh fish features strongly on the menu Michael takes pride in having introduced fresh seafood at a time when it wasn't popular locally, and aims to maintain the special reputation earned for fresh fish, including shellfish in season (or lobster from the fish tank) and freshwater fish like Lough Ree eel; a speciality that has stood the test of time especially well is a dish of pan-seared fresh scallops, with a garlic butter and balsamic reduction, sauté potatoes & deep-fried leeks. His cooking has long set the standard for the area and menus include many dishes perennially popular with regular guests and unlikely to be found on other menus, such as roast wild rabbit with a sauce of its own juices, deglazed with redcurrant jelly, fresh thyme and white wine, then set on a gnocchi with bacon lardons. There is a true love of food which, together with caring service under the supervision of Michael's sister Marie Brooks, who is restaurant manager, has attracted a well-earned loyal following. The wine list is balanced and informative; it includes seven house recommendations (€20-26) and nearly a dozen half bottles. The early dinner and Sunday lunch menus are especially good value. Toilets wheelchair accessible. Parking. Children welcome. **Seats 48.** D Tue -Sat 6-9.30; L Sun only 12.30-2.30. Set D €38.50, also à la carte; early D €27.50 (Tue-Fri, 6-7pm only). Set Sun L €24. House wines €20-27; SC discretionary. Closed D Sun, all Mon, 3 weeks mid Oct-early Nov, 3 days at Christmas. Amex, Diners, MasterCard, Visa, Laser. **Directions:** 8 km (5 miles) from Athlone on Longford/Cavan road (N55).

Glasson

☆ RESTAURANT WITH ROOMS

Wineport Lodge

Glasson Co Westmeath
Tel: 090 643 9010 Fax: 090 648 5471
Email: lodge@wineport.ie Web: www.wineport.ie

féile bia Ray Byrne and Jane English's lovely lakeside lodge styles itself 'Ireland's first wine hotel' and the accommodation - which now includes a further twenty beautiful rooms, hot tub and treatment rooms - is nothing less than stunning. A covered lakeside boardwalk leads to the front door: you enter your guest key card and step into a different world. A lofty residents lounge with a stove and its own bar simply oozes style and comfort, a hint of the high pamper quota waiting above in spacious suites and guest rooms, all with private balconies overlooking the lake. Superbly comfortable beds with goose down duvets and extra large pillows face the view, and seriously luxurious bathrooms have separate double-ended bath and walk-in shower. Wineport has a huge amount to offer discerning guests and has quickly become a hot choice for business and corporate events - every technological requirement has been thought of, and one look at meeting rooms which are dramatically planned to take full advantage of the beautiful location would sway anyone arranging a business event. Luxurious, romantic, beautiful, businesslike, this boutique hotel is a place of many moods: Wineport has everything. Ray and Jane were the Guide's Hosts of the Year in 1999, and Wineport was our Hideaway of the Year in 2003. Conference /banqueting 100/140. Children welcome (under 2 free in parents room, cot available free of charge, baby sitting arranged). Walking; fishing; garden. No pets. **Rooms 29** (5 suites, 8 junior suites, 3 superior, 1 family, 15 ground floor, 2 disabled, 2 shower only, all no smoking). B&B €97.50pps, ss €42.50; SC discretionary. No lift. Turndown service. All day room service. Masseuse (pre-booking required). Open all year except Christmas. **Restaurant:** Wineport Lodge began life as a restaurant, and faithful fans continue to beat a path to the door at the slightest excuse, to be treated to a fine meal, served with warmth and professionalism in this lovely contemporary restaurant - and what a setting! Regular guests find the combination of the view, the company and a good meal irresistible, and return bearing additions to the now famous Wineport collections (nauticalia, cats)... Head chef Feargal O'Donnell, who is a member of Euro-Toques and Féile Bia, presents well-balanced and strongly seasonal menus based on Quality Assured and local ingredients including game in season, eels, home-grown herbs and wild mushrooms. The number of dishes showcasing local and speciality produce is impressive, and constantly growing: local producers and suppliers listed on the menu include Abbey cheeses (Ballacolla, Co Laois), Reilly mushrooms (Glasson), Auburn Herbs (Athlone) and McBride's Butcher (Athlone) who is a specialist sausage maker, Donald Russell beef and lamb, Ballymahon - and, from further afield, Hick's pork products (Stillorgan), McGeough's smoked meats (Oughterad, Co Galway) and Lissadell Shellfish in Co Sligo. All this information, together with a stated commitment to the Féile Bia Charter is both interesting to read and very reassuring to guests, who will enjoy meals all the more in the knowledge that such care has been taken with sourcing the ingredients. The cooking style is diverse - international, with an occasional nod to traditional Irish themes - so you could begin a meal with a speciality starter such as McGeough's turf smoked lamb with wild rocket leaves & raspberries and bitter chocolate oil, or a delicious aromatic duck frisée salad with soft poached egg - and follow with dishes as diverse as baked turbot with cauliflower cream and oyster & mussel nage, or roast summer vegetables with herb gnocci & pesto butter. But this is beef country and it is fitting that a chargrilled 20 oz ribeye steak with smoked Ardrahan cheese & cracked pepper butter should top the bill, along with a mini-menu of beef (and lamb) dishes. After that you may well choose to finish with seasonal fruit and natural yoghurt or fromage frais as an alternative to a tempting selection of desserts... A separate children's menu is available. Wine is so closely intertwined with the history of Wineport that the list is very much a work in progress, but there are many suggestions for pairing wine and food throughout the menus offered; the main list include a value selection, organised by price. **Seats 100** (private room, 12; outdoor seating, 50). Toilets wheelchair accessible. Children welcome. Food service: Mon-Sat, 6-10; Sun 3-9; Set D €65, Gourmet Menu €95; otherwise à la carte; wines from €25. Closed 24-26 Dec. Amex, Diners, MasterCard, Visa, Laser. **Directions:** Midway between Dublin and Galway: take the Longford/Cavan exit off the Athlone relief road; fork left after 2.5 miles at the Dog & Duck; 1 mile, on the left.

Moate

E COUNTRY HOUSE

Temple Country Retreat & Spa

Horseleap Moate Co Westmeath
Tel: 057 933 5118 Fax: 057 933 5008
Email: reservations@templespa.ie Web: www.templespa.ie

Relaxation is the essence of Declan and Bernadette Fagan's philosophy at Temple, their charming and immaculately maintained 200 year-old farmhouse in the unspoilt Westmeath countryside. On its own farmland where guests are welcome to walk close to peat bogs, lakes and historical sites, outdoor activities such as walking, cycling and riding are all at hand. Relaxation programmes and healthy eating have always been available at Temple, but when they introduced the Spa, this side of the operation moved into a new phase, offering yoga, hydrotherapy, massage, reflexology and specialist treatments such as Yon-Ka spa facial and seaweed body contour wraps. the success of the Spa led to extensive developments recently, which have extended the premises, adding new bedrooms, a hydropool, gym and quiet relaxation areas - all opened in 2006. Temple is a member of the Health Farms of Ireland Association, which means that special attention is given to healthy eating guidelines; vegetarian, vegan and other special diets are catered for, and the best of local produce lamb from the farm, garden vegetables, best midland beef, cheese and yoghurts are used in good home cooking. An atmosphere of calm, good food, comfortable surroundings, gentle exercise and pampering therapies all contribute to a relaxing experience here - and the wide range of programmes offered include pampering weekends, 24 hour escape breaks, mother & daughter breaks and his & her weekends. Small Conferences/Banqueting (30/60). Destination Spa (hair dressing, massage, fitness room, treatment rooms, jacuzzi, sauna, steam room etc), garden, cycling, equestrian nearby. **Rooms 23** (all en-suite, 1 shower only, 1 junior suite, 1 suite, 1 for disabled, all no-smoking). B&B €115 pps, ss €50. Spa Package about €235 pps, (min 2-night stay at weekends). Spa weekends from about €300 pps (ss about €40). L & D Tue-Sat, 12.30-2, 7-9pm; set L €25; set Sun L €35, set D €45; also a la carte. Restaurant closed Sun D and Mon. Establishment closed Christmas. Amex, MasterCard, Visa, Laser. **Directions:** Just off N6, 1.6km (1 m) west of Horseleap.

MULLINGAR

This thriving midland town is really booming at the moment - the attractive old town-centre hotel, the **Greville Arms Hotel** (Tel 044 48563) continues to be the hub of local activities although, with well known chef Noel Kenny now proprietor of the **Austin Friar Hotel** (044 45777), his is the place to head for good food (informal at lunchtime, as little more dressed up at night). In the town centre also, **Canton Casey's** pub is a place for those who appreciate traditional bars (at its best at quiet times - it can get very busy); upstairs, over the bar, **Fat Cats Brasserie** (044 49969) offers informal dining. New restaurants - including several ethnic ones - are opening all the time, so it's worth taking a browse around the town. Lovers of Indian food should check out **Saagar** (044 40911), which is near the Dublin Bridge.

WWW.IRELAND-GUIDE.COM FOR THE BEST PLACES TO EAT, DRINK & STAY

Mullingar

E RESTAURANT

The Belfry Restaurant

Ballynegall Mullingar Co Westmeath
Tel: 044 934 2488 Fax: 044 934 0094
Email: belfryrestaurant@eircom.net Web: www.belfryrestaurant.com

The tall spire will lead you to this unusual restaurant in a magnificently converted church near Mullingar. The design is brilliant, with (excellent) toilets near the entrance, perfect for a quick freshen up before heading up thickly carpeted stairs to a mezzanine lounge which is luxuriously furnished with big lounge-around leather sofas, striking lamps and fresh flowers. A second staircase descends to the dining area, which is very striking and extremely atmospheric, especially when seen in candlight with a room full of people enjoying themselves, with background music from the grand piano where the altar used to be. Everything has been done to the very highest specifications, colours schemes are subtle and elegant - and the whole set-up is highly atmospheric. A new team, of head chef Damian Martin and front of house manager and sommelier Florence Servieres, took over The Belfry in 2005 and quickly earned a reputation well beyond the immediate area for their modern classical cooking and warm, professional and efficient service - just what this fine premises deserves. Damian offers well-priced lunch and early dinner menus and a more sophisticated à la carte; he is not afraid to have traditional dishes like oxtail, confit of belly pork or braised lamb neck on menus - and of course this is beef country, so offering tip top quality roast beef with Yorkshire pudding for Sunday lunch is a must - as well as the likes of foie gras en gelée with sweet & sour mango and brioche tuile, or seared salmon with crushed potato salad beetroot purée and sauce vierge. This down to earth quality in the cooking has won friends for the restaurant - and he has succeeded admirably in balancing the demands of an area where generous portions are de rigeur with the requirements of the fine dining guest. Florence is responsible for the wine list, which offers both treats and some interesting middle range bottles. Catering offered for private parties, small weddings (up to 75); private room for meetings. Cookery classes are offered - call the restaurant for details. **Seats 65** (private room 20); air conditioning; children welcome. D Wed-Sat, 6-9 (to 9.30 Fri-Sat); L Wed-Sat 12.30-2; Sun L only, 1-3.30. Early D €28.50 (6-7.30pm), otherwise D à la carte, Set Sun L about €30; house wine from €21. SC 10% on groups 6+. Closed Mon,Tue & may close for 2 weeks in Jan. MasterCard, Visa, Laser. **Directions:** Castlepollard road, off the Mullingar bypass. ◇

Mullingar

CAFÉ

Gallery 29 Café

16 Oliver Plunkett St Mullingar Co Westmeath **Tel: 044 49449**
Fax: 044 49449 Email: corbetstown@eircom.net

Ann & Emily Gray's smart black-painted traditionally-fronted premises is really bright and welcoming - and the buzz of an open kitchen and beautiful freshly cooked food on display draws people in. They're great bakers and, although there's much more on offer than that (and the choice is growing) their food reflects that interest - freshly baked breads, scones, muffins, baked puddings, tarts and gateaux are all on display. Good soups, salads (warm bacon salad with avocado, croutons & toasted pine nuts, perhaps), savoury tart of the day "tailor-made" sandwiches, fashionable focaccia with every imaginable filling and hot main courses, like oven-baked salmon with sweet chilli sauce, champ & salad and steak sandwich on ciabatta, with spicy salsa & mixed salad. It's a good place for any time of day, including breakfast (with freshly squeezed juice) and afternoon tea; it's very popular and often busy, but well-trained staff seem well able to cope. Outside catering, picnics and freshly made dishes for home freezing are also offered. Seats 50. Children welcome. Open Mon-Sat 9.30am-5.30pm (late opening with a bistro menu Thu-Fri evenings). All a la carte. Wine licence. Closed Sun, Christmas/New Year. **No Credit Cards. Directions:** From Dublin through traffic lights at Market Square in town centre. About 60m on right hand side. ◇

Mullingar

CAFÉ

Ilia A Coffee Experience

28 Oliver Plunkett Street Mullingar Co Westmeath **Tel: 044 934 0300**
Fax: 044 934 0050 Email: juliekenny@eircom.net

Julie Kenny's delightful 2-storey coffee house and informal restaurant in the centre of Mullingar is attractively set up - the first floor area is particularly pleasing, with a seating area of sofas, low tables and plants at the top of the stairs setting a relaxed tone and making a good place to wait for a friend, or to sip a cup of coffee while reading the paper at quiet times; the rest is more conventionally furnished in café style - and a more comfortable height for eating a real meal. Menus cater for all the changing moods though the day, beginning with an extensive breakfast (everything from porridge with brown sugar and cream to traditional breakfast, to toasted bagels (their Bagel Combo - toasted bagel with crispy bacon, poached egg, topped with melted cheddar & tomato relish 'just walks out of the door'!), then there are the mid-day bites like home-made soup, panini, steak baguettes, bruschetta, Ilia salad and much more (plenty for vegetarians) - and lots of pastries and desserts including a range of crêpes, both savoury and sweet. More predictably, there's a nice little drinks menu offering everything from big glasses of freshly squeezed orange juice through iced teas, smoothies, teas - and, of course, coffees (Java Republic), any way you like, including flavoured coffees. Everything is deliciously fresh and wholesome, staff are charming and efficient, prices reasonable - you'd be hard pushed to find much over €8. Takeaway also available. Wine licence.*"Ilia Gourmet" specialist food store (and outside catering) is across the road. **Seats 60.** Children welcome. Toilets wheelchair accessible. Air conditioning. Open Mon-Sat 9am-6pm. Closed Sun, Christmas & bank hols. Amex, MasterCard, Visa, Laser. **Directions:** Centre of Town.

Mullingar

HOTEL

Mullingar Park Hotel

Dublin Road Mullingar Co Westmeath
Tel: 044 934 4446 Fax: 044 930 4493

This large hotel on the Dublin side of Mullingar has brought quality accommodation and welcome facilities to the town - and it makes a very convenient journey break when travelling across the country. Although not especially appealing from the road, it is a spacious and friendly place - and has an unexpectedly pleasant outlook at the back, where the bar and conference areas open onto a large and sheltered courtyard style garden, well away from the road. Conference/banqueting (1000/700); business centre, secretarial services, video conferencing. Children welcome, under 4s free in parents' room, cot available without charge, baby sitting arranged. No pets. Garden, walking; leisure centre, swimming pool, spa, beauty salon. **Rooms 95** (1 suite, 2 junior suites, 2 disabled, 67 no smoking). 24 hr room service. B&B €95 pps, ss €25, no SC.*Short breaks offered. Restaurant open daily: B'fst 7.30-10.30; L 12.30-2.30; D 6.30-9.30. Bar meals available 12-5 daily. Amex, Diners, MasterCard, Visa, Laser, Switch. **Directions:** Off the N4 - take exit no. 9.

Mullingar
RESTAURANT

Oscars Restaurant

21 Oliver Plunkett Street Mullingar Co Westmeath
Tel: 044 44909 Fax: 044 44909

This smartly painted centrally located restaurant is extremely popular locally, pleasing people of all ages for its lively atmosphere and mix of traditional and contemporary favourites at reasonable prices. This is beef country, so a section of the menu given over to steaks should come as no surprise, but there's much else besides, ranging from '80s' classics like deep-fried mushrooms with garlic & cucumber dip, through spicy chicken wings to simple smoked salmon with lemon, capers & home-made bread. Main courses cover a similar range, also specialities which, apart from steaks various ways, offer everything from chicken Italienne to crispy Silver Hill duckling with cranberry stuffing and port & orange jus. Pastas and pizzas too - this is popular food, well executed at fair prices - the dearest main course is about €24.95 (large fillet steak) but the average is about €17.95 - and with cheerfully efficient service to match. An affordable outing with something for everyone and wines (from an accessible and informative list, with details on grape varieties as well as a well-balanced selection) starting at €17.95. **Seats 70.** Air conditioning. D daily, 6-9.30 (to 10 Fri/Sat, to 8.15 Sun), L Sun only, 12.30-2.15. A la carte D. Set Sun L €25. House wine €17.95. Closed 25/26 Dec, 1st 2 weeks Jan. MasterCard, Visa, Laser. **Directions:** Centre of town opposite town mall.

Mullingar Area
N PUB

Mary Lynch's Pub

MacNead's Bridge Coralstown Nr Mullingar Co Westmeath
Tel: 044 937 4501 Fax: 044 937 4743

John and Mary Moriarty's charming old-world pub a short distance east of Mullingar is tucked between the N4 and the Royal Canal, with a grandstand view of the new harbour works from the back of the bar. A blackboard menu offers traditional home-cooked dishes like soup of the day, fish pie, roast of the day and steak sandwiches, and there's likely to be live music at weekends too. It's a popular destination for locals, and a useful place for travellers to know about. Meals from noon daily. **Directions:** Between the N4 and the canal.◇

Multyfarnham
COUNTRY HOUSE

Mornington House

Mornington Multyfarnham Co Westmeath
Tel: 044 937 2191 Fax: 044 937 2191
Email: stay@mornington.ie Web: www.mornington.ie

Warwick and Anne O'Hara's gracious Victorian house is surrounded by mature trees and is just a meadow's walk away from Lough Derravarragh where the mythical Children of Lir spent 300 years of their 900 year exile - the lough is now occupied by a pleasing population of brown trout, pike, eels and other coarse fish. This has been the O'Hara family home since 1858, and is still furnished with much of the original furniture and family portraits - and, although centrally heated, log fires remain an essential feature. Bedrooms are typical of this kind of country house - spacious and well-appointed, with old furniture (three have brass beds) but with comfortable modern mattresses. Anne is well-known for her skills in the kitchen, and cooks proper country breakfasts and country house dinners for residents, using fresh fruit and vegetables from the walled garden and local produce (Westmeath beef cooked in Guinness is a speciality), while Warwick does the honours front-of-house. There is a wealth of wildlife around the house, and there are gardens and archaeological sites to visit nearby - this is a tranquil and restorative place for a short break. Pets allowed by arrangement. Garden, croquet; fishing. canoes, boats & bicycles can be hired. Equestrian: trekking & a cross-country course nearby. Golf nearby. Children welcome (cot available without charge, baby sitting arranged). **Rooms 5** (4 en-suite, 1 with private bathroom, 2 shower only, 1 family room, all no smoking). Turndown service. B&B about €70 pps, ss €20. Set residents D €42.50, at 8pm (book by 2pm). House wine €16. *Short breaks offered: 3-day stay (3 DB&B) from €275pps. Closed Nov-Mar. Amex, Diners, MasterCard, Visa, Laser. **Directions:** Exit N4 for Castlepollard.

COUNTY WEXFORD

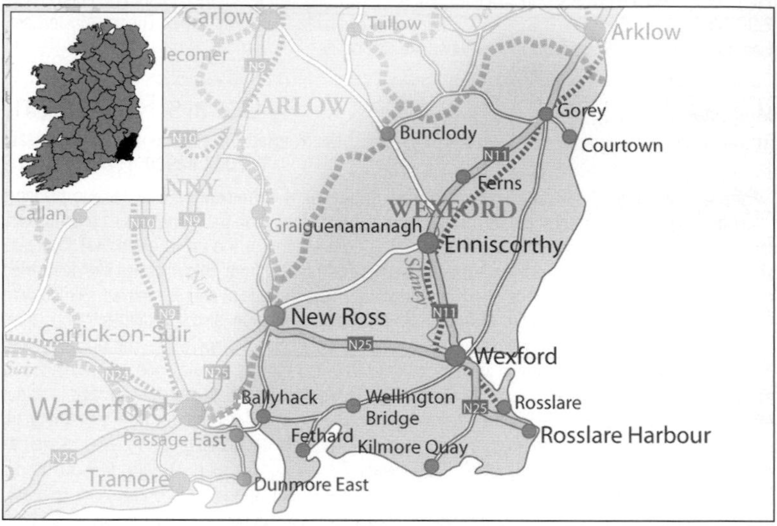

The popular vision of Wexford includes beaches, sunshine and opera. The longest continuous beach in all Ireland runs along the county's east coast, an astonishing 27 kilometres from Cahore Point near Courtown, south to Raven Point, which marks the northern side of the entrance to Wexford town's shallow harbour. As for sunshine, while areas further north along the east coast may record marginally less rainfall, in the very maritime climate of the "Sunny Southeast" around Wexford, the clouds seem to clear more quickly, so the chances of seeing the elusive orb are much improved.

And opera.....? Well, the annual Wexford Opera Festival every October is a byword for entertaining eccentricity - as international enthusiasts put it, "we go to Wexford town in the Autumn to enjoy operas written by people we've never heard of, and we have ourselves a thoroughly good time."

All of which is fine and dandy, but there's much more to this intriguing county than sun, sand and singing. Wexford itself is but one of three substantial towns in it, the other two being the market town of Enniscorthy, and the river port of New Ross. While much of the county is relatively low-lying, to the northwest it rises towards the handsome Blackstairs Mountains. There, the 793m peak of Mount Leinster may be just over the boundary in Carlow, but one of the most attractive little hill towns in all Ireland, Bunclody, is most definitely in Wexford.

In the north of the county, Gorey is a busy and prosperous place, while connoisseurs of coastlines will find the entire south coast of Wexford a fascinating area of living history, shellfish-filled shallow estuaries, and an excellent little harbour at the much-thatched village of Kilmore Quay inside the Saltee Islands.

Round the corner beyond the intriguing Hook Head, the peninsula marked by Ireland's oldest lighthouse, Wexford County faces west across its own shoreline along the beauties of Waterford estuary. Here, there's another fine beach, at Duncannon, while nearby other sheltered little ports of west Wexford - Arthurstown and Ballyhack - move at their own sweet and gentle pace.

In New Ross, where the authentic re-creation of a 19th Century emigrant ship - the impressive Dunbrody - is proving to be a very effective focal point for the revival of the picturesque waterfront, a fitting place for the lovely River Barrow to meet ships in from sea in an area with strong historical links to President John F Kennedy – his great-grandfather sailed from New Ross to America on the original Dunbrody.

Local Attractions and Information

Ballygarrett, Shrule Deer Farm 055 27277
Ballyhack, Ballyhack Castle 051 389468
Campile, Kilmokea Gardens 051 388109

Dunbrody, Abbey & Visitor Centre	051 388603
Duncannon, Duncannon Fort	051 388603
Enniscorthy, National 1798 Visitor Centre	054 37596
Enniscorthy, Tourism Information	054 34699
Enniscorthy, Wexford County Museum	054 46506
Ferrycarrig, National Heritage Park	053 20733
Gorey (Coolgreany), Ram House Gardens	0402 37238
Hook Head, Hook Head Lighthouse	051 397055
Johnstown, Castle Demesne & Agricultural Museum	053 42888
Kilmore Quay, Saltee Island Ferries	053 29684
New Ross, Dunbrody - re-creation of 19th C ship	051 425239
New Ross, Galley River Cruises	051 421723
New Ross, John F Kennedy Arboretum	051 388171
New Ross, John F Kennedy Homestead, Dunganstown	051 388264
New Ross, Tourism Information	051 421857
Rosslare Ferry Terminal	053 33622
Tintern Abbey (nr Saltmills)	051 562650
Wexford, North Slobs Wildfowl Reserve	053 23129
Wexford, Opera Festival (October)	053 22144
Wexford, Tourism Information	053 23111

Arthurstown

☆ HOTEL/RESTAURANT

Dunbrody Country House Hotel & Cookery School

Arthurstown Co Wexford **Tel: 051 389 600** Fax: 051 389 601
Email: dunbrody@indigo.ie Web: www.dunbrodyhouse.com

FÉILE BIA DISH OF THE YEAR AWARD

féile bia Set in twenty acres of parkland and gardens on the Hook Peninsula, just across the estuary from Waterford city, Catherine and Kevin Dundon's elegant Georgian manor was the ancestral home of the Chichester family and the long tradition of hospitality at this tranquil and luxurious retreat is very much alive and well. Well-proportioned public rooms, which include an impressive entrance hall and gracious drawing room, are all beautifully furnished and decorated with stunning flower arrangements and the occasional unexpectedly modern piece that brings life to a fine collection of antiques. Spacious bedrooms, including those in a newer wing which blends perfectly with the original building, generally have superb bathrooms and offer all the comforts expected of such a house - and fine views over the gardens. Constant improvement is the on-going quest at Dunbrody: recent developments include the conversion of outbuildings to create what must be Ireland's most stylish cookery school and, alongside it, a beautiful spa offering peace, relaxation and a full range of therapies and treatments. An outstanding breakfast offers a magnificent buffet - fresh juices, fruit compôtes, cheeses - as well as hot dishes from a tempting menu - and was the national winner of our Irish Breakfast Awards for 2004. While Dunbrody provides a wonderfully relaxing place for a leisure break, they also cater for business meetings, small conferences, product launches and incentive programmes (full details available on request). Conference/banqueting (30/110). Secretarial services; video conferencing. Cookery school. Spa & beauty salon. Garden, walking. Children welcome (under 5s free in parents' room; cot available without charge, baby sitting arranged). No pets. **Rooms 22** (7 suites, 7 junior suites, 7 superior). B&B€125 pps; ss €25. *A range of special breaks is offered (weekend, midweek, cookery, New Year); details on application. Open all year except Christmas. **The Harvest Room at Dunbrody:** The restaurant looks out onto a pleasure garden and, beyond, to a promisingly productive organic vegetable and fruit garden - an interesting place to browse around before dinner and, perhaps, hazard a guess as to what will be on the evening's menu. The dining room is a lovely well-proportioned room, with an open fire in winter and stunning flower arrangements all the time; it presents a striking blend of classic and contemporary style - bold choices which bring life to the room include some beautiful modern rugs, specially commissioned from Ceadogan Rugs at Wellington Bridge. Likewise, Kevin Dundon and his head chef, Gary Bourke, offer tempting à la carte and set menus that combine classical and international influences with local produce and Irish themes - and suppliers are given full credit: fresh fish is delivered daily from nearby Duncannon harbour, and shellfish from Kilmore Quay, and meats are supplied by Wallace's butchers, of Wellington Bridge - and organic fruit, vegetables and herbs are, as far as possible, home grown. Starters - which tend to showcase some unusual ingredients (tea-smoked chicken for example) and to be pretty and light - might include a lovely Wexford strawberry salad with a peppered Blackwater cheese basket: a perfect summer first course. Seafood dishes tend to the contemporary, as in Dublin Bay prawns with mead salsa. Kevin Dundon's 'eat local' philosophy comes through on all his menus, and local meats like rack of Wexford lamb often top the bill - in a terrific house speciality, Roast Rack of Lamb with an Irish Stew Consommé, for example, which is a modern twist on a very traditional theme, and a perfect example of what the Féile Bia Dish of the Year Award is all about: formal recognition of a dish that combines Irish produce, especially meat and vegetables, in an exceptionally creative way. (This dish was the main course of a modern Irish menu, cooked by Kevin, that wowed invited guests at a gala dinner during the St Patrick's Week Irish Food & Culture celebration in Boston, March 2006.) And meals at Dunbrody always end on a high note - so, whatever you do, make sure you save a little space for a spectacular dessert...Catherine leads a well-trained and efficient dining room staff with the charm and panache that typifies all aspects of the hospitality at this exceptional country house. An informative wine list which leans towards the classics includes a nice selection of half bottles and wines by the glass. The early dinner menu and Sunday lunch offer particularly good value. [Kevin Dundon's recent cookery book, 'Full On Irish', features many of the dishes from the restaurant and cookery school at Dunbrody, including the Féile Bia award-winning dish, Roast Rack of Lamb with an Irish Stew Consommé.] **Seats 70** (private room, 18). Reservations required. Toilets wheelchair accessible. D Mon-Sat 6.30-9.15. L Sun only 1.30-2.30. Set D €48/€60; 'Full On Irish' Tasting Menu €75, changes daily, offered with or without matching wines. House wines €21. SC discretionary. Not suitable for children after 8pm. Closed 22-26 Dec. Amex, Diners, MasterCard, Visa, Laser. **Directions:** N11 to Wexford, R733 from Wexford to Arthurstown.

Arthurstown
FARMHOUSE/B&B

Glendine Country House

Arthurstown New Ross Co Wexford
Tel: 051 389 500 Fax: 051 389 677
Email: glendinehouse@eircom.net Web: www.glendinehouse.com

Ann and Tom Crosbie's large nineteenth century farmhouse is approached up a driveway off the main road to Arthurstown, and has magnificent views across the estuary. It is a spacious house and makes a very comfortable and hospitable place to stay at a reasonable price; it would be ideal for a family holiday as there are sandy beaches nearby and there's a safe, enclosed playground for children beside the house - and they also enjoy the highland cows, Jacob sheep and horses which the Crosbies keep in paddocks around the house. A pleasant guest drawing room has plenty of comfortable seating and excellent views down to the harbour, and across the estuary, and the immaculately maintained bedrooms are very large, as are the en-suite bathrooms. Five new guest rooms have recently been completed and they are really lovely - large, bright and airy, they are individually decorated but the tone is quite contemporary and they have smart bathrooms; the original rooms are more traditional, with a cosy atmosphere, and all nine rooms have sea views. Service at Glendine House is a priority; the Crosbies take pride in giving their guests personal attention and lots of advice on local amenities - and sending everyone off well-fed for the day after a really good breakfast that offers home-baked breads, fresh and cooked fruits, organic porridge and a range of hot dishes include smoked salmon & scrambled eggs and French toast as well as the full Irish. *Glendine House was our Farmhouse of the Year in 2006.] Children welcome (cot available, baby sitting arranged; children's playground). Pets allowed by arrangement. Garden, walking. **Rooms 6** (1 suite, 4 shower only, 2 family rooms, all no smoking); turndown service offered; B&B €45 pps, ss €15. Room service (limited hours). Light meals (soup & home-baked bread, open sandwiches) available all day. *Off-season breaks offered. 2 self-catering cottages are also available - details on application. Closed at Christmas. MasterCard, Visa, Laser. **Directions:** From Wexford, turn right before Talbot Hotel, onto R733; 35km (22 m) to Arthurstown; entrance on right before village.

Arthurstown
Ⓝ B&B

Marsh Mere Lodge

Arthurstown New Ross Co Wexford **Tel: 051 389 186**
Email: sta@marshmerelodge.com Web: www.marshmerelodge.com

Maria McNamara's friendly almost-waterside bed and breakfast is beautifully located just outside Arthurstown and has lovely views out toward the Hook Head lighthouse. There's a sitting room for guests' use and the spacious, individually decorated en-suite rooms are very comfortably furnished. Marsh Mere complements other accommodation in the area and, as some rooms are suitable for families, this warm and welcoming place would make a relaxing base for a family break. Children welcome. Garden. Pets permitted. **Rooms 4** (all en suite). B&B €40 pps; family rooms from €90. **Directions:** from Wexford, R733 to Arthurstown via Wellingtonbridge; from Waterford, take Passage East-Ballyhack car ferry - coming off ferry turn right. House 1 km om left. ◇

Bunclody
HOTEL

Carlton Millrace Hotel

Carrigduff Bunclody Co Wexford **Tel: 053 937 5100** Fax: 053 937 5124
Email: info@millrace.ie Web: www.millrace.ie

The picturesque town of Bunclody is set in wonderful rolling countryside on the edge of the Hall-Dare estate, with magnificent parkland and riverside walks along the River Slaney. Ideally located for a break to explore this beautiful area, Bunclody is not much more than an hour's drive from either Dublin or Rosslare. This large hotel offers a wide range of facilities and, despite its size, is tucked quite neatly into a wooded site and, does not dominate the village too much. Individually furnished guest rooms, suites and family apartments are spacious and comfortably furnished for leisure and business guests and there are full spa facilities including and indoor swimming pool and a gym. A modern bar on the ground floor attracts local people as well as guests, and there is an impressive restaurant at the top of the building, which overlooks the town and opens onto a balcony - very pleasant on a summer evening, and handy for smokers. There's salmon fishing on site, walking in parkland and the nearby hills, and a number of championship golf courses including Carlow and Mount Wolseley are within an hours drive. Business facilities. Spa. **Rooms 60.** B&B from €85. Midweek specials from €99. Closed 24-27 Dec. MasterCard, Visa. **Directions:** On the N80 between Carlow and Enniscorthy. ◇

Bunclody
RESTAURANT

Chantry Restaurant

Bunclody Co Wexford
Tel: 053 937 7482 Fax: 053 937 6130

The Chantry is especially attractively situated within the little town of Bunclody. Originally a Wesleyan chapel, it enjoys a position of unexpected serenity above its own lovely waterside gardens, where guests can relax and enjoy the fine trees and plants, including many rare species. The restaurant is in a high room with a little gallery (just the right size for a grand piano) but, with its deep red walls, chandeliers and fascinating collection of old photographs and pictures of local interest, it doesn't feel too churchy. Artwork on display around the building is for sale, and can include some very interesting work. Menus offered vary considerably depending on the time of day - all day food tends to be casual, with a carvery lunch from 12.30, but evening service is more formal. At dinner, the self-service buffet is removed and an à la carte menu with table service is offered instead. Typical main courses include a speciality of traditional honey-glazed baked Chantry ham, with fresh parsley sauce and vegetarian dishes like tofu & vegetable stirfry. Early bird specials are good value - and what all the various menus have in common is good home cooking. Several little marquees (where smoking is allowed) are set up in the garden for outside dining - a pretty spot, looking down over the gardens to the river. **Seats 50** (private room, 14). Children welcome. Toilets wheelchair accessible. Own parking. Pets allowed in some areas. Open 7 days; Mon-Sat from 9.30am to 6pm Mon, 7pm Tue-Thu, to 9pm Fri/Sat. Sun 10am-6pm. House wine about €16. All a la carte menus. SC discretionary. Open all year (a phone call to check opening times is advised). MasterCard, Visa. **Directions:** In town centre. ◇

Campile
€ CAFÉ

Dunbrody Abbey Tea Rooms

Dunbrody Visitor Centre Campile New Ross Co Wexford
Tel: 051 388933 Email: theneptune@eircom.net
Web: www.cookingireland.com

The 12th century Dunbrody Abbey, and adjacent Dunbrody Castle and visitor centre make an interesting place to break a journey, or an excellent destination for a family outing - children will find plenty to enjoy here, including a full size yew hedge maze in the castle gardens (one of only two in Ireland), a small museum containing the Dunbrody Castle Doll's House and much else of historical interest, also pitch & putt for when it's time to let off steam (clubs can be hired in the craft shop). It is also home to good home cooking, in the Tea Rooms run by well-known chefs Pierce & Valerie McAuliffe, who run cookery courses all year round, at the adjoining Dunbrody Abbey Cookery Centre. In summer, they bake up a range of treats every day to make sure there's a fresh supply of simple good things to delight and refresh: usually a home-made soup of the day with Guinness & walnut brown soda bread, a selection of fresh filled rolls or sandwiches, home-made biscuits, muffins, tarts and cakes and a choice of teas, coffees and hot chocolate. There's also a range of Dunbrody Abbey food products on sale (mustard dressing, ginger marmalade, hot pepper relish). **Seats 35.** Open: 11-6 in high season (Jul/Aug); 12-5 shoulder seasons (May-Jun & 1st half Sep). Tea Rooms closed late Sep-end Apr. Cookery Centre open all year. Amex, MasterCard, Visa. **Directions:** On main New Ross-Hook Peninsula road; 3 miles from John F Kennedy Memorial Park, 2 miles from Passage East car ferry. ◇

Campile

COUNTRY HOUSE/RESTAURANT

Kilmokea Country Manor

Great Island Campile Co Wexford
Tel: 051 388 109 Fax: 051 388 776
Email: kilmokea@eircom.net Web: www.kilmokea.com

Mark and Emma Hewlett's peaceful and relaxing late Georgian country house is set in 7 acres of Heritage Gardens, including formal walled gardens (open to the public, 9-5; refreshments, for guests and garden visitors, are served in The Pink Teacup Café in the Georgian conservatory). The house is elegantly and comfortably furnished, with a drawing room overlooking the Italian Loggia, an honesty library bar, and a restaurant in the dining room. The individually-designed and immaculately maintained bedrooms command lovely views over the gardens and towards the estuary beyond; they have no television to disturb the tranquillity (although there is one in the drawing room). In an adjoining coach house there are newer rooms and self-catering suites; they have a separate entrance and, although some have been completely refurbished to match the style and standard of the main house, others have a lighter, more contemporary atmosphere - as they are so different it is wise to discuss your preferences when booking. Mark and Emma also continue with their ongoing programme of improvements to the property - there is now a tennis court and an indoor swimming pool, plus a gym and aromatherapy treatment rooms (Emma is a trained aromatherapist). And work continues on a large organic vegetable garden, planted in the old potager design - it's great to see a revival of this charming fashion. Conferences/banqueting (60/60). Children welcome (under 3s free in parents' room, cots available without charge; baby sitting arranged). Pets allowed in some areas by arrangement. Gardens, fishing, tennis, walking; swimming pool, gym, spa, aromatherapy. **Rooms 6** (5 en-suite, 1 with private bathroom; 1 suite, 1 junior suite, 2 with separate bath and shower, 1 shower only, 2 ground floor, 1 family room 1 disabled, all no smoking). B&B €95 pps; ss €30. Self-catering also available. Light meals in conservatory Pink Teacup Café, 10-5 daily when house and gardens are open; gift shop. Open weekends only 5 Nov- 1 Feb. **Peacock Dining Room:** The dining room overlooks the lovely gardens at the back, and is a delightful place. A new head chef, Denise Bradley (previously at Squigl Restaurant in Duncannon) joined the team in 2006, and she offers seasonal menus, based on local ingredients - especially seafood and, of course, fresh garden produce. Denise is well known for her confident cooking - stylish , yet very down to earth and with the emphasis on flavour - you should eat well here. There is also an unusually extensive wine list, including some real treats. **Seats 24** (private room, 14). Reservations required (non-residents welcome). Children welcome. Toilets wheelchair accessible. D daily, 7-9 (Sun to 9.15); Light meals in conservatory Pink Teacup Café, 10-5 daily when house and gardens are open (L, 12-3); gift shop. A la carte. House wines from about €19.95. Amex, MasterCard, Visa, Laser, Switch. **Directions:** Take R733 south from New Ross to Ballyhack, signposted for Kilmokea Gardens.

Carne

PUB/RESTAURANT

The Lobster Pot

Ballyfane Carne Co Wexford
Tel: 053 913 1110 Fax: 053 913 1401

Near Carnsore Point and just over 5 miles from Rosslare ferry port, Ciaran and Anne Hearne's good-looking country pub in elegant dark green with lots of well-maintained plants is a welcome sight indeed. Inside the long, low building several interconnecting bar areas are furnished in simple, practical style, with sturdy furniture designed for comfortable eating. For fine summer days there are picnic tables outside at the front. One room is a slightly more formal restaurant, but the atmosphere throughout is very relaxed and the emphasis is on putting local seafood to good use, providing good value and efficient service. Daily deliveries ensure fresh fish supplies and, the catch dictates daily specials. Simple but carefully prepared meals are served all day in the bar, typically including an outstanding seafood chowder (salmon, crab, prawns, cod, cockles & mussels in a rich fish base), a wild Irish smoked salmon platter and delicious fresh crab salad. An extensive laminated evening menu (with the names of 21 fish listed in eight different languages) offers treats like River Rush oysters and lobsters from the tank, crab mornay and, for non seafood lovers, crispy duckling and various steaks, pork fillet and ever-popular rack of lamb. Friendly service, a relaxing atmosphere and carefully prepared fresh food should ensure an enjoyable visit here - and, on Wednesday nights off-season (Sep-May), a special dinner menu offers great value at € 32.95. No reservations in high season (Jun-Aug) or bank hol weekends, so avoid busy times if possible. **Seats 100** (private rooms 16/28; outdoor seating, 20). Toilets wheelchair accessible. Children welcome, but not under 10 after 5pm. Bar menu Tue-Sat, 12-9 (to 8.30 Sun, 7.30 off season). A la carte menu 6-9 (to 8.30 Sun, 7.30 off season). Closed Mon except bank hols, 25 Dec, all Jan Good Fri. Amex, MasterCard, Visa, Laser. **Directions:** 8 km (5 miles) south of Rosslare port; follow route to Carnsore Point.

Duncannon

ⒺRESTAURANT WITH ROOMS

Aldridge Lodge

Duncannon New Ross Co Wexford
Tel: 051 389116 Fax: 051 389116
Email: info@aldridgelodge.com Web: www.aldridgelodge.com

féile bia Euro-Toques chef Billy Whitty's good cooking attracted a following around the south-east in recent years, and now he and his partner Joanne Harding have their own restaurant and guesthouse. Their modern stone fronted dormer home, overlooking the picturesque fishing village of Duncannon, enjoys lovely views of the beach and mountains - and has quickly earned a reputation for excellence in fine modern Irish cooking. The restaurant is bright and airy, with patio doors out onto a deck area, tables smartly set up with white linen runners and comfortable high backed leather chairs. Billy's fine training shows through in the many delightful dishes on dinner menus which are changed daily and offer six or eight appealing dishes on each course, including steak, poultry and some imaginative vegetarian options, although the emphasis is on seafood. First class ingredients are cooked with skill - a moist, flavourful and deliciously crumbly Hook Head crab cake, for example, makes a wonderful starter, served with wilted spinach and crème fraîche, and lobster (which is offered at a very moderate supplement on the dinner menu) is a treat of a main course, perfectly baked and served with lemon & saffron butter sauce, with the head re-filled with and delicious pomme duchesse potatoes. Soups, breads and side vegetables are all lovely, and a tasting plate of half a dozen desserts (followed by a well-made espresso) rounds off a meal here nicely. The wine list is sensibly limited and offers good value. **Seats 32** (+12 outdoors;private room, €22). Reservations required. Toilets wheelchair accessible. Children welcome but not after 7pm. D daily in summer, 6.45-9.30. L Wed-Fri & Sun, 1-2.30. Early D, €25 (6.45-7.15); Set D 35; à la carte d and Vegetarian Menu also available. Weekday lunch €18, Set Sun L €22.50. SC discretionary. Closed Mon, 24-30 Dec. **Accommodation:** Four well-appointed bedrooms (one with full bath and shower, the others with shower only) are quiet and comfortable, with a residents lounge area on the landing. *Aldride Lodge was our Newcomer of the Year in 2006. Small conferences/banquets (30/34). **Rooms 4** (all en suite, 3 shower only, 1 junior suite, all no smoking, 1 family room). Turndown service. Pets allowed by arrangement. Garden. B&B €50 pps, no ss. MasterCard, Visa, Laser. **Directions:** 1/4 mile outside duncannon, overlooking beach on Fethard-on-Sea road.

Duncannon

RESTAURANT

Sqigl Restaurant & Roches Bar

Quay Road Duncannon New Ross Co Wexford **Tel: 051 389 188**
Fax: 051 389 346 Email: sqiglrestaurant@eircom.net

féile bia Bob and Eileen Roche's fine traditional bar in the centre of Duncannon village serves the local community (and discerning visitors) well. There's an old bar at the front, pleasingly free of improvements, and it gradually develops more towards the back which keeps the younger crowd and the oldies in their preferred spaces. The bar food menu offers a selection of hot dishes, salads and sandwiches, plus some daily specials - a well-balanced mixture of traditional (creamy chowder with home baked bread, or mixed grill with fries and mushrooms) and contemporary (panini, melts, toasties). There is something for everyone - and if the weather is fine, you can now enjoy it out in the beer garden. Bar Food served 12.30-6.45 daily. (*Self-catering accommodation offered, details on application). Pub closed 25 Dec, Good Fri. **Restaurant:** Sqigl (pronounced Squiggle) is located in a converted barn behind the pub and is run by Bob and Eileen's daughter Cindy Roche, supported by head chef Shanta Watte, who joined the team in 2005. Sqigl aims to make the most of local produce and does it well with a sensibly limited menu, particularly the white fish landed at the harbour round the corner, wild locally caught salmon and Wexford beef and lamb. Décor is light, bright and modern and the cooking style is modern too, except that portions are aimed at generous Wexford appetites: creamy South-East seafood chowder, or fresh mixed South-East seafood salad with lemon dressing, for example, make fine substantial starters. With local seafood the star, a seasonal speciality to keep an eye open for is whole grilled black sole, which is always a great treat; but meat lovers have plenty to look forward too - rack of Wexford spring lamb is a regular, for example, and there's always an interesting vegetarian option too. Finish off with a rich dessert like chocolate and pecan nut brownie with toffee sauce, or something lighter - how pleasing to find something as simple and refreshing as a fresh fruit salad on the menu. Cindy supervises a friendly front of house team. The wine list offers a couple of good, reasonably priced organic wines - also six half bottles and an unusually wide choice of a dozen or so quarter bottles. A sign of the times, perhaps. **Seats 36** (outside seating, 12). Reservations advised. D Tue-Sat, 7-9.30; house wines from €15. Closed D Sun (except bank hol Suns), Mon, Tue off season, 24-27 Dec & Jan. MasterCard, Visa, Laser. **Directions:** R733 from Wexford & New Ross. Centre of village.

ENNISCORTHY

The aptly named **Riverside Park Hotel** (Tel 053 92 37800; www.riversideparkhotel.com) has a pleasant riverside path in a linear park beside the hotel, this can be a useful place to break a journey to stretch the legs and have a bite, as is the stylish **Bailey Café Bar** (Tel 053 92 30353; www.thebailey.ie). **Woodbrook** (053 925 5114), on the other hand, is a large late Georgian house a few miles from Enniscorthy, with a spectacular 'flying' spiral staircase; set in its own parkland under the Blackstairs Mountains, it is owned by the FitHerbert family. It is open for guests in the summer months, and is a most unusual place to stay.

WWW-IRELAND-GUIDE.COM FOR THE BEST PLACES TO EAT, DRINK & STAY

Enniscorthy

Ballinkeele House

Ⓔ COUNTRY HOUSE

Ballymurn Enniscorthy Co Wexford **Tel: 053 913 8105**
Fax: 053 913 8468 Email: john@ballinkeele.com Web: www.ballinkeele.com

Set in 350 acres of parkland, game-filled woods and farmland, this historic house is a listed building; designed by Daniel Robertson, it has been the Maher family home since it was built in 1840 and remains at the centre of their working farm. It is a grand house, with a lovely old cut stone stable yard at the back and some wonderful features, including a lofty columned hall with a big open fire in the colder months, and beautifully proportioned reception rooms with fine ceilings and furnishings which have changed very little since the house was built. Nevertheless, it is essentially a family house and has a refreshingly hospitable and down-to-earth atmosphere. Large bedrooms are furnished with antiques and have wonderful countryside views - all are large and comfortably furnished but one has just been upgraded to a more luxurious standard, and now has a separate bath and shower. Margaret, who is a keen cook and a member of Euro-Toques, enjoys preparing 4-course dinners for guests (nice little wine list to accompany too). There's croquet on the lawn, a long sandy beach nearby at Curracloe, and bicycles (and wellingtons!) are available for guests' use; horse riding, fishing and golf can be organised nearby - and work continues in the leisure grounds, including a lake in that is to be stocked for coarse fishing. Garden. Not suitable for children under 3. No pets. **Rooms 5** (all en-suite, 2 shower only, all no smoking). B&B €85 pps; ss 20. Residents Set D €40 at 7.30 (book by noon); house wine from €16.50. Private parties up to 14. Closed 1 Nov-28 Feb. MasterCard, Visa, Laser. **Directions:** From Wexford N11, north to Oilgate Village, turn right at signpost.

Enniscorthy

Monfin House

COUNTRY HOUSE

St Johns Enniscorthy Co Wexford **Tel: 053 923 8582**
Fax: 053 923 8583 Email: info@monfinhouse.com Web: www.monfin.com

This classic Georgian house just outside Enniscorthy was built in 1823 and has all the simplicity and elegance of that period. Having carried out major refurbishment, Chris and Avril Stewart opened their home to guests in 2001, with the aim of providing a quiet and relaxing haven, with the emphasis on comfort. Guests are free to stroll around the grounds and see the walled garden (which is destined for restoration to its original design and purpose) and your bedroom will provide a tranquil sanctuary - spacious and very comfortably furnished with a whirlpool or antique bath, although kept without the worldly intrusion of amenities like television (phone and modem connection are available on request however). Although dinner is not offered, Avril sources food carefully for breakfast, using local and organic produce wherever possible - and it is served in a lovely dining room where an open fire may be lit on chilly mornings. You may well need a walk afterwards. Not suitable for children under 10. Pets permitted by arrangement.*Weekend/short breaks offered- call Avril for details. **Rooms 4** (all en-suite). B&B €75 pps, ss €10. Closed Dec. MasterCard, Visa. **Directions:** From Enniscorthy take New Ross road - turn left after Grain Mill, 1km (0.5 m) up on right hand side.

Enniscorthy

Salville House

COUNTRY HOUSE

Salville Enniscorthy Co Wexford **Tel: 053 923 5252**
Email: info@salvillehouse.com Web: www.salvillehouse.com

Set high on a hillside outside Enniscorthy, Gordon and Jane Parker's large mid-19th century house has sweeping views over the Slaney River Valley but the main point of interest is indoors in the dining room, where Gordon Parker's delicious dinners are served to guests around a communal table, elegantly set up with candles and fresh flowers in the evening - and where splendid breakfasts are served next morning. Seasonal dinners have an emphasis on local seafood and organic produce from the garden - but there isn't a formal menu with choices, so it's wise to mention any allergies or dislikes when booking. Gordon's cooking is modern and he seeks out superb ingredients, notably ultra fresh fish; a typical dinner might offer a fish satay of lemongrass, with coconut & ginger, or Kilmore Quay scallops with rocket & pancetta salad, then sea bream with tomato coulis or salmoriglio dressing, with a classical pudding like Eton mess to finish. After dinner, guests can relax in front of the drawing room fire, or play a game of backgammon before heading up to one of the three large rooms in the main house, which have views over the Slaney and are comfortably furnished with some style, or one of two in a self-contained apartment at the back. (All have tea/coffee making facilities, but no TV). A really good breakfast sends everyone on their way in good heart - freshly squeezed juice, lovely fruit compôtes, freshly-baked bread warm from the oven and hot dishes cooked to order, like undyed smoked haddock with rösti and poached eggs, or local smoked salmon with scrambled egg. Laid back hospitality, great food and good value make this comfortable house a fine base for exploring the area, or somewhere to break a journey. Children welcome. Pets allowed by arrangement. Garden. Croquet, Tennis, Boule. **Rooms 5** (3 en-suite, 2 with private bathrooms, 1 shower only, 2 family rooms). B&B €50-55, ss €10. 3-course Set D €35, at 8pm (book a day ahead - residents only; no D on Sun). BYO wine.*1/2 day weekend house party packages available for groups of 6+ (exclusive use of house). Closed Christmas. **No Credit Cards. Directions:** Off N11, 3km (2 m) from Enniscorthy on Wexford side (look out for the sign on river side of main road). Go up hill & turn left; house on left.

Enniscorthy Area

Monart Destination Spa

HOTEL

The Still Enniscorthy Co Wexford **Tel: 053 923 8999**
Fax: 053 923 0944 Email: info@monart.ie Web: www.monart.ie

Nestled on a hundred acres of private mature woodland and only an hour and a half from Dublin airport, south-east Ireland's first purpose-built destination spa is an adults only facility in a magical location, offering world class Spa facilities and treatments, accommodation in 70 luxurious guest rooms and suites, personalised and attentive service and exceptional dining. Whether to address a specific health or wellness need (such as detox, inch-loss, anti-ageing, post surgery recovery, athlete rejuvenation) or simply to rest, relax and rejuvenate, Monart is a wonderful destination. A 2400 sq. m Thermal Suite includes a Swedish sauna with ice grotto among its facilities, and day programmes are available to non-residents - who are also welcome to share an exceptional dining experience - enhanced by wonderful gardens, designed by Chelsea Flower Show gold medallist, Mary Reynolds. Not suitable for children. Broadband Wi/Fi;garden, fitness room, destination spa, indoor 'pool, walking, hairdressing, massage. **Rooms 70** (2 suites, all executive & no smoking); lift; B&B €230 pps, ss €40. Closed 24-27 Dec. Amex, MasterCard, Visa, Laser.

Ferrycarrig Bridge

Ferrycarrig Hotel

HOTEL/RESTAURANT

Ferrycarrig Bridge Co Wexford
Tel: 053 912 0999 Fax: 053 912 0982
Email: res.ferrycarrig@ferrycarrighotel.com Web: www.ferrycarrighotel.ie

This stylish modern hotel is in a lovely location overlooking the Slaney estuary and has excellent amenities, including a superb health and fitness club. Public areas include an appealing contemporary bar, the Dry Dock, has a large outside seating area where you can relax and enjoy the view; it is a popular meeting place for local people as well as residents, and imaginative bar food is served here - specialities include 'Texan' steak sandwich and sticky toffee pudding... Otherwise, informal dining is available in the Boathouse Bistro, and Reeds (see below) offers a fine dining option. Accommodation is contemporary in style, and very comfortable - unusually, all of the well-appointed bedrooms have splendid views across the water, and some also have balconies with wooden loungers. Staff are exceptionally welcoming and friendly, and special breaks are offered. Conference/banqueting (400/350). Leisure centre, swimming pool, beauty salon. Garden. Children welcome (cots available, baby sitting arranged; playroom - limited hours). No pets. **Rooms 102** (4 suites, 5 junior suites, 2 for disabled, 76 no smoking). Lift. All day room service. about B&B about €120 pps; ss €35. Open all year. **Reeds Restaurant**; Reeds offers discerning guests modern cooking in the atmosphere of an independent restaurant rather than an hotel dining room. It has its own reception/bar area, tables are set up to make the most of the waterside position and it is formally appointed with linen tablecloths and napkins, quality tableware, fresh flowers and chilled water in stoppered bottles. Imaginative and well-balanced à la carte menus are interesting and, although the style is international, there is real emphasis on local foods - Killurin lamb, fresh fish from Duncannon, and speciality cheeses from Wexford and Wicklow are likely to be among the produce named, for example, and the kitchen takes pride in producing their own homemade pasta and ice creams. The little niceties of a special meal are observed - desserts are followed by home-made chocolates, served with coffee (including cappuccino/espresso) or tea (herbal teas available) - creating a sense of occasion. Food presentation is fashionable but not over the top, and service is pleasant and professional. The wine list is organised mainly by grape variety, with informative and very readable side panels to help your selection; eight half bottles are offered, arranged helpfully by style, and there's also a list of quarter bottles. **Seats 160.** Air conditioning. D Mon Sun 6.00-9.45 pm (limited opening in winter). A la carte. House wines from about €20 sc discretionary. Not suitable for children after 7.30. Amex, Diners, MasterCard, Visa, Laser. **Directions:** Located on N11, 2 miles north of Wexford Town. ◇

GOREY

Conveniently situated midway between Dublin and Wexford, Gorey is a good shopping town and handy to the many sandy beaches for which the area is famous. The **Ashdown Park Hotel** (053 948 0500; www.ashdownparkhotel.com) offers quality accommodation and good facilities including a Leisure Centre. Nearby, Courtown Harbour is a popular family resort with an attractive harbour, and walks in the surrounding countryside. **Poole's Porterhouse** (053 942 1271), on the main street, serves above average bar food all day and can be good place to break a journey. Near Gorey, the new **Seafield Hotel & Spa** (053 942 4000; www.seafieldhotel.com) is due to open early in 2007, and will have attractive opening offers through the spring.

WWW-IRELAND-GUIDE.COM FOR THE BEST PLACES TO EAT, DRINK & STAY

Gorey

Marlfield House

☆ RESTAURANT/COUNTRY HOUSE

Courtown Road Gorey Co Wexford
Tel: 053 942 1124 Fax: 053 942 1572
Email: info@marlfieldhouse.ie Web: www.marlfieldhouse.com

féile bia Often quoted as 'the luxury country house hotel par excellence', this impressive house was once the residence of the Earls of Courtown, and is now an elegant oasis of unashamed luxury offering outstanding hospitality and service, where guests are cosseted and pampered in sumptuous surroundings. It was first opened as an hotel in 1978 by Mary and Ray Bowe who have lavished care and attention on this fine property ever since - imposing gates, a wooded drive, antiques and glittering chandeliers all promise guests a very special experience - and, although Mary and Ray are still very much involved, their daughters Margaret and Laura Bowe now continue the family tradition of hospitality established by their parents. The interior is luxurious in the extreme, with accommodation including six very grand state rooms, but the gardens are also a special point of interest: there is a lake and wildfowl reserve, a formal garden, kitchen garden, and beautiful woodland with extensive woodland walks - and a number of gardens open to the public are within easy access, including Mount Usher, Powerscourt, Altamont and Kilmokea. Conference/banqueting (40/30). Secretarial services. Dogs and children are welcome by prior arrangement (cots available without charge, baby sitting arranged). Tennis, cycling, walking. Garden. **Rooms 20** (6 state rooms, 14 superior, 8 ground floor, all no smoking). B&B €137.50pps. Room service (limited hours). Closed mid Dec-1 Feb. **Restaurant:** Dining is always an exceptional experience in Marlfield's fine restaurant, where the graceful dining room and Turner style conservatory merge into one, allowing views out across the gardens, including a fine kitchen garden that is a delight to the eye and provides a wide range of fresh produce for the restaurant. The conservatory, with its hanging baskets, plants and fresh flowers (not to mention the odd stone statue), is one of the most romantic spots in the whole of Ireland, further enhanced at night by candlelight a wonderful setting in which to enjoy chef Micheál MacCurtain's accomplished cooking. His strongly seasonal menus are changed daily and outline the produce available in the kitchen garden (which is Ray Bowe's particular point of pride), and the origin of other ingredients used. Although contemporary in style and presentation, there is a strong classical background to the cooking, and it is all the better for that. Specialities that indicate the style include an elegant starter terrine of braised ham and foie gras with celeriac roulade & thyme toast, and a luxurious main course of roasted Dunmore East lobster with basil potatoes, sauce vierge, sautéed green beans and garden leaves - and the ready supply of fresh garden produce inspires imaginative vegetarian choices too. Lovely puds reflect the best fruit in season at the time, and a cheese selection from Sheridans cheesemongers is served with a delectable little salad, caramelised walnuts and quince jelly. Then it's off to the drawing room for coffee and petits fours to round off the feast. Very professional service is a match for this fine food and an informative wine list, long on burgundies and clarets, offers a wine of the month and a page of special recommendations. Not suitable for children under 8 at D. **Seats 90** (private room, 20; outdoor,20). Reservations advised. Air conditioning. Toilets wheelchair accessible. D daily, 7-9 (Sat to 10, Sun to 8); L Sun only 12.30-2. Early D €42 (Sun-Thu, 6.30-7.45), also à la carte; Set Sun L €42. House wine €26. SC for parties 6+. Light à la carte lunches are served daily in Library, 12.30-5. Amex, Diners, MasterCard, Visa, Laser. **Directions:** 1 mile outside Gorey on Courtown Road (R742).

KILMORE QUAY

This picturesque fishing village is noted for its thatched cottages, as a base for sea angling and for the Maritime Museum in the harbour, which is in a lightship - the Guillemot - previously used by Irish Lights,

and still with all the original cabin furniture and fittings. It is a popular place for family holidays, and the nearby Saltee Islands are home to Ireland's largest bird sanctuary. There are several attractive pubs and restaurants in the village, including the characterful Kehoe's, which is well known for its seafood.
WWW-IRELAND-GUIDE.COM FOR THE BEST PLACES TO EAT, DRINK & STAY

Kilmore Quay

Hotel Saltees

HOTEL/RESTAURANT

Kilmore Quay Co Wexford **Tel: 053 912 9601**
Fax: 053 912 9602 Email: info@hotelsaltees.ie Web: www.hotelsaltees.ie

This friendly hotel in the pretty fishing village of Kilmore Quay has recently come under new management, who have undertaken a considerable amount of refurbishment. It is a popular area for family holidays and, with moderate prices and comfortable accommodation - all rooms are en-suite, with all the necessary facilities - it would be a relaxing choice, especially as there is a very pleasant bar, the Coningbeg, and an unusually good restaurant for a small hotel (see below). Children under 3 are free in parents' room (baby sitting arranged. **Rooms 10** (all shower only, all ground floor, 3 family rooms, 4 no smoking). TV, tea/coffee-making, iron/trouser press in rooms. All day room service. B&B about €45 (also special offers). Open all year except Christmas. **Le Saffron:** Dominique Dayot, who is well known the area from his previous restaurant at Campile, set up this French restaurant in the hotel in 2005, and it has become a magnet for food lovers visiting the area. There's an hospitable atmosphere although not too fancy, it has classy white linen, high backed chairs and fresh flowers - a comfortable setting for some good French cooking. Menus are well-judged to allow for varying tastes so - although you'll find a leaning towards local seafood in dishes like his trademark 'Rendez-vous de Poissons' (a combination dish of cod, salmon, lemon sole with Kilmore scallops and prawns, with a basil sauce), classic black sole, and lobster, when available - there are lots of Slaney Valley steak and lamb dishes, roast duckling and several vegetarian dishes to choose from. Vegetables are charged separately, but the freshness of ingredients, generous portions and good cooking make it good value, even at around €22-28 for a main course. Staff are very willing and helpful, and it's a relaxing place to enjoy good food. Le Saffron Restaurant: **Seats 52;** not suitable for children after 8pm; non-residents welcome by reservation; D daily 6-9pm, L Sun only, 12.30-2.30pm; set Sun L €26, value D €34, 6-7.45pm, also a la carte; house wine €18.95. Bar meals avilable daily. Establishment closed 25 Dec. **Directions:** N25 out of Wexford towards Rosslare, turn right on R739 for Kilmore Quay.

Kilmore Quay

Kilmore Quay Guest House

GUESTHOUSE

Quay Road Kilmore Quay Co Wexford **Tel: 053 912 9988**
Fax: 053 912 9808 Email: quayhome@iol.ie Web: www.quayhouse.net

Siobhan McDonnell's pristine guesthouse is centrally located in the village and is especially famous for its support of sea angling and diving there's an annexe especially geared for anglers with drying/storage room, fridges and freezers, live bait and tackle sales. Packed lunches can be provided and non-residents are welcome for breakfast. The whole place is ship shape, with attractive, slightly nautical bedrooms ("a place for everything and everything in its place"), practical pine floors and neat en-suite rooms (most shower only). Children welcome (under 2s free in parents' room, cots available without charge). Pets by arrangement. Garden. Walking; cycling. **Rooms 7** (all en-suite, 4 shower-only). B&B €50 pps. *Self-catering also available. Open all year. MasterCard, Visa, Laser, Switch. **Directions:** Wexford 14 miles, Rosslare Ferry route. ◇

NEW ROSS

This old town has much of interest to the visitor - especially, of course, its key attraction, the recreation of the nineteenth century sailing ship the Dunbrody. **Kennedy's Pub** (Tel 051 425188; www.kennedyspub.com), just opposite the Dunbrody, has recently been renovated with some style and offers tasty modern bar food (also a restaurant upstairs). Just outside the town, on a hillside site with river views, the **Brandon House Hotel** (Tel 051 421703; www.brandonhousehotel.ie) has been developed around a house of character and offers some surprises (including an interesting art collection) as well as much-needed facilities (conference; leisure centre; spa).
WWW-IRELAND-GUIDE.COM FOR THE BEST PLACES TO EAT, DRINK & STAY

New Ross

Café Nutshell

CAFÉ

In A Nutshell 8 South Street New Ross Co Wexford
Tel: 051 422 777 Fax: 051 422 777

A walk through the town to find Philip and Patsy Rogers' Emporium will be very rewarding for lovers of good food. The concept is a natural evolution from Philip's background in farming, and Patsy's love of cooking: traditional country methods, handed down recipes and a respect for fresh produce are at the heart of this delightful shop and café, where everything is freshly made every day - and 'chemically treated or pre-prepared foods are not welcome'. Choose from a wide range of delicious freshly-prepared dishes like warm salads, quiches, fresh seafood - and lots of other seasonal produce - and, perhaps, a perfectly brewed Illy coffee - then take time to browse around the shop, which has a vast range of goodies to take home, including complimentary medicines like homeopathic ad herbal remedies. Anyone staying in self-catering accommodation in the area should also check out the food to go, which offers the same high standards of genuinely home-cooked foods as Patsy serves in the café. A little treasure. **Seats 45.** No reservations. Children welcome (supervised). Open Mon-Sat 9-5.30. Closed Sun, bank hols. MasterCard, Visa, Laser. **Directions:** Town centre. ◇

New Ross

HOTEL

Creacon Lodge Hotel

Creacon Lower New Ross Co Wexford **Tel: 051 421 897**

Email: info@creaconlodge.com Web: www.creaconlodge.com

A pretty owner-run hotel of some character just outside New Ross, Creacon Lodge is set in lovely gardens. Recent renovations have been undertaken with care, with the aim of retaining the country house ambience - so, for example, although there is an official reception desk, and public areas in general do have a hotel atmosphere, each of the individually decorated bedrooms has its own personality. This would make a good base for anyone wishing to explore the historic New Ross area. Conference/banqueting 20/70. Children welcome (under 4s free in parents' room, cot available without charge, baby-sitting arranged). Pets by arrangement. Garden, walking. **Rooms 10** (8 shower only, 2 family rooms, 6 ground floor, all no smoking). Room service (limited hours). B&B €75 pps, ss €19. Special breaks offered. Closed 24-27 Dec. MasterCard, Visa, Laser. **Directions:** From New Ross, take the R733 for 4km (2.5 m); turn left; 1km (half a mile), on the right.

Rosslare Area

COUNTRY HOUSE

Churchtown House

Tagoat Rosslare Co Wexford **Tel: 053 913 2555** Fax: 053 913 2577

Email: info@churchtownhouse.com Web: www.churchtownhouse.com

Patricia and Austin Cody's Georgian house is extremely handy for the Rosslare ferryport, about four miles away, but it is a really lovely place and deserves a longer stay - it would make a beautifully relaxing base for a few days exploring the area. It's set in about eight and a half acres of wooded gardens and dates back to 1703 but it has been completely renovated by the Codys, and elegantly furnished to make a comfortable country house retreat for discerning guests. Public areas are spacious, with plenty of seating in rooms of different character allowing a choice of mood for guests. Bedrooms are equally pleasing - large, and furnished to the highest standards in country house style, with generous beds, phones, TV and well-finished bathrooms. The Codys are renowned for their hospitality and, if you're lucky enough to arrive at this well-run house at around teatime, you'll be served delicious home-made cake and tea in the drawing room. Good food is an important feature here and a fine Irish breakfast is served in the bright dining room, where dinner is also served to residents (at separate tables), by arrangement. Garden. Children welcome. No pets. **Rooms 12** (2 junior suite, 6 shower only, all no smoking, 1 family room, cot avail €15) Dining room closed Sun-Mon. House closed Nov - Mar. MasterCard, Visa, Laser. **Directions:** On R736 1 km (half mile) from N25, at Tagoat.

Rosslare Strand

HOTEL/RESTAURANT

Kelly's Resort Hotel

Rosslare Co Wexford **Tel: 053 913 2114**

Fax: 053 913 2222 Email: info@kellys.ie Web: www.kellys.ie

The history of this renowned family-run hotel spans three centuries - yet constant renovating, refurbishing and building work each winter keep raising standards ever higher. Quite simply, the hotel has everything, for both individuals and families, many of whom return year after year (the number of children is limited at any one time, to prevent creating an imbalance). The many public rooms range from a quiet reading room and the snooker room to a supervised crèche and gallery lounge: paintings (mostly modern) throughout the hotel form an outstanding art collection. Many of the bedrooms have sea views, some with balconies; all the expected amenities are there except tea/coffee making, which is available on request. Leisure facilities include two indoor swimming pools, a well-being centre 'SeaSpa' which has 11 treatment rooms, seawater vitality pool, steam room, rock sauna and much else besides, indoor tennis, and - a bit of fun for Francophiles - boules. Outside the summer holiday season (end June-early Sept), ask about special breaks (including special interest breaks - everything from wine appreciation to golf clinics), when rates are reduced. No conferences or functions are accepted. Fishing (sea). Snooker, pool table. Hair dressing. Children welcome (under 3 months free in parents' room, cot available without charge, baby sitting arranged). Supervised playroom & children's playground. Walking, cycling, pitch & putt. Garden. No pets. **Rooms 120** (2 suites,

2 junior suites, 2 superior, 20 ground floor, 2 disabled). Lift. Room service (limited hours). Turndown service offered. B&B €85, ss €10; SC10%. Hotel closed 10 Dec-mid Feb. **Beaches Restaurant:** This L shaped room, which has been run under the eagle eye of Pat Doyle since 1971, was completely redesigned in 2003 to retain a sense of traditional opulence yet with a fresh, almost gallery-esque approach - an ideal home for some favourites from the hotel's famous art collection. Executive Chef Jim Aherne has been pleasing guests with his classic cuisine for over thirty years now - and his menus reflect the value placed on fresh local produce: Rosslare mackerel, Slaney salmon and locally sourced vegetables, for example, are used in daily-changing menus that ensure variety for residents who may be staying for some time. The hotel's renowned wine list is meticulously sourced, always changing, and excellent value. Highly informative (and a good read), most wines are directly imported and there are many treats in the collection, which includes organic and bio-dynamic wines, and an exceptional choice of half bottles - and a page of magnums (2 bottles), jeraboams (4 bottles) and imperials (8 bottles), which are ideal for big parties and special celebrations. Seats 250 (private room 40); air conditioning. L &D daily: L1-2.15, D 7.30-9; Set L €25; Set D €45. House wine from €20; SC discretionary. **La Marine:** This informal restaurant has its own separate entrance and offers a relaxed alternative to the dining experience in Beaches Restaurant. A zinc bar imported from France is the focal point of the rather pubby bar, where you can have an aperitif - although the turnover in La Marine is brisk and it is better to go directly to your table if it is ready. Comfort is not a top priority: fashionably sparse tables have fresh flowers, good quality cutlery and paper napkins, but space is at a premium so be prepared for a bit of a squeeze. Head chef Eugene Callaghan's ingredients are carefully sourced, using local seasonal produce as much as possible, and a finely judged balancing act between traditional and contemporary fare is achieved on menus offering plenty of choice: a starter of Moroccan couscous salad with garlic croutons & roast vegetables rubs shoulders with classic grilled Bannow Bay mussels with garlic & parsley butter, while main courses include roasted rack of lamb with minted French beans & sweet potato gratin, but also offer a lively repertoire of colourful dishes - recently tending to be less Asian and more European in style. Desserts are deliciously updated-classic - lemon meringue baked Alaska, perhaps - and there's always a selection of Irish cheese. Service is swift and friendly. Sunday lunch, which is very good value, tends to be a little more traditional and may include upbeat versions of traditional roasts. As in the hotel, there is very good wine list. Booking strongly advised, especially at weekends. A light snack menu is also available every afternoon, 3-6pm. Wines reflecting the style of food, are fairly priced (selection off main list). Seats 70. L daily, 12.30-2.15; D 6.30-9. Amex, MasterCard, Visa, Laser. **Directions:** Take the signs for Wexford/Rosslare/Southeast. 20 km from Wexford Town alongside Rosslare Strand beach.

Rosslare Strand
RESTAURANT

Le Colleseo

Strand Road Rosslare Strand Co Wexford
Tel: 053 917 3975

This friendly family restaurant offers an enjoyably informal dining experience - there's a good understanding of Italian cooking and excellent value for money, especially considering the quality of the seafood. Lunches are good, but the dinner menu is much more ambitious and gives a fairer impression of the scope of the kitchen. Food is well presented and service is friendly and efficient - staff are attentive and knowledgeable. Wine list a little limited but house wine good value at about €14. Open all day from 12.30am-9pm, Wed-Sun. Reservations advised. Closed Mon, Tue. Amex, MasterCard, Visa, Laser. **Directions:** Beside Kelly's Hotel. ◇

Wexford
RESTAURANT

Forde's Restaurant

Crescent Quay Wexford Co Wexford
Tel: 053 912 3832 Fax: 053 912 2816

Happy customers and good lighting create a good atmosphere at this informal restaurant in a renovated building near the Ballast Office; on the first-floor, overlooking the harbour it has mirrors reflecting lots of candles and, as darkness falls, lights twinkling across the harbour are highly atmospheric. Although set up in the pared-down modern style, fresh flowers and candles on well-spaced polished tables create a caring feeling, and Liam Forde's varied seasonal set and à la carte menus offer value and a wide choice, with vegetarian (and vegan) options listed although there's an understandable leaning towards local seafood. Start, perhaps, with an old favourite like moules marinière, served in a big bowl with an unusual toasted garlic rye bread, while main courses might include rack of local lamb, perhaps served with rosemary and raspberry jus. Desserts might include a more-ish dark chocolate mousses - a good partner for a well-made espresso. Everything is made on the premises - stocks, pastas, ice creams - and well-trained, knowledgeable staff are courteous and efficient. Interesting, informative wine list. Sunday lunch and the short dinner menu offer especially good value. **Seats 80.** Reservations advised. Air conditioning. Children welcome. D daily, 6-10, L Sun only, 12-6pm. Early D €22 (2-course); Set Sun L €22. Also à la carte. House wine €18.50; SC discretionary. Closed 22-25 Dec. Diners, MasterCard, Visa, Laser. **Directions:** On the quay front, opposite statue. ◇

Wexford

La Dolce Vita

Best CAFÉ/RESTAURANT

6/7 Trimmers Lane Wexford Co Wexford
Tel: 053 917 0806 Fax: 053 912 0267

In an unexpected little oasis of calm just off North Main Street, one of Ireland's favourite Italian restaurateurs has a smashing daytime restaurant and deli that is so popular with the locals that lunchtime hopefuls must arrive early, or be prepared for a long wait. You'll spot the trademark stripy awning (and tables outside in summer) from either end of this unexpected oasis in the centre of town, then see through the big window a bright spacious eating area set up with smart lighted tables and chairs, surrounded by shelves stacked with Italian goodies. Good glasses and elegant tableware heighten the sense of anticipation - and so to Roberto Pons's seriously tempting menus, in Italian with English translations, arranged so that you can have as little or as much as you wish: just a bite, such as home-made Italian bread with oil (about €2), fresh soup of the day (about €4), or risotto of the day (About €8), perhaps, or Tuscan salad (one of six super salads, all under about €10), antipasto with roasted vegetables (a generous platter of top class authentic Italian salami and meats - enough for two to share as a starter), and a range of pasta dishes, all under about €10. Then there are some more 'serious' dishes, like grilled seabass with salmoriglio dressing or Italian sausage with lentils. Don't leave without tasting at least one of Roberto's lovely desserts too - a perfect pannacotta, orange & lemon tart - and, of course, a classic tiramisu, with a really good coffee. But, anyway, there's still the shopping to do - all sorts of Italian treats, including wines (16 are offered by the glass) are imported directly by Roberto and, should you be lucky enough to live nearby (or staying in self-catering accommodation), there's even a short take-away menu including delights like grilled chicken & courgette with creamy gorgonzola, and suckling pig with homemade chutney. Now that's style. **Seats 45;** Toilets Wheelchair Accesible; Open Mon-Sat, 9-5.30pm, L 12-4pm, no evening meals. Set L €10-12; House Wine from €13. Closed Sun, Mon, Bank Hols & 4 days Christmas. MasterCard, Visa, Laser. **Directions:** Off the northern end of the main street - look out for the big green, red & white canopy. ◇

Wexford

La Riva

☆ RESTAURANT

2 Henrietta Street Crescent Quay Wexford Co Wexford
Tel: 053 912 4330 Fax: 053 912 4330 Email: warrengillen@dol.ie

Warren Gillen's first floor restaurant is approached up rather steep stairs, creating a wonderful contrast as you emerge into a bright room which overlooks the quay and twinkling lights along the shore - and is imbued with that indefinably warm atmosphere of happy people dining. And those with their backs to the harbour get compensation a-plenty: as the complementary view is of Warren and his team at work in the kitchen, creating delicious things for you to enjoy. Welcoming staff show arriving guest to smartly appointed tables, and the opening details - really delicious breads and a complimentary amuse-bouche - are very impressive. Warren's aim is 'to serve non-pretentious seasonal food, that allows the best local ingredients to shine' and this he does very well, as some of the finest food in the south-east is to be found here: menus are quietly impressive; without resorting to long or flowery descriptions, titles like Kilmore crab risotto with chilli, ginger, mango & coriander, or fried Croghan Farm goats cheese, with salad of roast peppers & red onion are extremely appealing - and they consistently follow through on the plate, in memorable dishes which are beautifully balanced in presentation, flavour and texture. Given the location, seafood is hard to resist but local meats are well represented too - pan-fried pure Angus sirloin, for example, with a caramelised onion & Wicklow Blue fondue, red wine, black pepper & clove syrup; vegetarian dishes are creative enough to have mainstream appeal, and you can finish off what is sure to be a memorable meal with a lovely dessert, such as a warm chocolate & pistachio brownie with Baileys custard & buttermilk granita: simply superb. Well-trained, attentive staff complement the creative cooking - the wonder is how they can produce such outstanding food in a kitchen of this size; however, the success of this great little restaurant means that there are plans to extend it soon. A short wine list is expanded by a page of monthly specials and a page of bin ends; the two-course early dinner menu offers exceptional value. Seats 45; Air conditioning. Not suitable for children after 8pm. D, Mon-Sat, 6-10 (to 10.30 Fri/Sat). Open Sun of Bank Hols only. Early D €24 (6-7 Mon-Fri). Set D, 2/3 courses €33/37; also à la carte. House wine from €19.70; sc discretionary. Closed Sun (except on Bank Hol weekends), last week of Feb. MasterCard, Visa, Laser. **Directions:** Opposite Commodore Barry Statue.

Wexford

€ B&B

McMenamin's Townhouse

6 Glena Terrace Spawell Road Wexford Co Wexford
Tel: 053 914 6442 Fax: 053 914 6442
Email: mcmem@indigo.ie Web: www.wexford-bedandbreakfast.com

Seamus and Kay McMenamin's B&B has been one of the most highly-regarded places to stay in this area for many years, making a useful first or last night overnight stop for travellers on the Rosslare ferry (15 minutes), as a base for the Wexford Opera, or for a short break exploring this fascinating corner of Ireland. However, a change of location is underway as we go to press - this hospitable duo has upped sticks and moved around the corner to a beautiful Victorian terrace house that has been completely restored and beautifully furnished. Although not complete at the time of our most recent visit, you may be sure of having top quality beds and bedding, and everything that you need to be comfortable away from home, including TV and tea/coffee-making facilities. The McMenamins' extensive local knowledge is generously passed on to guests and this, together with a really good breakfast, gets you off to a good start and helps to make the most of every day: quite extensive menus include a range of fruits and juices, home-made yoghurts, old-fashioned treats like kippers and also fresh local fish such as delicious fillets of plaice, lambs' kidneys in sherry sauce, omelettes or pancakes - all served with a choice of several freshly baked breads and home-made preserves, including an excellent marmalade and unusual jams such as loganberry. A McMenamin breakfast is always beautifully prepared and presented, and cooked dishes served piping hot: you will want to return as soon as possible! Hunting, shooting, fishing, walking, nearby. Also scenic drives, historic walks, racing, boating, swimming & tennis. Children welcome (under 2s free in parents' room, cots available without charge). No pets. **Rooms 5** (2 family rooms, all en-suite, all no smoking). B&B €45 pps; ss €10. Private parking. Closed Dec. MasterCard, Visa. **Directions:** In town centre opposite County Hall.

Wexford

HOTEL

Riverbank House Hotel

The Bridge Wexford Co Wexford **Tel: 053 912 3611** Fax: 053 912 3342
Email: info@riverbankhousehotel.com Web: www.riverbankhousehotel.com

Those who prefer to be a little away from the bustle of the town will enjoy this pleasant hotel just across the bridge; the approach is encouraging, with well-tended gardens around the front door and a welcoming reception area with lovely flower arrangements and candles, which are a feature of all the public areas. An attractive Victorian style bar and restaurant has views of the river, and an adjacent conservatory area has character and interesting plants - somebody clearly takes pride in this side of the property and it contributes a lot to the atmosphere. Recent renovations have been done with deference to the character of the building, so guest rooms tend to be a little small - and do check that your room has been refurbished room when booking. A very nice breakfast is served in Windows restaurant - fresh flowers on all the tables, a good range of juices, excellent coffee, lovely breads and good hot dishes, especially the fresh fish. A little different from others in the area, this hotel offers a pleasingly personal style of hospitality and food service. Conference/banqueting 350/260); business centre. **Rooms 23** (14 shower only, 1 disabled, 8 no smoking, 6 family rooms). 24 hr room service. Children welcome (under 4s free in parents' room, cot available free of charge, baby sitting arranged). No pets. Garden, walking. *Short breaks, including golf breaks, offered. B&B €85pps, ss €25. No SC. Restaurant open daily L 12.30-2.30, D 6.30-9.30 (Sun to 9). Bar meals available 12.30-9 daily. Closed 25 Dec. Amex, Diners, MasterCard, Visa, Laser. **Directions:** Directly across the bridge in Wexford town.

Wexford

HOTEL

Talbot Hotel

Trinity St Wexford Co Wexford **Tel: 053 912 2566**
Fax: 053 912 3377 Email: talbotwx@eircom.net Web: talbothotel.ie

Sister to the Stillorgan Park Hotel in Dublin, this 1960s hotel actually dates back to 1905 and has undergone massive renovation during recent years. It is well-located on the harbour-front, and also convenient to the town centre - indeed, so many activities revolve around it that many would say the Talbot is the town centre. A warm welcome from friendly staff, plus the contented crowd that always seems to be milling around the foyer, immediately sets arriving guests at ease - and one is immediately struck by the range and quality of original paintings, which is a feature of great interest throughout the hotel. Bedrooms are inevitably somewhat limited by the age and style of the building, but are pleasant and comfortable, with phone, TV and tea/coffee trays as standard. The basement leisure centre is an unexpectedly characterful area, confirming the feeling that the Talbot will always spring a few surprises. Short breaks offered. Conference/banqueting facilities. Leisure centre, indoor swimming pool. Beauty salon. Children welcome. Wheelchair access. Own parking. No pets. **Rooms 99** (all en-suite, 2 for disabled) Lift. B&B about €80 pps, ss about €20. Open all year except Christmas. Amex, Diners, MasterCard, Visa. **Directions:** On harbour front.◇

Wexford

Westgate Design

RESTAURANT

22 North Main Street Wexford Co Wexford
Tel: 053 912 3787 Fax: 053 912 3506

This busy daytime restaurant is under the Design Centre (through the design shop and down a flight of stairs), in a long, narrow high-ceilinged room. It's a pleasantly rustic-feeling café, simply set up with oil-clothed tables - and offers fast food as it should be. There's a counter where you can get smoothies made to order, as well as juices, and everything on display looks appetising - good home-made salads (20 per day) and quiches, for example, and other popular dishes like lasagne and braised lamb shank with chive champ, or fish pie are all typical. Well-cooked food, efficient service and reasonable prices: winning formula. *Outside catering. **Seats 140;** Air conditioning; Children welcome; Open Mon-Sat, Food served all day, L11-5.30; Wine from €4.50 per glass. Closed Sun, Bank Hols, 25/6 Dec. Visa, Laser. **Directions:** Accessible from the main street or, through the lower level, at the back.

Wexford

Whites Hotel

HOTEL

Georges Street Wexford Co Wexford **Tel: 053 912 2311** Fax: 053 914 5000
Email: info@whiteshotel.iol.ie Web: www.whitesofwexford.ie

Wexford's most famous hotel, Whites re-opened in June 2006 after total reconstruction. Very different from the higgledy-piggledy building we had all grown fond of, this sleek new development may not seem to have quite the character expected of an hotel that goes back to 1795, but it is very comfortable, and the unbroken tradition of hospitality lives on. The consolation at what is now a very large hotel is in excellent facilities in all areas including on-site leisure activities and pampering treatments; White's now has the first Cryotherapy Clinic in Ireland, and an impressive swimming pool and Spa. Smart contemporary guest rooms and suites have all the bells and whistles: in addition to the usual facilities, all rooms have plasma screen television, in house movie & satellite channels, broadband in room safe and minibar. There's a choice of bars and restaurants too, and extensive conference facilities. At the time of going to press everything is very new it will seem more 'real' when it's seen one or two Wexford Opera Festival seasons. Conference/banqueting (1,000/800). Secretarial services. Parking. Children welcome (under 3s free in parents' room, cots available). Pets by arrangement. Lift. **Rooms 157** (all en-suite). B&B about €67.50 pps; ss €22. Open all year. Amex, Diners, MasterCard, Visa, Laser. **Directions:** Follow signs when leaving N25 or N11.◇

Wexford Area

Killiane Castle

Ⓝ FARMHOUSE

Drinagh Wexford Co Wexford **Tel: 053 915 8885** Fax: 053 915 8885
Email: killianecastle@yahoo.com Web: www.killianecastle.com

The past and present mix effortlessly in Killiane Castle, the Mernagh family's farm B&B. The farmhouse and Towerhouse are 17th century and some of the 13th century Norman Castle still stands; if you climb the stairs in the east wall of the castle, there are panoramic views of the surrounding countryside, including the famous Wexford slob lands. Killiane is just a few miles from Wexford town so it's ideal for an overnight on the way to or from Rosslare Harbour (about 10 minutes). From the main Rosslare road, the drive to the house passes by green fields where cattle graze contentedly - there is an air of seclusion and quietness as you approach the building. Inside there's a spacious entrance hall, an elegant, comfortably furnished residents' sitting-room with an open fire and a small room down a few steps is a TV room, with tea and coffee always available, Climb up the 17th century staircase to the second and third floors where individually designed bedrooms have comfortable beds, en-suite facilities and great views over the countryside to make bedtime a pleasure. Kathleen Mernagh serves her delicious breakfasts in a warm and cosy dining-room a buffet offers homemade yoghurts, fruits from the garden and porridge with a dash of whiskey. Fresh soda breads and Kathleen's preserves are tempting, and hot meals include baked eggs and real Irish breakfasts. The working farm, run by the Mernaghs' two sons, allows visitors learn the milking process and see a modern dairy; there's also a farm walk, a tennis court, and even a driving range - and courtyard apartments behind the farmhouse (courtyard guests are welcome for breakfast too at an additional charge). No dinners but Wexford Town is only a few miles, or Kathleen directs guests to a nearby restaurant. 10 bay driving range, croquet, cycling, garden, walking, golf and equestrian nearby. Children welcome (cots available free of charge). **Rooms 8** (1 shower only, 2 family rooms, all no smoking). B&B €50 pps, ss €15. *Self catering also available in 2 courtyard apartments. MasterCard, Visa, Laser. **Directions:** 6km (3 m) outside Wexford town on Rosslare Road.

COUNTY WICKLOW

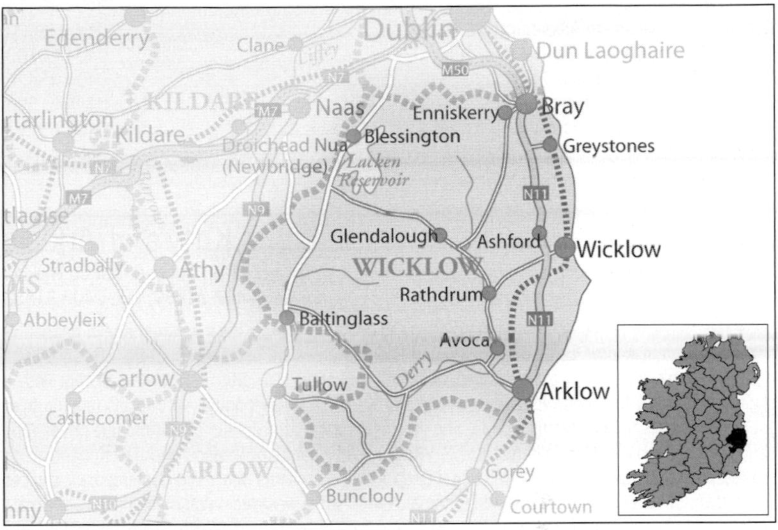

Wicklow is a miracle. Although the booming presence of Dublin is right next door, this spectacularly lovely county is very much its own place, an away-from-it-all world of moorland and mountain, farmland and garden, forest and lake, seashore and river. It's all right there, just over the nearest hill, yet it all seems so gloriously different.

In times past, the official perception of Wicklow – as seen from the viewpoint of the authorities in Dublin Castle – was the complex story of mountain strongholds where rebels and hermits alike could keep their distance from the capital. But modern Wicklow has no need to be in a state of rebellion, for it is an invigorating and inspiring place which captivates everyone who lives there, so much so that while many of its citizens inevitably work in Dublin, they're Wicklow people first, and associate Dubs - if at all - an extremely long way down the line.

Their attitude is easily understood, for even with today's traffic, it is only a short drive on notably handsome roads to transform your world from the crowded city streets right into the heart of some of the most beautiful scenery in all Ireland. Such scenery generates its own strong loyalties and sense of identity, and Wicklow folk are rightly and proudly a race apart. Drawing strength from their wonderful environment, they have a vigorous local life which keeps metropolitan blandness well at bay.

While being in a place so beautiful is almost sufficient reason for existence in itself, they're busy people too, with sheep farming and forestry and all sorts of light industries, while down in the workaday harbour of Arklow in the south of the county - a port with a long and splendid maritime history - they've been so successful in organising their own seagoing fleet of freighters that there are now more cargo ships registered in Arklow than any other Irish port.

Local Attractions and Information

Arklow, Tourism Information	0402 32484
Ashford, Mount Usher Gardens	0404 40116
Avoca, Tourism Information	0402 35788
Blessington, Russborough House & Gardens	045 865239
Bray, Kilruddery House & Gardens	01 2863405
Bray, National Sealife Centre	01 2866939
Derrynamuck, Dwyer McAllister Traditional Cottage	0404 45325
Enniskerry, Powerscourt House & Gardens	01 2046000
Glendalough Farm Market (second Suns)	0404 43885
Glendalough, Tourism Information	0404 45688
Glendalough, Visitor Centre	0404 45325
Kilmacanogue, Avoca Handweavers Garden	01 2867466

Kilquade, Nat. Garden Exhibition Centre 01 2819890
Macreddin Organic Market (first Suns month) 0402 36444
Rathdrum, Avondale House 0404 46111
Rathdrum, Kilmacurragh Arboretum 01 6473000
Wicklow County, Gardens Festival (May-July) 0404 20100
Wicklow Mountains, National Park 0404 45425
Wicklow Town, Wicklow Historic Gaol 0404 61599
Wicklow Town, Tourism Information 0404 69117

Arklow
BAR/RESTAURANT

Kitty's of Arklow

56 Main Street Arklow Co Wicklow
Tel: 0402 31669 Fax: 0402 31553

féile bia A big blue double-fronted building in the centre of town, Kitty's is something of an institution in Arklow. Large and airy ground floor bar areas are decorated in retro '50s style (with big comfortable chairs and old-fashioned radiators) and there's a lofty first floor restaurant with a slightly olde-world feel (open fireplaces and lots of wood). It's very popular with locals ranging from young commuters to large family groups, who like the informal atmosphere and affordable prices - the early evening menu is especially reasonable. Menus offer a range of seafood and descriptions aren't too fussy: typical starters include traditional deep fried mushrooms and more contemporary choices like a goat's cheese, black olive & sundried tomato tartlet with sweet red onion marmalade, while main courses include perennial favourites likes steaks and rack of lamb, and several fish dishes. There is a separate vegetarian menu, and coeliac options are also available on request. Cooking can be a little hit and miss, but generous portions and friendly, efficient and professional staff keep 'em coming back. Children welcome before 9pm. **Seats 110** (private room 24). Reservations required. Air conditioning. Food served: Mon-Fri, L 12-3, early D, 5.30-8 and D, 8-8.45pm; Sat, L 12-5pm, D, 6-9.45pm, Sun L 12-5.30pm and D, 5.30-8.45pm. Early D about €22. Set D about €37, also à la carte. House wine about €19. Closed 25 Dec & Good Fri. Amex, Diners, MasterCard, Visa, Laser. **Directions:** Off N11; centre of town, beside car park. ◇

Arklow
COUNTRY HOUSE

Plattenstown House

Coolgreaney Road Arklow Co Wicklow
Tel: 0402 37822 Fax: 0402 37822
Email: mcdpr@indigo.ie Web: www.wicklow.ie/farm/f-plattn.htm

About halfway between Dublin and Rosslare (each about an hour's drive away) and overlooking parkland, this quiet, peaceful place is set in 50 acres of land amidst its own lovely gardens close to the sea - and Margaret McDowell describes her period farmhouse well as having "the soft charm typical of the mid-19th century houses built in scenic Wicklow". There is plenty to do in the area, with the sea, golf, riding stables and forest walks all nearby, and places such as Glendalough and Avondale House to visit. There's a traditional drawing room furnished with family antiques overlooking the front garden, a TV lounge available for guests' use and a lovely dining room where breakfast is served - and evening meals are also offered by arrangement. Bedrooms vary in size and outlook according to their position in the house and have interestingly different characters, but all are comfortably furnished. A lovely, peaceful place. Children welcome (under 2s free in parents' room, cot available without charge, baby sitting arranged). No pets. **Rooms 4** (3 en-suite with shower only, 1 with private bathroom, all no smoking). B&B €40pps, ss €8. Weekend / mid-week breaks - details on application. Closed 23 Dec-2 Jan. MasterCard, Visa. **Directions:** Top of Arklow town, small roundabout, straight on to Coolgreaney Road. 5 km on left. ◇

Ashford
FARMHOUSE

Ballyknocken House & Cookery School

Gleanealy Ashford Co Wicklow
Tel: 0404 44627 Fax: 0404 44696
Email: info@ballyknocken.com Web: www.ballyknocken.com

féile bia Perfectly placed for walking holidays in the Wicklow Hills, playing golf, or simply for touring the area, Catherine Fulvio's charming Victorian farmhouse provides comfort, cosiness, home-cooked food and hospitality. The farm has been in the Byrne family for three generations and they have welcomed guests for over thirty years - Catherine took over in 1999, and she has since refurbished the house throughout in old country style. A gently Victorian theme prevails: bedrooms have been charmingly done up, with antique furniture and very good beds - and pretty bathrooms, five of which have Victorian baths. The dining room, parlour and sitting room are in a similar style and her energetic quest for perfection also extends to the garden, where new fruit tree, roses and herbs were planted, and her cookery school - which is in a renovated milking parlour in the grounds. Catherine cooks four course dinners for guests, based on local produce, including vegetables and herbs from the Ballyknocken farm (with wine list including some specially imported wines); the cooking style is modern and (influenced by her Italian husband Claudio) there's a Mediterranean flavour. All this, plus extensive breakfasts and a relaxing atmosphere ensure guests keep coming back for more. Short breaks are offered, also self-catering accommodation; details on these, and Ballyknocken Cookery School, on application. *Ballyknocken was our Farmhouse of the Year in 2004. **Rooms 7** (all en-suite, 1 shower only, 1 family room, all no smoking). B&B €59-65 pps, ss €30. Residents D Tue-Sat, at 7.30. Set 4-course D €39.50; houses wines €19.95. No D on Sun or Mon. Non-resident group (8+) lunches catered for, by arrangement. Closed Dec & Jan. MasterCard, Visa, Laser. **Directions:** From Dublin turn right after Texaco Petrol Station in Ashford. Continue for 5.5km (3 m).House on right.

Aughrim

COUNTRY HOUSE

Clone House

Aughrim Co Wicklow **Tel: 0402 36121** Fax: 0402 36029
Email: stay@clonehouse.com Web: www.clonehouse.com

The oldest part of Carla Edigati Watson's rambling country house in the lovely unspoilt south Wicklow countryside goes back to the 1600s, although it was largely rebuilt in 1805 after burning in the 1798 Rebellion. Today this elegantly furnished and hospitable house is full of comfort, providing a quiet and relaxing haven, away from the stresses of modern life. Open fires in every room are a particularly attractive feature - and thoughtful little touches abound, including fresh fruit and chocolates in each bedroom (some with four posters), as well as tea and coffee making facilities - and no television to intrude into this tranquil retreat. Landscaped gardens surround the house and are under continuous development; with lovely stonework in new pathways and walls echoing the old buildings beside the house, and many interesting features including ponds, the gardens are an attraction in themselves - although the natural countryside and mountain views would be difficult to upstage. Three comfortable guests' sitting rooms are comfortably furnished for relaxing in, and dinner is served in an elegant period dining room, also with an open fire. Carla, who is Italian, loves cooking and prepares traditional Tuscan dinners by arrangement - menus, changed daily, begin with a pre-starter - bruschetta, Kalamata olives and artichoke hearts, perhaps - followed by a soup (such as clam chowder with oregano croutons & parmigiano) or a choice of three other starters, such as grilled goat's cheese & Parma ham with honey roasted walnuts, pears and lettuce form the garden. Unusual main courses might include several poultry or game dishes - quail stuffed with spinach & Toulouse sausage, wrapped in bacon is typical- and delicious desserts tend to be simple and fruit-based - champagne sorbet with fresh peaches and strawberries, perhaps. Service is friendly and willing, but this is not a place to be clock-watching; Carla's food is simple and full of flavour - and different from other restaurants too, which adds to its appeal. A mainly Italian wine list complements the food well. This is a wonderful place to relax in beautiful, tranquil surroundings. *Short breaks are offered - details on application. Children under 3 free in parents' room (cot available). No pets. Gym, weight room, sauna; table tennis; garden. Banqueting (24). **Rooms 7** (5 en-suite, 2 private bathrooms, 4 shower only, all no smoking) B&B €75pps, ss €40. Dinner at 8pm by arrangement, €55-65. Wines about €24 (BYO corkage €8). 10% SC on dinners. Open all year. MasterCard, Visa, Laser. **Directions:** Follow brown house signs from Aughrim or Woodenbridge.

Avoca

CAFÉ

Avoca Handweavers

Avoca Village Co Wicklow **Tel: 0402 35105** Fax: 0402 35446
Email: info@avoca.ie Web: www.avoca.ie

Avoca handweavers, established in 1723, is Ireland's oldest business. It's a family owned craft design company which now has half a dozen branches throughout Ireland (most of which feature in this Guide) and the business originated here, at Avoca village, where you can watch the hand weavers who produce the lovely woven woollen rugs and fabrics which became the hallmark of the company in its early days. Today, the appeal of Avoca shops is much broader, as they are know not only for the high standard of crafts sold (and their beautiful locations) but also for their own ranges of clothing, restaurants with a well-earned reputation for imaginative, wholesome home-cooked food - and delicious deli products and speciality foods to take home. Garden. Parking. Children welcome. Pets allowed in some areas. **Seats 75.** Open all day (10-5) Mon-Sun. House wine about €12.50. No service charge. Wheelchair access. Closed 25-26 Dec. Amex, Diners, MasterCard, Visa, Laser. **Directions:** Leave N11 at Rathnew and follow signs for Avoca. ◇

Blessington

€ CAFÉ

Grangecon Café

Kilbride Road Blessington Co Wicklow
Tel: 045 857 892 Email: grangeconcafe@eircom.net

Wholesome aromas will draw you into Jenny and Richard Street's smashing café, which retained its name when re-locating from the charming village of Grangecon to the bustle of Blessington Here they are in an old building that has been given new life by a lovely renovation job, with gentle modern decor and natural materials that should never date. But the fundamentals remain unchanged: the stated aim has always been "to provide you with a really good food stop", and this they continue to do brilliantly. Everything on the menu is made on the premises, including the breads, pastries and ice cream; the ham hocks for the quiche lorraine are cooked here, the pork meat used in the sausage rolls is organic, fruit and vegetables come from Castleruddery organic farm, and all other ingredients are of the very best quality, many of them also organic and/or free range. The menu is understandably fairly brief, but the cooking is good, and flavours superb: the quiche, for example, is a little classic and comes with a scrumptious salad; similarly moist, freshly-baked brown bread arrives with home cooked ham, farm-house cheese (Sheridan's) and homemade chutney, also garnished with salad: simple and excellent - not for the first time, we say: why aren't there more places like this? No wine at the time of going to press, but a wine licence is expected soon - meanwhile you can opt for delicious chilled Crinnaughton apple juice, which comes from Cappoquin, instead and B-Y-O wine is fine. Luscious Illy coffee to finish and maybe a slice of chocolate cake. This is not cheap food - how could it be when the ingredients are of such high quality - but there s nothing on the menu over about 10 and it is extremely good value for money. **Seats 30.** Open all day Mon-Sat, 9am-5.30pm. Toilets wheelchair accessible; Baby Changing Facilities; Party Service; Closed Sun. Bank Hols & 25 Dec - 1 Jan. MasterCard, Visa, Laser. **Directions:** Centre of Blessington village, around the corner from Downshire House Hotel.

Delgany

HOTEL/RESTAURANT

Glenview Hotel

Glen O' The Downs Delgany Co Wicklow
Tel: 01 287 3399 Fax: 01 287 7511
Email: pkavanagh@glenviewhotel.com Web: www.glenviewhotel.com

Famous for its views over the luxuriantly green and leafy Glen O'The Downs, this well-located hotel has all the advantages of a beautiful rural location, yet is just a half hour's drive from Dublin and offers a wide range of facilities, including an excellent Health and Leisure Club (with beauty treatment and therapy rooms) and a state-of-the-art conference centre. Accommodation includes a penthouse suite, and all bedrooms are attractively furnished in warm colours and an undemanding modern style. Public areas include a pleasant, comfortably furnished conservatory bar, which is well situated for a casual meal (Conservatory Bistro menu, international cooking,12.30-9). For more formal meals, Woodlands Restaurant offers quite ambitious cooking - with forest views over Glen'O'The Downs from the dining room. All this, together with special breaks (golf, health and fitness, riding) offering good value, make the hotel a valuable asset to the area; it is a popular wedding venue. Conference/banqueting (250/180). Secretarial services, ISDN lines, video conferencing. Leisure centre (indoor swimming pool); beauty salon. Snooker room (adults only). Garden, woodland walks. Children welcome (under 2s free in parents' room, cots available without charge, play room). No pets. **Rooms 70** (all en-suite, 1 suite, 12 executive rooms). Lift. B&B from about €90, ss about €40. Restaurant seats 90; not suitable for children after 7.30pm; D daily, L Sun only; air conditioning; pianist some evenings. Open all year. Amex, Diners, MasterCard, Visa, Laser. **Directions:** On N11, turn left 2 miles southbound of Kilmacanogue. ◇

Dunlavin

COUNTRY HOUSE

Rathsallagh House, Golf & Country Club

Dunlavin Co Wicklow
Tel: 045 403 112 Fax: 045 403 343
Email: info@rathsallagh.com Web: www.rathsallagh.com

féile bia This large, rambling country house is just an hour from Dublin, but it could be in a different world. Although it's very professionally operated, the O'Flynn family insist it is not an hotel and - although there is an 18-hole golf course with clubhouse in the grounds - the gentle rhythms of life around the country house and gardens ensure that the atmosphere is kept decidedly low-key. Day rooms are elegantly furnished in classic country house style, with lots of comfortable seating areas and open fires. Bedrooms, as in all old houses do vary - some are spacious with lovely country views, while other smaller, simpler rooms in the stable yard have a special cottagey charm; and there are newer rooms, built discreetly behind the main courtyard, which very big and finished to a high standard, with luxurious bathrooms. Rathsallagh is renowned for its magnificent Edwardian breakfast buffet which was, for the second time, the overall national winner of our Irish Breakfast Awards in 2005. Breakfast at Rathsallagh offers every conceivable good thing, including silver chafing dishes, full of reminders of yesteryear. A large sideboard display offers such an array of temptations that it can be hard to decide where to start - fresh juices, fruits and home-bakes, local honey and home-made jams and chutneys...Irish farmhouse cheeses, Rathsallagh ham on the bone, salamis and smoked salmon...then there are the hot dishes, including the full Irish, and then some - less usual dishes like smoked salmon kedgeree, and Kay's devilled kidneys are specialities worth travelling for. And, for the faint-hearted, there's another whole menu devoted to the Healthy Option Breakfast. If golf is not your thing, there are plenty of other ways to work off this remarkable meal - the Wicklow Hills beckon walkers of all levels, for example, or you could at least fit in a gentle stroll around the charming walled gardens. Great food and service, warm hospitality, and surroundings that are quiet or romantic to suit the mood of the day - Rathsallagh has it all. *Ask about the relaxing bath menus. Conference/banqueting (130). Golf (18). Swimming pool. Gardens, tennis, cycling, walking. Pool table. Beauty salon. Pets allowed by arrangement. **Rooms 29** (1 suite, 9 ground floor, 20 separate bath & shower, 2 shower only, 2 for disabled, all no smoking). B&B about €135. *Short breaks (incl golf breaks) offered, details on application. Open all year. **Restaurant:** Have an aperitif in the old kitchen bar while considering daily-changing menus based on local and seasonal produce, much of it from Rathsallagh's own farm and gardens. Head Chef John Kosturk clearly relishes everything that is going on at Rathsallagh; his menus, which are interesting and change daily, are based on local and seasonal produce, much of it from Rathsallagh's own farm and walled garden. Menus are not over-complicated but offer a well-balanced range of about five dishes on each course, changed daily: a Duncannon scalops with Waldorf salad & carrot oil makes a lovely starter, for example, while main courses will usually include Wicklow lamb from Doyle's butchers - a roast rack, perhaps, served in summer with warm potato salad and red wine jus. Choices made, settle down in the graciously furnished dining room overlooking the gardens and the golf course to enjoy a series of dishes that are well-conceived and visually tempting but especially memorable for flavour. Leave room for luscious desserts, often based on fruit from the garden, which are served (generously) from a traditional trolley, or Irish farmhouse cheeses, before relaxing with coffee and petits fours in the drawing room or bar. An informative wine list offers many interesting bottles, notably in the Rathsallagh Cellar Collection, and includes a good choice of recommended wines under about €30. Helipad. **Seats 120** (private room, 55). Reservations essential. D daily, 7-9.30. Set D 2/3+ course €38/50; gourmet menu €65; house wine €25; SC discretionary. *Not suitable for children under 12. Lunch is available only for residents (12-4), but food is served at Rathsallagh Golf Club, 9-9 daily. Non-residents welcome for dinner, by reservation. Amex, Diners, MasterCard, Visa, Laser. **Directions:** 24km (15 miles) south of Naas off Carlow Road, take Kilcullen Bypass (M9), turn left 3km (2 miles) south of Priory Inn, follow signposts.

Enniskerry
CAFÉ/RESTAURANT

Powerscourt Terrace Café

Powerscourt House Enniskerry Co Wicklow **Tel: 01 204 6070**
Fax: 01 204 6072 Email: simon@avoca.ie Web: www.avoca.ie

féile bia Situated in a stunning location overlooking the famous gardens and fountains of Powerscourt House, the Pratt family of Avoca Handweavers opened this self-service restaurant in the summer of 1997. It is a delightfully relaxed space, with a large outdoor eating area as well as the 160-seater café, and the style and standard of food is similar to the original Avoca restaurant at Kilmacanogue: everything is freshly made, using as many local ingredients as possible including organic herbs and vegetables with lots of healthy food. Avoca cafés are renowned for interesting salads, home-bakes and good pastries, and also excellent vegetarian dishes many of which, such as oven-roasted vegetable and goat's cheese tart, have become specialities. Parking (some distance from the house). Children welcome. **Seats 160** (indoors; additional 140 outside terrace; private room 20-90). No-smoking area. Toilets wheelchair accessible. Open daily 10-5 (Sun to 5.30). House wine about €13. Closed 25-26 Dec. Amex, Diners, MasterCard, Visa, Laser. **Directions:** 2 miles from Enniskerry Village. ◇

Glendalough
B&B

Derrymore House

Lake Road Glendalough Co Wicklow **Tel: 0404 45493** Fax: 0404 45517
Email: patkelleher@eircom.net Web: http://homepage.eircom.net/~derrymore/

Very close to Glendalough, on a six-acre site of natural mountain woodland, Pat and Penny Kelleher's friendly B&B is in an unique position in the valley of Glendalough, overlooking the Lower Lake. It makes a quiet base for the outdoor pursuits which can be so enjoyable in the area - notably walking, fishing and horse riding - and seems like an oasis of calm when there are too many visitors around for comfort. Bedrooms are appropriately furnished in a fresh country style with antique furniture, TV and neat en-suite shower rooms. A guests' sitting room has multi-channel TV/VCR and a library of videos and, in fine weather, it is very pleasant to have a private garden to sit in. Home-baked bread for breakfast. Not suitable for children under 6. No pets. Walking, fishing. **Rooms 5** (all en-suite, shower only & no smoking, 1 family room). B&B €40 pps; ss €28. Closed Nov-Mar. **Directions:** Follow signs tor Glendalough - on the right as you approach.

Greystones
RESTAURANT

Chakra by Jaipur

1st Floor Meridian Point Church Road Greystones Co Wicklow
Tel: 01 201 7222 Fax: 01 201 7228
Email: info@chakra.ie Web: www.chakra.ie

This delightful younger sister to the successful Jaipur restaurants in Dalkey, Dublin & Malahide (see entries) occupies a custom designed restaurant space in and overlooking a modern shopping mall just off the main street of Greystones, and opened to some well-deserved acclaim in late 2005. It has a comfortable bar/reception within the spacious, high-ceilinged dining room which is very attractive, with lovely subdued warm-toned décor and, from the moment of arrival, service is unobtrusively attentive and charmingly friendly. The cooking maintains Jaipur's crisp, modern contemporary take on traditional Indian food colourful, delicious, well-flavoured dishes with a lot of eye-appeal. The vegetarian choices are numerous and appealing, and old favourites like tandoori prawns and succulent biryanis (in pastry-lidded individual pots) are served with splendid breads and delicious sauces. Unusually for an Indian restaurant, even the dessert menu is worth exploring. A fairly priced wine list has been carefully selected to complement Indian food. The shopping mall car park is available free for diners, who have their ticket validated by the restaurant. **Seats 90** (private room, 12); Air conditioning; Children welcome; D daily, 5-11pm; Early D €18, 5-7pm; Set D €30-45. House wine €19-21. Closed 25-26 Dec. MasterCard, Visa, Laser. **Directions:** Just off main street in new shopping centre, 2 minutes from DART station.

Greystones
RESTAURANT

The Hungry Monk

Church Road Greystones Co Wicklow
Tel: 01 287 5759 Fax: 01 287 7183
Email: info@thehungrymonk.ie Web: www.thehungrymonk.ie

Well-known wine buff Pat Keown has run this hospitable first floor restaurant on the main street since 1988. Pat is a great and enthusiastic host; his love of wine is infectious, the place is spick and span and the monk-related decor is a bit of fun. A combination of hospitality, great wines and interesting good quality food at affordable prices are at the heart of this restaurant's success and sheer generosity of spirit ensures value for money as well as a good meal. Seasonal menus offered include a well-priced all-day Sunday lunch and an evening à la carte menu, with fish the speciality in summer, and game in winter. Blackboard specials guaranteed to sharpen the appetite include the day's seafood dishes (usually a fine range of ultra-fresh fish just up from Greystones harbour), any special wine offers - and, perhaps, a special treat like suckling pig (a superb dish with a prune and apricot stuffing, apple sauce, a delicious jus and colcannon or champ). Menus give a slight nod to current trends - in dishes like a tian of Castletownbere crab with fresh ginger, apple & coriander flavoured coconut milk, for example - but there is no pretence at cutting edge style and you will also find faithful renditions of old favourites not often seen at the moment, like lambs kidneys dijonnaise. Vegetarian dishes and healthy heart options are highlighted on the menu and there is emphasis on high quality ingredients, including Angus steaks and Wicklow lamb as well as local seafood. The famous wine list ('The Thirsty Monk') is clearly a labour of love and, in turn, gives great pleasure to customers, especially as prices are very fair. Affordable favourites include a whole page of house wines listed by category - house wine Chile, house wine France, house wines organic, house champagne.... and so on - and also, of course, offers many special bottles for connoisseurs, from every great wine region in the world including a number of magnums and jeraboams (double magnums), which make a dramatic centre piece for a party and are great value for money. Two pages of half bottles too, and a couple of dozen pudding wines... Wine lovers should arrive early to allow the time to relish this list. Children welcome. **Restaurant Seats 45.** Reservations advised. Air conditioning. Food served Wed-Sun 12.30-9. à la carte; also Vegetarian Menu; Set Sun L €27. House wines from €19, SC 10%. Restaurant closed Mon & Tue. Closed 24-26 Dec. *Downstairs, The Hungry Monk Wine Bar offers an informal menu of bistro style dishes (Monk's famous burger, Dublin Bay prawn scampi & chips...) and a carefully selected short wine list. Wine Bar open daily, 5-12. Closed 25-26 Dec. Amex, MasterCard, Visa, Laser. **Directions:** Centre of Greystones village beside DART.

Greystones
Ⓝ RESTAURANT

The Three Q's

Gweedore Church Road Greystones Co Wicklow
Tel: 01 287 5477 Email: thethreeqs@gmail.com

The Three Qs is a small but stylish restaurant on the main street run by three brothers, Brian, Paul and Colin Quinn who bring together local foods and international inspiration to create innovative menus with real cutting edge style. The dinner menu has a smart edge, offering dishes like goats' curd, roasted beetroot & herb salad with a balsamic rhubarb dressing; saddle of rabbit with sage & black pudding stuffing and boulangère potatoes; and grilled brill with lemon verbena crust, creamed fennel and leeks. Lunch and brunch menus are more relaxed, offering tasty, fresh tasting combinations like a dish of corn fritters with crispy pancetta, avocado and tomato, along with both spring onions and the sharper red onions, rocket and flat leaf parsley - with plenty of zing and sweetness, this makes a perfect little summer brunch, and tomato and maple glazed rack of baby ribs is a dish attracting favourable mention too. Attention to detail is seen in good side orders including proper freshly cut chips and chunky sweetly spiced homemade tomato sauce. The flavours of North Africa and Arab cooking are seen in delicious desserts like Medjoul dates soaked in espresso, star anise and cinnamon, and served with vanilla mascarpone and shortbread. There's welcome originality here, also well informed service and fair pricing on both food and wine - a welcome newcomer among the fast-growing dining choices in Greystones. Not suitable for children after 6pm. **Seats 30** (outdoors, 8); food served daily 9am-11.30pm (Sun 9-3); L 12-4.30, D 6-10. A la carte. (Starters €4.95 to €9.95, main courses €16.95 to €26.95, desserts €6.95.); house wine €19. Closed Sun D, Christmas week. Amex, MasterCard, Visa, Laser. **Directions:** Main street Greystones, 100m from the Dart station.

Greystones
RESTAURANT

Vino Pasta

Church Road Greystones Co Wicklow
Tel: 01 287 4807 Fax: 01 287 4827

féile bia Attractive awnings and clear signage make a good impression at this popular Italian restaurant and, once past the tiny bar/reception area (which has just two seats), you'll find a warmly decorated room with bistro-style table settings - paper cloths & napkins - and a moderately priced menu, majoring in pastas and pizzas plus daily specials on a blackboard menu: lambs kidneys in a creamy mustard sauce with tagliatelle, perhaps, and fresh fish such as cod with a spicy chilli jam, or salmon with a herb crust. Efficient, friendly service, sound cooking and generous portions make this the kind of place that locals pop into frequently. Limited wine list. The early dinner is good value, and can include a fish special of the day. Seats 60; reservations required; air conditioning; not suitable for children under 6 or after 7pm. D Tue-Sat 5.30-10pm, Sun 5.30-9pm. Early D €19.95 (Tue-Fri 5-7, Sun 3-5.30). Also à la carte. House wine €16.95. Closed Mon; 24-25 Dec . Amex, MasterCard, Visa, Laser. **Directions:** End of Main Street beside DART station. ◇

Kilmacanogue
€ CAFÉ

Avoca Handweavers, Kilmacanogue

Kilmacanogue Bray Co Wicklow **Tel: 01 286 7466**
Fax: 01 286 2367 Email: reception@avoca.ie Web: www.avoca.ie

féile bia This large shop and restaurant, off the N11 south of Dublin, is the flagship premises of Ireland's most famous group of craft shops and, in recent years, they have become almost equally well known for the quality of their food - people come here from miles around to shop, and to tuck into wholesome home-cooked food, which is as healthy as it is delicious. The importance of sourcing only the very best ingredients has always been recognised at Avoca, where food is based as much as possible on local and artisan produce, and there is a commitment to using products from recognised Quality Assurance Schemes. (In recognition, Avoca Cafés were the recipients of the Féile Bia Award in 2003). The style at Avoca is eclectic and, although they are perhaps especially well-known for great baking and wholesome traditional dishes like beef and Guinness casserole, their salads and vegetables are also legendary - and their repertoire also includes a lot of dishes influenced by other cultures, notably Mediterranean and middle-eastern. There is also a wide range of excellent delicatessen fare for sale in the shop - and you can make many of their dishes at home too, using recipes given in the two handsome Avoca Café Cookbooks. *Also at: Avoca, Powerscourt, & Suffolk Street, Dublin 2 (see entries). *Also at: Avoca, Powerscourt, & Suffolk Street, Dublin 2 (see entries). Toilets Wheelchair Accessible; Children welcome. Seats 170 (+Outdoor Dining, 80). Air conditioning. Open daily, 9.30-5 (Sun 10-5). House wine from €20. No s.c. Closed 25-26 Dec. Amex, Diners, MasterCard, Visa, Laser. **Directions:** On N11 sign posted before Kilmacanogue Village.

Kiltegan

Barraderry Country House

E COUNTRY HOUSE

Barraderry Kiltegan Co Wicklow
Tel: 059 647 3209 Fax: 059 647 3209
Email: jo.hobson@oceanfree.net Web: www.barraderrycountryhouse.com

Olive and John Hobson's delightful Georgian house is in a quiet rural area close to the Wicklow Mountains and, once their family had grown up, the whole house was extensively refurbished and altered for the comfort of guests. Big bedrooms with country views are beautifully furnished with old family furniture and have well-finished shower rooms - and there's a spacious sitting room for guests' use too. Barraderry would make a good base for touring the lovely counties of Wicklow, Kildare, Carlow and Wexford and there's plenty to do nearby, with six golf courses within a half hour drive, several hunts and equestrian centres within easy reach and also Punchestown, Curragh and Naas racecourses - and, of course, walking in the lovely Wicklow Mountains. Garden; walking. Children welcome (cot available). Pets permitted in certain areas by arrangement. **Rooms 4** (all en-suite, shower only & no smoking). B&B €50 pps; ss €5. Closed 15 Dec-15 Jan. MasterCard, Visa. **Directions:** N81 Dublin-Baltinglass; R 747 to Kiltegan (7km).

Macreddin

The BrookLodge Hotel

HOTEL

Macreddin Village Co Wicklow **Tel: 0402 36444** Fax: 0402 36580
Email: brooklodge@macreddin.ie Web: www.brooklodge.com

Built on the site of a deserted village in a Wicklow valley, this extraordinary food, drink and leisure complex exists thanks to the vision of three brothers, Evan, Eoin and Bernard Doyle. The driving force is Evan, a pioneer of the new organic movement when he ran The Strawberry Tree restaurant in Killarney. Now their new hotel and restaurant has earned a national recognition for its strong position on organic food (BrookLodge won the Guide's Natural Food Award in association with Euro-Toques, in 2003), and their little "street" is thriving, with an olde-worlde pub (Actons), a café, a micro-brewery and gift shops selling home-made produce and related quality products. Organic food markets, held on the first Sunday of the month (first and third in summer) have also proved a great success. Spacious and welcoming, the hotel has elegant country house furnishings, open fires and plenty of places to sit quietly or meet for a sociable drink - and the accommodation choices are between the original rooms, which are furnished with quite traditional free standing furniture, and state-of-the-art mezzanine suites, which will please those who relish very modern high-tech surroundings. A luxurious spa centre, The Wells, features an indoor-to-outdoor swimming pool, gym, juice bar and a wide variety of exclusive beauty and health treatments. Midweek, weekend and low season special offers are good value, and staff are friendly and helpful. *A new development is The River Mews (4 conference suites and 8 bedrooms) a short stroll from the main hotel; also Macreddin Golf Club, designed by Irish Ryder Cup hero Paul McGinley, due to open summer 2007. Conference/banqueting (350/191). Secretarial services, video conferencing (by arrangement). Equestrian centre. Off road driving. Hot tub. Garden, walking. Snooker. Children welcome (under 4s free in parents' room, cot available without charge, baby sitting arranged). Pets allowed in some areas by arrangement. **Rooms 56** (13 suites, 3 junior suites, 3 superior rooms, 4 ground floor, 2 family, 4 disabled, 35 no smoking). Lift. B&B €130 pps; ss €50. Open all year. **The Strawberry Tree:** This is Ireland's only certified organic restaurant, reflecting the BrookLodge philosophy of sourcing only from producers using slow organic methods and harvesting in their correct season. Menus are not too long or too fussy: dishes have strong, simple names and, except when underlined on the menu as wild, everything offered is organic. Typical dishes might include starters like home smoked beef, with figs and balsamic dressing or grilled wild pollock with roast red pepper, and main courses such as slow cooked spring lamb with roast celeriac & garlic jus, or a vegetarian dish of wild mushroom and brie tart with wild garlic pesto. There's a great buzz associated with the commitment to organic production at BrookLodge, and it makes a natural venue for meetings of like-minded groups such as Euro-Toques and Slow Food, especially on market days. Dining at the Strawberry Tree is a unique experience - and good informal meals can be equally enjoyable at The Orchard Café and Actons pub (both open noon-9pm daily). Given the quality of ingredients used and the standard of cooking, meals at BrookLodge represent very good value. **Seats 145** (private room, 60, outdoor, 10). Air conditioning. Toilets wheelchair accessible. D daily 7-9.30 (to 9 Sun), L Sun only 1.30-3.30. Set D €60, Set Sun L €40. House wines €25. SC discretionary. *William Actons Pub - Bar food daily, 12.30-9; The Orchard Café, light meals in summer 12.30-9. Amex, Diners, MasterCard, Visa, Laser. **Directions:** Signed from Aughrim.

Newtownmountkennedy

HOTEL

Marriott Druids Glen Hotel & Country Club

Newtownmountkennedy Co Wicklow **Tel: 01 287 0800**
Fax: 01 287 0801 Email: mhrs.dubgs.reservations@marriotthotels.com
Web: www.marriottdruidsglen.com

féile bia Just 20 miles south of Dublin, in a stunning location between the sea and the mountains and adjacent to Druids Glen Golf Club, this luxurious hotel has a feeling of space throughout - beginning with the marbled foyer and its dramatic feature fireplace. Suites and guest rooms, many of them "double/doubles" (with two queen sized beds), are all generously-sized, with individual 'climate control' (heating and air conditioning), and all bathrooms have separate bath and walk-in shower. A wide range of recreational facilities on site includes the hotel's spa and health club (which has recently been refurbished and extended), while those nearby include horse riding, archery, quad biking - and, of course, the gentler attractions of the Wicklow Mountains National Park are on the doorstep. When dining in, choose between Flynns' Steakhouse (see below) and the bigger Druids Restaurant (where breakfast, carvery lunch and dinner are served daily). Bar meals also available in 'The Thirteenth' bar or, in fine weather, on a sheltered deck outside the two restaurants. Druids Glen Marriott was our Business Hotel of the Year in 2003 - and this is a place to relax and unwind, as well as do business. Conference/banqueting 250/220; business centre, secretarial services. Golf (2x18); leisure centre, swimming pool; spa, beauty/treatment rooms, walking, garden. **Rooms 148** (11 suites, 137 executive, 6 disabled). Lift. Children welcome (under 12s free in parents' room, cots available without charge; baby sitting arranged). 24 hr. room service, turndown service, laundry/valet service. B&B about €115, ss €30. Flynn's Steakhouse: Quite small and intimate, with an open log fire and candlelight, Flynn's has more atmosphere than the bigger daytime Druids Restaurant, and reservations are essential. American style steaks and grills are the speciality but, demonstrating a welcome commitment to using Irish produce, a supply of Certified Irish Angus is contracted for the hotel; just remember that American-style means big - 24oz porterhouse and ribeye, for example...Rack of Wicklow lamb is another speciality and there's a sprinkling of other dishes with an Irish flavour which might not be expected in an international hotel, like Dingle crab cakes, Guinness braised mussels - and an Irish cheese platter. **Seats 75** (private room 16). Reservations essential. Not suitable for children after 8. D daily, 6-10.30. Set D €40/50 2/3 course, also à la carte. House wine, from about €22; SC discretionary. *The larger Druid's Restaurant serves breakfast, lunch & dinner daily; L carvery, Druids Irish D Menu à la carte. Bar meals also available in 'The Thirteenth' bar or, in fine weather, on a sheltered deck outside the two restaurants. Amex, Diners, MasterCard, Visa, Laser. **Directions:** 36km (20 miles) south of Dublin on N11, at Newtownmountkennedy.

Rathdrum

GUESTHOUSE

Avonbrae Guesthouse

Rathdrum Co Wicklow **Tel: 0404 46198** Fax: 0404 46198
Email: info@avonbrae.com Web: www.avonbrae.com

Lovers of the outdoor life will find that Paddy Geoghegan's hospitable guesthouse makes a comfortable and relaxed base - walking, cycling, riding, pony-trekking, golf and fishing are major attractions to this beautiful area, but it's also ideal just for a quiet break. (Paddy offers weekly and weekend rates and off-season breaks which are very reasonable.) Simply furnished bedrooms vary in size and outlook but all have tea and coffee trays and en-suite facilities (only the smallest room has a bath). There are open fires as well as central heating and a comfortable guest sitting room. For fine weather, there's a tennis court in the well-kept garden and, although this perhaps sounds grander than it is, there is even a little indoor swimming pool. Children welcome (under 2s free in parent's room, cot available). Pets permitted by arrangement. **Rooms 7** (all en-suite, 1 with private bathroom). B&B €35 pps; ss €10. Evening meals about €22 at 6.30pm. House wine about €13.50. Packed lunches available by arrangement (€6). Closed 1 Dec-1 Mar. MasterCard, Visa. **Directions:** About 500 yards outside Rathdrum on Glendalough Road. ◇

Rathnew

E HOTEL/RESTAURANT

Hunter's Hotel

Newrath Bridge Rathnew Co Wicklow
Tel: 0404 40106 Fax: 0404 40338
Email: reception@hunters.ie Web: www.hunters.ie

A rambling old coaching inn set in lovely gardens alongside the River Vartry, this much-loved hotel has a long and fascinating history - it's one of Ireland's oldest coaching inns, with records indicating that it was built around 1720. In the same family now for five generations, the colourful Mrs Maureen Gelletlie takes pride in running the place on traditional lines with her sons Richard and Tom. This means old-fashioned comfort and food based on local and home-grown produce with the emphasis very much on 'old fashioned' which is where its charm and character lie. There's a proper little bar, with chintzy loose-covered furniture and an open fire, a traditional dining room with fresh flowers from the riverside garden where their famous afternoon tea is served in summer - and comfortable country bedrooms. There is nowhere else in Ireland like it. Conference (30). Garden. Parking. Children welcome. No pets. **Rooms 16** (1 junior suite, 1 shower only, 1 disabled). Wheelchair access. B&B from about €95 pps, ss about €20. **Restaurant:** In tune with the spirit of the hotel, the style is traditional country house cooking: simple food with a real home-made feeling about it - no mean achievement in a restaurant and much to be applauded. Seasonal lunch and dinner menus change daily, but you can expect classics such as chicken liver pâté with melba toast, soups based on fish or garden produce, traditional roasts rib beef, with Yorkshire pudding or old-fashioned roast stuffed chicken with bacon and probably several fish dishes, possibly including poached salmon with hollandaise and chive sauce. Desserts are often based on what the garden has to offer, and baking is good, so fresh raspberries and cream or baked apple and rhubarb tart could be wise choices. Delightful. **Seats 50.** Toilets wheelchair accessible. L daily, 1-3 (Sun 2 sittings: 12.45 & 2.30). D daily 7.30-9. Set D about €40. Set L about €22. No s.c. House wine about €16. Afternoon tea about €7.50. Closed 3 days at Christmas. Amex, Diners, MasterCard, Visa. **Directions:** Off N11 at Ashford or Rathnew. ◇

Rathnew

HOTEL/RESTAURANT

Tinakilly Country House & Restaurant

Rathnew Co Wicklow
Tel: 0404 69274 Fax: 0404 67806
Email: reservations@tinakilly.ie Web: www.tinakilly.ie

Josephine and Raymond Power have been running this fine hotel since January 2000 and they have retained those things which Raymond's parents, William and Bee Power, achieved to earn its reputation, while also bringing a new energy and enthusiasm which has lightened the atmosphere. Since opening for guests in 1983, after a sensitive restoration programme, caring owner-management and steadily improving amenities have combined to make it a favourite destination for both business and leisure. It's a place of great local significance, having been built in the 1870s for Captain Robert Halpin, a local man who became Commander of The Great Eastern, which laid the first telegraph cable linking Europe and America. Tinakilly is one of the country's top business and corporate venues, but there is also a romantic side to its nature as bedrooms have views across a bird sanctuary to the sea, and there are also period rooms, some with four-posters. To all this, add personal supervision by caring owners, friendly, well-trained staff, lovely grounds and a fine kitchen, and the recipe for success is complete. Conference/banqueting (65/80). Secretarial services. Fitness suite. Garden, walking, tennis. Golf nearby (brochure available on request). Children welcome (under 12s free in parents' room, cots available without charge, baby sitting arranged). No pets. **Rooms 51** (6 suites, 33 junior suites, 12 executive, 13 ground floor, 1 suitable for disabled). Lift. B&B €139pps; ss €61. Closed 24-26 Dec. **Brunel Restaurant:** This panelled split level restaurant is in the west wing of the house, which catches the evening sunlight, and it has a relaxed, intimate atmosphere. Comfort is the byword here, and tables are beautifully set up with lovely linen, stylish flowers and elegant glasses and china. Head chef Ross Quinn, who joined the team in 2004, presents refreshingly straightforward à la carte menus which are not overlong - half a dozen dishes on each course - yet offer plenty of choice. The best of local and home-grown ingredients are used in dishes showcasing local seafood (lobster salad with orange segments & raspberry vinaigrette), local meats (loin of Wicklow lamb with fondant potatoes, ratatouille & garden thyme) and venison (in season). In the Guide's experience, cooking is skilful and confident, with good attention to detail in, for example, the choice of freshly baked breads offered, and simple side vegetables, cooked al dente, which complement the main dishes well. An Irish cheese selection is offered, also some tempting desserts, usually including several based on seasonal fruits (local raspberries with lemon mascarpone, perhaps). Finish with tea or coffee from a short menu. Caring and professional service, under the direction of restaurant manager Conrad Robinson, match the high standard of food and cooking. **Seats 90** (private room, 30). Reservations required. Air conditioning. Toilets wheelchair accessible. D Brunel Restaurant Tue-Sat 7.30-9; 5-course D about €48, from à la carte menu. Sun & Mon shorter 'Tinakilly House' à la carte menu. L Sun and Mon from 1-8pm, otherwise light meals in bar. House wine from €21. SC discretionary. Closed 24-26 Dec. Amex, Diners, MasterCard, Visa, Laser. **Directions:** From N11(main Dublin - Wexford road) to Rathnew village; Tinakilly is 500 metres from village on R750 to Wicklow town.

Roundwood
RESTAURANT/PUB

Roundwood Inn

Roundwood Co Wicklow
Tel: 01 281 8107

PUB OF THE YEAR

féile bia Jurgen and Aine Schwalm have owned this atmospheric 17th century inn in the highest village in the Wicklow Hills for over 25 years and, during that time, caring hands-on managment backed up by dedicated long-serving staff have earned this unique bar and restaurant a lot of friends. There's a public bar at one end with a snug and an open fire and, in the middle of the building, the main bar food area has an enormous open fireplace with an ever-burning log fire, and is furnished in traditional style with wooden floors and big sturdy tables. Together with head chef Paul Taube, who has also been in the kitchen here for over 20 years, the style that the Schwalms have developed over the years is their own unique blend of Irish and German influences: excellent bar food includes Hungarian goulash, fresh crab bisque, Galway oysters, smoked Wicklow trout, smoked salmon and hearty hot meals, notably the delicious house variation on Irish stew. This has always been the way things are done at Roundwood; the food has always had a special character (unlike many of those johnny-come-lately 'gastropubs') and this, together with the place itself and its own special brand of hospitality, has earned the Roundwood Inn an enviable reputation with hillwalkers, Dubliners out for the day and visitors alike. Bar meals 12-9.30 daily. Bar closed 25 Dec, Good Fri. **Restaurant:** The restaurant is in the same style and only slightly more formal than the main bar, with fires at each end of the room (converted to gas here, alas), and is open by reservation. The menu choice leans towards more substantial dishes such as rack of Wicklow lamb, roast wild Wicklow venison, venison ragoût, pheasant and other game in season. German influences are again evident in long-established specialities such as smoked Westphalian ham and wiener schnitzel, but there are also classic specialities which cross all the usual boundaries: roast stuffed goose often appears on winter menus, especially around Christmas time, for example - and the roast suckling pig is not to be missed. An interesting mainly European wine list favours France and Germany, with many special bottles from Germany unlikely to be found elsewhere. Not suitable for children after 6.30. **Seats 45** (private room, 25). D Fri & Sat, 7.30-9; à la carte. L Sun only, 1-2. (Children welcome for lunch). House wine from about €16; SC discretionary; reservations advised. No SC. Restaurant closed L Mon-Sat, D Sun-Thu. Amex, MasterCard, Visa, Laser. **Directions:** N11, follow sign for Glendalough. ◇

Woodenbridge
HOTEL

Woodenbridge Hotel

Vale of Avoca Arklow Co Wicklow **Tel: 0402 35146** Fax: 0402 35573
Email: info@woodenbridgehotel.com Web: www.woodenbridgehotel.com

féile bia This pleasant country hotel lays claim to the title of Ireland's oldest hotel, with a history going back to 1608, when it was first licensed as a coaching inn on the old Dublin-Wexford highway - and later came to prominence when gold and copper were mined in the locality. Today, it is very popular for weddings and makes a friendly and relaxing base for a visit to this beautiful part of County Wicklow, or for a golfing break. The many other historical associations in the area include the home of Charles Stewart Parnell, nearby at Avondale. Woodenbridge Lodge, which opened in 2004, added forty new en-suite rooms overlooking the River Aughrim; older bedrooms in the hotel have all been refurbished and are comfortably furnished, with phone, TV and tea/coffee trays, and many of them overlook Woodenbridge golf course. As well as a more formal restaurant, food is available in the lively bar (traditional Irish music in summer). *Golf breaks are a speciality and discounted green fees are offered on a number of local golf courses, with other activities for non-golfing partners if required. Children welcome (under 12s free in parents' room; cots available without charge). No pets. **Rooms 62** (8 family rooms, 45 no smoking, 3 for disabled). B&B €50pps, ss €20. Food available 12.30-9. Amex, Diners, MasterCard, Visa, Laser. **Directions:** N11 to Arklow; turn off - 7km (4 miles).

NORTHERN IRELAND

BELFAST

The origins of the coastal cities of Ireland are usually found in 5th Century monastic centres which were overrun by the Vikings some four hundred or so years later to become trading settlements. These settlements in turn "had manners put on them" by the Normans two or three hundred years later. But Belfast is much newer than that. When the Vikings in the 9th century raided along the shores of what is now known as Belfast Lough, their target was the wealthy monastery at Bangor, and thus their beach-heads were at Ballyholme and Groomsport close to the eastward. Then, when the Normans held sway in the 13th Century, their main stronghold was at Carrickfergus on the northern shore of this commodious inlet, which was known for several centuries as Carrickfergus Bay.

At the head of that inlet beside the shallow River Lagan, the tiny settlement of beal feirste - the 'town at the mouth of the Farset or the sandspit' - wasn't named on maps at all until the late 15th Century. But Belfast proved to be the perfect greenfield site for rapid development as the Industrial Revolution got under way. Its rocketing growth began with linen manufacture in the 17th Century, and this was accelerated by the arrival of skilled Huguenot refugees after 1685.

There was also scope for ship-building on the shorelines in the valleymouth between the high peaks crowding in on the Antrim side on the northwest, and the Holywood Hills to the southeast, though the first shipyard of any significant size wasn't in being until 1791, when William and Hugh Ritchie opened for business. The Lagan Valley gave convenient access to the rest of Ireland for the increase of trade and commerce to encourage development of the port, while the prosperous farms of Down and Antrim fed a rapidly expanding population.

So, at the head of what was becoming known as Belfast Lough, Belfast took off in a big way, a focus for industrial ingenuity and manufacturing inventiveness, and a magnet for entrepreneurs and innovators from all of the north of Ireland, and the world beyond. Its population in 1600 had been less than 500, yet by 1700 it was 2,000, and by 1800 it was 25,000. The city's growth was prodigious, such that at the end of the 19th Century it could claim with justifiable pride to have the largest shipyard in the world, the largest ropeworks, the largest linen mills, the largest tobacco factory, and the largest heavy engineering works, all served by a greater mileage of quays than anywhere comparable. And it was an essentially Victorian expansion - the population in 1851 was 87,062, but by 1901 it was 349,l80 – in numerical terms, the largest city in Ireland.

Growth had become so rapid in the latter half of the 19th Century that it tended to obliterate the influence of the gentler intellectual and philosophical legacies inspired by the Huguenots and other earlier developers, a case in point being the gloriously flamboyant and baroque Renaissance-style City Hall, which was completed in 1906. It was the perfect expression of that late-Victorian energy and confidence in which Belfast shared with conspicuous enthusiasm. But its site had only become available because the City Fathers authorised the demolition of the quietly elegant White Linen Hall, which had been a symbol of Belfast's less strident period of development in the 18th Century.

However, Belfast Corporation was only fulfilling the spirit of the times. And in such a busy city, there was always a strongly human dimension to everyday life. Thus the City Hall may be on the grand scale, but it was nevertheless right at the heart of town. Equally, while the gantries of the shipyard may have loomed overheead, they did so near the houses of the workers in a manner which somehow softened their sheer size. Admittedly this theme of giving great projects a human dimension seems to have been forgotten in the later design and location of the imposing Government Building (completed 1932) at Stormont, east of the city. But back in the vibrant heart of Belfast, there is continuing entertainment and accessible interest in buildings as various as the Grand Opera House, St Anne's Cathedral, the Crown Liquor Saloon, Sinclair Seamen's Church, the Linenhall Library, and Smithfield Market, not to mention some of the impressive Victorian banking halls, while McHugh's pub on Queen's Square, and Tedford's Restaurant just round the corner on Donegall Quay, provide thoughtful reminders of the earlier, more restrained style.

Today, modern technologies and advanced engineering have displaced the old smokestack industries in the forefront of the city's work patterns, with the shipyard ceasing to build ships in 2003, though ship repair work continues. Shorts' aerospace factories are now the city's biggest employer, while parts of the former shipyard are being redeveloped as the Titanic Quarter in memory of the most famous ship built in Belfast. The energy of former times has been channeled into impressive urban regeneration along the River Lagan. Here, the flagship building is the Waterfront Hall, a large state-of-the-art concert venue which has won international praise, is complemented by the Odyssey Centre on the other side of the river. In the southern part of the city, Queen's University (founded 1845) is a beautifully balanced 1849 Lanyon building at the heart of a pleasant university district which includes the city's noted Lyric Theatre as well as the respected Ulster Museum & Art Gallery, while the university itself is particularly noted for its pioneering work in medicine and engineering.

Thus there's a buzz to Belfast which is expressed in its cultural and warmly sociable life, and reflected in the internationally-minded innovative energy of its young chefs. Yet in some ways it is still has marked elements of a country town and port strongly rooted in land and sea. The hills of Antrim can be glimpsed from most streets, and the farmland of Down makes its presence felt. They are quickly reached by a somewhat ruthlessly implemented motorway system, relished by those in a hurry who also find the increasingly busy and very accessible Belfast City Airport – renamed in honour of legendary footballer George Best - a convenient facility.. So although Belfast may have a clearly defined character, it is also very much part of the country around it, and is all the better for that. And in the final analysis, Belfast is uniquely itself.

Local Attractions and Information

Arts Council of Northern Ireland	028 90 385200
Belfast Castle & Zoo	028 90 776277
Belfast Crystal	028 90 622051
Belfast Festival at Queens (late Oct-early Nov)	028 90 665577
Belfast Welcome Centre	028 90 246609
City Airport	028 90 457745
City Hall	028 90 270456
Citybus Tours	028 90 458484
Fernhill House: The People's Museum	028 90 715599
Grand Opera House	028 90 241919
International Airport	028 94 484848
Kings Hall (exhibitions, concerts, trade shows)	028 90 665225
Lagan Valley Regional Park	028 90 491922
Linenhall Library	028 90 321707
Lyric Theatre	028 90 381081
National Trust Regional Office	028 97 510721
Northern Ireland Railways	028 90 899411
Odyssey (entertainment & sports complex)	028 90 451055
St Anne's Cathedral	028 90 328332
Sir Thomas & Lady Dixon Park (Rose Gardens)	028 90 320202
Tourism Information	028 90 246609
Ulster Historical Foundation (genealogical res.)	028 90 332288
Ulster Museum & Art Gallery	028 90 383000
Waterfront Hall (concert venue)	028 90 334455
West Belfast Festivals	028 90 313440

Belfast

Ⓔ RESTAURANT

Aldens Restaurant

229 Upper Newtownards Road Belfast Belfast BT4 3JF
Tel: 028 9065 0079 Fax: 028 9065 0032
Email: info@aldensrestaurant.com Web: www.aldensrestaurant.com

A neat canopy in aubergine-toned livery highlights the discreetly distinctive public face of Jonathan Davis's fine contemporary restaurant, an indication of the quality that lies within. Although the choice of location seemed unlikely at the time, Aldens was at the forefront of Belfast's first wave of chic, uncluttered modern restaurants when it opened in 1998, and it immediately became a destination address; Cath Gradwell, the head chef who had been with the restaurant since it opened, has now moved on to new pastures but she left the kitchen in very good order, as previous sous chef, Denise Hockey, inherited the mantle in 2006 and a recent visit confirms that she is succeeding in retaining Aldens' fine reputation - in the face of growing city centre competition. Aldens serves its area extremely well - it is convenient to Stormont, and there is a strong business following. A welcoming bar/reception area has comfortable seating and pleasing details - fresh flowers, choice of olives, newspapers and food guides to browse over a drink - while tables are smartly set up with quality linen, tapenade, olive oil and butter, along with several types of bread; opaque glass windows soften the light and give a sense of privacy, with strips of mirror adding reflections on painted walls. Lively international menus, changed daily, are admirably simple and use seasonal ingredients in cooking that especially emphasises flavour combinations, fish and local produce - and dishes are generally executed with flair. While not overlong, menus offer plenty of choice (including some luxurious dishes like seared foie gras with baby leaves and port jus); updated classics, like chicken liver paté with hot toast & red onion marmalade and steamed mussels with scallions, white wine and garlic sit happily alongside prime fish and meats (roast hake, sirloin steak), and humbler everyday foods like baked polenta with wild mushrooms and white asparagus (one of several mainstream vegetarian choices, usually also including a tempting twice-baked spinach & parmesan soufflé with chive cream), served with imaginative side dishes. Consistent cooking and professional service from smartly-uniformed staff under Jonathan Davis's personal direction make this one of Northern Ireland's finest restaurants and it offers very good value, notably the lunch specials and a short dinner menu. An interesting and informative wine list offers a great range of wines at very fair prices, including 14 house wines and - a sign of the times, perhaps - an exceptional choice of half bottles. **Seats 70.** Children welcome. No smoking area; air conditioning. L Mon-Fri,12-2.30; D Mon-Thu 6-10, Fri & Sat 6-11; Set D from £18.95 (Mon-Thu), à la carte. House wines from £11.95; sc discretionary. Closed L Sat, all Sun, Public Holidays, 2 weeks July. Amex, Diners, MasterCard, Visa, Switch. **Directions:** On the Upper Newtownards Road at junction with Sandown Road.

Belfast

€ GUESTHOUSE

An Old Rectory

148 Malone Road Belfast BT9 5LH
Tel: 028 9066 7882 Fax: 028 9068 3759
Email: info@anoldrectory.co.uk Web: www.anoldrectory.co.uk

Conveniently located near the King's Hall, Public Records Office, Lisburn Road and Queen's University, Mary Callan's lovely late Victorian house is set well back from the road in mature trees, with private parking. A former Church of Ireland rectory, it had the benefit of being in the Malone conservation area and retains many original features, including stained glass windows. There's a lovely drawing room with books, sofas, comfortable armchairs with cosy rugs over the arms - and a very hospitable habit of serving hot whiskey in the drawing room at 9 o'clock each night. Accommodation is on two storeys, every room individually decorated (and named) and each has both a desk and a sofa, magazines to browse, also beverage trays with hot chocolate and soup sachets as well as the usual tea and coffee; better still there's a fridge on each landing with iced water and fresh milk, helpful advice on eating out locally is available (including menus) and, although they don't do evening meals, pride is taken in providing a good breakfast. A ground floor room suitable for disabled guests is planned for 2007. Children welcome (under 5 free in parents' room). Garden, walking. No pets. **Rooms 5** (3 en-suite, 2 with private bathrooms - 2 shower only, 3 with bath & shower, all no smoking). B&B £25-33 pps, ss £12. Closed Christmas-New Year & Easter. **No Credit Cards**. **Directions:** 3km (2 miles) from city centre, between Balmoral Avenue and Stranmillis Road.

Belfast

RESTAURANT

The Bank Gallery

The Edge May's Meadow Belfast BT
Tel: 028 9032 2000

Right on the Lagan and just a short stroll along a walkway from the Waterfront, this gently contemporary first floor restaurant is over a designer bar, The Edge, with views of the famous Harland & Wolf cranes, and doors opening onto a small outside seating area on both levels - a pleasant spot which, thanks to Donal Keane's fine cooking, has earned a following. The decor is appealing: portholes in the double doors are repeated on chair backs and, with lightwood everywhere, recessed wall lights and dusky pinks and beiges used in voile curtains and upholstery, there's a softness that offsets the industrial exterior. Tables are set up smartly with black rubber mats and simply folded damask napkins, and professional black-aproned servers move speedily to bring breads (three, all delicious and gently warm) with tapenade. Donal Keane is a fine chef, especially known for a love of local produce and excellent fish cookery, so it is no surprise to find some old favourites on his very appealing and well-balanced menus - Ardglass crab among the starters (in a salad, with avocado, mango & home-made wheaten bread, perhaps), also naturally dyed smoked haddock (on a potato salad, with a cherry tomato & grain mustard dressing) and even an evening main course of Ballycastle lobster, which is cannily baked in combination with chicken in a thermidor sauce, glazed with Parmesan and served with boiled potatoes and mixed salad - ingenious, and great value at about £14.75. The lunch menu has no divisions, so you can mix & match from the dozen or so choices as you like - pretty, lusciously ripe galia melon with ruby grapefruit, honey & crème fraîche makes a perfect starter for weight-watchers, but Portavogie jumbo scampi is a tempting choice, and there's real comfort food in McCartneys famous pork & leek sausages, served on champ with an onion gravy. Desserts are also (unusually) well-balanced, considerately including a fresh fruit salad along with more fattening treats. This is a super place, where good food combines with caring service and value for money - a great combination by any standards. Parking (8). Disabled access; lift. Open Mon-Sat 11-'late'. L Mon-Fri 12-2.30; D Mon-Sat, 5.30-9.30. 2/3 course early D, £11.95/14.95 (5.30-6.45), otherwise à la carte. D reservations advised. Pianist - baby grand (Fri & Sat from 9pm). Closed Sun. MasterCard, Visa. **Directions:** Laganside. ◇

Belfast

Beatrice Kennedy

RESTAURANT

44 University Road Belfast BT7 1NJ **Tel: 028 9020 2290**
Fax: 028 9020 2291 Web: www.beatrice.kennedy.co.uk

Named after the lady whose home it once was, the dining area of this unusual restaurant begins in what would have been her front room and extends into adjoining areas towards the back, retaining something of the authentic lived-in feeling of a private period residence; although now furnished with white-damasked tables, it has a Victorian atmosphere with a small open fireplace and mantelpiece and a few books and leftover personal effects: softly-lit, atmospheric, intimate, it exudes an atmosphere of calm in which to enjoy proprietor-chef Jim McCarthy's accomplished cooking. Ingredients are carefully sourced, dishes are smoked on the premises and breads, desserts and ice creams are all home-made. The style is modern, with Thai and Chinese influences seen in dishes like red braised pork (with spiced aubergine salad) and Thai smoked duck, but also flavours closer to home in roast cod with crushed potato and sauce vierge. Presentation is very special, especially the desserts - which are minor works of art; desserts come with a BK signature in cocoa on the rim of each plate, then the motif is repeated on little home-made chocolate medallions served with coffee - a nice touch. **Seats 80** (private room 25). D Tue-Sun, 5-10.15 (Sun to 8.30pm); L Sun only 12-2.15. Early D £10 (5-7), Set Sun L about £15. Closed Mon, 24-26 Dec, 11-14 Jul. Amex, MasterCard, Visa, Switch. **Directions:** Adjacent to Queen's University. ◇

Belfast

Benedict's Hotel Belfast

Ⓝ HOTEL

7-21 Bradbury Place Belfast BT7 IRQ
Tel: 028 9059 1999 Fax: 028 9059 1990
Email: info@benedictsHotel.co.uk Web: www.benedictshotel.co.uk

Very conveniently located in Bradbury Place, just off Shaftsbury Square, this reasonably priced city centre hotel is situated in the heart of Belfast's "Golden Mile", and a wide range of attractions, including the Botanic Gardens, Queen's University, Queen's Film Theatre and Ulster Museum, are within a few minutes walk. Benedicts combines comfort and a degree of contemporary style with very moderate prices; the comfortable beds invariably come in for special praise, as do the warm and friendly staff on the downside, it can sometimes be noisy and there is no on-site parking although the hotel has an arrangement with a nearby carpark. Children welcome (cot available without charge). No private parking; no pets; free broadband WI/FI. **Rooms 32** (12 executive rooms, 2 shower only, 2 for disabled, 5 no smoking). Lift; all day room service. B&B from £35 pps, ss £25. Closed 24-25 Dec. Amex, Diners, MasterCard, Visa, Switch. **Directions:** City centre hotel situated in Bradbury Place - just off Shaftsbury Place in the heart of Belfast's "Golden Mile.".

Belfast

Bourbon

RESTAURANT

60 Great Victoria Street Belfast BT2 7BB **Tel: 028 9033 2121**
Email: info@bourbonrestaurant.com Web: www.bourbonrestaurant.com

Behind an unassuming entrance lies an amazingly theatrical interior: totally at home alongside neighbouring buildings like the Crown Liquor Saloon and the Grand Opera House, it features pillars, palms, ornate plaster work and wrought iron, chandeliers and statues - everything, in short, to convey sumptuousness. Not to everybody's taste, to be sure, but it works - and provides the perfect antidote for diners who've had an overdose of minimalism. But there's a bit of that here too - don't expect pristine white linen, silver and crystal: what you actually get is bare table tops, the ubiquitous black rubber place mats, and paper napkins. So it should come as no surprise that menus are modern, written in a no-nonsense style and offering a wide range of international contemporary crowd pleasers: starters of spicy chicken wings or goats cheese and caramelised onion tart are typical, for example, and an extensive selection of main courses includes half a dozen poultry dishes, pizzas and pasta, and a lot of meat - steaks various ways, homemade shepherd's pie, bangers & mash, a range of burgers...But vegetarians do get some choice from the pizza and pasta ranges, and there will be several main course fish dishes, such as roast cod with mash & parsley sauce. Helpful staff, competent cooking and - most of all - amazing atmosphere make this a place worth visiting. Definitely different. Open daily; No smoking area, air con. D Mon-Sun, 5-11 (Sun to 10); L Mon-Sat 12-5. Set 2-course D, £11.95 Value D £11; Value L £6. Also à la carte. House wine £14. Closed Sun L & 25-26 Dec. **Directions:** City centre.

Belfast
RESTAURANT

Café Altos

Unit 6 Anderson McCauley Building Belfast BT1 5EA
Tel: 028 9032 3087

Dieter Bergman's atmospheric café bar near the City Hall is a sister restaurant to his Italian Dublin restaurant, Il Primo, and is a very popular lunch spot. The stylish, high-ceilinged interior is alive with Mediterranean colour, and the high walls provide plenty of space for local art work; it's a casual place, offering smart informal cooking in a broadly Mediterranean style - and, in common with the Dublin restaurant, there should be treats to look forward on the wine list, including a good number by the glass. Mainly a daytime restaurant, it does a good breakfast, and stays open longer on Thursday for the late night shoppers. Prices are moderate. Wheelchair accessible, food served Mon-Wed, 10-5pm, Thu, 10-8pm, Fri-Sat 10-6pm. Closed Sun. **Directions:** City centre. ◇

Belfast
RESTAURANT

Café Conor

11A Stranmillis Road Belfast BT9 5AF
Tel: 028 9066 3266 Fax: 028 9020 0233

Just across the road from the Ulster Museum, Manus McConn's unusual high-ceilinged room is bright with natural light from a lantern roof and was originally the William Conor studio (1944-1959). The art theme is carried through to having original work always on show - there's a permanent exhibition of Neill Shawcross's bold and colourful work. Open for breakfast and brunch, through coffee, lunch, afternoon tea and eventually dinner, this is a casual place with a distinctive style - light wood booths along the walls and a long refectory-style table down the centre. Good coffee, home-baked scones, informal food such as warm chicken salad, hot paninis with mozzarella, modern European dishes including lots of pastas, comfort food (like fish & chips with mushy peas) and classic dishes such as moules mariniere and steak & Guinness pie are all worth dropping in for. Popular with locals, this place is a real find for those visiting the Museum (especially on Sundays); the only downside is that background music is sometimes too loud, which can make it difficult to converse. **Seats 50.** Open daily 9am-11pm, L menu from noon, D specials from 5pm. A la carte. Licensed. Closed July fortnight. MasterCard, Visa, Switch. **Directions:** Opposite Ulster Museum. ◇

Belfast
CAFÉ

Café Paul Rankin

27-29 Fountain Street Belfast BT1
Tel: 028 9031 5090 Fax: 028 9032 8340

Café Paul Rankin offers informal quality food (notably their speciality baking) throughout the day - be it for a quick cup of coffee or a more leisurely bite with a glass of wine, this is the in place for a shopping break. The breakfast menu is available all day and includes Jeanne's toasted muesli & yoghurt, while a wider range hot food on offer after 11 am includes the Rankin club sandwich and a range of quiches and salads. Smart pavement tables for fine weather - and food to go too. **Seats 50** (outside seating, 12). No reservations. No smoking. Open 7.30-5.30 (Thu to 7.30). Closed Sun; 25 Dec, 1 Jan, 12 Jul. *Also at 12-14 Arthur Street (times as Fountain St); Castlecourt Shopping Centre, on Royal Avenue (9-6, Thu to 9). MasterCard, Visa, Switch. **Directions:** Town centre, near City Hall. ◇

Belfast
CAFÉ

Cargoes Café

613 Lisburn Road Belfast BT9 7GT
Tel: 028 9066 5451

Radha Patterson's very special little delicatessen and café has maintained a great reputation over more than a decade in business - fine produce for the delicatessen side of the business is meticulously sourced, and the same philosophy applies to the food served in the café. Modern European, Thai and Indian influences work well together here; simple preparation and good seasonal ingredients dictate menus - where you might find dishes like smokey bacon & potato soup, Moroccan chicken with couscous, vegetarian dishes such as goat's cheese & tarragon tart or wild mushroom risotto. There are classic desserts like lemon tart or apple flan, and a range of stylish sandwiches. Children welcome. No smoking restaurant. **Seats 30.** Open Mon-Sat 9 am-5 pm, L 12-4. A la carte; sc discretionary. Toilets wheelchair accessible. MasterCard, Visa.

Belfast

Cayenne

Ⓔ RESTAURANT

7 Ascot House Shaftesbury Square BT2 7DB
Tel: 028 9033 1532 Fax: 028 9026 1575
Email: belinda@rankingroup.co.uk Web: www.rankingroup.co.uk

Paul and Jeanne Rankin's flagship restaurant is now much bigger than it was originally, with a more appealing reception-bar area, and two private rooms. But the aim remains the same and, together with head chef Danny Millar, they continue to offer a great mix of interesting and fashionable food in a cool urban atmosphere - and at very accessible prices. No corners have been cut with the furnishings and table appointments, however - the atmosphere may be funky and informal, but there's clearly a culinary experience in waiting here. Friendly, smartly uniformed staff are quick to settle arriving guests in and offer eclectic menus, which, in Danny Millar's adventurous and creative hands, are constantly evolving. Many of the Cayenne signature dishes are likely to feature - the ever-popular salt'n'chilli squid with napa slaw, chilli jam and aioli, for example, or a Japanese appetiser plate (prawn tempura, seafood spring roll, salmon teriyaki, crab sushi and cucumber & mirin salad), but nothing stands still here and even the most popular dishes are under constant review. There are a few dishes with a broadly international/Mediterranean tone - Strangford lobster & avocado salad, perhaps, with confit cherry tomatoes, lime and fresh coriander - but Asian flavours are dominant throughout the savoury sections of the menu, bringing a new dimension to local ingredients: dry aged Irish sirloin of beef comes with smoked chilli butter, shitake mushrooms and bok choy, for example, and roast skate wing is served with steamed Asian greens, new potatoes, Yuzu and cockle & soy vinaigrette. A separate vegetarian menu is offered too, although there's a sprinkling of appealing vegetarian dishes on the main menu - steamed asparagus with poached free range egg and lemon butter is a conservative (but delicious) example. The cooking here can be really exciting, and is generally backed efficiently up by smart, well-trained young staff; however this is a very popular restaurant, and both the kitchen and service can sometimes come under pressure. A very good wine wine list, organised by grape variety and style, offers a wide choice in both range and price, and includes a good choice of wines by the glass and half bottles, and also some fine wines; extensive drinks menu too. **Seats 120** (private room, 14). Reservations advised; children welcome. No smoking area; air conditioning; Toilets Wheelchair Accessible. L Mon-Fri 12-2.15, Set L from £15.50. Set D £15.50/19.50 2/3 course. D daily: Mon-Thu 6-10.15, Fri & Sat to 11.15, Sun to 8.45). A la carte & Vegetarian Menu. House wine from £14.95. sc discretionary (except 10% recommended on parties of 6+). Closed L Sat & L Sun, 25/26th Dec, 1 Jan, 12 July Amex, Diners, MasterCard, Visa, Switch. **Directions:** 5 mins from Europa Hotel at top of Great Victoria St.

Belfast

The Crescent Townhouse

HOTEL/RESTAURANT

13 Lower Crescent Belfast BT7 1NR
Tel: 028 9032 3349 Fax: 028 9032 0646
Email: info@crescenttownhouse.com Web: www.crescenttownhouse.com

This is an elegant building on the corner of Botanic Avenue, just a short stroll from the city centre. The ground floor is taken up by the Metro Brasserie and Bar/Twelve, a stylish club-like bar with oak panelling and snugs, which particularly lively and popular at night (necessitating 'greeters' for the entrance), so noise could be a problem in front bedrooms. The reception lounge is on the first floor. Spacious bedrooms - which include several superior grades, and six rooms fairly recently added - have phones with data points, TV and trouser press, and are comfortably furnished, with good tiled bathrooms. Suites and superior rooms are more elaborate and have luxurious bathrooms with roll-top baths and separate showers, but all rooms are regularly refurbished. A good choice for business visitors: fax, photocopying and secretarial services can be provided through reception. Breakfast is taken in the contemporary split-level Metro Brasserie, which is open for all meals: more than just a hotel dining room, this restaurant has a following for its good contemporary cooking. The early dinner menu is especially good value. Children welcome before 7pm (under 14s free in parents' room, cots available without charge, baby sitting arranged). No pets.*Weekend breaks offer good value. **Rooms 17** (1 suite, 2 junior suites, 5 superior, 6 shower only, 1 disabled, 2 no smoking). Wheelchair lift. Room service (limited hours). B&B £42.50 pps, ss £27.50. Metro Brasserie **Seats 70.** D daily 5.45-9.30 (Sat to 10; Sun 5.30-8), L Mon-Sat, 12-3. Early D from £11.50. Closed L Sun. Lunch also at BarTwelve: Mon-Sat 12-3. Amex, MasterCard, Visa, Switch. **Directions:** Opposite Botanic Railway Station. ◇

Belfast

Crown Liquor Saloon

PUB

46 Great Victoria Street Belfast BT2 7BA
Tel: 028 9027 9901 Fax: 028 9027 9902

Belfast's most famous pub, The Crown Liquor Saloon, was perhaps the greatest of all the Victorian gin palaces which once flourished in Britain's industrial cities. Remarkably, considering its central location close to the Europa Hotel, it survived The Troubles virtually unscathed. Although now owned by the National Trust (and run by Bass Leisure Retail) the Crown is far from being a museum piece and attracts a wide clientele of locals and visitors. A visit to one of its famous snugs for a pint and half a dozen oysters served on crushed ice, or a bowl of Irish Stew, is a must. The upstairs restaurant section, "Flannigans Eaterie & Bar", is built with original timbers from the SS Britannic, sister ship to the Titanic. Crown: bar food served Mon-Sat 12-3. Flannigans: 11-9. Closed 25-16 Dec. Diners, MasterCard, Visa. **Directions:** City centre, opposite Europa Hotel. ◇

Belfast

Deanes Brasserie

Ⓔ RESTAURANT

36-40 Howard Street Belfast BT1 6PF
Tel: 028 9056 0000 Fax: 028 9056 0001
Email: info@michaeldeane.co.uk Web: www.michaeldeane.co.uk

On the ground floor under Restaurant Michael Deane, this much larger restaurant is all buzz and offers an eclectic contemporary menu, with something for everybody. It is an impressive space with plenty of atmosphere, and always smartly maintained - and, with head chef Derek Creagh (previously at The Fat Duck in Bray) in the kitchen , this bustling brasseries is on peak form. Expect modish pre-starters like breads, oils, olives and almonds, and a stylish combination of luxurious dishes like foie gras & chicken liver parfait with spiced black fig chutney & toast, Dundrum Bay oysters, or pan fried scallops, contrasting with fashionable comfort food like cider braised belly of pork, lyonnaise sausages with choucroûte, or a dish of local cod with parsley mash, brown shrimp and pea & chardonnay emulsion. The cooking is great, prices are moderate, service slick and efficient, the wine list offers plenty under £20 - and the 2/3 course 'Menu Prix Fixe' offers great value at £12.95/15.95. **Seats 80** (private room, 40). Air conditioning; Toilets Wheelchair Accessible; Children welcome until 9pm. L Mon-Sat 12-3, D Mon-Sat 5.30-10.30. Early bird D £12.95 /15.95 (5.30-7) also A la carte; house wine GBp14.50-16; sc charge discretionary (10% on parties of 6+). Closed Sun; 24-26 Dec, Jul 12-14. ***'Deanes Deli'**, a New York style all day deli dining experience serving innovative and traditional food all day long (11.30am-10pm, Mon-Sat), is around the corner at 44 Bedford Street. It adds an extra twist with the sumptuous retail deli store adjacent to the restaurant where customers can re-create the dish of their choice by buying fresh ingredients and Deanes branded products to take home. Amex, MasterCard, Visa, Switch. **Directions:** From back of City Hall, about 150m towards M1, on left.

Belfast

Ginger

Ⓝ RESTAURANT

7-8 Hope Street Belfast BT12 5EE
Tel: 028 9024 4421 Web: www.gingerbistro.com

Chic and cheerful is the atmosphere at redhead Simon 'Ginger' McCance's bistro off Great Victoria Street. Carefully sourced ingredients have always been at the centre of this likeable chef's philosophy and, although you will find wide ranging influences on his constantly changing menus, you can be sure that the food that tastes so good will be local if possible. Menus are balanced, offering a good choice of vegetarian dishes alongside wholesome beef & puff pastry pie with home cut chips, for example, but seafood is what this chef likes to cook best - a big bowl of local mussels with a coconut curry sauce, for example, or warm salad of monkfish with rocket, confit of tomato, roasted baby potatoes, chorizo & merguez sausages and chilli butter. Finish with a classic dessert (lime pannacotta with berries, perhaps) or an Irish cheese selection. Reasonable prices generally are carried through onto a concise wine list, and there's a full bar list. Children welcome; reservations required. **Seats 35;** L & D Tue-Sat, 12-3pm, 5-10pm; set 3 course L £13; early D £9, 5-7pm; also a la carte L&D; house wine £11.75. Closed Sun, Mon, 2 weeks Jul, 2 weeks Christmas. MasterCard, Visa, Switch. **Directions:** Off Great Victoria street, 5 mins from Europa Hotel.

Belfast

Hastings Europa Hotel

HOTEL

Great Victoria Street Belfast BT2 7AP
Tel: 028 9027 1066 Fax: 028 9032 7800
Email: res@eur.hastingshotels.com Web: www.hastingshotels.com

This landmark 1970s city centre building is the largest hotel in Northern Ireland and particularly striking when illuminated at night. The location is exceptionally convenient, both to the business and commercial districts and the city's entertainment and shopping areas. It has undergone many changes since first opening in the '70s and has been renovated and refurbished to a high standard, including the addition of executive rooms, with air conditioning, ISDN lines and safe, as well as the usual facilities expected of a top hotel. Off the impressive tall-columned entrance foyer is an all-day brasserie and the lobby bar, featuring Saturday afternoon jazz and other live musical entertainment. Upstairs on the first floor you'll find the Gallery Lounge (afternoon teas served here to the accompaniment of a pianist) and a cocktail bar with circular marble-topped counter. But perhaps the hotel's greatest assets are the function suites, ranging from the Grand Ballroom to the twelfth floor Edinburgh Suite with its panoramic views of the city. Nearby parking (special rates apply) can be added to your account. Staff are excellent (porters offer valet parking) and, as in all the Hastings hotels, standards of housekeeping and maintenance are high. Conference/banqueting (750/600); business centre; secretarial services. Beauty salon; hairdressing. Children welcome (under 14s free in parents' room; cots available without charge, baby sitting arranged). Pets permitted by arrangement. **Rooms 240** (1 presidential suite, 4 junior suites, 56 executive rooms, 115 no smoking, 2 for disabled). Lifts. B&B about £97 pps, ss £30. Piano Bar Restaurant: D Mon-Sat (closed 24 Dec-2 Jan); Brasserie open all day 6am-11pm (Sun from 7 am). *Short breaks offered - details on application. Hotel closed 24-25 Dec. Amex, Diners, MasterCard, Visa, Switch. **Directions:** Located in the heart of Belfast. ◇

Belfast
HOTEL

Hastings Stormont Hotel

Upper Newtownards Road Belfast BT4 3LP
Tel: 028 9067 6012 Fax: 028 9048 0240
Email: sales@stor.hastingshotels.com Web: www.hastingshotels.com

A few miles east of the city centre, the hotel is directly opposite the imposing gates leading to Stormont Castle and Parliament Buildings and suits the business guest well. There's a huge entrance lounge, with stairs up to a more intimate mezzanine area overlooking the castle grounds, and the main restaurant and informal modern bistro are both pleasantly located. Spacious, practical bedrooms have good worktops and offer the usual facilities; several rooms are designated for female executives, and there is a relatively new executive floor. The hotel also has eight self-catering apartments with their own car parking area, featuring a twin bedroom, lounge and kitchen/dinette, available for short stays or long periods. The self-contained Confex Centre, comprising ten trade rooms, complements the function suites in the main building. Weekend rates and short breaks are good value. Conference/banqueting 500/350. Own parking (255). Wheelchair accessible. No pets. **Rooms 105** (2 suites, 23 executive rooms, 52 no-smoking, 1 for disabled). Lift. B&B about £40 pps, ss £20. Open all year. Amex, Diners, MasterCard, Visa, Switch. **Directions:** 3 miles east of Belfast city centre; take A20 towards Newtownards - directly opposite Stormont Parliament Buildings. ◇

Belfast
CAFÉ/RESTAURANT

Hawthorne Coffee Shop

Fulton's Fine Furnishings Boucher Crescent Belfast BT2 6HU
Tel: 028 90 384705 Fax: 028 384701

If you're shopping or have business in the area, this stylish contemporary café in a well known furniture store is a great place to know about, as they specialise in real home cooking and the art of scone making is alive and well here. There's nothing flashy about the food: expect lovely flavoursome dishes like home-made soup with wheaten bread, quiches - asparagus & salmon, vegetable - seafood pie and steak & mushroom hot-pot and several casseroles daily. There's always a large selection of salads and home-made desserts like banoffee and lemon meringue pie and there's free refills of coffee. An added attraction between 12 and 2 is to listen to the resident pianist play on the Steinway baby grand in the corner. **Seats 127.** Mon-Sat: morning coffee, lunch, afternoon tea. A la carte. MasterCard, Visa, Switch. **Directions:** Off M1, take Stockmans Lane exit off roundabout, left into Boucher Road, left again into Boucher Crescent. (At Fultons Fine Furnishings Store). *At the time of going to press Fulton's is moving to Boucher Road. ◇

Belfast
HOTEL

Hilton Belfast

4 Lanyon Place Belfast BT1 3LP **Tel: 028 9027 7000**
Fax: 028 9027 7277 Email: hilton_belfast@hilton.com

Occupying a prominent position on a rise beside the Waterfront Hall, the interior of this landmark hotel is impressive: the scale is grand, the style throughout is of contemporary clean-lined elegance - the best of modern materials have been used and the colour palette selected is delicious - and, best of all, it makes the best possible use of its superb waterside site, with the Sonoma Restaurant and several suites commanding exceptional views. Outstanding conference and business facilities include the state-of-the-art Hilton Meeting service tailored to individual requirements and three executive floors with a Clubroom. All rooms have air-conditioning, satellite TV, in-room movies, and no-stop check-out in addition to the usual facilities. Recreational facilities are also excellent. There is a multi-storey carpark next door, but it is not owned by the hotel. Conference/banqueting (400/260); secretarial services; business centre; video conferencing; ISDN lines. Leisure centre; indoor swimming pool; beauty salon. Children welcome (cots available). **Rooms 195** (6 suites, 7 junior suites, 38 executive rooms, 68 no-smoking, 10 for disabled). Lifts. Room rate (max. 2 guests) from about £100. Open all year. Amex, Diners, MasterCard, Visa, Switch. **Directions:** Belfast city centre, beside Waterfront Hall. ◇

Belfast
HOTEL

Holiday Inn Belfast

22 - 26 Ormeau Avenue Belfast BT2 8HS
Tel: 028 9032 8511 Fax: 028 9062 6546
Email: belfast@ichotelsgroup.com Web: www.belfast.holiday-inn.com

Conveniently located less than half a mile from most of the main city centre attractions, this contemporary hotel offers luxurious modern accommodation, with excellent business and health and leisure facilities. The style is classy and spacious; bedrooms are designed particularly with the business guest in mind - the decor is unfussy and warm, with comfort and relaxation to match its use as a workbase; superior rooms all have air conditioning, modem points, fridge, interactive TV with on-screen checkout facility and Sky Sports, trouser press, power shower, cotton bathrobe and quality toiletries, while suites have a hallway as well as a separate sitting/dining room. 'The Academy' offers state-of-the-art conference and training facilities, and business support. Conference/banqueting (120/100); business centre, secretarial services, video-conferencing. Children welcome (under 16s free in parents' room, cot available without charge). Leisure centre; swimming pool; beauty salon. **Rooms 170** (2 suites, 36 executive, 102 no smoking, 10 for disabled). Lift. 24 hour room service. B&B from about 85pps. Special weekend rates available. No private parking (NCP car park behind hotel). Open all year. Amex, Diners, MasterCard, Visa, Switch. **Directions:** Opposite BBC, 2 minutes walk from City Hall via Bedford Street. ◇

Belfast
☆RESTAURANT

James Street South

21 James Street South Belfast BT2 7GA
Tel: 028 9043 4310 Fax: 028 9043 4310
Email: info@jamesstreetsouth.co.uk Web: www.jamesstreetsouth.co.uk

Just across the road from the Europa Hotel, Niall and Joanne McKenna's cool modern restaurant is well located and well-appointed in a beautifully understated style with white walls and crisp white linen, relieved by fresh flowers and effective lighting - and, since opening in 2004, this talented team has not only brought something fresh and exceptionally good to Belfast, but their gem of a restaurant has thrived. Niall McKenna arrived at this address via Marco Pierre White's Canteen and two of Gary Rhodes' restaurants, Greenhouse and City Rhodes, and it shows in simple, evocative menus which are not long yet offer many a treat. There's a welcome European tone to menus that are classical / Mediterranean, with an emphasis on quality ingredients - and a merciful absence of fusion influences; menus are changed frequently and, although simply presented, there are plenty of very tempting options - including lovely vegetarian dishes like wild mushroom papardelle with crème fraîche, luxurious starters like sautéed foie gras with caramelised saffron pear and candied almonds, great seafood - as seen in a summer dish of sautéed halibut with artichoke and citrus juice - and utterly irresistible desserts including a delectable house fondue (to share) and choice of combination plates - a three crème brulée, for example, or a chocolate one with gorgeous white and dark chocolate creations... This is an exciting restaurant, and genuinely creative, beautifully judged cooking and excellent service by smartly-dressed and well trained staff should ensure a memorable meal here. Lunch and pre-theatre menus offer exceptional value. The wine list is arranged mainly by grape variety and includes regional varieties; although mainly under £30, there is also a short selection of fine wines. Gourmet wine evenings are sometimes held. **Seats 70.** Reservations advised. Air con. No smoking area (bar). Children welcome. L Mon-sat, 12-2.45; D daily, 5.45-10.45 (Sun 5.30-9.30). Set L £13.50. Pre theatre D Mon-Thu 5.45-6.45 £15.50, also A la Carte. Closed 25-26 Dec, 1 Jan, 11-12 July. Amex, MasterCard, Visa, Switch. **Directions:** City centre: located behind Belfast City Hall, between Bedford Stree and Brunswick street.

Belfast
BAR/RESTAURANT

The John Hewitt Bar & Restaurant

51 Donegall Street Belfast BT1
Tel: 028 9023 3768 Fax: 028 9096 1110
Email: info@thejohnhewitt.com Web: www.thejohnhewitt.com

The in-place pub for discerning Belfast people, who like the combination of traditional interior and good quality sassy modern food, The John Hewitt is owned by the Unemployment Resource Centre next door, which was originally opened by the poet and socialist John Hewitt in the 1980s. A few years ago they decided to open the premises (formerly the Newsletter offices) as a bar, and all profits go back to that worthy cause. High-ceilinged, with a marble bar, a snug and an open fire, there's a pleasing preference for conversation and civilised relaxation - an oasis for lovers of real Irish pubs and you'd think it had been here for a hundred years. It operates more or less as a restaurant by day - they serve lunch (a sassy mixture of traditional and modern food, all quality driven) every day except Sunday, and offer a light afternoon 'Talking Bowls' snack menu on Friday & Saturday afternoons. There are traditional music sessions three nights a week (Tue, Wed & Sat), live music every Thursday and jazz on Fridays - which leaves Mondays free for exhibition launches, usually for young or unemployed artists. The day's menu is posted on their website. A short wine list includes four wines by the glass and two bubblies. Open daily; food served Mon-Thu, 12-4pm, also short menu Fri & Sat 3.30-6pm. MasterCard, Visa, Switch. **Directions:** Belfast city centre; 3 doors from St Ann's Cathedral. ◇

Belfast

HOTEL

Jurys Inn Belfast

Fisherwick Place Great Victoria Street Belfast BT2 7AP
Tel: 028 9053 3500 Fax: 028 9053 3511
Email: jurysinnbelfast@jurysdoyle.com Web: www.book@jurysinn.com

Located in the heart of the city, close to the Grand Opera House and City Hall and just a couple of minutes walk from the major shopping areas of Donegall Place and the Castlecourt Centre, Jurys Belfast Inn offers comfortable accommodation in a central location at very reasonable prices. The high standards and good value of all Jurys Inns applies here too: all rooms are en-suite (with bath and shower) and spacious enough to accommodate two adults and two children (or three adults) at a fixed price. Rooms are well-designed and recently refurbished, with good amenities for a hotel in the budget class. **Rooms 190.** Room rate from about £78, (max 3 guests w/o b'fst). Restaurant. Closed 24-26 Dec. Amex, Diners, MasterCard, Visa. **Directions:** City centre, close to Opera House. ◇

Belfast

Ⓝ 🏛 HOTEL

Malmaison Hotel

34-38 Victoria Street Belfast BT1 3GH
Tel: 028 9022 0200 Email:belfast@malmaison.com
Web: www.malmaison-belfast.com

Previously the McCausland Hotel, this beautiful building (especially striking when lit up at night) was recently taken over by the stylish UK group Malmaison who have introduced a wow factor, beginning with the reception area where everything is black and white, with opulent drapes and large church candles. Friendly, efficient staff at reception set arriving guests at their ease and guest accommodation - spacious, contemporary, luxurious, with all the technical gizmos you could possibly want - is given a human dimension with the offer of early morning delivery of a quarter pint of fresh milk. The Brasserie offers simple wholesome fare (steaks from The Duke of Baccleuch's Scottish Estate, for example), good breakfasts are smartly served, and the bar (extensive cocktail menu, flat screen television, huge leather sofas, flickering lights, loud music) is an in-place at night. Multi storey car park nearby. **Rooms 62.** Brasserie: L & D daily. Amex, MasterCard, Visa, Switch. **Directions:** Centre of Belfast. ◇

Belfast

Ⓝ HOTEL

Malone Lodge

60 Eglantine Avenue Malone Road Belfast BT9 6DY
Tel: 028 9038 8000 Fax: 028 9038 8088
Email: info@malonelodgehotel.com Web: www.malonelodgehotel.com

This reasonably priced townhouse hotel near Queen's University is very pleasantly located if you like to be in a quiet area, yet convenient to the city centre. It offers comfortable accommodation in spacious smartly furnished en-suite rooms, with all the facilities required by business guests, both in-room and in the hotel itself. There are good conference and meeting facilities and plenty of parking space, and yet it is within walking distance of city centre restaurants and entertainment. Conferences (9 rooms, biggest caters for 140 delegates); Banqueting (30-140); ample parking, fitness suite, broadband. **Rooms 72** (standard or executive), B&B room rate from £89 mid-week to £109 weekends, single from £65-95. *Malone Lodge also has 22 apartments comprising of one, two and three bedroom suites. MasterCard, Visa, Switch. **Directions:** Between the Lisburn and Malone Roads in South Belfast. ◇

Belfast
PUB

McHugh's Bar & Restaurant

29-31 Queen's Square Belfast BT1 3FG
Tel: 028 9050 9999 Fax: 028 9050 9998
Email: info@mchughsbar.com Web: www.mchughsbar.com

This remarkable pub is in one of Belfast's few remaining 18th century buildings; built in 1711, it is the city's oldest listed building. It has been extensively and carefully renovated allowing the original bar (which has many interesting maps, photographs and other memorabilia of old Belfast) to retain its character while blending in a new café-bar and restaurant. It is worth a visit for its historical interest, and the modern food offered includes an interesting lunch menu ('open flame' wok cooking is a speciality), a slightly more formal evening menu and light food through the day. **Seats 100** (private room, 35). Air conditioning. L Sun-Fri,12-3; D daily 5-10.30 (Sun to 9); Set D £18, also à la carte. Bar food 12-10.30 daily. House wine from £11.45. Toilets wheelchair accessible. Parking in nearby carpark. Closed 25 Dec, 1 Jan, 12/13 Jul. Amex, MasterCard, Visa, Switch. **Directions:** Turn right at Albert Clock. ◇

Belfast
HOTEL/RESTAURANT

The Merchant Hotel

35-39 Waring Street Belfast BT1 2EW
Tel: 028 9023 4888 Email: www.themerchanthotel.com

The grandeur of a larger than life Victorian banking building is a fit setting for Belfast's newest, most dramatic and beautiful hotel. The exterior of the building is Italianate in style, with sculptures depicting Commerce, Justice and Britannia, looking down benignly from the apex of the magnificent facade. The entrance is up two flights of steps, through tall mahogany and glass revolving doors and then into a room of epic proportions with high ceilings, a central glassed dome with Tyrone crystal and brass chandelier, Corinthian columns, very tall doors painted black with bevelled glass panes and lovely windows with stained glass features at the back (where chunky bamboo plants give at least the appearance of garden outside.) The lobby - furnished with comfortable sofas and chairs, rich autumnal fabrics, antiques and curiosities - sets the tone for the whole hotel, which has an authentic period feeling throughout and, although very luxurious, is not ostentatious. The adjacent cocktail bar is equally beautifully furnished in the same style, with red velvet and deep, deep fringing and more of that autumnal velvet too on soft chairs; here, there are two beautiful windows overlooking the street. (On the other side of the front door, also with two beautiful windows, a residents' bar with modern furnishings seems less successful.) The bedrooms and suites are all named after a literary figure with Belfast associations (MacNeice, Heaney, Brian Friel, C.S. Lewis and Larkin etc); the geography of the building means there are features like lovely marble fireplaces with comfy chairs in lobbies and quaint corners en route to somewhere else - a world away from purpose built hotel accommodation with long corridors of doors. All guest rooms are elegantly and opulently appointed and offer air conditioning, black out curtains, WiFi, flat screen television, and spacious marbled bathrooms with many extras. Everything at the hotel is about luxury and indulgence - including the offer of The Merchant Bentley, which you can book to collect you from the airport or whatever. Three central steps take you from the lobby up to **The Great Room Restaurant** - a small antique reception desk and menu signal the transition; here, despite the great height and scale, low dividers give a sense of more intimate spaces without interrupting the view - and a bold choice, carried throughout the hotel, is the striped carpet. Although the hotel had not been open long at the time of our visit, the dining experience was most enjoyable; set menus are offered at various times, and also an à la carte typically, you might expect to find an assiette of fish (sea bass, scallops, crab ravioli, pea purée and tarragon cream), and classics like Gressingham duck, venison Wellington and tournedos rossini. The details are interesting here - an entertaining and practical house speciality is a canapé stand (also used for Afternoon Tea): a three-tier cake stand offering on two layers a selection of a single scallop, shredded duck in a little patty of flaky pastry, and a disc of wheaten bread with smoked salmon dressed with crème fraîche and chives, and, on the third layer, a little pot of foie gras to share - all with lovely breads to accompany. Coffee is beautifully served in art deco style silver pot with wicker handles and matching bowls (but no little treats). Business centre; meeting rooms. **Rooms 26** (5 suites, 21 deluxe). Suites from £290, deluxe from £220. Room service; laundry service. Great Room Restaurant: Open 7am-11pm daily; 2/3 course menus from £15.50/19.50. Also a la carte. Bar food also available in the hotel and in the Cloth Ear pub-bar nearby. Parking on site (35); valet parking offered. Amex, Diners, MasterCard, Visa. **Directions:** City centre. ◇

Belfast
Ⓝ RESTAURANT

Molly's Yard

1 College Green Mews Botanic Avenue Belfast BT7 1LW
Tel: 028 9032 2600 Fax: 028 9032 2777
Email: info@mollysyard.co.uk Web: www.mollysyard.co.uk

This atmospheric new restaurant on two floors - informal ground floor bistro with a more elegant dining room above - is on the site of former stables. Menus have a pleasingly down to earth tone - casual bistro fare downstairs with more 'grown up' versions upstairs. Barry Smyth, previously of the much-praised restaurant The Oriel of Gilford, in County Down, has been head chef during the set-up phase and has established a fine reputation for both the cooking and the philosophy of using carefully sourced ingredients, including as much local produce as possible. At the time of going to press Barry is handing over to new head chef Matthias Llorente - but the preparation work has been well done and this should be a restaurant that continues to please. An interesting drinks list has been one of the attractions here - including real ales from the renowned Hilden Brewery in Lisburn - and, in an exciting development which is due to be completed by the end of 2006, Belfast's first micro-brewery will be constructed on site. Children welcome before 6pm; Toilets wheelchair accessible. Outdoor seating for 20; L Mon-Fri, 12-2.30pm, D Mon-Fri, 5-9.30pm, Sat all day, 12-9.30pm; set D 2/3 course, £20/25; house wine £12.50. Closed Sun, 25-26 Dec, 1 Jan, 12-13 Jul. MasterCard, Visa, Switch. **Directions:** Beside Dukes hotel at back of Queen's University.

Belfast
Ⓝ BAR/RESTAURANT

Mourne Seafood Bar Belfast

34-36 Bank Street Belfast BT1 1HL
Tel: 028 9024 8544

A sandwich board sign will lead you to Mourne Seafood Bar, recently opened by Andy Rae, who was previously head chef with Paul Rankin at Roscoff and Cayenne, and business partner Bob McCoubrey, of the original Mourne Seafood Bar in Dundrum, Co Down, who have their own shellfish beds on Carlingford Lough. The Mourne is also a fish shop - you enter past a display of fish and shellfish on ice, manned by a fishmonger busy gutting and preparing fish for the restaurant and attending any customers that come along; there's a stainless steel fridge covered in drawings by kids who have been in the restaurant, and a dark brown painted door opens on to a long bar, with a counter running along one wall and wines displayed behind. The old walls are a mixture of red brick, and black areas acting as large blackboards for the menu and cocktail list, floorboards have been roughly painted black, tables are matt black with black cast iron pedestals, set simply with knife, fork and white paper napkin; it has an authentic Belfast feel, a world away from your designer bar concept - and all the better for that, since it reflects Andy's philosophy that food should be at the heart of the operation. It's attracting a complete cross section - business types, older couples who come for the battered fish, chips & mushy peas, arty types from nearby TV studios. Andy's passion for fish and shellfish is evident - starting with the sourcing. Like the restaurant in Dundrum, in the area where a lot of the fish cooked in Belfast is landed, he uses less popular local fish rather than trendy imports eg, as part of an excellent seafood platter, he makes a delicious brandade from conger eel, and may otherwise use ling. Everything is home made - including a really excellent mayonnaise and good wheaten bread, and the menu changes daily according to the catch; it offers a mix of dishes at varying prices, some priced as starter or mains, and the menu runs all day into the evening, with changes implemented should fish sell out. A daily specials board might offer 15 dishes priced from £4.50 to £15.00, including potted herrings, with crunchy fennel salad and wheaten bread, seafood casserole (a great dish), roast monkfish with bacon, root veg & barley risotto, organic salmon, haddock fishcakes, roast hake with papparelle pasta and prawn vinaigrette. And maybe just one meat dish to please a non fishy party member - dry aged rib eye steak, perhaps, with grilled veg and porcini whisky butter (£11.50). Nice desserts, good coffee to finish and lovely service. This is a new concept in Belfast dining and it's great to see it. *There's now a very informal menu downstairs, and more choice offered in a more recently opened room above the bar. Children welcome; toilets wheelchair accessible. **Seats 75** (private room, 30, outdoors, 30); air conditioning; food served Mon-Sat, 12-9.30pm, Sun, 1-6pm; vegetarian menu, also a la carte; housewine £12.95. Closed 25-26 Dec, 1 Jan. MasterCard, Visa, Switch. **Directions:** Beside Kelly's Bar on the corner of Royal Avenue and Bank Street.

Belfast
RESTAURANT/PUB

Nick's Warehouse

35-39 Hill Street Belfast BT1 2LB
Tel: 028 9043 9690 Fax: 028 9023 0514
Email: info@nickswarehouse.co.uk Web: www.nickswarehouse.co.uk

Nick and Kathy Price's long established restaurant is a clever conversion on two floors, with particularly interesting lighting and efficient aluminium duct air-conditioning. It's a lively spot, notable for attentive, friendly service and good food, in both the wine bar (where informal light meals and some hot dishes are served) and the restaurant (slightly more formal with structured à la carte menus). A network of trusted suppliers provide the superb ingredients that are the basis for lively contemporary menus offering a wide range of dishes which are consistently interesting and often offer unusual items - McCartney's famous sausages on mash, with house brown sauce, rare breed loin of pork - and game in season. There's always an imaginative selection of vegetarian dishes and menus are considerately marked with symbols indicating dishes containing nuts or oils and also shellfish. The cheese selection is interesting too - you can choose between continental house cheeses (Gorgonzola, Comte & Reblochon) or Irish cheeses (Cashel Blue, Durrus & Gubbeen). Wide choice of teas of coffees, and an informative, well-priced wine list that makes good reading - and includes a small selection of fine wines, a special Spanish listing and about eight keenly priced house wines. Children welcome before 9 pm. Air conditioning. **Seats 125** downstairs(+ 55 upstairs, available as private room at night). L Mon-Fri 12-3, D Tue-Sat 6-9.30 (Fri & Sat to 10). House wines from £12.95. Closed Sat L, all Sun, D Mon; 25-26 Dec, 12 July. Amex, Diners, MasterCard, Visa, Switch. **Directions:** Behind St.Anne's Cathedral, off Waring St.

Belfast
BAR

The Northern Whig

2 Bridge Street Belfast BT1 1LU
Tel: 028 9050 9888 Fax: 028 9050 9880
Email: info@thenorthernwhig.com Web: www.thenorthernwhig.com

Located in the former offices of the Northern Whig newspaper and convenient to the city's now fashionable Cathedral Quarter, this is an impressive bar venue of grand proportions. The high ceilings of the old press hall have been retained - and now look down on several gigantic statues that have been salvaged from Eastern Europe and are in keeping with the scale of the building. A long bar has comfortable contemporary seating in coffee and cream, where Belfast's trend-setters meet for drinks or a bite to eat - or you can take a pavement table on a sunny afternoon and watch the world go by, sipping cocktails or sampling something from the reasonably priced menu. Very popular with the local business fraternity for lunch and for a relaxing drink after work - and many stay on for a bite to eat. Expect upmarket bar food - pasta, risotto, tandoori chicken with wild rice - and good service from black-clad young staff. **Seats 160** (private room 40). No smoking area; air conditioning. Toilets wheelchair accessible. Children welcome. Open 10am-1am; bar food 12-9. MasterCard, Visa, Switch. **Directions:** From front of City Hall: walk to 2nd set of traffic lights, turn right, left at next lights; cross road - Northern Whig is on the corner. ◇

Belfast
CAFÉ

The Olive Tree Company

353 Ormeau Road Belfast BT7 3GL **Tel: 028 9064 8898**
Fax: 028 9064 8898 Web: www.olivetreecompany.com

This unique delicatessen/café specialises in freshly marinated olives, handmade cheeses and salamis - and also sells an exclusive range of French specialities, notably from Provence. The café offers authentic French patisserie and food with a Mediterranean flavour, mainly based on the best of local Irish produce. Think sandwiches with tapenade (olive paté with vine-ripened tomatoes & spring onions, or dolmades (vine leaves) salad with organic natural yoghurt and ciabatta bread and you'll get the flavour. Hot dishes include specialities like 'brodetto' a traditional Italian fish stew, or contemporary dishes such as warm duck salad with chilli & lime dressing. **Seats 26.** No smoking restaurant. Shop open daily: Mon-Sat 9am-6pm (café to 4.30pm), Sun 11-5. Hot food available Mon-Fri, 8.30-3.45pm, Sat, 9-3.45pm; (No wine but BYO allowed.) Closed 8-15 July, 24 Dec-2 Jan. **No Credit Cards. Directions:** From Belfast City Centre, take the direction for Newcastle/Downpatrick, cross the Ormeau Bridge - spot the Ormeau Bakery landmark and The Olive Tree Company is on the right. ◇

Belfast
RESTAURANT

Oxford Exchange Bar & Grill

1st floor St George's Market Oxford Street Belfast BT1 3NQ
Tel: 028 9024 0014 Fax: 028 9023 5675
Email: info@oxfordexchange.co.uk Web: www.oxfordexchange.co.uk

Dining in an historically interesting building has a certain cachet at any time, but this stylish venue over the renovated glass-roofed St. George's Market is particularly fascinating. The market is a redbrick listed Victorian building and Paul Horshcroft's successful conversion has created a pleasing restaurant with views of either the daytime market scene below or, at night, the attractively lit Laganside area. There's a small bar area, with comfortable seating, and a large restaurant with many striking features (including a designer gas fire) where interesting good-value lunches are served and, later, a fine dining dinner menu takes over. Ambitious dinner menus offer chargrills and traditional food with a modern twist; roast loin of wild boar may be served with with celeriac and mushroom purée and creamed onions; desserts are updated classics: steamed lemon pudding, perhaps, with raspberry sorbet and exotic fruit coulis. Stylish food, attractively presented, with professional service and (especially at lunch time) good value - no wonder this place is popular with a broad range of discerning diners, from visitors to the market to barristers from the nearby law courts. Quite convenient to Waterfront Hall for pre-theatre meals. Interesting wine list. **Seats 110.** Opening hours: Tue L only, 12-3, Wed/Thu, 12-8, Fri, 10-12 for coffee, 12-9pm meals, Sat, 5-9.30pm; pre-theatre menu, 5-7pm, also A la carte. House wine from about £11. SC discretionary (except 10% on parties of 8+). Closed Tue D, Sat L, all Sun, Mon; 25 Dec, 1 Jan, public holidays. MasterCard, Visa, Laser, Switch. **Directions:** Opposite Waterfront Hall. ◇

Belfast

HOTEL

Radisson SAS Hotel, Belfast

The Gasworks 3 Cromac Place Ormeau Road Belfast BT7 2JB
Tel: 028 9043 4065 Web: www.radissonsas.com

The hard red brick high-rise exterior may not be immediately pleasing, but you are in for a very pleasant surprise on entering this new hotel, which is uncompromisingly modern - and very impressive. Most strikingly, a highly original water feature seen through a glass wall has been created from the old 'grave dock' that was once a turning space for the boats coming up to the gasworks to deliver coal, and has ingeniously been incorporated into the design of the hotel - both restaurant and bar overlook this extraordinary feature, and it is worth a journey to see this alone. Other parts of the hotel may seem relatively unexciting by comparison with the public areas, but accommodation is designed and finished to the same high standard as other Radisson hotels - and, like them, a choice of room styles is offered: 'Urban' is warm and vibrant, in tones of reds and browns, while 'Nordic' is more restful, with soft blond wood surfaces, and gentle blues and browns. Suites and rooms have everything that the modern traveller could need, and more (the lavishly furnished Suite 7 is Belfast's largest one bedroom suite), and there's a welcome emphasis on customer service. Staff clearly take great pride in this hotel, and it is easy to see why. Conference/banqueting (150/40); secretarial services. Children welcome (cot available without charge, baby sitting arranged). No pets. **Rooms 120.** (1 suite, 7 junior suites, 18 executive, 94 no smoking, 6 disabled). Lift. 24 hour room service. B&B £about 78-95pps, ss £20. *Special offers / short breaks available. Filini Restaurant:L Mon-Sat, 12.30-2.30; D Mon-Sat, 6-10. Closed Sun. Bar meals 12-9 daily. Hotel open all year (not L 25 Dec). Parking (60). **Directions:** Belfast city centre, in the Cromac Wood Business Park development. ◇

Belfast

RESTAURANT

Rain City Café Grill

33-35 Malone Road Belfast BT9 6RU **Tel: 028 9068 2929**
Fax: 028 9068 2060 Web: www.rankingroup.co.uk

Another Paul Rankin enterprise, Rain City is on the corner of Malone Road and Eglantine Avenue and has the look of two terrace houses knocked into one, with attractive seating in the two bay windows. Walls stripped back to the original Belfast red brick alternating with walls done in cream paint are the main features of the decor and with wooden floors, pine tables laid out in a café style and colourful artworks, it has a lively yet relaxed atmosphere. Open all day, it offers a succession of menus through the day and evening; the style is international, the choice wide and accessible - but corners are not cut on ingredients (Angus burger and crispy duck confit are specialities). An extensive drinks menu includes liqueur coffees and a long list of cocktails. Presentation is attractive without any great frills, the portions are sizeable, the cooking is good and it represents good value too, so it's no surprise to find it a busy place. The family restaurant par excellence. **Seats 100** (private room, 50, outdoor, 25). Open daily 10am-10.30pm, L 12-4, D 5-10.30. Reservations accepted. Children welcome. Air conditioning. No smoking area. sc discretionary but 10% added on parties of 6+. Closed Christmas Day. Amex, Diners, MasterCard, Visa, Switch. **Directions:** Near Queens University.

Belfast

HOTEL

Ramada Hotel Belfast

117 Milltown Road Shaws Bridge Belfast BT8 7XP
Tel: 028 9092 3500 Fax: 028 9092 3600
Email: mail@ramadabelfast.com Web: www.ramadabelfast.com

This modern hotel near Shaws Bridge enjoys a beautiful setting in the Lagan Valley Regional Park, overlooking the River Lagan. Bedrooms are decorated in a fairly neutral modern style and have all the facilities expected of a new hotel, including in-room safes, TV with satellite and movie channels, telephone with voicemail and either a king-size bed or two singles. There are also executive suites available, intended mainly for business guests, and good conference and banqueting facilities. Leisure centre; steam room, spa and fitness suite; indoor swimming pool. Conference/banqueting 900/550. Garden, walking. No pets. Children welcome, (under 5s free in parents' room, cot available without charge). **Rooms 120** (4 suites, 116 executive, 83 no smoking, 6 for disabled). Lift. 24 hour room service. B&B about £70 pps, ss £15; room-only rate available. Belfast Bar & Grill, L&D daily. Parking (300). Open all year. Amex, Diners, MasterCard, Visa, Switch. **Directions:** In Lagan Valley Regional Park, near Shaws Bridge.◇

Belfast
€ GUESTHOUSE

Ravenhill House

690 Ravenhill Road Belfast BT6 0BZ
Tel: 028 9020 7444 Fax: 028 9028 2590
Email: info@ravenhillhouse.com Web: www.ravenhillhouse.com

Although it is beside a busy road, the Nicholson family home is a late Victorian redbrick house and has some sense of seclusion, with mature trees, private parking and a quiet tree-lined street alongside. A comfortable ground floor lounge has an open fireplace, a big sofa, lots of books and a PC for guests who want to use the Internet (at a modest charge). Bedrooms, which are a mixture of single, twin and double rooms, are comfortably furnished with style - beds and other furniture have been specially commissioned from an Islandmagee craftsman; all are en-suite, with tea/coffee making facilities and TV. After a good night's sleep, breakfast is sure to be the highlight of a visit here: served in a bay-windowed dining room with white-damasked tables, the breakfast buffet is displayed on the sideboard in a collection of Nicholas Mosse serving bowls - a feel for craft objects that is reflected elsewhere in the house. A printed breakfast menu shows a commitment to using local produce of quality and includes a vegetarian cooked breakfast; the Nicholsons buy most of the ingredients at the weekly St George's Farmers' Market, and support the concept behind it; eggs and meat are bought directly from known farms, and they make what they can on the premises, including marmalade and wheaten bread for breakfasts. All these good things, plus a particularly helpful attitude to guests, make this an excellent, reasonably priced base for a stay in Belfast. Children welcome (under 2s free in parents' room, cot available without charge). No pets. Garden. **Rooms 5** (all en-suite, 3 shower only, all no smoking). B&B £30 pps, single room £45. Open all year. MasterCard, Visa, Switch. **Directions:** Follow signs for A24 to Newcastle. 2 miles from city centre, located on corner of Ravenhill Road and Rosetta Park, close to junction with Ormeau Road (A24).

Belfast
★★ RESTAURANT

Restaurant Michael Deane

36-40 Howard Street Belfast BT1 6PF
Tel: 028 9033 1134 Fax: 028 9056 0001
Email: info@michaeldeane.co.uk Web: www.michaeldeane.co.uk

Michael Deane's reputation for offering meticulously prepared dishes, served with old world efficiency and charm in an elegant ambience remains unchallenged. This is exceptional food, based on great classic cooking, and the difference is on the plate: it always has been, and remains, on a different level to anything else in Belfast, and equal to the best in Ireland. Perhaps the contrast is all the more striking as, to reach the oasis of the restaurant, diners walk through the bustling Deane's Brasserie on the ground floor, climb the broad staircase and are admitted to the inner sanctum. Here all is comfort; the fin de siècle sitting room, the elegant dining room, the smart, attentive and knowledgeable staff and that open kitchen with the ever-present Deane meticulously controlling the pace of events and timing food to perfection. A two- or three-course dinner menu is offered, with four choices on each course - typically including a starter of roast scallops with potato bread, Clonakilty black pudding, cauliflower & brown butter, and a main of local lamb with crushed scallion potato, artichoke & Irish wholegrain mustard - and is extremely good value (about £35/£42); this will be a wonderful dining experience by any standards, allowing you to savour food cooked by the hand of the master. But to experience the sheer breadth and refinement of Michael Deane's cooking, the eight course Menu Prestige (about £62) is the yardstick against which all serious cooking in Northern Ireland should be judged: all the little niceties will be observed, leading off with an amuse bouche while you consider a menu that reads like a shopping list: monkfish; squab; scallop; foie gras; salmon; venison; cheese; dessert; chocolate. Simple on the page - simply superb on the plate; this is understatement taken to its extreme limit. Michael Deane was one of the first chefs in Ireland to cook fusion food - something in which he succeeded brilliantly, although it has failed in so many other hands - and, although it is now for his classical skills that he is (rightly) receiving recognition, he also blends fusion themes into classic menus. The wine list is grand as befits the standards of the restaurant and its food, yet not overawing, and the discreet advice given to match wines with the meal is outstanding. There is still no chef in Ireland who can surpass Michael Deane, and this small restaurant offers an increasingly rare alternative to the current fashion for informality. The first floor restaurant is only open for dinner on four evenings a week (except by arrangement for private parties at other times), so it may be necessary to make a reservation several weeks in advance. *Deanes Brasserie on the ground floor is open for L&D Mon-Sat. **Seats 30.** Air conditioning D Wed-Sat 7-9.30; L Fri only, 12.15-2. D £33-£59; sc discretionary (10% added to bills of 6+). Closed Sun-Tue, 10-25 July, 24 Dec-4 Jan. Amex, MasterCard, Visa, Switch. **Directions:** Tavelling towards M1 from rear of City Hall, about 150 m on left.

Belfast

E RESTAURANT

Roscoff Brasserie

7-11 Linenhall Street Belfast BT2 8AA
Tel: 028 9031 1150 Fax: 028 9031 1151
Email: belinda@rankingroup.co.uk Web: www.rankingroup.co.uk

In what has recently become something of a restaurant row - TENsq, Deane's and James Street South are all very close by - Belfast's original fine dining restaurant, the famous Roscoff, returned in a new guise in 2004. And, to the delight of those who admire the Rankins' cooking but don't enjoy the ambience, fine dining food is available once again, in a relaxed atmosphere. Avoiding sharp contemporary style, the decor is timelessly classic: with white linen-clad tables, soft neutral toned furnishings, effective lighting and sultry background jazz, the overall effect is attractively subdued and low key. You can slow down with a drink in the little reception bar, and smart well-trained staff are pleasant and hospitable, presenting menus that offer a wide choice of the more restrained, classical dishes that have been noticeable by their absence in many restaurants of late: starters like carpaccio of beef with artichoke, mustard cress and sauce 'cipriani', or smoked eel with roast beetroot & horseradish cream; and main courses like lemon sole with capers, and a comforting dish of beef short ribs with red wine, carrots & parsnip mash - or, perhaps, the supreme luxury dish, lobster thermidor, served with new potatoes and green beans. Head chef Conor McCann's cooking is accomplished, and well-conceived dishes both look and taste wonderful. There's a good ripened cheese plate and delicious desserts, which have always been a Roscoff tour de force, include good home-made ice creams and a dessert du jour - a boon for regular diners. Impressive, tasty cooking, soothing surroundings and excellent service add up to a winning combination - and a complete contrast to the Rankin flagship restaurant, Cayenne. **Seats 86.** Toilets Wheelchair Accessible; children welcome. L 12-2.15; D 6-10.15 (to 11.15 Fri/Sat). 3 course Set L, £19.50; Set 2/3 course D, £21.50/27.00, also á la carte. Separate vegetarian à la carte menu available. C losed Jan 1, Jul 12, Dec 25/26, Easter Sun/Mon. Amex, Diners, MasterCard, Visa. **Directions:** Near the City Hall.

Belfast

E RESTAURANT

Shu

253 Lisburn Road Belfast BT9 7EN
Tel: 028 9038 1655 Fax: 028 9068 1632
Email: eat@shu-restaurant.com Web: www.shu-restaurant.com

A smartly painted Victorian frontage and traditional arched windows provide a vivid contrast to the stainless steel efficiency of the bar and de rigeur 'on view' kitchen of this fashionable restaurant. After a courteous welcome, guests are led into a large L shaped room which is light and airy, with shiny metal softened by terracotta pillars and discreet covers. This is a smoothly run operation, with many regulars of all age groups. Head chef Brian McCann presents admirably simple menus based on carefully sourced ingredients, and offering a combination of classical and brasserie fare that is complemented by restaurant manager Julian Henry's marshalling of a tip top waiting staff. An outstanding bread selection will ease you through the menu stage, and may well be a highlight of the meal. Menus - à la carte, and a set dinner menu that is good value at £17.50 - are well balanced, allowing equally for the adventurous and more conservative diner. The ubiquitous salt & chilli squid (surely Belfast's favourite starter) makes its mandatory appearance, for example, but is well cooked and presented (and makes a beautiful light lunch dish), while a deliciously well-flavoured vegetarian penne pasta with tomatoes, fennel & rocket is one of a number of dishes offered as starter or main course portions. Dry aged sirloin will be a treat for those who cannot envisage a meal without steak but, judging by the success of a perfectly cooked and flavoursome dish of hake with white bean purée, ragôut of beans and mushrooms and pea & truffle velouté, fish may be an equally good choice. Upbeat classical desserts to finish, or cheese (not necessarily Irish farmhouse) with classy crackers. Cooking seems to go on getting better - and, together with great atmosphere, efficient service and good value for money this adds up to a restaurant that is always busy. If cocktails and tapas are your thing, head for the basement. Children welcome. **Seats 80** (private room, 24). Air conditioning. L Mon-Sat, 12-2.30, D Mon-Sat 6-9 (Sat to 9.30). 2-course menu £17.50, 3 course £25; otherwise à la carte (average main course £14), also Vegetarian Menu. House wines £14.50; s.c. discretionary (10% on parties of 6+). Bar open Fri & Sat 7-1. Closed Sun, 24-26 Dec, 11-13 Jul. Amex, MasterCard, Visa, Switch. **Directions:** Half mile south on Lisburn Road.

Belfast
RESTAURANT

Sun Kee Restaurant

38 Donegall Pass Belfast BT7 1BS
Tel: 028 9031 2016 Fax: 028 9024 2849

The Lo family's little place just off Shaftesbury Square has earned widespread recognition as one of Ireland's most authentic Chinese restaurants. What you get here is a combination of the classic Chinese dishes which are already familiar - but created in uncompromising Chinese style, without the usual "blanding down" typical of most oriental restaurants. They also offer more unusual dishes, which offer a genuine challenge to the jaded western palate: be prepared to be adventurous. It is unlicensed (but you may bring your own). The main difficulty is getting a reservation, as it's an extremely popular spot and invariably busy. Children welcome. **Seats 60.** L Mon-Sat, 12-2.30pm, D daily 5-11.30pm; range of 'banquet' menus for varying numbers (from £22 per person), also à la carte. Closed Sun L & Jul. **No Credit Cards. Directions:** Beside Police Station. QNR

Belfast
Ⓝ CAFÉ

Swantons Gourmet Foods

639 Lisburn Road Belfast BT9 7GT
Tel: 028 9068 3388 Fax: 028 9068 3388
Email: swantons@aol.com Web: www.swantons.com

Run by husband and wife team Stewart and Gloria Swanton, this speciality food store and café has earned a following amongst discerning Belfast people - even in an area that is especially well served with good places to shop and eat, it stands out for dedication to quality and value. As well as offering a carefully selected range of deli fare, the food freshly cooked on site is delicious. You can see the chefs at work in the kitchen at the back (always reassuring), and a changing selection through the day begins with breakfasts that include lovely options such as fruits with yoghurt and so on then, from late morning the lunch menu offers really good home made soups, custom made sandwiches in a variety of good breads, salads, hot dishes like quiches and spinach & filo pastry layer, plus one or two specials. Baking is a speciality - beautiful home baked desserts and tarts - and tray bakes with tea and coffees on the afternoon menu. It's a small place, so you may have to wait for a table at peak times, but you are not hurried or hassled once you get served. **Seats 20.** Open Mon-Sat, 9-5. Closed Sun.

Belfast
BAR/RESTAURANT

Ta Tu

701 Lisburn Road Belfast BT9 7GU
Tel: 028 9038 0818 Fax: 028 9038 0828

This fashionable bar and grill found an immediate niche when it opened in 2000, and is always packed at weekends. The design incorporates an ultra-modern high-roofed 'warehouse' with a long bar where the bright young things meet and greet and, at the rear, a more intimate restaurant area reminiscent of photographs depicting pre-war airship lounges. Menus change monthly and the food is, as one might expect, youthful and well presented; an all-day menu offers a wide range of dishes in various practical combinations and a reasonably priced evening Bistro Menu includes a range of gourmet pizzas, with an option of 1/2 carafe house red or white for only £5 extra. Well trained waiting staff really know the menus; the wine list offers a wide range of carefully chosen wines at very fair prices and there's plenty to choose from by the glass. Cocktail menu. DJ music. No children after 7pm. *The very trendy **Bar Bacca** in Franklin Street is in the same ownership. **Restaurant Seats 90.** Air conditioning. Food served daily all day. L 12-6, D 6-9.45 (Sun to 8.45). All day menu and a la carte. House wines from about £9.95. Bar food served 12-9.30 daily. *There are plans to close for a complete revamp early in 2007 and re-open with new head chef, Cath Gradwell. Closed 25 Dec. MasterCard, Visa. **Directions:** From the city centre, take Lisburn Road - about 1 mile on the right. ◇

Belfast
RESTAURANT

Tedfords Restaurant

5 Donegall Quay Belfast BT1 3EF
Tel: 028 9043 4000 Fax: 028 9024 8889

Sailing folk may remember Tedfords as a ship's chandlers - you can almost smell the sisal even now, especially as there are reminders a-plenty of this listed building's venerable maritime past. An informal ground floor restaurant has old charts papered on the walls and numerous other nautical artefacts including ship's lanterns, and bare-topped tables with linen napkins are pleasantly arranged on two levels with a railing around the upper one, allowing staff to move around the tables without disturbing diners too much - although many prefer the more sophisticated dining room upstairs, which is used only at weekends and lends a sense of occasion to a meal here. There's an appropriate emphasis on things from the sea in dishes like seafood & shellfish chowder (a tasty, rather creamy take on the classic), and a fresh seafood platter with crab mash & buttered asparagus: seafood is the star and accounts for about half of the menu - and Tedfords has a growing reputation for producing some of the best seafood in Belfast. But there's plenty else to choose from - especially certified Irish angus steaks. Vegetarian are not overlooked, however, and may be offered dishes like a goats cheese beignet with globe artichoke, or main course wild mushroom risotto with asparagus. Good desserts might include a Moorish hazelnut & chocolate parfait with vanilla cream, or there's an Irish cheeseboard, followed by cafetière coffee. Service is caring, and the food is imaginative and well cooked - good enough to earn a following. A very reasonably priced wine list includes half a dozen house wines, all under £12. *The basement lounge area is due for refurbishment early in 2007. **Seats 45.** Reservations required. L Tue-Fri, 12-2.30; D Tue-Sat, 5-9.30. Pre-theatre D Tue-Sat, £18.95 (5-6.30). Otherwise à la carte. House wine from £13; sc discretionary. Toilets wheelchair accessible. Children welcome. Parking in multi-storey carpark next door. Closed Sun-Mon, July fortnight, 1 week Christmas. Amex, MasterCard, Visa, Switch. **Directions:** 3 minute walk from Waterfront Hall, next to multi storey car park.

Belfast

Ten Square Hotel

HOTEL/RESTAURANT

10 Donegall Square South Belfast BT1 5JD
Tel: 028 9024 1001 Fax: 028 9024 3210
Email: reservations@tensquare.co.uk Web: www.tensquare.co.uk

This delightful boutique hotel has established a special niche for discerning visitors to Belfast: it is situated in a particularly attractive listed Victorian building and the location - just opposite the City Hall, and within walking distance of the whole city centre area - is superb. The interior is refreshingly contemporary, and has been achieved with sensitivity to the original building: a striking feature, for example, is the lovely old stained glass in many of the original windows, which is now subtly echoed in the interior design. Accommodation - in generous high-windowed rooms, theatrically decorated in an uncompromisingly modern style - is simple yet very luxurious; even the most dyed-in-the-wool traditionalist would be won over by the sheer style of these rooms and they have wonderful bathrooms to match. Features include well-planned lighting, state-of-the-art entertainment systems and - going a stage further than the usual mini-bar (which, however, includes fresh milk for your freshly brewed tea or coffee) - a collection of drinks, nibbles and bits and pieces that would be worthy of a small corner shop, all neatly tucked away out of sight. Conference/banqueting 100/150. Not suitable for children. No pets. **Rooms 23** (1 suite, 21 superior, 2 for disabled). Lift. 24 hour room service. Turndown service. Air conditioning, safe, ISDN, TV/DVD/video channel, tea/coffee-making facilities, iron & trouser press. B&B room rate £165 (max 2 guests). Closed 24-25 Dec. **Restaurant:** The stylishly informal Grill Room & Bar, which occupies the whole of the ground floor, has become one of Belfast's most popular restaurants and is always busy with non-residents, which gives the hotel a great buzz; the Grill Room is the perfect antidote to other fashionable restaurants in the city, as the focus is firmly on wholesome traditional all-day fare and very reasonable prices. The theme is colonial and, although there is actually quite a wide range offered on menus that smack of retro, red meat is king here (and very good meat it is too); char-grilled steaks and burgers are served with super chips and well-made classic sauces and other comforting dishes include 'knife & fork' barbecued ribs. The timing was perfect for the return of this down to earth food - the Grill Room's instant success is the proof. Staff are warm, welcoming and generally efficient, with none of the stuffiness sometimes encountered in exclusive hotels. All round, this accomplished hotel is retaining its well-earned its reputation as a top destination in Belfast for discerning travellers. **Seats 120** (private room, 30, outdoor, 48); Live music Wed & Sun. Food served daily 12-10pm (Sun, 8 am-10pm); L 12-3, D 6-10. A la carte. SC discretionary. Amex, MasterCard, Visa, Switch. **Directions:** Corner of Linenhall Street at rear of City Hall.

Belfast

The Water Margin

RESTAURANT

159-161 Donegall Pass Belfast BT7 1DP
Tel: 028 9032 6888 Fax: 028 9032 7333

This 200-seater emporium in a converted church at the bottom of the Ormeau Road is the biggest Chinese restaurant in Ireland. Inside, East meets West - a comfortable reception lounge with red leather sofas leads into the large open dining space with round tables of various sizes, lots of artificial plants and garish stained glass windows, all bright reds and greens and mythical beasts. An open bar runs the length of the inside wall and the dining area is divided between the ground floor and a gallery with a purple painted vaulted ceiling and an adjoining opaque glass walled function room. The menu is massive and it pays to either know Chinese food really well or have inside information to find your way about. An extensive Dim Sum menu offers uncompromising authentic Chinese dishes such as steamed ox tripe and steamed fish head (in black bean sauce), a reminder that there is a large Chinese community in Belfast. Finally you arrive at the safe haven of the set banquets, and the familiar territory of Western favourites: aromatic duck, sesame toast, sweet and sours, sizzlings and fried rice are all here - also desserts like chocolate gateau, mango pudding with cream and the fresh orange segments. At this level, the food is pretty average (and by no means cheap), but there is plenty of noisy atmosphere, and the Water Margin is somewhere to experience on a busy night for that alone. [There is a sister restaurant in Coleraine, Co. Londonderry.] **Seats 200.** Open daily, 12-11pm. Set menus from about £20 per person. House wine about £20. Open all year. MasterCard, Visa, Laser. **Directions:** Bottom of Ormeau Road. ◇

Belfast
HOTEL

The Wellington Park Hotel

2 Malone Road Belfast BT9 6RU
Tel: 028 9038 1111 Fax: 028 9066 5410
Email: info@wellingtonparkhotel.com Web: www.wellingtonparkhotel.com

Located in the fashionable Malone Road area close to the University, just five minutes from the city centre, this friendly, family-owned and managed hotel is quite a Belfast institution. Many regard it as the only place to stay when in the city, and it is certainly near most of the city's cultural attractions - Ulster Museum, Botanic Gardens, Odyssey Arena, Waterfront Hall, the Grand Opera House and St George's Market are all within walking distance on a fine day, or just a short taxi ride. It is also a popular conference venue and has all the most up to date audio-visual equipment and conference facilities, but private guests need not worry about being overrun by conference delegates, since one of the bars is exclusively for their use. The spacious foyer and public areas are comfortably furnished, as are the refurbished bedrooms, featuring the usual facilities, some with modem points and voice-mail. Guests have free use of Queen's University sports centre, a few minutes from the hotel. The Dunadry Hotel & Country Club, a fifteen minute drive from the city, is in the same ownership, also the new Armagh City Hotel (see entries). Conference/banqueting (400/300); business centre, secretarial services; video conferencing. Parking. Wheelchair accessible. Children welcome (under 12 free in parents' room; cots available without charge, baby sitting arranged). No pets. **Rooms 75** (all en-suite, 30 no smoking, 2 for disabled). Lift. 24 hour room service. B&B from about £40 pps. Restaurant open for L&D daily; Art Café, 7am-11pm daily. *Short breaks offered. Closed 24-26 Dec. Amex, Diners, MasterCard, Visa, Switch. **Directions:** From Queen's University, head south up Malone Road, hotel is on the right hand side.

BELFAST INTERNATIONAL AIRPORT

Although dining out at airport restaurants was once all the rage, airports and good food have not often been seen together recently - but Paul & Jeanne Rankin have done their best ensure that passengers going through Belfast can look forward to something a cut above the rest at **Café Paul Rankin** (028 9445 4992), which is in the Departure Lounge and offers wide range of quiches, salads, gourmet sandwiches and pasta dishes, and an upmarket all-day breakfast menu: Eggs Benedict, home-made pancakes, free range scrambles egg & toast, as well as their version of the traditional fry. For accommodation near the airport, **Hilton Templepatrick** (028 944 3500; www.templepatrickhilton.com) is nearby, on the Castle Upton Estate; it has excellent facilities, including golf.

WWW-IRELAND-GUIDE.COM FOR THE BEST PLACES TO EAT, DRINK & STAY

COUNTY ANTRIM

The Antrim Coast may be timeless in its beauty, but today its picturesque ports are enjoying the fruits of restoration and development at places as various as Ballycastle, Glenarm and Carrickfergus.

With its boundaries naturally defined by the sea, the River Bann, the extensive lake of Lough Neagh, and the River Lagan, County Antrim has always had a strong sense of its own clearcut geographical identity. This is further emphasised by the extensive uplands of the Antrim Plateau, wonderful for the sense of space with the moorland rising to heights such as Trostan (551m) and the distinctive Slemish (438m), famed for its association with St Patrick.

The plateau eases down to fertile valleys and bustling inland towns such as Ballymena, Antrim and Ballymoney, while the coastal towns ring the changes between the traditional resort of Portrush in the far north, the ferryport of Larne in the east, and historic Carrickfergus in the south.

In the spectacularly beautiful northeast of the county, the most rugged heights of the Plateau are softened by the nine Glens of Antrim, havens of beauty descending gently from the moorland down through small farms to hospitable villages clustered at the shoreline, and connected by the renowned Antrim Coast Road. Between these sheltered bays at the foot of the Glens, the sea cliffs of the headlands soar with remarkable rock formations which, on the North Coast, provide the setting for the Carrick-a-Rede rope bridge and the Giant's Causeway. From the charming town of Ballycastle, Northern Ireland's only inhabited offshore island of Rathlin is within easy reach by ferry, a mecca for ornithologists and perfect for days away from the pressures of mainland life.

Local Attractions and Information

Antrim town, Lough Neagh cruises	028 94 481312
Antrim town, Shanes Castle	028 94 428216
Antrim town, Tourism Information	028 94 428331
Ballycastle, Carrick-a-Rede Rope Bridge	028 20 731582
Ballymena, Tourism Information	028 25 660300
Ballymoney (Dervock), Benvarden Garden	028 20 741331
Ballymoney, Leslie Hill Open Farm	028 27 666803
Bushmills, Antrim Coast and Glens	028 20 731582
Bushmills Irish Whiskey-World's Oldest Distillery	028 20 731521
Carnlough, AlwaysIreland Activity Holidays	028 28 885995
Carrickfergus Castle	028 93 351273
Carrickfergus Waterfront	028 93 366455
Carrickfergus, Andrew Jackson Centre	028 93 366455
Dunluce Castle Visitor Centre	028 20 731938
Giants Causeway	028 20 731855

Giants Causeway & Bushmills Railway	028 20 741157
Glenariff Forest Park	028 21 758232
Larne, Carnfunnock Country Park	028 28 270451
Larne Ferryport	028 28 872100
Larne, Tourism Information	028 28 260088
Lisburn, Irish Linen Centre & Lisburn Museum	028 92 663377
Lisburn, Tourism Information	028 92 660038
Portrush, Tourism Information	028 70 823333
Rathlin Island Ferries	028 20 769299
Rathlin Island Visitor Centre	028 20 763951
Templepatrick, Patterson's Spade Mill	028 94 433619

Ballintoy

RESTAURANT/COUNTRY HOUSE

Whitepark House

150 Whitepark Road Ballintoy Ballycastle Co Antrim BT54 6NH **Tel: 028 2073 1482**
Email: bob@whiteparkhouse.com Web: www.whiteparkhouse.com

A warm welcome from chatty and well-informed hosts Bob and Siobhán Isles awaits visitors to this pretty old house, which is set in well-maintained gardens and enjoys stunning views of Whitepark Bay, and has a path down to the beach straight across the road. The three bedrooms have only one bathroom between them but Bob and Siobhán are considering adding en-suite bathrooms along with other necessary changes planned shortly; whether or not that happens, this is a house of great charm and character, and guests do not find it too difficult to forfeit a little convenience for the pleasure of being here. Bedrooms all have distinctive colour themes and lots of exotic touches to give each its special personality, and there is a lovely feeling of being surrounded by a well-loved garden. There's also a very comfortable and homely sitting room looking onto the garden, with couches, easy chairs and an open fire to relax beside - and, as elsewhere in the house, much of interest for the interested guest. Bob likes see guests well prepared for the day ahead and, as a vegetarian, he's well placed to make a great vegetarian breakfast in addition to the traditional Ulster Fry. Not suitable for children under 12. No pets. Garden, walking. **Rooms 3** (one bathroom for all; all no smoking). B&B from £30 pps, ss £5. 5% surcharge on credit card payments. MasterCard, Visa. **Directions:** On Antrim coast road A2, 9km (6m) East of Bushmills; on east side of Whitepark Bay.

Ballycastle

N RESTAURANT

Cellar Restaurant

11b The Diamond Ballycastle Co Antrim BT54 6AW
Tel: 028 2076 3037 Web: www.thecellarrestaurant.co.uk

Chris McCauley's atmospheric little restaurant just up the street from The House of McDonnell has an unusual barrel vaulted roof and cosy snugs separated by traditional etched glass dividers. Seafood, especially lobster, is the speciality on chef Nuala Mitchell's daily specials menu, where you will find starters like trout and smoked salmon terrine or 'petit fruit de mer' (seafood selection grilled in garlic butter and served with salad and lemon) and main courses including monkfish tails on crushed new potatoes, and whole Ballyvcastle lobster - which is available grilled with garlic butter or cold with mayonnaise, and reasonably priced at £22.95. The regular menu also includes some seafood but it offers a wider choice, including good steaks (have the best of both worlds with the surf'n'turf of charred fillet steak and half a Rathlin lobster...) and several vegetarian dishes - roast vegetable focccacia stuffed with Mediterranean roast vegetables and mozzarella cheese, for example, or vegetable fajitas. Charming staff provide good service under the direction of Chris McCauley and, although the seating is a little cramped, a meal here should be a thoroughly enjoyable outing. **Seats 46;** Air conditioning; Children welcome before 7pm; Food served daily in Summer: 12-10; L 12-3.30, D 3.30-10; Sun D only; L&D a la carte. House wine from £10. Open at 5pm in winter. Closed Sun L & last Mon-Tue in August, 25-26 Dec, 1 Jan. MasterCard, Visa, Switch.

Ballycastle

PUB

The House of McDonnell

71 Castle Street Ballycastle Co Antrim BT54 6AS
Tel: 028 2076 2975 Fax: 028 2076 2586
Email: toms1744@aol.com Web: www.houseofmcdonnell.com

The House of McDonnell has been in the caring hands of Tom and Eileen O'Neill since 1979 and in Tom's mother's family for generations before that they can even tell you not just the year, but the month the pub first opened (April 1766). Tom and Eileen delight in sharing the history of their long, narrow premises with its tiled floor and mahogany bar: it was once a traditional grocery-bar, and is now a listed building. The only real change in the last hundred years or so, says Tom, was the addition of a toilet block "but outside the premises you understand" and, more recently, some old photographs which came to light have been put on display. Music is important too they have a good traditional music session every Friday and love to see musicians coming along and joining in. But sessions attract large numbers, many of them smokers - and 'to comply with anti-smoking regulations' they are to provide a 'suitable area' at the rear of the bar. As Tom and Eileen rightly take pride in the fact that this is the only old bar in Ballycastle to have resisted 'refurbishment and makeover', you can rest assured that any changes will be completed with a very light touch. Not suitable for children after 8pm. They're usually open from 11 am until "late" at weekends, but only in the evenings midweek, although times might vary in winter; it's worth checking out at weekends anyway, all year. **Directions:** Town centre, near the Diamond.

Ballygally
HOTEL

Hastings Ballygally Castle Hotel

Coast Road Ballygally Co Antrim BT40 2QZ
Tel: 028 2858 1066 Fax: 028 2858 3681
Email: res@bgc.hastingshotels.com Web: www.hastingshotels.com

This coastal hotel really has got a (very) old castle at the heart of it - and they've even got a ghost. (You can visit her room at the top of the castle). The whole thing is quite unlike any of the other Hastings hotels and, although ongoing investment is dramatically improving standards, the hotel still has character; some of the older rooms are literally shaped by the castle itself, and are quite romantic. Cosy chintzy wing chairs and open fires make welcoming lounge areas to relax in - and the beach is just a stone's throw away, across the road. Conference/banqueting (200/120). Children welcome; (under 14 free in parents' room; cots available without charge). Wheelchair accessible. Parking. No pets. **Rooms 44** (3 junior suites, 4 executive, 4 shower only, 5 family rooms, 8 no smoking, 1 for disabled) B&B £65pps, ss £35; no SC. Meals: Rest D, 5-9; buffet L 12.30-2.30. *Short breaks offered - details on application. Open all year. Amex, Diners, MasterCard, Visa, Switch. **Directions:** Situated on the coast road between Larne and Glenarm (5km /3 miles from Larne on A2).

Ballygally
RESTAURANT

Lynden Heights Restaurant

97 Drumnagreagh Rd Ballygally nr Larne Co Antrim BT40 2RR
Tel: 028 2858 3560 Fax: 028 2858 3560

On a clear day, the Doran family's restaurant high up above the coast road has the most amazing views - and the dining room is in a conservatory, to make the most of it. There's a cosy bar, where orders are taken by friendly, neatly uniformed waiting staff. Well-balanced menus offer a wide choice of dishes on every course, with seafood the main strength, and also game in season - although this is less obvious on the set menus where the choice is more limited. On the carte, three of the seven starters and three main courses are seafood dishes, cooked in a fairly classic style and given the occasional contemporary twist. Steaks get a predictably good showing too, and also Ballymoney ham, with traditional parsley cream sauce; vegetarian dishes are not much in evidence, but a separate menu is available on request. Good carefully sourced ingredients, sound cooking, hearty portions and efficient service all complement this restaurant's natural appeal. An interesting, informative and well-priced wine list is changed monthly. [The Dorans are hoping to add bedroosm in the near furture.] Parking. **Seats 60** (private room, 26). Reservations advised. D Fri-Sun, 5-9 (Sun to 8); L Sun only, 12.30-3. Set D from £19.50, also à la carte; Set Sun L £15.95. Children welcome. Toilets wheelchair accessible. House wine £13.50. Closed Mon-Wed. Amex, MasterCard, Visa, Switch. **Directions:** Situated between Larne and Glenarm - signed off the coast road.

Ballymena
HOTEL

Galgorm Manor Hotel

136 Fenaghy Road Ballymena Co Antrim BT42 1EA
Tel: 028 2588 1001 Fax: 028 2588 0080
Email: sales@galgorm.com Web: www.galgorm.com

Set amidst beautiful scenery, with the River Maine running through the grounds, this previous gentleman's residence is now one of Northern Ireland's leading country house hotels. Approaching through well-tended parkland, guests pass the separate banqueting and conference facilities to arrive at the front door of the original house, (which is a mere 100 yards from the river). Except for the banqueting suites, the whole hotel has been closed recently for major development that will add extra bedrooms, conference and leisure facilities in 2007, and the old house has also undergone major renovation; at the time of going to press the hotel has partially re-opened - for updates, contact the hotel directly, or visit their website. The main house has a very pleasant atmosphere, with a welcoming fire in the foyers and an elegant drawing room and a traditional bar, as well as the more casual Ghillies Bar in a characterful converted buildings at the back of the hotel (where informal meals are also served). Accommodation includes some suites and rooms in the old house, most with views over the river, and 48 new bedrooms in the old walled garden area. Conference/banqueting (500); golf (9/18); fishing; horse-riding; walking; garden. Children welcome (under 4s free in parents room, cot £10, babysitting arranged). Wheelchair accessible. No pets. **Rooms 24** (3 suites, 2 disabled) B&B about £55 pps, ss about £40. L &D available daily. Open all year. Amex, Diners, MasterCard, Visa. **Directions:** From the Galgorm roundabout, take the third exit for Cullybackey (Feneghy road). About 2 miles, on the left. ◇

Ballymena

COUNTRY HOUSE

Marlagh Lodge

71, Moorfields Rd Ballymena Co Antrim BT42 3BU
Tel: 028 2563 1505 Fax: 028 2564 1590
Email: info@marlaghlodge.com Web: www.marlaghlodge.com

Robert and Rachel Thompson left their well-known country house The Moat Inn at Templepatrick in 2003, to move to a neglected early Victorian house on the edge of Ballymena, which they have painstakingly restored and opened for guests. It was no easy task, but they took on the restoration with characteristic determination and verve, cutting no corners along the way and, although close to the road, the result is truly impressive. Originally built as the Dower House for the O'Hara family of nearby Crebilly House, the Lodge is a classic of its era, double fronted with spacious, high-ceilinged reception rooms of human proportions on either side of the entrance hall, and bedrooms which have lent themselves remarkably well to the architectural gymnastics needed in order to provide en-suite bathrooms in an old house. The three rooms - The Blue Room, The Chintz Room and The Print Room - are all large and comfortably furnished with interesting antiques, but otherwise very different. Architectural salvage must have done well out of this job but, however difficult, it is clear that Robert and Rachel also had a lot of fun along the way. As they did at The Moat, Robert and Sarah also offer dinner for residents - and non-residents are welcome too, by reservation. The repertoire is quite extensive, and a typical summer menu might include griddled peach and feta salad, with or without frizzled Parma ham; a soup or sorbet; loin of pork fillet with apricots, mint & almonds; strawberry and mascarpone tart;and a selection of Irish and continental cheese; as everything is home made each day, the amount of choice depends on the number expected for dinner, but there will always be some choice. Special gourmet evenings are sometimes held, with wine paired with each course. Marlagh Lodge is within easy reach of the main airports and ferry ports, and all the attractions of the north Antrim coast. Banqueting (20). Children welcome (u 5s free in parents' room, cot available, free of charge). No pets. Golf nearby. **Rooms 3** (2 en-suite, 1 with private bathroom, all no smoking). B&B £35-40 pps, no ss. D Mon-Sat, 8pm (book by noon); Non residents welcome on Fri-Sat by reservations; Set D £31.50. Wines from £14.50. "Closed occasionally," please ring ahead off-season. MasterCard, Visa, Switch. **Directions:** On A36, 1km (0.6 m) from Larne Road roundabout and visible from the road.

Ballymoney

RESTAURANT WITH ROOMS

Harmony Hill Country House

Balnamore Ballymoney Co Antrim BT53 7PS
Tel: 028 2766 3459 Fax: 028 2766 3740
Email: webmaster@harmonyhill.net Web: www.harmonyhill.net

Trish and Richard Wilson's unusual restaurant is peacefully situated in a 5-acre woodland garden, with a mill race bordering and lots of bird life in the old mill building. The house itself is something of an enigma, single storey, with an interesting and rather grand eighteenth century section - including a beautiful light-filled drawing room, and broad raised verandah outside it - on the left as you go in, and, at the end of a mysterious plant-filled passage towards the back of the house, there is quite a substantial restaurant which, again, divides into two areas of very different character. One section is divided into booths, providing a homely spot for solitary guests dining in the company of a good book, or for times when the restaurant is not busy enough to use all the scrubbed pine tables; the other section is more open, with traditional dining tables, but the whole set-up is very appealing. Open fires play a major part in the life of this house - there's a big fire in the drawing room and one in the restaurant too - the logistics of running so many fires must be quite a challenge, but they give the house great atmosphere. The menu, incidentally, is also most unusual: instead of simply naming the dishes, they are presented as little recipes, hence 'Soused Trout: Gently poach the freshest trout fillets in white wine vinegar & court bouillon peppered with star anise & pickling spice, chill well then serve with a light salad of mixed leaves, radish and quail's eggs'. Ingenious. **Restaurant: Seats 50.** Non-residents welcome by reservation. D Wed-Sat, 6.30-9.30; Set D about £25. L Sun, 12.30-2. House wine about £10.95. Restaurant closed Mon, Tue; 25-26 Dec. **Accommodation:** Across the hall from the elegant eighteenth century drawing room, accommodation is in a very different style: six generous, rather low-key rooms have steps up to optional sleeping platforms (not necessarily used - but you could accommodate a family of five in one room). Bathroom arrangements are a little complicated (some rooms are en-suite, others have private bathrooms or showers). An unusual feature is that every bedroom has a working fireplace, where an open peat fire can be lit - not your average country house accommodation, but it could be fun for a family, or a group of friends. Garden. (B&B is about 36pps, ss £6.) The house open all year. MasterCard, Visa, Switch. **Directions:** Off A26, 1.5 miles outside Ballymoney. ◇

Bushmills

Bushmills Inn

Ⓔ HOTEL/RESTAURANT

9 Dunluce Rd Bushmills Co Antrim BT57 8QG
Tel: 028 2073 3000 Fax: 028 2073 2048
Email: mail@bushmillsinn.com Web: www.bushmillsinn.com

Originally a 19th-century coaching inn, recent developments have been undertaken with sensitivity, improving amenities without loss of character. The tone is set by the turf fire and country seating in the hall and public rooms bars, the famous circular library, the restaurant, even the Pine Room conference room carry on the same theme. Bedrooms are individually furnished in a comfortable cottage style and even have "antiqued" bathrooms but it's all very well done and avoids a theme park feel. It's hard to think of a better base for a holiday playing the famous golf courses of the area (Royal Portrush is just four miles away) - or simply exploring this beautiful coastline and its hinterland; taking the Magilligan-Greencastle ferry, day trips can comfortably include a visit to the beautiful Inishowen peninsula in Co. Donegal. Garden. Fishing. Children welcome (cot available, £10). No pets. **Rooms 32:** 22 in Mill House, 10 in Coaching Inn; (6 superior, 7 shower only, all no smoking, 1 for disabled) B&B from £84 pps.*Short breaks offered. Restaurant: The inn is known for its wholesome food and makes a good place to plan a break when touring, as it offers both day and evening menus in cosy surroundings (the only disadvantage is that coaches often make a lunchtimestop here for the same reasons). Pride in Irish ingredients is seen in A Taste of Ulster menus that offer a range of traditional dishes with a modern twist: an unusual speciality, for example, is Dalriada cullen skink, a 'meal in a soup bowl' based on smoked haddock and topped with an (optional) poached egg; another is onion & Guinness soup, which is topped with a cheese croûton like the French soup that inspired it - and, of course 'Bushmills coffee', which is better than a dessert any day. Wheelchair accessible. **Seats 110** (private room, 40, outdoor, 14). Reservations advised. Not suitable for children after 6pm. L&D á la carte; D daily 6-9.30; L daily, Day Menu 12-6.00; (Sun: carvery from 12.30-3pm and day menu to 6pm); bar food Sun only 12-4 (soup & sandwiches). House wines from £14; SC discretionary. Closed Dec 24/25. MasterCard, Visa, Switch. **Directions:** On the A4 Antrim coast road, in Bushmills village, as it crosses the river.

Bushmills

The Distillers Arms

BAR/RESTAURANT

140 Main Street Bushmills Co Antrim BT57 8QE
Tel: 028 2073 1044 Fax: 028 2073 2843
Email: simon@distillersarms.com Web: www.distillersarms.com

Simon Clarke's stylish modern bar and restaurant is housed in a renovated 18th century building which was once the home of the distillery owners. The bar - which leads into the restaurant at the far end - has smart modern lightwood bar stools with comfortable curved backs and a warm atmosphere is created by fresh flowers on the bar, the use of different woods and table lamps which soften the lighting, all emphasised by comfortably domestic seating groups and sofas inside the door. The restaurant is more rustic by comparison, with open stonework and a fireplace giving it an old-world character. As much as half of the menu could be seafood, with imports like tiger prawns and sea bass listed as well as local catches, including lobster and crab from nearby Rathlin Island. steamed Irish mussels in cider cream - and a speciality dish of salmon cured with old Bushmills whiskey; main courses also offer a good choice o seafood, but there will also be some good meat and poultry dishes (traditionally inspired pan seared chicken supreme with cabbage & bacon, fondant potatoes & grain mustard cream, perhaps), and mainstream vegetarian dishes are especially appealing. Lunch and early evening menus offer particularly good value and the wine list, which offers many bottles sourced directly from auction and sold with only a small mark up, includes a fair choice of house wines and half bottles. Toilets wheelchair accessible. Children welcome before 9pm. **Seats 76** (outdoor seating, 6, private room, 25). Open daily in summer: L12.30-3, D 5.30-9 (to 9.30 Fri/Sat); early D £10, 5.30-6.30. Sun L £15, otherwise à la carte. House wines from £10. Closed Mon-Tue off-season (Oct-Mar); 25 Dec. MasterCard, Visa, Switch. **Directions:** 300 yards from Old Bushmills Distillery.

Carnlough
HOTEL

Londonderry Arms Hotel

20 Harbour Road Carnlough Co Antrim BT44 0EU
Tel: 028 2888 5255 Fax: 028 2888 5263
Email: lda@glensofantrim.com Web: www.glensofantrim.com

Carnlough, with its charming little harbour and genuinely old-fashioned atmosphere (they still sell things like candyfloss in the little shops) is one of the most delightful places in Northern Ireland. The Londonderry Arms Hotel, built by the Marchioness of Londonderry in 1848 as a coaching inn, was inherited by her great grandson, Sir Winston Churchill, in 1921. Since 1948 it has been in the caring hands of the O'Neill family. The original building and interior remain intact, giving the hotel great character. They do good home-made bar meals, or afternoon tea. which you can have in the bar or beside the fire in a comfortably old fashioned lounge; in the evening, that great Northern Irish speciality High Tea is served in the restaurant, before dinner service begins. Bedrooms - which all have full baths and include 14 newer ones added at the back of the hotel - are comfortable and well-furnished in keeping with the character of the building. Many of the older rooms have sea views, and it is worthwhile discussing the type and location of your room when booking as one or two are badly positioned for a restful night's sleep. The hotel is a good conference venue and makes a very pleasant base for a short break exploring the Glens of Antrim. Conferences/banqueting (100/80). Parking. Wheelchair accessible. Children welcome (under 12s free in parents' room; cots available without charge). No pets. Walking.*Off season short breaks offered - details on application. **Rooms 35** (all en-suite, 10 no smoking, 2 for disabled). Lift. B&B £45 pps, ss £14. Restaurant: D 7-9 (5-8 Sun), L Sun only, 12-3. Bar food served daily, 12-9. Closed 24-25 Dec. Amex, MasterCard, Visa, Switch. **Directions:** On the A2 Antrim coast road, 24km (14 miles) north of Larne.

Carrickfergus
HOTEL

Clarion Hotel Carrickfergus

75 Belfast Road Carrickfergus Co Antrim BT38 8BX
Tel: 028 9336 4556 Fax: 028 9335 1620
Email: info@clarioncarrick.com Web: www.clarioncarrick.com

Conveniently located to Belfast airport (10 miles) and the scenic attractions of the Antrim coast, this modern hotel makes a comfortable base for business and leisure visitors. It has good conference facilities (600), meeting rooms (max. 60) and in-room amenities (desk, fax/modem line) for business guests. Bedrooms include three suitable for disabled guests, two suites, two junior suites and 20 non-smoking rooms; all are furnished to a high standard with well-finished en-suite bathrooms (all with bath and shower). **Rooms 68.** B&B from about £45 pps, ss about £30. Open all year except Christmas. Amex, Diners, MasterCard, Visa, Switch. **Directions:** Main Coast Road exit Belfast North (8 miles). ◇

Dunadry
HOTEL

Dunadry Hotel & Country Club

2 Islandreagh Drive Dunadry Co Antrim BT41 2HA
Tel: 028 9443 4343 Fax: 028 9443 3389
Email: info@dunadry.com Web: www.dunadry.com

This attractive riverside hotel is well-located close to Belfast International Airport and only about 15 minutes from the city centre. It was formerly a mill and it succeeds very well in combining the character of the old buildings with the comfort and efficiency of an international hotel. It has excellent facilities and is surrounded by ten acres of grounds, making it a good choice as a business and conference venue - and, equally, as a weekend retreat. Stylish, spacious bedrooms include three suites and eleven executive rooms all have good amenities, including satellite TV, and executive rooms have computer points and fax machines. The most desirable rooms have French windows opening on to the gardens or the inner courtyard and an informal restaurant, The Mill Race Bistro, makes the most of its situation overlooking the river. Leisure facilities within the grounds include a professional croquet lawn, fun bowling, trout fishing and cycling, as well as a leisure centre with fitness equipment, indoor swimming pool and professional beauty therapist. *Sister hotel to the Wellington Park Hotel in Belfast city and the new Armagh City Hotel (see entries). Conference/banqueting 350/300. Children welcome (under 12s free in parents' room cot available without charge, baby sitting arranged). **Rooms 83** (all en-suite, 2 for disabled). No pets. Garden, walking, fishing, cycling; leisure centre, beauty salon. B&B from £40pps; room-only rate also available.*Short breaks offered. Linen Mill Restaurant (fine dining): D Sat only, 7.30-10.30. Bistro: open all day. Closed 24-26 Dec. Amex, Diners, MasterCard, Visa, Switch. **Directions:** Near Belfast airport; look for signs to Antrim/Dunadry.

Portballintrae
BAR/RESTAURANT

Sweeney's Public House & Wine Bar

Seaport Avenue Portballintrae Co Antrim BT57 8SB
Tel: 028 2073 2404 Fax: 028 2073 1850 Email: seaport@freeuk.com

Seymour Sweeney's bar is in an attractive stone building is on the sea side of the road as you drive into Portballintrae, and is very handy to both the Royal Portrush Golf Club and the Giant's Causeway. It's a pleasant place, with a welcoming open fire in the bar and a choice of places to drink or have a bite to eat. Unpretentious food is in the modern international café/bar style; seafood platter and 'Wellington Bomber' are specialities... . Although likely to suit all age groups during the day, it can get very busy during the evening, especially on live music nights (folk & country; there is a late licence to 1 am on Friday and Saturday). A useful place to break a day exploring the area, although a phone call is advised. Children welcome, wheelchair accessible. **Seats 120** (+50 outside, +32 private room). Air con. Food daily, 12-9. Set L £9.50, set Sun L £12.50, also A la carte. Closed 25 Dec. Amex, Diners, MasterCard, Visa, Switch. **Directions:** Centre of village overlooking bay & harbour. ◇

PORTRUSH

Portrush is a popular seaside holiday resort, golfing destination and a good base area for exploring the beautiful Antrim coast. The most spectacularly located hotel in the area is the **Royal Court** (028 7082 2236; www.royalcourthotel.co.uk) on the coast road and, in the town, those in the know head for the smart **Comfort Hotel Portrush** (028 782 6100; www.comforthotelportrush.com). Nearby **'55 North'** (028 7082 2811; www.55-north.com) is in an attractive modern building with sea views, offering a useful all-day café on the ground floor and a restaurant with beautiful views serving eclectic food above it.

WWW-IRELAND-GUIDE.COM FOR THE BEST PLACES TO EAT, DRINK & STAY

Portrush
€ B&B/FARMHOUSE

Maddybenny Farmhouse

Loguestown Road Portrush Coleraine Co Antrim BT52 2PT
Tel: 028 7082 3394 Email: beds@maddybenny.com
Web: www.maddybenny.com

Just two miles from Portrush, the White family's Plantation Period farmhouse was built before 1650. Since extended, and now modernised, it makes a very comfortable and exceptionally hospitable place to stay, with a family-run equestrian centre nearby (including stabling for guests' own horses). There is also snooker, a games' room and quiet sitting places, as well as a a garden and an area for outdoor children's games. The accommodation is just as thoughtful. The bedrooms are all en-suite and there are all sorts of useful extras electric blankets, a comfortable armchair, hospitality tray complete with tea cosy, a torch and alarm clock beside the bed, trouser press, hair dryer and, on the landing, an ironing board, fridge and pay phone for guest use. Across the yard there are also six self-catering cottages, open all year (one wheelchair friendly). No evening meals, but guests are guided to the local eating places that will suit them best - and her breakfasts are legendary, so make sure you allow plenty of time to start the day with a feast the like of which you are unlikely to encounter again. Maddybenny was the Guide's Farmhouse of the Year in 2000. Golf, fishing, tennis and pitch & putt nearby. Equestrian, walking; snooker. Children welcome (cot available £2 charge). No pets. Garden. **Rooms 3** (all en-suite, 2 family rooms) B&B £22.50pps, ss £5 (children £10),no ss . Closed 25-26 Dec. MasterCard, Visa. **Directions:** Signposted off A29 Portrush/Coleraine road.

Portrush
€ RESTAURANT

The Ramore Restaurant & Wine Bar

6 The Harbour Road Portrush Co Antrim BT56 8BN
Tel: 028 7082 6969 Fax: 028 7082 3194
Email: ramore@btconnect.com Web: www.ramorerestaurants.co.uk

The wonderful Ramore Restaurant was once the leading light of cosmopolitan fine dining in Northern Ireland and, after a long spell concentrating exclusively on quality fast food, George and Jane McAlpin have brought back the spirit of the old Ramore in an 80-seater fine dining restaurant that now complements the three existing casual eating places and - unlike any of their other eating areas - it is bookable. The new restaurant is on the top floor, above the wine bar (and not clearly signed); it is in two areas - one a large square room overlooking the harbour, which is very noisy (hard surfaces without sound-dampening fabrics - and no tablecloths) and a quieter area in a room along the bar, with a mixture of long tables and high stools and high tables area. The design is very plain and, like the food, modern Asian. Anyone expecting a recreation of the old Ramore - in terms of menu or style - is doomed to disappointment, but it was a cutting edge restaurant in its day and its successor is in the same mould and, although the menu may now be Asian, you'll still get the same good choice of wines at very fair prices. Dishes enjoyed on a recent visit included fried crispy monkfish (with mango salad, nanjim, aoïli, mint & coriander), and sliced steak teriyaki (served with prawn spring rolls, oriental salad & sesame dressing, also a delicious side dish of wok fried vegetables. The cooking is as good as hoped, presentation is very attractive and service, as far as possible considering how busy this restaurant can get, is quick and attentive - wine service, especially, under the direction of sommelier Sam Stevenson who has been with the company since 1982, is impressive. And yet... with table cleaning beginning at 10.45 as the restaurant begins to empty, and the toilets showing signs of pressure after a busy evening, this is not the old Ramore - but it is very welcome all the same. **Ramore Wine Bar:** This informal restaurant is on the first floor, underneath the new Ramore, and above the pasta restaurant, and it remains very popular with the holiday market and with the young - teenagers, families with young children - who appreciate the fun & friendly atmosphere, the speed and prices which are reasonable for the quality of food. Menus offer a wide selection of contemporary dishes ranging from tortilla chips with dips, through bang bang chicken with oriental salad, peanut & garlic dips, chilli steak in pitta with salad & garlic mayo or lamb steaks with red pepper & cherry tomato salsa on bruschetta to jumbo prawn salad or vegetarian options like cheese & spinach flan. Prices are very accessible - almost everything is still around £10 - but the downside is noise, discomfort and scanty service. *The nearby Harbour Bar is in the same ownership; the old front retains its original characte (L&D served daily). Ramore Restaurant: **seats 80;** D Wed-Sat, 6.30-10.30pm, Sun 6-9.30pm; house wine from £9.95. Closed Mon&Tue. Ramore Wine Bar Seats 170. L&D daily: L12.15-2.15pm, D 5-10 (Sun,12.30-3 & 5-9); Coast Italiano Seats 90 (Mon-Sat 4-10.30, Sun 3-9.30). Wine bar & toilets on ground floor wheelchair accessible. Closed 25 Dec. MasterCard, Visa, Switch. **Directions:** At the harbour in Portrush.

COUNTY ARMAGH

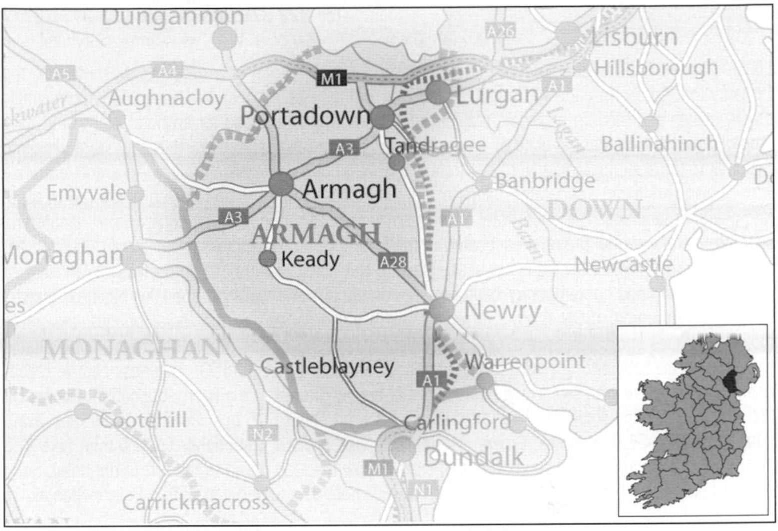

Mention Armagh, and most people will think of apples and archbishops. In the more fertile northern part of the county, orchards are traditionally important in the local economy, with the lore of apple growing and their use a part of County Armagh life and tradition. And the pleasant cathedral city of Armagh itself is of course the ecclesiastical capital of all Ireland, and many a mitre is seen about it.

But in fact Armagh city's significance long pre-dates Christian times. Emhain Macha - Navan Fort- to the west of the town, was a royal stronghold and centre of civilisation more than 4,000 years ago. Marking the county's northern coastline, the inland freshwater sea of Lough Neagh provides sand for the construction industry, eels for gourmets, and recreational boating of all sorts. In times past, it was part of the route which brought coal to Dublin from the mines in Coalisland in Tyrone, the main link to the seaport of Newry being the canal from Portadown which, when opened in 1742, was in the forefront of canal technology.

That County Armagh was a leader in canal technology is only one of its many surprises. The discerning traveller will find much of interest, whether it be in the undulating farmland and orchards, the pretty villages, or the handsome uplands rising to Carrigatuke above Newtownhamilton, and on towards the fine peak of Slieve Gullion in the south of the county, down to Forkhill and Crossmaglen and the Gaelic football heartlands.

Local Information and Attractions

Annaghmore (nr Portadown), Ardress (NT house)	028 38 851236
Armagh, County Museum	028 37 523070
Armagh, Planetarium	028 37 523689
Armagh, Astronomical Observatory	028 37 522928
Armagh, Palace Stables Heritage Centre	028 37 529629
Armagh, St Patrick's Trian Visitor Centre	028 37 521801
Bessbrook, Derrymore House	028 30 830353
Forkhill (Slieve Gullion)Ti chulainn Cultural Centre	028 30 888828
Loughgall, Loughgall Country Park	028 38 892900
Lough Neagh, Discovery Centre, Oxford Island	028 38 322205
Markethill, Gosford Forest Park	028 37 551277
Moy, The Argory (NT Mansion)	028 87 784753
Newry, Derrymore House	028 30 830353
Portadown, Moneypenny's Lock (Newry Canal)	028 37 521800
Scarva, Newry Canal Visitor Centre	028 38 832163
Slieve Gullion Forest Park	028 30 848226

Armagh
HOTEL

Armagh City Hotel

2 Friary Road Armagh Co Armagh BT60 4FR
Tel: 028 3751 8888 Fax: 028 3751 2777
Email: info@armaghcityhotel.com Web: www.armaghcityhotel.com

Located at the heart of the "orchard county" of Armagh, this hotel is a sister establishment to the Dunadry Inn, Co. Antrim and Wellington Park Hotel, Belfast (see entries). While its uncompromisingly blocky design and modern materials may surprise those who had hoped for an hotel that would have empathy with the traditional style of Ireland's historic ecclesiastical capital, it has brought welcome facilities to the area, including Northern Ireland's largest hotel conference facility. An events entrance with its own parking area separates delegates from other guests and has an impressive foyer, with separate check-in facilities. The main hotel entrance may seem disappointing by comparison - a cafeteria style 'Deli' and informal dining area located in the foyer give a poor impression on arrival - but the bar and more formal restaurant areas are at the back of the hotel, looking out onto pleasant landscaped gardens. Clean-lined contemporary bedrooms are practical - and well-equipped for business guests, with air conditioning, ISDN lines, safe and TV with video as well as the usual phones, tea/coffee making facilities and trouser press. Children welcome (under 12s free in parents' room, cot available without charge, baby sitting arranged). Conference/banqueting (1,200/650); business centre, broadband; leisure centre with swimming pool. *Special breaks offered - details on application. **Rooms 82** (10 executive, 30 no smoking, 4 for disabled). B&B from about £45 pps. Room-only rate also available. Closed 24-26 Dec. Amex, Diners, MasterCard, Visa, Switch. **Directions:** From Dublin take A28 to Armagh City, when the police station is in sight, follow the road round to the left to the hotel. From Belfast take M1 to Junction 11, then M12 on to A3 , hotel is situated just before Palace Stables.

Armagh
RESTAURANT

Manor Park Restaurant

2 College Hill The Mall Armagh Co Armagh BT61 9DF
Tel: 028 375 15353 Email: manorparkrestaurant@yahoo.ie
Web: www.manorparkrestaurant.com

An attractive early nineteenth century stone-fronted building beside the entrance to the Observatory is the home of Pascale Brissaud's French restaurant; it is a building of character - low-ceilinged, with a period fireplace, antique furnishings and silver - and makes an interesting setting for a busy restaurant. Arriving guests are greeted by one of all-French staff, and may have an aperitif in the little bar (just a few seats and, surprisingly, plastic flowers), or go straight to their table. Several different menus are offered at various times, and they make a good read - ingredients are very good quality and Pascale, who is originally from Perpignan, clearly takes pride in the produce of his adopted country: Kilkeel scallops, Donegal blue lobster and Lough Erne perch all feature, for example, and there are many more. Specialities include dishes like a classic Burgundy snail timbale with a fresh garlic soufflé & Chablis nut butter. Although dinner can be expensive, lunch and early dinner menus offer good value for money; the early dinner, for example, offers a choice of six or seven starters - possibly including a speciality gratin of Dublin Bay prawns with fresh garlic & almond butter - and a similar number of main courses, including local meats - sirloin beef, perhaps, and a tasty dish of stuffed leg of lamb with a honey, thyme and rosemary reduction - and perhaps less usual ingredients such as black Lyon duck, served with a traditional orange & Grand Marnier sauce. The full à la carte is much grander, and offers game in season, and specialities with a sense of occasion, such as a croustade of Kilkeel scallops with champagne butter sauce, and Combination of Roasted Piglet: the leg, stuffed with plum; the rack, with white wine cream; mignon, with cider & Calvados sauce. An extensive wine list includes many big names and offers good value, also an unusually wide selection of half bottles. *There are plans to open a second restaurant, with accommodation, on the shores of Upper Lough Erne, in spring 2007. Children welcome. **Seats 60** (private room 26). Reservations required. L & D daily: L 12-2.30, D 5.30-10. Set L from £5.95, Set Sun L £15.45; Early D £15.45 (Mon-Fri, 5-6.30), Set D from £19.95. L & D also à la carte. House wines from £15. Closed 24 & 26 Dec & 1 Jan. MasterCard, Visa, Laser, Switch. **Directions:** On the mall, beside the Courthouse.

Craigavon
COUNTRY HOUSE

Newforge House

58 Newforge Road Magheralin Craigavon
Co Armagh BT67 0QL **Tel: 028 9261 1255**
Fax: 028 9261 2823 Email: enquiries@newforgehouse.com
Web: www.newforgehouse.com

John and Louise Mathers' fine Georgian country house is less than half an hour's drive south west of Belfast, and handy to both Belfast International and City airports and Ferry Terminal - yet, in a wonderful setting of mature trees, gardens and green fields on the edge of the quiet village of Magheralin, it feels like worlds away. The property - which is substantial - was built around 1785 and has been in the Mathers family for six generations; after major renovations the Mathers opened John's former family home as a guesthouse in 2005, and it now offers luxurious en-suite accommodation in stylish, individually decorated rooms (all with beautiful bathrooms, five of which have separate bath and shower), a period drawing room with an open log fire and a fine dining room where John takes pride in presenting meals based mostly on local and organic produce - which can be taken at separate tables or as a group. It is a lovely spot for a short break and makes a perfect setting for special occasions, including weddings (which can be in a marquee in the garden for larger numbers), smaller celebrations, or corporate events. Free Broadband Wi/FI. **Rooms 6** (5 with separate bath & shower, 1 shower only, all no smoking). B&B £60 pps,, ss £15. Wheelchair accessible on ground floor, including toilet facilities; bedrooms upstairs not wheelchair accessible. Dining Room **seats 24.** D daily 7-8.30 (to 9 Fri/Sat); Sun & Mon light dinner only; Set D £28; Vegetarian meals on request; House wine £12. No smoking house. Closed 24 Dec - 8 Jan. MasterCard, Visa, Switch. **Directions:** M1 from Belfast to Craigavon until junction for A3 to Moira; through Moira to Magheralin then turn left at Byrnes Pub (on the corner) onto Newforge Road. Continue for 2 minutes until the National Speed Limit signs; black and white sign for Newforge House on the left. Next left through entrance in stone wall, take first right turn and park in front of the house.

Lurgan
€ RESTAURANT

The Brindle Beam Tea Rooms

House of Brindle 20 Windsor Avenue Lurgan
Co Armagh BT67 9BG **Tel: 028 3832 1721**

This in-store self-service restaurant is a real one-off. Nothing is bought in and the kitchen team, puts the emphasis firmly on real home cooking. There are two freshly-made soups each day and hot dishes like beef stew, made with well trimmed fat-free chump steak - with no onions. None of the pies or casseroles contain onions as some customers don't like them, but they're still full of flavour. Their salad cart is a special attraction, with anything up to 30 different salads served each day, and several different hot dishes including baked or grilled chicken breasts, salmon and always some vegetarian dishes too. There's also a huge variety of tray bakes and desserts - and only real fresh cream is used. Scrupulously clean, with reasonable prices (not cheap, but good value for the quality) and real home cooking, this place is a gem. **Seats 110** (private room 50). No smoking restaurant, Open Mon-Sat, 10-5, L 12-2.30, Aft Tea 2-4.30 (Sat to 4.45). A la carte self-service except special set menus, e.g. Christmas. Unlicensed. Closed Sun, 25-26 Dec, Easter, 12-13 Jul. MasterCard, Visa. **Directions:** Town centre; located in The House of Brindle Store. ◇

Portadown
CAFÉ

Café Paul Rankin

High Street Mall Portadown Co Armagh BT62 1HX
Tel: 028 3839 8818 Fax: 028 3839 8808

Anyone familiar with the Paul Rankin cafés will make a beeline here for a tasty daytime bite: Caesar salad, penne à la romana, chunky chicken chowder are the kind of dishes to expect, along with gourmet sandwiches like ham & cheese toasties, and roast Mediterranean vegetable & goats' cheese panini. Children welcome. Wheelchair accessible. **Seats 40.** No smoking area. Open Mon-Sat, 9-6; Sun 1-6. Closed 25 Dec, 1 Jan, Easter Sun. MasterCard, Visa, Switch. **Directions:** Town centre.

Portadown
HOTEL

Seagoe Hotel

Upper Church Lane Portadown Co Armagh BT63 5JE
Tel: 028 3833 3076 Fax: 028 3835 0210
Email: info@seagoe.com Web: www.seagoe.com

Attractively situated in its own grounds on the edge of Portadown, this fine hotel has been in the same ownership for many years but underwent a complete makeover a few years ago. The design is innovative and exceptionally easy on the eye and, once inside, the tone of the whole development is set by stylish public areas which are outstanding for grace and scale of design, and also the use of very high quality materials in construction, furnishing and decor. Easy wheelchair access throughout the building has been thought through in detail (the pay phone in the lobby is wheelchair accessible, for example). Bedrooms have contemporary simplicity teamed with warm, rich fabrics and good work space for business guests; executive rooms also have modem and fax facilities. Business/conference facilities are equally special - but it's not all work, as there's a separate function entrance (popular for weddings as well as conferences), with its own dramatic lobby/reception area - and there are two superb honeymoon suites. Bar and restaurant areas are designed with equal care, looking on to a delightful courtyard garden in the centre of the building. Own parking. Garden. **Rooms 34** (all en-suite, 2 disabled with shower only). Room only Mon-Thur about £70 single, £96 double, Fri/Sat/Sun all rooms about £50. Lift. Restaurant open for lunch and dinner daily. 12-2.30 & 5-9.30 (Sun to 9) and bar meals (panini, ciabatta, steak etc.) are available at the same times. Closed 25 Dec. Amex, Diners, MasterCard, Visa, Switch. **Directions:** Off A27 (Old Lurgan Road). ◇

Portadown
€ CAFÉ

Yellow Door Deli, Bakery & Café

74 Woodhouse Street Portadown Co Armagh BT62 1JL
Tel: 028 3835 3528 Fax: 028 3833 9012
Email: info@yellowdoordeli.co.uk Web: www.yellowdoordeli.co.uk

Previously well known for a restaurant of the same name in Gilford, Co Down, Simon Dougan opened the Yellow Door Deli in 1998 and it immediately became such a success that the restaurant was sold a couple of years later to allow time to focus on the new venture. It has an in-house bakery, producing some of the finest bread in Northern Ireland (an area renowned for its good home baking) and, as well as retailing a wide selection of the best speciality foods from Ireland and abroad, they also have a number of home-made specialities, including patés, terrines, chutneys, salads and ice cream, which are sold in the shop and served in the café - discerning customers from all over the north home in on this smashing shop, to top up with goodies and have a tasty bite of lunch. *A new soft seating area, complete with cookery book library, is due for completion in spring 2007. (Also at: 427 Lisburn Road, Belfast.) **Café seats 75.** Breakfast from 9am, L 12-2.30pm, otherwise food from deli all day until 5pm; house wine £8. Closed Mon, 12-13 Jul, 25-26 Dec, "some" Bank Hols. MasterCard, Visa, Switch. **Directions:** Off Main St. on left only street on left as the traffic flows one way.

COUNTY DOWN

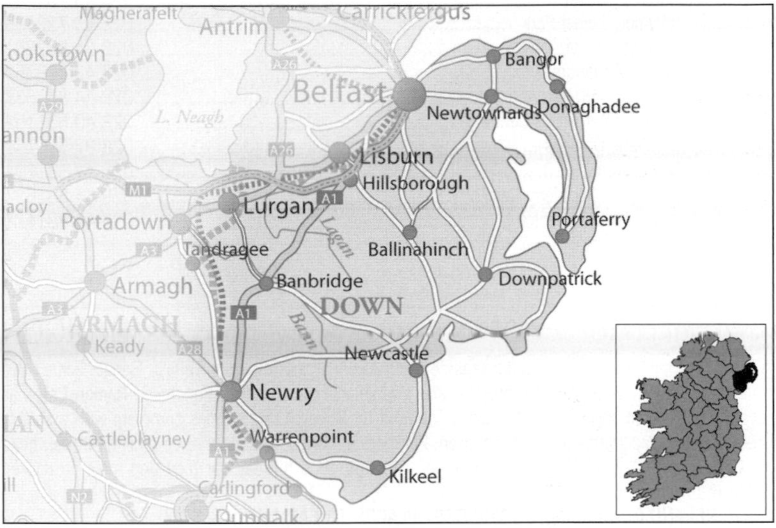

County Down rings the changes in elegant style, from its affluent shoreline along Belfast Lough - the "Gold Coast" - through the rolling drumlin country which provides Strangford Lough's many islands, and on then past the uplands around Slieve Croob, with the view southward being increasingly dominated by the purple slopes of the Mountains of Mourne.

The Mournes soar to Northern Ireland's highest peak of Slieve Donard (850m), and provide excellent hill-walking and challenging climbing. When seen across Down's patchwork of prosperous farmland, however, they have a gentleness which is in keeping with the county's well-groomed style. In the same vein, Down is home to some of Ireland's finest gardens, notably Mount Stewart on the eastern shore of Strangford Lough, and Rowallane at Saintfield, while the selection of forest and country parks is also exceptional.

Within the contemporary landscape, history is much in evidence. St Patrick's grave is in Downpatrick, while the Ulster Folk and Transport Museum at Cultra near Holywood provides an unrivalled overview of the region's past. The coastline is much-indented, so much so that, when measured in detail, County Down provides more than half of Northern Ireland's entire shoreline. Within it, the jewel of Strangford Lough is an unmatched attraction for naturalists and boat enthusiasts, while Portaferry has one of Ireland's longest-established saltwater aquariums in Exploris, and a convenient car ferry to Strangford across The Narrows.

In the south of the county, the increasingly prosperous former port town of Newry on the river inland from Carlingford Lough is – with Lisburn in County Antrim – one of Ireland's two newer cities under a re-designation of 2003, Newry has responded with enthusiasm to its enhanced status, and the urban regeneration of this interesting canalside centre is intriguing to watch.

Local Attractions and Information

Bangor, Events Office	028 91 278051
Bangor, Tourism Information	028 91 270069
Bangor, North Down Heritage Centre	028 91 271200
Castle Espie Wildfowl and Wetlands Centre	028 91 874146
Cultra, Ulster Folk & Transport Museum	028 90 428428
Downpatrick, Down Cathedral	028 44 614922
Downpatrick, St Patrick Centre	028 44 619000
Dromore, Kinallen Craft Centre	028 97 533733
Dundrum, Murlough National Nature Reserve	028 43 751467
Greyabbey, Mount Stewart House	028 42 788387
Hillsborough, Hillsborough Castle Gardens	028 92 681300

Kilkeel, Nautilus Centre	028 41 765555
Millisle, Ballycopeland Windmill	028 91 861413
Mourne Mountains, Guided Wildlife Walks	028 43 751467
Newcastle, Tollymore Forest Park	028 43 722428
Newtownards, Kingdoms of Down Tourism	028 91 822881
Portaferry, Exploris Aquarium	028 42 728062
Portaferry, Strangford-Portaferry Car Ferry	028 44 881637
Rathfriland, Bronte Interpretive Centre	028 40 631152
Saintfield, Rowallane Gardens	028 97 510131
Strangford, Castle Ward	028 44 881204
Strangford, Strangford-Portaferry Car Ferry	028 44 881637
Strangford Lough, Wildlife Centre	028 44 881411

BANGOR

A thriving shopping town and popular seaside resort easily accessible from Belfast, Bangor has a three mile seafront with extensive promenades, and a large marina. The first franchised **Rankin Café** has recently opened on High Street; the café, operated by Robert Craig, comes complete with a sound-proof play area facilitating up to 40 children. For more a more dining experience on High Street, head for **Coyle's pub** (028 9129 0362), where you will find good midday bar food and more structured meals in the evening.

WWW-IRELAND-GUIDE.COM FOR THE BEST PLACES TO EAT, DRINK & STAY

Bangor

HOTEL

Clandeboye Lodge Hotel

10 Estate Road Clandeboye Bangor Co Down BT19 1UR

Tel: 028 9185 2500 Fax: 028 9185 2772

Email: info@clandeboyelodge.co.uk Web: www.clandeboyelodge.com

Set in woodland on the edge of the Clandeboye estate, this comfortable modern hotel fits in well with its rural surroundings. The stylish foyer creates a good impression, with a welcoming fire and plentiful seating areas. Off it is the Lodge Restaurant with gothic-style windows and furnishings, where breakfast is also served. Good-sized bedrooms have neat, well-planned bathrooms (suites have whirlpool baths); standard amenities include phones with voicemail and fax/modem points. A country-style pub, The Poacher's Arms, is in an original Victorian building beside the hotel. *Developments recently completed at the hotel include major refurbishment of bedrooms, restaurant, conference and banqueting areas. Conference/banqueting (450/350) Golf (18/9), walking & garden available. Children welcome (under 12s free in parents' room; cots available at no charge). Wheelchair accessible. No Pets. Credit card numbers are taken when booking - and the deduction may be made before your arrival. Parking. Weekend specials. **Rooms 43** (all en-suite, 2 junior suites, 13 executive, 2 family rooms, 7 no smoking, 13 ground floor, 2 for disabled) Lift. B&B from £57.50 pps, ss £22.50. 24 hour room service. Closed 24-26 Dec. Amex, Diners, MasterCard, Visa, Switch. **Directions:** 15 minutes from Belfast, on outskirts of Bangor off A2.

Bangor

(N) RESTAURANT

Jeffers by the Marina

7 Grays Hill Bangor Co Down BT20 2BB **Tel: 028 9185 9555**

Email: info@stephenjeffers.com Web: www.stephenjeffers.com

Stephen Jeffers is one of Northern Ireland's top chefs and it was a happy day for Bangor when he decided to open this smart little harbour front restaurant overlooking the marina. Although not large, clever use of mirror creates a feeling of space - and also introduces a view by reflecting a waterside path across the road which, with a palm tree in the frame, suddenly makes the setting seem unexpectedly exotic...Bare tables, café chairs and uncurtained windows make for an uncluttered look too, although the downside is that there's not a lot to absorb noise, so the decibels can rise at busy times. Friendly staff are quick to settle new arrivals in with the wine list (informative, interesting, good vaue) and everything is very relaxed, with unstructured menus offering an eclectic choice of modern dishes, including sharing plates that get a meal off to a sociable start, and quite a few that are available as starter or main course portions. You might begin with Jeffers plate - a combination starter of houmous, organic feta meze, sweet purple olive jam and flat bread sticks, that is perfect to share or to nibble while waiting for a friend (and why not order the cocktail of the month while you're at it, a blackberry spritzer perhaps...) Although there are constants through the year, there's always a seasonal twist, and winter dishes that have attracted special praise include a lovely fresh-tasting salad of baby spinach with Stilton, pear & pecan nuts and a homely comfort dish of richly flavoured Portavogie Estate game sausage, with creamy colcannon and a green peppercorn cream. Menus change throughout the day - there's an afternoon tea menu, for example with a good choice of teas and coffees and treats like Victoria sponge with butter cream and fresh raspberry jam - and a proper children's menu, offering real food. Sunday brunch is especially popular here, but this really is an any-time pace, and all the better for it. And Stephen Jeffers has something else up his sleeve too, The Boathouse 'launching soon'... Open Mon 9-4.30pm, Tue-Sat, 9am-10pm, Su, 11-8pm. A la carte D. ◇

Bangor
HOTEL

Marine Court Hotel

18-20 Quay Street Bangor Co Down BT20 5ED
Tel: 028 9145 1100 Fax: 028 9145 1200
Email: marinecourt@btconnect.com Web: www.marinecourthotel.net

Excellent leisure facilities at the Marine Court's Oceanis Health & Fitness Club are this hotel's greatest asset these include an 18 metre pool, steam room, whirlpool and sunbeds, plus a well-equipped, professionally-staffed gym. The hotel overlooks the marina (beyond a public carpark) but the first-floor Lord Nelson's Bistro restaurant is the only public room with a real view. Only a few bedrooms are on the front most overlook (tidy) service areas - but all rooms have recently been refurbished and they are spacious, with plenty of worktop and tea/coffee tray, hair dryer and trouser press as standard in all rooms. Conference/banqueting (350/220). Leisure centre; swimming pool. Children welcome (cots available without charge; baby sitting arranged). Private parking 30. No Pets. **Rooms 52** (3 junior suites, 15 executive rooms, 3 family rooms, 16 no smoking, 1 for disabled). Lift. 24 hour room service. B&B £50pps, ss £20. * Short/off season breaks offered - details on application. Closed 25 Dec Amex, Diners, MasterCard, Visa, Switch. **Directions:** 23km (14 miles) from Belfast/ 16km (10 miles) Belfast City Airport, A2.

Bangor
Ⓝ BAR/RESTAURANT

More Brasserie Bar & Grill

150 Crawfordsburn Rd Bangor Co Down BT19 1GB
Tel: 028 9185 2599

This new restaurant is in the premises previously occupied by the renowned restaurant, Shanks. Proprietor-chef Jason More (hence the name) had worked for some years with the late Robbie Millar and, although he was running a group of gastropubs in Thailand at the time of Robbie's untimely death, he decided to return and has now taken on the lease for both the restaurant and upstairs bar, where bar food is served for golfers and casual visitors. Wisely, More does not attempt to emulate Shanks, but is a more commercial enterprise, offering accessible, lively menus in both bar and restaurant. The restaurant downstairs, now a brasserie, has been given a more informal look and is a pleasant room with the kitchen visible through a glass screen at the end - but the big draw here is the More Supper Menu which offers extremely good value and (no easy task) keeps the restaurant busy throughout the week. The Supper Menu at £29 offers a 3-course meal with a bottle of wine, and is based on two people sharing; for this you get a choice of three starters (typically crispy bacon & chicken Caesar salad or chicken liver parfait - and perhaps a 'fritto misto' seafood collection at a £3 supplement) and four main courses (roast chicken, a vegetarian pasta dish, salmon with fondant potatoes - and sirloin steak, at £4.50 supplement). The dishes sound ordinary enough, but the cooking is predictably good: the delicious homemade parfait is served with red onion marmalade and gorgeous French toast; fritto misto is a fine selection of seafood (scallops, salmon, prawns, squid, haddock) delicately coated and served with a tasty seasame, soy & ginger dipping sauce; roast chicken with creamy mash & rosemary jus is full of flavour - and very generous; penne pasta is a robust, tasty dish with honey ham, mushrooms, pine nuts & parmesan. Side vegetables are particularly good - a selection of small poached potatoes, diced beetroot, mangetout, peas and carrots, perhaps, each perfectly cooked. Of the desserts, really home made flavours come thriough in a delicious subtly spiced apple crumble, and there's a cheeseboard option too (£2.50 supplement). The à la carte includes dishes on the Supper Menu but offers a much wider choice; although seen as more of a weekend special meal out menu, it is interesting and very accessible, with most main courses around the £14.50 mark. The cooking is really good, and the offering is well-judged and appealing; service can be a little hit and miss but, all round, this enterprise has got off to a good start and deserves to succeed. **Seats 60.** D à la carte;Supper Menu (Tue-Fri, 3-course & wine £29). Infrmal meals served in fist floor bar. ◇

Bangor
HOTEL

Royal Hotel

26/28 Quay Street Bangor Co Down BT20 5ED
Tel: 028 9127 1866 Fax: 028 9146 7810
Email: royalhotelbangor@aol.com Web: www.the-royal-hotel.com

This old hotel near the marina came into new ownership a few years ago, but is still family-run and has lost none of its friendliness or old-fashioned charm. There's a warm personal welcome, a clear willingness to help guests in any way possible and the building has some endearing idiosyncrasies - although, alas, the early 20th century lift with folding grille doors and a mind of its own, was replaced by a sleek new early 21st century one. Rooms vary, but all have been refurbished quite recently - the best are the new ones on the front, overlooking the marina. Small conferences (40); Children welcome (under 5s free in parents' room; cots available). No Pets. **Rooms 50** (7 executive, 8 shower only, 1 for disabled). Lift. B&B about £30-40pps, ss £15. Special offers sometimes available. Nearby parking. Closed 25-26 Dec. Amex, Diners, MasterCard, Visa. **Directions:** A2 from Belfast, at bottom of Main Street turn right (keeping in left lane). Hotel is 300 yards on right facing marina. ◇

Crawfordsburn
(E) HOTEL/RESTAURANT

The Old Inn

11-15 Main Street Crawfordsburn Co Down BT19 1JH
Tel: 028 9185 3255 Fax: 028 9185 2775
Email: info@theoldinn.com Web: www.theoldinn.com

The pretty village setting of this famous and hospitable 16th century inn the oldest in continuous use in all Ireland belies its convenient location close to Belfast and its City Airport, and the Ulster Folk & Transport Museum and the Royal Belfast Golf Club are also nearby. Oak beams, antiques and gas lighting emphasise the natural character of the building, an attractive venue for business people and private guests alike. A welcoming fire and friendly staff in the cosy reception area set the tone for the whole hotel, which is full of charm, very comfortable - and always smartly presented. Bedrooms are individually decorated and, due to the age of the building, vary in size and style - most have antiques, some have romantic four-posters and a few have private sitting rooms. There are several dining options in the hotel: '1614' is the fine dining restaurant, informal evening meals are served in the Churn Bistro, and food is also served in the bar during afternoon and early evening. Conference/banqueting (100/125). Ample parking. Garden, walking. Children welcome (under 12s free in parents' room; cot available, £10). No pets. **Rooms 32** (1 suite, 3 junior suites, 12 superior). 24 hr room service. Room rate about £85.Open all year except Christmas. **'1614' Restaurant:** After an aperitif in the bar or the large and comfortable residents' lounge, a meal in this characterful old-world dining room should be very enjoyable. Interesting menus offer plenty of choice and, in the Guide's recent experience, the standard of cooking is well above that normally expected of hotel dining rooms; service can be a little uneven but this is offset by the high quality of food and cooking, plus the pleasant surroundings. Typical dishes might include pan-fried foie gras with sweet & sour red onion or a retro starter of '1614' prawn cocktail, with cherry tomatoes, avocado, salad & homemade tomato ketchup, and perhaps an unusual and attractively presented main course of pork fillet with puy lentils. A nice dessert menu offers more refreshing fruit-based dishes than usual, and coffee is served in the lounge. '1614' Restaurant: D Mon-Sat, 7-9, L Sun only 12.30-2; closed D Sun. Churn Bistro: D Mon-Sat, 7-9.30; closed Sun. Bar meals: 12 noon-7pm daily. *Short breaks offered. Closed 25 Dec. Amex, MasterCard, Visa, Switch. **Directions:** Off A2 Belfast-Bangor, 6 miles after Holywood (exit B20 for Crawfordsburn). ◇

Donaghadee
PUB/RESTAURANT

Grace Neill's

33 High Street Donaghadee Co Down BT21 0AH
Tel: 028 9188 4595 Fax: 028 9188 9631
Email: info@graceneills.com Web: www.graceneills.com

Dating back to 1611, Grace Neill's lays a fair claim to be one of the oldest inns in all Ireland; Grace Neill herself was born when the pub was more than two hundred years old and died in 1916 at the age of 98. Extensions and improvements in recent ownership have been completed with due sensitivity to the age and character of the original front bar, which has been left simple and unspoilt. The back of the building is contemporary: a bright, high-ceilinged restaurant area has elegant nautically-inspired decor - and, in recent years, this stylish informal restaurant has become a magnet for discerning diners who relish the delicious, easy-going food and relaxed atmosphere. Favourites that keep people going back include dishes available as starter or main course portions - smoked chicken Caesar, for example, or goats cheese & chargrilled artichoke - and ever-popular mains like Cumberland sausage & mash, and homemade beef burgers with handcut chips and ketchup. Good, imaginative food, efficient service and (fairly) reasonable prices make this a place people keep coming back. Sunday Brunch is a speciality, with live jazz. *A new head chef, Jonathan Feming, took over shortly before the guide went to press. Children welcome before 8pm. No smoking restaurant. Live Jazz Fri-Sat, 9.30-12.30, Sun,1.30-4.30. **Seats 80.** L & D daily (early D £30 Mon-Thurs 5.30-7, also à la carte, set Sun L £19.95); sc discretionary. Closed 25 Dec, 12 Jul. MasterCard, Visa, Switch. **Directions:** Centre of Donaghadee.

Downpatrick
PUB

Denvirs

14 English Street Downpatrick Co Down BT30 6AB
Tel: 028 4461 2012

What a gem this ancient place is. It's a wonderful pub wlth two old bars and an interesting informal restaurant, genuinely olde-worlde with an amazing original fireplace and chimney discovered during renovations. There's also delightful accommodation in sympathetically updated rooms. And there's a first floor room, with some remarkable original features, suitable for meetings or private parties. Go and see it - there can't be another place in Ireland quite like it. Private room available for conferences/meetings etc. (70). Wheelchair accessible. Children welcome. Accommodation offered. Bar/Restaurant: Food served L daily & D Mon-Fri. Closed 25 Dec. Amex, Diners, MasterCard, Visa. **Directions:** On same street as Cathedral and Courthouse in Downpatrick. ◇

Downpatrick
HOTEL/RESTAURANT

The Mill At Ballydugan

Drumcullen Road Ballydugan Downpatrick Co Down BT30 8HZ
Tel: 028 4461 3654 Fax: 028 4483 9754
Email: info@ballyduganmill.com Web: www.ballyduganmill.com

Hidden away in rolling County Down countryside just outside Downpatrick, the site of this 18th century flour mill is very atmospheric: looking out onto ruined stone outbuildings, it is almost like being in a medieval castle courtyard. The Mill would be worth a visit if only to see the magnificent restoration undertaken by the owner, Noel Killen, over more than fifteen years - but the building now houses a bistro/coffee shop on the ground floor, a more formal restaurant on the first floor and, above it, function rooms and accommodation. Bedrooms are appropriately furnished in traditional country style, with exposed beams and brass-and-iron beds, but have also the convenience of phones, TV with video channel, tea/coffee-making facilities and safe. The restaurant is open to non-residents, and is frequently used for private functions, mainly weddings. Conference/banqueting (120/86); secretarial service. Garden. Children welcome, under 5s free in parents' room (cots available free of charge). **Rooms 10** (1 shower only, 6 no smoking, 1 for disabled); B&B about £35 pps. Restaurant **seats 50.** MasterCard, Visa, Switch. **Directions:** Downpatrick enroute to Newcastle past race course take first right hand turn and follow road to the Mill. ◇

Downpatrick
COUNTRY HOUSE

Pheasants Hill Farm

37 Killyleagh Road Downpatrick Co Down BT30 9BL
Tel: 028 4461 7246 Fax: 028 4461 7246
Email: info@pheasantshill.com Web: www.pheasantshill.com

In 'St Patrick's country', Pheasants' Hill was a small Ulster farmstead for over 165 years until it was rebuilt in the mid-'90s - and is now a comfortable country house on a seven-acre organic small-holding within sight of the Mourne Mountains, 12 miles away. It is in an area of outstanding natural beauty and abundant wildlife bordering the Quoile Pondage (a wetland wildlife reserve and favoured fishing spot), and the property is right on the Ulster Way walking trail. Although very close to the road, it is otherwise an idyllic spot, as guests soon discover when they are welcomed with tea in front of the fire, or in the orchard on fine summer afternoons. The bedrooms, which are named after flowers and herbs, differ in character and outlook but are all comfortably furnished with generous beds and the advantages of modern facilities, including television, radio alarm clock, tea/coffee making facilities, quality toiletries, hair dryer and books and magazines to read; rooms away from the road at the back are quieter, and two new suites are due for completion in summer 2007. Breakfast is a major event and worth factoring in as a main meal in your day - the extensive menu even includes a vegetarian cooked breakfast mini-menu within it, although anyone who is not a dedicated vegetarian will find it hard to resist dry-cured bacon and home-made sausages made with their own free range Tamworth pork and many other serious temptations (you will be asked to make a selection the night before). *Farm shop: rare breed free range pork, bacon, lamb, beef & organic poultry, fruit, vegetables sold. Open Mon-Sat 9-6 & Sun 12-6. Delivery service available. Also farm shop & butchers shop in Comber, Mon-Sat 9-6. Children welcome. Garden, fishing, walking. **Rooms 5** (1 ground floor, 1 family room, 3 shower-only, all no smoking). B&B £32, ss £10. Closed 1 Nov-16 Mar. Amex, MasterCard, Visa, Switch. **Directions:** On A22, 4km (2.5 miles) north of Downpatrick, 4km south of Killyleagh.

Dundrum
RESTAURANT

The Buck's Head Inn

77 Main Street Dundrum Co Down BT33 OLU
Tel: 028 4375 1868 Fax: 028 44 811033
Email: buckshead1@aol.com Web: www.thebucksheaddundrum.com

Michael and Alison Crothers have developed this attractive, welcoming place from a pub with bar food and a restaurant, to its present position as a restaurant with bar. Alison is in charge of the kitchen and sources local produce, especially seafood, including oysters from Dundrum Bay, which might be baked with a garlic & cheddar crust and Kilkeel cod, with mushy peas and chips. Well-balanced and interesting menus have a pleasing sense of place - aside from the seafood, county Down beef is used for the Sunday roast sirloin and steaks on the dinner menu, lamb is from the Mournes, the famous butchers McCartneys of Moira supply sausages for the traditional bangers & champ; many tempting dishes are offered and, although there has been a move towards more global dishes, the range of styles ensures there is something to please all tastes. desserts are tempting and a short but imaginative vegetarian menu is also offered. At lunch time there's a shortish à la carte (often including excellent salads - try the fresh Dublin Bay prawns...) and daily blackboard specials - and they are open for high tea as well as dinner. Regular visits here confirm that the cooking is consistently good (and, indeed, always becoming more interesting) and service under the direction of the proprietor Michael Crothers, is friendly and efficient. The atmosphere is always relaxed and each dining space has its own personality and is quite intimate - a dining room at the back (formerly a conservatory) overlooks a walled garden and is particularly pleasant. This is a fine restaurant, providing an admirably comprehensive service: well worth planning a journey around. Interesting wines are supplied by the highly respected wine merchant James Nicholson. Children welcome. *Ask about accommodation - a previous owner, Maureen Griffith, offers B&B next door. **Seats 80** (private room, 50) No smoking area L 12-2.30, High Tea 5-6.30, D7-9 (Sun to 8.30). Set Sun L from £13; Set D from £17.50, otherwise à la carte. House wine from £11; sc discretionary. Closed Mon off-season (Oct-Apr); 25 Dec. Amex, MasterCard, Visa, Switch. **Directions:** On the main Belfast-Newcastle road, approx 3 miles from Newcastle. ◇

Dundrum
Ⓝ B&B

The Carriage House

71 Main St Dundrum Co Down BT33 OLU
Tel: 028 437 51635 Email: inbox@carriagehousedundrum.com
Web: www.carriagehousedundrum.com

Maureen Griffith, a previous owner of The Buck's Head inn, offers well-hidden bed and breakfast accommodation in her unusual house which is next door to the inn. Her home has great style, and is furnished mainly with antiques but she has an eye for unusual items and you will find modern pieces amongst them, and also quirky decorative little bits and pieces among the lovely paintings and prints - and some not so little, as a full size horse sculpture at the back of the house is the item that guests find most fascinating. The three guest rooms include one away from the road at the back of the house, and all are quietly luxurious with beautiful bedding and delightful details. No dinner is offered but a lovely breakfast is served in a sun room overlooking a walled garden, prettily planted with wild flowers and herbs. Fishing, equestrian, garden visits, walking and golf nearby (Royal County Down golf club). **Rooms 3** (all en-suite and no smoking); B&B £30 pps, ss £10 **No Credit Cards. Directions:** A24 from Belfast, Dundrum. The violet blue house next to The Bucks Head (no sign: name etched in glass on top of front door).

Dundrum
Ⓝ RESTAURANT

Mourne Seafood Bar

10 Main Street Dundrum Co Down BT33 OLY
Tel: 028 4375 1377 Fax: 028 4375 1161
Email: bob@mourneseafood.com Web: www.mourneseafood.com

A prominent black and white 19th century terrace building in the centre of Dundrum, Robert and Joanne McCoubrey's lively and informal seafood restaurant and fish shop is appreciated by the many happy punters who enjoy ultra fresh seafood which is allowed to be itself. They specialise in fresh fish from local ports of Keel and Annalong, and mussels, oysters and cockles from their own shellfish beds on Carlingford Lough - and, like the new sister restaurant run by Any Rae in Belfast (see entry), they use local fish that is not under threat such as gurnard and ling, helping to take the pressure off species like cod, so their extensive menu changes according to what is caught. Crab claws and haddock & chips were much enjoyed on a recent visit - also half a lobster, which is good value these days at £12.75. Very friendly, family-tolerant staff deserve special mention, and the wine list is short and interesting - and the sparkling water offered was San Pelligrino, a detail which is always a good sign of someone who is thinking about the best. Children welcome until 9pm; Toilets wheelchair accessible. **Seats 45** (outdoors, 20). Food served daily, 12-9.30pm; a la carte; house wine £11. Closed Mon in winter. MasterCard, Visa, Switch. **Directions:** Main Street of village.

Hillsborough
RESTAURANT/PUB

The Plough Inn

3 The Square Hillsborough Co Down BT26 6AG
Tel: 028 9268 2985 Fax: 028 9268 2472
Web: www.barretro.com

Established in 1752, this former coaching inn is owned by the Patterson family who have built up a national reputation for hospitality and good food, especially seafood. Somehow they manage to run three separate food operations each day, so pleasing customers looking for a casual daytime meal and more serious evening diners. The evening restaurant is in the old stables at the back of the pub, and renowned for seafood and fine steaks, booking is required. Recent developments and makeovers mercifully left the characterful old bar intact (fairly traditional bar food is still available there) and also the original Plough Restaurant, which has a separate entrance from the carpark. However the rest of the pub, including the adjacent building, is now stylishly contemporary and comprises the trendy Barretro Café & Bistro, which is open most of the day. The bistro is above the old bar and offers more substantial international dishes; bookings are taken there for business lunches, but not in the evening. Lots of cool leather seating, interesting lighting, incorporating existing features like the old mahogany bar into a design which is uncompromisingly modern, yet warm and welcoming, are just some of the attractions. While there is obvious youth appeal, people of all ages feel comfortable here and the staff, who are clearly very proud of it, are friendly and helpful. It is very extensive, so allow yourself time to have a good look around and get your bearings before settling down to eat. [The Plough Inn was our Pub of the Year in 2004]. *The Pheasant Inn at Annahilt is a sister establishment. Children welcome in the café, but the bar is unsuitable for children. Sun terrace. Parking. **Seats 200** (private room, 20) No smoking area. Air conditioning. L daily, 12-2.30 (Sun to 5) D 5-9.30 daily. Closed 25 Dec (no food 26 Dec). Amex, Diners, MasterCard, Visa, Switch. **Directions:** Off the main Dublin-Belfast road, turn off at Hillsborough roundabout; in village square.

Holywood
CAFÉ/RESTAURANT

Bay Tree Coffee House & Restaurant

118 High Street Holywood Co Down BT18 9HW
Tel: 028 90 421419 Email: suefarmer@utvinternet.com

Since 1988, The Bay Tree has been attracting people from miles around to its delightful craft shop and coffee house on the main street. The craft shop, which sells exclusively Irish wares, is a busy, colourful place specialising in pottery, with over two dozen Irish potters represented. There is also a gallery exhibiting the work of Irish artists and perhaps best of all Sue Farmer's delicious food. Baking is a strength, especially the cinnamon scones which are a house speciality. There's quite a strong emphasis on vegetarian dishes and organic salads, especially in summer, when you can also eat out on a patio in fine weather. No reservations for lunch, but they are required on Friday evenings, when the Bay Tree is open for dinner. *Sue Farmer has just published a book of Bay Tree recipes, available directly from the restaurant. Children welcome. Parking. Wheelchair accessible (not to toilets). No smoking restaurant. **Seats 55** (outdoors, 8). Open all day: Mon-Sat, 8-4.30, (Sat from 9.30); D Fri only, 7-9.30. L Mon-Sat,12-3; Set D Fri only 2/3 course £19.50/£22.50. Sun Brunch 10-3. House wine £12.50. SC 10% on Fri D. Closed Christmas 4 days, Easter 3 days & 12 July 4 days. MasterCard, Visa, Switch. **Directions:** Opposite the police station.

Holywood
RESTAURANT

Fontana Restaurant

61A High Street Holywood Co Down BT18 9AE
Tel: 028 90 809908 Fax: 028 90 809912
Email: colleen@btopenworld.com Web: www.fontanasrestaurant.com/.co.uk

A first floor restaurant over a classy kitchen shop ("down the alley & up the stairs"), Fontana is fresh and bright, with clear yellow walls which work well with lightwood chairs and vinyl banquette seating. Proprietor-chef Colleen Bennett was one of the first of the new wave of chefs who have taken Northern Ireland by storm in recent years and she offers lovely zesty Cal-Ital cooking, and loosely structured menus that suit the atmosphere of the room. Starters and main courses tend to overlap, with small and large portions of some dishes offered. A dish like Caesar salad with char-grilled chicken, black olives & Parmesan might come in two sizes, for example, and appear on both the lunch and dinner menus - and there's a vegetarian version offered. Vegetables and salads are used with great panache and seafood is usually strongly represented - consistently accomplished cooking, stylishly simple presentation and clear flavours make an appealing combination. Imaginative use of fresh produce (locally sourced where possible) is a striking characteristic of the food at Fontana - and vegetarian choices are highlighted. Outside eating area. Toilets wheelchair accessible. On street parking. Children welcome. **Seats 54** L Mon-Fri 12-2.30 (Sun brunch 11-2.30), D Mon-Fri 5-9.30, D Sat, 6.30-10pm. Set 2/3 course D about £13.50/16.50, otherwise à la carte (average meal about £25); house wine about £12.50; SC discretionary, except 10% added on tables of 6+. Closed L Sat, D Sun, all Mon, 25-26 Dec & 1 Jan. MasterCard, Visa, Switch. **Directions:** Three doors from Maypole flag pole. ◇

Holywood

HOTEL/RESTAURANT

Hastings Culloden Estate & Spa

Bangor Road Holywood Co Down BT18 0EX
Tel: 028 9042 1066 Fax: 028 9042 6777
Email: guest@cull.hastingshotels.com Web: www.hastingshotels.com

Formerly the official palace for the Bishops of Down, Hastings Hotels' flagship property is a fine example of 19th-century Scottish Baronial architecture with plasterwork ceilings, stained glass windows and an imposing staircase. It is set in beautifully maintained gardens and woodland overlooking Belfast Lough and the County Antrim coastline. Period furniture and fine paintings in spacious high ceilinged rooms give a soothing feeling of exclusivity, and comfortable drawing rooms overlook the lough. Spacious, lavishly decorated guest rooms include a large proportion of suites and a Presidential Suite, with the best view; all are lavishly furnished and decorated with splendid bathrooms and details such as bathrobes, a welcoming bowl of fruit, and nice touches like ground coffee and a cafetière on the hospitality tray. Wireless internet access is available in all areas, and there are video/DVD players in suites. The hotel has an association with The Royal Belfast Golf Club, four minutes away by car (book the complimentary hospitality limousine) also a fine health club; the 'Cultra Inn', a bar and informal restaurant in the grounds, offers an alternative to The Mitre Restaurant. The hotel is licensed to hold weddings on the premises. Conference/banqueting (1,000/600); business centre, secretarial services. Leisure centre (swimming pool; spa; beauty salon; hairdressing). Garden. Children welcome (under 3s free in parents' room; cot available without charge, baby sitting arranged). No pets. **Rooms 79** (2 suites, 17 junior suites, 22 executive rooms, 2 disabled, 40 no-smoking). Lift. Air conditioning. 24 hr room service B&B about £100 pps, ss about £60.* Short breaks offered. Parking (500). Helipad. Open all year. **The Mitre Restaurant:** The fine dining restaurant is in a long room overlooking the lough, with a discreet and luxurious ambience - and, with well-padded and very comfortable upholstered chairs, conducive to lingering. Tables are beautifully appointed in classic style, and extensive menus live up to their promise: there may be a perfectly cooked starter crown of asparagus, for example, presented standing up with little jewels of tapenade around it, and a speciality main course, of tender saddle of venison from nearby Clandeboye Estate, comes with crushed root vegetables and buttered greens. Classic cooking, lovely surroundings and correct, attentive service all make this a restaurant with a sense of occasion. Extensive wine list to match. **Seats 110** (private room, 50). Reservations required. No smoking restaurant. Children welcome. Toilets wheelchair accessible. Piano & Jazz Fri/Sat/Sun. D daily, 7-9.30, Set D £32.50; L Sun only, 12.30-2.30. Set Sun L, £28. House wine £17. Amex, Diners, MasterCard, Visa, Switch. **Directions:** 6 miles from Belfast city centre on A2 towards Bangor.

Holywood

COUNTRY HOUSE

Rayanne Country House

60 Demesne Road Holywood Co Down B18 9EX
Tel: 028 9042 5859 Fax: 028 9042 5859
Email: rayannehouse@hotmail.com Web: www.rayannehouse.co.uk

Situated almost next to the Holywood Golf Club and Redburn Country Park, and with views across Belfast Lough, the McClellands' family-run country house is a tranquil spot in which to unwind, and a fine alternative to impersonal hotels. Bedrooms, some with views of Belfast Lough, are individually decorated to a high standard with phones and television - and little extras like fresh fruit, spring water, sewing kit, stationery and a hospitality tray with bedtime drinks and home-made shortbread as well as the usual tea & coffee facilities. It's a relaxing place, with friendly staff and a great breakfast, offering a wide range, including unusual dishes such as prune soufflé, French toast topped with black and white pudding & served with a spiced apple compôte, grilled kippers and a 'healthy house grill' (with nothing fried). Friendly staff are helpful and make families with children most welcome; beach, shops and restaurants are all just a few minutes' walk away. *An extension completed just before the guide went to press has provided an additional three rooms; a disabled bedroom, and a bathroom for the use of all guests, is to be completed before Christmas 2006. **Restaurant:** Conor McClelland, who returned to take over Rayanne with 15 years as an international chef under his belt, cooks for up to 30 guests in their restaurant D'Vine Dining, which is open to non-residents by reservation (closed only 24-25 Dec). Small conferences/banqueting (15/34). Parking (14). Children welcome (under 2s free in parents room, cot available without charge). Pets allowed by arrangement. Garden, walking. **Rooms 11** (4 shower only, 2 family rooms, all no smoking). B&B £45pps, ss £22.50. D £39.50, by reservation. Short breaks offered. Open all year. MasterCard, Visa, Switch. **Directions:** Take A2 out of Belfast towards Holywood 10km (6 miles), up to top of My Ladys Mile; turn right; 200 metres.

Holywood

RESTAURANT

Sullivans Restaurant

2 Sullivan Place Holywood Co Down BT18 9JF **Tel: 028 9042 1000**
Fax: 028 9042 6664 Web: www.sullivansrestaurant.co.uk

Simon Shaw's bright, friendly and informal bar, restaurant & café is now well over a decade in business - and consistently excellent food, varied menus, a lively atmosphere and fair prices are the secret of his success. Lively lunch and sandwich menus range from a choice of home-made soups served with crusty bread to Sullivans Caesar salad (three variations) or a trio of seafood Asian style with chilli noodles. Quality ingredients have always been the building blocks of his cooking and he seeks out interesting produce from trusted suppliers like Helen's Bay Organics and Finnebroge (venison); vegetarians do well here, with interesting choices on the regular menus as well as a separate vegetarian menu. A nice departure from today's muddled up 'international' cuisine is seen in a menu that lists dishes by country - thus you may have a dish of venison with hot & sour red cabbage & mulled wine jus from Norway, or sea bream with tempura, prawn & ginger rice balls from Hong King; a welcome move that could help to take the con from fusion. Interesting, well-priced wine list too. **Seats 65.** Air conditioning. L daily 12-2.30, D Tue-Thu 6-9, Fri & Sat 5-10, Sun 5-8.30. Set D from D £12.50, also à la carte; house wine from £12; sc 10%, only on parties of 8+. Closed D Mon, 2 days Christmas,12-13 Jul. MasterCard, Visa, Switch. **Directions:** Just off main Belfast-Bangor dual carriageway. ◇

Holywood Area

B&B

Beech Hill Country House

23 Ballymoney Road Craigantlet Holywood Co Down BT23 4TG
Tel: 028 9042 5892 Fax: 028 9042 5892
Email: info@beech-hill.net Web: www.beech-hill.net

Victoria Brann's attractive Georgian style house is set in the peaceful Holywood Hills. It has great style - and the benefit of an exceptionally hospitable hostess, who does everything possible to ensure that guests have everything they need. Ground floor bedrooms have panoramic views over the North Down countryside and are furnished with antique furniture - and, believe it or not, the beds are made up with fine Irish linen; all also have en-suite bathrooms with lots of special little extras. Breakfast is a meal worth allowing time to enjoy - and it is served in a spacious conservatory overlooking a croquet lawn. *Self catering accommodation is also available inn The Colonel's Lodge, in Beech Hill garden (also available for B&B). **Rooms 3** (all en-suite, 1 shower only, all no smoking, all ground floor). B&B £35.00pps. ss £15.00. Pets permitted by arrangement. Open all year. *Self-catering accommodation or B&B also offered in The Colonel's Lodge (£280-£380 per week self catering, £70 per night B&B). Amex, MasterCard, Visa, Switch. **Directions:** A2 from Belfast; bypass Holywood; 3km (1.5 miles) from bridges at Ulster Folk Museum, turn right up Ballymoney Road signed Craigantlet - 3km (1.5) miles on left.

Killinchy

RESTAURANT/PUB

Balloo House

1 Comber Road Killinchy Co Down BT23 6PA
Tel: 028 9754 1210 Fax: 028 9754 1683
Email: info@balloohouse.com

This famous old 19th century coaching inn fell into great hands when Ronan and Jennie Sweeney took it over in 2004 with extensive experience in the hospitality industry behind them (Ronan had worked front of house with Paul Rankin at both Cayenne and Roscoff, then as restaurant manager at Bill Wolsey's Ta Tu, and Jennie has left a career in the wine trade). They were determined to restore Balloo's reputation as one of the finest country dining pubs in Northern Ireland. And this, as a growing band of loyal followers would testify, they are achieving very nicely. The place has oodles of genuine character and the old kitchen bar, with its flagstones and traditional range, makes a great setting for excellent bistro fare like fresh Kilkeel scampi & chips, dry-aged locally reared steaks and home-made burgers. Head chef Billy Burns (who trained with the late Robbie Millar, and is now in the unusual position of training his own boss in the Balloo kitchen) takes obvious care with menus that offer a finely balanced choice of pub grub and finer fare, are admirably simply worded and demonstrate a commitment to quality local produce. And, at the time of going to print, the downstairs bistro experience is about to be expanded as a first floor restaurant nears completion: it will have a private bar and, with an open fire and original stone walls, it should have a lovely atmosphere; as in the bar, great local ingredients and simplicity will shape menus specialising in fresh seafood and 'the best beef in the country'! And, with the combined knowledge of Jennie and new restaurant manager Nicola Walls (ex Roscoff), the wine list promises to be a treat. Children welcome; toilets wheelchair accessible; free broadband WI/FI; air conditioning. Downstairs bistro **seats 60** (private room, 40, outdoors, 12); live music (Blue Grass) Wed 9pm. Food served daily 12-9 (to 8pm on Sun); Early D £11.95, Mon-Thu 5-7pm; house wine £10.95. Closed 25 Dec. MasterCard, Visa, Switch. **Directions:** At Balloo crossroads on main road from Comber to Killyleagh.

Killyleagh
CAFÉ

Picnic

Killyleagh Co Down BT1 **Tel: 028 4482 8525**

Just beside the castle in Killyleagh, this smashing little deli and café is well worth knowing about: lovely simple daytime food to enjoy while you're there - and a great range of carefully sourced goodies to take home. Open Mon-Fri 7am-7pm, Sat 10-4. Last orders in café 6.30. Closed Sun off season. **Directions:** Beside the castle in Killyleagh. QNR

Kircubbin
RESTAURANT WITH ROOMS

Paul Arthurs Restaurant

62-66 Main Street Kircubbin Newtownards
Co Down BT22 2SP **Tel: 028 4273 8192**
Web: www.paularthurs.com

Paul Arthurs' restaurant is a simple modern room on the first floor, with an open kitchen where you can watch the great man at work. Very simply laid tables give one or two hints that this place might not be quite what it first seems - linen napkins, for example. Unusually for Northern Ireland, there is a menu in the window advising dishes offered that evening: duck breast with foie gras, brioche & figs is a typically luxurious starter, for example, and there will probably be mussels and various shellfish; you'll also likely to find local venison or wood pigeon, in season. Modern menus are interesting and the cooking is good: fresh lobster bisque will be full of flavour, and the grilled ribeye steak with roast shallots, bacon mushrooms & thyme has not had far to travel as the beef is from the Arthurs family's farm. There's a good range of dishes offered, including more meat and poultry than fish - although there is always a catch of the day; vegetarian options are listed separately (fresh potato gnocchi with gorgonzola, peas & parmesan, perhaps) and there's even a vegan choice. This great little place is a real asset to the area, prices are very fair and there are some tables in the garden too, allowing for al fresco dining in fine weather. **Accommodation**: Seven simply furnished en-suite bedrooms are offered, including 2 for disabled guests. (Make sure you have arrangements firmly in place before arriving, as there may be nobody on site, and the telephone is not always answered.) No smoking restaurant. Toilets accessible by wheelchair. **Seats 55** (outdoor, 20), air con. D Tue-Sat, 5-9.30; L Sun, 12-2.30. A la carte. House wine £11.95. **Rooms 7** (all en-suite, 3 ground floor, 2 disabled); B&B £35pps, ss £15.Closed D Sun, all Mon, & Jan Amex, MasterCard, Visa, Switch. **Directions:** On main street, 1st floor, opposite supermarket.

Newcastle
HOTEL

Burrendale Hotel & Country Club

51 Castlewellan Road Newcastle Co Down BT33 0JY
Tel: 028 4372 2599 Fax: 028 4372 2328
Email: reservations@burrendale.com Web: www.burrendale.com

Just outside the traditional seaside holiday town of Newcastle, and close to the championship links of the Royal County Down golf course, this area on the edge of the Mourne mountains has a remote atmosphere yet it is just an hour's drive from Belfast. Public areas in this friendly hotel are spacious and include the Cottage Bar with an open log fire, welcome on chilly days. Well-appointed accommodation includes family rooms and all rooms are well-equipped with phone, writing desk, TV with video, tea/coffee making facilities and trouser press; new superior rooms are furnished to a higher standard, and have air conditioning. Golf is a major attraction to the area, but a varied programme of other special breaks is also offered throughout the year and it is a popular conference venue. Well-trained, efficient staff are courteous, making this a pleasant place to stay. Conference/banqueting (300 /280); business centre, secretarial services; video conferencing available, broadband WI/Fi. Leisure centre, swimming pool; beauty salon. Snooker, pool table. Children welcome (under 2s free in parents' room; cots available without charge). Garden, walking, cycling. **Rooms 69** (3 suites, 18 executive rooms, 6 family rooms, 20 no smoking, 10 for disabled). Lift. 24 hour room service. B&B £60 pps, ss £15. Bar and restaurant meals available daily (phone to check restaurant times). Open all year. Amex, Diners, MasterCard, Visa, Switch. **Directions:** On A50 Castlewellan Road.

Newcastle
HOTEL

Hastings Slieve Donard Hotel

Downs Road Newcastle Co Down BT33 0AH
Tel: 028 4372 1066 Fax: 028 4372 4830
Email: res@sdh.hastingshotels.com Web: www.hastingshotels.com

This famous hotel stands beneath the Mournes in six acres of public grounds, adjacent to the beach and the Royal County Down Golf Links. The Victorian holiday hotel par excellence, the Slieve Donard first opened in 1897 and has been the leading place to stay in Newcastle ever since. Recent years have seen great improvements in both the public rooms and accommodation. Bedrooms are finished to a high standard and all the bathrooms sport one of the famous yellow Hastings' ducks. The nearby Tollymore

Forest Park provides excellent walking on clearly marked trails, just one of the many outdoor pursuits that attract guests; should the weather be unsuitable, the Elysium health club has enough facilities to keep the over-energetic occupied for weeks. The hotel is also well known for its wide range of special short breaks, which can be very good value. *A major upgrade, including the installation of 16 helicopter pads, was completed ahead of the 2006 Ryder Cup. Golf nearby (18). Conference/banqueting (825/440). Business centre; secretarial services. Leisure centre, swimming pool, spa, beauty salon. Pitch & putt. Ample parking. Children welcome (under 4s free in parents' room; cots available without charge, baby sitting arranged). No pets. **Rooms 124** (8 junior suites, 2 executive rooms, 3 for disabled). 2 Lifts. B&B about £87.50 pps, ss £25. Open all year. Helipad. Amex, Diners, MasterCard, Visa, Laser, Switch. **Directions:** Situated 32 miles south east of Belfast. ◇

Newcastle
CAFÉ/RESTAURANT

Sea Salt Bistro

51 Central Promenade Newcastle Co Down BT33 0HH
Tel: 028 4372 5027

A good meal will add greatly to your enjoyment of a visit to this traditional holiday town on the sea edge of the Mountains of Mourne, so make a point of seeking out Caroline (front of house) and Andrew (the chef) Fitzpatrick's restaurant in a seafront terrace, wedged between an ice-cream parlour and a chemist's shop. Sea Salt opened in 1997 as a delicatessen and café, seating only a dozen or so at lunch time, and it was then re-designed several years later in a classy contemporary style inspired by the sea, and re-opened with more ambitious aims. A commitment to using local produce creatively in global cooking has always been at the heart of the philosophy and well-sourced ingredients feature in daytime snacks like gourmet sandwiches - wraps, baguettes, ciabatta with salads - and an extensive hot and cold drinks menu that includes a choice of coffees, teas and refreshing juices like organic lemonade and pure fruit smoothies. Lunch and dinner menus are more substantial, but the ethos is carried through. Seafood stars in popular dishes like Dundrum Bay mussels Thai style with chilli, garlic, coriander & ginger, and seafood chowder with Ardglass crab, salmon & prawns - but you'll also find all-time favourites like chicken liver paté with brandy and rosemary (served with crisp ciabatta slices and green salad) and duck confit with caramelised red onion heading up main courses as diverse as Co. Down sirloin steak with creamy Ulster champ & brandy peppercorn sauce and a vegetarian dish of aubergine & buffalo mozzarella galette with red pepper pesto & salad. With no drinks licence and a modest £1 corkage, everyone brings their own and part of the charm of the evening is to see what diners on adjoining tables have brought in their carrier bags. Booking is essential. **Seats 30.** No smoking area; air conditioning. Open daily in summer from 9am: L 12-4 daily, D Thu-Sat, 7-9 (Fri & Sat only in winter). Set D about £21.50. Closed Mon in winter. MasterCard, Visa, Switch. **Directions:** Seafront Newcastle, foot of Mournes. ◇

Newcastle Area
RESTAURANT/COUNTRY HOUSE

Glassdrumman Lodge

85 Mill Road Annalong Co Down BT34 4RH
Tel: 028 4376 8451 Fax: 028 4376 7041
Email: info@glassdrummanlodge.com Web: www.glassdrummanlodge.com

In a dramatic hillside location just outside the coastal village of Annalong, and close to the great forest parks of Tollymore and Castlewellan, Glassdrumman Lodge is in the heart of one of Ireland's most picturesque mountain districts, the ancient 'Kingdom of Mourne'. It has been developed by the present owners, Graeme and Joan Hall, from what was once a typical Mourne farmhouse into an unusual country house, where fresh produce for delicious dinners comes from their own gardens, and local seafood from nearby ports. Comfortable guest rooms and suites offer a peaceful base for golfers wishing to play the Royal County Down Golf Course - and for fishing folk, who may prefer casting for trout on the well-stocked lake, to other more energetic outdoor activities like walking and climbing. The fine dining restaurant is also open to non-residents, by reservation. **Rooms 10.** Memories Restaurant **seats 45** (private room, 20); Non-smoking restaurant; D Daily at 8pm £40. Small conferences/banqueting 16/50; Rooms 10 (all en-suite, 2 junior suites, 2 suites, 1 ground floor); Children welcome (cots avail free of charge); B&B £50 pps, ss £30. Amex, Diners, MasterCard, Visa, Switch. **Directions:** A2 coast road between Newcastle and Kilkeel. Take right at Halfway House pub, 1.6km (1 mile) up Mill road.

NEWRY

Newry - now a city - has a canal as its central feature, and Canal Court Hotel (028 3025 1234; www.canalcourt.com) is the leading establishment of the area. Restaurants to check out nearby include the smart **Soho Place**, across the canal, on The Mall (028 308 33333; www.sohoplace.co.uk) and **The Bank** (028 3083 5501), a stylish big café-bar near the bridge, on Trevor Hill.

Newtownards

B&B/COUNTRY HOUSE

Edenvale House

130 Portaferry Road Newtownards Co Down BT22 2AH
Tel: 028 9181 4881 Email: edenvalehouse@hotmail.com
Web: www.edenvalehouse.com

Diane Whyte's charming Georgian house is set peacefully in seven acres of garden and paddock, with views over Strangford Lough to the Mourne mountains and a National Trust wildfowl reserve. The house has been sensitively restored and modernised, providing a high standard of accommodation and hospitality. Guests are warmly welcomed and well fed, with excellent traditional breakfasts and afternoon tea with homemade scones. For evening meals, Diane directs guests to one of the local restaurants. Edenvale is close to the National Trust property Mount Stewart, renowned for its gardens, and also convenient to Rowallan and Castle Ward. Children welcome (under-5s free in parents' room; cots available without charge). Pets permitted by arrangement. Garden. **Rooms 3** (all en-suite, 1 junior suite, 1 superior, 1 shower only, 1 family room, all no-smoking). B&B £40 pps, ss £10. Closed Christmas. MasterCard, Visa. **Directions:** 3.5 km (2 m) from Newtownards on A20 going towards Portaferry.

Portaferry

HOTEL/RESTAURANT

Portaferry Hotel

The Strand Portaferry Co Down BT22 1PE
Tel: 028 427 28231 Fax: 028 427 28999
Email: info@portaferryhotel.com Web: www.portaferryhotel.com

HOTEL BREAKFAST OF THE YEAR

This 18th-century waterfront terrace presents a neat, traditional exterior overlooking the lough towards the attractive village of Strangford and the National Trust property, Castleward, home to an opera festival each June. The inn is now one of the most popular destinations in Northern Ireland - not least for its reputation for good food, including their excellent lunchtime bar meals: an extensive menu is offered, everything is freshly-prepared and attractively presented and it is good value. The ground floor the bar, a comfortable sitting room, and the restaurant has a cosy, well-kept old-fashioned feeling to it and, whiule not luxurious, accommodation is comfortable and most of the individually decorated en-suite bedrooms have views of the water - those on the front attract a small supplement. The hotel is beautifully kept and maintained, a lovely place with personality, and friendly, helpful staff. Small conference/private parties (35/80); parking. Children (Under 16s free in parents' room; cots available at no charge). No pets. **Rooms 14** (all en-suite, 2 shower only, 4 family rooms, all no-smoking) B&B £65 pps, ss £20. **Restaurant:** A slightly cottagey style provides the perfect background for good unpretentious food. Local produce features prominently in prime Ulster beef, Mourne lamb and game from neighbouring estates but it is, of course, the seafood from daily landings at the nearby fishing villages of Ardglass and Portavogie that take pride of place. Well-balanced table d'hôte lunch and dinner menus are offered, plus a short carte, providing plenty of choice although majoring on local seafood. Excellent breakfasts are served in the restaurant a particularly good menu is offered, giving plenty of choice including fresh and smoked fish as a feature. This may not be the gargantuan spread that some country houses lay on for guests, but it is all freshly cooked to order and really delicious - and efficiently served by friendly staff: exactly what the perfect hotel breakfast should be. Small conference/private parties (35/80); parking. Children (Under 16s free in parents' room; cots available at no charge). No pets. **Rooms 14** (all en-suite, 2 shower only, 4 family rooms, all no-smoking) B&B £65 pps, ss £20. Restaurant: A slightly cottagey style provides the perfect background for good unpretentious food. Local produce features prominently in prime Ulster beef, Mourne lamb and game from neighbouring estates but it is, of course, the seafood from daily landings at the nearby fishing villages of Ardglass and Portavogie that take pride of place. Well-balanced table d'hôte lunch and dinner menus are offered, plus a short carte, providing plenty of choice although majoring on local seafood. An excellent breakfast is also served in the restaurant. **Seats 65.** Children welcome. L daily, 12.30-2.30; D daily 5.30-9 (to 8.30 Sun). D Value Menu nightly 5.30-6.30. Set menu Sun L £18.50. Á la carte and childrens menu also available; house wine from about £10.50; sc discretionary. Toilets wheelchair accessible. Open all year except Christmas. Amex, Diners, MasterCard, Visa. **Directions:** On Portaferry seafront.

Saintfield

RESTAURANT

Edgars Restaurant

Main Street Saintfield Co Down BT24 7AA
Tel: 028 9751 1755

In an attractive traditional terrace at the centre of Saintfield, Colin Edgar and Emma Noblett's smart contemporary café-style restaurant offers a wide-ranging bistro style menu all day. Then, at the weekends (Friday and Saturday nights from 6-9), it shifts up a gear and an enticing contemporary dinner à la carte dinner menu comes on stream. The lovely double-height room is simply furnished with wooden tables, comfortable chairs with a selection of newspapers and magazines to read. Depending on the time of day you can order anything from fry-ups and other breakfast dishes, through an interesting selection of lunchtime panini, stuffed potatoes, open sandwiches, and salads. The bistro menu offers a bread selection with tapenade and spiced hummus, crostini, chicken liver pate with toast - and mains like fresh cod, scampi, homemade burgers, rib-eye steak and chicken, all served with thick-cut homemade chips. On weekend dinner menus the style gears up to include more ambitious dishes - starters like shellfish linguini with light Thai cream sauce, Roquefort, pear & walnut tart, or smoked chicken parfait with orange coulis, and mains including Shetland salmon with shrimp butter, medallions of pork with pan jus & apricot pomme purée. Run by an enthusiastic young couple, Edgars is a charming place (the kind every small town deserves) that offers friendly service, good quality, freshly prepared and correctly cooked food. Open Tues-Sat.10 am-9.30pm, all day bistro menu. Fri & Sat. A la carte Dinner menu. Sun Brunch 10-1; Roast lunch 1-2.30. MasterCard, Visa. ◇

Strangford Village

PUB/GUESTHOUSE

The Cuan

6-10 The Square Strangford Village Co Down BT30 7ND

Tel: 028 4488 1222 Fax: 028 4488 1770

Email: info@thecuan.com Web: www.thecuan.com

On the square, just up from the car ferry that goes over to Portaferry, Peter and Caroline McErlean's friendly village inn presents a neat, inviting face to the world. Over a century old, it has character with open fires, cosy lounges and a homely bar, where food is available every day. Bedrooms, including two family rooms, are comfortably furnished with good bathrooms (nearly all with bath and shower), television and tea/coffee making facilities. Short breaks offered. Small conferences/banqueting (60/80). Children welcome (under 10s free in parents' room, cots available without charge, baby sitting arranged). **Rooms 9** (2 shower only, all no smoking, 1 for disabled). Limited room service (on request). B&B about £40 pps, ss £5. Special breaks offered; SC discretionary. Food available 12.30-9 daily. Closed 25 Dec. MasterCard, Visa, Switch. **Directions:** 7 miles from Downpatrick on the A25; on the square, near the ferry. ◇

Warrenpoint

RESTAURANT

Copper Restaurant

4 Duke Street Warrenpoint Co Down BT34 3JY

Tel: 028 4175 3047 Email: info@copperrestaurant.co.uk

Web: www.copperrestaurant.co.uk

Just off the diamond in the centre of Warrenoint, Neil and Sarah Meaney's appealing restaurant lies behind a smart understated façade there's a welcoming bar with comfy seating, a fine high-ceilinged dining room decorated in warm reds, and also a minstrels' gallery for use on busy evenings. Tables are welcomingly set up with classic white linen and all the nice little touches that convey a quality feeling, including great breads. Neil, well known from previous stints in top Belfast restaurants including Cayenne and Ta Tu Bar & Grill (where he was Head Chef), offers imaginative but admirably concise set menus as well as a more extensive à la carte. Typically delicious offerings might include a deeply-flavoured soup such as celeriac (served with crunchy freshly-made croûtons and snipped chives); seafood bourride (a magnificent seafood stew of mixed fish, brimming with luscious juices) and perhaps some moreish comfort food like beef bourguignon - a fine rendition of the classic casserole with mature flavours and melt-in-the-mouth meat, baby onions, mushrooms, and a mash of character. Clearly talented yet displaying a refreshing lack of attitude, this is a chef who likes to send customers away happy and, time permitting, there's a flexible approach to orders taken from the short menus (eg a dish offered as a main course may be served as a starter and vice versa), and portions are generous. An interesting and fairly priced wine list, great coffee and charming service under Sarah's direction all this and a pleasant surprise when the bill arrives. Lucky south Down - another great choice for discerning diners. Warrenpoint is well worth a detour. Toilets wheelchair accessible. **Seats 42.** Air conditioning; no smoking area, children welcome. L Tue-Fri & Sun 12-3; D Tue-Sun 5.30-9.30 (to 10.30 Fri/Sat). Set L £15; Earl dinner £15 5.30-7; Set D £23.50, also á la carte L&D. House wine £ 13-15. Closed Sat L, Mon & 25-26 Dec. Amex, MasterCard, Visa, Switch. **Directions:** Just off main square in Warrenpoint.

Warrenpoint

Ⓝ RESTAURANT

Restaurant 23

23 Church St Warrenpoint Co Down BT34 3HN

Tel: 028 4175 3222 Fax: 028 4177 4323

Email: restaurant23@btconnect.com

Right in the busy town centre of Warrenpoint, a traditional exterior gives little clue to what lies within: once part of a very large traditional pub (which still serves, through an internal door, as a welcoming and comfortable reception area in which to enjoy an aperitif and study the menu), a long L-shaped room has roof lights and mirrors allowing daylight to reach every corner of the cool creams and soft burgundies that tone with polished wooden tables - in what is now a beautifully crafted contemporary restaurant. The proprietors, Raymond McArdle (renowned executive chef at the Nuremore Hotel, Co Monaghan and a previous winner of our Chef of the Year Award) and his wife, Louisa, have assembled a great team led by talented head chef Trevor Cunningham, who offers an enticing menu based on carefully sourced and of the highest quality. His eclectic mix of modern interpretations of traditional dishes and cutting edge contemporary cuisine is presented with flair and style, and in tune with the current mood for less structured dining - many dishes are available in starter or main course portions: expect light tasty dishes like crab, avocado purée & a micro salad; roast tomato & basil soup; smoked salmon Caesar salad; delicious crisp spiced pork with a mango-mayonnaise or comfort food like Cumberland sausage, champ & red onion sauce, or lamb shank, champ & ratatouille sauce. Excellent attention to detail includes lovely freshly baked breads, and desserts that are both tempting and beautiful - and the same care is reflected in the wine list. Vegetarians are well catered for, and the service brings an easy blend of Northern friendliness and professional skill. With a talented and confident chef in the kitchen, a lovely ambience and good value, this new restaurant provides another reason for a detour to Warrenpoint - whether for a light and tasty lunch, or a leisurely dinner in a welcoming and relaxing atmosphere. Toilets wheelchair accessible. **Seats 60** (private room, 30); air conditioning; open Tue-Sat, L 12.15-2.30, D 6-9.30 (to 10 Fri/Sat), Sun 12.30-8. Set Sun L £14.95; set D 2/3 course, £18/23; also a la carte; House wine £12-14. Closed Mon, Tue off season (from Oct), 25 Dec, 2-9 Jan. Amex, MasterCard, Visa, Switch.

Warrenpoint

RESTAURANT

The Duke Restaurant

7 Duke Street Warrenpoint Co Down BT34 3JY **Tel: 028 4175 2084**
Fax: 028 4175 2084 Web: www.thedukerestaurant.com

Seafood straight from Kilkeel harbour and most other produce sourced with a ten mile radius is the foundation for Ciaran Gallagher's success at his popular restaurant, which occupies the whole of the first floor over pleasantly traditional pub, The Duke. Arriving up the (rather steep) stairs, guests are met promptly and efficiently, seated at tables laid with the familiar black rubber place mats, good contemporary cutlery, heavy paper napkins and plain white plates. A comfortable mixture of traditional and modern styles, divisions that lend some intimacy, the busy atmosphere and friendly service all add up to a relaxed ambience. Like the surroundings, menus are balanced and well-tailored to the clientèle; the midweek set menu is exceptionally good value and goes down well, keeping the restaurant full all week - and there will be four or five daily fish specials at accessible prices. Crowd pleasers like surf'n'turf and chicken kiev take their regular places alongside some more ambitious dishes for discerning diners, like hake fillet grilled with lemon butter, steamed courgette flower with prawn mousseline & lobster cream sauce - or roast venison with roast vegetables and shallots & cranberry jus. The cooking is as accomplished as it is generous, the staff cheerful and attentive and the value is terrific: who could ask for more? **Seats 65.** Air conditioning. D Tue-Sun, 6-9.30pm. Midweek Special Set D £12.95, also à la carte. House wine from £8.95. No SC. Closed Mon. Amex, MasterCard, Visa, Switch. **Directions:** Just off town square. ◇

COUNTY FERMANAGH

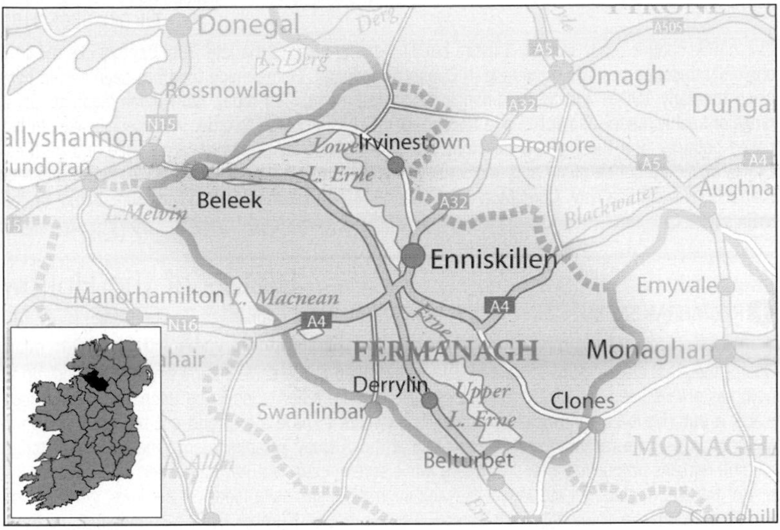

Ireland is a watery place of many lakes, rivers and canals. So it's quite an achievement to be the most watery county of all. Yet this is but one of Fermanagh's many claims to distinction. It is the only county in Ireland in which you can travel the complete distance between its furthest extremities within the heart of its territory entirely by boat. Elsewhere, rivers often divide one county from another, but Fermanagh is divided - or linked if you prefer - throughout its length by the handsome waters of the River Erne, both river and lake.

Southeast of the county town of Enniskillen, Upper Lough Erne is a maze of small waterways. Northwest of the historic and characterful town, the riverway opens out into the broad spread of Lower Lough Erne, a magnificent inland sea set off against the spectacular heights of the Cliffs of Magho. It's a stunningly beautiful county with much else of interest, including the Marble Arch caves, and the great houses of Castle Coole and Florence Court, the latter with its own forest park nestling under the rising heights of Cuilcagh (667m).

And if you think lakes are for fishing rather than floating over, then in western Fermanagh the village of Garrison gives access to Lough Melvin, an angler's heaven. You just can't escape from water in this county. So much so, in fact, that Fermanagh folk will tell you that during the more summery nine months of the year, the lakes are in Fermanagh, but in the damper three months of winter, Fermanagh is in the lakes.

Local Attractions and Information

Belleek, Porcelain and Explore Erne Exhibition 028 68 659300
Bellanaleck, Sheelin Lace Museum 028 66 348052
Enniskillen, Ardhowen Lakeside Theatre 028 66 325440
Enniskillen, Castle Coole House & Parkland 028 66 322690
Enniskillen, Enniskillen Castle 028 66 325000
Enniskillen, Florence Court 028 66 348249
Enniskillen, Lakelands Tourism 028 66 346736
Enniskillen, Lough Erne Cruises 028 66 322882
Enniskillen, Tourism Information 028 66 323110
Enniskillen, Waterways Ireland 028 66 323004
Florence Court, House and garden 028 66 348249
Florencecourt, Marble Arch Caves 028 66 348855
Garrison, Lough Melvin Activity Holiday Centre 028 68 658142
Kesh, Ardess Craft Centre 028 68 631267
Kesh, Castle Archdale Country Park 028 68 621588
Newtownbutler, Crom Castle 028 67 738174

Belleek
CAFÉ

The Thatch

Belleek Co Fermanagh BT93
Tel: 028 6865 8181

This coffee shop is really special: a listed building dating back to the late 18th century, it's the only originally thatched building remaining in County Fermanagh. Home-made food has been served here since the early 1900s and the tradition is being well-maintained today, with home-made soups, a range of freshly made sandwiches and toasted sandwiches all made to order, hot specials like stuffed baked potatoes and (best of all) delicious bakes like chocolate squares, carrot cake and muffins. Drinks include a coffee menu and, more unusually, you can also buy fishing tackle, hire a bike - or even a holiday cottage here. Open Mon-Sat. 9-5 (from 10 off-season). Closed Sun. **Directions:** On the main street.◇

Enniskillen
Ⓔ RESTAURANT/PUB

Blakes of the Hollow

6 Church Street Enniskillen Co Fermanagh BT74 6JE
Tel: 028 6632 0918 Fax: 028 6632 0918

One of the great classic pubs of Ireland, Blakes has been in the same family since 1887 and, up to now, has always been one of the few places that could be relied upon to be unchanged. Not a food place, a pub. Maybe a sandwich, but mainly somewhere to have a pint and put the world to rights. Major changes have recently been taking place at this historic establishment. The original Victorian bar still remains untouched after 115 years, while several extra features have been developed on the rest of the site, including Café Merlot (serving informal, bistro-style food) on the lower ground floor, and The Atrium - a gothic style bar spread over two floors. **Number 6:** The combination of Gerry Russell's ambitious cooking, a relaxed fine dining atmosphere and caring service under the knowledgeable supervision of Johnny Donnelly add up to one of the most interesting dining experiences in the area. It's an attractive space right up at the top of the house with a comfortably furnished reception area where you can wind down and ponder the choices on a concise à la carte menu. The restaurant is elegantly appointed for fine dining. With all the little extras, that give guests that pampered feeling. Imaginatively updated classics may include charred dry aged fillet (beef), a deliciously modern take on the nation's favourite dish, and you may find a speciality of roast belly pork with langoustines, black pudding, creamed cabbage & puy lentils doing something similar for surf'n'turf. Fish cookery is very good and side dishes are taken unusually seriously. Wine is Johnny Donnelly's passion, and this is reflected in both an interesting list, and interested guidance and service. **Café Merlot** (casual dining), L daily 12-3.30; D daily 5-9.30; a la carte, also 2-course early D £11.95 (5.30-7.30). No 6: D Fri-Sat 6-10; A la carte; will open any day for parties 12+. Open all year. MasterCard, Visa, Laser, Switch. **Directions:** Town centre.◇

Enniskillen
Ⓔ RESTAURANT/COUNTRY HOUSE

Ferndale Country House & Restaurant

139 Irvinestown Road Enniskillen
Co Fermanagh BT74 4RN **Tel: 028 6632 8374**
Fax: 028 6632 5706 Email: ferndalechandr@gmail.com
Web: www.ferndalecountryhouseandrestaurant.com

Peter Mills' took over this restaurant (previously Le Chateau) in 2004, and the decor is quite restrained providing a good backdrop for striking modern paintings, and there are open fires in both the reception room and restaurant. Menus are simply written, confidently offering five or six choices on each course: starters are relatively straightforward - warm organic salmon with broad beans and rosemary, or risotto 'primavera' - but main courses promise real punch: cannon of lamb is a speciality, served with a sweetbread beignet and confit shoulder, for example. Everything on the plate lives up to the subtle promise of the menu, and desserts could include a speciality hot fondant which takes 15 minutes to prepare, meanwhile, the canny guest will have a little taste of Irish speciality cheeses. Service, mainly by friendly local staff, is willing and helpful. Peter Mills is a skilled and creative chef, and has gathered a fine team around him - Ferndale offers excellent food and a sense of occasion at realistic prices. **Seats 50** (private room, 30). No smoking restaurant. D Wed-Sun, D 7-9.30, L Sun only 12-2.30. Set 2/3 course Sun L about £16.50/20.95; Set 2/3/6 course D about £27/33/38. House wines from about £10.95. SC discretionary. Vegetarian menu available. Closed Mon, Tue. *Accommodation is offered in six individually decorated rooms, and is in keeping with the country house feel: two of the bedrooms have four-posters and all are comfortably appointed. **Rooms 6** (all en-suite & no smoking). Children welcome (under 4s free in parents' room, cot available without charge, baby sitting arranged). B&B about £27.50 pps, (£37.50 pps for deluxe room with 4 poster bed) ss £10. *Weekend / golfing breaks offered. A dinner bed & breakfast offer is great value. MasterCard, Visa, Switch. **Directions:** On the edge of town, signed on main Enniskillen-Irvinestown road.◇

Enniskillen
RESTAURANT

Franco's Restaurant

Queen Elizabeth Road Enniskillen Co Fermanagh BT74
Tel: 028 6632 4183

If what you want is buzz and relaxed bustle, this is the place for you - there is no other restaurant in town that can even begin to match the ambience. You get a fair hint of this on arrival, as the exterior facing the Queen Elizabeth Road is always attractively maintained, with a pleasing mix of red brick and glass, and an eye-catching display of plants and creepers - and all expertly lit after dark too. Informal meals, including pizzas, pastas and barbecues, are the order of the day - and it's all done with great style, using quality ingredients. The range is impressive and really does offer something to everyone, with a long pizza menu (14 choices) pasta dishes (5 choices), a wide-ranging selection of other popular dishes - and a Special Menu listing more sophisticated items including (organic Glenarm) salmon wrapped in Parma ham, black sole, chargrilled rack of lamb and dry aged beef. Seafood from Donegal and Sligo is a speciality (fresh grilled Mullaghmore lobster is reasonably priced at around £18.95), also new age pizzas with Mediterranean style toppings like goat's cheese, smoked chicken, spinach & pesto. No side vegetables, except potato dishes, alas, but vegetarians have plenty to choose from in every section of the menu. Smart staff, efficient service and fairly reasonable prices keep this place busy, all the time. Popular wine list too (mainly under about £15), but it's a pity to hear staff referring to wines by number. **Seats 140** (private room, 60). Toilets wheelchair accessible. Children welcome. Open Mon-Sat, 12-11 (Sun to 10.30 pm). A la carte. Houses wines from about £10. Closed 25 Dec Amex, MasterCard, Visa, Switch. **Directions:** ◇

Enniskillen
HOTEL/RESTAURANT

Killyhevlin Hotel

Killyhevlin Enniskillen Co Fermanagh BT74 6RW
Tel: 028 66 32 3481 Fax: 028 66 32 4726
Email: info@killyhevlin.com Web: www.killyhevlin.com

Just south of Enniskillen, on the A4, this spacious, modern hotel on the banks of the Erne is a popular choice for business guests and would make a relaxing base from which to explore this fascinating and unspoilt area - and it's also a pleasant place to break a journey as there is food available all day, and the soothing river views from the Boathouse Grill Bar are lovely. A major refurbishment programme is now complete, and recent developments have added 27 new rooms and a new state-of-the art health and beauty spa with gymnasium & fitness suite, indoor swimming pool, outdoor hot tub, hydro therapy pool, treatment suites, sauna, and steam room. Outdoor activities such as golf and horse-riding are available nearby but, given the location, fishing and river cruising are particular attractions and the hotel gardens reach down to the riverbank and their own pontoon, where visiting cruisers can berth. Lakeshore self-catering chalets also available, with full use of hotel facilities. Conference/banqueting facilities (400/250); secretarial services. There are also some holiday chalets in the grounds, with private jetties. Ample parking. Children welcome (under 12s free in parents' room; cots available free of charge; baby sitting arranged). Wheelchair accessible. Pets permitted by arrangement. Garden, cycling. **Rooms 70** (4 suites, 3 junior suites, 2 for disabled, 50 no smoking). B&B £68.50 pps, ss £30; SC incl. Closed 24-25 Dec. Amex, Diners, MasterCard, Visa, Switch. **Directions:** On the A4 just south of Enniskillen.

Enniskillen
COUNTRY HOUSE

Rossahilly House

Rossahilly Enniskillen Co Fermanagh BT94 2FP **Tel: 028 6632 2352**
Email: info@rossahilly.com Web: www.rossahilly.com

Just three miles from Enniskillen, the approach to Monica Poole and Eric Bell's beautifully located 1930s guesthouse is on an elevated site with panoramic views overlooking Lower Lough Erne: "A little bit of heaven" is what one guest called it and it's easy to see why. The entrance is through a neat conservatory style entrance, with comfortable seating overlooking manicured lawns towards the lough - and there's a lovely traditionally tiled hallway too, setting the tone for a house that has been furnished with character. Accommodation in individually decorated bedrooms has been thoughtfully organised for the maximum comfort and security of guests - not only with phone, TV with video, tea/coffee making and pressing facilities, but also a safe and fax available on request. There is a lot to do in the area - they're specialists in fly-fishing holidays - and there is a tennis court on site. The dining room is only open to residents (and parties by arrangement), offering good home cooking (notably excellent baking). Everything is meticulously sourced (home grown vegetables, Fermanagh beef, Erne bacon and pork, Lough Erne trout) and well cooked - presentation is attractive and service, by local waiting staff, both efficient and friendly. Licensed. Children welcome (under 4s free in parents' room, cot available, £5, baby sitting arranged). No pets. Garden, walking, tennis, fishing. Golf nearby. **Rooms 7** (6 suite,

3 junior suites, 3 superior, all no smoking). B&B £35pps, ss £10; suite £45 pps. Room service all day. No smoking dining room, **seats 20** (outdoor seating, 10). Residents D 7-8, by arrangement. Set D about £28. House wine from about £12. MasterCard, Visa, Switch. **Directions:** 3 miles from Enniskillen on Kesh Road. ◇

Enniskillen
COUNTRY HOUSE

Rossfad House

Killadeas Ballinamallard Enniskillen Co Fermanagh BT94 2LS
Tel: 028 6638 8505 Fax: 028 6638 8505
Email: rossfadhouse@aol.com

Lois and John Williams' lovely house is approached up a curving drive, lined with mature trees, with horses grazing in the paddock. The present house is Georgian, built in 1776 on the site of an older Plantation house, and guest accommodation is in a Victorian wing which is at the back, but well-situated overlooking the garden and lake - Lois meets guests at the front door and directs them around to the back where there is parking, right at the door. While decor and furnishings are not lavish, the accommodation is very comfortable and there is a period feel with some nice antique pieces - and its location within the building gives a sense of privacy for both guests and hosts. Breakfast is served in a lovely light and airy room overlooking the garden and lake, which is attractively furnished in a natural, homely mixture of styles, and doubles as a sitting room. It's a beautiful, peaceful place to stay and, apart from the appeal of the location and the Williams' gentle hospitality, it would be of special interest to anyone with a feel for history - it's very close to Lough Erne Yacht Club (the oldest racing sailing club in the Ireland) and, nearby at Castle Archdale, there's an interesting display about the significance of the area in the Second World War. Golf, fishing and garden visits nearby. Children welcome (babies free; cot available without charge, baby siting arranged). Pets allowed in some areas. Garden, walking, equestrian. **Rooms 2** (1 en suite, 1 with private bathroom, both no smoking). B&B £25 pps, ss £5. Closed Nov-Feb. **No Credit Cards. Directions:** 5 miles from Enniskillen on Kesh Road, A32, for 2 miles to Trory Cross; then take B82 for 3 miles; entrance on left, opposite the Whitehill Cross road. ◇

Enniskillen
RESTAURANT/WINE BAR

Scoffs Restaurant & Uno Wine Bar

17 Belmore Street Enniskillen Co Fermanagh BT74 6AA
Tel: 028 663 42622 Fax: 028 663 42622
Email: info@scoffsuno.com Web: www.scoffsuno.com

Just a few minutes walk from the town centre, Gavin Murphy and Lesie Wilkin's popular bistro-style restaurant and wine bar has been pleasing a wide range of customers for several years. Early evening opening and Gavin's wide-ranging menus - offering everything from inexpensive pastas to more serious (but still moderately priced) 'dinner' dishes such as pan fried Blacklion duck breast with a compôte of vegetables, passion fruit & redcurrant sauce & carrot crisps (about £13.50) - partly explain the wide appeal, but consistent cooking, friendly, attentive staff and an atmosphere of relaxed informality are equally attractive. Although menus may include some choices from afar such as ostrich and kangaroo, some local produce features and interesting vegetarian options - which, like those with nuts or flour, are considerately highlighted. Modern classics like slow cooked lamb shank with brunoise of vegetables & creamy mash are well cooked and stylishly presented, and the only down side is that dishes charged extra at £2.50 can add significantly to the costs of a meal. **Seats 147** (private room, 57). Reservations accepted. No smoking area. Toilets wheelchair accessible. Children welcome. D only daily, 5-'late'. D à la carte, from about £20. House wine about £10. Closed 24-26 Dec. Diners, MasterCard, Visa, Laser. **Directions:** Access from main shopping centre.

Enniskillen Area
Ⓝ FARMHOUSE

Arch House

Tullyhona Florencecourt Enniskillen Co Fermanagh
Tel: 028 6634 8452 Email: info@archhouse.com
Web: www.archhouse.com

Located near Marble Arch Caves and Florencecourt House, Rosemary Armstrong's friendly farm guesthouse has six pretty en-suite bedrooms and a big comfortably furnished sitting room with lots of room for guests to relax. Good food is very important at Arch House and, not only does she serve a varied breakfast in the big dining room, but quite an extensive à la carte evening menu is offered too, and it is is open to non-residents by arrangement. Rosemary also has scone and bread making demonstrations in her kitchen - and home produce is on sale in their own shop. Children are very welcome, and there's a children's menu and high chair available. Farm shop, walking; Fishing, golf, tennis, equestrian boating and marble arch caves nearby. **Rooms 6** (3 family rooms, 2 twin, 1 double, all en-suite), children welcome (play ground, toys & games, baby listening); B&B £25 pps, £10ss. MasterCard, Visa.

Directions: From Enniskillen follow the A4 (Sligo Road) for 4km (2.5 m) on to A32 (Swanlinbar road). Follow signs for the Marble Arch Caves. Turn right at posting for National Trust Property at Florencecourt, 3km (2m) on. ◇

ENNISKILLEN AREA

Beautifully situated between two channels of the river joining Upper and Lower Lough Erne, Enniskillen has developed as a holiday centre in recent years, and is especially popular with fisher-folk and anyone with an interest in life on the river. Interesting waterside establishments nearby include the aptly-named **Waterfront Restaurant,** at Rosigh (028 686 21938), and the famous old thatched place, **The Sheelin** (028 6634 8232), which has been run as a restaurant for some years but, at the time of going to press, is expected to become more of a country pub doing informal food. Enniskillen is also famously associated with Oscar Wilde, who attended Portora Royal School; **Oscar's** (028 6632 7037) restaurant celebrates that connnection (with menus that read well and praise local ingredients) while, nearby, **Picasso's** (028 6632 2226) develops a different artistic theme (and has a wine list by James Nicholson).

WWW-IRELAND-GUIDE.COM FOR THE BEST PLACES TO EAT, DRINK & STAY

Kesh
HOTEL

Lough Erne Hotel

Main Street Kesh Co Fermanagh BT93 1TF
Tel: 028 6863 1275 Fax: 028 6863 1921
Email: info@loughernehotel.com Web: www.loughernehotel.com

In a very attractive location on the banks of the Glendurragh River, this friendly town centre hotel has twelve comfortable rooms with en-suite bath/shower rooms, TV and tea/coffee facilities. The hotel is understandably popular for weddings, as the bar and function rooms overlook the river and have access to a paved riverside walkway and garden. Food is above average for an hotel, and wholesome fare, helpful staff, good value and a soothing view make this a relaxing place to break a journey. Popular for fishing holidays, it would also make a good base for a family break; there is plenty to do in this lovely and unspoilt area, including golf, watersports and horse-riding. Conference/banqueting(200/180). Fishing, cycling, walking. Off-season breaks and self-catering accommodation in one and two bedroom cottages (from about £250 pw) also on offer. Garden. Limited wheelchair access. Own parking. Children welcome. Pets permitted in some areas. **Rooms 12** (all en-suite) B&B about £35pps, ss about £5; sc discretionary. Bar L Mon-Sat, 12.30-2; Grill Menu daily 2.30-8 (Sun 5-8). Restaurant D only except L Sun. Light snacks available all day. Closed 25 Dec. Amex, Diners, MasterCard, Visa, Switch. **Directions:** From Dublin N3 to Belturbet, A509 to Enniskillen, A35 to Kesh. ◇

Kesh
BAR/RESTAURANT/B&B

Lusty Beg Island

Boa Island Kesh Co Fermanagh BT93 8AD
Tel: 028 6863 3300 Fax: 028 6863 2033
Email: info@lustybegisland.com Web: www.lustybegisland.com

If you arrive by road, a little ferry takes you over to the island (leave your car on the mainland unless you will be staying on the island), or of course, you can call in by boat. It's an unusual place and worth a visit, if only to call into the pleasant waterside pub for a drink, a cup of tea or an informal bite such as smoked salmon and brown bread. However, you could stay much longer as accommodation is available in lodges, chalets and a motel, all spread relatively inconspicuously around the wooded island. Conferences, corporate entertaining and management training are specialities and all sorts of activity breaks are offered. Visiting boats are welcome; phone ahead for details of barbecues and other theme nights; music Saturday nights. Bar food available daily in summer, may be weekends only off season (phone ahead for details). Conference/banqueting (300/200). **Rooms 40** (all shower only, 23 family rooms, 10 ground floor, 2 for disabled, all no smoking) Children welcome (under 5s free in parents' room; cot available £5. Leisure centre: swimming pool, sauna, tennis, pool table. Football pitch, canoes, bike hire, archery, clay pigeon shooting, equestrian & fly fishing nearby. B&B £45 pps. ss £20. Closed Christmas week. MasterCard, Visa, Switch. **Directions:** Located off the main Kesh - Belleek Road A47.

Killadeas
HOTEL/RESTAURANT

Manor House Resort Hotel

Killadeas Co Fermanagh BT94 1NY
Tel: 028 6862 2211 Fax: 028 6862 1545
Email: info@manor-house-hotel.com Web: www.manor-house-hotel.com

This impressive lakeside period house makes a fine hotel. The scale of the architecture and the style of furnishings and decor lean very much towards the luxurious in both public areas and accommodation. Spacious bedrooms range from interconnecting family rooms to deluxe doubles and romantic suites with canopied four-poster beds and front rooms have stunning views. Recent changes have included extensive refurbishments and the addition of an impressive new conference and banqueting area with its own separate entrance, which has been discreetly added to the side and rear of the original building and, despite its large size and more contemporary approach, in no way detracts from the appeal of the old house. Conference/banqueting. Leisure centre, indoor swimming pool; beauty salon. Children under 3 free in parents' room. No pets. **Rooms 81** (all en-suite, 6 suites) B&B about £55pps, ss about £30. Special breaks offered. **The Belleek Restaurant:** Formally appointed in the old style, the restaurant is well positioned to make the most of the lovely view. Quite classical dinner menus offer a generous choice of about nine dishes on each course; typical examples recently enjoyed include a duck and green peppercorn terrine with red onion marmalade, followed by a little complimentary blackcurrant sorbet; main courses will probably include the ever popular fillet steak (with truffle mash and red wine jus perhaps), and fish choices such as sea bass beurre blanc - finish with desserts like raspberry bavarois or pear & orange gateau, or cheeses selected from a trolley. While not aiming to be cutting edge, cooking is accomplished and presentation well-judged (simple but attractive), and service by a well-trained team is exemplary. Both food and service are in tune with the grand surroundings, making this a good choice for a special evening out. Bar meals available 12.30-9 pm daily, 12.30-3.30 and 6.30-9.30. Restaurant seats 65 (private room 30). Non-smoking restaurant. Air Conditioning. L&D daily. Set D about £25. Set Sun L about £25. [*Information on the nearby Inishclare restaurant, bar & marina complex is available from the hotel, which is in common ownership.] Open all year. Amex, MasterCard, Visa. **Directions:** 6 miles from Enniskillen on the B82. ◇

Lisbellaw

Belle Isle Castle

CASTLE / HISTORIC HOUSE

Belle Isle Estate Lisbellaw Co Fermanagh BT94 5HG
Tel: 028 6638 7231 Fax: 028 6638 7261
Email: accommodation@belleisle-estate.com Web: www.belleislecastle.com

Belle Isle is owned by the Duke of Abercorn, and magically situated on one of eleven islands on Upper Lough Erne that are owned by the Estate; the original castle dates back to 1680 and has mid-19th century additions, including a courtyard and coach house which have been converted to make very appealing self-catering accommodation. The castle itself has a delightfully exclusive away-from-it-all country house atmosphere and is impressively furnished with antiques, striking paintings and dramatic colour schemes (the work of the internationally renowned interior designer, David Hicks); in addition to the eight romantic bedrooms, which all have their special character, guests have use of a magnificent drawing room and also the Grand Hall, complete with minstrels' gallery, where dinner is served. Under the eagle-eyed supervision of hosts Charles and Fiona Plunket, maintenance and housekeeping are immaculate throughout - and this romantic places could be the perfect choice for a small wedding: they are licensed to hold civil weddings. There are many wonderful things to do in this idyllically beautiful area - fishing is an obvious first choice but there are also golf courses nearby, field sports can be arranged and there are historic houses and gardens to visit. But, most tempting of all, perhaps, might be a course at the Belle Isle School of Cookery, which is very professionally operated and offers an extensive range of courses of varying lengths throughout the year. **Cookery School:** Tel 028 6638 7231; www.irishcookeryschool.com. Small weddings (30). Children welcome (under 5s free in parents' room, cot available without charge; playground). Pets allowed in some areas. Garden, walking, fishing, tennis **Rooms 8** (1 en-suite, 7 with private bathrooms, 1 shower only, all no smoking). B&B £70 pps, ss £15. No SC. Residents D daily, 8pm, £28/30; wines from £10. *Self-catering also offered in 10 apartments & 3 cottages, with 1-3 bedrooms; larger groups may use both castle & apartments. Open all year. Amex, Diners, MasterCard, Visa, Laser, Switch. **Directions:** From Belfast, take A4 to Lisbellaw - follow signs to Carrybridge.

COUNTY LONDONDERRY

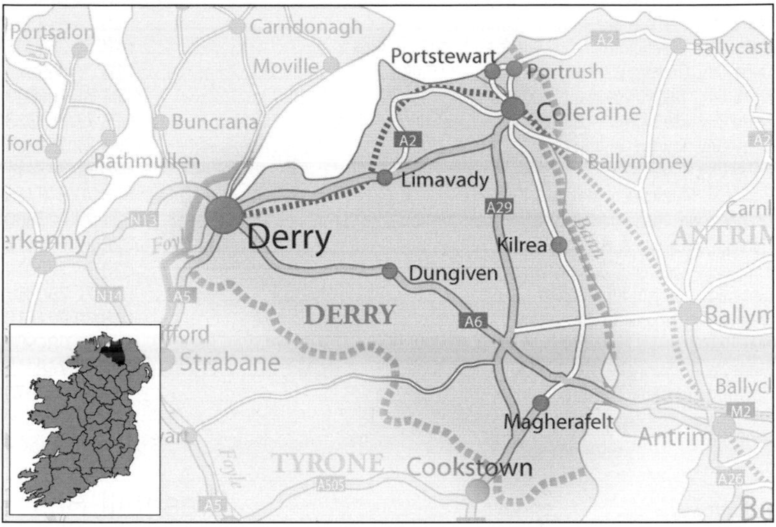

When its boundaries were first defined for "modern" times, this was known as the County of Coleraine, named for the busy little port on the River Bann a few miles inland from the Atlantic coast. It was an area long favoured by settlers, for Mountsandel - on the salmon-rich Bann a mile south of Coleraine - is where the 9,000 year old traces of the site of some of the oldest-known houses in Ireland have been found.

Today, Coleraine is the main campus of the University of Ulster, with the vitality of student life spreading to the nearby coastal resorts of Portstewart and Portrush in the area known as the "Golden Triangle", appropriately fringed to the north by the two golden miles of Portstewart Strand. Southwestward from Coleraine, the county - which was re-named after the City of Derry became Londonderry in 1613 - offers a fascinating variety of places and scenery, with large areas of fine farmland being punctuated by ranges of hills, while the rising slopes of the Sperrin Mountains dominate the County's southern boundary.

The road from Belfast to Derry sweeps through the Sperrins by way of the stirringly-named Glenshane Pass, and from its heights you begin to get the first glimpses westward of the mountains of Donegal. This is an appropriate hint of the new atmosphere in the City of Derry itself. This lively place could reasonably claim to be the most senior of all Ireland's contemporary cities, as it can trace its origins directly back to a monastery of St Colmcille, otherwise Columba, founded in 546AD. Today, the historic city, its ancient walls matched by up-dated port facilities on the River Foyle and a cheerfully restored urban heart, is moving into a vibrant future in which it thrives on the energy drawn from its natural position as the focal point of a larger catchment area which takes in much of Donegal County to the west in addition to County Londonderry to the east.

The area eastward of Lough Foyle is increasingly popular among discerning visitors, the Roe Valley through Dungiven and Limavady being particularly attractive. The ferry between Magilligan Point and Greencastle in Donegal across the narrow entrance to Lough Foyle gives an extra dimension to the region's infrastructure, as does the up-grading of the increasingly busy City of Derry Airport at Eglinton.

Local Attractions and Information

Bellaghy, Bellaghy Bawn (Seamus Heaney centre) 028 79 386812
Castlerock, Hezlett House 028 70 848567
City of Derry Airport 028 71 810784
Coleraine, Guy L Wilson Daffodil Garden 028 70 344141
Coleraine, Tourism Information 028 70 344723
Derry City, The Fifth Province - Celtic culture 028 71 373177
Derry City, Foyle Arts Centre 028 71 266657

Derry City, Foyle Cruises (year round)	028 71 362857
Derry City, Foyle Valley Railway Centre	028 71 265234
Derry City, The Guildhall	028 71 377335
Derry City, Harbour Museum	028 71 377331
Derry City, Millennium Forum Theatre	028 71 264426
Derry City, Orchard Gallery	028 71 269675
Derry City, The Playhouse	028 71 268027
Derry City, St Columb's Cathedral	028 71 267313
Derry City, Tourism Information	028 71 267284
Derry City, Tower Museum	028 71 372411
Downhill, Mussenden Temple & Gardens	028 70 848728
Draperstown, Plantation of Ulster Visitor Centre	028 79 627800
Garvagh, Museum & Heritage Centre	028 29 558216
Limavady, Roe Valley & Ness Wood Country Parks	028 77 722074
Limavady, Tourism Information	028 77 760307
Magherafelt, Tourism Information	028 79 631510
Magilligan, Lough Foyle Ferry (to Donegal) (ROI t.n.)	077 81901
Moneymore, Springhill (NT house)	028 86 748210
Sperrin Mountains, Sperrins Tourism	028 79 634570

Aghadowey
FARMHOUSE

Greenhill House

24 Greenhill Rd Aghadowey Coleraine Co Londonderry BT51 4EU
Tel: 028 7086 8241 Fax: 028 7086 8365
Email: greenhill.house@btinternet.com Web: www.greenhill-house.co.uk

Framed by trees with lovely country views, the Hegarty family's Georgian farmhouse is at the centre of a large working farm. In true Northern tradition, Elizabeth Hegarty is a great baker and greets guests in the drawing room with an afternoon tea which includes a vast array of home-made teabreads, cakes and biscuits - and home baking is also a highlight of wonderful breakfasts that are based on tasty local produce like bacon, sausages, mushrooms, free range eggs, smoked salmon, strawberries and preserves. There are two large family rooms and, although not luxurious, the thoughtfulness that has gone into furnishing bedrooms makes them exceptionally comfortable everything is in just the right place to be convenient - and Elizabeth is constantly maintaining and improving the decor and facilities. Bedrooms now have direct dial telephones, and little touches - like fresh flowers, a fruit basket, After Eights, tea & coffee making facilities, hair dryer, bathrobe, good quality clothes hangers and even a torch - are way above the standard expected of farmhouse accommodation. There's also internet access, a safe, fax machine, iron and trouser press available for guests' use on request. Guests have been welcomed to Greenhill House since 1980 and, wonderfully comforting and hospitable as it is, Elizabeth constantly seeks ways of improvement, big and small: this lovely house and the way it is run demonstrate rural Irish hospitality at its best. [Greenhill House was our Farmhouse of the Year Award for 2003.] *There are plans to convert some of the outhouses, for self-catering accommodation. Children welcome, cot available. No pets. Garden. **Rooms 6** (all en-suite, 2 shower only, 2 bath only, 2 family rooms, all no smoking). B&B £30 pps, ss £10. Closed Nov-Feb. Amex, MasterCard, Visa, Switch. **Directions:** On B66 Greenhill Road off A29, 10.5km (7 miles) south of Coleraine, 5km (3 m) north of Garvagh.

Aghadowey
E HOTEL/RESTAURANT

The Brown Trout Golf & Country Inn

209 Agivey Road Aghadowey Co Londonderry BT51 4AD
Tel: 028 7086 8209 Fax: 028 7086 8878
Email: jane@browntroutinn.com Web: www.browntroutinn.com

Golf is one of the major attractions at this lively family-run country inn, both on-site and in the locality, but it's a pleasant and hospitable place for anyone to stay. and golfers and non-golfers alike will soon find friends in the convivial bar, where food is served from noon to 10 pm every day - and outside in a pleasant barbecue too, in fine weather. Accommodation is not especially luxurious, but very comfortable, in good-sized en-suite rooms which are all on the ground floor, arranged around the main courtyard, and have plenty of space for golfing gear. New cottage suites overlooking the golf course (just 100 yards from the main building) are the first of this standard to be completed in Northern Ireland. As well as bar food, there's an evening restaurant up a steep staircase (with chair lift for the less able), overlooking the garden end of the golf course. A dedicated kitchen team aims to produce good home cooking with local fresh ingredients for daytime food (soups, freshly made sandwiches and open sandwiches, baked potatoes, pasta) and evening meals like hot garlic Aghadowey mushrooms or ribeye steak with a Bushmills whiskey sauce. Free Broadband WI/FI. Small conference/private parties (50). Tennis, horse-riding, golf (9), fishing. Gym. Children welcome (under 4s free in parents' room; cots available without charge, baby sitting arranged). Pets permitted. Garden, walking. Traditional music in bar (Sat). **Rooms 15** (all en-suite; 1 for disabled & most wheelchair friendly). B&B £50 pps, ss £20. Stair lift. Toilets wheelchair accessible. No smoking restaurant, house no smoking from 2007. Bar meals, 12-9.30 daily (to 10 in summer). Restaurant D only, 5-9.30. A la carte; house wine £9.95; sc discretionary. Bar meals: 12-9.30. Open all year. Amex, Diners, MasterCard, Visa, Switch. **Directions:** Intersection of A54/B66,11km (7 m) south of Coleraine.

Castledawson

N E RESTAURANT/GUESTHOUSE

The Inn at Castledawson

47 Main Street Castledawson Co Londonderry BT45 8AA
Tel: 028 7946 9777 Fax: 028 7946 9888
Email: info@theinnatcastledawson.co.uk Web: www.theinnatcastledawson.co.uk

Built around the 200 year old Castledawson House, Simon Toye and Kathy Tully's latter day inn is a delightful place - and, thanks to Simon's excellent cooking and their 'nothing is too much trouble' policy, a visit here sure to be memorable and relaxed. The Inn is most attractive, with a modern bar where smart informal dining is offered at neat round darkwood tables with cream leather armchairs and banquettes and, beyond it, a lovely tiered light-filled restaurant with a huge arched window overlooks the River Moyola and has doors leading out to a decked waterside balcony. Concise, well-constructed à la carte bar menus offer a tempting choice including seriously good soups and breads, lovely pasta dishes and outstanding fish cooking as in a memorable dish of undyed smoked haddock with a mustard cream sauce and mash. The restaurant menu offers a fine choice of 6-8 dishes on each course, some of them dressier developments of the delicious bar food; specialities to look out for include smoked salmon and other fish from Walter Ewing's renowned Belfast fishmongers, Finnebrogue 'Oisin' venison from Downpatrick, and rare breed pork dishes. The restaurant conveys a natural sense of occasion and is stylishly furnished, with hardwood flooring, warm red high-backed chairs, crisp white linen and gleaming glasses - it is a beautiful room in which to enjoy the good food and service for which the Inn already has a well-earned reputation. And it is a true inn, offering food, drink and a (very relaxing) place to lay your head: there are twelve chic contemporary bedrooms with river or courtyard views, including a suite with its own riverside balcony. With a spa next door, and golf, equestrian and fishing all nearby, this is a very appealing place for a short break. Children welcome. Wheelchair accessible. Wheelchair accessible. Small conferences/banqueting 90/80. **Restaurant Seats 80** (+20 outside). L Sun-Fri 12-2.30; D Mon-Sat 6-10, D Sun 5-8. House wine £11.95. Restaurant closed Sat L. **Rooms 12** (6 shower only, all no smoking, 2 disabled); children welcome (under 5s free in parents room, cot available with no charge) B&B £39.95, ss £10. MasterCard, Visa, Switch. **Directions:** On main street of Castledawson, on the main Belfast-Derry road (M2-M22-A6).

Coleraine

N RESTAURANT

Water Margin

The Boat House Hanover Place Coleraine Co Londonderry BT52 1EB
Tel: 028 7034 2222

An impressive first floor restaurant above the Boat Club, this magnificently located Chinese restaurant predated its famous Belfast sister (the largest Chinese restaurant in Ireland) by many a year and, with its fine river views, plush bar and a rather luxuriously appointed dining room to enhance cooking which has enjoyed a great reputation in the area over a long period, it has all the ingredients for a special meal out. Extensive menus offer all the familiar set 'banquets' and western favourites like aromatic duck, sesame toast, sweet & sours and sizzling dishes, but the more adventurous diner will find that there are many unusual dishes available too - and made all the more enjoyable by good service, provided by helpful, smartly-dressed staff. L Mon-Sat, 12.30-2pm, D daily,5-10.30pm, Sun 1-10pm. MasterCard, Visa, Switch. **Directions:** Above the boat club in Coleraine. ◇

Feeny

€ COUNTRY HOUSE

Drumcovitt House

704 Feeny Road Feeny Co Londonderry BT47 4SU
Tel: 028 7778 1224 Fax: 028 7778 1224
Email: drumcovitt.feeny@btinternet.com Web: www.drumcovitt.com

Drumcovitt is an intriguing house with an impressive Georgian front dating from 1796 - and, behind it a much older farmhouse, built about 1680. It is a listed building and many of the windows and wonderful interior features have been retained but, however interesting its history, today's creature comforts are very much in evidence - central heating extends throughout the house and an adjacent converted barn, and there are big log fires to relax beside while enjoying a fine collection of books, or making a jigsaw. Outdoor pursuits aplenty too: this unspoilt area is perfect for walking, bird-watching, visiting archaeological sites in the Sperrins and much else besides - horse riding, golf and angling are all available nearby and the Giants Causeway, beaches, Bushmills, Derry city and much of Donegal are within easy striking distance. The three guest rooms in the house are the two main front bedrooms (both with a double/ king-size bed and single) and a twin in the older part; in true country house fashion bathrooms are not en-suite, but two good modern showers (one over bath) are shared by the three rooms and there are plans to improve the bathrooms; all the rooms are spacious and comfortably furnished with tea/coffee-making, television and phone. The Sloan family are solicitous but relaxed hosts, who enjoy sharing their unique home and the area around it with guests; Chris Sloan and his partner Sarah Wallis took over day to day running of the house in 2005, but Chris's mother, Florence, is still involved and cooks for guests. This is a delightful place, but not one to rush through so allow more than one night if you can. Fax, safe and ironing facilities available for guests' use. Family celebrations/reunions up to about 20 can be catered for in house and three barn cottages, which are available for self-catering. **Rooms 3** (with ISDN, phone, tv). Children welcome (cot available without charge; games room). B&B £29, no ss. Closed Christmas. Amex, Diners, MasterCard, Visa, Switch. **Directions:** Half a mile east of Feeny Village on B74 off A6.

Limavady

E RESTAURANT

Lime Tree Restaurant

60 Catherine Street Limavady Co Londonderry BT49 9DB
Tel: 028 7776 4300 Email: info@limetreerest.com
Web: www.limetreerest.com

Loyal customers come from far and wide for the pleasure of dining at Stanley and Maria Matthews' restaurant on the handsome, wide main street of this attractive town. And no wonder, as it is always a pleasant place to be, Stanley is a fine chef and Maria a welcoming and solicitous hostess. Ingredients are carefully sourced, many of them local; menus are generous, with a classical base that Stanley works on to give popular dishes a new twist. Specialities include their own home-made wheaten bread, which is the perfect accompaniment for a chowder of Atlantic fish & local potatoes, or Irish smoked salmon (supplied by Donegal prime Fish), with cucumber salad, while main course favourites include Sperrin lamb (with honey & rosemary) fillet or sirloin steak (from the award-winning local butcher, Hunters) and seafood thermidor (Stanley's selection of fresh fish with a mild cheese & brandy sauce). Menus are not over-extensive, but change frequently to suit different occasions - there's an attractive early dinner menu which is exceptional value, followed by a dressier set dinner for the main evening menu, which also has an accompanying (and more adventurous) à la carte. Stanley's cooking is refreshingly down-to-earth - new dishes are often introduced, but if it's on the menu it's because it works: there are no gimmicks. Good cooking and good value go hand in hand with warm hospitality here and it is always a pleasure to visit The Lime Tree - indeed, many discerning guests enjoy it so much that they plan journeys around a meal here. Children welcome. A concise, interesting wine list also offers predictably good value. **Seats 30.** Reservations advised. Children welcome before 8pm. Toilets wheelchair accessible. D Tue-Sat, 6-9 (Sat to 9.30). Early D £10.50 (6-7pm only, excl Sat). Set D £18.25/21.50 2/3 course; also à la carte; house wine £11.50; sc discretionary. Non smoking restaurant. Closed Sun & Mon, 25/6 Dec, 1 week around 12 July. Amex, MasterCard, Visa, Switch. **Directions:** On the outskirts of town, main Derry-Limavady road.

Limavady

N HOTEL

Radisson SAS Roe Park Resort

Roe Park Limavady Co Londonderry BT47 2 AH
Tel: 028 7772 2222 Fax: 028 7772 2313
Email: reservations@radissonroepark.com Web: www.radissonroepark.com

Built on rising ground in lovely rolling countryside, this imposing hotel dates back to the eighteenth century when a Captain Richard Babington built the original house from which today's extensive hotel has grown. There is a pleasant air of relaxed luxury - the tone is set in an impressive foyer, with columns and a curved gallery overlooking a seating area smartly set up with comfortable sofas and armchairs in strong contemporary colours. Conferences play a major part in present-day business - and the surrounding greensward provides relaxation for delegates, along with many others who come here specifically to enjoy the excellent leisure facilities. Spacious bedrooms, in more restful shades, are designed in the modern classic mode with double and single beds and all the features expected of this type of hotel (all have desk areas, some with computers) and well-finished bathrooms - and all look out over the golf course or a courtyard garden. Dining options allow for different moods: formal dining in Greens Restaurant (dinner daily and lunch on Sunday) or a more relaxed style in The Coach House Brasserie.

Separate vegetarian menu offered. Conferences/banqueting (450/275). Leisure centre (indoor swimming pool, spa). Golf (18 hole), fishing. Children welcome (under 5 free in parents' room; cot available, baby sitting arranged, playroom). No pets. Garden, walking, cycling. Pool table. **Rooms 118** (7 suites, 3 junior suites, 108 executive, 2 disabled). Lift. 24 hr room service. B&B £55 pps, ss £25. *Wide range of special breaks offered. Open all year. Amex, Diners, MasterCard, Visa, Laser, Switch. **Directions:** On the A2 L'Derry-Limavady road, 1 miles from Limavady (Derry City 16 miles).

Londonderry
HOTEL/RESTAURANT

Beech Hill Country House Hotel

32 Ardmore Road Londonderry Co Londonderry BT47 3QP
Tel: 028 7134 9279 Fax: 028 7134 5366
Email: info@beech-hill.com Web: www.beech-hill.com

Beech Hill is just a couple of miles south of Londonderry, in a lovely setting of 42 acres of peaceful woodland, waterfalls and gardens. Built in 1729, the house has retained many of its original details and proprietor Patsy O'Kane makes an hospitable and caring hostess. Comfortable bedrooms vary in size and outlook many overlook the gardens but all are thoughtfully and attractively furnished with Mrs O'Kane's ever-growing collection of antiques. Public rooms include a good-sized bar, a fine restaurant (in what was originally the snooker room, now extended into a conservatory overlooking the gardens) and, unusually, a private chapel, now used for meetings, private parties or small weddings. Facilities include picnic areas in the grounds for fine weather and a fitness suite with sauna, steam room, jacuzzi and weight room. The US Marines had their headquarters here in World War II and an informative small museum of the US Marine Friendship Association is housed within the hotel. Conference/banqueting (100/90); secretarial services. Fitness centre, beauty salon. Tennis. Golf, fishing, equestrian nearby. Children welcome (under 3s free in parents' room cot available without charge, babysitting arranged). Pets allowed by arrangement; garden, walking. **Rooms 27** (2 suites, 3 junior suites, 10 executive rooms, 10 shower only, 1 for disabled). Lift. B&B about £60pps, ss about £10; SC discretionary. Closed 24/25 Dec. **Ardmore Restaurant**: The restaurant has always been a particularly attractive feature of Beech Hill: it is elegantly appointed in traditional style and well-positioned overlooking gardens (which is particularly pleasant at breakfast time) - and, although the head chef has changed from time to time, there is a tradition of using local ingredients to advantage in updated classical French cuisine, and the combination of high standards of cooking and caring service has earned a loyal local following. Various combinations of menus are offered, with specialities such as a smoked brie & chicken tart, with rocket salad & wholegrain mustard indicating the style - and there's a separate vegetarian listing of five or six interesting dishes which can be served as a starter or main course. The wine list offers good value - and a number of famous New World wines with Northern Ireland connections. **Seats 100.** Reservations accepted. No smoking restaurant. Children welcome. Toilets wheelchair accessible. L daily, 12-2; D daily 6.30-9. Set L about £17.95, Set Sun L about £17.95. Set 2/3 course D, about £21.95/27.95. A la carte and vegetarian menu also available. House wines (6), about £12.95. SC discretionary. Amex, MasterCard, Visa, Switch. **Directions:** Main Londonderry road A6. ◇

Londonderry
Ⓔ RESTAURANT

Browns Restaurant, Bar & Brasserie

1-2 Bonds Hill Londonderry Co Londonderry BT47 6DW
Tel: 028 7134 5180 Fax: 028 7134 5180
Email: eat@brownsrestaurant.com Web: www.brownsrestaurant.com

The city's leading contemporary restaurant has a devoted local following. Always immaculate, inside and out, it's a relaxed space with subtle blends of natural colours, textures and finishes - proprietor-chef Ivan Taylor's cool cooking keeps them coming back for more; his approach to food never stands still, and the cooking is consistently creative. Wide-ranging menus offer a range of fresh-flavoured dishes, including delicious starters like spiced crumbled beef served in a light vegetable broth with pecorino, and a perfectly judged main dish of char-grilled rare-breed sirloin steak on a fine balsamic onion gravy with a horesradish Yorkshire pudding & pea puree and braised root vegetables - one of several examples of classics that have been modernised without forgetting the basics. Desserts also ring some changes with the classics - or espresso, vin santo & home-made biscotti might make a pleasing alternative. All round, there's imagination, a certain amount of style, dedication and consistency - not bad after more than 20 years in business. *Browns2Go service offered, for boardroom lunches and corporate entertaining. L Tue-Fri, 12-2.15; D Tue-Sat, 5.30-Late. Early Set D Tue-Fri, about £10.95 (5.30-7.15). House wine about £11.95. Closed Sun & Mon, 1st 2 weeks Aug. Amex, MasterCard, Visa, Laser, Switch. **Directions:** In a cul-de-sac pposite the old Waterside railway station : Belfast-Derry road (A6), turn left at Melrose Terrace & branch right at sign. (Or park at station and walk across). ◇

Londonderry
HOTEL

City Hotel

Queens Quay Londonderry Co Londonderry BT48 7AS **Tel: 028 7136 5800**
Fax: 028 7136 5801 Email: res@derry-gsh.com Web: www.gshotels.com

Centrally located on a quayside site overlooking the River Foyle, Derry's newest hotel is bright and contemporary, and would make an equally attractive base for a leisure visit or for business - executive rooms have a workstation with modem/PC connections, voice mail, interactive TV systems and mini-bar and there's a business centre providing secretarial services for guests. Well-located close to the old city, business districts and main shopping areas, it also has free private parking for guests and on-site leisure facilities. Conference/banqueting (450/350). **Rooms 145** (1 suite, 4 junior suites). Lift. 24 hour room service. Children welcome (under 2s free in parents' room, cot available without charge). Leisure centre: swimming pool, Jacuzzi, steam room, sauna, dance suite, gym, hydrotherapy). B&B about £50pps. Room rate about £100 (max 3 guests). Amex, Diners, MasterCard, Visa, Laser. **Directions:** In Derry city centre, overlooking River Foyle. ◇

Londonderry
RESTAURANT

Exchange Restaurant & Wine Bar

Queens Quay Londonderry Co Londonderry BT48 7AY
Tel: 028 7127 3990 Fax: 028 7127 3991

Just outside the walled city, the contemporary design of this popular bar and restaurant makes a great contrast to the age of nearby landmarks. Although seriously modern, this is a friendly and welcoming place that appeals to all age groups and their colourful, fresh-flavoured food suits the mood perfectly. They seem to have a winning formula here as prices are reasonable, ingredients are sourced locally as far as possible and the cooking hits the mark. At first glance the menu seems very international but close examination reveals plenty to please traditionalists too and blackboard specials reflect the same desire to please a wide range of customers. **Seats 120.** Toilets wheelchair accessible. Children welcome. Air conditioning. L Mon-Sat, 12-2.30; D daily 5.30-10 (Sun to 9.30). A la carte. House wine about £10. SC discretionary. Closed L Sun, 25 Dec. Amex, MasterCard, Visa, Laser, Switch. **Directions:** Opposite City Hotel. ◇

Londonderry
RESTAURANT/WINE BAR

Fitzroys Bistro

2-4 Bridge Street Londonderry Co Londonderry BT48 6JZ
Tel: 028 7126 6211 Fax: 028 7137 0966
Email: info@fitzroysrestaurant.com Web: www.fitzroysrestaurant.com

This large modern restaurant beside the Foyle Shopping Centre is on two floors and very handy for shoppers, visitors or pre- and post-theatre meals. Recent refurbishment has revamped the interior, but the central philosophy of providing good quality, reasonably priced food in enjoyably informal surroundings remains unchanged. Menus change through the day and offer a wide range of food in the current international fashion - lamb cutlets with herb crust, champ, red onion confit, and red wine jus indicates the evening style while the daytime menu ranges from soup of the day and designer sandwiches (sweet chilli chicken & roast peppers panini) to house favourites like Cajun chicken tagliatelle. A conveniently located, family-friendly restaurant - handy to know about. A choice of sixteen wines is offered at a flat rate, and with notes and a useful flavour key, indicating style. **Seats 80.** Reservations accepted. Open daily, 10 - 10 (Sun 12-'late'). Value D Mon-Thurs 7-10 £ 12.95, also à la carte; Sun brasserie menus all day. House wines (4) £10.95. Closed 25 Dec. MasterCard, Visa, Switch. **Directions:** City centre, opposite main entrance to Foyleside Shopping Centre.

Londonderry
HOTEL

Hastings Everglades Hotel

Prehen Road Londonderry Co Londonderry BT47 2NH
Tel: 028 7132 1066 Fax: 028 7134 9200
Email: res@egh.hastingshotels.com Web: www.hastingshotels.com

Situated on the banks of the River Foyle, close to City of Derry airport and quite convenient to the city, this modern hotel is well located for business and pleasure in a quieter situation than more central alternatives. As at all the Hastings Hotels, an on-going system of refurbishment and upgrading pays off in comfortable, well-maintained bedrooms, and public areas which never feel dated. Accommodation is all of a high standard, with good amenities including air conditioning and a spacious desk area, although recently replaced beds are only standard size which is now unusual in a hotel of this class (and unnecessary as rooms are generally spacious); most of the bathrooms have also been recently renewed. The hotel is well located for golf, with the City of Derry course just a couple of minutes away and six other courses, including Royal Portrush, within easy driving distance. Conference/banqueting (400/320); secretarial services; video conferencing (on request). Wheelchair accessible. Own parking (200). Children under 14 free in parents' room; cots available; baby sitting arranged. No pets. **Rooms 64** (2 suites, 1 junior suite, 4 executive, 40 no-smoking, 1 for disabled). Lift. B&B about £57.50 pps, ss about £15; no sc. *Short breaks & golfing breaks offered. Closed 24-25 Dec. Amex, Diners, MasterCard, Visa, Switch. **Directions:** From Belfast follow M2; hotel is on A5 approx 1 mile from city. ◇

Londonderry
RESTAURANT

Mange 2

2 Clarendon Street Londonderry Co Londonderry BT48 7ES
Tel: 028 7136 1222 Fax: 028 7136 1122
Email: dine@mange2derry.com Web: www.mange2derry.com

John O'Connell and Kieran McGuinness's restaurant off the Strand Road has just been smartly refurbished, giving a better impression on arrival than previously - a better setting for Kieran's creative good cooking. Keen, knowledgeable staff are quick to welcome arriving guests, offering menus with plenty of choice, in a pleasingly straightforward modern style - there are some updated classics in there alongside the spicy dishes - chicken liver paté, for example, is served in quenelles, with raspberry & orange coulis, and you may well find other old favourites, like garlic mussels. Prices are reasonable and some dishes, such as moules marinière, are offered as starters (about £3.95) or main courses (about £10.95). There is some emphasis on fish and seafood, and vegetarians have a fair choice (mainly salads and pastas), but you will also find less usual ingredients, perhaps including game in season - Finnebrogue venison is a speciality, served in an upbeat style with roasted vegetables, red onion marmalade & red wine jus. Everything is home made on the premises, including desserts - what you get here is wholesome food, served in generous portions and with style. Look out for special promotions, such as a midweek early dinner with a bottle of wine for two, which is very good value. The wine list is limited but well priced. Toilets wheelchair accessible. **Seats 55;** air conditioning; children welcome. Open daily: D, 5.30-10.L, 12-3. A la carte; Set Sun L £11.95. Value D £31.95, 3 course D & bottle of wine, 5-7pm. House wines £10.95. Closed 3 days Christmas. Amex, MasterCard, Visa, Laser, Switch. **Directions:** Off Strand Road.

Londonderry
HOTEL

Tower Hotel Derry

Off The Diamond Londonderry Co Londonderry BT48 6HL
Tel: 028 7137 1000 Fax: 028 7137 1234
Email: reservations@thd.ie Web: wwwtowerhotelderry.com

This attractive new hotel has the distinction of being the only one to have been built inside the city walls and, while this does have its disadvantages (the constraints of the site restricted the amount of parking provided, for example), these are offset by wonderful views over the river and a real sense of being at the real heart of the city. Accommodation and facilities have obvious appeal for both leisure and business visitors - the style throughout is bright and sassy, and rooms are pleasingly decorated, with all the necessary modern facilities, including phones/ISDN, hospitality trays, TV, trouser press etc. (also a safe in suites). A fitness suite with gym and sauna has a great view across the city. An attractive bistro restaurant off the lobby has the potential to appeal to non-residents as well as hotel guests. Conference/banqueting 250/180). Parking (limited). **Rooms 90** (3 suites, 4 disabled). Lift. Room service (limited hours). Children welcome (cot available without charge). B&B about £35pps, ss about £20. Closed 24-27 Dec. Amex, Diners, MasterCard, Visa, Laser. **Directions:** City centre - old town. ◇

Magherafelt
Ⓝ RESTAURANT

Gardiners Restaurant

7 Garden Street Magherafelt Co Londonderry BT45 5DD
Tel: 028 7930 0333 Fax: 028 7930 0093
Email: gardiners2000@hotmail.com Web: www.gardiners.net

Local man Sean Owens trained at the renowned Portrush hotel & catering college then, after travelling the world, returned to settle in Magherafelt where, with his wife Helen, he opened this impressive restaurant in 1999. The premises was formerly a rugby club and the change of use must have been quite a design challenge - yet now, clever use of space has transformed what is basically a big boxy room into an interesting, smart and atmospheric dining room, with a proper bar to gladden the heart of every Irishman walking through the door, good use of colour - bright blue accents to enliven the warmer tones - beautiful flowers, and effective lighting all creating a fine setting for that special meal. The stated aim is to bring quality local food and service to the people of the area, and this is achieved remarkably well, through accessible menus that offer really good variations of many popular dishes: ever-popular prawn cocktail, for example, deep fried Ulster button mushrooms with garlic aoili and (who could resist?) real spaghetti bolognaise with parmesan croûte...Sean is a committed supporter of local produce and suppliers ("local people support Gardiners, so Gardiners supports them"), and you will find some unusual specialities here too - Lough Neagh smoked eel, for example (a parfait, perhaps, on roasted soda bread), and dishes inspired by traditional rural products, like blackthorn gravad lax with sloe gin and sweet Swedish senap mustard. All menus are good value (including a Celebrations Menu, offered occasionally to give the kitchen a good stretch, which is also keenly priced), and an early dinner menu offering plenty of choice with nothing over £9.95 is a snip. A carefully selected (and thoroughly tasted) wine list is also well priced. But it's not just good food that attracts people to Gardiners - it's a good night out. And that is exactly what you'll get here, especially at weekends when the buzz is mighty. There's a room upstairs for private parties too, and an outside catering service. Gardiners is a great neighbourhood restaurant - and plenty come from other neighbourhoods to enjoy a night out here. Children welcome; toilets wheelchair accessible; air conditioning. **Seats 90** (private room, 105); D Tue-Sun, 5.30-10pm; Sun L £15, value D £15, 5.30-7pm, set D £20, gourmet D £30, also a la carte; house wine from £10.95. Closed Mon, 25-26 Dec, 12-13 Jul. MasterCard, Visa, Switch. **Directions:** To diamond in Magherafelt, down Rainey St., first right into Garden St.

Portstewart

Cromore Halt Inn

RESTAURANT/GUESTHOUSE

158 Station Road Portstewart Co Londonderry BT55 7PU
Tel: 028 7083 6888 Fax: 028 7083 1910
Email: info@cromore.com Web: www.cromore.com

This friendly, family-owned guesthouse and restaurant has been managed by Niall O'Boyle and his wife Kate since it opened in 1994 and it feels like a small hotel. It would make an equally good base for a business or leisure visit as the rooms are furnished to hotel standard in an uncluttered modern style and have all the expected facilities, including satellite television, direct dial phone with computer line, tea & coffee making, trouser press, keycard & safety deposit box - and there's a quiet first floor residents' lounge too. The restaurant, in a large, pleasant room furnished in a relaxed informal style, is open for lunch and dinner every day, and has earned a great reputation in the locality for quality, value and good service. Clearly written menus offer plenty of choice and are well organised by ingredient - there are no great surprises, but ingredients are carefully sourced and there is a welcome honesty of tone that translates to the plate; vegetarians get a choice of about four main courses. Helpful, fairly priced wine list. Small conferences (25). No pets. **Rooms 12** (all en-suite & no smoking, 1 disabled). No room service. Lift. Children welcome (under 3s free in parents' room, cot available free of charge). B&B about £45, ss about £10. Restaurant: L daily, 12.15-2.25(Sun from 12.30), D daily 5-9.30 (Sun to 8.30); Children's Menu available, L & early D (5-7). House wine about £9.25. *Short breaks offered. Closed 24-26 Dec. MasterCard, Visa, Switch. **Directions:** M2 Belfast -Ballymena; A26 to Coleraine, then B185 to Portstewart.Cromore Halt on left as you enter Portstewart. ◇

Upperlands

Ardtara Country House

COUNTRY HOUSE

8 Gorteade Road Upperlands Maghera Co Londonderry BT46 5SA
Tel: 028 7964 4490 Fax: 028 7964 5080
Email: valerie_ferson@ardtara.com Web: www.ardtara.com

Former home to the Clark linen milling family, Ardtara is now an attractive, elegantly decorated Victorian country house with a genuinely hospitable atmosphere. Well-proportioned rooms have antique furnishings and fresh flowers, and all the large, luxuriously furnished bedrooms enjoy views of the garden and surrounding countryside and have king size beds, original fireplaces and LCD TV and DVDs, while bathrooms combine practicality with period details, some including free-standing baths and fireplaces. Breakfast should be a high point, so allow time to enjoy it. Ardtara would make an excellent base for exploring this beautiful and unspoilt area. Tennis, golf practice tee. Pets allowed by arrangement. Garden, woodland walk. Conferences/Banqueting (50). **Rooms 8** (3 suites) B&B about £75pps, ss about £10. *Short breaks offered. **Restaurant:** The dining room was previously a snooker room and still has the full Victorian skylight and original hunting frieze, making an unusual setting for fine dining. Head chef, Olivier Boudon, joined the team here in 2005, bringing experience from countries as diverse as China and Poland, so you may expect some unusual influences in the cooking and presentation (including a number of 'gala servings' such as serving caviar on ice), although the main influence is classical French. Olivier presents daily-changed menus offering three or four choices on each course - smoked salmon & fish terrine with salmon roe & fresh cream; pan-fried fillet of local beef (from McKees' butchers) with gratin dauphinoise, ratatouille and morel & armagnac sauce; and passion fruit parfait with blackcurrant sauce are typical - and you may finish with Irish cheeses & the famous locally-made Ditty's biscuits. However, there is also an extensive and much more ambitious à la carte menue offered, which is quite unlike anything you are likely to find in the neighbourhood. **Seats 65** (private room,30). Reservations required. No smoking restaurant. Children welcome. Toilets wheelchair accessible. L Daily 12-2.30, Sun L 12-4. Set L about £24, Set Sun L about £20. D daily 6.30-9.30 (to 9 Sun). Set 2/3 course D about £24/30. House wines from about £11.65. Amex, MasterCard, Visa, Switch. **Directions:** M2 from from Belfast to A6. A29 to Maghera. B75 to Kilrea. ◇

COUNTY TYRONE

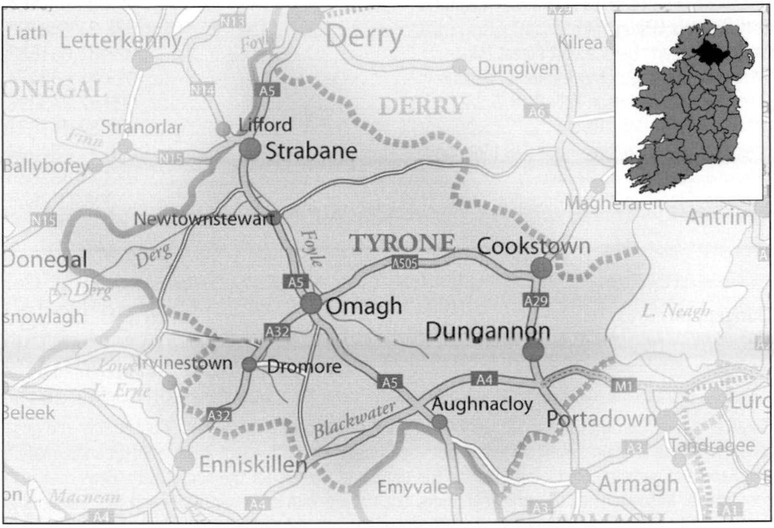

People in Ireland identify strongly with their counties. This is as it should be. The county boundaries may have evolved in many ways over a very long period, often in obscure ways. But in the 21st Century, Irish counties – for all that they vary enormously in size – seem to provide their people with a sense of place and pride which survives modern efforts to create newer administrative structures. The enduring spirit of Tyrone well expresses this, and never more so than when a county team is playing in a national final at Croke Park in Dublin.

Tyrone is Northern Ireland's largest county, so it is something of a surprise for the traveller to discover that its geography appears to be dominated by a range of mountains of modest height, and nearly half of these peaks seem to be in the neighbouring county of Londonderry.

Yet such is the case with Tyrone and the Sperrins. The village of Sperrin itself towards the head of Glenelly may be in Tyrone, but the highest peak of Sawel (678 m), which looms over it, is on the county boundary. But much of the county is upland territory and moorland, giving the impression that the Sperrins are even more extensive than is really the case.

In such a land, the lower country and the fertile valleys gleam like jewels, and there's often a vivid impression of a living - and indeed, prosperity - being wrested from a demanding environment. It's a character-forming sort of place, so it's perhaps understandable that it was the ancestral homeland of a remarkable number of early American Presidents, and this connection is commemorated in the Ulster American Folk Park a few miles north of the county town of Omagh.

Forest parks abound, while attractive towns like Castlederg and Dungannon, as well as villages in the uplands and along the charming Clogher Valley, provide entertainment and hospitality for visitors refreshed by the wide open spaces of the moorlands and the mountains.

Local Attractions and Information

Ardboe Kinturk (Lough Neagh) Cultural Centre	028 86 736512
Benburb, Benburb Castle and Valley Park	028 37 548241
Castlederg, Visitor Centre (Davy Crockett links)	028 81 670795
Clogher, Clogher Valley Rural Centre	028 85 548872
Coagh, Kinturk Cultural Centre	028 86 736512
Cookstown, Drum Manor Forest Park	028 86 762774
Cookstown, Wellbrook Beetling Mill (Corkhill)	028 86 748210
Cranagh (Glenelly), Sperrin Heritage Centre	028 81 648142
Creggan (nr Carrickmore), Visitor Centre	028 80 761112
Dungannon, Heritage Centre	028 87 724187
Dungannon, Tourism Information	028 87 767259

Dungannon, Tyrone Crystal 028 87 725335
Dungannon, Ulysses S Grant Ancestral Homestead 028 85 557133
Fivemiletown, Clogher Valley Railway Exhibition 028 89 521409
Gortin, Ulster History Park 028 81 648188
Newtownstewart, Baronscourt Forest Park 028 81 661683
Newtownstewart, Gateway Centre & Museum 028 81 662414
Omagh, Ulster-American Folk Park 028 82 243292
Omagh, Tourism Information 028 82 247831
Strabane, Gray's Printing Press (US Independence) 028 71 884094
Strabane, Tourism Information 028 71 883735
Strabane, President Wilson Ancestral Home 028 71 3844

Dungannon

COUNTRY HOUSE

Grange Lodge

7 Grange Road Dungannon Co Tyrone BT71 7EJ
Tel: 028 8778 4212 Fax: 028 8778 4313
Email: stay@grangelodgecountryhouse.com Web: www.grangelodgecountryhouse.com

Norah and Ralph Brown's renowned Georgian retreat offers comfort, true family hospitality and good food. The house is on an elevated site just outside Dungannon, with about 20 acres of grounds; mature woodland and gardens (producing food for the table and flowers for the house) with views over lush countryside. Improvements over the years have been made with great sensitivity and the feeling is of gentle organic growth, culminating in the present warm and welcoming atmosphere. Grange Lodge is furnished unselfconsciously, with antiques and family pieces throughout. Bedrooms (and bathrooms) are exceptionally comfortable and thoughtful in detail. Norah is well known for her home cooking and they will cater for groups of 10-30. Grange Lodge is fully licensed and dinner menus change daily (in consultation with guests). Resident dinner (from about £26) must be pre-booked, especially if you want to dine on the day of arrival. Breakfasts are also outstanding, so allow time to indulge: a fine buffet beautifully set out on a polished dining table might typically include a large selection of juices, fruit and cereals and porridge is a speciality, served with a tot of Bushmills whiskey, brown sugar and cream - and that's before you've even reached the cooked breakfast menu, served with lovely fresh breads and toast and home-made preserves. *"Cook with Norah" cookery classes have been running since 2002, and are now very successful; details on application. Conferences/banqueting (20/30). Garden, walking, snooker. Not suitable for children under 12. Pets allowed by arrangement. **Rooms 5** (3 shower only, all no smoking). Room service (limited hours). Turndown service. B&B £39 pps, ss £20. Residents D Mon-Sat, 7.30pm, by arrangement; Set D from £28. Closed 13 Dec-1 Feb. MasterCard, Visa, Switch. **Directions:** 1 mile from M1 junction 15. On A29 to Armagh, follow "Grange Lodge" signs.

Moygashel

CAFÉ

The Loft @ The Linen Green

Moygashel Co Tyrone BT71 7HB
Tel: 028 8775 3761

A long space with high ceilings, attractive windows and painted metal beams - all vaguely reminiscent of an industrial past - with a gallery area overlooking the gift shop below, this is a good place to have a bite when shopping, or to break a journey. Good baking - fresh scones, tray bakes - salads (curried chicken, sweetcorn, tomatoes), sandwiches and desserts like lemon meringue pie and apple tart. Cosmopolitan snacks like panini too, and a good selection of hot drinks. Open Mon-Sat, 10am-5pm. ◇